Microsoft® OFFICE 2013

BRIEF

Misty E. Vermaat

Contributing Authors
Steven M. Freund
Raymond E. Enger
Susan L. Sebok
Mali B. Jones
Philip J. Pratt
Mary Z. Last
Corinne L. Hoisington

CENGAGE
Learning®

SHELLY
CASHMAN
SERIES®

Australia • Brazil • Japan • Korea • Mexico • Singapore • Spain • United Kingdom • United States

Microsoft® Office 2013: Brief
Misty E. Vermaat

Executive Editor: Kathleen McMahon

Product Manager: Jon Farnham

Associate Product Manager: Crystal Parenteau

Editorial Assistant: Sarah Ryan

Print Buyer: Julio Esperas

Director of Production: Patty Stephan

Content Project Manager: Matthew Hutchinson

Development Editors: Lyn Markowicz, Deb Kaufmann, Amanda Brodkin, Lisa Ruffolo

Senior Brand Manager: Elinor Gregory

Market Development Manager: Kristie Clark

Market Development Manager: Gretchen Swann

Marketing Coordinator: Amy McGregor

QA Manuscript Reviewers: Jeffrey Schwartz, John Freitas, Serge Palladino, Susan Pedicini, Danielle Shaw, Susan Whalen

Art Director: GEX Publishing Services, Inc.

Text Design: Joel Sadagursky

Cover Design: Lisa Kuhn, Curio Press, LLC

Cover Photo: Tom Kates Photography

Compositor: PreMediaGlobal

Copyeditor: Foxxe Editorial

Proofreader: Kim Kosmatka

Indexer: Rich Carlson

Microsoft and the Office logo are either registered trademarks or trademarks of Microsoft Corporation in the United States and/or other countries. Cengage Learning is an independent entity from the Microsoft Corporation, and not affiliated with Microsoft in any manner.

For product information and technology assistance, contact us at **Cengage Learning Customer & Sales Support, 1-800-354-9706**

For permission to use material from this text or product, submit all requests online at **cengage.com/permissions**
Further permissions questions can be emailed to **permissionrequest@cengage.com**

Library of Congress Control Number: 2013935964

softcover binding:
ISBN-13: 978-1-285-16613-1
ISBN-10: 1-285-16613-2

softcover spiral binding:
ISBN-13: 978-1-285-16616-2
ISBN-10: 1-285-16616-7

Cengage Learning
20 Channel Center Street
Boston, MA 02210
USA

Cengage Learning is a leading provider of customized learning solutions with office locations around the globe, including Singapore, the United Kingdom, Australia, Mexico, Brazil, and Japan. Locate your local office at: **international.cengage.com/region**

Cengage Learning products are represented in Canada by Nelson Education, Ltd.

To learn more about Cengage Learning, visit **www.cengage.com**

Purchase any of our products at your local college bookstore or at our preferred online store at **www.CengageBrain.com**

Printed in the United States of America
2 3 4 5 6 7 14

Microsoft® OFFICE 2013 BRIEF

Contents

Preface x

Microsoft Office 2013 and Windows 8

Office 2013 and Windows 8: Essential Concepts and Skills

Objectives	**OFF 1**
Roadmap	OFF 2
Introduction to the Windows 8 Operating System	**OFF 2**
Using a Touch Screen and a Mouse	OFF 3
Scrolling	OFF 5
Keyboard Shortcuts	OFF 6
Starting Windows	OFF 6
To Sign In to an Account	OFF 7
The Windows Start Screen	OFF 8
Introduction to Microsoft Office 2013	**OFF 9**
Microsoft Office 2013 Apps	OFF 9
Microsoft Office 2013 Suites	OFF 9
Running and Using an App	**OFF 10**
Word	OFF 10
To Run an App from the Start Screen	OFF 11
Windows Desktop	OFF 13
To Switch between an App and the Start Screen	OFF 13
To Maximize a Window	OFF 14
Word Document Window, Ribbon, and Elements Common to Office Apps	OFF 14
To Display a Different Tab on the Ribbon	OFF 18
To Collapse and Expand the Ribbon and Use Full Screen Mode	OFF 19
To Use a Shortcut Menu to Relocate the Quick Access Toolbar	OFF 20
To Customize the Quick Access Toolbar	OFF 22
To Enter Text in a Document	OFF 23
Saving and Organizing Files	**OFF 23**
Organizing Files and Folders	OFF 24
To Create a Folder	OFF 25
Folder Windows	OFF 27
To Create a Folder within a Folder	OFF 27
To Create the Remaining Folders	OFF 28
To Expand a Folder, Scroll through Folder Contents, and Collapse a Folder	OFF 29
To Switch from One App to Another	OFF 30
To Save a File in a Folder	OFF 31
Navigating in Dialog Boxes	OFF 34
To Minimize and Restore a Window	OFF 34
To Save a File on SkyDrive	OFF 36
To Sign Out of a Microsoft Account	OFF 38
Screen Resolution	**OFF 39**
To Change the Screen Resolution	OFF 40
To Exit an Office App with One Document Open	OFF 42
To Copy a Folder to a USB Flash Drive	OFF 43
Additional Microsoft Office Apps	**OFF 44**
PowerPoint	OFF 45
To Run an App Using the Search Box	OFF 46
The PowerPoint Window and Ribbon	OFF 48
To Enter Content in a Title Slide	OFF 49
To Save a File in a Folder	OFF 50
To Create a New Office Document from the Backstage View	OFF 51
To Enter Content in a Title Slide of a Second PowerPoint Presentation	OFF 53
To Save a File in a Folder	OFF 53
To Close an Office File Using the Backstage View	OFF 54
To Open a Recent Office File Using the Backstage View	OFF 54
To Exit an Office App	OFF 55
Excel	OFF 55
To Create a New Blank Office Document from File Explorer	OFF 56
To Run an App from File Explorer and Open a File	OFF 57
Unique Features of Excel	OFF 59
To Enter a Worksheet Title	OFF 60
To Save an Existing Office File with the Same File Name	OFF 61
To Save a File with a New File Name	OFF 62
To Exit an Office App	OFF 62
Access	OFF 63
To Run an App	OFF 63
Unique Elements in Access	OFF 64
To Create an Access Database	OFF 64
To Close an Office File	OFF 66
To Open an Existing Office File	OFF 66
To Exit an Office App	OFF 67
Other Office Apps	**OFF 67**
Outlook	OFF 68
Publisher	OFF 69
OneNote	OFF 71

Renaming, Moving, and Deleting Files OFF 72
 To Rename a File OFF 72
 To Move a File OFF 73
 To Delete a File OFF 74
Microsoft Office and Windows Help **OFF 75**
 To Open the Help Window in an Office App OFF 75
 Moving and Resizing Windows OFF 75
 To Move a Window by Dragging OFF 76
 To Resize a Window by Dragging OFF 76
 Using Office Help OFF 77
 To Obtain Help Using the
 'Search online help' Text Box OFF 77
 To Obtain Help Using Help Links OFF 78
 Obtaining Help while Working
 in an Office App OFF 79
 Using Windows Help and Support OFF 79
 To Use Windows Help and Support OFF 80
Chapter Summary **OFF 81**
Apply Your Knowledge **OFF 83**
Extend Your Knowledge **OFF 84**
Analyze, Correct, Improve **OFF 85**
In the Labs **OFF 85**
Consider This: Your Turn **OFF 87**
Learn Online **OFF 88**

Microsoft **Office 365**

Office 365 Essentials

Objectives CLD 1
Introduction to Office 365 CLD 2
 Cloud Computing CLD 2
What Is Office 365? CLD 3
 Office 2013 and Office 365 Features Comparison CLD 4
 Subscription-Based Office 365 Plans CLD 5
First look at Office 365 CLD 6
 Productivity Tools CLD 6
 Email and Calendars CLD 7
 Online Meetings CLD 7
 File Sharing CLD 7
 Website Creation CLD 8
Synchronization CLD 8
 Multiple Device Access to Office 365 CLD 8
Teams Using Office 365 in Business CLD 9
 Email Communication Using Exchange CLD 10
 Collaboration Using SharePoint CLD 10
 Website Design Using SharePoint CLD 11
 Real-Time Communications Using Lync CLD 11
Chapter Summary CLD 15
Consider This: Your Turn CLD 15

Microsoft **Word 2013**

CHAPTER ONE
Creating, Formatting, and Editing
a Word Document with a Picture

Objectives WD 1
Introduction WD 2
Project — Flyer with a Picture WD 2
 Roadmap WD 4
 To Run Word and Create a Blank Document WD 4

Entering Text **WD 5**
 To Type Text WD 5
 To Display Formatting Marks WD 6
 To Insert a Blank Line WD 7
 To Zoom Page Width WD 7
 Wordwrap WD 8
 To Wordwrap Text as You Type WD 9
 Spelling and Grammar Check WD 9
 To Check Spelling and Grammar as You Type WD 10
 To Enter More Text WD 11
 Navigating a Document WD 12
 To Save a Document WD 12
Formatting Paragraphs and Characters **WD 13**
 Font, Font Sizes, and Themes WD 14
 To Center a Paragraph WD 15
 To Center Another Paragraph WD 15
 Formatting Single versus Multiple Paragraphs
 and Characters WD 16
 To Select a Line WD 16
 To Change the Font Size of Selected Text WD 17
 To Change the Font of Selected Text WD 18
 To Change the Case of Selected Text WD 19
 To Apply a Text Effect to Selected Text WD 20
 To Shade a Paragraph WD 21
 To Select Multiple Lines WD 22
 To Change the Font Size of Selected Text WD 22
 To Bullet a List of Paragraphs WD 23
 To Undo and Redo an Action WD 24
 To Italicize Text WD 25
 To Color Text WD 26
 To Use the Mini Toolbar to Format Text WD 27
 To Select a Group of Words WD 28
 To Underline Text WD 29
 To Bold Text WD 29
 To Zoom One Page WD 30
 To Change Theme Colors WD 31
 To Zoom Page Width WD 32
 Selecting Text WD 32
 To Save an Existing Document with
 the Same File Name WD 33
Inserting and Formatting a Picture
** in a Word Document** **WD 33**
 To Center Another Paragraph WD 33
 To Insert a Picture WD 34
 To Zoom the Document WD 35
 To Resize a Graphic WD 36
 To Zoom 100% WD 37
 To Apply a Picture Style WD 38
 To Apply Picture Effects WD 39
 Enhancing the Page WD 40
 To Add a Page Border WD 41
 To Zoom One Page WD 42
 To Change Spacing before and after Paragraphs WD 42
 To Center Page Contents Vertically WD 43
 To Save an Existing Document with the
 Same File Name WD 44
 Document Properties WD 44
 To Sign Out of a Microsoft Account WD 45
 To Exit Word WD 46
Correcting Errors and Revising a Document **WD 46**
 Types of Changes Made to Documents WD 46
 To Run Word WD 46
 To Open a Document from Word WD 47

To Zoom the Document WD 47
To Insert Text in an Existing Document WD 48
To Delete Text .. WD 48
To Move Text ... WD 49
To Save an Existing Document with
 the Same File Name WD 50
Printing or Reading a Document **WD 50**
To Print a Document WD 51
To Switch to Read Mode WD 52
To Switch to Print Layout View WD 53
To Exit Word .. WD 53
Chapter Summary **WD 54**
Apply Your Knowledge **WD 55**
Extend Your Knowledge **WD 56**
Analyze, Correct, Improve **WD 57**
In the Labs ... **WD 58**
Consider This: Your Turn **WD 63**
Learn Online ... **WD 64**

CHAPTER TWO
Creating a Research Paper with References and Sources
Objectives .. **WD 65**
Introduction ... **WD 66**
Project — Research Paper **WD 66**
Roadmap .. WD 68
MLA Documentation Style WD 68
Changing Document Settings **WD 69**
To Run Word and Create a Blank Document ... WD 69
To Display Formatting Marks WD 70
Styles .. WD 70
To Modify a Style .. WD 70
Adjusting Line and Paragraph Spacing WD 72
To Change Line Spacing WD 72
To Remove Space after a Paragraph WD 73
To Update a Style to Match a Selection WD 73
Creating a Header **WD 74**
To Switch to the Header WD 74
To Right-Align a Paragraph WD 75
To Enter Text ... WD 76
To Insert a Page Number WD 76
To Close the Header WD 77
Typing the Research Paper Text **WD 78**
To Enter Name and Course Information WD 78
To Click and Type .. WD 79
Keyboard Shortcuts WD 80
To Format Text Using a Keyboard Shortcut ... WD 81
To Save a Document WD 81
To Display the Rulers WD 82
To First-Line Indent Paragraphs WD 82
To AutoCorrect as You Type WD 84
To Use the AutoCorrect Options Button WD 85
To Create an AutoCorrect Entry WD 85
The AutoCorrect Dialog Box WD 87
To Enter More Text WD 88
Citations ... WD 88
To Change the Bibliography Style WD 89
To Insert a Citation and Create Its Source ... WD 89
To Enter More Text WD 91
To Save an Existing Document with
 the Same File Name WD 92
Footnotes ... WD 92
To Insert a Footnote Reference Mark WD 92
To Enter Footnote Text WD 93

To Insert a Citation Placeholder WD 93
Footnote Text Style WD 94
To Modify a Style Using a Shortcut Menu ... WD 94
To Edit a Source ... WD 96
To Edit a Citation .. WD 98
Working with Footnotes and Endnotes WD 99
To Enter More Text WD 100
To Count Words ... WD 100
Automatic Page Breaks WD 101
To Enter More Text and Insert a
 Citation Placeholder WD 101
To Hide and Show White Space WD 102
To Edit a Source ... WD 103
To Enter More Text WD 104
To Save an Existing Document with
 the Same File Name WD 104
Creating an Alphabetical Works Cited Page ... **WD 104**
To Page Break Manually WD 105
To Apply a Style ... WD 105
To Center Text ... WD 106
To Create the Bibliographical List WD 106
To Save an Existing Document with
 the Same File Name WD 108
Proofreading and Revising the Research Paper ... **WD 108**
To Modify a Source WD 109
To Update a Field .. WD 110
To Go to a Page ... WD 111
Copying, Cutting, and Pasting WD 111
To Copy and Paste WD 112
To Display the Paste Options Menu WD 113
To Find Text ... WD 113
To Replace Text ... WD 114
Find and Replace Dialog Box WD 115
To Find and Insert a Synonym WD 116
To Check Spelling and Grammar at Once ... WD 116
The Main and Custom Dictionaries WD 118
To Look Up Information WD 119
Research Task Pane Options WD 120
To Save an Existing Document with
 the Same File Name WD 120
To Zoom Multiple Pages WD 120
To Change Read Mode Color WD 121
To Print a Document WD 122
To Exit Word .. WD 122
Chapter Summary **WD 123**
Apply Your Knowledge **WD 124**
Extend Your Knowledge **WD 125**
Analyze, Correct, Improve **WD 127**
In the Labs ... **WD 128**
Consider This: Your Turn **WD 135**
Learn Online ... **WD 136**

Microsoft PowerPoint 2013

CHAPTER ONE
Creating and Editing a Presentation with Pictures

Objectives .. **PPT 1**
Introduction ... **PPT 2**
Project — Presentation with a Bulleted List,
 Photos, and an Illustration **PPT 2**
Roadmap .. PPT 4
To Run PowerPoint PPT 4

Choosing a Document Theme and Variant **PPT 5**
To Choose a Document Theme and Variant PPT 5
Creating a Title Slide **PPT 7**
To Enter the Presentation Title PPT 7
Correcting a Mistake When Typing PPT 8
Paragraphs PPT 8
To Enter the Presentation Subtitle Paragraph PPT 9
To Zoom a Slide PPT 10
Formatting Characters in a Presentation **PPT 10**
Fonts and Font Styles PPT 10
To Select a Paragraph PPT 11
To Italicize Text PPT 11
To Increase Font Size PPT 12
To Select a Word PPT 12
To Change the Text Color PPT 13
To Save a Presentation with a New File Name PPT 14
Adding a New Slide to a Presentation **PPT 15**
To Add a New Text Slide with a Bulleted List PPT 15
Creating a Text Slide with a Multilevel Bulleted List **PPT 17**
To Enter a Slide Title PPT 17
To Select a Text Placeholder PPT 18
To Type a Multilevel Bulleted List PPT 18
To Type the Remaining Text for Slide 2 PPT 20
To Select a Group of Words PPT 20
To Bold Text PPT 21
To Increase Font Size PPT 22
Adding New Slides, Changing Slide Layouts,
and Changing the Theme **PPT 22**
To Add a Slide with the Title Only Layout PPT 23
To Enter a Slide Title PPT 24
To Add a New Slide and Enter
a Slide Title and Headings PPT 24
To Change the Theme PPT 26
To Change the Variant PPT 27
To Save an Existing Presentation with
the Same File Name PPT 28
PowerPoint Views **PPT 28**
To Move to Another Slide in Normal View PPT 29
Inserting Photos and Illustrations into Slides **PPT 30**
To Insert a Picture from Office.com
into the Title Slide PPT 31
To Insert a Picture from Office.com into a Slide
without a Content Placeholder PPT 33
To Insert an Illustration from Office.com into
a Slide without a Content Placeholder PPT 33
To Insert a Picture from Office.com
into a Content Placeholder PPT 34
Resizing Photos and Illustrations **PPT 35**
To Proportionally Resize Pictures PPT 36
To Nonproportionally Resize
the Photograph on Slide 2 PPT 37
To Resize the Illustration on Slide 3 PPT 38
To Move Pictures PPT 39
Ending a Slide Show with a Closing Slide **PPT 40**
To Duplicate a Slide PPT 41
To Arrange a Slide PPT 42
Making Changes to Slide Text Content **PPT 42**
Replacing Text in an Existing Slide PPT 43
Deleting Text PPT 43
To Delete Text in a Placeholder PPT 43
Adding a Transition **PPT 45**
To Add a Transition between Slides PPT 45
Document Properties PPT 48

Viewing the Presentation in Slide Show View **PPT 49**
To Start Slide Show View PPT 49
To Move Manually through Slides in a Slide Show PPT 50
Printing a Presentation **PPT 52**
To Print a Presentation PPT 52
To Sign Out of a Microsoft Account PPT 55
To Exit PowerPoint PPT 55
Chapter Summary **PPT 56**
Apply Your Knowledge **PPT 57**
Extend Your Knowledge **PPT 58**
Analyze, Correct, Improve **PPT 59**
In the Labs **PPT 61**
Consider This: Your Turn **PPT 69**
Learn Online **PPT 71**

CHAPTER TWO
Enhancing a Presentation with
Pictures, Shapes, and WordArt
Objectives **PPT 73**
Introduction **PPT 74**
Project — Presentation with Pictures, Shapes,
and WordArt **PPT 74**
Roadmap PPT 76
To Run PowerPoint PPT 76
Downloading a Theme and Editing Slides **PPT 77**
To Search for and Download an Online Theme PPT 77
To Delete a Slide PPT 79
To Create a Title Slide PPT 81
To Create the First Text Slide PPT 81
To Create the Second Text Slide PPT 82
To Save a Presentation PPT 82
Inserting and Formatting Pictures in a Presentation **PPT 83**
To Insert a Picture into a Slide
without a Content Placeholder PPT 83
To Change a Picture PPT 85
To Correct a Picture PPT 87
To Apply a Picture Style PPT 87
To Add a Picture Border PPT 88
To Change a Picture Border Color PPT 89
To Apply Picture Effects PPT 90
Inserting and Formatting a Shape **PPT 91**
To Add a Shape PPT 92
To Resize a Shape PPT 93
To Add Other Shapes PPT 94
To Apply a Shape Style PPT 95
To Apply Another Style PPT 97
To Add Text to a Shape PPT 97
To Change the Font PPT 98
To Format the Text PPT 100
Format Painter PPT 100
To Format Text Using the Format Painter PPT 101
To Copy and Paste a Shape PPT 101
Inserting and Formatting WordArt **PPT 103**
To Insert WordArt PPT 103
To Change the WordArt Shape PPT 104
To Apply a WordArt Text Fill PPT 106
To Change the Weight of the WordArt Outline PPT 106
To Change the Color of the WordArt Outline PPT 107
Formatting Slide Backgrounds **PPT 108**
To Insert a Picture to Create a Background PPT 108
To Format the Background Picture
Fill Transparency PPT 109
To Insert a Texture Fill PPT 110

To Format the Background Texture
 Fill Transparency PPT 111
To Insert a Gradient Fill PPT 111
Reviewing and Revising Individual Slides **PPT 113**
Replace Dialog Box PPT 113
To Find and Replace Text PPT 113
To Find and Insert a Synonym PPT 114
To Add Notes PPT 115
Checking Spelling PPT 116
To Check Spelling PPT 117
To Insert a Slide Number PPT 118
To Add a Transition between Slides PPT 119
To Print Speaker Notes PPT 121
To Save the Presentation, Sign Out of a
 Microsoft Account, and Exit PowerPoint PPT 125
Chapter Summary **PPT 125**
Apply Your Knowledge **PPT 127**
Extend Your Knowledge **PPT 130**
Analyze, Correct, Improve **PPT 133**
In the Labs **PPT 135**
Consider This: Your Turn **PPT 143**
Learn Online **PPT 144**

Microsoft **Excel 2013**

CHAPTER ONE
Creating a Worksheet and a Chart

Objectives **EX 1**
Introduction **EX 2**
Project — Worksheet and a Chart **EX 2**
Roadmap EX 4
To Run Excel and Create a Blank Workbook EX 5
Selecting a Cell **EX 6**
Entering Text **EX 6**
To Enter the Worksheet Titles EX 7
AutoCorrect EX 9
To Enter Column Titles EX 9
To Enter Row Titles EX 11
Entering Numbers **EX 12**
To Enter Numbers EX 12
Calculating a Sum **EX 14**
To Sum a Column of Numbers EX 14
Using the Fill Handle to Copy a Cell to Adjacent Cells **EX 15**
To Copy a Cell to Adjacent Cells in a Row EX 16
To Determine Multiple Totals at the Same Time EX 18
To Enter a Formula Using the Keyboard EX 20
To Copy a Cell to Adjacent Cells in a Row EX 21
To Save a Workbook with a New File Name EX 21
Formatting the Worksheet **EX 22**
Font Style, Size, and Color EX 23
To Change a Cell Style EX 24
To Change the Font EX 25
To Bold a Cell EX 26
To Increase the Font Size of a Cell Entry EX 27
To Change the Font Color of a Cell Entry EX 28
To Center Cell Entries across Columns
 by Merging Cells EX 29
To Format Rows Using Cell Styles EX 30
To Format Numbers in the Worksheet EX 32
To Adjust the Column Width EX 34
To Use the Name Box to Select a Cell EX 35
Other Ways to Select Cells EX 36

Adding a Pie Chart to the Worksheet **EX 37**
To Add a 3-D Pie Chart EX 38
To Apply a Style to a Chart EX 40
Changing the Sheet Tab Names **EX 41**
To Move a Chart to a New Sheet EX 41
To Change the Worksheet Tab Name EX 42
Document Properties EX 44
To Save an Existing Workbook with the
 Same File Name EX 45
Printing a Worksheet **EX 45**
To Preview and Print a Worksheet
 in Landscape Orientation EX 46
To Open a Document from Excel EX 48
AutoCalculate **EX 48**
To Use the AutoCalculate Area
 to Determine a Maximum EX 48
Correcting Errors **EX 49**
Correcting Errors while Entering Data into a Cell EX 50
Correcting Errors after Entering Data into a Cell EX 50
Undoing the Last Cell Entry EX 51
Clearing a Cell or Range of Cells EX 52
Clearing the Entire Worksheet EX 52
To Sign Out of a Microsoft Account EX 53
To Exit Excel EX 53
Chapter Summary **EX 54**
Apply Your Knowledge **EX 55**
Extend Your Knowledge **EX 57**
Analyze, Correct, Improve **EX 58**
In the Labs **EX 59**
Consider This: Your Turn **EX 63**
Learn Online **EX 64**

CHAPTER TWO
Formulas, Functions, and Formatting

Objectives **EX 65**
Introduction **EX 66**
Project — Worksheet with Formulas and Functions **EX 66**
Roadmap EX 68
To Run Excel and Create a Blank Workbook EX 69
Entering the Titles and Numbers into the Worksheet **EX 70**
To Enter the Worksheet Title and Subtitle EX 70
To Enter the Column Titles EX 70
To Enter the Salary Data EX 71
To Enter the Row Titles EX 72
To Change the Worksheet Tab Name and Color
 and Save the Workbook EX 72
Entering Formulas **EX 73**
To Enter a Formula Using the Keyboard EX 73
Arithmetic Operations EX 75
Order of Operations EX 75
To Enter Formulas Using Point Mode EX 76
To Copy Formulas Using the Fill Handle EX 78
Option Buttons **EX 79**
To Determine Totals Using the Sum Button EX 80
To Determine the Total Tax Percentage EX 81
Using the AVERAGE, MAX, and MIN Functions **EX 81**
To Determine the Highest Number in
 a Range of Numbers Using the Insert
 Function Box EX 82
To Determine the Lowest Number in a Range
 of Numbers Using the Sum Menu EX 84
To Determine the Average of a Range
 of Numbers Using the Keyboard EX 86

To Copy a Range of Cells Across Columns to an Adjacent Range Using the Fill Handle	EX 87
To Save a Workbook Using the Same File Name	EX 88
Verifying Formulas Using Range Finder	**EX 89**
To Verify a Formula Using Range Finder	EX 89
Formatting the Worksheet	**EX 89**
To Change the Workbook Theme	EX 91
To Format the Worksheet Titles	EX 92
To Change the Background Color and Apply a Box Border to the Worksheet Title and Subtitle	EX 93
To Apply a Cell Style to the Column Headings and Format the Total Rows	EX 95
To Format Dates and Center Data in Cells	EX 96
Formatting Numbers Using the Ribbon	EX 97
To Apply an Accounting Number Format and Comma Style Format Using the Ribbon	EX 97
To Apply a Currency Style Format with a Floating Dollar Sign Using the Format Cells Dialog Box	EX 98
To Apply a Percent Style Format and Use the Increase Decimal Button	EX 99
Conditional Formatting	EX 100
To Apply Conditional Formatting	EX 100
Conditional Formatting Operators	EX 103
Changing Column Width and Row Height	EX 103
To Change Column Width	EX 103
To Change Row Height	EX 106
Checking Spelling	**EX 107**
To Check Spelling on the Worksheet	EX 108
Additional Spell Checker Considerations	EX 109
Printing the Worksheet	**EX 110**
To Change the Worksheet's Margins, Header, and Orientation in Page Layout View	EX 110
To Print a Worksheet	EX 113
To Print a Section of the Worksheet	EX 114
Displaying and Printing the Formulas Version of the Worksheet	**EX 115**
To Display the Formulas in the Worksheet and Fit the Printout on One Page	EX 115
To Change the Print Scaling Option Back to 100%	EX 117
To Sign Out of a Microsoft Account	EX 117
To Save the Workbook and Exit Excel	EX 118
Chapter Summary	**EX 118**
Apply Your Knowledge	**EX 119**
Extend Your Knowledge	**EX 121**
Analyze, Correct, Improve	**EX 122**
In the Labs	**EX 123**
Consider This: Your Turn	**EX 127**
Learn Online	**EX 128**

Microsoft **Access 2013**

CHAPTER ONE

Databases and Database Objects: An Introduction

Objectives	**AC 1**
Introduction	**AC 2**
Project — Database Creation	**AC 2**
Roadmap	AC 5
To Run Access	AC 5
Creating a Database	**AC 6**
To Create a Database	AC 6
The Access Window	**AC 7**
Navigation Pane and Access Work Area	AC 8
Determining Tables and Fields	**AC 8**
Naming Tables and Fields	AC 8
Determining the Primary Key	AC 8
Determining Data Types for the Fields	AC 9
Creating a Table	**AC 10**
To Modify the Primary Key	AC 11
To Define the Remaining Fields in a Table	AC 14
Making Changes to the Structure	AC 15
To Save a Table	AC 16
To View the Table in Design View	AC 17
Checking the Structure in Design View	AC 18
To Change a Field Size in Design View	AC 18
To Close the Table	AC 20
To Add Records to a Table	AC 20
Making Changes to the Data	AC 23
To Close a Table	AC 24
To Exit Access	AC 24
Starting Access and Opening a Database	AC 24
To Run Access	AC 25
To Open a Database from Access	AC 25
To Add Records to a Table that Contains Data	AC 26
To Resize Columns in a Datasheet	AC 28
Previewing and Printing the Contents of a Table	**AC 29**
To Preview and Print the Contents of a Table	AC 30
Importing or Linking Data from Other Applications to Access	**AC 32**
To Import an Excel Worksheet	AC 33
Modifying the Table	AC 37
To Modify a Table in Design View	AC 37
Correcting Errors in the Structure	AC 39
To Close the Table	AC 39
To Resize Columns in a Datasheet	AC 39
Additional Database Objects	**AC 40**
Creating Queries	AC 40
To Use the Simple Query Wizard to Create a Query	AC 40
Using Queries	AC 42
To Use a Criterion in a Query	AC 43
To Print the Results of a Query	AC 45
Creating and Using Forms	AC 45
To Create a Form	AC 45
Using a Form	AC 47
Creating and Printing Reports	AC 48
To Create a Report	AC 48
Using Layout View in a Report	AC 50
To Modify Report Column Headings and Resize Columns	AC 50
To Add Totals to a Report	AC 53
To Print a Report	AC 54
Database Properties	**AC 54**
To Sign Out of a Microsoft Account	AC 55
To Exit Access	AC 56
Special Database Operations	**AC 56**
Backup and Recovery	AC 56
Compacting and Repairing a Database	AC 57
Additional Operations	AC 57
Database Design	**AC 58**
Database Requirements	AC 58
Database Design Process	AC 60

Identifying the Tables AC 60
Determining the Primary Keys AC 60
Determining Additional Fields AC 61
Determining and Implementing
 Relationships Between the Tables AC 62
Determining Data Types for the Fields AC 62
Identifying and Removing Redundancy AC 62
Chapter Summary **AC 64**
Apply Your Knowledge **AC 65**
Extend Your Knowledge **AC 66**
Analyze, Correct, Improve **AC 67**
In the Labs **AC 68**
Consider This: Your Turn **AC 71**
Learn Online **AC 72**

CHAPTER TWO
Querying a Database
Objectives **AC 73**
Introduction **AC 74**
Project — Querying a Database **AC 74**
Roadmap AC 76
To Run Access AC 76
To Open a Database from Access AC 77
Creating Queries **AC 77**
To Create a Query in Design View AC 78
To Add Fields to the Design Grid AC 79
Determining Criteria AC 80
Running the Query AC 80
To Use Text Data in a Criterion AC 81
Using Saved Queries AC 82
Wildcards AC 83
To Use a Wildcard AC 83
To Use Criteria for a Field Not Included
 in the Results AC 85
Creating a Parameter Query AC 86
To Create and View a Parameter Query AC 87
To Use a Parameter Query AC 88
To Use a Number in a Criterion AC 89
Comparison Operators AC 89
To Use a Comparison Operator in
 a Criterion AC 90
Using Compound Criteria AC 91
To Use a Compound Criterion Involving AND AC 91
To Use a Compound Criterion Involving OR AC 92
Special Criteria AC 92

Sorting **AC 93**
To Clear the Design Grid AC 93
To Sort Data in a Query AC 94
To Omit Duplicates AC 94
To Sort on Multiple Keys AC 96
To Create a Top-Values Query AC 98
Joining Tables **AC 99**
To Join Tables AC 100
To Change Join Properties AC 101
To Create a Report from a Query AC 103
To Print a Report AC 105
Creating a Form for a Query **AC 105**
To Create a Form for a Query AC 105
Using a Form AC 107
**Exporting Data from Access to Other
 Applications** **AC 107**
To Export Data to Excel AC 107
Text Files AC 110
Adding Criteria to a Join Query **AC 111**
To Restrict the Records in a Join AC 111
Calculations **AC 112**
To Use a Calculated Field in a Query AC 112
To Change a Caption AC 114
To Calculate Statistics AC 115
To Use Criteria in Calculating Statistics AC 117
To Use Grouping AC 118
Crosstab Queries **AC 118**
To Create a Crosstab Query AC 119
Customizing the Navigation Pane **AC 121**
To Customize the Navigation Pane AC 122
To Sign Out of a Microsoft Account AC 123
To Exit Access AC 124
Chapter Summary **AC 124**
Apply Your Knowledge **AC 125**
Extend Your Knowledge **AC 127**
Analyze, Correct, Improve **AC 128**
In the Labs **AC 129**
Consider This: Your Turn **AC 133**
Learn Online **AC 135**

Index **IND 1**

Quick Reference Summary **QR 1**

Important Notes for Windows 7 Users **W7 1**

Preface

The Shelly Cashman Series® offers the finest textbooks in computer education. We are proud that since Microsoft Office 4.3, our series of Microsoft Office textbooks have been the most widely used books in education. With each new edition of our Office books, we make significant improvements based on the software and comments made by instructors and students. For this Microsoft Office 2013 text, the Shelly Cashman Series development team carefully reviewed our pedagogy and analyzed its effectiveness in teaching today's Office student. Students today read less, but need to retain more. They need not only to be able to perform skills, but to retain those skills and know how to apply them to different settings. Today's students need to be continually engaged and challenged to retain what they're learning.

With this Microsoft Office 2013 text, we continue our commitment to focusing on the users and how they learn best.

Objectives of This Textbook

Microsoft Office 2013: Brief is intended for a course that includes a brief introduction to Office 2013. No experience with a computer is assumed, and no mathematics beyond the high school freshman level is required. The objectives of this book are:

- To teach the fundamentals of Microsoft Windows 8, Microsoft Word 2013, Microsoft PowerPoint 2013, Microsoft Excel 2013, and Microsoft Access 2013
- To expose students to practical examples of the computer as a useful tool
- To acquaint students with the proper procedures to create documents, presentations, worksheets, and databases suitable for coursework, professional purposes, and personal use
- To help students discover the underlying functionality of Office 2013 so they can become more productive
- To develop an exercise-oriented approach that allows learning by doing

The Shelly Cashman Approach

A Proven Pedagogy with an Emphasis on Project Planning Each chapter presents a practical problem to be solved within a project planning framework. The project orientation is strengthened by the use of the Roadmap, which provides a visual framework for the project. Step-by-step instructions with supporting screens guide students through the steps. Instructional steps are supported by the Q&A, Experimental Step, and BTW features.

A Visually Engaging Book that Maintains Student Interest The step-by-step tasks, with supporting figures, provide a rich visual experience for the student. Call-outs on the screens that present both explanatory and navigational information provide students with information they need when they need to know it.

Supporting Reference Materials With the Quick Reference, students can quickly look up information about a single task, such as keyboard shortcuts, and find page references to where in the book the task is illustrated.

Integration of the World Wide Web The World Wide Web is integrated into the Office 2013 learning experience with (1) BTW annotations; (2) BTW, Q&A, and Quick Reference Summary Web pages; and (3) the Learn Online resources for each chapter.

End-of-Chapter Student Activities Extensive end-of-chapter activities provide a variety of reinforcement opportunities for students to apply and expand their skills through individual and group work. To complete some of these assignments, you will be required to use the Data Files for Students. Visit www.cengage.com/ct/studentdownload for detailed access instructions or contact your instructor for information about accessing the required files.

New to this Edition

Enhanced Coverage of Critical Thinking Skills A New Consider This element poses thought-provoking questions throughout each chapter, providing an increased emphasis on critical thinking and problem-solving skills. Also, every task in the project now includes a reason *why* the students are performing the task and *why* the task is necessary.

Enhanced Retention and Transference A new Roadmap element provides a visual framework for each project, showing students where they are in the process of creating each project, and reinforcing the context of smaller tasks by showing how they fit into the larger project.

Integration of Office with Cloud and Web Technologies A new Lab focuses entirely on integrating cloud and web technologies with Office 2013, using technologies like blogs, social networks, and SkyDrive.

More Personalization Each chapter project includes an optional instruction for the student to personalize his or her solution, if required by an instructor, making each student's solution unique.

More Collaboration A new Research and Collaboration project has been added to the Consider This: Your Turn assignment at the end of each chapter.

Instructor Resources

The Instructor Resources include both teaching and testing aids and can be accessed via CD-ROM or at www.cengage.com/login.

Instructor's Manual Includes lecture notes summarizing the chapter sections, figures and boxed elements found in every chapter, teacher tips, classroom activities, lab activities, and quick quizzes in Microsoft Word files.

Syllabus Easily customizable sample syllabi that cover policies, assignments, exams, and other course information.

Figure Files Illustrations for every figure in the textbook in electronic form.

Powerpoint Presentations A multimedia lecture presentation system that provides slides for each chapter. Presentations are based on chapter objectives.

Solutions to Exercises Includes solutions for all end-of-chapter and chapter reinforcement exercises.

Test Bank & Test Engine Test banks include 112 questions for every chapter, featuring objective-based and critical thinking question types, and including page number references and figure references, when appropriate. Also included is the test engine, Exam-View, the ultimate tool for your objective-based testing needs.

Data Files for Students Includes all the files that are required by students to complete the exercises.

Additional Activities for Students Consists of Chapter Reinforcement Exercises, which are true/false, multiple-choice, and short answer questions that help students gain confidence in the material learned.

Learn Online

CengageBrain.com is the premier destination for purchasing or renting Cengage Learning textbooks, eBooks, eChapters, and study tools at a significant discount (eBooks up to 50% off Print). In addition, CengageBrain.com provides direct access to all digital products, including eBooks, eChapters, and digital solutions, such as CourseMate and SAM, regardless of where purchased. The following are some examples of what is available for this product on www.cengagebrain.com.

Student Companion Site The Student Companion Site reinforces chapter terms and concepts using true/false questions, multiple choice questions, short answer questions, flash cards, practice tests, and learning games, all available for no additional cost at www.cengagebrain.com.

SAM: Skills Assessment Manager Get your students workplace-ready with SAM, the market-leading proficiency-based assessment and training solution for Microsoft Office! SAM's active, hands-on environment helps students master Microsoft Office skills and computer concepts that are essential to academic and career success, delivering the most comprehensive online learning solution for your course! Through skill-based assessments, interactive trainings, business-centric projects, and comprehensive remediation, SAM engages students in mastering the latest Microsoft Office programs on their own, giving instructors more time to focus on teaching. Computer concepts labs supplement instruction of important technology-related topics and issues through engaging simulations and interactive, auto-graded assessments. With enhancements including streamlined course setup, more robust grading and reporting features, and the integration of fully interactive MindTap Readers containing Cengage Learning's premier textbook content, SAM provides the best teaching and learning solution for your course.

MindLinks MindLinks is a new Cengage Learning Service designed to provide the best possible user experience and facilitate the highest levels of learning retention and outcomes, enabled through a deep integration of Cengage Learning's digital suite into an instructor's Learning Management System (LMS). MindLinks works on any LMS that supports the IMS Basic LTI open standard. Advanced features, including gradebook exchange, are the result of active, enhanced LTI collaborations with industry-leading LMS partners to drive the evolving technology standards forward.

CourseNotes

course|notes™
quick reference guide

Cengage Learning's CourseNotes are six-panel quick reference cards that reinforce the most important and widely used features of a software application in a visual and user-friendly format. CourseNotes serve as a great reference tool during and after the course. CourseNotes are available for software applications, such as Microsoft Office 2013. There are also topic-based CourseNotes available, such as Best Practices in Social Networking, Hot Topics in Technology, and Web 2.0. Visit www.cengagebrain.com to learn more!

Textbook Walk-Through

The Shelly Cashman Series Pedagogy: Project-Based — Step-by-Step — Variety of Assessments

Roadmaps provide a visual framework for each project, showing the students where they are in the process of creating each project.

Step-by-step instructions provide a context beyond the point-and-click. Each step provides information on why students are performing each task and what will occur as a result.

Explanatory callouts summarize what is happening on screen.

Navigational callouts in red show students where to click.

Consider This boxes pose thought-provoking questions with answers throughout each chapter, promoting critical thought along with immediate feedback.

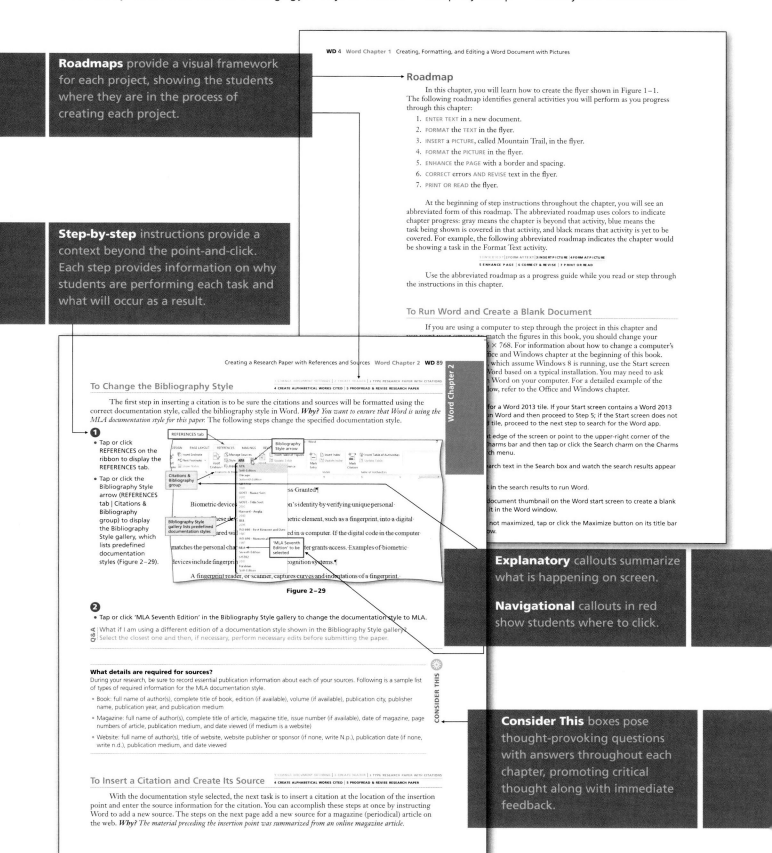

Consider This: **Plan Ahead** box presents a single master planning guide that students can use as they create documents on their own.

Apply Your Knowledge This exercise usually requires students to open and manipulate a file that parallels the activities learned in the chapter.

Chapter Summary A listing of the tasks completed within the chapter, grouped into major task categories in an outline format.

Databases and ...

Apply Your Knowledge

Reinforce the skills and apply the concepts you learne...

Adding a Caption, Changing a Data Type, Creating ...

Note: To complete this assignment, you will be required t... www.cengage.com/ct/studentdownload for detailed instru... mation about accessing the required files.

Instructions: Cosmetics Naturally Inc. manufactures and sells beauty and skin care products made with only natural ingredients. The company's products do not contain any synthetic chemicals, artificial fragrances, or chemical preservatives. Cosmetics Naturally has a database that keeps track of its sales representatives and customers. Each customer is assigned to a single sales rep, but each sales rep may be assigned to many customers. The database has two tables. The Customer table contains data on the customers who purchase Cosmetics Naturally products. The Sales Rep table contains data on the sales reps. You will add a caption, change a data type, create two queries, a form, and a report, as shown in Figure 1–83 on the next page.

Perform the following tasks:
1. Start Access, open the Apply Cosmetics Naturally database from the Data Files for Students, and enable the content.
2. Open the Sales Rep table in Datasheet view, add SR # as the caption for the Sales Rep Number field, and resize all columns to best fit the data. Save the changes to the layout of the table and close the table.
3. Open the Customer table in Design view and change the data type for the Postal Code field to Short Text. Change the field size for the field to 5. Save the changes to the table and close the table.
4. Use the Simple Query Wizard to create a query for the Customer table that contains the Customer Number, Customer Name, Amount Paid, Balance, and Sales Rep Number. The query is a detail query. Use the name Customer Query for the query and close the query.
5. Create a simple form for the Sales Rep table. Save the form and use the name Sales Rep for the form. Close the form.
6. Create the report shown in Figure 1–83 for the Customer table. The report includes totals for both the Amount Paid and Balance fields. Be sure the totals appear completely. You might need to expand the size of the total controls. Move the page number so that it is within the margins. Save the report as Customer Financial Report.
7. If requested by your instructor, add your last name to the title of the report, that is, change the title to Customer Financial Report LastName where LastName is your actual last name.
8. Compact and repair the database.
9. Submit the revised database in the format specified by your instructor.
10. ⊛ How would you change the field name of the Balance field in the Customer table to Current Balance?

Continued >

How should you submit solutions to questions in the ass...
a ⊛ symbol?
Every assignment in this book contains one or more questions identified...
you to think beyond the assigned database. Present your solutions to th...
instructor. Possible formats may include one or more of these options: ...
contains the answer; present your answer to the class; discuss your ans...
or video using a webcam, smartphone, or portable media player, or po...

Chapter Summary

In this chapter you have learned to create an Access database, create tables and add records to a database, print the contents of tables, import data, create queries, create reports, create forms, and change database properties. You also have learned how to design a database. The items listed below include all the new Access skills you have learned in this chapter, with tasks grouped by activity.

Report Creation
Create a Report (AC 48)
Modify Report Column Headings and Resize Columns (AC 50)
Add Totals to a Report (AC 53)
Print a Report (AC 54)

Query Creation
Use the Simple Query Wizard to Create a Query (AC 40)
Use a Criterion in a Query (AC 43)
Print the Results of a Query (AC 45)

Table Creation
Modify the Primary Key (AC 11)
Define the Remaining Fields in a Table (AC 14)
Save a Table (AC 16)
View the Table in Design View (AC 17)
Change a Field Size in Design View (AC 18)
Close the Table (AC 20)
Resize Columns in a Datasheet (AC 28)
Modify a Table in Design View (AC 37)

Table Update
Add Records to a Table (AC 20)
Add Records to a Table that Contains Data (AC 26)

Run Access (AC 5)

File Management
Create a Database (AC 6)
Create a Database Using a Template (AC 7)
Exit Access (AC 24)
Open a Database from Access (AC 25)
Back Up a Database (AC 56)
Compact and Repair a Database (AC 57)
Close a Database without Exiting Access (AC 57)
Save a Database with Another Name (AC 57)

Database Properties
Change Database Properties (AC 55)

Database Object Management
Rename an Object in the Database (AC 58)
Delete a Table or Other Object in the Database (AC 58)

Form Creation
Create a Form (AC 45)

Import Data
Import an Excel Worksheet (AC 33)

Print Objects
Preview and Print the Contents of a Table (AC 30)

⊛ **CONSIDER THIS**

What decisions will you need to make when creating your next database?
Use these guidelines as you complete the assignments in this chapter and create your own databases outside of this class.

1. Identify the tables that will be included in the database.
2. Determine the primary keys for each of the tables.
3. Determine the additional fields that should be included in each of the tables.
4. Determine relationships between the tables.
 a) Identify the "one" table.
 b) Identify the "many" table.
 c) Include the primary key of the "one" table as a field in the "many" table.
5. Determine data types for the fields in the tables.
6. Determine additional properties for fields.
 a) Determine if a special caption is warranted.
 b) Determine if a special description is warranted.
 c) Determine field sizes.
 d) Determine formats.
7. Identify and remove any unwanted redundancy.
8. Determine a storage location for the database.
9. Determine the best method for distributing the database objects.

Apply Your Knowledge *continued*

| Customer Financial Report | | | Monday, September 15, 2014 |
| | | | 9:24:56 PM |

Customer Number	Customer Name	Amount Paid	Balance	Sales Rep Number
AS24	Ashley's Salon	$1,789.65	$236.99	34
UR23	U R Beautiful	$0.00	$1,235.00	39
		$14,786.17	$5,617.78	

Figure 1–83

Extend Your Knowledge

Extend the skills you learned in this chapter and experiment with new skills. You may need to use Help to complete the assignment.

Using a Database Template to Create a Contacts Database

Note: To complete this assignment, you will be required to use the Data Files for Students. Visit www.cengage.com/ct/studentdownload for detailed instructions or contact your instructor for information about accessing the required files.

Instructions: Access includes both desktop database templates and web-based templates. You can use a template to create a beginning database that can be modified to meet your specific needs. You will use a template to create a Contacts database. The database template includes sample tables, queries, forms, and reports. You will modify the database and create the Contacts Query shown in Figure 1–84.

Perform the following tasks:

1. Start Access.

2. Select the Desktop contacts template in the temp[late] file name Extend Contacts.

3. Enable the content. If requested to do so by your Started with Contacts dialog box. Close the Gett[ing]

4. Close the Contact List form.

5. Open the Contacts table in Datasheet view and d[elete] Attachments field in the table. The Attachments

6. Change the data type for the ID field to Short Te[xt] and change the field size to 4. Change the colum[n] displayed.

7. Save the changes to the Contacts table and close

8. Use the Simple Query Wizard to create the Con[tacts] query.

Figure 1[–84]

9. Open the Phone Book report in Layout view. Delete the control containing the date. Change the title of the report to Contact Phone List.

10. Save the changes to the report.

11. If requested to do so by your instructor, add your first and last names to the end of the title and save the changes to the report.

12. Submit the revised database in the format specified by your instructor.

13. a. Why would you use a template instead of creating a database from scratch with just the fields you need?

 b. The Attachment data type allows you to attach files to a database record. If you were using this database for a job search, what specific documents might you attach to a Contacts record?

Analyze, Correct, Improve

Analyze a database, correct all errors, and improve the design.

Correcting Errors in the Table Structure

Note: To complete this assignment, you will be required to use the Data Files for Students. Visit www.cengage.com/ct/studentdownload for detailed instructions or contact your instructor for information about accessing the required files.

Instructions: Analyze SciFi Movies is a database containing information on classic science fiction movies that your film professor would like to use for teaching. The Movie table shown in Figure 1–85 contains errors to the table structure. Your professor has asked you to correct the errors and make some improvements to the database. Start Access and open the Analyze SciFi Movies database from the Data Files for Students.

Figure 1–85

1. Correct Movie Number should be the primary key for the Movie table. The ID field should not be a field in the table. The Rating field represents a numerical rating system of one to four to indicate the quality of the movie. Your instructor wants to be able to find the average rating for films directed by a particular director. Only integers should be stored in both the Rating and the Length (Minutes) fields.

2. Improve The default field size for Short Text fields is 255. Changing the field size to more accurately represent the maximum number of characters that can be stored in a field is one way to improve the accuracy of the data. The Movie Number, Director Number, and Awards fields should have a maximum size of 3 characters. The Year Made field should have a maximum field size of 4. The Movie Name and Studio fields should have a maximum field size of 50. If instructed to do so by your instructor, rename the Movie table as Movie Last Name where Last Name is your last name. Submit the revised database in the format specified by your instructor.

3. The Awards field currently has a data type of Short Text, but the only values that will be stored in that field are Yes and No to indicate whether the movie won any awards. What would be a more appropriate data type for this field?

✳ Consider This: Your Turn

Apply your creative thinking and problem solving skills to design and implement a solution.

Note: To complete these assignments, you may be required to use the Data Files for Students. Visit www.cengage.com/ct/studentdownload for detailed instructions or contact your instructor for information about accessing the required files.

Personal

1: Design and Create a Photography Club Flyer

Part 1: As secretary of your school's Photography Club, you are responsible for creating and distributing flyers announcing the club. The flyer should contain two digital pictures appropriately resized; the Data Files for Students contains two pictures called Photography 1 and Photography 2, or you can use your own digital pictures if they are appropriate for the topic of the flyer. The flyer should contain the headline, Photography Club, and this signature line: Questions? Call Emily at (883) 555-0901. The body copy consists of the following text, in any order: Do you love photography? This is the club for you! All skill levels are welcome. Meetings every Tuesday at 5:00 p.m. in the Student Center (room 232). Bring your camera. We look forward to seeing you at our next meeting!

Use the concepts and techniques presented in this chapter to create and format this flyer. Be sure to check spelling and grammar. Submit your assignment and answers to the critical thinking questions in the format specified by your instructor.

Part 2: 🔄 You made several decisions while creating the flyer in this assignment: where to place text, how to format the text (i.e., font, font size, paragraph alignment, bulleted paragraphs, underlines, italics, bold, color, etc.), which graphics to use, where to position the graphics, how to format the graphics, and which page enhancements to add (i.e., borders and spacing). What was the rationale behind each of these decisions? When you proofread the document, what further revisions did you make and why? How would you recommend distributing this flyer?

Professional

2: Design and Create a Hot Air Balloon Rides Flyer

Part 1: As a part-time employee at Galaxy Recreations, your boss has asked you to create and distribute flyers announcing hot air balloon rides. The flyer should contain two digital pictures appropriately resized; the Data Files for Students contains two pictures called Hot Air Balloon 1 and Hot Air Balloon 2, or you can use your own digital pictures if they are appropriate for the topic of the flyer. The flyer should contain the headline, Hot Air Balloon Rides, and this signature line: For reservations, call (485) 555-2295. The body copy consists of the following text, in any order: Amazing sights from incredible heights! The experience of a lifetime. Fun for the whole family. No pets. Bring your camera. Open seven days a week from 10:00 a.m. to 4:00 p.m. Book your private tour with Galaxy Recreations today!

Use the concepts and techniques presented in this chapter to create and format this flyer. Be sure to check spelling and grammar. Submit your assignment in the format specified by your instructor.

Part 2: 🔄 You made several decisions while creating the flyer in this assignment: where to place text, how to format the text (i.e., font, font size, paragraph alignment, bulleted paragraphs, underlines, italics, bold, color, etc.), which graphics to use, where to position the graphics, how to format the graphics, and which page enhancements to add (i.e., borders and spacing). What was the rationale behind each of these decisions? When you proofread the document, what further revisions did you make and why? How would you recommend distributing this flyer?

< Continued >

Table 1–6 Data for Service Rep Table

Service Rep Number	Last Name	First Name	Street	City
21	Kelly	Jenna	25 Paint St.	Kyle
45	Scott	Josh	1925 Pine Rd.	Byron
24	Liu	Mia	265 Marble Dr.	Kyle
37	Martinez	Mike	31 Steel St.	Georgetown

Instructions: Perform the following tasks:

1. Start Access and open the Lab 1 Dart Offsite Se...
2. Open the Service Rep table in Datasheet view a... the table. The field has the Currency data type. Number field.
3. Add the records shown in Table 1–6.
4. Resize the columns to best fit the data. Save the

Note: To complete this assignment, you will be required to use the Data Files for Students. Visit www.cengage.com/ct/studentdownload for detailed information about accessing the required files.

Lab 1: Creating Objects for the Dart Offsite Services Database

Problem: Dart Offsite Services is a local company that provides offsite data services and solutions. The company provides remote data backup, disaster recovery planning and services, website backup, and offsite storage of paper documents for small businesses and nonprofit organizations. Service representatives are responsible for communicating data solutions to the client, scheduling backups and other tasks, and resolving any conflicts. The company recently decided to store its client and service rep data in a database. Each client is assigned to a single service rep, but each service rep may be assigned many clients. The database and the Service Rep table have been created, but the Monthly Salary field needs to be added to the table. The records shown in Table 1–6 must be added to the Service Rep table. The company plans to import the Client table from the Excel worksheet shown in Figure 1–86. Dart would like to finish storing this data in a database and has asked you to help.

	A	B	C	D	E	F	G	H	I	J	K
1	Client Number	Client Name	Street	City	State	Postal Code	Amount Paid	Balance Due	Service Rep Number		
2	889J2	Bavant CPA Firm	464 Linwood Dr.	Austin	SC	28796	$1,526.00	$2,565.24			
15	WEG03	Weiburg Beverly Company	12 Polk St.	Weiburg	NC	28819	$1,200.00	$3,567.45			
16	WSC01	Wood Sports Complex	578 Central Ave.	Weiburg	NC	28819	$1,600.00	$2,250.00			

Figure 1–86

In the Labs

Design, create, modify, and/or use a database following the guidelines, concepts, and skills presented in this chapter. Labs are listed in order of increasing difficulty. Labs 1 and 2, which increase in difficulty, require you to create solutions based on what you learned in the chapter; Lab 3 requires you to create a solution, which uses cloud and web technologies, by learning and investigating on your own from general guidance.

Office 2013 and Windows 8: Essential Concepts and Skills

Microsoft product screen shots used with permission from Microsoft Corporation.

Objectives

You will have mastered the material in this chapter when you can:

- Use a touch screen
- Perform basic mouse operations
- Start Windows and sign in to an account
- Identify the objects in the Windows 8 desktop
- Identify the apps in and versions of Microsoft Office 2013
- Run an app
- Identify the components of the Microsoft Office ribbon

- Create folders
- Save files
- Change screen resolution
- Perform basic tasks in Microsoft Office apps
- Manage files
- Use Microsoft Office Help and Windows Help

Office 2013 and Windows 8: Essential Concepts and Skills

This introductory chapter covers features and functions common to Office 2013 apps, as well as the basics of Windows 8.

Roadmap

In this chapter, you will learn how to perform basic tasks in Windows and the Office apps. The following roadmap identifies general activities you will perform as you progress through this chapter:

1. SIGN IN to an account
2. USE WINDOWS
3. USE Office APPS
4. FILE and Folder MANAGEMENT
5. SWITCH between APPS
6. SAVE and Manage FILES
7. CHANGE SCREEN RESOLUTION
8. EXIT Office APPS
9. USE ADDITIONAL Office APPS
10. USE Office and Windows HELP

At the beginning of the step instructions throughout the chapter, you will see an abbreviated form of this roadmap. The abbreviated roadmap uses colors to indicate chapter progress: gray means the chapter is beyond that activity, blue means the task being shown is covered in that activity, and black means that activity is yet to be covered. For example, the following abbreviated roadmap indicates the chapter would be showing a task in the Use Apps activity.

1 SIGN IN | 2 USE WINDOWS | 3 USE APPS | 4 FILE MANAGEMENT | 5 SWITCH APPS | 6 SAVE FILES
7 CHANGE SCREEN RESOLUTION | 8 EXIT APPS | 9 USE ADDITIONAL APPS | 10 USE HELP

Use the abbreviated roadmap as a progress guide while you read or step through the instructions in this chapter.

Introduction to the Windows 8 Operating System

Windows 8 is the newest version of Microsoft Windows, which is a popular and widely used operating system. An **operating system** is a computer program (set of computer instructions) that coordinates all the activities of computer hardware,

such as memory, storage devices, and printers, and provides the capability for you to communicate with the computer.

The Windows operating system simplifies the process of working with documents and apps by organizing the manner in which you interact with the computer. Windows is used to run apps. An **app** (short for application) consists of programs designed to make users more productive and/or assist them with personal tasks, such as word processing or browsing the web.

The Windows 8 interface begins with the **Start screen**, which shows tiles (Figure 1). A **tile** is a shortcut to an app or other content. The tiles on the Start screen include installed apps that you use regularly. From the Start screen, you can choose which apps to run using a touch screen, mouse, or other input device.

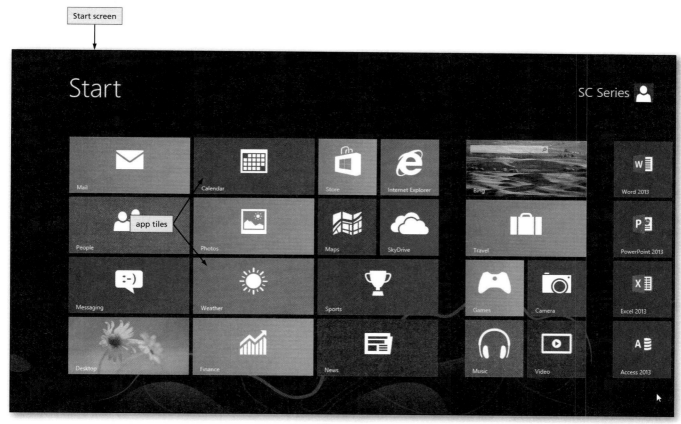

Figure 1

Using a Touch Screen and a Mouse

Windows users who have computers or devices with touch screen capability can interact with the screen using gestures. A **gesture** is a motion you make on a touch screen with the tip of one or more fingers or your hand. Touch screens are convenient because they do not require a separate device for input. Table 1 on the next page presents common ways to interact with a touch screen.

If you are using your finger on a touch screen and are having difficulty completing the steps in this chapter, consider using a stylus. Many people find it easier to be precise with a stylus than with a finger. In addition, with a stylus you see the pointer. If you still are having trouble completing the steps with a stylus, try using a mouse.

Table 1 Touch Screen Gestures

Motion	Description	Common Uses
Tap	Quickly touch and release one finger one time.	Activate a link (built-in connection) Press a button Run a program or an app
Double-tap	Quickly touch and release one finger two times.	Run a program or an app Zoom in (show a smaller area on the screen, so that contents appear larger) at the location of the double-tap
Press and hold	Press and hold one finger to cause an action to occur, or until an action occurs.	Display a shortcut menu (immediate access to allowable actions) Activate a mode enabling you to move an item with one finger to a new location
Drag, or slide	Press and hold one finger on an object and then move the finger to the new location.	Move an item around the screen Scroll
Swipe	Press and hold one finger and then move the finger horizontally or vertically on the screen.	Select an object Swipe from edge to display a bar such as the Charms bar, Apps bar, and Navigation bar (all discussed later)
Stretch	Move two fingers apart.	Zoom in (show a smaller area on the screen, so that contents appear larger)
Pinch	Move two fingers together.	Zoom out (show a larger area on the screen, so that contents appear smaller)

© 2014 Cengage Learning

BTW

BTWs

For a complete list of the BTWs found in the margins of this book, visit the BTW resource on the Student Companion Site located on www.cengagebrain.com. For detailed instructions about accessing available resources, visit www.cengage.com/ct/studentdownload or contact your instructor for information about accessing the required files.

BTW

Touch Screen Differences

The Office and Windows interfaces may vary if you are using a touch screen. For this reason, you might notice that the function or appearance of your touch screen differs slightly from this chapter's presentation.

CONSIDER THIS

Will your screen look different if you are using a touch screen?

The Windows and Microsoft Office interface varies slightly if you are using a touch screen. For this reason, you might notice that your screen looks slightly different from the screens in this chapter.

Windows users who do not have touch screen capabilities typically work with a mouse that has at least two buttons. For a right-handed user, the left button usually is the primary mouse button, and the right mouse button is the secondary mouse button. Left-handed people, however, can reverse the function of these buttons.

Table 2 explains how to perform a variety of mouse operations. Some apps also use keys in combination with the mouse to perform certain actions. For example, when you hold down the CTRL key while rolling the mouse wheel, text on the screen may become larger or smaller based on the direction you roll the wheel. The function of the mouse buttons and the wheel varies depending on the app.

Table 2 Mouse Operations

Operation	Mouse Action	Example*
Point	Move the mouse until the pointer on the desktop is positioned on the item of choice.	Position the pointer on the screen.
Click	Press and release the primary mouse button, which usually is the left mouse button.	Select or deselect items on the screen or run an app or app feature.
Right-click	Press and release the secondary mouse button, which usually is the right mouse button.	Display a shortcut menu.
Double-click	Quickly press and release the primary mouse button twice without moving the mouse.	Run an app or app feature.
Triple-click	Quickly press and release the primary mouse button three times without moving the mouse.	Select a paragraph.
Drag	Point to an item, hold down the primary mouse button, move the item to the desired location on the screen, and then release the mouse button.	Move an object from one location to another or draw pictures.
Right-drag	Point to an item, hold down the right mouse button, move the item to the desired location on the screen, and then release the right mouse button.	Display a shortcut menu after moving an object from one location to another.
Rotate wheel	Roll the wheel forward or backward.	Scroll vertically (up and down).
Free-spin wheel	Whirl the wheel forward or backward so that it spins freely on its own.	Scroll through many pages in seconds.
Press wheel	Press the wheel button while moving the mouse.	Scroll continuously.
Tilt wheel	Press the wheel toward the right or left.	Scroll horizontally (left and right).
Press thumb button	Press the button on the side of the mouse with your thumb.	Move forward or backward through webpages and/or control media, games, etc.

*Note: The examples presented in this column are discussed as they are demonstrated in this chapter.

© 2014 Cengage Learning

Scrolling

A **scroll bar** is a horizontal or vertical bar that appears when the contents of an area may not be visible completely on the screen (Figure 2). A scroll bar contains **scroll arrows** and a **scroll box** that enable you to view areas that currently cannot be seen on the screen. Tapping or clicking the up and down scroll arrows moves the screen content up or down one line. You also can tap or click above or below the scroll box to move up or down a section, or drag the scroll box up or down to move to a specific location.

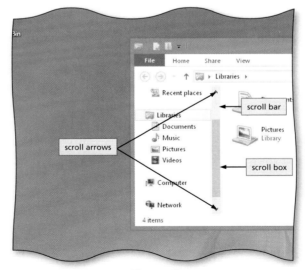

Figure 2

BTW

Pointer

If you are using a touch screen, the pointer may not appear on the screen as you perform touch gestures. The pointer will reappear when you begin using the mouse.

BTW

Minimize Wrist Injury

Computer users frequently switch between the keyboard and the mouse during a word processing session; such switching strains the wrist. To help prevent wrist injury, minimize switching. For instance, if your fingers already are on the keyboard, use keyboard keys to scroll. If your hand already is on the mouse, use the mouse to scroll. If your hand is on the touch screen, use touch gestures to scroll.

What should you do if you are running Windows 7 instead of Windows 8?

Although Windows 8 includes several user interface and feature enhancements, many of the steps in this chapter work in both Windows 7 and Windows 8. If you have any questions about differences between the two operating systems or how to perform tasks in an earlier version of Windows, contact your instructor.

CONSIDER THIS

Keyboard Shortcuts

In many cases, you can use the keyboard instead of the mouse to accomplish a task. To perform tasks using the keyboard, you press one or more keyboard keys, sometimes identified as a **keyboard shortcut**. Some keyboard shortcuts consist of a single key, such as the F1 key. For example, to obtain help in many apps, you can press the F1 key. Other keyboard shortcuts consist of multiple keys, in which case a plus sign separates the key names, such as CTRL+ESC. This notation means to press and hold down the first key listed, press one or more additional keys, and then release all keys. For example, to display the Start screen, press CTRL+ESC, that is, hold down the CTRL key, press the ESC key, and then release both keys.

Starting Windows

It is not unusual for multiple people to use the same computer in a work, educational, recreational, or home setting. Windows enables each user to establish a **user account**, which identifies to Windows the resources, such as apps and storage locations, a user can access when working with the computer.

Each user account has a user name and may have a password and an icon, as well. A **user name** is a unique combination of letters or numbers that identifies a specific user to Windows. A **password** is a private combination of letters, numbers, and special characters associated with the user name that allows access to a user's account resources. An icon is a small image that represents an object, thus a **user icon** is a picture associated with a user name.

When you turn on a computer, Windows starts and displays a **lock screen** consisting of the time and date (Figure 3a). To unlock the screen, swipe up or click the lock screen. Depending on your computer's settings, Windows may or may not display a sign-in screen that shows the user names and user icons for users who have accounts on the computer (Figure 3b). This **sign-in screen** enables you to sign in to your user account and makes the computer available for use. Tapping or clicking the user icon begins the process of signing in, also called logging on, to your user account.

At the bottom of the sign-in screen is the 'Ease of access' button and a Shut down button. Tapping or clicking the 'Ease of access' button displays the Ease of access menu, which provides tools to optimize a computer to accommodate the needs of the mobility, hearing, and vision impaired users. Tapping or clicking the Shut down

Figure 3a

Figure 3b

button displays a menu containing commands related to restarting the computer, putting it in a low-power state, and shutting it down. The commands available on your computer may differ.

- The Sleep command saves your work, turns off the computer fans and hard disk, and places the computer in a lower-power state. To wake the computer from sleep mode, press the power button or lift a laptop's cover, and sign in to your account.
- The Shut down command exits running apps, shuts down Windows, and then turns off the computer.
- The Restart command exits running apps, shuts down Windows, and then restarts Windows.

BTW
Q&As
For a complete list of the Q&As found in many of the step-by-step sequences in this book, visit the Q&A resource on the Student Companion Site located on www.cengagebrain.com. For detailed instructions about accessing available resources, visit www.cengage.com/ct/studentdownload or contact your instructor for information about accessing the required files.

1 SIGN IN │ 2 USE WINDOWS │ 3 USE APPS │ 4 FILE MANAGEMENT │ 5 SWITCH APPS │ 6 SAVE FILES
7 CHANGE SCREEN RESOLUTION │ 8 EXIT APPS │ 9 USE ADDITIONAL APPS │ 10 USE HELP

To Sign In to an Account

The following steps, which use SC Series as the user name, sign in to an account based on a typical Windows installation. *Why? After starting Windows, you might be required to sign in to an account to access the computer's resources.* You may need to ask your instructor how to sign in to your account. If you are using Windows 7, skip these steps and instead perform the steps in the yellow box that immediately follows these Windows 8 steps.

1

- Swipe up or click the lock screen (shown in Figure 3a) to display a sign-in screen (shown in Figure 3b).

- Tap or click the user icon (for SC Series, in this case) on the sign-in screen, which depending on settings, either will display a second sign-in screen that contains a Password text box (Figure 4) or will display the Windows Start screen (shown in Figure 5 on the next page).

Q&A

Why do I not see a user icon?
Your computer may require you to type a user name instead of tapping or clicking an icon.

What is a text box?
A text box is a rectangular box in which you type text.

Why does my screen not show a Password text box?
Your account does not require a password.

Figure 4

- If Windows displays a sign-in screen with a Password text box, type your password in the text box.

2

- Tap or click the Submit button (shown in Figure 4 on the previous page) to sign in to your account and display the Windows Start screen (Figure 5).

Q&A

Why does my Start screen look different from the one in Figure 5? The Windows Start screen is customizable, and your school or employer may have modified the screen to meet its needs. Also, your screen resolution, which affects the size of the elements on the screen, may differ from the screen resolution used in this book. Later in this chapter, you learn how to change screen resolution.

Figure 5

How do I type if my tablet has no keyboard?
You can use your fingers to press keys on a keyboard that appears on the screen, called an on-screen keyboard, or you can purchase a separate physical keyboard that attaches to or wirelessly communicates with the tablet.

TO SIGN IN TO AN ACCOUNT USING WINDOWS 7

If you are using Windows 7, perform these steps to sign in to an account instead of the previous steps that use Windows 8.

1. Click the user icon on the Welcome screen; depending on settings, this either will display a password text box or will sign in to the account and display the Windows 7 desktop.

2. If Windows 7 displays a password text box, type your password in the text box and then click the arrow button to sign in to the account and display the Windows 7 desktop.

The Windows Start Screen

The Windows Start screen provides a scrollable space for you to access apps that have been pinned to the Start screen (shown in Figure 5). Pinned apps appear as tiles on the Start screen. In addition to running apps, you can perform tasks such as pinning apps (placing tiles) on the Start screen, moving the tiles around the Start screen, and unpinning apps (removing tiles) from the Start screen.

If you swipe up from the bottom of or right-click an open space on the Start screen, the App bar will appear. The **App bar** includes a button that enables you to display all of your apps. When working with tiles, the App bar also provides options for manipulating the tiles, such as resizing them.

CONSIDER THIS

How do you pin apps, move tiles, and unpin apps?

- To pin an app, swipe up from the bottom of the Start screen or right-click an open space on the Start screen to display the App bar, tap or click the All apps button on the App bar to display the Apps list, swipe down on or right-click the app you want to pin, and then tap or click the 'Pin to Start' button on the App bar. One way to return to the Start screen is to swipe up from the bottom or right-click an open space in the Apps list and then tap or click the All apps button again.

- To move a tile, drag the tile to the desired location.

- To unpin an app, swipe down on or right-click the app to display the App bar and then tap or click the 'Unpin from Start' button on the App bar.

Introduction to Microsoft Office 2013

Microsoft Office 2013 is the newest version of Microsoft Office, offering features that provide users with better functionality and easier ways to work with the various files they create. These features include enhanced design tools, such as improved picture formatting tools and new themes, shared notebooks for working in groups, mobile versions of Office apps, broadcast presentations for the web, and a digital notebook for managing and sharing multimedia information.

Microsoft Office 2013 Apps

Microsoft Office 2013 includes a wide variety of apps such as Word, PowerPoint, Excel, Access, Outlook, Publisher, OneNote, InfoPath, SharePoint Workspace, and Lync:

- **Microsoft Word 2013**, or Word, is a full-featured word processing app that allows you to create professional-looking documents and revise them easily.

- **Microsoft PowerPoint 2013**, or PowerPoint, is a complete presentation app that enables you to produce professional-looking presentations and then deliver them to an audience.

- **Microsoft Excel 2013**, or Excel, is a powerful spreadsheet app that allows you to organize data, complete calculations, make decisions, graph data, develop professional-looking reports, publish organized data to the web, and access real-time data from websites.

- **Microsoft Access 2013**, or Access, is a database management system that enables you to create a database; add, change, and delete data in the database; ask questions concerning the data in the database; and create forms and reports using the data in the database.

- **Microsoft Outlook 2013**, or Outlook, is a communications and scheduling app that allows you to manage email accounts, calendars, contacts, and access to other Internet content.

- **Microsoft Publisher 2013**, or Publisher, is a desktop publishing app that helps you create professional-quality publications and marketing materials that can be shared easily.

- **Microsoft OneNote 2013**, or OneNote, is a note taking app that allows you to store and share information in notebooks with other people.

- **Microsoft InfoPath Designer 2013**, or InfoPath, is a form development app that helps you create forms for use on the web and gather data from these forms.

- **Microsoft SharePoint Workspace 2013**, or SharePoint, is a collaboration app that allows you to access and revise files stored on your computer from other locations.

- **Microsoft Lync 2013** is a communications app that allows you to use various modes of communications such as instant messaging, videoconferencing, and sharing files and apps.

Microsoft Office 2013 Suites

A **suite** is a collection of individual apps available together as a unit. Microsoft offers a variety of Office suites, including a stand-alone desktop app (boxed software), Microsoft Office 365, and Microsoft Office Web Apps. **Microsoft Office 365**, or Office 365, provides plans that allow organizations to use Office in a mobile setting while also being able to communicate and share files, depending upon the type of plan selected by the organization. **Microsoft Office Web Apps**, or Web Apps, are apps that allow you to edit and share files on the web using the familiar Office interface. Table 3 on the next page outlines the differences among these Office suites.

Table 3 Office Suites					
Apps/ Licenses	Office 365 Home Premium	Office 365 Small Business Premium	Office Home & Student	Office Home & Business	Office Professional
Word	✔	✔	✔	✔	✔
PowerPoint	✔	✔	✔	✔	✔
Excel	✔	✔	✔	✔	✔
Access	✔	✔			✔
Outlook	✔	✔		✔	✔
Publisher	✔	✔			✔
Lync		✔			
OneNote			✔	✔	✔
InfoPath		✔			
Licenses	5	5	1	1	1

© 2014 Cengage Learning

During the Office 365 installation, you select a plan, and depending on your plan, you receive different apps and services. Office Web Apps do not require a local installation and are accessed through SkyDrive and your browser. **SkyDrive** is a cloud storage service that provides storage and other services, such as Office Web Apps, to computer users.

CONSIDER THIS

How do you sign up for a SkyDrive account?

• Use your browser to navigate to skydrive.live.com.

• Create a Microsoft account by tapping or clicking the 'Sign up now' link and then entering your information to create the account.

• Sign in to SkyDrive using your new account or use it in Office to save your files on SkyDrive.

Apps in a suite, such as Microsoft Office, typically use a similar interface and share features. Once you are comfortable working with the elements and the interface and performing tasks in one app, the similarity can help you apply the knowledge and skills you have learned to another app(s) in the suite. For example, the process for saving a file in Word is the same in PowerPoint, Excel, and the other Office apps. While briefly showing how to use several Office apps, this chapter illustrates some of the common functions across the apps and identifies the characteristics unique to these apps.

Running and Using an App

To use an app, you must instruct the operating system to run the app. Windows provides many different ways to run an app, one of which is presented in this section (other ways to run an app are presented throughout this chapter). After an app is running, you can use it to perform a variety of tasks. The following pages use Word to discuss some elements of the Office interface and to perform tasks that are common to other Office apps.

Word

Word is a full-featured word processing app that allows you to create many types of personal and business documents, including flyers, letters, memos, resumes, reports, fax cover sheets, mailing labels, and newsletters. Word also provides tools that enable you to create webpages and save these webpages directly on a web server. Word has many features designed to simplify the production of documents and add visual appeal. Using Word, you easily can change the shape, size, and color of text. You also can include borders, shading, tables, images, pictures, charts, and web addresses in documents.

To Run an App from the Start Screen

The Start screen contains tiles that allow you to run apps, some of which may be stored on your computer. *Why? When you install an app, for example, tiles are added to the Start screen for the various Office apps included in the suite.*

The following steps, which assume Windows is running, use the Start screen to run an Office app based on a typical installation. You may need to ask your instructor how to run an Office app on your computer. Although the steps illustrate running the Word app, the steps to run any Office app are similar. If you are using Windows 7, skip these steps and instead perform the steps in the yellow box that immediately follows these Windows 8 steps.

1

- If necessary, scroll to display the Word tile on the Start screen (Figure 6).

Q&A Why does my Start screen look different?
It may look different because of your computer's configuration. The Start screen may be customized for several reasons, such as usage requirements or security restrictions.

What if the app I want to run is not on the Start screen?
You can display all installed apps by swiping up from the bottom of the Start screen or right-clicking an open space on the Start screen and then tapping or clicking the All apps button on the App bar.

How do I scroll on a touch screen?
Use the slide gesture; that is, press and hold your finger on the screen and then move your finger in the direction you wish to scroll.

Figure 6

2

- Tap or click the Word 2013 tile to run the Word app and display the Word start screen (Figure 7).

Figure 7

3

- Tap or click the Blank document thumbnail on the Word start screen to create a blank Word document in the Word window (Figure 8).

Q&A

What happens when you run an app?

Some apps provide a means for you to create a blank document, as shown in Figure 7 on the previous page; others immediately display a blank document in an app window, such as the Word window shown in Figure 8. A **window** is a rectangular area that displays data and information. The top of a window has a **title bar**, which is a horizontal space that contains the window's name.

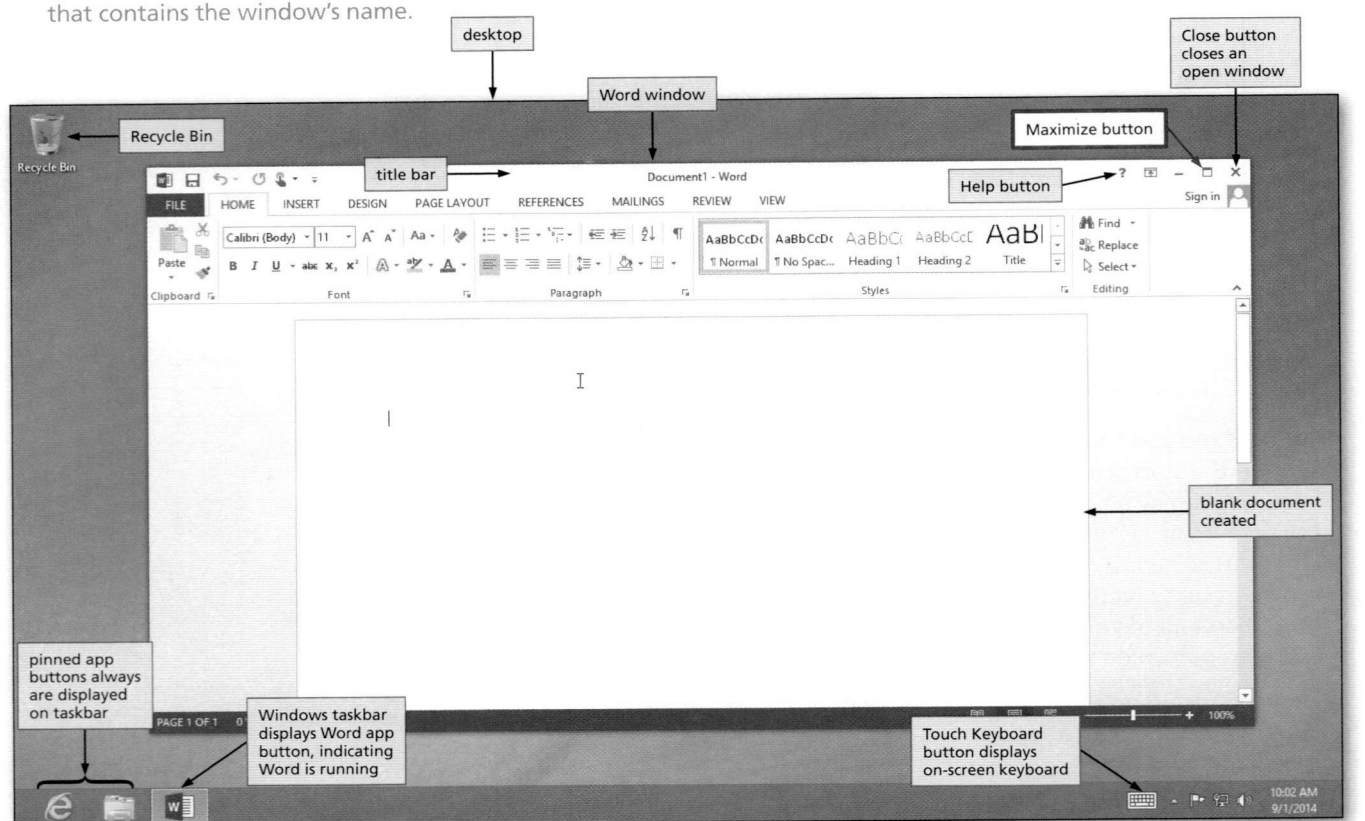

Figure 8

Other Ways

1. Tap or click Search charm on Charms bar, type app name in search box, tap or click app name in results list
2. Double-tap or double-click file created in app you want to run

TO RUN AN APP USING THE START MENU USING WINDOWS 7

BTW

Touch Keyboard
To display the on-screen touch keyboard, tap the Touch Keyboard button on the Windows taskbar. When finished using the touch keyboard, tap the X button on the touch keyboard to close the keyboard.

If you are using Windows 7, perform these steps to run an app using the Start menu instead of the previous steps that use Windows 8.

1. Click the Start button on the Windows 7 taskbar to display the Start menu.
2. Click All Programs at the bottom of the left pane on the Start menu to display the All Programs list.
3. If the app you wish to start is located in a folder, click, or scroll to and then click, the folder in the All Programs list to display a list of the folder's contents.
4. Click, or scroll to and then click, the app name in the list to run the selected app.

Windows Desktop

When you run an app in Windows, it may appear in an on-screen work area app, called the **desktop** (shown in Figure 8). You can perform tasks such as placing objects in the desktop, moving the objects around the desktop, and removing items from the desktop.

Some icons also may be displayed in the desktop. For instance, the icon for the **Recycle Bin**, the location of files that have been deleted, appears in the desktop by default. A **file** is a named unit of storage. Files can contain text, images, audio, and video. You can customize your desktop so that icons representing apps and files you use often appear in the desktop.

To Switch between an App and the Start Screen

1 SIGN IN | 2 USE WINDOWS | 3 USE APPS | 4 FILE MANAGEMENT | 5 SWITCH APPS | 6 SAVE FILES
7 CHANGE SCREEN RESOLUTION | 8 EXIT APPS | 9 USE ADDITIONAL APPS | 10 USE HELP

While working with an app or in the desktop, you easily can return to the Start screen. The following steps switch from the desktop to the Start screen. *Why? Returning to the Start screen allows you to run any of your other apps.* If you are using Windows 7, read these steps without performing them because Windows 7 does not have a Start screen.

- Swipe in from the left edge of the screen, and then back to the left, or point to the lower-left corner of the desktop to display a thumbnail of the Start screen (Figure 9).

Figure 9

- Tap or click the thumbnail of the Start screen to display the Start screen (Figure 10).

- Tap or click the Desktop tile to redisplay the desktop (shown in Figure 8).

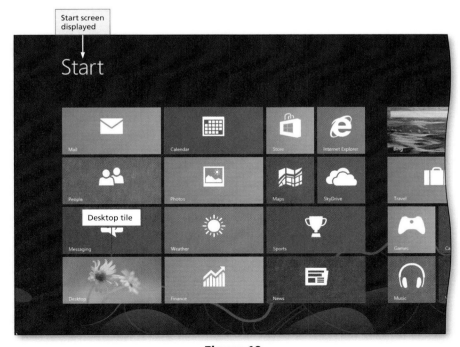

Figure 10

Other Ways

1. Press WINDOWS key to display Start screen

To Maximize a Window

Sometimes content is not visible completely in a window. One method of displaying the entire contents of a window is to **maximize** it, or enlarge the window so that it fills the entire screen. The following step maximizes the Word window; however, any Office app's window can be maximized using this step. *Why? A maximized window provides the most space available for using the app.*

1

- If the app window is not maximized already, tap or click the Maximize button (shown in Figure 8 on page OFF 12) next to the Close button on the window's title bar (the Word window title bar, in this case) to maximize the window (Figure 11).

Figure 11

Q&A

What happened to the Maximize button?
It changed to a Restore Down button, which you can use to return a window to its size and location before you maximized it.

How do I know whether a window is maximized?
A window is maximized if it fills the entire display area and the Restore Down button is displayed on the title bar.

Other Ways

1. Double-tap or double-click title bar 2. Drag title bar to top of screen

Word Document Window, Ribbon, and Elements Common to Office Apps

The Word window consists of a variety of components to make your work more efficient and documents more professional. These include the document window, ribbon, mini toolbar, shortcut menus, Quick Access Toolbar, and Microsoft Account area. Most of these components are common to other Microsoft Office apps; others are unique to Word.

You view a portion of a document on the screen through a **document window** (Figure 12). The default (preset) view is **Print Layout view**, which shows the document on a mock sheet of paper in the document window.

Scroll Bars You use a scroll bar to display different portions of a document in the document window. At the right edge of the document window is a vertical scroll bar. If a document is too wide to fit in the document window, a horizontal scroll bar also appears at the bottom of the document window. On a scroll bar, the position of the scroll box reflects the location of the portion of the document that is displayed in the document window.

Status Bar The **status bar**, located at the bottom of the document window above the Windows taskbar, presents information about the document, the progress of current tasks, and the status of certain commands and keys; it also provides controls for viewing the document. As you type text or perform certain tasks, various indicators and buttons may appear on the status bar.

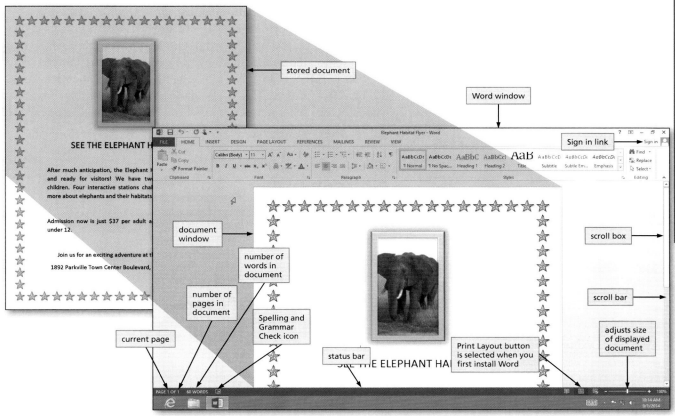

Figure 12

The left side of the status bar in Figure 12 shows the current page followed by the total number of pages in the document, the number of words in the document, and an icon to check spelling and grammar. The right side of the status bar includes buttons and controls you can use to change the view of a document and adjust the size of the displayed document.

Ribbon The ribbon, located near the top of the window below the title bar, is the control center in Word and other Office apps (Figure 13). The ribbon provides easy, central access to the tasks you perform while creating a document. The ribbon consists of tabs, groups, and commands. Each **tab** contains a collection of groups, and each **group** contains related commands. When you run an Office app, such as Word, it initially displays several main tabs, also called default or top-level tabs. All Office apps have a HOME tab, which contains the more frequently used commands.

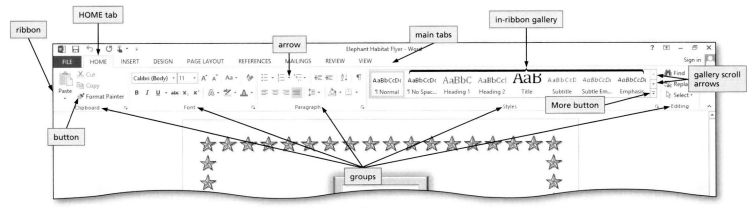

Figure 13

In addition to the main tabs, the Office apps display **tool tabs**, also called contextual tabs (Figure 14), when you perform certain tasks or work with objects such as pictures or tables. If you insert a picture in a Word document, for example, the PICTURE TOOLS tab and its related subordinate FORMAT tab appear, collectively referred to as the PICTURE TOOLS FORMAT tab. When you are finished working with the picture, the PICTURE TOOLS FORMAT tab disappears from the ribbon. Word and other Office apps determine when tool tabs should appear and disappear based on tasks you perform. Some tool tabs, such as the TABLE TOOLS tab, have more than one related subordinate tab.

Figure 14

Figure 15

Items on the ribbon include buttons, boxes, and galleries (shown in Figure 13 on the previous page). A **gallery** is a set of choices, often graphical, arranged in a grid or in a list. You can scroll through choices in an in-ribbon gallery by tapping or clicking the gallery's scroll arrows. Or, you can tap or click a gallery's More button to view more gallery options on the screen at a time.

Some buttons and boxes have arrows that, when tapped or clicked, also display a gallery; others always cause a gallery to be displayed when tapped or clicked. Most galleries support **live preview**, which is a feature that allows you to point to a gallery choice and see its effect in the document — without actually selecting the choice (Figure 15). Live preview works only if you are using a mouse; if you are using a touch screen, you will not be able to view live previews.

Figure 16

Some commands on the ribbon display an image to help you remember their function. When you point to a command on the ribbon, all or part of the command glows in a shade of blue, and a ScreenTip appears on the screen. A **ScreenTip** is an on-screen note that provides the name of the command, available keyboard shortcut(s), a description of the command, and sometimes instructions for how to obtain help about the command (Figure 16).

Some groups on the ribbon have a small arrow in the lower-right corner, called a **Dialog Box Launcher**, that when tapped or clicked, displays a dialog box or a task pane with additional options for the group (Figure 17). When presented with a dialog box, you make selections and must close the dialog box before returning to the document. A **task pane**, in contrast to a dialog box, is a window that can remain open and visible while you work in the document.

BTW
Touch Mode
The Office and Windows interfaces may vary if you are using Touch mode. For this reason, you might notice that the function or appearance of your touch screen differs slightly from this chapter's presentation.

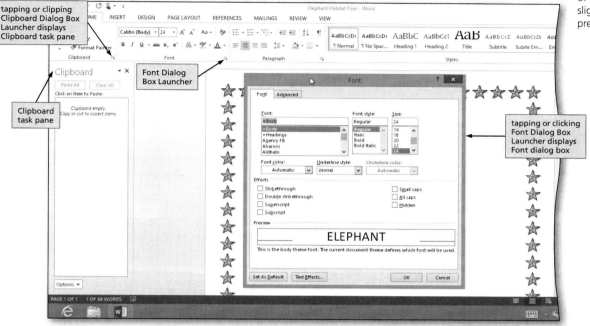

Figure 17

Mini Toolbar The **mini toolbar**, which appears automatically based on tasks you perform, contains commands related to changing the appearance of text in a document (Figure 18). If you do not use the mini toolbar, it disappears from the screen. The buttons, arrows, and boxes on the mini toolbar vary, depending on whether you are using Touch mode versus Mouse mode. If you press and hold or right-click an item in the document window, Word displays both the mini toolbar and a shortcut menu, which is discussed in a later section in this chapter.

All commands on the mini toolbar also exist on the ribbon. The purpose of the mini toolbar is to minimize hand or mouse movement.

Figure 18

Quick Access Toolbar The **Quick Access Toolbar**, located initially (by default) above the ribbon at the left edge of the title bar, provides convenient, one-tap or one-click access to frequently used commands (shown in Figure 16). The commands on the Quick Access Toolbar always are available, regardless of the task you are performing. The Touch/ Mouse Mode button on the Quick Access Toolbar allows you to switch between Touch mode and Mouse mode. If you primarily are using touch gestures, Touch mode will add

BTW
Turning Off the Mini Toolbar
If you do not want the mini toolbar to appear, tap or click FILE on the ribbon to open the Backstage view, tap or click Options in the Backstage view, tap or click General (Options dialog box), remove the check mark from the 'Show Mini Toolbar on selection' check box, and then tap or click the OK button.

more space between commands in menus and on the ribbon so that they are easier to tap. While touch gestures are convenient ways to interact with Office apps, not all features are supported when you are using Touch mode. If you are using a mouse, Mouse mode will not add the extra space between buttons and commands. The Quick Access Toolbar is discussed in more depth later in the chapter.

KeyTips If you prefer using the keyboard instead of the mouse, you can press the ALT key on the keyboard to display **KeyTips**, or keyboard code icons, for certain commands (Figure 19). To select a command using the keyboard, press the letter or number displayed in the KeyTip, which may cause additional KeyTips related to the selected command to appear. To remove KeyTips from the screen, press the ALT key or the ESC key until all KeyTips disappear, or tap or click anywhere in the app window.

Microsoft Account Area In this area, you can use the Sign in link to sign in to your Microsoft account. Once signed in, you will see your account information as well as a picture if you have included one in your Microsoft account.

Figure 19

To Display a Different Tab on the Ribbon

1 SIGN IN | 2 USE WINDOWS | 3 USE APPS | 4 FILE MANAGEMENT | 5 SWITCH APPS | 6 SAVE FILES
7 CHANGE SCREEN RESOLUTION | 8 EXIT APPS | 9 USE ADDITIONAL APPS | 10 USE HELP

When you run Word, the ribbon displays nine main tabs: FILE, HOME, INSERT, DESIGN, PAGE LAYOUT, REFERENCES, MAILINGS, REVIEW, and VIEW. The tab currently displayed is called the **active tab**. The following step displays the INSERT tab, that is, makes it the active tab. *Why? When working with an Office app, you may need to switch tabs to access other options for working with a document.*

1

- Tap or click INSERT on the ribbon to display the INSERT tab (Figure 20).

🔍 **Experiment**

- Tap or click the other tabs on the ribbon to view their contents. When you are finished, tap or click INSERT on the ribbon to redisplay the INSERT tab.

Q&A If I am working in a different Office app, such as PowerPoint or Access, how do I display a different tab on the ribbon? Follow this same procedure; that is, tap or click the desired tab on the ribbon.

Figure 20

To Collapse and Expand the Ribbon and Use Full Screen Mode

To display more of a document or other item in the window of an Office app, some users prefer to collapse the ribbon, which hides the groups on the ribbon and displays only the main tabs, or to use **Full Screen mode**, which hides all the commands and just displays the document. Each time you run an Office app, the ribbon appears the same way it did the last time you used that Office app. The chapters in this book, however, begin with the ribbon appearing as it did at the initial installation of the software.

The following steps collapse, expand, and restore the ribbon in an Office app and then switch to Full Screen mode. *Why? If you need more space on the screen to work with your document, you may consider collapsing the ribbon or switching to Full Screen mode to gain additional workspace.*

1

- Tap or click the 'Collapse the Ribbon' button on the ribbon (shown in Figure 20) to collapse the ribbon (Figure 21).

Q&A | What happened to the groups on the ribbon?
When you collapse the ribbon, the groups disappear so that the ribbon does not take up as much space on the screen.

What happened to the 'Collapse the Ribbon' button?
The 'Pin the ribbon' button replaces the 'Collapse the Ribbon' button when the ribbon is collapsed. You will see the 'Pin the ribbon' button only when you expand a ribbon by tapping or clicking a tab.

Figure 21

2

- Tap or click HOME on the ribbon to expand the HOME tab (Figure 22).

Q&A | Why would I click the HOME tab?
If you want to use a command on a collapsed ribbon, tap or click the main tab to display the groups for that tab. After you select a command on the ribbon, the groups will be collapsed once again. If you decide not to use a command on the ribbon, you can collapse the groups by tapping or clicking the same main tab or tapping or clicking in the app window.

Experiment

- Tap or click HOME on the ribbon to collapse the groups again. Tap or click HOME on the ribbon to expand the HOME tab.

Figure 22

3

- Tap or click the 'Pin the ribbon' button on the expanded HOME tab to restore the ribbon.

- Tap or click the 'Ribbon Display Options' button to display the Ribbon Display Options menu (Figure 23).

Figure 23

4

- Tap or click Auto-hide Ribbon to hide all the commands from the screen (Figure 24).

- Tap or click the ellipsis to temporarily display the ribbon.

- Tap or click the 'Ribbon Display Options' button to display the Ribbon Display Options menu (shown in Figure 23).

- Tap or click 'Show Tabs and Commands' to exit Full Screen mode.

Figure 24

Other Ways
1. Double-tap or double-click a main tab on the ribbon 2. Press CTRL+F1

To Use a Shortcut Menu to Relocate the Quick Access Toolbar

1 SIGN IN | 2 USE WINDOWS | 3 USE APPS | 4 FILE MANAGEMENT | 5 SWITCH APPS | 6 SAVE FILES
7 CHANGE SCREEN RESOLUTION | 8 EXIT APPS | 9 USE ADDITIONAL APPS | 10 USE HELP

When you press and hold or right-click certain areas of the Word and other Office app windows, a shortcut menu will appear. A **shortcut menu** is a list of frequently used commands that relate to an object. *Why? You can use shortcut menus to access common commands quickly.* When you press and hold or right-click the status bar, for example, a shortcut menu appears with commands related to the status bar. When you press and hold or right-click the Quick Access Toolbar, a shortcut menu appears with commands related to the Quick Access Toolbar. The following steps use a shortcut menu to move the Quick Access Toolbar, which by default is located on the title bar.

- Press and hold or right-click the Quick Access Toolbar to display a shortcut menu that presents a list of commands related to the Quick Access Toolbar (Figure 25).

Q&A

What if I cannot make the shortcut menu appear using the touch instruction?

When you use the press and hold technique, be sure to release your finger when the circle appears on the screen to display the shortcut menu. If the technique still does not work, you might need to add more space around objects on the screen, making it easier for you to press or tap them. Click the 'Customize Quick Access Toolbar' button and then click Touch/Mouse Mode on the menu.

Figure 25

- Tap or click 'Show Quick Access Toolbar Below the Ribbon' on the shortcut menu to display the Quick Access Toolbar below the ribbon (Figure 26).

Figure 26

- Press and hold or right-click the Quick Access Toolbar to display a shortcut menu (Figure 27).

④

- Tap or click 'Show Quick Access Toolbar Above the Ribbon' on the shortcut menu to return the Quick Access Toolbar to its original position (shown in Figure 25).

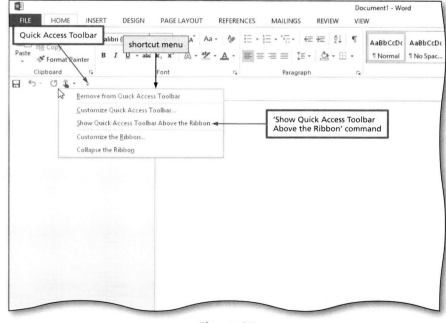

Figure 27

Other Ways

1. Tap or click 'Customize Quick Access Toolbar' button on Quick Access Toolbar, tap or click 'Show Below the Ribbon' or 'Show Above the Ribbon'

To Customize the Quick Access Toolbar

The Quick Access Toolbar provides easy access to some of the more frequently used commands in the Office apps. By default, the Quick Access Toolbar contains buttons for the Save, Undo, and Redo commands. You can customize the Quick Access Toolbar by changing its location in the window, as shown in the previous steps, and by adding more buttons to reflect commands you would like to access easily. The following steps add the Quick Print button to the Quick Access Toolbar. *Why? Adding the Quick Print button to the Quick Access Toolbar speeds up the process of printing.*

❶

- Tap or click the 'Customize Quick Access Toolbar' button to display the Customize Quick Access Toolbar menu (Figure 28).

Q&A Which commands are listed on the Customize Quick Access Toolbar menu?
It lists commands that commonly are added to the Quick Access Toolbar.

What do the check marks next to some commands signify?
Check marks appear next to commands that already are on the Quick Access Toolbar. When you add a button to the Quick Access Toolbar, a check mark will be displayed next to its command name.

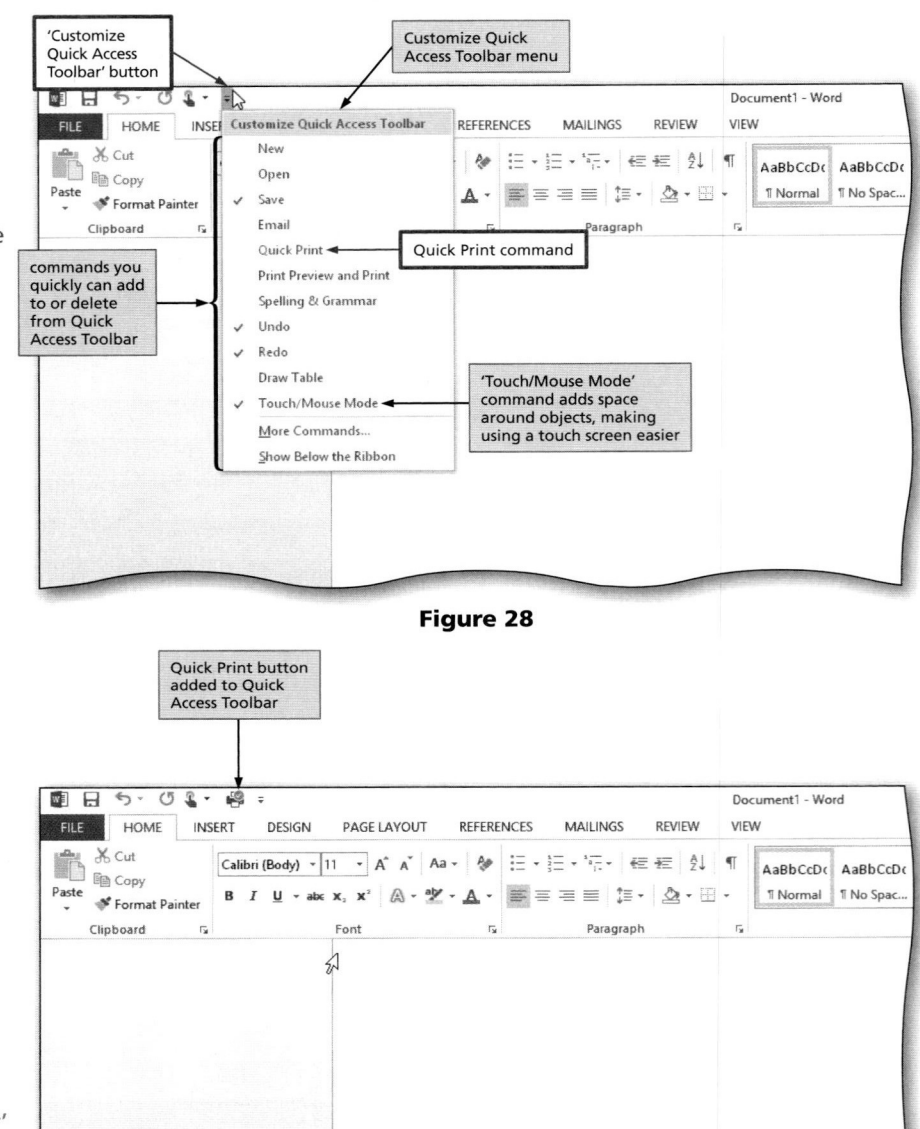

Figure 28

❷

- Tap or click Quick Print on the Customize Quick Access Toolbar menu to add the Quick Print button to the Quick Access Toolbar (Figure 29).

Q&A How would I remove a button from the Quick Access Toolbar?
You would press and hold or right-click the button you wish to remove and then tap or click 'Remove from Quick Access Toolbar' on the shortcut menu or tap or click the 'Customize Quick Access Toolbar' button on the Quick Access Toolbar and then click the button name in the Customize Quick Access Toolbar menu to remove the check mark.

Figure 29

To Enter Text in a Document

The first step in creating a document is to enter its text by typing on the keyboard. By default, Word positions text at the left margin as you type. The following steps type this first line of a flyer. *Why? To begin creating a flyer, for example, you type the headline in the document window.*

1

- Type **SEE THE ELEPHANT HABITAT** as the text (Figure 30).

Q&A What is the blinking vertical bar to the right of the text?
The blinking bar is the insertion point, which indicates where text, graphics, and other items will be inserted in the document. As you type, the insertion point moves to the right, and when you reach the end of a line, it moves down to the beginning of the next line.

What if I make an error while typing?
You can press the BACKSPACE key until you have deleted the text in error and then retype the text correctly.

Why does a circle appear below the insertion point?
If you are using a touch screen, a selection handle (small circle) appears below the text so that you can format the text easily.

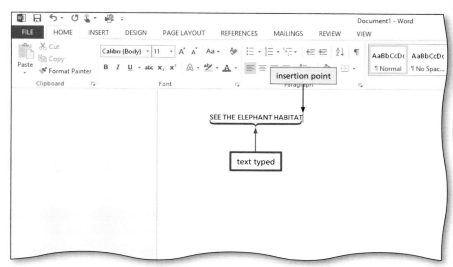

Figure 30

2

- Press the ENTER key to move the insertion point to the beginning of the next line (Figure 31).

Q&A Why did blank space appear between the entered text and the insertion point?
Each time you press the ENTER key, Word creates a new paragraph and inserts blank space between the two paragraphs. Depending on your settings, Office may or may not insert a blank space between the two paragraphs.

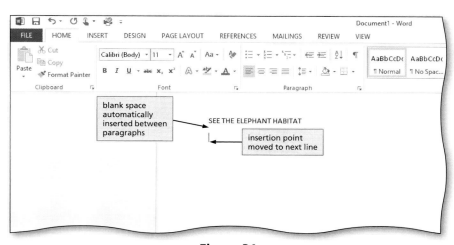

Figure 31

Saving and Organizing Files

While you are creating a document, the computer stores it in memory. When you save a document, the computer places it on a storage medium such as a hard disk, solid state drive (SSD), USB flash drive, or optical disc. The storage medium can be permanent in your computer, may be portable where you remove it from your computer, or may be on a web server you access through a network or the Internet.

BTW

File Type
Depending on your Windows settings, the file type .docx may be displayed immediately to the right of the file name after you save the file. The file type .docx is a Word 2013 document.

A saved document is referred to as a file. A **file name** is the name assigned to a file when it is saved. When saving files, you should organize them so that you easily can find them later. Windows provides tools to help you organize files.

How often should you save a document?
It is important to save a document frequently for the following reasons:

• The document in memory might be lost if the computer is turned off or you lose electrical power while an app is running.

• If you run out of time before completing a project, you may finish it at a future time without starting over.

Organizing Files and Folders

A file contains data. This data can range from a research paper to an accounting spreadsheet to an electronic math quiz. You should organize and store files in folders to avoid misplacing a file and to help you find a file quickly.

If you are taking an introductory computer class (CIS 101, for example), you may want to design a series of folders for the different subjects covered in the class. To accomplish this, you can arrange the folders in a hierarchy for the class, as shown in Figure 32.

The hierarchy contains three levels. The first level contains the storage medium, such as a hard disk. The second level contains the class folder (CIS 101, in this case), and the third level contains seven folders, one each for a different Office app that will be covered in the class (Word, PowerPoint, Excel, Access, Outlook, Publisher, and OneNote).

When the hierarchy in Figure 32 is created, the storage medium is said to contain the CIS 101 folder, and the CIS 101 folder is said to contain the separate Office folders (i.e., Word, PowerPoint, Excel, etc.). In addition, this hierarchy easily can be expanded to include folders from other classes taken during additional semesters.

The vertical and horizontal lines in Figure 32 form a pathway that allows you to navigate to a drive or folder on a computer or network. A **path** consists of a drive letter (preceded by a drive name when necessary) and colon, to identify the storage device, and one or more folder names. A hard disk typically has a drive letter of C. Each drive or folder in the hierarchy has a corresponding path.

By default, Windows saves documents in the Documents library, music in the Music library, photos in the Pictures library, and videos in the Videos library. A **library** helps you manage multiple folders stored in various locations on a computer and devices. It does not store the folder contents; rather, it keeps track of their locations so that you can access the folders and their contents quickly. For example, you can save pictures from a digital camera in any folder on any storage location on a computer. Normally, this would make organizing the different folders difficult. If you add

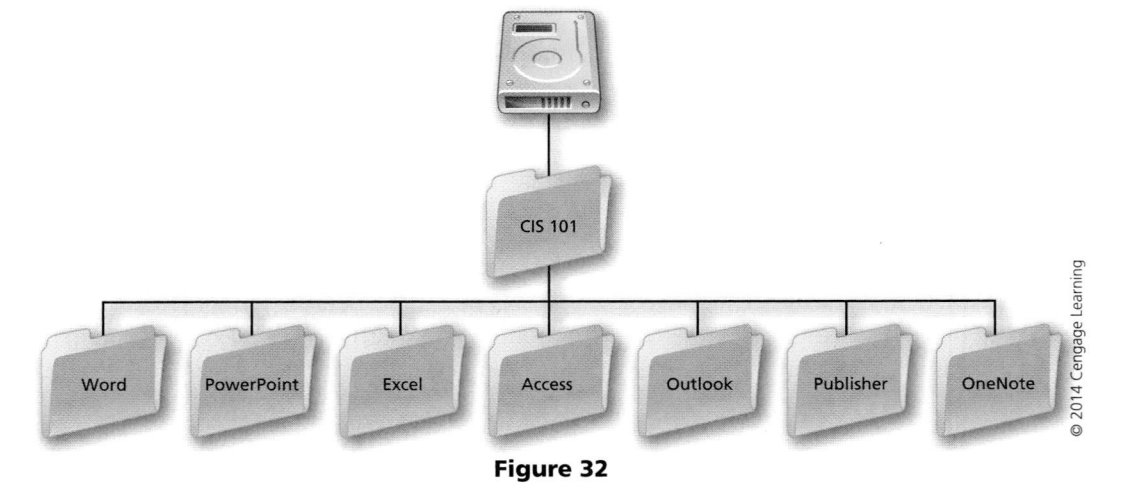

Figure 32

the folders to a library, however, you can access all the pictures from one location regardless of where they are stored.

The following pages illustrate the steps to organize the folders for this class and save a file in one of those folders:

1. Create the folder identifying your class.
2. Create the Word folder in the folder identifying your class.
3. Create the remaining folders in the folder identifying your class (one each for PowerPoint, Excel, Access, Outlook, Publisher, and OneNote).
4. Save a file in the Word folder.
5. Verify the location of the saved file.

To Create a Folder

1 SIGN IN | 2 USE WINDOWS | 3 USE APPS | 4 FILE MANAGEMENT | 5 SWITCH APPS | 6 SAVE FILES
7 CHANGE SCREEN RESOLUTION | 8 EXIT APPS | 9 USE ADDITIONAL APPS | 10 USE HELP

When you create a folder, such as the CIS 101 folder shown in Figure 32, you must name the folder. A folder name should describe the folder and its contents. A folder name can contain spaces and any uppercase or lowercase characters, except a backslash (\), slash (/), colon (:), asterisk (*), question mark (?), quotation marks ("), less than symbol (<), greater than symbol (>), or vertical bar (|). Folder names cannot be CON, AUX, COM1, COM2, COM3, COM4, LPT1, LPT2, LPT3, PRN, or NUL. The same rules for naming folders also apply to naming files.

The following steps create a class folder (CIS 101, in this case) in the Documents library. *Why? When storing files, you should organize the files so that it will be easier to find them later.* If you are using Windows 7, skip these steps and instead perform the steps in the yellow box that immediately follows these Windows 8 steps.

● Tap or click the File Explorer app button on the taskbar to run the File Explorer app (Figure 33).

Q&A | Why does the title bar say Libraries?
File Explorer, by default, displays the name of the selected library or folder on the title bar.

Figure 33

2

- Tap or click the Documents library in the navigation pane to display the contents of the Documents library in the file list (Figure 34).

Q&A What if my screen does not show the Documents, Music, Pictures, and Videos libraries?
Double-tap or double-click Libraries in the navigation pane to expand the list.

Figure 34

3

- Tap or click the New folder button on the Quick Access Toolbar to create a new folder with the name, New folder, selected in a text box (Figure 35).

Q&A Why is the folder icon displayed differently on my computer?
Windows might be configured to display contents differently on your computer.

Figure 35

4

- Type CIS 101 (or your class code) in the text box as the new folder name.

If requested by your instructor, add your last name to the end of the folder name.

- Press the ENTER key to change the folder name from New folder to a folder name identifying your class (Figure 36).

Q&A What happens when I press the ENTER key?
The class folder (CIS 101, in this case) is displayed in the file list, which contains the folder name, date modified, type, and size.

Figure 36

Other Ways

1. Press CTRL+SHIFT+N 2. Tap or click the New folder button (Home tab | New group)

To Create a Folder Using Windows 7

If you are using Windows 7, perform these steps to create a folder instead of the previous steps that use Windows 8.

1. Click the Windows Explorer button on the taskbar to run Windows Explorer.
2. Click the Documents library in the navigation pane to display the contents of the Documents library in the file list.
3. Click the New folder button on the toolbar to display a new folder icon with the name, New folder, selected in a text box.
4. Type CIS 101 (or your class code) in the text box to name the folder.
5. Press the ENTER key to create the folder.

Folder Windows

The Documents window (shown in Figure 36) is called a folder window. Recall that a folder is a specific named location on a storage medium that contains related files. Most users rely on **folder windows** for finding, viewing, and managing information on their computers. Folder windows have common design elements, including the following (shown in Figure 36).

- The **address bar** provides quick navigation options. The arrows on the address bar allow you to visit different locations on the computer.
- The buttons to the left of the address bar allow you to navigate the contents of the navigation pane and view recent pages.
- The **Previous Locations arrow** displays the locations you have visited.
- The **Refresh button** on the right side of the address bar refreshes the contents of the folder list.
- The **search box** contains the dimmed words, Search Documents. You can type a term in the search box for a list of files, folders, shortcuts, and elements containing that term within the location you are searching. A **shortcut** is an icon on the desktop that provides a user with immediate access to an app or file.
- The **ribbon** contains five tabs used to accomplish various tasks on the computer related to organizing and managing the contents of the open window. This ribbon works similarly to the ribbon in the Office apps.
- The **navigation pane** on the left contains the Favorites area, Libraries area, Homegroup area, Computer area, and Network area.
- The **Favorites area** shows your favorite locations. By default, this list contains only links to your Desktop, Downloads, and Recent places.
- The **Libraries area** shows folders included in a library.

To Create a Folder within a Folder

1 SIGN IN | 2 USE WINDOWS | 3 USE APPS | 4 FILE MANAGEMENT | 5 SWITCH APPS | 6 SAVE FILES
7 CHANGE SCREEN RESOLUTION | 8 EXIT APPS | 9 USE ADDITIONAL APPS | 10 USE HELP

With the class folder created, you can create folders that will store the files you create using each Office app. The following steps create a Word folder in the CIS 101 folder (or the folder identifying your class). *Why? To be able to organize your files, you should create a folder structure.* If you are using Windows 7, skip these steps and instead perform the steps in the yellow box that immediately follows these Windows 8 steps.

- Double-tap or double-click the icon or folder name for the CIS 101 folder (or the folder identifying your class) in the file list to open the folder (Figure 37).

Figure 37

2

- Tap or click the New folder button on the Quick Access Toolbar to create a new folder with the name, New folder, selected in a text box folder.

- Type **Word** in the text box as the new folder name.

- Press the ENTER key to rename the folder (Figure 38).

Figure 38

Other Ways

1. Press CTRL+SHIFT+N

2. Tap or click the New folder button (Home tab | New group)

TO CREATE A FOLDER WITHIN A FOLDER USING WINDOWS 7

If you are using Windows 7, perform these steps to create a folder within a folder instead of the previous steps that use Windows 8.

1. Double-click the icon or folder name for the CIS 101 folder (or the folder identifying your class) in the file list to open the folder.

2. Click the New folder button on the toolbar to display a new folder icon and text box for the folder.

3. Type **Word** in the text box to name the folder.

4. Press the ENTER key to create the folder.

To Create the Remaining Folders

The following steps create the remaining folders in the folder identifying your class (in this case, CIS 101). If you are using Windows 7, skip these steps and instead perform the steps in the yellow box that immediately follows these Windows 8 steps.

1 Tap or click New folder button on the Quick Access Toolbar to create a new folder with the name, New folder, selected in a text box.

2 Type **PowerPoint** in the text box as the new folder name.

3 Press the ENTER key to rename the folder.

4 Repeat Steps 1 through 3 to create each of the remaining folders, using Excel, Access, Outlook, Publisher, and OneNote as the folder names (Figure 39).

Figure 39

TO CREATE THE REMAINING FOLDERS USING WINDOWS 7

If you are using Windows 7, perform these steps to create the remaining folders instead of the previous steps that use Windows 8.

1. Click the New folder button on the toolbar to create a new folder with the name, New folder, selected in a text box.
2. Type **PowerPoint** in the text box as the new folder name.
3. Press the ENTER key to rename the folder.
4. Repeat Steps 1 through 3 to create each of the remaining folders, using Excel, Access, Outlook, Publisher, and OneNote as the folder names.

To Expand a Folder, Scroll through Folder Contents, and Collapse a Folder

1 SIGN IN | 2 USE WINDOWS | 3 USE APPS | 4 FILE MANAGEMENT | 5 SWITCH APPS | 6 SAVE FILES
7 CHANGE SCREEN RESOLUTION | 8 EXIT APPS | 9 USE ADDITIONAL APPS | 10 USE HELP

Folder windows display the hierarchy of items and the contents of drives and folders in the file list. You might want to expand a library or folder in the navigation pane to view its contents, slide or scroll through its contents, and collapse it when you are finished viewing its contents. *Why? When a folder is expanded, you can see all the folders it contains. By contrast, a collapsed folder hides the folders it contains.* The following steps expand, slide or scroll through, and then collapse the folder identifying your class (CIS 101, in this case).

1

- Double-tap or double-click the Documents library in the navigation pane, which expands the library to display its contents and displays a black arrow to the left of the Documents library icon (Figure 40).

Figure 40

2

- Double-tap or double-click the My Documents folder, which expands the folder to display its contents and displays a black arrow to the left of the My Documents folder icon.

Q&A | What is the My Documents folder? When you save files on your hard disk, the My Documents folder is the default save location.

- Double-tap or double-click the CIS 101 folder, which expands the folder to display its contents and displays a black arrow to the left of the folder icon (Figure 41).

Figure 41

 Experiment

- Slide the scroll bar down or click the down scroll arrow on the vertical scroll bar to display additional folders at the bottom of the navigation pane. Slide the scroll bar up or click the scroll bar above the scroll box to move the scroll box to the top of the navigation pane. Drag the scroll box down the scroll bar until the scroll box is halfway down the scroll bar.

3

- Double-tap or double-click the folder identifying your class (CIS 101, in this case) to collapse the folder (Figure 42).

Q&A

Why are some folders indented below others?

A folder contains the indented folders below it.

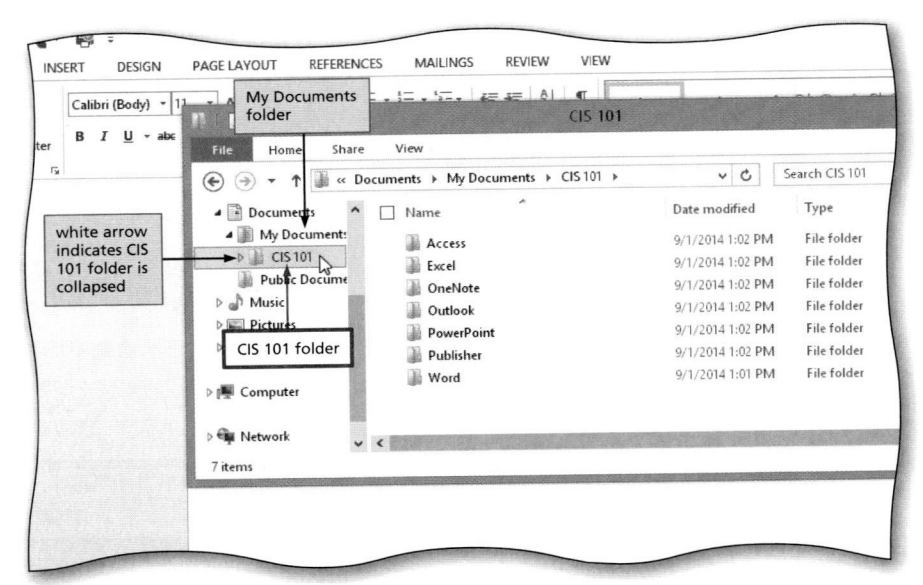

Figure 42

Other Ways

1. Point to display arrows in navigation pane, tap or click white arrow to expand or tap or click black arrow to collapse

2. Select folder to expand or collapse using arrow keys, press RIGHT ARROW to expand; press LEFT ARROW to collapse.

1 SIGN IN | 2 USE WINDOWS | 3 USE APPS | 4 FILE MANAGEMENT | 5 SWITCH APPS | 6 SAVE FILES
7 CHANGE SCREEN RESOLUTION | 8 EXIT APPS | 9 USE ADDITIONAL APPS | 10 USE HELP

To Switch from One App to Another

The next step is to save the Word file containing the headline you typed earlier. Word, however, currently is not the active window. You can use the app button on the taskbar and live preview to switch to Word and then save the document in the Word document window.

Why? By clicking the appropriate app button on the taskbar, you can switch to the open app you want to use. The steps below switch to the Word window; however, the steps are the same for any active Office app currently displayed as an app button on the taskbar.

1

- If you are using a mouse, point to the Word app button on the taskbar to see a live preview of the open document(s) or the window title(s) of the open document(s), depending on your computer's configuration (Figure 43).

Figure 43

• Tap or click the app button or the live preview to make the app associated with the app button the active window (Figure 44).

Q&A

What if multiple documents are open in an app?
Tap or click the desired live preview to switch to the window you want to use.

Figure 44

To Save a File in a Folder

1 SIGN IN | 2 USE WINDOWS | 3 USE APPS | 4 FILE MANAGEMENT | 5 SWITCH APPS | 6 SAVE FILES
7 CHANGE SCREEN RESOLUTION | 8 EXIT APPS | 9 USE ADDITIONAL APPS | 10 USE HELP

With the folders for storing your files created, you can save the Word document. *Why? Without saving a file, you may lose all the work you have done and will be unable to reuse or share it with others later.* The following steps save a file in the Word folder contained in your class folder (CIS 101, in this case) using the file name, Elephant Habitat.

• Tap or click the Save button (shown in Figure 44) on the Quick Access Toolbar, which depending on settings, will display either the Save As gallery in the Backstage view (Figure 45) or the Save As dialog box (Figure 46 on the next page).

What is the Backstage view?
The **Backstage view** contains a set of commands that enable you to manage documents and data about the documents.

What if the Save As gallery is not displayed in the Backstage view?
Tap or click the Save As tab to display the Save As gallery.

How do I close the Backstage view?
Tap or click the Back button in the upper-left corner of the Backstage view to return to the app window.

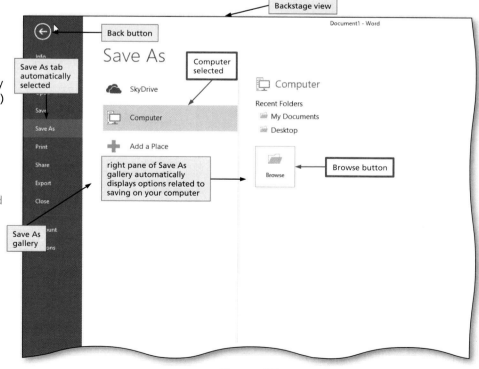

Figure 45

2

- If your screen displays the Backstage view, tap or click Computer, if necessary, to display options in the right pane related to saving on your computer; if your screen already displays the Save As dialog box, proceed to Step 3.

Q&A What if I wanted to save on SkyDrive instead?
You would tap or click SkyDrive. Saving on SkyDrive is discussed in a later section in this chapter.

- Tap or click the Browse button in the right pane to display the Save As dialog box (Figure 46).

Q&A Why does a file name already appear in the File name box?
Word automatically suggests a file name the first time you save a document. The file name normally consists of the first few words contained in the document. Because the suggested file name is selected, you do not need to delete it; as soon as you begin typing, the new file name replaces the selected text.

Figure 46

3

- Type **Elephant Habitat** in the File name box (Save As dialog box) to change the file name. Do not press the ENTER key after typing the file name because you do not want to close the dialog box at this time (Figure 47).

Q&A What characters can I use in a file name?
The only invalid characters are the backslash (\), slash (/), colon (:), asterisk (*), question mark (?), quotation mark ("), less than symbol (<), greater than symbol (>), and vertical bar (|).

Figure 47

4

- Navigate to the desired save location (in this case, the Word folder in the CIS 101 folder [or your class folder] in the My Documents folder in the Documents library) by performing the tasks in Steps 4a and 4b.

4a

- If the Documents library is not displayed in the navigation pane, slide to scroll or drag the scroll bar in the navigation pane until Documents appears.

- If the Documents library is not expanded in the navigation pane, double-tap or double-click Documents to display its folders in the navigation pane.

- If the My Documents folder is not expanded in the navigation pane, double-tap or double-click My Documents to display its folders in the navigation pane.

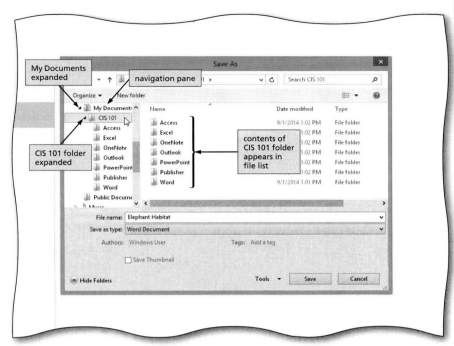

Figure 48

- If your class folder (CIS 101, in this case) is not expanded, double-tap or double-click the CIS 101 folder to select the folder and display its contents in the navigation pane (Figure 48).

Q&A | What if I do not want to save in a folder?
Although storing files in folders is an effective technique for organizing files, some users prefer not to store files in folders. If you prefer not to save this file in a folder, select the storage device on which you wish to save the file and then proceed to Step 5.

4b

- Tap or click the Word folder in the navigation pane to select it as the new save location and display its contents in the file list (Figure 49).

Figure 49

5

- Tap or click the Save button (Save As dialog box) to save the document in the selected folder in the selected location with the entered file name (Figure 50).

Q&A How do I know that the file is saved?

While an Office app is saving a file, it briefly displays a message on the status bar indicating the amount of the file saved. In addition, the file name appears on the title bar.

Figure 50

Other Ways

1. Tap or click FILE on ribbon, tap or click Save As in Backstage view, tap or click Computer, tap or click Browse button, type file name (Save As dialog box), navigate to desired save location, tap or click Save button

2. Press F12, type file name (Save As dialog box), navigate to desired save location, tap or click Save button

Navigating in Dialog Boxes

Navigating is the process of finding a location on a storage device. While saving the Elephant Habitat file, for example, Steps 4a and 4b on the previous page navigated to the Word folder located in the CIS 101 folder in the My Documents folder in the Documents library. When performing certain functions in Windows apps, such as saving a file, opening a file, or inserting a picture in an existing document, you most likely will have to navigate to the location where you want to save the file or to the folder containing the file you want to open or insert. Most dialog boxes in Windows apps requiring navigation follow a similar procedure; that is, the way you navigate to a folder in one dialog box, such as the Save As dialog box, is similar to how you might navigate in another dialog box, such as the Open dialog box. If you chose to navigate to a specific location in a dialog box, you would follow the instructions in Steps 4a and 4b.

To Minimize and Restore a Window

1 SIGN IN | **2 USE WINDOWS** | 3 USE APPS | 4 FILE MANAGEMENT | 5 SWITCH APPS | 6 SAVE FILES
7 CHANGE SCREEN RESOLUTION | 8 EXIT APPS | 9 USE ADDITIONAL APPS | 10 USE HELP

Before continuing, you can verify that the Word file was saved properly. To do this, you will minimize the Word window and then open the CIS 101 window so that you can verify the file is stored in the CIS 101 folder on the hard disk. A **minimized window** is an open window that is hidden from view but can be displayed quickly by clicking the window's app button on the taskbar.

In the following example, Word is used to illustrate minimizing and restoring windows; however, you would follow the same steps regardless of the Office app you are using. *Why? Before closing an app, you should make sure your file saved correctly so that you can find it later.*

The following steps minimize the Word window, verify that the file is saved, and then restore the minimized window. If you are using Windows 7, skip these steps and instead perform the steps in the yellow box that immediately follows these Windows 8 steps.

1

- Tap or click the Minimize button on the app's title bar (shown in Figure 50) to minimize the window (Figure 51).

 Is the minimized window still available?
The minimized window, Word in this case, remains available but no longer is the active window. It is minimized as an app button on the taskbar.

- If the File Explorer window is not open on the screen, tap or click the File Explorer app button on the taskbar to make the File folder window the active window.

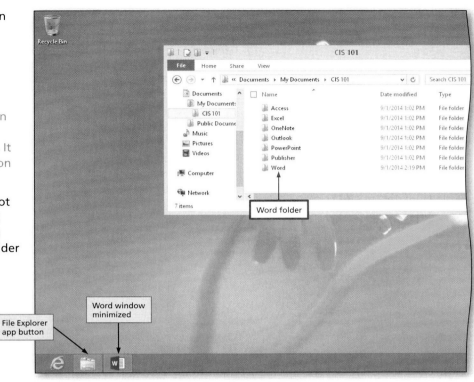

Figure 51

2

- Double-tap or double-click the Word folder in the file list to select the folder and display its contents (Figure 52).

 Why does the File Explorer app button on the taskbar change?
A selected app button indicates that the app is active on the screen. When the button is not selected, the app is running but not active.

3

- After viewing the contents of the selected folder, tap or click the Word app button on the taskbar to restore the minimized window (as shown in Figure 50).

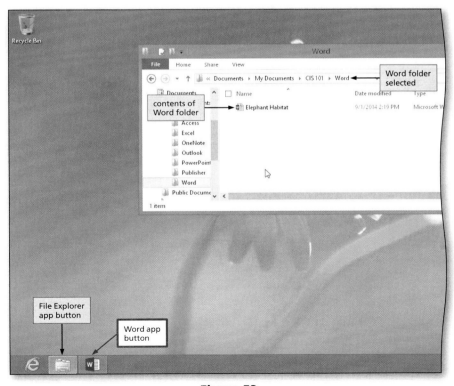

Figure 52

Other Ways

1. Press and hold or right-click title bar, tap or click Minimize on shortcut menu, tap or click taskbar button in taskbar button area

2. Press WINDOWS+M, press WINDOWS+SHIFT+M

To Minimize and Restore a Window Using Windows 7

If you are using Windows 7, perform these steps to minimize and restore a window instead of the previous steps that use Windows 8.

1. Click the Minimize button on the app's title bar to minimize the window.
2. If the Windows Explorer window is not open on the screen, click the Windows Explorer button on the taskbar to make the Windows Explorer window the active window.
3. Double-click the Word folder in the file list to select the folder and display its contents.
4. After viewing the contents of the selected folder, click the Word button on the taskbar to restore the minimized window.

To Save a File on SkyDrive

1 SIGN IN | 2 USE WINDOWS | 3 USE APPS | 4 FILE MANAGEMENT | 5 SWITCH APPS | 6 SAVE FILES
7 CHANGE SCREEN RESOLUTION | 8 EXIT APPS | 9 USE ADDITIONAL APPS | 10 USE HELP

One of the features of Office is the capability to save files on SkyDrive so that you can use the files on multiple computers without having to use external storage devices such as a USB flash drive. Storing files on SkyDrive also enables you to share files more efficiently with others, such as when using Office Web Apps and Office 365.

In the following example, Word is used to save a file to SkyDrive. *Why? Storing files on SkyDrive provides more portability options than are available from storing files in the Documents library.*

You can save files directly to SkyDrive from within Word, PowerPoint, and Excel. The following steps save the current Word file to the SkyDrive. These steps require you have a Microsoft account and an Internet connection.

1

- Tap or click FILE on the ribbon to open the Backstage view (Figure 53).

Q&A What is the purpose of the FILE tab?
The FILE tab opens the Backstage view for each Office app.

Figure 53

- Tap or click the Save As tab in the Backstage view to display the Save As gallery.

- Tap or click SkyDrive to display SkyDrive saving options or a Sign In button, if you are not signed in already to your Microsoft account (Figure 54).

Q&A What if my Save As gallery does not display SkyDrive as a save location?

Tap or click 'Add a Place' and proceed to Step 3.

Figure 54

- If your screen displays a Sign In button, tap or click it to display the Sign in dialog box (Figure 55).

Q&A What if the Sign In button does not appear?

If you already are signed into your Microsoft account, the Sign In button will not be displayed. In this case, proceed to Step 5.

Figure 55

4

- Type your Microsoft account user name and password in the text boxes and then tap or click the Sign in button (Sign in dialog box) to sign in to SkyDrive.

5

- Tap or click your SkyDrive to select your SkyDrive as the storage location (Figure 56).

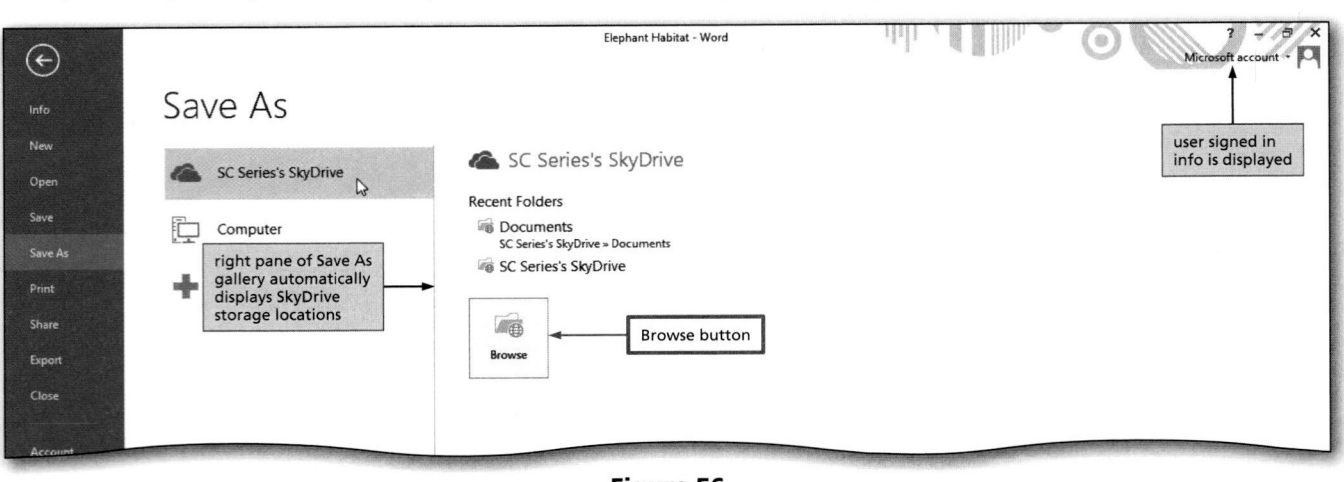

Figure 56

6

- Tap or click the Browse button to contact the SkyDrive server (which may take some time, depending on the speed of your Internet connection) and then display the Save As dialog box (Figure 57).

Q&A Why does the path in the address bar contain various letters and numbers?
The letters and numbers in the address bar uniquely identify the location of your SkyDrive files and folders.

7

- Tap or click the Save button (Save As dialog box) to save the file on SkyDrive.

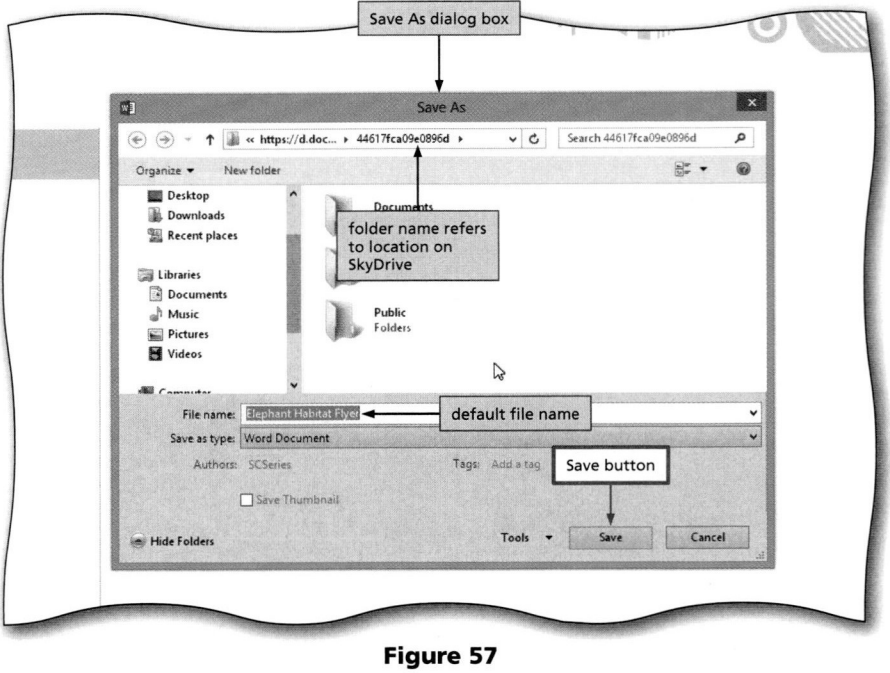

Figure 57

To Sign Out of a Microsoft Account

If you are using a public computer or otherwise wish to sign out of your Microsoft account, you should sign out of the account from the Accounts gallery in the Backstage view. Signing out of the account is the safest way to make sure that nobody else can access online files or settings stored in your Microsoft account. *Why?* *For security reasons, you should sign out of your Microsoft account when you are finished using a public or shared computer. Staying signed in to your Microsoft account might enable others to access your files.*

The following steps sign out of a Microsoft account from Word. You would use the same steps in any Office app. If you do not wish to sign out of your Microsoft account, read these steps without performing them.

1 Tap or click FILE on the ribbon to open the Backstage view.

2 Tap or click the Account tab to display the Account gallery (Figure 58).

3 Tap or click the Sign out link, which displays the Remove Account dialog box. If a Can't remove Windows accounts dialog box appears instead of the Remove Account dialog box, click the OK button and skip the remaining steps.

Q&A Why does a Can't remove Windows accounts dialog box appear?
If you signed in to Windows using your Microsoft account, then you also must sign out from Windows, rather than signing out from within Word. When you are finished using Windows, be sure to sign out at that time.

4 Tap or click the Yes button (Remove Account dialog box) to sign out of your Microsoft account on this computer.

Q&A Should I sign out of Windows after removing my Microsoft account?
When you are finished using the computer, you should sign out of Windows for maximum security.

5 Tap or click the Back button in the upper-left corner of the Backstage view to return to the document.

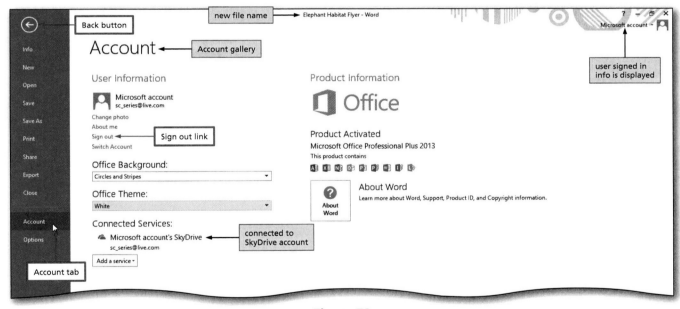

Figure 58

Screen Resolution

Screen resolution indicates the number of pixels (dots) that the computer uses to display the letters, numbers, graphics, and background you see on the screen. When you increase the screen resolution, Windows displays more information on the screen, but the information decreases in size. The reverse also is true: as you decrease the screen resolution, Windows displays less information on the screen, but the information increases in size.

Screen resolution usually is stated as the product of two numbers, such as 1366 × 768 (pronounced "thirteen sixty-six by seven sixty-eight"). A 1366 × 768 screen resolution results in a display of 1366 distinct pixels on each of 768 lines, or

about 1,050,624 pixels. Changing the screen resolution affects how the ribbon appears in Office apps and some Windows dialog boxes. Figure 59 shows the Word ribbon at screen resolutions of 1366 × 768 and 1024 × 768. All of the same commands are available regardless of screen resolution. The app (Word, in this case), however, makes changes to the groups and the buttons within the groups to accommodate the various screen resolutions. The result is that certain commands may need to be accessed differently depending on the resolution chosen. A command that is visible on the ribbon and available by tapping or clicking a button at one resolution may not be visible and may need to be accessed using its Dialog Box Launcher at a different resolution.

Comparing the two ribbons in Figure 59, notice the changes in content and layout of the groups and galleries. In some cases, the content of a group is the same in each resolution, but the layout of the group differs. For example, the same gallery and buttons appear in the Styles groups in the two resolutions, but the layouts differ. In other cases, the content and layout are the same across the resolution, but the level of detail differs with the resolution.

Figure 59a

Figure 59b

To Change the Screen Resolution

1 SIGN IN | 2 USE WINDOWS | 3 USE APPS | 4 FILE MANAGEMENT | 5 SWITCH APPS | 6 SAVE FILES
7 CHANGE SCREEN RESOLUTION | 8 EXIT APPS | 9 USE ADDITIONAL APPS | 10 USE HELP

If you are using a computer to step through the chapters in this book and you want your screen to match the figures, you may need to change your screen's resolution. *Why? The figures in this book use a screen resolution of 1366 × 768.* The following steps change the screen resolution to 1366 × 768. Your computer already may be set to 1366 × 768. Keep in mind that many computer labs prevent users from changing the screen resolution; in that case, read the following steps for illustration purposes.

1

- Tap or click the Show desktop button, which is located at the far-right edge of the taskbar, to display the Windows desktop.

 Q&A I cannot see the Show desktop button. Why not?
When you point to the far-right edge of the taskbar, a small outline appears to mark the Show desktop button.

- Press and hold or right-click an empty area on the Windows desktop to display a shortcut menu that contains a list of commands related to the desktop (Figure 60).

 Q&A Why does my shortcut menu display different commands?
Depending on your computer's hardware and configuration, different commands might appear on the shortcut menu.

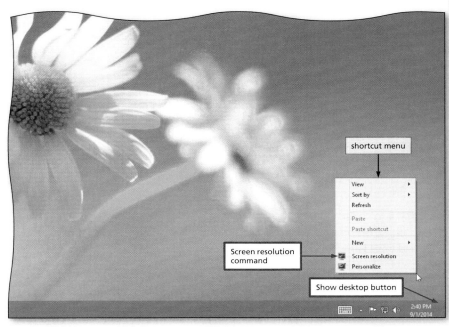

Figure 60

2

- Tap or click Screen resolution on the shortcut menu to open the Screen Resolution window (Figure 61).

3

- Tap or click the Resolution button in the Screen Resolution window to display the resolution slider.

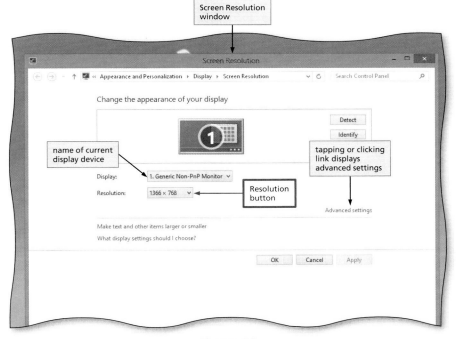

Figure 61

4

- If necessary, drag the resolution slider until the desired screen resolution (in this case, 1366 × 768) is selected (Figure 62).

Q&A What if my computer does not support the 1366 × 768 resolution?
Some computers do not support the 1366 ×768 resolution. In this case, select a resolution that is close to the 1366 × 768 resolution.

What is a slider?
A **slider** is an object that allows users to choose from multiple predetermined options. In most cases, these options represent some type of numeric value. In most cases, one end of the slider (usually the left or bottom) represents the lowest of available values, and the opposite end (usually the right or top) represents the highest available value.

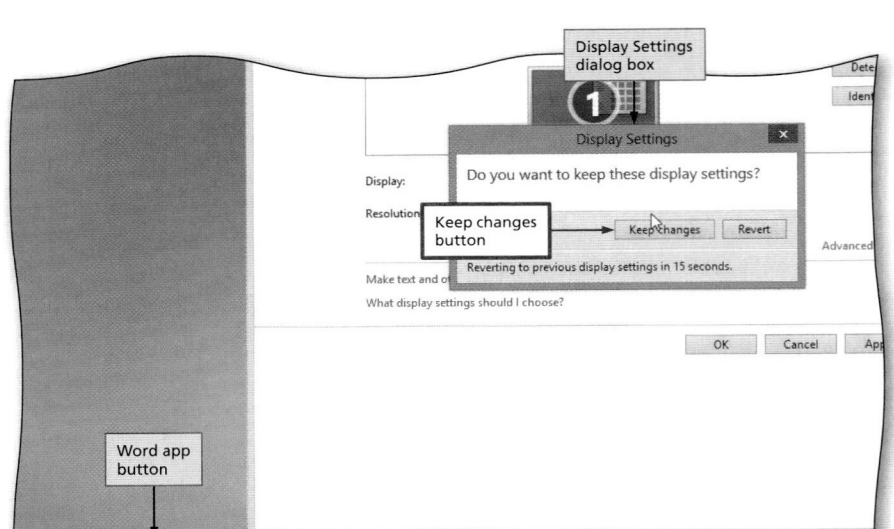

Figure 62

5

- Tap or click an empty area of the Screen Resolution window to close the resolution slider.

- Tap or click the OK button to change the screen resolution and display the Display Settings dialog box (Figure 63).

- Tap or click the Keep changes button (Display Settings dialog box) to accept the new screen resolution.

Q&A Why does a message display stating that the image quality can be improved?
Some computer monitors or screens are designed to display contents better at a certain screen resolution, sometimes referred to as an optimal resolution.

Figure 63

To Exit an Office App with One Document Open

1 SIGN IN | 2 USE WINDOWS | 3 USE APPS | 4 FILE MANAGEMENT | 5 SWITCH APPS | 6 SAVE FILES
7 CHANGE SCREEN RESOLUTION | 8 EXIT APPS | 9 USE ADDITIONAL APPS | 10 USE HELP

When you exit an Office app, such as Word, if you have made changes to a file since the last time the file was saved, the Office app displays a dialog box asking if you want to save the changes you made to the file before it closes the app window. *Why? The dialog box contains three buttons with these resulting actions: the Save button saves the changes and then exits the Office app, the Don't Save button exits the Office app without saving changes, and the Cancel button closes the dialog box and redisplays the file without saving the changes.*

If no changes have been made to an open document since the last time the file was saved, the Office app will close the window without displaying a dialog box.

The following steps exit an Office app. In the following example, Word is used to illustrate exiting an Office app; however, you would follow the same steps regardless of the Office app you were using.

- If necessary, tap or click the Word app button on the taskbar to display the Word window on the desktop.

- If you are using a mouse, point to the Close button on the right side of the app's title bar, Word in this case (Figure 64).

Figure 64

- Tap or click the Close button to close the document and exit Word.

Q&A What if I have more than one document open in an Office app?
You could click the Close button for each open document. When you click the last open document's Close button, you also exit the Office app. As an alternative that is more efficient, you could press and hold or right-click the app button on the taskbar and then tap or click 'Close all windows' on the shortcut menu, or press ALT+F4 to close all open documents and exit the Office app.

- If a Microsoft Word dialog box appears, tap or click the Save button to save any changes made to the document since the last save.

Other Ways

1. Press and hold or right-click the Office app button on Windows taskbar, click Close window on shortcut menu 2. Press ALT + F4

1 SIGN IN | 2 USE WINDOWS | 3 USE APPS | **4 FILE MANAGEMENT** | 5 SWITCH APPS | 6 SAVE FILES
7 CHANGE SCREEN RESOLUTION | 8 EXIT APPS | **9 USE ADDITIONAL APPS** | 10 USE HELP

To Copy a Folder to a USB Flash Drive

To store files and folders on a USB flash drive, you must connect the USB flash drive to an available USB port on a computer. The following steps copy your CIS 101 folder to a USB flash drive. **Why?** *It often is good practice to have a backup of your files. Besides SkyDrive, you can save files to a portable storage device, such as a USB flash drive.* If you are using Windows 7, skip these steps and instead perform the steps in the yellow box that immediately follows these Windows 8 steps.

- Insert a USB flash drive in an available USB port on the computer to connect the USB flash drive.

Q&A How can I ensure the USB flash drive is connected?
In File Explorer, you can use the navigation bar to find the USB flash drive. If it is not showing, then it is not connected properly.

Figure 65

2

- Tap or click the File Explorer app button on the taskbar to make the folder window the active window.

- If necessary, navigate to the CIS 101 folder in the File Explorer window (see Step 4a on page OFF 33 for instructions about navigating to a folder location).

- Press and hold or right-click the CIS 101 folder to display a shortcut menu (Figure 65).

③

- Tap or point to Send to, which causes a submenu to appear (Figure 66).

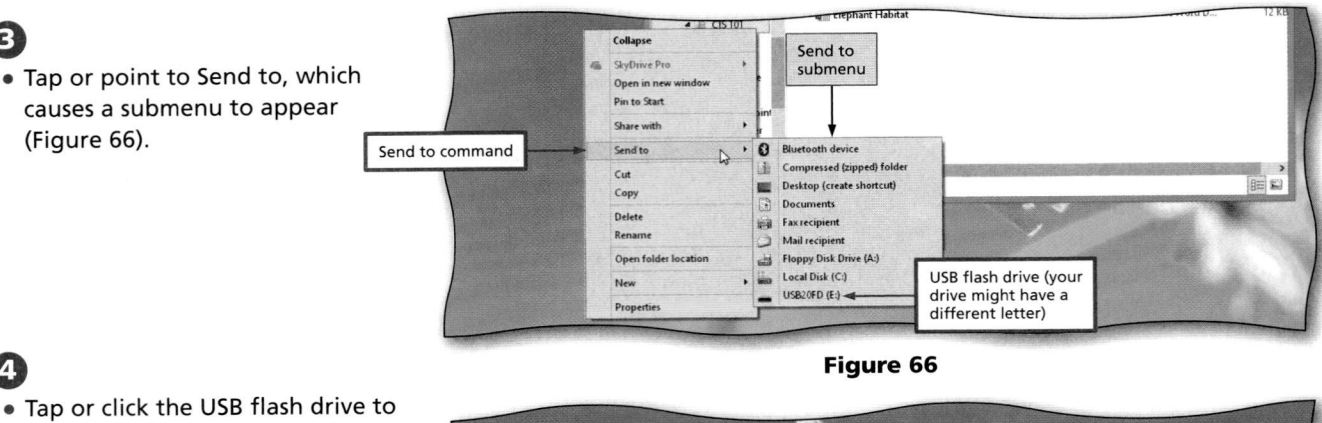

Figure 66

④

- Tap or click the USB flash drive to copy the folder to the USB flash drive (Figure 67).

Q&A Why does the drive letter of my USB flash drive differ?
Windows assigns the next available drive letter to your USB flash drive when you connect it. The next available drive letter may vary by computer, depending on the number of storage devices that currently are connected.

Figure 67

TO COPY A FOLDER TO A USB FLASH DRIVE USING WINDOWS 7

If you are using Windows 7, perform these steps to copy a folder to a USB flash drive instead of the previous steps that use Windows 8.

1. Insert a USB flash drive in an available USB port on the computer to open the AutoPlay window.
2. Click the 'Open folder to view files' link in the AutoPlay window to open the Windows Explorer window.
3. Navigate to the Documents library.
4. Right-click the CIS 101 folder to display a shortcut menu.
5. Point to Send to, which causes a submenu to appear.
6. Click the USB flash drive to copy the folder to the USB flash drive.

Break Point: If you wish to take a break, this is a good place to do so. To resume at a later time, continue to follow the steps from this location forward.

Additional Microsoft Office Apps

The previous section used Word to illustrate common features of Office and some basic elements unique to Word. The following sections present elements unique to PowerPoint, Excel, and Access, as well as illustrate additional common features of Office.

In the following pages, you will learn how to do the following:

1. Run an Office app (PowerPoint) using the search box.
2. Create two small documents in the same Office app (PowerPoint).
3. Close one of the documents.
4. Reopen the document just closed.
5. Create a document in a different Office app (Excel).
6. Save the document with a new file name.
7. Create a file in a different Office app (Access).
8. Close the file and then open the file.

PowerPoint

PowerPoint is a full-featured presentation app that allows you to produce compelling presentations to deliver and share with an audience (Figure 68). A PowerPoint **presentation** also is called a **slide show**. PowerPoint contains many features to design, develop, and organize slides, including formatting text, adding and editing video and audio clips, creating tables and charts, applying artistic effects to pictures, animating graphics, and collaborating with friends and colleagues. You then can turn your presentation into a video, broadcast your slide show on the web, or create a photo album.

Figure 68

(a) Slide 1 (Title)

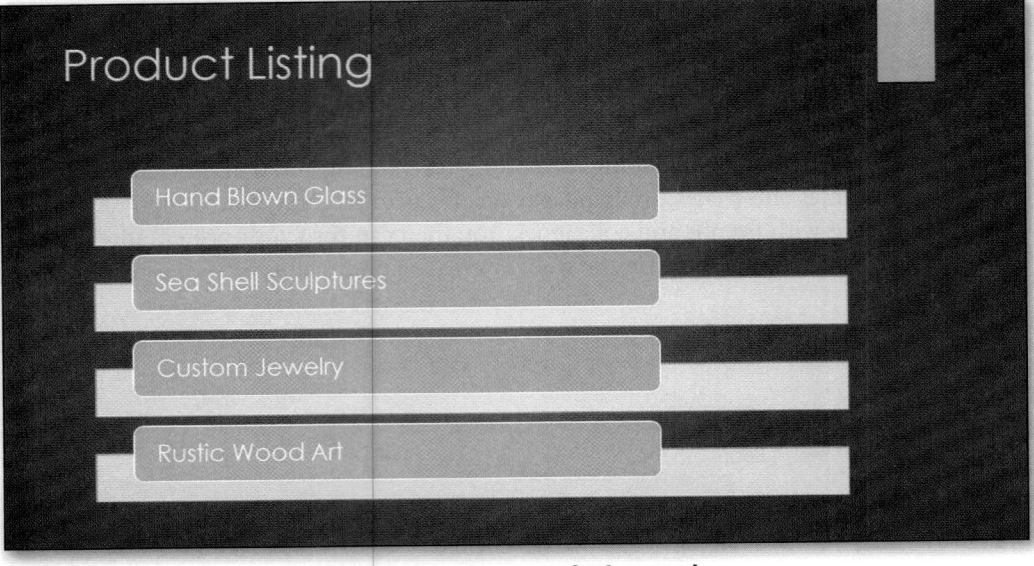

(b) Slide 2 (Text and Diagram)

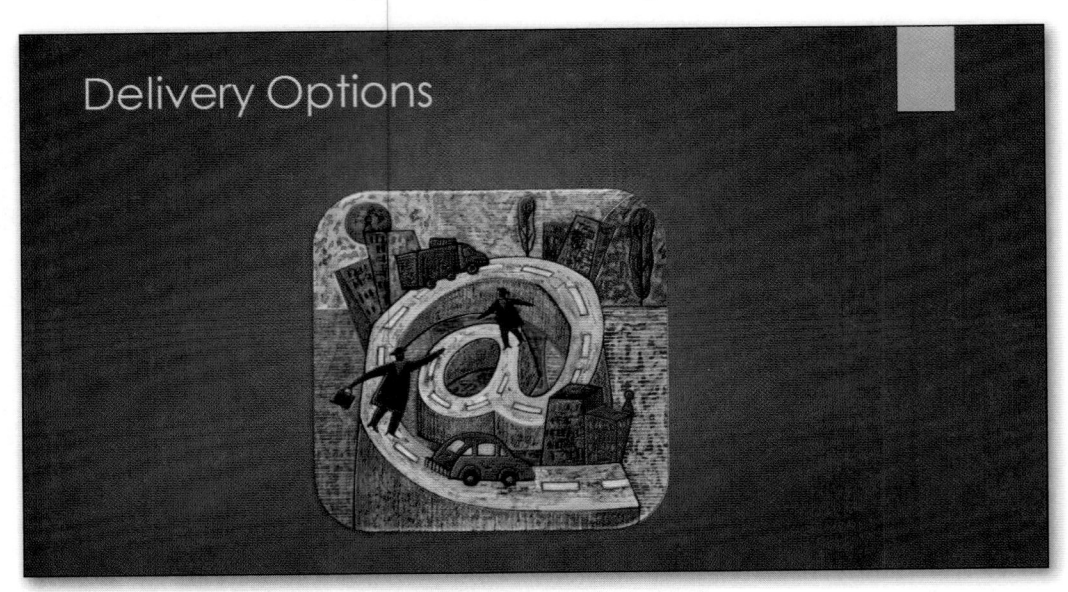

(c) Slide 3 (Text and Picture)

Figure 68 (Continued)

To Run an App Using the Search Box

1 SIGN IN | 2 USE WINDOWS | 3 USE APPS | 4 FILE MANAGEMENT | 5 SWITCH APPS | 6 SAVE FILES
7 CHANGE SCREEN RESOLUTION | 8 EXIT APPS | 9 USE ADDITIONAL APPS | **10 USE HELP**

The following steps, which assume Windows is running, use the search box to run the PowerPoint app based on a typical installation; however, you would follow similar steps to run any Office app. *Why? Sometimes an app does not appear on the Start screen, so you can find it quickly by searching.* You may need to ask your instructor how to run apps for your computer. If you are using Windows 7, skip these steps and instead perform the steps in the yellow box that immediately follows these Windows 8 steps.

1

- Swipe in from the right edge of the screen or point to the upper-right corner of the screen to display the Charms bar (Figure 69).

Figure 69

2

• Tap or click the Search charm on the Charms bar to display the Search menu (Figure 70).

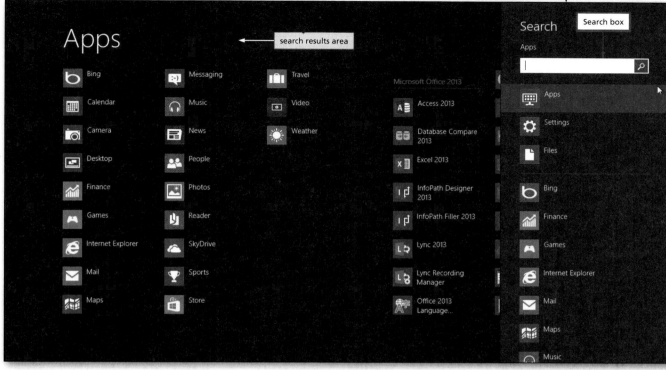

Figure 70

3

• Type **PowerPoint 2013** as the search text in the Search box and watch the search results appear in the Apps list (Figure 71).

Q&A Do I need to type the complete app name or use correct capitalization?
No, you need to type just enough characters of the app name for it to appear in the Apps list. For example, you may be able to type PowerPoint or powerpoint, instead of PowerPoint 2013.

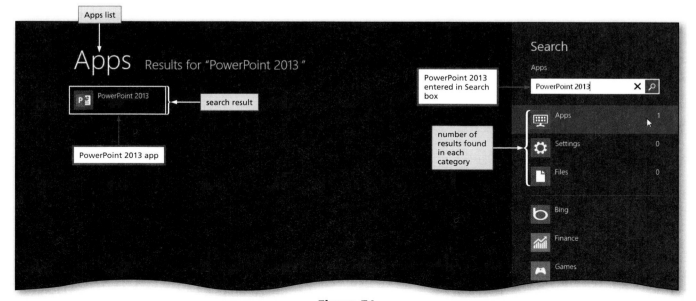

Figure 71

4

- Tap or click the app name, PowerPoint 2013 in this case, in the search results to run PowerPoint.
- Tap or click the Blank Presentation thumbnail to create a blank presentation and display it in the PowerPoint window.
- If the app window is not maximized, tap or click the Maximize button on its title bar to maximize the window (Figure 72).

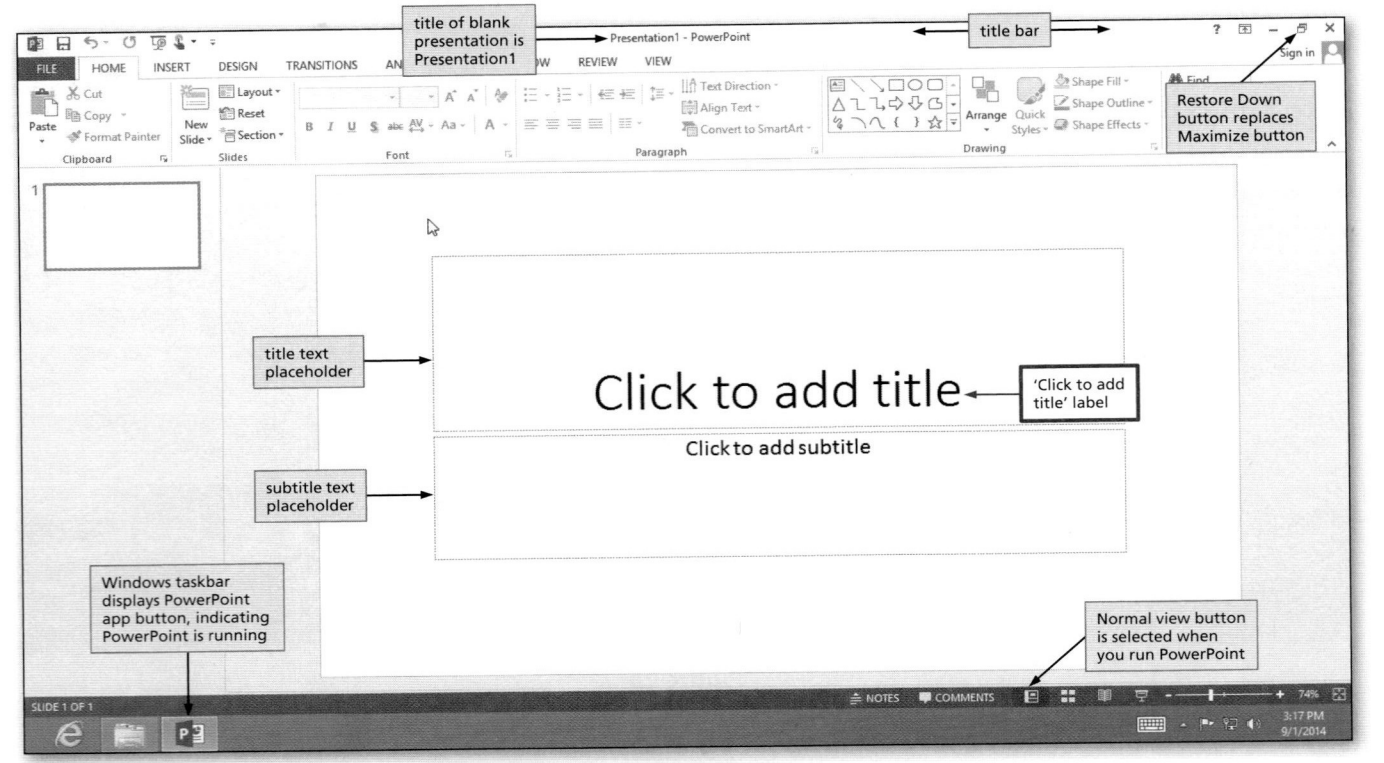

Figure 72

To Run an App Using the Search Box Using Windows 7

If you are using Windows 7, perform these steps to run an app using the search box instead of the previous steps that use Windows 8.

1. Click the Start button on the Windows 7 taskbar to display the Start menu.

2. Type **PowerPoint 2013** as the search text in the 'Search programs and files' text box and watch the search results appear on the Start menu.

3. Click the app name, PowerPoint 2013 in this case, in the search results on the Start menu to run PowerPoint.

4. Click the Blank Presentation thumbnail to create a blank presentation and display it in the PowerPoint window.

5. If the app window is not maximized, click the Maximize button on its title bar to maximize the window.

The PowerPoint Window and Ribbon

The PowerPoint window consists of a variety of components to make your work more efficient and documents more professional: the window, ribbon, mini toolbar, shortcut menus, Quick Access Toolbar, and Microsoft Account area. Many of these components are common to other Office apps and have been discussed earlier in this chapter. Other components, discussed in the following paragraphs and later in subsequent chapters, are unique to PowerPoint.

The basic unit of a PowerPoint presentation is a **slide**. A slide may contain text and objects, such as graphics, tables, charts, and drawings. **Layouts** are used to position this content on the slide. When you create a new presentation, the default **Title Slide** layout appears (shown in Figure 72). The purpose of this layout is to introduce the presentation to the audience. PowerPoint includes several other built-in standard layouts.

The default slide layouts are set up in **landscape orientation**, where the slide width is greater than its height. In landscape orientation, the slide size is preset to 10 inches wide and 7.5 inches high when printed on a standard sheet of paper measuring 11 inches wide and 8.5 inches high.

Placeholders **Placeholders** are boxes with dashed or solid borders that are displayed when you create a new slide. All layouts except the Blank slide layout contain placeholders. Depending on the particular slide layout selected, title and subtitle placeholders are displayed for the slide title and subtitle; a content placeholder is displayed for text or a table, chart, picture, graphic, or movie. The title slide in Figure 73 has two text placeholders for the main heading, or title, and the subtitle.

Figure 73

Ribbon The ribbon in PowerPoint is similar to the one in Word and the other Microsoft Office apps. When you run PowerPoint, the ribbon displays nine main tabs: FILE, HOME, INSERT, DESIGN, TRANSITIONS, ANIMATIONS, SLIDE SHOW, REVIEW, and VIEW.

To Enter Content in a Title Slide

1 SIGN IN | 2 USE WINDOWS | 3 USE APPS | 4 FILE MANAGEMENT | 5 SWITCH APPS | 6 SAVE FILES
7 CHANGE SCREEN RESOLUTION | 8 EXIT APPS | 9 USE ADDITIONAL APPS | 10 USE HELP

With the exception of a blank slide, PowerPoint assumes every new slide has a title. Many of PowerPoint's layouts have both a title text placeholder and at least one content placeholder. To make creating a presentation easier, any text you type after a new slide appears becomes title text in the title text placeholder. As you begin typing text in the title text placeholder, the title text also is displayed in the Slide 1 thumbnail in the Thumbnail pane. The title for this presentation is Kelitestone Crafts. The steps on the next page enter a presentation title on the title slide. *Why? In general, every presentation should have a title to describe what the presentation will be covering.*

①

- Tap or click the 'Click to add title' label located inside the title text placeholder (shown in Figure 72 on page OFF 48) to select the placeholder (Figure 74).

Q&A What are the white squares that appear around the title text placeholder as I type the presentation title?

The white squares are sizing handles, which you can drag to change the size of the title text placeholder. Sizing handles also can be found around other placeholders and objects within an Office app.

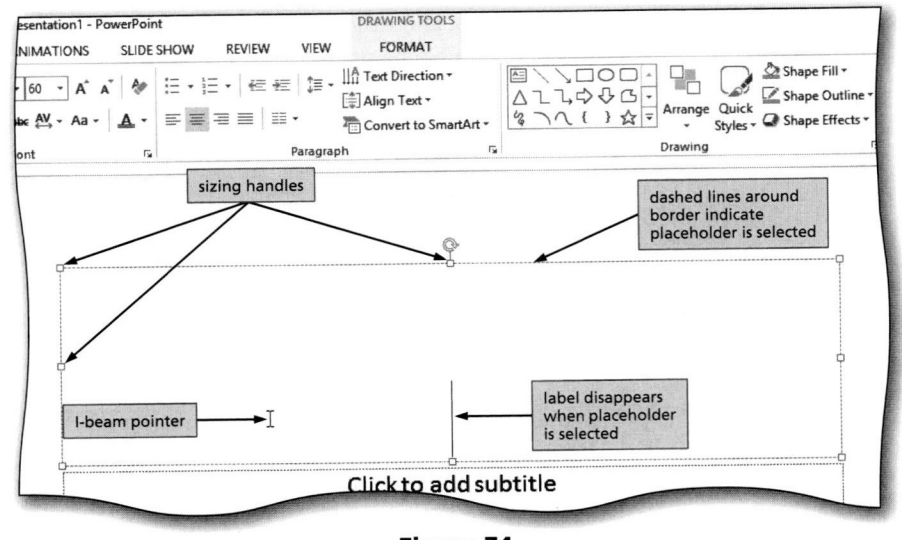

Figure 74

②

- Type **Kelitestone Crafts** in the title text placeholder. Do not press the ENTER key because you do not want to create a new line of text (Figure 75).

Figure 75

To Save a File in a Folder

The following steps save the presentation in the PowerPoint folder in the class folder (CIS 101, in this case) in the My Documents folder in the Documents library using the file name, Kelitestone Crafts.

① Tap or click the Save button on the Quick Access Toolbar (shown in Figure 75), which depending on settings will display either the Save As gallery in the Backstage view or the Save As dialog box.

② If your screen displays the Backstage view, tap or click Computer, if necessary, to display options in the right pane related to saving on your computer; if your screen already displays the Save As dialog box, proceed to Step 4.

③ Tap or click the Browse button in the right pane to display the Save As dialog box.

4 If necessary, type `Kelitestone Crafts` in the File name box (Save As dialog box) to change the file name. Do not press the ENTER key after typing the file name because you do not want to close the dialog box at this time.

5 Navigate to the desired save location (in this case, the PowerPoint folder in the CIS 101 folder [or your class folder] in the My Documents folder in the Documents library). For specific instructions, perform the tasks in Steps 5a through 5e.

5a If the Documents library is not displayed in the navigation pane, slide to scroll or drag the scroll bar in the navigation pane until Documents appears.

5b If the Documents library is not expanded in the navigation pane, double-tap or double-click Documents to display its folders in the navigation pane.

5c If the My Documents folder is not expanded in the navigation pane, double-tap or double-click My Documents to display its folders in the navigation pane.

5d If your class folder (CIS 101, in this case) is not expanded, double-tap or double-click the CIS 101 folder to select the folder and display its contents in the navigation pane.

5e Tap or click the PowerPoint folder in the navigation pane to select it as the new save location and display its contents in the file list.

6 Tap or click the Save button (Save As dialog box) to save the presentation in the selected folder in the selected location with the entered file name.

To Create a New Office Document from the Backstage View

1 SIGN IN | 2 USE WINDOWS | 3 USE APPS | 4 FILE MANAGEMENT | 5 SWITCH APPS | 6 SAVE FILES
7 CHANGE SCREEN RESOLUTION | 8 EXIT APPS | 9 USE ADDITIONAL APPS | **10 USE HELP**

As discussed earlier, the Backstage view contains a set of commands that enable you to manage documents and data about the documents. ***Why?*** *From the Backstage view in PowerPoint, for example, you can create, open, print, and save presentations. You also can share documents, manage versions, set permissions, and modify document properties. In other Office 2013 apps, the Backstage view may contain features specific to those apps.* The following steps create a file, a blank presentation in this case, from the Backstage view.

1

• Tap or click FILE on the ribbon to open the Backstage view (Figure 76).

Q&A What is the purpose of the Info tab in the Backstage view?

The Info tab, which is selected by default when you click FILE on the ribbon, allows you to protect your document, inspect your document, and manage versions of your document as well as view all the file properties such as when the file was created.

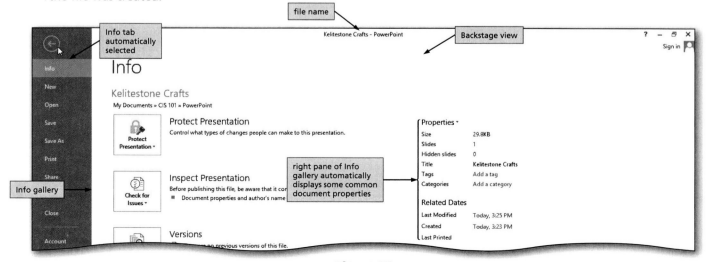

Figure 76

2

- Tap or click the New tab in the Backstage view to display the New gallery (Figure 77).

Q&A

Can I create documents through the Backstage view in other Office apps?

Yes. If the Office app has a New tab in the Backstage view, the New gallery displays various options for creating a new file.

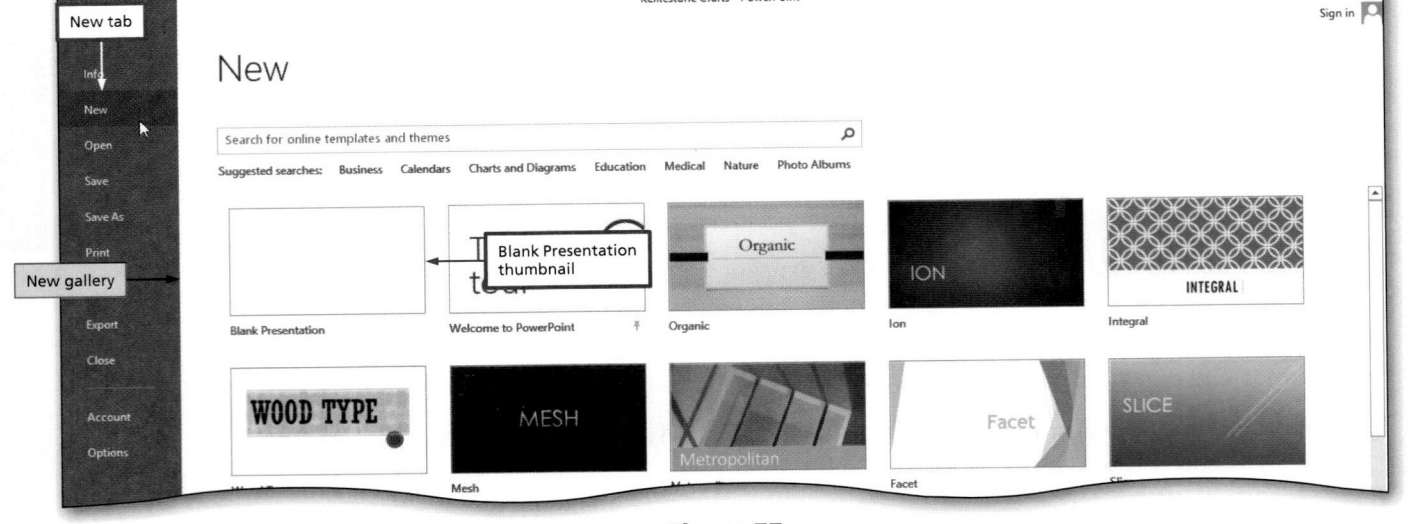

Figure 77

3

- Tap or click the Blank Presentation thumbnail in the New gallery to create a new presentation (Figure 78).

Figure 78

Other Ways

1. Press CTRL+N

To Enter Content in a Title Slide of a Second PowerPoint Presentation

The presentation title for this presentation is Elephant Habitat Opening. The following steps enter a presentation title on the title slide.

① Tap or click the title text placeholder (shown in Figure 78) to select it.

② Type `Elephant Habitat Opening` in the title text placeholder. Do not press the ENTER key (Figure 79).

Figure 79

To Save a File in a Folder

The following steps save the second presentation in the PowerPoint folder in the class folder (CIS 101, in this case) in the My Documents folder in the Documents library using the file name, Elephant Habitat Opening.

① Tap or click the Save button on the Quick Access Toolbar (shown in Figure 79), which depending on settings will display either the Save As gallery in the Backstage view or the Save As dialog box.

② If your screen displays the Backstage view, tap or click Computer, if necessary, to display options in the right pane related to saving on your computer; if your screen already displays the Save As dialog box, proceed to Step 4.

③ Tap or click the Browse button in the right pane to display the Save As dialog box.

④ If necessary, type `Elephant Habitat Opening` in the File name box (Save As dialog box) to change the file name. Do not press the ENTER key after typing the file name because you do not want to close the dialog box at this time.

⑤ If necessary, navigate to the desired save location (in this case, the PowerPoint folder in the CIS 101 folder [or your class folder] in the My Documents folder in the Documents library). For specific instructions, perform the tasks in Steps 5a through 5e on page OFF 51.

⑥ Tap or click the Save button (Save As dialog box) to save the presentation in the selected folder on the selected drive with the entered file name.

To Close an Office File Using the Backstage View

Sometimes, you may want to close an Office file, such as a PowerPoint presentation, entirely and start over with a new file. **Why else would I close a file?** *You also may want to close a file when you are finished working with it so that you can begin a new file.* The following steps close the current active Office file, that is, the Elephant Habitat Opening presentation, without exiting the active app (PowerPoint, in this case).

1
- Tap or click FILE on the ribbon (shown in Figure 79 on the previous page) to open the Backstage view (Figure 80).

2
- Tap or click Close in the Backstage view to close the open file (Elephant Habitat Opening, in this case) without exiting the active app.

Q&A What if the Office app displays a dialog box about saving?
Tap or click the Save button if you want to save the changes, tap or click the Don't Save button if you want to ignore the changes since the last time you saved, and tap or click the Cancel button if you do not want to close the document.

Can I use the Backstage view to close an open file in other Office apps, such as Word and Excel?
Yes.

Figure 80

Other Ways

1. Press CTRL+F4

To Open a Recent Office File Using the Backstage View

You sometimes need to open a file that you recently modified. **Why?** *You may have more changes to make such as adding more content or correcting errors.* The Backstage view allows you to access recent files easily. The following steps reopen the Elephant Habitat Opening file just closed.

1
- Tap or click FILE on the ribbon to open the Backstage view.
- Tap or click the Open tab in the Backstage view to display the Open gallery (Figure 81).

2
- Tap or click the desired file name in the Recent Presentations list, Elephant Habitat Opening in this case, to open the file (shown in Figure 79 on the previous page).

Q&A Can I use the Backstage view to open a recent file in other Office apps, such as Word and Excel?
Yes, as long as the file name appears in the list of recent files.

Open gallery

Open tab

Open

New
Open
Save
Save As
Print
Share
Export
Close

Account
Options

Kelitestone Crafts - PowerPoint

? — ⟋ ✕
Sign in

Recent Presentations list

Recent Presentations

🕐 Recent Presentations

☁ SkyDrive

Recent Presentations automatically selected

➕ Add a Place

Recent Presentations

Elephant Habitat Opening
My Documents » CIS 101 » PowerPoint

Elephant Habitat Opening presentation

Kelitestone Crafts
My Documents » CIS 101 » PowerPoint

Figure 81

Other Ways

1. Tap or click FILE on ribbon, tap or click Open in Backstage view, tap or click Computer, tap or click Browse, navigate to file (Open dialog box), tap or click Open button

To Exit an Office App

You are finished using PowerPoint. Thus, you should exit this Office app. The following steps exit PowerPoint.

1 If you have one Office document open, tap or click the Close button on the right side of the title bar to close the document and exit the Office app; or if you have multiple Office documents open, press and hold or right-click the app button on the taskbar and then tap or click 'Close all windows' on the shortcut menu, or press ALT+F4 to close all open documents and exit the Office app.

Q&A If I am using a touch screen, could I press and hold the Close button until all windows close and the app exits?
Yes.

2 If a dialog box appears, tap or click the Save button to save any changes made to the document since the last save.

Excel

Excel is a powerful spreadsheet app that allows users to organize data, complete calculations, make decisions, graph data, develop professional-looking reports (Figure 82), publish organized data to the web, and access real-time data from websites. The four major parts of Excel are:

- **Workbooks and Worksheets:** A **workbook** is like a notebook. Inside the workbook are sheets, each of which is called a **worksheet**. Thus, a workbook is a collection of worksheets. Worksheets allow users to enter, calculate, manipulate, and analyze data such as numbers and text. The terms worksheet and spreadsheet are interchangeable.

- **Charts:** Excel can draw a variety of charts such as column charts and pie charts.

- **Tables:** Tables organize and store data within worksheets. For example, once a user enters data into a worksheet, an Excel table can sort the data, search for specific data, and select data that satisfies defined criteria.

• **Web Support:** Web support allows users to save Excel worksheets or parts of a worksheet in a format that a user can view in a browser, so that a user can view and manipulate the worksheet using a browser. Excel web support also provides access to real-time data, such as stock quotes, using web queries.

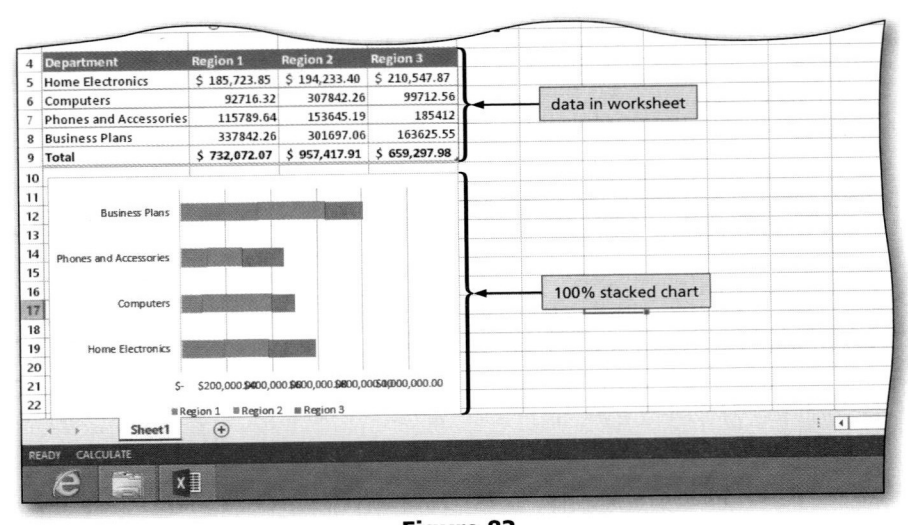

4	Department	Region 1	Region 2	Region 3
5	Home Electronics	$ 185,723.85	$ 194,233.40	$ 210,547.87
6	Computers	92716.32	307842.26	99712.56
7	Phones and Accessories	115789.64	153645.19	185412
8	Business Plans	337842.26	301697.06	163625.55
9	Total	$ 732,072.07	$ 957,417.91	$ 659,297.98

Figure 82

To Create a New Blank Office Document from File Explorer

1 SIGN IN | 2 USE WINDOWS | 3 USE APPS | 4 FILE MANAGEMENT | 5 SWITCH APPS | 6 SAVE FILES
7 CHANGE SCREEN RESOLUTION | 8 EXIT APPS | 9 USE ADDITIONAL APPS | 10 USE HELP

File Explorer provides a means to create a blank Office document without running an Office app. The following steps use File Explorer to create a blank Excel document. *Why? Sometimes you might need to create a blank document and then return to it later for editing.* If you are using Windows 7, skip these steps and instead perform the steps in the yellow box that immediately follows these Windows 8 steps.

1

• If necessary, double-tap or double-click the File Explorer app button on the taskbar to make the folder window the active window.

• If necessary, double-tap or double-click the Documents library in the navigation pane to expand the Documents library.

• If necessary, double-tap or double-click the My Documents folder in the navigation pane to expand the My Documents folder.

• If necessary, double-tap or double-click your class folder (CIS 101, in this case) in the navigation pane to expand the folder.

• Tap or click the Excel folder in the navigation pane to display its contents in the file list.

• With the Excel folder selected, press and hold or right-click an open area in the file list to display a shortcut menu.

• Tap or point to New on the shortcut menu to display the New submenu (Figure 83).

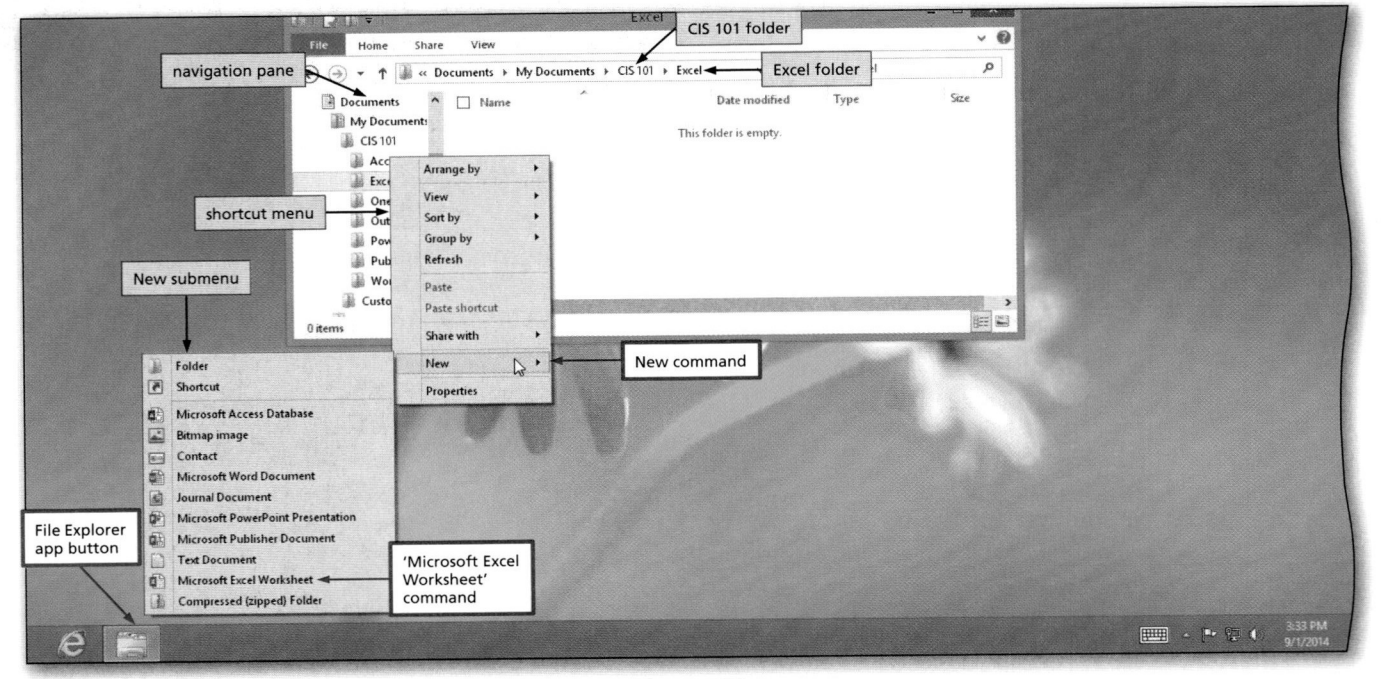

Figure 83

2

- Tap or click 'Microsoft Excel Worksheet' on the New submenu to display an icon and text box for a new file in the current folder window with the file name, New Microsoft Excel Worksheet, selected (Figure 84).

Figure 84

3

- Type **Iverstonit Electronics** in the text box and then press the ENTER key to assign a new name to the new file in the current folder (Figure 85).

Figure 85

TO CREATE A NEW BLANK OFFICE DOCUMENT FROM WINDOWS EXPLORER USING WINDOWS 7

If you are using Windows 7, perform these steps to create a new blank Office document from Windows Explorer instead of the previous steps that use Windows 8.

1. If necessary, click the Windows Explorer button on the taskbar to make the folder window the active window.

2. If necessary, double-click the Documents library in the navigation pane to expand the Documents library.

3. If necessary, double-click the My Documents folder in the navigation pane to expand the My Documents folder.

4. If necessary, double-click your class folder (CIS 101, in this case) in the navigation pane to expand the folder.

5. Click the Excel folder in the navigation pane to display its contents in the file list.

6. With the Excel folder selected, right-click an open area in the file list to display a shortcut menu.

7. Point to New on the shortcut menu to display the New submenu.

8. Click 'Microsoft Excel Worksheet' on the New submenu to display an icon and text box for a new file in the current folder window with the name, New Microsoft Excel Worksheet, selected.

9. Type **Iverstonit Electronics** in the text box and then press the ENTER key to assign a new name to the new file in the current folder.

To Run an App from File Explorer and Open a File

1 SIGN IN | 2 USE WINDOWS | 3 USE APPS | 4 FILE MANAGEMENT | 5 SWITCH APPS | 6 SAVE FILES
7 CHANGE SCREEN RESOLUTION | 8 EXIT APPS | 9 USE ADDITIONAL APPS | 10 USE HELP

Previously, you learned how to run an Office app using the Start screen and the Search charm. The steps on the next page, which assume Windows is running, use File Explorer to run the Excel app based on a typical installation. *Why? Another way to run an Office app is to open an existing file from File Explorer, which causes the app in which the file was created to run and then open the selected file.* You may need to ask your instructor how to run Office apps for your computer. If you are using Windows 7, follow the steps in the yellow box that immediately follows these Windows 8 steps.

1

- If necessary, display the file to open in the folder window in File Explorer (shown in Figure 85 on the previous page).

- Press and hold or right-click the file icon or file name (Iverstonit Electronics, in this case) to display a shortcut menu (Figure 86).

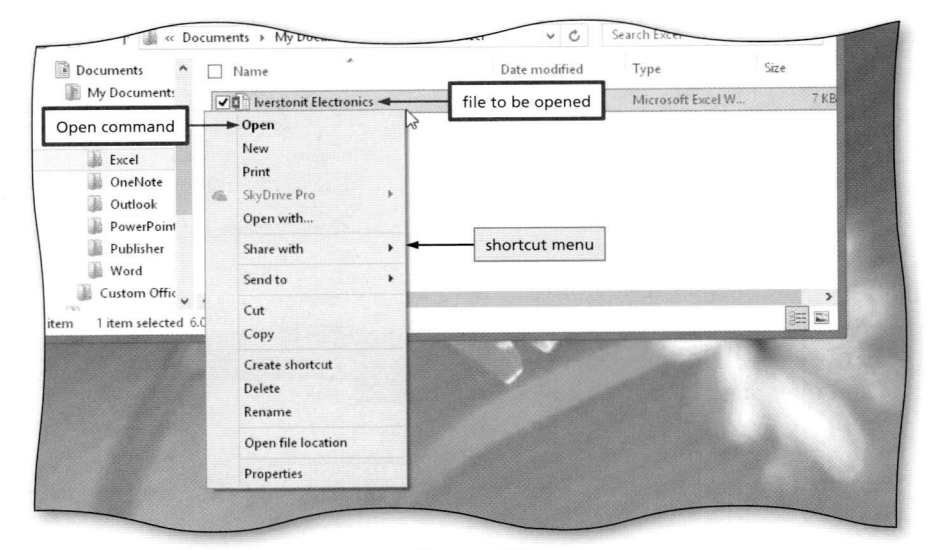

Figure 86

2

- Tap or click Open on the shortcut menu to open the selected file in the app used to create the file, Excel in this case (Figure 87).

- If the app window is not maximized, tap or click the Maximize button on the title bar to maximize the window.

Q&A Instead of using File Explorer, can I run Excel using the same method shown previously for Word and PowerPoint?
Yes, you can use any method of running an Office app to run Excel.

Figure 87

TO RUN AN APP FROM WINDOWS EXPLORER AND OPEN A FILE USING WINDOWS 7

If you are using Windows 7, perform these steps to run an app from Windows Explorer and open a file instead of the previous steps that use Windows 8.

1. Display the file to open in the folder window in Windows Explorer.
2. Right-click the file icon or file name (Iverstonit Electronics, in this case) to display a shortcut menu.
3. Click Open on the shortcut menu to open the selected file in the app used to create the file, Excel in this case.
4. If the app window is not maximized, click the Maximize button on the title bar to maximize the window.

Unique Features of Excel

The Excel window consists of a variety of components to make your work more efficient and worksheets more professional. These include the document window, ribbon, mini toolbar and shortcut menus, Quick Access Toolbar, and Microsoft Account area. Some of these components are common to other Office apps; others are unique to Excel.

Excel opens a new workbook with one worksheet. If necessary, you can add additional worksheets as long as your computer has enough memory to accommodate them.

Each worksheet has a sheet name that appears on a **sheet tab** at the bottom of the workbook. For example, Sheet1 is the name of the active worksheet displayed in the Iverstonit Electronics workbook. You can add more sheets to the workbook by clicking the New sheet button.

The Worksheet The worksheet is organized into a rectangular grid containing vertical columns and horizontal rows. A column letter above the grid, also called the **column heading**, identifies each column. A row number on the left side of the grid, also called the **row heading**, identifies each row. With the screen resolution set to 1366×768 and the Excel window maximized, Excel displays 20 columns (A through T) and 23 rows (1 through 23) of the worksheet on the screen, as shown in Figure 87.

The intersection of each column and row is a cell. A **cell** is the basic unit of a worksheet into which you enter data. Each worksheet in a workbook has 16,384 columns and 1,048,576 rows for a total of 17,179,869,180 cells. Only a small fraction of the active worksheet appears on the screen at one time.

A cell is referred to by its unique address, or **cell reference**, which is the coordinates of the intersection of a column and a row. To identify a cell, specify the column letter first, followed by the row number. For example, cell reference E2 refers to the cell located at the intersection of column E and row 2 (Figure 87).

One cell on the worksheet, designated the **active cell**, is the one into which you can enter data. The active cell in Figure 87 is A1. The active cell is identified in three ways. First, a heavy border surrounds the cell; second, the active cell reference shows immediately above column A in the Name box; and third, the column heading A and row heading 1 are highlighted so that it is easy to see which cell is active (Figure 87).

The horizontal and vertical lines on the worksheet itself are called **gridlines**. Gridlines make it easier to see and identify each cell in the worksheet. If desired, you can turn the gridlines off so that they do not show on the worksheet. While learning Excel, gridlines help you to understand the structure of the worksheet.

BTW

The Worksheet Size and Window
The 16,384 columns and 1,048,576 rows in Excel make for a huge worksheet that — if you could imagine — takes up the entire side of a building to display in its entirety. Your computer screen, by comparison, is a small window that allows you to view only a minute area of the worksheet at one time. While you cannot see the entire worksheet, you can move the window over the worksheet to view any part of it.

BTW

Customizing the Ribbon
In addition to customizing the Quick Access Toolbar, you can add items to and remove items from the ribbon. To customize the ribbon, click FILE on the ribbon to open the Backstage view, click Options in the Backstage view, and then click Customize Ribbon in the left pane of the Options dialog box. More information about customizing the ribbon is presented in a later chapter.

The pointer in Figure 87 on page OFF 58 has the shape of a block plus sign. The pointer appears as a block plus sign whenever it is located in a cell on the worksheet. Another common shape of the pointer is the block arrow. The pointer turns into the block arrow when you move it outside the worksheet or when you drag cell contents between rows or columns. The other pointer shapes are described when they appear on the screen.

Ribbon When you run Excel, the ribbon displays eight main tabs: FILE, HOME, INSERT, PAGE LAYOUT, FORMULAS, DATA, REVIEW, and VIEW. The FORMULAS and DATA tabs are specific to Excel. The FORMULAS tab allows you to work with Excel formulas, and the DATA tab allows you to work with data processing features such as importing and sorting data.

Formula Bar As you type, Excel displays the entry in the **formula bar**, which appears below the ribbon (Figure 88). You can make the formula bar larger by dragging the sizing handle at the bottom of the formula bar or tapping or clicking the expand button to the right of the formula bar. Excel also displays the active cell reference in the **Name box** on the left side of the formula bar.

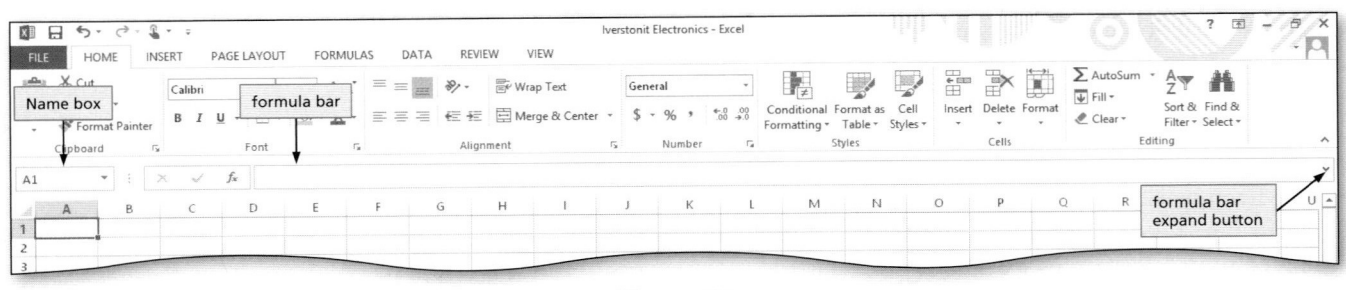

Figure 88

To Enter a Worksheet Title

1 SIGN IN | 2 USE WINDOWS | 3 USE APPS | 4 FILE MANAGEMENT | 5 SWITCH APPS | 6 SAVE FILES
7 CHANGE SCREEN RESOLUTION | 8 EXIT APPS | 9 USE ADDITIONAL APPS | 10 USE HELP

To enter data into a cell, you first must select it. The easiest way to select a cell (make it active) is to tap the cell or use the mouse to move the block plus sign pointer to the cell and then click. An alternative method is to use the arrow keys that are located just to the right of the typewriter keys on the keyboard. An arrow key selects the cell adjacent to the active cell in the direction of the arrow on the key.

In Excel, any set of characters containing a letter, hyphen (as in a telephone number), or space is considered text. **Text** is used to place titles, such as worksheet titles, column titles, and row titles, on the worksheet. The following steps enter the worksheet title in cell A1. **Why?** *A title informs others as to the contents of the worksheet, such as information regarding a company.*

1

- If it is not already the active cell, tap or click cell A1 to make it the active cell (Figure 89).

Figure 89

Office 2013 and Windows 8 Chapter

2

- Type **Inverstonit Electronics** in cell A1 (Figure 90).

Q&A Why did the appearance of the formula bar change?

Excel displays the title in the formula bar and in cell A1. When you begin typing a cell entry, Excel displays two additional boxes in the formula bar: the Cancel box and the Enter box. Tapping or clicking the Enter box completes an entry. Tapping or clicking the Cancel box cancels an entry.

Figure 90

3

- Tap or click the Enter box to complete the entry and enter the worksheet title in cell A1 (Figure 91).

Q&A Why do some commands on the ribbon appear dimmed?

Excel dims the commands that are unavailable for use at the current time.

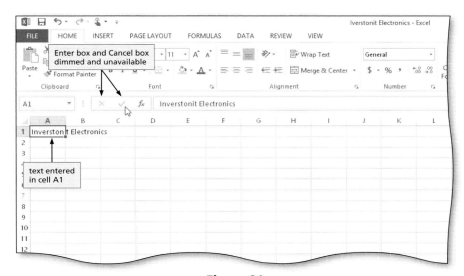

Figure 91

Other Ways

1. To complete entry, tap or click any cell other than active cell
2. To complete entry, press ENTER, HOME, PAGE UP, PAGE DOWN, END, UP ARROW, DOWN ARROW, LEFT ARROW, or RIGHT ARROW

To Save an Existing Office File with the Same File Name

1 SIGN IN | 2 USE WINDOWS | 3 USE APPS | 4 FILE MANAGEMENT | 5 SWITCH APPS | 6 SAVE FILES
7 CHANGE SCREEN RESOLUTION | 8 EXIT APPS | 9 USE ADDITIONAL APPS | 10 USE HELP

Saving frequently cannot be overemphasized. *Why? You have made modifications to the file (spreadsheet) since you created it. Thus, you should save again. Similarly, you should continue saving files frequently so that you do not lose the changes you have made since the time you last saved the file.* You can use the same file name, such as Iverstonit Electronics, to save the changes made to the document. The step on the next page saves a file again with the same file name.

1

• Tap or click the Save button on the Quick Access Toolbar to overwrite the previously saved file (Iverstonit Electronics, in this case) in the Excel folder (Figure 92).

Figure 92

Other Ways

1. Press CTRL+S or press SHIFT+F12

To Save a File with a New File Name

You might want to save a file with a different name or to a different location. For example, you might start a homework assignment with a data file and then save it with a final file name for submission to your instructor, saving it to a location designated by your instructor. The following steps save a file with a different file name.

1 Tap or click the FILE tab to open the Backstage view.

2 Tap or click the Save As tab to display the Save As gallery.

3 If necessary, tap or click Computer to display options in the right pane related to saving on your computer.

4 Tap or click the Browse button in the right pane to display the Save As dialog box.

5 Type **Iverstonit Electronics Rental Summary** in the File name box (Save As dialog box) to change the file name. Do not press the ENTER key after typing the file name because you do not want to close the dialog box at this time.

6 If necessary, navigate to the desired save location (in this case, the Excel folder in the CIS 101 folder [or your class folder] in the My Documents folder in the Documents library). For specific instructions, perform the tasks in Steps 5a through 5e on page OFF 51, replacing the PowerPoint folder with the Excel folder.

7 Tap or click the Save button (Save As dialog box) to save the worksheet in the selected folder on the selected drive with the entered file name.

To Exit an Office App

You are finished using Excel. The following steps exit Excel.

1 If you have one Office document open, tap or click the Close button on the right side of the title bar to close the document and exit the Office app; or if you have multiple Office documents open, press and hold or right-click the app button on the taskbar and then tap or click 'Close all windows' on the shortcut menu, or press ALT+F4 to close all open documents and exit the Office app.

2 If a dialog box appears, tap or click the Save button to save any changes made to the file since the last save.

Access

The term **database** describes a collection of data organized in a manner that allows access, retrieval, and use of that data. **Access** is a database management system. A **database management system** is software that allows you to use a computer to create a database; add, change, and delete data in the database; create queries that allow you to ask questions concerning the data in the database; and create forms and reports using the data in the database.

To Run an App

The following steps, which assume Windows is running, run the Access app based on a typical installation. You may need to ask your instructor how to run apps for your computer. If you are using Windows 7, skip these steps and instead perform the steps in the yellow box that immediately follows these Windows 8 steps.

1 Swipe in from the right edge of the screen or point to the upper-right corner of the screen to display the Charms bar.

2 Tap or click the Search charm on the Charms bar to display the Search menu.

3 Type **Access 2013** as the search text in the Search box and watch the search results appear in the Apps list.

4 Tap or click the app name, Access 2013 in this case, in the search results to run Access.

5 If the app window is not maximized, tap or click the Maximize button on its title bar to maximize the window (Figure 93).

Figure 93

Q&A Do I have to run Access using these steps?
No. You can use any previously discussed method of running an Office app to run Access.

TO RUN AN APP USING WINDOWS 7

If you are using Windows 7, perform these steps to run an app instead of the previous steps that use Windows 8.

1. Click the Start button on the Windows 7 taskbar to display the Start menu.

2. Type **Access 2013** as the search text in the 'Search programs and files' text box and watch the search results appear on the Start menu.

3. Click the app name, Access 2013 in this case, in the search results on the Start menu to run Access.

4. If the app window is not maximized, click the Maximize button on its title bar to maximize the window.

Unique Elements in Access

You work on objects such as tables, forms, and reports in the **Access work area**. Figure 94 shows a work area with multiple objects open. **Object tabs** for the open objects appear at the top of the work area. You select an open object by tapping or clicking its tab. In the figure, the Asset List table is the selected object. To the left of the work area is the Navigation Pane, which contains a list of all the objects in the database. You use this pane to open an object. You also can customize the way objects are displayed in the Navigation Pane.

Because the Navigation Pane can take up space in the window, you may not have as much open space for working as you would with Word or Excel. You can use the 'Shutter Bar Open/Close Button' to minimize the Navigation Pane when you are not using it, which allows more space to work with tables, forms, reports, and other database elements.

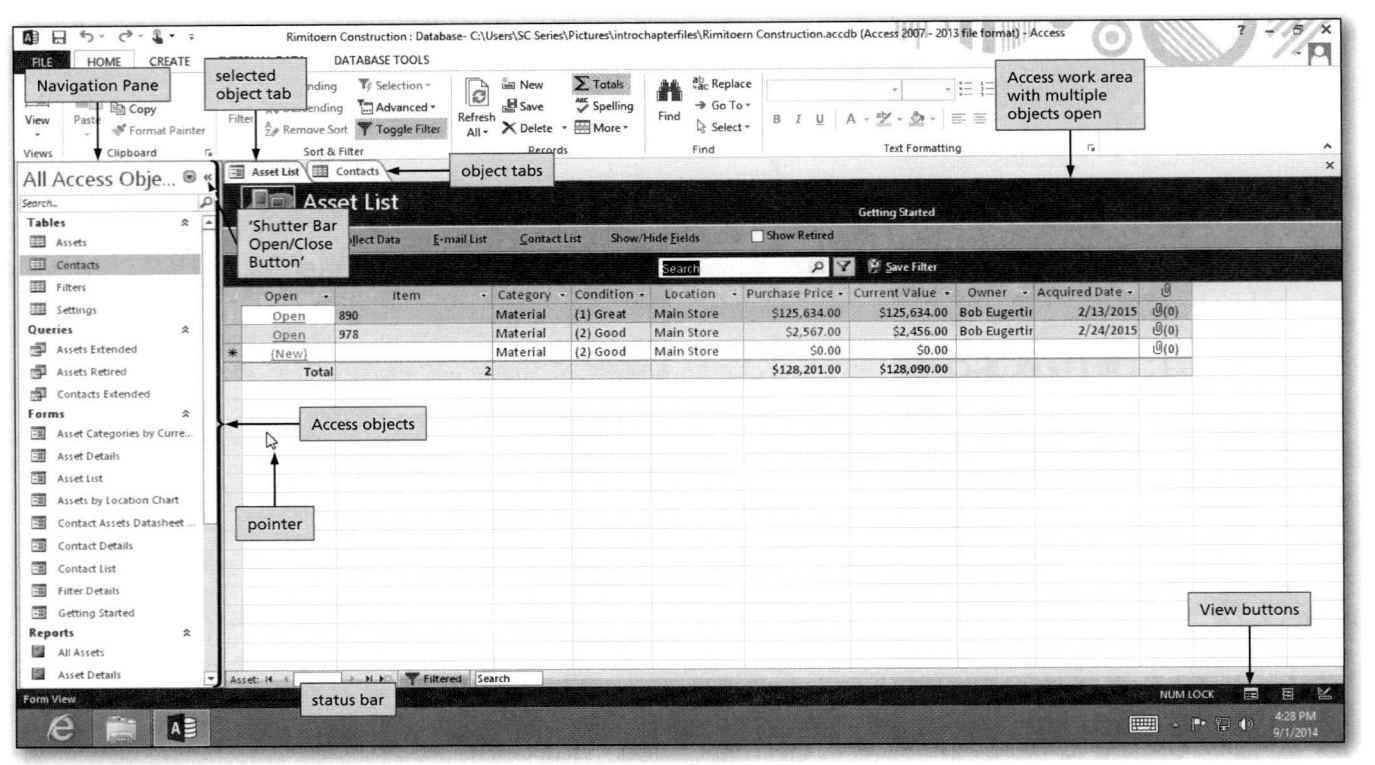

Figure 94

Ribbon When you run Access, the ribbon displays five main tabs: FILE, HOME, CREATE, EXTERNAL DATA, and DATABASE TOOLS. Access has unique groupings such as Sort & Filter and Records that are designed specifically for working with databases. Many of the formatting options are reserved for the tool tabs that appear when you are working with forms and reports.

To Create an Access Database

1 SIGN IN | 2 USE WINDOWS | 3 USE APPS | 4 FILE MANAGEMENT | 5 SWITCH APPS | 6 SAVE FILES
7 CHANGE SCREEN RESOLUTION | 8 EXIT APPS | 9 USE ADDITIONAL APPS | **10 USE HELP**

Unlike the other Office apps, Access saves a database when you first create it. When working in Access, you will add data to an Access database. As you add data to a database, Access automatically saves your changes rather than waiting until you manually save the database or exit Access. Recall that in Word and Excel, you entered the data first and then saved it.

Because Access automatically saves the database as you add and change data, you do not always have to click the Save button on the Quick Access Toolbar. Instead, the Save button in Access is used for saving the objects (including tables, queries, forms, reports, and other database objects) a database contains. You can use either the 'Blank desktop database' option or a template to create a new database. If you already know the

organization of your database, you would use the 'Blank desktop database' option. If not, you can use a template. Templates can guide you by suggesting some commonly used database organizations.

The following steps use the 'Blank desktop database' option to create a database named Rimitoein Construction in the Access folder in the class folder (CIS 101, in this case) in the Documents library. *Why? You have decided to use Microsoft Access to maintain large amounts of data.*

- Tap or click the 'Blank desktop database' thumbnail (shown in Figure 93 on page OFF 63) to select the database type.

- Type **Rimitoein Construction** in the File Name box to enter the new file name. Do not press the ENTER key after typing the file name because you do not want to create the database at this time (Figure 95).

Figure 95

- Tap or click the 'Browse for a location to put your database' button to display the File New Database dialog box.

- Navigate to the location for the database, that is, the Documents library, the My Documents folder, then to the folder identifying your class (CIS 101, in this case), and then to the Access folder (Figure 96). For specific instructions, perform the tasks in Steps 5a through 5e on page OFF 51, replacing the PowerPoint folder with the Access folder.

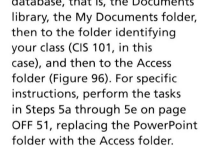

Q&A | Why does the 'Save as type' box say Microsoft Access 2007-2013 Databases?
Microsoft Access database formats change with some new versions of Microsoft Access. The most recent format is the Microsoft Access 2007-2013 Databases format, which was released with Access 2007 and Access 2013.

Figure 96

- Tap or click the OK button (File New Database dialog box) to select the Access folder as the location for the database and close the dialog box (Figure 97).

Figure 97

4

- Tap or click the Create button to create the database on the selected drive in the selected folder with the file name, Rimitoein Construction (Figure 98).

Q&A
How do I know that the Rimitoein Construction database is created?
The file name of the database appears on the title bar.

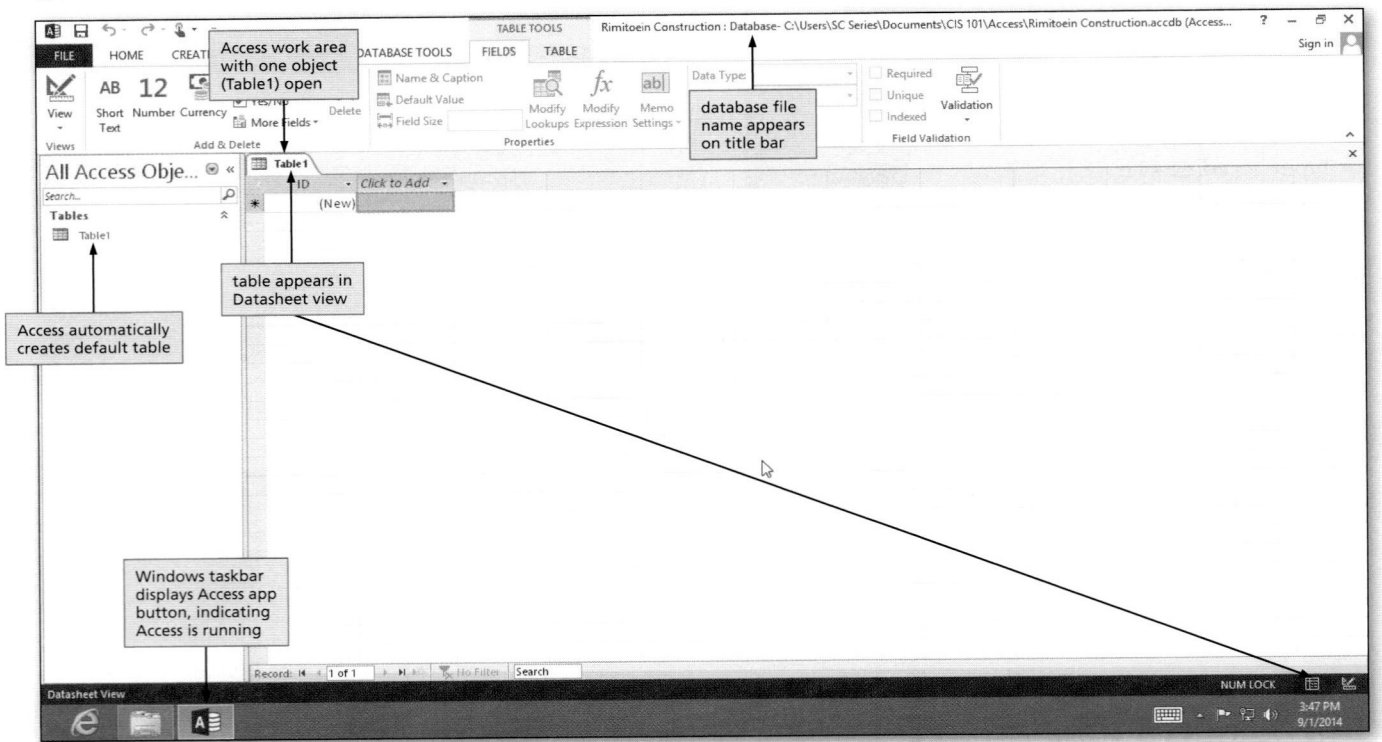

Figure 98

To Close an Office File

Assume you need to close the Access database and return to it later. The following step closes an Office file.

1 Tap or click FILE on the ribbon to open the Backstage view and then tap or click Close in the Backstage view to close the open file (Rimitoein Construction, in this case) without exiting the active app.

Q&A
Why is Access still on the screen?
When you close a database, the app remains running.

To Open an Existing Office File

1 SIGN IN | 2 USE WINDOWS | 3 USE APPS | 4 FILE MANAGEMENT | 5 SWITCH APPS | 6 SAVE FILES
7 CHANGE SCREEN RESOLUTION | 8 EXIT APPS | 9 USE ADDITIONAL APPS | 10 USE HELP

Assume you wish to continue working on an existing file, that is, a file you previously saved. Earlier in this chapter, you learned how to open a recently used file through the Backstage view. The following step opens a database, specifically the Rimitoein Construction database, that recently was saved. *Why? Because the file has been created already, you just need to reopen it.*

- Tap or click FILE on the ribbon to open the Backstage view and then tap or click Open in the Backstage view to display the Open gallery in the Backstage view.

- Tap or click Computer to display recent folders accessed on your computer.

- Tap or click the Browse button to display the Open dialog box.

- If necessary, navigate to the location of the file to open.

- Tap or click the file to open, Rimitoein Construction in this case, to select the file.

- Tap or click the Open button (Open dialog box) to open the file. If necessary, tap or click the Enable Content button (Figure 99).

Q&A | Why did the Security Warning appear?
The Security Warning appears when you open an Office file that might contain harmful content. The files you create in this chapter are not harmful, but you should be cautious when opening files from other people.

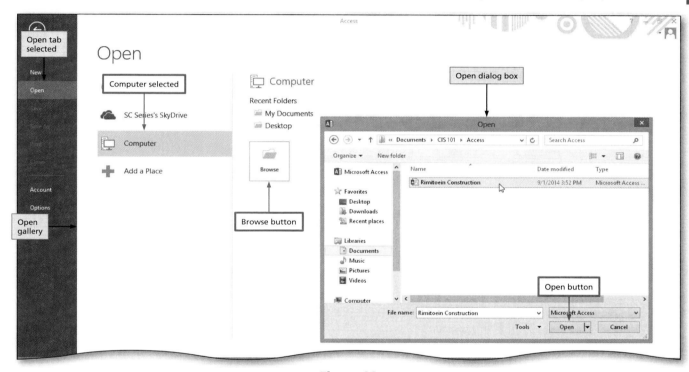

Figure 99

Other Ways
1. Press CTRL+O 2. Navigate to file in File Explorer window, double-tap or double-click file

To Exit an Office App

You are finished using Access. The following step exits Access.

1 Tap or click the Close button on the right side of the title bar to close the file and exit the Office app.

Other Office Apps

In addition to the Office apps discussed thus far, three other apps are useful when collaborating and communicating with others: Outlook, Publisher, and OneNote.

Outlook

Outlook is a powerful communications and scheduling app that helps you communicate with others, keep track of contacts, and organize your calendar. Apps such as Outlook provide a way for individuals and workgroups to organize, find, view, and share information easily. Outlook allows you to send and receive email messages and provides a means to organize contacts. Users can track email messages, meetings, and notes related to a particular contact. Outlook's Calendar, People, Tasks, and Notes components aid in this organization. Contact information readily is available from the Outlook Calendar, Mail, People, and Task components by accessing the Search Contacts feature.

Email is the transmission of messages and files over a computer network. Email has become an important means of exchanging information and files between business associates, classmates and instructors, friends, and family. Businesses find that using email to send documents electronically saves both time and money. Parents with students away at college or relatives who live across the country find that communicating by email is an inexpensive and easy way to stay in touch with their family members. Exchanging email messages is a widely used service of the Internet.

The Outlook Window Figure 100 shows an Outlook window, which is divided into three panes: the Folder pane, the Inbox message pane to the left of center, and the Reading Pane to the right of center.

When an email message is open in Outlook, it is displayed in a Message window (Figure 101). When you open a message, the Message tab on the ribbon appears, which contains the more frequently used commands.

Figure 100

Figure 101

Publisher

Publisher is a powerful desktop publishing (DTP) app that assists you in designing and producing professional-quality documents that combine text, graphics, illustrations, and photos. DTP software provides additional tools beyond those typically found in word processing apps, including design templates, graphic manipulation tools, color schemes or libraries, advanced layout and printing tools, and web components. For large jobs, businesses use DTP software to design publications that are camera ready, which means the files are suitable for outside commercial printing. In addition, DTP software can be used to create webpages and interactive web forms.

Publisher is used by people who regularly produce high-quality color publications, such as newsletters, brochures, flyers, logos, signs, catalogs, cards, and business forms. Saving publications as webpages or complete websites is a powerful component of Publisher. All publications can be saved in a format that easily is viewed and manipulated using a browser.

Publisher has many features designed to simplify production and make publications visually appealing. Using Publisher, you easily can change the shape, size, and color of text and graphics. You can include many kinds of graphical objects, including mastheads, borders, tables, images, pictures, charts, and web objects in publications, as well as integrate spreadsheets and databases.

The Publisher Window Publisher initially displays a list of publication types. **Publication types** are typical publications used by desktop publishers. The more popular types are displayed in the center of the window.

Once you select a publication type, a dialog box is displayed to allow you to create the publication (Figure 102 on the next page). Some templates are installed with Publisher, and others are available online. In Figure 102, the Brochure publication dialog box is displayed.

BTW
Running Publisher
When you first run Publisher, the New templates gallery usually is displayed in the Backstage view. If it is not displayed, click FILE on the ribbon, click Options in the Backstage view, click General (Publisher Options dialog box), and then click 'Show the New template gallery when starting Publisher' to select the check box in the right pane.

Figure 102

When you click the template, Publisher creates the document and sets it up for you to edit. Figure 103 shows the Brochure document that Publisher creates when default options are selected.

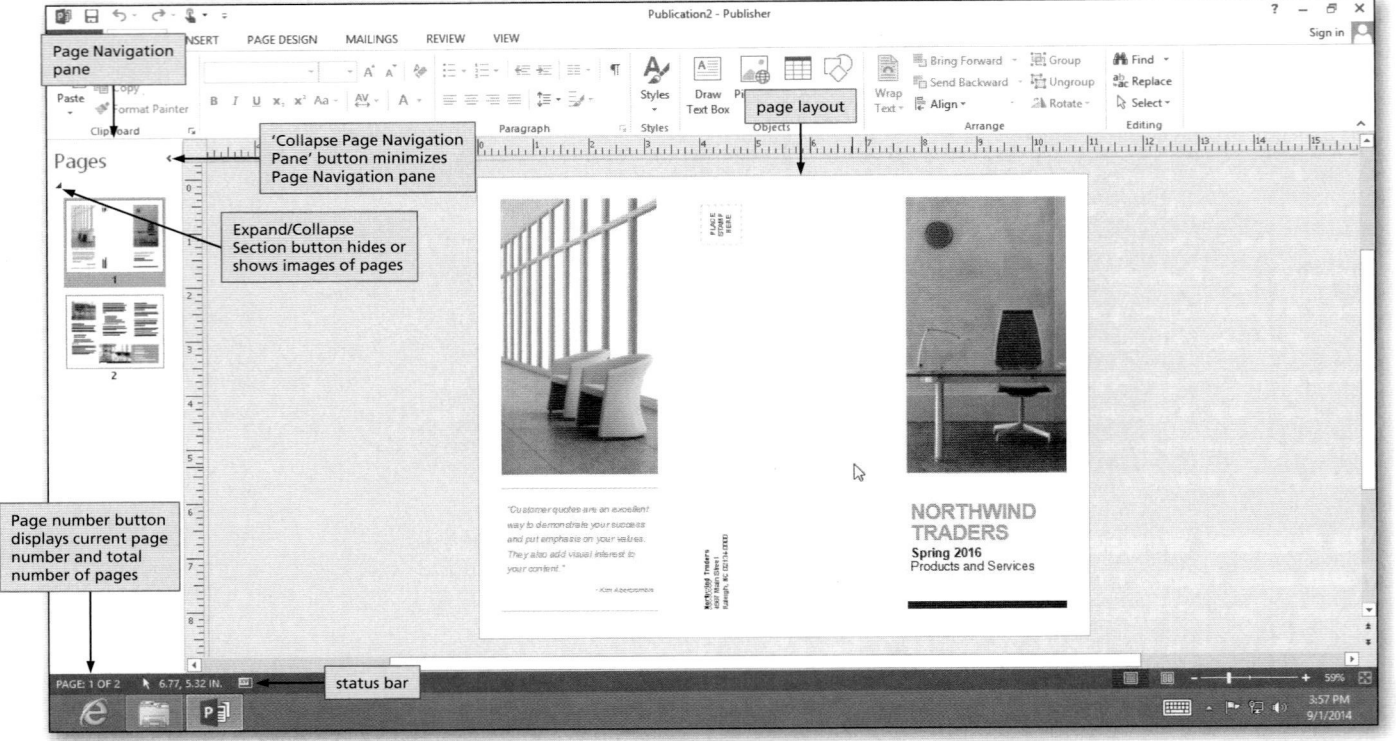

Figure 103

OneNote

OneNote is a note taking app that assists you in entering, saving, organizing, searching, and using notes. It enables you to create pages, which are organized in sections, just as in a physical notebook. In OneNote, you can type notes anywhere on a page and then easily move the notes around on the page. You can create lists and outlines, use handwriting to enter notes, and create drawings. If you use a tablet to add handwritten notes to a document, OneNote can convert the handwriting to text. It also can perform searches on the handwritten entries. Pictures and data from other apps easily are incorporated in your notes.

In addition to typing and handwriting, you can take audio notes. For example, you could record conversations during a meeting or lecture. As you record, you can take additional notes. When you play back the audio notes, you can synchronize the additional notes you took; that is, OneNote will show you during playback the exact points at which you added the notes. A variety of note flags, which are symbols that call your attention to notes on a page, enable you to flag notes as being important. You then can use the Note Flags summary to view the flagged notes, which can be sorted in a variety of ways.

OneNote includes tools to assist you with organizing a notebook and navigating its contents. It also includes a search feature, making it easy to find the specific notes in which you are interested. For short notes that you always want to have available readily, you can use Side Notes, which are used much like the sticky notes that you might use in a physical notebook.

OneNote Window All activity in OneNote takes place in the **notebook** (Figure 104). Like a physical notebook, the OneNote notebook consists of notes that are placed on **pages**. The pages are grouped into **sections**, which can be further grouped into **folders**. (No folders are shown in the notebook in the figure.) You can use the Search box to search for specific text in your notes.

You can add pages to the notebook using the Add Page button in the Page Tabs pane. If Page Tabs are displayed, you can switch to a page by tapping or clicking its tab. Figure 104 shows the Quick Notes page being displayed for the notebook.

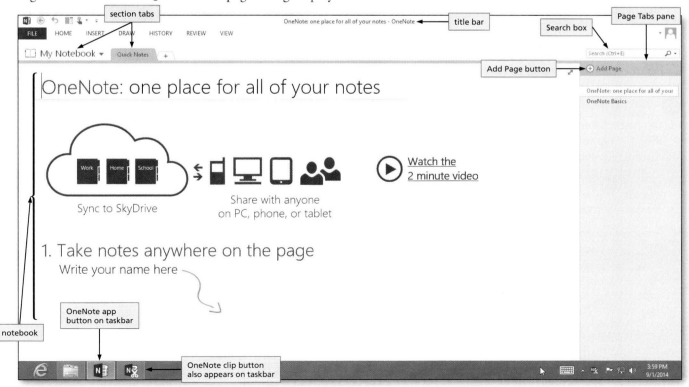

Figure 104

Break Point: If you wish to take a break, this is a good place to do so. To resume at a later time, continue to follow the steps from this location forward.

Renaming, Moving, and Deleting Files

Earlier in this chapter, you learned how to organize files in folders, which is part of a process known as **file management**. The following sections cover additional file management topics including renaming, moving, and deleting files.

To Rename a File

1 SIGN IN | 2 USE WINDOWS | 3 USE APPS | **4 FILE MANAGEMENT** | 5 SWITCH APPS | 6 SAVE FILES
7 CHANGE SCREEN RESOLUTION | 8 EXIT APPS | 9 USE ADDITIONAL APPS | **10 USE HELP**

In some circumstances, you may want to change the name of, or rename, a file or a folder. ***Why? You may want to distinguish a file in one folder or drive from a copy of a similar file, or you may decide to rename a file to better identify its contents.*** The Word folder shown in Figure 67 on page OFF 44 contains the Word document, Elephant Habitat. The following steps change the name of the Elephant Habitat file in the Word folder to Elephant Habitat Flyer. If you are using Windows 7, skip these steps and instead perform the steps in the yellow box that immediately follows these Windows 8 steps.

1

- If necessary, tap or click the File Explorer app button on the taskbar to make the folder window the active window.

- Navigate to the location of the file to be renamed (in this case, the Word folder in the CIS 101 [or your class folder] folder in the My Documents folder in the Documents library) to display the file(s) it contains in the file list.

- Press and hold or right-click the Elephant Habitat icon or file name in the file list to select the Elephant Habitat file and display a shortcut menu that presents a list of commands related to files (Figure 105).

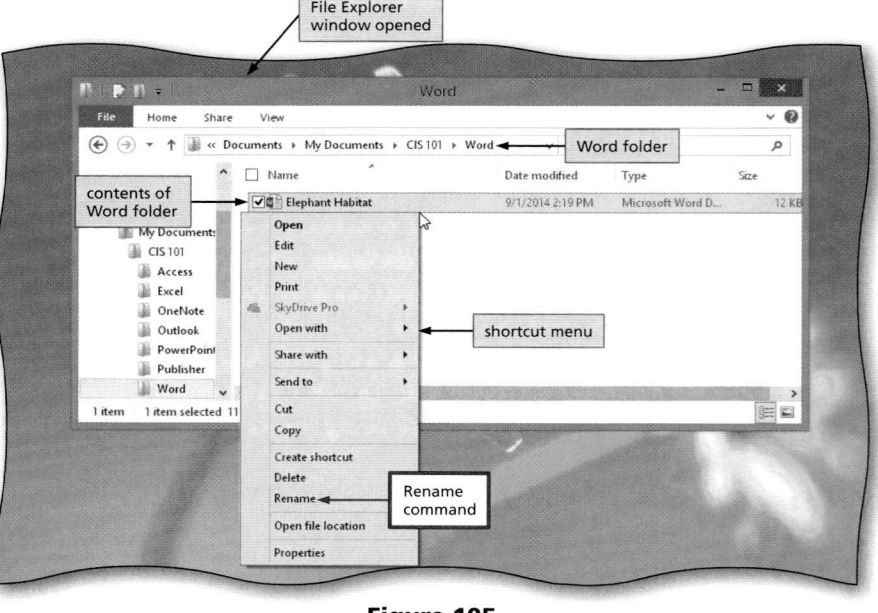

Figure 105

2

- Tap or click Rename on the shortcut menu to place the current file name in a text box.

- Type **Elephant Habitat Flyer** in the text box and then press the ENTER key (Figure 106).

Figure 106

Q&A
Are any risks involved in renaming files that are located on a hard disk?
If you inadvertently rename a file that is associated with certain apps, the apps may not be able to find the file and, therefore, may not run properly. Always use caution when renaming files.

Can I rename a file when it is open?
No, a file must be closed to change the file name.

Other Ways

1. Select file, press F2, type new file name, press ENTER 2. Select file, tap or click Rename (Home tab | Organize group), type new file name, press ENTER

TO RENAME A FILE USING WINDOWS 7

If you are using Windows 7, perform these steps to rename a file instead of the previous steps that use Windows 8.

1. If necessary, click the Windows Explorer app button on the taskbar to make the folder window the active window.
2. Navigate to the location of the file to be renamed (in this case, the Word folder in the CIS 101 [or your class folder] folder in the My Documents folder in the Documents library) to display the file(s) it contains in the file list.
3. Right-click the Elephant Habitat icon or file name in the file list to select the Elephant Habitat file and display a shortcut menu that presents a list of commands related to files.
4. Click Rename on the shortcut menu to place the current file name in a text box.
5. Type **Elephant Habitat Flyer** in the text box and then press the ENTER key.

To Move a File

1 SIGN IN | 2 USE WINDOWS | 3 USE APPS | **4 FILE MANAGEMENT** | 5 SWITCH APPS | 6 SAVE FILES
7 CHANGE SCREEN RESOLUTION | 8 EXIT APPS | 9 USE ADDITIONAL APPS | **10 USE HELP**

Why? *At some time, you may want to move a file from one folder, called the source folder, to another, called the destination folder.* When you move a file, it no longer appears in the original folder. If the destination and the source folders are on the same media, you can move a file by dragging it. If the folders are on different media, then you will need to press and hold and then drag, or right-drag the file, and then click Move here on the shortcut menu. The following step moves the Iverstonit Electronics Rental Summary file from the Excel folder to the OneNote folder. If you are using Windows 7, skip these steps and instead perform the steps in the yellow box that immediately follows these Windows 8 steps.

- In File Explorer, navigate to the location of the file to be moved (in this case, the Excel folder in the CIS 101 folder [or your class folder] in the Documents library).

- Tap or click the Excel folder in the navigation pane to display the files it contains in the right pane (Figure 107).

- Drag the Iverstonit Electronics Rental Summary file in the right pane to the OneNote folder in the navigation pane.

 Experiment

- Click the OneNote folder in the navigation pane to verify that the file was moved.

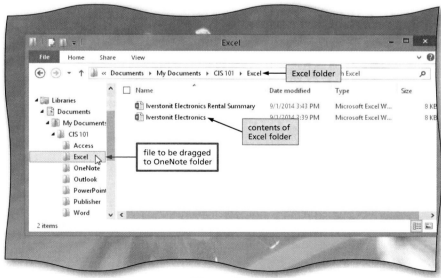

Figure 107

Other Ways

1. Press and hold or right-click file to move, tap or click Cut on shortcut menu, press and hold or right-click destination folder, tap or click Paste on shortcut menu

2. Select file to move, press CTRL+X, select destination folder, press CTRL+V

To Move a File Using Windows 7

If you are using Windows 7, perform these steps to move a file instead of the previous steps that use Windows 8.

1. In Windows Explorer, navigate to the location of the file to be moved (in this case, the Excel folder in the CIS 101 folder [or your class folder] in the Documents library).
2. Click the Excel folder in the navigation pane to display the files it contains in the right pane.
3. Drag the Iverstonit Electronics Rental Summary file in the right pane to the OneNote folder in the navigation pane.

To Delete a File

1 SIGN IN | 2 USE WINDOWS | 3 USE APPS | **4 FILE MANAGEMENT** | 5 SWITCH APPS | 6 SAVE FILES
7 CHANGE SCREEN RESOLUTION | 8 EXIT APPS | 9 USE ADDITIONAL APPS | **10 USE HELP**

A final task you may want to perform is to delete a file. Exercise extreme caution when deleting a file or files. When you delete a file from a hard disk, the deleted file is stored in the Recycle Bin where you can recover it until you empty the Recycle Bin. If you delete a file from removable media, such as a USB flash drive, the file is deleted permanently. The next steps delete the Elephant Habitat Opening file from the PowerPoint folder. *Why? When a file no longer is needed, you can delete it to conserve space in your storage location.* If you are using Windows 7, skip these steps and instead perform the steps in the yellow box that immediately follows these Windows 8 steps.

1

- In File Explorer, navigate to the location of the file to be deleted (in this case, the PowerPoint folder in the CIS 101 folder [or your class folder] in the Documents library).

- Press and hold or right-click the Elephant Habitat Opening icon or file name in the right pane to select the file and display a shortcut menu (Figure 108).

2

- Tap or click Delete on the shortcut menu to delete the file.

- If a dialog box appears, tap or click the Yes button to delete the file.

Q&A Can I use this same technique to delete a folder?
Yes. Right-click the folder and then click Delete on the shortcut menu. When you delete a folder, all of the files and folders contained in the folder you are deleting, together with any files and folders on lower hierarchical levels, are deleted as well.

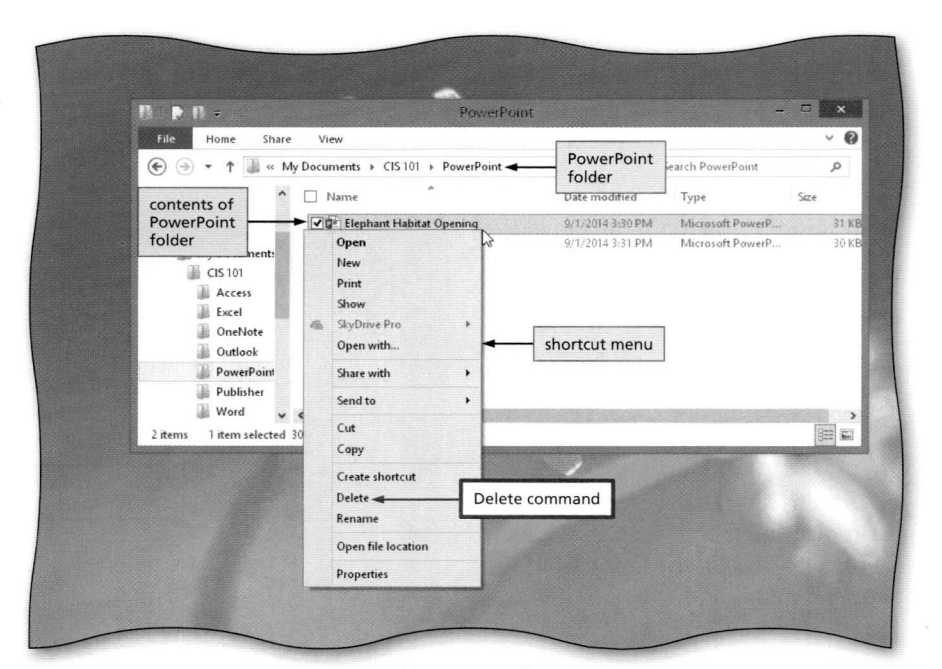

Figure 108

Other Ways

1. Select icon, press DELETE

To Delete a File Using Windows 7

If you are using Windows 7, perform these steps to delete a file instead of the previous steps that use Windows 8.

1. In Windows Explorer, navigate to the location of the file to be deleted (in this case, the PowerPoint folder in the CIS 101 folder [or your class folder] in the Documents library).
2. Right-click the Elephant Habitat Opening icon or file name in the right pane to select the file and display a shortcut menu.
3. Click Delete on the shortcut menu to delete the file.
4. If a dialog box appears, click the Yes button to delete the file.

Microsoft Office and Windows Help

At any time while you are using one of the Office apps, you can use Office Help to display information about all topics associated with the app. To illustrate the use of Office Help, this section uses Word. Help in other Office apps operates in a similar fashion.

In Office, Help is presented in a window that has browser-style navigation buttons. Each Office app has its own Help home page, which is the starting Help page that is displayed in the Help window. If your computer is connected to the Internet, the contents of the Help page reflect both the local help files installed on the computer and material from Microsoft's website.

To Open the Help Window in an Office App

1 SIGN IN | 2 USE WINDOWS | 3 USE APPS | **4 FILE MANAGEMENT** | 5 SWITCH APPS | 6 SAVE FILES
7 CHANGE SCREEN RESOLUTION | 8 EXIT APPS | 9 USE ADDITIONAL APPS | **10 USE HELP**

The following step opens the Word Help window. **Why?** *You might not understand how certain commands or operations work in Word, so you can obtain the necessary information using help.*

1

- Run an Office app, in this case Word.

- Tap or click the Office app's Help button near the upper-right corner of the app window (the 'Microsoft Word Help' button, in this case) to open the app's Help window (Figure 109).

Figure 109

Other Ways
1. Press F1

Moving and Resizing Windows

At times, it is useful, or even necessary, to have more than one window open and visible on the screen at the same time. You can resize and move these open windows so that you can view different areas of and elements in the window. In the case of the Help window, for example, it could be covering document text in the Word window that you need to see.

To Move a Window by Dragging

You can move any open window that is not maximized to another location on the desktop by dragging the title bar of the window. ***Why?*** *You might want to have a better view of what is behind the window or just want to move the window so that you can see it better.* The following step drags the Word Help window to the upper-left corner of the desktop.

1

- Drag the window title bar (the Word Help window title bar, in this case) so that the window moves to the upper-left corner of the desktop, as shown in Figure 110.

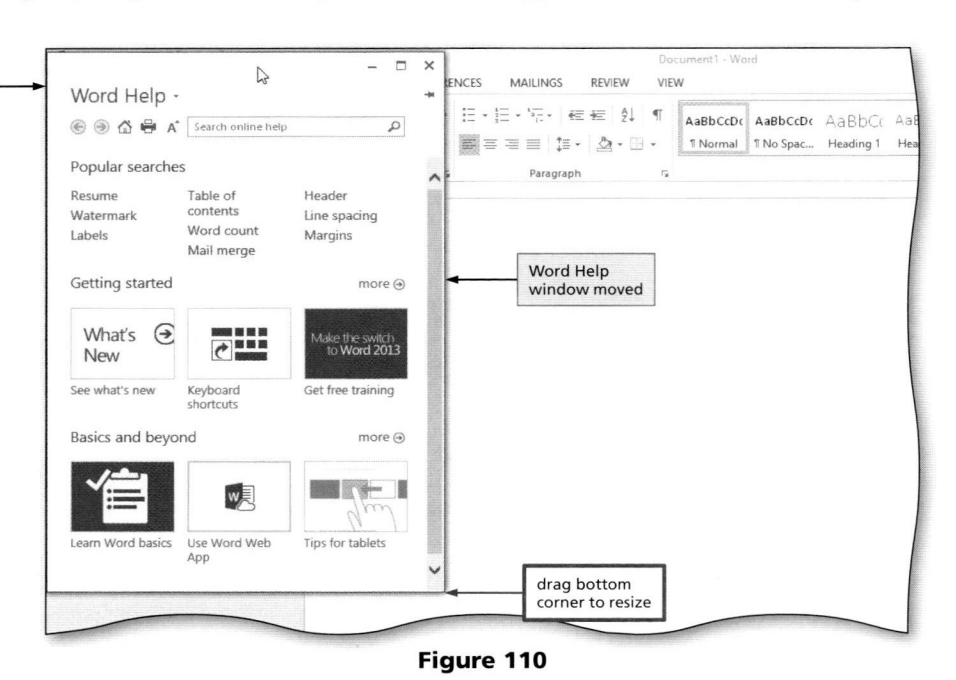

Figure 110

To Resize a Window by Dragging

A method used to change the size of the window is to drag the window borders. The following step changes the size of the Word Help window by dragging its borders. ***Why?*** *Sometimes, information is not visible completely in a window, and you want to increase the size of the window.*

1

- If you are using a mouse, point to the lower-right corner of the window (the Word Help window, in this case) until the pointer changes to a two-headed arrow.

- Drag the bottom border downward to display more of the active window (Figure 111).

Q&A

Can I drag other borders on the window to enlarge or shrink the window?

Yes, you can drag the left, right, and top borders and any window corner to resize a window.

Will Windows remember the new size of the window after I close it?

Yes. When you reopen the window, Windows will display it at the same size it was when you closed it.

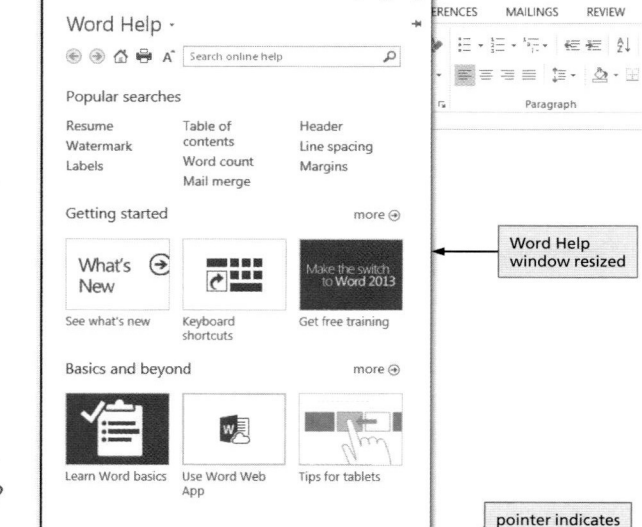

Figure 111

Using Office Help

Once an Office app's Help window is open, several methods exist for navigating Help. You can search for help by using any of the three following methods from the Help window:

1. Enter search text in the 'Search online help' text box.
2. Click the links in the Help window.
3. Use the Table of Contents.

To Obtain Help Using the 'Search online help' Text Box

1 SIGN IN | 2 USE WINDOWS | 3 USE APPS | 4 FILE MANAGEMENT | 5 SWITCH APPS | 6 SAVE FILES
7 CHANGE SCREEN RESOLUTION | 8 EXIT APPS | 9 USE ADDITIONAL APPS | 10 USE HELP

Assume for the following example that you want to know more about fonts. The following steps use the 'Search online help' text box to obtain useful information about fonts by entering the word, fonts, as search text. *Why? You may not know the exact help topic you are looking to find, so using keywords can help narrow your search.*

1

- Type **fonts** in the 'Search online help' text box at the top of the Word Help window to enter the search text.

- Tap or click the 'Search online help' button to display the search results (Figure 112).

Q&A Why do my search results differ?
If you do not have an Internet connection, your results will reflect only the content of the Help files on your computer. When searching for help online, results also can change as material is added, deleted, and updated on the online Help webpages maintained by Microsoft.

Why were my search results not very helpful?
When initiating a search, be sure to check the spelling of the search text; also, keep your search specific to return the most accurate results.

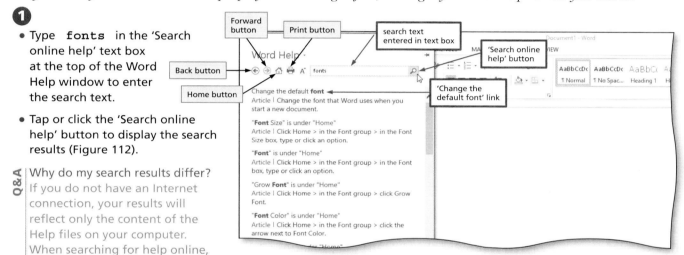

Figure 112

2

- Tap or click the 'Change the default font' link to display the Help information associated with the selected topic (Figure 113).

Figure 113

- Tap or click the Home button in the Help window to clear the search results and redisplay the Help home page (Figure 114).

Figure 114

To Obtain Help Using Help Links

1 SIGN IN | 2 USE WINDOWS | 3 USE APPS | 4 FILE MANAGEMENT | 5 SWITCH APPS | 6 SAVE FILES
7 CHANGE SCREEN RESOLUTION | 8 EXIT APPS | 9 USE ADDITIONAL APPS | 10 USE HELP

If your topic of interest is listed in the Help window, you can click the link to begin browsing the Help categories instead of entering search text. *Why?* *You browse Help just as you would browse a website. If you know which category contains your Help information, you may wish to use these links.* The following step finds the Resume information using the Resume link from the Word Help home page.

1

- Tap or click the Resume link on the Help home page (shown in Figure 114) to display the Resume help links (Figure 115).

2

- After reviewing the page, tap or click the Close button to close the Help window.

- Tap or click the Office app's Close button (Word, in this case) to exit the Office app.

Figure 115

Obtaining Help while Working in an Office App

Help in the Office apps provides you with the ability to obtain help directly, without opening the Help window and initiating a search. For example, you may be unsure about how a particular command works, or you may be presented with a dialog box that you are not sure how to use.

Figure 116 shows one option for obtaining help while working in an Office app. If you want to learn more about a command, point to its button and wait for the ScreenTip to appear. If the Help icon appears in the ScreenTip, press the F1 key while pointing to the button to open the Help window associated with that command.

Figure 117 shows a dialog box that contains a Help button. Pressing the F1 key while the dialog box is displayed opens a Help window. The Help window contains help about that dialog box, if available. If no help file is available for that particular dialog box, then the main Help window opens.

Figure 116

Figure 117

Using Windows Help and Support

One of the more powerful Windows features is Windows Help and Support. **Windows Help and Support** is available when using Windows or when using any Microsoft app running in Windows. The same methods used for searching Microsoft Office Help can be used in Windows Help and Support. The difference is that Windows Help and Support displays help for Windows, instead of for Microsoft Office.

OFF 80 **Office 2013 and Windows 8 Chapter** Essential Concepts and Skills

1 SIGN IN | 2 USE WINDOWS | 3 USE APPS | 4 FILE MANAGEMENT | 5 SWITCH APPS | 6 SAVE FILES
7 CHANGE SCREEN RESOLUTION | 8 EXIT APPS | 9 USE ADDITIONAL APPS | 10 USE HELP

To Use Windows Help and Support

The following steps use Windows Help and Support and open the Windows Help and Support window, which contains links to more information about Windows. *Why? This feature is designed to assist you in using Windows or the various apps.* If you are using Windows 7, skip these steps and instead perform the steps in the yellow box that immediately follows these Windows 8 steps.

- Swipe in from the right edge of the screen or point to the upper-right corner of the screen to display the Charms bar (Figure 118).

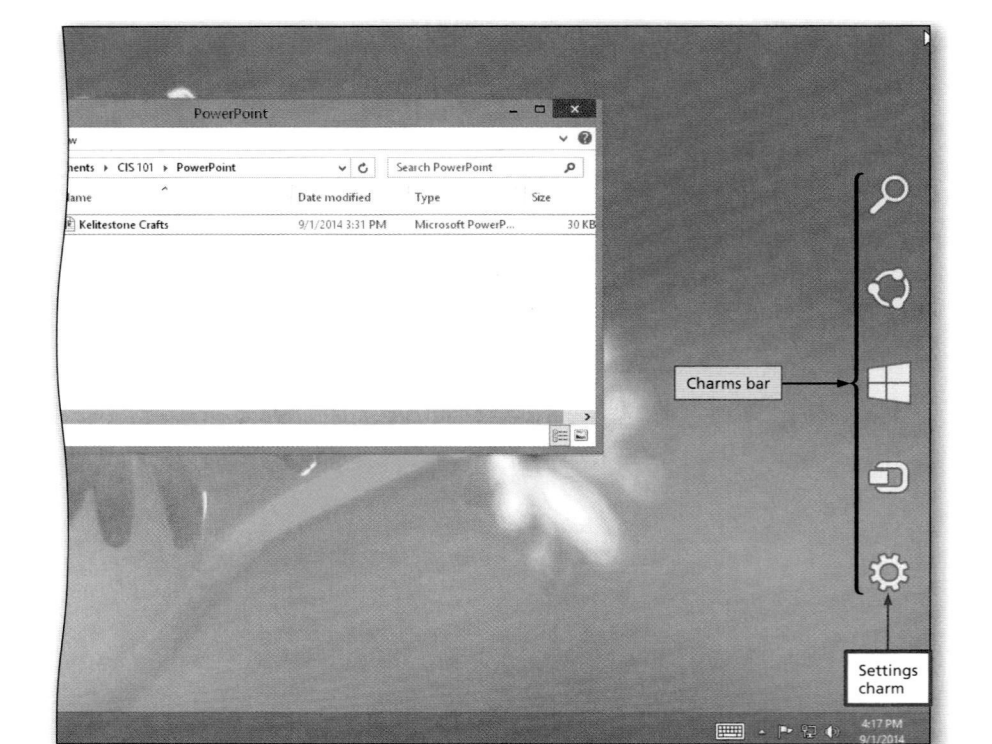

Figure 118

2

- Tap or click the Settings charm on the Charms bar to display the Settings menu (Figure 119).

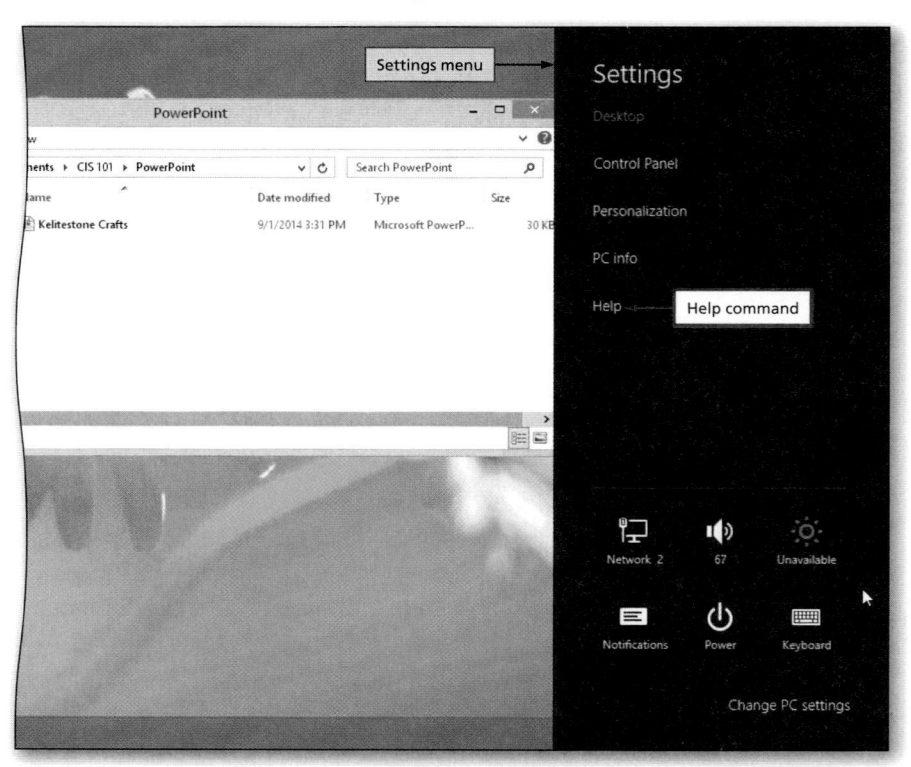

Figure 119

❸

- Tap or click Help to open the Windows Help and Support window (Figure 120).

❹

- After reviewing the Windows Help and Support window, tap or click the Close button to close the Windows Help and Support window.

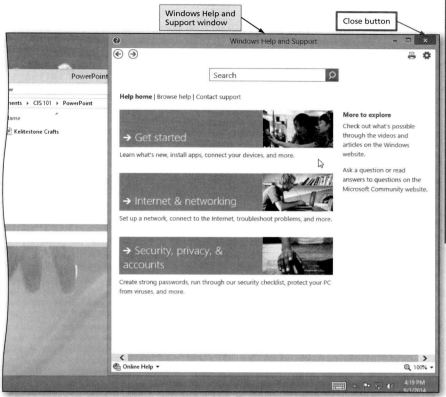

Figure 120

Other Ways

1. Press WINDOWS + F1

TO USE WINDOWS HELP AND SUPPORT WITH WINDOWS 7

If you are using Windows 7, perform these steps to start Windows Help and Support instead of the previous steps that use Windows 8.

1. Click the Start button on the taskbar to display the Start menu.
2. Click Help and Support on the Start menu to open the Windows Help and Support window.
3. After reviewing the Windows Help and Support window, click the Close button to exit Windows Help and Support.

Chapter Summary

In this chapter, you learned how to use the Windows interface, several touch screen and mouse operations, file and folder management, some basic features of some Microsoft Office apps, including Word, PowerPoint, Excel, and Access, and discovered the common elements that exist among these different Office apps, and additional Office apps, including Office, Publisher, and OneNote. The items listed on the next page include all of the new Windows and Office apps skills you have learned in this chapter, with the tasks grouped by activity.

BTW

Certification
The Microsoft Office Specialist (MOS) program provides an opportunity for you to obtain a valuable industry credential — proof that you have the Microsoft Office 2013 skills required by employers. For more information, visit the Certification resource on the Student Companion Site located on www.cengagebrain.com. For detailed instructions about accessing available resources, visit www.cengage .com/ct/studentdownload or contact your instructor for information about accessing the required files.

BTW

Quick Reference
For a table that lists how to complete the tasks covered in this book using touch gestures, the mouse, ribbon, shortcut menu, and keyboard, see the Quick Reference Summary at the back of this book, or visit the Quick Reference resource on the Student Companion Site located on www.cengagebrain.com. For detailed instructions about accessing available resources, visit www.cengage .com/ct/studentdownload or contact your instructor for information about accessing the required files.

Change Screen Resolution
Change the Screen Resolution (OFF 40)

Exit Apps
Exit an Office App with One Document Open (OFF 42)

File Management
Create a Folder (OFF 25)
Create a Folder within a Folder (OFF 27)
Expand a Folder, Scroll through Folder Contents, and Collapse a Folder (OFF 29)
Copy a Folder to a USB Flash Drive (OFF 43)
Rename a File (OFF 72)
Move a File (OFF 73)
Delete a File (OFF 74)

Save and Manage Files
Save a File in a Folder (OFF 31, 53)
Save a File on SkyDrive (OFF 36)

Sign In
Sign In to an Account (OFF 7)

Switch Apps
Switch from One App to Another (OFF 30)

Use Apps
Display a Different Tab on the Ribbon (OFF 18)
Collapse and Expand the Ribbon and Use Full Screen Mode (OFF 19)
Use a Shortcut Menu to Relocate the Quick Access Toolbar (OFF 20)
Customize the Quick Access Toolbar (OFF 22)

Enter Text in a Document (OFF 23)
Run an App Using the Search Box (OFF 46)
Enter Content in a Title Slide (OFF 49)
Create a New Office Document from the Backstage View (OFF 51)
Close an Office File Using the Backstage View (OFF 54)
Open a Recent Office File Using the Backstage View (OFF 54)
Create a New Blank Office Document from File Explorer (OFF 56)
Run an App from File Explorer and Open a File (OFF 57)
Enter a Worksheet Title (OFF 60)
Save an Existing Office File with the Same File Name (OFF 61)
Create an Access Database (OFF 64)
Open an Existing Office File (OFF 66)

Use Help
Open the Help Window in an Office App (OFF 75)
Obtain Help Using the Search online help Text Box (OFF 77)
Obtain Help Using Help Links (OFF 78)
Use Windows Help and Support (OFF 80)

Use Windows
Run an App from the Start Screen (OFF 11)
Switch between an App and the Start Screen (OFF 13)
Maximize a Window (OFF 14)
Minimize and Restore a Window (OFF 34)
Move a Window by Dragging (OFF 76)
Resize a Window by Dragging (OFF 76)

CONSIDER THIS: PLAN AHEAD

What guidelines should you follow to plan your projects?

The process of communicating specific information is a learned, rational skill. Computers and software, especially Microsoft Office 2013, can help you develop ideas and present detailed information to a particular audience and minimize much of the laborious work of drafting and revising projects. No matter what method you use to plan a project, it is beneficial to follow some specific guidelines from the onset to arrive at a final product that is informative, relevant, and effective. Use some aspects of these guidelines every time you undertake a project, and others as needed in specific instances.

1. Determine the project's purpose.
 a) Clearly define why you are undertaking this assignment.
 b) Begin to draft ideas of how best to communicate information by handwriting ideas on paper; composing directly on a laptop, tablet, or mobile device; or developing a strategy that fits your particular thinking and writing style.

2. Analyze your audience.
 a) Learn about the people who will read, analyze, or view your work.
 b) Determine their interests and needs so that you can present the information they need to know and omit the information they already possess.
 c) Form a mental picture of these people or find photos of people who fit this profile so that you can develop a project with the audience in mind.

3. Gather possible content.
 a) Locate existing information that may reside in spreadsheets, databases, or other files.
 b) Conduct a web search to find relevant websites.
 c) Read pamphlets, magazine and newspaper articles, and books to gain insights of how others have approached your topic.
 d) Conduct personal interviews to obtain perspectives not available by any other means.
 e) Consider video and audio clips as potential sources for material that might complement or support the factual data you uncover.

4. Determine what content to present to your audience.
 a) Write three or four major ideas you want an audience member to remember after reading or viewing your project.
 b) Envision your project's endpoint, the key fact you wish to emphasize, so that all project elements lead to this final element.
 c) Determine relevant time factors, such as the length of time to develop the project, how long readers will spend reviewing your project, or the amount of time allocated for your speaking engagement.
 d) Decide whether a graph, photo, or artistic element can express or enhance a particular concept.
 e) Be mindful of the order in which you plan to present the content, and place the most important material at the top or bottom of the page, because readers and audience members generally remember the first and last pieces of information they see and hear.

How should you submit solutions to questions in the assignments identified with a symbol?
Every assignment in this book contains one or more questions identified with a symbol. These questions require you to think beyond the assigned file. Present your solutions to the questions in the format required by your instructor. Possible formats may include one or more of these options: write the answer; create a document that contains the answer; present your answer to the class; discuss your answer in a group; record the answer as audio or video using a webcam, smartphone, or portable media player; or post answers on a blog, wiki, or website.

CONSIDER THIS

Apply Your Knowledge

Reinforce the skills and apply the concepts you learned in this chapter.

Creating a Folder and a Document
Instructions: You will create a Word folder and then create a Word document and save it in the folder.

Perform the following tasks:

1. Open the File Explorer window and then double-tap or double-click to open the Documents library.
2. Tap or click the New folder button on the Quick Access Toolbar to display a new folder icon and text box for the folder name.
3. Type **Word** in the text box to name the folder. Press the ENTER key to create the folder in the Documents library.
4. Run Word.
5. Enter the text shown in Figure 121 in a new blank document.
6. Tap or click the Save button on the Quick Access Toolbar. Navigate to the Word folder in the Documents library and then save the document using the file name, Apply 1 Class List.
7. If your Quick Access Toolbar does not show the Quick Print button, add the Quick Print button to the Quick Access Toolbar. Print the document using the Quick Print button on the Quick Access Toolbar. When you are finished printing, remove the Quick Print button from the Quick Access Toolbar.
8. Submit the printout to your instructor.
9. Exit Word.
10. What other commands might you find useful to include on the Quick Access Toolbar?

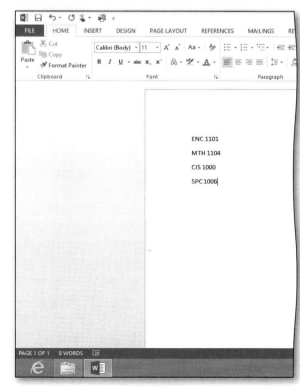

Figure 121

Extend Your Knowledge

Extend the skills you learned in this chapter and experiment with new skills. You will use Help to complete the assignment.

Using Help

Instructions: Use Office Help to perform the following tasks.

Perform the following tasks:

1. Run Word.
2. Tap or click the Microsoft Word Help button to open the Word Help window (Figure 122).
3. Search Word Help to answer the following questions.
 a. What are the steps to add a new group to the ribbon?
 b. What are Quick Parts?
4. With the Word app still running, run PowerPoint.
5. Tap or click the Microsoft PowerPoint Help button on the title bar to open the PowerPoint Help window.
6. Search PowerPoint Help to answer the following questions.
 a. What is a slide master?
 b. How do you copy slides from another presentation into the existing presentation?
7. Exit PowerPoint.
8. Run Excel.
9. Tap or click the Microsoft Excel Help button to open the Excel Help window.
10. Search Excel Help to answer the following questions.
 a. What are three different functions available in Excel?
 b. What are sparklines?
11. Exit Excel.
12. Run Access.
13. Tap or click the Microsoft Access Help button to open the Access Help window.
14. Search Access Help to answer the following questions.
 a. What is SQL?
 b. What is a data macro?
15. Exit Access.
16. Type the answers from your searches in a new blank Word document. Save the document with a new file name and then submit it in the format specified by your instructor.
17. Exit Word.
18. ✳ What search text did you use to perform the searches above? Did it take multiple attempts to search and locate the exact information for which you were searching?

Figure 122

Analyze, Correct, Improve

Analyze a file structure, correct all errors, and improve the design.

Organizing Vacation Photos

Note: To complete this assignment, you will be required to use the Data Files for Students. Visit www.cengage.com/ct/studentdownload for detailed instructions or contact your instructor for information about accessing the required files.

Instructions: Traditionally, you have stored photos from past vacations together in one folder. The photos are becoming difficult to manage, and you now want to store them in appropriate folders. You will create the folder structure shown in Figure 123. You then will move the photos to the folders so that they will be organized properly.

1. Correct Create the folder structure in Figure 123 so that you are able to store the photos in an organized manner.

2. Improve View each photo and drag it to the appropriate folder to improve the organization.

3. ✺ Think about the files you have stored on your computer. What folder hierarchy would be best to manage your files?

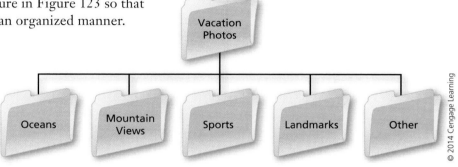

Figure 123

© 2014 Cengage Learning

In the Labs

Use the guidelines, concepts, and skills presented in this chapter to increase your knowledge of Windows 8 and Office 2013. Labs 1 and 2, which increase in difficulty, require you to create solutions based on what you learned in the chapter; Lab 3 requires you to create a solution, which uses cloud and web technologies, by learning and investigating on your own from general guidance.

Lab 1: **Creating Folders for a Video Store**

Problem: Your friend works for Ebaird Video. He would like to organize his files in relation to the types of videos available in the store. He has six main categories: drama, action, romance, foreign, biographical, and comedy. You are to create a folder structure similar to Figure 124 on the next page.

Instructions: Perform the following tasks:
1. Insert a USB flash drive in an available USB port and then open the USB flash drive window.
2. Create the main folder for Ebaird Video.
3. Navigate to the Ebaird Video folder.
4. Within the Ebaird Video folder, create a folder for each of the following: Drama, Action, Romance, Foreign, Biographical, and Comedy.
5. Within the Action folder, create two additional folders, one for Science Fiction and the second for Western.
6. Submit the assignment in the format specified by your instructor.
7. ✺ Think about how you use your computer for various tasks (consider personal, professional, and academic reasons). What folders do you think will be required on your computer to store the files you save?

Continued >

In the Labs *continued*

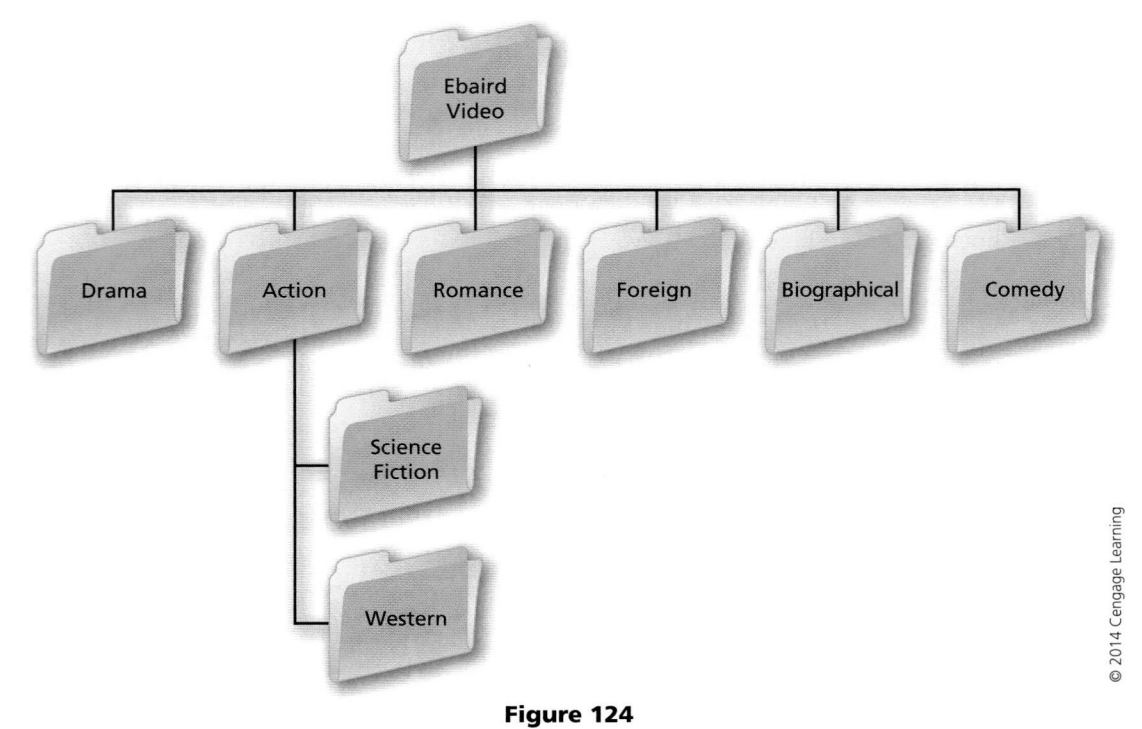

Figure 124

Lab 2: **Saving Files in Folders**

Creating Office Documents

Problem: You are taking a class that requires you to create a Word, PowerPoint, Excel, and Access file. You will save these files to folders named for four different Office apps (Figure 125).

Instructions: Create the folders shown in Figure 125. Then, using the respective Office app, create a small file to save in each folder (i.e., create a Word document to save in the Word folder, a PowerPoint presentation to save in the PowerPoint folder, and so on).

1. Create a Word document containing the text, First Word Assignment.

2. In the Backstage view, tap or click Save As and then tap or click Computer.

3. Tap or click the Browse button to display the Save As dialog box.

4. Tap or click Documents to open the Documents library. Next, create the folder structure shown in Figure 125 using the New folder button.

5. Navigate to the Word folder and then save the file in the Word folder.

6. Create a PowerPoint presentation with one slide containing the title text, Sample PowerPoint Presentation, and then save it in the PowerPoint folder.

7. Create an Excel spreadsheet containing the text, My First Budget Excel Spreadsheet, in cell A1 and then save it in the Excel folder.

8. Save an Access database named, My Music Database, in the Access folder.

9. Submit the assignment in the format specified by your instructor.

10. ☀ Based on your current knowledge of Word, PowerPoint, Excel, and Access, which app do you think you will use most frequently? Why?

Figure 125

Lab 3: Expand Your World: Cloud and Web Technologies
Creating Office Web App Documents

Problem: You are taking a class that requires you to create a file in Word, PowerPoint, and Excel. You will save these files to folders named for three different Office Web apps (Figure 126).

Instructions: Create the folders shown in Figure 126. Then, using the respective Office Web app, create a small file to save in each folder (i.e., create a Word document to save in the Word folder, a PowerPoint presentation to save in the PowerPoint folder, and so on).

1. Sign in to SkyDrive in your browser.

2. Use the Create button to create the folder structure shown in Figure 126.

3. In the Word folder, use the Create button to create a Word document with the file name, Notes, and containing the text, Important Test on Tuesday.

4. Save the document and then exit the app.

5. Navigate to the PowerPoint folder.

6. Create a PowerPoint presentation called Kirek Sales with one slide containing the title text, Online Presentation, and then exit the app.

7. Navigate to the Excel folder.

8. Create an Excel spreadsheet, called Kirek Sales Analysis, containing the text, Sales Cost Analysis, in cell A1, and then exit the app.

9. Submit the assignment in the format specified by your instructor.

10. ✺ Based on your current knowledge of SkyDrive, do you think you will use it? What about the Web apps?

© 2014 Cengage Learning

Figure 126

✺ Consider This: Your Turn

Apply your creative thinking and problem solving skills to design and implement a solution.

1: Creating Beginning Files for Classes

Personal

You are taking the following classes: Introduction to Sociology, Chemistry, Calculus, and Marketing. Create folders for each of the classes. Create a folder structure that will store the documents for each of these classes. Use Word to create a Word document with the name of each class and the class meeting locations and times. Use PowerPoint to begin creating a simple lab presentation for your chemistry class. It should begin with a title slide containing the text, Chemical Reactions. Create and save a database named Companies for your marketing class. The database does not need to contain any data. In the Calculus folder, create an Excel spreadsheet with the text, Excel Formulas, in cell A1. Use the concepts and techniques presented in this chapter to create the folders and files, and store the files in their respective locations. Submit your assignment in the format specified by your instructor.

✺ You made several decisions while determining the folder structure in this assignment. What was the rationale behind these decisions? Are there any other decisions that also might have worked?

Continued >

Consider This: Your Turn *continued*

2: Creating Folders

Professional

Your boss at the music store where you work part-time has asked for help with organizing his files. After looking through the files, you decided upon a file structure for her to use, including the following folders: CDs, DVDs, and general merchandise. Think about the different types of CDs, DVDs, and general merchandise that might be sold at your store, and create a folder structure that will be used to store information about the three types of items (CDs, DVDs, and general merchandise), and also can organize the different types of each item. For example, general merchandise might include items such as clothing, portable media players, and accessories. Use the concepts and techniques presented in this chapter to create the folders. Submit your assignment in the format specified by your instructor.

☀ You made several decisions while determining the folder structure in this assignment. What was the rationale behind these decisions? Justify why you feel this folder structure will help your boss organize her files.

3: Using Help

Research and Collaboration

You have just installed a new computer with the Windows operating system and want to be sure that it is protected from the threat of viruses, so you ask two of your friends to help research computer viruses, virus prevention, and virus removal. In a team of three people, each person should choose a topic (computer viruses, virus prevention, and virus removal) to research. Use the concepts and techniques presented in this chapter to use Help to find information regarding these topics. Create a Word document that contains steps to properly safeguard a computer from viruses, ways to prevent viruses, as well as the different ways to remove a virus should your computer become infected. Submit your assignment in the format specified by your instructor.

☀ You made several decisions while searching Windows Help and Support for this assignment. What decisions did you make? What was the rationale behind these decisions? How did you locate the required information about viruses in help?

Learn Online

Reinforce what you learned in this chapter with games, exercises, training, and many other online activities and resources.

Student Companion Site Reinforcement activities and resources are available at no additional cost on www.cengagebrain.com. Visit www.cengage.com/ct/studentdownload for detailed instructions about accessing the resources available at the Student Companion Site.

SAM Put your skills into practice with SAM Projects! If you have a SAM account, go to www.cengage.com/sam2013 to access SAM assignments for this chapter.

Office 365 Essentials

Microsoft product screen shots used with permission from Microsoft Corporation.

Objectives

You will have mastered the material in this chapter when you can:

- Describe the components of Office 365
- Compare Office 2013 to Office 365 subscription plans
- Understand the productivity tools of Office 365
- Sync multiple devices using Office 365
- Describe how business teams collaborate using SharePoint
- Describe how to use a SharePoint template to design a public website
- Describe how to conduct an online meeting with Lync

Explore Office 365

Introduction to Office 365

Microsoft Office 365 uses the cloud to deliver a subscription-based service offering the newest Office suite and much more. The Microsoft cloud provides Office software and information stored on remote servers all over the world. Your documents are located online or on the cloud, which provides you access to your information anywhere using a PC, Mac, tablet, mobile phone, or other device with an Internet connection. For businesses and students alike, Office 365 offers significant cost savings compared to the traditional cost of purchasing Microsoft Office 2013. In addition to the core desktop Office suite, Office 365 provides access to email, calendars, conferencing, file sharing, and website design, which sync across multiple devices.

Cloud Computing

Cloud computing refers to a collection of computer servers that house resources users access through the Internet (Figure 1). These resources include email messages, schedules, music, photos, videos, games, websites, programs, apps, servers, storage, and more. Instead of accessing these resources on your computer or mobile device, you access them on the cloud.

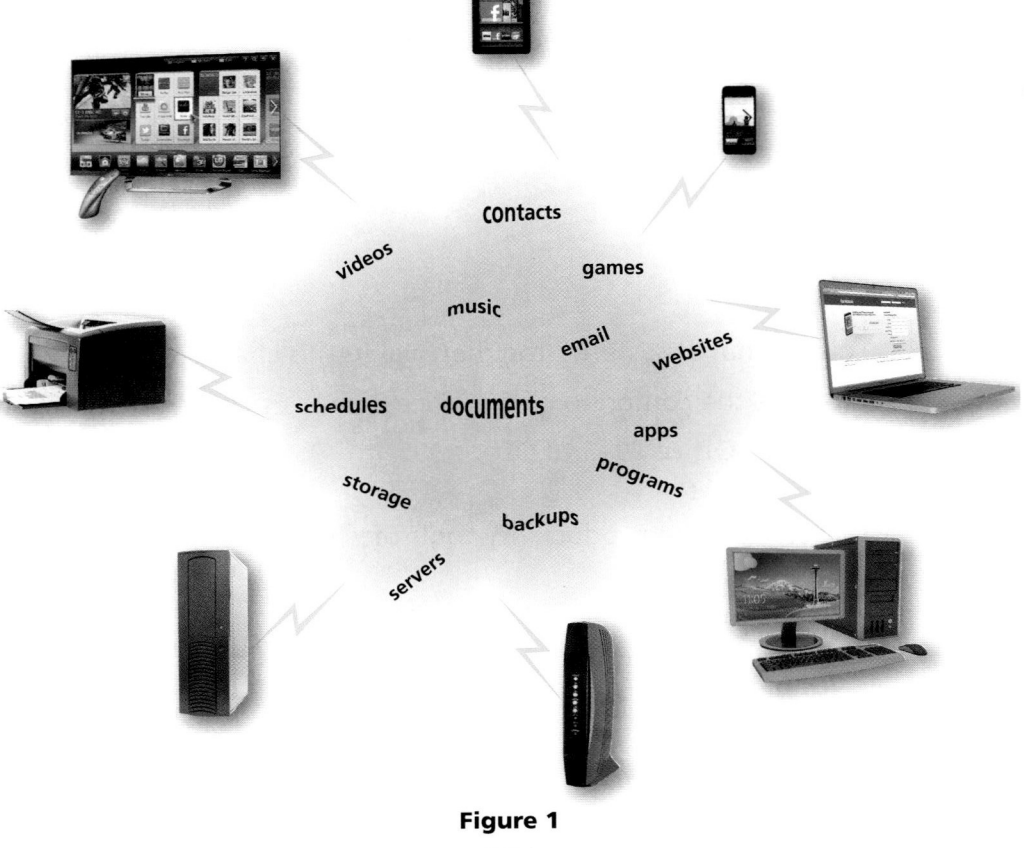

contacts
videos
games
music
email
websites
schedules
documents
apps
storage
programs
backups
servers

Figure 1

CLD 2

Cloud computing can help businesses be more efficient and save them money by shifting usage and the consumption of resources, such as servers and programs, from a local environment to the Internet. For example, an employee working during the day in California could use computing resources located in an office in London that is closed for the evening. When the company in California uses the computing resources, it pays a fee that is based on the amount of computing time and other resources it consumes, much in the same way that consumers pay utility companies for the amount of electricity they use.

Cloud computing is changing how users access and pay for software applications. Fading fast are the days when software packages were sold in boxes at a physical store location with a one-time purchase software license fee. Instead, the new pricing structure is a subscription-based model, where users pay a monthly or annual fee for the software that you can use on multiple devices. The cloud-based Office 365 offers the Office suite with added features that allow you to communicate and collaborate with others in real time.

When you create a free Microsoft account, do you get free cloud storage space?
Yes, when you create a free Microsoft account at Outlook.com, you have access to 7 GB of cloud storage for any type of files.

CONSIDER THIS

What Is Office 365?

Office 365 (Office365.com) is a collection of programs and services, which includes the Microsoft Office 2013 suite, file storage, online collaboration, and file synchronization, as shown in Figure 2 on the next page. You can access these services using your computer, browser, or supported mobile device. For example, a business has two options for providing Office to their employees. A business could purchase Office 2013 and install the software on company computers and servers; however, this traditional Office 2013 package with perpetual licensing does not include the communication and collaboration tools. Employees could not access the Office software if they were not using their work computers. In contrast, if the business purchases a monthly subscription to Office 365, each employee has access to the Office suite on up to five different computers, whether at home or work; company-wide email; web conferencing; website creation capabilities; cloud storage; and shared files. For a lower price, Office 365 provides many more features. In addition, a business may prefer a subscription plan with predictable monthly costs and no up-front infrastructure costs.

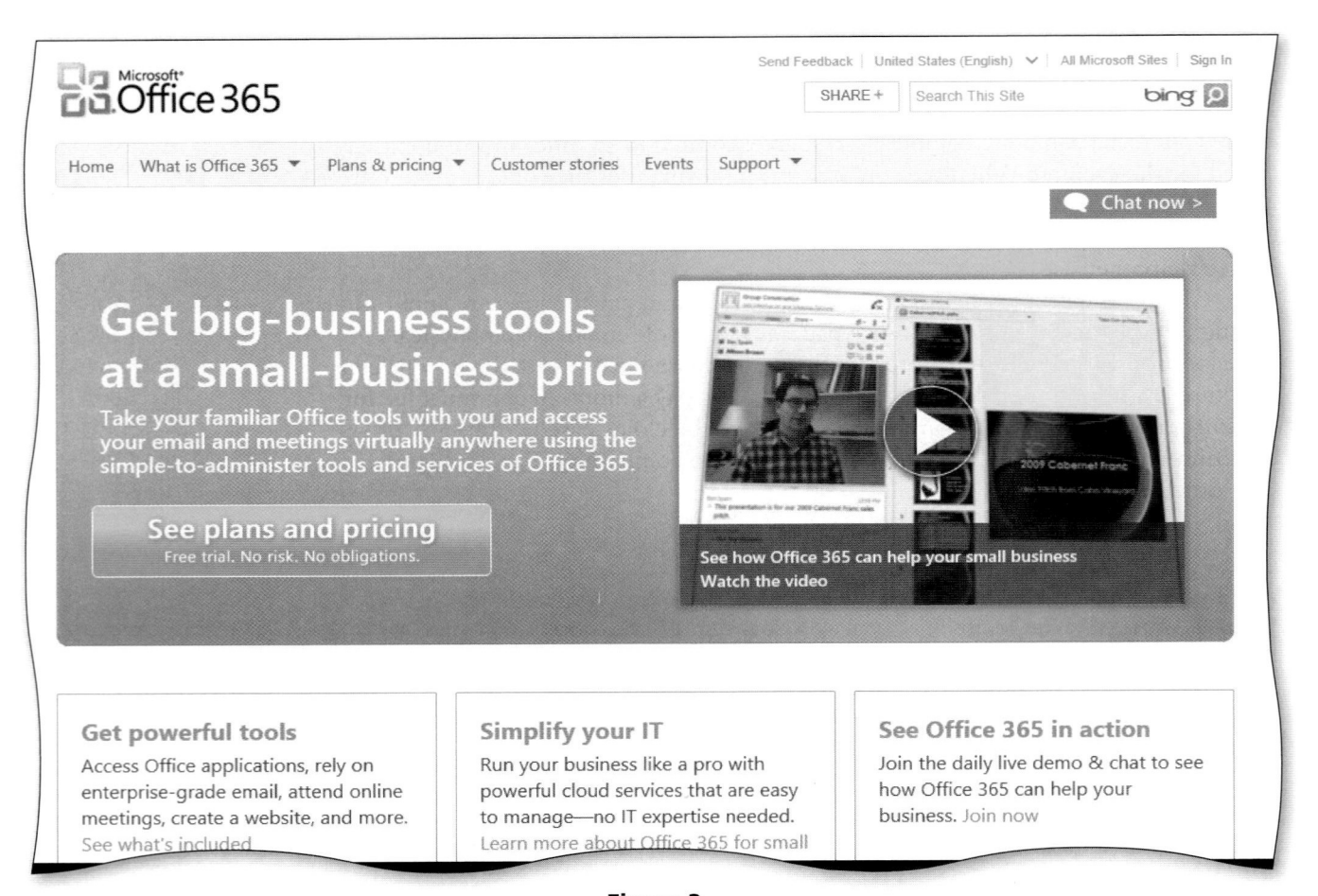

Figure 2

Office 2013 and Office 365 Features Comparison

Office 2013 is the name of the perpetual software package that includes individual applications that can be installed on a single computer. An Office 365 subscription comes with a license to install the software on multiple PCs or Macs at the same time, giving you more flexibility to use your Office products in your home, school, or workplace, whether on a computer or a mobile device. Office 365 provides the Office 2013 programs as part of a subscription service that includes online storage, sharing, and syncing via Microsoft cloud services as shown in Table 1.

Office 365 is available in business, consumer, education, and government editions. Office 365 combines the full version of the Microsoft Office desktop suite with cloud-based versions of Microsoft's communications and collaboration services. The subscription package includes:

- Microsoft Exchange online for shared email and calendars
- Microsoft SharePoint Online for shared file access and public website creation
- Microsoft Office Web apps for browser viewing
- Microsoft Lync Online for communication services

Table 1 Office 2013 and Office 365 Feature Comparison

Office 2013 Professional (Installed on a single device)	Office 365 Subscription (Installed on 2 to 5 devices)
Microsoft Word	Microsoft Word
Microsoft Excel	Microsoft Excel
Microsoft PowerPoint	Microsoft PowerPoint
Microsoft Access	Microsoft Access
Microsoft Outlook	Microsoft Outlook
Microsoft Publisher	Microsoft Publisher
Microsoft OneNote	Microsoft OneNote
	email and calendars (Exchange Online)
	file sharing (SharePoint Online)
	public website design and publishing (SharePoint Online)
	browser-based Office Web Apps
	instant messaging (Lync Online)
	audio and video web conferencing (Lync Online)
	screen sharing with shared control (Lync Online)
	technical support

© 2014 Cengage Learning

Subscription-Based Office 365 Plans

Microsoft provides various subscription plans for Office 365 with different benefits for each individual or organization. Subscription plans include Office 365 Home Premium for home users, Office 365 University for students, Office 365 Small Business, Office 365 Small Business Premium, Office 365 Midsize Business, and Office 365 Enterprise and Government. During the Office 365 sign-up process, you create a Microsoft email address and password to use on your multiple devices. A single subscription to an Office 365 Home Premium account can cover an entire household. The Office 365 Home Premium subscription allows up to five concurrent installations by using the same email address and password combination. This means that your mother could be on the main family computer while you use your tablet and smartphone at the same time. You each can sign in with your individual Microsoft accounts using your settings and accessing your own documents using a single Office 365 subscription.

The Office 365 University subscription plan is designed for higher-education full-time and part-time students, faculty, and staff. By submitting the proper credentials, such as a school email address, students and faculty can purchase Office 365 University, including Word, PowerPoint, Excel, Access, Outlook, Publisher, and OneNote. A one-time payment covers a four-year subscription. In addition, Office 365 University provides users with 27 GB of SkyDrive cloud storage rather than the free 7 GB provided by a Microsoft account, and 60 Skype world minutes per month for videoconferencing. Students have the option of renewing for another four years, for a total of eight years. The Office 365 University edition is limited to two computers (PC or Mac).

The Microsoft Office 365 Business Plans can provide full support for employees to work from any location, whether they are in their traditional business office, commuting to and from work across the country, or working from a home office. Office 365 small business plans (Small Business and Small Business Premium) are best for companies with up to 10 employees, but can accommodate up to 25 users. Office 365 Midsize Business accommodates from 11 to 300 users. Office 365 Enterprise Plan fits organizations ranging in size from a single employee to 50,000-plus users. Each employee can install Microsoft Office 365 on five different computers.

First Look at Office 365

Microsoft Office 365 subscription plans offer all the same applications that are available in the Microsoft Office Professional 2013 suite in addition to multiple communication and collaboration tools. With Office 365 you can retrieve, edit, and save Office documents on the Office 365 cloud, coauthor documents in real time with others, and quickly initiate computer-based calls, instant messages, and web conferences with others.

Productivity Tools

Whether you are inserting audio and video into a Word document to create a high-impact business plan proposal or utilizing the visualization tools in Excel to chart the return on investment of a new mobile marketing program, Office 365 premium plans deliver the full Office product with the same features as the latest version of Microsoft Office. Office 365 uses a quick-start installation technology, called **Click-to-Run**, that downloads and installs the basics within minutes, so that users are able to start working almost immediately. It also includes **Office on Demand**, which streams Office to Windows 7- and Windows 8-based PCs for work performed on public computers. The single-use copy that is installed temporarily on the Windows computer does not count toward the device limit. No installation is necessary when using Office on Demand, and the applications disappear from the computer once you are finished using them. If you have a document on a USB drive or on SkyDrive that you need to edit on another PC, you can use Office on Demand to get the full version of Word in just a few minutes.

In effect, the Office 365 subscription provides access to the full Office applications wherever you are working. When you access your Office 365 account management panel, three choices are listed: 32- and 64-bit versions of Office 2013, and Office for Mac. Selecting the third option will initiate a download of an installer that must be run in the standard OS X fashion. When you install Office 365 on a Mac, the most current Mac version of Office is installed.

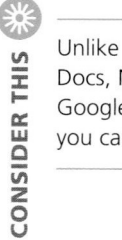

CONSIDER THIS

Unlike Google, which offers online documents, spreadsheets, and presentations called Google Docs, Microsoft Office 365 installs locally on your computer in addition to being available online. Google Docs is entirely browser based, which means if you are not connected to the Internet, you cannot access your Google Docs files.

Email and Calendars

In business, sharing information is essential to meeting the needs of your customers and staff. Office 365 offers shared access to business email, calendars, and contacts using **Exchange Online** from a computer, tablet, phone, and browser. The cloud-based Exchange Online enables business people to access Outlook information from anywhere at any time, while eliminating the cost of purchasing and maintaining servers to store data. If you need to meet with a colleague about a new project, you can compare calendars to view availability, confirm conference room availability, share project contacts, search email messages related to the project, and send email invitations to the project meeting. Exchange Online also allows you to search and access your company's address list.

Online Meetings

When you are working with a team on a project that requires interaction, email and text communications can slow the communications process. Microsoft Lync connects you with others by facilitating real-time, interactive presentations and meetings over the Internet using both video and audio calling. As shown in Figure 3, you can conduct an online meeting with a team member or customer that includes an instant messaging conversation, audio, high-definition video, virtual whiteboards, and screen sharing. If the customer does not have an Office 365 subscription, they still can join the meeting through the invitation link, which runs the Lync Web App.

Skype is another tool in the Office 365 subscription, which enables users to place video calls to computers and smartphones and voice calls to landlines. Skype also supports instant message and file sharing to computers and mobile devices. While Skype may be adequate for simple communication, Lync provides for more robust, comprehensive communications. These robust features include high-definition (HD) videoconferencing capabilities, a whiteboard, and a larger audience. Using Lync, meeting attendees simultaneously can view up to five participants' video, identify the active speaker, and associate names with faces. Lync supports up to 250 attendees per meeting. Unlike Skype, Lync meetings can be recorded for replaying at a later time. This enables businesses and schools to schedule meetings or organize online classes using Lync capabilities.

File Sharing

Office 365 includes a team site, which is a password-protected portal that supports sharing of large, difficult-to-email files and provides a single location for the latest versions of documents. In business, for example, colleagues working on common projects can save valuable time by being able to access instantly the latest master copy of each document. Security can be managed through different

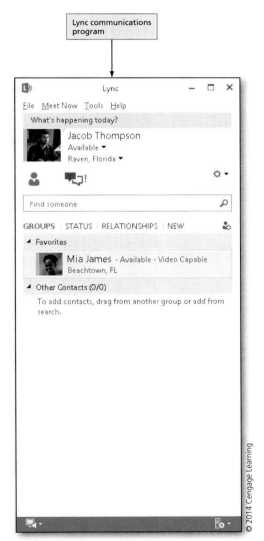

Lync communications program

Figure 3

levels of user access so that users see only what they are supposed to see. Office 365 provides access to shared files using the cloud, making writing, editing, and sharing documents easier. If a construction company creates a commercial bid for a building project, the customers can be invited to view an Excel spreadsheet bid, construction timetable with a shared calendar, and an Access database of all the materials needed using the file sharing feature online.

Website Creation

Office 365 business plan subscriptions include a built-in hosted public website, where customers and clients can find an online storefront of a company. This public website, called the Website, can be customized to market a company by using various templates within the Office 365 cloud. The website creation tools include those for adding a theme, graphics, fonts, maps, directions, blogs, stock tickers, slide shows, PayPal, weather, and videos to interact with the website's visitors.

Synchronization

Office 365 subscription plans provide a central place to store and access your documents and business information. A feature of Office 365 ensures the original and backup computer files in two or more locations are identical through a process called **Active Directory Synchronization**. For example, if you open a PowerPoint presentation on your smartphone while you are riding a city bus and then add a new slide as you head to school, the PowerPoint presentation automatically is synced with Office 365. When you arrive on campus and open the PowerPoint presentation on a school computer, your new slide already is part of the finished slide show. By storing your files in Office 365, you can access your files on another computer if your home computer fails, with no loss of time or important information. When using your mobile phone's data plan, you do not need to search for a Wi-Fi hot spot to connect to the Office 365 cloud. Computer labs in schools can be configured to synchronize automatically all student files to Office 365 online.

Multiple Device Access to Office 365

With a single sign-in process, Office 365 provides access to multiple computers and mobile devices, including Android smartphones and tablets, Apple iPhones and iPads, Windows phones, and Blackberry phones. After you configure your devices' email settings, you can view your Microsoft account calendar, contacts, and email. Your personalized settings, preferences, and documents can be synchronized among all the different devices included in your Office 365 premium subscription. With the mobility of Office 365, students and employees can work anywhere, accessing information and responding to email requests immediately. If you lose your phone, Office 365 includes a feature that allows you to remotely wipe your phone clean of any data. By wiping your phone's data, you can prevent any unauthorized access to sensitive information, such as your banking information, passwords, and contacts, as well as discourage identity theft. Because your phone contacts and other information are stored on the Microsoft cloud, damaged or lost equipment is never a problem.

A thief can be quite resourceful if he or she steals your phone. Before you can alert your parents or spouse to the theft, they might receive a text from "you" asking for your ATM or credit card PIN number. Your parents or spouse might then reply with the PIN number. Your bank account could be emptied in minutes.

Teams Using Office 365 in Business

In the business world, rarely does an employee work in isolation. Companies need their employees to collaborate, whether they work in the same office or in locations around the world. Telecommuters working from home can communicate as if they were on-site by using a common team website and conferencing software. SharePoint Online and Lync Online provide seamless communication.

Small business subscription plans as low as $6.00 per user per month allow employees to create and store Word documents, Excel spreadsheets, and PowerPoint presentations online and communicate with one another via email, instant messaging, or video chat as they work on projects together. As shown in Figure 4, a team portal page is shown when you subscribe at https://portal.microsoftonline.com. Larger companies and those requiring more features can take advantage of the Office 365 business premium package, which, in addition to the features listed above, provides access to the Office 365 portal website and eliminates the effort and cost of the users maintaining their own costly computer servers.

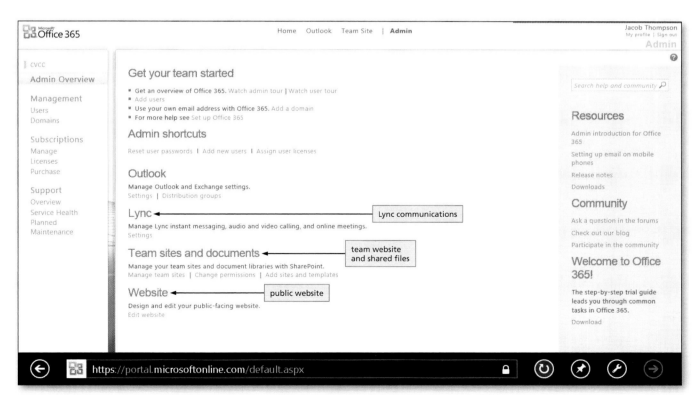

Figure 4

Email Communication Using Exchange

Office 365 includes Exchange Online, an email-based collaborative communications server for business. Exchange enables employees to be more productive by effectively managing email across multiple devices and facilitating teamwork.

Collaboration Using SharePoint

SharePoint Online, a part of Office 365 subscription plans, allows employees to collaborate with one another, share documents, post announcements, and track tasks, as shown in Table 2.

Table 2 Office 365 SharePoint Features	
Team Site Feature	**Description**
Calendar	Track important dates
Shared Document Library	Store related documents according to topic; picture, report, and slide libraries often are included
Task List	Track team tasks according to who is responsible for completion
Team Discussion Board	Discuss the topics at hand in an open forum
Contacts List	Share contact lists of employees, customers, contractors, and suppliers

© 2014 Cengage Learning

Office 365 provides the tools to plan meetings. Users can share calendars side by side, view availability, and suggest meeting times from shared calendars. Typically, a SharePoint team administrator or website owner establishes a folder structure to share and manage documents. The team website is fully searchable online, making locating and sharing data more efficient than using a local server. With a team website, everyone on the team has a central location to store and find all the information for a project, client, or department, as shown in Figure 5.

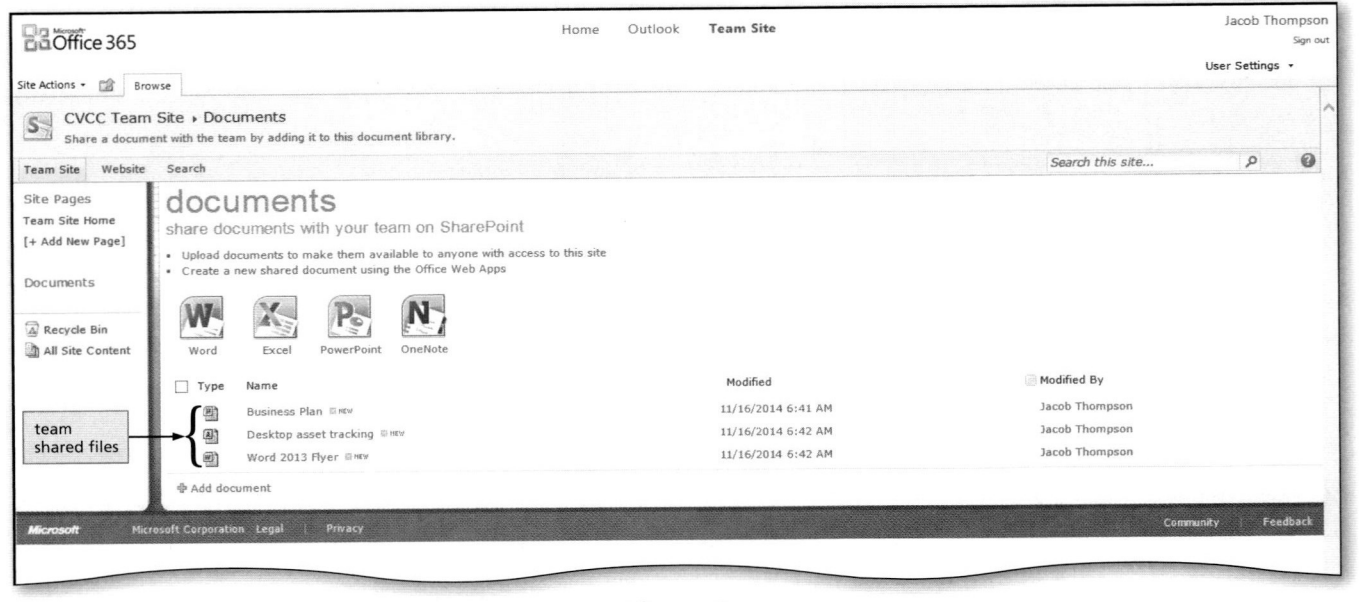

Figure 5

Website Design Using SharePoint

SharePoint provides templates to create a professional looking, public website for an online presence to market your business. As shown in Figure 6, a local pet sitting business is setting up a business website by customizing a SharePoint template. SharePoint Public Website includes features within the Design Manager that you use to customize and design your website by adding your own images, forms, style sheets, maps, themes, and social networking tools. When you finish customizing your business site, you can apply your own domain name to the site. A **domain** is a unique web address that identifies where your website can be found. Office 365 SharePoint hosts your website as part of your subscription. Your customers easily can find your business online and learn about your services.

BTW
Creating SharePoint Intranet Sites
A SharePoint website also can be customized to serve as an internal company website for private communications within the company.

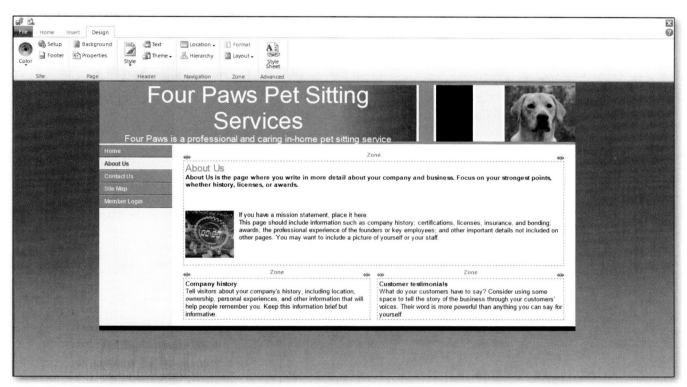

Figure 6

Real-Time Communications Using Lync

Lync Online is Microsoft's server platform for online team communications and comes bundled with Office 365 business subscriptions. As shown in Figure 7, Lync connects in real time to allow instant messaging, videoconferencing, and voice communications; it also integrates with email and Microsoft Office applications.

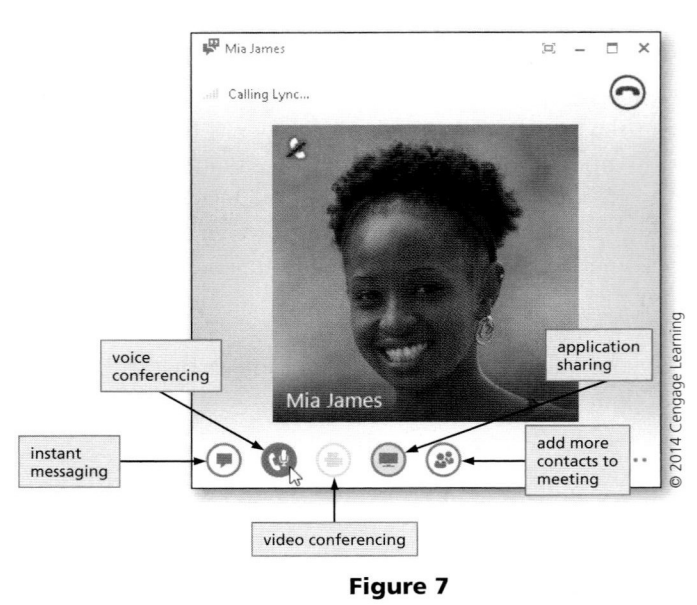

Figure 7

Lync allows you to connect with staff at remote locations using instant messaging capabilities, desktop sharing, videoconferencing, and shared agendas or documents. Lync is integrated into Office 365, which allows staff to start communicating from within the applications in which they currently are working. For example, while an employee is creating a PowerPoint presentation for a new product line, as shown in Figure 8, Lync enables him or her to collaborate with the entire team about the details of the product presentation. The team can view the presenter's screen displaying the PowerPoint presentation. The presenter can share control with any member of the team and can share his or her screen at any time during the Lync meeting.

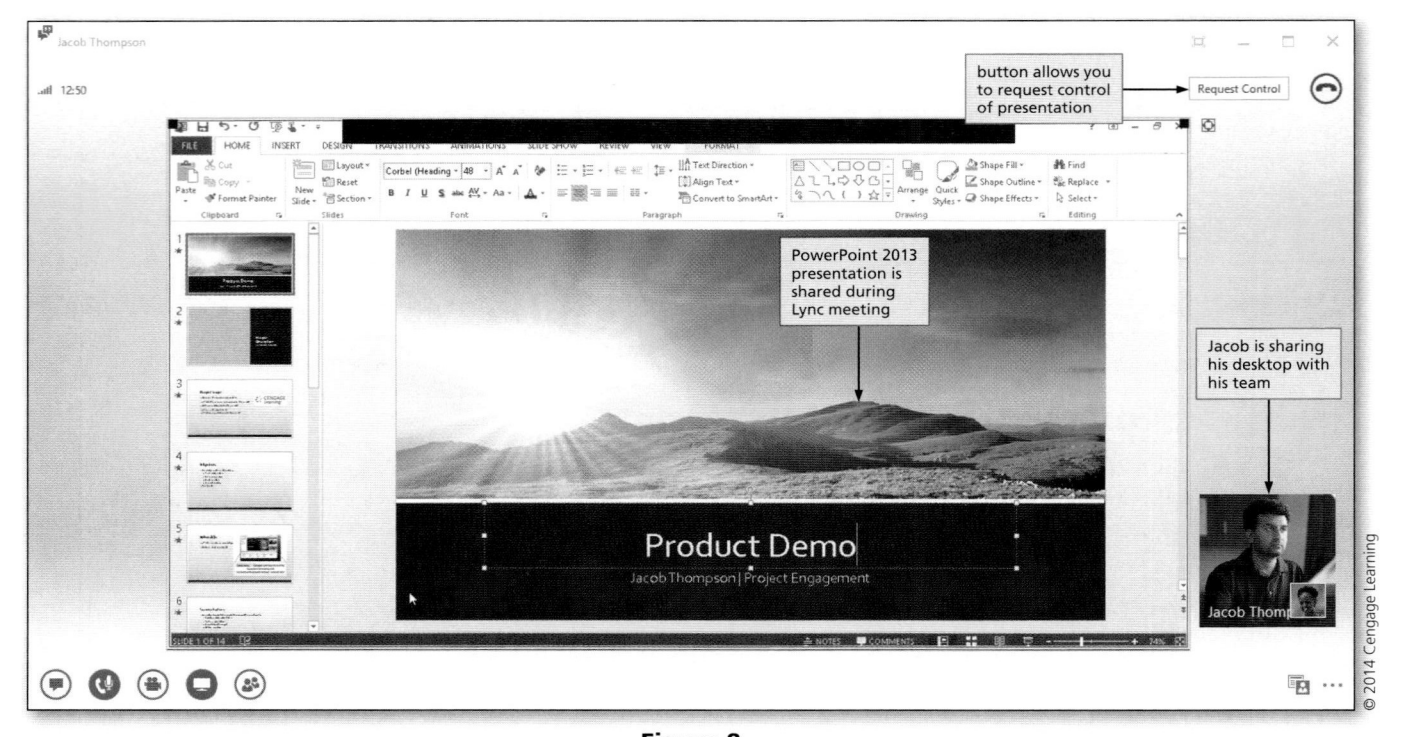

Figure 8

Users can send a Lync meeting request to schedule a team meeting, or an impromptu conversation can be started immediately using the Meet Now feature. Participants receive a Lync meeting request link via an email message, and when they click the meeting request link, Lync automatically connects them to the online conference. If the participant does not have Lync installed, the Lync Web App automatically connects to the Lync meeting through the user's PC or Mac OS X browser. If a participant is away from his or her computer, he or she still can participate using the Lync Mobile apps for Windows Phone, iOS, and Android. As shown in Figure 9, Lync utilizes **instant messaging** (IM), allowing two or more people to share text messages. They can communicate in real time, similar to a voice conversation. In addition to a simple instant message, Lync provides a feature called **persistent chat**, which allows end-users to participate in a working session of instant messages that is persistent or sustained over a specified amount of time in a moderated chat room. Consider having an instant messaging session with a group of colleagues in different parts of your organization, regardless of geographic region, where you all are working on the same project. Over the course of the project, different people post questions and concerns, and others are able to respond to all those who have subscribed to your topic or been admitted to the chat room. Instead of a long trail of email messages, a team can keep information in a controlled environment with a full history of the discussion in one location.

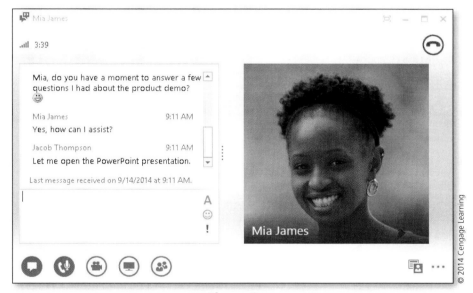

Figure 9

Lync also delivers support for full high-definition (HD) videoconferencing, so that a team can have a clear view of the participants, products, and demos. Before you join the video feed, you can preview your video feed to make sure your video camera is at the correct angle, your image is centered within the video frame, and that your room lighting provides for a clear image. The Lync preview option is important in creating a positive first impression over video. Your audio devices can be tested for clarity to make sure your headset, microphone, and speakers are functioning properly.

Lync provides a polling feature that presenters can use to ask the participants' opinions during a meeting (Figure 10). The poll question can consist of up to seven possible choices. The presenter has the option to view the results privately or share the results with the entire group.

Figure 10

Finally, by enabling the recording feature, Lync meetings and conversations can be captured for viewing at a later time. For instance, you can capture the audio, video, instant messaging (IM), screen sharing, Microsoft PowerPoint presentations, whiteboard, and polling portions of the Lync session and then play them back just as they transpired during the live Lync event. The meeting recordings can be made available to others so that they can view all or part of the Lync event. Instructors can record Lync online class sessions for students who were unable to attend the original presentation. The recording starts in Microsoft Lync; recordings then can be viewed within the Recording Manager feature.

Chapter Summary

In this chapter, you have learned how to subscribe to Office 365, which provides local and online access to Office applications, email, document sharing, web conferencing, and business websites. You also learned how a business can utilize Office 365 features on the cloud to facilitate teamwork. Finally, you learned about the features of SharePoint and Lync, which provide collaboration and communications for business teams using Office 365.

✷ Consider This: Your Turn

Apply your creative thinking and problem solving skills to design and implement a solution.

1: Comparing Office 365 Personal Plans

Personal

Part 1: You are a freshman in college living at home with your family. You are considering if it would be a better value to subscribe to Office 365 University or Office 365 Home Premium. Write a one-page document comparing the pros and cons of the two subscription plans. Research the different subscriptions in detail at Office365.com. Submit your assignment in the format specified by your instructor.

Part 2: ✷ Which type of computer and/or devices would you use with your Office 365 subscription? If you are at a friend's home that does not have Office 365, how could you access your Office files if you do not have your computer or mobile device with you?

2: Upgrading a Local Business to Office 365

Professional

Part 1: You are an employee at Impact Digital Marketing, a small marketing firm with 12 employees. The firm is setting up an Office 365 Small Business subscription next week, and you need to compose an email message with multiple paragraphs to explain the features of this new subscription plan to the members of your firm. Research the Office 365 Small Business subscription plan in detail at Office365.com, and compile your findings in an email message. Submit your assignment in the format specified by your instructor.

Part 2: ✷ Give three examples of how a marketing firm could use Lync. How could a marketing firm use the SharePoint Websites feature?

3: Conducting a Lync Meeting

Research and Collaboration

* Students need an Office 365 subscription to complete the following assignment.

Part 1: Using your Office 365 subscription, conduct a meeting using Lync. Working with a partner, use your Office 365 subscription to research how to use Lync. Then, conduct a 15-minute Lync meeting, including instant messaging, to discuss the features of Lync. Use the concepts and techniques presented in this chapter to create the Lync meeting. Submit your assignment in the format specified by your instructor.

Part 2: ✷ When using Lync in business, when would the video feature best be utilized?

1 Creating, Formatting, and Editing a Word Document with a Picture

Microsoft product screen shots used with permission from Microsoft Corporation.

Objectives

You will have mastered the material in this chapter when you can:

- Enter text in a Word document
- Check spelling as you type
- Format paragraphs
- Format text
- Undo and redo commands or actions
- Change theme colors
- Insert digital pictures in a Word document

- Format pictures
- Add a page border
- Adjust spacing
- Change document properties
- Correct errors and revise a document
- Print and read a document

Creating, Formatting, and Editing a Word Document with a Picture

Introduction

To advertise a sale, promote a business, publicize an event, or convey a message to the community, you may want to create a flyer and hand it out in person or post it in a public location. Libraries, schools, religious organizations, grocery stores, coffee shops, and other places often provide bulletin boards or windows for flyers. You also see flyers posted on webpages or as email messages.

Flyers announce personal items for sale or rent (car, boat, apartment); garage or block sales; services being offered (animal care, housecleaning, lessons, tours); membership, sponsorship, or donation requests (club, religious organization, charity); and other messages, such as a lost or found pet.

Project — Flyer with a Picture

Individuals and businesses create flyers to gain public attention. Flyers, which usually are a single page in length, are an inexpensive means of reaching the community. Many flyers, however, go unnoticed because they are designed poorly.

The project in this chapter follows general guidelines and uses Word to create the flyer shown in Figure 1–1. This colorful, eye-catching flyer announces tour adventures. The picture of the tour group on the mountain trail, taken with a digital camera, entices passersby or viewers to stop and look at the flyer. The headline on the flyer is large and colorful to draw attention into the text. The body copy below the picture briefly describes the tours, along with a bulleted list that concisely highlights important tour information. The signature line of the flyer calls attention to the contact phone number. The word, breathtaking, and the signature line are in a different color so that they stand apart from the rest of the text on the flyer. Finally, the graphical page border nicely frames and complements the contents of the flyer.

For an introduction to Office and instruction about how to perform basic tasks in Office apps, read the Office and Windows chapter at the beginning of this book, where you can learn how to run an application, use the ribbon, save a file, open a file, exit an application, use Help, and much more.

page border

ADVENTURE!

headline

digital picture of mountain trail tour

Explore scenic trails with *breathtaking* views as you travel through meadows, forests, streams, and mountains in an **off-road** vehicle.

bulleted list

- Self-guided tours available
- All vehicles and gear provided
- Open March through October

body copy

To book your adventure, call 555-8928!

signature line

Figure 1–1

Roadmap

In this chapter, you will learn how to create the flyer shown in Figure 1–1. The following roadmap identifies general activities you will perform as you progress through this chapter:

1. ENTER TEXT in a new document.
2. FORMAT the TEXT in the flyer.
3. INSERT a PICTURE, called Mountain Trail, in the flyer.
4. FORMAT the PICTURE in the flyer.
5. ENHANCE the PAGE with a border and spacing.
6. CORRECT errors AND REVISE text in the flyer.
7. PRINT OR READ the flyer.

At the beginning of step instructions throughout the chapter, you will see an abbreviated form of this roadmap. The abbreviated roadmap uses colors to indicate chapter progress: gray means the chapter is beyond that activity, blue means the task being shown is covered in that activity, and black means that activity is yet to be covered. For example, the following abbreviated roadmap indicates the chapter would be showing a task in the 2 FORMAT TEXT activity.

1 ENTER TEXT | **2 FORMAT TEXT** | **3 INSERT PICTURE** | **4 FORMAT PICTURE**
5 ENHANCE PAGE | **6 CORRECT & REVISE** | **7 PRINT OR READ**

Use the abbreviated roadmap as a progress guide while you read or step through the instructions in this chapter.

To Run Word and Create a Blank Document

If you are using a computer to step through the project in this chapter and you want your screens to match the figures in this book, you should change your screen's resolution to 1366 × 768. For information about how to change a computer's resolution, refer to the Office and Windows chapter at the beginning of this book.

The following steps, which assume Windows 8 is running, use the Start screen or the Search box to run Word based on a typical installation. You may need to ask your instructor how to run Word on your computer. For a detailed example of the procedure summarized below, refer to the Office and Windows chapter.

1 Scroll the Start screen for a Word 2013 tile. If your Start screen contains a Word 2013 tile, tap or click it to run Word and then proceed to Step 5; if the Start screen does not contain the Word 2013 tile, proceed to the next step to search for the Word app.

2 Swipe in from the right edge of the screen or point to the upper-right corner of the screen to display the Charms bar and then tap or click the Search charm on the Charms bar to display the Search menu.

3 Type **Word** as the search text in the Search box and watch the search results appear in the Apps list.

4 Tap or click Word 2013 in the search results to run Word.

5 Tap or click the Blank document thumbnail on the Word start screen to create a blank document and display it in the Word window.

6 If the Word window is not maximized, tap or click the Maximize button on its title bar to maximize the window.

For an introduction to Windows and instruction about how to perform basic Windows tasks, read the Office and Windows chapter at the beginning of this book, where you can learn how to resize windows, change screen resolution, create folders, move and rename files, use Windows Help, and much more.

One of the few differences between Windows 7 and Windows 8 occurs in the steps to run Word. If you are using Windows 7, click the Start button, type **Word** in the 'Search programs and files' box, click Word 2013, and then, if necessary, maximize the Word window. For detailed steps to run Word in Windows 7, refer to the Office and Windows chapter at the beginning of this book. For a summary of the steps, refer to the Quick Reference located at the back of this book.

7 If the Print Layout button on the status bar is not selected (shown in Figure 1–2), tap or click it so that your screen is in Print Layout view.

Q&A What is Print Layout view?

The default (preset) view in Word is **Print Layout view**, which shows the document on a mock sheet of paper in the document window.

8 If Normal (HOME tab | Styles group) is not selected in the Styles gallery (shown in Figure 1–2), tap or click it so that your document uses the Normal style.

Q&A What is the Normal style?

When you create a document, Word formats the text using a particular style. The default style in Word is called the **Normal style**, which is discussed later in this book.

What if rulers appear on my screen?

Tap or click VIEW on the ribbon to display the VIEW tab and then remove the check mark from the View Ruler check box (VIEW tab | Show group).

BTW
The Word Window
The chapters in this book begin with the Word window appearing as it did at the initial installation of the software. Your Word window may look different depending on your screen resolution and other Word settings.

Entering Text

The first step in creating a document is to enter its text. With the projects in this book, you enter text by typing on the keyboard. By default, Word positions text you type at the left margin. In a later section of this chapter, you will learn how to format, or change the appearance of, the entered text.

To Type Text

1 ENTER TEXT | 2 FORMAT TEXT | 3 INSERT PICTURE | 4 FORMAT PICTURE
5 ENHANCE PAGE | 6 CORRECT & REVISE | 7 PRINT OR READ

To begin creating the flyer in this chapter, type the headline in the document window. *Why? The headline is the first line of text in the Adventure Flyer.* The following steps type the first line of text in the document.

1

• Type **Adventure!** as the headline (Figure 1–2).

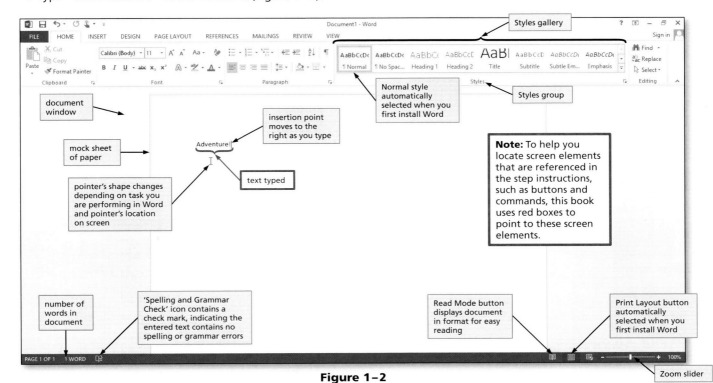

Figure 1–2

Q&A What if I make an error while typing?

You can press the BACKSPACE key until you have deleted the text in error and then retype the text correctly.

What is the purpose of the Spelling and Grammar Check icon on the status bar?

The **Spelling and Grammar Check icon** displays either a check mark to indicate the entered text contains no spelling or grammar errors, or an X to indicate that it found potential errors. Word flags potential errors in the document with a red, green, or blue wavy underline. Later in this chapter, you will learn how to fix flagged errors.

2

- Press the ENTER key to move the insertion point to the beginning of the next line (Figure 1–3).

Q&A Why did blank space appear between the headline and the insertion point?

Each time you press the ENTER key, Word creates a new paragraph and inserts blank space between the two paragraphs. Later in this chapter, you will learn how to increase and decrease the spacing between paragraphs.

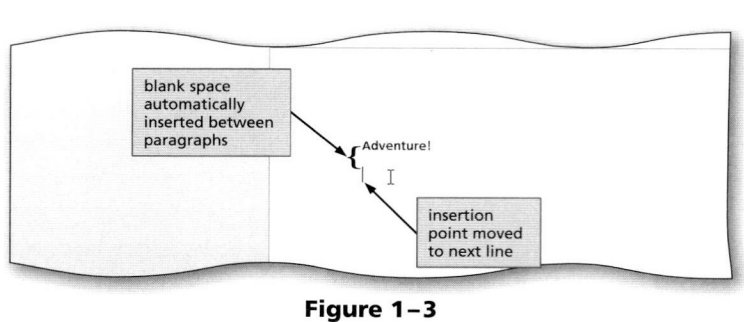

Figure 1–3

CONSIDER THIS

How do you use the touch keyboard with a touch screen?

To display the on-screen touch keyboard, tap the Touch Keyboard button on the Windows taskbar. When finished using the touch keyboard, tap the X button on the touch keyboard to close the keyboard.

To Display Formatting Marks

1 ENTER TEXT | 2 FORMAT TEXT | 3 INSERT PICTURE | 4 FORMAT PICTURE
5 ENHANCE PAGE | 6 CORRECT & REVISE | 7 PRINT OR READ

You may find it helpful to display formatting marks while working in a document. *Why? Formatting marks indicate where in a document you press the* ENTER *key,* SPACEBAR, *and other nonprinting characters.* A **formatting mark** is a character that Word displays on the screen but is not visible on a printed document. For example, the paragraph mark (¶) is a formatting mark that indicates where you pressed the ENTER key. A raised dot (·) shows where you pressed the SPACEBAR. Formatting marks are discussed as they appear on the screen.

Depending on settings made during previous Word sessions, your Word screen already may display formatting marks (Figure 1–4). The following step displays formatting marks, if they do not show already on the screen.

1

- If the HOME tab is not the active tab, tap or click HOME on the ribbon to display the HOME tab.

- If it is not selected already, tap or click the 'Show/Hide ¶' button (HOME tab | Paragraph group) to display formatting marks on the screen (Figure 1–4).

BTW

Zooming

If text is too small for you to read on the screen, you can zoom the document by dragging the Zoom slider on the status bar or tapping or clicking the Zoom Out or Zoom In buttons on the status bar. Changing the zoom has no effect on the printed document.

Figure 1–4

Q&A What if I do not want formatting marks to show on the screen?
You can hide them by tapping or clicking the 'Show/Hide ¶' button (HOME tab | Paragraph group) again. It is recommended that you display formatting marks so that you visually can identify when you press the ENTER key, SPACEBAR, and other keys associated with nonprinting characters. Most of the document windows presented in this book, therefore, show formatting marks.

Other Ways

1. Press CTRL+SHIFT+*

To Insert a Blank Line

1 ENTER TEXT | 2 FORMAT TEXT | 3 INSERT PICTURE | 4 FORMAT PICTURE
5 ENHANCE PAGE | 6 CORRECT & REVISE | 7 PRINT OR READ

In the flyer, the digital picture of the mountain trail appears between the headline and body copy. You will not insert this picture, however, until after you enter and format all text. *Why? Although you can format text and insert pictures in any order, for illustration purposes, this chapter formats all text first before inserting the picture. Thus, you leave a blank line in the document as a placeholder for the picture.*

To enter a blank line in a document, press the ENTER key without typing any text on the line. The following step inserts one blank line below the headline.

1

• Press the ENTER key to insert a blank line in the document (Figure 1–5).

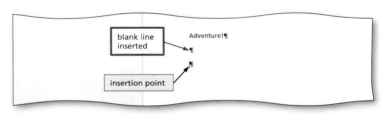

Figure 1–5

To Zoom Page Width

1 ENTER TEXT | 2 FORMAT TEXT | 3 INSERT PICTURE | 4 FORMAT PICTURE
5 ENHANCE PAGE | 6 CORRECT & REVISE | 7 PRINT OR READ

The next step in creating this flyer is to enlarge the contents that appear on the screen. *Why? You would like the text on the screen to be larger so that it is easier to read.* The document currently displays at 100% (shown in Figure 1–6). With Word, you can zoom page width, which zooms (enlarges or shrinks) the mock sheet of paper on the screen so that it is the width of the Word window. The following steps zoom page width.

1

• Tap or click VIEW on the ribbon to display the VIEW tab.

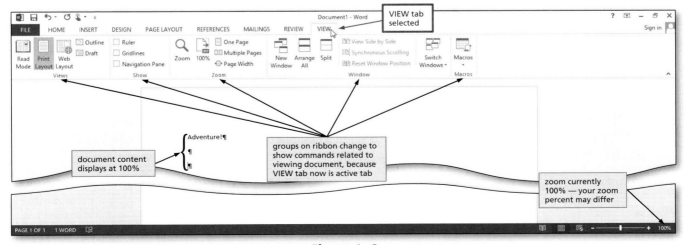

Figure 1–6

2

- Tap or click the Page Width button (VIEW tab | Zoom group) to display the page the same width as the document window (Figure 1–7).

Q&A

If I change the zoom, will the document print differently?
Changing the zoom has no effect on the printed document.

What are the other predefined zoom options?
Through the VIEW tab | Zoom group or the Zoom dialog box (Zoom button in Zoom group), you can zoom to one page (an entire single page appears in the document window), many pages (multiple pages appear at once in the document window), page width, text width, and a variety of set percentages. Whereas page width zoom places the edges of the page at the edges of the document window, text width zoom places the document contents at the edges of the document window.

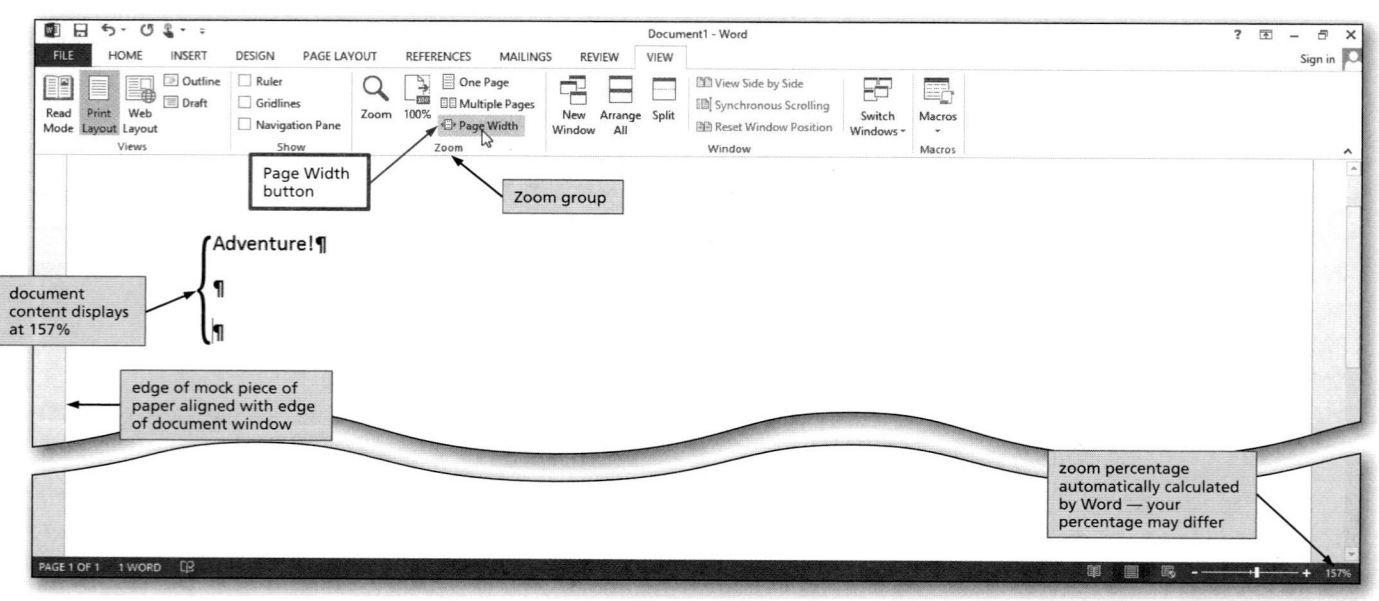

Figure 1–7

Other Ways

1. Tap or click Zoom button (VIEW tab | Zoom group), tap or click Page width (Zoom dialog box), tap or click OK button

BTW

The Ribbon and Screen Resolution

Word may change how the groups and buttons within the groups appear on the ribbon, depending on the computer's screen resolution. Thus, your ribbon may look different from the ones in this book if you are using a screen resolution other than 1366 × 768.

Wordwrap

Wordwrap allows you to type words in a paragraph continually without pressing the ENTER key at the end of each line. As you type, if a word extends beyond the right margin, Word also automatically positions that word on the next line along with the insertion point.

Word creates a new paragraph each time you press the ENTER key. Thus, as you type text in the document window, do not press the ENTER key when the insertion point reaches the right margin. Instead, press the ENTER key only in these circumstances:

1. To insert a blank line(s) in a document (as shown in the previous steps)
2. To begin a new paragraph
3. To terminate a short line of text and advance to the next line
4. To respond to questions or prompts in Word dialog boxes, task panes, and other on-screen objects

To Wordwrap Text as You Type

1 ENTER TEXT | 2 FORMAT TEXT | 3 INSERT PICTURE | 4 FORMAT PICTURE
5 ENHANCE PAGE | 6 CORRECT & REVISE | 7 PRINT OR READ

The next step in creating the flyer is to type the body copy. ***Why?*** *In many flyers, the body copy text appears below the headline.* The following steps illustrate how the body copy text wordwraps as you enter it in the document.

- Type the first sentence of the body copy: `Explore scenic trails with breathtaking views as you travel through meadows, forests, streams, and mountains in an off-road vehicle.`

Q&A Why does my document wrap on different words?
The printer connected to a computer is one factor that can control where wordwrap occurs for each line in a document. Thus, it is possible that the same document could wordwrap differently if printed on different printers.

②

- Press the ENTER key to position the insertion point on the next line in the document (Figure 1–8).

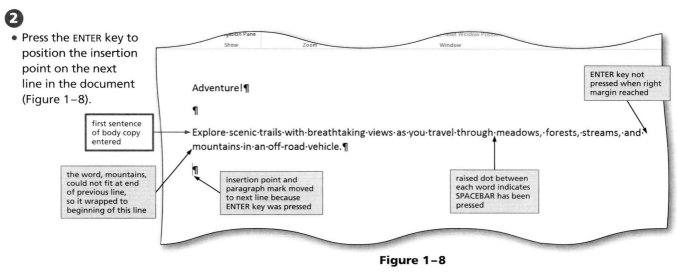

Figure 1–8

Spelling and Grammar Check

As you type text in a document, Word checks your typing for possible spelling and grammar errors. If all of the words you have typed are in Word's dictionary and your grammar is correct, as mentioned earlier, the Spelling and Grammar Check icon on the status bar displays a check mark. Otherwise, the icon shows an X. In this case, Word flags the potential error in the document window with a red, green, or blue wavy underline. A red wavy underline means the flagged text is not in Word's dictionary (because it is a proper name or misspelled). A green wavy underline indicates the text may be incorrect grammatically. A blue wavy underline indicates the text may contain a contextual spelling error, such as the misuse of homophones (words that are pronounced the same but that have different spellings or meanings, such as one and won). Although you can check the entire document for spelling and grammar errors at once, you also can check flagged errors as they appear on the screen.

A flagged word is not necessarily misspelled. For example, many names, abbreviations, and specialized terms are not in Word's main dictionary. In these cases, you can instruct Word to ignore the flagged word. As you type, Word also detects duplicate words while checking for spelling errors. For example, if your document contains the phrase, to the the store, Word places a red wavy underline below the second occurrence of the word, the.

BTW
Automatic Spelling Correction
As you type, Word automatically corrects some misspelled words. For example, if you type recieve, Word automatically corrects the misspelling and displays the word, receive, when you press the SPACEBAR or type a punctuation mark. To see a complete list of automatically corrected words, click FILE on the ribbon to open the Backstage view, click Options in the Backstage view, click Proofing in the left pane (Word Options dialog box), click the AutoCorrect Options button, and then scroll through the list near the bottom of the dialog box.

To Check Spelling and Grammar as You Type

In the following steps, the word, tours, has been misspelled intentionally as tuors. ***Why?*** *These steps illustrate Word's check spelling as you type feature. If you are completing this project on a computer, your flyer may contain different or no misspelled words, depending on the accuracy of your typing.*

1

- Type **Self-guided tuors** and then press the SPACEBAR, so that a red wavy line appears below the misspelled word (Figure 1–9).

Q&A What if Word does not flag my spelling and grammar errors with wavy underlines?

To verify that the check spelling and grammar as you type features are enabled, tap or click FILE on the ribbon to open the Backstage view and then tap or click Options in the Backstage view. When the Word Options dialog box is displayed, tap or click Proofing in the left pane, and then ensure the 'Check spelling as you type' and 'Mark grammar errors as you type' check boxes contain check marks. Also ensure the 'Hide spelling errors in this document only' and 'Hide grammar errors in this document only' check boxes do not contain check marks. Tap or click the OK button.

Figure 1–9

2

- Press and hold or right-click the flagged word (tuors, in this case) to display a shortcut menu that presents a list of suggested spelling corrections for the flagged word (Figure 1–10).

Q&A What if, when I press and hold or right-click the misspelled word, my desired correction is not in the list on the shortcut menu?

You can tap or click outside the shortcut menu to close the shortcut menu and then retype the correct word.

What if a flagged word actually is, for example, a proper name and spelled correctly?

Press and hold or right-click it and then tap or click Ignore All on the shortcut menu to instruct Word not to flag future occurrences of the same word in this document.

Figure 1–10

3

- Tap or click tours on the shortcut menu to replace the misspelled word in the document with a correctly spelled word (Figure 1–11).

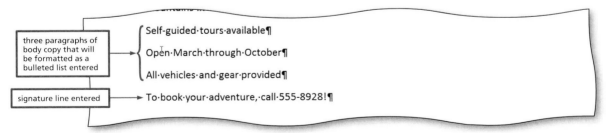

Explore·scenic·trails·with·breathtaking·views·as·you·travel·through·meadows,·forests,·streams,·and mountains·in·an·off-road·vehicle.¶

Self-guided·tours·¶

> flagged word replaced with word selected on shortcut menu

> 'Spelling and Grammar Check' icon now shows check mark because no errors are flagged in document

22 WORDS

Figure 1–11

Other Ways

1. Tap or click 'Spelling and Grammar Check' icon on status bar, tap or click desired word in Spelling pane, tap or click Change button, tap or click OK button

To Enter More Text

In the flyer, the text yet to be entered includes the remainder of the body copy, which will be formatted as a bulleted list, and the signature line. The next steps enter the remainder of text in the flyer.

1 Press the END key to move the insertion point to the end of the current line.

2 Type `available` and then press the ENTER key.

3 Type `Open March through October` and then press the ENTER key.

4 Type `All vehicles and gear provided` and then press the ENTER key.

5 Type the signature line in the flyer (Figure 1–12): `To book your adventure, call 555-8928!`

If requested by your instructor, enter your phone number instead of 555-8928 in the signature line.

BTW

Character Widths
Many word processing documents use variable character fonts, where some characters are wider than others; for example, the letter w is wider than the letter i.

> three paragraphs of body copy that will be formatted as a bulleted list entered

Self-guided·tours·available¶

Open·March·through·October¶

All·vehicles·and·gear·provided¶

> signature line entered

To·book·your·adventure,·call·555-8928!¶

Figure 1–12

CONSIDER THIS

How should you organize text in a flyer?

The text in a flyer typically is organized into three areas: headline, body copy, and signature line.

- The **headline** is the first line of text on the flyer. It conveys the product or service being offered, such as a car for sale, personal lessons, or sightseeing tours, or the benefit that will be gained, such as a convenience, better performance, greater security, higher earnings, or more comfort, or it can contain a message, such as a lost or found pet.

- The **body copy** consists of text between the headline and the signature line. This text highlights the key points of the message in as few words as possible. It should be easy to read and follow. While emphasizing the positive, the body copy must be realistic, truthful, and believable.

- The **signature line**, which is the last line of text on the flyer, contains contact information or identifies a call to action.

Navigating a Document

BTW
Minimize Wrist Injury
Computer users frequently switch among touch gestures, the keyboard, and the mouse during a word processing session; such switching strains the wrist. To help prevent wrist injury, minimize switching. For instance, if your fingertips already are on the screen, use your finger to slide the document to a new location. If your fingers are already on the keyboard, use keyboard keys to scroll. If your hand already is on the mouse, use the mouse to scroll.

You view only a portion of a document on the screen through the document window. At some point when you type text or insert graphics, Word probably will **scroll** the top or bottom portion of the document off the screen. Although you cannot see the text and graphics once they scroll off the screen, they remain in the document.

You can use touch gestures, the keyboard, or a mouse to scroll to a different location in a document and/or move the insertion point around a document. If you are using a touch screen, simply use your finger to slide the document up or down to display a different location in the document and then tap to move the insertion point to a new location. When you use the keyboard, the insertion point automatically moves when you press the desired keys. For example, the previous steps used the END key to move the insertion point to the end of the current line. Table 1–1 outlines various techniques to navigate a document using the keyboard.

With the mouse, you can use the scroll arrows or the scroll box on the scroll bar to display a different portion of the document in the document window and then click the mouse to move the insertion point to that location. Table 1–2 explains various techniques for using the scroll bar to scroll vertically with the mouse.

Table 1–1 Moving the Insertion Point with the Keyboard

Insertion Point Direction	Key(s) to Press	Insertion Point Direction	Key(s) to Press
Left one character	LEFT ARROW	Up one paragraph	CTRL+UP ARROW
Right one character	RIGHT ARROW	Down one paragraph	CTRL+DOWN ARROW
Left one word	CTRL+LEFT ARROW	Up one screen	PAGE UP
Right one word	CTRL+RIGHT ARROW	Down one screen	PAGE DOWN
Up one line	UP ARROW	To top of document window	ALT+CTRL+PAGE UP
Down one line	DOWN ARROW	To bottom of document window	ALT+CTRL+PAGE DOWN
To end of line	END	To beginning of document	CTRL+HOME
To beginning of line	HOME	To end of document	CTRL+END

© 2014 Cengage Learning

Table 1–2 Using the Scroll Bar to Scroll Vertically with the Mouse

Scroll Direction	Mouse Action	Scroll Direction	Mouse Action
Up	Drag the scroll box upward.	Down one screen	Click anywhere below the scroll box on the vertical scroll bar.
Down	Drag the scroll box downward.	Up one line	Click the scroll arrow at the top of the vertical scroll bar.
Up one screen	Click anywhere above the scroll box on the vertical scroll bar.	Down one line	Click the scroll arrow at the bottom of the vertical scroll bar.

© 2014 Cengage Learning

To Save a Document

You have performed many tasks while creating this document and do not want to risk losing work completed thus far. Accordingly, you should save the document on your hard disk, SkyDrive, or a location that is most appropriate to your situation.

The following steps assume you already have created folders for storing your files, for example, a CIS 101 folder (for your class) that contains a Word folder (for your assignments). Thus, these steps save the document in the Word folder in the

CIS 101 folder on your desired save location. For a detailed example of the procedure for saving a file in a folder or saving a file on SkyDrive, refer to the Office and Windows chapter at the beginning of this book.

1 Tap or click the Save button on the Quick Access Toolbar, which depending on settings, will display either the Save As gallery in the Backstage view or the Save As dialog box.

2 To save on a hard disk or other storage media on your computer, proceed to Step 2a. To save on SkyDrive, proceed to Step 2b.

2a If your screen opens the Backstage view and you want to save on storage media on your computer, tap or click Computer in the left pane, if necessary, to display options in the right pane related to saving on your computer. If your screen already displays the Save As dialog box, proceed to Step 4.

2b If your screen opens the Backstage view and you want to save on SkyDrive, tap or click SkyDrive in the left pane to display SkyDrive saving options or a Sign In button. If your screen displays a Sign In button, tap or click it and then sign in to SkyDrive.

3 Tap or click the Browse button in the right pane to display the Save As dialog box associated with the selected save location (i.e., Computer or SkyDrive).

4 Type **Adventure Flyer** in the File name box to change the file name. Do not press the ENTER key after typing the file name because you do not want to close the dialog box at this time.

5 Navigate to the desired save location (in this case, the Word folder in the CIS 101 folder [or your class folder] on your computer or SkyDrive).

6 Tap or click the Save button (Save As dialog box) to save the document in the selected folder on the selected save location with the entered file name.

BTW
Organizing Files and Folders
You should organize and store files in folders so that you easily can find the files later. For example, if you are taking an introductory computer class called CIS 101, a good practice would be to save all Word files in a Word folder in a CIS 101 folder. For a discussion of folders and detailed examples of creating folders, refer to the Office and Windows chapter at the beginning of this book.

Formatting Paragraphs and Characters

With the text for the flyer entered, the next step is to **format**, or change the appearance of, its text. A paragraph encompasses the text from the first character in the paragraph up to and including its paragraph mark (¶). **Paragraph formatting** is the process of changing the appearance of a paragraph. For example, you can center or add bullets to a paragraph. Characters include letters, numbers, punctuation marks, and symbols. **Character formatting** is the process of changing the way characters appear on the screen and in print. You use character formatting to emphasize certain words and improve readability of a document. For example, you can color, italicize, or underline characters. Often, you apply both paragraph and character formatting to the same text. For example, you may center a paragraph (paragraph formatting) and underline some of the characters in the same paragraph (character formatting).

Although you can format paragraphs and characters before you type, many Word users enter text first and then format the existing text. Figure 1–13a on the next page shows the flyer in this chapter before formatting its paragraphs and characters. Figure 1–13b on the next page shows the flyer after formatting. As you can see from the two figures, a document that is formatted is easier to read and looks more professional. The following pages discuss how to format the flyer so that it looks like Figure 1–13b.

If you are using your finger on a touch screen and are having difficulty completing the steps in this chapter, consider using a stylus. Many people find it easier to be precise with a stylus than with a finger. In addition, with a stylus you see the pointer. If you still are having trouble completing the steps with a stylus, try using a mouse.

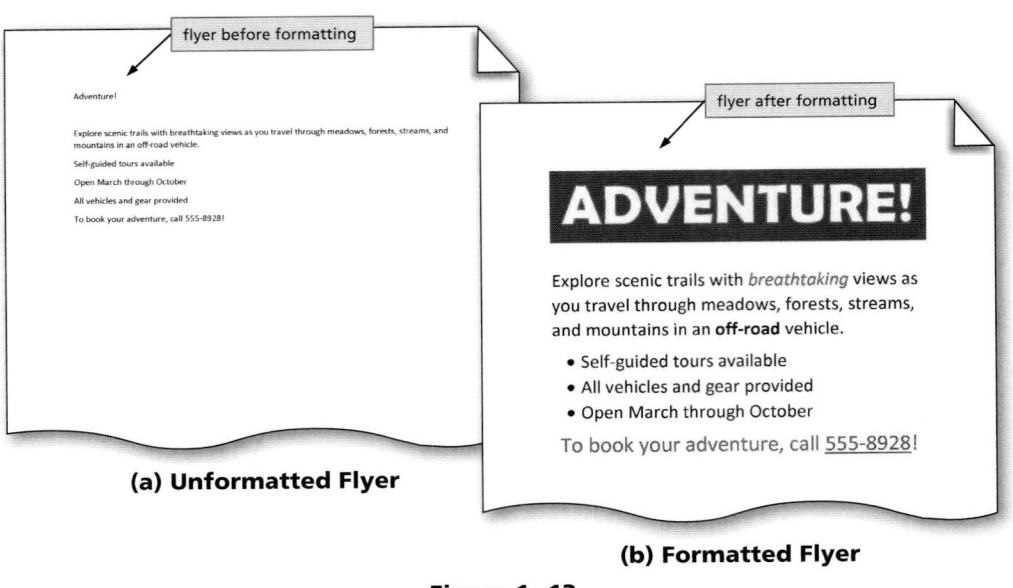

(a) Unformatted Flyer

(b) Formatted Flyer

Figure 1–13

Font, Font Sizes, and Themes

Characters that appear on the screen are a specific shape and size. The **font**, or typeface, defines the appearance and shape of the letters, numbers, and special characters. In Word, the default font usually is Calibri (shown in Figure 1–14). You can leave characters in the default font or change them to a different font. **Font size** specifies the size of the characters and is determined by a measurement system called points. A single **point** is about 1/72 of one inch in height. The default font size in Word typically is 11 (Figure 1–14). Thus, a character with a font size of 11 is about 11/72 or a little less than 1/6 of one inch in height. You can increase or decrease the font size of characters in a document.

A document **theme** is a set of unified formats for fonts, colors, and graphics. Word includes a variety of document themes to assist you with coordinating these visual elements in a document. The default theme fonts are Calibri Light for headings and Calibri for body text. By changing the document theme, you quickly can give your document a new look. You also can define your own document themes.

CONSIDER THIS

How do I know which formats to use in a flyer?
In a flyer, consider the following formatting suggestions.

- **Increase the font size of characters.** Flyers usually are posted on a bulletin board or in a window. Thus, the font size should be as large as possible so that passersby easily can read the flyer. To give the headline more impact, its font size should be larger than the font size of the text in the body copy. If possible, make the font size of the signature line larger than the body copy but smaller than the headline.

- **Change the font of characters.** Use fonts that are easy to read. Try to use only two different fonts in a flyer; for example, use one for the headline and the other for all other text. Too many fonts can make the flyer visually confusing.

- **Change the paragraph alignment.** The default alignment for paragraphs in a document is **left-aligned**, that is, flush at the left margin of the document with uneven right edges. Consider changing the alignment of some of the paragraphs to add interest and variety to the flyer.

- **Highlight key paragraphs with bullets.** A bulleted paragraph is a paragraph that begins with a dot or other symbol. Use bulleted paragraphs to highlight important points in a flyer.

- **Emphasize important words.** To call attention to certain words or lines, you can underline them, italicize them, or bold them. Use these formats sparingly, however, because overuse will minimize their effect and make the flyer look too busy.

- **Use color.** Use colors that complement each other and convey the meaning of the flyer. Vary colors in terms of hue and brightness. Headline colors, for example, can be bold and bright. Signature lines should stand out more than body copy but less than headlines. Keep in mind that too many colors can detract from the flyer and make it difficult to read.

To Center a Paragraph

The headline in the flyer currently is left-aligned (Figure 1–14). ***Why?*** *Word, by default left-aligns text, unless you specifically change the alignment.* You want the headline to be **centered**, that is, positioned horizontally between the left and right margins on the page. Recall that Word considers a single short line of text, such as the one-word headline, a paragraph. Thus, you will center the paragraph containing the headline. The following steps center a paragraph.

- Tap or click HOME on the ribbon to display the HOME tab.

- Tap or click somewhere in the paragraph to be centered (in this case, the headline) to position the insertion point in the paragraph to be formatted (Figure 1–14).

Figure 1–14

- Tap or click the Center button (HOME tab | Paragraph group) to center the paragraph containing the insertion point (Figure 1–15).

Q&A What if I want to return the paragraph to left-aligned?
You would tap or click the Center button again or tap or click the Align Left button (HOME tab | Paragraph group).

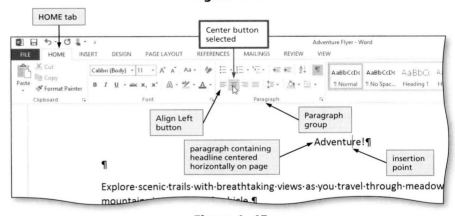

Figure 1–15

Other Ways

1. Tap 'Show Context Menu' button on mini toolbar or right-click paragraph, tap or click Paragraph on shortcut menu, tap or click Indents and Spacing tab (Paragraph dialog box), tap or click Alignment arrow, tap or click Centered, tap or click OK button

2. Tap or click Paragraph Settings Dialog Box Launcher (HOME tab or PAGE LAYOUT tab | Paragraph group), tap or click Indents and Spacing tab (Paragraph dialog box), tap or click Alignment arrow, tap or click Centered, tap or click OK button

3. Press CTRL+E

To Center Another Paragraph

In the flyer, the signature line is to be centered to match the paragraph alignment of the headline. The following steps center the signature line.

1 Tap or click somewhere in the paragraph to be centered (in this case, the signature line) to position the insertion point in the paragraph to be formatted.

2 Tap or click the Center button (HOME tab | Paragraph group) to center the paragraph containing the insertion point (shown in Figure 1–16 on the next page).

BTW
File Type
Depending on your Windows settings, the file type .docx may be displayed on the title bar immediately to the right of the file name after you save the file. The file type .docx identifies a Word 2013 document.

BTW
Touch Screen
Differences
The Office and Windows interfaces may vary if you are using a touch screen. For this reason, you might notice that the function or appearance of your touch screen differs slightly from this chapter's presentation.

Formatting Single versus Multiple Paragraphs and Characters

As shown on the previous pages, to format a single paragraph, simply move the insertion point in the paragraph to make it the current paragraph, and then format the paragraph. Similarly, to format a single word, position the insertion point in the word to make it the current word, and then format the word.

To format multiple paragraphs or words, however, you first must select the paragraphs or words you want to format and then format the selection.

1 ENTER TEXT | 2 FORMAT TEXT | 3 INSERT PICTURE | 4 FORMAT PICTURE
5 ENHANCE PAGE | 6 CORRECT & REVISE | 7 PRINT OR READ

To Select a Line

The default font size of 11 point is too small for a headline in a flyer. To increase the font size of the characters in the headline, you first must select the line of text containing the headline. *Why? If you increase font size of text without selecting any text, Word will increase the font size only of the word containing the insertion point.* The following steps select a line.

1

- If you are using a mouse, move the pointer to the left of the line to be selected (in this case, the headline) until the pointer changes to a right-pointing block arrow (Figure 1–16).

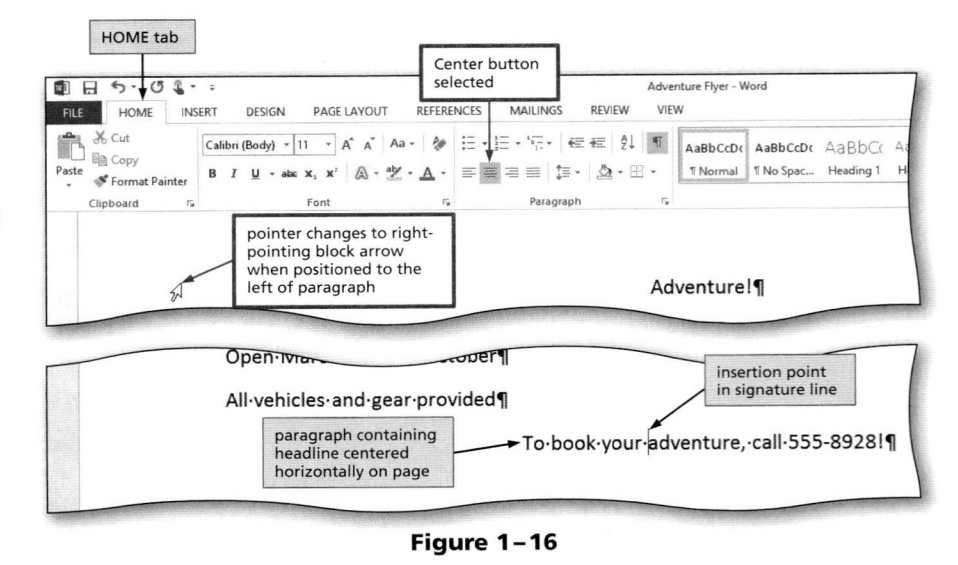

Figure 1–16

2

- If you are using a touch screen, double-tap to the left of the line to be selected to select the line; if you are using a mouse, while the pointer is a right-pointing block arrow, click the mouse to select the entire line to the right of the pointer (Figure 1–17).

Q&A Why is the selected text shaded gray?
If your screen normally displays dark letters on a light background, which is the default setting in Word, then selected text displays with a light shading color, such as gray, on the dark letters. Note that the selection that appears on the text does not print.

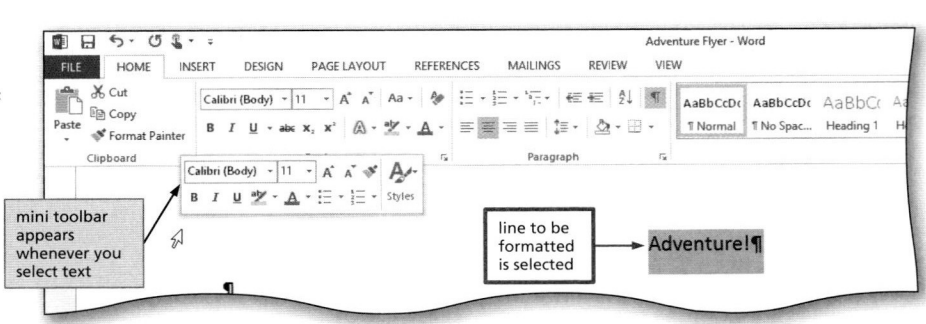

Figure 1–17

Other Ways

1. Drag pointer through line
2. With insertion point at beginning of desired line, press SHIFT+DOWN ARROW

To Change the Font Size of Selected Text

The next step is to increase the font size of the characters in the selected headline. *Why? You would like the headline to be as large as possible and still fit on a single line, which in this case is 72 point.* The following steps increase the font size of the headline from 11 to 72 point.

1

- With the text selected, tap or click the Font Size arrow (HOME tab | Font group) to display the Font Size gallery (Figure 1–18).

Q&A Why are the font sizes in my Font Size gallery different from those in Figure 1–18?
Font sizes may vary depending on the current font and your printer driver.

What happened to the mini toolbar?
The mini toolbar disappears if you do not use it. These steps use the Font Size arrow on the HOME tab instead of the Font Size arrow on the mini toolbar.

Figure 1–18

2

- If you are using a mouse, point to 72 in the Font Size gallery to display a live preview of the selected text at the selected point size (Figure 1–19).

Q&A Can I use live preview on a touch screen?
Live preview is not available on a touch screen.

Experiment

- If you are using a mouse, point to various font sizes in the Font Size gallery and watch the font size of the selected text change in the document window.

Figure 1–19

3

- Tap or click 72 in the Font Size gallery to increase the font size of the selected text.

Other Ways

| 1. Tap or click Font Size arrow on mini toolbar, tap or click desired font size in Font Size gallery | 2. Tap 'Show Context Menu' button on mini toolbar or right-click selected text, tap or click Font on shortcut menu, tap or click Font tab (Font dialog box), select desired font size in Size list, tap or click OK button | 3. Tap or click Font Dialog Box Launcher, tap or click Font tab (Font dialog box), select desired font size in Size list, tap or click OK button | 4. Press CTRL+D, tap or click Font tab (Font dialog box), select desired font size in Size list, tap or click OK button |

To Change the Font of Selected Text

The default theme font for headings is Calibri Light and for all other text, called body text in Word, is Calibri. Many other fonts are available, however, so that you can add variety to documents.

The following steps change the font of the headline from Calibri to Berlin Sans FB Demi. **Why?** *To draw more attention to the headline, you change its font so that it differs from the font of other text in the flyer.*

❶

- With the text selected, tap or click the Font arrow (HOME tab | Font group) to display the Font gallery (Figure 1–20).

Q&A

Will the fonts in my Font gallery be the same as those in Figure 1–20?
Your list of available fonts may differ, depending on the type of printer you are using and other settings.

What if the text no longer is selected?
Follow the steps on page WD 16 to select a line.

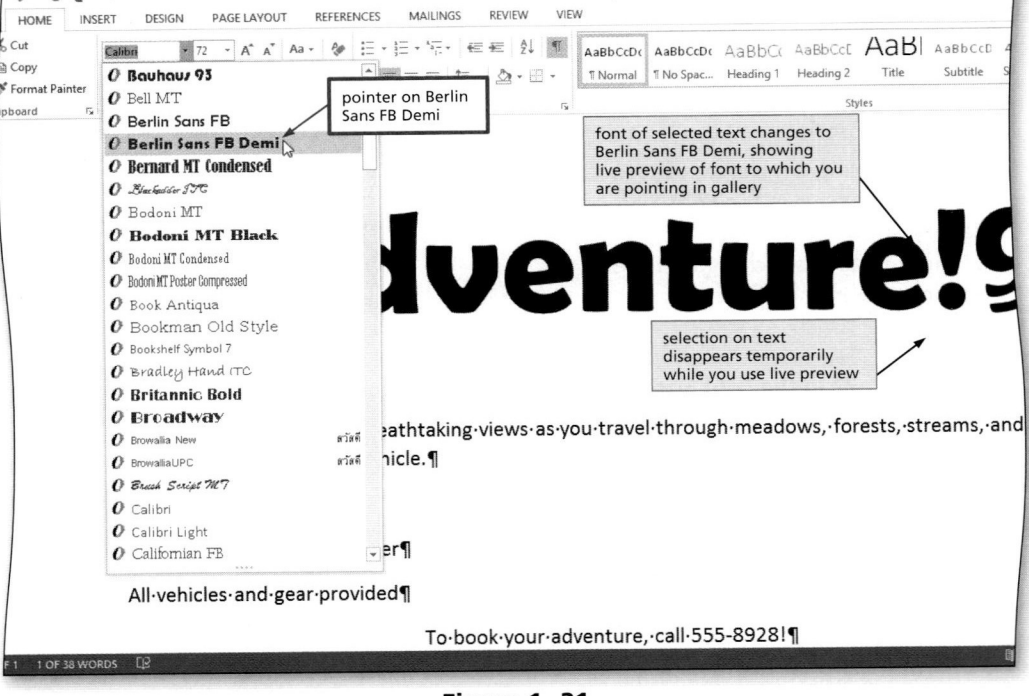

Figure 1–20

❷

- If necessary, scroll through the Font gallery to display Berlin Sans FB Demi (or a similar font).

- If you are using a mouse, point to Berlin Sans FB Demi (or a similar font) to display a live preview of the selected text in the selected font (Figure 1–21).

 Experiment

- If you are using a mouse, point to various fonts in the Font gallery and watch the font of the selected text change in the document window.

Figure 1–21

- Tap or click Berlin Sans FB Demi (or a similar font) to change the font of the selected text.

Q&A If the font I want to use appears in the Recently Used Fonts list in the Font gallery, could I tap or click it there instead?

Yes.

Other Ways

1. Tap or click Font arrow on mini toolbar, tap or click desired font in Font gallery

2. Tap 'Show Context Menu' button on mini toolbar or right-click selected text, tap or click Font on shortcut menu, tap or click Font tab (Font dialog box), select desired font in Font list, tap or click OK button

3. Tap or click Font Dialog Box Launcher (HOME tab | Font group), tap or click Font tab (Font dialog box), select desired font in Font list, tap or click OK button

4. Press CTRL+D, tap or click Font tab (Font dialog box), select desired font in Font list, tap or click OK button

To Change the Case of Selected Text

1 ENTER TEXT | 2 FORMAT TEXT | 3 INSERT PICTURE | 4 FORMAT PICTURE
5 ENHANCE PAGE | 6 CORRECT & REVISE | 7 PRINT OR READ

The headline currently shows the first letter in each word capitalized, which sometimes is referred to as initial cap. The following steps change the headline to uppercase. *Why? To draw more attention to the headline, you would like the entire line of text to be capitalized, or in uppercase letters.*

- With the text selected, tap or click the Change Case button (HOME tab | Font group) to display the Change Case gallery (Figure 1–22).

Figure 1–22

- Tap or click UPPERCASE in the Change Case gallery to change the case of the selected text (Figure 1–23).

Q&A What if a ruler appears on the screen or the pointer shape changes?

If you are using a mouse, depending on the position of your pointer and locations you click on the screen, a ruler may automatically appear or the pointer's shape may change. Simply move the mouse and the ruler should disappear and/or the pointer shape will change.

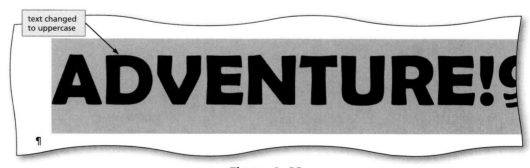

Figure 1–23

Other Ways

1. Tap 'Show Context Menu' button on mini toolbar or right-click selected text, tap or click Font on shortcut menu, tap or click Font tab (Font dialog box), select All caps in Effects area, tap or click OK button

2. Tap or click Font Dialog Box Launcher (HOME tab | Font group), tap or click Font tab (Font dialog box), select All caps in Effects area, tap or click OK button

3. Press SHIFT+F3 repeatedly until text is desired case

To Apply a Text Effect to Selected Text

Word provides many text effects to add interest and variety to text. The following steps apply a text effect to the headline. *Why? You would like the text in the headline to be even more noticeable.*

1

- With the text selected, tap or click the 'Text Effects and Typography' button (HOME tab | Font group) to display the Text Effects and Typography gallery (Figure 1–24).

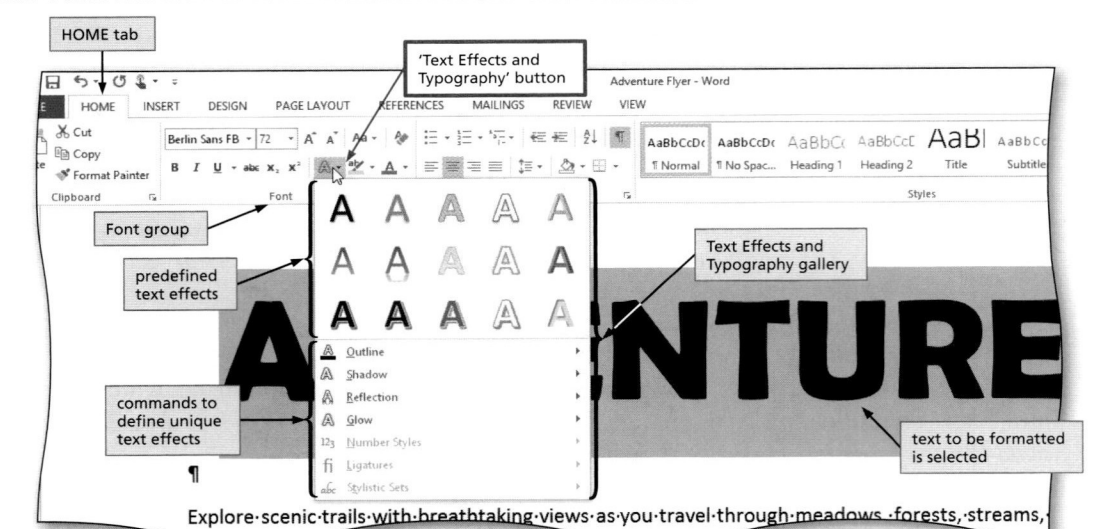

Figure 1–24

2

- If you are using a mouse, point to 'Fill - White, Outline - Accent 1, Glow - Accent 1' (fourth text effect in second row) to display a live preview of the selected text in the selected text effect (Figure 1–25).

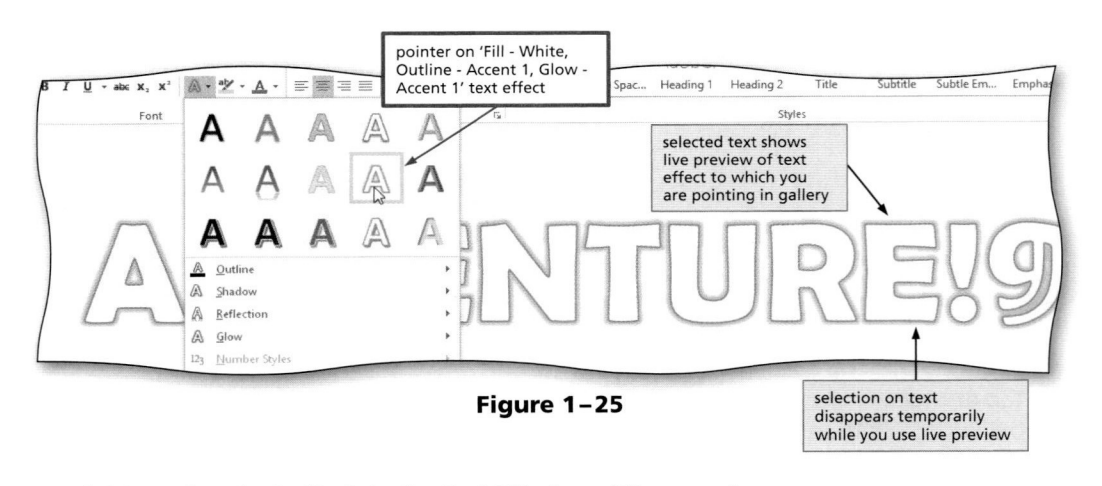

Figure 1–25

Experiment

- If you are using a mouse, point to various text effects in the Text Effects and Typography gallery and watch the text effects of the selected text change in the document window.

3

- Tap or click 'Fill - White, Outline - Accent 1, Glow - Accent 1' to change the text effect of the selected text.

4

- Tap or click anywhere in the document window to remove the selection from the selected text.

Other Ways

1. Tap 'Show Context Menu' button on mini toolbar or right-click selected text, tap or click Font on shortcut menu, tap or click Font tab (Font dialog box), tap or click Text Effects button, expand TEXT FILL or TEXT OUTLINE section and then select the desired text effect(s) (Format Text Effects dialog box), tap or click OK button, tap or click OK button

2. Tap or click Font Dialog Box Launcher (HOME tab | Font group), tap or click Font tab (Font dialog box), tap or click Text Effects button, expand TEXT FILL or TEXT OUTLINE section and then select desired text effect (Format Text Effects dialog box), tap or click OK button, tap or click OK button

To Shade a Paragraph

When you **shade** text, Word colors the rectangular area behind any text or graphics. If the text to shade is a paragraph, Word shades the area from the left margin to the right margin of the current paragraph. To shade a paragraph, place the insertion point in the paragraph. To shade any other text, you must first select the text to be shaded.

This flyer uses green as the shading color for the headline. *Why? To make the headline of the flyer more eye-catching, you shade it.* The following steps shade a paragraph.

1
- Tap or click somewhere in the paragraph to be shaded (in this case, the headline) to position the insertion point in the paragraph to be formatted.

- Tap or click the Shading arrow (HOME tab | Paragraph group) to display the Shading gallery (Figure 1–26).

Figure 1–26

Q&A If I am using a mouse, what if I click the Shading button by mistake?
Click the Shading arrow and proceed with Step 2. If you are using a touch screen, you may not have a separate Shading button.

Experiment
- If you are using a mouse, point to various colors in the Shading gallery and watch the shading color of the current paragraph change.

2
- Tap or click 'Green, Accent 6, Darker 25%' (rightmost color in fifth row) to shade the current paragraph (Figure 1–27).

Q&A What if I apply a dark shading color to dark text?
When the font color of text is Automatic, it usually is black. If you select a dark shading color, Word automatically may change the text color to white so that the shaded text is easier to read.

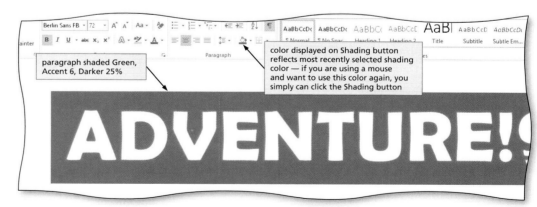

Figure 1–27

Other Ways
1. Tap or click Borders arrow (HOME tab | Paragraph group), tap or click Borders and Shading, tap or click Shading tab (Borders and Shading dialog box), tap or click Fill arrow, select desired color, tap or click OK button

To Select Multiple Lines

The next formatting step for the flyer is to increase the font size of the characters between the headline and the signature line. ***Why?*** *You want this text to be easier to read from a distance.*

To change the font size of the characters in multiple lines, you first must select all the lines to be formatted. The following steps select multiple lines.

1

- Scroll, if necessary, so that all text below the headline is displayed on the screen.

- If you are using a touch screen, tap to position the insertion point in the text to select; if you are using a mouse, move the pointer to the left of the first paragraph to be selected until the pointer changes to a right-pointing block arrow (Figure 1–28).

Figure 1–28

2

- If you are using a touch screen, drag the selection handle(s) as necessary to select the text that will be formatted; if you are using a mouse, while the pointer is a right-pointing block arrow, drag downward to select all lines that will be formatted (Figure 1–29).

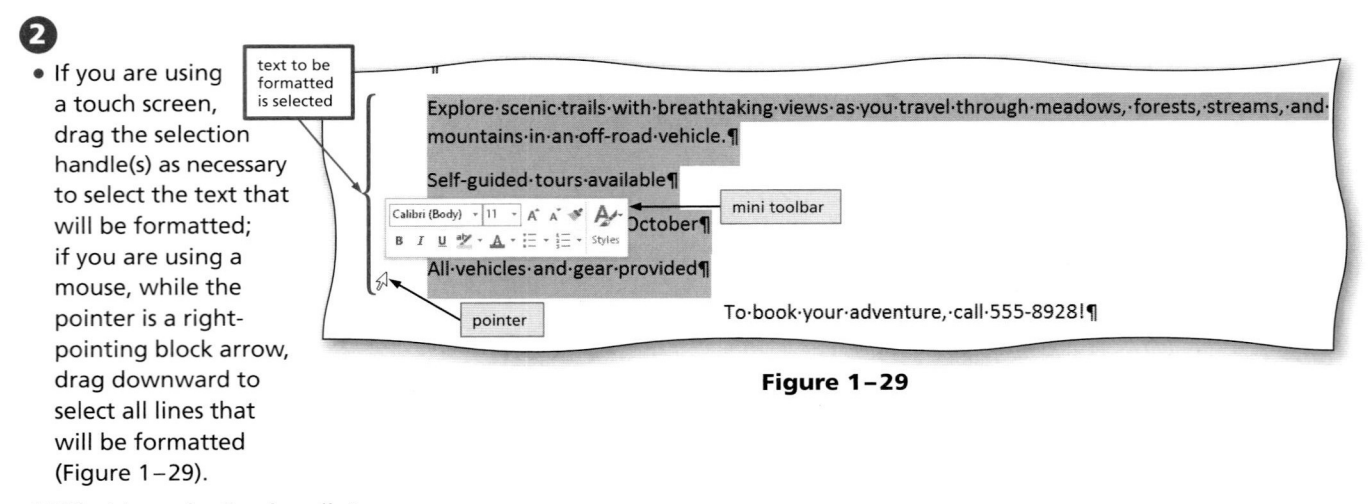

Figure 1–29

Q&A | What is a selection handle?
When working on a touch screen, a **selection handle** (small circle) appears below the insertion point. Using a fingertip, you drag a selection handle to select text.

Other Ways

1. With insertion point at beginning of desired line, press SHIFT+DOWN ARROW repeatedly until all lines are selected

To Change the Font Size of Selected Text

The characters between the headline and the signature line in the flyer currently are 11 point. To make them easier to read from a distance, this flyer uses a 24-point font size for these characters. The following steps change the font size of the selected text.

1 With the text selected, tap or click the Font Size arrow (HOME tab | Font group) to display the Font Size gallery.

2 Tap or click 24 in the Font Size gallery to increase the font size of the selected text.

3 Tap or click anywhere in the document window to remove the selection from the text.

4 If necessary, scroll so that you can see all the resized text on the screen (Figure 1–30).

Figure 1–30

To Bullet a List of Paragraphs

1 ENTER TEXT | 2 FORMAT TEXT | 3 INSERT PICTURE | 4 FORMAT PICTURE
5 ENHANCE PAGE | 6 CORRECT & REVISE | 7 PRINT OR READ

A **bulleted list** is a series of paragraphs, each beginning with a bullet character. The next step is to format the three paragraphs about the tours that are above the signature line in the flyer as a bulleted list.

To format a list of paragraphs with bullets, you first must select all the lines in the paragraphs. ***Why?*** *If you do not select all paragraphs, Word will place a bullet only in the paragraph containing the insertion point.* The following steps bullet a list of paragraphs.

1

- If you are using a touch screen, tap to position the insertion point in the text to select; if you are using a mouse, move the pointer to the left of the first paragraph to be selected until the pointer changes to a right-pointing block arrow.

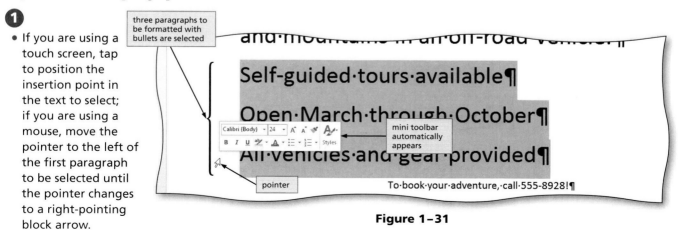

Figure 1–31

- If you are using a touch screen, drag the selection handle(s) as necessary to select the text that will be formatted; if you are using a mouse, drag downward until all paragraphs that will be formatted with a bullet character are selected (Figure 1–31).

2

- Tap or click the Bullets button (HOME tab | Paragraph group) to place a bullet character at the beginning of each selected paragraph (Figure 1–32).

Q&A

What if my screen displays a Bullets gallery?
If you are using a touch screen, you may not have a separate Bullets button and Bullets arrow. In this case, select the desired bullet style in the Bullets gallery.

If I am using a mouse, what if I accidentally click the Bullets arrow?
Press the ESCAPE key to remove the Bullets gallery from the screen and then repeat Step 2. If you are using a touch screen, you may not have a separate Bullets button and Bullets arrow.

How do I remove bullets from a list or paragraph?
Select the list or paragraph and then tap or click the Bullets button again.

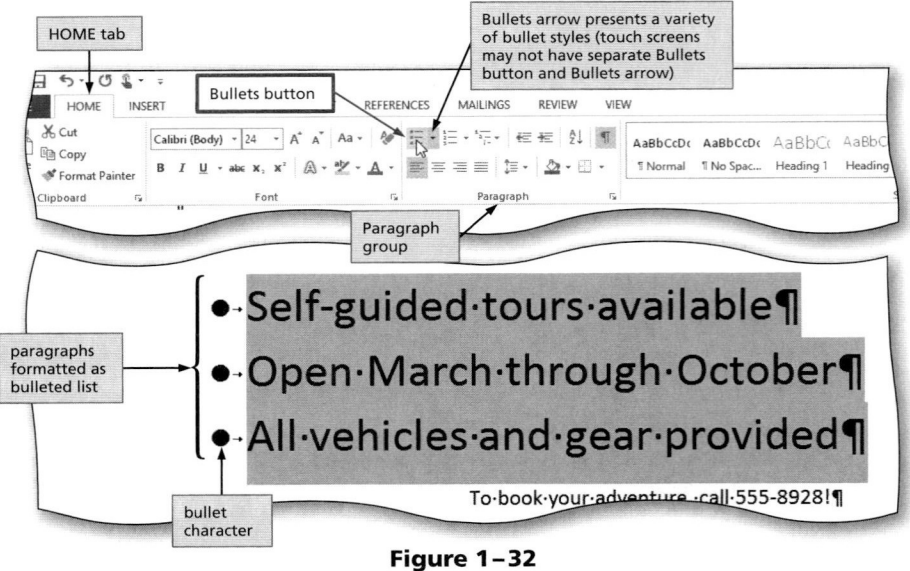

Figure 1–32

Other Ways

1. Press and hold or right-click selected paragraphs, tap or click Bullets button on mini toolbar, if necessary select bullet style in Bullets gallery

To Undo and Redo an Action

1 ENTER TEXT | 2 FORMAT TEXT | **3 INSERT PICTURE** | **4 FORMAT PICTURE**
5 ENHANCE PAGE | **6 CORRECT & REVISE** | **7 PRINT OR READ**

Word provides a means of canceling your recent command(s) or action(s). For example, if you format text incorrectly, you can undo the format and try it again. When you point to the Undo button, Word displays the action you can undo as part of a ScreenTip.

If, after you undo an action, you decide you did not want to perform the undo, you can redo the undone action. Word does not allow you to undo or redo some actions, such as saving or printing a document. The following steps undo the bullet format just applied and then redo the bullet format. *Why?* *These steps illustrate the undo and redo actions.*

1

- Tap or click the Undo button on the Quick Access Toolbar to reverse your most recent action (in this case, remove the bullets from the paragraphs) (Figure 1–33).

Figure 1–33

● Tap or click the Redo button on the Quick Access Toolbar to reverse your most recent undo (in this case, place a bullet character on the paragraphs again) (shown in Figure 1–32).

Other Ways

1. Press CTRL+Z to undo; press CTRL+Y to redo

1 ENTER TEXT | 2 FORMAT TEXT | 3 INSERT PICTURE | 4 FORMAT PICTURE
5 ENHANCE PAGE | 6 CORRECT & REVISE | 7 PRINT OR READ

To Italicize Text

Italic text has a slanted appearance. The next step is to italicize the word, breathtaking, in the flyer to further emphasize it. As with a single paragraph, if you want to format a single word, you do not need to select it. *Why?* *To format a single word, you simply position the insertion point somewhere in the word and apply the desired format.* The following step italicizes a word.

● Tap or click somewhere in the word to be italicized (breathtaking, in this case) to position the insertion point in the word to be formatted.

● Tap or click the Italic button (HOME tab | Font group) to italicize the word containing the insertion point (Figure 1–34).

Q&A

How would I remove an italic format?
You would tap or click the Italic button a second time, or you immediately could tap or click the Undo button on the Quick Access Toolbar or press CTRL+Z.

Figure 1–34

How can I tell what formatting has been applied to text?
The selected buttons and boxes on the HOME tab show formatting characteristics of the location of the insertion point. With the insertion point in the word, breathtaking, the HOME tab shows these formats: 24-point Calibri italic font.

Why did the appearance of the Redo button change?
It changed to a Repeat button. When it is a Repeat button, you can tap or click it to repeat your last action. For example, you can select different text and then click the Repeat button to apply (repeat) the italic format to the selected text.

Other Ways

1. Tap or click Italic button on mini toolbar	2. Tap 'Show Context Menu' button on mini toolbar or right-click selected text, tap or click Font on shortcut menu, tap or click Font tab (Font dialog box), tap or click Italic in Font style list, tap or click OK button	3. Tap or click Font Dialog Box Launcher (HOME tab \| Font group), tap or click Font tab (Font dialog box), tap or click Italic in Font style list, tap or click OK button	4. Press CTRL+I

To Color Text

The following steps change the color of the word, breathtaking. *Why? To emphasize the word even more, you change its color to a shade of orange.*

1

- With the insertion point in the word to format, tap or click the Font Color arrow (HOME tab | Font group) to display the Font Color gallery (Figure 1–35).

Q&A If I am using a mouse, what if I click the Font Color button by mistake? Click the Font Color arrow and then proceed with Step 2. If you are using a touch screen, you may not have a separate Font Color button.

Figure 1–35

Experiment

- If you are using a mouse, point to various colors in the Font Color gallery and watch the color of the current word change.

2

- Tap or click 'Orange, Accent 2, Darker 25%' (sixth color in fifth row) to change the color of the text (Figure 1–36).

Q&A How would I change the text color back to black? You would position the insertion point in the word or select the text, tap or click the Font Color arrow (HOME tab | Font group) again, and then tap or click Automatic in the Font Color gallery.

Figure 1–36

Other Ways

1. Tap or click Font Color arrow on mini toolbar, tap or click desired color	2. Tap 'Show Context Menu' button on mini toolbar or right-click selected text, tap or click Font on shortcut menu, tap or click Font tab (Font dialog box), tap or click Font color arrow, tap or click desired color, tap or click OK button	3. Tap or click Font Dialog Box Launcher (HOME tab	Font group), tap or click Font tab (Font dialog box), tap or click Font color arrow, tap or click desired color, tap or click OK button

To Use the Mini Toolbar to Format Text

Recall from the Office and Windows chapter at the beginning of this book that the mini toolbar automatically appears based on certain tasks you perform. *Why? Word places commonly used buttons and boxes on the mini toolbar for your convenience. If you do not use the mini toolbar, it disappears from the screen.* All commands on the mini toolbar also exist on the ribbon.

The following steps use the mini toolbar to change the color and font size of text in the signature line of the flyer.

1

• If you are using a touch screen, double-tap to the left of the line to be selected to select the line, and then tap the selection to display the mini toolbar; if you are using a mouse, move the pointer to the left of the line to be selected until the pointer changes to a right-pointing block arrow and then click to select the line and display the mini toolbar (Figure 1–37).

Figure 1–37

Why does my mini toolbar look different than the one in Figure 1–37?

If you are using a touch screen, the buttons and boxes on the mini toolbar differ. For example, it contains a 'Show Context Menu' button at the far-right edge, which you tap to display a shortcut menu.

2

• Tap or click the Font Size arrow on the mini toolbar to display the Font Size gallery.

• If you are using a mouse, point to 28 in the Font Size gallery to display a live preview of the selected font size (Figure 1–38).

3

• Tap or click 28 in the Font Size gallery to increase the font size of the selected text.

Figure 1–38

4

- With the text still selected and the mini toolbar still displayed, tap or click the Font Color arrow on the mini toolbar to display the Font Color gallery.

- If you are using a mouse, point to 'Orange, Accent 2, Darker 25%' (sixth color in the fifth row) to display a live preview of the selected font color (Figure 1–39).

5

- Tap or click 'Orange, Accent 2, Darker 25%' to change the color of the selected text.

- Tap or click anywhere in the document window to remove the selection from the text.

Figure 1–39

To Select a Group of Words

1 ENTER TEXT | 2 FORMAT TEXT | 3 INSERT PICTURE | 4 FORMAT PICTURE
5 ENHANCE PAGE | 6 CORRECT & REVISE | 7 PRINT OR READ

To emphasize the contact phone number (555-8928), this text is underlined in the flyer. Because the phone number is separated with a hyphen, Word considers it a group of words. To format a group of words, you first must select them. ***Why?*** *If you underline text without selecting any text first, Word will underline only the word containing the insertion point.* The following steps select a group of words.

1

- If you are using a touch screen, tap to position the insertion point in the text you want to select; if you are using a mouse, position the pointer immediately to the left of the first character of the text to be selected, in this case, the 5 in 555 (Figure 1–40).

Figure 1–40

Q&A Why did the shape of the pointer change?
The pointer's shape is an I-beam when positioned in unselected text in the document window.

2

- If you are using a touch screen, drag the selection handle(s) to select the text to be formatted; if you are using a mouse, drag the pointer through the last character of the text to be selected, in this case, the 8 in the phone number (Figure 1–41).

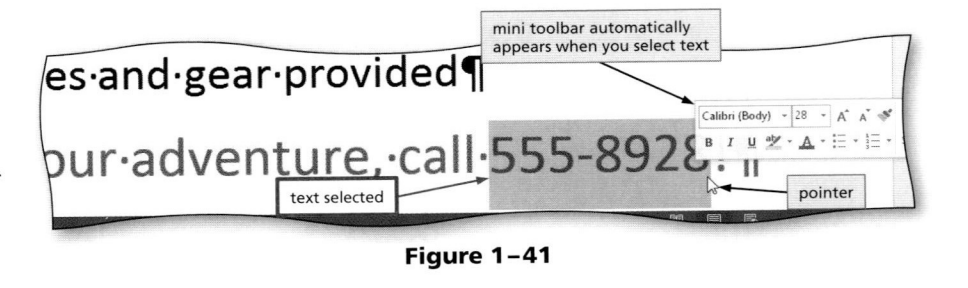

Figure 1–41

Q&A Why did the pointer shape change again?
When the pointer is positioned in selected text, its shape is a left-pointing block arrow.

Other Ways

1. With insertion point at beginning of first word in group, press CTRL+SHIFT+RIGHT ARROW repeatedly until all words are selected

To Underline Text

Underlined text prints with an underscore (_) below each character. In the flyer, the contact phone number, 555-8928, in the signature line is underlined. *Why? Underlines are used to emphasize or draw attention to specific text.* The following step formats selected text with an underline.

- With the text selected, tap or click the Underline button (HOME tab | Font group) to underline the selected text (Figure 1–42).

Q&A What if my screen displays an Underline gallery?
If you are using a touch screen, you may not have a separate Underline button and Underline arrow. In this case, select the desired underline style in the Underline gallery.

If a button exists on the mini toolbar, can I tap or click that instead of using the ribbon?
Yes.

Figure 1–42

How would I remove an underline?
You would tap or click the Underline button a second time, or you immediately could tap or click the Undo button on the Quick Access Toolbar.

Other Ways				
1. Tap or click Underline button on mini toolbar	2. Tap 'Show Context Menu' button on mini toolbar or right-click text, tap or click Font on shortcut menu, tap or click Font tab (Font dialog box), tap or click Underline style box arrow, tap or click desired underline style, tap or click OK button	3. Tap or click Font Dialog Box Launcher (HOME tab	Font group), tap or click Font tab (Font dialog box), tap or click Underline style arrow, tap or click desired underline style, tap or click OK button	4. Press CTRL+U

To Bold Text

Bold characters appear somewhat thicker and darker than those that are not bold. The steps on the next page format the text, off-road, in bold characters. *Why? To further emphasize this text, it is bold in the flyer.* Recall that if you want to format a single word, you simply position the insertion point in the word and then format the word. To format text that consists of more than one word, as you have learned previously, you select the text first.

- Select the text to be formatted (the text, off-road, in this case); that is, if you are using a touch screen, tap to position the insertion point in the text you want to select and then drag the selection handle(s) to select the text to be formatted; if you are using a mouse, position the pointer immediately to the left of the first character of the text to be selected and then drag the pointer through the last character of the text to be selected.

2

- With the text selected, tap or click the Bold button (HOME tab | Font group) to bold the selected text (Figure 1–43).

Q&A How would I remove a bold format?
You would tap or click the Bold button a second time, or you immediately could tap or click the Undo button on the Quick Access Toolbar.

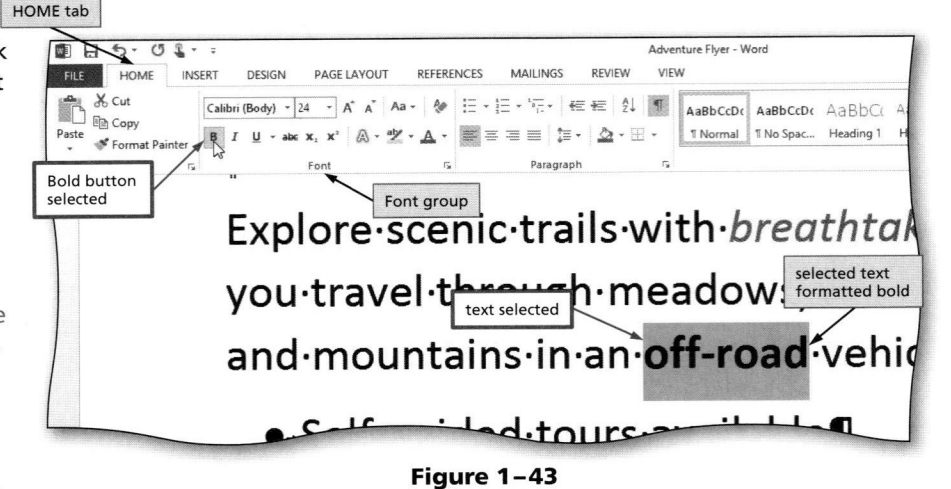

Figure 1–43

3

- Tap or click anywhere in the document window to remove the selection from the screen.

Other Ways

1. Tap or click Bold button on mini toolbar	2. Tap 'Show Context Menu' button on mini toolbar or right-click selected text, tap or click Font on shortcut menu, tap or click Font tab (Font dialog box), tap or click Bold in Font style list, tap or click OK button	3. Tap or click Font Dialog Box Launcher (HOME tab	Font group), tap or click Font tab (Font dialog box), tap or click Bold in Font style list, tap or click OK button	4. Press CTRL+B

To Zoom One Page

1 ENTER TEXT | 2 FORMAT TEXT | 3 INSERT PICTURE | 4 FORMAT PICTURE
5 ENHANCE PAGE | 6 CORRECT & REVISE | 7 PRINT OR READ

Earlier in this chapter, you changed the zoom to page width so that the text on the screen was larger and easier to read. In the next set of steps, you want to see the entire page (mock sheet of paper) on the screen at once. *Why? You want be able to see the effect of adjusting colors in the document as a whole.* The next step displays a single page in its entirety in the document window as large as possible.

1

- Tap or click VIEW on the ribbon to display the VIEW tab.

- Tap or click the One Page button (VIEW tab | Zoom group) to display the entire page in the document window as large as possible (Figure 1–44).

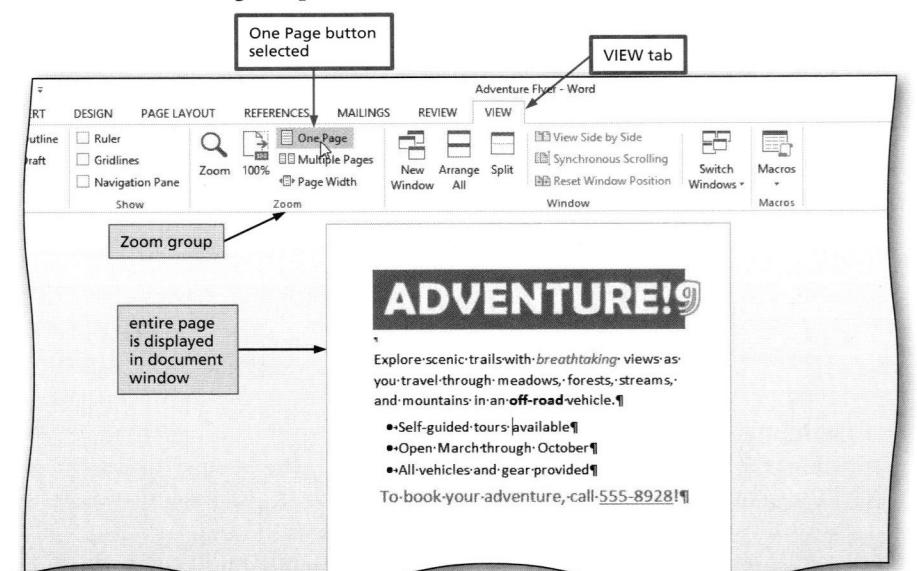

Figure 1–44

Other Ways

1. Tap or click Zoom button (VIEW tab | Zoom group), tap or click Whole page (Zoom dialog box), tap or click OK button

What colors should I choose when creating documents?

When choosing color, associate the meaning of the color with your message:

- Red expresses danger, power, or energy and often is associated with sports or physical exertion.

- Brown represents simplicity, honesty, and dependability.

- Orange denotes success, victory, creativity, and enthusiasm.

- Yellow suggests sunshine, happiness, hope, liveliness, and intelligence.

- Green symbolizes growth, healthiness, harmony, blooming, and healing and often is associated with safety or money.

- Blue indicates integrity, trust, importance, confidence, and stability.

- Purple represents wealth, power, comfort, extravagance, magic, mystery, and spirituality.

- White stands for purity, goodness, cleanliness, precision, and perfection.

- Black suggests authority, strength, elegance, power, and prestige.

- Gray conveys neutrality and, thus, often is found in backgrounds and other effects.

To Change Theme Colors

1 ENTER TEXT | 2 FORMAT TEXT | 3 INSERT PICTURE | 4 FORMAT PICTURE
5 ENHANCE PAGE | 6 CORRECT & REVISE | 7 PRINT OR READ

A **color scheme** in Word is a document theme that identifies 12 complementary colors for text, background, accents, and links in a document. With more than 20 predefined color schemes, Word provides a simple way to coordinate colors in a document.

The default color scheme is called Office. In the flyer, you will change the color scheme from Office to Green. *Why? You want the colors in the flyer to suggest growth, harmony, blooming, trust, and stability, which are conveyed by shades of greens and blues. In Word, the Green color scheme uses these colors.* The following steps change theme colors.

- Tap or click DESIGN on the ribbon to display the DESIGN tab.

- Tap or click the Theme Colors button (DESIGN tab | Document Formatting group) to display the Theme Colors gallery.

- If you are using a mouse, point to Green in the Theme Colors gallery to display a live preview of the selected theme color (Figure 1–45).

Figure 1–45

Experiment

- If you are using a mouse, point to various color schemes in the Theme Colors gallery and watch the colors change in the document.

❷

• Tap or click Green in the Colors gallery to change the document theme colors.

Q&A What if I want to return to the original color scheme?
You would tap or click the Theme Colors button again and then tap or click Office in the Theme Colors gallery.

BTW
Selecting Nonadjacent Items
In Word, you can use keyboard keys to select nonadjacent items, that is, items not next to each other. This is helpful when you are applying the same formatting to multiple items. To select nonadjacent items (text or graphics), select the first item, such as a word or paragraph, as usual; then, press and hold down the CTRL key. While holding down the CTRL key, select additional items.

To Zoom Page Width

Because the document contents are small when displayed at one page, the next steps zoom page width again.

❶ Tap or click VIEW on the ribbon to display the VIEW tab.

❷ Tap or click the Page Width button (VIEW tab | Zoom group) to display the page the same width as the document window (shown in Figure 1–46 on page WD 34).

Selecting Text

In many of the previous steps, you have selected text. Table 1–3 summarizes the techniques used to select various items.

Table 1–3 Techniques for Selecting Text			
Item to Select	**Touch**	**Mouse**	**Keyboard (where applicable)**
Block of text	Tap to position insertion point in text to select and then drag selection handle(s) to select text.	Click at beginning of selection, scroll to end of selection, position pointer at end of selection, hold down SHIFT key, and then click; or drag through text.	
Character(s)	Tap to position insertion point in text to select and then drag selection handle(s) to select text.	Drag through character(s).	SHIFT+RIGHT ARROW or SHIFT+LEFT ARROW
Document		Move pointer to left of text until pointer changes to right-pointing block arrow and then triple-click.	CTRL+A
Graphic	Tap the graphic.	Click the graphic.	
Line	Double-tap to left of line to be selected.	Move pointer to left of line until pointer changes to right-pointing block arrow and then click.	HOME, then SHIFT+END or END, then SHIFT+HOME
Lines	Tap to position insertion point in text to select and then drag selection handle(s) to select text.	Move pointer to left of first line until pointer changes to right-pointing block arrow and then drag up or down.	HOME, then SHIFT+DOWN ARROW or END, then SHIFT+UP ARROW
Paragraph	Tap to position insertion point in text to select and then drag selection handle(s) to select text.	Triple-click paragraph; or move pointer to left of paragraph until pointer changes to right-pointing block arrow and then double-click.	CTRL+SHIFT+DOWN ARROW or CTRL+SHIFT+UP ARROW
Paragraphs	Tap to position insertion point in text to select and then drag selection handle(s) to select text.	Move pointer to left of paragraph until pointer changes to right-pointing block arrow, double-click, and then drag up or down.	CTRL+SHIFT+DOWN ARROW or CTRL+SHIFT+UP ARROW repeatedly
Sentence	Tap to position insertion point in text to select and then drag selection handle(s) to select text.	Press and hold down CTRL key and then click sentence.	
Word	Double-tap word.	Double-click word.	CTRL+SHIFT+RIGHT ARROW or CTRL+SHIFT+LEFT ARROW
Words	Tap to position insertion point in text to select and then drag selection handle(s) to select text.	Drag through words.	CTRL+SHIFT+RIGHT ARROW or CTRL+SHIFT+LEFT ARROW repeatedly

To Save an Existing Document with the Same File Name

You have made several modifications to the document since you last saved it. Thus, you should save it again. The following step saves the document again. For an example of the step listed below, refer to the Office and Windows chapter at the beginning of this book.

1 Tap or click the Save button on the Quick Access Toolbar to overwrite the previously saved file.

Break Point: If you wish to take a break, this is a good place to do so. You can exit Word now (refer to page WD 46 for instructions). To resume at a later time, run Word (refer to pages WD 46 to WD 47 for instructions), open the file called Adventure Flyer (refer to page WD 47 for instructions), and continue following the steps from this location forward.

Inserting and Formatting a Picture in a Word Document

With the text formatted in the flyer, the next step is to insert a digital picture in the flyer and format the picture. Flyers usually contain a graphical image(s), such as a picture, to attract the attention of passersby. In the following pages, you will perform these tasks:

1. Insert a digital picture into the flyer and then reduce its size.
2. Enlarge the size of the picture.
3. Change the look of the picture.

CONSIDER THIS

How do I locate a graphic file to use in a document?

To use a graphic in a Word document, the image must be stored digitally in a file. Files containing graphics are available from a variety of sources:

- Microsoft has free digital images on the web for use in a document. Other websites also have images available, some of which are free, while others require a fee.
- You can take a picture with a digital camera or camera phone and **download** it, which is the process of copying the digital picture from the camera or phone to your computer.
- With a scanner, you can convert a printed picture, drawing, or diagram to a digital file.

If you receive a picture from a source other than yourself, do not use the file until you are certain it does not contain a virus. A **virus** is a computer program that can damage files and programs on your computer. Use an antivirus program to verify that any files you use are virus free.

To Center Another Paragraph

In the flyer, the digital picture of a mountain trail tour group should be centered on the blank line below the headline. The blank paragraph below the headline currently is left-aligned. The following steps center this paragraph.

1 Tap or click HOME on the ribbon to display the HOME tab.

2 Tap or click somewhere in the paragraph to be centered (in this case, the blank line below the headline) to position the insertion point in the paragraph to be formatted.

3 Tap or click the Center button (HOME tab | Paragraph group) to center the paragraph containing the insertion point (shown in Figure 1–46 on the next page).

BTW
BTWs
For a complete list of the BTWs found in the margins of this book, visit the BTW resource on the Student Companion Site located on www.cengagebrain.com. For detailed instructions about accessing available resources, visit www.cengage.com/ct/studentdownload or contact your instructor for information about accessing the required files.

To Insert a Picture

The next step in creating the flyer is to insert a digital picture of a mountain trail tour group in the flyer on the blank line below the headline. The picture, which was taken with a digital camera, is available on the Data Files for Students. Visit www.cengage.com/ct/studentdownload for detailed instructions or contact your instructor for information about accessing the required files.

The following steps insert a picture, which, in this example, is located in the Chapter 01 folder in the Word folder in the Data Files for Students folder. *Why? It is good practice to organize and store files in folders so that you easily can find the files at a later date.*

1

- If necessary, position the insertion point at the location where you want to insert the picture (in this case, on the centered blank paragraph below the headline).

- Tap or click INSERT on the ribbon to display the INSERT tab (Figure 1–46).

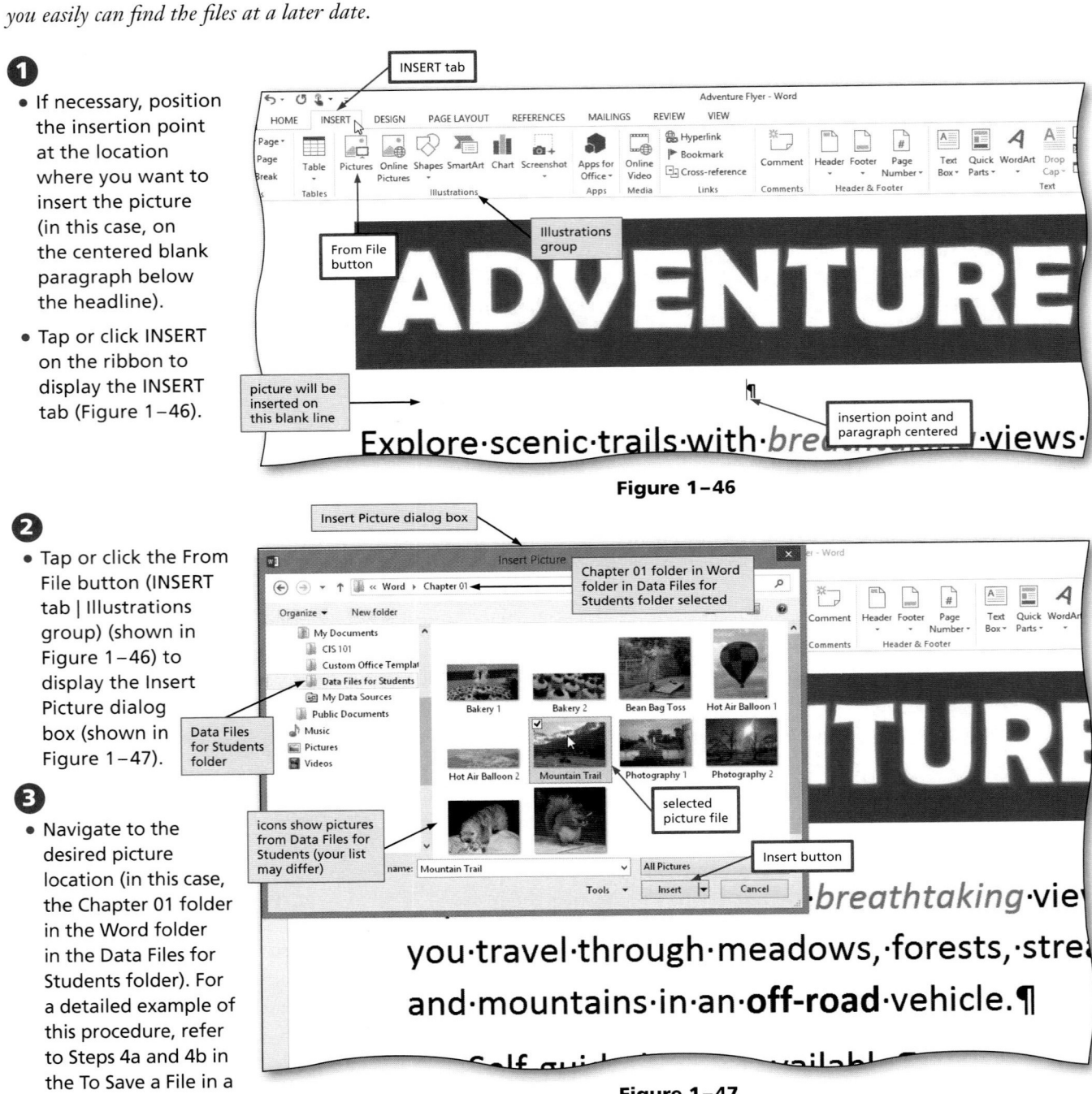

Figure 1–46

2

- Tap or click the From File button (INSERT tab | Illustrations group) (shown in Figure 1–46) to display the Insert Picture dialog box (shown in Figure 1–47).

3

- Navigate to the desired picture location (in this case, the Chapter 01 folder in the Word folder in the Data Files for Students folder). For a detailed example of this procedure, refer to Steps 4a and 4b in the To Save a File in a Folder section in the Office and Windows chapter at the beginning of this book.

- Tap or click Mountain Trail to select the file (Figure 1–47).

Figure 1–47

4

- Tap or click the Insert button (Insert Picture dialog box) to insert the picture at the location of the insertion point in the document (Figure 1–48).

Q&A | What are the symbols around the picture?

A selected graphic appears surrounded by a **selection rectangle**, which has small squares and circles, called **sizing handles**, at each corner and middle location.

What is the purpose of the Layout Options button?

When you tap or click the Layout Options button, Word provides options for changing how the graphic is positioned with text in the document.

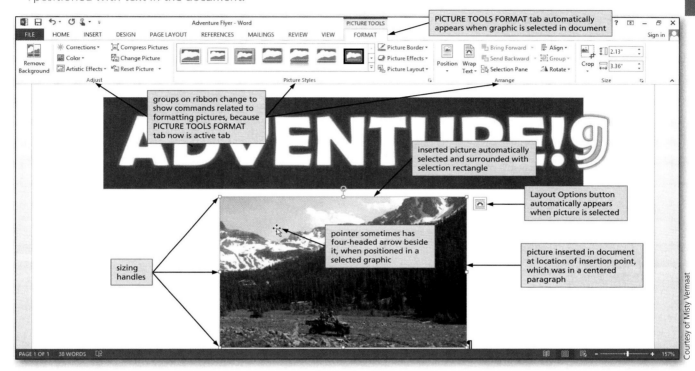

Figure 1–48

How do you know where to position a graphic on a flyer?

The content, size, shape, position, and format of a graphic should capture the interest of passersby, enticing them to stop and read the flyer. Often, the graphic is the center of attention and visually the largest element on a flyer. If you use colors in the graphical image, be sure they are part of the document's color scheme.

CONSIDER THIS

1 ENTER TEXT | 2 FORMAT TEXT | 3 INSERT PICTURE | **4 FORMAT PICTURE**
5 ENHANCE PAGE | 6 CORRECT & REVISE | 7 PRINT OR READ

To Zoom the Document

In the steps on the following pages, you will work with the picture just inserted. The next task is to adjust the zoom percentage. *Why? Currently, you can see only a small amount of text with the picture. Seeing more of the document at once helps you determine the appropriate size for the picture.* The following step zooms the document.

Experiment

- If you are using a mouse, repeatedly click the Zoom Out and Zoom In buttons on the status bar and watch the size of the document change in the document window.

- If you are using a touch screen, repeatedly pinch (move two fingers together) and stretch (move two fingers apart) and watch the size of the document change in the document window.

- Pinch and stretch or click the Zoom Out or Zoom In button as many times as necessary until the Zoom button on the status bar displays 80% on its face (Figure 1–49).

Figure 1–49

Other Ways

1. Drag Zoom slider on status bar
2. Tap or click Zoom level button on status bar, select desired zoom percent or type (Zoom dialog box), tap or click OK button
3. Tap or click Zoom button (VIEW tab | Zoom group), select desired zoom percent or type (Zoom dialog box), tap or click OK button

To Resize a Graphic

1 ENTER TEXT | 2 FORMAT TEXT | 3 INSERT PICTURE | **4 FORMAT PICTURE**
5 ENHANCE PAGE | **6 CORRECT & REVISE** | **7 PRINT OR READ**

Resizing includes both increasing and reducing the size of a graphic. The next step is to resize the picture so that it is larger in the flyer. **Why?** *You want the graphic as large as possible on a single page flyer to draw the attention of passersby.* The following steps resize a selected graphic.

1

- Be sure the graphic still is selected.

Q&A What if my graphic (picture) is not selected?
To select a graphic, tap or click it.

- If you are using a mouse, point to the lower-left corner sizing handle on the picture so that the pointer shape changes to a two-headed arrow (Figure 1–50).

Figure 1–50

- Drag the sizing handle diagonally outward until the lower-left corner of the picture is positioned approximately as shown in Figure 1–51. Do not lift your finger or release the mouse button at this point.

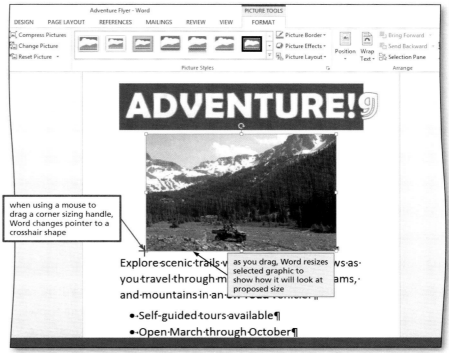

- Release your finger or the mouse button to resize the graphic, which in this case, should have a height of about 3.26" and a width of about 5.04".

Q&A

How can I see the height and width measurements?
Look in the Size group on the PICTURE TOOLS FORMAT tab to see the height and width measurements of the currently selected graphic (shown in Figure 1–49).

What if the graphic is the wrong size?
Repeat Steps 1, 2, and 3, or enter the desired height and width values in the Shape Height and Shape Width boxes (PICTURE TOOLS FORMAT tab | Size group).

What if I want to return a graphic to its original size and start again?
With the graphic selected, tap or click the Size Dialog Box Launcher (PICTURE TOOLS FORMAT tab | Size group), tap or click the Size tab (Layout dialog box), tap or click the Reset button, and then tap or click the OK button.

Figure 1–51

Callout: when using a mouse to drag a corner sizing handle, Word changes pointer to a crosshair shape

Callout: as you drag, Word resizes selected graphic to show how it will look at proposed size

Courtesy of Misty Vermaat

Other Ways

1. Enter height and width of graphic in Shape Height and Shape Width boxes (PICTURE TOOLS FORMAT tab | Size group)
2. Tap or click Advanced Layout: Size Dialog Box Launcher (PICTURE TOOLS FORMAT tab | Size group), tap or click Size tab (Layout dialog box), enter desired height and width values in boxes, tap or click OK button

To Zoom 100%

1 ENTER TEXT | 2 FORMAT TEXT | 3 INSERT PICTURE | **4 FORMAT PICTURE**
5 ENHANCE PAGE | 6 CORRECT & REVISE | 7 PRINT OR READ

In the next series of steps, you will format the picture. Earlier in this chapter, you changed the zoom to 80% so that you could see more of the page while resizing the graphic. The step on the next page zooms the screen to 100%. **Why?** *You want the contents of the image to be enlarged a bit, while still seeing some of the text in the document.*

1

- Tap or click VIEW on the ribbon to display the VIEW tab.

- Tap or click the 100% button (VIEW tab | Zoom group) to display the page at 100% in the document window (Figure 1–52).

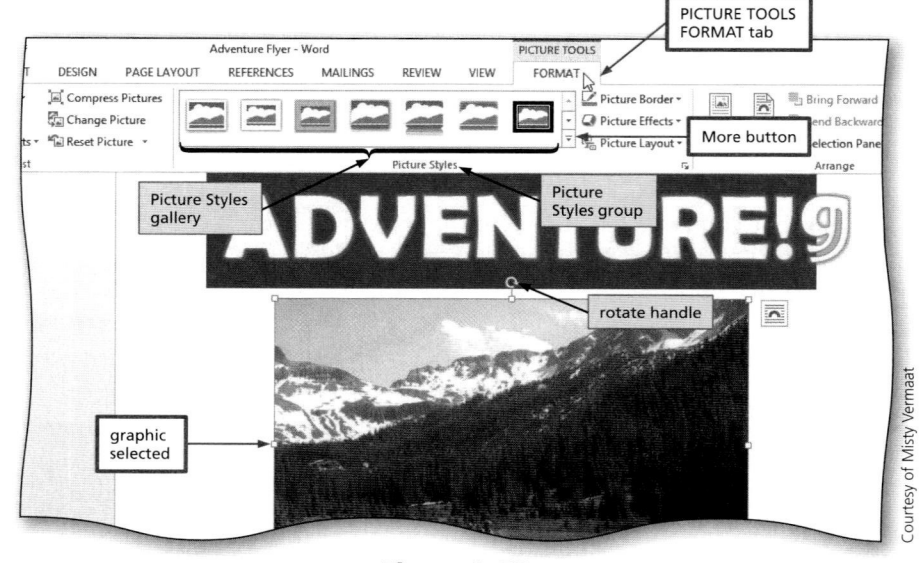

Figure 1–52

Other Ways

1. Tap or click Zoom button (VIEW tab | Zoom group), tap or click 100% (Zoom dialog box), tap or click OK button

To Apply a Picture Style

1 ENTER TEXT | 2 FORMAT TEXT | 3 INSERT PICTURE | 4 FORMAT PICTURE
5 ENHANCE PAGE | 6 CORRECT & REVISE | 7 PRINT OR READ

A **style** is a named group of formatting characteristics. Word provides more than 25 picture styles. *Why?* *Picture styles enable you easily to change a picture's look to a more visually appealing style, including a variety of shapes, angles, borders, and reflections.* The flyer in this chapter uses a style that applies a drop shadow to the picture. The following steps apply a picture style to a picture.

1

- Tap or click PICTURE TOOLS FORMAT on the ribbon to display the PICTURE TOOLS FORMAT tab.

- Be sure the graphic still is selected (Figure 1–53).

Q&A What if my graphic (picture) is not selected?
To select a graphic, tap or click it.

What is the white circle attached to top of the selected graphic?
It is called a rotate handle. When you drag a graphic's **rotate handle**, the graphic moves in either a clockwise or counterclockwise direction.

Figure 1–53

2

- Tap or click the More button in the Picture Styles gallery (PICTURE TOOLS FORMAT tab | Picture Styles group) (shown in Figure 1–53) to expand the gallery.

- If you are using a mouse, point to 'Drop Shadow Rectangle' in the Picture Styles gallery to display a live preview of that style applied to the picture in the document (Figure 1–54).

 Experiment

- If you are using a mouse, point to various picture styles in the Picture Styles gallery and watch the style of the picture change in the document window.

3

- Tap or click 'Drop Shadow Rectangle' in the Picture Styles gallery (fourth style in first row) to apply the style to the selected picture.

Figure 1–54

Other Ways

1. Press and hold or right-click picture, tap or click 'Picture Quick Styles' on mini toolbar, select desired style

To Apply Picture Effects

1 ENTER TEXT | 2 FORMAT TEXT | 3 INSERT PICTURE | **4 FORMAT PICTURE**
5 ENHANCE PAGE | **6 CORRECT & REVISE** | **7 PRINT OR READ**

Word provides a variety of picture effects, such as shadows, reflections, glow, soft edges, bevel, and 3-D rotation. The difference between the effects and the styles is that each effect has several options, providing you with more control over the exact look of the image.

In this flyer, the picture has a slight green glow effect and beveled edges. The following steps apply picture effects to the selected picture. *Why? Picture effects enable you to further customize the a picture.*

1

- With the picture still selected, tap or click the Picture Effects button (PICTURE TOOLS FORMAT tab | Picture Styles group) to display the Picture Effects menu.

- Tap or point to Glow on the Picture Effects menu to display the Glow gallery.

- If you are using a mouse, point to 'Turquoise, 5 pt glow, Accent color 6' in the Glow Variations area (rightmost glow in first row) to display a live preview of the selected glow effect applied to the picture in the document window (Figure 1–55).

 Experiment

- If you are using a mouse, point to various glow effects in the Glow gallery and watch the picture change in the document window

Figure 1–55

2

- Tap or click 'Turquoise, 5 pt glow, Accent color 6' in the Glow gallery to apply the selected picture effect.

Q&A

What if I wanted to discard formatting applied to a picture?

You would tap or click the Reset Picture button (PICTURE TOOLS FORMAT tab | Adjust group). To reset formatting and size, you would tap or click the Reset Picture arrow (PICTURE TOOLS FORMAT tab | Adjust group) and then tap or click 'Reset Picture & Size' on the Reset Picture menu.

3

- Tap or click the Picture Effects button (PICTURE TOOLS FORMAT tab | Picture Styles group) to display the Picture Effects menu again.

- Tap or point to Bevel on the Picture Effects menu to display the Bevel gallery.

- If you are using a mouse, point to Angle in the Bevel area (first effect in second row) to display a live preview of the selected bevel effect applied to the picture in the document window (Figure 1–56).

🔍 **Experiment**

- If you are using a mouse, point to various bevel effects in the Bevel gallery and watch the picture change in the document window.

4

- Tap or click Angle in the Bevel gallery to apply the selected picture effect.

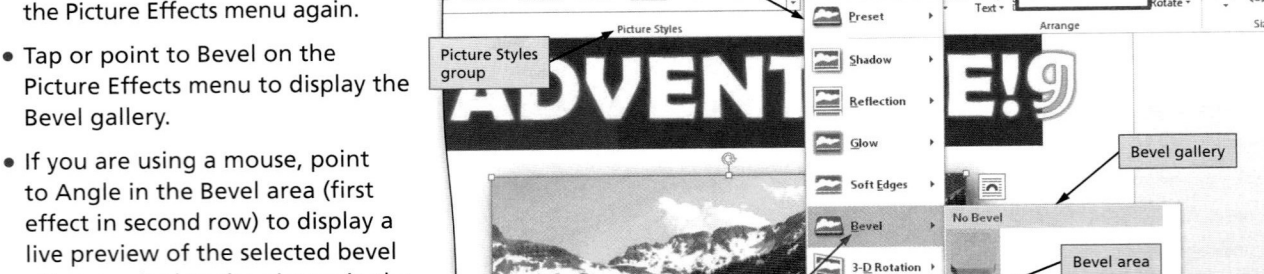

Figure 1–56

Courtesy of Misty Vermaat

Other Ways

1. Tap 'Show Context Menu' button on mini toolbar or right-click picture, tap or click Format Object or Format Picture on shortcut menu, tap or click Effects button (Format Picture task pane), select desired options, tap or click Close button

2. Tap or click Format Shape Dialog Box Launcher (PICTURE TOOLS FORMAT tab | Picture Styles group), tap or click Effects button (Format Picture task pane), select desired options, tap or click Close button

Enhancing the Page

With the text and graphics entered and formatted, the next step is to look at the page as a whole and determine if it looks finished in its current state. As you review the page, answer these questions:

- Does it need a page border to frame its contents, or would a page border make it look too busy?

- Is the spacing between paragraphs and graphics on the page adequate? Do any sections of text or graphics look as if they are positioned too closely to the items above or below them?

- Does the flyer have too much space at the top or bottom? Should the contents be centered vertically?

You determine that a graphical, color-coordinated border would enhance the flyer. You also notice that the flyer would look better proportioned if it had a little more space above and below the picture. You also want to ensure that the contents are centered vertically. The following pages make these enhancements to the flyer.

To Add a Page Border

In Word, you can add a border around the perimeter of an entire page. The flyer in this chapter has a light green border. *Why? This border color complements the color of the flyer contents.* The following steps add a page border.

1

- Tap or click DESIGN on the ribbon to display the DESIGN tab.

- Tap or click the 'Borders and Shading' button (DESIGN tab | Page Background group) to display the Borders and Shading dialog box (Figure 1–57).

Figure 1–57

2

- Tap or click the second border style in the Style list (Borders and Shading dialog box) to select the style.

- Tap or click the Color arrow to display a Color palette (Figure 1–58).

Figure 1–58

3

- Tap or click 'Lime, Accent 2, Lighter 80%' (sixth color in second row) in the Color palette to select the color for the page border.

- Tap or click the Width arrow to display the Width list and then tap or click 4 ½ pt to select the thickness of the page border (Figure 1–59).

4

- Tap or click the OK button to add the border to the page (shown in Figure 1–60).

Q&A What if I wanted to remove the border?
You would tap or click None in the Setting list in the Borders and Shading dialog box.

Figure 1–59

To Zoom One Page

1 ENTER TEXT | 2 FORMAT TEXT | 3 INSERT PICTURE | 4 FORMAT PICTURE
5 ENHANCE PAGE | 6 CORRECT & REVISE | 7 PRINT OR READ

The next steps zoom one page so that you can see the entire page on the screen at once.

1 Tap or click VIEW on the ribbon to display the VIEW tab.

2 Tap or click the One Page button (VIEW tab | Zoom group) to display the entire page in the document window as large as possible.

To Change Spacing before and after Paragraphs

1 ENTER TEXT | 2 FORMAT TEXT | 3 INSERT PICTURE | 4 FORMAT PICTURE
5 ENHANCE PAGE | 6 CORRECT & REVISE | 7 PRINT OR READ

The default spacing above (before) a paragraph in Word is 0 points and below (after) is 8 points. In the flyer, you want to increase the spacing below the paragraph containing the headline and above the signature line. *Why? The flyer spacing will look more balanced with spacing increased above and below these paragraphs.* The following steps change the spacing above and below a paragraph.

1

- Position the insertion point in the paragraph to be adjusted, in this case, the paragraph containing the headline.

Q&A What happened to the PICTURE TOOLS FORMAT tab?
When you tap or click outside of a graphic or press a key to scroll through a document, Word deselects the graphic and removes the PICTURE TOOLS FORMAT tab from the screen. That is, this tab appears only when a graphic is selected.

- Tap or click PAGE LAYOUT on the ribbon to display the PAGE LAYOUT tab.

- If you are using a touch screen, tap the Spacing After box (PAGE LAYOUT tab | Paragraph group) and then type 12 to change the spacing below the paragraph; if you are using a mouse, click the Spacing After up arrow (PAGE LAYOUT tab | Paragraph group) so that 12 pt is displayed in the Spacing After box to increase the space below the current paragraph (Figure 1–60).

Figure 1–60

2

- Position the insertion point in the paragraph to be adjusted, in this case, the paragraph containing the signature line.

- If you are using a touch screen, tap the Spacing Before box (PAGE LAYOUT tab | Paragraph group) and then type 12 to change the spacing above the paragraph; if you are using a mouse, click the Spacing Before up arrow (PAGE LAYOUT tab | Paragraph group) as many times as necessary so that 12 pt is displayed in the Spacing Before box to increase the space above the current paragraph (Figure 1–61).

- If the text flows to two pages, reduce the spacing above and below paragraphs as necessary.

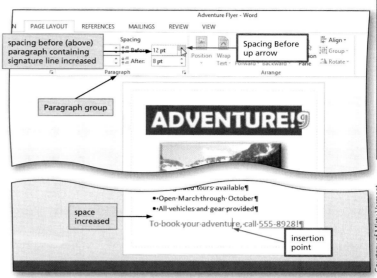

Courtesy of Misty Vermaat

Figure 1–61

Other Ways

1. Tap 'Show Context Menu' button on mini toolbar or right-click paragraph, tap or click Paragraph on shortcut menu, tap or click Indents and Spacing tab (Paragraph dialog box), enter spacing before and after values, tap or click OK button

2. Tap or click Paragraph Settings Dialog Box Launcher (HOME tab or PAGE LAYOUT tab | Paragraph group), tap or click Indents and Spacing tab (Paragraph dialog box), enter spacing before and after values, tap or click OK button

To Center Page Contents Vertically

1 ENTER TEXT | 2 FORMAT TEXT | 3 INSERT PICTURE | 4 FORMAT PICTURE
5 ENHANCE PAGE | 6 CORRECT & REVISE | 7 PRINT OR READ

In Word, you can center the page contents vertically. *Why? This places the same amount of space at the top and bottom of the page.* The following steps center page contents vertically.

1

- If necessary, tap or click PAGE LAYOUT on the ribbon to display the PAGE LAYOUT tab.

- Tap or click the Page Setup Dialog Box Launcher (PAGE LAYOUT tab | Page Setup group) to display the Page Setup dialog box.

- Tap or click the Layout tab (Page Setup dialog box) to display the Layout sheet (Figure 1–62).

Figure 1–62

- Tap or click the Vertical alignment arrow (Page Setup dialog box) to display the list of alignment options and then tap or click Center in the list (Figure 1–63).

- Tap or click the OK button to center the page contents vertically on the screen (shown in Figure 1–1 on page WD 3).

Q&A What if I wanted to change the alignment back?
You would select the Top vertical alignment from the Vertical alignment list in the Layout sheet (Page Setup dialog box).

Figure 1–63

To Save an Existing Document with the Same File Name

You have made several modifications to the document since you last saved it. Thus, you should save it again. The following step saves the document again. For an example of the step listed below, refer to the Office and Windows chapter at the beginning of this book.

1 Tap or click the Save button on the Quick Access Toolbar to overwrite the previously saved file.

Document Properties

Word helps you organize and identify your files by using **document properties**, which are the details about a file such as the project author, title, and subject. For example, a class name or document topic can describe the file's purpose or content.

CONSIDER THIS

Why would you want to assign document properties to a document?
Document properties are valuable for a variety of reasons:

- Users can save time locating a particular file because they can view a file's document properties without opening the document.
- By creating consistent properties for files having similar content, users can better organize their documents.
- Some organizations require Word users to add document properties so that other employees can view details about these files.

The more common document properties are standard and automatically updated properties. **Standard properties** are associated with all Microsoft Office files and include author, title, and subject. **Automatically updated properties** include file system properties, such as the date you create or change a file, and statistics, such as the file size.

To Change Document Properties

To change document properties, you would follow these steps.

1. Tap or click FILE on the ribbon to open the Backstage view and then, if necessary, tap or click the Info tab in the Backstage view to display the Info gallery.

2. If the property you wish to change is displayed in the Properties list in the right pane of the Info gallery, try to tap or click to the right of the property. If a text box appears to the right of the property, type the text for the property in the text box, and then tap or click the Back button in the upper-left corner of the Backstage view to return to the Word window. Skip the remaining steps.

3. If the property you wish to change is not displayed in the Properties list in the right pane of the Info gallery or you cannot change it in the Info gallery, tap or click the Properties button in the right pane to display the Properties menu, and then tap or click 'Show Document Panel' on the Properties menu to close the Backstage view and display the Document Information Panel in the Word document window.

Q&A Why are some of the document properties in my Document Information Panel already filled in?
The person who installed Office 2013 on your computer or network may have set or customized the properties.

4. Type the desired text in the appropriate property text boxes.

Q&A What if the property I want to change is not displayed in the Document Information Panel?
Tap or click the Document Properties button in the Document Information Panel and then tap or click Advanced Properties on the menu to display the Properties dialog box. If necessary, tap or click the Summary tab (Properties dialog box) to display the Summary sheet, fill in the appropriate text boxes, and then tap or click the OK button.

5. Tap or click the 'Close the Document Information Panel' button at the right edge of the Document Information Panel so that the panel no longer appears in the Word document window.

To Sign Out of a Microsoft Account

If you are signed in to a Microsoft account and are using a public computer or otherwise wish to sign out of your Microsoft account, you should sign out of the account from the Account gallery in the Backstage view before exiting Word. Signing out of the account is the safest way to make sure that nobody else can access SkyDrive files or settings stored in your Microsoft account. The following steps sign out of a Microsoft account from Word. For a detailed example of the procedure summarized below, refer to the Office and Windows chapter at the beginning of this book.

1 If you wish to sign out of your Microsoft account, tap or click FILE on the ribbon to open the Backstage view and then tap or click the Account tab to display the Account gallery.

2 Tap or click the Sign out link, which displays the Remove Account dialog box. If a Can't remove Windows accounts dialog box appears instead of the Remove Account dialog box, tap or click the OK button and skip the remaining steps.

Q&A Why does a Can't remove Windows accounts dialog box appear?
If you signed in to Windows using your Microsoft account, then you also must sign out from Windows, rather than signing out from within the Word. When you are finished using Windows, be sure to sign out at that time.

3 Tap or click the Yes button (Remove Account dialog box) to sign out of your Microsoft account on this computer.

Q&A Should I sign out of Windows after signing out of my Microsoft account?
When you are finished using the computer, you should sign out of your account for maximum security.

4 Tap or click the Back button in the upper-left corner of the Backstage view to return to the document.

BTW
Q&As
For a complete list of the Q&As found in many of the step-by-step sequences in this book, visit the Q&A resource on the Student Companion Site located on www.cengagebrain.com. For detailed instructions about accessing available resources, visit www.cengage.com/ ct/studentdownload or contact your instructor for information about accessing the required files.

To Exit Word

Although you still need to make some edits to this document, you want to exit Word and resume working on the project at a later time. Thus, the following steps exit Word. For a detailed example of the procedure summarized below, refer to the Office and Windows chapter at the beginning of this book.

1a If you have one Word document open, tap or click the Close button on the right side of the title bar to close the open document and exit Word.

1b If you have multiple Word documents open, press and hold or right-click the Word app button on the taskbar and then tap or click 'Close all windows' on the shortcut menu to close all open documents and exit Word.

Q&A Could I press and hold or repeatedly click the Close button to close all open documents and exit Word?
Yes.

2 If a Microsoft Word dialog box appears, tap or click the Save button to save any changes made to the document since the last save.

Break Point: If you wish to take a break, this is a good place to do so. To resume at a later time, continue following the steps from this location forward.

Correcting Errors and Revising a Document

After creating a document, you may need to change it. For example, the document may contain an error, or new circumstances may require you to add text to the document.

Types of Changes Made to Documents

The types of changes made to documents normally fall into one of the three following categories: additions, deletions, or modifications.

Additions Additional words, sentences, or paragraphs may be required in a document. Additions occur when you omit text from a document and want to insert it later. For example, you may want to add your email address to the flyer.

Deletions Sometimes, text in a document is incorrect or no longer is needed. For example, you may discover that the tours no longer provide gear. In this case, you would delete the words, and gear, from the flyer.

Modifications If an error is made in a document or changes take place that affect the document, you might have to revise a word(s) in the text. For example, the tours may start in April instead of March.

To Run Word

Once you have created and saved a document, you may need to retrieve it from your storage medium. For example, you might want to revise the document or print it. The following steps, which assume Windows 8 is running, use the Start screen or the Search box to run Word based on a typical installation. You may need to ask your instructor how to run Word on your computer. For a detailed example of the procedure summarized below, refer to the Office and Windows chapter.

BTW
Certification
The Microsoft Office Specialist (MOS) program provides an opportunity for you to obtain a valuable industry credential — proof that you have the Word 2013 skills required by employers. For more information, visit the Certification resource on the Student Companion Site located on www.cengagebrain.com. For detailed instructions about accessing available resources, visit www.cengage.com/ct/studentdownload or contact your instructor for information about accessing the required files.

1 Scroll the Start screen for a Word 2013 tile. If your Start screen contains a Word 2013 tile, tap or click it to run Word and then proceed to Step 5; if the Start screen does not contain the Word 2013 tile, proceed to the next step to search for the Word app.

2 Swipe in from the right edge of the screen or point to the upper-right corner of the screen to display the Charms bar and then tap or click the Search charm on the Charms bar to display the Search menu.

3 Type **Word** as the search text in the Search box and watch the search results appear in the Apps list.

4 Tap or click Word 2013 in the search results to run Word.

5 Tap or click the Blank document thumbnail on the Word start screen to create a blank document and display it in the Word window.

6 If the Word window is not maximized, tap or click the Maximize button on its title bar to maximize the window.

To Open a Document from Word

Earlier in this chapter you saved your flyer using the file name, Adventure Flyer. The following steps open the Adventure Flyer file from the Word folder in the CIS 101 folder. For a detailed example of the procedure summarized below, refer to the Office and Windows chapter at the beginning of this book.

1 Tap or click FILE on the ribbon to open the Backstage view and then tap or click the Open tab in the Backstage view to display the Open gallery.

2 If the file you wish to open is displayed in the Recent Documents list, tap or click the file name to open the file and display the opened document in the Word window; then, skip the remaining steps. If the file you wish to open is not displayed in the Recent Documents list, proceed to the next step to locate the file.

3 Tap or click Computer, SkyDrive, or another location in the left pane, tap or click the Browse button, and then navigate to the location of the file to be opened (in this case the Word folder in the CIS 101 folder).

4 Tap or click Adventure Flyer to select the file to be opened.

5 Tap or click the Open button (Open dialog box) to open the selected file and display the opened document in the Word window.

To Zoom the Document

While modifying the document, you prefer the document at 100% so that it is easier to read. Thus, the following step changes the zoom back to 100%.

1 Tap or click VIEW on the ribbon to display the VIEW tab.

2 Tap or click the 100% button (VIEW tab | Zoom group) to display the page at 100% in the document window.

BTW
Quick Reference
For a table that lists how to complete the tasks covered in this book using touch gestures, the mouse, ribbon, shortcut menu, and keyboard, see the Quick Reference Summary at the back of this book, or visit the Quick Reference resource on the Student Companion Site located on www.cengagebrain.com. For detailed instructions about accessing available resources, visit www.cengage.com/ct/studentdownload or contact your instructor for information about accessing the required files.

To Insert Text in an Existing Document

1 ENTER TEXT | 2 FORMAT TEXT | 3 INSERT PICTURE | 4 FORMAT PICTURE
5 ENHANCE PAGE | 6 CORRECT & REVISE | **7 PRINT OR READ**

Word inserts text to the left of the insertion point. The text to the right of the insertion point moves to the right and downward to fit the new text. The following steps insert the word, today, to the left of the word, with, in the flyer. **Why?** *These steps illustrate the process of inserting text.*

1

- Scroll through the document and then tap or click to the left of the location of text to be inserted (in this case, the w in with) to position the insertion point where text should be inserted (Figure 1–64).

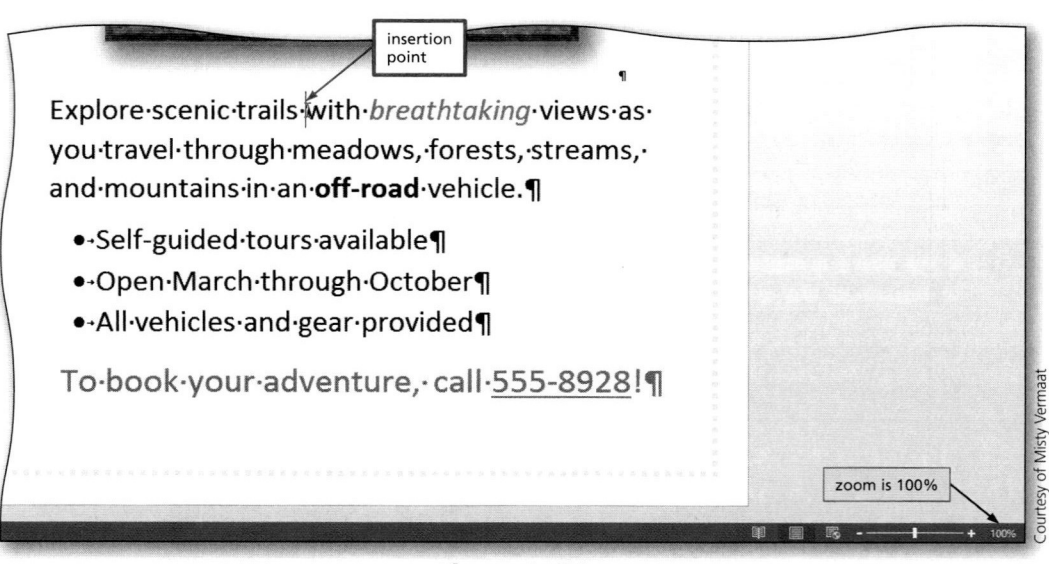

Figure 1–64

2

- Type **today** and then press the SPACEBAR to insert the word to the left of the insertion point (Figure 1–65).

Q&A

Why did the text move to the right as I typed?

In Word, the default typing mode is **insert mode**, which means as you type a character, Word moves all the characters to the right of the typed character one position to the right.

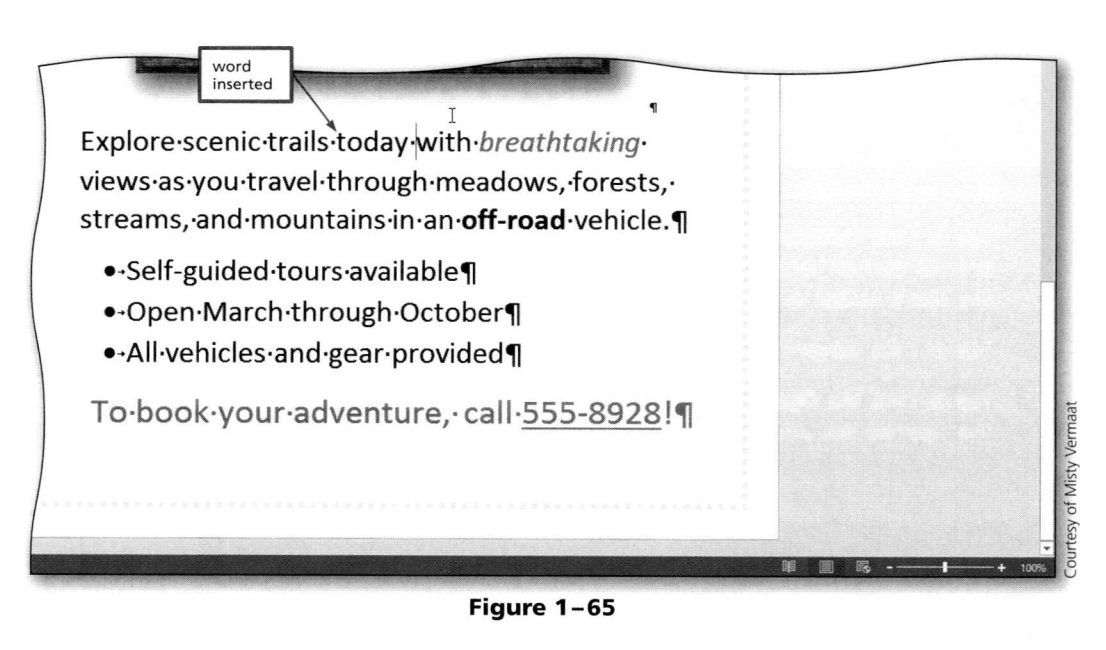

Figure 1–65

To Delete Text

1 ENTER TEXT | 2 FORMAT TEXT | 3 INSERT PICTURE | 4 FORMAT PICTURE
5 ENHANCE PAGE | **6 CORRECT & REVISE** | **7 PRINT OR READ**

It is not unusual to type incorrect characters or words in a document. As discussed earlier in this chapter, you can tap or click the Undo button on the Quick Access Toolbar to undo a command or action immediately — this includes typing. Word also provides other methods of correcting typing errors.

To delete an incorrect character in a document, simply tap or click next to the incorrect character and then press the BACKSPACE key to erase to the left of the insertion point, or press the DELETE key to erase to the right of the insertion point.

To delete a word or phrase, you first must select the word or phrase. The following steps select the word, today, which was just added in the previous steps and then delete the selection. ***Why?*** *These steps illustrate the process of selecting a word and then deleting selected text.*

- Double-tap or double-click the word to be selected (in this case, today) to select the word (Figure 1–66).

- If you are using a touch screen, tap the selected text to display the mini toolbar and then tap the Cut button on the mini toolbar to delete the selected text; if you are using a keyboard, with the text selected, press the DELETE key to delete the selected text.

Courtesy of Misty Vermaat

Figure 1–66

Other Ways

1. Press and hold or right-click selected item, tap Cut on mini toolbar or click Cut on shortcut menu
2. Select item, press BACKSPACE to delete to left of insertion point or press DELETE to delete to right of insertion point
3. Select item, press CTRL+X

To Move Text

1 ENTER TEXT | 2 FORMAT TEXT | 3 INSERT PICTURE | 4 FORMAT PICTURE | 5 ENHANCE PAGE | 6 CORRECT & REVISE | 7 PRINT OR READ

An efficient way to move text a short distance is drag-and-drop editing. With **drag-and-drop editing**, you select the item to be moved, drag the selected item to the new location, and then drop, or insert, it in the new location. Another technique for moving text is the cut-and-paste technique, which is discussed in the next chapter.

The following steps use drag-and-drop editing to move text. ***Why?*** *While proofreading the flyer, you realize that the body copy would read better if the last two bulleted paragraphs were reversed.*

- If you are using a mouse, position the pointer in the paragraph to be moved (in this case, the last bulleted item) and then triple-click to select the paragraph.

- If you are using a mouse, with the pointer in the selected text, press and hold down the mouse button, which displays a small dotted box with the pointer (Figure 1–67).

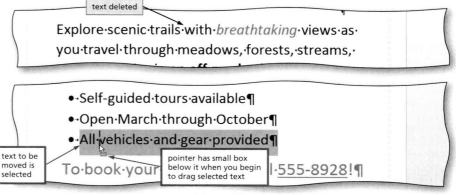

Figure 1–67

- If you are using a mouse, drag the insertion point to the location where the selected text is to be moved, as shown in Figure 1–68.

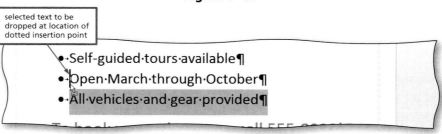

Figure 1–68

3

- If you are using a mouse, release the mouse button to move the selected text to the location of the dotted insertion point (Figure 1–69).

Q&A
What if I accidentally drag text to the wrong location?

Tap or click the Undo button on the Quick Access Toolbar and try again.

Can I use drag-and-drop editing to move any selected item?

Yes, you can select words, sentences, phrases, and graphics and then use drag-and-drop editing to move them.

What is the purpose of the Paste Options button?

If you are using a mouse and click the Paste Options button, a menu appears that allows you to change the format of the item that was moved. The next chapter discusses the Paste Options menu.

- Tap or click anywhere in the document window to remove the selection from the bulleted item.

Q&A
What if I am using a touch screen?

If you have a stylus, you can follow Steps 1 through 3 using the stylus. If you are using your finger, you will need to use the cut-and-paste technique: tap to position the insertion point in the text to be moved and then drag the selection handles as necessary to select the text that you want to move; tap the selection to display the mini toolbar and then tap the Cut button on the mini toolbar to remove the text; tap to position the insertion point at the location where you want to move the text; display the HOME tab and then tap the Paste button on the HOME tab to place the text at the location of the insertion point. The next chapter discusses this procedure in more depth.

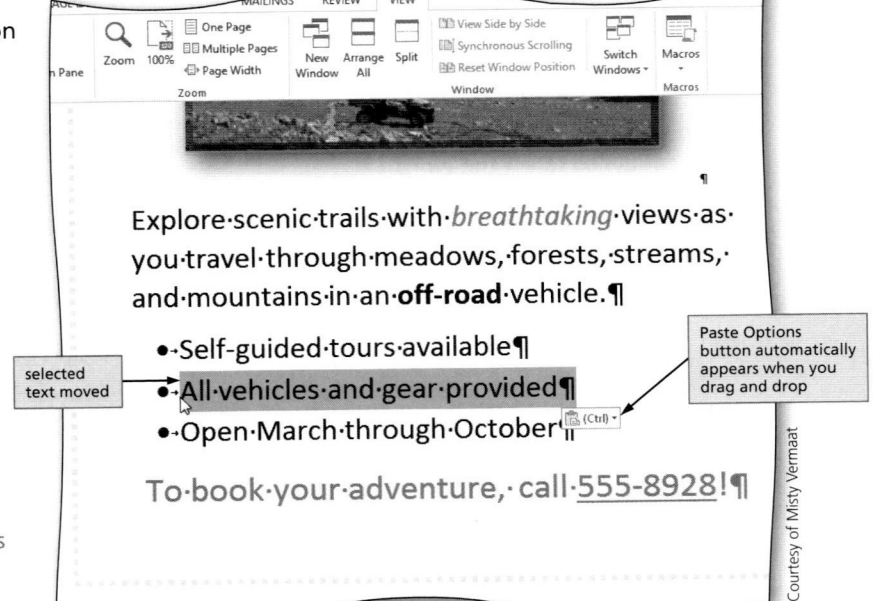

Figure 1–69

Other Ways

1. Tap or click Cut button (HOME tab | Clipboard group), tap or click where text or object is to be pasted, tap or click Paste button (HOME tab | Clipboard group)
2. Press and hold or right-click selected text, tap or click Cut on mini toolbar or shortcut menu, press and hold or right-click where text or object is to be pasted, tap Paste on mini toolbar or click Keep Source Formatting on shortcut menu
3. Press CTRL+X, position insertion point where text or object is to be pasted, press CTRL+V

To Save an Existing Document with the Same File Name

You have made several modifications to the document since you last saved it. Thus, you should save it again. The following step saves the document again. For an example of the step listed below, refer to the Office and Windows chapter at the beginning of this book.

1 Tap or click the Save button on the Quick Access Toolbar to overwrite the previously saved file.

Printing or Reading a Document

After creating a document, you may want to print it or read it on-screen. Printing a document enables you to distribute it to others in a form that can be read or viewed but typically not edited. It is a good practice to save a document before printing it, in the event you experience difficulties printing. Some users prefer reading a document on-screen instead of on paper.

What is the best method for distributing a document?

The traditional method of distributing a document uses a printer to produce a hard copy. A **hard copy** or **printout** is information that exists on a physical medium such as paper. Hard copies can be useful for the following reasons:

- Some people prefer proofreading a hard copy of a document rather than viewing it on the screen to check for errors and readability.

- Hard copies can serve as a backup reference if your storage medium is lost or becomes corrupted and you need to recreate the document.

Instead of distributing a hard copy of a document, users can distribute the document as an electronic image that mirrors the original document's appearance. The electronic image of the document can be sent as an email attachment, posted on a website, or copied to a portable storage medium such as a USB flash drive. Two popular electronic image formats, sometimes called fixed formats, are PDF by Adobe Systems and XPS by Microsoft. In Word, you can create electronic image files through the Save As dialog box and the Export, Share, and Print tabs in the Backstage view. Electronic images of documents, such as PDF and XPS, can be useful for the following reasons:

- Users can view electronic images of documents without the software that created the original document (e.g., Word). Specifically, to view a PDF file, you use a program called Adobe Reader, which can be downloaded free from Adobe's website. Similarly, to view an XPS file, you use a program called XPS Viewer, which is included in the latest versions of Windows and Internet Explorer.

- Sending electronic documents saves paper and printer supplies. Society encourages users to contribute to **green computing**, which involves reducing the electricity consumed and environmental waste generated when using computers, mobile devices, and related technologies.

To Print a Document

1 ENTER TEXT | 2 FORMAT TEXT | 3 INSERT PICTURE | 4 FORMAT PICTURE
5 ENHANCE PAGE | 6 CORRECT & REVISE | 7 PRINT OR READ

With the completed document saved, you may want to print it. *Why? Because this flyer is being posted, you will print a hard copy on a printer.* The following steps print a hard copy of the contents of the saved Adventure Flyer document.

1
- Tap or click FILE on the ribbon to open the Backstage view.

- Tap or click the Print tab in the Backstage view to display the Print gallery (Figure 1–70).

Q&A
How can I print multiple copies of my document?
Increase the number in the Copies box in the Print gallery.

What if I decide not to print the document at this time?
Tap or click the Back button in the upper-left corner of the Backstage view to return to the document window.

2
- Verify that the printer listed on the Printer Status button will print a hard copy of the document. If necessary, click the Printer Status button to display a list of available printer options and then click the desired printer to change the currently selected printer.

Figure 1–70

● Tap or click the Print button in the Print gallery to print the document on the currently selected printer.

● When the printer stops, retrieve the hard copy (Figure 1–71).

Q&A Do I have to wait until my document is complete to print it?
No, you can follow these steps to print a document at any time while you are creating it.

What if I want to print an electronic image of a document instead of a hard copy?
You would click the Printer Status button in the Print gallery and then select the desired electronic image option, such as Microsoft XPS Document Writer, which would create an XPS file.

What if one or more of my borders do not print?
Tap or click the Page Borders button (DESIGN tab | Page Background group), tap or click the Options button (Borders and Shading dialog box), tap or click the Measure from arrow and click Text, change the four text boxes to 15 pt, and then tap or click the OK button in each dialog box. Try printing the document again. If the borders still do not print, adjust the boxes in the dialog box to a number smaller than 15 point.

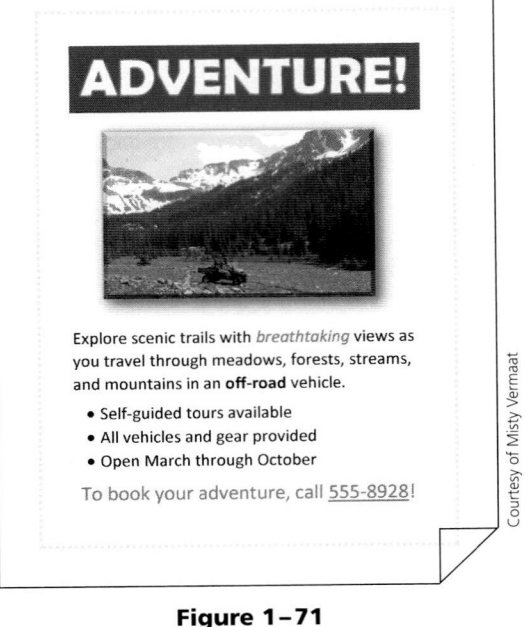

Figure 1–71

1 ENTER TEXT | 2 FORMAT TEXT | 3 INSERT PICTURE | 4 FORMAT PICTURE
5 ENHANCE PAGE | 6 CORRECT & REVISE | **7 PRINT OR READ**

To Switch to Read Mode

The next steps switch from Print Layout view to Read mode. *Why? If you are not composing a document, you can switch to **Read mode**, which hides the ribbon and other writing tools so that more content fits on the screen. Read mode is intended to make it easier to read a document.* The following step switches to Read mode.

● Tap or click the Read Mode button on the status bar to switch to Read mode (Figure 1–72).

Experiment

● Tap or click the arrows to advance forward and then move backward through the document.

Q&A Besides reading, what can I do in Read mode?
You can zoom, copy text, highlight text, search, add comments, and more.

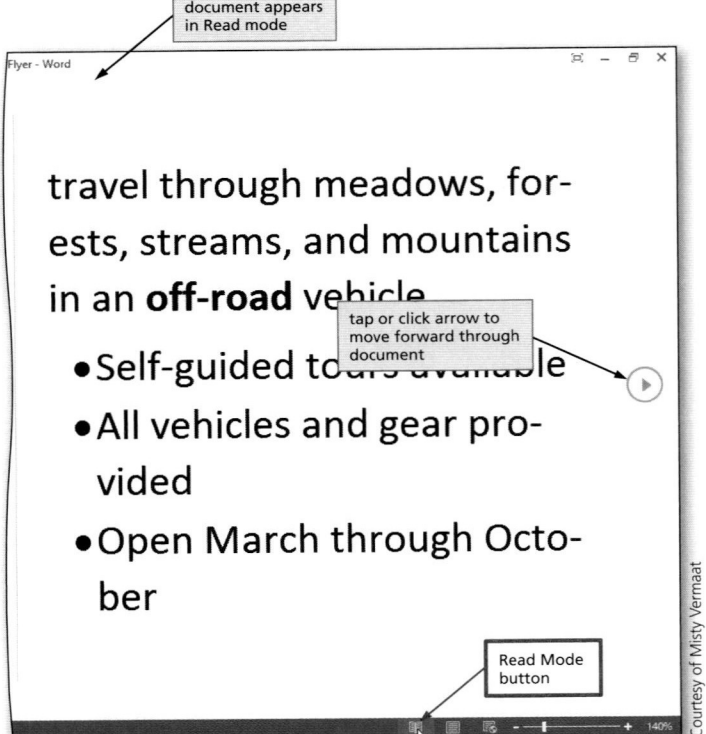

Figure 1–72

Other Ways

1. Tap or click Read Mode button (VIEW tab | Views group) 2. Tap or click VIEW on the ribbon, tap or click Edit Document

To Switch to Print Layout View

The next steps switch back to Print Layout view. **Why?** *If you want to show the document on a mock sheet of paper in the document window, along with the ribbon and other writing tools, you should switch to Print Layout view.* The following step switches to Print Layout view.

1

- Tap or click the Print Layout button on the status bar to switch to Print Layout view (Figure 1–73).

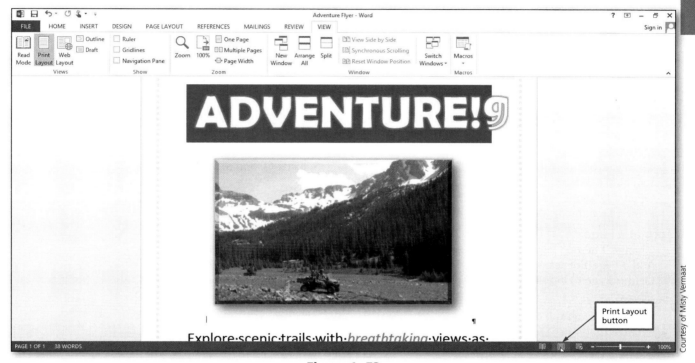

Figure 1–73

> **Other Ways**
>
> 1. Tap or click Print Layout button (VIEW tab | Views group)

To Exit Word

This project now is complete. The following steps exit Word. For a detailed example of the procedure summarized below, refer to the Office and Windows chapter at the beginning of this book.

1a If you have one Word document open, tap or click the Close button on the right side of the title bar to close the open document and exit Word.

1b If you have multiple Word documents open, press and hold or right-click the Word app button on the taskbar and then tap or click 'Close all windows' on the shortcut menu to close all open documents and exit Word.

2 If a Microsoft Word dialog box appears, tap or click the Save button to save any changes made to the document since the last save.

BTW
Printing Document Properties
To print document properties, tap or click FILE on the ribbon to open the Backstage view, tap or click the Print tab in the Backstage view to display the Print gallery, tap or click the first button in the Settings area to display a list of options specifying what you can print, tap or click Document Info in the list to specify you want to print the document properties instead of the actual document, and then tap or click the Print button in the Print gallery to print the document properties on the currently selected printer.

Chapter Summary

In this chapter, you have learned how to enter text in a document, format text, insert and format a picture, add a page border, adjust paragraph and page spacing, and print and read a document. The items listed below include all the new Word skills you have learned in this chapter, with the tasks grouped by activity.

Enter and Edit Text
Type Text (WD 5)
Insert a Blank Line (WD 7)
Wordwrap Text as You Type (WD 9)
Check Spelling and Grammar as You Type (WD 10)
Insert Text in an Existing Document (WD 48)
Delete Text (WD 48)
Move Text (WD 49)

File Management
Run Word (WD 4)
Save a Document (WD 12)
Save an Existing Document with the Same File Name (WD 33)
Change Document Properties (WD 44)
Exit Word (WD 46)
Open a Document from Word (WD 47)
Print a Document (WD 51)

Format a Page
Change Theme Colors (WD 31)
Add a Page Border (WD 41)
Center Page Contents Vertically (WD 43)

Format Text
Center a Paragraph (WD 15)
Change the Font Size of Selected Text (WD 17)
Change the Font of Selected Text (WD 18)
Change the Case of Selected Text (WD 19)
Apply a Text Effect to Selected Text (WD 20)

Shade a Paragraph (WD 21)
Bullet a List of Paragraphs (WD 23)
Undo and Redo an Action (WD 24)
Italicize Text (WD 25)
Color Text (WD 26)
Use the Mini Toolbar to Format Text (WD 27)
Underline Text (WD 29)
Bold Text (WD 29)
Change Spacing before and after Paragraphs (WD 42)

Select Text
Select a Line (WD 16)
Select Multiple Lines (WD 22)
Select a Group of Words (WD 28)

Word Settings
Display Formatting Marks (WD 6)
Zoom Page Width (WD 7)
Zoom One Page (WD 30)
Zoom the Document (WD 35)
Zoom 100% (WD 37)
Switch to Read Mode (WD 52)
Switch to Print Layout View (WD 53)

Work with Graphics (Pictures)
Insert a Picture (WD 34)
Resize a Graphic (WD 36)
Apply a Picture Style (WD 38)
Apply Picture Effects (WD 39)

CONSIDER THIS: PLAN AHEAD

What decisions will you need to make when creating your next flyer?

Use these guidelines as you complete the assignments in this chapter and create your own flyers outside of this class.

1. Choose the text for the headline, body copy, and signature line — using as few words as possible to make a point.

2. Format various elements of the text.

 a) Select appropriate font sizes for text in the headline, body copy, and signature line.

 b) Select appropriate fonts for text in the headline, body copy, and signature line.

 c) Adjust paragraph alignment, as appropriate.

 d) Highlight key paragraphs with bullets.

 e) Emphasize important words.

 f) Use color to convey meaning and add appeal.

3. Find an eye-catching graphic(s) that conveys the overall message and meaning of the flyer.

4. Establish where to position and how to format the graphical image(s) so that the image grabs the attention of passersby and draws them into reading the flyer.

5. Determine whether the flyer needs enhancements such as a graphical, color-coordinated border or spacing adjustments to improve readability or overall appearance.

6. Correct errors and revise the document as necessary.

 a) Post the flyer on a wall and make sure all text and images are legible from a distance.

 b) Ask someone else to read the flyer and give you suggestions for improvements.

7. Determine the best method for distributing the document such as printing, sending via email, or posting on the web.

How should you submit solutions to questions in the assignments identified with a ✸ symbol?
Every assignment in this book contains one or more questions identified with a ✸ symbol. These questions require you to think beyond the assigned document. Present your solutions to the questions in the format required by your instructor. Possible formats may include one or more of these options: write the answer; create a document that contains the answer; present your answer to the class; discuss your answer in a group; record the answer as audio or video using a webcam, smartphone, or portable media player; or post answers on a blog, wiki, or website.

Apply Your Knowledge

Reinforce the skills and apply the concepts you learned in this chapter.

Modifying Text and Formatting a Document

Note: To complete this assignment, you will be required to use the Data Files for Students. Visit www.cengage.com/ct/studentdownload for detailed instructions or contact your instructor for information about accessing the required files.

Instructions: Run Word. Open the document, Apply 1-1 County Park Flyer Unformatted, from the Data Files for Students. The document you open is an unformatted flyer. You are to modify text, format paragraphs and characters, and insert a picture in the flyer to create the flyer shown in Figure 1–74.

Perform the following tasks:

1. Delete the word, below, in the sentence below the headline.

2. Insert the word, Valley, between the words, Green County, in the second to last line of the flyer.

3. Change the period to an exclamation point in the last line so that the text reads: Thank You!

4. If requested by your instructor, change the phone number in the flyer to your phone number.

5. Center the headline and the last two paragraphs of the flyer.

6. Select the third, fourth, and fifth paragraphs in the flyer and add bullets to the selected paragraphs.

7. Change the theme colors to the Red Orange color scheme.

8. Change the font and font size of the headline to 48-point Franklin Gothic Heavy, or a similar font. Change the case of the headline text to uppercase letters. Apply the text effect called Fill - Black, Text 1, Outline - Background 1, Hard Shadow - Background 1 to the headline. Change the font color of the headline text to Dark Red, Accent 6.

headline →

PLEASE DO NOT FEED THE WILDLIFE!

Follow these guidelines to keep our wildlife healthy and our environment clean.

bulleted list →

- Do **not** feed the wildlife.
- Never leave food unattended.
- Discard *all* trash in provided containers.

Questions? Call Green Valley County Park at 329-555-1020.

Thank You!

Courtesy of Misty Vermaat

Figure 1–74

Continued >

Apply Your Knowledge *continued*

9. Change the font size of the sentence below the headline, the bulleted list, and the last line of flyer to 26 point.

10. Use the mini toolbar to change the font size of the sentence below the bulleted list to 18 point.

11. Select the words, Follow these guidelines, in the paragraph below the headline and underline them.

12. Bold the word, not, in the first bulleted paragraph. Change the font color of this same word to Dark Red, Accent 6.

13. Italicize the word, all, in the second bulleted item. Undo this change and then redo the change.

14. Switch the last two bulleted paragraphs. That is, select the 'Never leave food unattended' bullet and move it so that it is the second bulleted paragraph.

15. Bold the text, Thank You!, in the last line of the flyer. Shade this same paragraph Dark Red, Accent 6, Darker 25%. If the font color does not automatically change to a lighter color, change its color to White, Background 1.

16. Change the zoom so that the entire page is visible in the document window.

17. Insert the picture of the squirrel eating the sucker centered on the blank line below the headline. The picture is called Squirrel and is available on the Data Files for Students. Apply the Soft Edge Oval picture style to the inserted picture.

18. Change the spacing before the first bulleted paragraph to 12 point and the spacing after the last bulleted paragraph to 24 point.

19. The entire flyer should fit on a single page. If it flows to two pages, resize the picture or decrease spacing before and after paragraphs until the entire flyer text fits on a single page.

20. Change the zoom to text width, then page width, then 100% and notice the differences.

21. If requested by your instructor, enter the text, Green Valley, as the keywords in the document properties. Change the other document properties, as specified by your instructor.

22. Click FILE on the ribbon and then click Save As. Save the document using the file name, Apply 1-1 County Park Flyer Formatted.

23. Print the document. Switch to Read Mode and browse pages through the document. Switch to Print Layout view.

24. Submit the revised document, shown in Figure 1–74, in the format specified by your instructor.

25. Exit Word.

26. ✳ If this flyer were announcing the park reopening instead of including a warning, which color scheme would you apply and why?

Extend Your Knowledge

Extend the skills you learned in this chapter and experiment with new skills. You may need to use Help to complete the assignment.

Modifying Text and Picture Formats and Adding Page Borders

Note: To complete this assignment, you will be required to use the Data Files for Students. Visit www.cengage.com/ct/studentdownload for detailed instructions or contact your instructor for information about accessing the required files.

Instructions: Run Word. Open the document, Extend 1-1 Baseball Tryouts Flyer Draft, from the Data Files for Students. You will enhance the look of the flyer shown in Figure 1–75.
Hint: Remember, if you make a mistake while formatting the picture, you can reset it by using the Reset Picture button or Reset Picture arrow (PICTURE TOOLS FORMAT tab | Adjust group).

Perform the following tasks:

1. Use Help to learn about the following: remove bullets, grow font, shrink font, art page borders, decorative underline(s), picture bullets, picture border shading, picture border color, shadow picture effects, and color saturation and tone.

2. Remove the bullet from the last line of the flyer.

3. Select the text, August 30, and use the 'Increase Font Size' button (HOME tab | Font group) to increase its font size.

4. Add an art page border to the flyer. If the border is not in color, add color to it.

5. Change the solid underline below the word, Travel, to a decorative underline. Change the color of the underline.

6. Change the style of the bullets to picture bullet(s). Adjust the hanging indent, if necessary, to align the text in bulleted list.

7. Change the color of the picture border. Add the Perspective Right 3-D Rotation picture effect to the picture.

8. Change the color saturation and color tone of the picture.

9. If requested by your instructor, change the name of the field (High Crop) to your last name.

10. Save the revised document with the file name, Extend 1-1 Baseball Tryouts Flyer Final, and then submit it in the format specified by your instructor.

11. ☀ In this assignment you added an art page border to the flyer. Which border did you select and why?

Figure 1–75

Analyze, Correct, Improve

Analyze a document, correct all errors, and improve it.

Correcting Spelling and Grammar Errors and Adding Color

Note: To complete this assignment, you will be required to use the Data Files for Students. Visit www.cengage.com/ct/studentdownload for detailed instructions or contact your instructor for information about accessing the required files.

Instructions: Run Word. Open the document, Analyze 1-1 Beauty Salon Flyer Draft, from the Data Files for Students. The document is a flyer that contains spelling and grammar errors, as shown in Figure 1–76 on the next page. It also could include color to make it more visually appealing.

Continued >

Analyze, Correct, Improve *continued*

1. Correct You are to correct each spelling (red wavy underline) and grammar (green and blue wavy underlines) error by pressing and holding or right-clicking the flagged text and then clicking the appropriate correction on the shortcut menu.

If your screen does not display the wavy underlines, tap or click FILE on the ribbon and then tap or click Options in the Backstage view. When the Word Options dialog box is displayed, tap or click Proofing in the left pane, be sure the 'Hide spelling errors in this document only' and 'Hide grammar errors in this document only' check boxes do not contain check marks, and then tap or click the OK button. If your screen still does not display the wavy underlines, redisplay the Word Options dialog box, tap or click Proofing, and then tap or click the Recheck Document button.

2. Improve Enhance the flyer by (a) adding a shading color to the first and last lines (paragraphs) on the flyer, (b) changing the color of the text in the first line and last line of the flyer, and (c) adding a color glow effect to the three pictures in the flyer.

If requested by your instructor, change the street name in the flyer to your first name. Save the revised document with the file name, Extend 1-1 Beauty Salon Flyer Final, and then submit it in the format specified by your instructor.

3. ✳ In this assignment, you selected color to add to the flyer. Which color(s) did you select and why?

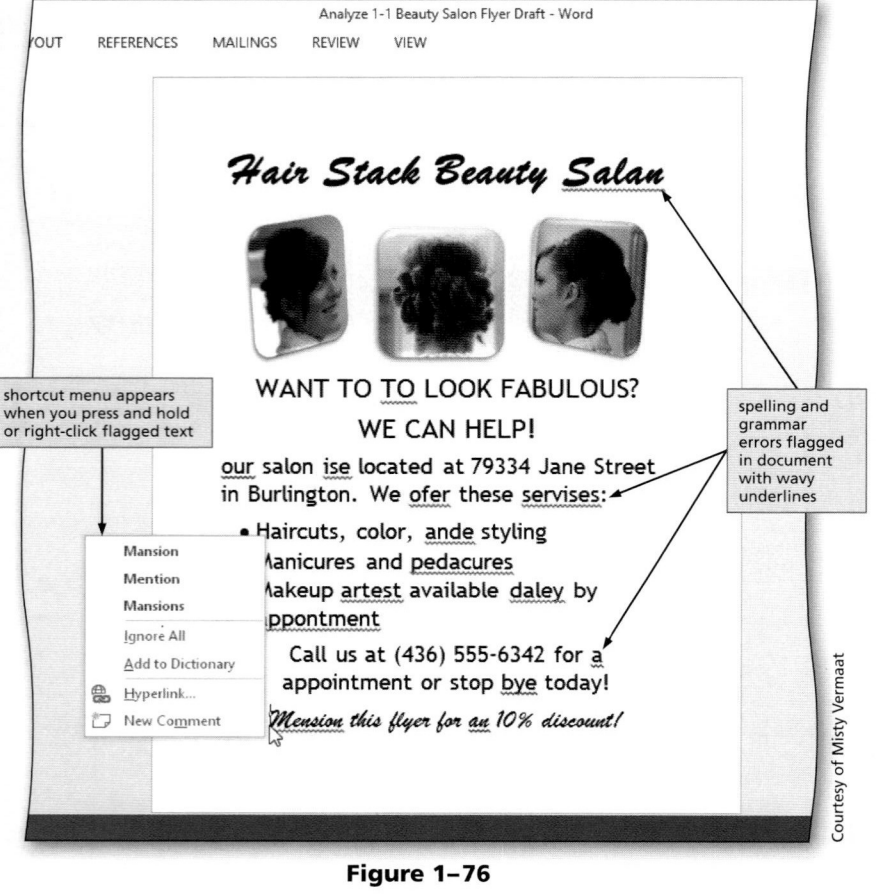

Figure 1–76

In the Labs

Design and/or create a document using the guidelines, concepts, and skills presented in this chapter. Labs 1 and 2, which increase in difficulty, require you to create solutions based on what you learned in the chapter; Lab 3 requires you to create a solution, which uses cloud and web technologies, by learning and investigating on your own from general guidance.

Lab 1: Creating a Flyer with a Picture

Problem: Your friend asked you to prepare a flyer that advertises the puppy she has for sale. First, you prepare the unformatted flyer shown in Figure 1–77a, and then you format it so that it looks like Figure 1–77b on page WD 60. *Hint:* Remember, if you make a mistake while formatting the flyer, you can use the Undo button on the Quick Access Toolbar to undo your last action.

Note: To complete this assignment, you will be required to use the Data Files for Students. Visit www.cengage.com/ct/studentdownload for detailed instructions or contact your instructor for information about accessing the required files.

Instructions: Perform the following tasks:

1. Run Word. Display formatting marks on the screen.
2. Type the flyer text, unformatted, as shown in Figure 1–77a, inserting a blank line between the headline and the body copy. If Word flags any misspelled words as you type, check their spelling and correct them.
3. Save the document using the file name, Lab 1-1 Puppy for Sale Flyer.
4. Center the headline and the signature line.
5. Change the theme colors to Aspect.
6. Change the font size of the headline to 72 point and the font to Gil Sans Ultra Bold Condensed, or a similar font. Apply the text effect called Fill - Dark Purple, Accent 1, Outline - Background, Hard Shadow - Accent 1.
7. Change the font size of body copy between the headline and the signature line to 22 point.
8. Change the font size of the signature line to 20 point.
9. Change the font of the body copy and signature line to Comic Sans MS.
10. Bullet the three lines (paragraphs) of text above the signature line.
11. Change the color of the words, purebred American Cocker Spaniel, to Dark Green, Accent 4, Darker 50%.
12. Italicize the word, and, in the third bulleted paragraph.
13. Bold the text in the signature line. Shade this paragraph containing the signature line in Dark Purple, Accent 5, Lighter 80%.
14. Underline the phone number in the signature line.
15. Change the zoom so that the entire page is visible in the document window.
16. Insert the picture centered on a blank line below the headline. The picture is called Puppy and is available on the Data Files for Students.
17. Apply the Rotated, White picture style to the inserted picture. Apply the glow effect called Dark Purple, 5 pt glow, Accent color 5 to the picture.

Puppy for Sale

blank line →

Own this six-month-old male, potty-trained, purebred American Cocker Spaniel puppy.

Fun, smart, cuddly, and playful

Needs a loving home

Knows these commands: sit, down, stay, heel, and leave it

If interested, call Vivian at (356) 555-7733.

(a) Unformatted Text
Figure 1–77 (Continued)

Continued >

In the Labs continued

(b) Formatted Document
Figure 1–77 (Continued)

18. Change the spacing after the paragraph containing the headline to 0 pt. Change the spacing above (before) the signature line to 18 pt. The entire flyer should fit on a single page. If it flows to two pages, resize the picture or decrease spacing before and after paragraphs until the entire flyer text fits on a single page.

19. Add a 6-pt Dark Green, Accent 4, Lighter 60% page border, as shown in Figure 1–77b.

20. If requested by your instructor, change the contact name in the flyer to your first name.

21. Save the flyer again with the same file name. Submit the document, shown in Figure 1–77b, in the format specified by your instructor.

22. ✸ Why do you think this flyer used shades of purple and green?

Lab 2: **Creating a Flyer with a Resized Pictures**

Problem: Your boss at Junior's Wedding Bakery has asked you to prepare a flyer that promotes its business. You prepare the flyer shown in Figure 1–78. *Hint:* Remember, if you make a mistake while formatting the flyer, you can use the Undo button on the Quick Access Toolbar to undo your last action.

Note: To complete this assignment, you will be required to use the Data Files for Students. Visit www.cengage.com/ct/studentdownload for detailed instructions or contact your instructor for information about accessing the required files.

Instructions: Perform the following tasks:
1. Run Word. Type the flyer text, unformatted. If Word flags any misspelled words as you type, check their spelling and correct them.

2. Save the document using the file name, Lab 1-2 Wedding Bakery Flyer.

3. Change the theme colors to the Marquee color scheme.

4. Add bullets to the three paragraphs shown in the figure. Center all paragraphs, except the paragraphs containing the bulleted list.

5. Change the font size of the headline to 36 point and the font to Franklin Gothic Heavy, or a similar font. Apply the text effect called Fill - Orange, Accent 3, Sharp Bevel.

6. Change the font size of body copy between the headline and signature line to 20 point, except for line above the bulleted list, which is 24 point.

7. Change the font size of the signature line to 22 point. Bold the text in the signature line. Change the font color of the text in the signature line to Orange, Accent 3.

8. Italicize the word, personalize.

9. Bold the text above the bulleted list.

10. Underline the text, Junior's Wedding Bakery.

11. Shade the line above the bulleted list to the Orange, Accent 3 color. If the font color does not automatically change to a lighter color, change it to White, Background 1.

12. Change the zoom so that the entire page is visible in the document window.

13. Insert the first picture on a blank line below the headline and the second picture on a blank line below the bulleted list. The pictures are called Bakery 1 and Bakery 2, respectively, and are available on the Data Files for Students.

14. Resize the top picture so that it is approximately 2.8" × 5.39". Apply the Soft Edge Oval picture style to the top inserted picture. Apply the Offset Right Shadow picture effect to the top picture. Resize the bottom picture so that it is approximately 1.5" × 4.05". Apply the Simple Frame, Black picture style to the bottom inserted picture.

15. Change the spacing after the paragraph containing the bakery name to 0 pt and the spacing after the last bulleted paragraph to 12 pt. The entire flyer should fit on a single page. If it flows to two pages, resize the picture or decrease spacing before and after paragraphs until the entire flyer text fits on a single page.

16. Add the page border shown in Figure 1–78, using the color Gold, Accent 5.

17. Center the page contents vertically.

18. If requested by your instructor, change the bakery name to your last name.

19. Save the flyer again with the same file name. Submit the document, shown in Figure 1–78, in the format specified by your instructor.

20. ✳ Why do you think this flyer used shades of orange and yellow?

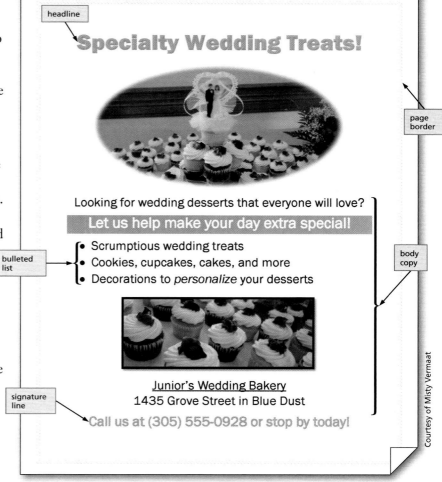

Figure 1–78

Courtesy of Misty Vermaat

Lab 3: Expand Your World: Cloud and Web Technologies
Using the Word Web App to Create a Flyer with a Picture

Problem: You have a side business where you build bean bag toss boards. You would like to create a flyer that promotes this business. You will use the Word Web App to prepare a flyer. The text for the unformatted flyer is shown in Figure 1–79.

Note: To complete this assignment, you will be required to use the Data Files for Students. Visit www.cengage.com/ct/studentdownload for detailed instructions or contact your instructor for information about accessing the required files.

Instructions: Perform the following tasks:
1. Run a browser. Search for the text, Word Web App, using a search engine. Visit several websites to learn about the Word Web App. Navigate to the Office Web Apps website. You will need to sign in to your SkyDrive account.
2. Use the Create button to begin creating a Word document using the Word Web App. Name the document Lab 1-3 Bean Bag Toss Flyer.
3. Notice the differences between the Word Web App and the Word desktop app you used to create the project in this chapter.
4. Enter the text in the flyer, shown in Figure 1–79, checking spelling as you type.

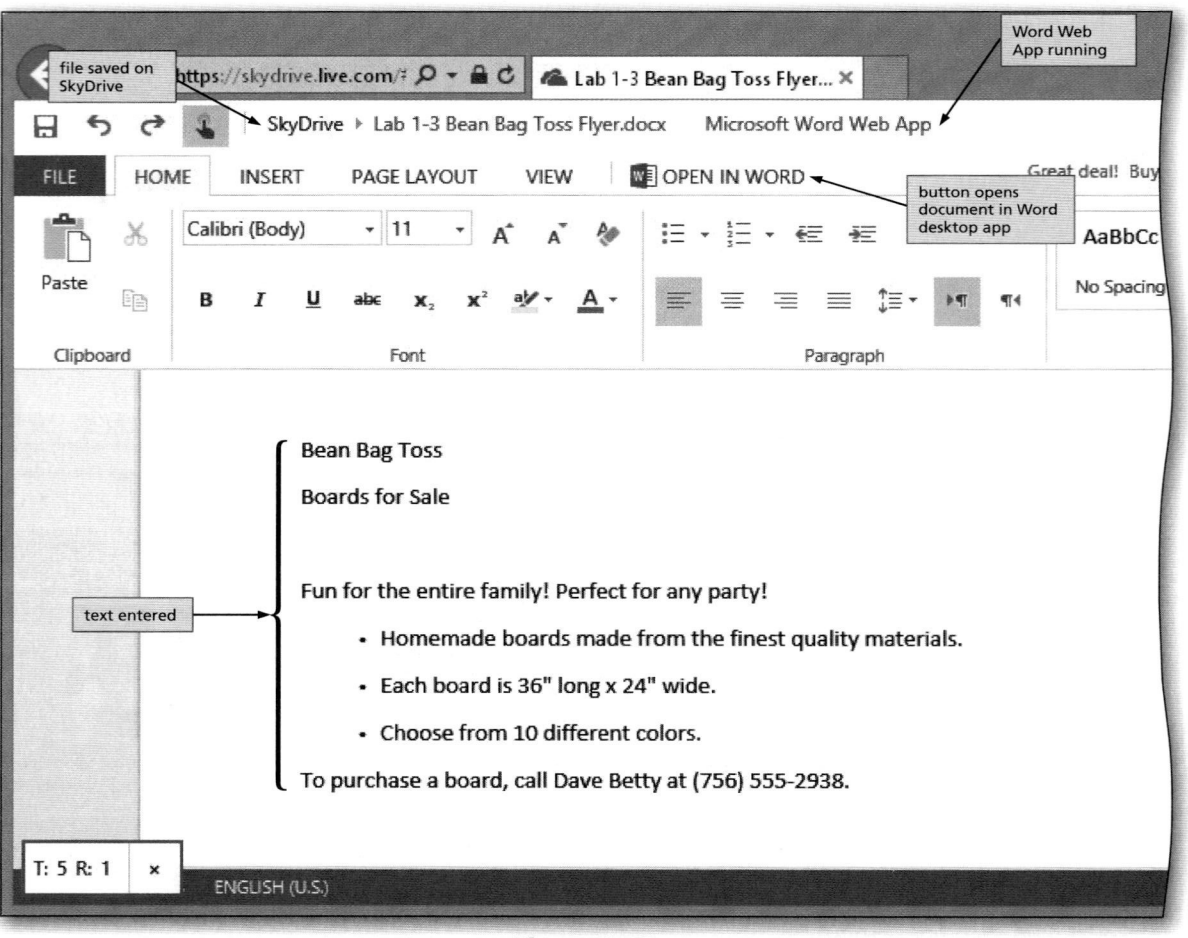

Figure 1–79

5. Insert the picture called Bean Bag Toss, which is located on the Data Files for Students.

6. Use the features available in the Word Web App, along with the concepts and techniques presented in this chapter, to format this flyer. Be sure to change the font and font size of text, center a paragraph(s), italicize text, color text, underline text, and apply a picture style. Adjust spacing above and below paragraphs as necessary. Resize the picture, if necessary.

7. If requested by your instructor, replace the contact name in the flyer with your name.

8. Save the document again. Tap or click the button to open the document in the Word desktop app. If necessary, sign in to your Microsoft account when prompted. Notice how the document appears in the Word desktop app.

9. Using either the Word Web App or Word desktop app, submit the document in the format requested by your instructor. Exit the Word Web App (FILE tab | Exit). Sign out of your SkyDrive account. Sign out of the Microsoft account in Word.

10. ✳ What is the Word Web App? Which features that are covered in this chapter are not available in the Word Web App? Do you prefer using the Word Web App or the Word desktop app? Why?

✳ Consider This: Your Turn

Apply your creative thinking and problem solving skills to design and implement a solution.

Note: To complete these assignments, you may be required to use the Data Files for Students. Visit www.cengage.com/ct/studentdownload for detailed instructions or contact your instructor for information about accessing the required files.

1: Design and Create a Photography Club Flyer
Personal

Part 1: As secretary of your school's Photography Club, you are responsible for creating and distributing flyers announcing the club. The flyer should contain two digital pictures appropriately resized; the Data Files for Students contains two pictures called Photography 1 and Photography 2, or you can use your own digital pictures if they are appropriate for the topic of the flyer. The flyer should contain the headline, Photography Club, and this signature line: Questions? Call Emily at (883) 555-0901. The body copy consists of the following text, in any order: Do you love photography? This is the club for you! All skill levels are welcome. Meetings every Tuesday at 5:00 p.m. in the Student Center (room 232). Bring your camera. We look forward to seeing you at our next meeting!

Use the concepts and techniques presented in this chapter to create and format this flyer. Be sure to check spelling and grammar. Submit your assignment and answers to the critical thinking questions in the format specified by your instructor.

Part 2: ✳ You made several decisions while creating the flyer in this assignment: where to place text, how to format the text (i.e., font, font size, paragraph alignment, bulleted paragraphs, underlines, italics, bold, color, etc.), which graphics to use, where to position the graphics, how to format the graphics, and which page enhancements to add (i.e., borders and spacing). What was the rationale behind each of these decisions? When you proofread the document, what further revisions did you make and why? How would you recommend distributing this flyer?

2: Design and Create a Hot Air Balloon Rides Flyer
Professional

Part 1: As a part-time employee at Galaxy Recreations, your boss has asked you to create and distribute flyers announcing hot air balloon rides. The flyer should contain two digital pictures appropriately resized; the Data Files for Students contains two pictures called Hot Air Balloon 1

Continued >

Consider This: Your Turn *continued*

and Hot Air Balloon 2, or you can use your own digital pictures if they are appropriate for the topic of the flyer. The flyer should contain the headline, Hot Air Balloon Rides, and this signature line: For reservations, call (485) 555-2295. The body copy consists of the following text, in any order: Amazing sights from incredible heights! The experience of a lifetime. Fun for the whole family. No pets. Bring your camera. Open seven days a week from 10:00 a.m. to 4:00 p.m. Book your private tour with Galaxy Recreations today!

Use the concepts and techniques presented in this chapter to create and format this flyer. Be sure to check spelling and grammar. Submit your assignment in the format specified by your instructor.

Part 2: ☀ You made several decisions while creating the flyer in this assignment: where to place text, how to format the text (i.e., font, font size, paragraph alignment, bulleted paragraphs, underlines, italics, bold, color, etc.), which graphics to use, where to position the graphics, how to format the graphics, and which page enhancements to add (i.e., borders and spacing). What was the rationale behind each of these decisions? When you proofread the document, what further revisions did you make and why? How would you recommend distributing this flyer?

3: Design and Create a Water Park Flyer

Research and Collaboration

Part 1: As a part-time employee at a local water park, your boss has asked you and two other employees to create and distribute flyers for the upcoming water park season. Form a three-member team to compose and create this flyer. Research a local water park: its location, hours, prices, rules, specials, etc. As a group, determine the text for the flyer's headline, body copy, and signature line. Your team also will need to obtain at least two digital pictures appropriate for the content of this flyer. You could take the pictures with a digital camera or search for public-domain images on the web.

Use the concepts and techniques presented in this chapter to create and format this flyer. Be sure to check spelling and grammar. Submit your team assignment in the format specified by your instructor.

Part 2: ☀ You made several decisions while creating the flyer in this assignment: text to use, where to place text, how to format the text (i.e., font, font size, paragraph alignment, bulleted paragraphs, underlines, italics, bold, color, etc.), which graphics to use, where to position the graphics, how to format the graphics, and which page enhancements to add (i.e., borders and spacing). What was the rationale behind each of these decisions? When you proofread the document, what further revisions did you make and why? What research methods did you use to create the flyer? Where did you obtain your pictures? How would you recommend distributing this flyer?

Learn Online

Reinforce what you learned in this chapter with games, exercises, training, and many other online activities and resources.

Student Companion Site Reinforcement activities and resources are available at no additional cost on www.cengagebrain.com. Visit www.cengage.com/ct/studentdownload for detailed instructions about accessing the resources available at the Student Companion Site.

SAM Put your skills into practice with SAM Projects! If you have a SAM account, go to www.cengage.com/sam2013 to access SAM assignments for this chapter.

2 | Creating a Research Paper with References and Sources

Microsoft product screen shots used with permission from Microsoft Corporation.

Objectives

You will have mastered the material in this chapter when you can:

- Describe the MLA documentation style for research papers
- Modify a style
- Change line and paragraph spacing in a document
- Use a header to number pages of a document
- Apply formatting using keyboard shortcuts
- Modify paragraph indentation
- Insert and edit citations and their sources

- Add a footnote to a document
- Insert a manual page break
- Create a bibliographical list of sources
- Cut, copy, and paste text
- Find text and replace text
- Find a synonym
- Check spelling and grammar at once
- Look up information

2 | Creating a Research Paper with References and Sources

Introduction

In both academic and business environments, you will be asked to write reports. Business reports range from proposals to cost justifications to five-year plans to research findings. Academic reports focus mostly on research findings.

A **research paper** is a document you can use to communicate the results of research findings. To write a research paper, you learn about a particular topic from a variety of sources (research), organize your ideas from the research results, and then present relevant facts and/or opinions that support the topic. Your final research paper combines properly credited outside information along with personal insights. Thus, no two research papers — even if they are about the same topic — will or should be the same.

Project — Research Paper

When preparing a research paper, you should follow a standard documentation style that defines the rules for creating the paper and crediting sources. A variety of documentation styles exists, depending on the nature of the research paper. Each style requires the same basic information; the differences in styles relate to requirements for presenting the information. For example, one documentation style uses the term bibliography for the list of sources, whereas another uses references, and yet a third prefers the title works cited. Two popular documentation styles for research papers are the **Modern Language Association of America (MLA)** and **American Psychological Association (APA)** styles. This chapter uses the MLA documentation style because it is used in a wide range of disciplines.

The project in this chapter follows research paper guidelines and uses Word to create the short research paper shown in Figure 2–1. This paper, which discusses biometric devices, follows the MLA documentation style. Each page contains a page number. The first two pages present the name and course information (student name, instructor name, course name, and paper due date), paper title, an introduction with a thesis statement, details that support the thesis, and a conclusion. This section of the paper also includes references to research sources and a footnote. The third page contains a detailed, alphabetical list of the sources referenced in the research paper. All pages include a header at the upper-right edge of the page.

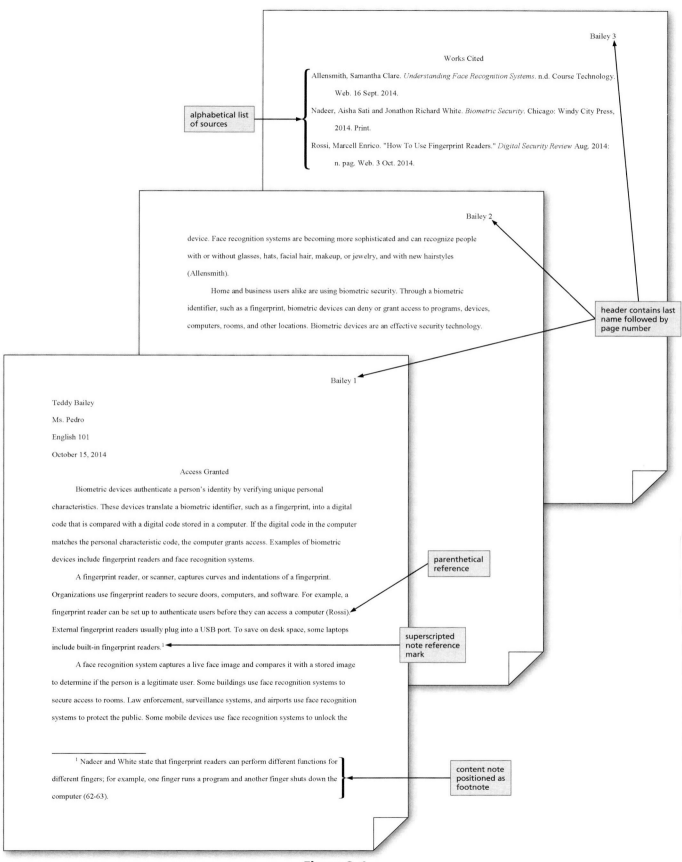

Bailey 3

Works Cited

Allensmith, Samantha Clare. *Understanding Face Recognition Systems*. n.d. Course Technology. Web. 16 Sept. 2014.

Nadeer, Aisha Sati and Jonathon Richard White. *Biometric Security*. Chicago: Windy City Press, 2014. Print.

Rossi, Marcell Enrico. "How To Use Fingerprint Readers." *Digital Security Review* Aug. 2014: n. pag. Web. 3 Oct. 2014.

alphabetical list of sources

header contains last name followed by page number

Bailey 2

device. Face recognition systems are becoming more sophisticated and can recognize people with or without glasses, hats, facial hair, makeup, or jewelry, and with new hairstyles (Allensmith).

Home and business users alike are using biometric security. Through a biometric identifier, such as a fingerprint, biometric devices can deny or grant access to programs, devices, computers, rooms, and other locations. Biometric devices are an effective security technology.

Bailey 1

Teddy Bailey

Ms. Pedro

English 101

October 15, 2014

Access Granted

Biometric devices authenticate a person's identity by verifying unique personal characteristics. These devices translate a biometric identifier, such as a fingerprint, into a digital code that is compared with a digital code stored in a computer. If the digital code in the computer matches the personal characteristic code, the computer grants access. Examples of biometric devices include fingerprint readers and face recognition systems.

A fingerprint reader, or scanner, captures curves and indentations of a fingerprint. Organizations use fingerprint readers to secure doors, computers, and software. For example, a fingerprint reader can be set up to authenticate users before they can access a computer (Rossi). External fingerprint readers usually plug into a USB port. To save on desk space, some laptops include built-in fingerprint readers.[1]

A face recognition system captures a live face image and compares it with a stored image to determine if the person is a legitimate user. Some buildings use face recognition systems to secure access to rooms. Law enforcement, surveillance systems, and airports use face recognition systems to protect the public. Some mobile devices use face recognition systems to unlock the

parenthetical reference

superscripted note reference mark

[1] Nadeer and White state that fingerprint readers can perform different functions for different fingers; for example, one finger runs a program and another finger shuts down the computer (62-63).

content note positioned as footnote

Figure 2–1

For an introduction to Windows and instruction about how to perform basic Windows tasks, read the Office and Windows chapter at the beginning of this book, where you can learn how to resize windows, change screen resolution, create folders, move and rename files, use Windows Help, and much more.

Roadmap

In this chapter, you will learn how to create the research paper shown in Figure 2–1 on the previous page. The following roadmap identifies general activities you will perform as you progress through this chapter:

1. CHANGE the DOCUMENT SETTINGS.
2. CREATE the HEADER for each page of the research paper.
3. TYPE the RESEARCH PAPER text WITH CITATIONS.
4. CREATE an ALPHABETICAL WORKS CITED page.
5. PROOFREAD AND REVISE the RESEARCH PAPER.

At the beginning of step instructions throughout the chapter, you will see an abbreviated form of this roadmap. The abbreviated roadmap uses colors to indicate chapter progress: gray means the chapter is beyond that activity, blue means the task being shown is covered in that activity, and black means that activity is yet to be covered. For example, the following abbreviated roadmap indicates the chapter would be showing a task in the 2 CREATE HEADER activity.

1 CHANGE DOCUMENT SETTINGS | 2 CREATE HEADER | 3 TYPE RESEARCH PAPER WITH CITATIONS
4 CREATE ALPHABETICAL WORKS CITED | 5 PROOFREAD & REVISE RESEARCH PAPER

Use the abbreviated roadmap as a progress guide while you read or step through the instructions in this chapter.

MLA Documentation Style

The research paper in this project follows the guidelines presented by the MLA. To follow the MLA documentation style, use a 12-point Times New Roman or similar font. Double-space text on all pages of the paper using one-inch top, bottom, left, and right margins. Indent the first word of each paragraph one-half inch from the left margin. At the right margin of each page, place a page number one-half inch from the top margin. On each page, precede the page number with your last name.

The MLA documentation style does not require a title page. Instead, place your name and course information in a block at the left margin beginning one inch from the top of the page. Center the title one double-spaced line below your name and course information.

In the text of the paper, place author references in parentheses with the page number(s) of the referenced information. The MLA documentation style uses in-text **parenthetical references** instead of noting each source at the bottom of the page or at the end of the paper. In the MLA documentation style, notes are used only for optional content or bibliographic notes.

If used, content notes elaborate on points discussed in the paper, and bibliographic notes direct the reader to evaluations of statements in a source or provide a means for identifying multiple sources. Use a superscript (raised number) both to signal that a note exists and to sequence the notes (shown in Figure 2–1). Position notes at the bottom of the page as footnotes or at the end of the paper as endnotes. Indent the first line of each note one-half inch from the left margin. Place one space following the superscripted number before beginning the note text. Double-space the note text (shown in Figure 2–1).

The MLA documentation style uses the term, **works cited,** to refer to the bibliographic list of sources at the end of the paper. The works cited page

BTW
APA Documentation Style
In the APA style, a separate title page is required instead of placing name and course information on the paper's first page. Double-space all pages of the paper with one-inch top, bottom, left, and right margins. Indent the first word of each paragraph one-half inch from the left margin. In the upper-right margin of each page, including the title page, place a running head that consists of the page number preceded by a brief summary of the paper title.

alphabetically lists sources that are referenced directly in the paper. Place the list of sources on a separate numbered page. Center the title, Works Cited, one inch from the top margin. Double-space all lines. Begin the first line of each source at the left margin, indenting subsequent lines of the same source one-half inch from the left margin. List each source by the author's last name, or, if the author's name is not available, by the title of the source.

Changing Document Settings

The MLA documentation style defines some global formats that apply to the entire research paper. Some of these formats are the default in Word. For example, the default left, right, top, and bottom margin settings in Word are one inch, which meets the MLA documentation style. You will modify, however, the font, font size, and line and paragraph spacing.

To Run Word and Create a Blank Document

If you are using a computer to step through the project in this chapter and you want your screens to match the figures in this book, you should change your screen's resolution to 1366 × 768. For information about how to change a computer's resolution, refer to the Office and Windows chapter at the beginning of this book.

The following steps, which assume Windows 8 is running, use the Start screen or the Search box to run Word based on a typical installation. You may need to ask your instructor how to run Word on your computer. For a detailed example of the procedure summarized below, refer to the Office and Windows chapter.

1 Scroll the Start screen for a Word 2013 tile. If your Start screen contains a Word 2013 tile, tap or click it to run Word and then proceed to Step 5; if the Start screen does not contain the Word 2013 tile, proceed to the next step to search for the Word app.

2 Swipe in from the right edge of the screen or point to the upper-right corner of the screen to display the Charms bar and then tap or click the Search charm on the Charms bar to display the Search menu.

3 Type **Word** as the search text in the Search box and watch the search results appear in the Apps list.

4 Tap or click Word 2013 in the search results to run Word.

5 Tap or click the Blank document thumbnail on the Word start screen to create a blank document and display it in the Word window.

6 If the Word window is not maximized, tap or click the Maximize button on its title bar to maximize the window.

7 If the Print Layout button on the status bar is not selected (shown in Figure 2–2 on the next page), tap or click it so that your screen is in Print Layout view.

8 If Normal (HOME tab | Styles group) is not selected in the Styles gallery (shown in Figure 2–2), tap or click it so that your document uses the Normal style.

9 To display the page the same width as the document window, if necessary, tap or click the Page Width button (VIEW tab | Zoom group).

For an introduction to Office and instruction about how to perform basic tasks in Office apps, read the Office and Windows chapter at the beginning of this book, where you can learn how to run an application, use the ribbon, save a file, open a file, exit an application, use Help, and much more.

One of the few differences between Windows 7 and Windows 8 occurs in the steps to run Word. If you are using Windows 7, click the Start button, type **Word** in the 'Search programs and files' box, click Word 2013, and then, if necessary, maximize the Word window. For detailed steps to run Word in Windows 7, refer to the Office and Windows chapter at the beginning of this book. For a summary of the steps, refer to the Quick Reference located at the back of this book.

To Display Formatting Marks

BTW
Style Formats
To see the formats assigned to a particular style in a document, tap or click the Styles Dialog Box Launcher (HOME tab | Styles group) and then tap or click the Style Inspector button in the Styles task pane. Position the insertion point in the style in the document and then point to the Paragraph formatting or Text level formatting areas in the Style Inspector task pane to display a ScreenTip describing formats assigned to the location of the insertion point. You also can tap or click the Reveal Formatting button in the Style Inspector task pane or press SHIFT+F1 to display the Reveal Formatting task pane.

As discussed in Chapter 1, it is helpful to display formatting marks that indicate where in the document you press the ENTER key, SPACEBAR, and other keys. The following steps display formatting marks.

1 If the HOME tab is not the active tab, tap or click HOME on the ribbon to display the HOME tab.

2 If the 'Show/Hide ¶' button (HOME tab | Paragraph group) is not selected already, tap or click it to display formatting marks on the screen.

Styles

When you create a document, Word formats the text using a particular style. A **style** is a named group of formatting characteristics, including font and font size. The default style in Word is called the **Normal style**, which most likely uses an 11-point Calibri font. If you do not specify a style for text you type, Word applies the Normal style to the text. In addition to the Normal style, Word has many other built-in, or predefined, styles that you can use to format text. Styles make it easy to apply many formats at once to text. You can modify existing styles and create your own styles. Styles are discussed as they are used in this book.

To Modify a Style

1 CHANGE DOCUMENT SETTINGS | 2 CREATE HEADER | 3 TYPE RESEARCH PAPER WITH CITATIONS
4 CREATE ALPHABETICAL WORKS CITED | 5 PROOFREAD & REVISE RESEARCH PAPER

The MLA documentation style requires that all text in the research paper use a 12-point Times New Roman or similar font. If you change the font and font size using buttons on the ribbon, you will need to make the change many times during the course of creating the paper. *Why? Word formats various areas of a document based on the Normal style, which uses an 11-point Calibri font. For example, body text, headers, and bibliographies all display text based on the Normal style.*

Thus, instead of changing the font and font size for various document elements, a more efficient technique is to change the Normal style for this document to use a 12-point Times New Roman font. *Why? By changing the Normal style, you ensure that all text in the document will use the format required by the MLA.* The following steps change the Normal style.

1
- Press and hold or right-click Normal in the Styles gallery (HOME tab | Styles group) to display a shortcut menu related to styles (Figure 2–2).

Figure 2–2

2

- Tap or click Modify on the shortcut menu to display the Modify Style dialog box (Figure 2–3).

Figure 2–3

3

- Tap or click the Font arrow (Modify Style dialog box) to display the Font list. Scroll to and then click Times New Roman in the list to change the font for the style being modified.

- Tap or click the Font Size arrow (Modify Style dialog box) and then tap or click 12 in the Font Size list to change the font size for the style being modified.

- Ensure that the 'Only in this document' option button is selected (Figure 2–4).

Q&A

Will all future documents use the new font and font size?
No, because the 'Only in this document' option button is selected. If you wanted all future documents to use a new setting, you would select the 'New documents based on this template' option button.

Figure 2–4

4

- Tap or click the OK button (Modify Style dialog box) to update the Normal style to the specified settings.

Other Ways

1. Tap or click Styles Dialog Box Launcher, tap or click arrow next to style name, tap or click Modify on menu, change settings (Modify Style dialog box), tap or click OK button

2. Press ALT+CTRL+SHIFT+S, tap or click arrow next to style name, tap or click Modify on menu, change settings (Modify Style dialog box), tap or click OK button

BTW
Line Spacing
If the top of a set of characters or a graphical image is chopped off, then line spacing may be set to Exactly. To remedy the problem, change line spacing to 1.0, 1.15, 1.5, 2.0, 2.5, 3.0, or At least (in the Paragraph dialog box), all of which accommodate the largest font or image.

Adjusting Line and Paragraph Spacing

Line spacing is the amount of vertical space between lines of text in a paragraph. **Paragraph spacing** is the amount of space above and below a paragraph. By default, the Normal style places 8 points of blank space after each paragraph and inserts a vertical space equal to 1.08 lines between each line of text. It also automatically adjusts line height to accommodate various font sizes and graphics.

The MLA documentation style requires that you **double-space** the entire research paper. That is, the amount of vertical space between each line of text and above and below paragraphs should be equal to one blank line. The next sets of steps adjust line spacing and paragraph spacing according to the MLA documentation style.

To Change Line Spacing

1 CHANGE DOCUMENT SETTINGS | 2 CREATE HEADER | 3 TYPE RESEARCH PAPER WITH CITATIONS
4 CREATE ALPHABETICAL WORKS CITED | 5 PROOFREAD & REVISE RESEARCH PAPER

The following steps change the line spacing to 2.0 to double-space lines in a paragraph. *Why? The lines of the research paper should be double-spaced, according to the MLA documentation style.*

1
- Tap or click the 'Line and Paragraph Spacing' button (HOME tab | Paragraph group) to display the Line and Paragraph Spacing gallery (Figure 2–5).

Q&A What do the numbers in the Line and Paragraph Spacing gallery represent?
The options 1.0, 2.0, and 3.0 set line spacing to single, double, and triple, respectively. Similarly, the 1.15, 1.5, and 2.5 options set line spacing to 1.15, 1.5, and 2.5 lines. All of these options adjust line spacing automatically to accommodate the largest font or graphic on a line.

Figure 2–5

2
- Tap or click 2.0 in the Line and Paragraph Spacing gallery to change the line spacing at the location of the insertion point.

Q&A Can I change the line spacing of existing text?
Yes. Select the text first and then change the line spacing as described in these steps.

Other Ways

1. Tap 'Show Context Menu' on mini toolbar or right-click paragraph, tap or click Paragraph on shortcut menu, tap or click Indents and Spacing tab (Paragraph dialog box), tap or click Line spacing arrow, select desired spacing, tap or click OK button

2. Tap or click Paragraph Settings Dialog Box Launcher (HOME tab or PAGE LAYOUT tab | Paragraph group), tap or click Indents and Spacing tab (Paragraph dialog box), tap or click Line spacing arrow, select desired spacing, tap or click OK button

3. Press CTRL+2 for double-spacing

To Remove Space after a Paragraph

The following steps remove space after a paragraph. *Why? The research paper should not have additional blank space after each paragraph, according to the MLA documentation style.*

- Tap or click the 'Line and Paragraph Spacing' button (HOME tab | Paragraph group) to display the Line and Paragraph Spacing gallery (Figure 2–6).

Q&A
Why is there a check mark to the left of 2.0 in the gallery?
The check mark indicates the currently selected line spacing.

- Tap or click 'Remove Space After Paragraph' in the Line and Paragraph Spacing gallery so that no blank space appears after paragraphs.

Q&A
Can I remove space after existing paragraphs?
Yes. Select the paragraphs first and then remove the space as described in these steps.

Figure 2–6

Other Ways

1. Adjust Spacing After arrows (PAGE LAYOUT tab | Paragraph group) until 0 pt is displayed
2. Tap 'Show Context Menu' on mini toolbar or right-click paragraph, tap or click Paragraph on shortcut menu, tap or click Indents and Spacing tab (Paragraph dialog box), adjust After arrows until 0 pt is displayed, tap or click OK button
3. Tap or click Paragraph Settings Dialog Box Launcher (HOME tab or PAGE LAYOUT tab | Paragraph group), tap or click Indents and Spacing tab (Paragraph dialog box), adjust After arrows until 0 pt is displayed, tap or click OK button

To Update a Style to Match a Selection

To ensure that all paragraphs in the paper will be double-spaced and do not have space after the paragraphs, you want the Normal style to include the line and paragraph spacing changes made in the previous two sets of steps. The following steps update the Normal style. *Why? You can update a style to reflect the settings of the location of the insertion point or selected text. Because no text has yet been typed in the research paper, you do not need to select text prior to updating the Normal style.*

- Press and hold or right-click Normal in the Styles gallery (HOME tab | Styles group) to display a shortcut menu (Figure 2–7).

- Tap or click 'Update Normal to Match Selection' on the shortcut menu to update the selected (or current) style to reflect the settings at the location of the insertion point.

Figure 2–7

Other Ways

1. Tap or click Styles Dialog Box Launcher, tap or click arrow next to style name, tap or click 'Update Normal to Match Selection'
2. Press ALT+CTRL+SHIFT+S, tap or click arrow next to style name, tap or click 'Update Normal to Match Selection'

Creating a Header

A **header** is text and/or graphics that print at the top of each page in a document. Similarly, a **footer** is text and/or graphics that print at the bottom of every page. In Word, headers print in the top margin one-half inch from the top of every page, and footers print in the bottom margin one-half inch from the bottom of each page, which meets the MLA documentation style. In addition to text and graphics, headers and footers can include document information such as the page number, current date, current time, and author's name.

In this research paper, you are to precede the page number with your last name placed one-half inch from the upper-right edge of each page. The procedures on the following pages enter your name and the page number in the header, as specified by the MLA documentation style.

BTW

The Ribbon and Screen Resolution
Word may change how the groups and buttons within the groups appear on the ribbon, depending on the computer's screen resolution. Thus, your ribbon may look different from the ones in this book if you are using a screen resolution other than 1366 × 768.

To Switch to the Header

1 CHANGE DOCUMENT SETTINGS | 2 CREATE HEADER | 3 TYPE RESEARCH PAPER WITH CITATIONS
4 CREATE ALPHABETICAL WORKS CITED | 5 PROOFREAD & REVISE RESEARCH PAPER

The following steps switch from editing the document text to editing the header. **Why?** *To enter text in the header, you instruct Word to edit the header.*

1

- Tap or click INSERT on the ribbon to display the INSERT tab.

- Tap or click the 'Add a Header' button (INSERT tab | Header & Footer group) to display the Add a Header gallery (Figure 2–8).

Experiment

- Tap or click the down scroll arrow in the Add a Header gallery to see the available built-in headers.

Q&A
Can I use a built-in header for this research paper?
None of the built-in headers adheres to the MLA documentation style. Thus, you enter your own header content instead of using a built-in header for this research paper.

How would I remove a header from a document?
You would tap or click Remove Header in the Add a Header gallery. Similarly, to remove a footer, you would tap or click Remove Footer in the Add a Footer gallery.

Figure 2–8

2

- Tap or click Edit Header in the Add a Header gallery to switch from the document text to the header, which allows you to edit the contents of the header (Figure 2–9).

Q&A How do I remove the HEADER & FOOTER TOOLS DESIGN tab from the ribbon?
When you are finished editing the header, you will close it, which removes the HEADER & FOOTER TOOLS DESIGN tab.

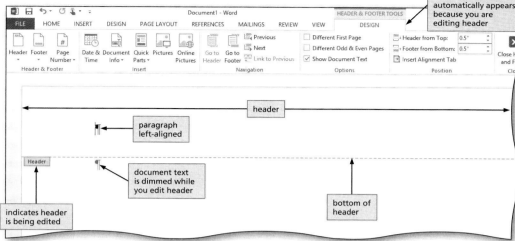

Figure 2–9

Other Ways

1. Double-tap or double-click dimmed header
2. Press and hold or right-click header in document, tap or click Edit Header button that appears

To Right-Align a Paragraph

1 CHANGE DOCUMENT SETTINGS | 2 CREATE HEADER | 3 TYPE RESEARCH PAPER WITH CITATIONS
4 CREATE ALPHABETICAL WORKS CITED | 5 PROOFREAD & REVISE RESEARCH PAPER

The paragraph in the header currently is left-aligned (Figure 2–9). The following steps right-align this paragraph. *Why? Your last name and the page number should print **right-aligned**; that is, they should print at the right margin, according to the MLA documentation style.*

1

- Tap or click HOME on the ribbon to display the HOME tab.

2

- Tap or click the Align Right button (HOME tab | Paragraph group) to right-align the current paragraph (Figure 2–10).

Q&A What if I wanted to return the paragraph to left-aligned?
Tap or click the Align Right button again, or tap or click the Align Left button (HOME tab | Paragraph group).

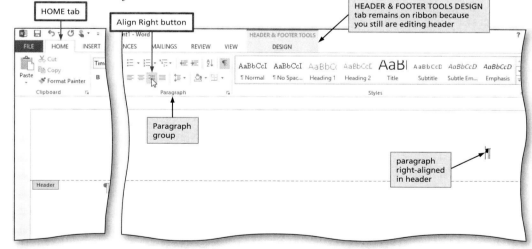

Figure 2–10

Other Ways

1. Tap 'Show Context Menu' button on mini toolbar or right-click paragraph, tap or click Paragraph on shortcut menu, tap or click Indents and Spacing tab (Paragraph dialog box), tap or click Alignment arrow, tap or click Right, tap or click OK button
2. Tap or click Paragraph Settings Dialog Box Launcher (HOME tab or PAGE LAYOUT tab | Paragraph group), tap or click Indents and Spacing tab (Paragraph dialog box), tap or click Alignment arrow, tap or click Right, tap or click OK button
3. Press CTRL+R

BTW
Footers
If you wanted to create a footer, you would click the Footer button (INSERT tab | Header & Footer group) and then select the desired built-in footer or click Edit Footer to create a customized footer; or, you could double-tap or double-click the dimmed footer.

To Enter Text

The following step enters the last name right-aligned in the header area.

1 Type **Bailey** and then press the SPACEBAR to enter the last name in the header.

If requested by your instructor, enter your last name instead of Bailey in the header.

1 CHANGE DOCUMENT SETTINGS | 2 CREATE HEADER | 3 TYPE RESEARCH PAPER WITH CITATIONS
4 CREATE ALPHABETICAL WORKS CITED | 5 PROOFREAD & REVISE RESEARCH PAPER

To Insert a Page Number

The following steps insert a page number at the location of the insertion point. **Why?** *The MLA documentation style requires a page number following the last name in the header.*

1
- Tap or click HEADER & FOOTER TOOLS DESIGN on the ribbon to display the HEADER & FOOTER TOOLS DESIGN tab.
- Tap or click the 'Add Page Numbers' button (HEADER & FOOTER TOOLS DESIGN tab | Header & Footer group) to display the Add Page Numbers menu.

Q&A | Why does the button name in the step differ from the name on the face of the button in the figure?
The text that appears on the face of the button may vary, depending on screen resolution. The name that appears in the ScreenTip (when you point to the button), however, never changes. For this reason, this book uses the name that appears in the ScreenTip to identify buttons, boxes, and other on-screen elements.

- Tap or point to Current Position on the Add Page Numbers menu to display the Current Position gallery (Figure 2–11).

 Experiment
- Tap or click the down scroll arrow in the Current Position gallery to see the available page number formats.

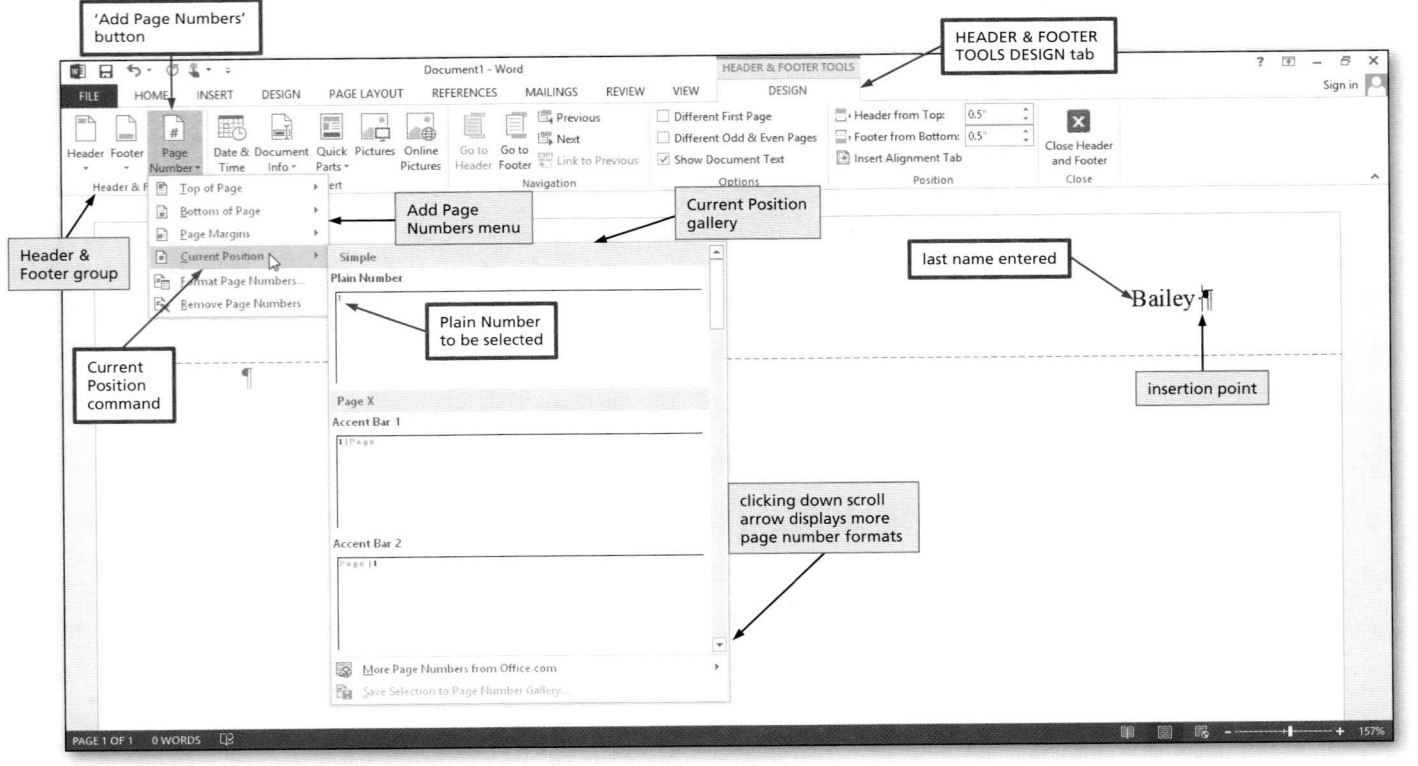

Figure 2–11

2

- If necessary, scroll to the top of the Current Position gallery.

- Tap or click Plain Number in the Current Position gallery to insert an unformatted page number at the location of the insertion point (Figure 2–12).

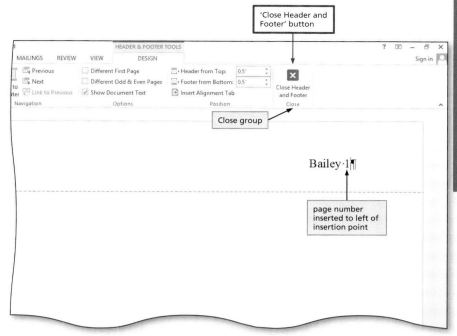

'Close Header and Footer' button

Close group

Bailey·1¶

page number inserted to left of insertion point

Figure 2–12

To Close the Header

1 CHANGE DOCUMENT SETTINGS | 2 CREATE HEADER | 3 TYPE RESEARCH PAPER WITH CITATIONS
4 CREATE ALPHABETICAL WORKS CITED | 5 PROOFREAD & REVISE RESEARCH PAPER

The next task is to switch back to the document text. *Why? You are finished entering text in the header.* The following step closes the header.

1

- Tap or click the 'Close Header and Footer' button (HEADER & FOOTER TOOLS DESIGN tab | Close group) (shown in Figure 2–12) to close the header and switch back to the document text (Figure 2–13).

Q&A | How do I make changes to existing header text?
Switch to the header using the steps described on page WD 74, edit the header as you would edit text in the document window, and then switch back to the document text.

HEADER & FOOTER TOOLS DESIGN tab disappears from screen when you switch back to document text

document text will be bright when you type it because you switched back to document text

header is dim when you switch back to document text

Bailey·1¶

Figure 2–13

Typing the Research Paper Text

The text of the research paper in this chapter encompasses the first two pages of the paper. You will type the text of the research paper and then modify it later in the chapter, so that it matches Figure 2–1 on page WD 67.

CONSIDER THIS

What should you consider when writing the first draft of a research paper?

As you write the first draft of a research paper, be sure it includes the proper components, uses credible sources, and does not contain any plagiarized material.

- **Include an introduction, body, and conclusion.** The first paragraph of the paper introduces the topic and captures the reader's attention. The body, which follows the introduction, consists of several paragraphs that support the topic. The conclusion summarizes the main points in the body and restates the topic.

- **Evaluate sources for authority, currency, and accuracy.** Be especially wary of information obtained on the web. Any person, company, or organization can publish a webpage on the Internet. Ask yourself these questions about the source:

 - Authority: Does a reputable institution or group support the source? Is the information presented without bias? Are the author's credentials listed and verifiable?

 - Currency: Is the information up to date? Are dates of sources listed? What is the last date revised or updated?

 - Accuracy: Is the information free of errors? Is it verifiable? Are the sources clearly identified?

- **Acknowledge all sources of information; do not plagiarize.** Sources of research include books, magazines, newspapers, and the Internet. As you record facts and ideas, list details about the source: title, author, place of publication, publisher, date of publication, etc. When taking notes, be careful not to **plagiarize**. That is, do not use someone else's work and claim it to be your own. If you copy information directly, place it in quotation marks and identify its source. Not only is plagiarism unethical, but it is considered an academic crime that can have severe punishments such as failing a course or being expelled from school.

 When you summarize, paraphrase (rewrite information in your own words), present facts, give statistics, quote exact words, or show a map, chart, or other graphic, you must acknowledge the source. Information that commonly is known or accessible to the audience constitutes common knowledge and does not need to be acknowledged. If, however, you question whether certain information is common knowledge, you should document it — just to be safe.

To Enter Name and Course Information

As discussed earlier in this chapter, the MLA documentation style does not require a separate title page for research papers. Instead, place your name and course information in a block at the top of the page, below the header, at the left margin. The following steps enter the name and course information in the research paper.

BTW

Date Formats
The MLA style prefers the day-month-year (15 October 2014) or month-day-year (October 15, 2014) format.

1 Type **Teddy Bailey** as the student name and then press the ENTER key.

2 Type **Ms. Pedro** as the instructor name and then press the ENTER key.

3 Type **English 101** as the course name and then press the ENTER key.

4 Type **October 15, 2014** as the paper's due date and then press the ENTER key (Figure 2–14).

If requested by your instructor, enter your name and course information instead of the information shown above.

Q&A Why did the word, October, appear on the screen as I began typing the month name?
Word has an AutoComplete feature, where it predicts some words or phrases as you are typing and displays its prediction in a ScreenTip. If the AutoComplete prediction is correct, you can tap the ScreenTip or press the ENTER key to instruct Word to finish your typing with the word or phrase that appears in the ScreenTip.

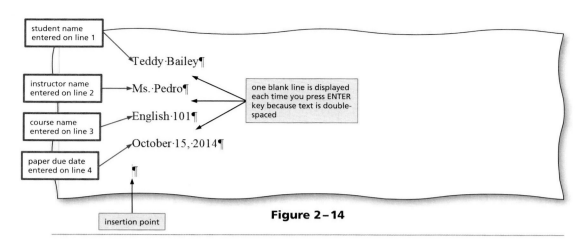

student name entered on line 1

Teddy·Bailey¶

instructor name entered on line 2

Ms.·Pedro¶

one blank line is displayed each time you press ENTER key because text is double-spaced

course name entered on line 3

English·101¶

paper due date entered on line 4

October·15,·2014¶

¶

insertion point

Figure 2–14

To Click and Type

1 CHANGE DOCUMENT SETTINGS | 2 CREATE HEADER | **3 TYPE RESEARCH PAPER WITH CITATIONS**
4 CREATE ALPHABETICAL WORKS CITED | 5 PROOFREAD & REVISE RESEARCH PAPER

The next task is to enter the title of the research paper centered between the page margins. In Chapter 1, you used the Center button (HOME tab | Paragraph group) to center text and graphics. As an alternative, if you are using a mouse, you can use Word's Click and Type feature to format and enter text, graphics, and other items. *Why?* With ***Click and Type***, *you can double-click a blank area of the document window and Word automatically formats the item you type or insert according to the location where you double-clicked.* If you are using a mouse, the following steps use Click and Type to center and then type the title of the research paper. If you are using a touch screen, you will use a different method.

- If you are using a touch screen, tap the Center button (HOME tab | Paragraph group) and then proceed to Step 3 because the Click and Type feature does not work with a touch screen.

🔍 Experiment

- If you are using a mouse, move the pointer around the document below the entered name and course information and observe the various icons that appear with the I-beam.

- If you are using a mouse, position the pointer in the center of the document at the approximate location for the research paper title until a center icon appears below the I-beam (Figure 2–15).

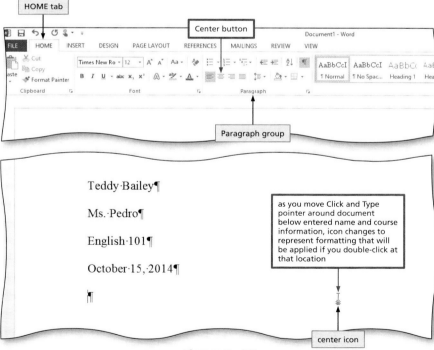

HOME tab

Center button

Document1 - Word

Paragraph group

Teddy·Bailey¶

Ms.·Pedro¶

English·101¶

October·15,·2014¶

¶

as you move Click and Type pointer around document below entered name and course information, icon changes to represent formatting that will be applied if you double-click at that location

center icon

Figure 2–15

Q&A What are the other icons that appear in the Click and Type pointer?
A left-align icon appears to the right of the I-beam when the Click and Type pointer is in certain locations on the left side of the document window. A right-align icon appears to the left of the I-beam when the Click and Type pointer is in certain locations on the right side of the document window.

- If you are using a mouse, double-click to center the paragraph mark and insertion point between the left and right margins.

3

- Type **Access Granted** as the paper title and then press the ENTER key to position the insertion point on the next line (Figure 2–16).

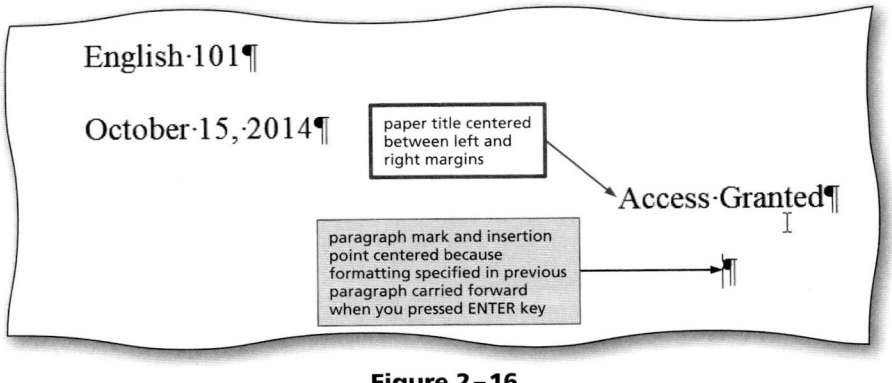

English·101¶

October·15,·2014¶

paper title centered between left and right margins

Access·Granted¶

paragraph mark and insertion point centered because formatting specified in previous paragraph carried forward when you pressed ENTER key

¶

Figure 2–16

Keyboard Shortcuts

Word has many **keyboard shortcuts**, sometimes called shortcut keys or keyboard key combinations, for your convenience while typing. Table 2–1 lists the common keyboard shortcuts for formatting characters. Table 2–2 lists common keyboard shortcuts for formatting paragraphs.

Table 2–1 Keyboard Shortcuts for Formatting Characters

Character Formatting Task	Keyboard Shortcut	Character Formatting Task	Keyboard Shortcut
All capital letters	CTRL+SHIFT+A	Italic	CTRL+I
Bold	CTRL+B	Remove character formatting (plain text)	CTRL+SPACEBAR
Case of letters	SHIFT+F3	Small uppercase letters	CTRL+SHIFT+K
Decrease font size	CTRL+SHIFT+<	Subscript	CTRL+EQUAL SIGN
Decrease font size 1 point	CTRL+[Superscript	CTRL+SHIFT+PLUS SIGN
Double-underline	CTRL+SHIFT+D	Underline	CTRL+U
Increase font size	CTRL+SHIFT+>	Underline words, not spaces	CTRL+SHIFT+W
Increase font size 1 point	CTRL+]		

© 2014 Cengage Learning

Table 2–2 Keyboard Shortcuts for Formatting Paragraphs

Paragraph Formatting	Keyboard Shortcut	Paragraph Formatting	Keyboard Shortcut
1.5 line spacing	CTRL+5	Justify paragraph	CTRL+J
Add/remove one line above paragraph	CTRL+0 (ZERO)	Left-align paragraph	CTRL+L
Center paragraph	CTRL+E	Remove hanging indent	CTRL+SHIFT+T
Decrease paragraph indent	CTRL+SHIFT+M	Remove paragraph formatting	CTRL+Q
Double-space lines	CTRL+2	Right-align paragraph	CTRL+R
Hanging indent	CTRL+T	Single-space lines	CTRL+1
Increase paragraph indent	CTRL+M		

© 2014 Cengage Learning

To Format Text Using a Keyboard Shortcut

The paragraphs below the paper title should be left-aligned, instead of centered. Thus, the next step is to left-align the paragraph below the paper title. When your fingers are already on the keyboard, you may prefer using keyboard shortcuts to format text as you type it.

The following step left-aligns a paragraph using the keyboard shortcut CTRL+L. (Recall from Chapter 1 that a notation such as CTRL+L means to press the letter L on the keyboard while holding down the CTRL key.)

1 Press CTRL+L to left-align the current paragraph, that is, the paragraph containing the insertion point (shown in Figure 2–17 on the next page).

Q&A Why would I use a keyboard shortcut instead of the ribbon to format text?
Switching between the mouse and the keyboard takes time. If your hands are already on the keyboard, use a keyboard shortcut. If your hand is on the mouse, use the ribbon.

To Save a Document

You have performed many tasks while creating this research paper and do not want to risk losing work completed thus far. Accordingly, you should save the document. The following steps assume you already have created folders for storing your files, for example, a CIS 101 folder (for your class) that contains a Word folder (for your assignments). Thus, these steps save the document in the Word folder in the CIS 101 folder using the file name, Biometric Devices Paper.

1 Tap or click the Save button on the Quick Access Toolbar, which depending on settings, will display either the Save As gallery in the Backstage view or the Save As dialog box.

2 To save on a hard disk or other storage media on your computer, proceed to Step 2a. To save on SkyDrive, proceed to Step 2b.

2a If your screen opens the Backstage view and you want to save on storage media on your computer, tap or click Computer in the left pane, if necessary, to display options in the right pane related to saving on your computer. If your screen already displays the Save As dialog box, proceed to Step 4.

2b If your screen opens the Backstage view and you want to save on SkyDrive, tap or click SkyDrive in the left pane to display SkyDrive saving options or a Sign In button. If your screen displays a Sign In button, tap or click it and then sign in to SkyDrive.

3 Tap or click the Browse button in the right pane to display the Save As dialog box associated with the selected save location (i.e., Computer or SkyDrive).

4 Type **Biometric Devices Paper** in the File name box to change the file name. Do not press the ENTER key after typing the file name because you do not want to close the dialog box at this time.

5 Navigate to the desired save location (in this case, the Word folder in the CIS 101 folder [or your class folder] on your computer or SkyDrive).

6 Tap or click the Save button (Save As dialog box) to save the research paper in the selected folder on the selected save location with the entered file name.

BTW

Keyboard Shortcuts
To print a complete list of keyboard shortcuts in Word, tap or click the Microsoft Word Help button near the upper-right corner of the Word window, type **keyboard shortcuts** in the 'Search online help' text box at the top of the Word Help window, press the ENTER key, tap or click the Keyboard shortcuts for Microsoft Word link, tap or click the Show All link in the upper-right corner of the Help window, tap or click the Print button in the Help window, and then tap or click the Print button in the Print dialog box.

BTW

Organizing Files and Folders
You should organize and store files in folders so that you easily can find the files later. For example, if you are taking an introductory computer class called CIS 101, a good practice would be to save all Word files in a Word folder in a CIS 101 folder. For a discussion of folders and detailed examples of creating folders, refer to the Office and Windows chapter at the beginning of this book.

To Display the Rulers

According to the MLA documentation style, the first line of each paragraph in the research paper is to be indented one-half inch from the left margin. Although you can use a dialog box to indent paragraphs, Word provides a quicker way through the **horizontal ruler**. This ruler is displayed at the top edge of the document window just below the ribbon. Word also provides a **vertical ruler** that is displayed along the left edge of the Word window. The following step displays the rulers. *Why? You want to use the horizontal ruler to indent paragraphs.*

1

- If necessary, scroll the document so that the research paper title is at the top of the document window.

- Tap or click VIEW on the ribbon to display the VIEW tab.

- If the rulers are not displayed, tap or click the View Ruler check box (VIEW tab | Show group) to place a check mark in the check box and display the horizontal and vertical rulers on the screen (Figure 2–17).

Q&A | What tasks can I accomplish using the rulers?
You can use the rulers to indent paragraphs, set tab stops, change page margins, and adjust column widths.

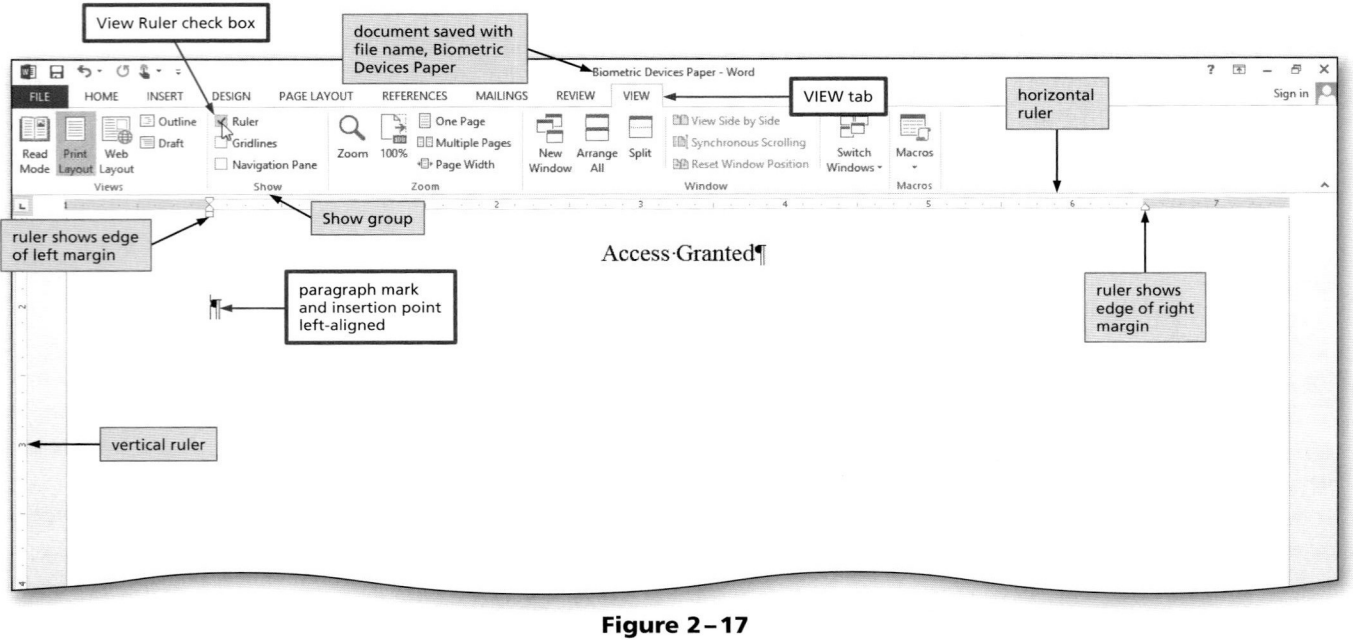

Figure 2–17

To First-Line Indent Paragraphs

If you are using a mouse, you can use the horizontal ruler, usually simply called the **ruler**, to indent just the first line of a paragraph, which is called a **first-line indent**. The left margin on the ruler contains two triangles above a square. The '**First Line Indent' marker** is the top triangle at the 0" mark on the ruler (Figure 2–18). The bottom triangle is discussed later in this chapter. The small square at the 0" mark is the Left Indent marker. The **Left Indent marker** allows you to change the entire left margin, whereas the 'First Line Indent' marker indents only the first line of the paragraph.

The next steps first-line indent paragraphs in the research paper. *Why? The first line of each paragraph in the research paper is to be indented one-half inch from the left margin, according to the MLA documentation style.*

- If you are using a mouse, with the insertion point on the paragraph mark below the research paper title, point to the 'First Line Indent' marker on the ruler (Figure 2–18).

Figure 2–18

- If you are using a mouse, drag the 'First Line Indent' marker to the .5" mark on the ruler to display a vertical dotted line in the document window, which indicates the proposed indent location of the first line of the paragraph (Figure 2–19).

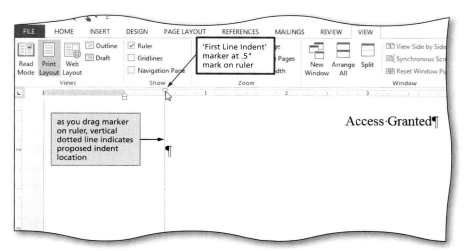

Figure 2–19

- If you are using a mouse, release the mouse button to place the 'First Line Indent' marker at the .5" mark on the ruler, or one-half inch from the left margin (Figure 2–20).

- If you are using a touch screen, you cannot drag the 'First Line Indent' marker and must follow these steps instead: tap the Paragraph Settings Dialog Box Launcher (HOME tab or PAGE LAYOUT tab | Paragraph group) to display the Paragraph dialog box, tap the Indents and Spacing tab (Paragraph dialog box), tap the Special arrow, tap First line, and then tap the OK button.

Figure 2–20

- Type **Biometric devices authenticate a person's identity by verifying unique personal characteristics.** and notice that Word automatically indented the first line of the paragraph by one-half inch (Figure 2–21).

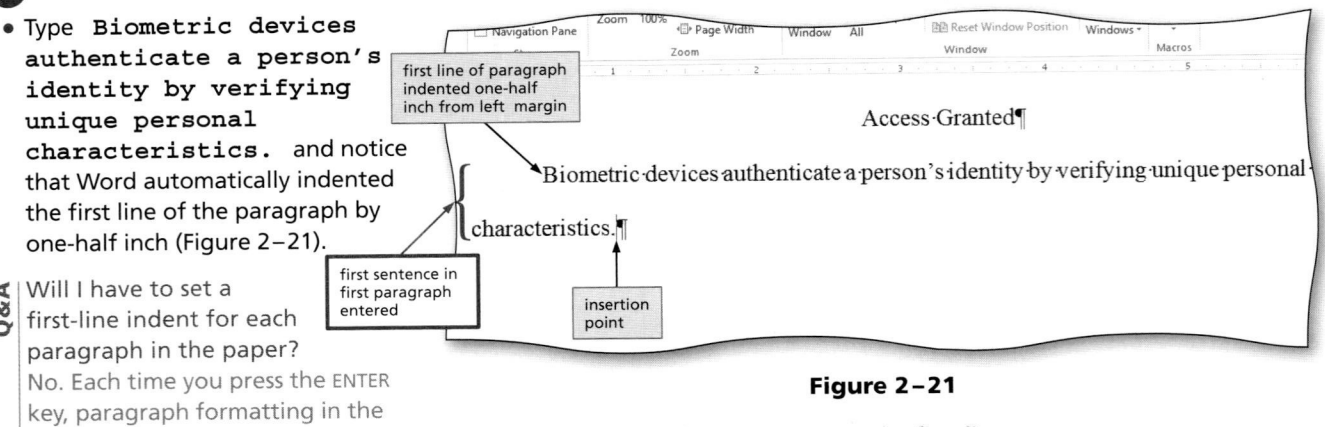

Figure 2–21

Q&A

Will I have to set a first-line indent for each paragraph in the paper?

No. Each time you press the ENTER key, paragraph formatting in the previous paragraph carries forward to the next paragraph. Thus, once you set the first-line indent, its format carries forward automatically to each subsequent paragraph you type.

Other Ways

1. Tap 'Show Context Menu' button on mini toolbar or right-click paragraph, tap or click Paragraph on shortcut menu, tap or click Indents and Spacing tab (Paragraph dialog box), tap or click Special arrow, tap or click First line, tap or click OK button

2. Tap or click Paragraph Settings Dialog Box Launcher (HOME tab or PAGE LAYOUT tab | Paragraph group), tap or click Indents and Spacing tab (Paragraph dialog box), tap or click Special arrow, tap or click First line, tap or click OK button

To AutoCorrect as You Type

1 CHANGE DOCUMENT SETTINGS | 2 CREATE HEADER | **3 TYPE RESEARCH PAPER WITH CITATIONS**
4 CREATE ALPHABETICAL WORKS CITED | 5 PROOFREAD & REVISE RESEARCH PAPER

Word has predefined many commonly misspelled words, which it automatically corrects for you. ***Why?*** *As you type, you may make typing, spelling, capitalization, or grammar errors. Word's **AutoCorrect** feature automatically corrects these kinds of errors as you type them in the document. For example, if you type ahve, Word automatically changes it to the correct spelling, have, when you press the SPACEBAR or a punctuation mark key such as a period or comma.* The following steps intentionally misspell the word, that, as taht to illustrate the AutoCorrect feature.

1

- Press the SPACEBAR.

- Type the beginning of the next sentence, misspelling the word, that, as follows: **These devices translate a biometric element, such as a fingerprint, into a digital code taht** (Figure 2–22).

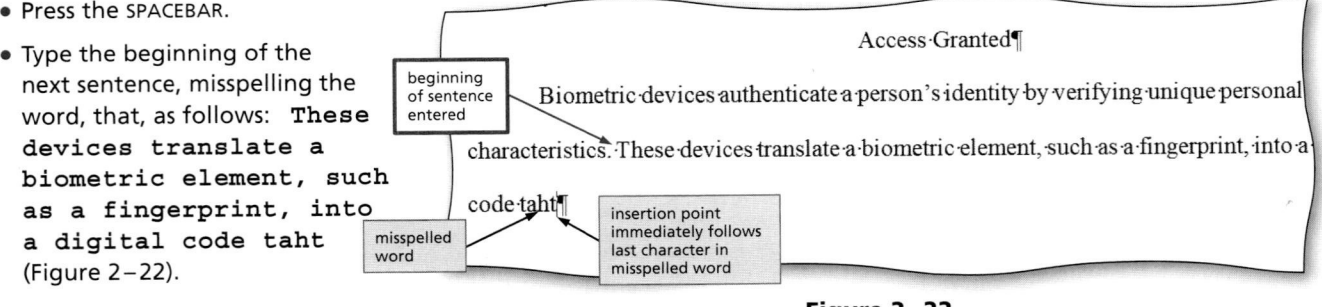

Figure 2–22

2

- Press the SPACEBAR and watch Word automatically correct the misspelled word.

- Type the rest of the sentence (Figure 2–23): **is compared with a digital code stored in a computer.**

Figure 2–23

To Use the AutoCorrect Options Button

The following steps illustrate the AutoCorrect Options button and menu. *Why? If you are using a mouse, when you position the pointer on text that Word automatically corrected, a small blue box appears below the text. If you point to the small blue box, Word displays the AutoCorrect Options button. When you tap or click the **AutoCorrect Options button**, Word displays a menu that allows you to undo a correction or change how Word handles future automatic corrections of this type. If you are using a touch screen, read these steps without performing them.*

- If you are using a mouse, position the pointer in the text automatically corrected by Word (the word, that, in this case) to display a small blue box below the automatically corrected word (Figure 2–24).

Figure 2–24

- Point to the small blue box to display the AutoCorrect Options button.

- Click the AutoCorrect Options button to display the AutoCorrect Options menu (Figure 2–25).

- Press the ESCAPE key to remove the AutoCorrect Options menu from the screen.

Q&A Do I need to remove the AutoCorrect Options button from the screen?
No. When you move the pointer, the AutoCorrect Options button will disappear from the screen. If, for some reason, you wanted to remove the AutoCorrect Options button from the screen, you could press the ESCAPE key a second time.

Figure 2–25

To Create an AutoCorrect Entry

The next steps create an AutoCorrect entry. *Why? In addition to the predefined list of AutoCorrect spelling, capitalization, and grammar errors, you can create your own AutoCorrect entries to add to the list. For example, if you tend to mistype the word computer as comptuer, you should create an AutoCorrect entry for it.*

1

- Tap or click FILE on the ribbon (shown in Figure 2–25 on the previous page) to open the Backstage view (Figure 2–26).

Figure 2–26

2

- Tap or click Options in the Backstage view to display the Word Options dialog box.
- Tap or click Proofing in the left pane (Word Options dialog box) to display proofing options in the right pane.
- Tap or click the AutoCorrect Options button in the right pane to display the AutoCorrect dialog box.
- When Word displays the AutoCorrect dialog box, type **comptuer** in the Replace text box.
- Press the TAB key and then type **computer** in the With text box (Figure 2–27).

Q&A How would I delete an existing AutoCorrect entry?
You would select the entry to be deleted in the list of defined entries in the AutoCorrect dialog box and then tap or click the Delete button (AutoCorrect dialog box).

Figure 2–27

- Tap or click the Add button (AutoCorrect dialog box) to add the entry alphabetically to the list of words to correct automatically as you type. (If your dialog box displays a Replace button instead, tap or click it and then tap or click the Yes button in the Microsoft Word dialog box to replace the previously defined entry.)

- Tap or click the OK button (AutoCorrect dialog box) to close the dialog box.

- Tap or click the OK button (Word Options dialog box) to close the dialog box.

The AutoCorrect Dialog Box

In addition to creating AutoCorrect entries for words you commonly misspell or mistype, you can create entries for abbreviations, codes, and so on. For example, you could create an AutoCorrect entry for asap, indicating that Word should replace this text with the phrase, as soon as possible.

If, for some reason, you do not want Word to correct automatically as you type, you can turn off the Replace text as you type feature by tapping or clicking Options in the Backstage view, tapping or clicking Proofing in the left pane (Word Options dialog box), tapping or clicking the AutoCorrect Options button in the right pane (Figure 2–27), removing the check mark from the 'Replace text as you type' check box, and then tapping or clicking the OK button in each open dialog box.

The AutoCorrect sheet in the AutoCorrect dialog box (Figure 2–27) contains other check boxes that correct capitalization errors if the check boxes are selected:

- If you type two capital letters in a row, such as TH, Word makes the second letter lowercase, Th.

- If you begin a sentence with a lowercase letter, Word capitalizes the first letter of the sentence.

- If you type the name of a day in lowercase letters, such as tuesday, Word capitalizes the first letter in the name of the day, Tuesday.

- If you leave the CAPS LOCK key on and begin a new sentence, such as aFTER, Word corrects the typing, After, and turns off the CAPS LOCK key.

If you do not want Word to automatically perform any of these corrections, simply remove the check mark from the appropriate check box in the AutoCorrect dialog box.

Sometimes you do not want Word to AutoCorrect a particular word or phrase. For example, you may use the code WD. in your documents. Because Word automatically capitalizes the first letter of a sentence, the character you enter following the period will be capitalized (in the previous sentence, it would capitalize the letter i in the word, in). To allow the code WD. to be entered into a document and still leave the AutoCorrect feature turned on, you would set an exception. To set an exception to an AutoCorrect rule, tap or click Options in the Backstage view, tap or click Proofing in the left pane (Word Options dialog box), tap or click the AutoCorrect Options button in the right pane, tap or click the Exceptions button (Figure 2–27), tap or click the appropriate tab in the AutoCorrect Exceptions dialog box, type the exception entry in the text box, tap or click the Add button, tap or click the Close button (AutoCorrect Exceptions dialog box), and then tap or click the OK button in each of the remaining dialog boxes.

To Enter More Text

The next task is to continue typing text in the research paper up to the location of the in-text parenthetical reference. The following steps enter this text.

1 With the insertion point positioned at the end of the first paragraph in the paper, as shown in Figure 2–25 on page WD 85, press the SPACEBAR and then type these two sentences, intentionally misspelling the word readers as raders: `If the digital code in the computer matches the personal characteristic code, the computer grants access. Examples of biometric devices include fingerprint raders and face recognition systems.`

Q&A Why is the word, readers, misspelled?
Later in this chapter, you will use Word's check spelling and grammar at once feature to check the entire document for errors.

2 Press the ENTER key to start a new paragraph.

3 Type `A fingerprint reader, or scanner, captures curves and indentations of a fingerprint. Organizations use fingerprint readers to secure doors, computers, and software. For example, a fingerprint reader can be set up to authenticate users before they can access a computer` and then press the SPACEBAR (Figure 2–28).

Figure 2–28

- code that is compared with a digital code stored in a computer. If the digital code in the computer matches the personal characteristic code, the computer grants access. Examples of biometric devices include fingerprint raders and face recognition systems.¶
- A fingerprint reader, or scanner, captures curves and indentations of a fingerprint. Organizations use fingerprint readers to secure doors, computers, and software. For example, a fingerprint reader can be set up to authenticate users before they can access a computer¶

Callouts: *word intentionally misspelled*; *first line of subsequent paragraph indented automatically when you pressed ENTER key*; *text entered*; *insertion point*

Citations

Both the MLA and APA guidelines suggest the use of in-text parenthetical references (placed at the end of a sentence), instead of footnoting each source of material in a paper. These parenthetical references, called citations in Word, guide the reader to the end of the paper for complete information about the source.

Word provides tools to assist you with inserting citations in a paper and later generating a list of sources from the citations. With a documentation style selected, Word automatically formats the citations and list of sources according to that style. The process for adding citations in Word is as follows:

1. Modify the documentation style, if necessary.
2. Insert a citation placeholder.
3. Enter the source information for the citation.

You can combine Steps 2 and 3, where you insert the citation placeholder and enter the source information at once. Or, you can insert the citation placeholder as you write and then enter the source information for the citation at a later time. While creating the research paper in this chapter, you will use both methods.

BTW
Spacing after Punctuation
Because word processing documents use variable character fonts, it often is difficult to determine in a printed document how many times someone has pressed the SPACEBAR between sentences. Thus, the rule is to press the SPACEBAR only once after periods, colons, and other punctuation marks.

BTW
BTWs
For a complete list of the BTWs found in the margins of this book, visit the BTW resource on the Student Companion Site located on www.cengagebrain.com. For detailed instructions about accessing available resources, visit www.cengage.com/ct/studentdownload or contact your instructor for information about accessing the required files.

To Change the Bibliography Style

The first step in inserting a citation is to be sure the citations and sources will be formatted using the correct documentation style, called the bibliography style in Word. *Why? You want to ensure that Word is using the MLA documentation style for this paper.* The following steps change the specified documentation style.

- Tap or click REFERENCES on the ribbon to display the REFERENCES tab.

- Tap or click the Bibliography Style arrow (REFERENCES tab | Citations & Bibliography group) to display the Bibliography Style gallery, which lists predefined documentation styles (Figure 2–29).

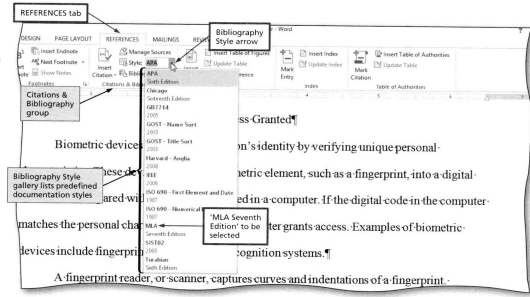

Figure 2–29

2

- Tap or click 'MLA Seventh Edition' in the Bibliography Style gallery to change the documentation style to MLA.

Q&A What if I am using a different edition of a documentation style shown in the Bibliography Style gallery?
Select the closest one and then, if necessary, perform necessary edits before submitting the paper.

What details are required for sources?

During your research, be sure to record essential publication information about each of your sources. Following is a sample list of types of required information for the MLA documentation style.

- Book: full name of author(s), complete title of book, edition (if available), volume (if available), publication city, publisher name, publication year, and publication medium

- Magazine: full name of author(s), complete title of article, magazine title, issue number (if available), date of magazine, page numbers of article, publication medium, and date viewed (if medium is a website)

- Website: full name of author(s), title of website, website publisher or sponsor (if none, write N.p.), publication date (if none, write n.d.), publication medium, and date viewed

CONSIDER THIS

To Insert a Citation and Create Its Source

With the documentation style selected, the next task is to insert a citation at the location of the insertion point and enter the source information for the citation. You can accomplish these steps at once by instructing Word to add a new source. The steps on the next page add a new source for a magazine (periodical) article on the web. *Why? The material preceding the insertion point was summarized from an online magazine article.*

1

- Tap or click the Insert Citation button (REFERENCES tab | Citations & Bibliography group) to display the Insert Citation menu (Figure 2–30).

Figure 2–30

2

- Tap or click 'Add New Source' on the Insert Citation menu to display the Create Source dialog box (Figure 2–31).

Q&A

What are the Bibliography Fields in the Create Source dialog box?
A **field** is a placeholder for data whose contents can change. You enter data in some fields; Word supplies data for others. In this case, you enter the contents of the fields for a particular source, for example, the author name in the Author field.

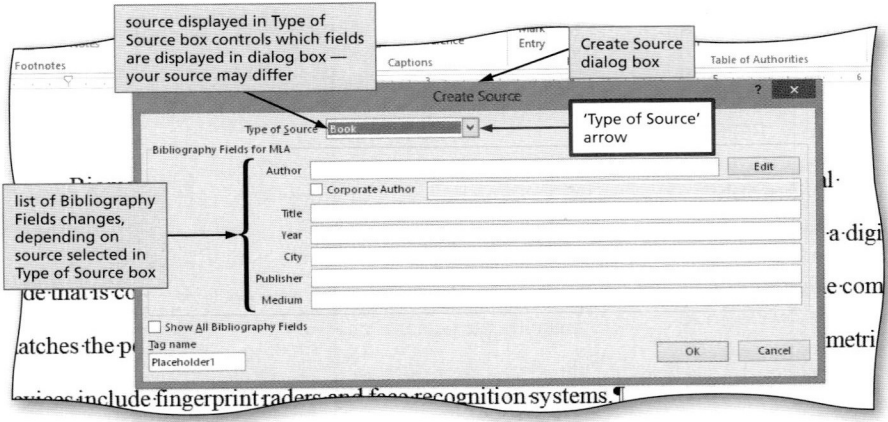

Figure 2–31

Experiment

- Tap or click the 'Type of Source' arrow and then tap or click one of the source types in the list, so that you can see how the list of fields changes to reflect the type of source you selected.

3

- If necessary, tap or click the 'Type of Source' arrow (Create Source dialog box) and then tap or click 'Article in a Periodical', so that the list shows fields required for a magazine (periodical).

- Tap or click the Author text box. Type **Rossi, Marcell Enrico** as the author.

- Tap or click the Title text box. Type **Understanding How to Use Fingerprint Readers** as the article title.

- Press the TAB key and then type **Digital Security Review** as the periodical title.

- Press the TAB key and then type **2014** as the year.

- Press the TAB key and then type **Aug.** as the month.

- Press the TAB key twice and then type **n. pag.** as the number of pages.

- Press the TAB key and then type **Web** as the medium (Figure 2–32).

Figure 2–32

Q&A

Why is the month abbreviated?
The MLA documentation style abbreviates all months, except May, June, and July, when they appear in a source.

What does the n. pag. entry mean in the Pages text box?
The MLA documentation style uses the abbreviation n. pag. for no pagination, which indicates the source has no page references. This is common for web sources.

4

- Place a check mark in the 'Show All Bibliography Fields' check box so that Word displays all fields available for the selected source, including the date viewed (accessed) fields.

- If necessary, scroll to the bottom of the Bibliography Fields list to display the date viewed (accessed) fields.

- Tap or click the Year Accessed text box. Type **2014** as the year.

- Press the TAB key and then type **Oct.** as the month accessed.

- Press the TAB key and then type **3** as the day accessed (Figure 2–33).

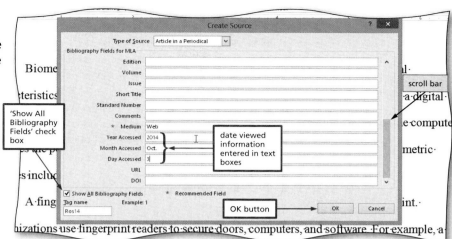

Figure 2–33

What if some of the text boxes disappear as I enter the fields?
With the 'Show All Bibliography Fields' check box selected, the dialog box may not be able to display all fields at the same time. In this case, some may scroll up off the screen.

5

- Tap or click the OK button to close the dialog box, create the source, and insert the citation in the document at the location of the insertion point.

- Press the END key to move the insertion point to the end of the line, which also deselects the citation.

- Press the PERIOD key to end the sentence (Figure 2–34).

Figure 2–34

To Enter More Text

The next task is to continue typing text in the research paper up to the location of the footnote. The following steps enter this text.

1 Press the SPACEBAR.

2 Type the next sentences (Figure 2–35): **External fingerprint readers usually plug into a USB port. To save on desk space, some laptops include built-in fingerprint readers.**

fingerprint·reader·can·be·set·up·to·authenticate·users·before·they·can·access·a·computer·(Rossi).·

External·fingerprint·readers·usually·plug·into·a·USB·port.·To·save·on·desk·space,·some·laptops·

include·built-in·fingerprint·readers.¶

Figure 2–35

To Save an Existing Document with the Same File Name

You have made several modifications to the document since you last saved it. Thus, you should save it again. The following step saves the document again. For an example of the step listed below, refer to the Office and Windows chapter at the beginning of this book.

1 Tap or click the Save button on the Quick Access Toolbar to overwrite the previously saved file.

Footnotes

As discussed earlier in this chapter, notes are optional in the MLA documentation style. If used, content notes elaborate on points discussed in the paper, and bibliographic notes direct the reader to evaluations of statements in a source or provide a means for identifying multiple sources. The MLA documentation style specifies that a superscript (raised number) be used for a **note reference mark** to signal that a note exists either at the bottom of the page as a **footnote** or at the end of the document as an **endnote**.

In Word, **note text** can be any length and format. Word automatically numbers notes sequentially by placing a note reference mark both in the body of the document and to the left of the note text. If you insert, rearrange, or remove notes, Word renumbers any subsequent note reference marks according to their new sequence in the document.

To Insert a Footnote Reference Mark

1 CHANGE DOCUMENT SETTINGS | 2 CREATE HEADER | 3 TYPE RESEARCH PAPER WITH CITATIONS
4 CREATE ALPHABETICAL WORKS CITED | 5 PROOFREAD & REVISE RESEARCH PAPER

The following step inserts a footnote reference mark in the document at the location of the insertion point and at the location where the footnote text will be typed. *Why? You will insert a content note elaborating on fingerprint reader functions, which you want to position as a footnote.*

1

• With the insertion point positioned as shown in Figure 2–35 on the previous page, tap or click the Insert Footnote button (REFERENCES tab | Footnotes group) to display a note reference mark (a superscripted 1) in two places: (1) in the document window at the location of the insertion point and (2) at the bottom of the page where the footnote will be positioned, just below a separator line (Figure 2–36).

Q&A
What if I wanted notes to be positioned as endnotes instead of as footnotes?
You would tap or click the Insert Endnote button (REFERENCES tab | Footnotes group), which places the separator line and the endnote text at the end of the document, instead of at the bottom of the page containing the reference.

Figure 2–36

Other Ways

1. Press ALT+CTRL+F

To Enter Footnote Text

The following step types the footnote text to the right of the note reference mark below the separator line.

1 Type the footnote text up to the citation (shown in Figure 2–37): `Nadeer and White state that fingerprint readers can perform different functions for different fingers; for example, one finger runs a program and another finger shuts down the computer` and then press the SPACEBAR.

To Insert a Citation Placeholder

1 CHANGE DOCUMENT SETTINGS | 2 CREATE HEADER | 3 TYPE RESEARCH PAPER WITH CITATIONS
4 CREATE ALPHABETICAL WORKS CITED | 5 PROOFREAD & REVISE RESEARCH PAPER

Earlier in this chapter, you inserted a citation and its source at once. In Word, you also can insert a citation without entering the source information. **Why?** *Sometimes, you may not have the source information readily available and would prefer to enter it at a later time.*

The following steps insert a citation placeholder in the footnote, so that you can enter the source information later.

1

- With the insertion point positioned as shown in Figure 2–37, tap or click the Insert Citation button (REFERENCES tab | Citations & Bibliography group) to display the Insert Citation menu (Figure 2–37).

Figure 2–37

2

- Tap or click 'Add New Placeholder' on the Insert Citation menu to display the Placeholder Name dialog box.

- Type **Nadeer** as the tag name for the source (Figure 2–38).

Figure 2–38

Q&A What is a tag name?
A tag name is an identifier that links a citation to a source. Word automatically creates a tag name when you enter a source. When you create a citation placeholder, enter a meaningful tag name, which will appear in the citation placeholder until you edit the source.

3

- Tap or click the OK button (Placeholder Name dialog box) to close the dialog box and insert the entered tag name in the citation placeholder in the document (shown in Figure 2–39).

- Press the PERIOD key to end the sentence.

Q&A What if the citation is in the wrong location?

Tap or click the citation to select it and then drag the citation tab (on the upper-left corner of the selected citation) to any location in the document.

If you are using your finger on a touch screen and are having difficulty completing the steps in this chapter, consider using a stylus. Many people find it easier to be precise with a stylus than with a finger. In addition, with a stylus you see the pointer. If you still are having trouble completing the steps with a stylus, try using a mouse.

Footnote Text Style

When you insert a footnote, Word formats it using the Footnote Text style, which does not adhere to the MLA documentation style. For example, notice in Figure 2–37 on the previous page that the footnote text is single-spaced, left-aligned, and a smaller font size than the text in the research paper. According to the MLA documentation style, notes should be formatted like all other paragraphs in the paper.

You could change the paragraph formatting of the footnote text to first-line indent and double-spacing and then change the font size from 10 to 12 point. If you use this technique, however, you will need to change the format of the footnote text for each footnote you enter into the document.

A more efficient technique is to modify the format of the Footnote Text style so that every footnote you enter in the document will use the formats defined in this style.

To Modify a Style Using a Shortcut Menu

1 CHANGE DOCUMENT SETTINGS | 2 CREATE HEADER | 3 TYPE RESEARCH PAPER WITH CITATIONS
4 CREATE ALPHABETICAL WORKS CITED | 5 PROOFREAD & REVISE RESEARCH PAPER

The Footnote Text style specifies left-aligned single-spaced paragraphs with a 10-point font size for text. The following steps modify the Footnote Text style. *Why? To meet MLA documentation style, the footnotes should be double-spaced with a first line indent and a 12-point font size for text.*

1

- If you are using a touch screen, press and hold the note text in the footnote and then tap the 'Show Context Menu' button on the mini toolbar; if you are using a mouse, right-click the note text in the footnote to display a shortcut menu related to footnotes (Figure 2–39).

Figure 2–39

2

- Tap or click Style on the shortcut menu to display the Style dialog box. If necessary, tap or click the Category arrow, tap or click All styles in the Category list, and then tap or click Footnote Text in the Styles list to select the style to modify.

- Tap or click the Modify button (Style dialog box) to display the Modify Style dialog box.

- Tap or click the Font Size arrow (Modify Style dialog box) to display the Font Size list and then tap or click 12 in the Font Size list to change the font size.

- Tap or click the Double Space button to change the line spacing.

- Tap or click the Format button to display the Format menu (Figure 2–40).

Figure 2–40

3

- Tap or click Paragraph on the Format menu (Modify Style dialog box) to display the Paragraph dialog box.

- Tap or click the Special arrow (Paragraph dialog box) and then tap or click First line (Figure 2–41).

Figure 2–41

4

- Tap or click the OK button (Paragraph dialog box) to close the dialog box.

- Tap or click the OK button (Modify Style dialog box) to close the dialog box.

- Tap or click the Apply button (Style dialog box) to apply the style changes to the footnote text (Figure 2–42).

Q&A Will all footnotes use this modified style?

Yes. Any future footnotes entered in the document will use a 12-point font with the paragraphs first-line indented and double-spaced.

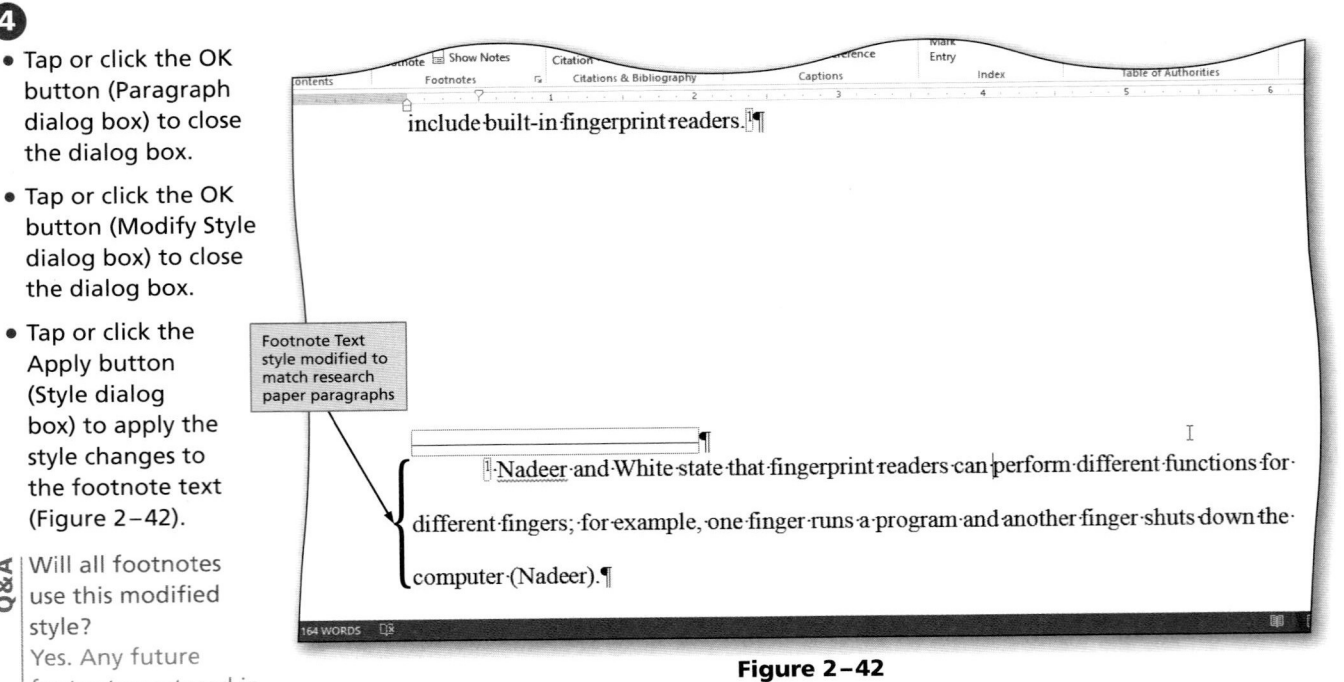

Figure 2–42

Other Ways

1. Tap or click Styles Dialog Box Launcher (HOME tab | Styles group), tap or point to style name in list, tap or click style name arrow, tap or click Modify, change settings (Modify Style dialog box), tap or click OK button

2. Tap or click Styles Dialog Box Launcher (HOME tab | Styles group), tap or click Manage Styles button in task pane, select style name in list, tap or click Modify button (Manage Styles dialog box), change settings (Modify Style dialog box), tap or click OK button in each dialog box

To Edit a Source

1 CHANGE DOCUMENT SETTINGS | 2 CREATE HEADER | 3 TYPE RESEARCH PAPER WITH CITATIONS
4 CREATE ALPHABETICAL WORKS CITED | 5 PROOFREAD & REVISE RESEARCH PAPER

When you typed the footnote text for this research paper, you inserted a citation placeholder for the source. The following steps edit a source. *Why? Assume you now have the source information and are ready to enter it.*

1

- Tap or click somewhere in the citation placeholder to be edited, in this case (Nadeer), to select the citation placeholder.

- Tap or click the Citation Options arrow to display the Citation Options menu (Figure 2–43).

Q&A What is the purpose of the tab to the left of the selected citation?

If, for some reason, you wanted to move a citation to a different location in the document, you would select the citation and then drag the citation tab to the desired location.

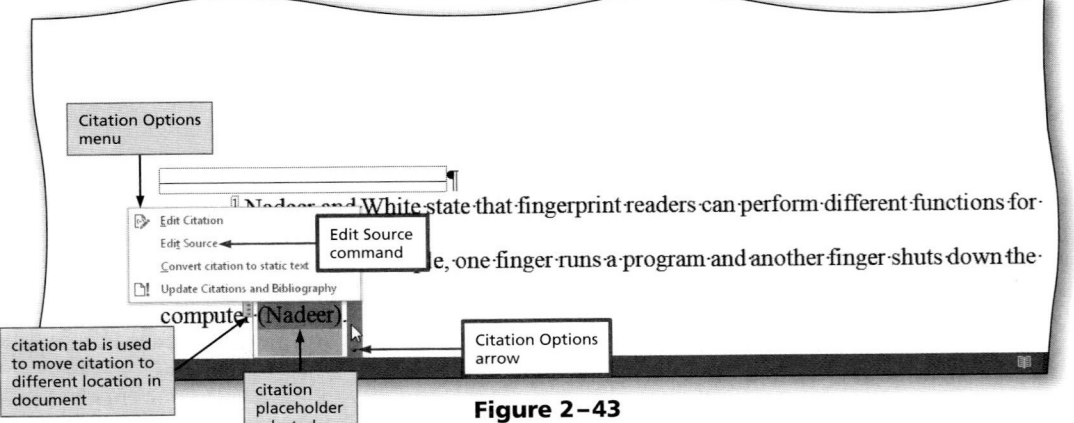

Figure 2–43

2

- Tap or click Edit Source on the Citation Options menu to display the Edit Source dialog box.

- If necessary, tap or click the 'Type of Source' arrow (Edit Source dialog box) and then tap or click Book, so that the list shows fields required for a book.

- Because this source has two authors, tap or click the Edit button to display the Edit Name dialog box, which assists you with entering multiple author names.

- Type **Nadeer** as the first author's last name; press the TAB key and then type **Aisha** as the first name; press the TAB key and then type **Sati** as the middle name (Figure 2–44).

Q&A What if I already know how to punctuate the author entry properly?
You can enter the name directly in the Author box.

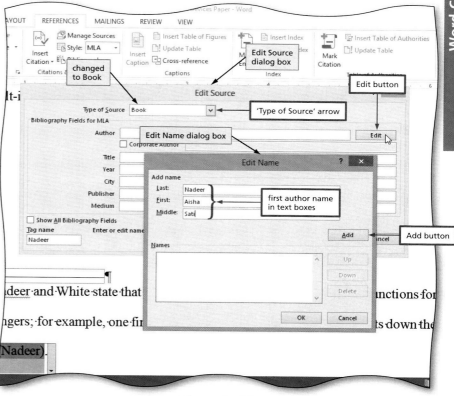

Figure 2–44

3

- Tap or click the Add button (Edit Name dialog box) to add the first author name to the Names list.

- Type **White** as the second author's last name; press the TAB key and then type **Jonathon** as the first name; press the TAB key and then type **Richard** as the middle name.

- Tap or click the Add button to add the second author name to the Names list (Figure 2–45).

Figure 2–45

4

- Tap or click the OK button (Edit Name dialog box) to add the author names that appear in the Names list to the Author box in the Edit Source dialog box.

- Tap or click the Title text box (Edit Source dialog box). Type **Biometric Security** as the book title.

- Press the TAB key and then type **2014** as the year.

- Press the TAB key and then type **Chicago** as the city.

- Press the TAB key and then type **Windy City Press** as the publisher.

- Press the TAB key and then type **Print** as the medium (Figure 2–46).

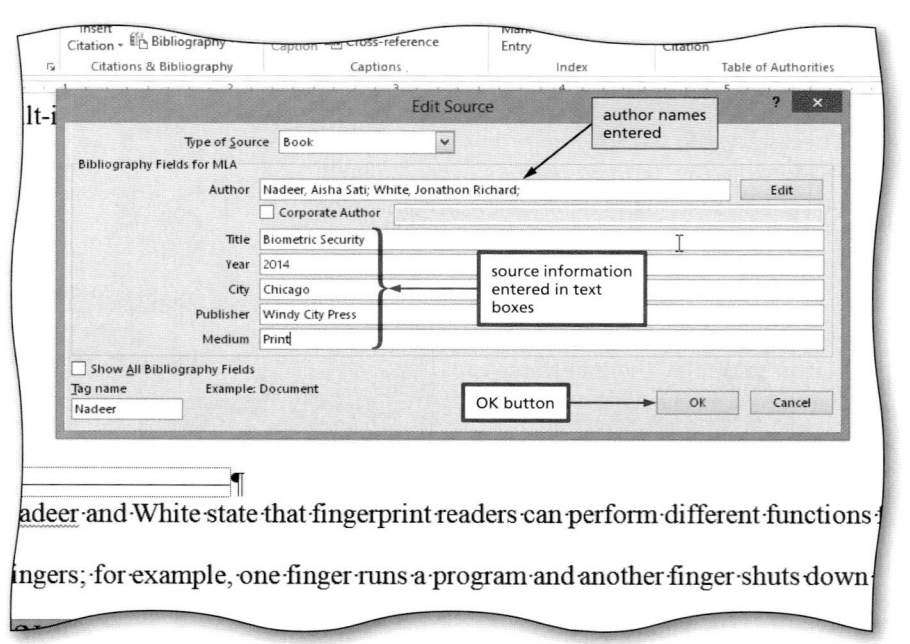

Figure 2–46

5

- Tap or click the OK button to close the dialog box, create the source, and update the citation to display both author last names (shown in Figure 2–47).

Other Ways

1. Tap or click Manage Sources button (REFERENCES tab | Citations & Bibliography group), tap or click placeholder source in Current List, tap or click Edit button (Source Manager dialog box)

To Edit a Citation

1 CHANGE DOCUMENT SETTINGS | 2 CREATE HEADER | 3 TYPE RESEARCH PAPER WITH CITATIONS
4 CREATE ALPHABETICAL WORKS CITED | 5 PROOFREAD & REVISE RESEARCH PAPER

In the MLA documentation style, if a source has page numbers, you should include them in the citation. Thus, Word provides a means to enter the page numbers to be displayed in the citation. Also, if you reference the author's name in the text, you should not list it again in the parenthetical citation. Instead, just list the page number(s) in the citation. To do this, you instruct Word to suppress author and title. **Why?** *If you suppress the author, Word automatically displays the title, so you need to suppress both the author and title if you want just the page number(s) to be displayed.* The following steps edit the citation, suppressing the author and title but displaying the page numbers.

1

- If necessary, tap or click somewhere in the citation to be edited, in this case somewhere in (Nadeer and White), which selects the citation and displays the Citation Options arrow.

- Tap or click the Citation Options arrow to display the Citation Options menu (Figure 2–47).

Figure 2–47

- Tap or click Edit Citation on the Citation Options menu to display the Edit Citation dialog box.

- Type 62–63 in the Pages text box (Edit Citation dialog box).

- Tap or click the Author check box to place a check mark in it.

- Tap or click the Title check box to place a check mark in it (Figure 2–48).

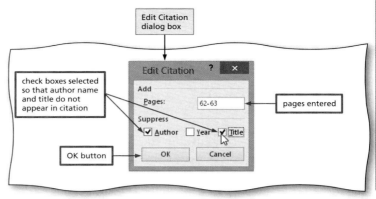

Figure 2–48

- Tap or click the OK button to close the dialog box, remove the author names from the citation in the footnote, suppress the title from showing, and add page numbers to the citation.

- Press the END key to move the insertion point to the end of the line, which also deselects the citation (Figure 2–49).

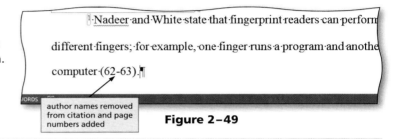

Figure 2–49

Working with Footnotes and Endnotes

You edit footnote text just as you edit any other text in the document. To delete or move a note reference mark, however, the insertion point must be in the document text (not in the footnote text).

To delete a note, select the note reference mark in the document text (not in the footnote text) by dragging through the note reference mark and then tap or click the Cut button (HOME tab | Clipboard group). Or, tap or click immediately to the right of the note reference mark in the document text and then press the BACKSPACE key twice, or tap or click immediately to the left of the note reference mark in the document text and then press the DELETE key twice.

To move a note to a different location in a document, select the note reference mark in the document text (not in the footnote text), tap or click the Cut button (HOME tab | Clipboard group), tap or click the location where you want to move the note, and then tap or click the Paste button (HOME tab | Clipboard group). When you move or delete notes, Word automatically renumbers any remaining notes in the correct sequence.

If you are using a mouse and position the pointer on the note reference mark in the document text, the note text is displayed above the note reference mark as a ScreenTip. To remove the ScreenTip, move the pointer.

If, for some reason, you wanted to change the format of note reference marks in footnotes or endnotes (i.e., from 1, 2, 3, to A, B, C), you would tap or click the Footnote & Endnote Dialog Box Launcher (REFERENCES tab | Footnotes group) to display the Footnote and Endnote dialog box, tap or click the Number format arrow (Footnote and Endnote dialog box), tap or click the desired number format in the list, and then tap or click the Apply button.

If, for some reason, you wanted to change a footnote number, you would tap or click the Footnote & Endnote Dialog Box Launcher (REFERENCES tab | Footnotes group) to display the Footnote and Endnote dialog box, enter the desired number in the Start at box, and then tap or click the Apply button (Footnote and Endnote dialog box).

If, for some reason, you wanted to convert footnotes to endnotes, you would tap or click the Footnote & Endnote Dialog Box Launcher (REFERENCES tab | Footnotes group) to display the Footnote and Endnote dialog box, tap or click the

BTW
Footnote and Endnote Location
You can change the location of footnotes from the bottom of the page to the end of the text by tapping or clicking the Footnote & Endnote Dialog Box Launcher (REFERENCES tab | Footnotes group), tapping or clicking the Footnotes arrow (Footnote and Endnote dialog box), and then tapping or clicking Below text. Similarly, tapping or clicking the Endnotes arrow (Footnote and Endnote dialog box) enables you to change the location of endnotes from the end of the document to the end of a section.

Convert button (Footnote and Endnote dialog box), select the 'Convert all footnotes to endnotes' option button, tap or click the OK button, and then tap or click the Close button (Footnote and Endnote dialog box).

To Enter More Text

The next task is to continue typing text in the body of the research paper. The following steps enter this text.

1 Position the insertion point after the note reference mark in the document and then press the ENTER key.

2 Type the first three sentences in the third paragraph of the research paper (shown in Figure 2–50): `A face recognition system captures a live face image and compares it with a stored image to determine if the person is a legitimate user. Some buildings use face recognition systems to secure access to rooms. Law enforcement, surveillance systems, and airports use face recognition systems to protect the public.`

1 CHANGE DOCUMENT SETTINGS | 2 CREATE HEADER | **3 TYPE RESEARCH PAPER WITH CITATIONS**
4 CREATE ALPHABETICAL WORKS CITED | 5 PROOFREAD & REVISE RESEARCH PAPER

To Count Words

Often when you write papers, you are required to compose the papers with a minimum number of words. The minimum requirement for the research paper in this chapter is 275 words. You can look on the status bar and see the total number of words thus far in a document. For example, Figure 2–50 shows the research paper has 214 words, but you are not sure if that count includes the words in your footnote. The following steps display the Word Count dialog box. ***Why?*** *You want to verify that the footnote text is included in the count.*

1
- Tap or click the Word Count indicator on the status bar to display the Word Count dialog box.
- If necessary, place a check mark in the 'Include textboxes, footnotes and endnotes' check box (Word Count dialog box) (Figure 2–50).

Q&A Why do the statistics in my Word Count dialog box differ from those in Figure 2–50?
Depending on the accuracy of your typing, your statistics may differ.

Figure 2–50

• Tap or click the Close button to close the dialog box.

Q&A Can I display statistics for just a section of the document?
Yes. Select the section and then click the Word Count indicator on the status bar to display statistics about the selected text.

Other Ways

1. Tap or click Word Count button (REVIEW tab | Proofing group) 2. Press CTRL+SHIFT+G

Automatic Page Breaks

As you type documents that exceed one page, Word automatically inserts page breaks, called **automatic page breaks** or **soft page breaks**, when it determines the text has filled one page according to paper size, margin settings, line spacing, and other settings. If you add text, delete text, or modify text on a page, Word recalculates the location of automatic page breaks and adjusts them accordingly.

Word performs page recalculation between the keystrokes, that is, in between the pauses in your typing. Thus, Word refers to the automatic page break task as **background repagination**. An automatic page break will occur in the next set of steps.

To Enter More Text and Insert a Citation Placeholder

The next task is to type the remainder of the third paragraph in the body of the research paper. The following steps enter this text and a citation placeholder at the end of the paragraph.

1 With the insertion point positioned at the end of the third sentence in the third paragraph, as shown in Figure 2–50, press the SPACEBAR.

2 Type the rest of the third paragraph: `Some mobile devices use face recognition systems to unlock the device. Face recognition systems are becoming more sophisticated and can recognize people with or without glasses, hats, facial hair, makeup, or jewelry, and with new hairstyles` and then press the SPACEBAR.

Q&A Why does the text move from the second page to the first page as I am typing?
Word, by default, will not allow the first line of a paragraph to be by itself at the bottom of a page (an **orphan**) or the last line of a paragraph to be by itself at the top of a page (a **widow**). As you type, Word adjusts the placement of the paragraph to avoid orphans and widows.

3 Tap or click the Insert Citation button (REFERENCES tab | Citations & Bibliography group) to display the Insert Citation menu. Tap or click 'Add New Placeholder' on the Insert Citation menu to display the Placeholder Name dialog box.

4 Type `Allensmith` as the tag name for the source.

5 Tap or click the OK button to close the dialog box and insert the tag name in the citation placeholder.

6 Press the PERIOD key to end the sentence.

BTW
Page Break Locations
As you type, your page break may occur at different locations depending on Word settings and the type of printer connected to the computer.

To Hide and Show White Space

With the page break and header, it is difficult to see the entire third paragraph at once on the screen. With the screen in Print Layout view, you can hide white space, which is the space that is displayed at the top and bottom of pages (including headers and footers) and also the space between pages. The following steps hide white space, if your screen displays it, and then shows white space. *Why? You want to see the as much of the third paragraph as possible at once, which spans the bottom of the first page and the top of the second page.*

1

- If you are using a mouse, position the pointer in the document window in the space between pages so that the pointer changes to a 'Hide White Space' button (Figure 2–51).

2

- If you are using a touch screen, double-tap in the space between pages; if you are using a mouse, double-click while the pointer is a 'Hide White Space' button to hide white space.

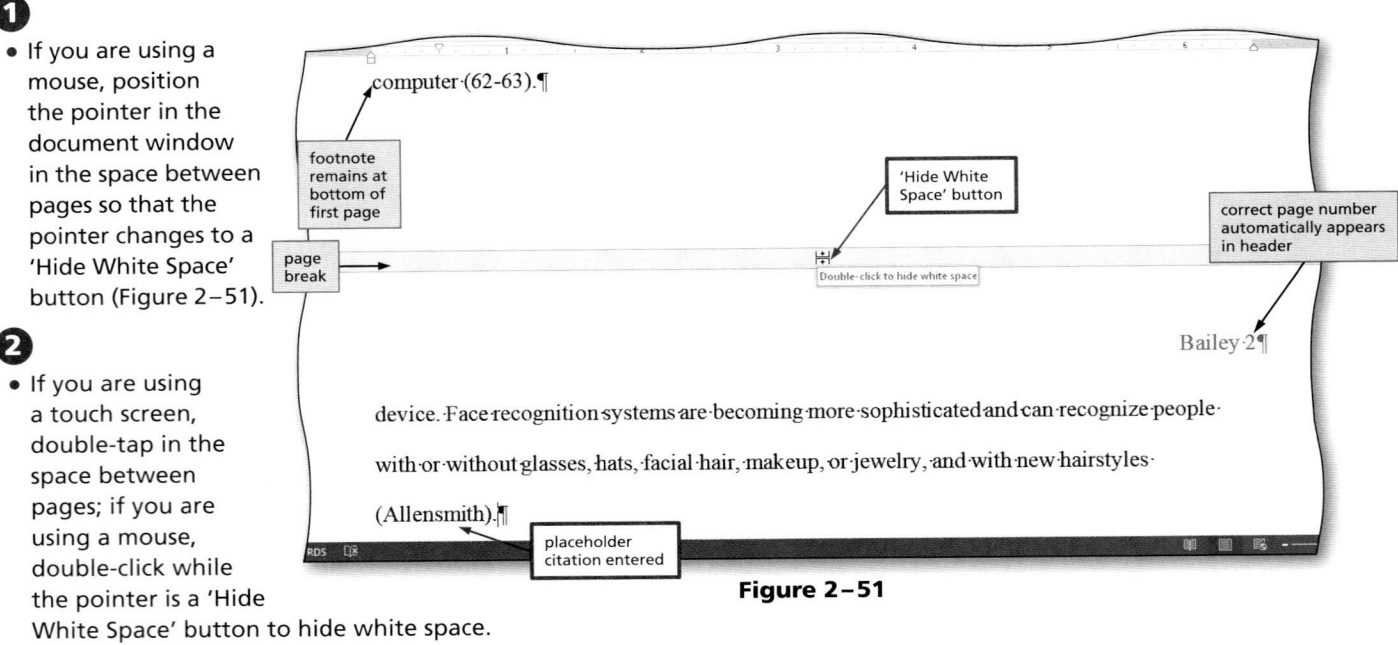

Figure 2–51

Q&A Does hiding white space have any effect on the printed document?
No.

3

- If you are using a mouse, position the pointer in the document window on the page break between pages so that the pointer changes to a 'Show White Space' button (Figure 2–52).

4

- If you are using a touch screen, double-tap the page break; if you are using a mouse, double-click while the pointer is a 'Show White Space' button to show white space.

Figure 2–52

Other Ways

1. Tap or click FILE on ribbon, tap or click Options in Backstage view, tap or click Display in left pane (Word Options dialog box), remove or select check mark from 'Show white space between pages in Print Layout view' check box, tap or click OK button

To Edit a Source

When you typed the third paragraph of the research paper, you inserted a citation placeholder, Allensmith, for the source. You now have the source information, which is for a website, and are ready to enter it. The following steps edit the source for the Allensmith citation placeholder.

1 Tap or click somewhere in the citation placeholder to be edited, in this case (Allensmith), to select the citation placeholder.

2 Tap or click the Citation Options arrow to display the Citation Options menu.

3 Tap or click Edit Source on the Citation Options menu to display the Edit Source dialog box.

4 If necessary, tap or click the Type of Source arrow (Edit Source dialog box); scroll to and then click Web site, so that the list shows fields required for a Web site.

5 Place a check mark in the 'Show All Bibliography Fields' check box to display more fields related to Web sites.

6 Tap or click the Author text box. Type **Allensmith, Samantha Clare** as the author.

7 Tap or click the Name of Web Page text box. Type **Understanding Face Recognition Systems** as the webpage name.

8 Tap or click the Production Company text box. Type **Course Technology** as the production company.

9 Tap or click the Year Accessed text box. Type **2014** as the year accessed (Figure 2–53).

10 Press the TAB key and then type **Sept.** as the month accessed.

11 Press the TAB key and then type **16** as the day accessed.

12 Press the TAB key and then type **Web** as the Medium.

Q&A Do I need to enter a web address (URL)?
The latest MLA documentation style update does not require the web address in the source.

13 Tap or click the OK button to close the dialog box and create the source.

BTW

Q&As
For a complete list of the Q&As found in many of the step-by-step sequences in this book, visit the Q&A resource on the Student Companion Site located on www.cengagebrain.com. For detailed instructions about accessing available resources, visit www.cengage.com/ct/studentdownload or contact your instructor for information about accessing the required files.

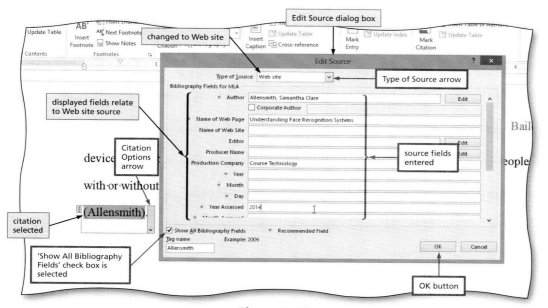

Figure 2–53

BTW
Printing Document Properties
To print document properties, tap or click FILE on the ribbon to open the Backstage view, tap or click the Print tab in the Backstage view to display the Print gallery, tap or click the first button in the Settings area to display a list of options specifying what you can print, tap or click Document Info in the list to specify you want to print the document properties instead of the actual document, and then tap or click the Print button in the Print gallery to print the document properties on the currently selected printer.

To Enter More Text

The next task is to type the last paragraph of text in the research paper. The following steps enter this text.

1 Press the END key to position the insertion point at the end of the third paragraph and then press the ENTER key.

2 Type the last paragraph of the research paper (Figure 2–54): `Home and occupational users alike are using biometric security. Through a biometric element, such as a fingerprint, devices can deny or grant access to programs, devices, computers, rooms, and other locations. Biometric devices are an effective security technology.`

Bailey 2

device. Face recognition systems are becoming more sophisticated and can recognize people with or without glasses, hats, facial hair, makeup, or jewelry, and with new hairstyles (Allensmith).¶

Home and occupational users alike are using biometric security. Through a biometric element, such as a fingerprint, devices can deny or grant access to programs, devices, computers, rooms, and other locations. Biometric devices are an effective security technology.¶

last paragraph entered

word count now meets minimum required

289 WORDS

insertion point

Figure 2–54

To Save an Existing Document with the Same File Name

You have made several modifications to the document since you last saved it. Thus, you should save it again. The following step saves the document again.

1 Tap or click the Save button on the Quick Access Toolbar to overwrite the previously saved file.

Break Point: If you wish to take a break, this is a good place to do so. You can exit Word now (refer to page WD 46 for instructions). To resume at a later time, run Word (refer to page WD 46 for instructions), open the file called Biometric Devices Paper (refer to page WD 47 for instructions), and continue following the steps from this location forward.

Creating an Alphabetical Works Cited Page

According to the MLA documentation style, the **works cited page** is a list of sources that are referenced directly in a research paper. You place the list on a separate numbered page with the title, Works Cited, centered one inch from the top margin. The works are to be alphabetized by the author's last name or, if the work has no author, by the work's title. The first line of each entry begins at the left margin. Indent subsequent lines of the same entry one-half inch from the left margin.

What is a bibliography?

A **bibliography** is an alphabetical list of sources referenced in a paper. Whereas the text of the research paper contains brief references to the source (the citations), the bibliography lists all publication information about the source. Documentation styles differ significantly in their guidelines for preparing a bibliography. Each style identifies formats for various sources, including books, magazines, pamphlets, newspapers, websites, television programs, paintings, maps, advertisements, letters, memos, and much more. You can find information about various styles and their guidelines in printed style guides and on the web.

To Page Break Manually

1 CHANGE DOCUMENT SETTINGS | 2 CREATE HEADER | 3 TYPE RESEARCH PAPER WITH CITATIONS
4 CREATE ALPHABETICAL WORKS CITED | 5 PROOFREAD & REVISE RESEARCH PAPER

The next step is to insert a manual page break following the body of the research paper. *Why? According to the MLA documentation style, the works cited are to be displayed on a separate numbered page.*

A **manual page break**, or **hard page break**, is one that you force into the document at a specific location. Word never moves or adjusts manual page breaks. Word, however, does adjust any automatic page breaks that follow a manual page break. Word inserts manual page breaks immediately above or to the left of the location of the insertion point. The following step inserts a manual page break after the text of the research paper.

- Verify that the insertion point is positioned at the end of the text of the research paper, as shown in Figure 2–54.

- Tap or click INSERT on the ribbon to display the INSERT tab.

- Tap or click the 'Insert a Page Break' button (INSERT tab | Pages group) to insert a manual page break immediately to the left of the insertion point and position the insertion point immediately below the manual page break (Figure 2–55).

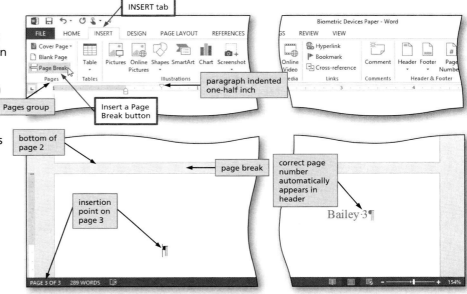

Figure 2–55

Other Ways

1. Press CTRL+ENTER

To Apply a Style

1 CHANGE DOCUMENT SETTINGS | 2 CREATE HEADER | 3 TYPE RESEARCH PAPER WITH CITATIONS
4 CREATE ALPHABETICAL WORKS CITED | 5 PROOFREAD & REVISE RESEARCH PAPER

The works cited title is to be centered between the margins of the paper. If you simply issue the Center command, the title will not be centered properly. *Why? It will be to the right of the center point because earlier you set the first-line indent for paragraphs to one-half inch.*

To properly center the title of the works cited page, you could drag the 'First Line Indent' marker back to the left margin before centering the paragraph, or you could apply the Normal style to the location of the insertion point. Recall that you modified the Normal style for this document to 12-point Times New Roman with double-spaced, left-aligned paragraphs that have no space after the paragraphs.

To apply a style to a paragraph, first position the insertion point in the paragraph and then apply the style. The step on the next page applies the modified Normal style to the location of the insertion point.

- Tap or click HOME on the ribbon to display the HOME tab.
- With the insertion point on the paragraph mark at the top of page 3 (as shown in Figure 2–55 on the previous page) even if Normal is selected, tap or click Normal in the Styles gallery (HOME tab | Styles group) to apply the Normal style to the paragraph containing the insertion point (Figure 2–56).

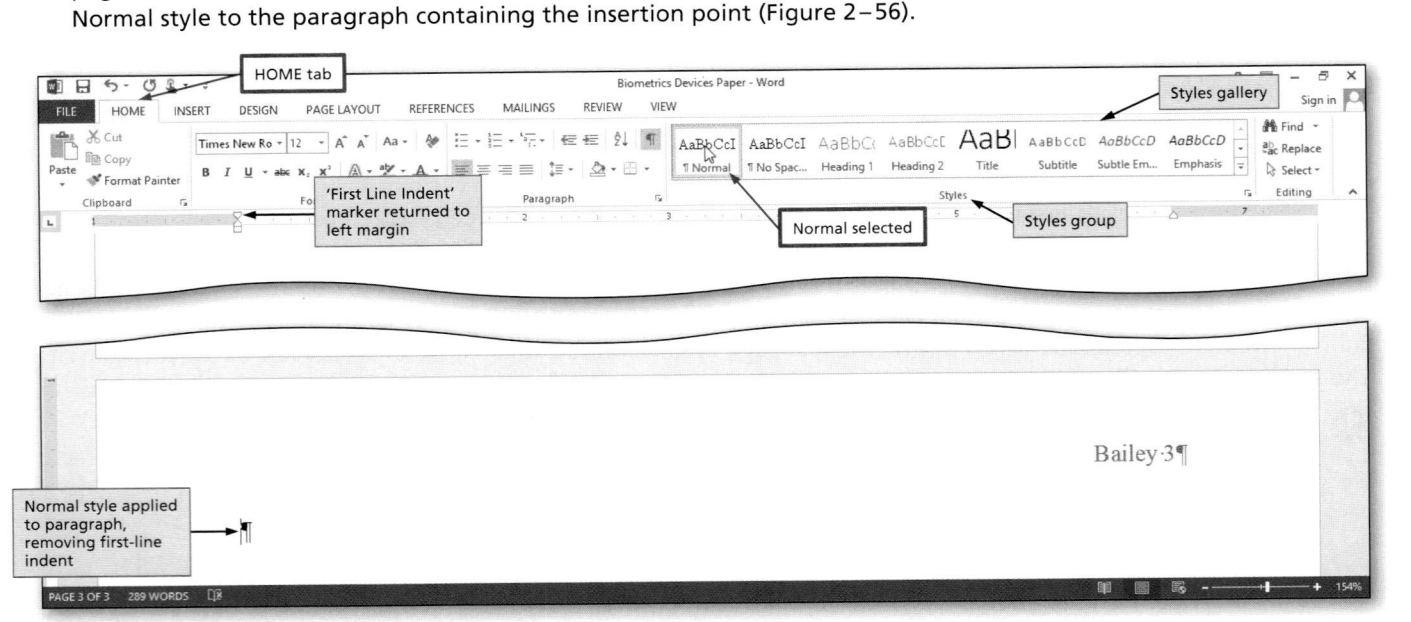

Figure 2–56

Other Ways

1. Tap or click Styles Dialog Box Launcher (HOME tab | Styles group), select desired style in Styles task pane

2. Press CTRL+SHIFT+S, tap or click Style Name arrow in Apply Styles task pane, select desired style in list

To Center Text

The next task is to enter the title, Works Cited, centered between the margins of the paper. The following steps use a keyboard shortcut to format the title.

1 Press CTRL+E to center the paragraph mark.

2 Type **Works Cited** as the title.

3 Press the ENTER key.

4 Press CTRL+L to left-align the paragraph mark (shown in Figure 2–57).

To Create a Bibliographical List

1 CHANGE DOCUMENT SETTINGS | 2 CREATE HEADER | 3 TYPE RESEARCH PAPER WITH CITATIONS
4 CREATE ALPHABETICAL WORKS CITED | **5 PROOFREAD & REVISE RESEARCH PAPER**

While typing the research paper, you created several citations and their sources. The next task is to use Word to format the list of sources and alphabetize them in a **bibliographical list**. *Why? Word can create a bibliographical list with each element of the source placed in its correct position with proper punctuation, according to the specified style, saving you time looking up style guidelines. For example, in this research paper, the book source will list, in this order, the author name(s), book title, publisher city, publishing company name, and publication year with the correct punctuation between each element according to the MLA documentation style.* The next steps create an MLA-styled bibliographical list from the sources previously entered.

1

- Tap or click REFERENCES on the ribbon to display the References tab.

- With the insertion point positioned as shown in Figure 2–56, tap or click the Bibliography button (REFERENCES tab | Citations & Bibliography group) to display the Bibliography gallery (Figure 2–57).

Will I select the Works Cited option from the Bibliography gallery? No. The title it inserts is not formatted according to the MLA documentation style. Thus, you will use the Insert Bibliography command instead.

Figure 2–57

2

- Tap or click Insert Bibliography in the Bibliography gallery to insert a list of sources at the location of the insertion point.

- If necessary, scroll to display the entire list of sources in the document window (Figure 2–58).

What is the n.d. in the first work? The MLA documentation style uses the abbreviation n.d. for no date (for example, no date appears on the webpage).

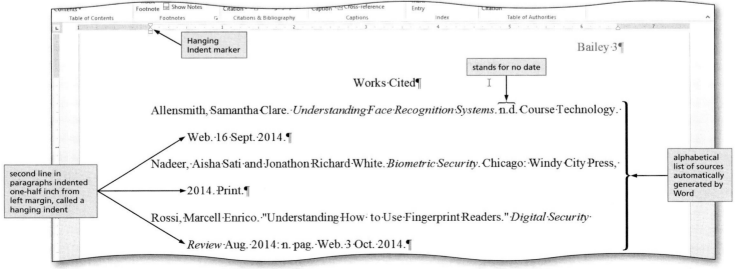

Figure 2–58

To Format Paragraphs with a Hanging Indent

Notice in Figure 2–58 on the previous page that the first line of each source entry begins at the left margin, and subsequent lines in the same paragraph are indented one-half inch from the left margin. In essence, the first line hangs to the left of the rest of the paragraph; thus, this type of paragraph formatting is called a **hanging indent**. The Bibliography style in Word automatically formats the works cited paragraphs with a hanging indent.

If you wanted to format paragraphs with a hanging indent, you would use one of the following techniques.

- With the insertion point in the paragraph to format, drag the **Hanging Indent marker** (the bottom triangle) on the ruler to the desired mark on the ruler (i.e., .5") to set the hanging indent at that location from the left margin.

or

- Tap the 'Show Context Menu' button on the mini toolbar or right-click the paragraph to format, tap or click Paragraph on shortcut menu, tap or click the Indents and Spacing tab (Paragraph dialog box), tap or click the Special arrow, tap or click Hanging, and then tap or click the OK button.

or

- Tap or click the Paragraph Dialog Box Launcher (HOME tab or PAGE LAYOUT tab | Paragraph group), tap or click the Indents and Spacing tab (Paragraph dialog box), tap or click the Special arrow, tap or click Hanging, and then tap or click the OK button.

or

- With the insertion point in the paragraph to format, press CTRL+T.

To Save an Existing Document with the Same File Name

You have made several modifications to the document since you last saved it. Thus, you should save it again. The following step saves the document again. For an example of the step listed below, refer to the Office and Windows chapter at the beginning of this book.

1 Tap or click the Save button on the Quick Access Toolbar to overwrite the previously saved file.

Proofreading and Revising the Research Paper

As discussed in Chapter 1, once you complete a document, you might find it necessary to make changes to it. Before submitting a paper to be graded, you should proofread it. While **proofreading**, ensure all the source information is correct and look for grammatical errors and spelling errors. Also ensure that transitions between sentences flow smoothly and the sentences themselves make sense.

To assist you with the proofreading effort, Word provides several tools. You can go to a page, copy text, find text, replace text, insert a synonym, check spelling and grammar, and look up information. The following pages discuss these tools.

BTW
Certification
The Microsoft Office Specialist (MOS) program provides an opportunity for you to obtain a valuable industry credential — proof that you have the Word 2013 skills required by employers. For more information, visit the Certification resource on the Student Companion Site located on www.cengagebrain.com. For detailed instructions about accessing available resources, visit www.cengage.com/ct/studentdownload or contact your instructor for information about accessing the required files.

What should you consider when proofreading and revising a paper?

As you proofread the paper, look for ways to improve it. Check all grammar, spelling, and punctuation. Be sure the text is logical and transitions are smooth. Where necessary, add text, delete text, reword text, and move text to different locations. Ask yourself these questions:

- Does the title suggest the topic?

- Is the thesis clear?

- Is the purpose of the paper clear?

- Does the paper have an introduction, body, and conclusion?

- Does each paragraph in the body relate to the thesis?

- Is the conclusion effective?

- Are sources acknowledged correctly?

- Are all sources acknowledged?

To Modify a Source

1 CHANGE DOCUMENT SETTINGS | 2 CREATE HEADER | 3 TYPE RESEARCH PAPER WITH CITATIONS
4 CREATE ALPHABETICAL WORKS CITED | **5 PROOFREAD & REVISE RESEARCH PAPER**

While proofreading the paper, you notice an error in the magazine title; specifically, the first word (Understanding) should be removed. If you modify the contents of any source, the list of sources automatically updates. ***Why?*** *Word automatically updates the contents of fields, and the bibliography is a field.* The following steps delete a word from the title of the magazine article.

- Tap or click the Manage Sources button (REFERENCES tab | Citations & Bibliography group) to display the Source Manager dialog box.

- Tap or click the source you wish to edit in the Current List, in this case the article by Rossi, to select the source.

- Tap or click the Edit button (Source Manager dialog box) to display the Edit Source dialog box.

- In the Title text box, delete the word, Understanding, from the beginning of the title (Figure 2–59).

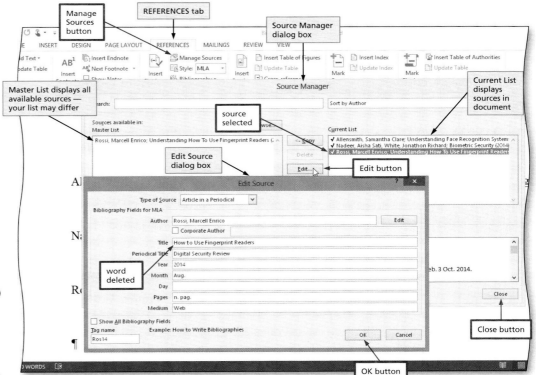

Figure 2–59

2

- Tap or click the OK button (Edit Source dialog box) to close the dialog box.

- If a Microsoft Word dialog box appears, tap or click its Yes button to update all occurrences of the source.

- Tap or click the Close button (Source Manager dialog box) to update the list of sources and close the dialog box.

To Update a Field

Depending on settings, the bibliography field may not automatically reflect the edited magazine title. Thus, the following steps update the bibliography field. **Why?** *Because the bibliography is a field, you may need to instruct Word to update its contents.*

1

- If you are using a touch screen, press and hold anywhere in the bibliography text and then tap the 'Show Context Menu' button on the mini toolbar; if you are using a mouse, right-click anywhere in the bibliography text to display a shortcut menu related to fields (Figure 2–60).

Q&A Why are all the words in the bibliography shaded gray?
By default, Word shades selected fields gray.

What if the bibliography field is not shaded gray?
Tap or click FILE on the ribbon to open the Backstage view, tap or click Options in the Backstage view, tap or click Advanced in the left pane (Word Options dialog box), scroll to the 'Show document content' area, tap or click the Field shading arrow, tap or click When selected, and then tap or click the OK button.

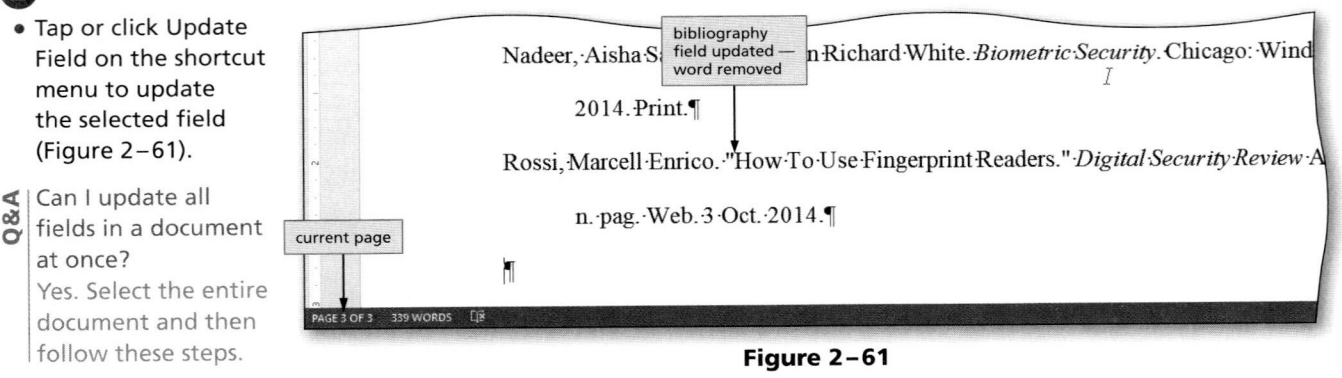

Figure 2–60

2

- Tap or click Update Field on the shortcut menu to update the selected field (Figure 2–61).

Q&A Can I update all fields in a document at once?
Yes. Select the entire document and then follow these steps.

Nadeer, Aisha S. [bibliography field updated — word removed] n Richard White. *Biometric Security.* Chicago: Wind
2014. Print.¶

Rossi, Marcell Enrico. "How To Use Fingerprint Readers." *Digital Security Review A*

n. pag. Web. 3 Oct. 2014.¶

¶

PAGE 3 OF 3 339 WORDS

Figure 2–61

Other Ways

1. Select the field, press F9

TO CONVERT A FIELD TO REGULAR TEXT

If, for some reason, you wanted to convert a field, such as the bibliography field, to regular text, you would perform the following steps. Keep in mind, though, once you convert the field to regular text, it no longer is a field that can be updated.

1. Tap or click somewhere in the field to select it, in this case, somewhere in the bibliography.

2. Press CTRL+SHIFT+F9 to convert the selected field to regular text.

To Go to a Page

The next task in revising the paper is to modify text on the second page of the document. *Why? You want to copy text from one location to another on the second page.* You could scroll to the desired location in the document, or you can use the Navigation Pane to browse through pages in a document. The following steps display the top of the second page in the document window and position the insertion point at the beginning of that page.

- Tap or click VIEW on the ribbon to display the VIEW tab.

- Place a check mark in the 'Open the Navigation Pane' check box (VIEW tab | Show group) to open the Navigation Pane on the left side of the Word window.

- If necessary, tap or click the PAGES tab in the Navigation Pane to display thumbnails of the pages in the document.

- Scroll to and then tap or click the thumbnail of the second page to display the top of the selected page in the top of the document window (Figure 2–62).

Q&A What is the Navigation Pane?
The **Navigation Pane** is a window that enables you to browse through headings in a document, browse through pages in a document, or search for text in a document.

Figure 2–62

- Tap or click the Close button in the Navigation Pane to close the pane.

Other Ways

1. Tap or click Find arrow (HOME tab | Editing group), tap or click Go To on Find menu, tap or click Go To tab (Find and Replace dialog box), enter page number, tap or click Go To button

2. Tap or click Page Number indicator on status bar, tap or click PAGES tab in Navigation Pane, tap or click thumbnail of desired page (Navigation Pane)

3. Press CTRL+G, enter page number, tap or click Go To button

Copying, Cutting, and Pasting

While proofreading the research paper, you decide it would read better if the word, biometric, in the second sentence of the last paragraph also appeared in front of the word, devices, in the same sentence. You could type the word at the desired location, but because this is a difficult word to spell and type, you decide to use the Office Clipboard. The **Office Clipboard** is a temporary storage area that holds up to 24 items (text or graphics) copied from any Office program. The Office Clipboard works with the copy, cut, and paste commands:

- **Copying** is the process of placing items on the Office Clipboard, leaving the item in the document.

- **Cutting** removes the item from the document before placing it on the Office Clipboard.

- **Pasting** is the process of copying an item from the Office Clipboard into the document at the location of the insertion point.

BTW

Quick Reference
For a table that lists how to complete the tasks covered in this book using touch gestures, the mouse, ribbon, shortcut menu, and keyboard, see the Quick Reference Summary at the back of this book, or visit the Quick Reference resource on the Student Companion Site located on www.cengagebrain .com. For detailed instructions about accessing available resources, visit www.cengage.com/ct/ studentdownload or contact your instructor for information about accessing the required files.

To Copy and Paste

In the research paper, you copy a word from one location to another. *Why? The sentence reads better with the word, biometric, inserted before the word, devices.* The following steps copy and paste a word.

1
- Select the item to be copied (the word, biometric, in this case).
- Tap or click HOME on the ribbon to display the HOME tab.
- Tap or click the Copy button (HOME tab | Clipboard group) to copy the selected item in the document to the Office Clipboard (Figure 2–63).

2
- Position the insertion point at the location where the item should be pasted (immediately to the left of the word, devices, in this case) (Figure 2–64).

3
- Tap or click the Paste button (HOME tab | Clipboard group) to paste the copied item in the document at the location of the insertion point (Figure 2–65).

Q&A
What if I click the Paste arrow by mistake?
Click the Paste arrow again to remove the Paste menu and repeat Step 3.

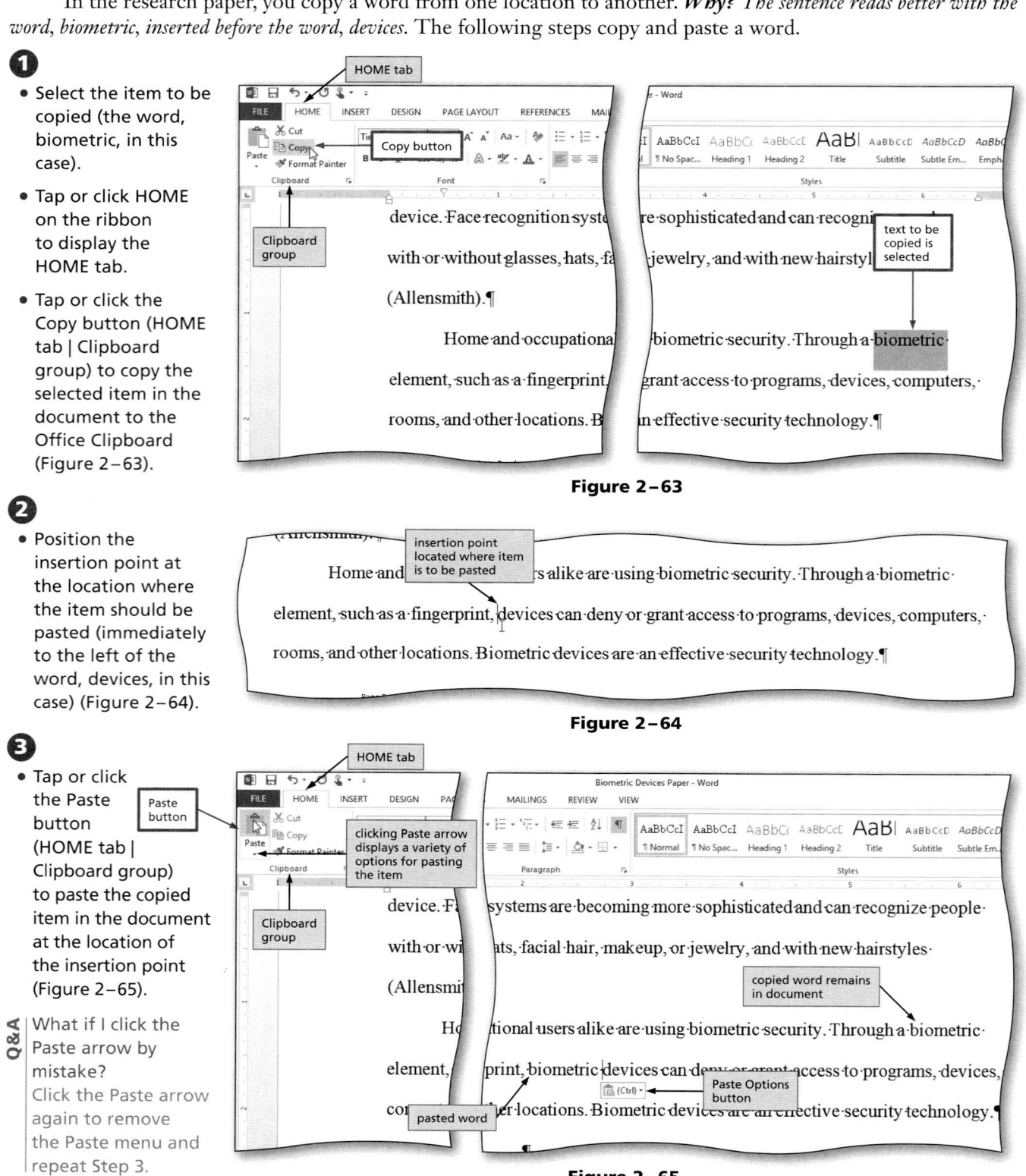

Figure 2–63

Figure 2–64

Figure 2–65

Other Ways

1. Press and hold or right-click selected item, tap Copy on mini toolbar or click Copy on shortcut menu, press and hold or right-click where item is to be pasted, tap Paste on mini toolbar or click Keep Source Formatting in Paste Options area on shortcut menu

2. Select item, press CTRL+C, position insertion point at paste location, press CTRL+V

To Display the Paste Options Menu

When you paste an item or move an item using drag-and-drop editing, which was discussed in the previous chapter, Word automatically displays a Paste Options button near the pasted or moved text (Figure 2–65). *Why?* *The Paste Options button allows you to change the format of a pasted item. For example, you can instruct Word to format the pasted item the same way as where it was copied (the source), or format it the same way as where it is being pasted (the destination).* The following steps display the Paste Options menu.

- Tap or click the Paste Options button to display the Paste Options menu (Figure 2–66).

Q&A

What are the functions of the buttons on the Paste Options menu?
In general, the left button indicates the pasted item should look the same as it did in its original location (the source). The second button formats the pasted text to match the rest of the item where it was pasted (the destination). The third button removes all formatting from the pasted item. The Set Default Paste command displays the Word Options dialog box. Keep in mind that the buttons shown on a Paste Options menu will vary, depending on the item being pasted.

Figure 2–66

- Tap or click anywhere to remove the Paste Options menu from the window.

Other Ways

1. CTRL (to remove the Paste Options menu)

To Find Text

While proofreading the paper, you would like to locate all occurrences of the word, element. *Why?* *You are contemplating changing occurrences of this word to the word, identifier.* The following steps find all occurrences of specific text in a document.

- If you are using a touch screen, tap the Find button (HOME tab | Editing group) and then tap Find on the menu; if you are using a mouse, click the Find button (HOME tab | Editing group) to display the Navigation Pane.

- If necessary, tap or click the RESULTS tab in the Navigation Pane, which displays a Search box where you can type text for which you want to search (Figure 2–67).

Figure 2–67

2

- Type **element** in the Navigation Pane Search box to display all occurrences of the typed text, called the search text, in the Navigation Pane and to highlight the occurrences of the search text in the document window (Figure 2–68).

3

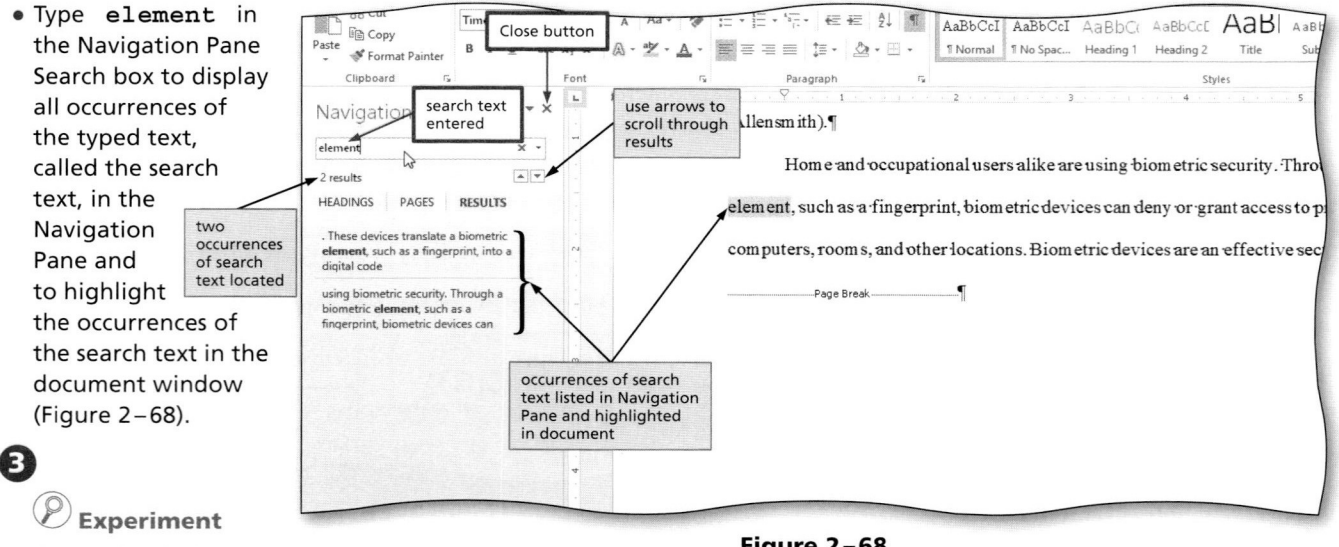

Experiment

- Tap or click both occurrences in the Navigation Pane and watch Word display the associated text in the document window.

- Type various search text in the Navigation Pane Search box, and watch Word both list matches in the Navigation Pane and highlight matches in the document window.

- Tap or click the Close button in the Navigation Pane to close the pane.

Figure 2–68

Other Ways

1. Tap or click Find arrow (HOME tab | Editing group), tap or click Find on Find menu, enter search text in Navigation Pane

2. Tap or click Page Number indicator on status bar, enter search text in Navigation Pane

3. Press CTRL+F, enter search text in Navigation Pane

To Replace Text

1 CHANGE DOCUMENT SETTINGS | 2 CREATE HEADER | 3 TYPE RESEARCH PAPER WITH CITATIONS
4 CREATE ALPHABETICAL WORKS CITED | 5 PROOFREAD & REVISE RESEARCH PAPER

You decide to change all occurrences of element to identifier. *Why? The text, biometric identifier, is a better description than biometric element.* Word's find and replace feature locates each occurrence of a word or phrase and then replaces it with text you specify. The following steps find and replace text.

1

- Tap or click the Replace button (HOME tab | Editing group) to display the Replace sheet in the Find and Replace dialog box.

- If necessary, type **element** in the Find what box (Find and Replace dialog box).

- Type **identifier** in the Replace with box (Figure 2–69).

Figure 2–69

2

- Tap or click the Replace All button to instruct Word to replace all occurrences of the Find what text with the Replace with text (Figure 2–70). If Word displays a dialog box asking if you want to continue searching from the beginning of the document, tap or click the Yes button.

Q&A Does Word search the entire document?
If the insertion point is at the beginning of the document, Word searches the entire document; otherwise, Word searches from the location of the insertion point to the end of the document and then displays a dialog box asking if you want to continue searching from the beginning. You also can search a section of text by selecting the text before tapping or clicking the Replace button.

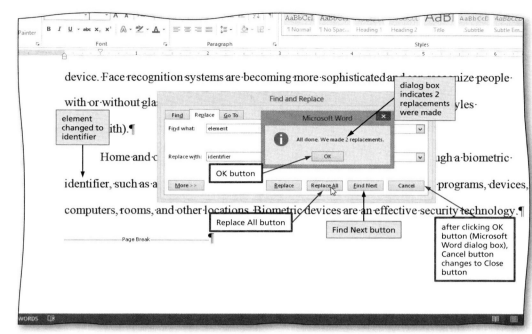

Figure 2–70

3

- Tap or click the OK button (Microsoft Word dialog box) to close the dialog box.
- Tap or click the Close button (Find and Replace dialog box) to close the dialog box.

Other Ways

1. Press CTRL+H

Find and Replace Dialog Box

The Replace All button (Find and Replace dialog box) replaces all occurrences of the Find what text with the Replace with text. In some cases, you may want to replace only certain occurrences of a word or phrase, not all of them. To instruct Word to confirm each change, tap or click the Find Next button (Find and Replace dialog box) (Figure 2–70), instead of the Replace All button. When Word locates an occurrence of the text, it pauses and waits for you to tap or click either the Replace button or the Find Next button. Tapping or clicking the Replace button changes the text; tapping or clicking the Find Next button instructs Word to disregard the replacement and look for the next occurrence of the Find what text.

If you accidentally replace the wrong text, you can undo a replacement by tapping or clicking the Undo button on the Quick Access Toolbar. If you used the Replace All button, Word undoes all replacements. If you used the Replace button, Word undoes only the most recent replacement.

BTW

Finding Formatting
To search for formatting or a special character, tap or click the More button in the Find and Replace dialog box (shown in Figure 2–69). To find formatting, use the Format button in the Find dialog box. To find a special character, use the Special button.

To Find and Insert a Synonym

In this project, you would like a synonym for the word, occupational, in the fourth paragraph of the research paper. **Why?** *When writing, you may discover that you used the same word in multiple locations or that a word you used was not quite appropriate, which is the case here.* In these instances, you will want to look up a **synonym**, or a word similar in meaning, to the duplicate or inappropriate word. A **thesaurus** is a book of synonyms. Word provides synonyms and a thesaurus for your convenience. The following steps find a suitable synonym.

❶

- If you are using a touch screen, press and hold the word for which you want a synonym and then tap the 'Show Context Menu' button on the mini toolbar; if you are using a mouse, right-click the word for which you want to find a synonym (in this case, occupational) to display a shortcut menu.

- Tap or point to Synonyms on the shortcut menu to display a list of synonyms for the word you right-clicked (Figure 2–71).

Figure 2–71

❷

- Tap or click the synonym you want (in this case, business) on the Synonyms submenu to replace the selected word in the document with the selected synonym (Figure 2–72).

Q&A

What if the synonyms list on the shortcut menu does not display a suitable word?

You can display the thesaurus in the Thesaurus task pane by tapping or clicking Thesaurus on the Synonyms submenu. The Thesaurus task pane displays a complete thesaurus, in which you can look up synonyms for various meanings of a word. You also can look up an **antonym,** or word with an opposite meaning.

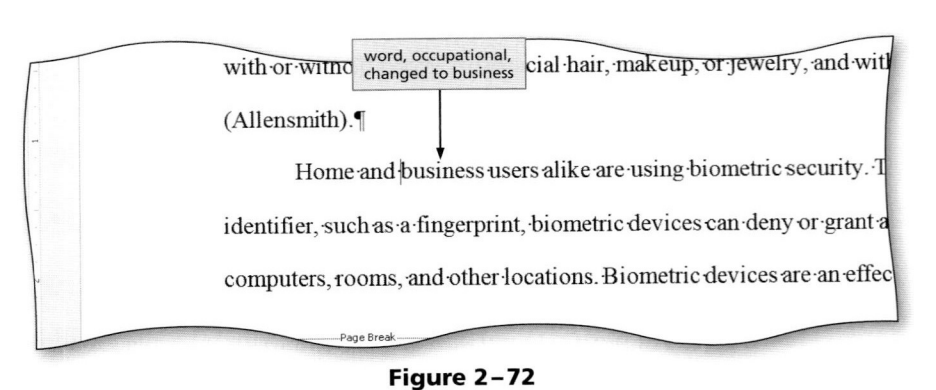

Figure 2–72

Other Ways

1. Click Thesaurus button (REVIEW tab | Proofing group) 2. Press SHIFT+F7

To Check Spelling and Grammar at Once

As discussed in Chapter 1, Word checks spelling and grammar as you type and places a wavy underline below possible spelling or grammar errors. Chapter 1 illustrated how to check these flagged words immediately. The next steps check spelling and grammar at once. **Why?** *Some users prefer to wait and check their entire document for spelling and grammar errors at once.*

Note: In the following steps, the word, readers, has been misspelled intentionally as raders to illustrate the use of Word's check spelling and grammar at once feature. If you are completing this project on a personal computer, your research paper may contain different misspelled words, depending on the accuracy of your typing.

- Press CTRL+HOME because you want the spelling and grammar check to begin from the top of the document.

- Tap or click REVIEW on the ribbon to display the REVIEW tab.

- Tap or click the Spelling & Grammar button (REVIEW tab | Proofing group) to begin the spelling and grammar check at the location of the insertion point, which, in this case, is at the beginning of the document.

- Tap or click the desired word in the list of suggestions in the Spelling pane (readers, in this case) (Figure 2–73).

Figure 2–73

- With the word, reader, selected in the list of suggestions, tap or click the Change button (Spelling task pane) to change the flagged word to the selected suggestion and then continue the spelling and grammar check until the next error is identified or the end of the document is reached (Figure 2–74).

- Because the flagged word is a proper noun and spelled correctly, tap or click the Ignore All button (Spelling task pane) to ignore this and future occurrences of the flagged proper noun and then continue the spelling and grammar check until the next error is identified or the end of the document is reached.

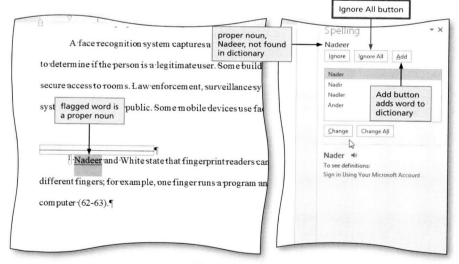

Figure 2–74

❹

- When the spelling and grammar check is finished and Word displays a dialog box, tap or click its OK button.

Q&A Can I check spelling of just a section of a document?
Yes, select the text before starting the spelling and grammar check.

Other Ways

1. Tap or click 'Spelling and Grammar Check' icon on status bar 2. Press F7

BTW
Readability Statistics
You can instruct Word to display readability statistics when it has finished a spelling and grammar check on a document. Three readability statistics presented are the percent of passive sentences, the Flesch Reading Ease score, and the Flesch-Kincaid Grade Level score. The Flesch Reading Ease score uses a 100-point scale to rate the ease with which a reader can understand the text in a document. A higher score means the document is easier to understand. The Flesch-Kincaid Grade Level score rates the text in a document on a U.S. school grade level. For example, a score of 10.0 indicates a student in the tenth grade can understand the material. To show readability statistics when the spelling check is complete, open the Backstage view, tap or click Options in the Backstage view, tap or click Proofing in the left pane (Word Options dialog box), place a check mark in the 'Show readability statistics' check box, and then click the OK button. Readability statistics will be displayed the next time you check spelling and grammar at once in the document.

The Main and Custom Dictionaries

As shown in the previous steps, Word may flag a proper noun as an error because the proper noun is not in its main dictionary. To prevent Word from flagging proper nouns as errors, you can add the proper nouns to the custom dictionary. To add a correctly spelled word to the custom dictionary, tap or click the Add button (Spelling task pane) or press and hold and then tap 'Show Context Menu' button on mini toolbar or right-click the flagged word and then tap or click Add to Dictionary on the shortcut menu. Once you have added a word to the custom dictionary, Word no longer will flag it as an error.

TO VIEW OR MODIFY ENTRIES IN A CUSTOM DICTIONARY

To view or modify the list of words in a custom dictionary, you would follow these steps.

1. Tap or click FILE on the ribbon and then tap or click Options in the Backstage view.
2. Tap or click Proofing in the left pane (Word Options dialog box).
3. Tap or click the Custom Dictionaries button.
4. When Word displays the Custom Dictionaries dialog box, place a check mark next to the dictionary name to view or modify. Tap or click the 'Edit Word List' button (Custom Dictionaries dialog box). (In this dialog box, you can add or delete entries to and from the selected custom dictionary.)
5. When finished viewing and/or modifying the list, tap or click the OK button in the dialog box.
6. Tap or click the OK button (Custom Dictionaries dialog box).
7. If the 'Suggest from main dictionary only' check box is selected in the Word Options dialog box, remove the check mark. Tap or click the OK button (Word Options dialog box).

TO SET THE DEFAULT CUSTOM DICTIONARY

If you have multiple custom dictionaries, you can specify which one Word should use when checking spelling. To set the default custom dictionary, you would follow these steps.

1. Tap or click FILE on the ribbon and then tap or click Options in the Backstage view.
2. Tap or click Proofing in the left pane (Word Options dialog box).
3. Tap or click the Custom Dictionaries button.
4. When the Custom Dictionaries dialog box is displayed, place a check mark next to the desired dictionary name. Tap or click the Change Default button (Custom Dictionaries dialog box).
5. Tap or click the OK button (Custom Dictionaries dialog box).
6. If the 'Suggest from main dictionary only' check box is selected in the Word Options dialog box, remove the check mark. Tap or click the OK button (Word Options dialog box).

To Look Up Information

If you are signed in to your Microsoft account, you can look up a definition by tapping or clicking the Define button (REVIEW tab | Proofing group). If you are not signed in to your Microsoft account but are connected to the Internet, you can use the Research task pane to search through various forms of reference information on the web. The following steps use the Research task pane to look up a definition of a word. *Why?* *Assume you want to know more about the word, legitimate, but are not signed in to your Microsoft account.*

1

- While holding down the ALT key, tap or click the word you want to look up (in this case, legitimate) to open the Research task pane and display a dictionary entry for the ALT+clicked word (Figure 2–75). Release the ALT key.

Q&A Why does my Research task pane look different?
Depending on your settings and Microsoft's website search settings, your Research task pane may appear different from the figures shown here.

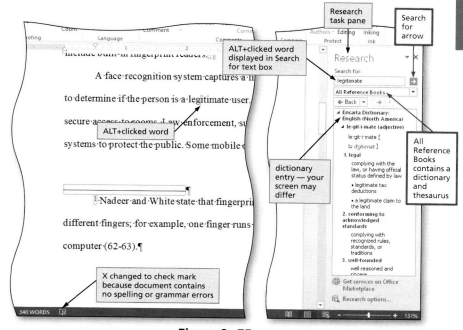

Figure 2–75

2

- Tap or click the Source arrow in the Research task pane to display a list of search locations and then tap or click 'All Research Sites' in the list (Figure 2–76).

Q&A Can I copy information from the Research task pane into my document?
Yes, you can use the Copy and Paste commands. When using Word to insert material from the Research task pane or any other online reference, however, be careful not to plagiarize.

3

- Tap or click the Close button in the Research task pane.

Figure 2–76

Other Ways

1. Press ALT+SHIFT+F7

Research Task Pane Options

When you install Word, it selects a series of services (reference books and websites) that it searches through when you use the Research task pane. You can view, modify, and update the list of services at any time.

Tapping or clicking the Research options link at the bottom of the Research task pane (shown in Figure 2–76 on the previous page) displays the Research Options dialog box, where you can view or modify the list of installed services. You can view information about any installed service by tapping or clicking the service in the list and then tapping or clicking the Properties button. To activate an installed service, tap or click the check box to its left; likewise, to deactivate a service, remove the check mark. To add a particular website to the list, tap or click the Add Services button, enter the web address in the Address text box, and then tap or click the Add button (Add Services dialog box). To update or remove services, tap or click the Update/Remove button, select the service in the list, tap or click the Update (or Remove) button (Update or Remove Services dialog box), and then tap or click the Close button. You also can install parental controls through the Parental Control button (Research Options dialog box), for example, if you want to prevent minor children who use Word from accessing the web.

BTW
Distributing a Document
Instead of printing and distributing a hard copy of a document, you can distribute the document electronically. Options include sending the document via email; saving it on cloud storage (such as SkyDrive) and sharing the file with others; posting it on a social networking site, blog, or other website; and sharing a link associated with an online location of the document. You also can create and share a PDF or XPS image of the document, so that users can view the file in Acrobat Reader or XPS Viewer instead of in Word.

To Save an Existing Document with the Same File Name

You have made several modifications to the document since you last saved it. Thus, you should save it again. The following step saves the document again. For an example of the step listed below, refer to the Office and Windows chapter at the beginning of this book.

1 Tap or click the Save button on the Quick Access Toolbar to overwrite the previously saved file.

To Zoom Multiple Pages

1 CHANGE DOCUMENT SETTINGS | 2 CREATE HEADER | 3 TYPE RESEARCH PAPER WITH CITATIONS
4 CREATE ALPHABETICAL WORKS CITED | 5 PROOFREAD & REVISE RESEARCH PAPER

The next steps display multiple pages in the document window at once. *Why? You want be able to see all pages in the research paper on the screen at the same time. You also hide formatting marks and the rulers so that the display is easier to view.*

- Tap or click HOME on the ribbon to display the HOME tab.
- If the 'Show/Hide ¶' button (HOME tab | Paragraph group) is selected, tap or click it to hide formatting marks.
- Tap or click VIEW on the ribbon to display the VIEW tab.
- If the rulers are displayed, tap or click the View Ruler check box (VIEW tab | Show group) to remove the check mark from the check box and remove the horizontal and vertical rulers from the screen.
- Tap or click the Multiple Pages button (VIEW tab | Zoom group) to display the all three pages at once in the document window (Figure 2–77).

Figure 2–77

②

- When finished, tap or click the Page Width button (VIEW tab | Zoom group) to return to the page width zoom.

To Change Read Mode Color

1 CHANGE DOCUMENT SETTINGS | 2 CREATE HEADER | 3 TYPE RESEARCH PAPER WITH CITATIONS
4 CREATE ALPHABETICAL WORKS CITED | **5 PROOFREAD & REVISE RESEARCH PAPER**

You would like to read the entire research paper using Read mode but would like to change the background color of the Read mode screen. *Why? You prefer a background that is easier on your eyes when reading on the screen.* The following steps change the color of the screen in Read mode.

①

- Tap or click the Read Mode button on the status bar to switch to Read mode.

- Tap or click the VIEW tab to display the VIEW menu.

- Tap or point to Page Color on the VIEW menu to display the Page Color menu (Figure 2–78).

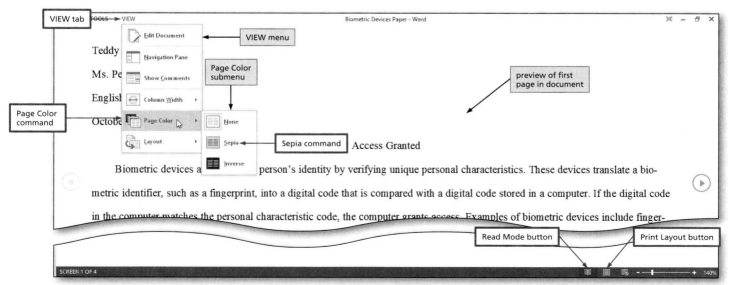

Figure 2–78

2

- Tap or click Sepia on the Page Color submenu to change the color of the Read mode screen to sepia (Figure 2–79).

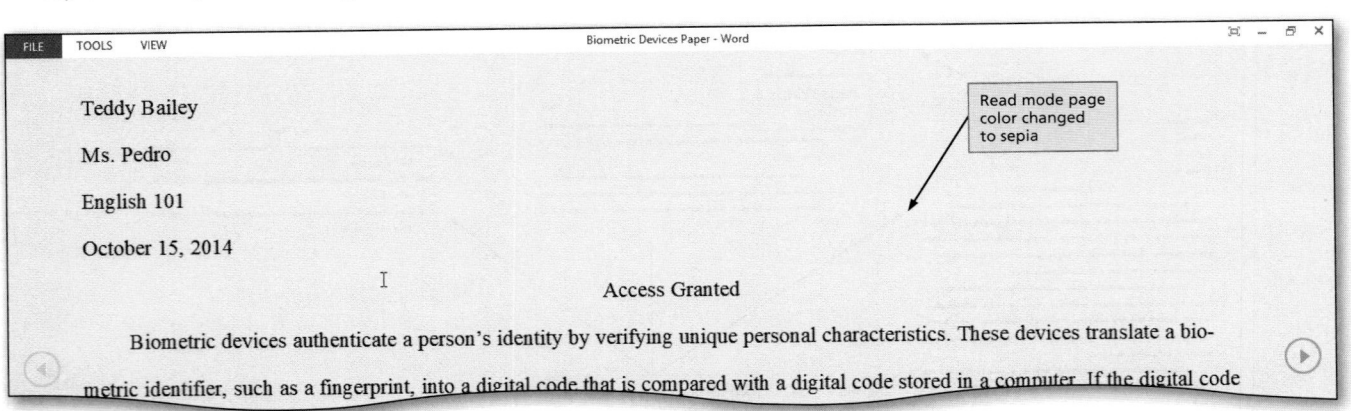

Figure 2–79

3

- When finished, tap or click the Print Layout button (shown in Figure 2–78 on the previous page) on the status bar to return to Print Layout view.

To Print a Document

If you want a hard copy of the research paper, perform the following steps.

1 Tap or click FILE on the ribbon to open the Backstage view.

2 Tap or click the Print tab in the Backstage view to display the Print gallery.

3 Verify that the printer listed on the Printer Status button will print a hard copy of the document. If necessary, tap or click the Printer Status button to display a list of available printer options and then tap or click the desired printer to change the currently selected printer.

4 Tap or click the Print button in the Print gallery to print the document on the currently selected printer.

5 When the printer stops, retrieve the hard copy (shown in Figure 2–1 on page WD 67).

To Exit Word

This project now is complete. The following steps exit Word. For a detailed example of the procedure summarized below, refer to the Office and Windows chapter at the beginning of this book.

1a If you have one Word document open, tap or click the Close button on the right side of the title bar to close the open document and exit Word.

1b If you have multiple Word documents open, press and hold or right-click the Word app button on the taskbar and then tap or click 'Close all windows' on the shortcut menu to close all open documents and exit Word.

2 If a Microsoft Word dialog box appears, tap or click the Save button to save any changes made to the document since the last save.

Chapter Summary

In this chapter, you have learned how to change document settings, use headers to number pages, modify a style, insert and edit citations and their sources, add footnotes, create a bibliographical list of sources, and use proofreading tools. The items listed below include all the new Word skills you have learned in this chapter, with the tasks grouped by activity.

Enter and Edit Text
AutoCorrect as You Type (WD 84)
Use the AutoCorrect Options Button (WD 85)
Create an AutoCorrect Entry (WD 85)
Count Words (WD 100)
Update a Field (WD 110)
Copy and Paste (WD 112)
Find Text (WD 113)
Replace Text (WD 114)
Find and Insert a Synonym (WD 115)
Check Spelling and Grammar at Once (WD 116)
View or Modify Entries in a Custom Dictionary (WD 118)
Set the Default Custom Dictionary (WD 118)

Format a Page
Switch to the Header (WD 74)
Insert a Page Number (WD 76)
Close the Header (WD 77)
Page Break Manually (WD 105)

Format Text
Modify a Style (WD 70)
Change Line Spacing (WD 72)
Remove Space after a Paragraph (WD 73)
Update a Style to Match a Selection (WD 73)

Right-Align a Paragraph (WD 75)
Click and Type (WD 79)
First-Line Indent Paragraphs (WD 82)
Modify a Style Using a Shortcut Menu (WD 94)
Apply a Style (WD 105)
Format Paragraphs with a Hanging Indent (WD 108)
Convert a Field to Regular Text (WD 110)
Display the Paste Options Menu (WD 113)

Word Settings
Display the Rulers (WD 82)
Hide and Show White Space (WD 102)
Go to a Page (WD 111)
Look Up Information (WD 119)
Zoom Multiple Pages (WD 120)
Change Read Mode Color (WD 121)

Work with Citations, Sources, and Footnotes
Change the Bibliography Style (WD 89)
Insert a Citation and Create Its Source (WD 89)
Insert a Footnote Reference Mark (WD 92)
Insert a Citation Placeholder (WD 93)
Edit a Source (WD 96)
Edit a Citation (WD 98)
Create a Bibliographical List (WD 106)
Modify a Source (WD 109)

What decisions will you need to make when creating your next research paper?
Use these guidelines as you complete the assignments in this chapter and create your own research papers outside of this class.

1. Select a topic.

 a) Spend time brainstorming ideas for a topic.

 b) Choose a topic you find interesting.

 c) For shorter papers, narrow the scope of the topic; for longer papers, broaden the scope.

 d) Identify a tentative thesis statement, which is a sentence describing the paper's subject matter.

2. Research the topic and take notes, being careful not to plagiarize.

3. Organize your notes into related concepts, identifying all main ideas and supporting details in an outline.

4. Write the first draft from the outline, referencing all sources of information and following the guidelines identified in the required documentation style.

5. Create the list of sources, using the formats specified in the required documentation style.

6. Proofread and revise the paper.

CONSIDER THIS: PLAN AHEAD

How should you submit solutions to questions in the assignments identified with a ✳ symbol?

Every assignment in this book contains one or more questions identified with a ✳ symbol. These questions require you to think beyond the assigned document. Present your solutions to the questions in the format required by your instructor. Possible formats may include one or more of these options: write the answer; create a document that contains the answer; present your answer to the class; discuss your answer in a group; record the answer as audio or video using a webcam, smartphone, or portable media player; or post answers on a blog, wiki, or website.

Apply Your Knowledge

Reinforce the skills and apply the concepts you learned in this chapter.

Revising Text and Paragraphs in a Document

Note: To complete this assignment, you will be required to use the Data Files for Students. Visit www.cengage.com/ct/studentdownload for detailed instructions or contact your instructor for information about accessing the required files.

Instructions: Run Word. Open the document, Apply 2 - 1 Virtual Reality Paragraph Draft, from the Data Files for Students. The document you open contains a paragraph of text. You are to revise the document as follows: move a word, move another word and change the format of the moved word, change paragraph indentation, change line spacing, find all occurrences of a word, replace all occurrences of a word with another word, locate a synonym, and edit the header.

Perform the following tasks:

1. Copy the text, VR, from the first sentence and paste it in the last sentence after the underlined word, potential.

2. Select the underlined word, potential, in the paragraph. If you are using a mouse, use drag-and-drop editing to move the selected word, potential, so that it is before the word, buyers, in the same sentence. If you are using a touch screen, use the cut and paste commands to move the word. Tap or click the Paste Options button that displays to the right of the moved word, potential. Remove the underline format from the moved sentence by tapping or clicking 'Keep Text Only' on the Paste Options menu.

3. Display the ruler, if necessary. If you are using a mouse, use the ruler to indent the first line of the paragraph one-half inch; otherwise, use the Paragraph dialog box.

4. Change the line spacing of the paragraph to double.

5. Use the Navigation Pane to find all occurrences of the word, VR. How many are there?

6. Use the Find and Replace dialog box to replace all occurrences of the word, 3D, with the word, 3-D. How many replacements were made?

7. Use the Navigation Pane to find the word, endless. Use Word's thesaurus to change the word, endless, to the word, infinite. What other words are in the list of synonyms?

8. Switch to the header so that you can edit it. In the first line of the header, change the word, Draft, to the word, Modified, so that it reads: VR Paragraph Modified.

9. In the second line of the header, insert the page number (with no formatting) one space after the word, Page.

10. Change the alignment of both lines of text in the header from left-aligned to right-aligned. Switch back to the document text.

11. If requested by your instructor, enter your first and last name on a separate line below the page number in the header.

12. Tap or click FILE on the ribbon and then tap or click Save As. Save the document using the file name, Apply 2 - 1 Virtual Reality Paragraph Modified.

13. Submit the modified document, shown in Figure 2–80, in the format specified by your instructor.

14. Use the Research task pane to look up the definition of the word, simulate, in the paragraph. Which dictionary was used? If you have a Microsoft account and are signed into it, use the Define button (REVIEW tab | Proofing group) to look up a definition of the word.

15. Change the search location to All Research Sites. Submit an article from one of the sites.

16. Display the Research Options dialog box. How many currently active Reference Books and Research Sites are in the list? If your instructor approves, activate one of the services.

17. ✸ Answer the questions posed in #5, #6, #7, #14, and #16. How would you find and replace a special character, such as a paragraph mark?

Figure 2–80

Extend Your Knowledge

Extend the skills you learned in this chapter and experiment with new skills. You may need to use Help to complete the assignment.

Working with References and Proofing Tools

Note: To complete this assignment, you will be required to use the Data Files for Students. Visit www.cengage.com/ct/studentdownload for detailed instructions or contact your instructor for information about accessing the required files.

Instructions: Run Word. Open the document, Extend 2 - 1 Cybercrime Paper Draft, from the Data Files for Students. You will add another footnote to the paper, convert the footnotes to endnotes, modify the Endnote Text style, change the format of the note reference marks, use Word's readability statistics, translate the document to another language (Figure 2–81 on the next page), and convert the document from MLA to APA documentation style.

Perform the following tasks:
1. Use Help to learn more about footers, footnotes and endnotes, readability statistics, bibliography styles, AutoCorrect, and the Mini Translator.

2. Delete the footer from the document.

Continued >

Extend Your Knowledge *continued*

Figure 2–81

3. Insert a second footnote at an appropriate place in the research paper. Use the following footnote text: Unscrupulous companies hire corporate spies, a practice known as corporate espionage, to gain a competitive advantage.

4. Change the location of the footnotes from bottom of page to below text. How did the placement of the footnotes change?

5. Convert the footnotes to endnotes. Where are the endnotes positioned?

6. Modify the Endnote Text style to 12-point Times New Roman font, double-spaced text with a hanging-line indent.

7. Change the format of the note reference marks to capital letters (A, B, etc.).

8. Add an AutoCorrect entry that replaces the word, perpetraters, with the word, perpetrators. Add this sentence as the last sentence in the paper, misspelling the word perpetrators to test the AutoCorrect entry: These perpetraters present a growing threat to society. Delete the AutoCorrect entry that replaces perpetraters with the word, perpetrators.

9. Display the Word Count dialog box. How many words, characters without spaces, characters with spaces, paragraphs, and lines are in the document? Be sure to include footnote and endnote text in the statistics.

10. Check spelling of the document, displaying readability statistics. What are the Flesch-Kincaid Grade Level, the Flesch Reading Ease score, and the percent of passive sentences? Modify the paper to lower the grade level, increase the reading ease score, and lower the percent of passive sentences. How did you modify the paper? What are the new statistics?

11. If requested by your instructor, change the student name at the top of the paper to your name, including the last name in the header.

12. Save the revised document with the file name, Extend 2-1 Cybercrime Paper Modified, and then submit it in the format specified by your instructor.

13. If you have an Internet connection, translate the research paper into a language of your choice using the Translate button (REVIEW tab | Language group). Submit the translated document in the format specified by your instructor. Use the Mini Translator to hear how to pronounce three words in your paper.

14. Select the entire document and then change the documentation style from MLA to APA. Save the APA version of the document with a new file name. Compare the APA version to the MLA version. If you have a hard copy of each and your instructor requests it, circle the differences between the two documents.

15. ✳ Answer the questions posed in #4, #5, #9, and #10. Where did you insert the second footnote and why?

Analyze, Correct, Improve

Analyze a document, correct all errors, and improve it.

Inserting Missing Elements in an MLA-Styled Research Paper

Note: To complete this assignment, you will be required to use the Data Files for Students. Visit www.cengage.com/ct/studentdownload for detailed instructions or contact your instructor for information about accessing the required files.

Instructions: Run Word. Open the document, Analyze 2 - 1 Internet Filters Paper Draft, from the Data Files for Students. The document is a research paper that is missing several elements. You are to insert these missing elements, all formatted according to the MLA documentation style: header with a page number, name and course information, paper title, footnote, and source information for a citation.

1. Correct In the research paper, correct the following items:

(a) Insert a header with a your own last name and page number and then type the course information (your name, your instructor's name, your course name, and today's date), and an appropriate paper title, all formatted according to the MLA documentation style.

(b) The Clark citation placeholder is missing its source information (shown in Figure 2–82 on the next page). Use the following information to edit the source: book titled *Internet Protection*, written by Addison Lee Clark, publication year is 2014, publication city is New York, publisher is Journey Press, medium is Print. Edit the citation so that it displays the author name and the page numbers of 35–37 for this reference.

(c) Modify the website author name to include his middle name: Robert Timothy Lane. Also, change the medium in this same source from Print to Web.

(d) Use the Navigation Pane to display page 2. Insert a page break before the Works Cited heading. Use Word to insert the bibliographical list (bibliography) below the Works Cited heading.

2. Improve Enhance the paper by inserting a footnote with the note reference at an appropriate place in the paper, formatted according to the MLA documentation style, that gives a statistic about spam. (You will need to do research to obtain this statistic.) Change the Footnote Text style to 12-point Times New Roman, double-spaced paragraphs with a first-line indent. Add a citation and source for your new footnote. Be sure to update the works cited page after you add the citation and source. Save the modified document with the file name, Analyze 2 - 1 Internet Filters Paper Modified, and then submit it in the format specified by your instructor.

3. ✳ In this assignment you inserted a statistic from a web source. Why did you select that website?

Continued >

Analyze, Correct, Improve *continued*

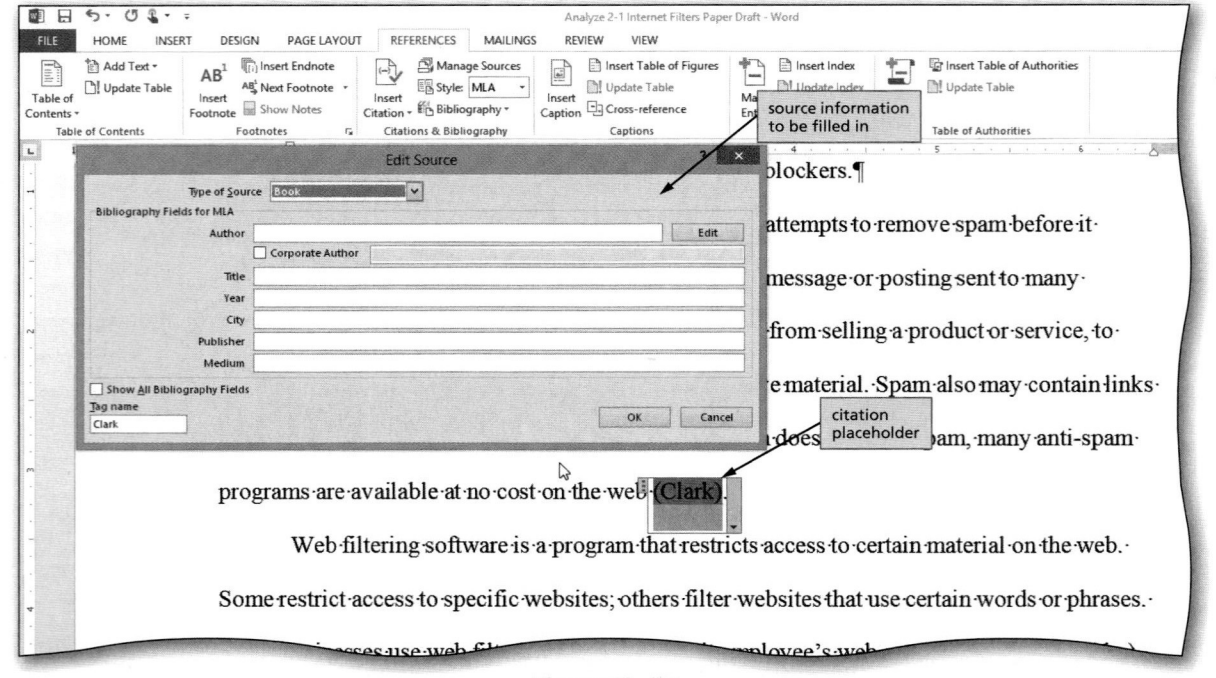

Figure 2–82

In the Labs

Design and/or create a document using the guidelines, concepts, and skills presented in this chapter. Labs 1 and 2, which increase in difficulty, require you to create solutions based on what you learned in the chapter; Lab 3 requires you to create a solution, which uses cloud and web technologies, by learning and investigating on your own from general guidance.

Lab 1: Preparing a Short Research Paper

Problem: You are a college student currently enrolled in an introductory English class. Your assignment is to prepare a short research paper (350–450 words) in any area of interest to you. The requirements are that the paper be presented according to the MLA documentation style and have three references. At least one of the three references must be from the web. You prepare the paper shown in Figure 2–83, which discusses health risks associated with technology.

Instructions: Perform the following tasks:
1. Run Word. If necessary, display formatting marks on the screen.
2. Modify the Normal style to the 12-point Times New Roman font.
3. Adjust line spacing to double.
4. Remove space below (after) paragraphs.
5. Update the Normal style to reflect the adjusted line and paragraph spacing.
6. Create a header to number pages.
7. Type the name and course information at the left margin. If requested by your instructor, use your name and course information instead of the information shown in Figure 2–83a. Center and type the title.
8. Set a first-line indent to one-half inch for paragraphs in the body of the research paper.

Delhi 1

Rajesh Delhi

Ms. June

English 102

November 9, 2014

Health Risks Associated with Technology

The widespread use of technology has led to some important user health concerns. Some of the more common physical health risks are repetitive strain injuries, computer vision syndrome, and muscular pain. These injuries are on the rise for users of technology.

A repetitive strain injury (RSI) is an injury or disorder of the muscles, nerves, tendons, ligaments, and joints. Technology-related RSIs include tendonitis and carpal tunnel syndrome (CTS). Tendonitis is inflammation of a tendon due to repeated motion or stress on that tendon. CTS is inflammation of the nerve that connects the forearm to the palm. Repeated or forceful bending of the wrist can cause tendonitis or CTS of the wrist. Factors that cause these disorders include prolonged typing or mouse usage and continual shifting between a mouse and keyboard (Jones 45-48). If untreated, these disorders can lead to permanent physical damage.

Computer vision syndrome (CVS) affects eyesight. Symptoms of CVS are sore, tired, burning, itching, or dry eyes; blurred or double vision; distance blurred vision after prolonged staring at a display device; headache or sore neck; difficulty shifting focus between a display device and documents; difficulty focusing on a screen image; color fringes or afterimages when looking away from a display device; and increased sensitivity to light. Eyestrain associated with CVS is not thought to have serious or long-term consequences (Anderson and Dean).

People who spend their workday using the computer sometimes complain of lower back pain, muscle fatigue, and emotional fatigue. Lower back pain sometimes is caused from poor

(a) Page 1

Figure 2–83

Continued >

In the Labs continued

Delhi 2

posture. It is advisable to sit properly in a chair while working and take periodic breaks. Users

also should be sure their workplace is designed ergonomically. Ergonomic studies have shown

that using the correct type and configuration of chair, keyboard, display device, and work surface

helps users work comfortably and efficiently and helps protect their health (Sanchez).

Many physical health risks are associated with using technology. These risks include

repetitive strain injuries, computer vision syndrome, and muscular pain. Users should take as

many preventive measures as possible to avoid these risks.

(b) Page 2
Figure 2–83 (Continued)

9. Type the research paper as shown in Figures 2–83a and 2–83b. Change the bibliography style to MLA. As you insert citations, enter their source information (shown in Figure 2–83c). Edit the citations so that they are displayed according to Figures 2–83a and 2–83b.

10. At the end of the research paper text, press the ENTER key and then insert a manual page break so that the Works Cited page begins on a new page. Enter and format the works cited title (Figure 2–83c). Use Word to insert the bibliographical list (bibliography).

11. Check the spelling and grammar of the paper at once.

12. Save the document using Lab 2‑1 Technology Health Risks Paper as the file name. Submit the document, shown in Figure 2–83, in the format specified by your instructor.

13. ✳ Read the paper in Print Layout view. Switch to Read mode and scroll through the pages. Do you prefer reading in Print Layout view or Read mode. Why? In Read mode, which of the page colors do you like best and why?

Delhi 3

Works Cited

Anderson, Cricket Finley and Stacey Anne Dean. "Computer Pains." *The Medical Update* Aug.

2014: n. pag. Web. 2 October 2014.

Jones, Jacob Lee. *Medical Concerns of the 21st Century*. Chicago: Smiley Incorporated, 2014.

Print.

Sanchez, Jorge Mario. *Aches and Pains*. 30 Sept. 2014. Course Technology. Web. 5 Aug. 2014.

(c) Page 3
Figure 2–83 (Continued)

Lab 2: **Preparing a Research Report with a Footnote**

Problem: You are a college student enrolled in an introductory technology class. Your assignment is to prepare a short research paper (350–450 words) in any area of interest to you. The requirements are that the paper be presented according to the MLA documentation style, contain at least one note positioned as a footnote, and have three references. At least one ne of the three references must be from the Internet. You prepare a paper about protecting mobile devices (Figure 2–84).

Instructions: Perform the following tasks:
 1. Run Word. Modify the Normal style to the 12-point Times New Roman font. Adjust line spacing to double and remove space below (after) paragraphs. Update the Normal style to include the adjusted line and paragraph spacing. Create a header to number pages. Type the name and course information at the left margin. If requested by your instructor, use your name and course information instead of the information shown in Figure 2–84a on the next page. Center and type the title. Set a first-line indent for paragraphs in the body of the research paper.

Continued >

In the Labs *continued*

Tanner 1

Camryn Tanner

Dr. Bai

Technology 101

October 16, 2014

Mobile Device Protection

 The consequences of losing a smartphone or other mobile device are significant because these devices store personal and business data. The goal, therefore, for mobile device users is to make their data as secure as possible. Techniques include avoiding unsafe links, using caution when downloading apps, turning off GPS tracking, and installing mobile security software.

 A high percentage of users follow unknown links, which can lead to a malicious website. Malicious links can inject malware on a mobile device. The malware may steal personal information or create toll fraud, which secretly contacts wireless messaging services that impose steep fees on a monthly bill (Bao). Users should avoid tapping or clicking unknown links.

 Any device that connects to the Internet is susceptible to mobile malware.[1] Popular games are likely candidates to house malware, and it often is difficult to distinguish the legitimate apps from the fake apps. Users should check the reliability of the seller, the descriptions and reviews of the app, and the requested permissions before downloading.

 GPS technology can track the mobile device's location as long as it is transmitting and receiving signals to and from satellites. Although this feature may be helpful, serious privacy concerns can arise when the technology is used in malicious ways, such as to stalk individuals or trace their whereabouts (Fields). It is best to keep this feature disabled until needed.

 [1] According to Jameson and Bennett, cyberthieves target apps on popular devices (72).

(a) Page 1

Figure 2–84

2. Type the research paper as shown in Figures 2–84a and 2–84b. Insert the footnote as shown in Figure 2–84a. Change the Footnote Text style to the format specified in the MLA documentation style. Change the bibliography style to MLA. As you insert citations, use the following source information, entering it according to the MLA style:

a. Type of Source: Article in a Periodical
 Author: He Gao Bao
 Article Title: Securing Mobile Devices
 Periodical Title: Technology Today
 Year: 2014
 Month: Sept.
 Pages: no pages used
 Medium: Web
 Year Accessed: 2014
 Month Accessed: Oct.
 Day Accessed: 1

b. Type of Source: Web site
 Author: Charlotte Fields
 Name of webpage: Secure Your Mobile Device
 Year/Month/Date: none given
 Medium: Web
 Year Accessed: 2014
 Month Accessed: Sept.
 Day Accessed: 22

c. Type of Source: Book
 Author: Lewis Taylor Jameson and Kathryn Leona Bennett
 Title: Mobile Technologies
 Year: 2014
 City: New York
 Publisher: Maxwell Press
 Medium: Print

3. At the end of the research paper text, press the ENTER key once and insert a manual page break so that the Works Cited page begins on a new page. Enter and format the works cited title. Use Word to insert the bibliographical list.

4. Check the spelling and grammar of the paper.

5. Save the document using Lab 2 - 2 Mobile Devices Protection Paper as the file name. Submit the document, shown in Figure 2–84, in the format specified by your instructor.

6. ✺ This paper uses web sources. What factors should you consider when selecting web sources?

Tanner 2

Users can enable the password feature on their mobile device as the first step in stopping prying eyes from viewing contents. More protection is necessary, however, to stop viruses and spyware and to safeguard personal and business data. Mobile security apps can lock a mobile device remotely, erase its memory, and activate its GPS function (Bao).

Some techniques users can take to protect their mobile devices include avoiding unsafe links, using caution when downloading, turning off GPS tracking, and using mobile security software. Users should take these measures to protect their mobile devices.

(b) Page 2
Figure 2–84 (Continued)

Continued >

In the Labs *continued*

Lab 3: Expand Your World: Cloud and Web Technologies
Using an Online Bibliography Tool to Create a List of Sources

Problem: Assume you are using a mobile device or computer that does not have Word but has Internet access. To make use of time between classes, you will use an online bibliography tool to create a list of sources that you can copy and paste into the Works Cited pages of a research paper due tomorrow.

Instructions: Perform the following tasks:

1. Run a browser. Search for the text, online bibliography tool, using a search engine. Visit several of the online bibliography tools and determine which you would like to use to create a list of sources. Navigate to the desired online bibliography tool.

2. Use the online bibliography tool to enter list of sources shown below (Figure 2–85):

Dayton, Lacey Marie and Sally Louise Walsh. *The Wireless Revolution*. New York: New Artists Press, 2014. Print.

Dover, Guy Sean. *Communications of Today*. Los Angeles: Sunshine Works, 2014. Print.

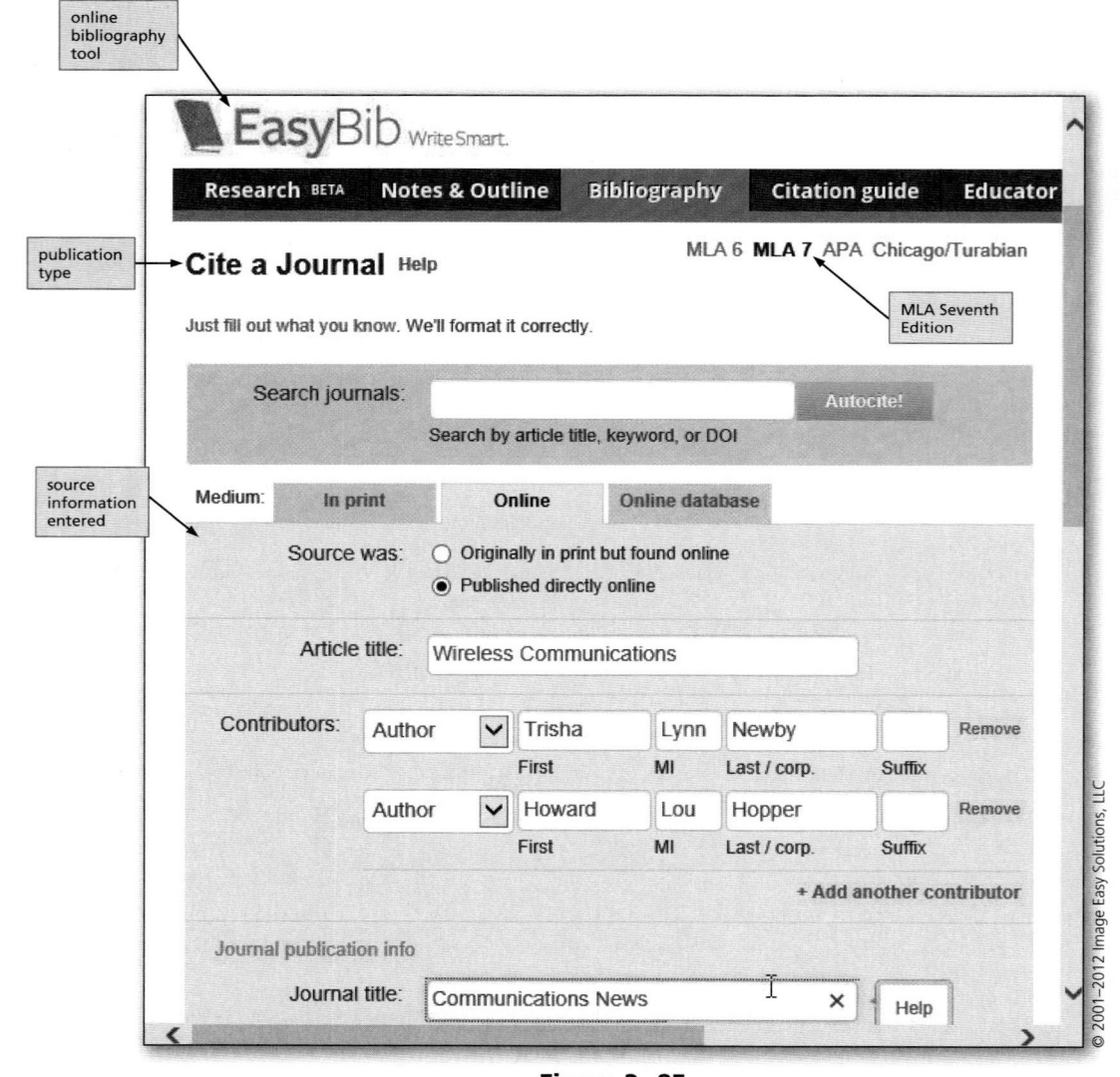

Figure 2–85

© 2001–2012 Image Easy Solutions, LLC

James. "The Wireless Era." *Computers and Networks* Aug. 2014. Web. 29

James. *Wireless Trends*. Aug. 2014. Course Technology. Web. 8 Sept. 2014.

Lynn and Howard Lou Hopper. "Wireless Communications." *Communications* 4. Web. 4 Oct. 2014.

iam Jared. *The Amazing Wireless World*. Sept. 2014. Course Technology. Web. 28

your instructor, replace the name in one of the sources above with your name.

ther source that discusses wireless communications. Add that source.

e the list of sources into a Word document.

nent with the name Lab 1-3 Wireless Communications Sources. Submit the he format specified by your instructor.

line bibliography tools did you evaluate? Which one did you select to use and prefer using the online bibliography tool or Word to create sources? Why? ences, if any, did you notice between the list of sources created with the online bib. y tool and the lists created when you use Word?

✹ Consider This: Your Turn

Apply your creative thinking and problem solving skills to design and implement a solution.

Note: To complete these assignments, you may be required to use the Data Files for Students. Visit www.cengage.com/ct/studentdownload for detailed instructions or contact your instructor for information about accessing the required files.

1: Create a Research Paper about Laptops, Tablets, and Desktops
Personal

Part 1: As a student in an introductory computer class, your instructor has assigned a brief research paper that discusses types of computers. The source for the text in your research paper is in a file called Your Turn 2 - 1 Computer Notes, which is located on the Data Files for Students. If your instructor requests, use the Research task pane to obtain information from another source and include that information as a note positioned as a footnote in the paper, along with entering its corresponding source information as appropriate. Add an AutoCorrect entry to correct a word you commonly mistype. If necessary, set the default dictionary. Add one of the source last names to the dictionary.

Using the concepts and techniques presented in this chapter, organize the notes in the text in the file on the Data Files for Students, rewording as necessary, and then create and format this research paper according to the MLA documentation style. Be sure to check spelling and grammar of the finished paper. Submit your assignment and answers to the critical thinking questions in the format specified by your instructor.

Part 2: ✹ You made several decisions while creating the research paper in this assignment: how to organize the notes, where to place citations, how to format sources, and which source on the web to use for the footnote text (if requested by your instructor). What was the rationale behind each of these decisions? When you proofread the document, what further revisions did you make and why?

Continued >

Consider This: Your Turn *continued*

2: Create a Research Paper about POS Terminals, ATMs, and Self-Service Kiosks
Professional

Part 1: As a part-time employee at an advertising firm that specializes in marketing for technology, your boss has asked you to write a brief research paper that discusses types of terminals. The source for the text in your research paper is in a file called Your Turn 2 - 2 Terminals Notes, which is located on the Data Files for Students. If your instructor requests, use the Research task pane to obtain information from another source and include that information as a note positioned as a footnote in the paper, and enter its corresponding source information as appropriate. Add an AutoCorrect entry to correct a word you commonly mistype. If necessary, set the default dictionary. Add one of the source last names to the dictionary.

Using the concepts and techniques presented in this chapter, organize the notes in the file on the Data Files for Students, rewording as necessary, and then create and format this research paper according to the MLA documentation style. Be sure to check spelling and grammar of the finished paper. Submit your assignment and answers to the critical thinking questions in the format specified by your instructor.

Part 2: ✹ You made several decisions while creating the research paper in this assignment: how to organize the notes, where to place citations, how to format sources, and which source on the web to use for the footnote text (if requested by your instructor). What was the rationale behind each of these decisions? When you proofread the document, what further revisions did you make and why?

3: Create a Research Paper about Social Media Sites
Research and Collaboration

Part 1: Because all local youth groups will be creating a page on a social media site, you and two other leaders of local youth groups have been asked to prepare a research paper comparing and contrasting three different social media sites. Form a three-member team to research, compose, and create this paper. Research three separate social media sites: features, capabilities, typical uses, privacy settings, etc. Each team member should write the supporting paragraphs for the social media site he or she researched, including all citations and sources. As a group, write the introduction and conclusion. Be sure to include your team's recommendation in the conclusion.

Use the concepts and techniques presented in this chapter to create and format this paper according to the MLA documentation style. Be sure to check spelling and grammar of the finished paper. Submit your team notes and research paper in the format specified by your instructor.

Part 2: ✹ You made several decisions while creating the research paper in this assignment: the sources to use, which notes to take from the sources, how to organize the notes, how to organize each team member's submissions, what text to write for the introduction and conclusion, where to place citations, and how to format sources. What was the rationale behind each of these decisions? When you proofread the document, what further revisions did you make and why?

Learn Online

Reinforce what you learned in this chapter with games, exercises, training, and many other online activities and resources.

Student Companion Site Reinforcement activities and resources are available at no additional cost on www.cengagebrain.com. Visit www.cengage.com/ct/studentdownload for detailed instructions about accessing the resources available at the Student Companion Site.

SAM Put your skills into practice with SAM! If you have a SAM account, go to www.cengage.com/sam2013 to access SAM assignments for this chapter.

1 Creating and Editing a Presentation with Pictures

Microsoft product screenshots used with permission from Microsoft Corporation.

Objectives

You will have mastered the material in this chapter when you can:

- Select and change a document theme and variant
- Create a title slide and a text slide with a multilevel bulleted list
- Add new slides and change slide layouts
- Insert photos and illustrations into slides with and without content placeholders
- Move and resize photos and illustrations

- Change font size and color
- Bold and italicize text
- Duplicate a slide
- Arrange slides
- Select slide transitions
- View a presentation in Slide Show view
- Print a presentation

Creating and Editing a Presentation with Pictures

Introduction

A PowerPoint **presentation,** also called a **slide show,** can help you deliver a dynamic, professional-looking message to an audience. PowerPoint allows you to produce slides to use in an academic, business, or other environment. The collection of slides in a presentation is called a **deck,** resembling a deck of cards that are stacked on top of each other. A common use of slide decks is to enhance an oral presentation. A speaker might desire to convey information, such as urging students to volunteer at a fund-raising event, explaining changes in employee compensation packages, or describing a new laboratory procedure. The PowerPoint slides should reinforce the speaker's message and help the audience retain the information presented. Custom slides can fit your specific needs and contain diagrams, charts, tables, pictures, shapes, video, sound, and animation effects to make your presentation more effective. An accompanying handout gives audience members reference notes and review material for your presentation.

Project — Presentation with a Bulleted List, Photos, and an Illustration

In this chapter's project, you will follow proper design guidelines and learn to use PowerPoint to create, save, and print the slides shown in Figures 1–1a through 1–1e. The objective is to produce a presentation, titled Keeping Hydrated, to help athletes understand the need to drink water before, during, and after a workout. This slide show has a variety of pictures and visual elements to add interest and give facts about proper hydration. Some of the text has formatting and color enhancements. Transitions help one slide flow gracefully into the next during a slide show. In addition, you will print a handout of your slides to distribute to audience members.

(a) Slide 1 (Title Slide with Photo)

(b) Slide 2 (Multilevel Bulleted List with Photo)

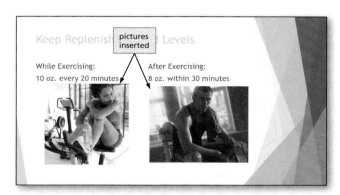

(c) Slide 3 (Title and Illustration)

(d) Slide 4 (Comparison Layout and Photos)

(e) Slide 5 (Closing Slide)

Figure 1–1

Roadmap

For an introduction to Windows and instruction about how to perform basic Windows tasks, read the Office and Windows chapter at the beginning of this book, where you can learn how to resize windows, change screen resolution, create folders, move and rename files, use Windows Help, and much more.

In this chapter, you will learn how to create the slides shown in Figure 1–1 on the previous page. The following roadmap identifies general activities you will perform as you progress through this chapter:

1. INSERT the four PRESENTATION SLIDES, using various layouts.
2. ENTER the TEXT for the slides.
3. FORMAT the TEXT on each slide.
4. INSERT GRAPHICAL ELEMENTS, including photos and an illustration.
5. SIZE AND POSITION the graphical elements.
6. ENHANCE the SLIDE SHOW by adding a closing slide and transition.
7. DISPLAY AND PRINT the SLIDES and a handout.

At the beginning of step instructions throughout the chapter, you will see an abbreviated form of this roadmap. The abbreviated roadmap uses colors to indicate chapter progress: gray means the chapter is beyond that activity; blue means the task being shown is covered in that activity, and black means that activity is yet to be covered. For example, the following abbreviated roadmap indicates the chapter would be showing a task in the 5 Size & Position activity.

1 INSERT PRESENTATION SLIDES | 2 ENTER TEXT | 3 FORMAT TEXT | 4 INSERT GRAPHICAL ELEMENTS
5 SIZE & POSITION | 6 ENHANCE SLIDE SHOW | 7 DISPLAY & PRINT SLIDES

Use the abbreviated roadmap as a progress guide while you read or step through the instructions in this chapter.

To Run PowerPoint

One of the few differences between Windows 7 and Windows 8 occurs in the steps to run PowerPoint. If you are using Windows 7, click the Start button, type **PowerPoint** in the 'Search programs and files' box, click PowerPoint 2013, and then, if necessary, maximize the PowerPoint window. For detailed steps to run PowerPoint in Windows 7, refer to the Office and Windows chapter at the beginning of this book. For a summary of the steps, refer to the Quick Reference located at the back of this book.

If you are using a computer to step through the project in this chapter and you want your screens to match the figures in this book, you should change your screen's resolution to 1366 × 768. For information about how to change a computer's resolution, refer to the Office and Windows chapter at the beginning of this book.

The following steps, which assume Windows 8 is running, use the Start screen or the search box to run PowerPoint based on a typical installation. You may need to ask your instructor how to run PowerPoint on your computer. For a detailed example of the procedure summarized below, refer to the Office and Windows chapter.

1 Scroll the Start screen for a PowerPoint 2013 tile. If your Start screen contains a PowerPoint 2013 tile, tap or click it to run PowerPoint and then proceed to Step 5; if the Start screen does not contain the PowerPoint 2013 tile, proceed to the next step to search for the PowerPoint app.

2 Swipe in from the right edge of the screen or point to the upper-right corner of the screen to display the Charms bar and then tap or click the Search charm on the Charms bar to display the Search menu.

3 Type **PowerPoint** as the search text in the Search box and watch the search results appear in the Apps list.

4 Tap or click PowerPoint 2013 in the search results to run PowerPoint.

5 If the PowerPoint window is not maximized, tap or click the Maximize button on its title bar to maximize the window.

Choosing a Document Theme and Variant

You easily can give the slides in a presentation a professional and integrated appearance by using a theme. A document **theme** is a specific design with coordinating colors, fonts, and special effects such as shadows and reflections. Several themes are available when you run PowerPoint, each with a specific name. Using one of the formatted themes makes creating a professional-looking presentation easier and quicker than using the Blank Presentation template, where you would need to make all design decisions.

Each theme has a set of four alternate designs, called **variants.** Each variant has the same overall composition, but the colors, fonts, and design elements differ. Once you select a theme, you then can select a variation that best fits your overall design needs. If you later decide that another theme or variant would better fit the presentation's general theme, you can change these elements while you are developing slides.

To Choose a Document Theme and Variant

1 INSERT PRESENTATION SLIDES | 2 ENTER TEXT | 3 FORMAT TEXT | 4 INSERT GRAPHICAL ELEMENTS
5 SIZE & POSITION | 6 ENHANCE SLIDE SHOW | 7 DISPLAY & PRINT SLIDES

When you begin creating a new PowerPoint presentation, you need to select a theme. You either can start with no design elements by using the Blank Presentation, or you select one of the available professionally designed themes. The following steps apply the Ion theme and then change the variant. *Why? The title slide will have text and a photo, so you want to select a theme, like Ion, with an uncluttered background. The presentation discusses the importance of drinking water while exercising, and blue is the color commonly associated with water in lakes and oceans. The default Ion theme is predominantly green and white, but one of its variants is blue and is an appropriate choice to relate to the water concept.*

• Press and hold or point to the Ion theme on the New screen (Figure 1–2).

Q&A Why are my theme images, called thumbnails, displaying in a different order?

PowerPoint places the themes you have used recently in the first rows. You may need to scroll down to locate the Ion theme.

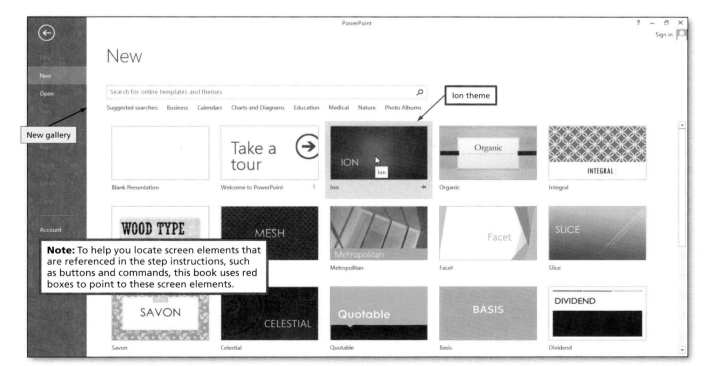

Figure 1–2

2

- Tap or click the Ion theme to display a theme preview dialog box with a thumbnail view of the theme and its variants (Figure 1–3).

◄ | Can I see previews of other themes?
Q&A | Yes. Tap or click the right or left arrows on the sides of the theme preview dialog box.

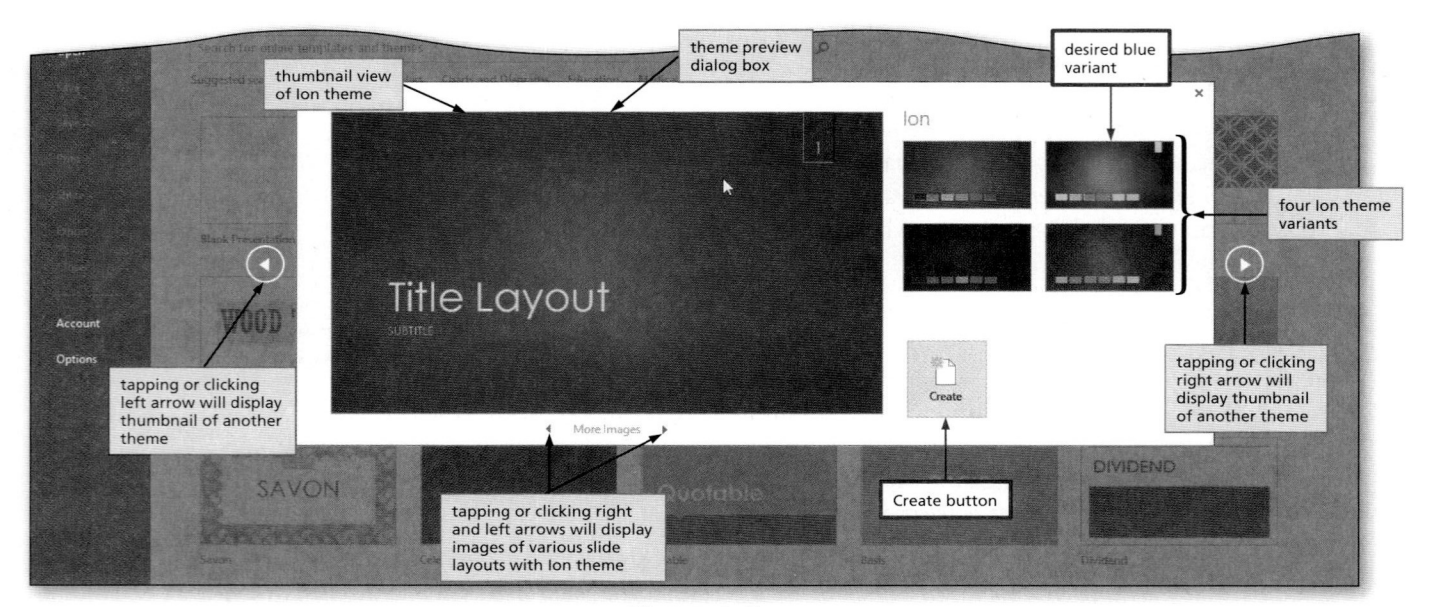

Figure 1–3

3

- Tap or click the upper-right (blue) variant to view previews of that style applied to the thumbnail.

◄ | Can I see previews of the Ion theme and blue variant applied to layouts other than the title slide?
Q&A | Yes. Tap or click the right or left arrows beside the words, More Images, below the thumbnail. Three other layouts will be displayed: Title and Content, Two Content, and Photo.

- Tap or click the Create button to apply the Ion theme and blue variant to the presentation and to display Slide 1 (Figure 1–4).

Figure 1–4

Creating a Title Slide

When you open a new presentation, the default **Title Slide** layout appears. The purpose of this layout is to introduce the presentation to the audience. PowerPoint includes other standard layouts for each of the themes. The slide layouts are set up in **landscape orientation**, where the slide width is greater than its height. In landscape orientation, the slide size is preset to 10 inches wide and 7.5 inches high when printed on a standard sheet of paper measuring 11 inches wide and 8.5 inches high.

Placeholders are boxes with dotted or hatch-marked borders that are displayed when you create a new slide. Most layouts have both a title text placeholder and at least one content placeholder. Depending on the particular slide layout selected, title and subtitle placeholders are displayed for the slide title and subtitle; a content text placeholder is displayed for text, art, or a table, chart, picture, graphic, or movie. The title slide has two text placeholders where you can type the main heading, or title, of a new slide and the subtitle.

With the exception of the Blank slide layout, PowerPoint assumes every new slide has a title. To make creating a presentation easier, any text you type after a new slide appears becomes title text in the title text placeholder. The following steps create the title slide for this presentation.

Choose the words for the slide.
All presentations should follow the 7 × 7 rule, which states that each slide should have a maximum of seven lines, and each line should have a maximum of seven words. PowerPoint designers must choose their words carefully and, in turn, help viewers read the slides easily.

Avoid line wraps. Your audience's eyes want to stop at the end of a line. Thus, you must plan your words carefully or adjust the font size so that each point displays on only one line.

CONSIDER THIS

To Enter the Presentation Title

1 INSERT PRESENTATION SLIDES | 2 ENTER TEXT | 3 FORMAT TEXT | 4 INSERT GRAPHICAL ELEMENTS
5 SIZE & POSITION | 6 ENHANCE SLIDE SHOW | 7 DISPLAY & PRINT SLIDES

The presentation title for Project 1 is Healthy Hydration. *Why? The presentation discusses the importance of drinking water while exercising, and blue is the color associated with water.* The following step creates the slide show's title.

- Tap or click the label, 'Tap to add title', or, 'Click to add title', located inside the title text placeholder to select the placeholder (Figure 1–5).

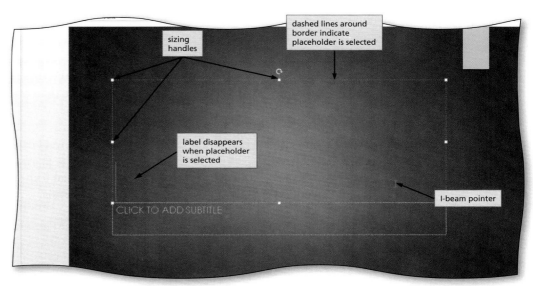

Figure 1–5

2

- Type **Healthy Hydration** in the title text placeholder. Do not press the ENTER key (Figure 1–6).

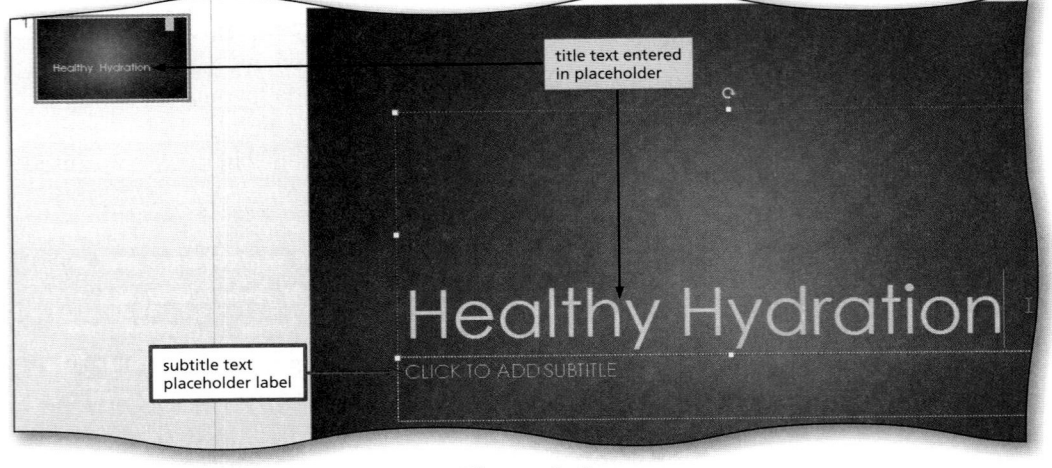

Figure 1–6

BTW
Q&As
For a complete list of the Q&As found in many of the step-by-step sequences in this book, visit the Q&A resource on the Student Companion Site located on www.cengagebrain.com. For detailed instructions about accessing available resources, visit www.cengage.com/ct/studentdownload or see the inside back cover of this book.

For an introduction to Office and instruction about how to perform basic tasks in Office apps, read the Office and Windows chapter at the beginning of this book, where you can learn how to run an application, use the ribbon, save a file, open a file, exit an application, use Help, and much more.

Correcting a Mistake When Typing

If you type the wrong letter, press the BACKSPACE key to erase all the characters back to and including the one that is incorrect. If you mistakenly press the ENTER key after typing the title and the insertion point is on the new line, simply press the BACKSPACE key to return the insertion point to the right of the letter in the word, Water.

When you install PowerPoint, the default setting allows you to reverse up to the last 20 changes by tapping or clicking the Undo button on the Quick Access Toolbar. The ScreenTip that appears when you point to the Undo button changes to indicate the type of change just made. For example, if you type text in the title text placeholder and then point to the Undo button, the ScreenTip that appears is Undo Typing. For clarity, when referencing the Undo button in this project, the name displaying in the ScreenTip is referenced. You can reapply a change that you reversed with the Undo button by tapping or clicking the Redo button on the Quick Access Toolbar. Tapping or clicking the Redo button reverses the last undo action. The ScreenTip name reflects the type of reversal last performed.

Paragraphs

Text in the subtitle text placeholder supports the title text. It can appear on one or more lines in the placeholder. To create more than one subtitle line, you press the ENTER key after typing some words. PowerPoint creates a new line, which is the second paragraph in the placeholder. A **paragraph** is a segment of text with the same format that begins when you press the ENTER key and ends when you press the ENTER key again. This new paragraph is the same level as the previous paragraph. A **level** is a position within a structure, such as an outline, that indicates the magnitude of importance. PowerPoint allows for five paragraph levels.

PowerPoint Chapter 1

How do you use the touch keyboard with a touch screen?

To display the on-screen touch keyboard, tap the Touch Keyboard button on the Windows taskbar. When finished using the touch keyboard, tap the X button on the touch keyboard to close the keyboard.

To Enter the Presentation Subtitle Paragraph

1 INSERT PRESENTATION SLIDES | 2 ENTER TEXT | 3 FORMAT TEXT | 4 INSERT GRAPHICAL ELEMENTS
5 SIZE & POSITION | 6 ENHANCE SLIDE SHOW | 7 DISPLAY & PRINT SLIDES

The first subtitle paragraph links to the title. *Why? The subtitle gives additional detail that the presentation will focus on water consumption while exercising.* The following steps enter the presentation subtitle.

- Tap or click the label, 'Tap to add subtitle', or, 'Click to add subtitle', located inside the subtitle text placeholder to select the placeholder (Figure 1–7).

Figure 1–7

- Type **Drinking Water While Exercising** but do not press the ENTER key (Figure 1–8).

Q&A Why does the text display with capital letters despite the fact I am typing uppercase and lowercase letters? The Ion theme uses the All Caps effect for the subtitle text. This effect converts lowercase letters to uppercase letters.

Figure 1–8

To Zoom a Slide

You will be modifying the text and other slide components as you create the presentation, so you can enlarge the slide on the screen. *Why? Zooming the slide can help you see slide elements more clearly so that you can position them precisely where desired.* The following step changes the zoom to 80 percent.

1

Figure 1–9

Experiment

- Repeatedly tap or click the Zoom In and Zoom Out buttons on the status bar and watch the size of the slide change in the Slide pane.

- Tap or click the Zoom In or Zoom Out button as many times as necessary until the Zoom button on the status bar displays 80% on its face (Figure 1–9).

Q&A If I change the zoom percentage, will the slide display differently when I run the presentation?
No. Changing the zoom helps you develop the slide content and does not affect the slide show.

Other Ways

1. Drag Zoom slider on status bar	2. Tap or click Zoom level button on status bar, select desired zoom percent or type (Zoom dialog box), tap or click OK button	3. Tap or click Zoom button (VIEW tab \| Zoom group), select desired zoom percent or type (Zoom dialog box), tap or click OK button	4. For touch screens: Pinch two fingers together in Slide pane (zoom out) or stretch two fingers apart (zoom in)

Formatting Characters in a Presentation

BTW
BTWs
For a complete list of the BTWs found in the margins of this book, visit the BTW resource on the Student Companion Site located on www.cengagebrain.com. For detailed instructions about accessing available resources, visit www.cengage.com/ct/ studentdownload or see the inside back cover of this book.

Recall that each document theme determines the color scheme, font set, and layout of a presentation. You can use a specific document theme and then change the characters' formats any time before, during, or after you type the text.

Fonts and Font Styles

Characters that appear on the screen are a specific shape and size. Examples of how you can modify the appearance, or **format**, of these typed characters on the screen and in print include changing the font, style, size, and color. The **font**, or typeface, defines the appearance and shape of the letters, numbers, punctuation marks, and symbols. **Style** indicates how the characters are formatted. PowerPoint's text font styles include regular, italic, bold, and bold italic. **Size** specifies the height of the characters and is gauged by a measurement system that uses points. A **point** is 1/72 of an inch in height. Thus, a character with a font size of 36 is 36/72 (or 1/2) of an inch in height. **Color** defines the hue of the characters.

This presentation uses the Ion document theme, which has particular font styles and font sizes. The Ion document theme default title text font is named Century Gothic. It has no special effects, and its size is 54 point. The Ion default subtitle text font also is Century Gothic with a font size of 18 point.

To Select a Paragraph

1 INSERT PRESENTATION SLIDES | 2 ENTER TEXT | 3 FORMAT TEXT | 4 INSERT GRAPHICAL ELEMENTS
5 SIZE & POSITION | 6 ENHANCE SLIDE SHOW | 7 DISPLAY & PRINT SLIDES

You can use many techniques to format characters. When you want to apply the same formats to multiple words or paragraphs, it is helpful to select these words. *Why? It is efficient to select the desired text and then make the desired changes to all the characters simultaneously.* The first formatting change you will make will apply to the title slide subtitle. The following step selects this paragraph.

- If you are using a touch screen, tap to position the insertion point in the text to select, and then drag the selection handles as necessary to select the entire paragraph; if you are using a mouse, triple-click the paragraph, Drinking Water While Exercising, in the subtitle text placeholder to select the paragraph (Figure 1–10).

Figure 1–10

Q&A What is the selection handle?

When working on a touch screen, a **selection handle** (small circle) appears below the insertion point. Using a fingertip, you drag the selection handle to select text.

Other Ways

1. Position pointer to left of first paragraph and drag to end of line

To Italicize Text

1 INSERT PRESENTATION SLIDES | 2 ENTER TEXT | 3 FORMAT TEXT | 4 INSERT GRAPHICAL ELEMENTS
5 SIZE & POSITION | 6 ENHANCE SLIDE SHOW | 7 DISPLAY & PRINT SLIDES

Different font styles often are used on slides. *Why? These style changes make the words more appealing to the reader and emphasize particular text.* **Italicized** text has a slanted appearance. Used sparingly, it draws the readers' eyes to these characters. The following step adds emphasis to the line of the subtitle text by changing regular text to italic text.

- With the subtitle text still selected, tap or click the Italic button on the mini toolbar to italicize that text on the slide (Figure 1–11).

Figure 1–11

Q&A If I change my mind and decide not to italicize the text, how can I remove this style?

Tap or click the Italic button a second time, immediately tap or click the Undo button on the Quick Access Toolbar, or press CTRL+Z.

Other Ways

1. Tap 'Show Context Menu' button on mini toolbar or right-click selected text, tap or click Font on shortcut menu, tap or click Font tab (Font dialog box), tap or click Italic in Font style list, tap or click OK button

2. Select text, tap or click Italic button (HOME tab | Font group)

3. Tap or click Font dialog box launcher (HOME tab | Font group), tap or click Font tab (Font dialog box), tap or click Italic in Font style list, tap or click OK button

4. Select text, press CTRL+I

To Increase Font Size

Why? *To add emphasis, you increase the font size for the subtitle text.* The Increase Font Size button on the mini toolbar increases the font size in preset increments. The following step uses this button to increase the font size.

1
- Tap or click the 'Increase Font Size' button on the mini toolbar three times to increase the font size of the selected text from 20 to 32 point (Figure 1–12).

Figure 1–12

Other Ways

1. Tap or click Font Size arrow on mini toolbar, tap or click desired font size in Font Size gallery	2. Tap or click Increase Font Size button (HOME tab \| Font group)	3. Tap or click Font Size arrow (HOME tab \| Font group), tap or click desired font size in Font size gallery	4. Press CTRL+SHIFT+>

To Select a Word

PowerPoint designers use many techniques to emphasize words and characters on a slide. To accentuate the word, Water, on your slide, you want to increase the font size and change the font color to dark blue for the word, WATER, in the subtitle text. To make these changes, you should begin by selecting the word, WATER. *Why?* *You could perform these actions separately, but it is more efficient to select the word and then change the font attributes.* The following steps select a word.

1
- Position the pointer somewhere in the word to be selected (in this case, in the word, WATER) (Figure 1–13).

Figure 1–13

- Double-tap or double-click the word to select it (Figure 1–14).

entire word is selected

Figure 1–14

Other Ways

1. Position pointer before first character, press CTRL+SHIFT+RIGHT ARROW

To Change the Text Color

1 INSERT PRESENTATION SLIDES | 2 ENTER TEXT | 3 FORMAT TEXT | 4 INSERT GRAPHICAL ELEMENTS
5 SIZE & POSITION | 6 ENHANCE SLIDE SHOW | 7 DISPLAY & PRINT SLIDES

PowerPoint allows you to use one or more text colors in a presentation. You decide to change the color of the word you selected, WATER. *Why? The color, blue, is associated with water, and you want to add more emphasis, subtly, to that word in your subtitle slide text.* The following steps add emphasis to this word by changing the font color from green to blue.

- With the word, WATER, selected, tap or click the Font Color arrow on the mini toolbar to display the Font Color gallery, which includes Theme Colors and Standard Colors (Figure 1–15).

Q&A If the mini toolbar disappears from the screen, how can I display it once again?
Press and hold or right-click the text, and the mini toolbar should appear.

Experiment

- If you are using a mouse, point to various colors in the gallery and watch the word's font color change.

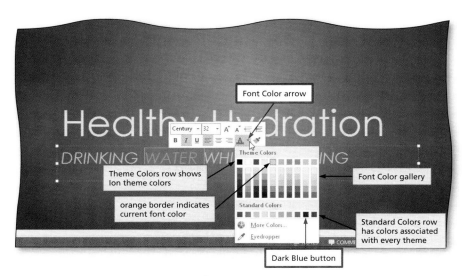

Font Color arrow

Theme Colors row shows Ion theme colors

orange border indicates current font color

Font Color gallery

Standard Colors row has colors associated with every theme

Dark Blue button

Figure 1–15

2

• Tap or click Dark Blue in the Standard Colors row on the mini toolbar (second color from right) to change the font color to Dark Blue (Figure 1–16).

Q&A
Why did I select the color Dark Blue?
Dark Blue is one of the 10 standard colors associated with every document theme, and it is a universal color representing the natural resource of water. The color will emphasize the fact that the presentation focuses on water.

What is the difference between the colors shown in the Theme Colors area and the Standard Colors?
The 10 colors in the top row of the Theme Colors area are two text, two background, and six accent colors in the Ion theme; the five colors in each column under the top row display different transparencies. The Standard Colors are available in every document theme.

Figure 1–16

3

• Tap or click outside the selected area to deselect the word.

Other Ways
1. Tap 'Show Context Menu' button on mini toolbar or right-click selected text, tap or click Font on shortcut menu, tap or click Font Color button, tap or click Dark Blue in Standard Colors row 2. Tap or click Font Color arrow (HOME tab

BTW
Organizing Files and Folders
You should organize and store files in folders so that you easily can find the files later. For example, if you are taking an introductory computer class called CIS 101, a good practice would be to save all PowerPoint files in a PowerPoint folder in a CIS 101 folder. For a discussion of folders and detailed examples of creating folders, refer to the Office and Windows chapter at the beginning of this book.

To Save a Presentation with a New File Name

You have performed many tasks while creating this presentation and do not want to risk losing work completed thus far. Accordingly, you should save the presentation on your hard disk, SkyDrive, or a location that is most appropriate to your situation.

The following steps assume you already have created folders for storing your files, for example, a CIS 101 folder (for your class) that contains a PowerPoint folder (for your assignments). Thus, these steps save the presentation in the PowerPoint

folder in the CIS 101 folder on your desired save location. For a detailed example of the procedure for saving a file in a folder or saving a file on SkyDrive, refer to the Office and Windows chapter at the beginning of this book.

1 Tap or click the Save button on the Quick Access Toolbar, which depending on settings, will display either the Save As gallery in the Backstage view or the Save As dialog box.

2 To save on a hard disk or other storage media on your computer, proceed to Step 2a. To save on SkyDrive, proceed to Step 2b.

2a If your screen opens the Backstage view and you want to save on storage media on your computer, tap or click Computer in the left pane, if necessary, to display options in the right pane related to saving on your computer. If your screen already displays the Save As dialog box, proceed to Step 3.

2b If your screen opens the Backstage view and you want to save on SkyDrive, tap or click SkyDrive in the left pane to display SkyDrive saving options or a Sign In button. If your screen displays a Sign In button, tap or click it and then sign in to SkyDrive.

3 Tap or click the Browse button in the right pane to display the Save As dialog box associated with the selected save location (i.e., Computer or SkyDrive).

4 Type **Keeping Hydrated** in the File name box to change the file name. Do not press the ENTER key after typing the file name because you do not want to close the dialog box at this time.

5 Navigate to the desired save location (in this case, the PowerPoint folder in the CIS 101 folder [or your class folder] on your computer or SkyDrive).

6 Tap or click the Save button (Save As dialog box) to save the presentation in the selected folder on the selected save location with the entered file name.

BTW
The Ribbon and Screen Resolution
PowerPoint may change how the groups and buttons within the groups appear on the ribbon, depending on the computer's screen resolution. Thus, your ribbon may look different from the ones in this book if you are using a screen resolution other than 1366 × 768.

Adding a New Slide to a Presentation

With the text for the title slide for the presentation created, the next step is to add the first text slide immediately after the title slide. Usually, when you create a presentation, you add slides with text, pictures, graphics, or charts. Some placeholders allow you to double-tap or double-click the placeholder and then access other objects, such as videos, charts, diagrams, and organization charts. You can change the layout for a slide at any time during the creation of a presentation.

To Add a New Text Slide with a Bulleted List

1 INSERT PRESENTATION SLIDES | 2 ENTER TEXT | 3 FORMAT TEXT | **4 INSERT GRAPHICAL ELEMENTS**
5 SIZE & POSITION | 6 ENHANCE SLIDE SHOW | 7 DISPLAY & PRINT SLIDES

When you add a new slide, PowerPoint uses the Title and Content slide layout. This layout provides a title placeholder and a content area for text, art, charts, and other graphics. A vertical scroll bar appears in the Slide pane when you add the second slide. *Why?* *The scroll bar allows you to move from slide to slide easily.* A small image of this slide also appears in the Thumbnail pane. The step on the next page adds a new slide with the Title and Content slide layout.

1

- Tap or click the New Slide button (HOME tab | Slides group) to insert a new slide with the Title and Content layout (Figure 1–17).

Q&A

Why does the bullet character display a green triangle?
The Ion document theme determines the bullet characters. Each paragraph level has an associated bullet character.

I clicked the New Slide arrow instead of the New Slide button. What should I do?
Tap or click the Title and Content slide thumbnail in the Ion layout gallery.

How do I know which slide number I am viewing?
The left edge of the status bar shows the current slide number followed by the total number of slides in the document. In addition, the slide number is displayed to the left of the slide thumbnail.

What are those six icons grouped in the middle of the Slide pane?
You can tap or click one of the icons to insert a specific type of content: table, chart, SmartArt graphic, pictures, online pictures, or video.

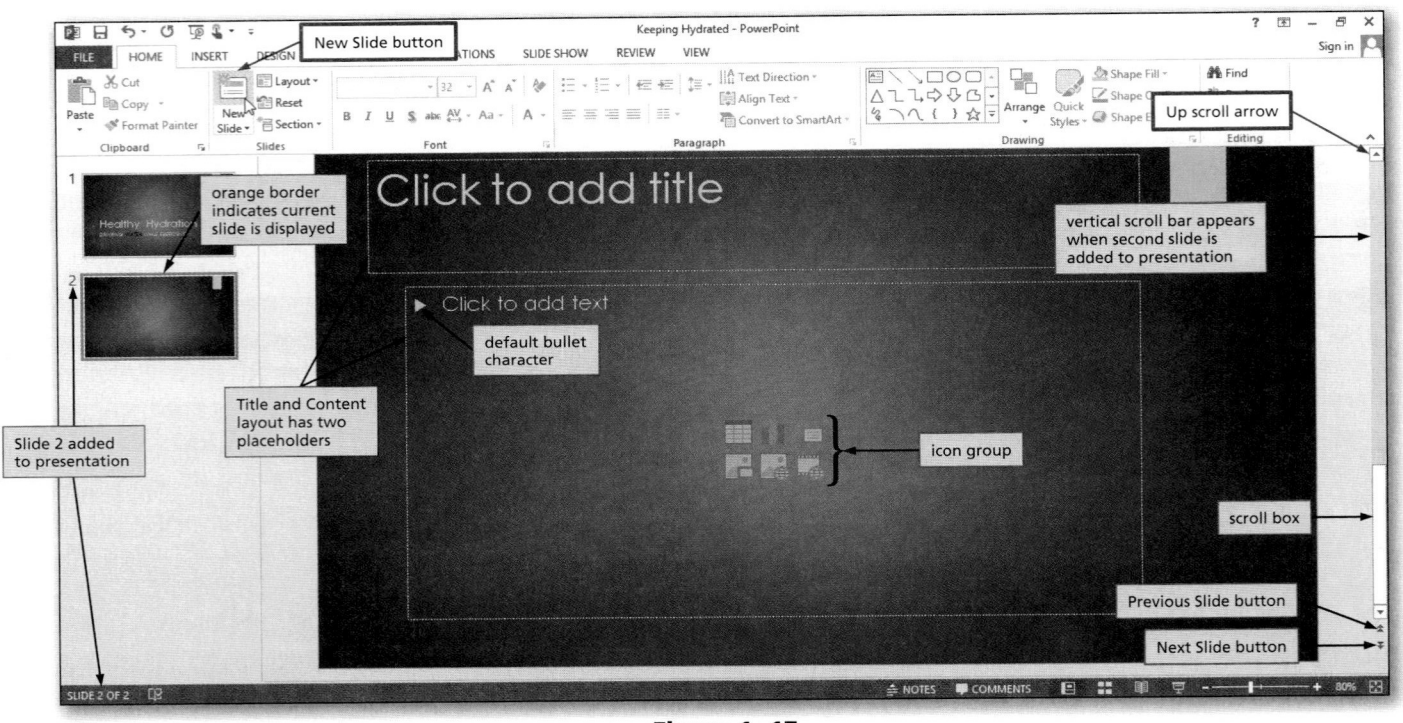

Figure 1–17

Other Ways

1. Press CTRL+M

Creating a Text Slide with a Multilevel Bulleted List

The information in the Slide 2 text placeholder is presented in a bulleted list with three levels. A **bulleted list** is a list of paragraphs, each of which may be preceded by a bullet character, such as a dot, arrow, or checkmark. Some themes, such as the Ion theme, do not display a bullet character at the start of a paragraph by default. A slide that consists of more than one level of bulleted text is called a **multilevel bulleted list slide**. In a multilevel bulleted list, a lower-level paragraph is a subset of a higher-level paragraph. It usually contains information that supports the topic in the paragraph immediately above it.

As you can see in Figure 1–1b on page PPT 3, two of the Slide 2 paragraphs appear at the same level, called the first level: Cushions and protects vital organs, and Regulates body temperature. Beginning with the second level, each paragraph indents to the right of the preceding level and is pushed down to a lower level. For example, if you increase the indent of a first-level paragraph, it becomes a second-level paragraph. The second, fourth, and fifth paragraphs on Slide 2 are second-level paragraphs. The last paragraph, Can cause muscle fatigue and heat stroke, is a third-level paragraph.

Creating a text slide with a multilevel bulleted list requires several steps. Initially, you enter a slide title in the title text placeholder. Next, you select the content text placeholder. Then, you type the text for the multilevel bulleted list, increasing and decreasing the indents as needed. The next several sections add a slide with a multilevel bulleted list.

BTW
Touch Screen Differences
The Office and Windows interfaces may vary if you are using a touch screen. For this reason, you might notice that the function or appearance of your touch screen differs slightly from this chapter's presentation.

To Enter a Slide Title

1 INSERT PRESENTATION SLIDES | 2 ENTER TEXT | 3 FORMAT TEXT | 4 INSERT GRAPHICAL ELEMENTS
5 SIZE & POSITION | 6 ENHANCE SLIDE SHOW | 7 DISPLAY & PRINT SLIDES

PowerPoint assumes every new slide has a title. *Why? The audience members read the title and then can begin to focus their attention on the information being presented on that slide.* The title for Slide 2 is Water: Your Essential Nutrient. The following step enters this title.

1

• Tap or click the label, 'Tap to add title', or, 'Click to add title', to select it and then type **Water: Your Essential Nutrient** in the title text placeholder. Do not press the ENTER key (Figure 1–18).

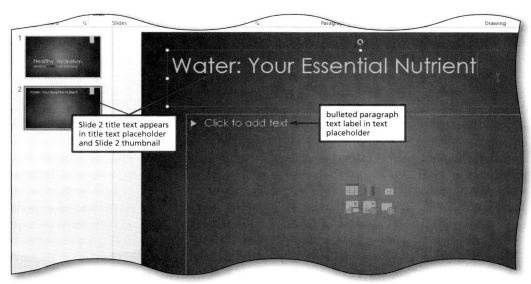

Figure 1–18

To Select a Text Placeholder

Why? *Before you can type text into a content placeholder, you first must select it.* The following step selects the text placeholder on Slide 2.

1

- Tap or click the label, 'Tap to add text', or 'Click to add text', to select the content placeholder (Figure 1–19).

Q&A Why does my pointer have a different shape?
If you move the pointer away from the bullet, it will change shape.

Figure 1–19

Other Ways

1. Press CTRL+ENTER

To Type a Multilevel Bulleted List

The content placeholder provides an area for the text characters. When you tap or click inside a placeholder, you then can type or paste text. As discussed previously, a bulleted list is a list of paragraphs, each of which is preceded by a bullet. A paragraph is a segment of text ended by pressing the ENTER key. The theme determines the bullets for each level. *Why?* *The bullet variations are determined by the specific paragraph levels, and they generally vary in size, shape, and color.*

The content text placeholder is selected, so the next step is to type the multilevel bulleted list that consists of six paragraphs, as shown in Figure 1–1b on page PPT 3. Creating a lower-level paragraph is called **demoting** text; creating a higher-level paragraph is called **promoting** text. The following steps create a multilevel bulleted list consisting of three levels.

1

- Type **Cushions and protects vital organs** and then press the ENTER key (Figure 1–20).

Figure 1–20

- Tap or click the 'Increase List Level' button (HOME tab | Paragraph group) to indent the second paragraph below the first and create a second-level paragraph (Figure 1–21).

Q&A Why does the bullet for this paragraph have a different size?
A different bullet is assigned to each paragraph level.

Figure 1–21

- Type **Transports nutrients and oxygen to cells** and then press the ENTER key (Figure 1–22).

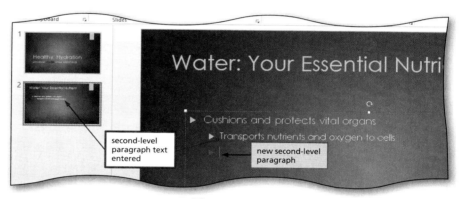

Figure 1–22

- Tap or click the 'Decrease List Level' button (HOME tab | Paragraph group) so that the second-level paragraph becomes a first-level paragraph (Figure 1–23).

Q&A Can I delete bullets on a slide?
Yes. If you do not want bullets to display in a particular paragraph, tap or click the Bullets button (HOME tab | Paragraph group) or press and hold or right-click the paragraph and then tap or click the Bullets button on the shortcut menu.

Figure 1–23

Other Ways

1. Press TAB to promote paragraph; press SHIFT+TAB to demote paragraph

To Type the Remaining Text for Slide 2

The following steps complete the text for Slide 2.

1 Type **Regulates body temperature** and then press the ENTER key.

2 Tap or click the 'Increase List Level' button (HOME tab | Paragraph group) to demote the paragraph to the second level.

3 Type **Dehydrated body cannot cool itself** and then press the ENTER key to add a new paragraph at the same level as the previous paragraph.

4 Tap or click the 'Increase List Level' button (HOME tab | Paragraph group) to demote the paragraph to the third level.

5 Type **Can cause muscle fatigue and heat stroke** but do not press the ENTER key (Figure 1–24).

Q&A I pressed the ENTER key in error, and now a new bullet appears after the last entry on this slide. How can I remove this extra bullet?
Press the BACKSPACE key twice.

Figure 1–24

To Select a Group of Words

1 INSERT PRESENTATION SLIDES | 2 ENTER TEXT | 3 FORMAT TEXT | 4 INSERT GRAPHICAL ELEMENTS
5 SIZE & POSITION | 6 ENHANCE SLIDE SHOW | 7 DISPLAY & PRINT SLIDES

PowerPoint designers use many techniques to emphasize words and characters on a slide. To highlight your slide show's concept of the dangers of not drinking water while exercising, you want to bold and increase the font size of the words, cannot cool itself, in the body text. The following steps select three words. *Why? You could perform these actions separately, but it is more efficient to select the words and then change the font attributes.*

1

- Position the pointer immediately to the left of the first character of the text to be selected (in this case, the c in the word, cannot) (Figure 1–25).

Figure 1–25

- Drag the pointer through the last character of the text to be selected (in this case, the f in the word, itself) (Figure 1–26).

text to be formatted is selected

Figure 1–26

Other Ways

1. Press CTRL+SHIFT+RIGHT ARROW repeatedly until desired words are selected

To Bold Text

1 INSERT PRESENTATION SLIDES | 2 ENTER TEXT | 3 FORMAT TEXT | 4 INSERT GRAPHICAL ELEMENTS
5 SIZE & POSITION | 6 ENHANCE SLIDE SHOW | 7 DISPLAY & PRINT SLIDES

Why? Bold characters display somewhat thicker and darker than those that display in a regular font style. Tapping or clicking the Bold button on the mini toolbar is an efficient method of bolding text. To add more emphasis to the fact that the body needs water for cooling purposes, you want to bold the words, cannot cool itself. The following step bolds this text.

- With the words, cannot cool itself, selected, tap or click the Bold button on the mini toolbar to bold the three words (Figure 1–27).

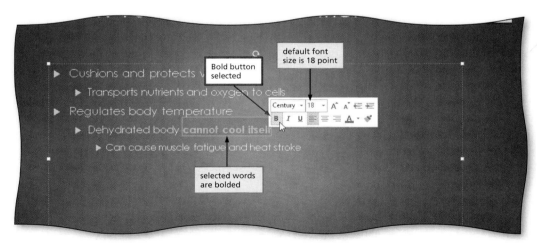

Bold button selected

default font size is 18 point

selected words are bolded

Figure 1–27

Other Ways

1. Tap 'Show Context Menu' button on mini toolbar or right-click selected text, tap or click Font on shortcut menu, tap or click Font tab (Font dialog box), tap or click Bold in Font style list, tap or click OK button

2. Select text, tap or click Bold button (HOME tab | Font group)

3. Tap or click Font dialog box launcher (HOME tab | Font group), tap or click Font tab (Font dialog box), tap or click Bold in Font style list, tap or click OK button

4. Select text, press CTRL+B

To Increase Font Size

Why? *To add emphasis, you increase the font size for the words, cannot cool itself.* The following steps increase the font size from 18 to 20 point.

1 With the words, cannot cool itself, still selected, tap or click the 'Increase Font Size' button on the mini toolbar once (Figure 1–28).

2 Tap or click outside the selected area to deselect the three words.

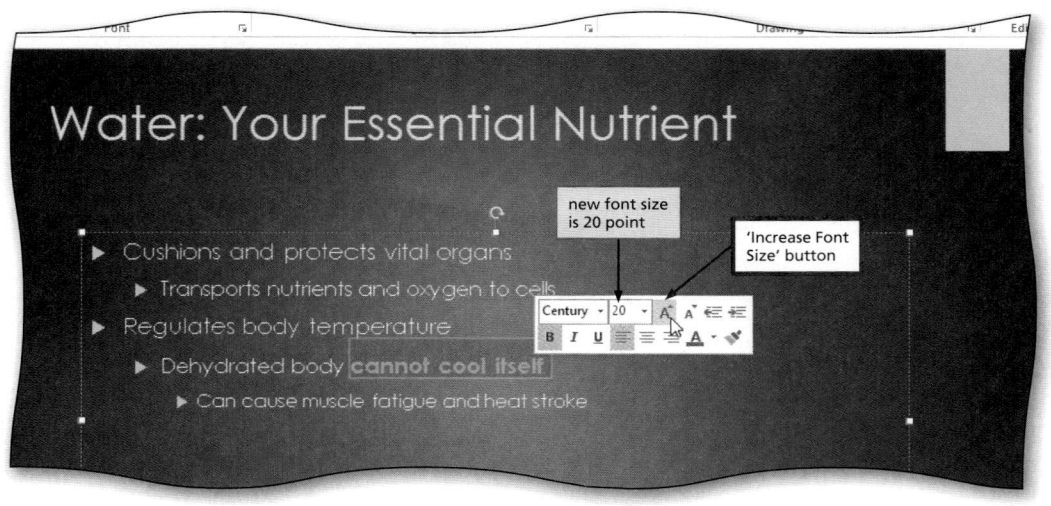

Figure 1–28

Adding New Slides, Changing Slide Layouts, and Changing the Theme

BTW
**Customizing
a Slide Layout**
PowerPoint provides a wide variety of slide layouts for each theme, but you can customize the layouts to make your deck unique. Display the VIEW tab, tap or click Slide Master (VIEW tab | Master Views group), select the thumbnail below the slide master in the left pane that you would like to customize, and then make the desired modifications.

Slide 3 in Figure 1–1c on page PPT 3 contains an illustration of a character drinking water and does not contain a bulleted list. When you add a new slide, PowerPoint applies the Title and Content layout. This layout, along with the Title Slide layout for Slide 1, are the default styles. A **layout** specifies the arrangement of placeholders on a slide. These placeholders are arranged in various configurations and can contain text, such as the slide title or a bulleted list, or they can contain content, such as SmartArt graphics, photos, charts, tables, and shapes. The placement of the text, in relationship to content, depends on the slide layout. You can specify a particular slide layout when you add a new slide to a presentation or after you have created the slide.

Using the **layout gallery**, you can choose a slide layout. The nine layouts in this gallery have a variety of placeholders to define text and content positioning and formatting. Three layouts are for text: Title Slide, Section Header, and Title Only. Five are for text and content: Title and Content, Two Content, Comparison, Content with Caption, and Picture with Caption. The Blank layout has no placeholders. If none of these standard layouts meets your design needs, you can create a **custom layout**. A custom layout specifies the number, size, and location of placeholders, background content, and optional slide and placeholder-level properties.

When you change the layout of a slide, PowerPoint retains the text and objects and repositions them into the appropriate placeholders. Using slide layouts eliminates the need to resize objects and the font size because PowerPoint automatically sizes the objects and text to fit the placeholders. At any time when creating the slide content, you can change the theme and variant to give the presentation a different look and feel.

To Add a Slide with the Title Only Layout

The following steps add Slide 3 to the presentation with the Title Only slide layout style. *Why? The only text on the slide is the title, and the majority of the slide content is the illustration.*

1
- If necessary, tap or click HOME on the ribbon to display the HOME tab.
- Tap or click the New Slide arrow (HOME tab | Slides group) to display the Ion layout gallery (Figure 1–29).

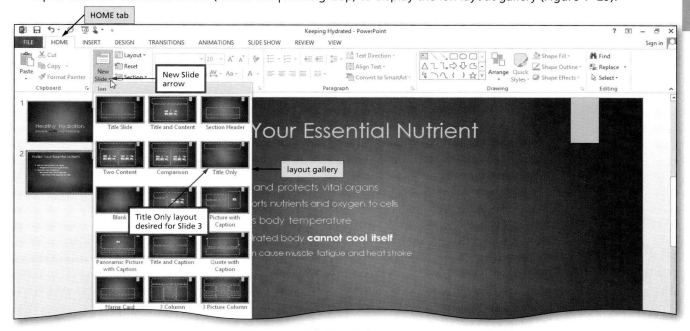

Figure 1–29

2
- Tap or click Title Only to add a new slide and apply that layout to Slide 3.
- If necessary, swipe up or click the Up scroll arrow several times until the title text placeholder is visible (Figure 1–30).

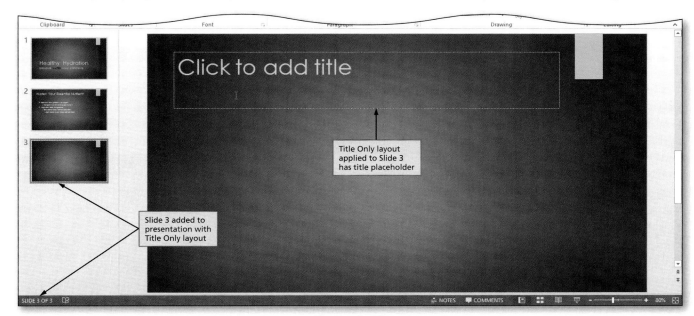

Figure 1–30

To Enter a Slide Title

The only text on Slide 3 is the title. The following step enters the title text for this slide.

1 Type **Begin Workout with Plenty of Water** as the title text but do not press the ENTER key (Figure 1–31).

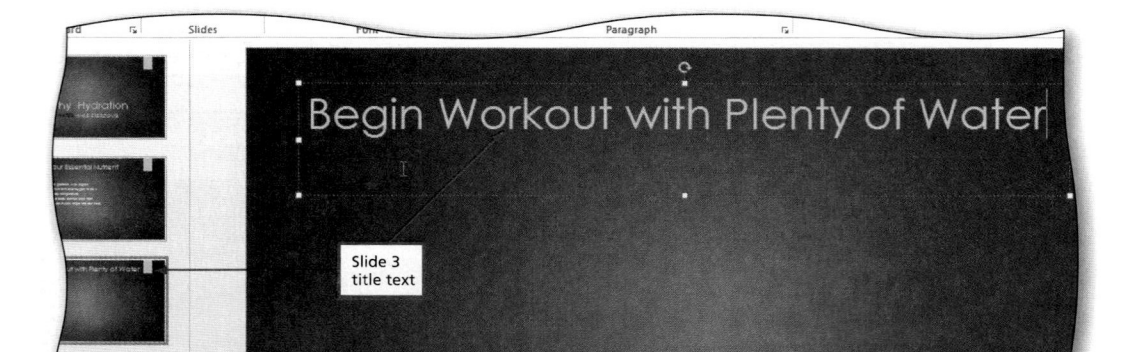

Figure 1–31

To Add a New Slide and Enter a Slide Title and Headings

1 INSERT PRESENTATION SLIDES | 2 ENTER TEXT | 3 FORMAT TEXT | 4 INSERT GRAPHICAL ELEMENTS
5 SIZE & POSITION | 6 ENHANCE SLIDE SHOW | 7 DISPLAY & PRINT SLIDES

The text on Slide 4 in Figure 1–1d on page PPT 3 consists of a title and two headings. The appropriate layout for this slide is named Comparison. ***Why?*** *The Comparison layout has two headings and two text placeholders adjacent to each other, so an audience member easily can compare and contrast the items shown side by side.* The following steps add Slide 4 to the presentation with the Comparison layout and then enter the title and heading text for this slide.

1

- Tap or click the New Slide arrow in the Slides group to display the Ion layout gallery (Figure 1–32).

Figure 1–32

2

- Tap or click Comparison to add Slide 4 and apply that layout (Figure 1–33).

Figure 1–33

3

- Type **Keep Replenishing Fluid Levels** in the title text placeholder.

- Tap or click the left heading placeholder with the label, 'Tap to add text', or 'Click to add text', to select this placeholder (Figure 1–34).

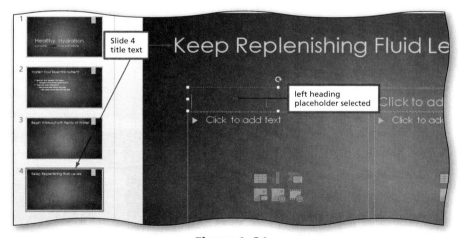

Figure 1–34

4

- Type **While Exercising:** and then press the ENTER key.

- Type **10 oz. every 20 minutes** but do not press the ENTER key.

- Select the right heading placeholder and then type **After Exercising:** and press the ENTER key.

- Type **8 oz. within 30 minutes** but do not press the ENTER key (Figure 1–35).

Figure 1–35

Q&A

What is the white box with the arrow between the placeholders?

The text is too large to fit in the placeholder using the default font and paragraph attributes, so PowerPoint adjusts the text so it displays properly. That icon informs you that the font was altered.

To Change the Theme

A theme provides consistency in design and color throughout the entire presentation by setting the color scheme, font set, and layout of a presentation. This collection of formatting choices includes a set of colors (the Theme Colors group), a set of heading and content text fonts (the Theme Fonts group), and a set of lines and fill effects (the Theme Effects group). These groups allow you to choose and change the appearance of all the slides or individual slides in your presentation. *Why? At any time while creating the slide deck, you may decide to switch the theme so that the slides have a totally different appearance.* The following steps change the theme for this presentation from Ion to Facet.

1

- Tap or click DESIGN on the ribbon to display the DESIGN tab (Figure 1–36).

Figure 1–36

2

- Tap or click the More button (DESIGN tab | Themes group) to expand the gallery, which shows more theme gallery options (Figure 1–37).

Experiment

- If you are using a mouse, point to various document themes in the Themes gallery and watch the colors and fonts change on the title slide.

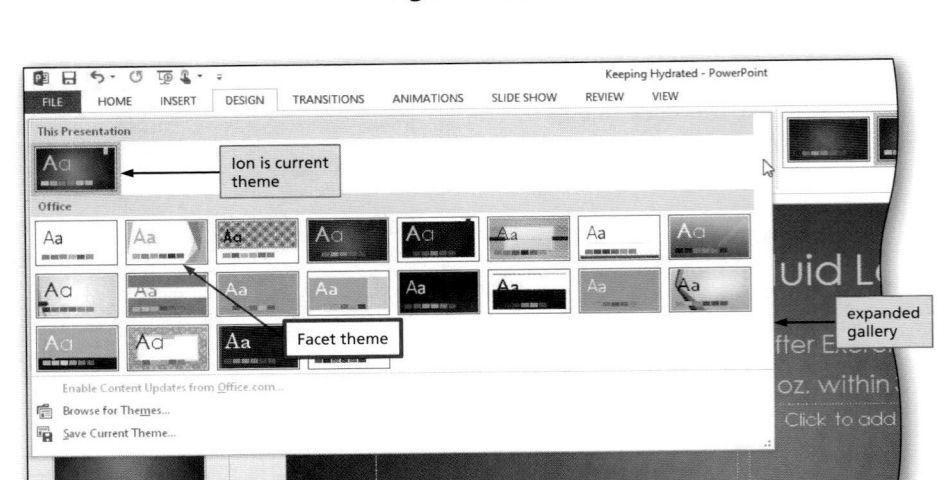

Figure 1–37

Q&A Are the themes displayed in a specific order?

They are listed in alphabetical order in two groups: Facet to Wisp beginning in the first row and Banded to Wood Type beginning in the second row. If you are using a mouse and point to a theme, a ScreenTip with the theme's name appears on the screen.

3

- Tap or click the Facet theme to apply this theme to all four slides (Figure 1–38).

Q&A The Facet theme is visible in the first row of the gallery, so why did I click the More button to expand the gallery?

While it is not necessary to view all the thumbnails, it sometimes is helpful to see all possible themes when deciding which one best fits the presentation.

If I decide at some future time that this design does not fit the theme of my presentation, can I apply a different design?

Yes. You can repeat these steps at any time while creating your presentation.

Figure 1–38

To Change the Variant

1 INSERT PRESENTATION SLIDES | 2 ENTER TEXT | 3 FORMAT TEXT | 4 INSERT GRAPHICAL ELEMENTS
5 SIZE & POSITION | 6 ENHANCE SLIDE SHOW | 7 DISPLAY & PRINT SLIDES

When you began creating this presentation, you selected the Ion theme and then chose a blue variant. You can change the color variation at any time for any theme. *Why? The new Facet theme has a default green color, but you want to emphasize the blue color associated with water, just like you initially did when you chose the blue variant for the Ion theme.* The following steps change the variant from green to blue.

- If you are using a mouse, point to the blue variation (DESIGN tab | Variants group) to see a preview of the blue variation on Slide 4 (Figure 1–39).

Experiment

- If you are using a mouse, point to the pink and black variants and watch the colors change on the slide.

Figure 1–39

2
- Tap or click the blue variant to apply this color to all four slides (Figure 1–40).

Q&A If I decide at some future time that this color variation does not fit the theme of my presentation, can I apply a different variant?
Yes. You can repeat these steps at any time while creating your presentation.

Figure 1–40

To Save an Existing Presentation with the Same File Name

You have made several modifications to the presentation since you last saved it. Thus, you should save it again. The following step saves the presentation again. For an example of the step listed below, refer to the Office and Windows chapter at the beginning of this book.

1 Tap or click the Save button on the Quick Access Toolbar to overwrite the previously saved file.

Break Point: If you wish to take a break, this is a good place to do so. You can exit PowerPoint now (refer to page PPT 55 for instructions). To resume at a later time, run PowerPoint (refer to page PPT 4 for instructions), open the file called Keeping Hydrated, and continue following the steps from this location forward.

BTW
Welcome Back!
If you are designing a slide in your deck other than Slide 1 and then save and close the document, PowerPoint's new Welcome back! feature allows you to continue where you left off at the last save when you open the document. You may need to adjust the zoom if you are working at a different level than the default setting.

PowerPoint Views

The PowerPoint window display varies depending on the view. A **view** is the mode in which the presentation appears on the screen. You will use some views when you are developing slides and others when you are delivering your presentation. When creating a presentation, you most likely will use Normal, Slide Sorter, Notes Page, and Outline views. When presenting your slides to an audience, you most likely will use Slide Sorter, Presenter, and Reading views.

The default view is **Normal view**, which is composed of three areas that allow you to work on various aspects of a presentation simultaneously. The large area in the middle, called the **Slide pane**, displays the slide you currently are developing and allows you to enter text, tables, charts, graphics, pictures, video, and other elements. As you create the slides, miniature views of the individual slides, called thumbnails, are displayed in the **Thumbnail pane**. You can rearrange the thumbnails in this pane. The **Notes pane**, by default, is hidden at the bottom of the window. If you want to type notes to yourself or remarks to share with your audience, you can click the Notes button in the status bar to open the Notes pane. After you have created at least two slides, a scroll bar containing **scroll arrows** and **scroll boxes** will appear on the right edge of the window.

To Move to Another Slide in Normal View

Why? *When creating or editing a presentation in Normal view (the view you are currently using), you often want to display a slide other than the current one.* Before continuing with developing this project, you want to display the title slide. If you are using a touch screen, you can tap the desired slide in the Thumbnail pane; if you are using a mouse, you can click the desired slide in the Thumbnail pane or drag the scroll box on the vertical scroll bar. When you drag the scroll box, the **slide indicator** shows the number and title of the slide you are about to display. Releasing shows the slide. The following steps move from Slide 4 to Slide 1 using the scroll box in the Slide pane.

- Position the pointer on the scroll box.
- Press and hold down the mouse button so that Slide: 4 of 4 Keep Replenishing Fluid Levels appears in the slide indicator (Figure 1–41).

Figure 1–41

❷

- Drag the scroll box up the vertical scroll bar until Slide: 1 of 4 Healthy Hydration appears in the slide indicator (Figure 1–42).

Figure 1–42

3

- Release so that Slide 1 appears in the Slide pane and the Slide 1 thumbnail has an orange border in the Thumbnail pane (Figure 1–43).

Figure 1–43

Other Ways

1. Click Next Slide button or Previous Slide button to move forward or back one slide
2. Tap or click slide in Thumbnail pane
3. Press PAGE DOWN or PAGE UP to move forward or back one slide

Inserting Photos and Illustrations into Slides

A **clip** is a single media file, such as a photo, illustration, sound, or video. Adding a clip can help increase the visual and audio appeal of many slides and can offer a quick way to add professional-looking graphics and multimedia to a presentation without creating these files yourself. This material is contained in the **Office.com Clip Art** collection of drawings, photos, sounds, and other media files shared among Microsoft Office applications.

You also can add your own clips to slides. These images may include scanned photos, illustrations, and artwork from storage media, such as USB flash drives, hard disks, and memory cards. If you have a Microsoft account, you can add photos from other websites, including Flickr and SkyDrive.

You can add images from Office.com to your presentation in two ways. One way is by selecting one of the slide layouts that includes a content placeholder with an Online Pictures button. A second method is by tapping or clicking the Online Pictures button in the Images area on the INSERT tab. Tapping or clicking the Online Pictures button opens the Insert Pictures dialog box. The **Insert Pictures dialog box** allows you to search for clip art by using descriptive keywords. Clips have one or more keywords associated with various entities, activities, labels, and emotions.

If you have an active connection to the Internet, clips from the Microsoft Office.com website will display automatically as the result of your search. Microsoft constantly revises the content of Office.com, so you may not be able to locate the pictures used in this chapter. Contact your instructor if you need the photos and illustration used in the following steps.

CONSIDER THIS

How can you design a title slide that holds your audience's attention?

Develop a slide that reflects the content of your presentation but does so in a thought-provoking way. A title, at the very least, should prepare your audience for the material they are about to see and hear. Look for ways to focus attention on your theme and the method in which you plan to present this theme. A unique photograph or graphic can help generate interest. You may decide to introduce your topic with a startling fact, a rhetorical question, or a quotation. The device you choose depends upon your audience, the occasion, and the presentation's purpose.

To Insert a Picture from Office.com into the Title Slide

1 INSERT PRESENTATION SLIDES | 2 ENTER TEXT | 3 FORMAT TEXT | **4 INSERT GRAPHICAL ELEMENTS**
5 SIZE & POSITION | 6 ENHANCE SLIDE SHOW | 7 DISPLAY & PRINT SLIDES

Slide 1 uses the Title Slide layout, which has two placeholders for text but none for graphical content. You desire to place a graphic on Slide 1. *Why? It is likely that your viewers will see an image on this slide before they read any text, so you want to include a photo to create interest in the presentation and introduce your audience to the topic. For this presentation,* you will locate a photo of a person holding a water bottle and then insert this photo in this slide. Later in this chapter, you will resize and position the photo in an appropriate location. The following steps add a photo to Slide 1.

- Tap or click INSERT on the ribbon to display the INSERT tab.

- Tap or click the Online Pictures button (INSERT tab | Images group) to display the Insert Pictures dialog box.

- With the insertion point in the Office.com Clip Art area, type **water bottle** in the search box (Figure 1–44).

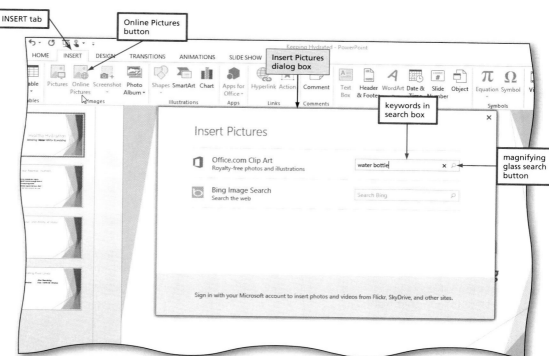

Figure 1–44

2

- Tap or click the Search button (the magnifying glass) or press the ENTER key so that Office.com will search for and display all clips having the keywords, water bottle.

◄ | Why does the x button display when I begin typing the search terms?
Q&A | Clicking the x button deletes all letters in the box.

3

- If necessary, slide or scroll down the list to display the photo shown in Figure 1–45.

- Tap or click the photo to select it (Figure 1–45).

◄ | What if the water bottle image
Q&A | displayed in Figure1–45 is not shown in my Office.com Clip Art dialog box?
Select a similar photo. Microsoft updates the files in the Office.com Clip art collection, so the images change constantly.

What are the words and numbers in the lower-left corner of the dialog box?
The words are the keywords associated with this photo, and the figures are the number of pixels associated with the width and height of the clip.

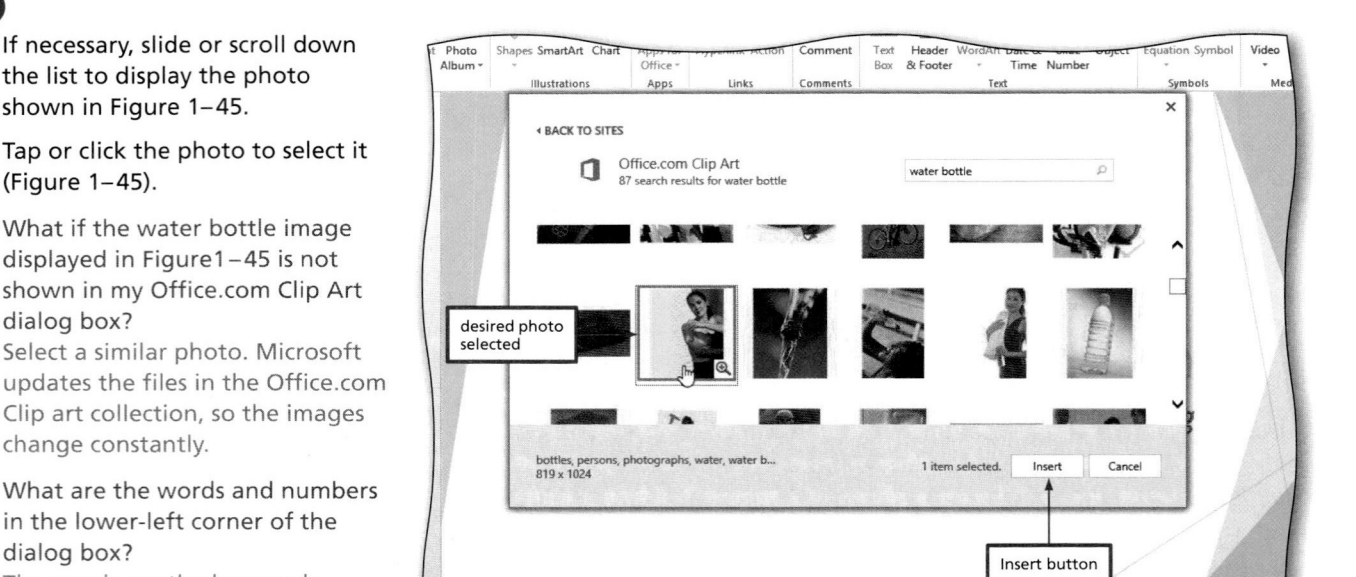

Figure 1–45

4

- Tap or click the Insert button to download the photo and insert it into the slide (Figure 1–46).

◄ | Can I double-tap or double-click
Q&A | the photo instead of selecting it and then tap or click the Insert button?
Yes. Either method downloads and inserts the photo.

Why is this photo displayed in this location on the slide?
The slide layout does not have a content placeholder, so PowerPoint inserts the file in the center of the slide.

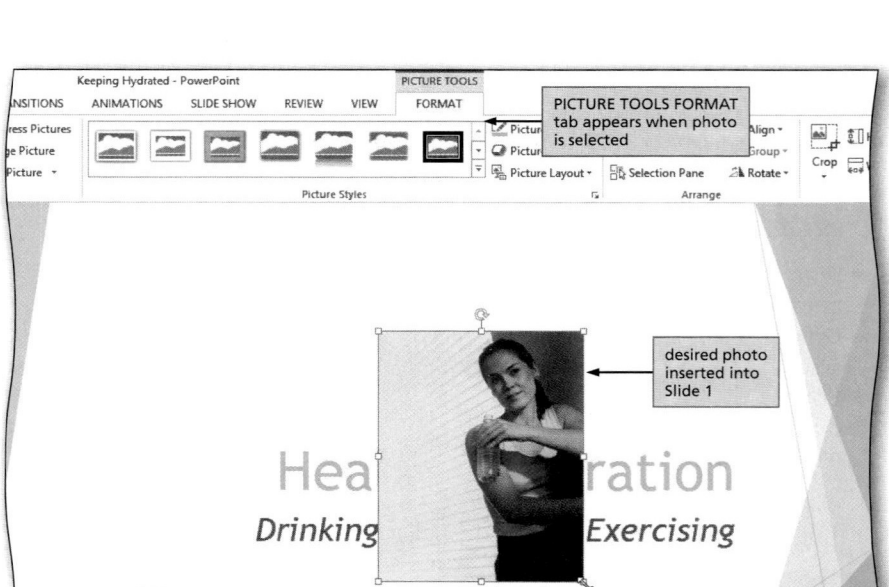

Figure 1–46

To Insert a Picture from Office.com into a Slide without a Content Placeholder

The next step is to add a water bottle photo to Slide 2. This slide has a bulleted list in the text placeholder, so the icon group does not display in the center of the placeholder. Later in this chapter, you will resize the inserted photo. The following steps add one photo to Slide 2.

1 Tap or click the Slide 2 thumbnail in the Thumbnail pane to display Slide 2.

2 Tap or click INSERT on the ribbon to display the INSERT tab and then tap or click the Online Pictures button (INSERT tab | Images group) to display the Insert Pictures dialog box.

3 Type **water bottle** in the Office.com Clip Art search box and then tap or click the Search button.

4 If necessary, slide or scroll down the list to display the water bottle photo shown in Figure 1–47, tap or click the photo to select it, and then tap or click the Insert button to download and insert the photo into Slide 2 (Figure 1–47).

Q&A | Why is my photo a different size from the one shown in Figure1–1b on page PPT 3? The clip was inserted into the slide and not into a content placeholder. You will resize the photo later in this chapter.

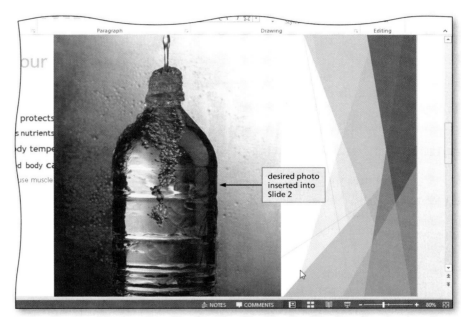

Figure 1–47

To Insert an Illustration from Office.com into a Slide without a Content Placeholder

Next, you will add an illustration to Slide 3. You will not insert this file into a content placeholder, so it will display in the center of the slide. Later in this chapter, you will resize this illustration. You locate and download illustrations in the same manner you used to locate and download photos. The following steps add an illustration to Slide 3.

1 Tap or click the Slide 3 thumbnail in the Thumbnail pane.

2 Display the INSERT tab, tap or click the Online Pictures button, type **drinking water** as the search text, and then tap or click the Search button.

3 If necessary, slide or scroll down the list to display the picture of a character drinking water shown in Figure 1–48 and then insert it into Slide 3 (Figure 1–48).

Figure 1–48

To Insert a Picture from Office.com into a Content Placeholder

1 INSERT PRESENTATION SLIDES | 2 ENTER TEXT | 3 FORMAT TEXT | **4 INSERT GRAPHICAL ELEMENTS**
5 SIZE & POSITION | 6 ENHANCE SLIDE SHOW | 7 DISPLAY & PRINT SLIDES

Slide 4 uses the Comparison layout, which has a content placeholder below each of the two headings. You desire to insert photos into both content placeholders. *Why? You want to reinforce the concept that people should drink water during and after workouts.* The following steps insert photos of a female into the left content placeholder and a male into the right content placeholder on Slide 4.

1
- Tap or click the Slide 4 thumbnail in the Thumbnail pane to display Slide 4 (Figure 1–49).

Figure 1–49

- Tap or click the Online Pictures icon in the left content placeholder to select that placeholder and to open the Insert Pictures dialog box.

- Tap or click the search box, type **women bottled water** as the search text, and then press the ENTER key.

- If necessary, slide or scroll down the list to display the photo shown in Figure 1–50.

- Select the photo and then double-tap or double-click to download and insert it into the left content placeholder (Figure 1–50).

Figure 1–50

❸

- Tap or click the Online Pictures icon in the right content placeholder to select that placeholder and to open the Insert Pictures dialog box.

- Tap or click the search box, type **men exercises hydration** as the search text, and press or tap the ENTER key.

- If necessary, slide or scroll down the list to display the photo shown in Figure 1–51.

- Insert the photo into the right content placeholder (Figure 1–51).

Figure 1–51

Break Point: If you wish to take a break, this is a good place to do so. You can save your presentation and then exit PowerPoint now. To resume at a later time, run PowerPoint, open the file called Keeping Hydrated, and continue following the steps from this location forward.

Resizing Photos and Illustrations

Sometimes it is necessary to change the size of photos and illustrations. **Resizing** includes enlarging or reducing the size of a graphic. You can resize these images using a variety of techniques. One method involves changing the size of a picture by specifying exact dimensions in a dialog box. Another method involves sliding or dragging one of the graphic's sizing handles to the desired location. A selected graphic appears surrounded by a **selection rectangle**, which has small squares and circles, called **sizing handles** or move handles, at each corner and middle location.

BTW
PowerPoint Help
At any time while using PowerPoint, you can find answers to questions and display information about various topics through PowerPoint Help. Used properly, this form of assistance can increase your productivity and reduce your frustrations by minimizing the time you spend learning how to use PowerPoint. For instruction about PowerPoint Help and exercises that will help you gain confidence in using it, read the Office and Windows chapter at the beginning of this book.

To Proportionally Resize Pictures

Why? *On Slides 1, 2, and 3, the photo and illustration sizes are either too small or too large to display aesthetically on the slides. The photo and illustration on Slides 1 and 3 are too small, and the photo on Slide 2 is too large.* The photo on Slide 1 is of a person, so it generally is important to maintain the proportions. To change the size of a photo and keep the width and height in proportion to each other, drag the corner sizing handles to view how the image will look on the slide. Using these corner handles maintains the graphic's original proportions. If, however, the proportions do not need to be maintained, as with the water bottle on Slide 2, drag the square sizing handles to alter the proportions so that the graphic's height and width become larger or smaller. The following steps proportionally increase the size of the Slide 1 photo using a corner sizing handle.

1

- Click the Slide 1 thumbnail in the Thumbnail pane to display Slide 1.

- Tap or click the photo to select it and display the selection rectangle.

- Point to the upper-right corner sizing handle on the illustration so that the pointer changes to a two-headed arrow (Figure 1–52).

Q&A I am using a touch screen and do not see a two-headed arrow when I press and hold the upper-right sizing handle. Why?
Touch screens may not display pointers; you can just press and slide sizing handles to resize.

Figure 1–52

2

- Drag the sizing handle diagonally toward the upper-right corner of the slide until the upper-right sizing handle or the crosshair is positioned approximately as shown in Figure 1–53.

Q&A What if the illustration is not the same size as the one shown in Figure 1–53?
Repeat Steps 1 and 2.

Figure 1–53

- Release to resize the illustration.

- Tap or click outside the illustration to deselect it (Figure 1–54).

Q&A What happened to the PICTURE TOOLS FORMAT tab?

When you tap or click outside the illustration, PowerPoint deselects the illustration and removes the PICTURE TOOLS FORMAT tab from the screen.

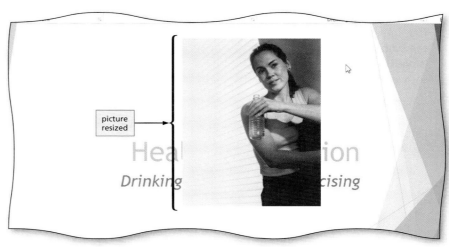

Figure 1–54

To Nonproportionally Resize the Photograph on Slide 2

1 INSERT PRESENTATION SLIDES | 2 ENTER TEXT | 3 FORMAT TEXT | 4 INSERT GRAPHICAL ELEMENTS
5 SIZE & POSITION | **6 ENHANCE SLIDE SHOW** | 7 DISPLAY & PRINT SLIDES

Why? *The height of the water bottle photo in Slide 2 extends from the top to the bottom of the slide. The width, however, will cover some of the text when the photo is positioned on the right side of the slide.* The width of this photo can be decreased slightly without negatively distorting the original image. You can decrease the width of a photo by sliding or dragging one of the square sizing handles on the sides of the image. The following steps resize the width of the water bottle photo using a sizing handle along the side of the image.

- Display Slide 2 and then tap or click the water bottle photo to select it and display the selection rectangle.

- Tap or click the Zoom Out button as many times as necessary until the Zoom level is 60%.

- Press or point to the sizing handle on the left side of the photo so that the pointer changes to a two-headed arrow (Figure 1–55).

Figure 1–55

- Drag the sizing handle toward the right side of the slide until the sizing handle or crosshair is positioned approximately as shown in Figure 1–56.

Q&A What if the illustration is not the same size as the one shown in Figure 1–56?
Repeat Steps 1 and 2.

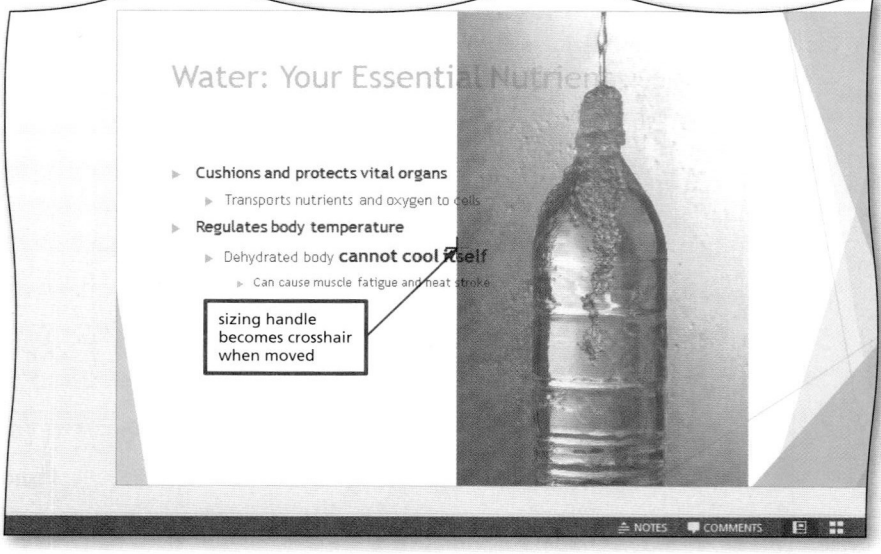

Figure 1–56

- Release to resize the photo.
- Tap or click outside the photo to deselect it (Figure 1–57).

Q&A What if I want to return the photo to its original size and start again?
With the photo selected, tap or click the Reset Picture arrow (PICTURE TOOLS FORMAT tab | Adjust group) and then click Reset Picture & Size in the Reset Picture gallery.

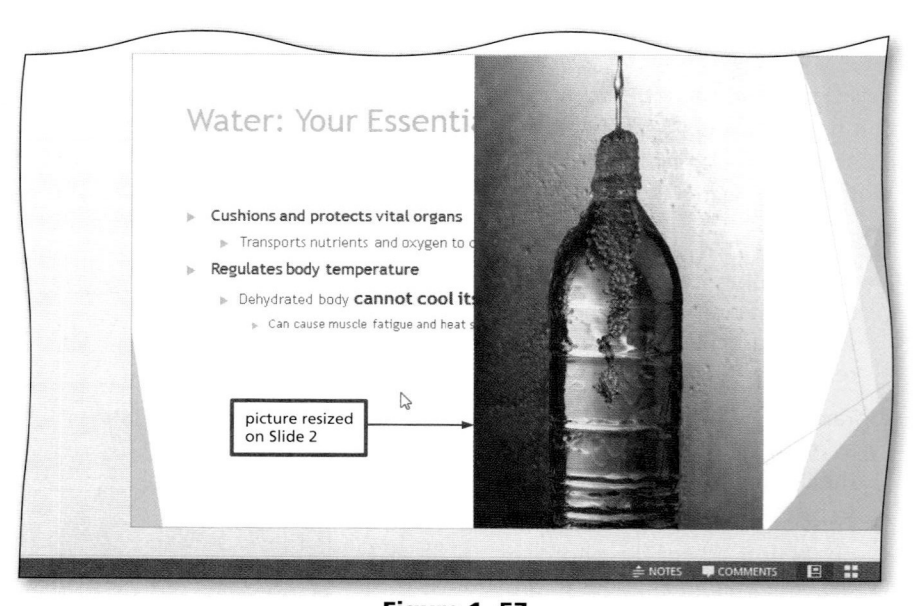

Figure 1–57

To Resize the Illustration on Slide 3

The illustration on Slide 3 can be reduced slightly to fit entirely on the slide. You resize an illustration in the same manner that you resize a photo. You want to maintain the proportions of the character and water in this illustration, so you will drag one of the corner sizing handles. The following steps resize this illustration using a corner sizing handle.

1 Display Slide 3 and then tap or click the character drinking water illustration to select it.

2 Drag the lower-left corner sizing handle on the illustration diagonally outward until the illustration is resized approximately as shown in Figure 1–58.

Figure 1–58

To Move Pictures

1 INSERT PRESENTATION SLIDES | 2 ENTER TEXT | 3 FORMAT TEXT | 4 INSERT GRAPHICAL ELEMENTS
5 SIZE & POSITION | 6 ENHANCE SLIDE SHOW | 7 DISPLAY & PRINT SLIDES

Why? *After you insert a photo or an illustration on a slide, you might want to reposition it. The female athlete photo on Slide 1 could be moved to the left side of the slide, the water bottle on Slide 2 could be moved to the right side of the slide, and the illustration on Slide 3 could be positioned in the center of the slide.* PowerPoint displays **Smart Guides** automatically when a photo, illustration, shape, or other object is close to lining up with another slide element. For example, a Smart Guide will display to help you align the right or left edge of a picture in relation to a text placeholder or to another picture. The following steps move the photos on Slides 1 and 2 and center the illustration on Slide 3.

1

- If necessary, tap or click the character illustration on Slide 3 to select it.

- Drag the illustration upward until the horizontal Smart Guide is displayed under the title text placeholder and the vertical Smart Guide is displayed through the center of the slide, as shown in Figure 1–59, and then release.

- If necessary, select the photo and then use the ARROW keys to position it precisely as shown in Figure 1–59.

Q&A The illustration still is not located exactly where I want it to display. What can I do to align the image? Press the CTRL key while you press the ARROW keys. This key combination moves the illustration in smaller increments than when you press only an ARROW key.

Figure 1–59

2

- Display Slide 2 and then tap or click the water bottle photo to select it.

- Drag the photo to align with the right edge of the slide (Figure 1–60).

Q&A My water bottle photo is covering some of the title text on the slide. What should I do?
Either resize the photo to make it narrower or move the photo to the right so that it is hanging slightly off the side of the slide.

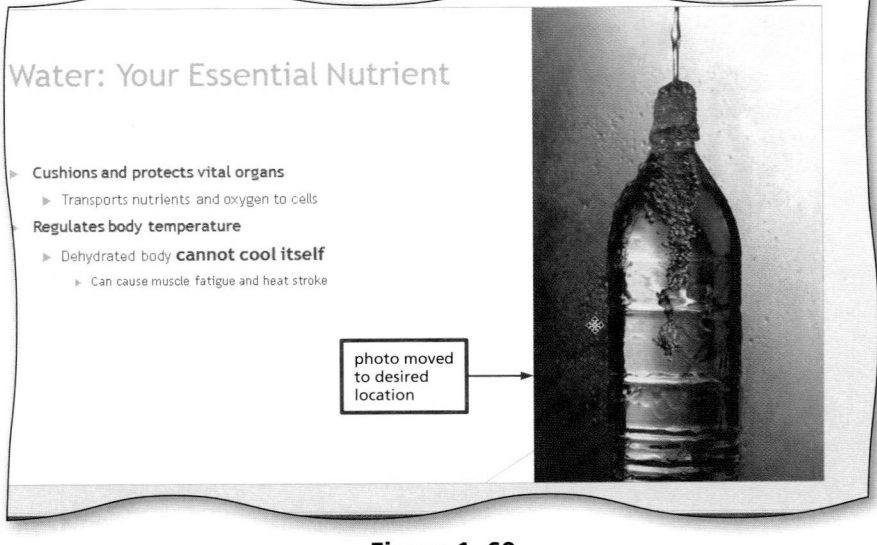

Figure 1–60

3

- Display Slide 1 and then tap or click the athlete photo to select it.

- Drag the photo to the left and either upward or downward until the horizontal center Smart Guide is displayed, as shown in Figure 1–61, and then release.

4

- Tap or click outside the photo to deselect it.

Figure 1–61

Q&A The athlete photo is too wide and is covering some of the text on the slide. What should I do?
Changing the width of a photo showing a person generally is not advisable because the altered proportions make the person appear tall and thin or short and overweight. In this case, move the photo to the left so that it is hanging slightly off the side of the slide, as shown in Figure1–61.

Ending a Slide Show with a Closing Slide

All the text for the slides in the Healthy Hydration slide show has been entered. This presentation thus far consists of a title slide, one text slide with a multilevel bulleted list, a third slide for a photo, and a fourth slide with a Comparison layout. A closing slide that resembles the title slide is the final slide to create.

What factors should you consider when developing a closing slide for the presentation?
After the last slide appears during a slide show, the default PowerPoint setting is to end the presentation with a **black slide**. This black slide appears only when the slide show is running and concludes the slide show, so your audience never sees the PowerPoint window. It is a good idea, however, to end your presentation with a final closing slide to display at the end of the presentation. This slide ends the presentation gracefully and should be an exact copy, or a very similar copy, of your title slide. The audience will recognize that the presentation is drawing to a close when this slide appears. It can remain on the screen when the audience asks questions, approaches the speaker for further information, or exits the room.

To Duplicate a Slide

Why? *When two slides contain similar information and have the same format, duplicating one slide and then making minor modifications to the new slide saves time and increases consistency.*

Slide 5 will have the same layout and design as Slide 1. The most expedient method of creating this slide is to copy Slide 1 and then make minor modifications to the new slide. The following steps duplicate the title slide.

1

• With Slide 1 selected, tap or click the New Slide arrow (HOME tab | Slides group) to display the Facet layout gallery (Figure 1–62).

Figure 1–62

2

• Tap or click 'Duplicate Selected Slides' in the Facet layout gallery to create a new Slide 2, which is a duplicate of Slide 1 (Figure 1–63).

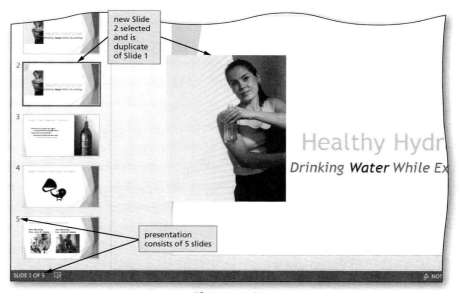

Figure 1–63

Break Point: If you wish to take a break, this is a good place to do so. Be sure to save the Keeping Hydrated file again and then you can exit PowerPoint. To resume at a later time, run PowerPoint, open the file called Keeping Hydrated, and continue following the steps from this location forward.

PPT 42 **PowerPoint Chapter 1** Creating and Editing a Presentation with Pictures

1 INSERT PRESENTATION SLIDES | 2 ENTER TEXT | 3 FORMAT TEXT | 4 INSERT GRAPHICAL ELEMENTS
5 SIZE & POSITION | 6 ENHANCE SLIDE SHOW | 7 DISPLAY & PRINT SLIDES

To Arrange a Slide

The new Slide 2 was inserted directly below Slide 1 because Slide 1 was the selected slide. This duplicate slide needs to display at the end of the presentation directly after the final title and content slide. *Why? It is a closing slide that reinforces the concept presented in Slide 1 and indicates to your audiences that your presentation is ending.*

Changing slide order is an easy process and is best performed in the Thumbnail pane. When you tap or click the thumbnail and begin to drag it to a new location, the remaining thumbnails realign to show the new sequence. When you release, the slide drops into the desired location. Hence, this process of sliding or dragging and then dropping the thumbnail in a new location is called **drag and drop**. You can use the drag-and-drop method to move any selected item, including text and graphics. The following step moves the new Slide 2 to the end of the presentation so that it becomes a closing slide.

1

- With Slide 2 selected, drag the Slide 2 slide thumbnail below the last slide in the Thumbnail pane (Figure 1–64).

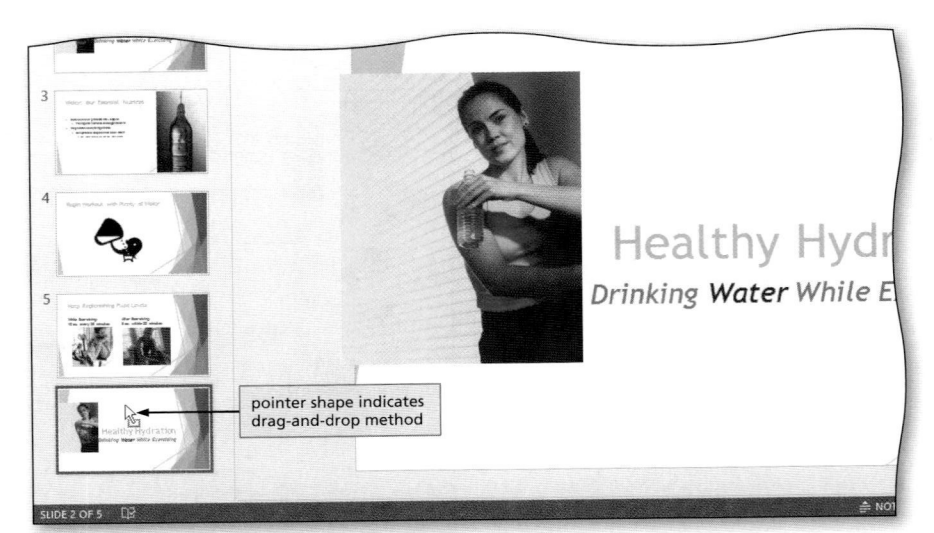

Figure 1–64

Other Ways

1. Tap or click Slide Sorter button on status bar, drag thumbnail to new location

2. Tap or click Slide Sorter button (VIEW tab | Presentation Views group), tap or click slide thumbnail, drag thumbnail to new location

Making Changes to Slide Text Content

After creating slides in a presentation, you may find that you want to make changes to the text. Changes may be required because a slide contains an error, the scope of the presentation shifts, or the style is inconsistent. This section explains the types of changes that commonly occur when creating a presentation.

You generally make three types of changes to text in a presentation: additions, replacements, and deletions.

- Additions are necessary when you omit text from a slide and need to add it later. You may need to insert text in the form of a sentence, word, or single character. For example, you may want to add the presenter's middle name on the title slide.

- Replacements are needed when you want to revise the text in a presentation. For example, you may want to substitute the word, *their*, for the word, *there*.

- Deletions are required when text on a slide is incorrect or no longer is relevant to the presentation. For example, a slide may look cluttered. Therefore, you may want to remove one of the bulleted paragraphs to add more space.

Editing text in PowerPoint basically is the same as editing text in a word processing program. The following sections illustrate the most common changes made to text in a presentation.

Replacing Text in an Existing Slide

When you need to correct a word or phrase, you can replace the text by selecting the text to be replaced and then typing the new text. As soon as you press any key on the keyboard, the selected text is deleted and the new text is displayed.

PowerPoint inserts text to the left of the insertion point. The text to the right of the insertion point moves to the right (and shifts downward if necessary) to accommodate the added text.

Deleting Text

You can delete text using one of many methods. One is to use the BACKSPACE key to remove text just typed. The second is to position the insertion point to the left of the text you want to delete and then press the DELETE key. The third method is to drag through the text you want to delete and then tap or click the Cut button on the mini toolbar, press DELETE or BACKSPACE key, or press CTRL + X. Use the third method when deleting large sections of text.

To Delete Text in a Placeholder

1 INSERT PRESENTATION SLIDES | 2 ENTER TEXT | 3 FORMAT TEXT | 4 INSERT GRAPHICAL ELEMENTS
5 SIZE & POSITION | 6 ENHANCE SLIDE SHOW | **7 DISPLAY & PRINT SLIDES**

Why? To keep the ending slide clean and simple, you want to delete a few words in the slide title and subtitle text. The following steps change Healthy Hydration to Be Healthy and then change Drinking Water While Exercising to Drink Water.

- With Slide 5 selected, position the pointer immediately to the right of the last character of the text to be selected in the title text placeholder (in this case, the n in the word, Hydration).

- Drag the pointer through the first character of the text to be selected (in this case, the space after the word, Healthy) (Figure 1–65).

Q&A
I am having difficulty selecting the required text. Can I drag from left to right or right to left?
Yes. You may need several attempts to select the correct characters.

Could I also have selected the word, Hydration, by double-tapping or double-clicking it?
Yes. Either method works to select a word.

Figure 1–65

- Tap or click the Cut button (HOME tab | Clipboard group) to delete the selected text and space.

- Position the pointer to the left of the word, Healthy, and then type **Be** and press the SPACEBAR as the first word in the title text placeholder (Figure 1–66).

- If requested by your instructor, add your mother's first name after the word, Healthy, in the title text placeholder.

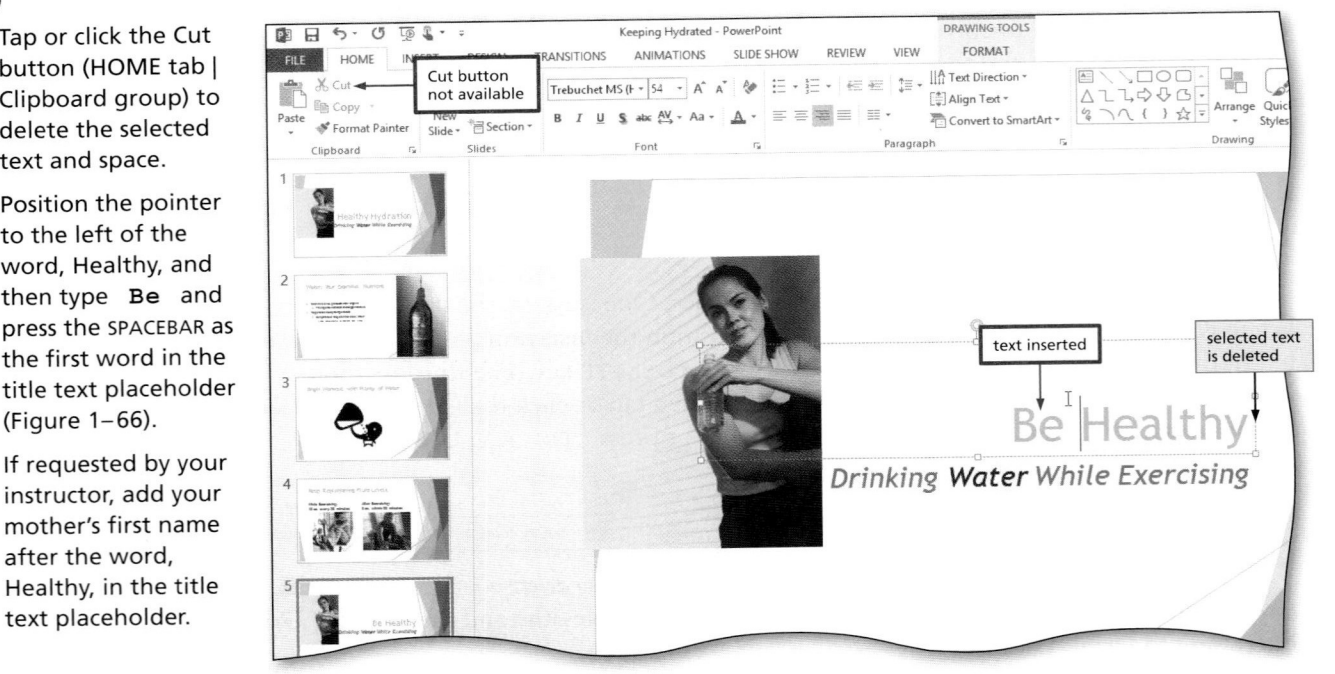

Figure 1–66

- Position the pointer immediately to the right of the last character of the text to be selected in the subtitle text placeholder (in this case, the g in the word, Exercising).

- Drag the pointer to the left through the last character of the text to be selected (in this case, the space after the word, Water) (Figure 1–67).

Figure 1–67

- Tap or click the Cut button.

- Select the letters, ing, in the word, Drinking.

- Tap or click the Cut button (Figure 1–68).

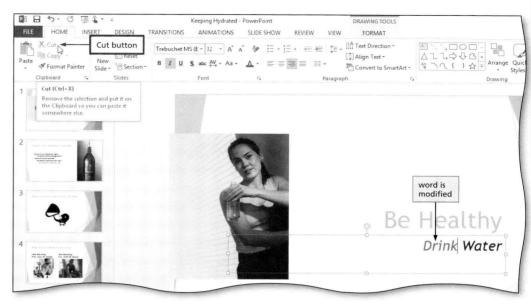

Figure 1–68

Other Ways

1. Tap 'Show Context Menu' button on mini toolbar or right-click selected text, tap or click Cut on shortcut menu
2. Select text, press DELETE or BACKSPACE key
3. Select text, press CTRL+X

Adding a Transition

PowerPoint includes a wide variety of visual and sound effects that can be applied to text or content. A **slide transition** is a special effect used to progress from one slide to the next in a slide show. You can control the speed of the transition effect and add a sound.

To Add a Transition between Slides

1 INSERT PRESENTATION SLIDES | 2 ENTER TEXT | 3 FORMAT TEXT | 4 INSERT GRAPHICAL ELEMENTS
5 SIZE & POSITION | 6 ENHANCE SLIDE SHOW | **7 DISPLAY & PRINT SLIDES**

Why? *Transitions add interest when you advance the slides in a presentation and make a slide show presentation look professional.* In this presentation, you apply the Switch transition in the Exciting category to all slides and change the transition speed from 1.25 seconds to 2 seconds. The following steps apply this transition to the presentation.

1

- Tap or click the TRANSITIONS tab on the ribbon and then point to the More button (TRANSITIONS tab | Transition to This Slide group) in the Transition to This Slide gallery (Figure 1–69).

Figure 1–69

 Is a transition applied now?

No. None, the first slide icon in the Transition to This Slide group, is selected, which indicates no transition has been applied.

②

- Tap or click the More button to expand the Transitions gallery.

- Point to the Switch transition in the Exciting category in the Transitions gallery (Figure 1–70).

Figure 1–70

③

- Tap or click Switch in the Exciting category in the Transitions gallery to apply this transition to the closing slide.

Q&A Why does a star appear next to Slide 5 in the Thumbnail pane?
The star indicates that a transition animation effect is applied to that slide.

- Tap or click the Duration up arrow (TRANSITIONS tab | Timing group) seven times to change the transition speed from 01.25 seconds to 03.00 seconds (Figure 1–71).

Q&A Why did the time change from the default 2.00 to 1.25?
Each transition has a default duration time. The default Switch transition time is 01.25 seconds.

Figure 1–71

4

• Tap or click the Preview Transitions button (TRANSITIONS tab | Preview area) to view the transition and the new transition time (Figure 1–72).

Q&A Can I adjust the duration time I just set?

Yes. Tap or click the Duration up or down arrows or type a speed in the Duration box and preview the transition until you find the time that best fits your presentation.

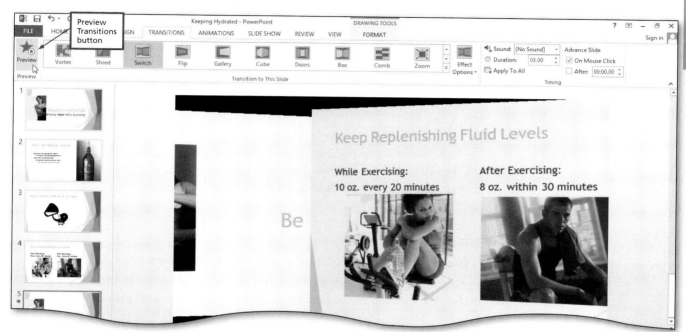

Figure 1–72

5

• Tap or click the 'Apply To All' button (TRANSITIONS tab | Timing group) to apply the Switch transition and the increased transition time to Slides 1 through 4 in the presentation (Figure 1–73).

Q&A What if I want to apply a different transition and duration to each slide in the presentation?

Repeat Steps 2 and 3 for each slide individually.

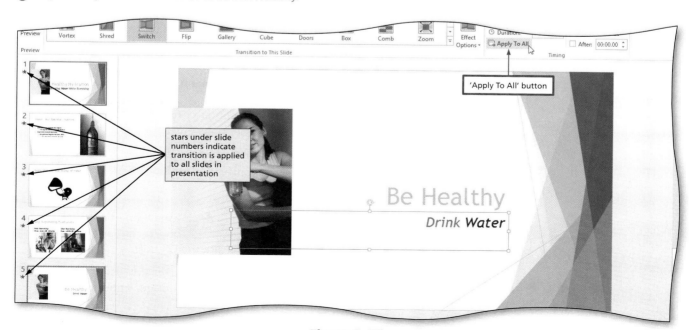

Figure 1–73

Document Properties

PowerPoint helps you organize and identify your files by using **document properties**, which are the details about a file such as the project author, title, and subject. For example, a class name or presentation topic can describe the file's purpose or content.

CONSIDER THIS

Why would you want to assign document properties to a presentation?

Document properties are valuable for a variety of reasons:

- Users can save time locating a particular file because they can view a file's document properties without opening the presentation.

- By creating consistent properties for files having similar content, users can better organize their presentations.

- Some organizations require PowerPoint users to add document properties so that other employees can view details about these files.

The more common document properties are standard and automatically updated properties. **Standard properties** are associated with all Microsoft Office files and include author, title, and subject. **Automatically updated properties** include file system properties, such as the date you create or change a file, and statistics, such as the file size.

TO CHANGE DOCUMENT PROPERTIES

BTW

Printing Document Properties

PowerPoint 2013 does not allow you to print document properties. This feature, however, is available in other Office 2013 apps, including Word and Excel.

To change document properties, you would follow these steps.

1. Tap or click FILE on the ribbon to open the Backstage view and then, if necessary, tap or click the Info tab in the Backstage view to display the Info gallery.

2. If the property you wish to change is displayed in the Properties list in the right pane of the Info gallery, try to tap or click to the right of the property. If a box appears to the right of the property, type the text for the property in the box, and then tap or click the Back button in the upper-left corner of the Backstage view to return to the PowerPoint window. Skip the remaining steps.

3. If the property you wish to change is not displayed in the Properties list in the right pane of the Info gallery or you cannot change it in the Info gallery, tap or click the Properties button in the right pane to display the Properties menu, and then tap or click 'Show Document Panel' on the Properties menu to close the Backstage view and display the Document Information Panel in the PowerPoint presentation window.

Q&A Why are some of the document properties in my Document Information Panel already filled in?

The person who installed Office 2013 on your computer or network may have set or customized the properties.

4. Type the desired text in the appropriate property boxes.

Q&A What if the property I want to change is not displayed in the Document Information Panel?

Tap or click the Document Properties button in the Document Information Panel and then tap or click Advanced Properties on the menu to display the Properties dialog box. If necessary, tap or click the Summary tab (Properties dialog box) to display the Summary sheet, fill in the appropriate boxes, and then tap or click the OK button.

5. Tap or click the 'Close the Document Information Panel' button at the right edge of the Document Information Panel so that the panel no longer appears in the PowerPoint presentation window.

Viewing the Presentation in Slide Show View

The Start From Beginning button, located in the Quick Access Toolbar, allows you to show a presentation using a computer. As the name implies, the first slide to be displayed always will be Slide 1. You also can run a presentation starting with the slide currently displaying when you tap or click the Slide Show button on the status bar. In either case, PowerPoint displays the slides on the full screen without any of the PowerPoint window objects, such as the ribbon. The full-screen slide hides the toolbars, menus, and other PowerPoint window elements.

To Start Slide Show View

1 INSERT PRESENTATION SLIDES | 2 ENTER TEXT | 3 FORMAT TEXT | 4 INSERT GRAPHICAL ELEMENTS
5 SIZE & POSITION | 6 ENHANCE SLIDE SHOW | **7 DISPLAY & PRINT SLIDES**

Why? *You run a presentation in for your audience so they can see the slides in their entirety and view any transitions or other effects added to the slides.* When making a presentation, you use **Slide Show view**. You can start Slide Show view from Normal view or Slide Sorter view. Slide Show view begins when you tap or click the Start From Beginning button or the Slide Show button. The following steps start Slide Show view starting with Slide 1.

- If you are using a touch screen, proceed to Step 2. If you are using a mouse, point to the Start From Beginning button (Figure 1–74).

Q&A | What would have displayed if I had tapped or clicked the Slide Show button instead of the Start From Beginning button?
When you tap or click the Slide Show button to start the presentation, PowerPoint begins the show with the currently displayed slide, which in this case is Slide 5. Only Slide 5 would display during the slide show.

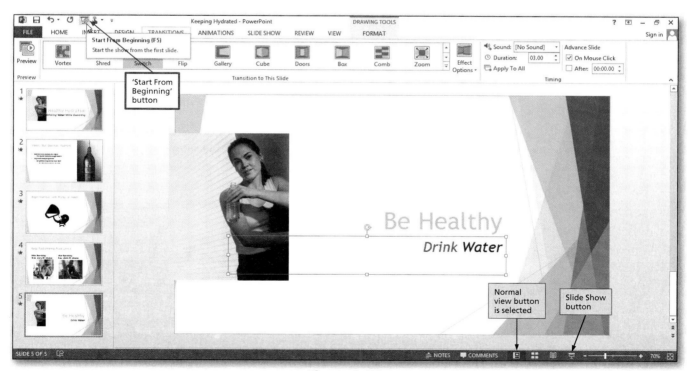

Figure 1–74

2

- Tap or click the Start From Beginning button to display the title slide (Figure 1–75).

Q&A | Where is the PowerPoint window?
When you run a slide show, the PowerPoint window is hidden. It will reappear once you end your slide show.

Figure 1–75

Other Ways
1. Display Slide 1, tap or click Slide Show button on status bar

To Move Manually through Slides in a Slide Show

1 INSERT PRESENTATION SLIDES | 2 ENTER TEXT | 3 FORMAT TEXT | 4 INSERT GRAPHICAL ELEMENTS
5 SIZE & POSITION | 6 ENHANCE SLIDE SHOW | **7 DISPLAY & PRINT SLIDES**

After you begin Slide Show view, you can move forward or backward through the slides. PowerPoint allows you to advance through the slides manually or automatically. During a slide show, each slide in the presentation shows on the screen, one slide at a time. Each time you tap or click, the next slide appears. The following steps move manually through the slides. *Why? You can control the length of time each slide is displayed and change the preset order if you need to review a slide already shown or jump ahead to another slide designed to display later in the presentation.*

❶

- Swipe forward on or click each slide until Slide 5 (Be Healthy) is displayed (Figure 1–76).

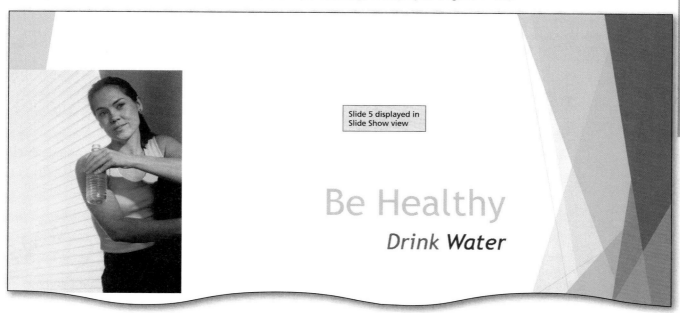

Figure 1–76

❷

- Swipe forward on or click Slide 5 so that the black slide appears with a message announcing the end of the slide show (Figure 1–77).

Q&A I see a small toolbar in the lower-left corner of my slide. What is this toolbar?
The Slide Show toolbar appears when you begin running a slide show and then tap a slide or move the pointer. The buttons on this toolbar allow you to navigate to the next slide, the previous slide, to mark up the current slide, or to change the current display.

Figure 1–77

3

- Swipe forward on or click the black slide to return to Normal view in the PowerPoint window.

Other Ways

1. Press PAGE DOWN to advance one slide at a time, or press PAGE UP to go back one slide at a time

2. Press RIGHT ARROW or DOWN ARROW to advance one slide at a time, or press LEFT ARROW or UP ARROW to go back one slide at a time

3. If Slide Show toolbar is displayed, tap or click Next Slide or Previous Slide button on toolbar

Printing a Presentation

After creating a presentation, you may want to print it. Printing a presentation enables you to distribute it to others in a form that can be read or viewed but typically not edited. It is a good practice to save a presentation before printing it, in the event you experience difficulties printing.

CONSIDER THIS

What is the best method for distributing a presentation?

The traditional method of distributing a presentation uses a printer to produce a hard copy. A **hard copy** or **printout** is information that exists on a physical medium such as paper. Hard copies can be useful for the following reasons:

- Some people prefer proofreading a hard copy of a presentation rather than viewing it on the screen to check for errors and readability.

- Hard copies can serve as a backup reference if your storage medium is lost or becomes corrupted and you need to recreate the presentation.

 Instead of distributing a hard copy of a presentation, users can distribute the presentation as an electronic image that mirrors the original presentation's appearance. The electronic image of the presentation can be sent as an email attachment, posted on a website, or copied to a portable storage medium such as a USB flash drive. Two popular electronic image formats, sometimes called fixed formats, are PDF by Adobe Systems and XPS by Microsoft. In PowerPoint, you can create electronic image files through the Save As dialog box and the Export, Share, and Print tabs in the Backstage view. Electronic images of presentations, such as PDF and XPS, can be useful for the following reasons:

- Users can view electronic images of presentations without the software that created the original presentation (e.g., PowerPoint). Specifically, to view a PDF file, you use a program called Adobe Reader, which can be downloaded free from Adobe's website. Similarly, to view an XPS file, you use a program called XPS Viewer, which is included in the latest versions of Windows and Internet Explorer.

- Sending electronic presentations saves paper and printer supplies. Society encourages users to contribute to **green computing**, which involves reducing the electricity consumed and environmental waste generated when using computers, mobile devices, and related technologies.

To Print a Presentation

1 INSERT PRESENTATION SLIDES | 2 ENTER TEXT | 3 FORMAT TEXT | 4 INSERT GRAPHICAL ELEMENTS | 5 SIZE & POSITION | 6 ENHANCE SLIDE SHOW | **7 DISPLAY & PRINT SLIDES**

With the completed presentation saved, you may want to print it. *Why? You could distribute a handout of the slides to your audience members, or you might want to keep a printed copy as a backup in the event you experience technical difficulties before or during your speech. You, therefore, will print a hard copy on a printer.* The following steps print a hard copy of the contents of the saved Keeping Hydrated presentation.

- Tap or click FILE on the ribbon to open the Backstage view.

- Tap or click the Print tab in the Backstage view to display the Print gallery (Figure 1–78).

Q&A | How do I preview Slides 2 through 5?
Tap or click the Next Page button in the Print gallery to scroll forward through pages in the document; similarly, tap or click the Previous Page button to scroll backward through pages.

How can I print multiple copies of my presentation?
Increase the number in the Copies box in the Print gallery.

What if I decide not to print the presentation at this time?
Tap or click the Back button in the upper-left corner of the Backstage view to return to the presentation window.

2

- Verify that the printer listed on the Printer Status button will print a hard copy of the presentation. If necessary, click the Printer Status button to display a list of available printer options and then click the desired printer to change the currently selected printer.

Q&A | The selected printer is a black-and-white laser printer, so the preview is grayscale and shows varying shades of gray. If I change the currently selected printer to a color printer, will the preview display in color?
Yes, the preview will match the printer output.

BTW
Conserving Ink and Toner
If you want to conserve ink or toner, you can instruct PowerPoint to print draft quality documents by tapping or clicking FILE on the ribbon to open the Backstage view, tapping or clicking Options in the Backstage view to display the PowerPoint Options dialog box, tapping or clicking Advanced in the left pane (PowerPoint Options dialog box), sliding or scrolling to the Print area in the right pane, not placing a check mark in the High quality check box, and then tapping or clicking the OK button. Then, use the Backstage view to print the document as usual.

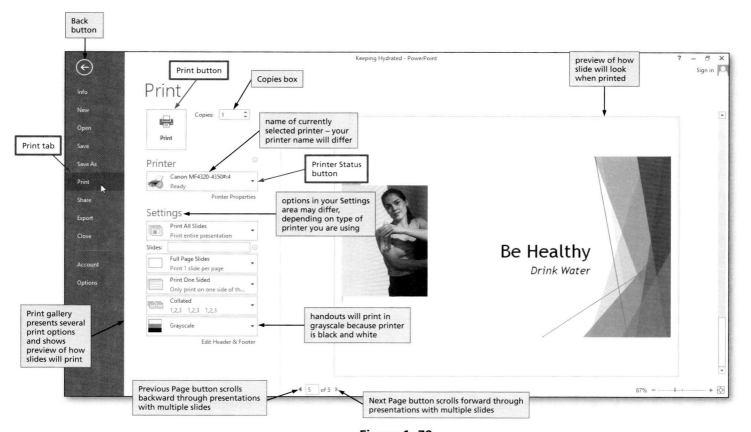

Figure 1–78

3

- Tap or click the Print button in the Print gallery to print the presentation on the currently selected printer.

- When the printer stops, retrieve the hard copy (Figure 1–79).

◄ | Do I have to wait until my presentation is complete to print it?
Q&A | No, you can follow these steps to print a presentation at any time while you are creating it.

What if I want to print an electronic image of a presentation instead of a hard copy?
You would click the Printer Status button in the Print gallery and then select the desired electronic image option, such as Microsoft XPS Document Writer, which would create an XPS file.

Healthy Hydration
Drinking Water While Exercising

(a) Slide 1

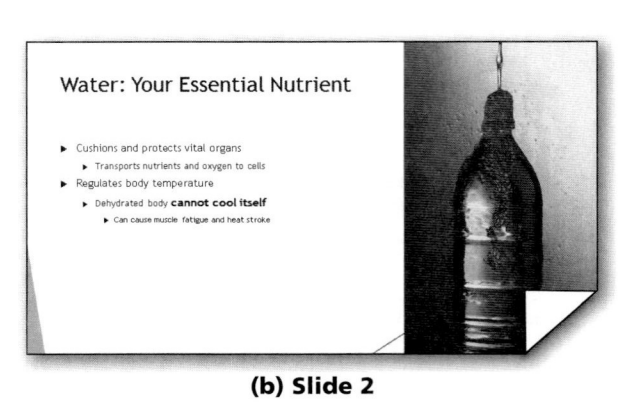

Water: Your Essential Nutrient

- Cushions and protects vital organs
 - Transports nutrients and oxygen to cells
- Regulates body temperature
 - Dehydrated body **cannot cool itself**
 - Can cause muscle fatigue and heat stroke

(b) Slide 2

Begin Workout with Plenty of Water

(c) Slide 3

Keep Replenishing Fluid Levels

While Exercising:	After Exercising:
10 oz. every 20 minutes	8 oz. within 30 minutes

(d) Slide 4

Be Healthy
Drink Water

(e) Slide 5

Figure 1–79 (Handouts printed using a black-and-white printer)

Other Ways

1. Press CTRL+P, press ENTER

To Sign Out of a Microsoft Account

If you are signed in to a Microsoft account and are using a public computer or otherwise wish to sign out of your Microsoft account, you should sign out of the account from the Accounts gallery in the Backstage view before exiting PowerPoint. Signing out of the account is the safest way to make sure that nobody else can access SkyDrive files or settings stored in your Microsoft account. The following steps sign out of a Microsoft account from PowerPoint. For a detailed example of the procedure summarized below, refer to the Office and Windows chapter at the beginning of this book.

1 If you wish to sign out of your Microsoft account, tap or click FILE on the ribbon to open the Backstage view and then tap or click the Account tab to display the Account gallery.

2 Tap or click the Sign out link, which displays the Remove Account dialog box. If a Can't remove Windows accounts dialog box appears instead of the Remove Account dialog box, click the OK button and skip the remaining steps.

Q&A Why does a Can't remove Windows accounts dialog box appear?
If you signed in to Windows using your Microsoft account, then you also must sign out from Windows, rather than signing out from within PowerPoint. When you are finished using Windows, be sure to sign out at that time.

3 Tap or click the Yes button (Remove Account dialog box) to sign out of your Microsoft account on this computer.

Q&A Should I sign out of Windows after signing out of my Microsoft account?
When you are finished using the computer, you should sign out of your account for maximum security.

4 Tap or click the Back button in the upper-left corner of the Backstage view to return to the presentation.

BTW
Certification
The Microsoft Office Specialist (MOS) program provides an opportunity for you to obtain a valuable industry credential — proof that you have the PowerPoint 2013 skills required by employers. For more information, visit the Certification resource on the Student Companion Site located on www.cengagebrain.com. For detailed instructions about accessing available resources, visit www.cengage.com/ct/studentdownload or see the inside back cover of this book.

To Exit PowerPoint

This project now is complete. The following steps exit PowerPoint. For a detailed example of the procedure summarized below, refer to the Office and Windows chapter at the beginning of this book.

1a If you have one PowerPoint presentation open, tap or click the Close button on the right side of the title bar to close the open document and exit PowerPoint.

1b If you have multiple PowerPoint presentations open, press and hold or right-click the PowerPoint app button on the taskbar and then tap or click 'Close all windows' on the shortcut menu, or press ALT+F4 to close all open presentations and exit PowerPoint.

Q&A Could I press and hold or repeatedly click the Close button to close all open documents and exit PowerPoint?
Yes.

2 If a Microsoft PowerPoint dialog box appears, tap or click the Save button to save any changes made to the presentation since the last save.

BTW
Quick Reference
For a table that lists how to complete the tasks covered in this book using touch gestures, the mouse, ribbon, shortcut menu, and keyboard, see the Quick Reference Summary at the back of this book, or visit the Quick Reference resource on the Student Companion Site located on www.cengagebrain.com. For detailed instructions about accessing available resources, visit www.cengage.com/ct/studentdownload or see the inside back cover of this book.

Chapter Summary

In this chapter you have learned how to apply and change a document theme and variant, create a title slide and text slides with a bulleted list, insert photos and an illustration and then resize and move them on a slide, format and edit text, add a slide transition, view the presentation in Slide Show view, and print slides as handouts. The items listed below include all the new PowerPoint skills you have learned in this chapter, with the tasks grouped by activity.

Enter and Edit Text
Enter the Presentation Title (PPT 7)
Enter the Presentation Subtitle Paragraph (PPT 9)
Zoom a Slide (PPT 10)
Add a New Text Slide with a Bulleted List (PPT 15)
Enter a Slide Title (PPT 17)
Type a Multilevel Bulleted List (PPT 18)
Add a Slide with the Title Only Layout (PPT 23)
Add a New Slide and Enter a Slide Title and Headings (PPT 24)
Move to Another Slide in Normal View (PPT 29)
Duplicate a Slide (PPT 41)
Arrange a Slide (PPT 42)
Delete Text in a Placeholder (PPT 43)

Format a Slide
Choose a Document Theme and Variant (PPT 5)
Change the Theme (PPT 26)
Change the Variant (PPT 27)

Format Text
Italicize Text (PPT 11)
Increase Font Size (PPT 12, 22)

Change the Text Color (PPT 13)
Bold Text (PPT 21)

Enhance Slides with Pictures and a Transition
Insert a Picture from Office.com into the Title Slide (PPT 31)
Insert a Picture from Office.com into a Content Placeholder (PPT 34)
Proportionally Resize Pictures (PPT 36)
Move Pictures (PPT 39)
Add a Transition between Slides (PPT 45)

Run and Print a Slide Show
Change Document Properties (PPT 48)
Start Slide Show View (PPT 49)
Move Manually through Slides in a Slide Show (PPT 50)
Print a Presentation (PPT 52)

Select Text and Slide Elements
Select a Paragraph (PPT 11)
Select a Word (PPT 12)
Select a Text Placeholder (PPT 18)
Select a Group of Words (PPT 20)

CONSIDER THIS

What decisions will you need to make when creating your next presentation?
Use these guidelines as you complete the assignments in this chapter and create your own slide show decks outside of this class.

1. Determine the content you want to include on your slides.

2. Determine which theme and variant are appropriate.

3. Identify the slide layouts that best communicate your message.

4. Format various text elements to emphasize important points.

 a) Select appropriate font sizes.

 b) Emphasize important words with bold or italic type and color.

5. Locate graphical elements, such as photos and illustrations, that reinforce your message.

 a) Size and position them aesthetically on slides.

6. Determine a storage location for the presentation.

7. Determine the best method for distributing the presentation.

How should you submit solutions to questions in the assignments identified with a ✳ symbol?

Every assignment in this book contains one or more questions identified with a ✳ symbol. These questions require you to think beyond the assigned presentation. Present your solutions to the questions in the format required by your instructor. Possible formats may include one or more of these options: write the answer; create a document that contains the answer; present your answer to the class; discuss your answer in a group; record the answer as audio or video using a webcam, smartphone, or portable media player; or post answers on a blog, wiki, or website.

Apply Your Knowledge

Reinforce the skills and apply the concepts you learned in this chapter.

Modifying Character Formats and Paragraph Levels and Moving an Illustration

Note: To complete this assignment, you will be required to use the Data Files for Students. Visit www.cengage.com/ct/studentdownload for detailed instructions or contact your instructor for information about accessing the required files.

Instructions: Run PowerPoint. Open the presentation, Apply 1-1 Effective Writing, from the Data Files for Students.

The two slides in the presentation discuss steps to follow when writing a persuasive essay. The document you open is an unformatted presentation. You are to modify the document theme, indent the paragraphs, resize and move the photo, and format the text so the slides look like Figure 1–80 on this page and the next page.

Perform the following tasks:

1. Change the document theme to Ion.
2. On the title slide, use your name in place of Student Name and bold and italicize your name.
3. If requested by your instructor, change your first name to your grandmother's first name on the title slide.
4. Increase the title text font size to 60 point. Size and position the photo using the Smart Guides to align the image with the bottom of the title placeholder, as shown in Figure 1–80a.

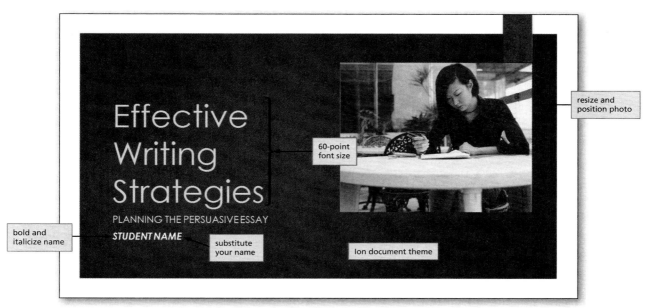

(a) Slide 1 (Title Slide with a Picture)
Figure 1–80

Continued >

Apply Your Knowledge *continued*

5. On Slide 2, increase the indent of the third and fourth paragraphs to second-level paragraphs. Then combine paragraphs six and seven (To change readers' minds? and To confirm opinions?) to read, To change readers' minds or confirm opinions?, as shown in Figure 1–80b. Increase the indent of this paragraph to second level.

6. Save the presentation using the file name, Apply 1-1 Effective Writing Strategies.

7. Submit the revised document in the format specified by your instructor.

8. ✳ In Step 5 you combined two paragraphs. How did this action improve the slide content?

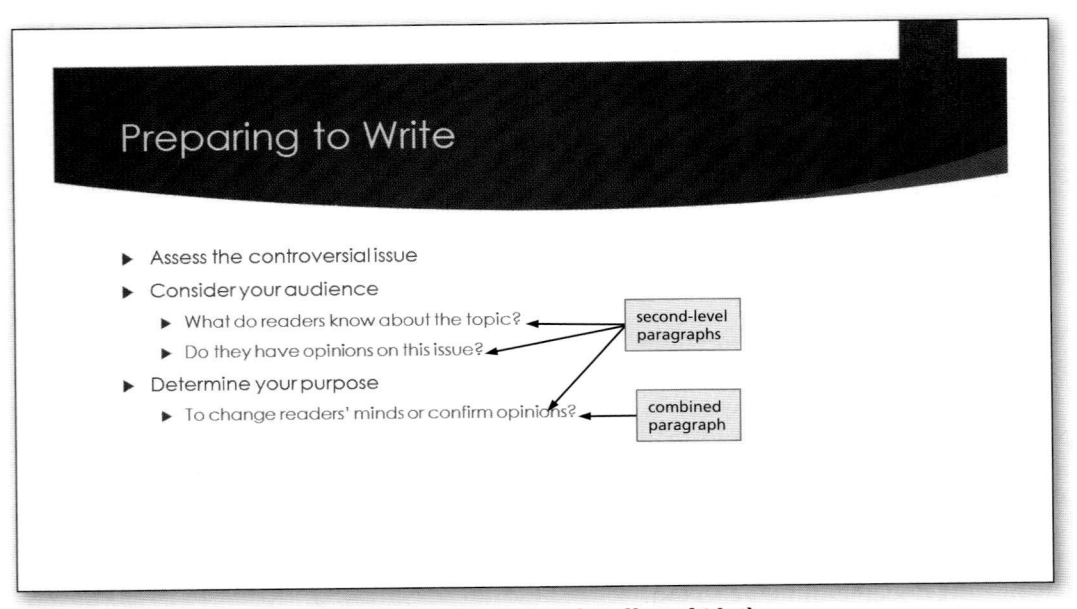

(b) Slide 2 (Multilevel Bulleted List)
Figure 1–80 (Continued)

Extend Your Knowledge

Extend the skills you learned in this chapter and experiment with new skills. You may need to use Help to complete the assignment.

Changing Slide Theme, Layout, and Text

Note: To complete this assignment, you will be required to use the Data Files for Students. Visit www.cengage.com/ct/studentdownload for detailed instructions or contact your instructor for information about accessing the required files.

Instructions: Run PowerPoint. Open the presentation that you are going to prepare for your brother's horseback riding business, Extend 1-1 Horseback Riding, from the Data Files for Students. You will choose a theme, format slides, and create a closing slide.

Perform the following tasks:

1. Apply an appropriate document theme.

2. On Slide 1 (Figure 1–81), use your name in place of Student Name. Format the text on this slide using techniques you learned in this chapter, such as changing the font size and color and bolding and italicizing words.

3. Delete the bullets in the subtitle text.

4. Resize the photo and move it to an appropriate area on the slide.

5. On Slide 2, add bullets to the paragraphs in the Beginners and Advanced boxes, and then change the look of the default bullets.

6. On Slide 3, create paragraphs and adjust the paragraph levels to create a bulleted list. Edit the text so that the slide meets the 7 × 7 rule, which states that each line should have a maximum of seven words, and each slide should have a maximum of seven lines.

7. Create an appropriate closing slide using the title slide as a guide. Change the title text to, See you at the Trails!

8. The slides contain a variety of pictures downloaded from Office.com. Size and move them when necessary.

9. Apply an appropriate transition to all slides.

10. Save the presentation using the file name, Extend 1-1 Horseback Riding Lessons.

11. Submit the revised document in the format specified by your instructor.

12. If requested by your instructor, replace the word, you, with your mother's first name on the closing slide.

13. ✷ In this assignment, you changed the bullet style on Slide 2. Which bullet style did you select and why?

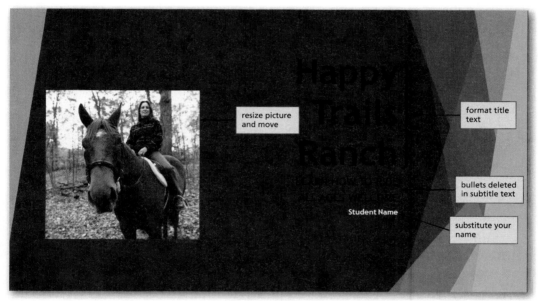

Figure 1–81

Analyze, Correct, Improve

Analyze a presentation, correct all errors, and improve it.

Correcting Formatting and List Levels

Note: To complete this assignment, you will be required to use the Data Files for Students. Visit www.cengage.com/ct/studentdownload for detailed instructions or contact your instructor for information about accessing the required files.

Instructions: Run PowerPoint. Open the presentation, Analyze 1-1 Math Tutor, from the Data Files for Students. As a part-time job while attending college, you decide to tutor students who are struggling with math. You decide to create a presentation promoting your service and begin with this document. Modify the slides by making the indicated corrections and improvements.

Continued >

Analyze, Correct, Improve *continued*

1. Correct

a. Change the document theme from Office Theme Dark, shown in Figure 1–82, to Organic with the rightmost color variant.

b. If requested by your instructor, change the Southtown Library Room number, 201, to your birth year on Slide 2.

c. Correct the spelling errors on Slides 2 and 3.

d. Use your name in place of Student Name on Slide 1.

2. Improve

a. Adjust the size of the picture on Slide 1 and move it to the left of the subtitle text.

b. Move Slide 2 to the end of the presentation so that it becomes the new Slide 3.

c. On Slide 2, increase the font size of the Slide 2 title text, A Math Tutor Is Your Answer, to 54 point. Increase the size of the picture and move it to fill the white space on the right of the bulleted list. Align the picture using the right and bottom Smart Guides.

d. On Slide 3, increase the font size of the title text, Schedule, to 60 point. Decrease the indent level for both bulleted lists to first level. Adjust the size of the picture and move it to the upper-right corner of the slide so that the upper edge of the image is aligned with the top edge of the title text placeholder.

e. Apply the same transition and duration to all slides.

f. Save the presentation using the file name, Analyze 1-1 – Math Tutor Info.

g. Submit the revised document in the format specified by your instructor.

3. ✳ Which errors existed in the starting file? How did decreasing the indent level of the bulleted lists on Slide 3 and increasing the title text on Slides 2 and 3 enhance the presentation? When you adjusted the pictures, how did you determine their final sizes?

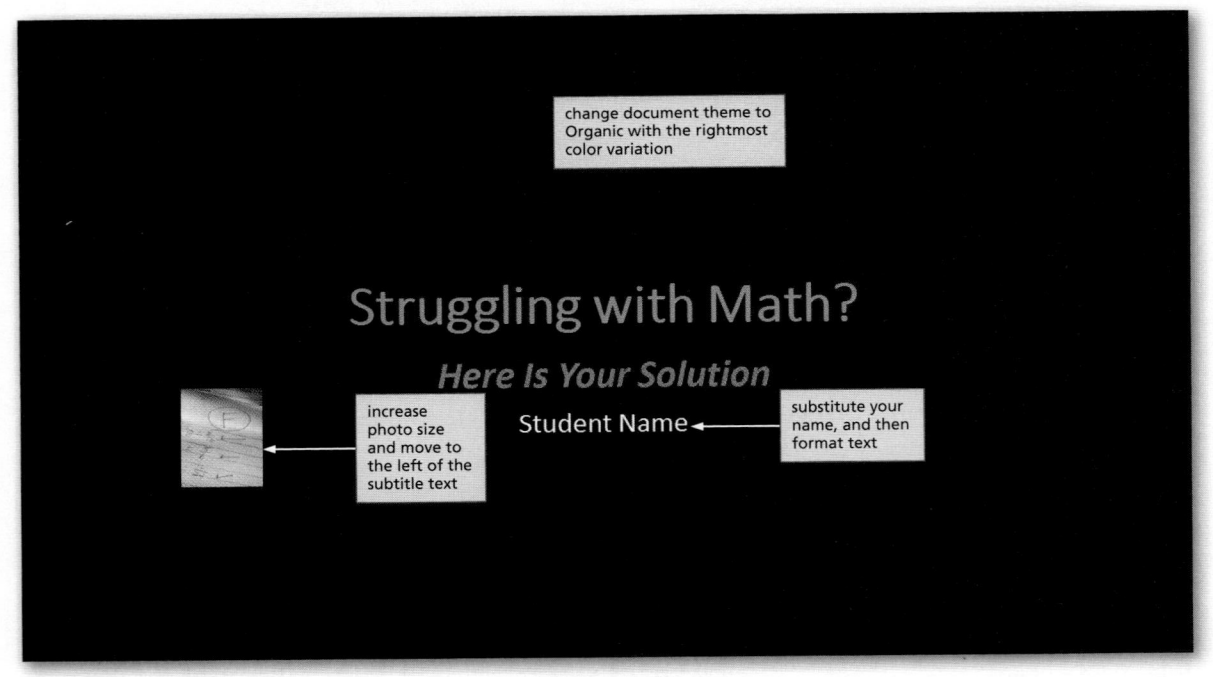

Figure 1–82

In the Labs

Design and/or create a presentation using the guidelines, concepts, and skills presented in this chapter. Labs 1 and 2, which increase in difficulty, require you to create solutions based on what you learned in the chapter; Lab 3 requires you to create a solution, which uses cloud and web technologies, by learning and investigating on your own from general guidance.

Lab 1: Creating a Presentation with Bulleted Lists, a Closing Slide, and Pictures

Problem: You are majoring in accounting and work part-time at a tax-filing service. Your clients have asked you numerous times what documents they should keep at home to support their tax returns. You decide to put together a presentation that would offer some basic guidelines about how to organize personal documents. You develop the outline shown in Figure 1–83 and then prepare the PowerPoint presentation shown in Figures 1–84a through 1–84e on pages PPT 62–64.

Files or Piles
　　Document Storage and Retention at Home

Store and Retain
　　In Home Office Safe
　　　　Tax records for six years
　　　　Pay stubs until W2 arrives
　　　　Credit card statements
　　　　Canceled checks
　　　　Utility bills
　　In Bank Safe Deposit Box
　　　　Wills, deeds, and titles
　　　　Birth and death certificates
　　　　Passports
　　　　Military records

Keep Indefinitely
　　Personal health records
　　Medical history
　　Retirement benefit statements

General Rules
　　Shred documents showing personal information
　　Organize and store chronologically
　　Keep list of important documents
　　　　State their location
　　　　Share with relative or friend

Figure 1–83

Continued >

In the Labs *continued*

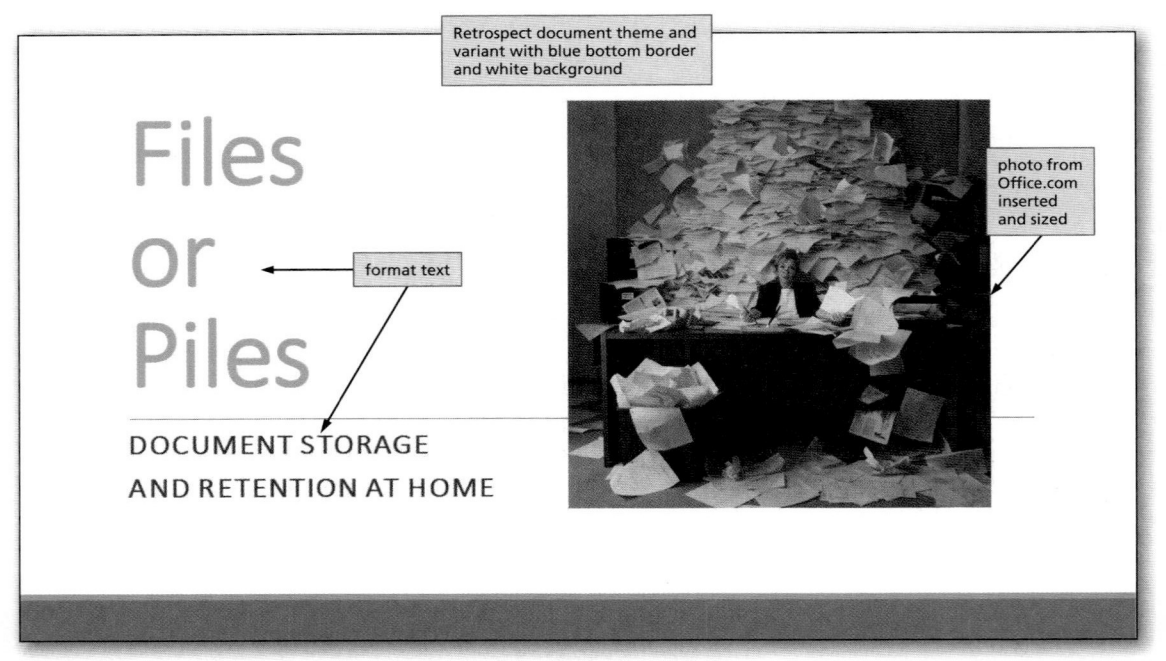

(a) Slide 1 (Title Slide)

(b) Slide 2

Figure 1–84

(c) Slide 3

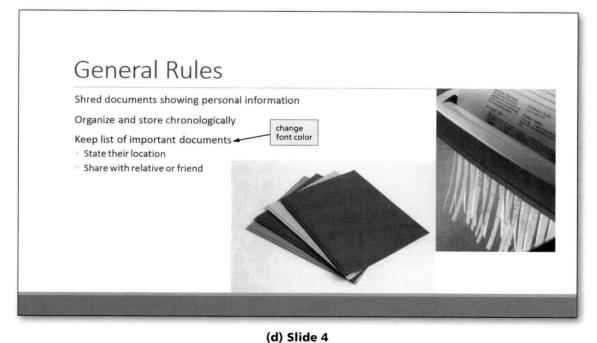

(d) Slide 4

Figure 1–84 (Continued)

Continued >

In the Labs *continued*

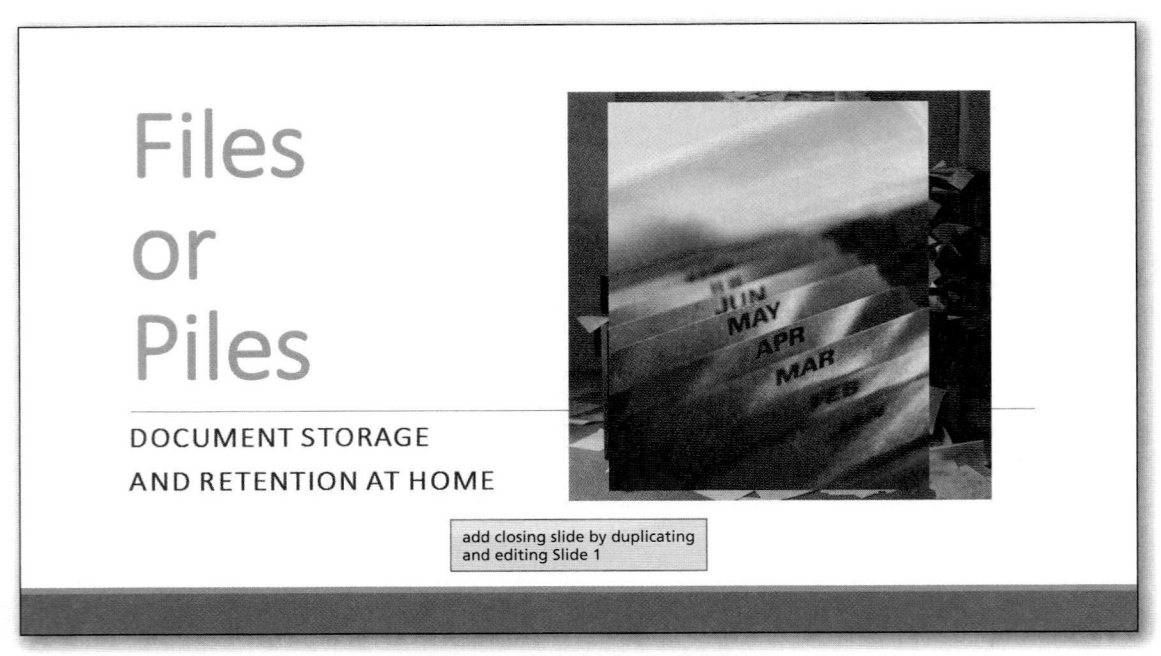

(e) Slide 5 (Closing Slide)
Figure 1–84 (Continued)

Instructions: Perform the following tasks:

1. Create a new presentation using the Retrospect document theme and select the variant with the blue bottom border and white background.

2. Using the typed outline illustrated in Figure 1–83 on page PPT 61, create the title slide shown in Figure 1–84a. Press the ENTER key to place each word on a separate line and divide the title into three lines, as shown in the figure. Increase the font size of the title text to 88 point and bold this text. Change the font color to Green (the sixth color from left in the Standard Colors row). Increase the font size of the subtitle text, DOCUMENT STORAGE AND RETENTION AT HOME, to 28 point and bold this text. Press the ENTER key to divide the subtitle into two lines, as shown in the figure. Find and insert the picture from the Office.com Clip Art collection. Size the picture and use the Smart Guides to position it as shown in the figure.

3. Using the typed outline in Figure 1–83, create the three text slides with lists and find and insert the pictures from the Office.com Clip Art collection. Size the pictures and use the Smart Guides to position these images, as shown in Figures 1–84b, 1–84c, and 1–84d. You may want to zoom the slides to help you align these graphic elements.

4. On Slide 2, change the font color in the left and right heading placeholders to Green and bold and italicize this text.

5. On Slides 2, 3 and 4, change the font color of the lists to Dark Blue (second color from right in the Standard Colors row).

6. Create a closing slide by duplicating Slide 1 and adding the photo using the Smart Guides to center it on top of the existing photo.

7. If requested by your instructor, use your father's first name in place of the word, Piles, and replace the word, or, with the word, for, on Slide 5.

8. Apply the Shred transition in the Exciting category to all slides. Change the duration to 4.5 seconds.

9. Tap or click the Start From Beginning button to start the show from the first slide. Then swipe or click to display each slide.

10. Save the presentation using the file name, Lab 1-1 Document Storage at Home.

11. Submit the document in the format specified by your instructor.

12. ✳ What is the significance of placing the neat file folders photo on top of the messy desk photo on the closing slide? Why did you change the font color on Slides 2, 3, and 4 to Dark Blue?

Lab 2: Creating a Presentation with Bulleted Lists and Pictures

Problem: The number of reported West Nile Virus (WNV) cases across the continental United States has been growing steadily. After a discussion in your biology class, your instructor assigned everyone in the class to research WNV and to outline the facts that were discussed. You use your class notes to create the outline shown in Figure 1–85 and then create the presentation shown in Figures 1–86a through 1–86d on pages PPT 66–68.

West Nile Virus (WNV)
Facts, Signs, and Prevention
Student Name

What Is WNV?
 Transmitted by mosquitoes that bit infected birds
 First identified in eastern Africa in 1937
 Now worldwide in tropical and temperate climates
 Appeared in United States in 1999
 Now reported in 48 states
 At risk: People with weak immune systems

What Are the Symptoms?
 Most commonly resemble the flu
 High fever
 Headache
 Body aches
 Nausea / vomiting
 Vision problems

How Can I Avoid WNV?
 Protect against mosquito bites
 Wear repellent with EPA-recommended ingredients
 Avoid being outdoors at dawn and dusk
 Wear clothes that cover skin
 Remove standing water from yard vessels
 Repair damaged window and door screens

Figure 1–85

Continued >

In the Labs *continued*

Instructions: Perform the following tasks:

1. Create a new presentation using the Facet document theme.

2. Using the outline illustrated in Figure 1–85 on the previous page, create the title slide shown in Figure 1–86a, using your name in place of Student Name.

3. If requested by your instructor, substitute the name of your hometown in place of your last name.

4. On Slide 1, bold the text, West Nile Virus (WNV). Decrease the font size of the text, Facts, Signs, and Prevention, to 44 point. Change the font color of all the title text to Red, Accent 5 (second color from right in the Theme Colors row).

5. Using the outline in Figure 1–85, create the three text slides with bulleted lists shown in Figures 1–86b, 1–86c, and 1–86d. Change the color of the title text on these three text slides to Red, Accent 5.

6. Add the pictures shown in Figures 1–86a through 1–86d from Office.com. Zoom the slide and then resize the pictures when necessary.

7. Apply the Page Curl transition in the Exciting category to all slides. Change the duration to 2.25 seconds.

8. Tap or click the Start From Beginning button to start the slide show and then display each slide.

9. Save the presentation using the file name, Lab 1–2 West Nile Virus.

10. Submit the revised document in the format specified by your instructor.

11. ✳ How does changing the font color to red help reinforce the West Nile Virus prevention concept? What is the significance of adding a mosquito illustration to every slide?

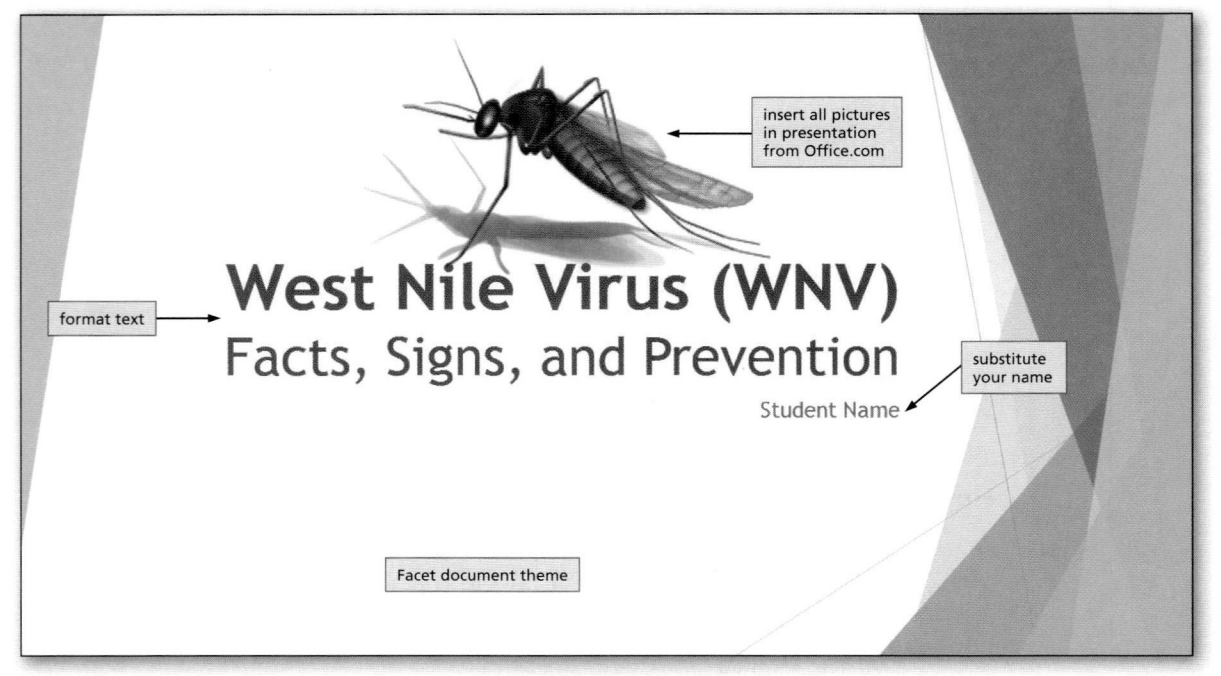

(a) Slide 1 (Title Slide)

Figure 1–86

(b) Slide 2

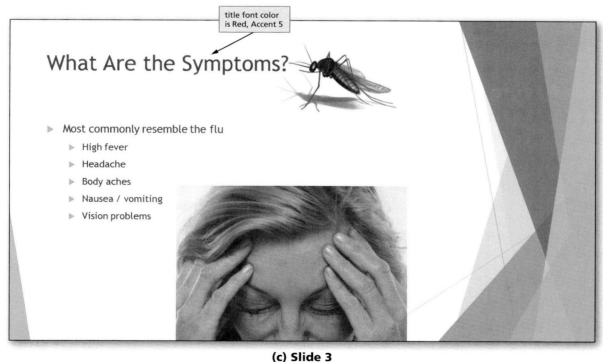

(c) Slide 3

Figure 1–86 (Continued)

Continued >

In the Labs *continued*

(d) Slide 4

Figure 1–86 (Continued)

Lab 3: Expand Your World: Cloud and Web Technologies
Modifying and Exporting a Presentation

Problem: Your local library is planning events to celebrate Hispanic Heritage Month, and you are part of a committee to publicize the event. You want to share the title slide of your preliminary PowerPoint presentation with fellow committee members, so you have decided to store the file on SkyDrive. You are going to modify the slide you have created thus far shown in Figure 1–87 and save it to SkyDrive.

Note: To complete this assignment, you will be required to use the Data Files for Students. Visit www.cengage.com/ct/studentdownload for detailed instructions or contact your instructor for information about accessing the required files.

Instructions:

1. Open the Lab 1–3 Hispanic Heritage file.

2. Insert another picture on the title slide in the area indicated in Figure 1–87.

3. If requested to do so by your instructor, change the city to the town where you were born.

4. Save the presentation using the file name, Lab 1–3 Heritage Month.

5. Export the file to your SkyDrive in the Chapter 01 folder in the PowerPoint folder.

6. Submit the assignment in the format specified by your instructor.

7. ✸ When would you save one of your files for school or your job to SkyDrive? Do you think using SkyDrive enhances collaboration efforts? Why?

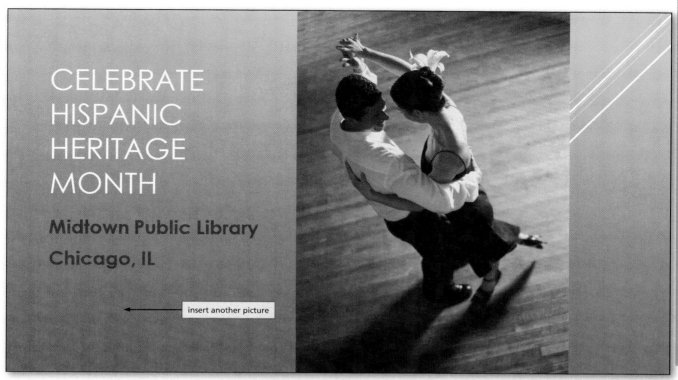

Figure 1–87 Slide 1 (Title Slide)

✺ Consider This: Your Turn

Apply your creative thinking and problem-solving skills to design and implement a solution.

1. Design and Create a Presentation about Mars Exploration

Personal

Part 1: Your astronomy class is studying the solar system, and you have been assigned the topic of the Mars Curiosity rover and its exploration of that planet. You have learned that the rover was launched from Cape Canaveral, Florida, on November 26, 2011, and landed in the Gale Crater on Mars on August 6, 2012. The mission was scheduled to last two years and had the major goal of assessing whether Mars was or is capable of supporting life. The Curiosity rover is the size of a car and has a MastCam equipped with two camera systems to take photos of the landscape as it maneuvers around the rocky surface. The rover also can scoop up samples of the Martian soil, fire a laser at rocks as far away as nine feet (2.7 meters), and make weather station readings. Use the concepts and techniques you learned in the chapter to create a PowerPoint presentation with a suitable theme, a title slide, and three text slides with bulleted lists. Add pictures from Office.com and apply a transition. Submit your assignment in the format specified by your instructor.

Part 2: ✺ You made several decisions while creating the presentation in this assignment: what theme to use, where to place text, how to format the text (font, font size, paragraph alignment, bulleted paragraphs, italics, bold, color). You also decided which graphical images to use, where to position the graphical images, if a closing slide would be useful, and which transition would be most effective. What was the rationale behind each of these decisions? When you proofed the document, what further revisions did you make and why? Where would you recommend showing this slide show?

Continued >

Consider This: Your Turn *continued*

2. Design and Create a Fire Department Safety Expo Presentation

Professional

Part 1: Your local fire department is sponsoring a Safety Expo one month from today at the local hardware store. The chief has asked you to prepare a slide show promoting the event, which will be held from noon to 5 p.m. A wide variety of demonstrations and informational booths will be present. They include: firefighters from your community's fire department, who will discuss home emergency planning, proper car seat installation, and fire extinguisher use; a local insurance agent, who will distribute tote bags filled with materials regarding adequate home and rental insurance coverage and also a nine-volt battery for a smoke alarm; and a children's workshop, where participants under 10 years of age can build a picture frame. Use the concepts and techniques presented in this chapter to develop and format this slide show with at least four slides with bulleted lists. Add pictures from Office.com and apply a transition. Submit your assignment in the format specified by your instructor.

Part 2: ✺ You made several decisions while creating the presentation in this assignment: what theme to use, where to place text, how to format the text (font, font size, paragraph alignment, bulleted paragraphs, italics, bold, color). You also decided which graphical images to use, where to position the graphical images, if a closing slide would be useful, and which transition would be most effective. What was the rationale behind each of these decisions? When you proofed the document, what further revisions did you make and why? Where would you recommend showing this slide show?

3. Design and Create a Presentation about Commemorative Postage Stamps

Research and Collaboration

Part 1: Stamp collecting is one of the world's more popular indoor hobbies. Collectors often seek postage stamps pertaining to a particular interest, such as birds, flowers, famous people, or ships. Have each member of your team gather information on these topics: stamp collecting equipment, popular commemorative stamps issued, current commemorative stamps for sale at your local post office, and rare stamps. After coordinating these facts, use the concepts and techniques presented in this chapter to prepare a presentation with a minimum of four slides that explore the subject of stamp collection. Select a suitable theme and include a title slide, bulleted lists, and a closing slide. Add pictures from Office.com and apply a transition. Submit your assignment in the format specified by your instructor.

Part 2: ✺ You made several decisions while creating the presentation in this assignment: what theme to use, where to place text, how to format the text (font, font size, paragraph alignment, bulleted paragraphs, italics, bold, color). You also decided which graphical images to use, where to position the graphical images, if a closing slide would be useful, and which transition would be most effective. What was the rationale behind each of these decisions? When you proofed the document, what further revisions did you make and why? Where would you recommend showing this slide show?

Learn Online

Reinforce what you learned in this chapter with games, exercises, training, and many other online activities and resources.

Student Companion Site Reinforcement activities and resources are available at no additional cost on www.cengagebrain.com. Visit www.cengage.com/ct/studentdownload for detailed instructions about accessing the resources available at the Student Companion Site.

 SAM Put your skills into practice with SAM! If you have a SAM account, go to www.cengage.com/sam2013 to access SAM assignments for this chapter.

2 | Enhancing a Presentation with Pictures, Shapes, and WordArt

Microsoft product screenshots used with permission from Microsoft Corporation.

Objectives

You will have mastered the material in this chapter when you can:

- Search for and download an online theme
- Insert and format pictures
- Insert and size a shape
- Apply effects to a shape
- Add text to a shape
- Change the text font

- Insert and format WordArt
- Insert a picture to create a background
- Format slide backgrounds
- Find and replace text and check spelling
- Add and print speaker notes

2 | Enhancing a Presentation with Pictures, Shapes, and WordArt

Introduction

In our visually oriented culture, audience members enjoy viewing effective graphics. Whether reading a document or viewing a PowerPoint presentation, people increasingly want to see photographs, artwork, graphics, and a variety of typefaces. Researchers have known for decades that documents with visual elements are more effective than those that consist of only text because the illustrations motivate audiences to study the material. People remember at least one-third more information when the document they are seeing or reading contains visual elements. These graphics help clarify and emphasize details, so they appeal to audience members with differing backgrounds, reading levels, attention spans, and motivations.

Project — Presentation with Pictures, Shapes, and WordArt

The project in this chapter focuses on helping families plan for emergencies. Children need to prepare for the unexpected by collecting supplies to make an emergency supply kit, developing a communication plan, and realizing the need to be ready for any unexpected situation that may arise. The presentation shown in Figure 2–1 follows graphical guidelines and has a variety of illustrations and visual elements that are colorful and appealing to children. For example, the pictures have particular shapes and effects. The enhanced type has a style that blends well with the formatted background and illustrations. Pictures and type are formatted using picture styles and WordArt, which give the presentation a professional look. You plan to present the material during community safety open houses at fire stations and local hardware stores, so you want to add notes explaining concepts you will be discussing during the meeting.

BTW

BTWs
For a complete list of the BTWs found in the margins of this book, visit the BTW resource on the Student Companion Site located on www.cengagebrain.com. For detailed instructions about accessing available resources, visit www.cengage.com/ct/studentdownload or see the inside back cover of this book.

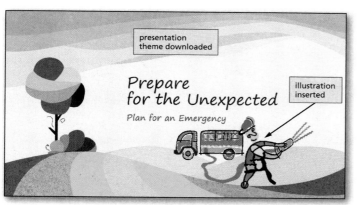

(a) Slide 1 (Title Slide)

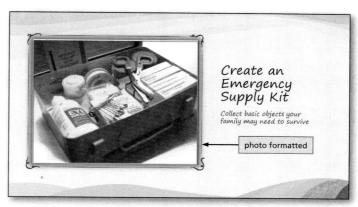

(b) Slide 2 (Formatted Picture)

(c) Slide 3 (Shapes Inserted and Formatted)

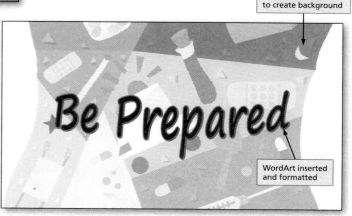

(d) Slide 4 (Picture Background)

Figure 2–1

Roadmap

In this chapter, you will learn how to create the slides shown in Figure 2–1 on the previous page. The following roadmap identifies general activities you will perform as you progress through this chapter:

1. DOWNLOAD a theme and SELECT SLIDES for the presentation.
2. INSERT and FORMAT PICTURES for the slides.
3. INSERT and FORMAT SHAPES on one slide.
4. INSERT and FORMAT WORDART by changing the shape, fill, and outline.
5. FORMAT SLIDE BACKGROUNDS with a gradient, texture, and picture fill.
6. REVIEW and REVISE SLIDES by finding a synonym and checking spelling.

At the beginning of step instructions throughout the chapter, you will see an abbreviated form of this roadmap. The abbreviated roadmap uses colors to indicate chapter progress: gray means the chapter is beyond that activity; blue means the task being shown is covered in that activity, and black means that activity is yet to be covered. For example, the following abbreviated roadmap indicates the chapter would be showing a task in the 5 FORMAT SLIDE BACKGROUNDS activity.

1 DOWNLOAD & SELECT SLIDES | 2 INSERT & FORMAT PICTURES | 3 INSERT & FORMAT SHAPES
4 INSERT & FORMAT WORDART | **5 FORMAT SLIDE BACKGROUNDS** | 6 REVIEW & REVISE SLIDES

Use the abbreviated roadmap as a progress guide while you read or step through the instructions in this chapter.

To Run PowerPoint

If you are using a computer to step through the project in this chapter and you want your screens to match the figures in this book, you should change your screen's resolution to 1366 × 768. For information about how to change a computer's resolution, refer to the Office and Windows chapter at the beginning of this book.

The following steps, which assume Windows 8 is running, use the Start screen or the search box to run PowerPoint based on a typical installation. You may need to ask your instructor how to run PowerPoint on your computer. For a detailed example of the procedure summarized below, refer to the Office and Windows chapter.

1 Scroll the Start screen for a PowerPoint 2013 tile. If your Start screen contains a PowerPoint 2013 tile, tap or click it to run PowerPoint and then proceed to Step 5; if the Start screen does not contain the PowerPoint 2013 tile, proceed to the next step to search for the PowerPoint app.

2 Swipe in from the right edge of the screen or point to the upper-right corner of the screen to display the Charms bar and then tap or click the Search charm on the Charms bar to display the Search menu.

3 Type **PowerPoint** as the search text in the Search box and watch the search results appear in the Apps list.

4 Tap or click PowerPoint 2013 in the search results to run PowerPoint.

5 If the PowerPoint window is not maximized, tap or click the Maximize button on its title bar to maximize the window.

Downloading a Theme and Editing Slides

In Chapter 1, you selected a theme and then typed the content for the title and text slides. In this chapter, you will type the slide content for the title and text slides, select a background, insert and format pictures and shapes, and then insert and format WordArt. To begin creating the four slides in this presentation, you will download a theme, delete unneeded slides in this downloaded presentation, and then enter text in three of the four slides.

To Search for and Download an Online Theme

1 DOWNLOAD & SELECT SLIDES | **2 INSERT & FORMAT PICTURES** | **3 INSERT & FORMAT SHAPES**
4 INSERT & FORMAT WORDART | **5 FORMAT SLIDE BACKGROUNDS** | **6 REVIEW & REVISE SLIDES**

PowerPoint displays many themes that are varied and appealing and give you an excellent start at designing a presentation. At times, however, you may have a specific topic and design concept and could use some assistance in starting to develop the presentation. Microsoft offers hundreds of predesigned themes and templates that could provide you with an excellent starting point. ***Why?*** *You can search for one of these ready-made presentations, or you can browse one of the predefined categories, such as business, medical, education, and nature. The themes and templates can save you time and help you develop content.* The following steps search for a theme that has an educational concept and is oriented toward children.

- Press and hold or point to Education in the Suggested searches list (Figure 2–2).

Q&A Why does a Recent Presentation list display on the left side of my screen?
You can specify the number of recent presentations to display in the Advanced tab of the PowerPoint Options dialog box.

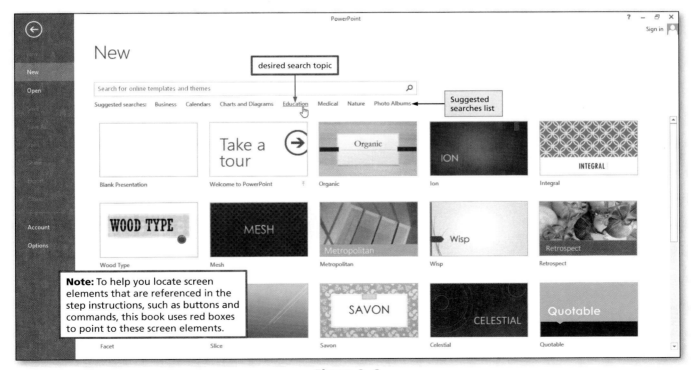

Figure 2–2

2

- Tap or click Education to search for themes with an academic subject.

Q&A Can I also use keywords to search for themes?
Yes. Tap or click the 'Search for online templates and themes' search box, type terms that relate to the topic of your presentation, and then click the Start searching button (the magnifying glass) or press the ENTER key so that Office.com will search for and display all themes with your keywords.

3

- Slide or scroll down about halfway through the theme thumbnails until the 'Colorful nature presentation, illustrated landscape design (widescreen)' theme, shown in Figure 2–3, is displayed.

Q&A Why are my theme thumbnails displaying in a different order?
Microsoft adds and modifies the themes, so the order may change.

4

- Tap or click the 'Colorful nature presentation, illustrated landscape design (widescreen)' theme to display a theme preview dialog box with a thumbnail view of the theme (Figure 2–3).

Q&A Can I see previews of the slides in this theme?
Yes. Click the right or left arrows beside the words, More Images, below the thumbnail. On some devices, a preview of all slides starts automatically after you tap the theme.

Figure 2–3

5

- Tap or click the Create button to download the theme and open a presentation with that theme in PowerPoint.

BTW

Additional Theme Information
You may see additional information regarding the theme in the theme preview dialog box if you are downloading the file for the first time. This information includes the provider (in this case, Microsoft Corporation), a description of the theme content and the intended audience, the file size (in this case, 2190 KB), and a rating.

To Delete a Slide

The downloaded theme has 13 slides with a variety of layouts. You will use four different layouts in your Be Prepared presentation, so you can delete the slides you downloaded that you will not need. *Why? Deleting the extra slides now helps reduce clutter and helps you focus on the layouts you will use.* The following steps delete the extra slides.

1

- If necessary, tap or click the Slide 1 thumbnail in the Thumbnail pane to select this slide.

- Swipe horizontally across each of the Slide 2, 3, and 4 thumbnails, or press and hold the SHIFT key and then click the thumbnail for Slide 4 to select slides 1 through 4 (Figure 2–4).

Q&A Why would I select Slide 1, the Title Slide layout, for deletion if I need a title slide for my presentation?
Slide 9 also will work well to format as the title slide (Slide 1) in this presentation.

Slide 1 thumbnail

four slides selected

Slide 4 thumbnail

Figure 2–4

2

- Press and hold or right-click any selected slide to display the shortcut menu (Figure 2–5).

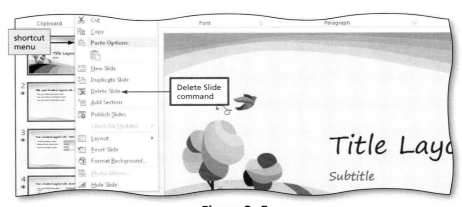

shortcut menu

Delete Slide command

Figure 2–5

3

- Tap Delete or click Delete Slide to delete the selected slides from the presentation (Figure 2–6).

Q&A How would I delete several slides simultaneously if they are not sequential?
Repeat this procedure except make a short swipe across each slide thumbnail you want to delete to select it, or press and hold the CTRL key while you tap or click each slide you want to delete.

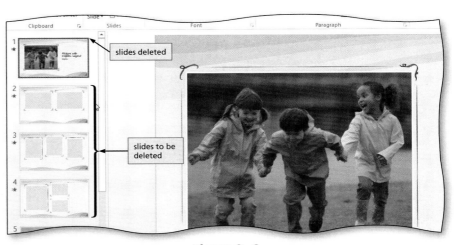

slides deleted

slides to be deleted

Figure 2–6

4

- Select the new Slides 2, 3, and 4, display the shortcut menu, and then delete these slides (Figure 2–7).

Q&A | Why am I selecting and then deleting these slides?
You want to use the current slides 1 and 5 in your presentation, so you need to delete the slides between these two slides.

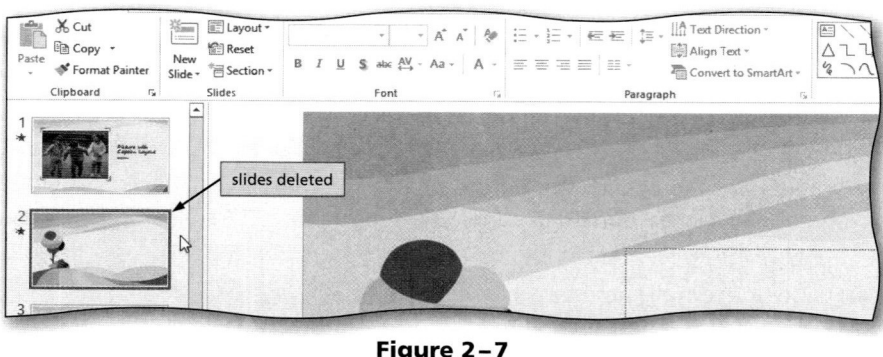

Figure 2–7

5

- Tap or click the Slide 3 thumbnail to select this slide.

- Scroll down and then swipe the Slide 6 thumbnail or press and hold the CTRL key and then click the thumbnail for Slide 6 to select both slides 3 and 6 (Figure 2–8).

Q&A | Why did I press and hold down the CTRL key instead of the SHIFT key?
Holding down the CTRL key selects only the slides you tap or click, whereas holding the SHIFT key selects consecutive slides between the first and last selected slides.

Why am I selecting and then deleting these slides?
You want to use the current slides 4 and 5 in your presentation, so you need to delete slides 3 and 6.

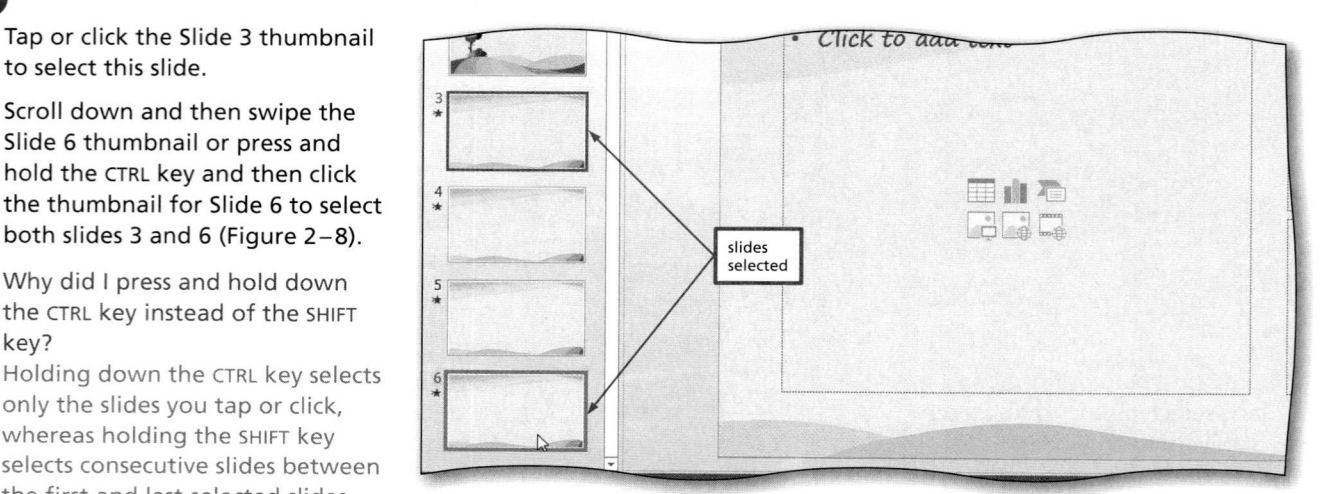

Figure 2–8

6

- Display the shortcut menu and then delete slides 3 and 6 (Figure 2–9).

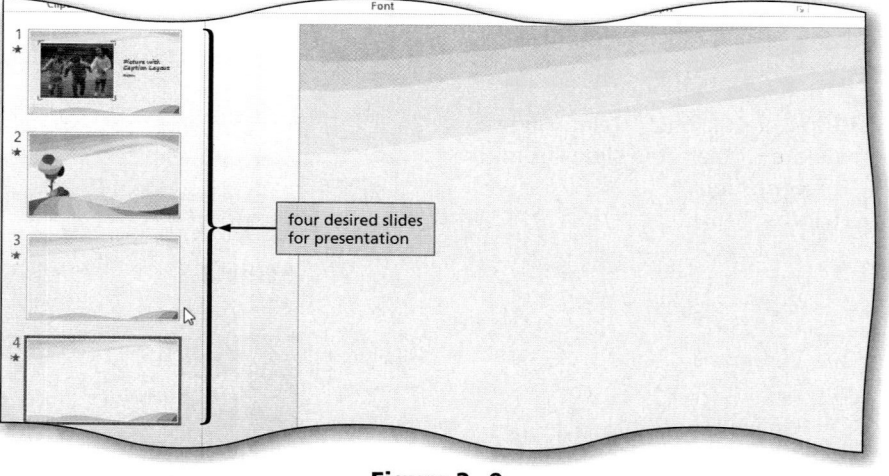

Figure 2–9

Other Ways

1. Select slide(s), press DELETE

To Create a Title Slide

Recall from Chapter 1 that the title slide introduces the presentation to the audience. In addition to introducing the presentation, this project uses the title slide to capture the audience's attention by using title text and an illustration. *Why? The presentation focuses on families and their need to work together to develop an emergency plan. The illustration of a fire truck and firefighter help introduce the concept.* The following steps rearrange Slide 1 and Slide 2 and then create the slide show's title slide.

1 Move Slide 2 in the Thumbnail pane above Slide 1 so that it becomes the first slide in the deck.

2 Type `Prepare` as the first text paragraph in the title text placeholder.

3 Press the ENTER key and then type `for the Unexpected` as the second paragraph in the title text placeholder.

4 Tap or click the subtitle text placeholder and then type `Plan for a Disaster` as the subtitle text (Figure 2–10).

Figure 2–10

To Create the First Text Slide

The first text slide you create in Chapter 2 emphasizes the need to make an emergency supply kit that contains supplies and other necessities for survival. The following steps create the Slide 2 text slide using the Picture with Caption layout.

1 Display Slide 2, select the text in the title text placeholder, and then type `Create a Disaster Supply Kit` in the placeholder.

2 Tap or click the caption placeholder and then type `Collect basic objects your family may need to stay alive` in this placeholder (Figure 2–11).

BTW
Q&As
For a complete list of the Q&As found in many of the step-by-step sequences in this book, visit the Q&A resource on the Student Companion Site located on www.cengagebrain.com. For detailed instructions about accessing available resources, visit www.cengage.com/ct/studentdownload or see the inside back cover of this book.

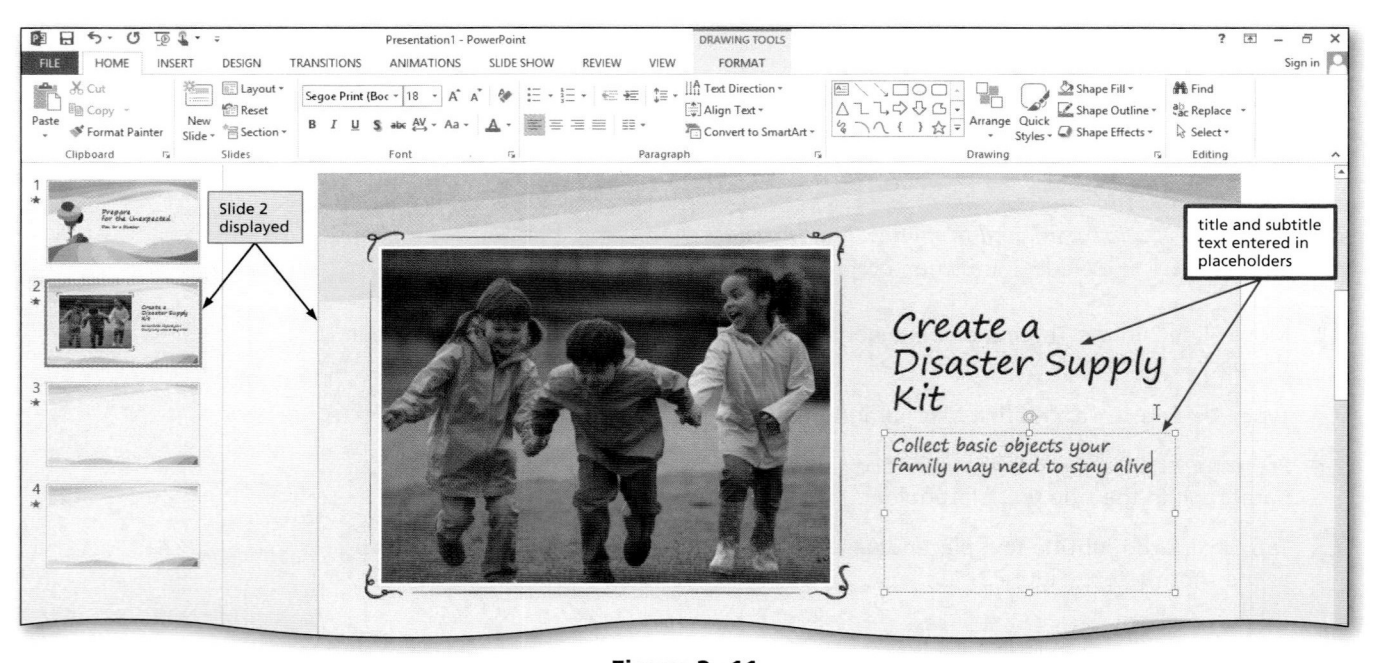

Figure 2–11

To Create the Second Text Slide

The second text slide you create shows two components of the family communication plan: carrying a contact list and arranging meeting places. The following step adds a title to Slide 3, which uses the Title Only layout.

Note: In the following step, the word, Communication, has been misspelled intentionally as Comunication to illustrate the use of PowerPoint's spell check feature. Your slides may contain different misspelled words, depending upon the accuracy of your typing.

1 Display Slide 3 and then type **Develop a Family Comunication Plan** in the title text placeholder. The word, Comunication, is intentionally misspelled; the red wavy line indicates the misspelling (Figure 2–12).

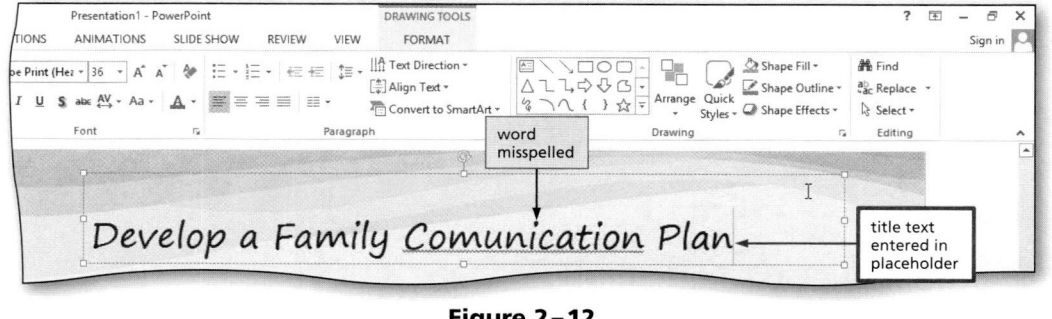

Figure 2–12

BTW
The Ribbon and Screen Resolution
PowerPoint may change how the groups and buttons within the groups appear on the ribbon, depending on the computer's screen resolution. Thus, your ribbon may look different from the ones in this book if you are using a screen resolution other than 1366 × 768.

To Save a Presentation

You have performed many tasks while creating this presentation and do not want to risk losing work completed thus far. Accordingly, you should save the presentation on your hard disk, SkyDrive, or a location that is most appropriate to your situation.

The following steps assume you already have created folders for storing your files, for example, a CIS 101 folder (for your class) that contains a PowerPoint folder

(for your assignments). Thus, these steps save the presentation in the PowerPoint folder in the CIS 101 folder on your desired save location. For a detailed example of the procedure for saving a file in a folder or saving a file on SkyDrive, refer to the Office and Windows chapter at the beginning of this book.

1 Tap or click the Save button on the Quick Access Toolbar, which depending on settings, will display either the Save As gallery in the Backstage view or the Save As dialog box.

2 To save on a hard disk or other storage media on your computer, proceed to Step 2a. To save on SkyDrive, proceed to Step 2b.

2a If your screen opens the Backstage view and you want to save on storage media on your computer, tap or click Computer in the left pane, if necessary, to display options in the right pane related to saving on your computer. If your screen already displays the Save As dialog box, proceed to Step 3.

2b If your screen opens the Backstage view and you want to save on SkyDrive, tap or click SkyDrive in the left pane to display SkyDrive saving options or a Sign In button. If your screen displays a Sign In button, tap or click it and then sign in to SkyDrive.

3 Tap or click the Browse button in the right pane to display the Save As dialog box associated with the selected save location (i.e., Computer or SkyDrive).

4 Type **Emergency Plan** in the File name box to change the file name. Do not press the ENTER key after typing the file name because you do not want to close the dialog box at this time.

5 Navigate to the desired save location (in this case, the PowerPoint folder in the CIS 101 folder [or your class folder] on your computer or SkyDrive).

6 Tap or click the Save button (Save As dialog box) to save the presentation in the selected folder on the selected save location with the entered file name.

Inserting and Formatting Pictures in a Presentation

With the text entered in three of the four slides, the next step is to insert pictures into Slides 1 and 2 and then format the pictures. These graphical images draw the viewers' eyes to the slides and help them retain the information presented.

In the following pages, you will perform these tasks:

1. Insert the illustration into Slide 1.
2. Resize the illustration.
3. Change the Slide 2 photo.
4. Change the photo's brightness and contrast.
5. Change the photo's style and effect.
6. Add and modify the photo's border.

BTW
Organizing Files and Folders
You should organize and store files in folders so that you easily can find the files later. For example, if you are taking an introductory computer class called CIS 101, a good practice would be to save all PowerPoint files in a PowerPoint folder in a CIS 101 folder. For a discussion of folders and detailed examples of creating folders, refer to the Office and Windows chapter at the beginning of this book.

To Insert a Picture into a Slide without a Content Placeholder

1 DOWNLOAD & SELECT SLIDES | 2 INSERT & FORMAT PICTURES | **3 INSERT & FORMAT SHAPES**
4 INSERT & FORMAT WORDART | 5 FORMAT SLIDE BACKGROUNDS | 6 REVIEW & REVISE SLIDES

In Chapter 1, you inserted photos and an illustration into slides without a content placeholder. *Why? Some slide layouts do not have a content placeholder, so you must insert and move the pictures to appropriate locations on the slide.* The illustration for Slide 1 is available on the Data Files for Students. Visit www.cengage.com/ct/studentdownload for detailed instructions or contact your instructor for information about accessing the

required files. The instructions in this chapter show the required files in the PowerPoint Chapter 2 folder in the CIS 101 folder on your computer. The following steps insert an illustration into the title slide.

1

- Display Slide 1 and then tap or click INSERT on the ribbon to display the INSERT tab.
- Tap or click the Pictures button (INSERT tab | Images group) to display the Insert Picture dialog box.

2

- If Computer is not displayed in the navigation pane, press and drag or drag the navigation pane scroll bar (Insert Picture dialog box) until Computer appears.
- Tap or click Computer in the navigation pane to display a list of available storage locations in the Insert Picture dialog box. If necessary, scroll through the dialog box until your class folder appears in the list.
- Double-tap or double-click your folder in the list of available storage locations to display a list of files and folders. Double-tap or double-click the Data Files for Students folder, double-tap or double-click the PowerPoint folder, and then double-tap or double-click the Chapter 02 folder to display a list of files in that folder.

- Slide or scroll down and then tap or click Fire Truck to select the file name (Figure 2–13).

What if the picture is not in the folder?
Use the same process, but select the location containing the Chapter 2 data file pictures or search for the picture on Office.com.

Why do I see thumbnails of the pictures along with the file names in my folder?
Your view is different from the view shown in Figure 2–13.

Figure 2–13

3

- Tap or click the Insert button (Insert Picture dialog box) to insert the illustration into Slide 1.
- Drag the upper-right sizing handle diagonally toward the upper-right corner of the slide until the crosshair is positioned approximately as shown in Figure 2–14.

Figure 2–14

- Release to resize the illustration.

- Drag the illustration downward until the horizontal Smart Guide is displayed under the title text placeholder and the vertical Smart Guide is displayed near the right side of the slide, as shown in Figure 2–15, and then release.

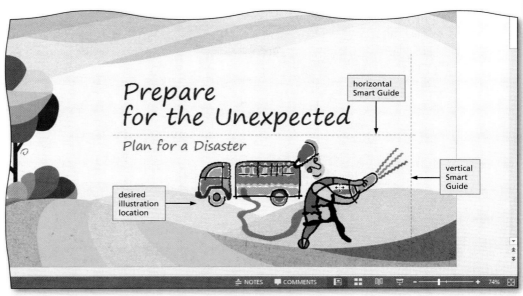

Figure 2–15

To Change a Picture

1 DOWNLOAD & SELECT SLIDES | 2 INSERT & FORMAT PICTURES | 3 INSERT & FORMAT SHAPES
4 INSERT & FORMAT WORDART | 5 FORMAT SLIDE BACKGROUNDS | 6 REVIEW & REVISE SLIDES

Why? *The downloaded theme included the photo of three children on Slide 2. You need to change the photo to reflect the emergency kit concept presented on this slide.* The next task in the presentation is to change the default picture on Slide 2 with one of the emergency pictures on the Data Files for Students. The following steps change the Slide 2 photo to the Emergency Kit photo, which, in this example, is located in the PowerPoint Chapter 02 folder that contains the saved presentation.

- Display Slide 2 and then press and hold or right-click the picture to display the shortcut menu (Figure 2–16).

Q&A Why are the Style and Crop buttons displayed above the shortcut menu on my screen?
These two buttons display either above or below the shortcut menu depending upon where you press and hold or right-click on the screen.

Figure 2–16

- Tap or click Change Picture to display the Insert Pictures dialog box (Figure 2–17).

Figure 2–17

- Tap or click the Browse button in the From a file area to display the Insert Pictures dialog box.

- If necessary, navigate to the PowerPoint Chapter 02 folder, slide or scroll down, and then click First Aid Kit to select the file name (Figure 2–18).

Figure 2–18

- Tap or click the Insert button (Insert Picture dialog box) to insert the photo into the Slide 2 picture placeholder (Figure 2–19).

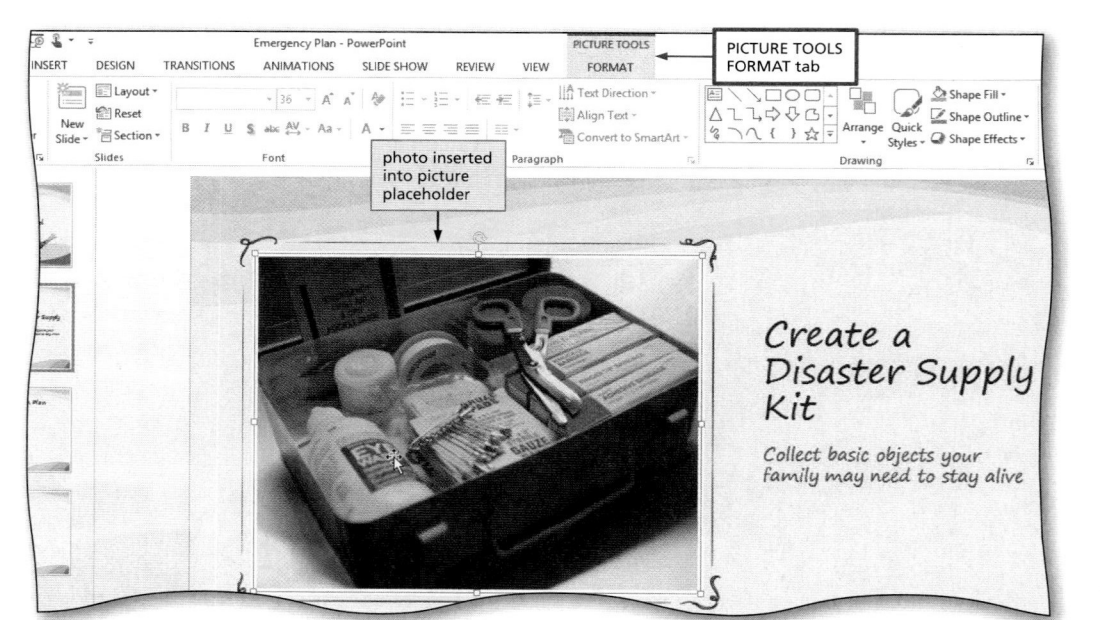

Figure 2–19

Other Ways

1. Tap or click Change Picture button (PICTURE TOOLS FORMAT tab | Adjust group)

To Correct a Picture

A photo's color intensity can be modified by changing the brightness and contrast. **Brightness** determines the overall lightness or darkness of the entire image, whereas **contrast** is the difference between the darkest and lightest areas of the image. The brightness and contrast are changed in predefined percentage increments. The following step increases the brightness and decreases the contrast. *Why? Altering the photo's brightness will coordinate with the vibrant colors in the slide design while decreasing the contrast will soften the image. It is important for the audience to recognize the first aid kit but not focus on each individual supply in the kit.*

- With the First Aid Kit photo on Slide 2 still selected, tap or click FORMAT on the ribbon to display the PICTURE TOOLS FORMAT tab.

- Tap or click the Corrections button (PICTURE TOOLS FORMAT tab | Adjust group) to display the Corrections gallery.

- If you are using a mouse, point to Brightness: +20% Contrast: −40% (the fourth picture in the first Brightness/Contrast row) to display a live preview of these corrections on the picture (Figure 2–20).

Figure 2–20

Q&A Can I use live preview on a touch screen?
Live preview is not available on a touch screen.

Why is a pink border surrounding the pictures in the center of the Sharpen/Soften and Brightness/Contrast areas of the gallery?
The image on Slide 2 currently has normal sharpness, brightness, and contrast (0%), which is represented by these center images in the gallery.

Experiment

- If you are using a mouse, point to various pictures in the Brightness and Contrast area and watch the brightness and contrast change on the picture in Slide 2.

- Tap or click Brightness: +20% Contrast: −40% to apply this correction to the First Aid Kit photo.

Q&A How can I remove all effects from the picture?
Tap or click the Reset Picture button (PICTURE TOOLS FORMAT tab | Adjust group).

Other Ways

1. Tap or click Picture Corrections Options (Corrections gallery), move Brightness or Contrast sliders or enter number in box next to slider (Format Picture task pane)

To Apply a Picture Style

A **style** is a named group of formatting characteristics. The picture on Slide 2 emphasizes the concept of assembling a supply kit, and you can increase its visual appeal by applying a style. *Why? PowerPoint provides more than 25 picture styles that enable you easily to change a picture's look to a more visually appealing style, including a variety of shapes, angles, borders, and reflections.* You want to use a style that applies a shadow to the First Aid Kit photo. The following steps apply a picture style to the Slide 2 photo.

①

- With the Slide 2 picture selected, if necessary tap or click the PICTURE TOOLS FORMAT tab and then tap or click the More button in the Picture Styles gallery (PICTURE TOOLS FORMAT tab | Picture Styles group) (shown in Figure 2–20) to expand the gallery.

- If you are using a mouse, point to Center Shadow Rectangle in the Picture Styles gallery (the sixth style in the second row) to display a live preview of that style applied to the picture in the document (Figure 2–21).

Figure 2–21

⊘ Experiment

- If you are using a mouse, point to various picture styles in the Picture Styles gallery and watch the style of the picture change in the document window.

②

- Tap or click Center Shadow Rectangle in the Picture Styles gallery to apply the style to the selected picture (Figure 2–22).

BTW

Touch Screen Differences

The Office and Windows interfaces may vary if you are using a touch screen. For this reason, you might notice that the function or appearance of your touch screen differs slightly from this chapter's presentation.

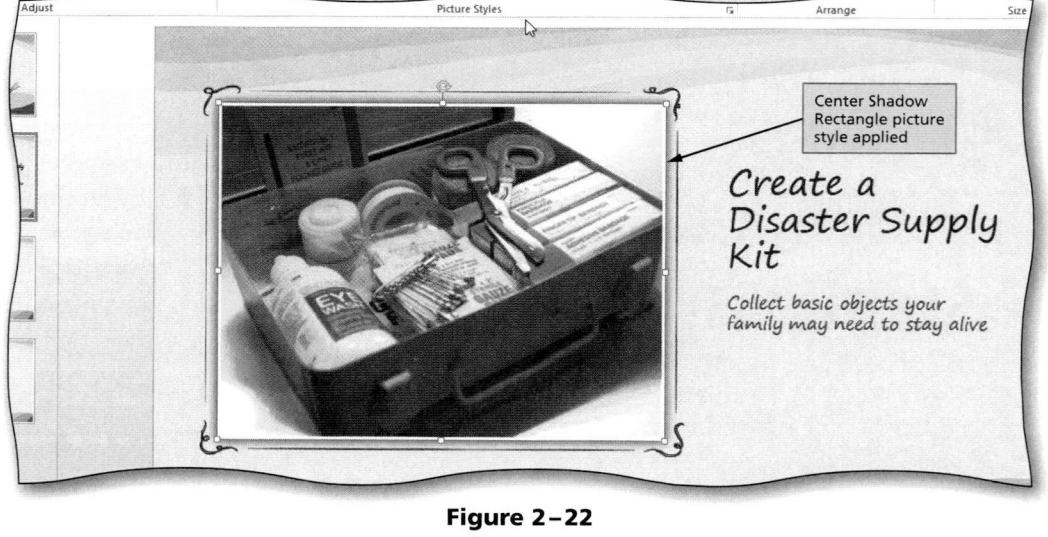

Figure 2–22

To Add a Picture Border

1 DOWNLOAD & SELECT SLIDES | 2 INSERT & FORMAT PICTURES | 3 INSERT & FORMAT SHAPES
4 INSERT & FORMAT WORDART | 5 FORMAT SLIDE BACKGROUNDS | 6 REVIEW & REVISE SLIDES

The next step is to add a border to the Slide 2 picture. *Why? Some picture styles do not have a border; others, such as the Center Shadow Rectangle style you applied to this picture, do have this edging. This border is small, and you want a larger edge around the photo to draw attention to the graphic.* The following steps add a border to the First Aid Kit picture.

- With the Slide 2 picture still selected, tap or click the Picture Border arrow (PICTURE TOOLS FORMAT tab | Picture Styles group) to display the Picture Border gallery.

Q&A What if the PICTURE TOOLS FORMAT tab no longer is displayed on my ribbon?
Tap or click the picture to display the PICTURE TOOLS FORMAT tab.

- Point to Weight on the Picture Border gallery to display the Weight gallery (Figure 2–23).

③

- If you are using a mouse, point to 3 pt to display a live preview of this line weight on the picture.

Q&A Can I make the line width more than 6 pt?
Yes. Tap or click More Lines, tap or click Solid line in the LINE section of the Format Picture task pane, and then increase the amount in the Width box.

Figure 2–23

Experiment

- If you are using a mouse, point to various line weights in the Weight gallery and watch the line thickness change.

- Tap or click 3 pt to add this line weight to the picture.

To Change a Picture Border Color

1 DOWNLOAD & SELECT SLIDES | 2 INSERT & FORMAT PICTURES | **3 INSERT & FORMAT SHAPES**
4 INSERT & FORMAT WORDART | 5 FORMAT SLIDE BACKGROUNDS | 6 REVIEW & REVISE SLIDES

The default color for the border you added to the Slide 2 picture is brown, but you will change the border color to light blue. *Why? The light blue color coordinates with other elements on the slide, especially the blue sky.* The following steps change the Slide 2 picture border color.

- With the Slide 2 photo still selected, tap or click the Picture Border arrow (PICTURE TOOLS FORMAT tab | Picture Styles group) to display the Picture Border gallery.

- If you are using a mouse, point to Light Blue, Background 2 (the third color in the first row) in the Picture Border gallery to display a live preview of that border color on the picture (Figure 2–24).

Figure 2–24

- If you are using a mouse, point to various colors in the Picture Border gallery and watch the border on the picture change in the slide.

❸

- Tap or click Light Blue, Background 2 in the Picture Border gallery to change the picture border color.

To Apply Picture Effects

Why? *The picture effect allows you to further customize a picture.* PowerPoint provides a variety of picture effects, including shadows, reflections, glow, soft edges, bevel, and 3-D rotation. The difference between the effects and the styles is that each effect has several options, providing you with more control over the exact look of the image.

In this presentation, the photo on Slide 2 has a blue glow effect and a bevel applied to its edges. The following steps apply picture effects to the selected picture.

❶

- With the Slide 2 picture selected, tap or click the Picture Effects button (PICTURE TOOLS FORMAT tab | Picture Styles group) to display the Picture Effects menu.

Q&A What if the PICTURE TOOLS FORMAT tab no longer is displayed on my ribbon?
Tap or double-click the picture to display the PICTURE TOOLS FORMAT tab.

- Point to Glow on the Picture Effects menu to display the Glow gallery.

Figure 2–25

- If you are using a mouse, point to Light Blue, 18 pt glow, Accent color 2 in the Glow Variations area (the second glow in the last row) to display a live preview of the selected glow effect applied to the picture in the document window (Figure 2–25).

- If you are using a mouse, point to various glow effects in the Glow gallery and watch the picture change in the document window.

❷

- Tap or click Light Blue, 18 pt glow, Accent color 2 in the Glow gallery to apply the selected picture effect.

- Tap or click the Picture Effects button (PICTURE TOOLS FORMAT tab | Picture Styles group) to display the Picture Effects menu again.

- Point to Bevel on the Picture Effects menu to display the Bevel gallery.

- If you are using a mouse, point to Relaxed Inset (the second bevel in the first row) to display a live preview of the selected bevel effect applied to the Slide 2 picture (Figure 2–26).

Figure 2–26

Experiment

- If you are using a mouse, point to various bevel effects in the Bevel gallery and watch the picture change in the slide.

- Tap or click Relaxed Inset in the Bevel gallery to apply the selected picture effect.

Other Ways

1. Press and hold or right-click picture, click Format Picture on shortcut menu, select desired options (Format Picture task pane), tap or click Close button

2. Tap or click Format Shape task pane launcher (PICTURE TOOLS FORMAT tab | Picture Styles group), select desired options (Format Picture task pane), tap or click Close button

Break Point: If you wish to take a break, this is a good place to do so. Be sure to save the Emergency Plan file again and then you can exit PowerPoint. To resume at a later time, run PowerPoint, open the file called Emergency Plan, and continue following the steps from this location forward.

Inserting and Formatting a Shape

One method of getting the audience's attention and reinforcing the major concepts being presented is to have graphical elements on the title slide. PowerPoint provides a wide variety of predefined shapes that can add visual interest to a slide. Shape elements include lines, basic geometrical shapes, arrows, equation shapes, flowchart symbols, stars, banners, and callouts. After adding a shape to a slide, you can change its default characteristics by adding text, bullets, numbers, and styles. You also can combine multiple shapes to create a more complex graphic.

Slide 3 in this presentation is enhanced in a variety of ways. First, a scroll and a plus shape are inserted on Slide 4. Then, a rectangle is added and copied, and text is added to each rectangle and then formatted.

To Add a Shape

Many of the shapes included in the Shapes gallery can direct the viewer to important aspects of the presentation. The following steps add a scroll shape to Slide 3. *Why? A scroll shape helps emphasize the presentation's theme of drafting and finalizing a plan for dealing with emergencies in the household.*

1

- Display Slide 3 and then display the HOME tab (Figure 2–27).

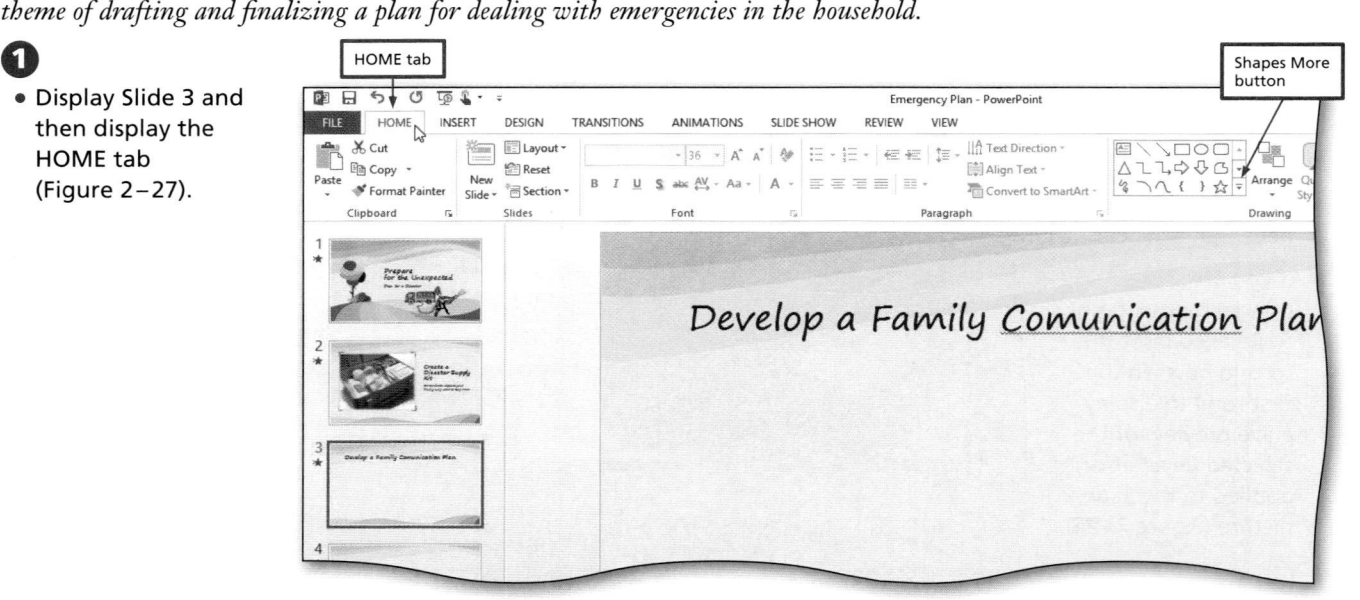

Figure 2–27

2

- Tap or click the Shapes More button (HOME tab | Drawing group) shown in Figure 2–27 to display the Shapes gallery (Figure 2–28).

Q&A I do not see a Shapes More button and the three rows of the shapes shown in Figure 2–28. Instead, I have a Shapes button. Why? Monitor dimensions and resolution affect how buttons display on the ribbon. Tap or click the Shapes button to display the entire Shapes gallery.

Figure 2–28

- Tap or click the Vertical Scroll shape in the Stars and Banners area of the Shapes gallery.

Q&A Why did my pointer change shape?
The pointer changed to a plus shape to indicate the Vertical Scroll shape has been added to the Clipboard.

- Position the pointer (a crosshair) below the word, Develop, as shown in Figure 2–29.

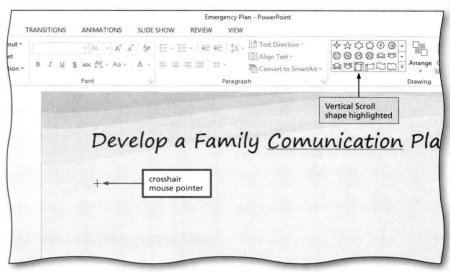

- Tap or click Slide 3 to insert the Vertical Scroll shape.

Figure 2–29

Other Ways

1. Tap or click Shapes button (INSERT tab | Illustrations group)

To Resize a Shape

1 DOWNLOAD & SELECT SLIDES | 2 INSERT & FORMAT PICTURES | 3 INSERT & FORMAT SHAPES
4 INSERT & FORMAT WORDART | 5 FORMAT SLIDE BACKGROUNDS | 6 REVIEW & REVISE SLIDES

The next step is to resize the Vertical Scroll shape. *Why? The shape should be enlarged so that it fills the middle area of the left side of the slide.* The following steps resize the selected Vertical Scroll shape.

- Press and hold down the SHIFT key and then drag the lower-right corner sizing handle until the Vertical Scroll shape is resized approximately as shown in Figure 2–30.

Q&A Why did I need to press the SHIFT key while enlarging the shape?
Holding down the SHIFT key while dragging keeps the proportions of the original shape.

What if my shape is not selected?
To select a shape, click it.

If I am using a touch screen, how can I maintain the shape's original proportion?
If you drag one of the corner sizing handles, the object should stay in proportion.

Figure 2–30

- Release to resize the shape.

- Drag the scroll shape until the vertical Smart Guide is displayed along the left side of the slide, as shown in Figure 2–31, and then release.

Q&A What if I want to move the shape to a precise location on the slide? With the shape selected, press the ARROW keys or the CTRL+ARROW keys to move the shape to the desired location.

Figure 2–31

Other Ways

1. Enter shape height and width in Height and Width boxes (DRAWING TOOLS FORMAT tab | Size group)

2. Tap or click Size and Position task pane launcher (DRAWING TOOLS FORMAT tab | Size group), tap or click Size tab, enter desired height and width values in boxes, tap or click Close button

To Add Other Shapes

1 DOWNLOAD & SELECT SLIDES | 2 INSERT & FORMAT PICTURES | 3 INSERT & FORMAT SHAPES
4 INSERT & FORMAT WORDART | 5 FORMAT SLIDE BACKGROUNDS | 6 REVIEW & REVISE SLIDES

Circles, squares, arrows, stars, and equation shapes are among the items included in the Shapes gallery. These shapes can be combined to show relationships among the elements, and they can help illustrate the basic concepts presented in your slide show. The following steps add the Plus and Rectangle shapes to Slide 3.

- Tap or click the Shapes More button (HOME tab | Drawing group) to display the Shapes gallery (Figure 2–32).

Figure 2–32

• Tap or click the Plus shape in the Equation Shapes area of the Shapes gallery.

• Position the pointer in the center of Slide 3 and then tap or click to insert the Plus shape.

• Press and hold down the SHIFT key and then drag a corner sizing handle until the Plus shape is the size shown in Figure 2–33.

Q&A If I am using a touch screen, how can I maintain the Plus shape's original proportion?
The object should stay in proportion when you drag one of the corner sizing handles.

• Drag the Plus shape until the horizontal Smart Guide is displayed in the middle of the two shapes and the vertical Smart Guide is displayed between the two shapes, as shown in Figure 2–33, and then release.

Figure 2–33

• Display the Shapes gallery and then tap or click the Rectangle shape in the Rectangles area of the gallery.

• Position the pointer toward the upper-right side of the Plus shape and then tap or click to insert the Rectangle shape.

• Resize the Rectangle shape so that it is the size shown in Figure 2–34.

• Drag the Rectangle shape until the horizontal Smart Guide is displayed below the title text and the vertical Smart Guide is displayed between the Plus and the Rectangle shapes, as shown in Figure 2–34, and then release.

Figure 2–34

To Apply a Shape Style

Formatting text in a shape follows the same techniques as formatting text in a placeholder. You can change font, font color and size, and alignment. You later will add contact information to the scroll, but now you want to apply a shape style to the scroll. *Why? The style will give depth to the object so that it appears three-dimensional.* The Quick Styles gallery has a variety of styles that change depending upon the theme applied to the presentation. The following steps apply a style to the Vertical Scroll shape.

1

- Tap or click the Vertical Scroll shape to select it and then tap or click the Quick Styles button (HOME tab | Drawing group) (Figure 2–35).

Figure 2–35

2

- If you are using a mouse, point to Subtle Effect – Lavender, Accent 6 in the Quick Styles gallery (the last shape in the fourth row) to display a live preview of that style applied to the Vertical Scroll shape in the slide (Figure 2–36).

🔎 **Experiment**

- If you are using a mouse, point to various styles in the Quick Styles gallery and watch the style of the shape change.

Figure 2–36

3

- Tap or click Subtle Effect – Lavender, Accent 6 in the Quick Styles gallery to apply the selected style to the Vertical Scroll shape.

Other Ways

1. Tap or click Shape Styles More button (DRAWING TOOLS FORMAT tab | Shape Styles group), select style
2. Press and hold or right-click shape, tap or click Format Shape on shortcut menu, select desired style (Format Shape task pane), tap or click Close button

To Apply Another Style

You later will add meeting place information to the rectangle, but now you want to format this shape. *Why? The formatting will add interest. In addition, the Plus shape helps join the scroll and the rectangle, both of which will contain components of the family communication plan. You can apply a coordinating shape style to the Plus sign.* The following steps apply styles to the Rectangle and Plus shapes.

1 Tap or click the Rectangle shape on Slide 3 to select it.

2 Tap or click the Quick Styles button (HOME tab | Drawing group) to display the Quick Styles gallery and then apply the Subtle Effect – Lavender, Accent 6 style to the Rectangle shape.

3 Tap or click the Plus shape on Slide 3 to select it and then tap or click the Quick Styles button.

4 Tap or click Colored Outline – Lavender, Accent 6 (the last style in the first row) to apply that style to the Plus shape (Figure 2–37).

Figure 2–37

To Add Text to a Shape

1 DOWNLOAD & SELECT SLIDES | 2 INSERT & FORMAT PICTURES | 3 INSERT & FORMAT SHAPES
4 INSERT & FORMAT WORDART | 5 FORMAT SLIDE BACKGROUNDS | 6 REVIEW & REVISE SLIDES

The scroll and rectangle shapes on Slide 3 help call attention to the key aspects of your presentation. *Why? Your goal is to urge families to develop a communication plan by gathering contact information and determining meeting locations.* The next step is to add this information to Slide 3. The following steps add text to the two shapes.

1

- Tap or click the Vertical Scroll shape to select it and then type `Contact names & phone numbers` in the shape.

2

- Tap or click the Rectangle shape to select it and then type `Meeting place near house` in the shape (Figure 2–38).

Figure 2–38

To Change the Font

1 DOWNLOAD & SELECT SLIDES | 2 INSERT & FORMAT PICTURES | **3 INSERT & FORMAT SHAPES**
4 INSERT & FORMAT WORDART | 5 FORMAT SLIDE BACKGROUNDS | 6 REVIEW & REVISE SLIDES

The default theme font is Segoe Print. To draw more attention to text in the shapes and to help differentiate these slide elements from the title text, you want to change the font to Courier New. *Why? This font resembles the letters that typewriters produced.* To change the font, you must select the letters you want to format. In Chapter 1, you selected a paragraph and then formatted the characters, and you follow the same procedure to change the font. The following steps change the text font in the shape.

1

- Be certain the Rectangle shape is selected. If you are using a touch screen, tap to position the insertion point in the text to select and then drag the selection handles as necessary until all the characters are selected and the mini toolbar is displayed; if you are using a mouse, triple-click the text to select all the characters and display the mini toolbar (Figure 2–39).

Figure 2–39

2

- Tap or click the Font arrow to display the Font gallery (Figure 2–40).

Q&A Will the fonts in my Font gallery be the same as those shown in Figure 2–40?
Your list of available fonts may differ, depending on what fonts you have installed and the type of printer you are using.

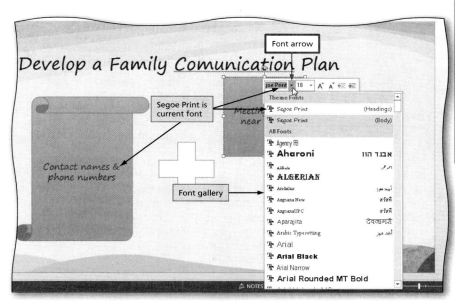

Figure 2–40

3

- If you are using a mouse, drag or scroll through the Font gallery and then point to Courier New (or a similar font) to display a live preview of the title text in the Courier New font (Figure 2–41).

Experiment

- If you are using a mouse, point to various fonts in the Font gallery and watch the subtitle text font change in the slide.

- Tap or click Courier New (or a similar font) to change the font of the selected text to Courier New.

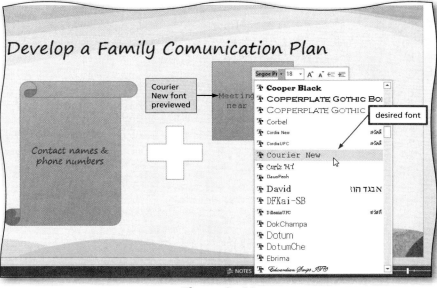

Figure 2–41

Other Ways

1. Tap or click Font arrow (HOME tab | Font group), tap or click desired font in Font gallery

2. Press and hold or right-click selected text, click Font on shortcut menu (Font dialog box), tap or click Font tab, select desired font in Font list, tap or click OK button

3. Tap or click Font dialog box launcher (HOME tab | Font group), tap or click Font tab (Font dialog box), select desired font in Font list, tap or click OK button

4. Press CTRL+SHIFT+F, click Font tab (Font dialog box), select desired font in the Font list, tap or click OK button

To Format the Text

To increase readability, you can format the Rectangle shape text by increasing the font size, bolding the characters, and changing the font color to black. The following steps format the Rectangle shape text.

1 With the Rectangle shape text selected, tap or click the Increase Font Size button (HOME tab | Font group) three times to increase the font size to 28 pt.

2 Tap or click the Bold button (HOME tab | Font group) to bold the text.

3 Tap or click the Font Color arrow and change the color to Black (the fourth color in the first row) (Figure 2–42).

Q&A Could I also add a shadow behind the text to add depth and help the letters display prominently?
Yes. Select the text and then tap or click the Text Shadow button (HOME tab | Font group).

Figure 2–42

Other Ways

1. Select text, tap 'Show Context Menu' button on mini toolbar or right-click selected text, tap or click desired text format button on mini toolbar

BTW
Shadowing Text
Adding a shadow to text adds depth and helps the letters display prominently by adding a shadow behind them. To add a shadow, select the text and then tap or click the Text Shadow button (HOME tab | Font group).

Format Painter

To save time and avoid formatting errors, you can use the Format Painter to apply custom formatting to other places in your presentation quickly and easily. You can use this feature in three ways:

• To copy only character attributes, such as font and font effects, select text that has these qualities.

• To copy both character attributes and paragraph attributes, such as alignment and indentation, select the entire paragraph.

• To apply the same formatting to multiple words, phrases, or paragraphs, double-tap or double-click the Format Painter button and then select each item you want to format. You then can press the ESC key or click the Format Painter button to turn off this feature.

To Format Text Using the Format Painter

Why? *To save time and duplicated effort, you quickly can use the Format Painter to copy formatting attributes from the Rectangle shape text and apply them to Vertical Scroll text.* The following steps use the Format Painter to copy formatting features.

- With the Rectangle shape text still selected, double-tap or double-click the Format Painter button (HOME tab | Clipboard group).

- Move the pointer off the ribbon (Figure 2–43).

Q&A Why did my pointer change shape?
The pointer changed shape by adding a paintbrush to indicate that the Format Painter function is active.

Figure 2–43

- Tap and drag the selection handles as necessary or triple-click the Vertical Scroll text to apply the format to all characters (Figure 2–44).

- Tap the Format Painter button or press the ESC key to turn off the Format Painter feature.

Figure 2–44

Other Ways

1. Select text, tap or click Format Painter button on mini toolbar

To Copy and Paste a Shape

When developing a communication plan, family members need to determine two meeting places: one near the house and a second outside the neighborhood. You already have created the shape stating the first meeting location. You now need to create a second shape with the instruction to decide where to meet away from the house. The following steps copy the Rectangle shape and then move the copy. **Why?** *You could repeat all the steps you performed to create the first rectangle, but it is much more efficient to duplicate the shape and then edit the text.*

- Select the Rectangle shape and then tap or click the Copy button (HOME tab | Clipboard group) (Figure 2–45).

Figure 2–45

2

- Tap or click the Paste button (HOME tab | Clipboard group) to insert a duplicate Rectangle shape on Slide 3.

- Drag the Rectangle shape below the first Rectangle shape (Figure 2–46).

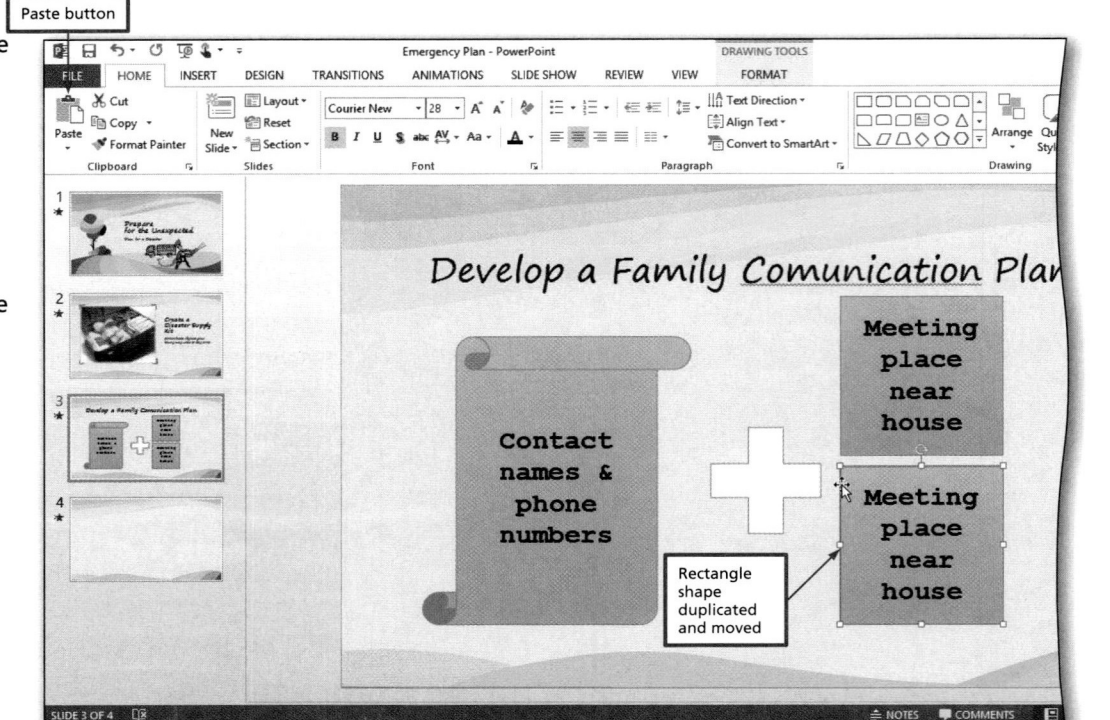

Figure 2–46

3

- In the second Rectangle shape, select the text, near house, and then type **away from vicinity** as the replacement text (Figure 2–47).

Figure 2–47

Other Ways

1. Press and hold or right-click selected shape, tap or click Copy on shortcut menu, press and hold or right-click, tap or click Paste on shortcut menu

2. Select shape, press CTRL+C, press CTRL+V

Break Point: If you wish to take a break, this is a good place to do so. Be sure to save the Emergency Plan file again and then you can exit PowerPoint. To resume at a later time, run PowerPoint, open the file called Emergency Plan, and continue following the steps from this location forward.

Inserting and Formatting WordArt

One method of adding appealing visual elements to a presentation is by using **WordArt** styles. This feature is found in other Microsoft Office applications, including Word and Excel. This gallery of decorative effects allows you to type new text or convert existing text to WordArt. You then can add elements such as fills, outlines, and effects.

WordArt **fill** in the interior of a letter can consist of a solid color, texture, picture, or gradient. The WordArt **outline** is the exterior border surrounding each letter or symbol. PowerPoint allows you to change the outline color, weight, and style. You also can add an **effect**, which helps add emphasis or depth to the characters. Some effects are shadows, reflections, glows, bevels, and 3-D rotations.

BTW
Undo Text Formatting Changes
To remove a formatting change you have made to text, such as an underline or bolding, select the text and then tap or click the button that originally applied the format. For example, to undo bolding, select the text and then click the Bold button. If you apply a format and then immediately decide to remove this effect, click the Undo button on the Quick Access Toolbar.

To Insert WordArt

1 DOWNLOAD & SELECT SLIDES | 2 INSERT & FORMAT PICTURES | 3 INSERT & FORMAT SHAPES
4 INSERT & FORMAT WORDART | 5 FORMAT SLIDE BACKGROUNDS | 6 REVIEW & REVISE SLIDES

Having a communication plan is of utmost importance to prepare for the unexpected. You want to emphasize this concept, and the last slide in the presentation is an excellent location to urge your audience to take action. *Why? Audience members remember the first and last things they see and hear.* You quickly can add a visual element to the slide by selecting a WordArt style from the WordArt Styles gallery and then applying it to some text. The following steps insert WordArt.

- Display Slide 4 and then display the INSERT tab.

- Tap or click the WordArt button (INSERT tab | Text group) to display the WordArt gallery (Figure 2–48).

Figure 2–48

- Tap or click Fill – Brown, Text 1, Outline – Background 1, Hard Shadow – Background 1 (the first style in the third row) to insert the WordArt object (Figure 2–49).

Figure 2–49

- Type **Be Prepared** in the object as the WordArt text (Figure 2–50).

Why did the DRAWING TOOLS FORMAT tab appear automatically in the ribbon?

It appears when you select text to which you could add a WordArt style or other effect.

Figure 2–50

To Change the WordArt Shape

Why? *The WordArt text is useful to emphasize the need to prepare for emergencies. You further can emphasize this text by changing its shape.* PowerPoint provides a variety of graphical shapes that add interest to WordArt text. The following steps change the WordArt shape to Inflate Bottom.

1

- With the WordArt object still selected, click the Text Effects button (DRAWING TOOLS FORMAT tab | WordArt Styles group) to display the Text Effects menu (Figure 2–51).

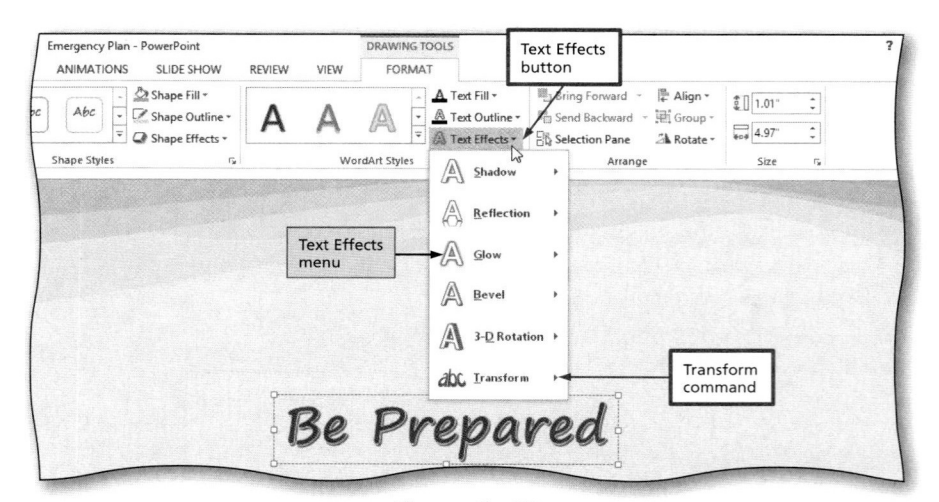

Figure 2–51

2

- Point to Transform in the Text Effects menu to display the WordArt Transform gallery (Figure 2–52).

Figure 2–52

- If you are using a mouse, point to the Inflate Bottom shape in the Warp area (the third shape in the last row) to display a live preview of that text effect applied to the WordArt object (Figure 2–53).

🔍 **Experiment**

- If you are using a mouse, point to various effects in the Transform gallery and watch the format of the text and borders change.

Q&A How can I see the preview of a Transform effect if the gallery is overlaying the WordArt letters?
Move the WordArt box to the left or right side of the slide and then repeat Steps 1 and 2.

Figure 2–53

- Tap or click the Inflate Bottom shape to apply this text effect to the WordArt object.

Q&A Can I change the shape I applied to the WordArt?
Yes. Position the insertion point in the box and then repeat Steps 1 and 2.

- Drag the upper-left sizing handle diagonally toward the upper-left corner of the slide until the crosshair is positioned approximately as shown in Figure 2–54.

Figure 2–54

6

- Release to resize the WordArt object.

- Drag the WordArt object toward the center of the slide until it is positioned approximately as shown in Figure 2–55.

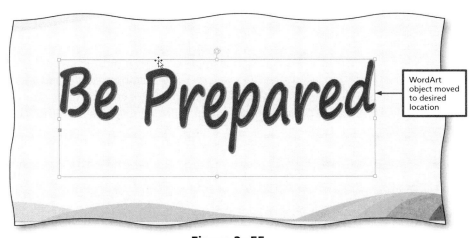

Figure 2–55

To Apply a WordArt Text Fill

Various texture fills are available to give your WordArt characters a unique look. The 24 pictures in the Texture gallery give the appearance of a physical object, such as water drops, sand, tissue paper, and a paper bag. The following steps add the Purple Mesh texture as a fill for the WordArt characters. *Why?* *Purple coordinates well with the shapes on Slide 3 and is similar to the color in the Slide1 flower and firefighter's hose.*

1

• With the WordArt object selected, click the Text Fill arrow (DRAWING TOOLS FORMAT tab | WordArt Styles group) to display the Text Fill gallery.

• Point to Texture in the Text Fill gallery to display the Texture gallery.

2

• If you are using a mouse, point to the Purple mesh texture (the third texture in the fifth row) to display a live preview of that texture applied to the WordArt object (Figure 2–56).

Experiment

• If you are using a mouse, point to various styles in the Texture gallery and watch the fill change.

3

• Tap or click the Purple mesh texture to apply this texture as the fill for the WordArt object.

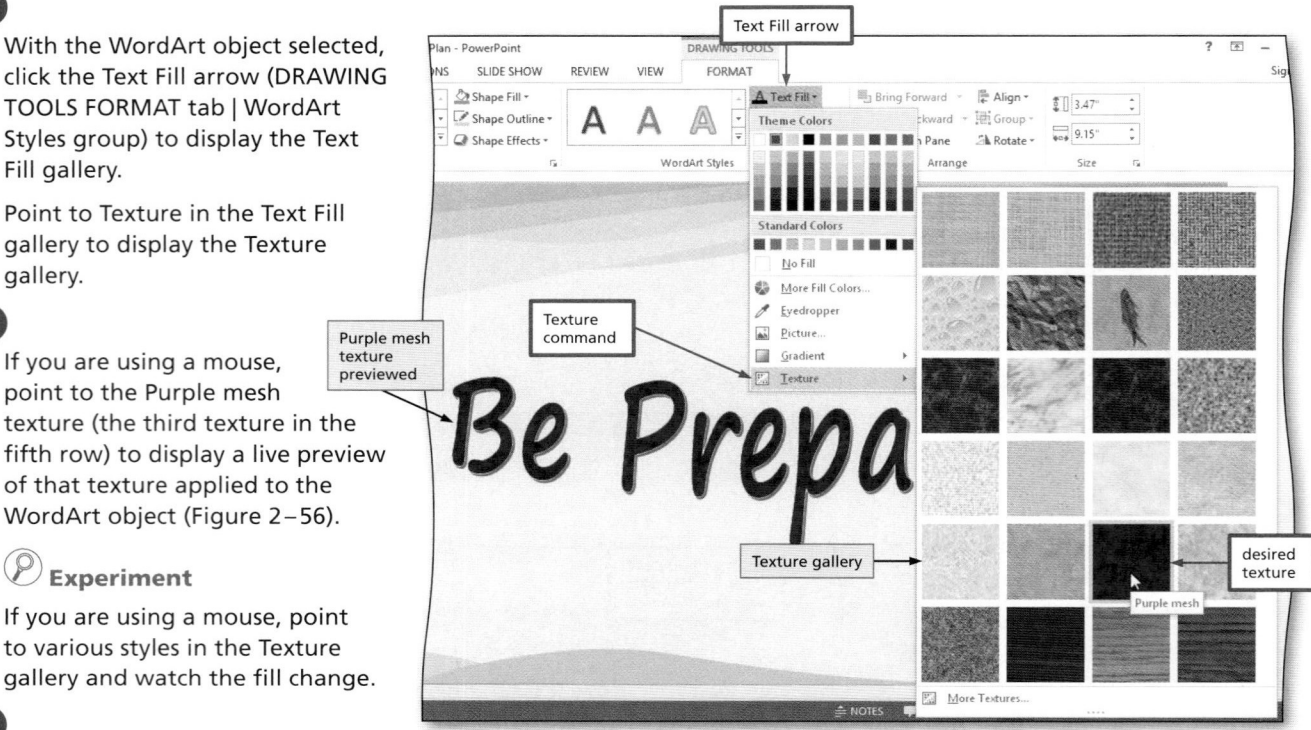

Figure 2–56

Q&A Can I apply this texture simultaneously to text that appears in more than one place on my slide?

Yes. If you are not using a touch screen, you can select one area of text, press and then hold the CTRL key while you select the other text, and then apply the texture.

To Change the Weight of the WordArt Outline

The letters in the WordArt style applied have an outline around the edges. You can increase the width of the lines. *Why?* *The thicker line will emphasize this characteristic and add another visual element.* As with fonts, lines also are measured in point size, and PowerPoint gives you the option to change the line **weight**, or thickness, starting with ¼ point (pt) and increasing in one-fourth-point increments. Other outline options include modifying the color and the line style, such as changing to dots or dashes or a combination of dots and dashes. The following steps change the WordArt outline weight to 3 pt.

- With the WordArt object still selected, click the Text Outline arrow (DRAWING TOOLS FORMAT tab | WordArt Styles group) to display the Text Outline gallery.

- Point to Weight in the gallery to display the Weight list.

- If you are using a mouse, point to 3 pt to display a live preview of this line weight on the WordArt text outline (Figure 2–57).

Q&A Can I make the line width more than 6 pt?
Yes. Tap or click More Lines and increase the amount in the Width box.

Experiment

- If you are using a mouse, point to various line weights in the Weight list and watch the line thickness change.

Figure 2–57

- Tap or click 3 pt to apply this line weight to the WordArt text outline.

Q&A Must my text have an outline?
No. To delete the outline, click No Outline in the Text Outline gallery.

To Change the Color of the WordArt Outline

1 DOWNLOAD & SELECT SLIDES | 2 INSERT & FORMAT PICTURES | 3 INSERT & FORMAT SHAPES
4 INSERT & FORMAT WORDART | 5 FORMAT SLIDE BACKGROUNDS | 6 REVIEW & REVISE SLIDES

Why? *The WordArt outline color and the slide background color are similar, so you can add contrast by changing one of these slide elements.* The following steps change the WordArt outline color.

- With the WordArt object still selected, display the Text Outline gallery.

- If you are using a mouse, point to Red (the second color in the Standard Colors row) to display a live preview of this outline color.

Experiment

- If you are using a mouse, point to various colors in the gallery and watch the outline colors change.

Figure 2–58

- Tap or click Red to apply this color to the WordArt outline.

- Tap or click outside of the WordArt box to deselect this slide element (Figure 2–58).

Formatting Slide Backgrounds

A slide's background is an integral part of a presentation because it can generate audience interest. Every slide can have the same background, or different backgrounds can be used in a presentation. This background is considered fill, which is the content that makes up the interior of a shape, line, or character. Four fills are available: solid, gradient, picture or texture, and pattern. **Solid fill** is one color used throughout the entire slide. **Gradient fill** is one color shade gradually progressing to another shade of the same color or one color progressing to another color. **Picture** or **texture fill** uses a specific file or an image that simulates a material, such as cork, granite, marble, or canvas. **Pattern fill** adds designs, such as dots or diamonds, that repeat in rows across the slide.

Once you add a fill, you can adjust its appearance. For example, you can adjust its **transparency**, which allows you to see through the background, so that any text on the slide is visible. You also can select a color that is part of the theme or a custom color. You can use **offsets**, another background feature, to move the background away from the slide borders in varying distances by percentage. **Tiling options** repeat the background image many times vertically and horizontally on the slide; the smaller the tiling percentage, the greater the number of times the image is repeated.

To Insert a Picture to Create a Background

1 DOWNLOAD & SELECT SLIDES | 2 INSERT & FORMAT PICTURES | 3 INSERT & FORMAT SHAPES
4 INSERT & FORMAT WORDART | 5 FORMAT SLIDE BACKGROUNDS | 6 REVIEW & REVISE SLIDES

Why? *For variety and interest, you want to use an illustration as the Slide 4 background.* This picture is stored on the Data Files for Students. PowerPoint will stretch the height and width of this picture to fill the slide area. The following steps insert the picture, Emergency Collage, on Slide 4 only.

1
- With Slide 4 displaying, display the DESIGN tab and then click the Format Background button (DESIGN tab | Customize group).

- With the FILL section displaying (Format Background task pane) and 'Picture or texture fill' selected, tap or click the File button to display the Insert Picture dialog box (Figure 2–59).

- If necessary, navigate to the PowerPoint Chapter 02 folder or the location where your Data Files for Students folder is located.

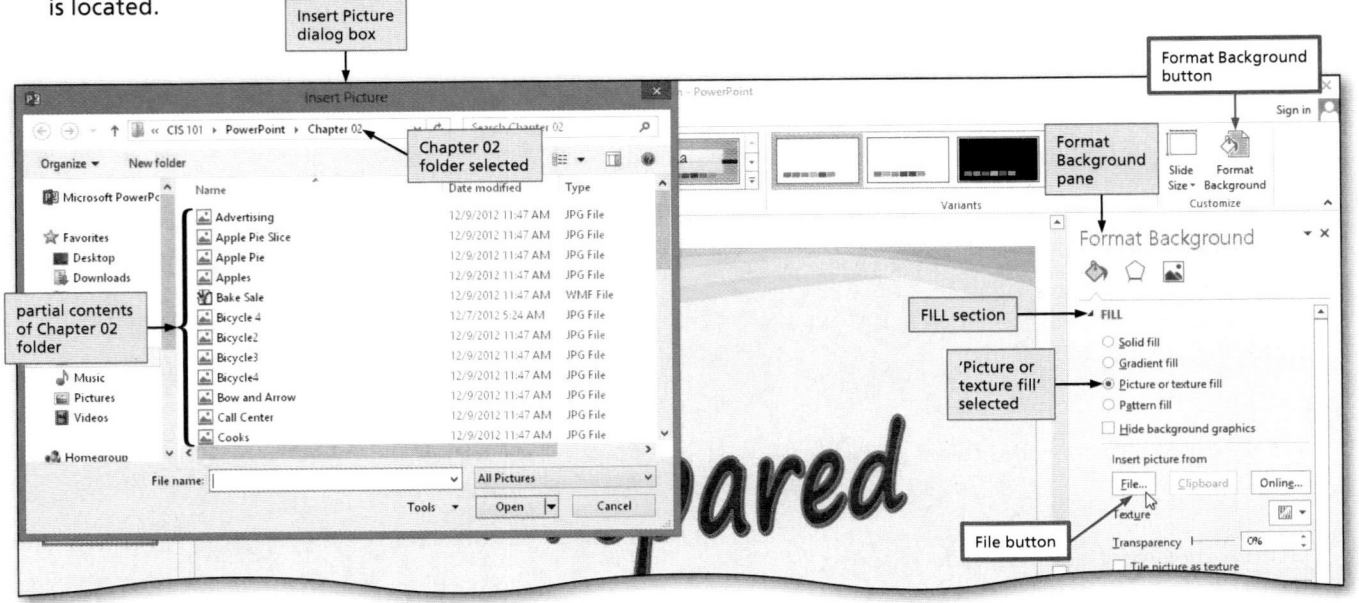

Figure 2–59

2

- If necessary, slide or scroll down and then click Emergency Collage to select the file name (Figure 2–60).

Figure 2–60

3

- Tap or click the Insert button (Insert Picture dialog box) to insert the Emergency Collage illustration as the Slide 4 background (Figure 2–61).

Q&A | What if I do not want to use this picture?
Tap or click the Undo button on the Quick Access Toolbar or tap or click the Reset Background button at the bottom of the Format Background task pane.

Figure 2–61

Other Ways

1. Tap or click Format Background on shortcut menu, click Picture or Texture Fill, Insert from File (Format Background pane)

To Format the Background Picture Fill Transparency

1 DOWNLOAD & SELECT SLIDES | 2 INSERT & FORMAT PICTURES | 3 INSERT & FORMAT SHAPES
4 INSERT & FORMAT WORDART | 5 FORMAT SLIDE BACKGROUNDS | 6 REVIEW & REVISE SLIDES

The Emergency Collage illustration on Slide 4 has vibrant colors and conflicts with the WordArt. One method of reducing this richness is to change the transparency. The **Transparency slider** indicates the amount of opaqueness. The default setting is 0, which is fully opaque. The opposite extreme is 100%, which is fully transparent. To change the transparency, you can move the Transparency slider or enter a number in the box next to the slider. The following step adjusts the transparency of the background picture to 60%.

1

- Tap or click the Transparency slider and drag it to the right until 60% is displayed in the Transparency box (Figure 2–62).

Q&A Can I move the slider in small increments so that I can get a precise percentage easily?
Yes. Tap or click the up or down arrows in the Transparency box to move the slider in one-percent increments.

Figure 2–62

To Insert a Texture Fill

You used a texture fill to add interest to the WordArt characters. These same fills are available to add as a slide background. You also can use your own texture pictures for custom backgrounds. The following steps insert the Bouquet fill on Slide 3 in the presentation.

1

- Display Slide 3 and, if necessary, tap or click the Format Background button (DESIGN tab | Customize group) to display the Format Background task pane.

- Tap or click the Texture button to display the Texture gallery (Figure 2–63).

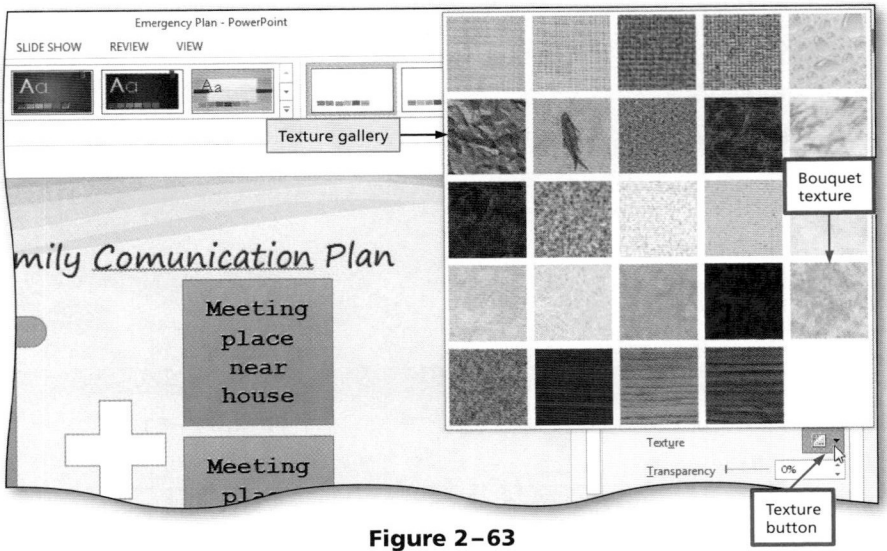

Figure 2–63

2

- Tap or click the Bouquet texture (the last texture in the fourth row) to insert this texture fill as the background on Slide 3 (Figure 2–64).

Q&A Is a live preview available to see the various textures on this slide?
No. Live preview is not an option with the background textures and fills.

Could I insert this background on all four slides simultaneously?
Yes. You would click the 'Apply to All' button to insert the Bouquet background on all slides.

Figure 2–64

Other Ways

1. Press and hold or right-click background, click Format Background on shortcut menu, select desired options (Format Background pane)

To Format the Background Texture Fill Transparency

1 DOWNLOAD & SELECT SLIDES | 2 INSERT & FORMAT PICTURES | 3 INSERT & FORMAT SHAPES
4 INSERT & FORMAT WORDART | **5 FORMAT SLIDE BACKGROUNDS** | **6 REVIEW & REVISE SLIDES**

The Bouquet texture on Slide 3 may detract from the three shapes because it does not offer sufficient contrast with the symbols and text. You can adjust the transparency of a slide texture in the same manner that you change a picture transparency. The following step adjusts the texture transparency to 35%.

1

- Click the Transparency slider and drag it to the right until 35% is displayed in the Transparency box (Figure 2–65).

Figure 2–65

To Insert a Gradient Fill

1 DOWNLOAD & SELECT SLIDES | 2 INSERT & FORMAT PICTURES | 3 INSERT & FORMAT SHAPES
4 INSERT & FORMAT WORDART | **5 FORMAT SLIDE BACKGROUNDS** | **6 REVIEW & REVISE SLIDES**

Although you selected Bouquet texture fill on Slide 3 and changed the transparency, you decide that another type of background may be more suitable for your presentation. *Why? The Bouquet texture is very colorful and may detract from the messages presented in the symbols.* For each theme, PowerPoint provides 30 preset **gradient fills** with five designs for each of the six major theme colors. Each fill has one dark color shade that gradually lightens to either another shade of the same color or another color. The following steps replace the texture fill on Slide 3 to a preset gradient fill.

1

- Tap or click Gradient fill in the Format Background pane and then click the Preset gradients button to display the Preset gradients gallery (Figure 2–66).

Q&A Are the backgrounds displayed in a specific order?

Yes. The first row has light colors at the top of the background; the middle rows have darker fills at the bottom; the bottom row has overall dark fills on all edges.

Is a live preview available to see the various gradients on this slide?

No. Live preview is not an option with the background textures and fills.

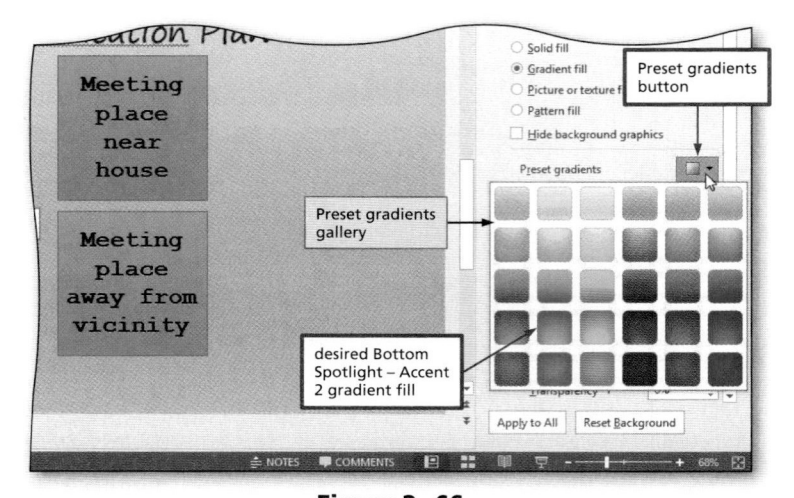

Figure 2–66

2

- Tap or click Bottom Spotlight – Accent 2 (the second fill in the fourth row) to apply that style to Slide 3 (Figure 2–67).

Q&A If I decide later that this background gradient does not fit the theme of my presentation, can I apply a different background?

Yes. You can repeat these steps at any time while creating your presentation.

What if I want to apply this background gradient to all slides in the presentation?

Tap or click the desired style or click the 'Apply to All' button at the bottom of the pane.

Figure 2–67

3

- Tap or click the Close button (Format Background pane) to close the pane and return to Slide 3.

Other Ways

1. Tap or click DESIGN tab on ribbon, tap or click Format Background button (Customize group), select desired options (Format Background pane)

2. Press and hold or right-click background, click Format Background on shortcut menu, select desired options (Format Background pane)

Reviewing and Revising Individual Slides

The text, pictures, and shapes for all slides in the Emergency Plan presentation have been entered. Once you complete a slide show, you might decide to change elements. PowerPoint provides several tools to assist you with making changes. They include finding and replacing text, inserting a synonym, and checking spelling. The following pages discuss these tools.

Replace Dialog Box

At times, you might want to change all occurrences of a word or phrase to another word or phrase. For example, an instructor may have one slide show to accompany a lecture for several introductory classes, and he wants to update slides with the particular class name and section that appear on several slides. He manually could change the characters, but PowerPoint includes an efficient method of replacing one word with another. The Find and Replace feature automatically locates specific text and then replaces it with desired text.

In some cases, you may want to replace only certain occurrences of a word or phrase, not all of them. To instruct PowerPoint to confirm each change, click the Find Next button in the Replace dialog box instead of the Replace All button. When PowerPoint locates an occurrence of the text, it pauses and waits for you to click either the Replace button or the Find Next button. Clicking the Replace button changes the text; clicking the Find Next button instructs PowerPoint to disregard that particular instance and look for the next occurrence of the Find what text.

To Find and Replace Text

1 DOWNLOAD & SELECT SLIDES | 2 INSERT & FORMAT PICTURES | 3 INSERT & FORMAT SHAPES
4 INSERT & FORMAT WORDART | 5 FORMAT SLIDE BACKGROUNDS | 6 REVIEW & REVISE SLIDES

While reviewing your slides, you realize that the word, Emergency, would be a better choice than the word, Disaster. To change these words throughout a presentation, you could view each slide, look for the word, Disaster, delete the word, and then type the replacement word, Emergency. A more efficient and effective method of performing this action is to use PowerPoint's Find and Replace feature, which automatically locates each occurrence of a word or phrase and then replaces it with specified text. The word, Disaster, displays twice in the presentation. The following steps use Find and Replace to replace all occurrences of the words, a Disaster, with the words, an Emergency.

- Display the HOME tab and then tap or click the Replace button (HOME tab | Editing group) to display the Replace dialog box.

- Type **a Disaster** in the Find what box (Replace dialog box).

- Tap or click the Replace with box and then type **an Emergency** in the box (Figure 2–68).

Figure 2–68

2

- Tap or click the Replace All button (Replace dialog box) to instruct PowerPoint to replace all occurrences of the Find what words, a Disaster, with the Replace with words, an Emergency (Figure 2–69).

Q&A If I accidentally replaced the wrong text, can I undo this replacement?
Yes. Tap or click the Undo button on the Quick Access Toolbar to undo all replacements. If you had tapped or clicked the Replace button instead of the Replace All button, PowerPoint would undo only the most recent replacement.

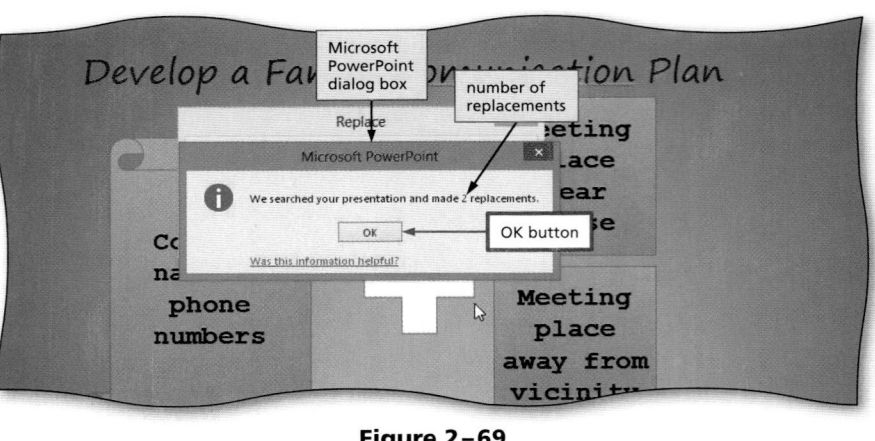

Figure 2–69

3

- Tap or click the OK button (Microsoft PowerPoint dialog box).

- Tap or click the Close btton (Replace dialog box).

BTW
Finding and Replacing Text
When finding and replacing text, you do not need to display the slide that contains the word for which you are searching. You can perform this action when any slide is displayed. To see the results of the search and replace action, however, you need to display the slide where the change occurred.

Other Ways
1. Press CTRL+H

To Find and Insert a Synonym

1 DOWNLOAD & SELECT SLIDES | 2 INSERT & FORMAT PICTURES | 3 INSERT & FORMAT SHAPES
4 INSERT & FORMAT WORDART | 5 FORMAT SLIDE BACKGROUNDS | 6 REVIEW & REVISE SLIDES

When reviewing your slide show, you may decide that a particular word does not express the exact usage you intended or that you used the same word on multiple slides. In these cases, you could find a **synonym**, or word similar in meaning, to replace the inappropriate or duplicate word. PowerPoint provides a **thesaurus**, which is a list of synonyms and antonyms, to help you find a replacement word.

In this project, you want to find a synonym to replace the words, stay alive, on Slide 2. The following steps locate an appropriate synonym and replace the word.

1

- Display Slide 2 and then select the words, stay alive.

- If you are using a mouse, right-click to display a shortcut menu related to the words you right-clicked. Then, point to Synonyms on the shortcut menu to display a list of synonyms for these words (Figure 2–70).

Q&A If I want to locate a synonym for only one word, do I need to select it?
No. You simply need to place the insertion point in the word and then press and hold or right-click to display the shortcut menu.

- If you are using a touch screen, tap the Thesaurus button (REVIEW tab | Proofing group) to display the Thesaurus task pane for the selected words. Then, in the task pane, tap the arrow next to the word survive if necessary to display a shortcut menu.

Figure 2–70

2

- Tap Insert or click the synonym you want (survive) on the Synonyms submenu to replace the words, stay alive, in the presentation with the word, survive (Figure 2–71).

Q&A What if a suitable word does not display in the Synonyms submenu?
You can display the Thesaurus task pane by tapping or clicking Thesaurus on the Synonyms submenu. A complete thesaurus with synonyms displays in the task pane along with an antonym, which is a word with an opposite meaning.

Figure 2–71

Other Ways

1. Tap or click Thesaurus (REVIEW tab | Proofing group) 2. Press SHIFT+F7

To Add Notes

1 DOWNLOAD & SELECT SLIDES | 2 INSERT & FORMAT PICTURES | 3 INSERT & FORMAT SHAPES
4 INSERT & FORMAT WORDART | 5 FORMAT SLIDE BACKGROUNDS | 6 REVIEW & REVISE SLIDES

As you create slides, you may find material you want to state verbally and do not want to include on the slide. You can type and format notes in the **Notes pane** as you work in Normal view and then print this information as **notes pages**. The Notes pane is hidden until you tap or click the Notes button on the status bar to open the pane. If you want to close the Notes pane, tap or click the Notes button again. After adding comments, you can print a set of speaker notes. These notes will print below a small image of the slide. Charts, tables, and pictures added to the Notes pane also print on these pages. The following steps add text to the Notes pane on Slides 2, 3, and 4.

Note: In the following step, the word, whistle, has been misspelled intentionally as wistle to illustrate the use of PowerPoint's spell check feature. Your slides may contain different misspelled words, depending upon the accuracy of your typing.

1

- Display Slide 2 and then if necessary tap or click the Notes button on the status bar to display the Notes pane.

Q&A Why might I need to tap or click the Notes pane?
By default, the Notes pane is closed when you begin a new presentation. Once you display the Notes pane for any slide, the Notes pane will remain open unless you tap or click the Notes button to close it.

- Tap or click the Notes pane and then type **The kit should include a flashlight, wistle, water, radio, batteries, three-day supply of food, three gallons of water for each family member, change of clothing, tools, and first aid kit.** (Figure 2–72).

Q&A What if I cannot see all the lines I typed?
You can drag the splitter bar up to enlarge the Notes pane. Clicking the Notes pane scroll arrows or swiping up or down on the Notes pane allows you to view the entire text.

Figure 2–72

②

- Display Slide 3, tap or click the Notes pane, and then type `One meeting place should be near the home, and the second should be outside the neighborhood. One out-of-state relative should be included in the contacts list.` (Figure 2–73).

Figure 2–73

③

- Display Slide 4 and then type `The Federal Emergency Management Agency (FEMA) has additional information about helping people prepare for emergency situations. Visit www.ready.gov.` in the Notes pane (Figure 2–74).

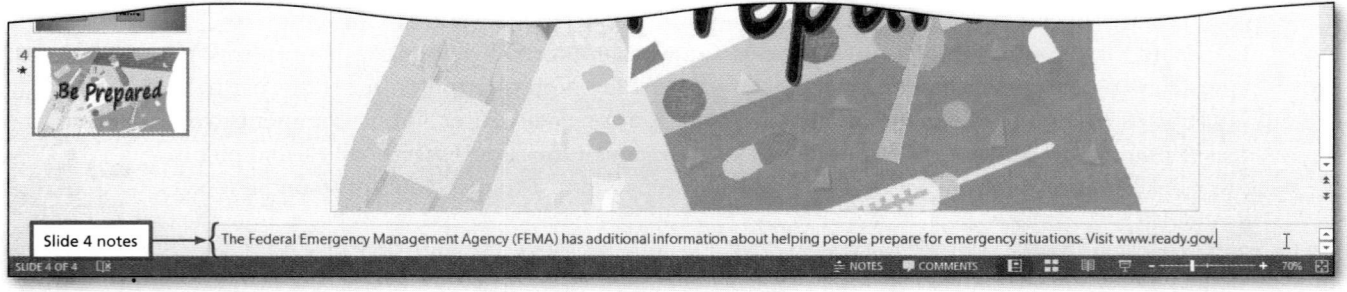

Figure 2–74

BTW
Formatting Notes Pane Text
You can format text in the Notes pane in the same manner you format text on a slide. For example, you can bold key words or change the font size and color to add emphasis.

BTW
Detecting Spelling Errors
The x in the Spell Check icon indicates PowerPoint detected a possible spelling error. A check mark in the icon indicates the entered text contains no spelling errors.

Checking Spelling

After you create a presentation, you should check it visually for spelling errors and style consistency. In addition, you use PowerPoint's Spelling tool to identify possible misspellings on the slides and in the notes. Do not rely on the spelling checker to catch all your mistakes. Although PowerPoint's spelling checker is a valuable tool, it is not infallible. You should proofread your presentation carefully by pointing to each word and saying it aloud as you point to it. Be mindful of commonly misused words such as its and it's, through and though, and to and too.

PowerPoint checks the entire presentation for spelling mistakes using a standard dictionary contained in the Microsoft Office group. This dictionary is shared with the other Microsoft Office applications such as Word and Excel. A custom dictionary is available if you want to add special words such as proper names, cities, and acronyms. When checking a presentation for spelling errors, PowerPoint opens the standard dictionary and the custom dictionary file, if one exists. When a word appears in the Spelling pane, you can perform one of several actions, as described in Table 2–1.

The standard dictionary contains commonly used English words. It does not, however, contain many proper names, abbreviations, technical terms, poetic contractions, or antiquated terms. PowerPoint treats words not found in the dictionaries as misspellings.

Table 2–1 Spelling Pane Buttons and Actions		
Button Name/Action	**When to Use**	**Action**
Ignore	Word is spelled correctly but not found in dictionaries	PowerPoint continues checking rest of the presentation but will flag that word again if it appears later in document.
Ignore All	Word is spelled correctly but not found in dictionaries	PowerPoint ignores all occurrences of the word and continues checking rest of presentation.
Add	Add word to custom dictionary	PowerPoint opens custom dictionary, adds word, and continues checking rest of presentation.
Change	Word is misspelled	Click proper spelling of the word in Suggestions list. PowerPoint corrects word, continues checking rest of presentation, but will flag that word again if it appears later in document.
Change All	Word is misspelled	Click proper spelling of word in Suggestions list. PowerPoint changes all occurrences of misspelled word and continues checking rest of presentation.
Listen to the pronunciation	To hear the pronunciation of a word	Tap or click the audio speaker icon next to the properly spelled word near the bottom of the Spelling pane.
View synonyms	See some synonyms for the correctly spelled word	View the bullet list of synonyms below the correctly spelled word near the bottom of the Spelling pane.
Close	Stop spelling checker	PowerPoint closes spelling checker and returns to PowerPoint window.

© 2014 Cengage Learning

To Check Spelling

1 DOWNLOAD & SELECT SLIDES | 2 INSERT & FORMAT PICTURES | 3 INSERT & FORMAT SHAPES
4 INSERT & FORMAT WORDART | 5 FORMAT SLIDE BACKGROUNDS | 6 REVIEW & REVISE SLIDES

The following steps check the spelling on all slides in the Emergency Plan presentation.

1
- Tap or click REVIEW on the Ribbon to display the REVIEW tab.
- Tap or click the Spelling button (REVIEW Tab | Proofing group) to start the spelling checker and display the Spelling pane (Figure 2–75).

Figure 2–75

- With the word, wistle, selected in the list, tap or click the Change button (Spelling pane) to replace the misspelled flagged word, wistle, with the selected correctly spelled word, whistle, and then continue the spelling check (Figure 2–76).

Q&A
Could I have tapped or clicked the Change All button instead of the Change button?
Yes. When you tap or click the Change All button, you change the current and future occurrences of the misspelled word. The misspelled word, wistle, appears only once in the presentation, so tapping or clicking the Change or the Change All button in this instance produces identical results.

Occasionally a correctly spelled word is flagged as a possible misspelled word. Why?
Your custom dictionary does not contain the word, so it is seen as spelled incorrectly. You can add this word to a custom dictionary to prevent the spelling checker from flagging it as a mistake.

Figure 2–76

- Replace the misspelled word, Comunication, with the word, Communication.

- Continue checking all flagged words in the presentation. When the Microsoft PowerPoint dialog box appears, tap or click the OK button (Microsoft PowerPoint dialog box) to close the spelling checker and return to the slide where a possible misspelled word appeared.

Other Ways

1. Tap or click Spell Check icon on status bar 2. Press and hold or right-click flagged word, tap or click correct word 3. Press F7

To Insert a Slide Number

1 DOWNLOAD & SELECT SLIDES | 2 INSERT & FORMAT PICTURES | 3 INSERT & FORMAT SHAPES
4 INSERT & FORMAT WORDART | 5 FORMAT SLIDE BACKGROUNDS | 6 REVIEW & REVISE SLIDES

PowerPoint can insert the slide number on your slides automatically to indicate where the slide is positioned within the presentation. The number location on the slide is determined by the presentation theme. You have the option to not display this slide number on the title slide. The following steps insert the slide number on all slides except the title slide.

1

- If necessary, display Slide 3 and then display the INSERT tab.

- Tap or click the Slide Number button (INSERT tab | Text group) to display the Header and Footer dialog box (Figure 2–77).

Q&A
Why might I need to tap or click the Thumbnail pane?
If the final flagged word had been located in the Notes pane during the spell check, the insertion point would have been in the Notes pane. The page number, consequently, would have been inserted in the Notes pane instead of on the slide.

Figure 2–77

2

- Tap or click the Slide number check box (Header and Footer dialog box) to place a check mark in it.

- Tap or click the 'Don't show on title slide' check box (Header and Footer dialog box) to place a check mark in it (Figure 2–78).

 Where does the slide number display on the slide?

Each theme determines where the slide number is displayed in the footer. In this theme, the slide number location is the left side of the footer, as indicated by the black box at the bottom of the Preview area.

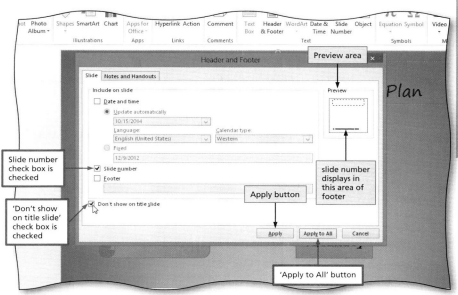

Figure 2–78

3

- Tap or click the Apply to All button (Header and Footer dialog box) to close the dialog box and insert the slide number on all slides except Slide 1 (Figure 2–79).

 How does tapping or clicking the Apply to All button differ from tapping or clicking the Apply button?

The Apply button inserts the slide number only on the currently displayed slide whereas the Apply to All button inserts the slide number on every slide.

Figure 2–79

Other Ways

1. Tap or click Header & Footer button (INSERT tab | Text group), tap or click Slide Number box (Header and Footer dialog box), tap or click 'Slide number' and 'Don't show on title slide' boxes, tap or click Apply to All button

To Add a Transition between Slides

A final enhancement you will make in this presentation is to apply the Fracture transition in the Exciting category to all slides and increase the transition duration. The following steps apply this transition to the presentation.

1 Tap or click TRANSITIONS on the ribbon. Tap or click the More button (TRANSITIONS tab | Transition to This Slide group) to expand the Transitions gallery.

2 Tap or click the Fracture transition in the Exciting category to apply this transition.

3 Tap or click the Duration up arrow in the Timing group four times to change the transition speed from 02.00 to 03.00.

BTW
Certification
The Microsoft Office Specialist (MOS) program provides an opportunity for you to obtain a valuable industry credential — proof that you have the PowerPoint 2013 skills required by employers. For more information, visit the Certification resource on the Student Companion Site located on www.cengagebrain.com. For detailed instructions about accessing available resources, visit www.cengage.com/ct/studentdownload or see the inside back cover of this book.

④ Tap or click the Preview Transitions button (TRANSITIONS tab | Preview area) to view the new transition time.

⑤ Tap or click the Apply To All button (TRANSITIONS tab | Timing group) to apply this transition and speed to all four slides in the presentation (Figure 2–80).

Q&A Can I apply a particular transition or duration to one slide and then change the transition or timing for a different slide in the presentation?

Yes. Select a slide and then select a transition and duration. Do not tap or click the Apply To All button. Repeat this process to apply the transition and duration to individual slides.

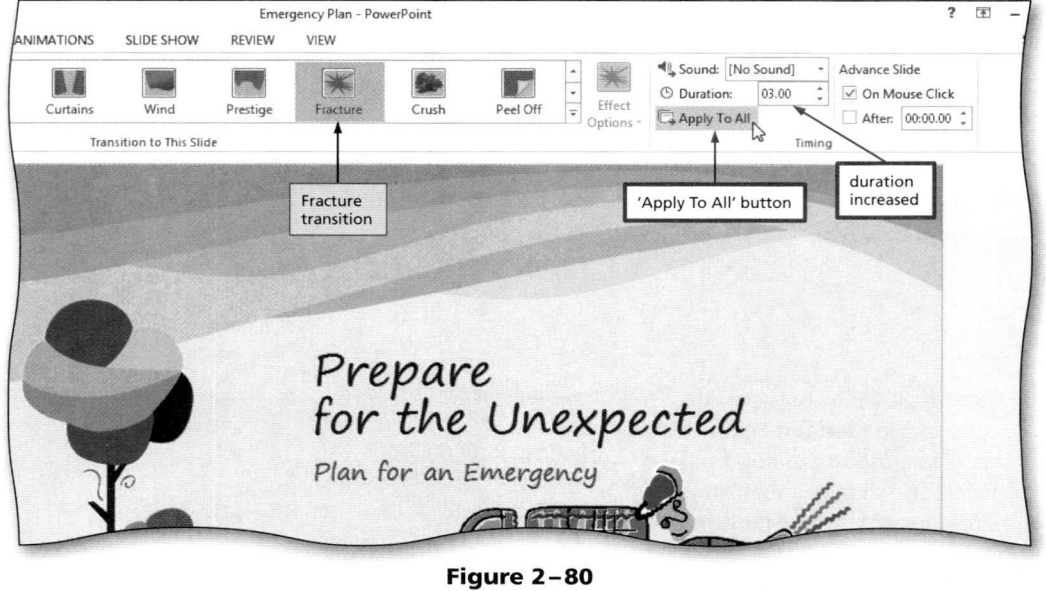

Figure 2–80

How can I use handouts to organize my speech?

As you develop a lengthy presentation with many visuals, handouts may help you organize your material. Print handouts with the maximum number of slides per page. Use scissors to cut each thumbnail and then place these miniature slide images adjacent to each other on a flat surface. Any type on the thumbnails will be too small to read, so the images will need to work with only the support of the verbal message you provide. You can rearrange these thumbnails as you organize your speech. When you return to your computer, you can rearrange the slides on your screen to match the order of your thumbnail printouts. Begin speaking the actual words you want to incorporate in the body of the talk. This process of glancing at the thumbnails and hearing yourself say the key ideas of the speech is one of the best methods of organizing and preparing for the actual presentation. Ultimately, when you deliver your speech in front of an audience, the images on the slides or on your note cards should be sufficient to remind you of the accompanying verbal message.

To Print Speaker Notes

Comments added to slides in the Notes pane give the speaker information that supplements the text on the slide. They will print with a small image of the slide at the top and the comments below the slide. The following steps print the speaker notes.

- Display Slide 1, tap or click FILE on the ribbon to open the Backstage view, and then tap or click the Print tab in the Backstage view to display Slide 1 in the Print gallery.

- Tap or click 'Full Page Slides' in the Settings area to display the Print gallery (Figure 2–81).

Q&A Why does the preview of my slide appear in color?
Your printer determines how the preview appears. If your printer is not capable of printing color images, the preview will not appear in color.

Figure 2–81

BTW

Distributing a Document
Instead of printing and distributing a hard copy of a document, you can distribute the document electronically. Options include sending the document via email; posting it on cloud storage (such as SkyDrive) and sharing the file with others; posting it on a social networking site, blog, or other website; and sharing a link associated with an online location of the document. You also can create and share a PDF or XPS image of the document, so that users can view the file in Acrobat Reader or XPS Viewer instead of in PowerPoint.

2

- Tap or click Notes Pages in the Print Layout area to select this option and then tap or click the Next Page button three times to display a preview of Slide 4 (Figure 2–82).

Q&A Can I preview Slides 1, 2, or 3 now?
Yes. Click the Previous Page button to preview the other slides.

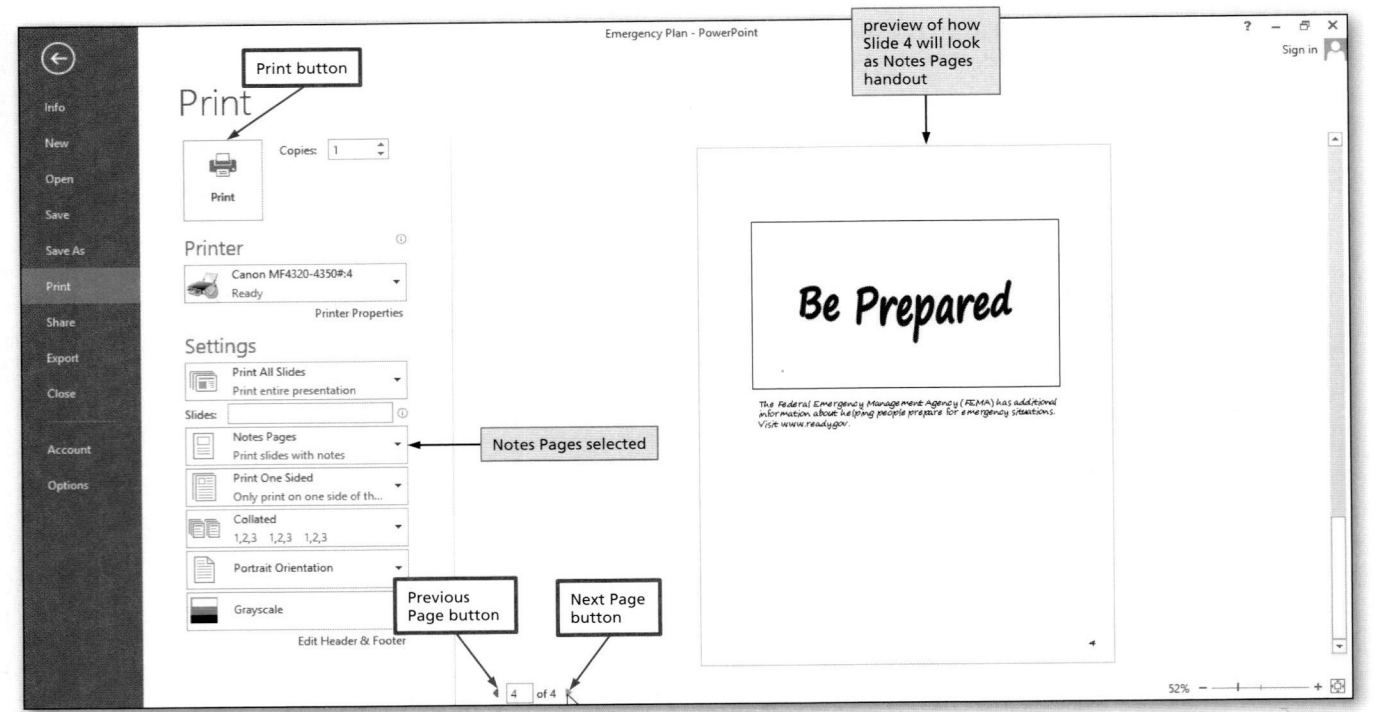

Figure 2–82

3

- Verify that the printer listed on the Printer Status button will print a hard copy of the presentation. If necessary, click the Printer Status button to display a list of available printer options and then click the desired printer to change the currently selected printer.

- Tap or click the Print button in the Print gallery to print the notes pages on the currently selected printer.

- When the printer stops, retrieve the hard copy (Figure 2–83).

Q&A Why does the background display on my printout but not in the figure?
Graphics are displayed depending upon the settings in the Print gallery. For example, the background will print if Color is specified whereas it will not with a Grayscale or Pure Black and White setting.

BTW
Printing Document Properties
To print document properties, tap or click FILE on the ribbon to open the Backstage view, tap or click the Print tab in the Backstage view to display the Print gallery, tap or click the first button in the Settings area to display a list of options specifying what you can print, tap or click Document Info in the list to specify you want to print the document properties instead of the actual document, and then tap or click the Print button in the Print gallery to print the document properties on the currently selected printer.

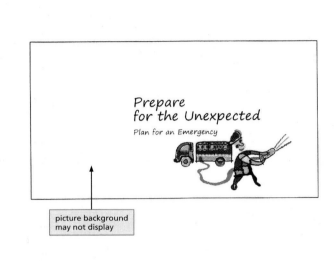

picture background
may not display

(a) Slide 1 – Speaker Notes

Create an
Emergency
Supply Kit

Collect basic objects your
family may need to survive

The kit should include a flashlight, whistle, water, radio, batteries,
three-day supply of food, three gallons of water for each family
member, change of clothing, tools, and first aid kit.

(b) Slide 2 – Speaker Notes

Figure 2–83 (Continued)

Develop a Family Communication Plan

One meeting place should be near the home, and the second should be outside the neighborhood. One out-of-state relative should be included in the contacts list.

3

(c) Slide 3 – Speaker Notes

Be Prepared

The Federal Emergency Management Agency (FEMA) has additional information about helping people prepare for emergency situations. Visit www.ready.gov.

4

(d) Slide 4 – Speaker Notes

Figure 2–83 (Handouts printed using a black-and-white printer) (Continued)

BTW

Conserving Ink and Toner
If you want to conserve ink or toner, you can instruct PowerPoint to print draft quality documents by tapping or clicking FILE on the ribbon to open the Backstage view, tapping or clicking Options in the Backstage view to display the PowerPoint Options dialog box, tapping or clicking Advanced in the left pane (PowerPoint Options dialog box), sliding or scrolling to the Print area in the right pane, placing a check mark in the 'Use draft quality' check box, and then tapping or clicking the OK button. Then, use the Backstage view to print the document as usual.

Other Ways

1. Press CTRL+P, press ENTER

To Save the Presentation, Sign Out of a Microsoft Account, and Exit PowerPoint

You have made several changes to the presentation since you last saved it. Thus, you should save it again. The following steps save the presentation, sign out of your Microsoft account, and exit PowerPoint.

1 Tap or click the Save button on the Quick Access Toolbar.

2 If you wish to sign out of your Microsoft account, open the Backstage view, tap or click the Account tab to display the Account gallery, and then tap or click the Sign out link, which displays the Remove Account dialog box. If a Can't remove Windows accounts dialog box appears instead of the Remove Account dialog box, click the OK button and skip the remaining steps.

3 Tap or click the Yes button (Remove Account dialog box) to sign out of your Microsoft account on this computer.

4 Tap or click the Back button in the upper-left corner of the Backstage view to return to the presentation.

5a If you have one PowerPoint presentation open, tap or click the Close button on the right side of the title bar to close the open document and exit PowerPoint.

5b If you have multiple PowerPoint presentations open, press and hold or right-click the PowerPoint app button on the taskbar and then tap or click 'Close all windows' on the shortcut menu, or press ALT+F4 to close all open presentations and exit PowerPoint.

BTW

Quick Reference
For a table that lists how to complete the tasks covered in this book using touch gestures, the mouse, ribbon, shortcut menu, and keyboard, see the Quick Reference Summary at the back of this book, or visit the Quick Reference resource on the Student Companion Site located on www.cengagebrain.com. For detailed instructions about accessing available resources, visit www.cengage.com/ct/studentdownload or see the inside back cover of this book.

Chapter Summary

In this chapter you have learned how to insert and format pictures, add and format shapes, insert and format WordArt, add slide backgrounds, find and replace text, check spelling, add notes, and print speaker notes. The items listed below include all the new PowerPoint skills you have learned in this chapter, with the tasks grouped by activity.

Download and Modify Themes
Search for and Download an Online Theme (PPT 77)
Delete a Slide (PPT 79)

Format Fonts
Change the Font (PPT 98)
Format Text Using the Format Painter (PPT 101)

Format Slide Backgrounds
Insert a Picture to Create a Background (PPT 108)
Format the Background Picture Fill Transparency (PPT 109)
Insert a Texture Fill (PPT 110)
Format the Background Texture Fill Transparency (PPT 111)
Insert a Gradient Fill (PPT 111)

Insert and Format Pictures
Insert a Picture into a Slide without a Content Placeholder (PPT 83)
Change a Picture (PPT 85)
Correct a Picture (PPT 87)
Apply a Picture Style (PPT 87)
Add a Picture Border (PPT 88)
Change a Picture Border Color (PPT 89)
Apply Picture Effects (PPT 90)

Insert and Format Shapes
Add a Shape (PPT 92)
Resize a Shape (PPT 93)
Add Other Shapes (PPT 94)
Apply a Shape Style (PPT 95)
Add Text to a Shape (PPT 97)
Copy and Paste a Shape (PPT 101)

Insert and Format WordArt
 Insert WordArt (PPT 103)
 Change the WordArt Shape (PPT 104)
 Apply a WordArt Text Fill (PPT 106)
 Change the Weight of the WordArt Outline
 (PPT 106)
 Change the Color of the WordArt Outline
 (PPT 107)

Review and Enhance Slides and Printouts
 Find and Replace Text (PPT 113)
 Find and Insert a Synonym (PPT 114)
 Add Notes (PPT 115)
 Check Spelling (PPT 117)
 Insert a Slide Number (PPT 118)
 Print Speaker Notes (PPT 121)

CONSIDER THIS

What decisions will you need to make when creating your next presentation?
Use these guidelines as you complete the assignments in this chapter and create your own slide show decks outside of this class.

1. Determine if an online theme can help you design and develop the presentation efficiently and effectively.

2. Identify personal pictures that would create interest and promote the message being presented.

3. Consider modifying pictures.

 a) Add corrections.

 b) Add styles.

 c) Add effects.

 d) Add and format borders.

4. Locate shapes that supplement the verbal and written message.

 a) Size and position them aesthetically on slides.

 b) Add styles.

5. Develop WordArt that emphasizes major presentation messages.

 a) Modify the shape.

 b) Change the weight and color to coordinate with slide elements.

6. Format individual slide backgrounds.

 a) Add and modify fills.

 b) Insert a picture.

7. Change fonts to emphasize particular slide components.

8. Search for synonyms that help express your thoughts.

9. Create speaker notes.

10. Check spelling.

How should you submit solutions to questions in the assignments identified with a ✳ symbol?

Every assignment in this book contains one or more questions identified with a ✳ symbol. These questions require you to think beyond the assigned presentation. Present your solutions to the questions in the format required by your instructor. Possible formats may include one or more of these options: write the answer; create a document that contains the answer; present your answer to the class; discuss your answer in a group; record the answer as audio or video using a webcam, smartphone, or portable media player; or post answers on a blog, wiki, or website.

Apply Your Knowledge

Reinforce the skills and apply the concepts you learned in this chapter.

Changing the Background and Adding Photos and WordArt

Note: To complete this assignment, you will be required to use the Data Files for Students. Visit www.cengage.com/ct/studentdownload for detailed instructions or contact your instructor for information about accessing the required files.

Instructions: Run PowerPoint. Open the presentation, Apply 2-1 Bicycle, from the Data Files for Students.

The five slides in the presentation discuss bicycle safety. The document you open is an unformatted presentation. You are to add photos, apply picture styles, add WordArt, change slide layouts, apply a transition, and use the Format Painter so the slides look like Figures 2–84a through 2–84e on pages PPT 127 through 130.

Perform the following tasks:

1. On the title slide, use your name in place of Student Name and bold and italicize your name.

2. If requested by your instructor, change your first name to your mother's first name on the title slide.

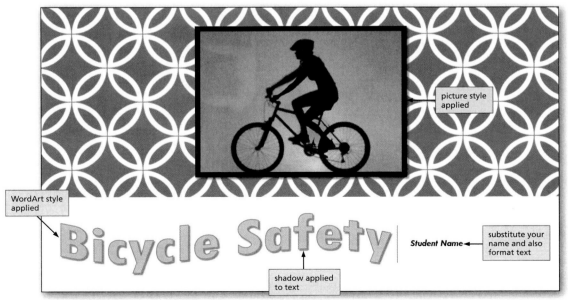

(a) Slide 1

Figure 2–84 (Continued)

Continued >

Apply Your Knowledge *continued*

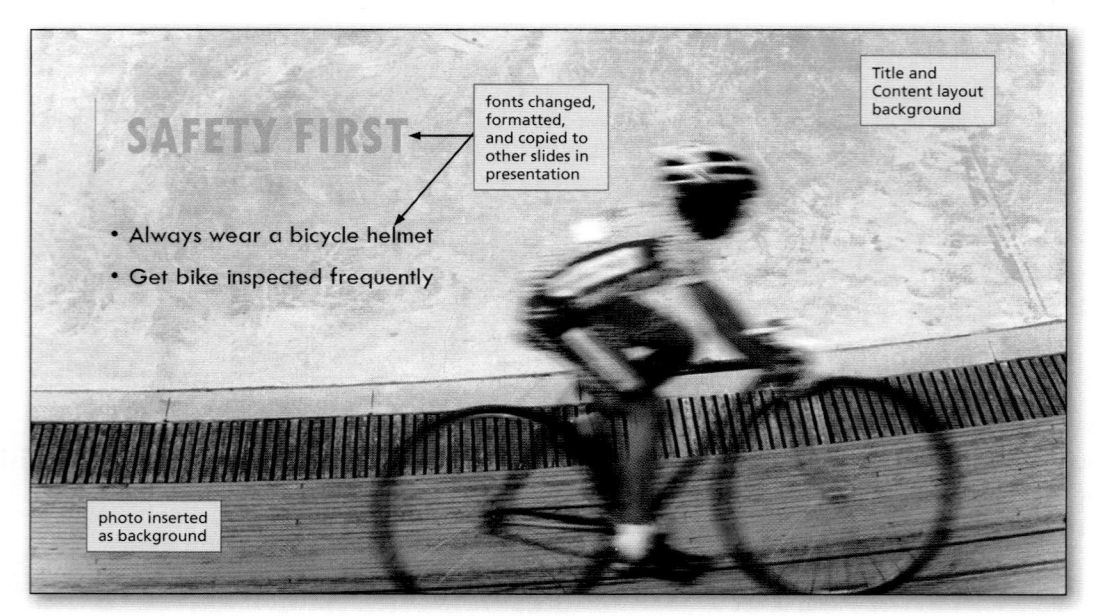

Title and Content layout background

fonts changed, formatted, and copied to other slides in presentation

photo inserted as background

(b) Slide 2

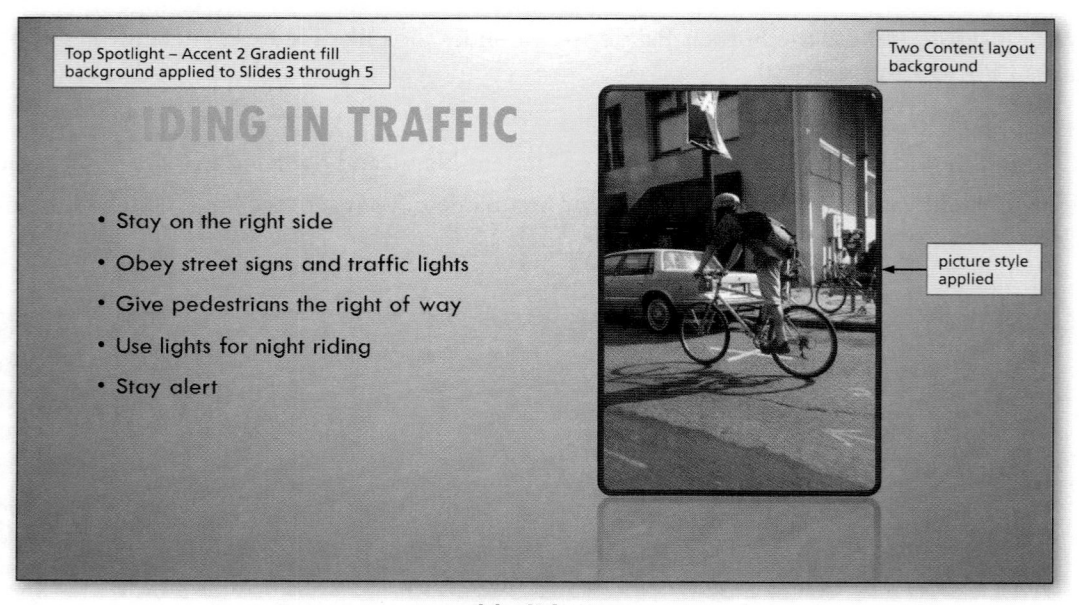

Top Spotlight – Accent 2 Gradient fill background applied to Slides 3 through 5

Two Content layout background

picture style applied

(c) Slide 3

Figure 2–84

3. Increase the title text font size to 60 point. Apply the WordArt style, Fill – Blue, Accent 2, Outline – Accent 2 (the third style in the first row). Apply the Transform text effect, Wave 2 (the second effect in the fifth Warp area row) to this text. Also add a shadow to this text.

4. Apply the Moderate Frame, Black picture style (the fifth style in the second row) to the photo on Slide 1, as shown in Figure 2–84a on the previous page.

5. On Slide 2, change the layout to Title and Content. Increase the title text font to 54 point, change the font color to Green (the sixth color in the Standard Colors row), and then bold this text. Increase the bulleted list font to 24 point, as shown in Figure 2–84b.

6. Create a background on Slide 2 by inserting the photo called Cyclist, which is available on the Data Files for Students.

7. On Slide 2, type **The average cost for a routine bike inspection is $20.** in the Notes pane.

8. On Slides 3 through 5, change the layout to Two Content. Insert the photos, as shown in Figures 2–84c through 2–84e on the next page. The photos to be inserted are called Bicycle2, Bicycle3, and Bicycle4 and are available on the Data Files for Students. Also, change the background to Top Spotlight – Accent 2 gradient fill (the second gradient in the second row) in the Preset gradients gallery on Slides 3 through 5.

9. On Slide 3, adjust the size of the photo and apply the Reflected Bevel, Black picture style (the fourth style in the fourth row) and change the photo brightness to +20% (the fourth picture in the third row in the Brightness and Contrast area).

10. On Slide 3, type **Laws for bicycles on the road vary in every state and country.** in the Notes pane.

11. On Slide 4, adjust the size of the photo, apply the Metal Oval picture style (the seventh style in the fourth row), and then change the photo border to Black, Text 1 (the second color in the first Theme Colors row), as shown in Figure 2–84d.

12. Use the thesaurus to change the word, suitable, to appropriate.

13. Type **Hydration is critical. Make sure your bike is equipped with a bottle holder.** in the Notes pane.

14. On Slide 5, adjust the size of the photo and apply the Bevel Perspective picture style (the first style in the fourth row) to the photo, as shown in Figure 2–84e on the next page.

15. Use the Format Painter to format the title text and the bulleted lists on Slides 3 through 5 with the same features as the title text and bulleted list on Slide 2.

16. Apply the Wind transition in the Exciting category to all slides. Change the duration to 2.50 seconds.

(d) Slide 4

Figure 2–84 (Continued)

Continued >

Apply Your Knowledge *continued*

(e) Slide 5
Figure 2–84 (Continued)

17. Save the presentation using the file name, Apply 2-1 Bicycle Safety.

18. Submit the revised document in the format specified by your instructor.

19. ☀ In Step 4 you applied the Moderate Frame, Black picture style. How did this style improve the slide?

Extend Your Knowledge

Extend the skills you learned in this chapter and experiment with new skills. You may need to use Help to complete the assignment.

Changing Slide Backgrounds, Inserting Shapes and WordArt, and Finding and Replacing Text

Note: To complete this assignment, you will be required to use the Data Files for Students. Visit www.cengage.com/ct/studentdownload for detailed instructions or contact your instructor for information about accessing the required files.

Instructions: Run PowerPoint. Open the presentation, Extend 2-1 Field Archery, from the Data Files for Students. You will create backgrounds including inserting a photo to create a background, apply a WordArt Style and Effect, and add shapes to create the presentation shown in Figure 2–85.

Perform the following tasks:

1. Change the theme to Wisp and choose the second variant.

2. Find and replace the words, Bow and Arrow, with the word, Archery, on all slides.

3. On Slides 2 through 4, change the background style to Top Spotlight – Accent 5 (the fifth style in the second Preset gradients row). Also, change the title text to bold and change the font color to Orange, Accent 1 (the fifth color in the first Theme Colors row) on Slides 2 through 4.

4. On the title slide (Figure 2–85a), create a background by inserting the photo called Bow and Arrow, which is available on the Data Files for Students. Change the transparency to 50%.

5. Apply the WordArt style, Fill - Orange, Accent 1, Shadow (the second style in the first row), to the title text, center the text, and increase the font size to 72 point. Apply the WordArt Transform text effect, Arch Up (the first effect in the first Follow Path row), and then bold this text. Also, move the title text above the archer in the photo on the title slide.

6. If requested by your instructor, add your current or previous pet's name as the Slide 1 subtitle text.

7. On Slides 2 through 4, increase the font size of the first-level bulleted text to 22 point and the second-level bulleted text to 20 point.

8. On Slide 2, enlarge the illustration to the size shown in Figure 2–85b on the next page, apply the Reflected Bevel, Black picture style (the fourth style in the fourth row), and then move it to the location shown in the figure.

9. On Slide 3, apply the Soft Edge Oval picture style (the sixth style in the third row) to the photo and move the photo to the upper-right area of the slide. Also, apply the Orange, 18 pt glow, Accent color 1 glow variation (the first variation in the fourth Glow Variations row) to this photo, as shown in Figure 2–85c on the next page.

10. On Slide 4, select the Oval shape and while holding down the Shift key, draw a circle 6" × 6", as shown in Figure 2–85d on page PPT 133. Fill this shape with Black, Text 1, Lighter 15% and then change the shape outline to No Outline. Then copy and paste this shape two times. Change the shape size of the first pasted circle to 4" × 4". Hint: Use the Size and Position group on the PICTURE TOOLS FORMAT tab to enter the exact measurement of the shape. Change the Shape Fill to White and then center this shape over the original black circle using the Smart Guides. Select the second pasted circle and change the shape size to 2" × 2", the Shape Fill to Black, Text 1, Lighter 15% and then center this shape over the white circle shape using the Smart Guides.

photo inserted as background and transparency changed

Field Archery

bold and shadow the WordArt text and move up to new location

color variant changed

Wisp document theme

(a) Slide 1

Figure 2–85 (Continued)

Continued >

Extend Your Knowledge *continued*

(b) Slide 2

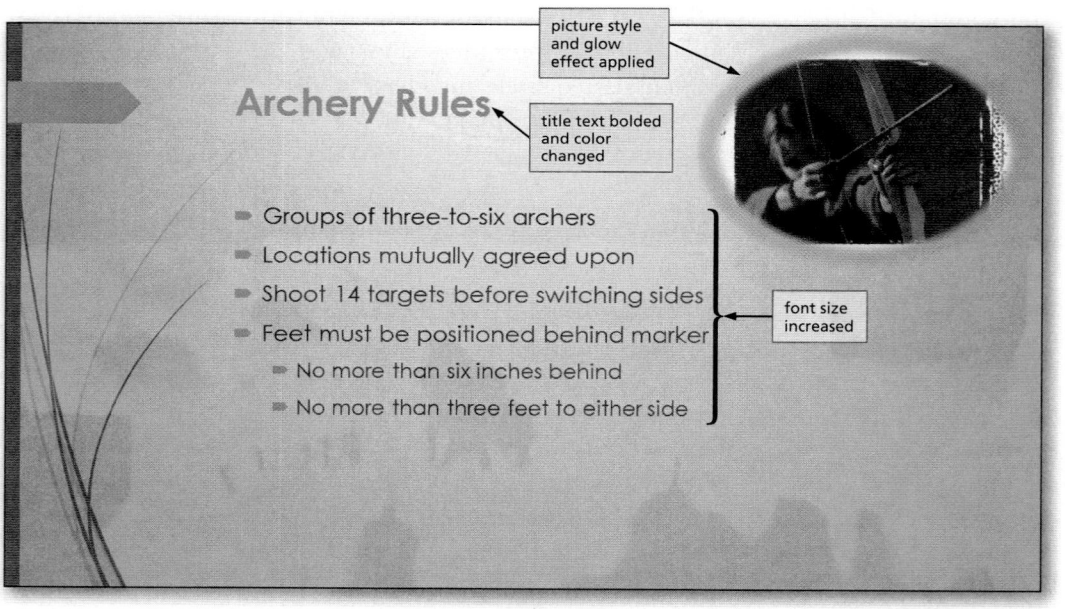

(c) Slide 3

Figure 2–85

11. Insert an arrow on Slide 4 by using the Right Arrow shape under Block Arrows. Size the arrow to 1.5" × 6" and then copy and paste this arrow shape two times. Copy and paste the three paragraphs from the bulleted list into the three arrow shapes. Select the text on one of these shapes, change the font size to 28 point, change the font color to black, center the text, and

(d) Slide 4
Figure 2–85 (Continued)

then bold the text. Use the Format Painter to format the text in the two arrows with the same features as the first arrow. Move the arrows so that each one points to the correct ring, as shown in Figure 2–85d. Delete the bulleted text in the text placeholder.

12. Apply an appropriate transition to all slides.

13. Save the presentation using the file name, Extend 2-1 Field Archery Scoring.

14. Submit the revised document in the format specified by your instructor.

15. ✳ In this assignment, you changed the transparency of the inserted background photo on the title slide to 50%. How did this transparency change enhance your title slide?

Analyze, Correct, Improve

Analyze a presentation, correct all errors, and improve it.

Correcting Formatting, Adding Slide Numbers, and Correcting Spelling

Note: To complete this assignment, you will be required to use the Data Files for Students. Visit www.cengage.com/ct/studentdownload for detailed instructions or contact your instructor for information about accessing the required files.

Instructions: Run PowerPoint. Open the presentation, Analyze 2-1 Avoid the Flu, from the Data Files for Students. This presentation contains four slides and explains why doctors recommend you should get an annual flu shot. Figure 2–86 on the next page shows the uncorrected title slide. Modify the slides by making the indicated corrections and improvements.

1. Correct

a. Change the variant to blue (the second variant in the gallery).

b. Decrease the font size of the Slide 1 title text and change the font color. Also, capitalize the letter F in the word, flu.

c. Use your name in place of Student Name on Slide 1.

Continued >

Analyze, Correct, Improve *continued*

d. If requested by your instructor, change your first name on Slide 1 to your mother's first name.

e. On Slides 2 through 4, adjust the photo sizes and move them so they do not overlap text and are the appropriate dimensions for the slide content.

f. On all slides, adjust font sizes and font color so they are the appropriate size and enhance the presentation.

g. Correct the spelling errors on all slides.

2. Improve

a. Increase the size of the medical symbol on the title slide and move the symbol to the right side of the slide.

b. On Slides 2 through 4, change the color of the title text and bold all the titles.

c. Change the photo border colors on all slides to make them more visually attractive.

d. Add the slide number to all slides except the title slide.

e. Apply the same transition and duration to all slides.

f. Save the presentation using the file name, Analyze 2-1 – Get Your Flu Shot.

g. Submit the revised document in the format specified by your instructor.

3. ✳ Which errors existed in the starting file? How did changing the variant color help? When you adjusted the photo sizes, how did you determine their final sizes?

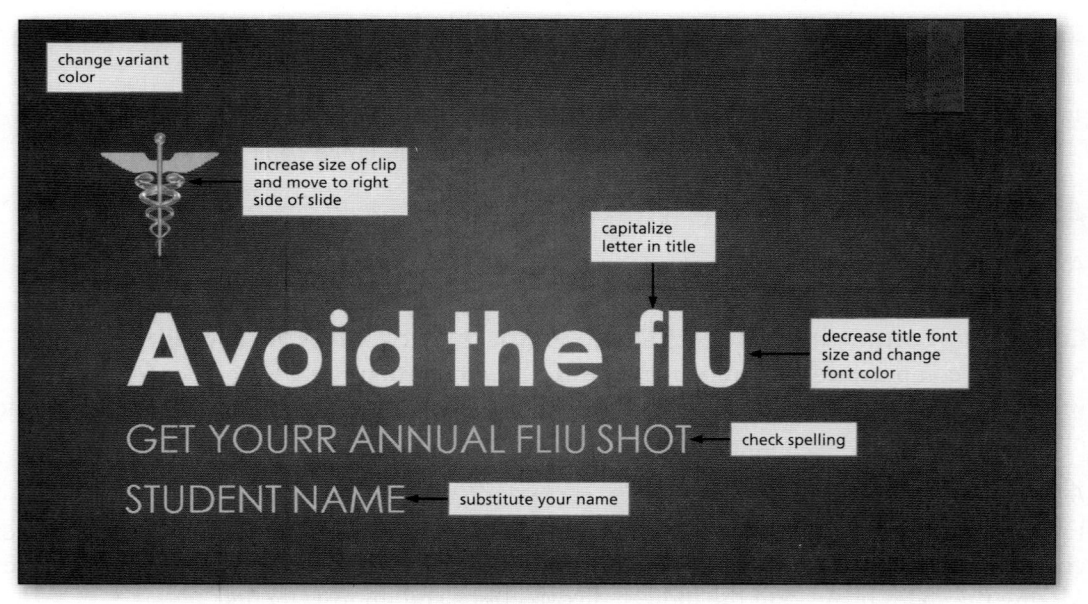

Slide 1

Figure 2–86

In the Labs

Design and/or create a presentation using the guidelines, concepts, and skills presented in this chapter. Labs 1 and 2, which increase in difficulty, require you to create solutions based on what you learned in the chapter; Lab 3 requires you to create a solution, which uses cloud and web technologies, by learning and investigating on your own from general guidance.

Lab 1: Creating a Presentation Inserting Photos, Applying Picture Styles, and Inserting Shapes

Problem: Your creative cooking class has volunteered to manage a bake sale to raise funds for victims of a tornado in a neighboring town. To encourage more students to participate in the bake sale, you decide to put together a presentation that would run in the cafeteria. You want to show your audience how easy it is to make an apple pie. Create the slides shown in Figure 2–87.

Instructions: Perform the following tasks:

1. Create a new presentation using the Retrospect theme. Do not change the brown variant.

2. On Slide 1, create a background by inserting the photo called Apple Pie from the Data Files for Students, as shown in Figure 2–87a. Change the transparency to 53%.

3. Type **Homemade Apple Pie** as the Slide 1 title text. Press the ENTER key after the word, Homemade, so the text is on two lines, and then center the text. Apply the WordArt style Fill – Orange, Accent 2, Outline – Accent 2 (the third style in the first row). Change the text fill to Dark Red (the first color in the Standard Colors row), and then change the text outline color to Green (the sixth color in the Standard Colors row) and the text outline weight to 3 pt. Also, apply the Transform text Effect, Chevron Up (the first effect in the second Warp row), to this text. Position this WordArt, as shown in Figure 2–87a. Type **BAKE SALE – SATURDAY JANUARY 20** in the subtitle placeholder. Change the font to MV Boli, increase the font size to 30 point, bold this text, and then center the text, as shown in the figure.

4. Create Slides 2 through 4 with the Two Content layout, Slide 5 with the Content with Caption layout, and Slide 6 with the Picture with Caption layout.

(a) Slide 1

Figure 2–87 (Continued)

Continued >

In the Labs *continued*

5. Type the title and content and insert all photos on Slides 2 through 5, as shown in Figures 2–87b through 2–87e. The photos to be inserted are called Apples, Ingredients, Cooks, and Apple Pie Slice, and are available on the Data Files for Students. Size the photos and then use the Smart Guides to position these images. You may want to zoom the slides to help you align these graphic elements.

6. On Slide 2, increase the title text size to 54 point, change the font color to Dark Red, and then bold this text. Use the Format Painter to apply these formatting changes to the title text on Slides 3 and 4. On Slide 2, change the list font size to 24 point. Apply the Bevel Perspective picture style (the first style in the fourth row) to the photo, change the border color to Light Green (the fifth color in the Standard Colors row), and then change the border weight to 6 pt, as shown in Figure 2–87b.

(b) Slide 2

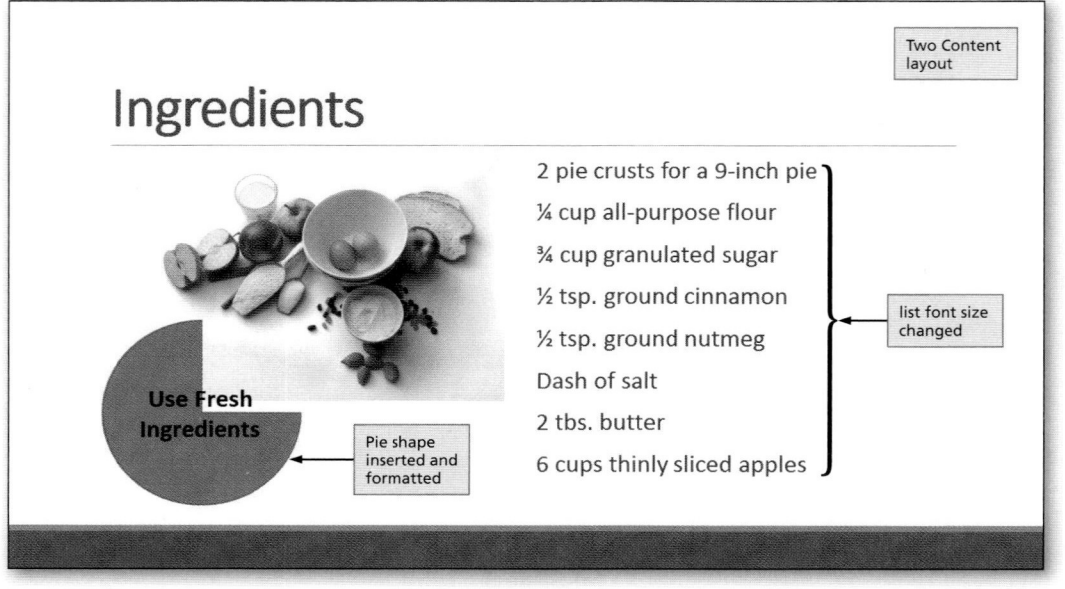

(c) Slide 3
Figure 2–87

7. On Slide 3, change the list font size to 24 point. Insert the Pie shape located in the Basic Shapes area to the lower-left corner of the slide. Apply the Colored Fill – Brown, Accent 4 (the eighth color in the first row) to the shape. Size the shape as shown in the figure. Type the text, **Use Fresh Ingredients** in the shape. Bold this text, and change the font size to 24 point, as shown in Figure 2–87c.

8. On Slide 4, change the list font size to 20 point. Apply the Snip Diagonal Corner, White picture style (the first style in the third row) to the photo, change the border color to Dark Red (the first color in the Standard Colors row), and then apply the Reflection picture effect, Tight Reflection, touching (the first effect in the first Reflection Variations row). Copy the pie shape from Slide 3 and paste it in the bottom center of the slide. Type the text, **Bake 40 to 50 Minutes,** as shown in Figure 2–87d.

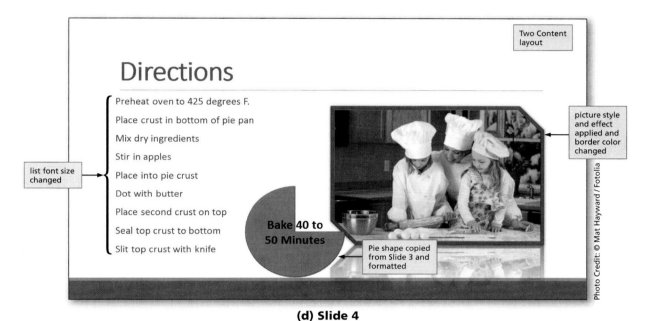

(d) Slide 4

(e) Slide 5

Figure 2–87 (Continued)

Continued >

In the Labs *continued*

9. On Slide 5, change the title text font to MV Boli, change the font size to 40 point, and then center this text. Apply the Simple Frame, White picture style (the first style in the first row) to the slice of pie photo and then change the border color to Orange, Accent 1 (the fifth color in the Theme Colors row), as shown in Figure 2–87e on the previous page.

10. On Slide 6, change the caption title font to MV Boli, change the font size to 32 point, and then bold this text. Select the photo, click the Change Picture button (PICTURE TOOLS FORMAT tab | Adjust group), and then insert the Bake Sale illustration from the Data Files for Students, as shown in Figure 2–87f.

11. If requested by your instructor, type the name of the city or county in which you were born into the subtitle text placeholder on Slide 6.

12. Apply the Peel Off transition in the Exciting category to all slides. Change the duration to 2.5 seconds.

13. Check the spelling and correct any errors. Save the presentation using the file name, Lab 2-1 Homemade Apple Pie.

14. Submit the document in the format specified by your instructor.

15. ✸ What is the significance of changing the transparency of the photo on the title slide? Why did you put a red border on the photo on Slide 4? Explain why you did not follow the 7 × 7 rule on Slides 3 and 4.

(f) Slide 6
Figure 2–87 (Continued)

Lab 2: Creating a Presentation Using an Online Theme Template, Shapes, and WordArt

Problem: Your local Chamber of Commerce is presenting a seminar to local business owners about ways to expand their business. Because you are majoring in business, your teacher thought that attending this meeting would be a good experience for you. He asked the Chamber of Commerce president if you could submit some ideas for the seminar. You decide to put together the presentation shown in Figure 2–88.

Instructions: Perform the following tasks:

1. Create a new presentation using the Business project plan presentation (widescreen) in the Business category under Suggested searches.

2. Delete Slides 7 through 14.

3. Apply the Two Content layout to Slide 2, the Alternate Content with Caption layout to Slide 3, the Content with Caption layout to Slide 4, the Title only layout to Slide 5, and the Section Header layout to Slide 6. Delete all titles and text content from Slides 2 through 6. Type the new title and text content for Slides 2, 3, and 4, as shown in Figures 2–88b through 2–88d on the next page.

4. Insert the photos and illustration shown in Figures 2–88b through 2–88e from the Data Files for Students. The photos and illustration are called Advertising, Delivery, Customer, and Call Center. Apply the Canvas texture fill (the second texture in the first row) to Slides 2 through 5 and change the transparency to 35%.

5. On the title slide, type the new title and subtitle content, increase the font size of the subtitle text to 28 point, and then change the font color to Orange (the third color in the Standard Colors row), as shown in Figure 2–88a.

6. If requested by your instructor, add the name of your hometown after the word, Business, in the subtitle placeholder. Type the word **in** before the name of your hometown.

7. On Slide 2, increase the font size of the title to 40 point, change the font color to Indigo, Text 2, Darker 25% (the fourth color in the fifth Theme Colors row), and then bold this text. Increase the font size of the bulleted list to 24 point. Apply the Perspective Shadow, White picture style (the fourth style in the third row) and resize the photo, as shown in Figure 2–88b.

8. On Slide 3, increase the font size of the title to 40 point and then bold this text. Increase the font size of the text to 24 point. Apply the Simple Frame picture style (the first style in the first row) to the photo, as shown in Figure 2–88c.

9. On Slide 4, increase the font size of the title text to 40 point, change the font color to Indigo, Text 2, Darker 25% (the fourth color in the fifth Theme Colors row), and then bold this text. Increase the font size of the bulleted list text to 24 point. Apply the Metal Frame picture style (the third style in the first row) to the photo, as shown in Figure 2–88d.

10. On Slide 5, increase the font size of the title to 40 point, change the font color to Indigo, Text 2, Darker 25% (the fourth color in the fifth Theme Colors row), and then bold this text. Move

(a) Slide 1

Figure 2–88 (Continued)

Continued >

In the Labs *continued*

(b) Slide 2

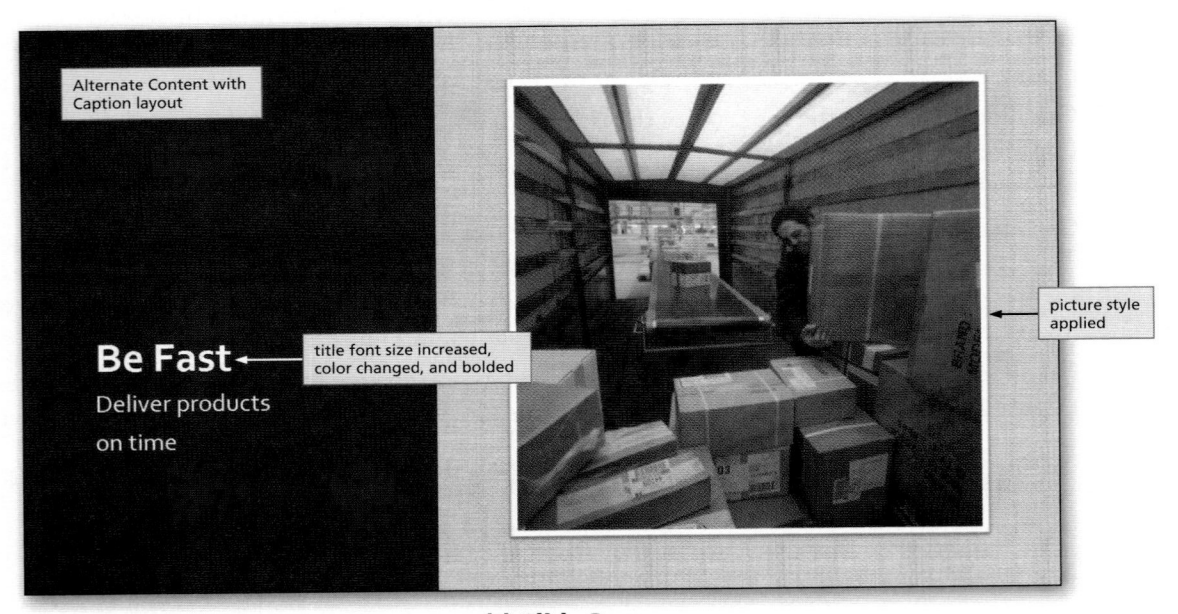

(c) Slide 3

Figure 2–88

the photo to the right side of the slide and then apply the Soft Edge Oval picture style (the sixth style in the third row) to the photo, as shown in Figure 2–88e.

11. Insert the Diamond shape located in the Basic Shapes area, resize the shape so that it is approximately 3.42" × 3.93", and then right-click the shape, click Style, and apply the Subtle Effect – Red, Accent 6 Shape Quick Style (the seventh style in the fourth row). Copy and paste the shape two times and move the shapes, as shown in Figure 2–88e. Type the text into the shape and then increase the text size to 24 point.

12. On Slide 6, type the new title and subtitle content, and create a background by inserting the Ladder photo from the Data Files for Students. Change the transparency to 40%. Decrease the title font size to 44 point, change the font color to Indigo, Text 2, Darker 25% (the fourth color in the fifth Theme Colors row), right-align the text, and then bold this text. Increase the font size of the subtitle text to 28 point, change the font color to Indigo, Text 2 (the fourth color in the first Theme

(d) Slide 4

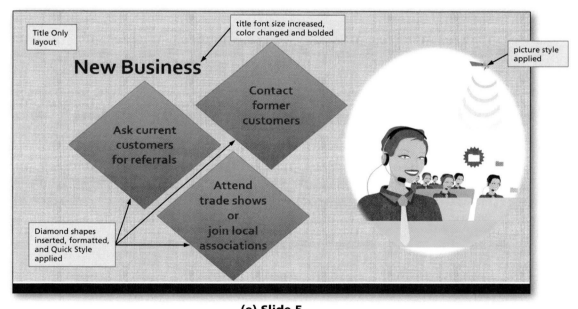

(e) Slide 5

Figure 2–88 (Continued)

Colors row), and then right-align this text, as shown in Figure 2–88f. Insert the Pentagon shape located in the Block Arrows area and then apply the Subtle Effect - Lime, Accent 1 Quick Style (the second style in the fourth row) to the shape. Type **Success** in the shape, change the font to Forte, change the font size to 60 point, and then change the font color to Gray – 80%, Text 1.

13. Change the transition to Doors in the Exciting category to all slides. Change the duration to 2.75 seconds.

14. Check spelling and correct all errors. Save the presentation using the file name, Lab 2-2 Small Business Seminar.

15. Submit the revised document in the format specified by your instructor.

16. ❋ You searched for an online theme under Business. Why? Do you think any of the other themes would have worked well for your presentation? How does changing the slide layouts help your presentation?

Continued >

In the Labs *continued*

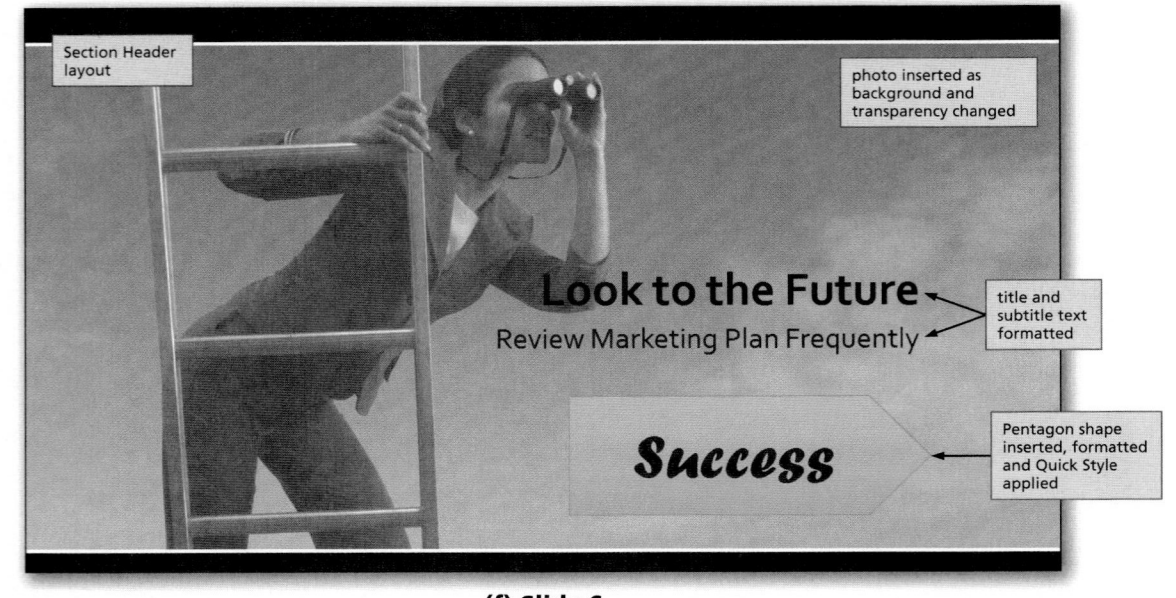

(f) Slide 6

Figure 2–88 (Continued)

Lab 3: Expand Your World: Cloud and Web Technologies
Modifying a Presentation Using the PowerPoint Web App

Problem: The fire chief in your community is planning a family security and safety workshop at your local hardware store. He has asked you to help him publicize the event, and he wants to focus on urging families to prepare for unexpected situations. You inform him that you have created an Emergency Plan presentation for your computer class, and he would like you to customize the content of these slides slightly to promote the workshop.

Instructions:

1. Sign in to your Microsoft account and run the PowerPoint web app.

2. Create a presentation with content similar to what you used for the Emergency Plan presentation.

3. On the title slide, add the name and address of the nearest hardware store. In addition, add the date that is exactly one month from today and a starting time of noon. Add the name of one of your elementary school teachers as the fire chief's name on this slide.

4. Save the presentation using the file name, Lab 2-3 Local Safety Workshop.

5. Submit the assignment in the format specified by your instructor.

6. ✳ Other than the content the chief asked you to include on the title slide, how does the presentation you created using the PowerPoint web app differ from the presentation you created in the Chapter 2 project? Which formatting features are not available in the web app? Do you think using the web app has sufficient functions to develop effective presentations? Why or why not?

Consider This: Your Turn

Apply your creative thinking and problem-solving skills to design and implement a solution.

1. Design and Create a Presentation about Skydiving from New Heights

Personal

Part 1: Members of your skydiving club are discussing free-falling records of new heights reached by skydivers over the past years. They've been following the news reports about the man from Austria, 43-year-old Felix Baumgartner, who broke a record by completing the highest skydive and traveling faster than the speed of sound without being in an aircraft. At a recent meeting with your fellow skydivers, many questions arose as to how this man was able to accomplish this, what risks were involved, and how long he trained for this venture. You researched facts about this record-breaking skydive and learned that the height he dove from (128,100 feet above Earth) was more than three times the cruising altitude of a passenger jet (hitting Mach 1.24 or 833.9 mph). It was the height at which water boils. If his pressurized spacesuit had malfunctioned, it would have been disastrous: a leak in his spacesuit would have caused his blood to boil instantly. Half of his nine-minute descent was a free fall of 119,846 feet. He trained for seven years. Use the concepts and techniques presented in this chapter to prepare a presentation with a minimum of four slides that explores this subject. Select a suitable theme, and include a title slide, bulleted lists, shapes, and WordArt. The presentation should contain photos and illustrations appropriately resized. Eight photos and illustrations are available on the Data Files for Students: Skydiving1, Skydiving2, Skydiving3, Skydiving4, Skydiving5, Skydiving6, Skydiving7, and Skydiving8. You can add your own digital photos or photos from Office.com if they are appropriate for this topic. Apply picture styles and effects. Add a title slide and closing slide to complete your presentation. Format the title slide with a shape. Format the background with at least one photo and apply a background texture to at least one slide. Review and revise your presentation as needed. Submit your assignment in the format specified by your instructor.

Part 2: You made several decisions while creating the presentation in this assignment: where to place text, how to format the text (such as font, font size, and where to use WordArt), which graphical image(s) to use, what styles and effects to apply, where to position the graphical image, how to format the graphical images, and which shapes to use to add interest to the presentation. What was the rationale behind each of these decisions? When you reviewed the document, what further revisions did you make and why? Where would you recommend showing this slide show?

2. Design and Create a Presentation about Teaching Geometry to Elementary Students

Professional

Part 1: You work part time for a tutoring agency. Because you are majoring in math, your boss asked if you would put together a teaching aid for teaching geometry to the elementary students. You decide to create a presentation with some basic shapes: squares, circles, and triangles. To make the slides appeal to your young students, you decide to use shapes and add photos and illustrations. Geometry for elementary students also can cover parallel lines, intersecting lines, and how intersecting lines form angles. You can show them shapes such as pentagons, heptagons, and octagons. They can look for shapes in their environment and draw them. You can teach them that even though a shape is turned upside down or rotated, it is still the same shape even if it looks different. Use the concepts and techniques presented in this chapter to create a presentation with at least four slides. Select a suitable theme, include a title slide, and add WordArt. Review and revise your presentation as needed. Submit your assignment in the format specified by your instructor.

Part 2: You made several decisions while creating the presentation in this assignment: where to place text, how to format the text (such as font, font size, and where to use WordArt), which graphical image(s) to use, what styles and effects to apply, where to position the graphical images,

Continued >

STUDENT ASSIGNMENTS

Consider This: Your Turn *continued*

and which shapes to use to add interest to the presentation. What was the rationale behind each of these decisions? When you reviewed the document, what further revisions did you make and why? Where would you recommend showing this slide show?

3. Design and Create a Presentation about Coyotes Roaming in Your Neighborhood
Research and Collaboration

Part 1: Many of your neighbors are concerned about the coyotes that have been spotted in your neighborhood. With the help of a friend who works part time at a local wildlife refuge, you suggest that each of you do some research about coyotes and discuss your findings and put together a presentation to share at the next town hall meeting. Your main concern is that the coyotes are finding outdoor food sources such as pet food, uncovered garbage cans, and areas near homes where rodents may be nesting. You want to make suggestions to your neighbors about how to deter the coyotes from staying in your neighborhood. You ask your friend who works at the wildlife refuge to research the habits of coyotes. You will gather information from the local newspaper where there have been articles written about the coyotes and your other neighbor will talk to other people in the neighbor about sightings of coyotes and possible photographs. After coordinating all the facts about the coyotes, use the concepts and techniques presented in this chapter to prepare a presentation with a minimum of four slides that explores the subject of coyotes. Summarize your research findings and type this information in the Notes pane of each slide. Select a suitable theme, include a title slide, bulleted lists, shapes, and WordArt. Seven photos and illustrations are available on the Data Files for Students: Coyote1, Coyote2, Coyote3, Coyote4, Coyote5, Coyote6, and Coyote7. Change the brightness and contrast for at least one photo. Insert shapes and WordArt to enhance your presentation. Apply a transition in the Subtle area to all slides and increase the duration. Review and revise your presentation as needed. Submit your assignment in the format specified by your instructor.

Part 2: ✹ You made several decisions while creating the presentation in this assignment: where to place text, how to format the text (such as font, font size, and where to use WordArt), which graphical image(s) to use, what styles and effects to apply, where to position the graphical image, what shapes to use to add interest to the presentation. What was the rationale behind each of these decisions? When you reviewed the document, what further revisions did you make and why? Where would you recommend showing this slide show?

Learn Online
Reinforce what you learned in this chapter with games, exercises, training, and many other online activities and resources.

Student Companion Site Reinforcement activities and resources are available at no additional cost on www.cengagebrain.com. Visit www.cengage.com/ct/studentdownload for detailed instructions about accessing the resources available at the Student Companion Site.

SAM Put your skills into practice with SAM! If you have a SAM account, go to www.cengage.com/sam2013 to access SAM assignments for this chapter.

1 Creating a Worksheet and a Chart

Microsoft product screenshots used with permission from Microsoft Corporation.

Objectives

You will have mastered the material in this chapter when you can:

- Describe the Excel worksheet
- Enter text and numbers
- Use the Sum button to sum a range of cells
- Enter a simple function
- Copy the contents of a cell to a range of cells using the fill handle
- Apply cell styles
- Format cells in a worksheet

- Create a 3-D pie chart
- Change a worksheet name and worksheet tab color
- Change document properties
- Preview and print a worksheet
- Use the AutoCalculate area to display statistics
- Correct errors on a worksheet

1 | Creating a Worksheet and a Chart

Introduction

Almost any organization collects vast amounts of data. Often, data is consolidated into a summary so that people in the organization better understand the meaning of the data. An Excel worksheet allows data to be summarized and charted easily. A chart conveys a visual representation of data. In this chapter, you will create a worksheet that includes a chart. The data in the worksheet and chart includes data for a personal budget worksheet that contains monthly estimates on budget amounts.

Project — Worksheet and a Chart

The project in this chapter follows proper design guidelines and uses Excel to create the worksheet and chart shown in Figure 1–1a and Figure 1–1b. The worksheet contains budget data for Bob Gleamin. He wants to estimate what his personal budget will look like for the year, so he has gathered together the information on how much he pays for various expenses and has a list of his current incomes. Now, he wants an easy-to-read worksheet using this information to see how much he will be ahead or behind each month to aid him in planning his budget. In addition, a 3-D pie chart is required that shows the estimated expenses portion for each of the 12 months.

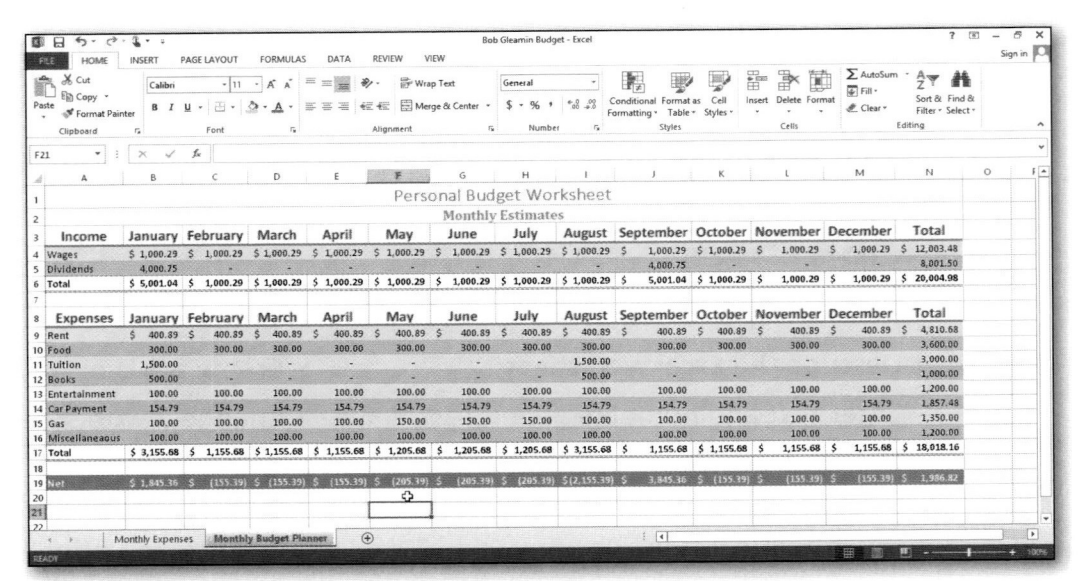

Figure 1–1 (a) Personal Budget Worksheet

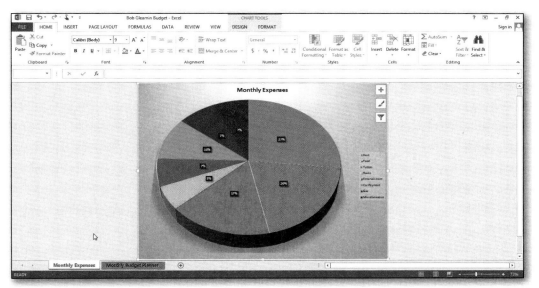

Figure 1–1 (b) Pie Chart Showing Monthly Expenses by Category

The first step in creating an effective worksheet is to make sure you understand what is required. The person or persons requesting the worksheet should supply their requirements in a requirements document. A requirements document includes a needs statement, a source of data, a summary of calculations, and any other special requirements for the worksheet, such as charting and web support. Figure 1–2 shows the requirements document for the new workbook to be created in this chapter.

Worksheet Title	Personal Budget Worksheet
Needs	A yearly projection of Bob Gleamin's personal budget
Source of data	The data supplied by Bob Gleamin includes monthly estimates, including income and expenses
Calculations	The following calculations must be made: 1. For each month, a total for incomes and expenses 2. For each budget item, a total for the item 3. A total for all incomes and expenses 4. Net = income – expenses

Figure 1–2

Roadmap

In this chapter, you will learn how to perform basic workbook tasks using Excel. The following roadmap identifies general activities you will perform as you progress through this chapter:

Descriptive, Overview Roadmap

1. ENTER TEXT in a blank worksheet.
2. CALCULATE SUMS AND USE FORMULAS in the worksheet.
3. SAVE the WORKBOOK using the file name, Bob Gleamin Budget.
4. FORMAT TEXT in the worksheet.
5. INSERT a pie CHART into the worksheet.
6. Assign a NAME to the worksheet TAB.
7. PREVIEW AND PRINT the WORKSHEET.

At the beginning of step instructions throughout the chapter, you will see an abbreviated form of this roadmap. The abbreviated roadmap uses colors to indicate chapter progress: gray means the chapter is beyond that activity, blue means the task being shown is covered in that activity, and black means that activity is yet to be covered. For example, the following abbreviated roadmap indicates the chapter would be showing a task in the Save Workbook activity.

1 ENTER TEXT | 2 CALCULATE SUMS & USE FORMULAS | 3 SAVE WORKBOOK | 4 FORMAT TEXT
5 INSERT CHART | 6 NAME TAB | 7 PREVIEW & PRINT WORKSHEET

The key to developing a useful worksheet is careful planning. Careful planning can reduce your effort significantly and result in a worksheet that is accurate, easy to read, flexible, and useful. When analyzing a problem and designing a worksheet solution, what steps should you follow?

• Define the problem, including need, source of data, calculations, charting, and web or special requirements.

• Design the worksheet.

• Enter the data and formulas.

• Test the worksheet.

For an introduction to Windows and instruction about how to perform basic Windows tasks, read the Office and Windows chapter at the beginning of this book, where you can learn how to resize windows, change screen resolution, create folders, move and rename files, use Windows Help, and much more.

After carefully reviewing the requirements document (Figure 1–2 on the previous page) and making the necessary decisions, the next step is to design a solution or draw a sketch of the worksheet based on the requirements, including titles, column and row headings, the location of data values, and the 3-D pie chart, as shown in Figure 1–3. The dollar signs and commas that you see in the sketch of the worksheet indicate formatted numeric values.

With a good understanding of the requirements document, an understanding of the necessary decisions, and a sketch of the worksheet, the next step is to use Excel to create the worksheet and chart.

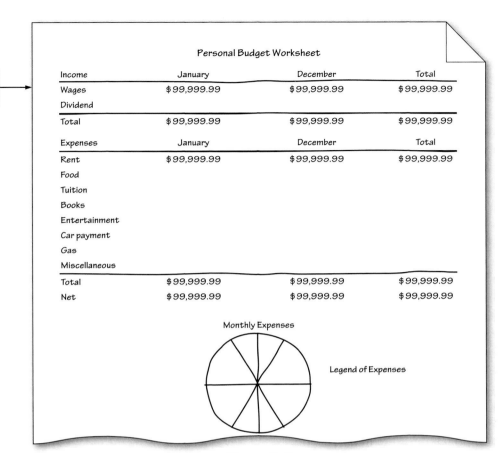

sketch of worksheet and chart

Figure 1–3

To Run Excel and Create a Blank Workbook

If you are using a computer to step through the project in this chapter and you want your screens to match the figures in this book, you should change your screen's resolution to 1366 × 768. For information about how to change a computer's resolution, refer to the Office and Windows chapter at the beginning of this book.

The following steps, which assume Windows is running, use the Start screen or the Search box to run Excel based on a typical installation. You may need to ask your instructor how to run Excel on your computer. For a detailed example of the procedure summarized below, refer to the Office and Windows chapter.

1 Scroll the Start screen for an Excel 2013 tile. If your Start screen contains an Excel 2013 tile, tap or click it to run Excel and then proceed to Step 5; if the Start screen does not contain the Excel 2013 tile, proceed to the next step to search for the Excel app.

2 Swipe in from the right edge of the screen or point to the upper-right corner of the screen to display the Charms bar and then tap or click the Search charm on the Charms bar to display the Search menu.

3 Type **Excel** as the search text in the Search box and watch the search results appear in the Apps list.

4 Tap or click Excel 2013 in the search results to run Excel.

5 Tap or click the Blank workbook thumbnail on the Excel start screen to create a blank workbook and display it in the Excel window.

6 If the Excel window is not maximized, tap or click the Maximize button on its title bar to maximize the window.

One of the few differences between Windows 7 and Windows 8 occurs in the steps to run Excel. If you are using Windows 7, click the Start button, type **Excel** in the 'Search programs and files' text box, click Excel 2013, and then, if necessary, maximize the Excel window. For detailed steps to run Excel in Windows 7, refer to the Office and Windows chapter at the beginning of this book. For a summary of the steps, refer to the Quick Reference located at the back of this book.

BTW
BTWs
For a complete list of the BTWs found in the margins of this book, visit the BTW resource on the Student Companion Site located on www.cengagebrain .com. For detailed instructions about accessing available resources, visit www.cengage .com/ct/studentdownload or contact your instructor for information about accessing the required files.

If you are using your finger on a touch screen and are having difficulty completing the steps in this chapter, consider using a stylus. Many people find it easier to be precise with a stylus than with a finger. In addition, with a stylus you see the pointer. If you still are having trouble completing the steps with a stylus, try using a mouse.

For an introduction to Office and instruction about how to perform basic tasks in Office apps, read the Office and Windows chapter at the beginning of this book, where you can learn how to run an application, use the ribbon, save a file, open a file, exit an application, use Help, and much more.

BTW

Touch Screen Differences

The Office and Windows interfaces may vary if you are using a touch screen. For this reason, you might notice that the function or appearance of your touch screen differs slightly from this chapter's presentation.

BTW

Q&As

For a complete list of the Q&As found in many of the step-by-step sequences in this book, visit the Q&A resource on the Student Companion Site located on www.cengagebrain.com. For detailed instructions about accessing available resources, visit www.cengage.com/ct/studentdownload or contact your instructor for information about accessing the required files.

Selecting a Cell

To enter data into a cell, you first must select it. The easiest way to **select** a cell (make it active) is to tap it or use the mouse to move the block plus sign pointer to the cell and then click.

An alternative method is to use the arrow keys that are located just to the right of the alphanumeric keys on a standard keyboard. An arrow key selects the cell adjacent to the active cell in the direction of the arrow on the key.

You know a cell is selected, or active, when a heavy border surrounds the cell and the active cell reference appears in the Name box on the left side of the formula bar. Excel also changes the active cell's column heading and row heading to a shaded color.

Entering Text

In Excel, any set of characters containing a letter, hyphen (as in a telephone number), or space is considered text. **Text** is used to place titles, such as worksheet titles, column titles, and row titles, on the worksheet.

Worksheet titles and subtitles should be as brief and meaningful as possible. A worksheet title could include the name of the organization, department, or a description of the content of the worksheet. A worksheet subtitle, if included, could include a more detailed description of the content of the worksheet. Examples of worksheet titles are December 2014 Payroll and Year 2015 Projected Budget, and examples of subtitles are Marketing Department and Rent and Utilities, respectively.

As shown in Figure 1–4, data in a worksheet often is identified by row and column titles so that the user of a worksheet easily can identify the meaning of the data. Rows typically contain information that is similar to items in a list. Columns typically contain descriptive information about items in rows or contain information that helps to group the data in the worksheet. Examples of row titles are Income and Total, and examples of column titles are Wages and Gas.

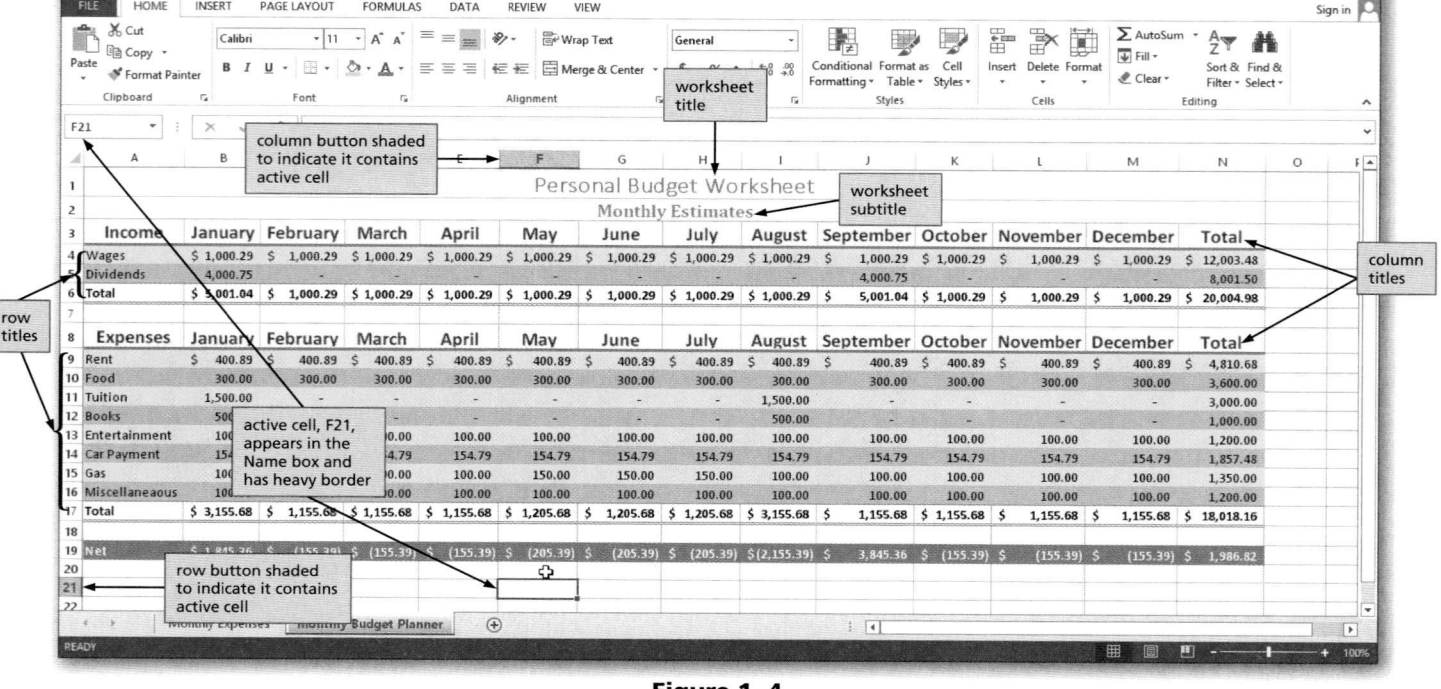

Figure 1–4

To Enter the Worksheet Titles

As shown in Figure 1–4, the worksheet title, Personal Budget Worksheet, identifies the purpose for which the worksheet is being created in Chapter 1. The worksheet subtitle, Monthly Estimates, identifies the type of data contained in the worksheet. *Why? A title and subtitle help the reader to understand clearly what the worksheet contains.*

The following steps enter the worksheet titles in cells A1 and A2. Later in this chapter, the worksheet titles will be formatted so that they appear as shown in Figure 1–4.

1

- If necessary, tap or click cell A1 to make cell A1 the active cell (Figure 1–5).

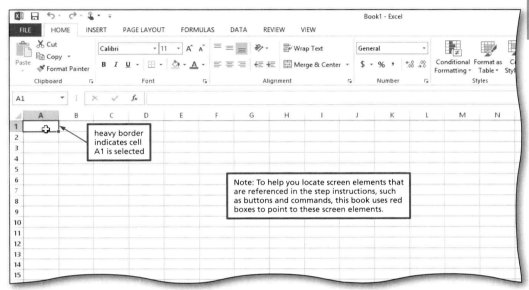

Figure 1–5

2

- Type **Personal Budget Worksheet** in cell A1 and then point to the Enter box in the formula bar to prepare to enter text in the active cell (Figure 1–6).

Q&A Why did the appearance of the formula bar change? Excel displays the title in the formula bar and in cell A1. When you begin typing a cell entry, Excel displays two additional boxes in the formula bar: the Cancel box and the Enter box. Tapping or clicking the **Enter box** completes an entry. Tapping or clicking the **Cancel box** cancels an entry.

Figure 1–6

③

- Tap or click the Enter box to complete the entry and enter the worksheet title (Figure 1–7).

Q&A Why does the entered text appear in three cells?

When the text is longer than the width of a cell, Excel displays the overflow characters in adjacent cells to the right as long as those adjacent cells contain no data. If the adjacent cells contain data, Excel hides the overflow characters. Excel displays the overflow characters in the formula bar whenever that cell is the active cell.

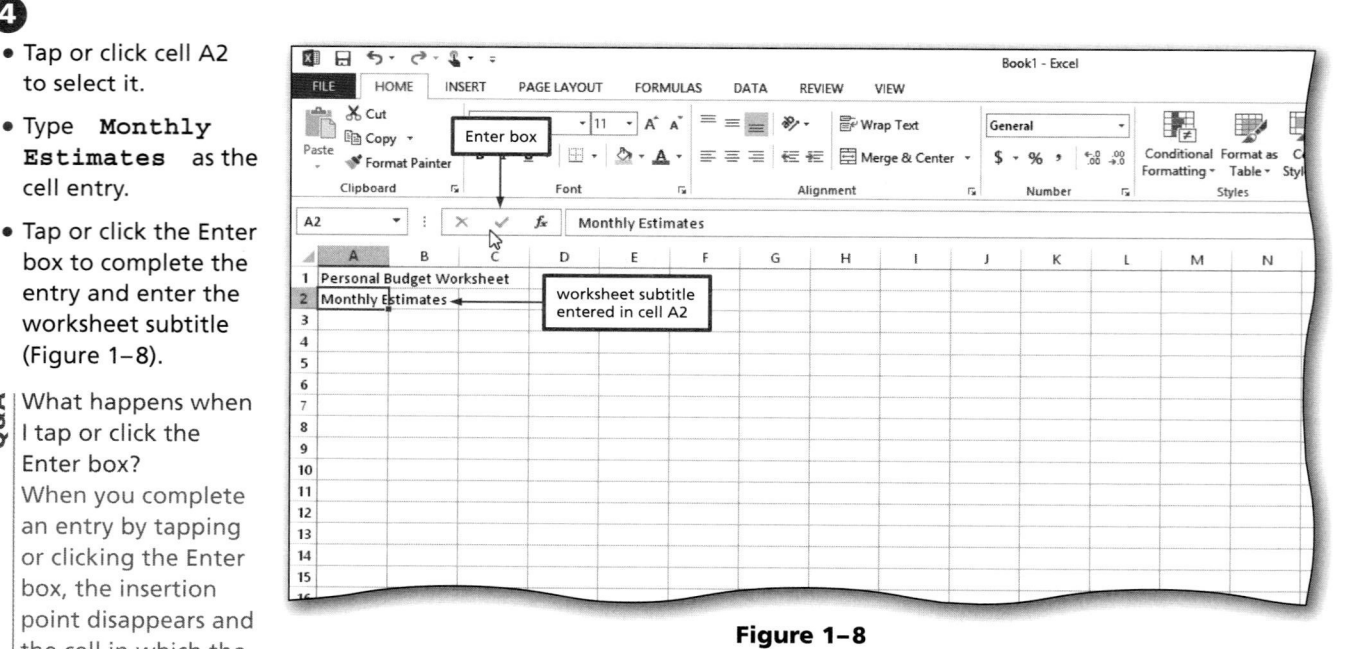

Figure 1–7

④

- Tap or click cell A2 to select it.

- Type **Monthly Estimates** as the cell entry.

- Tap or click the Enter box to complete the entry and enter the worksheet subtitle (Figure 1–8).

Q&A What happens when I tap or click the Enter box?

When you complete an entry by tapping or clicking the Enter box, the insertion point disappears and the cell in which the text is entered remains the active cell.

Figure 1–8

Other Ways

1. To complete entry, tap or click any cell other than active cell
2. To complete entry, press ENTER
3. To complete entry, press HOME, PAGE UP, PAGE DOWN, or END
4. To complete entry, press UP ARROW, DOWN ARROW, LEFT ARROW, or RIGHT ARROW

AutoCorrect

The **AutoCorrect feature** of Excel works behind the scenes, correcting common mistakes when you complete a text entry in a cell. AutoCorrect makes three types of corrections for you:

1. Corrects two initial uppercase letters by changing the second letter to lowercase.

2. Capitalizes the first letter in the names of days.

3. Replaces commonly misspelled words with their correct spelling. For example, it will change the misspelled word *recieve* to *receive* when you complete the entry. AutoCorrect will correct the spelling of hundreds of commonly misspelled words automatically.

BTW

The Ribbon and Screen Resolution
Excel may change how the groups and buttons within the groups appear on the ribbon, depending on the computer's screen resolution. Thus, your ribbon may look different from the ones in this book if you are using a screen resolution other than 1366 × 768.

To Enter Column Titles

1 ENTER TEXT | 2 CALCULATE SUMS & USE FORMULAS | 3 SAVE WORKBOOK | 4 FORMAT TEXT
5 INSERT CHART | 6 NAME TAB | 7 PREVIEW & PRINT WORKSHEET

The column titles in row 3 shown in Figure 1–4 (Income, January, February, March, April, May, June, July, August, September, October, November, December, and Total) identify the numbers in each column in the first part of the worksheet. The column titles in row 8 (Expenses, January, February, March, April, May, June, July, August, September, October, November, December, and Total) identify the numbers in each column in the second part of the worksheet. In the case of the Personal Budget Worksheet data, the month names identify the estimates for the budget for each month using the income or expense type, depending on which part you are reviewing.

To enter the column titles in row 3, select the appropriate cell and then enter the text. The following steps enter the column titles in row 3. ***Why?*** *Data entered in columns should be identified using column titles to identify what the column contains.*

1

- Tap or click cell A3 to make it the active cell.

- Type **Income** to begin entry of a column title in the active cell (Figure 1–9).

Q&A What is the vertical line in cell A1?
The text in cell A1 is followed by the insertion point. The **insertion point** is a blinking vertical line that indicates where the next typed character will appear.

Figure 1–9

2

- If you are using a touch screen, tap cell B3; if you are using a mouse, press the RIGHT ARROW key to enter a column title and make the cell to the right the active cell (Figure 1–10).

Why is the RIGHT ARROW key used to complete the entry in the cell?

If the next entry you want to enter is in an adjacent cell, use the arrow keys to complete the entry in a cell. When you press an arrow key to complete an entry, the adjacent cell in the direction of the arrow (up, down, left, or right) becomes the active cell. If the next entry is in a nonadjacent cell, complete the current entry by tapping or clicking the next cell in which you plan to enter data. You also can tap or click the Enter box or press the ENTER key and then tap or click the appropriate cell for the next entry.

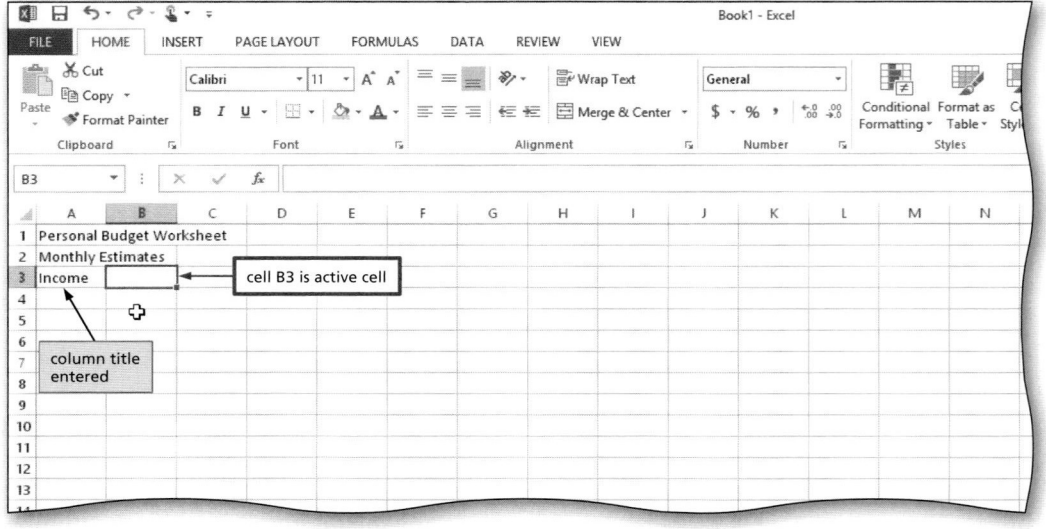

Figure 1–10

3

- Repeat Steps 1 and 2 to enter the remaining column titles; that is, enter **January** in cell B3, **February** in cell C3, **March** in cell D3, **April** in cell E3, **May** in cell F3, **June** in cell G3, **July** in cell H3, **August** in cell I3, **September** in cell J3, **October** in cell K3, **November** in cell L3, **December** in cell M3, and **Total** in cell N3 (complete the last entry in cell N3 by tapping or clicking the Enter box in the formula bar).

- Tap or click cell A8 to select it.

- Repeat Steps 1 and 2 to enter the remaining column titles; that is, enter **Expenses** in cell A8, **January** in cell B8, **February** in cell C8, **March** in cell D8, **April** in cell E8, **May** in cell F8, **June** in cell G8, **July** in cell H8, **August** in cell I8, **September** in cell J8, **October** in cell K8, **November** in cell L8, **December** in cell M8, and **Total** in cell N8 (complete the last entry in cell N8 by tapping or clicking the Enter box in the formula bar) (Figure 1–11).

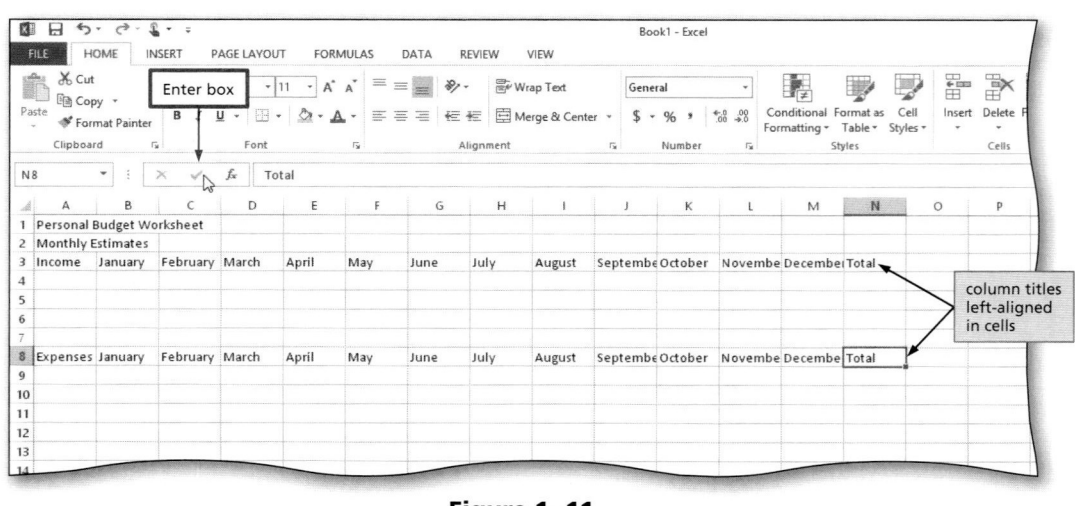

Figure 1–11

To Enter Row Titles

The next step in developing the worksheet for this project is to enter the row titles in column A. For the Personal Budget Worksheet data, the list of income types and expense types make up the row titles. It is likely that in the future, Bob Gleamin may add more income or expense items. Each income or expense item, therefore, should be placed in its own row. The row titles in column A for income (Wages, Dividends, and Total), expenses (Rent, Food, Tuition, Books, Entertainment, Car Payment, Gas, Miscellaneous, and Total), and net income (Net) identify the numbers in each row.

This process for entering row titles is similar to the process for entering column titles. The following steps enter the row titles in the worksheet.

1

- Tap or click cell A4 to select it.

- Type **Wages** and then tap cell A5 or press the DOWN ARROW key to enter a row title (Figure 1–12).

Figure 1–12

2

- Repeat Step 1 to enter the remaining row titles in column A; that is, enter **Dividends** in cell A5, **Total** in cell A6, **Rent** in cell A9, **Food** in cell A10, **Tuition** in cell A11, **Books** in cell A12, **Entertainment** in cell A13, **Car Payment** in cell A14, **Gas** in cell A15, **Miscellaneous** in cell A16, **Total** in cell A17, and **Net** in cell A19 (Figure 1–13).

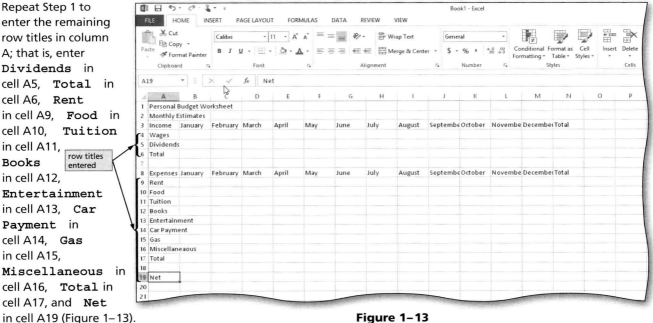

Figure 1–13

Q&A Why is the text left-aligned in the cells?

When you enter text, Excel automatically left-aligns the text in the cell. Excel treats any combination of numbers, spaces, and nonnumeric characters as text. For example, Excel recognizes the following entries as text: 401AX21, 921–231, 619 321, 883XTY

You can change the text alignment in a cell by realigning it. Other alignment techniques are discussed later in this chapter.

Entering Numbers

In Excel, you can enter numbers into cells to represent amounts. A **number** can contain only the following characters:

0 1 2 3 4 5 6 7 8 9 + – () , / . $ % E e

If a cell entry contains any other keyboard character (including spaces), Excel interprets the entry as text and treats it accordingly. The use of special characters is explained when they are used in this book.

To Enter Numbers

1 ENTER TEXT | 2 CALCULATE SUMS & USE FORMULAS | 3 SAVE WORKBOOK | 4 FORMAT TEXT
5 INSERT CHART | 6 NAME TAB | 7 PREVIEW & PRINT WORKSHEET

The Personal Budget Worksheet numbers used in Chapter 1 are summarized in Table 1–1. These numbers, which represent yearly income and expenses amounts, must be entered in rows 4–5 and 9–16.

Table 1–1 Personal Budget Worksheet

Income	January	February	March	April	May	June	July	August	September	October	November	December
Wages	1000.29	1000.29	1000.29	1000.29	1000.29	1000.29	1000.29	1000.29	1000.29	1000.29	1000.29	1000.29
Dividends	4000.75	0	0	0	0	0	0	0	4000.75	0	0	0

Expenses	January	February	March	April	May	June	July	August	September	October	November	December
Rent	400.89	400.89	400.89	400.89	400.89	400.89	400.89	400.89	400.89	400.89	400.89	400.89
Food	300	300	300	300	300	300	300	300	300	300	300	300
Tuition	1500	0	0	0	0	0	0	1500	0	0	0	0
Books	500	0	0	0	0	0	0	500	0	0	0	0
Entertainment	100	100	100	100	100	100	100	100	100	100	100	100
Car Payment	154.79	154.79	154.79	154.79	154.79	154.79	154.79	154.79	154.79	154.79	154.79	154.79
Gas	100	100	100	100	150	150	150	100	100	100	100	100
Miscellaneous	100	100	100	100	100	100	100	100	100	100	100	100

The following steps enter the numbers in Table 1–1 one row at a time.

1

- Tap or click cell B4 to select it.

- Type 1000.29 and then if you are using a touch screen, tap cell C4. If you are using a mouse, press the RIGHT ARROW key to enter the data in the selected cell and make the cell to the right (cell C4) the active cell (Figure 1–14).

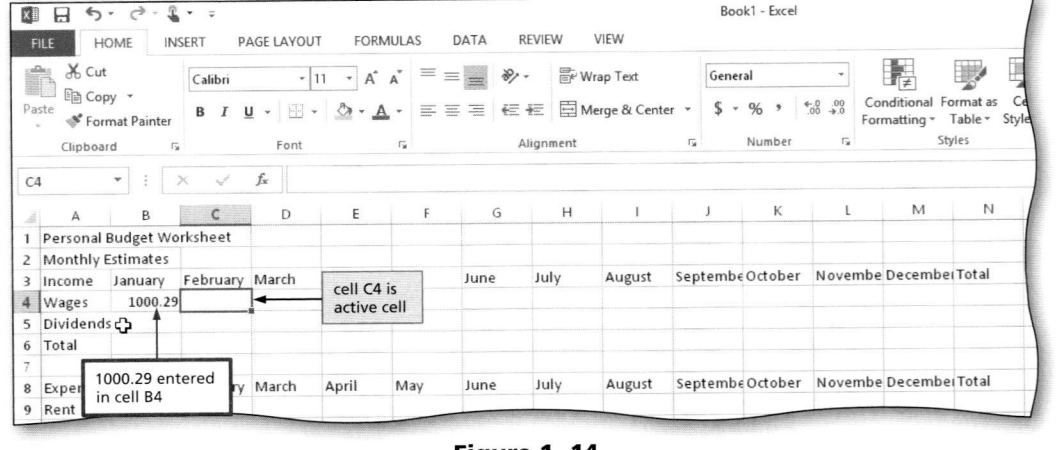

Figure 1–14

Do I need to enter dollar signs, commas, or trailing zeros for the amounts?
You are not required to type dollar signs, commas, or trailing zeros. When you enter a dollar value that has cents, however, you must add the decimal point and the numbers representing the cents. Later in this chapter, the numbers will be formatted to use dollar signs, commas, and trailing zeros to improve the appearance and readability of the numbers.

- Enter **1000.29** in cells C4, D4, E4, F4, G4, H4, I4, J4, K4, L4, and M4 to complete the first row of numbers in the worksheet (Figure 1–15).

Q&A

Why are the numbers right-aligned?

When you enter numeric data in a cell, Excel recognizes the values as numbers and right-aligns the values in order to properly vertically align decimal and integer values. For example, values entered below those entered in this step automatically will be right-aligned so that the decimals of the values properly align.

Figure 1–15

- Tap or click cell B5 to select it and complete the entry in the previously selected cell.

- Enter the remaining personal budget numbers provided in Table 1–1 on page EX 12 for each of the nine remaining budget items in rows 5 and 9–16 to finish entering numbers in the worksheet (Figure 1–16).

Q&A

Why did tapping or clicking cell B5 complete the entry in cell M4?

Selecting another cell completes the entry in the previously selected cell in the same way as pressing the ENTER key, pressing an arrow key, or tapping or clicking the Enter box in the formula bar. In the next set of steps, the entry of the number in cell B5 will be completed by selecting another cell.

Figure 1–16

Calculating a Sum

The next step in creating the worksheet is to perform any necessary calculations, such as calculating the column and row totals. When you use functions, Excel performs the calculations for you, which helps to prevent errors and allows you to work more efficiently.

To Sum a Column of Numbers

1 ENTER TEXT | 2 CALCULATE SUMS & USE FORMULAS | 3 SAVE WORKBOOK | 4 FORMAT TEXT
5 INSERT CHART | 6 NAME TAB | 7 PREVIEW & PRINT WORKSHEET

As stated in the requirements document in Figure 1–2 on page EX 3, totals are required for each month and each budget item. The first calculation is to determine the total income for the Wages and Dividends in the month of January in column B. To calculate this value in cell B6, Excel must add, or sum, the numbers in cells B4 and B5. The **SUM function** adds all the numbers in a range of cells. *Why? Excel's SUM function provides a convenient means to accomplish this task.*

A **range** is a series of two or more adjacent cells in a column or row or a rectangular group of cells. For example, the group of adjacent cells B4 and B5 is called a range. Many Excel operations, such as summing numbers, are performed on a range of cells.

After the total income for a month in column B is determined, the totals for the remaining months for income, the totals for the expenses, and the totals for budget item will be determined. The following steps sum the numbers in column B.

1

- Tap or click cell B6 to make it the active cell and complete the entry in the previously selected cell.

- Tap or click the Sum button (HOME tab | Editing group) to display a formula in the formula bar and in the active cell (Figure 1–17).

Q&A

What if my screen displays a Sum menu?
If you are using a touch screen, you may not have a separate Sum button and Sum arrow. In this case, select the desired option on the Sum menu.

How does Excel know which cells to sum?
When you enter the SUM function using the Sum button on the ribbon, Excel automatically selects what it considers to be your choice of the range to sum. When proposing the range to sum, Excel first looks for a range of cells with numbers above the active cell and then to the left. If Excel proposes the wrong range, you can correct it by dragging through the correct range before pressing the ENTER key. You also can enter the correct range by typing the beginning cell reference, a colon (:), and the ending cell reference.

Figure 1–17

2

- Tap or click the Enter box in the formula bar to enter a sum in the active cell.

Q&A What is the purpose of the Sum arrow?

If you tap or click the Sum arrow on the right side of the Sum button (HOME tab | Editing group) (shown in Figure 1–17), Excel displays a list of often-used functions from which you can choose. The list includes functions that allow you to determine the average, the number of items in the selected range, the maximum value, or the minimum value of a range of numbers.

3

- Repeat Steps 1 and 2 to enter the SUM function in cell B17 (Figure 1–18).

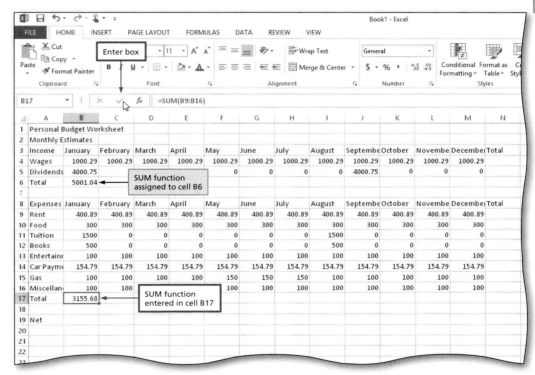

Figure 1–18

Other Ways

1. Tap or click Insert Function button in formula bar, select SUM in Select a function list, tap or click OK button (Insert Function dialog box),

 tap or click OK button (Function Arguments dialog box)

2. Tap or click Sum arrow (HOME tab | Editing group), tap or click More Functions in list, tap

 or click SUM (Insert Function dialog box), tap or click OK button, select range (Function Arguments dialog box), tap or click OK button

3. Type **=s** in cell, select SUM in list, select range, tap or click Enter box

4. Press ALT+EQUAL SIGN (=) twice

Using the Fill Handle to Copy a Cell to Adjacent Cells

Excel also must calculate the totals for income during each month in cells C6:M6. Table 1–2 on the next page illustrates the similarities between the entry in cell B6 and the entries required to sum the totals in cells C6, D6, E6, F6, G6, H6, I6, J6, K6, L6, and M6.

To place the SUM functions in range C6:M6, you could follow the same steps shown previously in Figure 1–17 and Figure 1–18. A second, more efficient method, however, is to copy the SUM function from cell B6 to the range C6:M6. The cell being copied is called the **source area** or **copy area**. The range of cells receiving the copy is called the **destination area** or **paste area**.

Table 1–2 Sum Function Entries in Row 6		
Cell	**SUM Function Entries**	**Result**
B6	=SUM(B4:B5)	Sums cells B4 and B5
C6	=SUM(C4:C5)	Sums cells C4 and C5
D6	=SUM(D4:D5)	Sums cells D4 and D5
E6	=SUM(E4:E5)	Sums cells E4 and E5
F6	=SUM(F4:F5)	Sums cells F4 and F5
G6	=SUM(G4:G5)	Sums cells G4 and G5
H6	=SUM(H4:H5)	Sums cells H4 and H5
I6	=SUM(I4:I5)	Sums cells I4 and I5
J6	=SUM(J4:J5)	Sums cells J4 and J5
K6	=SUM(K4:K5)	Sums cells K4 and K5
L6	=SUM(L4:L5)	Sums cells L4 and L5
M6	=SUM(M4:M5)	Sums cells M4 and M5

Although the SUM function entries in Table 1–2 are similar, they are not exact copies. The range in each SUM function entry uses cell references that are one column to the right of the previous column. When you copy formulas that include cell references, Excel automatically adjusts them for each new position, resulting in the SUM function entries illustrated in Table 1–2. Each adjusted cell reference is called a **relative reference**.

To Copy a Cell to Adjacent Cells in a Row

1 ENTER TEXT | 2 CALCULATE SUMS & USE FORMULAS | 3 SAVE WORKBOOK | 4 FORMAT TEXT
5 INSERT CHART | 6 NAME TAB | 7 PREVIEW & PRINT WORKSHEET

The easiest way to copy the SUM formula from cell B6 to cells C6:M6 is to use the fill handle. *Why? Using the fill handle means that Excel creates the formulas for you.* The **fill handle** is the small black square located in the lower-right corner of the heavy border around the active cell. The following steps use the fill handle to copy cell B6 to the adjacent cells C6:M6.

- With cell B6 active, if you are using a touch screen, press and hold cell B6 to display the mini toolbar, then tap AutoFill on the mini toolbar; if you are using a mouse, point to the fill handle to activate it (Figure 1–19).

Q&A Why is my fill handle not a black square? If you are using a touch screen, the fill handle appears as a black and white rectangle with a blue down arrow in it.

Figure 1–19

• Drag the fill handle to select the destination area, range C6:M6, to display a shaded border around the source area and the destination area (Figure 1–20). Do not lift your finger from the screen or release the mouse button.

Figure 1–20

• Lift your finger from the screen or release the mouse button to copy the SUM function from the active cell to the destination area and calculate the sums (Figure 1–21).

Q&A

What is the purpose of the 'Auto Fill Options' button?

When you copy one range to another, Excel displays an 'Auto Fill Options' button (Figure 1–21). The 'Auto Fill Options' button allows you to choose whether you want to copy the values from the source area to the destination area with formatting, do so without formatting, or copy only the format. To view the available fill options, tap or click the 'Auto Fill Options' button. The 'Auto Fill Options' button disappears when you begin another activity in Excel, such as typing data in another cell or applying formatting to a cell or range of cells.

Figure 1–21

- Repeat Steps 1–3 to copy the SUM function from cell B17 to the range C17:M17 (Figure 1–22).

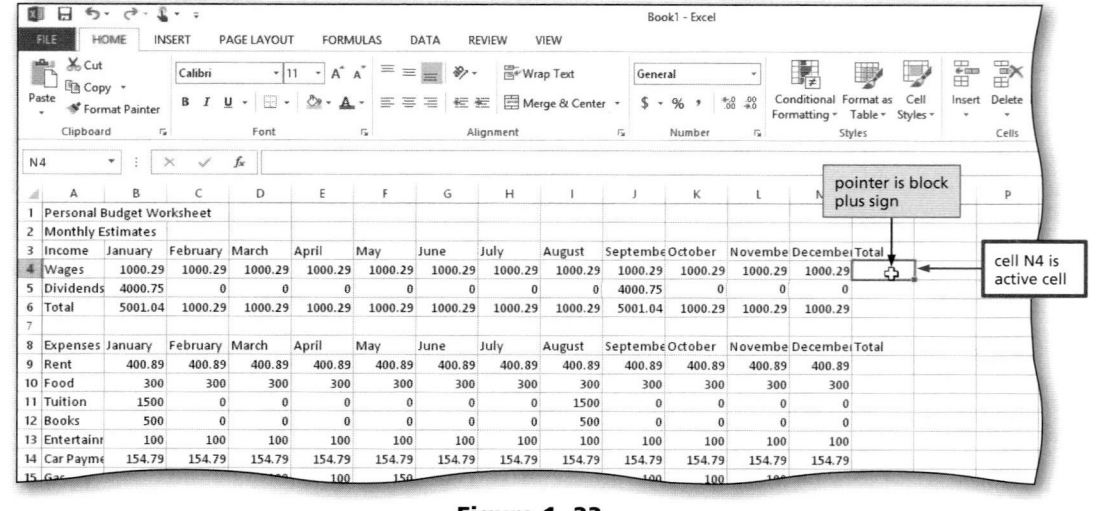

Figure 1–22

Other Ways

1. Select source area, tap or click Copy button (HOME tab | Clipboard group), select destination area, tap or click Paste button (HOME tab | Clipboard group)

2. Press and hold or right-click source area, tap or click Copy on shortcut menu; press and hold or right-click destination area, tap or click Paste on shortcut menu

To Determine Multiple Totals at the Same Time

1 ENTER TEXT | 2 CALCULATE SUMS & USE FORMULAS | 3 SAVE WORKBOOK | 4 FORMAT TEXT
5 INSERT CHART | 6 NAME TAB | 7 PREVIEW & PRINT WORKSHEET

The next step in building the worksheet is to determine the budget item totals for each budget item and total income and expenses in column N. To calculate these totals, you can use the SUM function much as it was used to total the budget items for each month in rows 6 and 17.

In this example, however, Excel will determine totals for all of the rows at the same time. *Why? By determining multiple totals at the same time, the number of steps to add totals is reduced.* The following steps sum multiple totals at once.

- Tap or click cell N4 to make it the active cell (Figure 1–23).

Figure 1–23

2

- If you are using a touch screen, drag the lower-right selection handle down to cell N6; if you are using a mouse, with the pointer in cell N4 and in the shape of a block plus sign, drag the pointer down to cell N6 to highlight the range with a transparent view (Figure 1–24).

Figure 1–24

3

- Tap or click the Sum button (HOME tab | Editing group) to calculate and display the sums of the corresponding rows (Figure 1–25).

Q&A ◄ How does Excel create unique totals for each row?
If each cell in a selected range is next to a row of numbers, Excel assigns the SUM function to each cell when you tap or click the Sum button.

Figure 1–25

4

- Repeat Steps 1–3 to select cells N9 to N17 and calculate and display the sums of the corresponding rows (Figure 1–26).

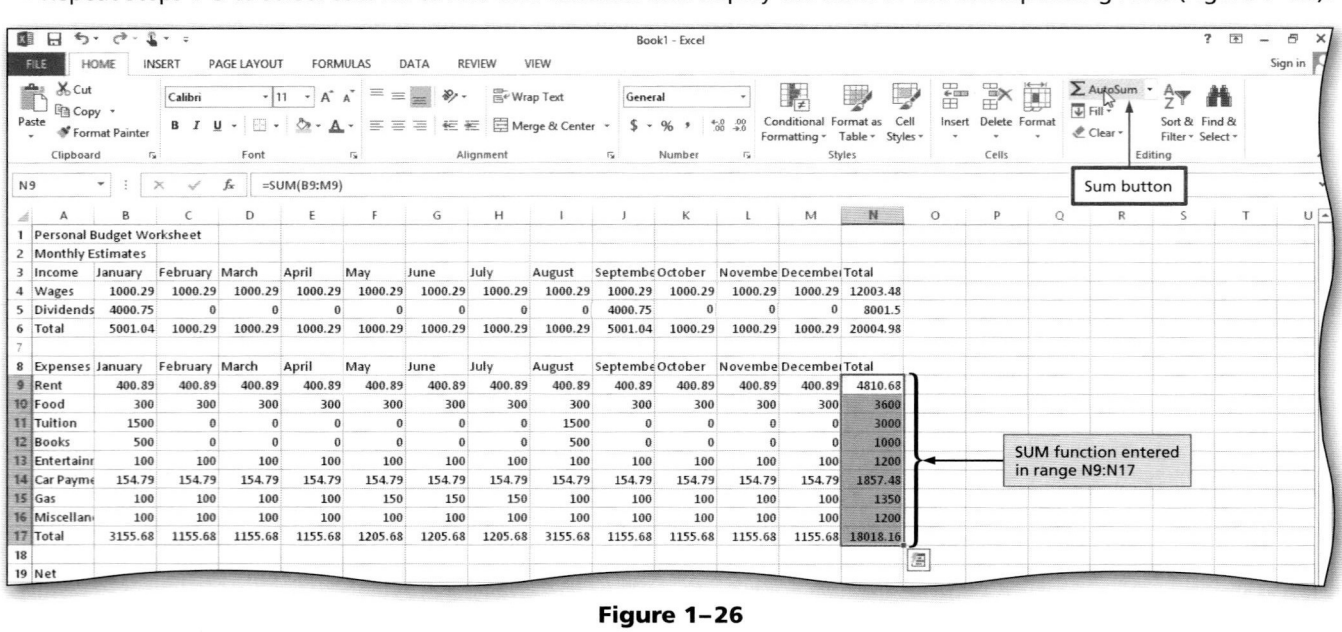

Figure 1–26

To Enter a Formula Using the Keyboard

1 ENTER TEXT | 2 CALCULATE SUMS & USE FORMULAS | 3 SAVE WORKBOOK | 4 FORMAT TEXT
5 INSERT CHART | 6 NAME TAB | 7 PREVIEW & PRINT WORKSHEET

The formulas needed in the worksheet are noted in the requirements document as follows:

 Net (row 19) = Income – Expenses

 The net for each month, which appears in row 19, is equal to the income total in row 6 minus the expense total in row 17. The following steps enter the initial net formula in cell B19 using the keyboard. **Why?** *Sometimes a predefined function does not fit your needs; therefore, you enter a formula of your own.*

1

- Select cell B19 to deselect the selected range.

- Type **=b6-b17** in the cell to display the formula in the formula bar and in the current cell and to display colored borders around the cells referenced in the formula (Figure 1–27).

Q&A What occurs on the worksheet as I enter the formula?

The **equal sign (=)** preceding b6–b17 in the formula alerts Excel that you are entering a

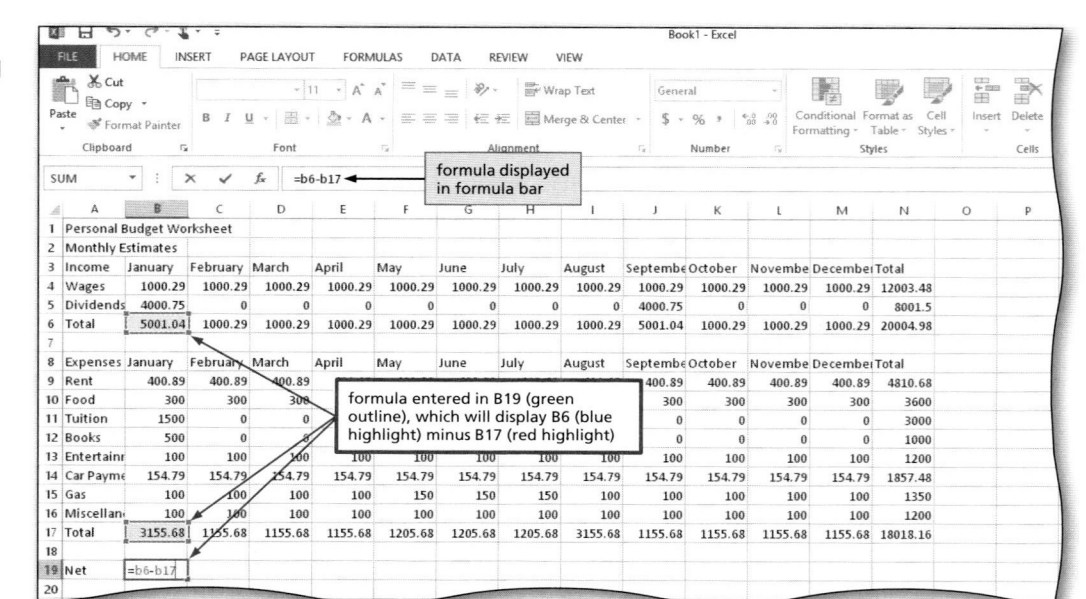

Figure 1–27

formula or function and not text. Because the most common error when entering a formula is to reference the wrong cell in a formula, Excel colors the borders of the cells referenced in the formula. The coloring helps in the reviewing process to ensure the cell references are correct. The **minus sign** (–) following b6 in the formula is the arithmetic operator that directs Excel to perform the subtraction operation.

2

- Tap or click cell C19 to complete the arithmetic operation indicated by the formula, to display the result in the worksheet, and to select the cell to the right (Figure 1–28).

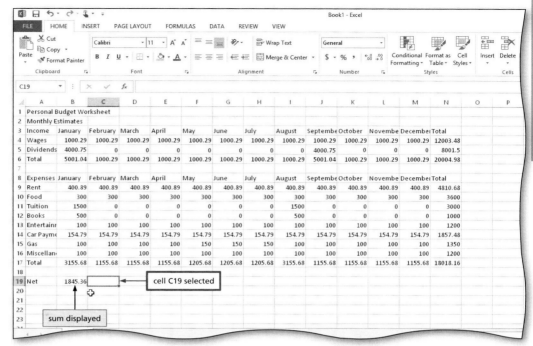

Figure 1–28

To Copy a Cell to Adjacent Cells in a Row

The easiest way to copy the SUM formula from cell B19 to cells C19, D19, E19, F19, G19, H19, I19, J19, K19, L19, M19, and N19 is to use the fill handle. The following steps use the fill handle to copy the formula in cell B19 to the adjacent cells C19:N19.

1 Select cell B19.

2 Drag the fill handle to select the destination area, range C19:N19, to display a shaded border around the source area and the destination area. Do not lift your finger or release the mouse button.

3 Lift your finger or release the mouse button to copy the simple formula function from the active cell to the destination area and calculate the results.

To Save a Workbook with a New File Name

You have performed many tasks while creating this workbook and do not want to risk losing work completed thus far. Accordingly, you should save the workbook on your hard disk, SkyDrive, or a location that is most appropriate to your situation.

The following steps assume you already have created folders for storing your files, for example, a CIS 101 folder (for your class) that contains an Excel folder (for your assignments). Thus, these steps save the workbook in the Excel folder in the CIS 101 folder on your desired save location. For a detailed example of the procedure for saving a file in a folder or saving a file on SkyDrive, refer to the Office and Windows chapter at the beginning of this book.

1 Tap or click the Save button on the Quick Access Toolbar, which depending on settings, will display either the Save As gallery in the Backstage view or the Save As dialog box.

2 To save on a hard disk or other storage media on your computer, proceed to Step 2a. To save on SkyDrive, proceed to Step 2b.

2a If your screen opens the Backstage view and you want to save on storage media on your computer, tap or click Computer in the left pane, if necessary, to display options in the right pane related to saving on your computer. If your screen already displays the Save As dialog box, proceed to Step 3.

2b If your screen opens the Backstage view and you want to save on SkyDrive, tap or click SkyDrive in the left pane to display SkyDrive saving options or a Sign In button. If your screen displays a Sign In button, tap or click it and then sign in to SkyDrive.

3 Tap or click the Browse button in the right pane to display the Save As dialog box associated with the selected save location (i.e., Computer or SkyDrive).

4 Type **Bob Gleamin Budget** in the File name box to change the file name. Do not press the ENTER key after typing the file name because you do not want to close the dialog box at this time.

5 Navigate to the desired save location (in this case, the Excel folder in the CIS 101 folder [or your class folder] on your computer or SkyDrive).

6 Tap or click the Save button (Save As dialog box) to save the workbook in the selected folder on the selected save location with the entered file name.

Break Point: If you wish to take a break, this is a good place to do so. You can exit Excel. To resume at a later time, run Excel, open the file called Bob Gleamin Budget, and continue following the steps from this location forward.

Formatting the Worksheet

The text, numeric entries, and functions for the worksheet now are complete. The next step is to format the worksheet. You **format** a worksheet to emphasize certain entries and make the worksheet easier to read and understand.

Figure 1–29a shows the worksheet before formatting. Figure 1–29b shows the worksheet after formatting. As you can see from the two figures, a worksheet that is formatted not only is easier to read but also looks more professional.

CONSIDER THIS

The key to formatting a worksheet is to consider the ways you can enhance the worksheet so that it appears professional. When formatting a worksheet, what steps should you consider?

• Identify how to format various elements of the worksheet.

• Increase the font size of cells.

• Change the font color of cells.

• Center the worksheet titles, subtitles, and column headings.

• Modify column widths to best fit text in cells.

• Change the font style of cells.

To change the unformatted worksheet in Figure 1–29a so that it appears like the formatted worksheet in Figure 1–29b, the following tasks must be completed:

1. Change the font, change the font style to bold, increase the font size, and change the font color of the worksheet titles in cells A1 and A2.

2. Center the worksheet titles in cells A1 and A2 across columns A through N.

(a) Unformatted Worksheet

(b) Formatted Worksheet

Figure 1–29

3. Format the body of the worksheet. The body of the worksheet, range A3:N19, includes the column titles, row titles, and numbers. Formatting the body of the worksheet changes the numbers to use a dollars-and-cents format, with dollar signs in rows 4 and 9 and the total rows (row 6 and 17); changes the styles of some rows; adds underlining that emphasizes portions of the worksheet; and modifies the column widths to fit the text in the columns and make the text and numbers readable.

The remainder of this section explains the process required to format the worksheet. Although the formatting procedures are explained in the order described above, you should be aware that you could make these format changes in any order. Modifying the column widths, however, usually is done last because other formatting changes may affect the size of data in the cells in the column.

Font Style, Size, and Color

The characters that Excel displays on the screen are a specific font, style, size, and color. The **font**, or font face, defines the appearance and shape of the letters, numbers, and special characters. Examples of fonts include Calibri, Cambria, Times New Roman, Arial, and Courier. **Font style** indicates how the characters are emphasized. Common font styles include regular, bold, underline, and italic. The **font size** specifies the size of the characters on the screen. Font size is gauged by a measurement system called points. A single point is about 1/72 of one inch in height. Thus, a character with a **point size** of 10 is about 10/72 of one inch in height. The **font color** defines the color of the characters. Excel can display characters in a wide variety of colors.

When Excel first runs, the preset font for the entire workbook is Calibri, with a font size, font style, and font color of 11–point regular black. Excel allows you to change the font characteristics in a single cell, a range of cells, the entire worksheet, or the entire workbook.

BTW
Organizing Files and Folders
You should organize and store files in folders so that you easily can find the files later. For example, if you are taking an introductory computer class called CIS 101, a good practice would be to save all Excel files in a Excel folder in a CIS 101 folder. For a discussion of folders and detailed examples of creating folders, refer to the Office and Windows chapter at the beginning of this book.

To Change a Cell Style

Excel includes the capability of changing several characteristics of a cell, such as the font, font size, and font color, all at once by assigning a predefined cell style to a cell. *Why? Using the predefined styles that Excel includes provides a consistent appearance to common portions of your worksheets, such as worksheet titles, worksheet subtitles, column headings, and total rows.* The following steps assign the Title cell style to the worksheet title in cell A1.

1

- Tap or click cell A1 to make cell A1 the active cell.

- Tap or click the Cell Styles button (HOME tab | Styles group) to display the Cell Styles gallery (Figure 1–30).

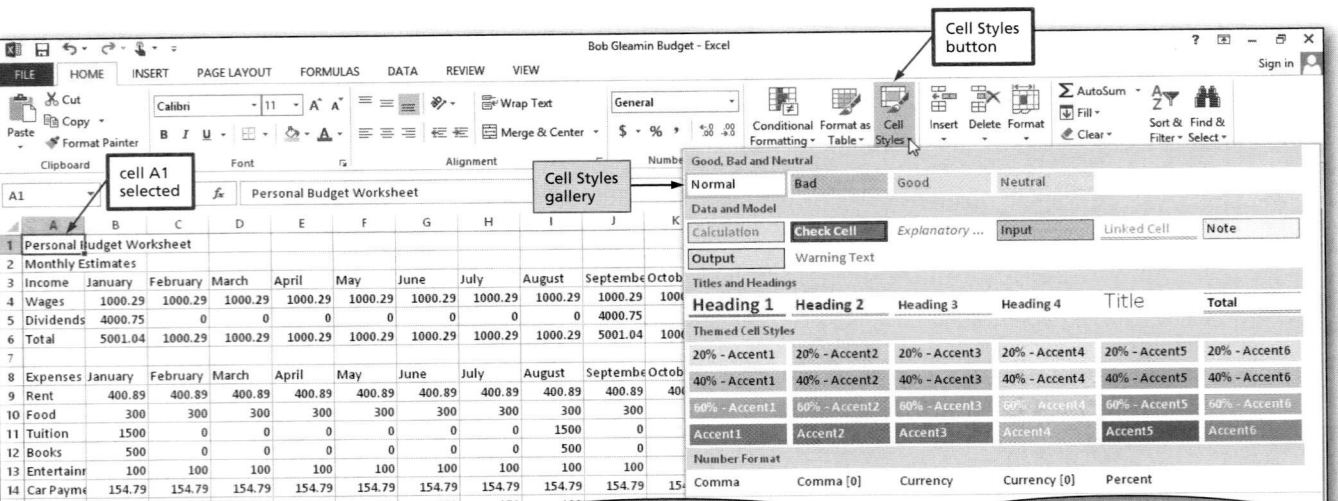

Figure 1–30

2

- If you are using a mouse, point to the Title cell style in the Titles and Headings area of the Cell Styles gallery to see a live preview of the cell style in the active cell (Figure 1–31).

Q&A Can I use live preview on a touch screen?
Live preview is not available on a touch screen.

Experiment

- If you are using a mouse, point to several other cell styles in the Cell Styles gallery to see a live preview of other cell styles in cell A1.

Figure 1–31

- Tap or click the Title cell style to apply the cell style to the active cell (Figure 1– 32).

Q&A Why do several items in the Font group on the ribbon change?

The changes to the Font box and Font Size box indicate the font changes applied to the active cell, cell A1, as a result of applying the Title cell style.

Figure 1–32

To Change the Font

1 ENTER TEXT | 2 CALCULATE SUMS & USE FORMULAS | 3 SAVE WORKBOOK | 4 FORMAT TEXT
5 INSERT CHART | 6 NAME TAB | 7 PREVIEW & PRINT WORKSHEET

Why? Different fonts often are used in a worksheet to make it more appealing to the reader and to relate or distinguish data in the worksheet. The following steps change the worksheet subtitle's font to Cambria.

- Tap or click cell A2 to make it the active cell.

- Tap or click the Font arrow (HOME tab | Font group) to display the Font gallery. If necessary, scroll to display Cambria.

- If you are using a mouse, point to Cambria in the Font gallery to see a live preview of the selected font in the active cell (Figure 1–33).

Experiment

- If you are using a mouse, point to several other fonts in the Font gallery to see a live preview of other fonts in the selected cell.

Figure 1–33

2

- Tap or click Cambria in the Font gallery to change the font of the worksheet subtitle to Cambria (Figure 1–34).

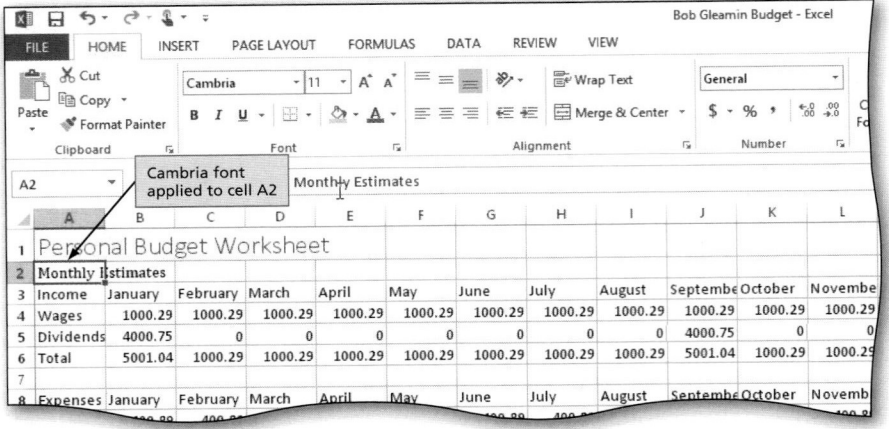

Figure 1–34

Other Ways

1. Tap or click Font Settings Dialog Box Launcher, tap or click Font tab (Format Cells dialog box), tap or click desired font in Font list, tap or click OK button

2. If you are using a mouse, click Font box arrow on mini toolbar, click desired font in Font gallery

3. Tap 'Show Context Menu' button on mini toolbar or right-click selected cell, tap or click Format Cells on shortcut menu, tap or click Font tab (Format Cells dialog box), tap or click desired font, tap or click OK button

1 ENTER TEXT | 2 CALCULATE SUMS & USE FORMULAS | 3 SAVE WORKBOOK | 4 FORMAT TEXT
5 INSERT CHART | 6 NAME TAB | 7 PREVIEW & PRINT WORKSHEET

To Bold a Cell

Bold text has a darker appearance than normal text. *Why? You bold an entry in a cell to emphasize it or make it stand out from the rest of the worksheet.* The following steps bold the worksheet title and subtitle.

1

- Tap or click cell A1 to make it active and then tap or click the Bold button (HOME tab | Font group) to change the font style of the active cell to bold (Figure 1–35).

Q&A

What if a cell already includes a bold style?
If the active cell already is bold, then Excel displays the Bold button with a transparent green background.

How do I remove the bold style from a cell?
Tapping or clicking the Bold button (HOME tab | Font group) a second time removes the bold style.

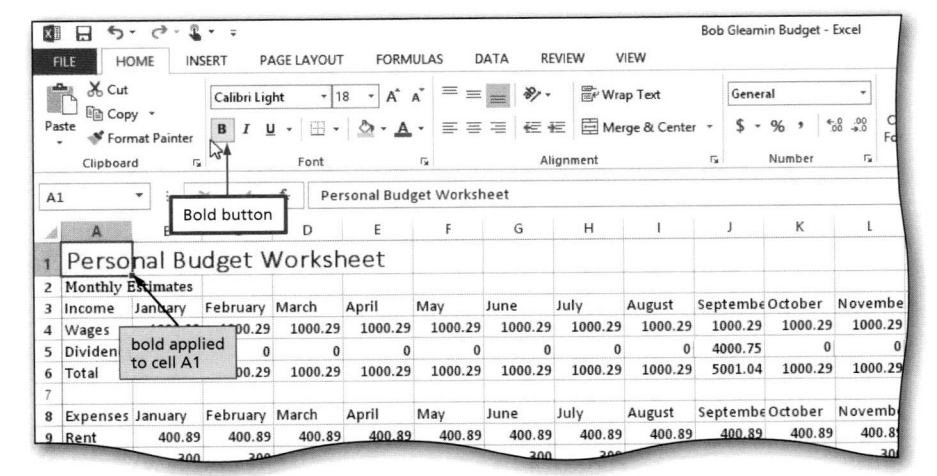

Figure 1–35

2

- Repeat Step 1 to bold cell A2.

Other Ways

1. Tap or click Font Settings Dialog Box Launcher, tap or click Font tab (Format Cells dialog box), tap or click Bold in Font style list, tap or click OK button

2. If you are using a mouse, click Bold button on mini toolbar

3. Tap 'Show Context Menu' button on mini toolbar or right-click selected cell, tap or click Format Cells on shortcut menu, tap or click Font tab (Format Cells dialog box), tap or click Bold, tap or click OK button

4. Press CTRL+B

To Increase the Font Size of a Cell Entry

Increasing the font size is the next step in formatting the worksheet subtitle. *Why? You increase the font size of a cell so that the entry stands out and is easier to read.* The following steps increase the font size of the worksheet subtitle in cell A2.

- With cell A2 selected, tap or click the Font Size arrow (HOME tab | Font group) to display the Font Size gallery.

- If you are using a mouse, point to 14 in the Font Size gallery to see a live preview of the active cell with the selected font size (Figure 1–36).

 Experiment

- If you are using a mouse, point to several other font sizes in the Font Size list to see a live preview of other font sizes in the selected cell.

Figure 1–36

- Tap or click 14 in the Font Size gallery to change the font size in the active cell (Figure 1–37).

Q&A Can I assign a font size that is not in the Font Size gallery?
Yes. An alternative to tapping or clicking a font size in the Font Size gallery is to tap or click the Font Size box (HOME tab | Font group), type the font size, and then press the ENTER key. This procedure allows you to assign a font size not available in the Font Size gallery to a selected cell entry.

Figure 1–37

Other Ways

1. Tap or click 'Increase Font Size' button (HOME tab | Font group) or 'Decrease Font Size' button (HOME tab | Font group)

2. Tap or click Font Settings Dialog Box Launcher, tap or click Font tab (Format Cells dialog box), tap or click desired size in Size list, tap or click OK button

3. Tap or click Font Size arrow on mini toolbar, tap or click desired font size in Font Size gallery

4. Tap 'Show Context Menu' button on mini toolbar or right-click selected cell, tap or click Format Cells on shortcut menu, tap or click Font tab (Format Cells dialog box), select font size in Size box, tap or click OK button

To Change the Font Color of a Cell Entry

The next step is to change the color of the font in cells A1 and A2 to blue. **Why?** *Changing the font color of cell entries can help the text stand out more.* The following steps change the font color of a cell entry.

1

- Tap or click cell A1 and then tap or click the Font Color arrow (HOME tab | Font group) to display the Font Color gallery.

- If you are using a mouse, point to 'Blue, Accent 1' (column 5, row 1) in the Theme Colors area of the Font Color gallery to see a live preview of the font color in the active cell (Figure 1–38).

🔍 **Experiment**

- If you are using a mouse, point to several other colors in the Font Color gallery to see a live preview of other font colors in the active cell.

Figure 1–38

Q&A Which colors does Excel make available in the Font Color gallery?
You can choose from more than 60 different font colors in the Font Color gallery. Your Font Color gallery may have more or fewer colors, depending on color settings of your operating system. The Theme Colors area contains colors that are included in the current workbook's theme.

2

- Tap or click 'Blue, Accent 1' (column 5, row 1) in the Font Color gallery to change the font color of the worksheet title in the active cell (Figure 1–39).

Q&A Why does the Font Color button change after I select the new font color?
When you choose a color on the Font Color gallery, Excel changes the Font Color button (HOME tab | Font group) to the chosen color. Thus, to change the font color of the cell entry in another cell to the same color, you need only to select the cell and then tap or click the Font Color button (HOME tab | Font group).

Figure 1–39

3

- Repeat Steps 1 and 2 to apply Blue, Accent 1 (column 5, row 1) to cell A2.

Other Ways

1. Tap or click Font Settings Dialog Box Launcher, tap or click Font tab (Format Cells dialog box), tap or click desired color in Color list, tap or click OK button

2. Tap or click Font Color arrow on mini toolbar, tap or click desired font color in the Font Color gallery

3. Tap 'Show Context Menu' button on mini toolbar or right-click selected cell, tap or click Format Cells on shortcut menu, tap or click Font tab (Format Cells dialog box), select color in Font Color gallery, tap or click OK button

To Center Cell Entries across Columns by Merging Cells

The final step in formatting the worksheet title and subtitle is to center them across columns A through N. **Why?** *Centering a title across the columns used in the body of the worksheet improves the worksheet's appearance.* To do this, the 14 cells in the range A1:N1 are combined, or merged, into a single cell that is the width of the columns in the body of the worksheet. The 14 cells in the range A2:N2 are merged in a similar manner. **Merging** cells involves creating a single cell by combining two or more selected cells. The following steps center the worksheet title and subtitle across columns by merging cells.

①

- Select cell A1 and then if you are using a touch screen, drag the selection handles as necessary to cell N1; if you are using a mouse, drag to cell N1 to highlight the range to be merged and centered (Figure 1–40).

Q&A What if a cell in the range B1:N1 contains data?
For the 'Merge & Center' button (HOME tab | Alignment group) to work properly, all the cells except the leftmost cell in the selected range must be empty.

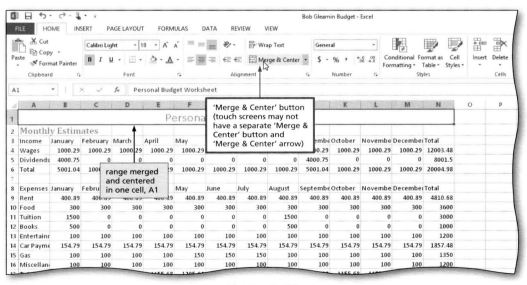

Figure 1–40

②

- Tap or click the 'Merge & Center' button (HOME tab | Alignment group) to merge cells A1 through N1 and center the contents of the leftmost cell across the selected columns (Figure 1–41).

Q&A What if my screen displays a Merge & Center menu?
If you are using a touch screen, you may not have a separate 'Merge & Center' button and 'Merge & Center' arrow. In this case, select the desired option on the Merge & Center menu.

Figure 1–41

What happened to cells B1 through N1?
After the merge, cells B1 through N1 no longer exist. The new cell A1 now extends across columns A through N.

3

- Repeat Steps 1 and 2 to merge and center the worksheet subtitle across cells A2 through N2 (Figure 1–42).

Q&A

Are cells B1 through N1 and B2 through N2 lost forever?

No. The opposite of merging cells is **splitting** a merged cell.

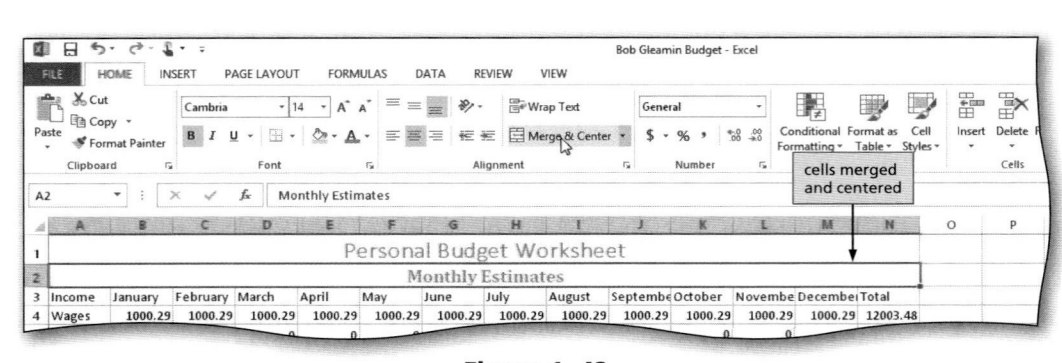

Figure 1–42

After you have merged multiple cells to create one merged cell, you can unmerge, or split, the merged cell to display the original cells on the worksheet. You split a merged cell by selecting it and tapping or clicking the 'Merge & Center' button. For example, if you tap or click the 'Merge & Center' button a second time in Step 2, it will split the merged cell A1 into cells A1, B1, C1, D1, E1, F1, G1, H1, I1, J1, K1, L1, M1, and N1.

Other Ways

1. If you are using a mouse, right-click selection, click 'Merge & Center' button on mini toolbar

2. Tap 'Show Context Menu' button on mini toolbar or right-click selected cell, tap or click Format Cells on shortcut menu, tap or click Alignment tab (Format Cells dialog box), select 'Center Across Selection' in Horizontal list, tap or click OK button

To Format Rows Using Cell Styles

1 ENTER TEXT | 2 CALCULATE SUMS & USE FORMULAS | 3 SAVE WORKBOOK | 4 FORMAT TEXT
5 INSERT CHART | 6 NAME TAB | 7 PREVIEW & PRINT WORKSHEET

The next step to format the worksheet is to format the rows. *Why? Row titles and the total row should be formatted so that anyone who views the worksheet can distinguish quickly the column titles and total row from the data in the body of the worksheet. Data rows can be formatted to make them easier to read, as well.* The following steps format the column titles and total row using cell styles in the default worksheet theme.

- Tap or click cell A3 and then drag to cell N3 to select the range.

- Tap or click the Cell Styles button (HOME tab | Styles group) to display the Cell Styles gallery.

- If you are using a mouse, point to the Heading 1 cell style in the Titles and Headings area of the Cell Styles gallery to see a live preview of the cell style in the selected range (Figure 1–43).

Experiment

- If you are using a mouse, point to other cell styles in the Titles and Headings area of the Cell Styles gallery to see a live preview of other cell styles in the selected range, A3:N3.

Figure 1–43

- Tap or click the Heading 1 cell style to apply the cell style to the selected range.

- Tap or click the Center button (HOME tab | Alignment group) to center the column headings in the selected range.

- Tap or click cell A8 and then drag the pointer to cell N8 to select the range (Figure 1–44).

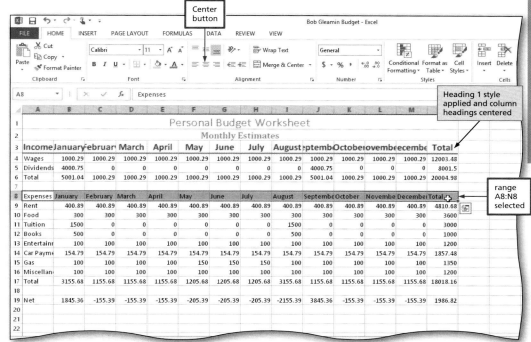

Figure 1–44

❸

- Use Steps 1 and 2 to center the column headings and format the range A8:N8 with the Heading 1 cell style format (Figure 1–45).

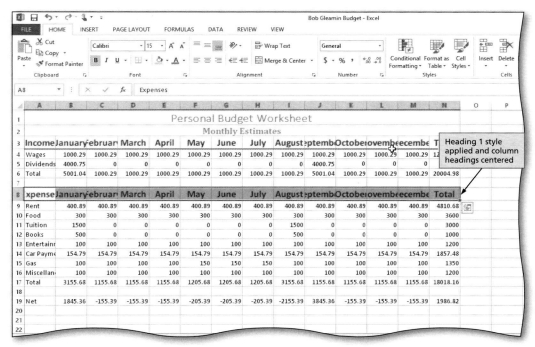

Figure 1–45

4

- Use Steps 1 and 2 to format the range A6:N6 and A17:N17 with the Total cell style format.

- Use Steps 1 and 2 to format the range A19:N19 with the Accent 1 cell style format.

- Use Steps 1 and 2 to format the range A4:N4, A9:N9, A11:N11, A13:N13, A15:N15 with the 20% - Accent 1 cell style format.

- Use Steps 1 and 2 to format the range A5:N5, A10:N10, A12:N12, A14:N14, A16:N16 with the 40% - Accent 1 cell style format (Figure 1–46).

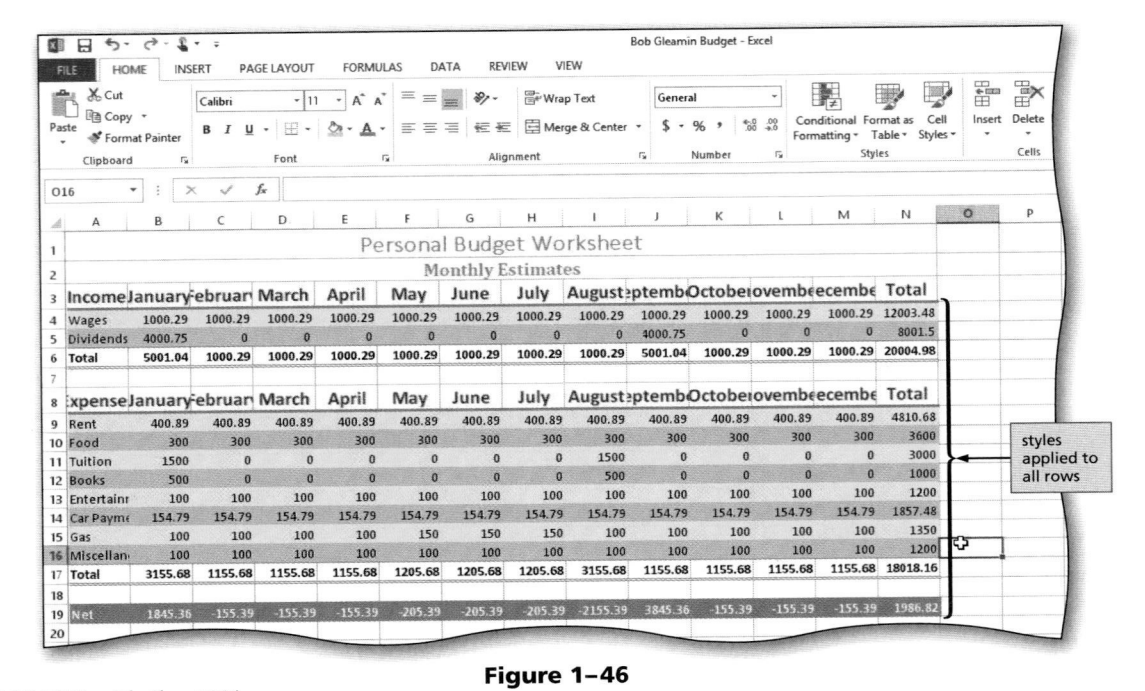

Figure 1–46

To Format Numbers in the Worksheet

1 ENTER TEXT | 2 CALCULATE SUMS & USE FORMULAS | 3 SAVE WORKBOOK | 4 FORMAT TEXT
5 INSERT CHART | 6 NAME TAB | 7 PREVIEW & PRINT WORKSHEET

Why? As previously noted, the numbers in the first row and last row of each section should be formatted to use a dollar-and-cents format, while the others use a comma format. Excel allows you to format numbers in a variety of ways, and these methods are discussed in other chapters in this book. The following steps use buttons on the ribbon to format the numbers in the worksheet.

1

- Select the range B4:N4.

- Tap or click the 'Accounting Number Format' button (HOME tab | Number group) to apply the accounting number format to the cells in the selected range.

Q&A What if my screen displays an Accounting Number Format menu? If you are using a touch screen, you may not have a separate 'Accounting Number Format' button and 'Accounting Number Format' arrow. In this case, select the desired option on the Accounting Number Format menu.

- Select the range B5:N5 (Figure 1– 47).

Figure 1–47

Q&A What effect does the accounting number format have on the selected cells?
The accounting number format causes the cells to be displayed with two decimal places so that decimal places in cells below the selected cells align vertically. Cell widths are adjusted automatically to accommodate the new formatting.

2

- Tap or click the Comma Style button (HOME tab | Number group) to apply the comma style format to the selected range.

- Select the range B6:N6 to make it the active range (Figure 1–48).

Q&A | What effect does the comma style format have on the selected cells?

The comma style format causes the cells to be displayed with two decimal places and commas as thousands separators.

Figure 1–48

3

- Tap or click the 'Accounting Number Format' button (HOME tab | Number group) to apply the accounting number format to the cells in the selected range.

- Select cell A7.

4

- Use Steps 1–3 to format the ranges B9:N9, B17:N17, and B19:N19 with the accounting number format.

- Use Steps 1–3 to format the range B10:N16 with the comma style format (Figure 1–49).

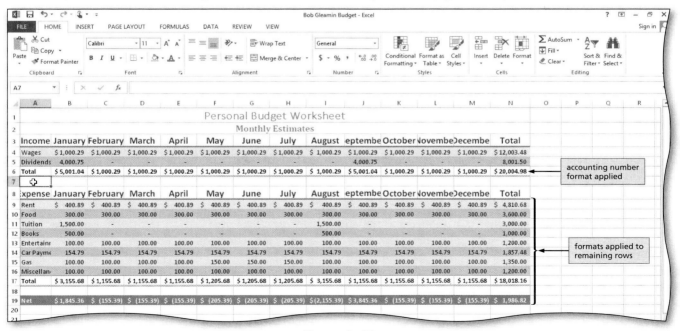

Figure 1–49

Other Ways

1. Tap or click 'Accounting Number Format' or Comma Style button on mini toolbar

2. Tap 'Show Context Menu' button on mini toolbar or right-click selected cell, tap or click Format Cells on shortcut menu, tap or click Number tab (Format Cells dialog box), select Accounting in Category list or select Number and tap or click 'Use 1000 Separator', tap or click OK button

To Adjust the Column Width

The last step in formatting the worksheet is to adjust the width of the columns so that all the titles can be seen clearly. *Why? To make a worksheet easy to read, the column widths should be adjusted appropriately.* Excel includes several methods for adjusting cell widths and row heights, and these methods are discussed later in this book. The following steps adjust the width of columns A through N so that the contents of the columns are seen clearly.

①

- If you are using a mouse, point to the boundary on the right side of the column A heading above row 1 to change the pointer to a split double arrow (Figure 1–50).

Figure 1–50

②

- If you are using a mouse, double-click the boundary to adjust the width of the column to the width of the largest item in the column (Figure 1–51).

Q&A

What if none of the items in column A extends through the entire width of the column?
If all of the items in column A were shorter in length than the width of the column when you double-tap or double-click the right side of the column A heading, then Excel still would adjust the column width to the largest item in the column. That is, Excel would reduce the width of the column to the largest item.

Figure 1–51

3

- Repeat Steps 1 and 2 to adjust the column width of columns B through N (Figure 1–52).

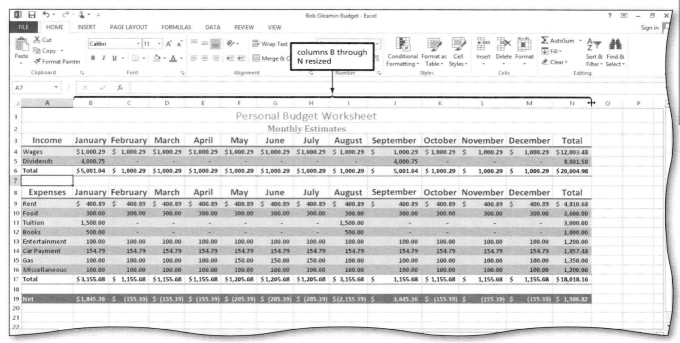

Figure 1–52

To Use the Name Box to Select a Cell

1 ENTER TEXT | 2 CALCULATE TOTALS | 3 SAVE WORKBOOK | **4 FORMAT TEXT**
5 INSERT CHART | 6 NAME TAB | 7 PREVIEW & PRINT WORKSHEET

The next step is to chart the monthly expenses. To create the chart, you first must select the cell in the upper-left corner of the range to chart (cell A3). Rather than tapping or clicking cell A3 to select it, the next section describes how to use the Name box to select the cell. The Name box is located on the left side of the formula bar. **Why?** *To select any cell, tap or click the Name box and enter the cell reference of the cell you want to select.* The following steps select cell A3 using the Name box.

- Tap or click the Name box in the formula bar and then type **a3** as the cell you want to select (Figure 1–53).

Q&A

Why is cell A7 still selected?
The current cell will remain selected until you press the ENTER key.

Figure 1–53

2

- Press the ENTER key to change the active cell in the Name box and make cell A3 the active cell (Figure 1–54).

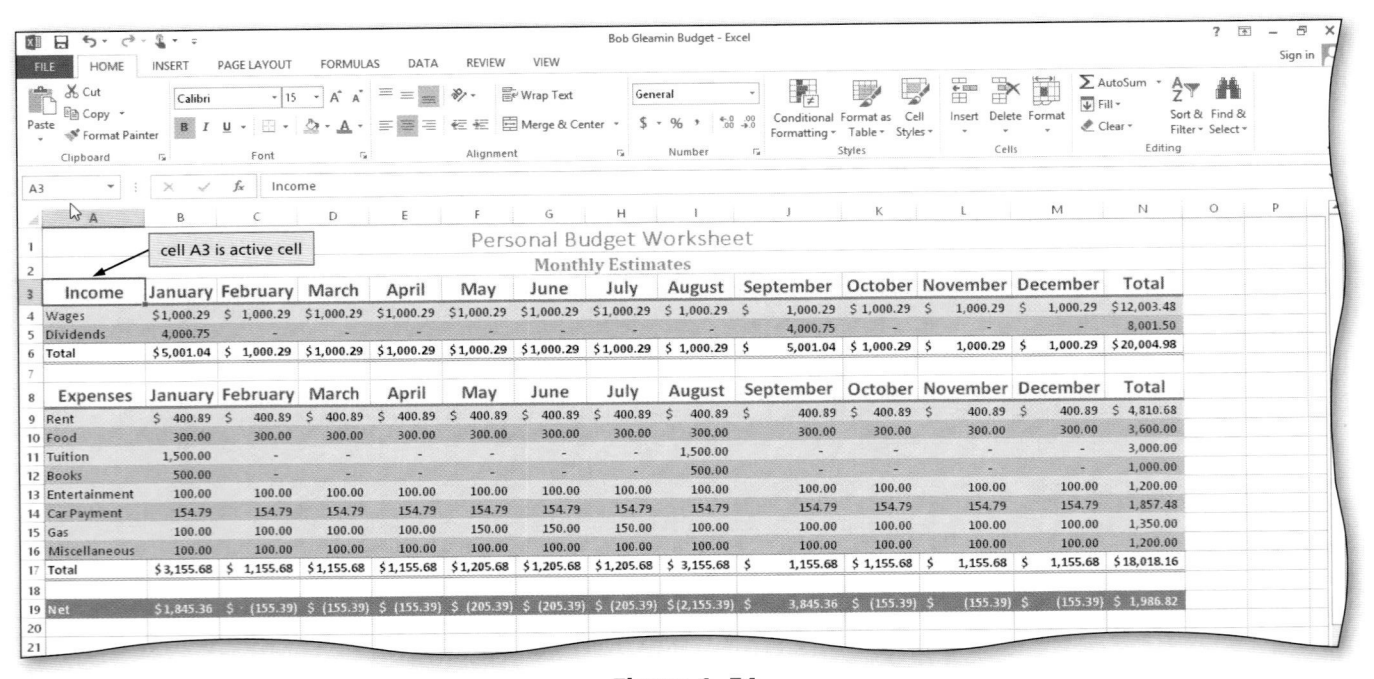

Figure 1–54

Other Ways to Select Cells

As you will see in later chapters, in addition to using the Name box to select any cell in a worksheet, you also can use it to assign names to a cell or range of cells. Excel supports several additional ways to select a cell, as summarized in Table 1–3.

Table 1–3 Selecting Cells in Excel

Key, Box, or Command	Function
ALT+PAGE DOWN	Selects the cell one worksheet window to the right and moves the worksheet window accordingly.
ALT+PAGE UP	Selects the cell one worksheet window to the left and moves the worksheet window accordingly.
ARROW	Selects the adjacent cell in the direction of the arrow on the key.
CTRL+ARROW	Selects the border cell of the worksheet in combination with the arrow keys and moves the worksheet window accordingly. For example, to select the rightmost cell in the row that contains the active cell, press CTRL+RIGHT ARROW. You also can press the END key, release it, and then press the appropriate arrow key to accomplish the same task.
CTRL+HOME	Selects cell A1 or the cell one column and one row below and to the right of frozen titles and moves the worksheet window accordingly.
Find command on Find and Select menu or SHIFT+F5	Finds and selects a cell that contains specific contents that you enter in the Find and Replace dialog box. If necessary, Excel moves the worksheet window to display the cell. You also can press CTRL+F to display the Find dialog box.
Go To command on Find and Select menu or F5	Selects the cell that corresponds to the cell reference you enter in the Go To dialog box and moves the worksheet window accordingly. You also can press CTRL+G to display the Go To dialog box.
HOME	Selects the cell at the beginning of the row that contains the active cell and moves the worksheet window accordingly.
Name box	Selects the cell in the workbook that corresponds to the cell reference you enter in the Name box.
PAGE DOWN	Selects the cell down one worksheet window from the active cell and moves the worksheet window accordingly.
PAGE UP	Selects the cell up one worksheet window from the active cell and moves the worksheet window accordingly.

Break Point: If you wish to take a break, this is a good place to do so. Be sure to save the Bob Gleamin Budget file again and then you can exit Excel. To resume at a later time, run Excel, open the file called Bob Gleamin Budget, and continue following the steps from this location forward.

Adding a Pie Chart to the Worksheet

Excel includes 10 chart types from which you can choose, including column, line, pie, bar, area, X Y (scatter), stock, surface, bubble, and radar. The type of chart you choose depends on the type of data that you have, how much data you have, and the message you want to convey.

A line chart often is used to illustrate changes in data over time. Pie charts show the contribution of each piece of data to the whole, or total, of the data. Area charts, like line charts, illustrate changes over time, but often are used to compare more than one set of data, and the area below the lines is filled in with a different color for each set of data. An X Y (scatter) chart is used much like a line chart, but each piece of data is represented by a dot and is not connected with a line. A stock chart provides a number of methods commonly used in the financial industry to show stock market data. A surface chart compares data from three columns and/or rows in a three-dimensional manner. A bubble chart is much like an X Y (scatter) chart, but a third set of data results indicates how large each individual dot, or bubble, is on the chart. A radar chart can compare several sets of data in a manner that resembles a radar screen, with each set of data represented by a different color. A column or cylinder chart is a good way to compare values side by side. A pie chart can go even further in comparing values across categories by showing each pie piece in comparison with the others.

As outlined in the requirements document in Figure 1–2 on page EX 3, the worksheet should include a pie chart to represent graphically the yearly expenses totals for the expenses budget items for Bob Gleamin's budget. The pie chart shown in Figure 1–55 is on its own sheet in the workbook. The pie chart resides on a separate sheet, called a **chart sheet**, which contains only the chart.

BTW

Excel Help
At any time while using Excel, you can find answers to questions and display information about various topics through Excel Help. Used properly, this form of assistance can increase your productivity and reduce your frustrations by minimizing the time you spend learning how to use Excel. For instruction about Excel Help and exercises that will help you gain confidence in using it, read the Office and Windows chapter at the beginning of this book.

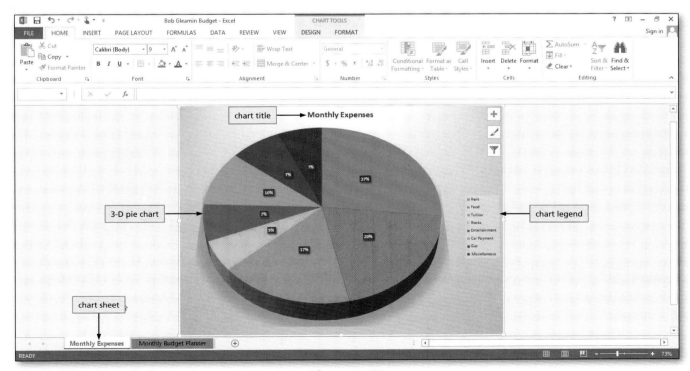

Figure 1–55

In this worksheet, the ranges to chart are the nonadjacent ranges A9:A16 (category names) and N9:N16 (yearly expense totals). The expense titles in the range A9:A16 will identify the slices of the pie chart; these entries are called **category names**. The range N9:N16 contains the data that determines the size of the slices in the pie; these entries are called the **data series**. Because eight budget items are being charted, the 3-D pie chart contains eight slices.

1 ENTER TEXT | 2 CALCULATE SUMS & USE FORMULAS | 3 SAVE WORKBOOK | 4 FORMAT TEXT
5 INSERT CHART | 6 NAME TAB | 7 PREVIEW & PRINT WORKSHEET

To Add a 3-D Pie Chart

Why? *When you want to see how each part relates to the whole, you use a pie chart.* The following steps draw the 3-D pie chart.

1

- Select the range A9:A16 to identify the range of the category names for the 3-D pie chart.

- While holding down the CTRL key, select the range N9:N16.

- Tap or click INSERT on the ribbon to display the INSERT tab.

- Tap or click the 'Insert Pie or Doughnut Chart' button (INSERT tab | Charts group) to display the Insert Pie or Doughnut Chart gallery (Figure 1–56).

◄ Why does the ribbon display extra tabs?
Q&A Excel displays additional tabs that provide options for use when you are working with certain objects, such as charts.

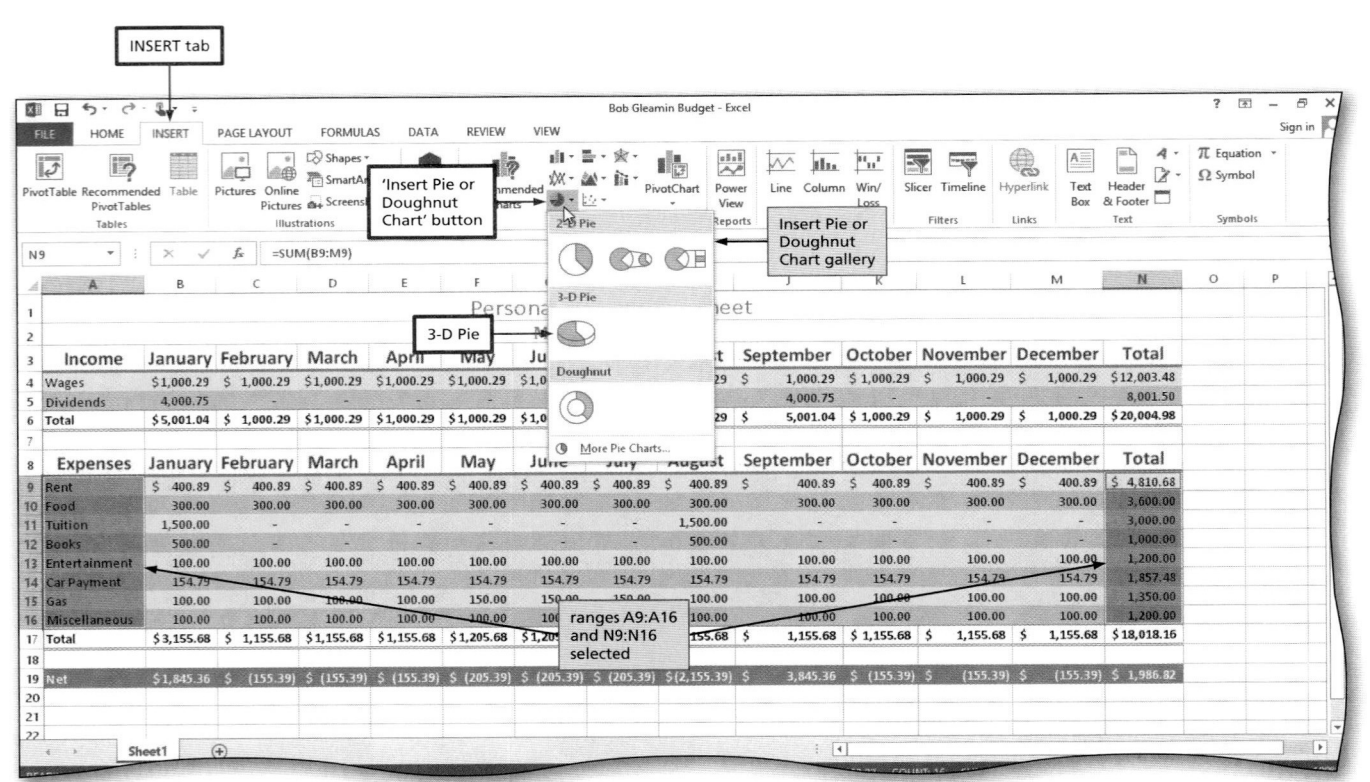

Figure 1–56

2

• Tap or click 3-D Pie in the Insert Pie or Doughnut Chart gallery to insert the chart in the worksheet (Figure 1–57).

Figure 1–57

3

• Tap or click the chart title to select it.

• Type **Monthly Expenses** and then press the ENTER key to change the title.

• Deselect the chart title (Figure 1–58).

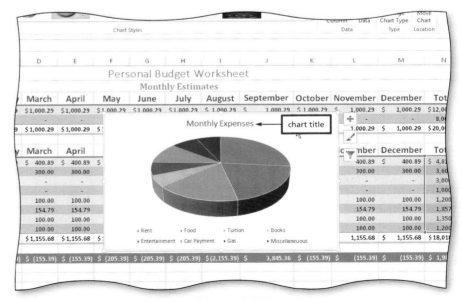

Figure 1–58

To Apply a Style to a Chart

Why? *If you want to make it clear how much of the pie each slice represents, you can use a style to include a percentage.* The following steps apply Style 3 to the 3-D pie chart.

1

- Tap or click the Chart Styles button to display the Chart Styles gallery (Figure 1–59).

Figure 1–59

- Tap or click Style 3 in the Chart Styles gallery to change the chart style to Style 3 (Figure 1– 60).

- Tap or click the Chart Styles button to close the Chart Styles gallery.

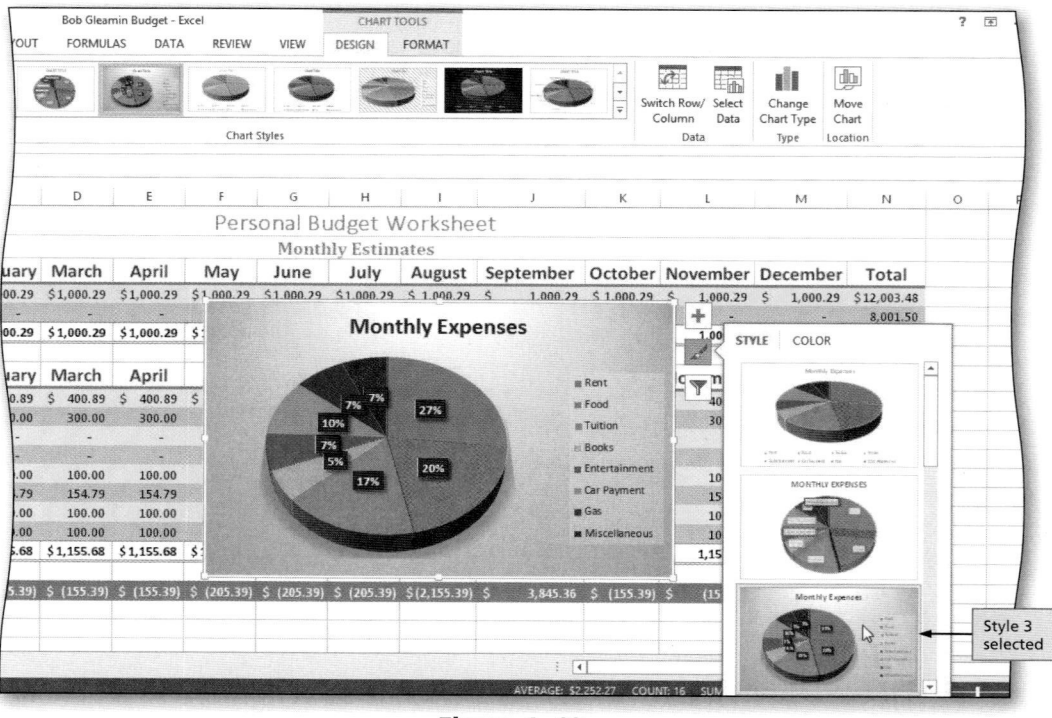

Figure 1–60

Changing the Sheet Tab Names

The sheet tabs at the bottom of the window allow you to view any worksheet in the workbook. You tap or click the sheet tab of the worksheet you want to view in the Excel window. By default, Excel presets the names of the worksheets to Sheet1, Sheet2, and so on. The worksheet names become increasingly important as you move toward more sophisticated workbooks, especially workbooks in which you reference cells between worksheets.

To Move a Chart to a New Sheet

1 ENTER TEXT | 2 CALCULATE SUMS & USE FORMULAS | 3 SAVE WORKBOOK | 4 FORMAT TEXT
5 INSERT CHART | 6 NAME TAB | **7 PREVIEW & PRINT WORKSHEET**

Why? *By moving a chart to its own sheet, the size will increase, which allows better viewing.* The following steps move the 3-D pie chart to a chart sheet named, Monthly Expenses.

- Tap or click the Move Chart button (CHART TOOLS DESIGN tab | Location group) to display the Move Chart dialog box (Figure 1–61).

Figure 1–61

2

- Tap or click New sheet to select it (Move Chart dialog box) and then type **Monthly Expenses** in the New sheet text box to enter a sheet tab name for the worksheet that will contain the chart.

- Tap or click the OK button (Move Chart dialog box) to move the chart to a new chart sheet with a new sheet tab name, Monthly Expenses in this case (Figure 1–62).

Figure 1–62

To Change the Worksheet Tab Name

1 ENTER TEXT | 2 CALCULATE SUMS & USE FORMULAS | 3 SAVE WORKBOOK | 4 FORMAT TEXT
5 INSERT CHART | 6 NAME TAB | 7 PREVIEW & PRINT WORKSHEET

You decide to change the name of the Sheet1 worksheet tab to Monthly Budget Planner. *Why? Use simple, meaningful names for each worksheet tab. Worksheet tab names often match the worksheet title. If a worksheet includes multiple titles in multiple sections of the worksheet, use a sheet tab name that encompasses the meaning of all of the sections.*

The following steps rename the worksheet tab.

1

- Double-tap or double-click the sheet tab labeled Sheet1 in the lower-left corner of the window.

- Type **Monthly Budget Planner** as the worksheet tab name and then press the ENTER key to display the new worksheet tab name on the sheet tab (Figure 1–63).

Q&A What is the maximum length for a sheet tab name?
Worksheet tab names can be up to 31 characters (including spaces) in length. Longer worksheet names, however, mean that fewer sheet tabs will show. If you have multiple sheets, you will be able to scroll through sheet tabs.

Figure 1–63

2

- Press and hold or right-click the sheet tab labeled, Monthly Budget Planner, in the lower-left corner of the window to display a shortcut menu.

- Tap or point to Tab Color on the shortcut menu to display the Tab Color gallery (Figure 1–64).

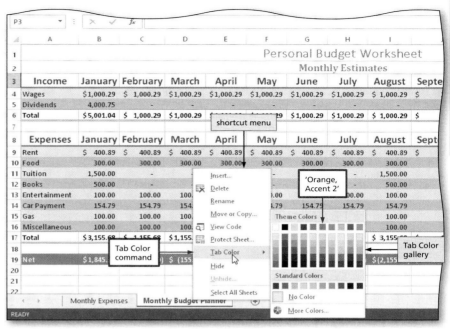

Figure 1–64

3

- Tap or click the color of your shirt in the Theme Colors area to change the color of the tab (Figure 1–65).

- If necessary, tap or click HOME on the ribbon to display the HOME tab.

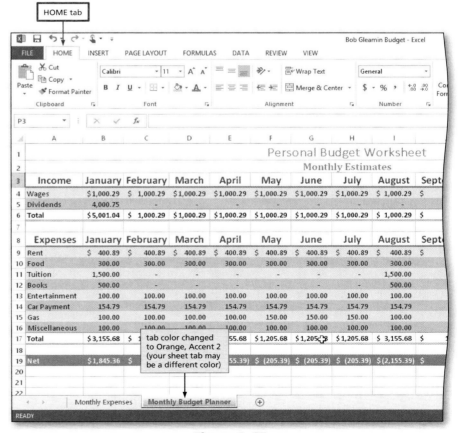

Figure 1–65

Document Properties

Excel helps you organize and identify your files by using **document properties**, which are the details about a file such as the project author, title, and subject. For example, a class name or workbook topic can describe the file's purpose or content.

Why would you want to assign document properties to a workbook?

Document properties are valuable for a variety of reasons:

• Users can save time locating a particular file because they can view a file's document properties without opening the workbook.

• By creating consistent properties for files having similar content, users can better organize their workbooks.

• Some organizations require Excel users to add document properties so that other employees can view details about these files.

The more common document properties are standard and automatically updated properties. **Standard properties** are associated with all Microsoft Office files and include author, title, and subject. **Automatically updated properties** include file system properties, such as the date you create or change a file, and statistics, such as the file size.

TO CHANGE DOCUMENT PROPERTIES

To change document properties, you would follow these steps.

1. Tap or click FILE on the ribbon to open the Backstage view and then, if necessary, tap or click the Info tab in the Backstage view to display the Info gallery.

2. If the property you wish to change is displayed in the Properties list in the right pane of the Info gallery, try to tap or click to the right of the property. If a text box appears to the right of the property, type the text for the property in the text box and then tap or click the Back button in the upper-left corner of the Backstage view to return to the Excel window. Skip the remaining steps.

3. If the property you wish to change is not displayed in the Properties list in the right pane of the Info gallery or you cannot change it in the Info gallery, tap or click the Properties button in the right pane to display the Properties menu, and then tap or click 'Show Document Panel' on the Properties menu to close the Backstage view and display the Document Information Panel in the Excel workbook window.

Q&A

Why are some of the document properties in my Document Information Panel already filled in?

The person who installed Office 2013 on your computer or network may have set or customized the properties.

4. Type the desired text in the appropriate property text boxes.

What if the property I want to change is not displayed in the Document Information Panel?

Tap or click the Document Properties button in the Document Information Panel and then tap or click Advanced Properties on the menu to display the Properties dialog box. If necessary, tap or click the Summary tab (Properties dialog box) to display the Summary sheet, fill in the appropriate text boxes, and then tap or click the OK button.

5. Tap or click the 'Close the Document Information Panel' button at the right edge of the Document Information Panel so that the panel no longer appears in the Excel workbook window.

To Save an Existing Workbook with the Same File Name

You have made several modifications to the workbook since you last saved it. Thus, you should save it again. The following step saves the workbook again. For an example of the step listed below, refer to the Office and Windows chapter at the beginning of this book.

 Tap or click the Save button on the Quick Access Toolbar to overwrite the previously saved file.

Printing a Worksheet

After creating a worksheet, you may want to print it. Printing a worksheet enables you to distribute the worksheet to others in a form that can be read or viewed but typically not edited. It is a good practice to save a workbook before printing a worksheet, in the event you experience difficulties printing.

BTW

Conserving Ink and Toner

If you want to conserve ink or toner, you can instruct Excel to print draft quality documents by tapping or clicking FILE on the ribbon to open the Backstage view, tapping or clicking Options in the Backstage view to display the Excel Options dialog box, tapping or clicking Advanced in the left pane (Excel Options dialog box), sliding or scrolling to the Print area in the right pane, placing a check mark in the 'Use draft quality' check box, and then tapping or clicking the OK button. Then, use the Backstage view to print the document as usual.

CONSIDER THIS

What is the best method for distributing a workbook?

The traditional method of distributing a workbook uses a printer to produce a hard copy. A **hard copy** or **printout** is information that exists on a physical medium such as paper. Hard copies can be useful for the following reasons:

• Some people prefer proofreading a hard copy of a workbook rather than viewing it on the screen to check for errors and readability.

• Hard copies can serve as a backup reference if your storage medium is lost or becomes corrupted and you need to recreate the workbook.

Instead of distributing a hard copy of a workbook, users can distribute the workbook as an electronic image that mirrors the original workbook's appearance. The electronic image of the workbook can be sent as an email attachment, posted on a website, or copied to a portable storage medium such as a USB flash drive. Two popular electronic image formats, sometimes called fixed formats, are PDF by Adobe Systems and XPS by Microsoft. In Excel, you can create electronic image files through the Save As dialog box and the Export, Share, and Print tabs in the Backstage view. Electronic images of workbooks, such as PDF and XPS, can be useful for the following reasons:

• Users can view electronic images of workbooks without the software that created the original workbook (e.g., Excel). Specifically, to view a PDF file, you use a program called Adobe Reader, which can be downloaded free from Adobe's website. Similarly, to view an XPS file, you use a program called XPS Viewer, which is included in the latest versions of Windows and Internet Explorer.

• Sending electronic workbooks saves paper and printer supplies. Society encourages users to contribute to **green computing**, which involves reducing the electricity consumed and environmental waste generated when using computers, mobile devices, and related technologies.

To Preview and Print a Worksheet in Landscape Orientation

Pages printed in portrait orientation have the short (8½") edge at the top of the printout; the printed page is taller than it is wide. Landscape orientation prints the long (11") edge at the top of the paper; the printed page is wider than it is tall. With the completed workbook saved, you may want to print it. *Why? Because the worksheet is included in a report, you will print a hard copy on a printer.* The following steps print a hard copy of the contents of the worksheet.

1

- Tap or click FILE on the ribbon to open the Backstage view.

- Tap or click the Print tab in the Backstage view to display the Print gallery (Figure 1–66).

Q&A How can I print multiple copies of my worksheet?
Increase the number in the Copies box in the Print gallery.

What if I decide not to print the worksheet at this time?
Tap or click the Back button in the upper-left corner of the Backstage view to return to the workbook window.

Figure 1–66

2

- Verify that the printer listed on the Printer Status button will print a hard copy of the workbook. If necessary, tap or click the Printer Status button to display a list of available printer options and then tap or click the desired printer to change the currently selected printer.

3

- Tap or click the Portrait Orientation button in the Settings area and then select Landscape Orientation to change the orientation of the page to landscape.

- Tap or click the No Scaling button and then select 'Fit Sheet on One Page' to print the entire worksheet on one page (Figure 1–67).

Figure 1–67

4

- Tap or click the Print button in the Print gallery to print the worksheet in landscape orientation on the currently selected printer.

- When the printer stops, retrieve the hard copy (Figure 1–68).

Q&A Do I have to wait until my worksheet is complete to print it?
No, you can follow these steps to print a document at any time while you are creating it.

Personal Budget Worksheet
Monthly Estimates

Income	January	February	March	April	May	June	July	August	September	October	November	December	Total
Wages	$1,000.29	$ 1,000.29	$1,000.29	$1,000.29	$1,000.29	$1,000.29	$1,000.29	$ 1,000.29	$ 1,000.29	$1,000.29	$ 1,000.29	$ 1,000.29	$12,003.48
Dividends	4,000.75	-	-	-	-	-	-	-	4,000.75	-	-	-	8,001.50
Total	**$5,001.04**	**$ 1,000.29**	**$1,000.29**	**$1,000.29**	**$1,000.29**	**$1,000.29**	**$1,000.29**	**$ 1,000.29**	**$ 5,001.04**	**$1,000.29**	**$ 1,000.29**	**$ 1,000.29**	**$ 20,004.98**

Expenses	January	February	March	April	May	June	July	August	September	October	November	December	Total
Rent	$ 400.89	$ 400.89	$ 400.89	$ 400.89	$ 400.89	$ 400.89	$ 400.89	$ 400.89	$ 400.89	$ 400.89	$ 400.89	$ 400.89	$ 4,810.68
Food	300.00	300.00	300.00	300.00	300.00	300.00	300.00	300.00	300.00	300.00	300.00	300.00	3,600.00
Tuition	1,500.00	-	-	-	-	-	-	1,500.00	-	-	-	-	3,000.00
Books	500.00	-	-	-	-	-	-	500.00	-	-	-	-	1,000.00
Entertainment	100.00	100.00	100.00	100.00	100.00	100.00	100.00	100.00	100.00	100.00	100.00	100.00	1,200.00
Car Payment	154.79	154.79	154.79	154.79	154.79	154.79	154.79	154.79	154.79	154.79	154.79	154.79	1,857.48
Gas	100.00	100.00	100.00	100.00	150.00	150.00	150.00	100.00	100.00	100.00	100.00	100.00	1,350.00
Miscellaneous	100.00	100.00	100.00	100.00	100.00	100.00	100.00	100.00	100.00	100.00	100.00	100.00	1,200.00
Total	**$3,155.68**	**$ 1,155.68**	**$1,155.68**	**$1,155.68**	**$1,205.68**	**$1,205.68**	**$1,205.68**	**$ 3,155.68**	**$ 1,155.68**	**$1,155.68**	**$ 1,155.68**	**$ 1,155.68**	**$ 18,018.16**

| Net | $1,845.36 | $ (155.39) | $ (155.39) | $ (155.39) | $ (205.39) | $ (205.39) | $ (205.39) | $(2,155.39) | $ 3,845.36 | $ (155.39) | $ (155.39) | $ (155.39) | $ 1,986.82 |

Figure 1–68

Other Ways

1. Press CTRL+P, press ENTER

To Open a Document from Excel

Earlier in this chapter you saved your workbook using the file name, Bob Gleamin Budget. The following steps open the Bob Gleamin Budget file from the Excel folder in the CIS 101 folder. For a detailed example of the procedure summarized below, refer to the Office and Windows chapter at the beginning of this book.

1. Tap or click FILE on the ribbon to open the Backstage view and then tap or click the Open tab in the Backstage view to display the Open gallery.

2. If the file you wish to open is displayed in the Recent Workbooks list, tap or click the file name to open the file and display the opened workbook in the Excel window; then skip the remaining steps. If the file you wish to open is not displayed in the Recent Workbooks list, proceed to the next step to locate the file.

3. Tap or click Computer, SkyDrive, or another location in the left pane and then navigate to the location of the file to be opened (in this case, the Excel folder in the CIS 101 folder).

4. Tap or click Bob Gleamin Budget to select the file to be opened.

5. Tap or click the Open button (Open dialog box) to open the selected file and display the opened workbook in the Excel window.

BTW

Printing Document Properties

To print document properties, tap or click FILE on the ribbon to open the Backstage view, tap or click the Print tab in the Backstage view to display the Print gallery, tap or click the first button in the Settings area to display a list of options specifying what you can print, tap or click Document Info in the list to specify you want to print the document properties instead of the actual document, and then tap or click the Print button in the Print gallery to print the document properties on the currently selected printer.

AutoCalculate

You easily can obtain a total, an average, or other information about the numbers in a range by using the **AutoCalculate area** on the status bar. First, select the range of cells containing the numbers you want to check. Next, press and hold or right-click the AutoCalculate area to display the Customize Status Bar shortcut menu (Figure 1–69). The check marks indicate that the calculations are included in the status bar; more than one may be selected. The functions of the AutoCalculate commands on the Customize Status Bar shortcut menu are described in Table 1–4.

Table 1–4 Commonly Used Status Bar Commands	
Command	**Function**
Average	AutoCalculate area displays the average of the numbers in the selected range
Count	AutoCalculate area displays the number of nonblank cells in the selected range
Numerical Count	AutoCalculate area displays the number of cells containing numbers in the selected range
Minimum	AutoCalculate area displays the lowest value in the selected range
Maximum	AutoCalculate area displays the highest value in the selected range
Sum	AutoCalculate area displays the sum of the numbers in the selected range

To Use the AutoCalculate Area to Determine a Maximum

1 ENTER TEXT | 2 CALCULATE SUMS & USE FORMULAS | 3 SAVE WORKBOOK | 4 FORMAT TEXT
5 INSERT CHART | 6 NAME TAB | 7 PREVIEW & PRINT WORKSHEET

The following steps display the largest total for the months in the budget. *Why? Sometimes, you want to see a quick analysis, which can be shown in the AutoCalculate area on the status bar.*

1

- Select the range B19:M19. Press and hold or right-click the status bar to display the Customize Status Bar shortcut menu (Figure 1–69).

Q&A What is displayed on the Customize Status Bar shortcut menu?

This shortcut menu includes several commands that allow you to control the items displayed on the Customize Status Bar shortcut menu. The AutoCalculate area includes six commands as well as the result of the associated calculation on the right side of the menu.

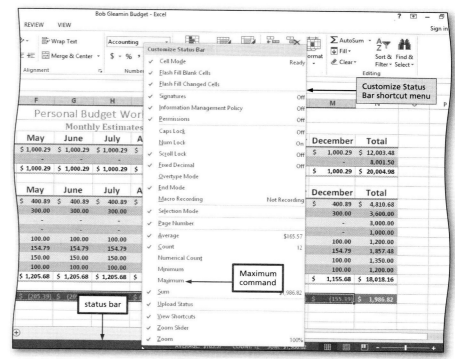

Figure 1–69

2

- Tap or click Maximum on the shortcut menu to display the Maximum value in the range B19:M19 in the AutoCalculate area of the status bar.

- Tap or click anywhere on the worksheet to cause the shortcut menu to disappear (Figure 1–70).

3

- Press and hold or right-click the AutoCalculate area and then tap or click Maximum on the shortcut menu to cause the Maximum value to no longer appear in the AutoCalculate area.

- Tap or click anywhere in the worksheet to cause the shortcut menu to disappear.

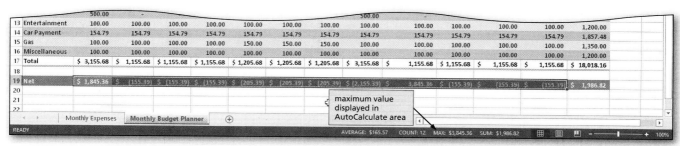

Figure 1–70

Correcting Errors

You can correct errors on a worksheet using one of several methods. The method you choose will depend on the extent of the error and whether you notice it while entering the data or after you have entered the incorrect data into the cell.

Correcting Errors while Entering Data into a Cell

If you notice an error while you are entering data into a cell, press the BACKSPACE key to erase the incorrect character(s) and then enter the correct character(s). If the error is a major one, tap or click the Cancel box in the formula bar or press the ESC key to erase the entire entry and then reenter the data from the beginning.

Correcting Errors after Entering Data into a Cell

If you find an error in the worksheet after entering the data, you can correct the error in one of two ways:

1. If the entry is short, select the cell, retype the entry correctly, and then tap or click the Enter box or press the ENTER key. The new entry will replace the old entry.
2. If the entry in the cell is long and the errors are minor, using Edit mode may be a better choice than retyping the cell entry. Use Edit mode as described below.

 a. Double-tap or double-click the cell containing the error to switch Excel to Edit mode. In **Edit mode**, Excel displays the active cell entry in the formula bar and a flashing insertion point in the active cell. With Excel in Edit mode, you can edit the contents directly in the cell — a procedure called **in-cell editing** (Figure 1–71).

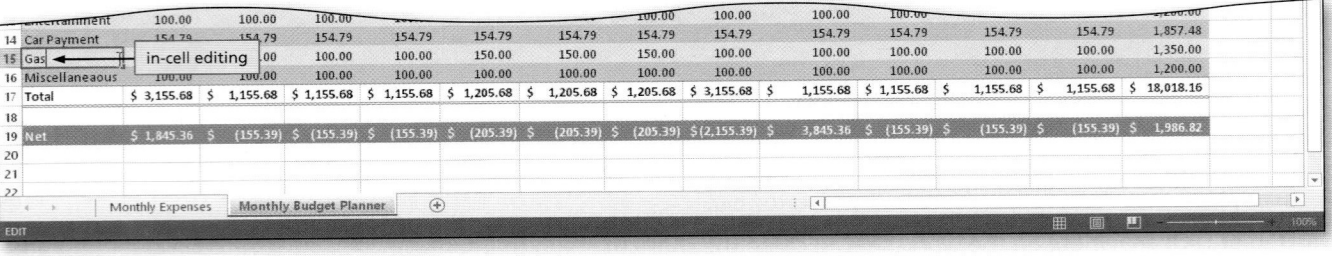

Figure 1–71

 b. Make changes using in-cell editing, as indicated below.

 (1) To insert new characters between two characters, place the insertion point between the two characters and begin typing. Excel inserts the new characters to the left of the insertion point.

 (2) To delete a character in the cell, move the insertion point to the left of the character you want to delete and then press the DELETE key, or place the insertion point to the right of the character you want to delete and then press the BACKSPACE key. You also can drag to select the character or adjacent characters you want to delete and then press the DELETE key or CTRL+X, or tap or click the Cut button (HOME tab | Clipboard group).

 (3) When you are finished editing an entry, tap or click the Enter box or press the ENTER key.

When Excel enters Edit mode, the keyboard usually is in Insert mode. In **Insert mode**, as you type a character, Excel inserts the character and moves all characters to the right of the typed character one position to the right. You can change to Overtype mode by pressing the INSERT key. In **Overtype mode**, Excel overtypes, or replaces, the character to the right of the insertion point. The INSERT key toggles the keyboard between Insert mode and Overtype mode.

While in Edit mode, you may have reason to move the insertion point to various points in the cell, select portions of the data in the cell, or switch from inserting characters to overtyping characters. Table 1–5 summarizes the more common tasks performed during in-cell editing.

Table 1–5 Summary of In-Cell Editing Tasks

	Task	Touch / Mouse	Keyboard
1.	Move the insertion point to the beginning of data in a cell.	Point to the left of the first character and tap or click.	Press HOME
2.	Move the insertion point to the end of data in a cell.	Point to the right of the last character and tap or click.	Press END
3.	Move the insertion point anywhere in a cell.	Point to the appropriate position and tap or click the character.	Press RIGHT ARROW or LEFT ARROW
4.	Highlight one or more adjacent characters.	Drag through adjacent characters.	Press SHIFT+RIGHT ARROW or SHIFT+LEFT ARROW
5.	Select all data in a cell.	Double-tap or double-click the cell with the insertion point in the cell if the data in the cell contains no spaces.	
6.	Delete selected characters.	Tap or click the Cut button (HOME tab \| Clipboard group).	Press DELETE
7.	Delete characters to the left of the insertion point.		Press BACKSPACE
8.	Delete characters to the right of the insertion point.		Press DELETE
9.	Toggle between Insert and Overtype modes.		Press INSERT

Undoing the Last Cell Entry

Excel provides the Undo button on the Quick Access Toolbar (Figure 1–72), which allows you to erase recent cell entries. Thus, if you enter incorrect data in a cell and notice it immediately, tap or click the Undo button and Excel changes the cell entry to what it was prior to the incorrect data entry.

Figure 1–72

Excel remembers the last 100 actions you have completed. Thus, you can undo up to 100 previous actions by tapping or clicking the Undo arrow to display the Undo list and then tapping or clicking the action to be undone (Figure 1–72). You can drag through several actions in the Undo list to undo all of them at once. If no actions are available for Excel to undo, then the Undo button is unavailable; its dimmed appearance indicates that it is unavailable.

The Redo button, next to the Undo button on the Quick Access Toolbar, allows you to repeat previous actions; that is, if you accidentally undo an action, you can use the Redo button to redo it.

Clearing a Cell or Range of Cells

If you enter data into the wrong cell or range of cells, you can erase, or clear, the data using one of the first four methods listed below. The fifth method clears the formatting from the selected cells. To clear a cell or range of cells, you would perform the following steps:

TO CLEAR CELL ENTRIES USING THE FILL HANDLE

1. Select the cell or range of cells and then point to the fill handle so that the pointer changes to a crosshair.
2. Drag the fill handle back into the selected cell or range until a shadow covers the cell or cells you want to erase.

TO CLEAR CELL ENTRIES USING THE SHORTCUT MENU

1. Select the cell or range of cells to be cleared.
2. Press and hold or right-click the selection.
3. Tap or click Clear Contents on the shortcut menu.

TO CLEAR CELL ENTRIES USING THE DELETE KEY

1. Select the cell or range of cells to be cleared.
2. Press the DELETE key.

TO CLEAR CELL ENTRIES AND FORMATTING USING THE CLEAR BUTTON

1. Select the cell or range of cells to be cleared.
2. Tap or click the Clear button (HOME tab | Editing group).
3. Tap or click Clear Contents on the menu.

TO CLEAR FORMATTING USING THE CELL STYLES BUTTON

1. Select the cell or range of cells from which you want to remove the formatting.
2. Tap or click the Cell Styles button (HOME tab | Styles group) and point to Normal.
3. Tap or click Normal in the Cell Styles gallery.

The Clear All command on the Clear menu is the only command that clears both the cell entry and the cell formatting. As you are clearing cell entries, always remember that you should *never press the SPACEBAR to clear a cell*. Pressing the SPACEBAR enters a blank character. A blank character is text and is different from an empty cell, even though the cell may appear empty.

Clearing the Entire Worksheet

If the required worksheet edits are extremely extensive or if the requirements drastically change, you may want to clear the entire worksheet and start over. To clear the worksheet or delete an embedded chart, you would use the following steps.

TO CLEAR THE ENTIRE WORKSHEET

1. Tap or click the Select All button on the worksheet.
2. Tap or click the Clear button (HOME tab | Editing group) and then tap or click Clear All on the menu to delete both the entries and formats.

BTW

Certification
The Microsoft Office Specialist (MOS) program provides an opportunity for you to obtain a valuable industry credential — proof that you have the Excel 2013 skills required by employers. For more information, visit the Certification resource on the Student Companion Site located on www.cengagebrain.com. For detailed instructions about accessing available resources, visit www.cengage.com/ct/studentdownload or contact your instructor for information about accessing the required files.

The Select All button selects the entire worksheet. Instead of tapping or clicking the Select All button, you can press CTRL+A. To clear an unsaved workbook, tap or click the Close Window button on the workbook's title bar or tap or click the Close button in the Backstage view. Tap or click the No button if the Microsoft Excel dialog box asks if you want to save changes. To start a new, blank workbook, tap or click the New button in the Backstage view.

To Sign Out of a Microsoft Account

If you are signed in to a Microsoft account and are using a public computer or otherwise wish to sign out of your Microsoft account, you should sign out of the account from the Account gallery in the Backstage view before exiting Excel. Signing out of the account is the safest way to make sure that nobody else can access SkyDrive files or settings stored in your Microsoft account. The following steps sign out of a Microsoft account from Excel. For a detailed example of the procedure summarized below, refer to the Office and Windows chapter at the beginning of this book.

1 If you wish to sign out of your Microsoft account, tap or click FILE on the ribbon to open the Backstage view and then tap or click the Account tab to display the Account gallery.

2 Tap or click the Sign out link, which displays the Remove Account dialog box. If a Can't remove Windows accounts dialog box appears instead of the Remove Account dialog box, click the OK button and skip the remaining steps.

Q&A Why does a Can't remove Windows accounts dialog box appear?
If you signed in to Windows using your Microsoft account, then you also must sign out from Windows, rather than signing out from within Excel. When you are finished using Windows, be sure to sign out at that time.

3 Tap or click the Yes button (Remove Account dialog box) to sign out of your Microsoft account on this computer.

Q&A Should I sign out of Windows after signing out of my Microsoft account?
When you are finished using the computer, you should sign out of your account for maximum security.

4 Tap or click the Back button in the upper-left corner of the Backstage view to return to the worksheet.

To Exit Excel

This project now is complete. The following steps exit Excel. For a detailed example of the procedure summarized below, refer to the Office and Windows chapter at the beginning of this book.

1a If you have one Excel workbook open, tap or click the Close button on the right side of the title bar to close the open workbook and exit Excel.

1b If you have multiple Excel workbooks open, press and hold or right-click the Excel app button on the taskbar and then tap or click 'Close all windows' on the shortcut menu, or press ALT+F4 to close all open workbooks and exit Excel.

Q&A Could I press and hold or repeatedly click the Close button to close all open documents and exit Excel?
Yes.

2 If a Microsoft Excel dialog box appears, tap or click the Save button to save any changes made to the workbook since the last save.

BTW
Quick Reference
For a table that lists how to complete the tasks covered in this book using touch gestures, the mouse, ribbon, shortcut menu, and keyboard, see the Quick Reference Summary at the back of this book, or visit the Quick Reference resource on the Student Companion Site located on www.cengagebrain.com. For detailed instructions about accessing available resources, visit www.cengage.com/ct/studentdownload or contact your instructor for information about accessing the required files.

Chapter Summary

In this chapter you have learned how to enter text and numbers to create a worksheet, select a range, use the Sum button, format cells, insert a chart, and preview and print a worksheet. The items listed below include all the new Excel skills you have learned in this chapter, with the tasks grouped by activity.

Clear Cells
Clear Cell Entries Using the Fill Handle (EX 52)
Clear Cell Entries Using the Shortcut Menu (EX 52)
Clear Cell Entries Using the DELETE Key (EX 52)
Clear Cell Entries and Formatting Using the Clear Button (EX 52)
Clear Cell Formatting Using the Cell Styles Button (EX 52)
Clear the Entire Worksheet (EX 52)

Display AutoCalculate Functions
Use the AutoCalculate Area to Determine a Maximum (EX 48)

Enter Data
Enter the Worksheet Titles (EX 7)
Enter Column Titles (EX 9)
Enter Row Titles (EX 11)
Enter Numbers (EX 12)

Enter Functions and Formulas
Sum a Column of Numbers (EX 14)
Copy a Cell to Adjacent Cells in a Row (EX 16)
Determine Multiple Totals at the Same Time (EX 18)
Enter a Formula Using the Keyboard (EX 20)

File Management
Change Document Properties (EX 44)

Format a Worksheet
Change a Cell Style (EX 24)
Change the Font (EX 25)
Bold a Cell (EX 26)
Increase the Font Size of a Cell Entry (EX 27)
Change the Font Color of a Cell Entry (EX 28)
Center Cell Entries across Columns by Merging Cells (EX 29)
Format Rows Using Cell Styles (EX 30)
Format Numbers in the Worksheet (EX 32)
Adjust the Column Width (EX 34)
Use the Name Box to Select a Cell (EX 35)

Insert a Chart
Add a 3-D Pie Chart (EX 38)
Apply a Style to a Chart (EX 40)

Manage Worksheets
Move a Chart to a New Sheet (EX 41)
Change the Worksheet Tab Name (EX 42)

Preview and Print Worksheets
Preview and Print a Worksheet in Landscape Orientation (EX 46)

CONSIDER THIS

What decisions will you need to make when creating workbooks and charts in the future?

1. Determine the workbook structure.

 a) Determine the data you will need for your workbook.

 b) Sketch a layout of your data and your chart.

2. Create the worksheet.

 a) Enter titles, subtitles, and headings.

 b) Enter data, functions, and formulas.

3. Format the worksheet.

 a) Format the titles, subtitles, and headings using styles.

 b) Format the totals.

 c) Format the numbers.

 d) Format the text.

4. Create the chart.

 a) Determine the type of chart to use.

 b) Determine the chart title and data.

 c) Format the chart.

How should you submit solutions to questions in the assignments identified with a ✵ symbol?
Every assignment in this book contains one or more questions identified with a ✵ symbol. These questions require you to think beyond the assigned file. Present your solutions to the questions in the format required by your instructor. Possible formats may include one or more of these options: write the answer; create a document that contains the answer; present your answer to the class; discuss your answer in a group; record the answer as audio or video using a webcam, smartphone, or portable media player; or post answers on a blog, wiki, or website.

Apply Your Knowledge

Reinforce the skills and apply the concepts you learned in this chapter.

Changing the Values in a Worksheet

Note: To complete this assignment, you will be required to use the Data Files for Students. Visit www.cengage.com/ct/studentdownload for detailed instructions or contact your instructor for information about accessing the required files.

Instructions: Run Excel. Open the workbook Apply 1–1 Treagle Market (Figure 1–73a on the next page).

1. Make the changes to the worksheet described in Table 1–6 so that the worksheet appears as shown in Figure 1–73b on the next page. As you edit the values in the cells containing numeric data, watch the totals in row 8, the totals in column G, and the chart change.

2. Change the worksheet title in cell A1 to the Title cell style and then merge and center it across columns A through G. Use buttons in the Font group on the HOME tab on the ribbon to change the worksheet subtitle in cell A2 to 14-point font and then center it across columns A through G. Use the Aqua, Accent 5 color (column 9, row 1 in the Font Color gallery) for the aqua font color.

3. Apply the worksheet name, Yearly Analysis, to the sheet tab and apply the Aqua, Accent 5 theme color to the sheet tab.

4. Move the chart to a new sheet called Sales Analysis Chart. Apply the Style 2 chart style to the chart (Figure 1–73c on the next page). Change the chart title to SALES ANALYSIS.

5. Replace Treagle in cell A1 with your last name. Save the workbook using the file name, Apply 1–1 Treagle Market Sales Analysis. Submit the revised workbook as specified by your instructor.

6. Exit Excel.

7. ✵ Besides the styles used in the worksheet, what other changes could you make to enhance the worksheet?

Table 1–6 New Worksheet Data	
Cell	**Change Cell Contents To**
A2	Yearly Sales Analysis
B7	3895.23
C5	26125.75
D6	30589.14
E7	35450.82
F6	6352.78

Continued >

Apply Your Knowledge *continued*

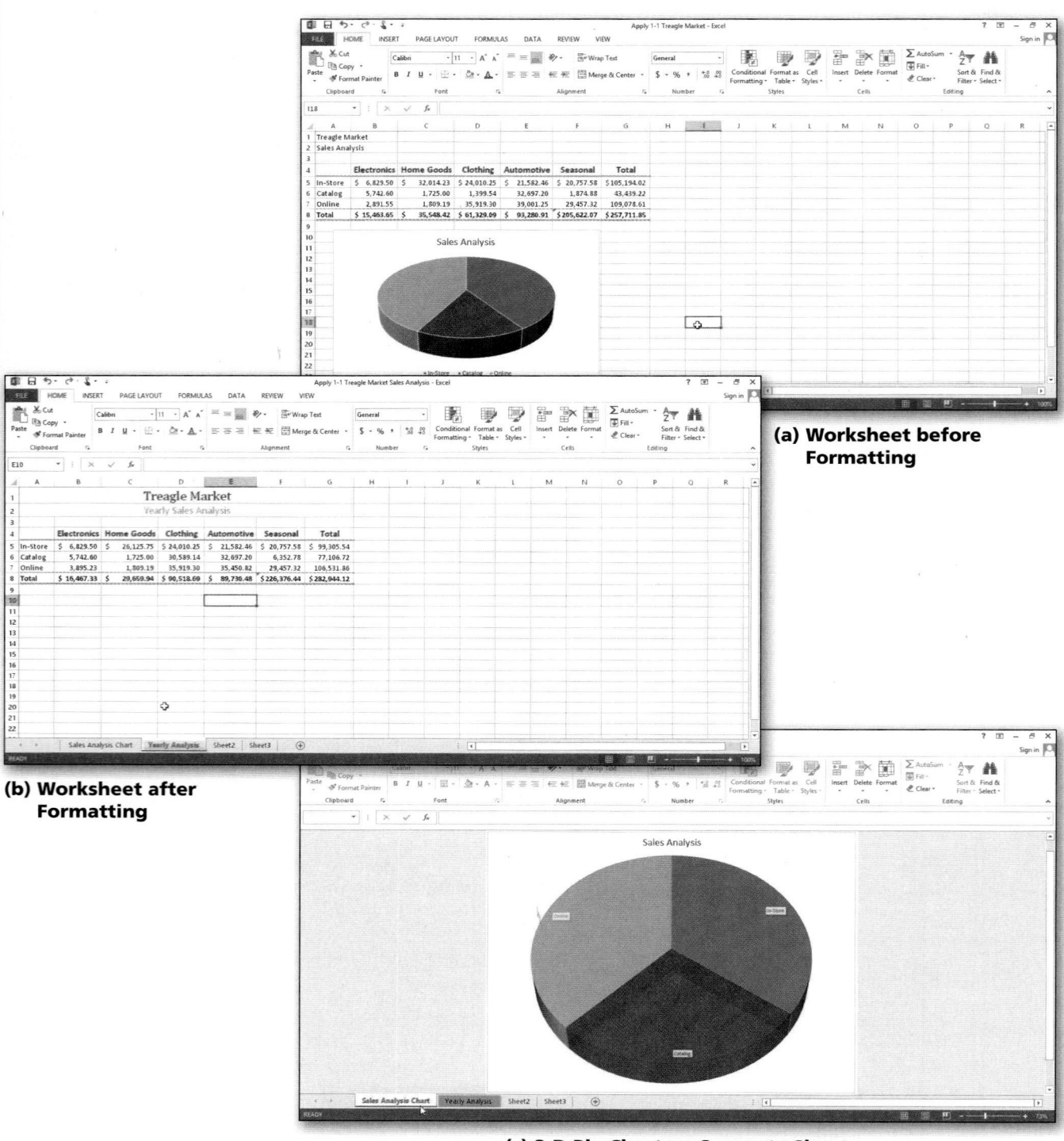

(a) **Worksheet before Formatting**

(b) **Worksheet after Formatting**

(c) **3-D Pie Chart on Separate Sheet**

Figure 1–73

Extend Your Knowledge

Extend the skills you learned in this chapter and experiment with new skills. You may need to use Help to complete the assignment.

Creating Styles and Formatting a Worksheet

Note: To complete this assignment, you will be required to use the Data Files for Students. Visit www.cengage.com/ct/studentdownload for detailed instructions or contact your instructor for information about accessing the required files.

Instructions: Run Excel. Open the workbook Extend 1–1 Kaseey Vehicles (Figure 1–74). Perform the following tasks to create styles and format a worksheet using them.

1. Select cell A4. Use the New Cell Style command in the Cell Styles gallery to create a style that fills only cell A4 using the Orange, Accent 2, Lighter 40% color (row 4, column 6). Name the style, MyHeadings.

2. Select cell A5. Use the New Cell style dialog box to create a style that fills only cell A5 using the Orange, Accent 2, Lighter 80% color. Name the style, MyRows.

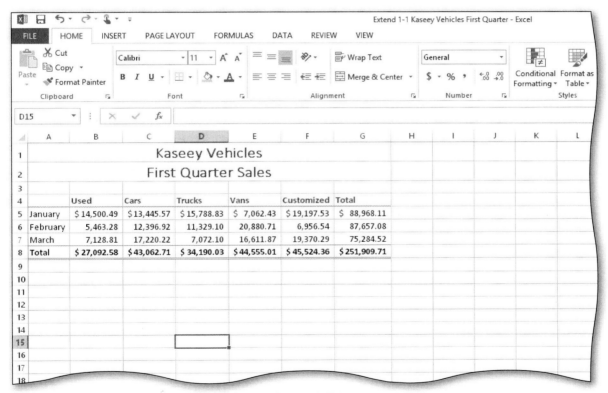

Figure 1–74

3. Select cell ranges B4:G4 and A5:A8. Apply the MyHeadings style to the cell ranges.

4. Select cell ranges B5:G5 and B7:G7. Apply the MyRows style to the cell ranges.

5. Apply a worksheet name to the sheet tab and apply a color of your choice to the sheet tab.

6. Change the font color for the text in cells A1 and A2 to the color of your eyes. Save the workbook using the file name, Extend 1–1 Kaseey Vehicles First Quarter. Submit the revised workbook as specified by your instructor.

7. Exit Excel.

8. ✹ What other styles would you create to improve the worksheet's appearance?

Analyze, Correct, Improve

Analyze a workbook and correct all errors and/or improve the design.

Fixing Formatting Problems and Data Errors in a Worksheet

Note: To complete this assignment, you will be required to use the Data Files for Students. Visit www.cengage.com/ct/studentdownload for detailed instructions or contact your instructor for information about accessing the required files.

Instructions: Run Excel. Open the workbook Analyze 1–1 CPJ Clothing. Correct the following formatting problems and data in the worksheet, while keeping in mind the guidelines presented in this chapter. Your worksheet should look like Figure 1–75 when it is corrected.

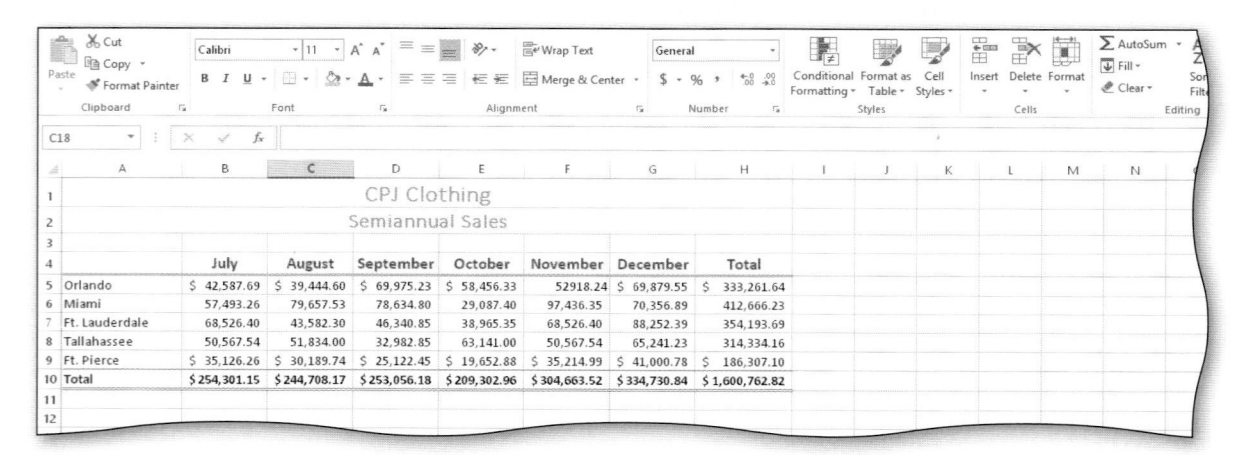

Figure 1–75

1. Correct

 a. Correct the spelling mistake in cell A2 by changing Semiannul to Semiannual. Correct the spelling mistake in cell A5 by changing Orlndo to Orlando.

 b. The SUM function in cell H7 does not sum all of the numbers in the column. Correct this error by editing the range for the SUM function in the cell.

2. Improve

 a. Merge and center the worksheet title and subtitle appropriately.

 b. Format the worksheet title and subtitle with appropriate cell styles. Change the font size of the subtitle to 16.

 c. Apply the Green, Accent 6 color to the title and subtitle and bold them.

 d. Add a title for totals row 10 and create the necessary totals in row 10.

 e. Apply proper formatting to the column headers and total row, including centering the column headers.

 f. Adjust the column sizes so that all data in each column is visible.

 g. Create the grand total for the annual cost of goods.

 h. Apply a worksheet name to the sheet tab and apply the Green, Accent 6 color to the sheet tab.

 i. Change the document properties as specified by your instructor. Save the workbook using the file name, Analyze 1–1 CPJ Clothing Sales. Submit the revised workbook as specified by your instructor.

 j. Change the city in cell A5 to the city you were born.

3. ✳ If you were going to create a pie chart of the expenses for each city, what data would you use?

In the Labs

Design and/or create a workbook using the guidelines, concepts, and skills presented in this chapter. Labs 1 and 2, which increase in difficulty, require you to create solutions based on what you learned in the chapter; Lab 3 requires you to create a solution, which uses cloud and web technologies, by learning and investigating on your own from general guidance.

Lab 1: **Fourth Quarter Revenue Analysis Worksheet**

Problem: You work as a spreadsheet specialist for Caitlyn's Candles, which has four regional shops in the state of California. Your manager has asked you to develop a fourth quarter revenue analysis similar to the one shown in Figure 1–76.

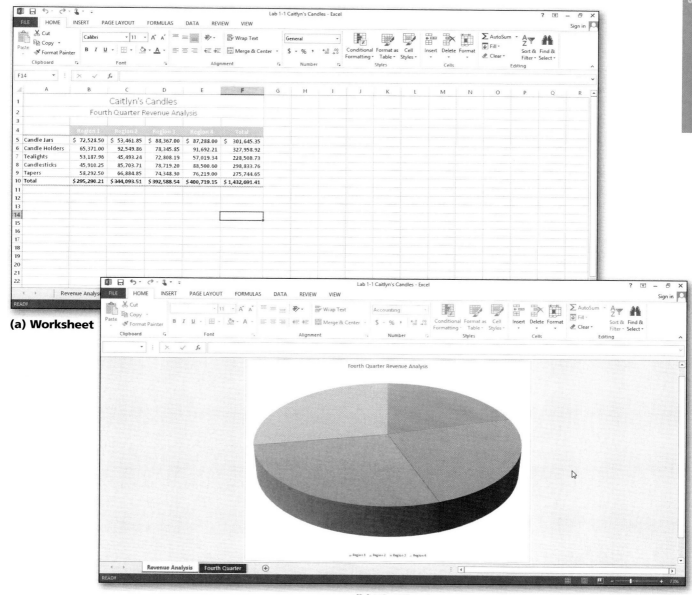

(a) Worksheet

(b) Pie Chart

Figure 1–76

Continued >

In the Labs *continued*

Instructions: Perform the following tasks.

1. Run Excel and create a new blank workbook. Enter the worksheet title, Caitlyn's Candles, in cell A1 and the worksheet subtitle, Fourth Quarter Revenue Analysis, in cell A2. Beginning in row 4, enter the region data shown in Table 1–7.

Table 1–7 Caitlyn's Candles				
	Region 1	**Region 2**	**Region 3**	**Region 4**
Candle Jars	72,528.50	53,461.85	88,367.00	87,288.00
Candle Holders	65,371.00	92,549.86	78,345.85	91,692.21
Tealights	53,187.96	45,493.24	72,808.19	57,019.34
Candlesticks	45,910.25	85,703.71	78,719.20	88,500.60
Tapers	58,292.50	66,884.85	74,348.30	76,219.00

2. Create totals for each region, product, and company grand total.

3. Format the worksheet title with the Title cell style. Center the title across columns A through F.

4. Format the worksheet subtitle to 14-point Calibri Light, and change the font color to Blue-Gray, Text 2. Center the subtitle across columns A through F.

5. Use Cell Styles to format the range A4:F4 with the Heading 2 cell style, the range B4:F4 with the 60% - Accent 4 cell style, and the range A10:F10 with the Total cell style. Center the column titles in row 4. Apply the accounting number format to the ranges B5:F5 and B10:F10. Apply the comma style format to the range B6:F9. Adjust any column widths to the widest text entry in each column.

6. Select the ranges B4:E4 and B10:E10 and then insert a 3-D pie chart. Apply the Style 4 chart style to the chart. Move the chart to a new worksheet named Revenue Analysis. Change the chart title to Fourth Quarter Revenue Analysis.

7. Rename the Sheet1 tab, Fourth Quarter, and apply the Purple color to the sheet tab. Change the document properties, as specified by your instructor.

8. Save the workbook using the file name, Lab 1-1 Caitlyn's Candles.

9. Preview and print the worksheet in landscape orientation.

10. Make the following two corrections to the Tealights: 55899.23 for Region 4 (cell E7) and 55,238.56 for Candle Jars for Region 2 (cell C5). After you enter the corrections, the total in cell F10 should equal $1,433,348.01.

11. Change the font color of the text in cells A1 and A2 to the color of the shirt you currently are wearing.

12. Preview and print the revised worksheet in landscape orientation. Close the workbook without saving the changes.

13. ✳ If you wanted to chart the item totals instead of the regions, which ranges would you use to create the chart?

14. Submit the assignment as specified by your instructor.

Lab 2: **Sales Analysis Worksheet**

Problem: As the chief accountant for CinCar Satellite, a satellite service serving seven states, you have been asked by the vice president to create a worksheet to analyze the yearly sales for each state (Figure 1–77). The packages and corresponding sales by state for the year are shown in Table 1–8 on the next page.

(a) Worksheet

(b) Pie Chart

Figure 1–77

Continued >

In the Labs *continued*

Instructions: Perform the following tasks.

1. Create the worksheet shown in Figure 1–77a on the previous page using the data in Table 1–8.

2. Use the SUM function to determine total revenue for the four packages, the totals for each state, and the company total. Add column and row headings for the totals row and totals column, as appropriate.

Table 1–8 CinCar Satellite				
	Package A	**Package B**	**Package C**	**Package D**
Florida	$882,159.71	$139,388.08	$282,893.78	$521,907.12
Georgia	424,831.57	644,502.14	378,930.88	504,893.62
Louisiana	51,992.60	402,543.65	779,472.20	84,159.19
Mississippi	917,288.79	648,651.15	493,499.41	266,127.38
North Carolina	897,478.89	653,663.92	326,152.40	290,625.29
South Carolina	374,888.19	429,976.17	455,069.28	627,464.72
Virginia	$791,763.66	$257,652.61	$384,759.74	$895,336.17

3. Format the worksheet title and subtitle with the Title cell style and center them across columns A through F. Use the Font group on the ribbon to format the worksheet subtitle as 14-point Cambria red. Format the title with Dark Red, bold font color. Center the titles across columns A through F.

4. Format the range B4:F4 with the Heading 3 cell style and center the text in the cells. Format the range A5:F11 with the 20% - Accent 1 cell style, and the range A12:F12 with the Total cell style. Format cells B5:F5 and B12:F12 with the accounting number format and cells B6:F11 with the comma style format.

5. Create a 3-D pie chart that shows the sales contributions of each state. Chart the state names (A5:A11) and corresponding totals (F5:F11). Insert the 3-D pie chart by using the 'Insert Pie or Doughnut Chart' button (INSERT tab | Charts group). Use the sheet tab name, Yearly Sales Chart. Apply a chart style of your choosing.

6. Change the Sheet1 tab name to Yearly Sales, and apply the Purple color to the sheet tab. Change the document properties, as specified by your instructor.

7. Save the workbook using the file name, Lab 1-2 CinCar Satellite. Print the worksheet in landscape orientation.

8. Two corrections to the figures were sent in from the accounting department. The correct sales figure is $151,992.60 for Package A sold in Louisiana (cell B7) and $183,573.67 for Package B sold in Virginia (cell C11). Print the revised worksheet in landscape orientation.

9. Use the Undo button to change the worksheet back to the original numbers in Table 1–8. Use the Redo button to change the worksheet back to the revised state.

10. Exit Excel without saving the latest changes to the workbook.

11. Change the state in cell A11 to the state in which you were born. If your state already is listed in the spreadsheet, choose a different state.

12. ✺ If you wanted to make a distinction between the rows in the table, what could you do?

13. Submit the assignment as specified by your instructor.

Lab 3: **Expand Your World: Cloud and Web Technologies Online**

Problem: You are tasked with creating a travel expense report for two trips you made to conferences during the past six months. You decide to download and use one of Excel's templates to create your worksheet.

Instructions Part 1: Tap or click the New tab in the Backstage view and then search for and tap or click the Travel expense report template to download it. Enter data for two trips, one to Las Vegas and one for San Diego, using the web to search for data. Save the file as Lab 1-3 Part 1 Travel Expenses. Print the worksheet. Submit the assignment as specified by your instructor.

Instructions Part 2: ✳ Which template would you use if you wanted to create a workout plan or a training plan for employees?

✳ **Consider This: Your Turn**

Apply your creative thinking and problem solving skills to design and implement a solution.

1: Create a Personal Budget

Personal

Part 1: To estimate your budget, you decide to create a worksheet listing your income and expenses. Create a worksheet that lists your incomes and your expenses using estimates for the next six months. Total your income and expenses. Calculate your net value using a simple formula. Use the concepts and techniques presented in this chapter to format your worksheet and create a 3-D pie chart for your net result for the six months. Submit your assignment in the format specified by your instructor.

Part 2: ✳ Now that you have looked over your results, did you neglect to include any income? How did you determine the values you used in your estimates? Did you anticipate possible changes in the near future?

2: Create a Sales Worksheet

Professional

Part 1: You are working for a popular sports restaurant that has five branches. Your boss has asked you to create a worksheet to show results for drinks, meals, games, and souvenir sales. Using estimates, create the worksheet for Sports & You. Include totals and averages. Use the concepts and techniques presented in this chapter to format the workbook. Include a chart to compare your revenues. Submit your assignment in the format specified by your instructor.

Part 2: ✳ What steps did you use to create your estimates? Based upon your knowledge of restaurants, do you think seasonal sales would be different, and if so, why?

3: Compare Car Prices

Research and Collaboration

Part 1: Working in a group, research current cars for sale. Create a worksheet that compares the type of cars and the base price for each model, as well as the costs to add various additional options. Calculate the average price for the cars and averages of the additional options. Use the concepts and techniques presented in this chapter to format the worksheet. Include a chart to compare the different car costs. Submit your assignment in the format specified by your instructor.

Part 2: ✳ Based upon the data you found, how could you chart the information to show the comparisons? Which chart would be the best to use?

STUDENT ASSIGNMENTS

Learn Online

Reinforce what you learned in this chapter with games, exercises, training, and many other online activities and resources.

Student Companion Site Reinforcement activities and resources are available at no additional cost on www.cengagebrain.com. Visit www.cengage.com/ct/studentdownload for detailed instructions about accessing the resources available at the Student Companion Site.

SAM Put your skills into practice with SAM! If you have a SAM account, go to www.cengage.com/sam2013 to access SAM assignments for this chapter.

2 Formulas, Functions, and Formatting

Microsoft product screenshots used with permission from Microsoft Corporation.

Objectives

You will have mastered the material in this chapter when you can:

- Enter formulas using the keyboard
- Enter formulas using Point mode
- Apply the MAX, MIN, and AVERAGE functions
- Verify a formula using Range Finder
- Apply a theme to a workbook
- Apply a date format to a cell or range

- Add conditional formatting to cells
- Change column width and row height
- Check the spelling on a worksheet
- Change margins and headers in Page Layout view
- Preview and print versions and sections of a worksheet

2 | Formulas, Functions, and Formatting

Introduction

In Chapter 1, you learned how to enter data, sum values, format a worksheet to make it easier to read, and draw a chart. This chapter continues to illustrate these topics and presents some new ones.

The new topics covered in this chapter include using formulas and functions to create a worksheet. A **function** is a prewritten formula that is built into Excel. Other new topics include option buttons, verifying formulas, applying a theme to a worksheet, borders, formatting numbers and text, conditional formatting, changing the widths of columns and heights of rows, spell checking, alternative types of worksheet displays and printouts, and adding page headers and footers to a worksheet. One alternative worksheet display and printout shows the formulas in the worksheet instead of the values. When you display the formulas in the worksheet, you see exactly what text, data, formulas, and functions you have entered into it.

Project — Worksheet with Formulas and Functions

The project in this chapter follows proper design guidelines and uses Excel to create the worksheet shown in Figure 2–1. HyperMass Online Storage established its online website to provide online storage for its customers. The owners pay employees to maintain the servers and handle customer requests. Before the owners pay the employees, they summarize the hours worked, pay rate, and tax information for each employee to ensure that the business properly compensates its employees. This summary includes information such as the employee names, number of dependents, hours worked, hourly pay rate, tax information, net pay, and hire date. As the complexity of the task of creating the summary increases, the owners want to use Excel to create a salary report.

Figure 2–1

Recall that the first step in creating an effective worksheet is to make sure you understand what is required. The people who will use the worksheet usually provide the requirements. The requirements document for the HyperMass Online Storage Salary Report worksheet includes the following needs: source of data, summary of calculations, and other facts about its development (Figure 2–2).

Worksheet Title	HyperMass Online Storage Salary Report
Needs	An easy-to-read worksheet that summarizes the company's salary report (Figure 2–3 on the next page). For each employee, the worksheet is to include the employee's name, dependents, hours worked, hourly pay rate, gross pay, federal tax, state tax, total tax percent, net pay, and hire date. The worksheet also should include totals and the highest value, lowest value, and average for the columns of numbers specified below.
Source of Data	The data supplied includes the employee names, dependents, hours worked, hourly pay rate, and hire dates.
Calculations	The following calculations must be made for each of the employees: 1. Gross Pay = Hours Worked × Hourly Pay Rate 2. Federal Tax = 0.22 × (Gross Pay − Dependents * 24.32) 3. State Tax = 0.04 × Gross Pay 4. Tax % = (Federal Tax + State Tax) / Gross Pay 5. Net Pay = Gross Pay − (Federal Tax + State Tax) 6. Compute the totals for hours worked, gross pay, federal tax, state tax, and net pay 7. Compute the total tax percent 8. Use the MAX and MIN functions to determine the highest and lowest values for dependents, hours worked, hourly pay rate, gross pay, federal tax, state tax, total tax percent, and net pay 9. Use the AVERAGE function to determine the average for hours worked, dependents, hourly pay rate, gross pay, federal tax, state tax, and net pay

Figure 2–2

In addition, using a sketch of the worksheet can help you visualize its design. The sketch for the HyperMass Online Storage Salary Report worksheet includes a title, a subtitle, column and row headings, and the location of data values (Figure 2–3). It also uses specific characters to define the desired formatting for the worksheet, as follows:

1. The row of Xs below the leftmost column heading defines the cell entries as text, such as employee names.

2. The rows of Zs and 9s with slashes, dollar signs, decimal points, commas, and percent signs in the remaining columns define the cell entries as numbers. The Zs indicate that the selected format should instruct Excel to suppress leading 0s. The 9s indicate that the selected format should instruct Excel to display any digits, including 0s.

3. The decimal point means that a decimal point should appear in the cell entry and indicates the number of decimal places to use.

4. The slashes in the last column identify the cell entry as a date.

5. The dollar signs that are adjacent to the Zs below the totals row signify a floating dollar sign, or one that appears next to the first significant digit.

6. The commas indicate that the selected format should instruct Excel to display a comma separator only if the number has sufficient digits (values in the thousandths) to the left of the decimal point.

7. The percent sign (%) in the Tax % column indicates a percent sign should appear after the number.

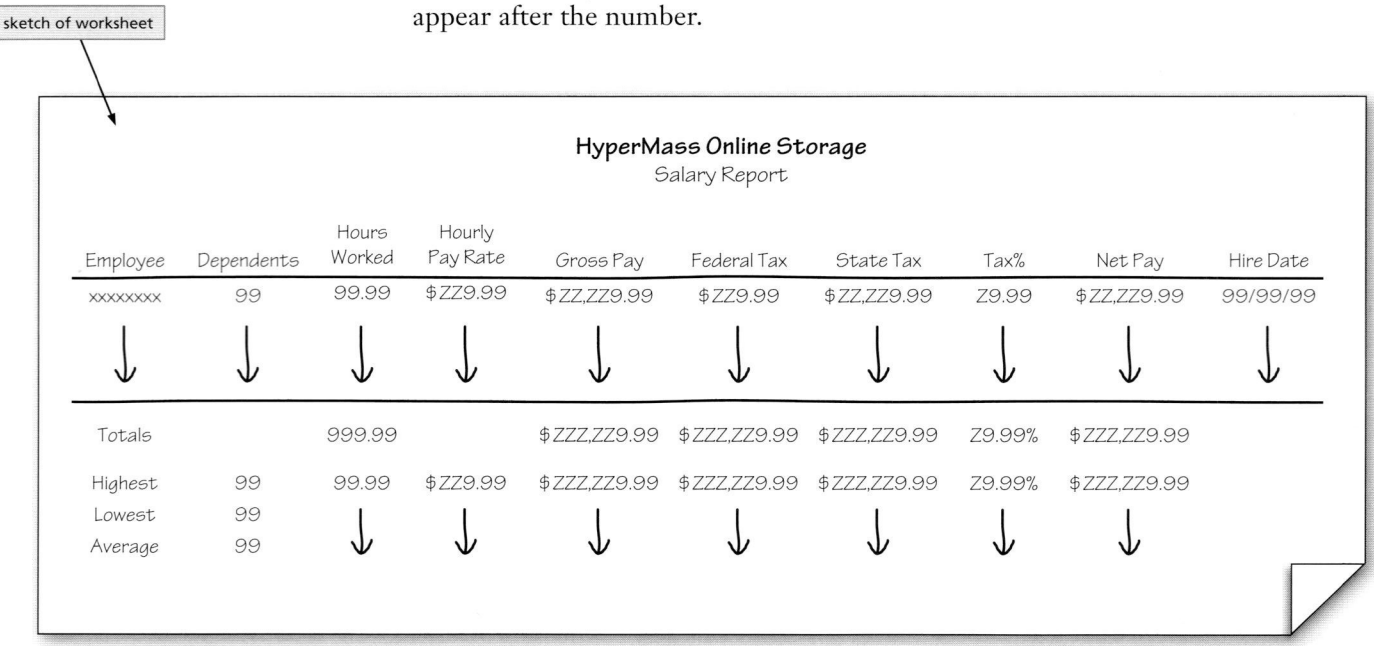

sketch of worksheet

Figure 2–3

Roadmap

In this chapter, you will learn how to use functions and create formulas. The following roadmap identifies general activities you will perform as you progress through this chapter:

1. ENTER FORMULAS in the worksheet.

2. ENTER FUNCTIONS in the worksheet.

3. VERIFY FORMULAS in the worksheet.

4. FORMAT the WORKSHEET.

5. CHECK SPELLING.

6. PRINT the WORKSHEET.

At the beginning of step instructions throughout the chapter, you will see an abbreviated form of this roadmap. The abbreviated roadmap uses colors to indicate chapter progress: gray means the chapter is beyond that activity, blue means the task being shown is covered in that activity, and black means that activity is yet to be covered. For example, the following abbreviated roadmap indicates the chapter would be showing a task in the 2 ENTER FUNCTIONS activity.

1 ENTER FORMULAS | 2 ENTER FUNCTIONS | **3 VERIFY FORMULAS**
4 FORMAT WORKSHEET | 5 CHECK SPELLING | 6 PRINT WORKSHEET

CONSIDER THIS

The function, or purpose, of a worksheet is to provide a user with direct ways to accomplish tasks. In designing a worksheet, functional considerations should supersede visual aesthetics. When designing your worksheet, what steps should be taken to ensure this?

• Avoid the temptation to use flashy or confusing visual elements within the worksheet.

• Understand the requirements document.

• Choose the proper functions and formulas.

• Build the worksheet.

To Run Excel and Create a Blank Workbook

If you are using a computer to step through the project in this chapter and you want your screens to match the figures in this book, you should change your screen's resolution to 1366 × 768. For information about how to change a computer's resolution, refer to the Office and Windows chapter at the beginning of this book.

The following steps, which assume Windows 8 is running, use the Start screen or the search box to run Excel based on a typical installation. You may need to ask your instructor how to run Excel on your computer. For a detailed example of the procedure summarized below, refer to the Office and Windows chapter.

1 Scroll the Start screen for an Excel 2013 tile. If your Start screen contains an Excel 2013 tile, tap or click it to run Excel and then proceed to Step 5; if the Start screen does not contain the Excel 2013 tile, proceed to the next step to search for the Excel app.

2 Swipe in from the right edge of the screen or point to the upper-right corner of the screen to display the Charms bar and then tap or click the Search charm on the Charms bar to display the Search menu.

3 Type **Excel** as the search text in the Search box and watch the search results appear in the Apps list.

4 Tap or click Excel 2013 in the search results to run Excel.

5 Tap or click the Blank workbook thumbnail on the Excel start screen to create a blank workbook and display it in the Excel window.

6 If the Excel window is not maximized, tap or click the Maximize button on its title bar to maximize the window.

For an introduction to Windows and instruction about how to perform basic Windows tasks, read the Office and Windows chapter at the beginning of this book, where you can learn how to resize windows, change screen resolution, create folders, move and rename files, use Windows Help, and much more.

For an introduction to Office and instruction about how to perform basic tasks in Office programs, read the Office and Windows chapter at the beginning of this book, where you can learn how to run a program, use the ribbon, save a file, open a file, exit a program, use Help, and much more.

Entering the Titles and Numbers into the Worksheet

The first step in creating the worksheet is to enter the titles and numbers into the worksheet. The following sets of steps enter the worksheet title and subtitle and then the salary report data shown in Table 2–1 on page EX 71.

To Enter the Worksheet Title and Subtitle

With a good comprehension of the requirements document, an understanding of the necessary decisions, and a sketch of the worksheet, the next step is to use Excel to create the worksheet.

The following steps enter the worksheet title and subtitle into cells A1 and A2.

1 If necessary, select cell A1. Type **HyperMass Online Storage** in the selected cell and then press the DOWN ARROW key to enter the worksheet title.

2 Type **Salary Report** in cell A2 and then press the DOWN ARROW key to enter the worksheet subtitle.

To Enter the Column Titles

The employee names and the row titles Totals, Average, Highest, and Lowest in the leftmost column begin in cell A4 and continue down to cell A16. The employee data is entered into rows 4 through 12 of the worksheet. The remainder of this section explains the steps required to enter the column titles, payroll data, and row titles, as shown in Figure 2–4, and then save the workbook.

The column titles in row 3 begin in cell A3 and extend through cell J3. Some of the column titles in Figure 2–4 include multiple lines of text, such as Hours Worked in cell C3. To start a new line in a cell, press ALT+ENTER after each line, except for the last line, which is completed by tapping or clicking the Enter box, pressing the ENTER key, or pressing one of the arrow keys. When you see ALT+ENTER in a step, press the ENTER key while holding down the ALT key and then release both keys. The following steps enter the column titles.

1 With cell A3 selected, type **Employee** and then press the RIGHT ARROW key to enter the column heading.

2 Type **Dependents** and then press the RIGHT ARROW key to enter the column heading.

3 In cell C3, type **Hours** and then press ALT+ENTER to enter the first line of the column heading. Type **Worked** and then press the RIGHT ARROW key to enter the column heading.

4 Type **Hourly** in cell D3 and then press ALT+ENTER to begin a new line in the cell. Type **Pay Rate** and then press the RIGHT ARROW key to enter the column heading.

5 Type **Gross Pay** in cell E3 and then press the RIGHT ARROW key to enter the column heading.

6 Type **Federal Tax** in cell F3 and then press the RIGHT ARROW key to enter the column heading.

7 Type **State Tax** in cell G3 and then press the RIGHT ARROW key to enter the column heading.

8 Type **Tax %** in cell H3 and then press the RIGHT ARROW key to enter the column heading.

9 Type **Net Pay** in cell I3 and then press the RIGHT ARROW key to enter the column heading.

10 Type **Hire Date** in cell J3 and then press the RIGHT ARROW key to enter the column heading.

To Enter the Salary Data

The salary data in Table 2–1 includes a hire date for each employee. Excel considers a date to be a number and, therefore, it displays the date right-aligned in the cell. The following steps enter the data for each employee: name, dependents, hours worked, hourly pay rate, and hire date.

1 Select cell A4. Type **Carl, Michael** and then press the RIGHT ARROW key to enter the employee name.

2 Type **3** in cell B4 and then press the RIGHT ARROW key to enter a number in the selected cell.

3 Type **60.45** in cell C4 and then press the RIGHT ARROW key to enter a number in the selected cell.

4 Type **19.50** in cell D4 and then press the RIGHT ARROW key to enter a number in the selected cell.

5 Type **4/5/10** in cell J4 and then tap or click cell A5 to select the cell.

6 Enter the payroll data in Table 2–1 for the eight remaining employees in rows 5 through 12 (shown in Figure 2–4 on page 72).

Q&A

In Step 5, why did the date that was entered change from 4/5/10 to 4/5/2010?
When Excel recognizes that you entered a date in mm/dd/yy format, it automatically formats the date as mm/dd/yyyy for you. Most professionals prefer to view dates in mm/dd/yyyy format as opposed to mm/dd/yy format because the latter can cause confusion regarding the intended year. For example, a date displayed as 3/3/50 could imply a date of 3/3/1950 or 3/3/2050. The use of a four-digit year eliminates this confusion.

Table 2–1 HyperMass Online Storage Salary Report Data

Employee	Dependents	Hours Worked	Hourly Pay Rate	Hire Date
Carl, Michael	3	60.45	19.50	4/5/10
Green, Sue	0	81.50	22.85	7/15/11
Fekir, Sith	1	69.50	17.36	1/13/09
Lane, Jon	2	65.25	19.45	3/1/12
Nichols, Peter	3	71.25	12.60	4/15/11
Pearson, Ada	3	44.65	22.45	10/31/08
Rodriquez, Juan	2	55.50	20.15	7/15/09
Williams, Sean	0	80.00	20.85	5/14/09
Yau, Xin	4	70.00	18.75	6/17/02

To Enter the Row Titles

The following steps add row titles for the rows that will contain the totals, highest, lowest, and average amounts.

1 Select cell A13. Type **Totals** and then press the DOWN ARROW key to enter a row header.

2 Type **Highest** in cell A14 and then press the DOWN ARROW key to enter a row header.

3 Type **Lowest** in cell A15 and then press the ENTER key to enter a row header.

4 Type **Average** in cell A16 and then press the DOWN ARROW key to enter a row header (Figure 2–4).

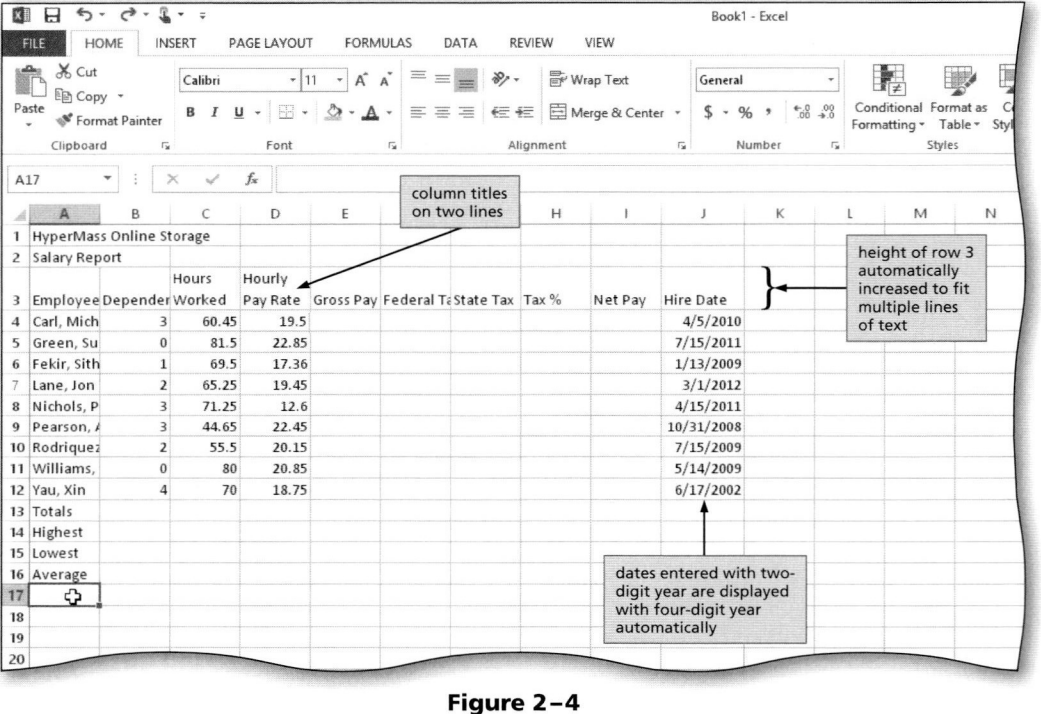

Figure 2–4

To Change the Worksheet Tab Name and Color and Save the Workbook

The following steps change the worksheet tab name to Salary Report, change the sheet tab color, and save the workbook in the Excel folder (for your assignments) using the file name, HyperMass Online Storage Salary Report.

1 Double-tap or double-click the Sheet1 tab and then enter **Salary Report** as the sheet tab name and then press the ENTER key.

2 Press and hold or right-click the sheet tab to display the shortcut menu.

3 Tap or point to Tab Color on the shortcut menu to display the Tab Color gallery. Tap or click Green, Accent 6, Darker 25% (column 10, row 5) in the Theme Colors area to apply a new color to the sheet tab.

4 Tap or click the Save button on the Quick Access Toolbar, which depending on settings, will display either the Save As gallery in the Backstage view or the Save As dialog box.

5 To save on a hard disk or other storage media on your computer, proceed to Step 5a. To save on SkyDrive, proceed to Step 5b.

5a If your screen opens the Backstage view and you want to save on storage media on your computer, tap or click Computer, if necessary, to display options in the right pane related to saving on your computer. If your screen already displays the Save As dialog box, proceed to Step 6.

5b If your screen opens the Backstage view and you want to save on SkyDrive, tap or click SkyDrive to display SkyDrive saving options or a Sign In button. If your screen displays a Sign In button, tap or click it and then sign in to SkyDrive.

6 Tap or click the Browse button in the right pane to display the Save As dialog box associated with the selected Save As Place (i.e., Computer or SkyDrive).

7 Type **HyperMass Online Storage Salary Report** in the File name box to change the file name. Do not press the ENTER key after typing the file name because you do not want to close the dialog box at this time.

8 Navigate to the desired save location (in this case, the Excel folder in the CIS 101 folder [or your class folder] on your computer or SkyDrive).

9 Tap or click the Save button (Save As dialog box) to save the document in the selected folder on the selected location with the entered file name.

Entering Formulas

One of the reasons Excel is such a valuable tool is that you can assign a **formula** to a cell, and Excel will calculate the result. Consider, for example, what would happen if you had to multiply 60.45 by 19.5 and then manually enter the product for Gross Pay, 1,178.78, in cell E4. Every time the values in cells C4 or D4 changed, you would have to recalculate the product and enter the new value in cell E4. By contrast, if you enter a formula in cell E4 to multiply the values in cells C4 and D4, Excel recalculates the product whenever new values are entered into those cells and displays the result in cell E4.

A formula in a cell that contains a reference back to itself is called a **circular reference**. Excel often warns you when you create a circular reference. In almost all cases, circular references are the result of an incorrect formula. A circular reference can be direct or indirect. For example, placing the formula =A1 in cell A1 results in a direct circular reference. An **indirect circular reference** occurs when a formula in a cell refers to another cell or cells that include a formula that refers back to the original cell.

To Enter a Formula Using the Keyboard

1 ENTER FORMULAS | 2 ENTER FUNCTIONS | 3 VERIFY FORMULAS
4 FORMAT WORKSHEET | 5 CHECK SPELLING | 6 PRINT WORKSHEET

The formulas needed in the worksheet are noted in the requirements document as follows:

1. Gross Pay (column E) = Hours Worked × Hourly Pay Rate
2. Federal Tax (column F) = 0.22 × (Gross Pay − Dependents × 24.32)
3. State Tax (column G) = 0.04 × Gross Pay
4. Tax % (column H) = (Federal Tax + State Tax) / Gross Pay
5. Net Pay (column I) = Gross Pay − (Federal Tax + State Tax)

The gross pay for each employee, which appears in column E, is equal to hours worked in column C times hourly pay rate in column D. Thus, the gross pay for Michael Carl in cell E4 is obtained by multiplying 60.45 (cell C4) by 19.50 (cell D4) or =C4 × D4. The following steps enter the initial gross pay formula in cell E4 using the keyboard. **Why?** *In order for Excel to perform the calculations, you must create formulas.*

1

- With cell E4 selected, type **=c4*d4** in the cell to display the formula in the formula bar and in the current cell and to display colored borders around the cells referenced in the formula (Figure 2–5).

Q&A

What occurs on the worksheet as I enter the formula?

The **equal sign** (=) preceding c4*d4 alerts Excel that you are entering a formula or function and not text. Because the most common error when entering a formula is to reference the wrong cell in a formula mistakenly, Excel colors the borders of the cells referenced in the formula. The coloring helps in the reviewing process to ensure the cell references are correct. The **asterisk** (*) following c4 is the arithmetic operator that directs Excel to perform the multiplication operation.

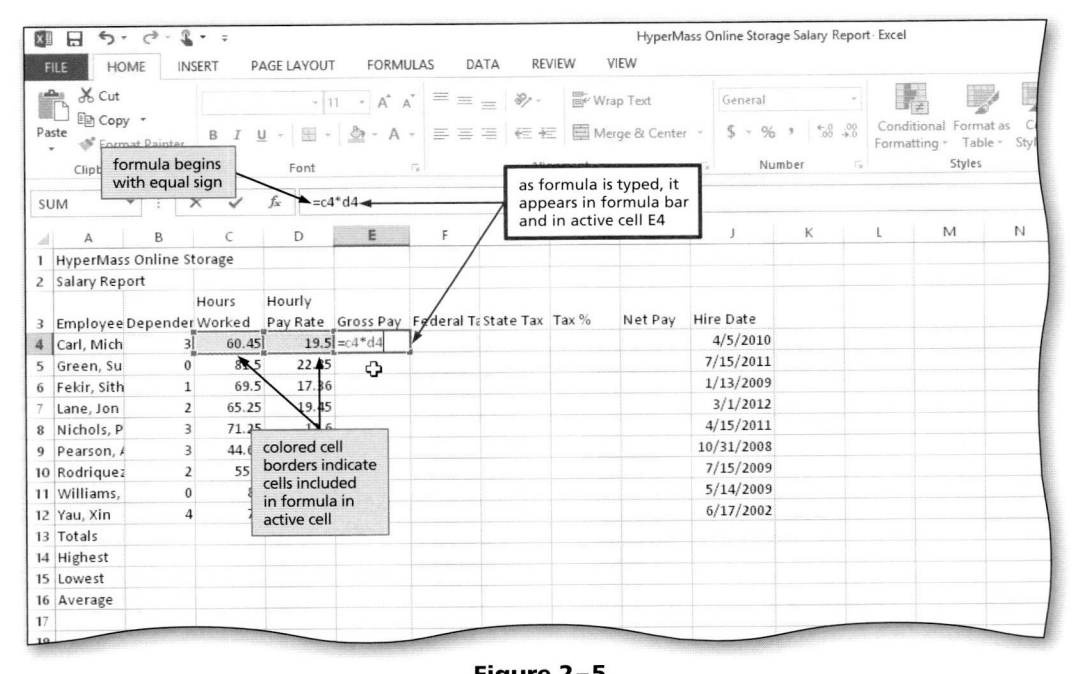

Figure 2–5

2

- Press the RIGHT ARROW key to complete the arithmetic operation indicated by the formula, to display the result in the worksheet, and to select the cell to the right (Figure 2–6). The number of decimal places shown in cell E4 may be different, but these values will be adjusted later in this chapter.

Figure 2–6

Arithmetic Operations

Excel provides powerful functions and capabilities that allow you to perform arithmetic operations easily and efficiently. Table 2–2 describes multiplication and other valid Excel arithmetic operators.

Arithmetic Operator	Meaning	Example of Usage	Result
−	Negation	−78	Negative 78
%	Percentage	=23%	Multiplies 23 by 0.01
^	Exponentiation	=3 ^ 4	Raises 3 to the fourth power
*	Multiplication	=61.5 * C5	Multiplies the contents of cell C5 by 61.5
/	Division	=H3 / H11	Divides the contents of cell H3 by the contents of cell H11
+	Addition	=11 + 9	Adds 11 and 9
−	Subtraction	=22 − F15	Subtracts the contents of cell F15 from 22

Table 2–2 Summary of Arithmetic Operators

Order of Operations

When more than one arithmetic operator is involved in a formula, Excel follows the same basic order of operations that you use in algebra. Moving from left to right in a formula, the **order of operations** is as follows: first negation (−), then all percentages (%), then all exponentiations (^), then all multiplications (*) and divisions (/), and finally, all additions (+) and subtractions (−).

As in algebra, you can use parentheses to override the order of operations. For example, if Excel follows the order of operations, 8 * 3 + 2 equals 26. If you use parentheses, however, to change the formula to 8 * (3 + 2), the result is 40, because the parentheses instruct Excel to add 3 and 2 before multiplying by 8. Table 2–3 illustrates several examples of valid Excel formulas and explains the order of operations.

Table 2–3 Examples of Excel Formulas

Formula	Result
=G15	Assigns the value in cell G15 to the active cell.
=2^4 + 7	Assigns the sum of 16 + 7 (or 23) to the active cell.
=100 + D2 or =D2 +100 or =(100 + D2)	Assigns 100 plus the contents of cell D2 to the active cell.
=25% * 40	Assigns the product of 0.25 times 40 (or 10) to the active cell.
− (K15 * X45)	Assigns the negative value of the product of the values contained in cells K15 and X45 to the active cell. You do not need to type an equal sign before an expression that begins with minus signs, which indicates a negation.
=(U8 − B8) * 6	Assigns the difference between the values contained in cells U8 and B8 times 6 to the active cell.
=J7 / A5 + G9 * M6 − Z2 ^ L7	Completes the following operations, from left to right: exponentiation (Z2 ^ L7), then division (J7 / A5), then multiplication (G9 * M6), then addition (J7 / A5) + (G9 * M6), and finally subtraction (J7 / A5 + G9 * M6) − (Z2 ^ L7). If cells A5 = 6, G9 = 2, J7 = 6, L7 = 4, M6 = 5, and Z2 = 2, then Excel assigns the active cell the value −5; that is, 6 / 6 + 2 * 5 − 2 ^ 4 = −5.

To Enter Formulas Using Point Mode

The sketch of the worksheet in Figure 2–3 on page EX 68 calls for the federal tax, state tax, tax percent, and net pay for each employee to appear in columns F, G, H, and I, respectively. All four of these values are calculated using formulas in row 4:

Federal Tax (cell F4) = 0.22 × (Gross Pay – Dependents × 24.32) or =0.22 * (E4 – B4 * 24.32)
State Tax (cell G4) = 0.04 × Gross Pay or =0.04 * E4
Tax % (cell H4) = (Federal Tax + State Tax) / Gross Pay or =(F4 + G4)/E4
Net Pay (cell I4) = Gross Pay – (Federal Tax + State Tax) or =E4 – (F4 + G4)

An alternative to entering the formulas in cells F4, G4, H4, and I4 using the keyboard is to enter the formulas using the pointer and Point mode. **Point mode** allows you to select cells for use in a formula by using your finger or the pointer. The following steps enter formulas using Point mode. *Why? Using Point mode makes it easier to create formulas without worrying about typographical errors when entering cell references.*

1
- With cell F4 selected, type =0.22*(to begin the formula and then tap or click cell E4 to add a cell reference in the formula (Figure 2–7).

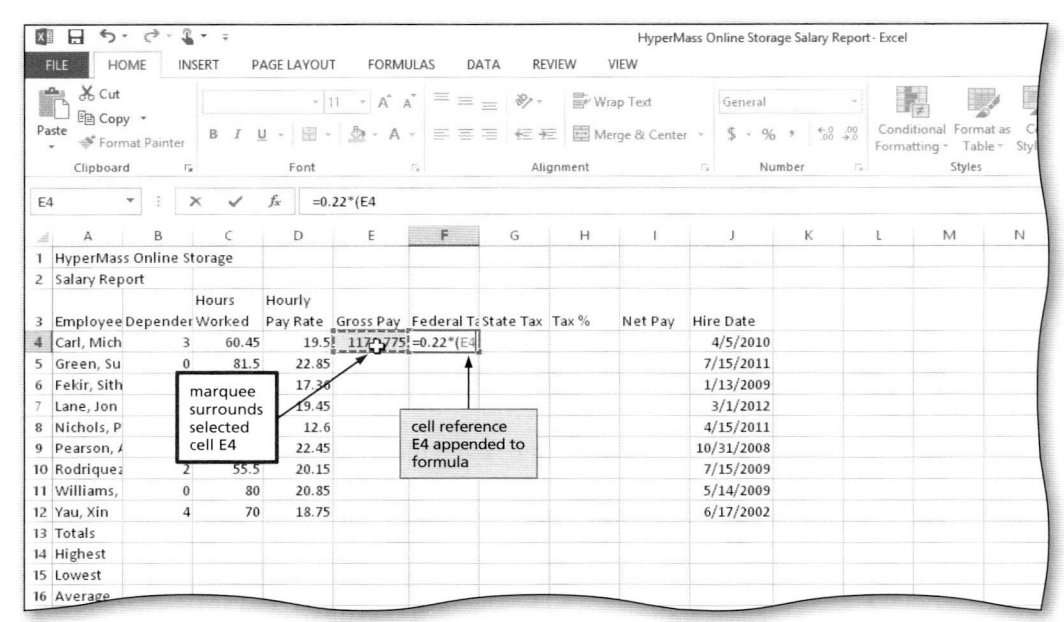

Figure 2–7

2
- Type – (minus sign) and then tap or click cell B4 to add a subtraction operator and a reference to another cell to the formula.

- Type *24.32) to complete the formula (Figure 2–8).

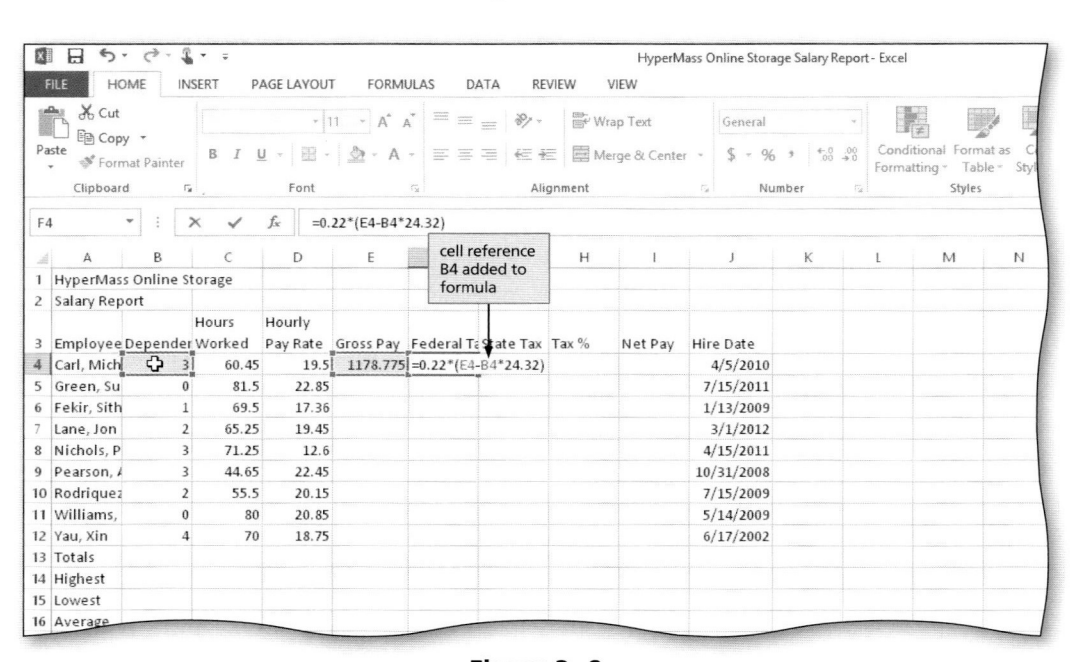

Figure 2–8

3

- Tap or click the Enter box in the formula bar and then select cell G4 to prepare to enter the next formula.

- Type **=0.04*** and then tap or click cell E4 to add a cell reference to the formula (Figure 2–9).

Q&A Why should I use Point mode to enter formulas?
Using Point mode to enter formulas often is faster and more accurate than using the keyboard to type the entire formula when the cell you want to select does not require you to scroll. In many instances, as in these steps, you may want to use both the keyboard and touch gestures or the pointer when entering a formula in a cell. You can use the keyboard to begin the formula, for example, and then use touch gestures or the pointer to select a range of cells.

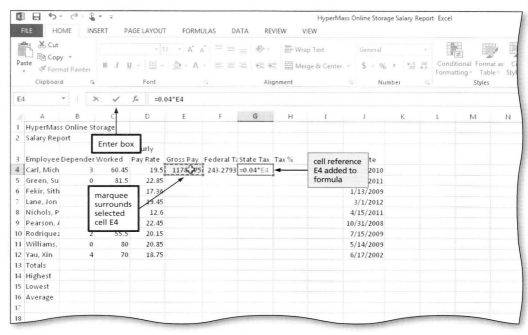

Figure 2–9

4

- Tap or click the Enter box in the formula bar to enter the formula in cell G4.

- Select cell H4. Type **=(** (equal sign followed by an open parenthesis) and then tap or click cell F4 to add a reference to the formula.

- Type **+** (plus sign) and then tap or click cell G4 to add a cell reference to the formula.

- Type **)/** (close parenthesis followed by a forward slash), and then tap or click cell E4 to add a cell reference to the formula.

- Tap or click the Enter box in the formula bar to enter the formula in cell H4 (Figure 2–10).

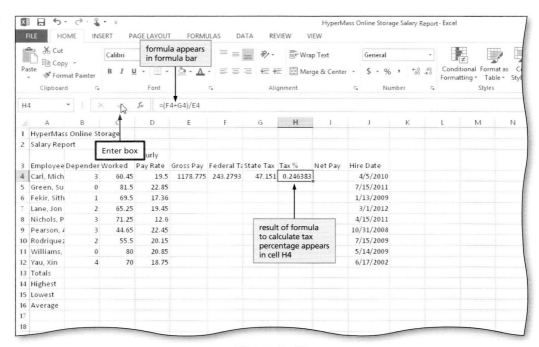

Figure 2–10

5

- Tap or click cell I4 to select cell I4 to prepare to enter the next formula.

- Type = (equal sign) and then tap or click cell E4 to begin the formula and add a cell reference to the formula.

- Type – ((minus sign followed by an open parenthesis) and then tap or click cell F4 to add a subtraction operator, open parenthesis, and cell reference to the formula.

- Type + (plus sign) and then tap or click cell G4 to add an addition operator and cell reference to the formula.

Figure 2–11

- Type) (close parenthesis) to complete the formula (Figure 2–11).

- Tap or click the Enter box in the formula bar to enter the formula.

To Copy Formulas Using the Fill Handle

The five formulas for Michael Carl in cells E4, F4, G4, H4, and I4 now are complete. The next step is to copy them to the range E5:I12. When performing copying operations in Excel, the source area is the cell, or range, from which data or formulas are being copied. When a range is used as a source, it sometimes is called the source range. The destination area is the cell, or range, to which data or formulas are being copied. When a range is used as a destination, it sometimes is called the destination range. Recall from Chapter 1 that the fill handle is a small black square in the lower-right corner of the active cell or active range. The following steps copy the formulas using the fill handle.

1 Select the source range, E4:I4 in this case, activate the fill handle, drag the fill handle down through cell I12, and then continue to hold your finger or the mouse button to select the destination range.

2 Lift your finger or release the mouse button to copy the formulas to the destination range (Figure 2–12).

Q&A How does Excel adjust the cell references in the formulas in the destination area?

Recall that when you copy a formula, Excel adjusts the cell references so that the new formulas contain references corresponding to the new location and perform calculations using the appropriate values. Thus, if you copy downward, Excel adjusts the row portion of cell references. If you copy across, then Excel adjusts the column portion of cell references. These cell references are called **relative cell references**.

Figure 2–12

Option Buttons

Excel displays Option buttons in a workbook while you are working on it to indicate that you can complete an operation using automatic features such as AutoCorrect, Auto Fill, error checking, and others. For example, the 'Auto Fill Options' button shown in Figure 2–12 appears after a fill operation, such as dragging the fill handle. When an error occurs in a formula in a cell, Excel displays the Trace Error button next to the cell and identifies the cell with the error by placing a green triangle in the upper left of the cell.

Table 2–4 summarizes the Option buttons available in Excel. When one of these buttons appears on your worksheet, tap or click its arrow to produce the list of options for modifying the operation or to obtain additional information.

Table 2–4 Option Buttons in Excel	
Name	**Menu Function**
'Auto Fill Options'	Gives options for how to fill cells following a fill operation, such as dragging the fill handle
AutoCorrect Options	Undoes an automatic correction, stops future automatic corrections of this type, or causes Excel to display the AutoCorrect Options dialog box
Insert Options	Lists formatting options following an insertion of cells, rows, or columns
Paste Options	Specifies how moved or pasted items should appear (for example, with original formatting, without formatting, or with different formatting)
Trace Error	Lists error-checking options following the assignment of an invalid formula to a cell

CONSIDER THIS

The Paste Options button provides powerful functionality. When performing copy and paste operations, the button allows you great freedom in specifying what it is you want to paste. You can choose from the following options:

- Paste an exact copy of what you copied, including the cell contents and formatting.
- Copy only formulas.
- Copy only formatting.
- Copy only values.
- Copy a combination of these options.
- Copy a picture of what you copied.

To Determine Totals Using the Sum Button

The next step is to determine the totals in row 13 for the hours worked in column C, gross pay in column E, federal tax in column F, state tax in column G, and net pay in column I. To determine the total hours worked in column C, the values in the range C4 through C12 must be summed. To do so, enter the function =sum(c4:c12) in cell C13 or select cell C13, tap or click the Sum button (HOME tab | Editing group), and then press the ENTER key. Recall that a function is a prewritten formula that is built into Excel. Similar SUM functions can be used in cells E13, F13, G13, and I13 to total gross pay, federal tax, state tax, and net pay, respectively. The following steps determine totals in cell C13, the range E13:G13, and cell I13.

1 Select the cell to contain the sum, cell C13 in this case. Tap or click the Sum button (HOME tab | Editing group) to sum the contents of the range C4:C12 in cell C13 and then tap or click the Enter box to display a total in the selected cell.

2 Select the range to contain the sums, range E13:G13 in this case. Tap or click the Sum button (HOME tab | Editing group) to display totals in the selected range.

3 Select the cell to contain the sum, cell I13 in this case. Tap or click the Sum button (HOME tab | Editing group) to sum the contents of the range I4:I12 in cell I13 and then tap or click the Enter box to display a total in the selected cell (Figure 2–13).

Q&A Why did I have to tap or click the Enter box?
When creating a sum for a single column, you tap or click the Enter box. If you are calculating the sum for multiple ranges, you tap or click the Sum button.

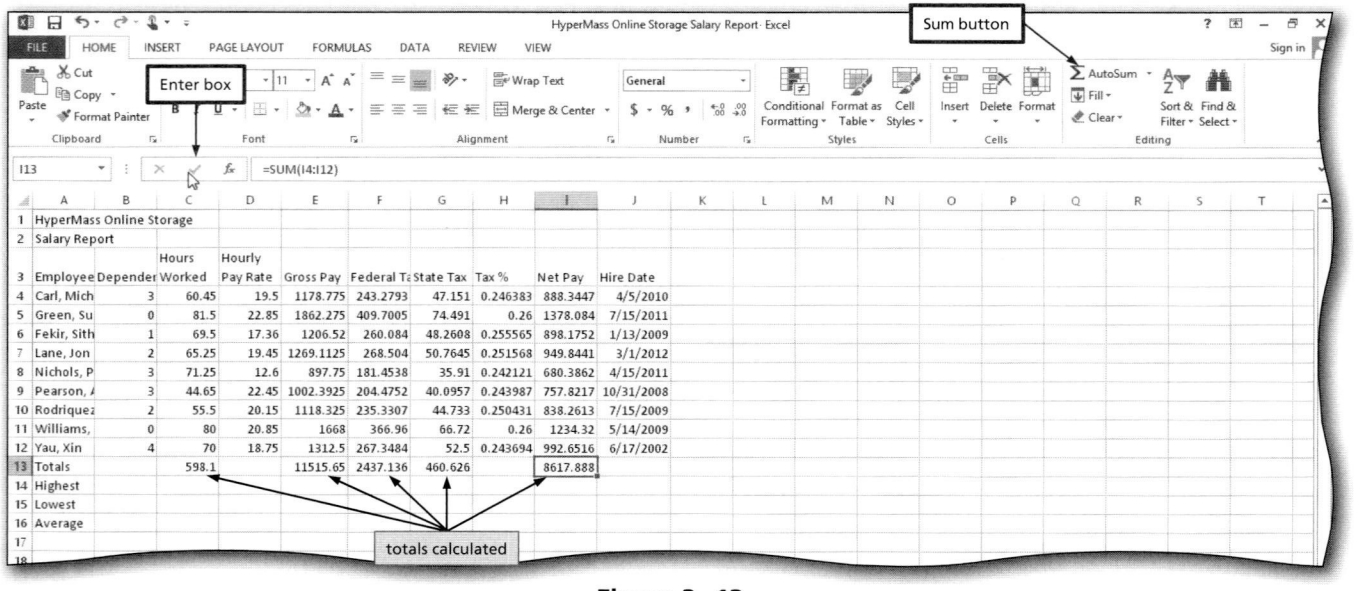

Figure 2–13

To Determine the Total Tax Percentage

With the totals in row 13 determined, the next step is to copy the tax percentage formula in cell H12 to cell H13. The following step copies the tax percentage formula.

1 Select the cell to be copied, H12 in this case, and then drag the fill handle down through cell H13 to copy the formula (Figure 2–14).

Q&A Why was the SUM function not used for tax percentage in H13?
The tax percentage is based off of the totals, not the sum, of the tax percentage column; therefore, there was no need to use the SUM function.

Figure 2–14

Using the AVERAGE, MAX, and MIN Functions

The next step in creating the HyperMass Online Storage Salary Report worksheet is to compute the highest value, lowest value, and average value for the number of dependents listed in the range B4:B12 using the MAX, MIN, and AVERAGE functions in the range B14:B16. Once the values are determined for column B, the entries can be copied across to the other columns.

With Excel, you can enter functions using one of five methods: (1) keyboard, touch gesture, or pointer; (2) the Insert Function box in the formula bar; (3) the Sum menu; (4) the Sum button (FORMULAS tab | Function Library group); and (5) the Name box area in the formula bar. The method you choose will depend on your typing skills and whether you can recall the function name and required arguments.

In the following sections, three of these methods will be used. The Insert Function box in the formula bar method will be used to determine the highest number of dependents (cell B14). The Sum menu will be used to determine the lowest number of dependents (cell B15). The keyboard and pointer will be used to determine the average number of dependents (cell B16).

To Determine the Highest Number in a Range of Numbers Using the Insert Function Box

The next step is to select cell B14 and determine the highest (maximum) number in the range B4:B12. Excel includes a function called the **MAX function** that displays the highest value in a range. The following steps use the Insert Function box in the formula bar to enter the MAX function. *Why? Although you could enter the MAX function using the keyboard and Point mode as described previously, an alternative method to entering the function is to use the Insert Function box in the formula bar.*

1

- Select the cell to contain the maximum number, cell B14 in this case.

- Tap or click the Insert Function box in the formula bar to display the Insert Function dialog box.

- If necessary, scroll to and then tap or click MAX in the Select a function list (Insert Function dialog box) to select it (Figure 2–15).

Q&A

What if the MAX function is not in the Select a function list?
Click the 'Or select a category' arrow to display the list of function categories, select All, and then scroll down and select the MAX function in the Select a function list.

How can I learn about other functions?
Excel has more than 400 additional functions that perform nearly every type of calculation you can imagine. These functions are categorized in the Insert Function dialog box shown in Figure 2–15. To view the categories, tap or click the 'Or select a category' arrow. To obtain a description of a selected function, select its name in the Insert Function dialog box. Excel displays the description of the function below the Select a function list in the dialog box.

Figure 2–15

2

- Tap or click the OK button (Insert Function dialog box) to display the Function Arguments dialog box.

- Type **b4:b12** in the Number1 box (Function Arguments dialog box) to enter the first argument of the function (Figure 2–16).

Q&A Why did numbers appear to the right of the Number 1 box in the Function Arguments dialog box?
As shown in Figure 2–16, Excel displays the value the MAX function will return to cell B14 in the Function Arguments dialog box. It also lists the first few numbers in the selected range, next to the Number1 box.

Figure 2–16

3

- Tap or click the OK button (Function Arguments dialog box) to display the highest value in the chosen range in the selected cell (Figure 2–17).

Q&A Why should I not just enter the highest value that I see in the range B4:B12 in cell B14?
In this example, rather than entering the MAX function, you visually could scan the range B4:B12, determine that the highest number of dependents is 4, and manually enter the number 4 as a constant in cell B14. Excel would display the number the same as in Figure 2–17. Because it contains a constant, however, Excel will continue to display 4 in cell B14, even if the values in the range change. If you use the MAX function, Excel will recalculate the highest value in the range each time a new value is entered into the worksheet.

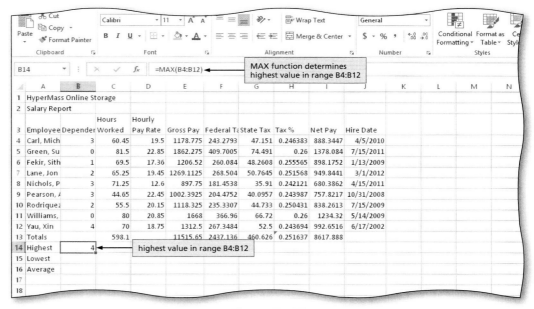

Figure 2–17

Other Ways

1. Tap or click Sum arrow (HOME tab | Editing group), tap or click Max
2. Tap or click Sum arrow (FORMULAS tab | Function Library group), tap or click Max
3. Type **=MAX** in cell, fill in arguments

To Determine the Lowest Number in a Range of Numbers Using the Sum Menu

The next step is to enter the **MIN function** in cell B15 to determine the lowest (minimum) number in the range B4:B12. Although you can enter the MIN function using the method used to enter the MAX function, the following steps illustrate an alternative method using the Sum button (HOME tab | Editing group). *Why?* *The Sum menu provides another way that you can insert functions, providing a menu from which you can choose.*

1

- Select cell B15 and then tap or click the Sum arrow (HOME tab | Editing group) to display the Sum menu (Figure 2–18).

Q&A Why should I use the Sum menu?
Using the Sum menu allows you to enter one of five often-used functions easily into a cell, without having to memorize its name or the required arguments.

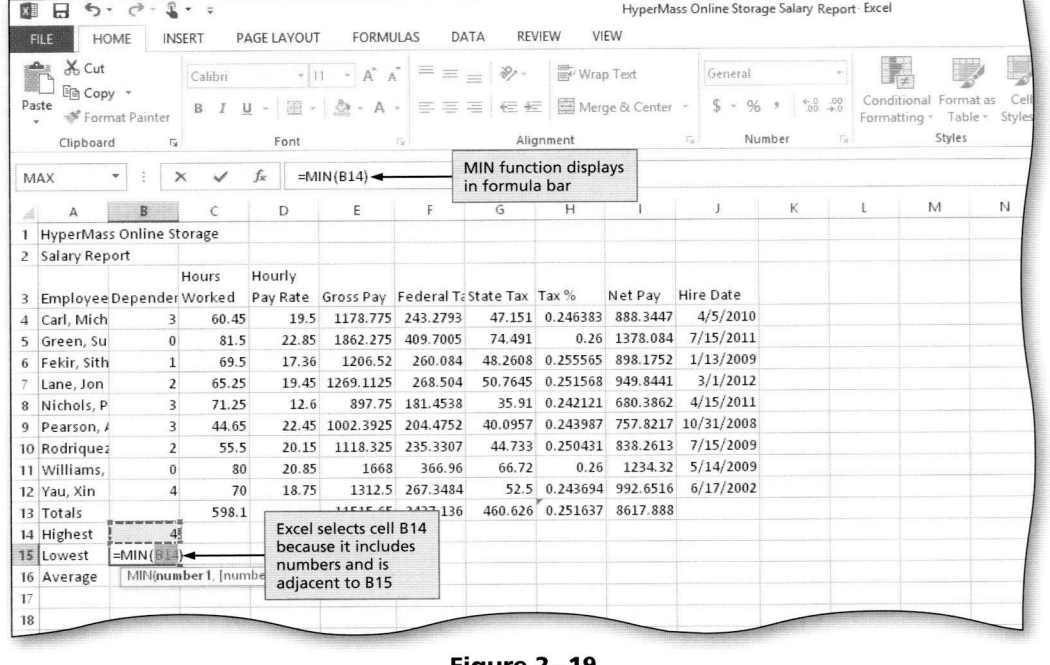

Figure 2–18

2

- Tap or click Min to display the MIN function in the formula bar and in the active cell (Figure 2–19).

Q&A Why does Excel select the incorrect range?
The range automatically selected by Excel is not always correct. Excel attempts to guess which cells you want to include in the function by looking for ranges that are adjacent to the selected cell and that contain numeric data.

Figure 2–19

● Tap or click cell
B4 and then drag
through cell B12 to
display the function
with the new range
in the formula bar
and in the selected
cell (Figure 2–20).

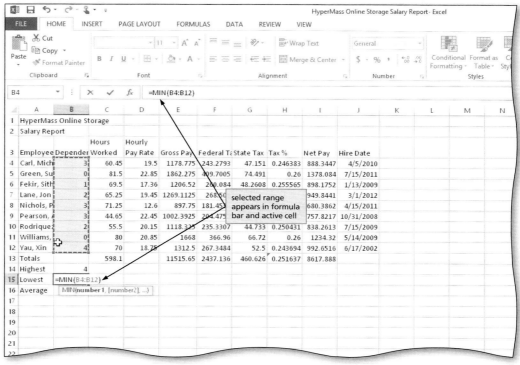

Figure 2–20

④
● Tap or click the Enter
box to determine
the lowest value in
the range B4:B12
and display the
result in the selected
cell (Figure 2–21).

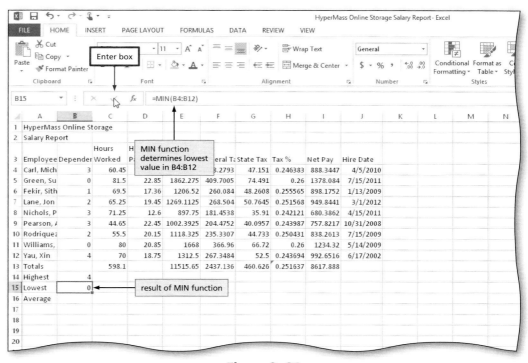

Figure 2–21

Other Ways

1. Tap or click Insert Function box in formula bar, if necessary, select Statistical category, tap or click MIN, specify arguments

2. Tap or click Sum arrow (FORMULAS tab | Function Library group), tap or click Min

3. Type `=MIN` in cell, fill in arguments

To Determine the Average of a Range of Numbers Using the Keyboard

The AVERAGE function sums the numbers in a specified range and then divides the sum by the number of cells with numeric values in the range. The following steps use the AVERAGE function to determine the average of the numbers in the range B4:B12. **Why?** *The AVERAGE function creates an accurate average automatically.*

1

- Select the cell to contain the average, cell B16 in this case.

- Type **=av** in the cell to display the Formula AutoComplete list. Press the DOWN ARROW key to highlight the required formula (Figure 2–22).

Q&A What is happening as I type?

As you type the equal sign followed by the characters in the name of a function, Excel displays the Formula AutoComplete list. This list contains those functions that alphabetically match the letters you have typed. Because you typed =av, Excel displays all the functions that begin with the letters, av.

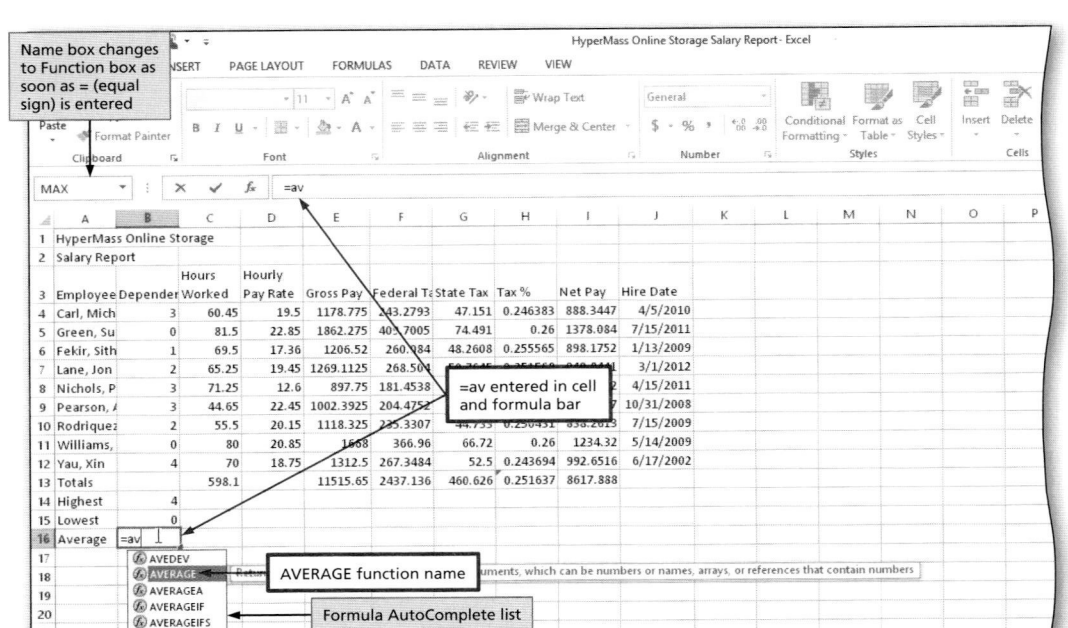

Figure 2–22

2

- Double-tap or double-click AVERAGE in the Formula AutoComplete list to select the function.

- Select the range to be averaged, B4:B12 in this case, to insert the range as the argument to the function (Figure 2–23).

Q&A As I drag, why does the function in cell B16 change?

When you tap or click cell B4, Excel appends cell B4 to the left parenthesis in the formula bar and surrounds cell B4 with a marquee. When you begin dragging, Excel appends to the argument a colon (:) and the cell reference of the cell where the pointer is located.

Figure 2–23

3

- Tap or click the Enter box to compute the average of the numbers in the selected range and display the result in the selected cell (Figure 2–24).

Q&A
Can I use the arrow keys to complete the entry instead?
No. When you use Point mode you cannot use the arrow keys to complete the entry. While in Point mode, the arrow keys change the selected cell reference in the range you are selecting.

What is the purpose of the parentheses in the function?
The AVERAGE function requires that the argument (in this case, the range B4:B12) be included within parentheses following the function name. Excel automatically appends the right parenthesis to complete the AVERAGE function when you tap or click the Enter box or press the ENTER key.

Function box changes back to Name box

Enter box

HyperMass Online Storage Salary Report - Excel

right parenthesis automatically appended when Enter box is tapped or clicked or ENTER key is pressed

B16 =AVERAGE(B4:B12)

	A	B	C	D	E	F	G				K	L	M	N
1	HyperMass Online Storage													
2	Salary Report													
3	Employee	Depender	Hours Worked	Hourly Pay Rate	Gross Pay	Federal Ta	State Tax	Tax %		Net Pay	Hire Date			
4	Carl, Mich	3	60.45	19.5	1178.775	243.2793	47.151	0.246383		888.3447	4/5/2010			
5	Green, Su	0	81.5	22.85	1862.275	409.7005	74.491	0.26		1378.084	7/15/2011			
6	Fekir, Sith	1	69.5	17.36	1206.52	260.084	48.2608	0.255565		898.1752	1/13/2009			
7	Lane, Jon	2	65.25	19.45	1269.1125	268.504	50.7645	0.251568		949.8441	3/1/2012			
8	Nichols, P	3	71.25	12.6	897.75	181.4538	35.91	0.242121		680.3862	4/15/2011			
9	Pearson, A	3	44.65	22.45	1002.3925	204.4752	40.0957	0.243987		757.8217	10/31/2008			
10	Rodriquez	2	55.5	20.15	1118.325	235.3307	44.733	0.250431		838.2613	7/15/2009			
11	Williams,	0	80	20.85	1668	366.96	66.72	0.26		1234.32	5/14/2009			
12	Yau, Xin	4	70	18.75	1312.5	267.3484	52.5	0.243694		992.6516	6/17/2002			
13	Totals		598.1		11515.65	2437.136	460.626	0.251637		8617.888				
14	Highest	4												
15	Lowest	0												
16	Average	2												
17														
18														
19														
20														
21														
22														

average number of dependents in cell B16

Figure 2–24

Other Ways

1. Tap or click Insert Function box in formula bar, select Statistical category, tap or click AVERAGE

2. Tap or click Sum arrow (HOME tab | Editing group), tap or click Average

3. Tap or click Sum arrow (FORMULAS tab | Function Library group), tap or click Average

To Copy a Range of Cells Across Columns to an Adjacent Range Using the Fill Handle

The next step is to copy the AVERAGE, MAX, and MIN functions in the range B14:B16 to the adjacent range C14:I16. The following steps use the fill handle to copy the functions.

1 Select the source range from which to copy the functions, in this case B14:B16.

2 Drag the fill handle in the lower-right corner of the selected range through cell I16 to copy the three functions to the selected range.

3 Select cell H16 and then press the DELETE key to delete the average of the tax % (Figure 2–25).

Q&A Why delete the formula in cell H16?

The average of the tax percentage in cell H16 is deleted because an average of percentages of this type is mathematically invalid.

How can I be sure that the function arguments are proper for the cells in range C14:I16? Remember that Excel adjusts the cell references in the copied functions so that each function refers to the range of numbers above it in the same column. Review the numbers in rows 14 through 16 in Figure 2–25. You should see that the functions in each column return the appropriate values, based on the numbers in rows 4 through 12 of that column.

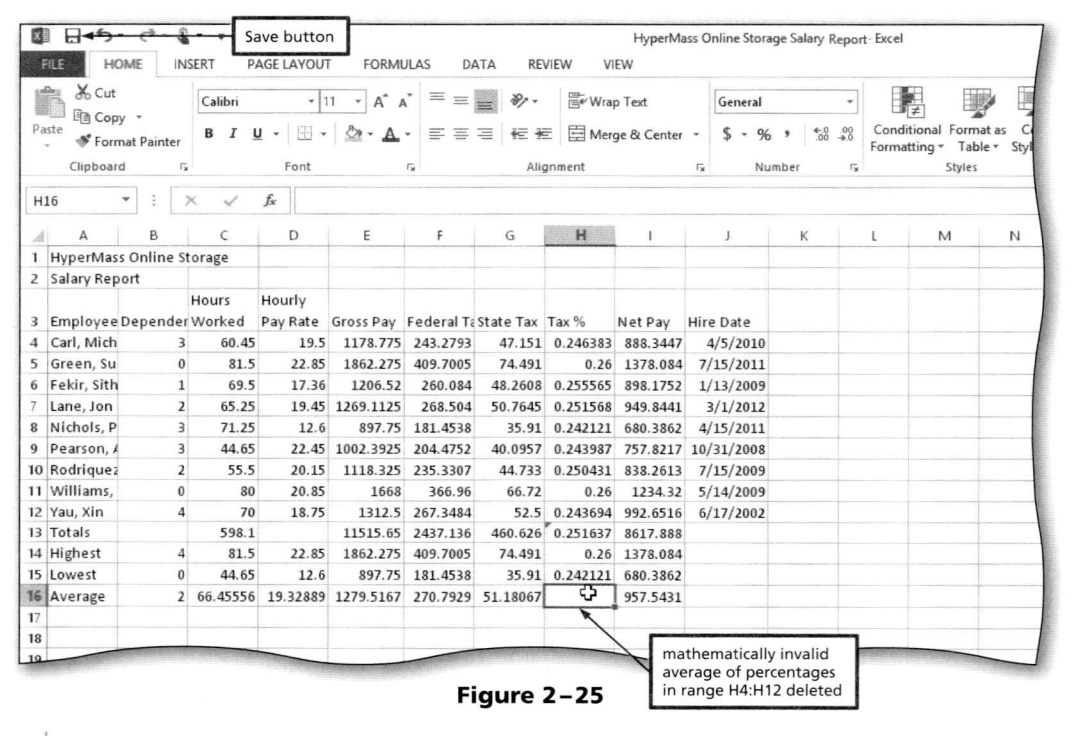

Figure 2–25

Other Ways

1. Select source area, tap or click Copy button (HOME tab \| Clipboard group), select destination area, tap or click Paste button (HOME tab \| Clipboard group)	2. Press and hold or right-click source area, tap or click Copy on shortcut menu; press and hold or right-click destination area, tap or click Paste icon on shortcut menu	3. Select source area and then point to border of range; while holding down CTRL, drag source area to destination area	4. Select source area, press CTRL+C, select destination area, press CTRL+V

To Save a Workbook Using the Same File Name

Earlier in this project, an intermediate version of the workbook was saved using the file name, HyperMass Online Storage Salary Report. The following step saves the workbook a second time, using the same file name.

1 Tap or click the Save button on the Quick Access Toolbar to overwrite the previously saved file.

Break Point: If you wish to take a break, this is a good place to do so. You can exit Excel now. To resume at a later time, run Excel, open the file called HyperMass Online Storage Salary Report, and continue following the steps from this location forward.

Verifying Formulas Using Range Finder

One of the more common mistakes made with Excel is to include an incorrect cell reference in a formula. An easy way to verify that a formula references the cells you want it to reference is to use Range Finder. **Range Finder** checks which cells are referenced in the formula assigned to the active cell.

To use Range Finder to verify that a formula contains the intended cell references, double-tap or double-click the cell with the formula you want to check. Excel responds by highlighting the cells referenced in the formula so that you can verify that the cell references are correct.

To Verify a Formula Using Range Finder

1 ENTER FORMULAS | 2 ENTER FUNCTIONS | 3 VERIFY FORMULAS
4 FORMAT WORKSHEET | 5 CHECK SPELLING | 6 PRINT WORKSHEET

Why? *Range Finder allows you to make immediate changes to the cells referenced in a formula.* The following steps use Range Finder to check the formula in cell H4.

- Double-tap or double-click cell H4 to activate Range Finder (Figure 2–26).

- Press the ESC key to quit Range Finder and then tap or click anywhere in the worksheet, such as cell A18, to deselect the current cell.

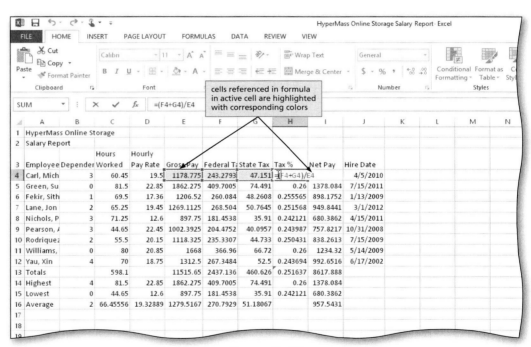

Figure 2–26

Formatting the Worksheet

Although the worksheet contains the appropriate data, formulas, and functions, the text and numbers need to be formatted to improve their appearance and readability.

In Chapter 1, cell styles were used to format much of the worksheet. This section describes how to change the unformatted worksheet in Figure 2–27a to the formatted worksheet in Figure 2–27b using a theme and other commands on the ribbon. The colors and fonts that are used in the worksheet shown in Figure 2–27b are those that are associated with the Basis theme.

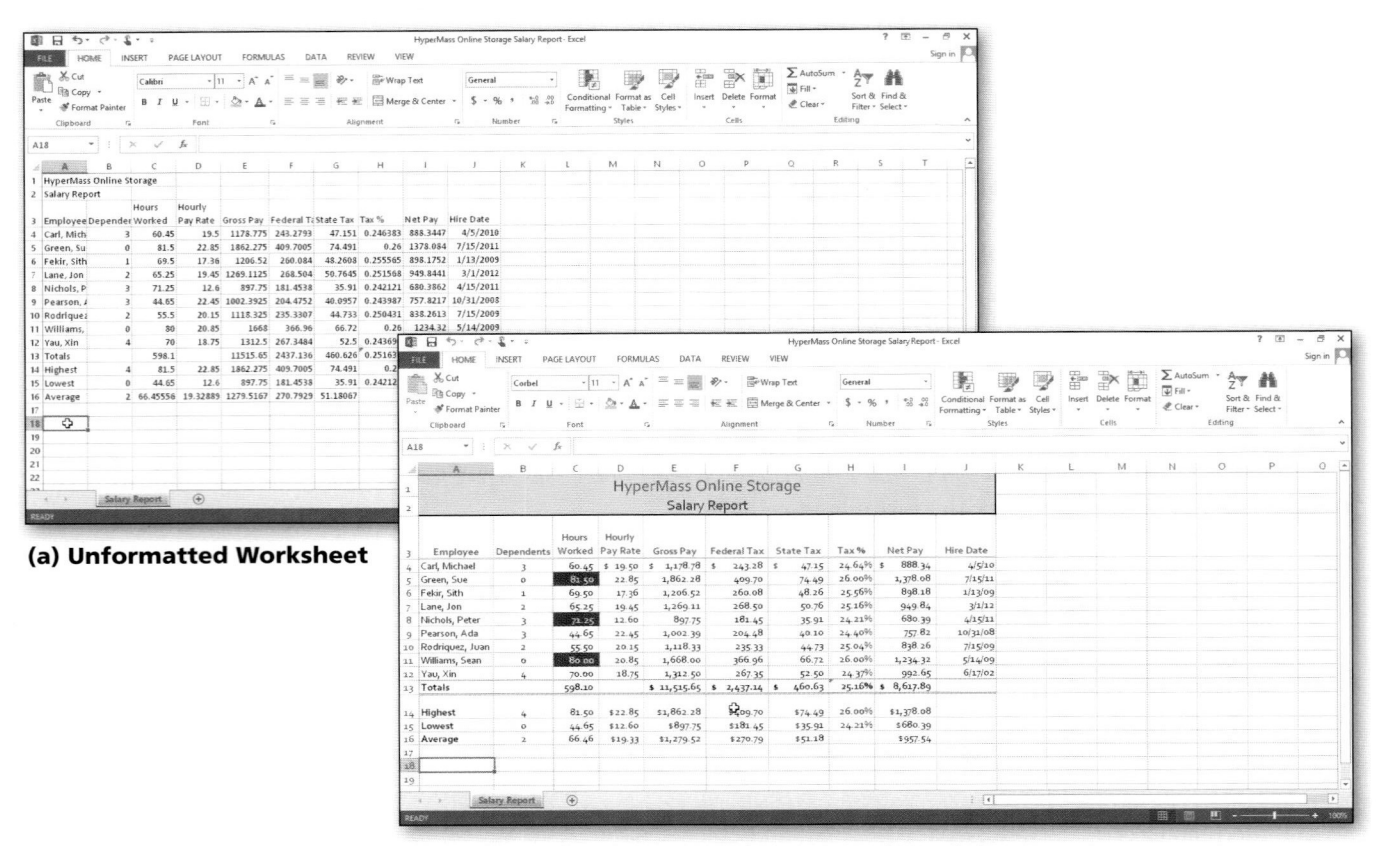

(a) Unformatted Worksheet

(b) Formatted Worksheet

Figure 2–27

The following outlines the formatting suggested in the sketch of the worksheet in Figure 2–3 on page EX 68.

1. Workbook theme — Basis
2. Worksheet title and subtitle
 a. Alignment — center across columns A through J
 b. Cell style — Title
 c. Font size — title 18; subtitle 16
 d. Background color (range A1:J2) — Green, Accent 1, Lighter 60%
 e. Border — thick box border around range A1:J2
3. Column titles
 a. Cell style — Heading 3
 b. Alignment — center
4. Data
 a. Dates in column J — mm/dd/yy format
 b. Alignment — center data in range B4:B16
 c. Numbers in column C — comma style and two decimal places; if a cell in range C4:C12 is greater than 70, then cell appears with background color of orange and a font color of white
 d. Numbers in top row (D4:G4, I4) — accounting number format
 e. Numbers below top row (D5:G12) — comma style and decimal places

5. Total line
 a. Cell style — Total
 b. Numbers — accounting number format

6. Highest, lowest, and average rows
 a. Font style of row titles in range A14:A16 — bold
 b. Numbers — currency style with floating dollar sign, comma style for Hours Worked

7. Percentages in column H
 a. Numbers — percentage style with two decimal places

8. Column widths
 a. Columns A and B — best fit
 b. Columns E, F, and I — 10.50 characters
 c. Column G — 10.25 characters
 d. Column C, D, and H — 7.50 characters

9. Row heights
 a. Row 3 — 48.00 points
 b. Row 14 — 27.00 points
 c. Remaining rows — default

To Change the Workbook Theme

1 ENTER FORMULAS | 2 ENTER FUNCTIONS | 3 VERIFY FORMULAS
4 FORMAT WORKSHEET | 5 CHECK SPELLING | 6 PRINT WORKSHEET

Why? *The Basis theme includes fonts and colors that provide the worksheet with a professional and subtly colored appearance.* The following steps change the workbook theme to the Basis theme.

1

- Display the PAGE LAYOUT tab.

- Tap or click the Themes button (PAGE LAYOUT tab | Themes group) to display the Themes gallery (Figure 2–28).

Experiment

- Point to several themes in the Themes gallery to see a live preview of the themes.

Q&A
Why should I change the theme of a workbook?
A company or department may standardize with a specific theme so that all of their documents have a similar appearance. Similarly, an individual may want to have a theme that sets his or her work apart from the work of others. Other Office programs, such as Word and PowerPoint, include the same themes included with Excel, meaning that all of your Microsoft Office documents can share a common theme.

Figure 2–28

②

- Tap or click Basis in the Themes gallery to change the workbook theme (Figure 2–29).

Q&A Why did the cells in the worksheet change?

The cells in the worksheet originally were formatted with the default font for the default Office theme. The default font for the Basis theme is different from that of the default font for the Office theme and, therefore, changed on the worksheet when you changed the theme. If you had modified the font for any of the cells, those cells would not be formatted with the default font for the Basis theme.

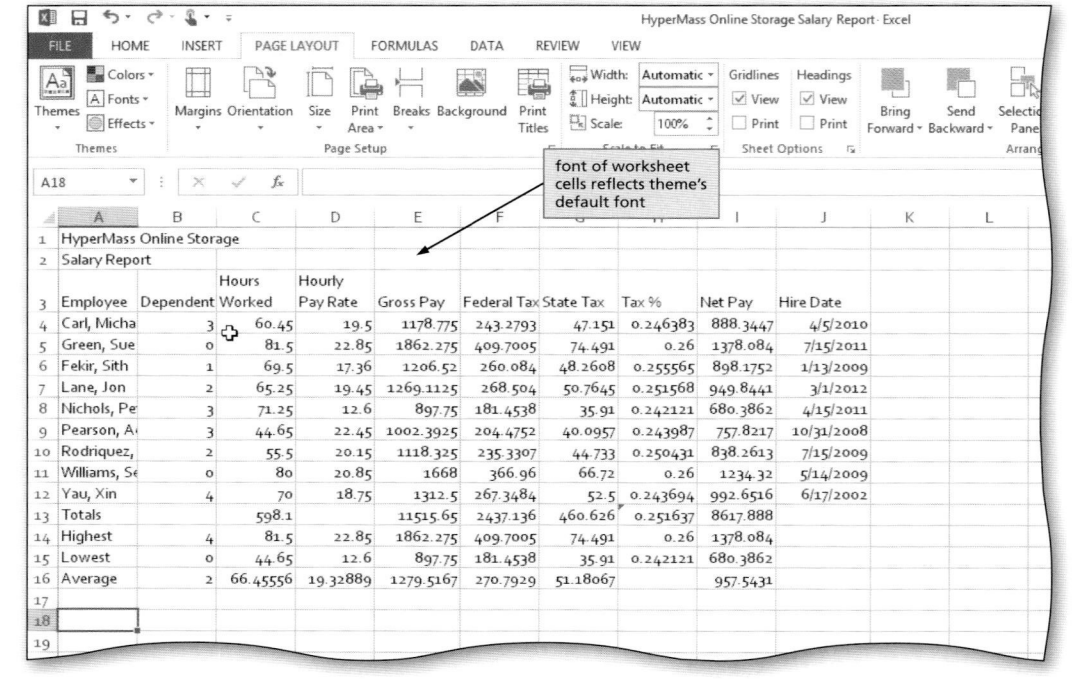

Figure 2–29

To Format the Worksheet Titles

The following steps merge and center the worksheet titles, apply the Title cells style to the worksheet titles, and decrease the font of the worksheet subtitle.

① Display the HOME tab.

② Select the range to be merged, A1:J1 in this case, and then tap or click the 'Merge & Center' button (HOME tab | Alignment group) to merge and center the text in the selected range.

③ Select the range A2:J2 and then tap or click the 'Merge & Center' button (HOME tab | Alignment group) to merge and center the text in the selected range.

④ Select the range to contain the Title cell style, in this case A1:A2, tap or click the Cell Styles button (HOME tab | Styles group) to display the Cell Styles gallery, and then tap or click the Title cell style in the Cell Styles gallery to apply the Title cell style to the selected range.

⑤ Select cell A2 and then tap or click the 'Decrease Font Size' button (HOME tab | Font group) to decrease the font size of the selected cell to the next lowest font size (Figure 2–30).

Q&A What is the effect of tapping or clicking the 'Decrease Font Size' button?

When you tap or click the 'Decrease Font Size' button, Excel assigns the next lowest font size in the Font Size gallery to the selected range. The 'Increase Font Size' button works in a similar manner, but causes Excel to assign the next highest font size in the Font Size gallery to the selected range.

Figure 2–30

Which colors should you select when formatting your worksheet?

Knowing how people perceive colors helps you emphasize parts of your worksheet. Warmer colors (red and orange) tend to reach toward the reader. Cooler colors (blue, green, and violet) tend to pull away from the reader. Bright colors jump out of a dark background and are easiest to see. White or yellow text on a dark blue, green, purple, or black background is ideal.

To Change the Background Color and Apply a Box Border to the Worksheet Title and Subtitle

1 ENTER FORMULAS | 2 ENTER FUNCTIONS | 3 VERIFY FORMULAS
4 FORMAT WORKSHEET | 5 CHECK SPELLING | 6 PRINT WORKSHEET

Why? *A background color and border can draw attention to the title of a worksheet.* The final formats assigned to the worksheet title and subtitle are the green background color and thick box border (Figure 2–27b on page EX 90). The following steps complete the formatting of the worksheet titles.

1

- Select the range A1:A2 and then tap or click the Fill Color arrow (HOME tab | Font group) to display the Fill Color gallery (Figure 2–31).

 Experiment

- Point to a number of colors in the Fill Color gallery to display a live preview of the color in the range A1:A2.

Figure 2–31

2

• Tap or click Green, Accent 1, Lighter 60% (column 5, row 3) in the Fill Color gallery to change the background color of the range of cells (Figure 2–32).

Figure 2–32

3

• Tap or click the Borders arrow (HOME tab | Font group) to display the Borders gallery (Figure 2–33).

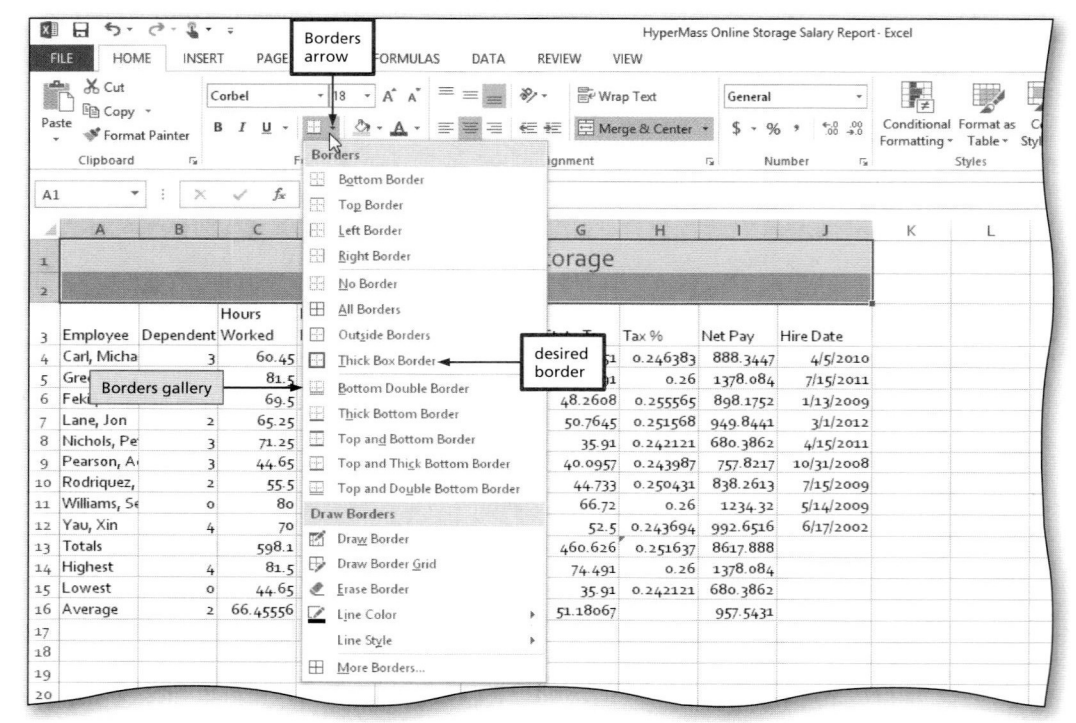

Figure 2–33

4

• Tap or click 'Thick Box Border' in the Borders gallery to display a thick box border around the selected range.

• Tap or click anywhere in the worksheet, such as cell A18, to deselect the current range (Figure 2–34).

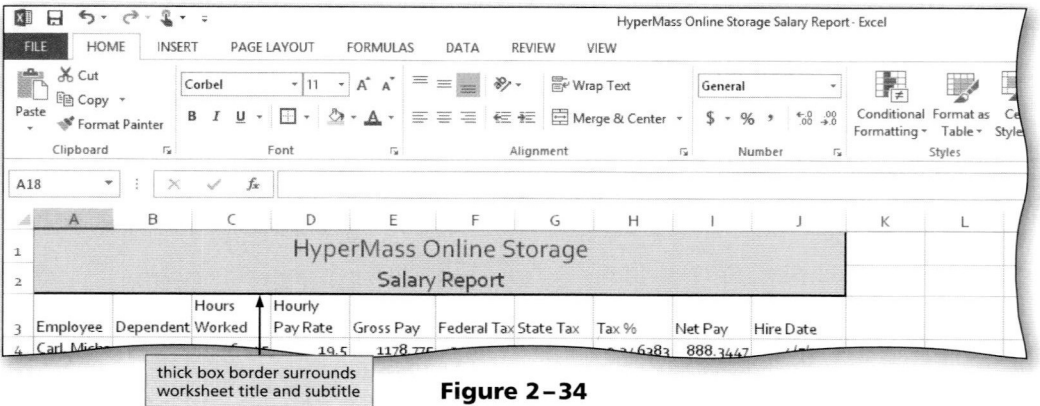

Figure 2–34

Other Ways

1. Tap or click Font Settings Dialog Box Launcher (HOME tab | Font group), tap or click Fill tab (Format Cells dialog box), tap or click desired fill, tap or click OK button

2. Press and hold or right-click range, tap or click Format Cells on shortcut menu, tap or click Fill tab (Format Cells dialog box), tap or click desired fill, tap or click OK button

3. Press CTRL+1, tap or click Fill tab (Format Cells dialog box), tap or click desired fill, tap or click OK button

To Apply a Cell Style to the Column Headings and Format the Total Rows

As shown in Figure 2–27b on page EX 90, the column titles (row 3) should have the Heading 3 cell style and the totals row (row 13) should have the Total cell style. The summary information headings in the range A14:A16 should be bold. The following steps assign these styles and formats to row 3 and row 13 and the range A14:A16.

1 Select the range to be formatted, cells A3:J3 in this case.

2 Use the Cell Styles gallery to apply the Heading 3 cell style to the range A3:J3.

3 Tap or click the Center button (HOME tab | Alignment group) to center the column headings.

4 Apply the Total cell style to the range A13:J13.

5 Bold the range A14:A16 (Figure 2–35).

Figure 2–35

To Format Dates and Center Data in Cells

Why? *With the column titles and total rows formatted, the next step is to format the dates in column J and center the dependents in column B.* The following steps format the dates in the range J4:J12 and center the data in the range B4:B16.

- Select the range to contain the new date format, cells J4:J12 in this case.

- Tap or click the Format Cells: Number Format Dialog Box Launcher (HOME tab | Number group) to display the Format Cells dialog box.

- If necessary, tap or click the Number tab (Format Cells dialog box), tap or click Date in the Category list, and then tap or click 3/14/12 in the Type list to choose the format for the selected range (Figure 2–36).

2

- Tap or click the OK button (Format Cells dialog box) to format the dates in the current column using the selected date format style.

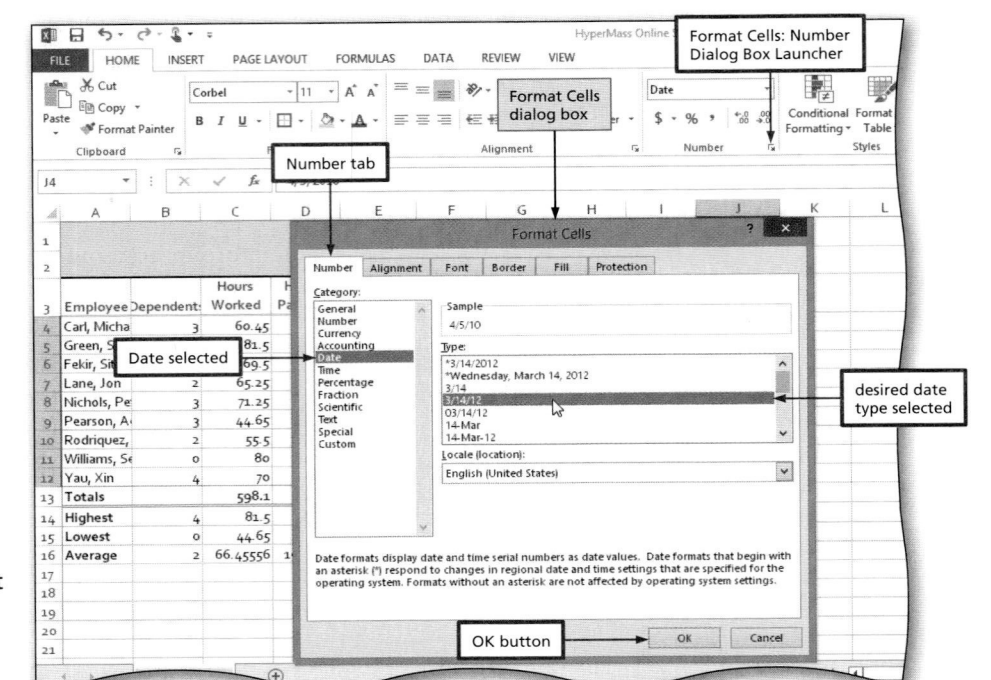

Figure 2–36

3

- Select the range B4:B16 and then tap or click the Center button (HOME tab | Alignment group) to center the data in the selected range.

- Select cell E4 to deselect the selected range (Figure 2–37).

Q&A
Can I format an entire column at once?

Yes. Rather than selecting the range B4:B16 in Step 3, you could have tapped or clicked the column B heading immediately above cell B1, and then tapped or clicked the Center button (HOME tab | Alignment group). In this case, all cells in column B down to the last cell in the worksheet would have been formatted to use center alignment. This same procedure could have been used to format the dates in column J.

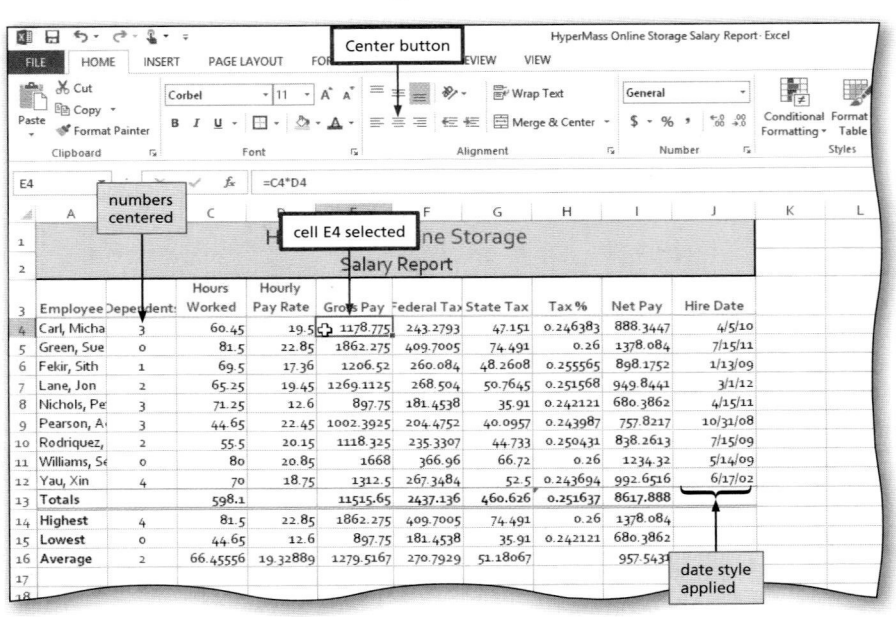

Figure 2–37

Other Ways

1. Press and hold or right-click range, tap or click Format Cells on shortcut menu, tap or click Number tab (Format Cells dialog box), tap or click desired number format, tap or click OK button

2. Press CTRL+1, tap or click Number tab (Format Cells dialog box), tap or click desired number format, tap or click OK button

Formatting Numbers Using the Ribbon

As shown in Figure 2–27b on page EX 90, the worksheet is formatted to resemble an accounting report. For example, in columns D through G and I, the numbers in the first row (row 4), the totals row (row 13), and the rows below the totals (rows 14 through 16) have dollar signs, while the remaining numbers (rows 5 through 12) in columns D through G and column I do not.

To Apply an Accounting Number Format and Comma Style Format Using the Ribbon

1 ENTER FORMULAS | 2 ENTER FUNCTIONS | 3 VERIFY FORMULAS
4 FORMAT WORKSHEET | 5 CHECK SPELLING | 6 PRINT WORKSHEET

The following steps assign formats using the 'Accounting Number Format' button and the Comma Style button. The accounting number format is applied to the currency amounts in rows 4 and 13. The comma style format is applied to the range E5:G12 and to range I5:I12, and to column C (Hours Worked). *Why? This gives the worksheet a more professional look.*

- Select the range to contain the accounting number format, cells D4:G4 in this case.

- While holding down the CTRL key, select cell I4, the range E13:G13, and cell I13 to select the nonadjacent ranges and cells.

- Tap or click the 'Accounting Number Format' button (HOME tab | Number group) to apply the accounting number format with fixed dollar signs to the selected nonadjacent ranges (Figure 2–38).

Q&A What is the effect of applying the accounting number format?

The 'Accounting Number Format' button assigns a fixed dollar sign to the numbers in the ranges. In each cell in these ranges, Excel displays the dollar sign to the far left with spaces between it and the first digit in the cell.

Figure 2–38

- Select the ranges to contain the comma style format, cells D5:G12 and I5:I12 in this case.

- Tap or click the Comma Style button (HOME tab | Number group) to assign the comma style format to the selected ranges (Figure 2–39).

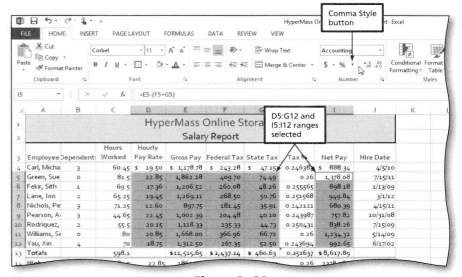

Figure 2–39

3

- Select the range to contain the comma style format, cells C4:C16 in this case.

- Tap or click the Comma Style button (HOME tab | Number group) to assign the comma style format to the selected range (Figure 2–40).

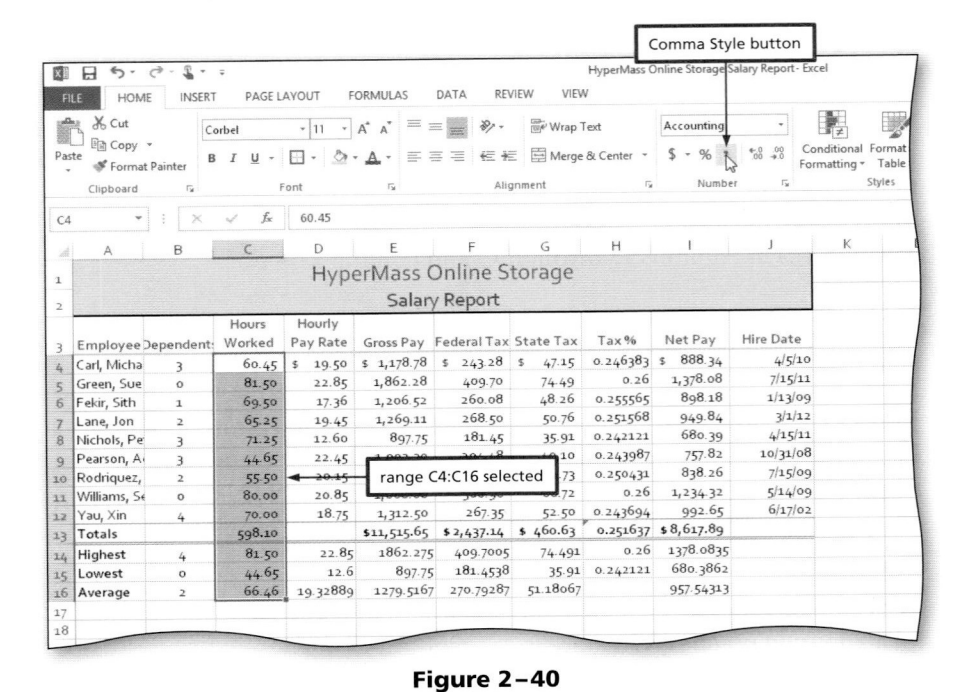

Figure 2–40

To Apply a Currency Style Format with a Floating Dollar Sign Using the Format Cells Dialog Box

1 ENTER FORMULAS | 2 ENTER FUNCTIONS | 3 VERIFY FORMULAS
4 FORMAT WORKSHEET | 5 CHECK SPELLING | 6 PRINT WORKSHEET

Why? The Format Cells dialog box can be used to apply formatting that is not available directly on the ribbon. The following steps use the Format Cells dialog box to apply the currency style format with a floating dollar sign to the numbers in the ranges D14:G16 and I14:I16.

1

- Select the ranges (D14:G16 and I14:I16) and then tap or click the Number Format Dialog Box Launcher (HOME tab | Number group) to display the Format Cells dialog box.

- If necessary, tap or click the Number tab to display the Number sheet (Format Cells dialog box).

- Tap or click Currency in the Category list to select the necessary number format category and then tap or click the third style ($1,234.10) in the Negative numbers list to select the desired currency format for negative numbers (Figure 2–41).

Q&A How do I select the proper format?

You can choose from 12 categories of formats. Once you select a category, you can select the number of decimal places, whether or not a dollar sign should be displayed, and how negative numbers should appear. Selecting the appropriate negative numbers format is important, because doing so adds a space to the right of the number in order to align the numbers in the worksheet on the decimal points. Some of the available negative number formats do not align the numbers in the worksheet on the decimal points.

Figure 2–41

2

- Tap or click the OK button (Format Cells dialog box) to assign the currency style format with a floating dollar sign to the selected ranges (Figure 2–42).

Q&A What is the difference between using the accounting number style and currency style?

When using the 'Accounting Number Format' button, recall that a floating dollar sign always appears immediately to the left of the first digit, and the fixed dollar sign always appears on the left side of the cell.

Figure 2–42

Other Ways

1. Press CTRL+1, tap or click Number tab (Format Cells dialog box), tap or click Currency in Category list, select format, tap or click OK button

2. Press CTRL+SHIFT+DOLLAR SIGN ($)

To Apply a Percent Style Format and Use the Increase Decimal Button

1 ENTER FORMULAS | 2 ENTER FUNCTIONS | 3 VERIFY FORMULAS
4 FORMAT WORKSHEET | 5 CHECK SPELLING | 6 PRINT WORKSHEET

The next step is to format the tax percentage in column H. *Why?* *Currently, Excel displays the numbers as decimal fractions when they should appear as percentages.* The following steps format the range H4:H16 to the percent style format with two decimal places.

1

- Select the range to format, cells H4:H16 in this case.

- Tap or click the Percent Style button (HOME tab | Number group) to display the numbers in the selected range as a rounded whole percent.

Q&A What is the result of tapping or clicking the Percent Style button?

The Percent Style button instructs Excel to display a value as a percentage, determined by multiplying the cell entry by 100, rounding the result to the nearest percent, and adding a percent sign. For example, when cell H4 is formatted using the Percent Style buttons, Excel displays the actual value 0.246383 as 25%.

Figure 2–43

2

- Tap or click the Increase Decimal button (HOME tab | Number group) two times to display the numbers in the selected range with two decimal places (Figure 2–43).

Other Ways

1. Press and hold or right-click selected range, tap or click Format Cells on shortcut menu, tap or click Number tab (Format Cells dialog box), tap or click Percentage in Category list, select format, tap or click OK button

2. Press CTRL+1, tap or click Number tab (Format Cells dialog box), tap or click Percentage in Category list, select format, tap or click OK button

3. Press CTRL+SHIFT+PERCENT SIGN (%)

Conditional Formatting

The next step is to emphasize the values greater than 70 in column C by formatting them to appear with an orange background and white font color (Figure 2–44).

To Apply Conditional Formatting

The following steps assign conditional formatting to the range C4:C12. *Why? After formatting, any cell value greater than 70 will cause Excel to display the number in the cell with an orange background and a white font color.*

1

- Select the range C4:C12.

- Tap or click the Conditional Formatting button (HOME tab | Styles group) to display the Conditional Formatting menu (Figure 2–44).

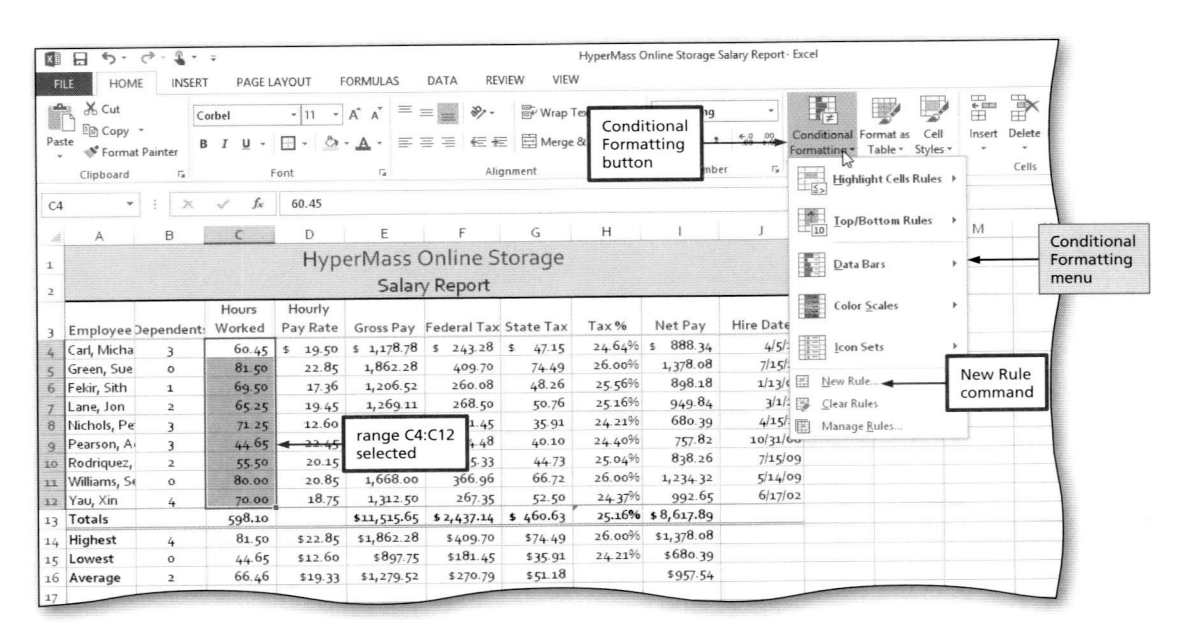

Figure 2–44

2

- Tap or click New Rule on the Conditional Formatting menu to display the New Formatting Rule dialog box.

- Tap or click 'Format only cells that contain' in the Select a Rule Type area (New Formatting Rule dialog box) to change the Edit the Rule Description area.

- In the Edit the Rule Description area, tap or click the arrow in the relational operator box (second box) to display a list of relational operators, and then select greater than to select the desired operator.

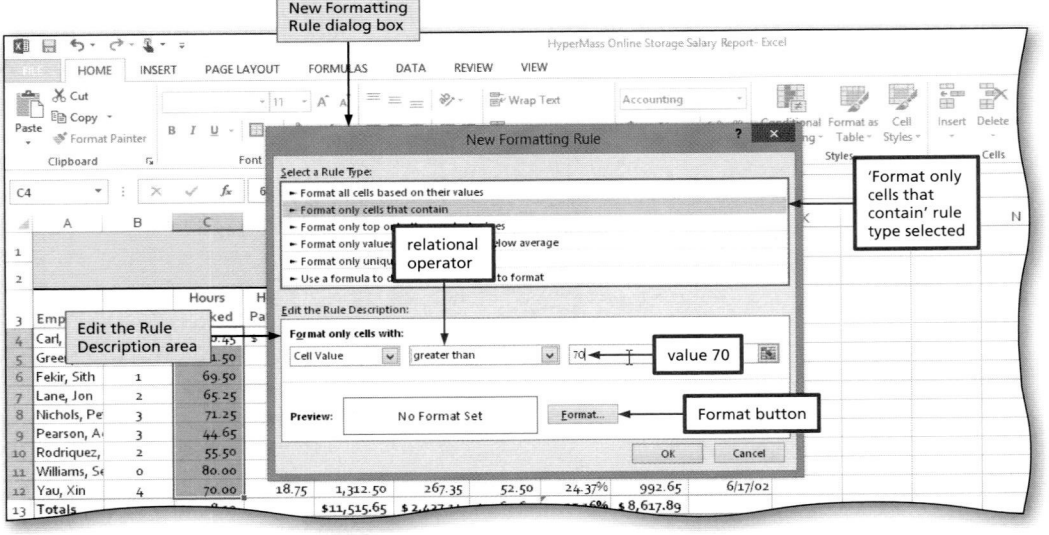

Figure 2–45

- Select the rightmost box, and then type 70 to enter the second value of the rule description (Figure 2–45).

Q&A What do the changes in the Edit the Rule Description area indicate?

The Edit the Rule Description area allows you to view and edit the rules for the conditional format. In this case, reading the area indicates that Excel should conditionally format only those cells with cell values greater than 70.

3

- Tap or click the Format button (New Formatting Rule dialog box) to display the Format Cells dialog box.

- If necessary, tap or click the Font tab (Format Cells dialog box) to display the Font sheet. Tap or click the Color arrow to display the Color gallery and then tap or click White, Background 1 (column 1, row 1) in the Color gallery to select the font color (Figure 2–46).

Figure 2–46

4

- Tap or click the Fill tab (Format Cells dialog box) to display the Fill sheet and then tap or click the orange color in column 6, row 5 to select the background color (Figure 2–47).

Figure 2–47

5

- Tap or click the OK button (Format Cells dialog box) to close the Format Cells dialog box and display the New Formatting Rule dialog box with the desired font and background colors displayed in the Preview box (Figure 2–48).

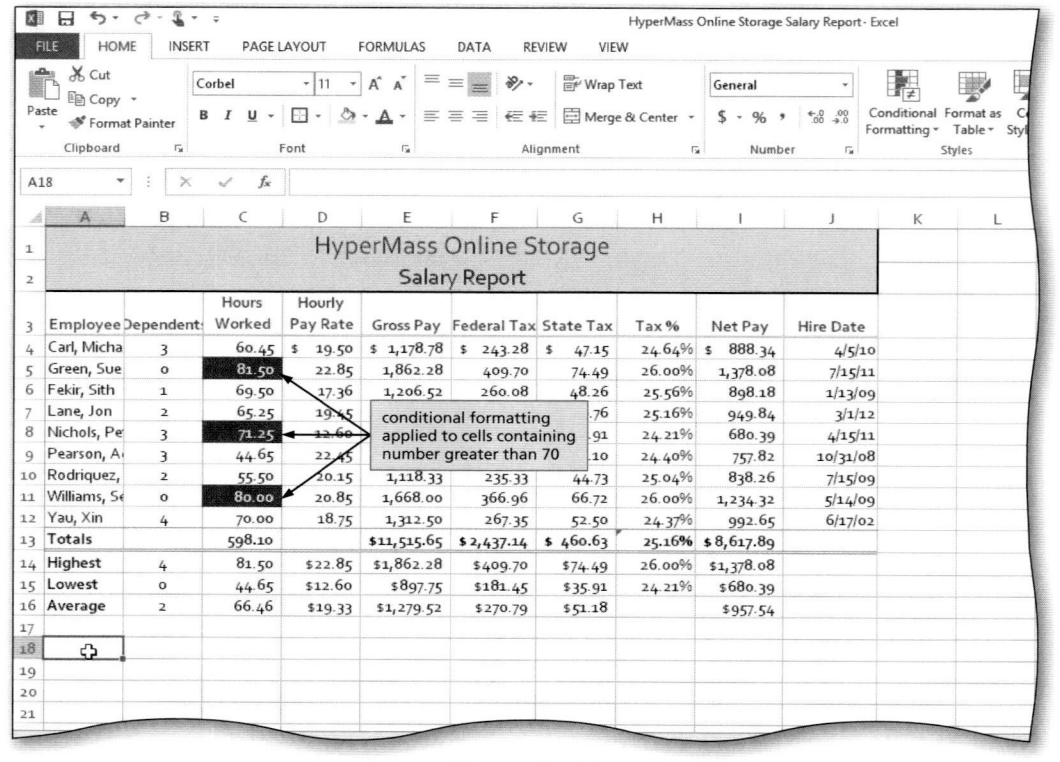

Figure 2–48

6

- Tap or click the OK button (New Formatting Rule dialog box) to assign the conditional format to the selected range.

- Tap or click anywhere in the worksheet, such as cell A18, to deselect the current range (Figure 2–49).

Figure 2–49

Conditional Formatting Operators

As shown in Figure 2–48, the second text box in the Edit the Rule Description area in the New Formatting Rule dialog box allows you to select a relational operator, such as less than, to use in the condition. The eight different relational operators from which you can choose for conditional formatting in the New Formatting Rule dialog box are summarized in Table 2–5.

Table 2–5 Summary of Conditional Formatting Relational Operators	
Relational Operator	**Description**
between	Cell value is between two numbers
not between	Cell value is not between two numbers
equal to	Cell value is equal to a number
not equal to	Cell value is not equal to a number
greater than	Cell value is greater than a number
less than	Cell value is less than a number
greater than or equal to	Cell value is greater than or equal to a number
less than or equal to	Cell value is less than or equal to a number

Changing Column Width and Row Height

When Excel starts and displays a blank worksheet on the screen, all of the columns have a default width of 8.43 characters, or 64 pixels. These values may change depending on the theme applied to the workbook. For example, in this chapter, the Basis theme was applied to the workbook, resulting in columns having a default width of 8.38 characters. A character is defined as a letter, number, symbol, or punctuation mark in 11-point Calibri font, the default font used by Excel. An average of 8.43 characters in 11-point Calibri font will fit in a cell.

Another measure of the height and width of cells is pixels. A **pixel**, which is short for picture element, is a dot on the screen that contains a color. The size of the dot is based on your screen's resolution. At the resolution of 1366 × 768 used in this book, 1366 pixels appear across the screen and 768 pixels appear down the screen for a total of 1,049,088 pixels. It is these 1,049,088 pixels that form the font and other items you see on the screen.

The default row height in a blank worksheet is 15 points (or 20 pixels). Recall from Chapter 1 that a point is equal to 1/72 of an inch. Thus, 15 points is equal to about 1/5 of an inch. You can change the width of the columns or height of the rows at any time to make the worksheet easier to read or to ensure that Excel displays an entry properly in a cell.

To Change Column Width

1 ENTER FORMULAS | 2 ENTER FUNCTIONS | 3 VERIFY FORMULAS
4 FORMAT WORKSHEET | 5 CHECK SPELLING | 6 PRINT WORKSHEET

When changing the column width, you can set the width manually or you can instruct Excel to size the column to best fit. **Best fit** means that the width of the column will be increased or decreased so that the widest entry will fit in the column. *Why? Sometimes, you may prefer more or less white space in a column than best fit provides. To change the white space, Excel allows you to change column widths manually.*

When the format you assign to a cell causes the entry to exceed the width of a column, Excel automatically changes the column width to best fit. If you do not assign a format to a cell or cells in a column, the column width will remain 8.43 characters. To set a column width to best fit, double-tap or double-click the right boundary of the column heading above row 1.

The steps on the following pages change the column widths as follows: column A and B to best fit; column G to 10.25 characters; columns C, D, and H to 7.50 characters; and columns E, F, and I to 10.50 characters.

1

- Drag through column headings A and B above row 1 to select the columns.

- Tap or point to the boundary on the right side of column heading B to cause the pointer to become a split double arrow (Figure 2–50).

Q&A What if I want to make a large change to the column width?

If you want to increase or decrease column width significantly, you can press and hold or right-click a column heading and then use the Column Width command on the shortcut menu to change the column's width. To use this command, however, you must select one or more entire columns.

Figure 2–50

2

- Double-tap or double-click the right boundary of column heading B to change the width of the selected columns to best fit.

- Tap or point to the right boundary of the column G heading above row 1.

- When the pointer changes to a split double arrow, drag until the ScreenTip indicates Width: 10.25 (87 pixels). Do not lift your finger or release the mouse button (Figure 2–51).

Figure 2–51

Q&A What happens if I change the column width to zero (0)?

If you decrease the column width to 0, the column is hidden. **Hiding cells** is a technique you can use to hide data that might not be relevant to a particular report or sensitive data that you do not want others to see. To instruct Excel to display a hidden column, position the mouse pointer to the right of the column heading boundary where the hidden column is located and then drag to the right.

- Lift your finger or release the mouse button to change the column width.

- Tap or click the column C heading above row 1 to select the column.

- While holding down the CTRL key, tap or click the column D heading and then the column H heading above row 1 so that nonadjacent columns are selected.

- Tap or point to the boundary on the right side of the column H heading above row 1.

- Drag until the ScreenTip indicates Width: 7.50 (65 pixels). Do not lift your finger or release the mouse button (Figure 2–52).

Figure 2–52

- Lift your finger or release the mouse button to change the column widths.

- Tap or click the column E heading and drag to select the column F heading.

- While holding down the CTRL key, tap or click the column I heading above row 1 so that nonadjacent columns are selected.

- Drag the right boundary of column F until the ScreenTip indicates Width: 10.50 (89 pixels). Lift your finger or release the mouse button to change the column widths.

- Tap or click anywhere in the worksheet, such as cell A18, to deselect the columns (Figure 2–53).

Figure 2–53

Other Ways

1. Press and hold or right-click column heading or drag through multiple column headings, press and hold or right-click selected heading, tap or click Column Width on shortcut menu, enter desired column width, tap or click OK button

To Change Row Height

Why? You also can increase or decrease the height of a row manually to improve the appearance of the worksheet. When you increase the font size of a cell entry, such as the title in cell A1, Excel automatically increases the row height to best fit so that it can display the characters properly. Recall that Excel did this earlier when multiple lines were entered in a cell in row 3, and when the cell style of the worksheet title and subtitle was changed. The following steps improve the appearance of the worksheet by increasing the height of row 3 to 48.00 points and increasing the height of row 14 to 27.00 points.

1

- Tap or point to the boundary below row heading 3 until the pointer displays the split double arrow.

- Drag down until the ScreenTip indicates Height: 48.00 (64 pixels). Do not apply the change yet (Figure 2–54).

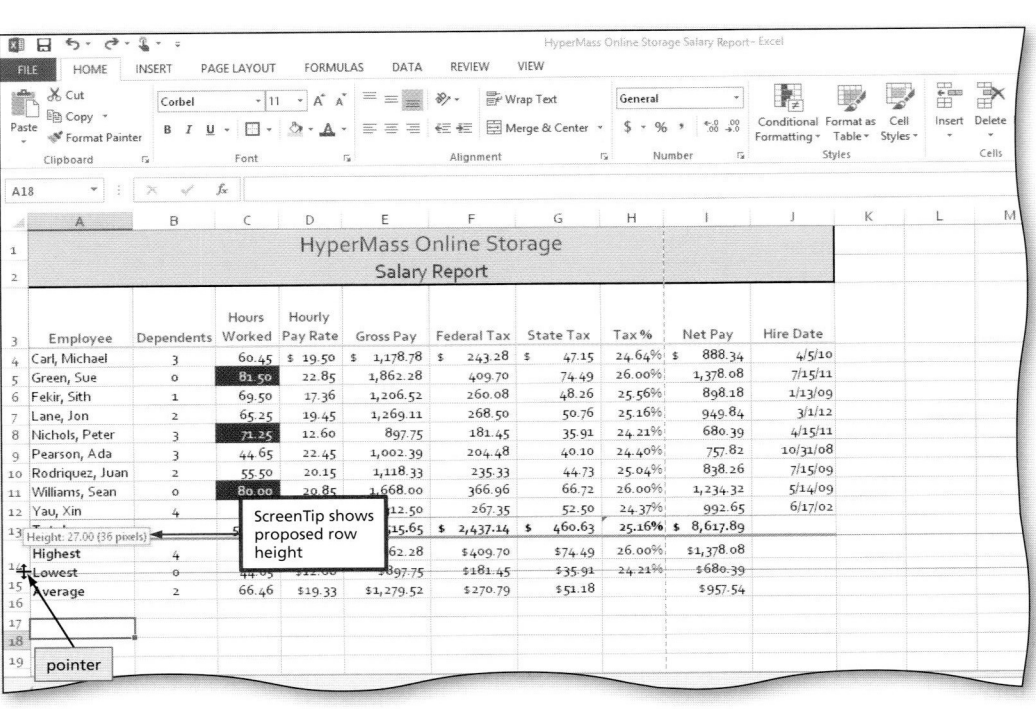

Figure 2–54

2

- Lift your finger or release the mouse button to change the row height.

- Tap or point to the boundary below row heading 14 until the pointer displays the split double arrow and then drag downward until the ScreenTip indicates Height: 27.00 (36 pixels). Do not lift your finger or release the mouse button (Figure 2–55).

Figure 2–55

3

- Lift your finger or release the mouse button to change the row height.

- Tap or click anywhere in the worksheet, such as cell A18, to deselect the current cell (Figure 2–56).

Q&A
Can I hide a row?
Yes. As with column widths, when you decrease the row height to 0, the row is hidden. To instruct Excel to display a hidden row, position the pointer just below the row heading boundary where the row is hidden and then drag downward. To set a row height to best fit, double-tap or double-click the bottom boundary of the row heading.

Figure 2–56

Other Ways

1. Press and hold or right-click row heading or drag through multiple row headings, press and hold or right-click selected heading, tap or click Row Height on shortcut menu, enter desired row height, tap or click OK button

Break Point: If you wish to take a break, this is a good place to do so. Be sure to save the HyperMass Online Storage Salary Report file again and then you can exit Excel. To resume at a later time, run Excel, open the file called HyperMass Online Storage Salary Report, and continue following the steps from this location forward.

Checking Spelling

Excel includes a **spell checker** you can use to check a worksheet for spelling errors. The spell checker looks for spelling errors by comparing words on the worksheet against words contained in its standard dictionary. If you often use specialized terms that are not in the standard dictionary, you may want to add them to a custom dictionary using the Spelling dialog box.

When the spell checker finds a word that is not in either dictionary, it displays the word in the Spelling dialog box. You then can correct it if it is misspelled.

Does the spell checker catch all spelling mistakes?

While Excel's spell checker is a valuable tool, it is not infallible. You should proofread your workbook carefully by pointing to each word and saying it aloud as you point to it. Be mindful of misused words such as its and it's, through and though, and to and too. Nothing undermines a good impression more than a professional looking report with misspelled words.

CONSIDER THIS

To Check Spelling on the Worksheet

Why? *Everything on a worksheet should be spell checked to make sure it is as accurate as possible.* To illustrate how Excel responds to a misspelled word, the following steps purposely misspell the word, Employee, in cell A3 as the word, Empolyee, as shown in Figure 2–57.

1
- Tap or click cell A3 and then type **Empolyee** to misspell the word, Employee.
- Select cell A2 so that the spell checker begins checking at the selected cell.
- Tap or click REVIEW on the ribbon to display the REVIEW tab.
- Tap or click the Spelling button (REVIEW tab | Proofing group) to run the spell checker and display the misspelled word in the Spelling dialog box (Figure 2–57).

Q&A What happens when the spell checker finds a misspelled word?
When the spell checker identifies that a cell contains a word not in its standard or custom dictionary, it selects that cell as the active cell and displays the Spelling dialog box. The Spelling dialog box lists the word not found in the dictionary and a list of suggested corrections (Figure 2–58).

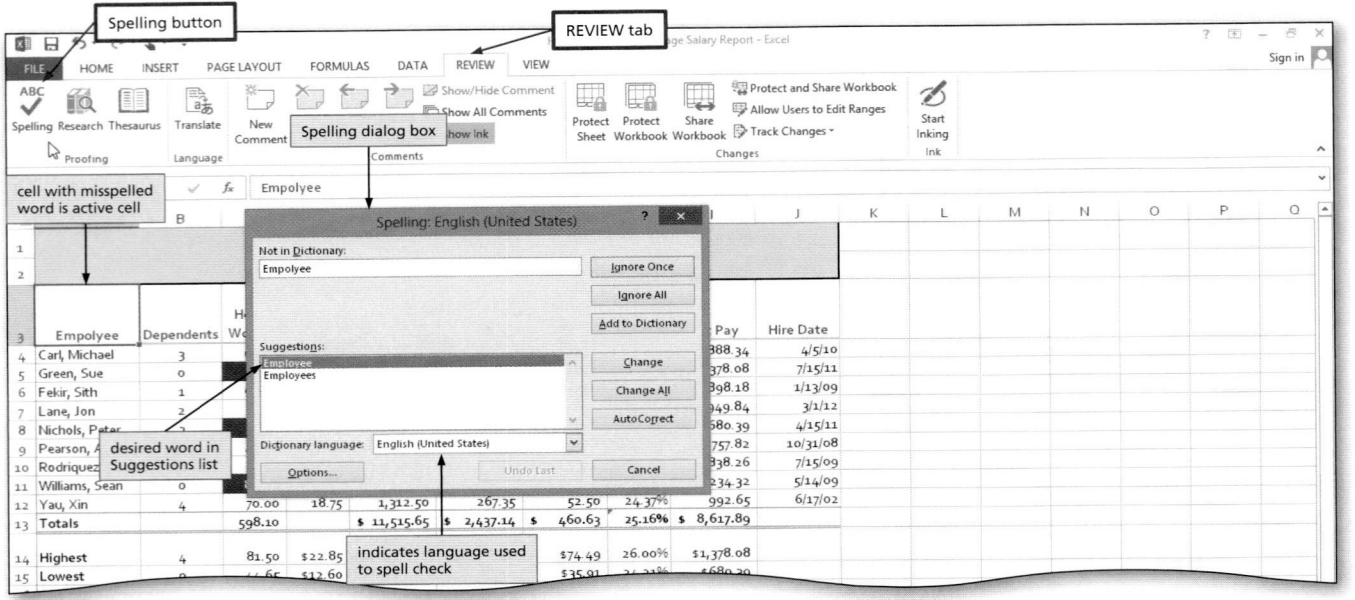

Figure 2–57

2
- Tap or click the Change button (Spelling dialog box) to change the misspelled word to the correct word (Figure 2–58).
- Tap or click the Close button to close the Spelling dialog box.
- If a Microsoft Excel dialog box is displayed, tap or click the OK button.

3
- Tap or click anywhere in the worksheet, such as cell A18, to deselect the current cell.
- Display the HOME tab.
- Tap or click the Save button on the Quick Access Toolbar to save the workbook.

Q&A What other actions can I take in the Spelling dialog box?
If one of the words in the Suggestions list is correct, tap or click it and then tap or click the Change button. If none of the suggestions is correct, type the correct word in the Not in Dictionary text box and then tap or click the Change button. To change the word throughout the worksheet, tap or click the Change All button instead of the Change button. To skip correcting the word, tap or click the Ignore Once button. To have Excel ignore the word for the remainder of the worksheet, tap or click the Ignore All button.

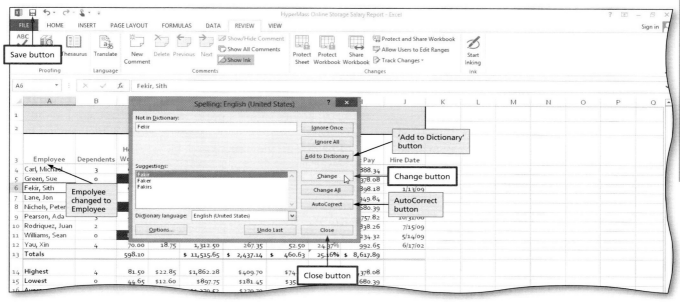

Figure 2–58

Other Ways

1. Press F7

Additional Spell Checker Considerations

Consider these additional guidelines when using the spell checker:

- To check the spelling of the text in a single cell, double-tap or double-click the cell to make the formula bar active and then tap or click the Spelling button (REVIEW tab | Proofing group).

- If you select a single cell so that the formula bar is not active and then start the spell checker, Excel checks the remainder of the worksheet, including notes and embedded charts.

- If you select a cell other than cell A1 before you start the spell checker, Excel will display a dialog box when the spell checker reaches the end of the worksheet, asking if you want to continue checking at the beginning.

- If you select a range of cells before starting the spell checker, Excel checks the spelling of the words only in the selected range.

- To check the spelling of all the sheets in a workbook, press and hold or right-click any sheet tab, tap or click 'Select All Sheets' on the sheet tab shortcut menu, and then start the spell checker.

- To add words to the dictionary, such as your last name, tap or click the 'Add to Dictionary' button in the Spelling dialog box (shown in Figure 2–58) when Excel flags the word as not being in the dictionary.

- Tap or click the AutoCorrect button (shown in Figure 2–58) to add the misspelled word and the correct version of the word to the AutoCorrect list. For example, suppose that you misspell the word, do, as the word, dox. When the spell checker displays the Spelling dialog box with the correct word, do, in the Suggestions list, tap or click the AutoCorrect button. Then, anytime in the future that you type the word, dox, Excel automatically will change it to the word, do.

Printing the Worksheet

Excel allows for a great deal of customization in how a worksheet appears when printed. For example, the margins on the page can be adjusted. A header or footer can be added to each printed page, as well. A **header** is text and graphics that print at the top of each page. Similarly, a **footer** is text and graphics that print at the bottom of each page. Excel also has the capability to work on the worksheet in Page Layout view. **Page Layout view** allows you to create or modify a worksheet while viewing how it will look in printed format. The default view that you have worked in up until this point in the book is called **Normal view**.

To Change the Worksheet's Margins, Header, and Orientation in Page Layout View

1 ENTER FORMULAS | 2 ENTER FUNCTIONS | 3 VERIFY FORMULAS
4 FORMAT WORKSHEET | 5 CHECK SPELLING | **6 PRINT WORKSHEET**

The following steps change to Page Layout view, narrow the margins of the worksheet, change the header of the worksheet, and set the orientation of the worksheet to landscape. *Why? Often, you may want to reduce margins so that the printed worksheet better fits the page. Changing the header helps to identify the content on each page, and changing the orientation can help you fit wider printouts across a sheet of paper.* **Margins** are those portions of a printed page outside the main body of the printed document and always are blank when printed. The current worksheet is too wide for a single page and requires landscape orientation to fit on one page in a readable manner.

1

- Tap or click the Page Layout button on the status bar to view the worksheet in Page Layout view (Figure 2–59).

Q&A What are some key features of Page Layout view?

Page Layout view shows the worksheet divided into pages. A gray background separates each page. The white areas surrounding each page indicate the print margins. The top of each page includes a Header area, and the bottom of each page includes a Footer area. Page Layout view also includes a ruler at the top of the page that assists you in placing objects on the page, such as charts and pictures.

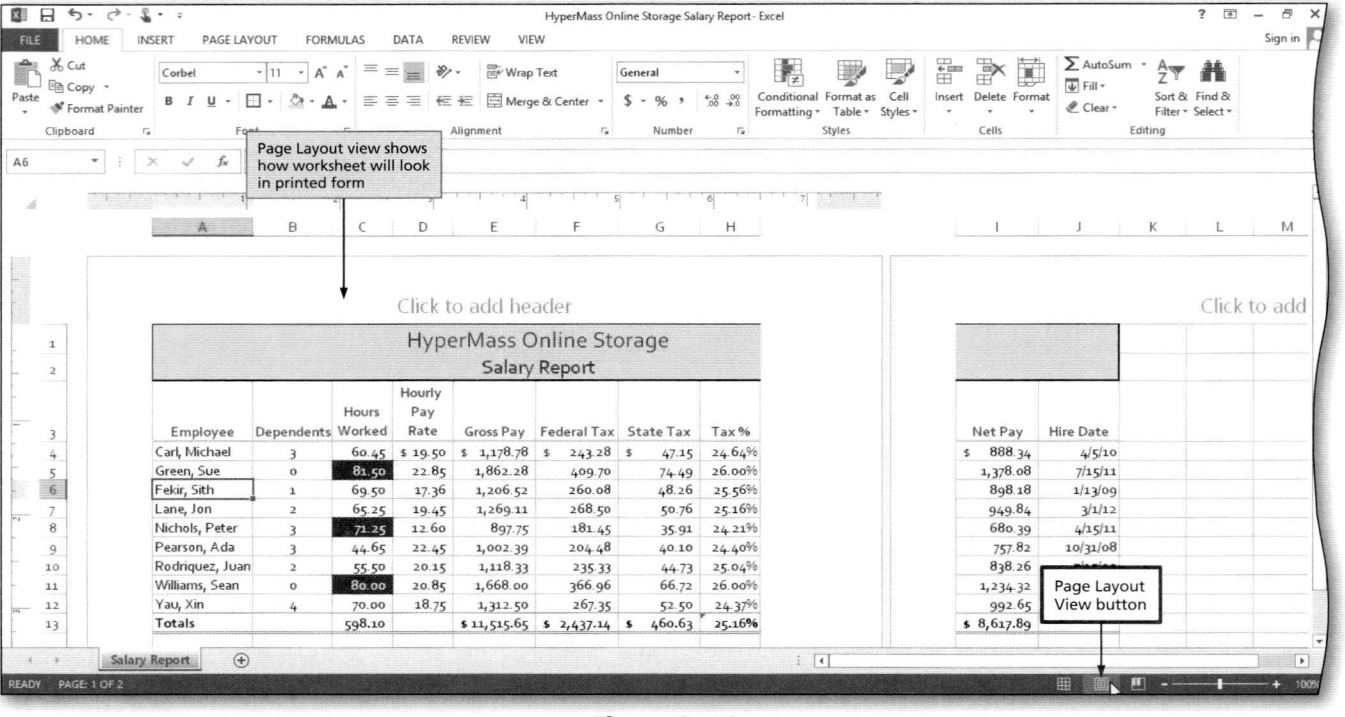

Figure 2–59

2

- Display the PAGE LAYOUT tab.

- Tap or click the Adjust Margins button (PAGE LAYOUT tab | Page Setup group) to display the Margins gallery (Figure 2–60).

Figure 2–60

3

- Tap or click Narrow in the Margins gallery to change the worksheet margins to the Narrow margin style.

- Select cell A6 to deselect the header. Tap or click above the worksheet title in cell A1 in the center area of the Header area.

- Type **John Simon** and then press the ENTER key. Type **Chief Financial Officer** to complete the worksheet header (Figure 2–61).

If requested by your instructor, type your name instead of John Simon.

- Select cell A6 to deselect the header.

Figure 2–61

Q&A

What else can I place in a header?

You can add text, page number information, date and time information, the file path of the workbook, the file name of the workbook, the sheet name of the workbook, and pictures to a header.

4

- Display the PAGE LAYOUT tab.

- Tap or click the 'Change Page Orientation' button (PAGE LAYOUT tab | Page Setup group) to display the Change Page Orientation gallery (Figure 2–62).

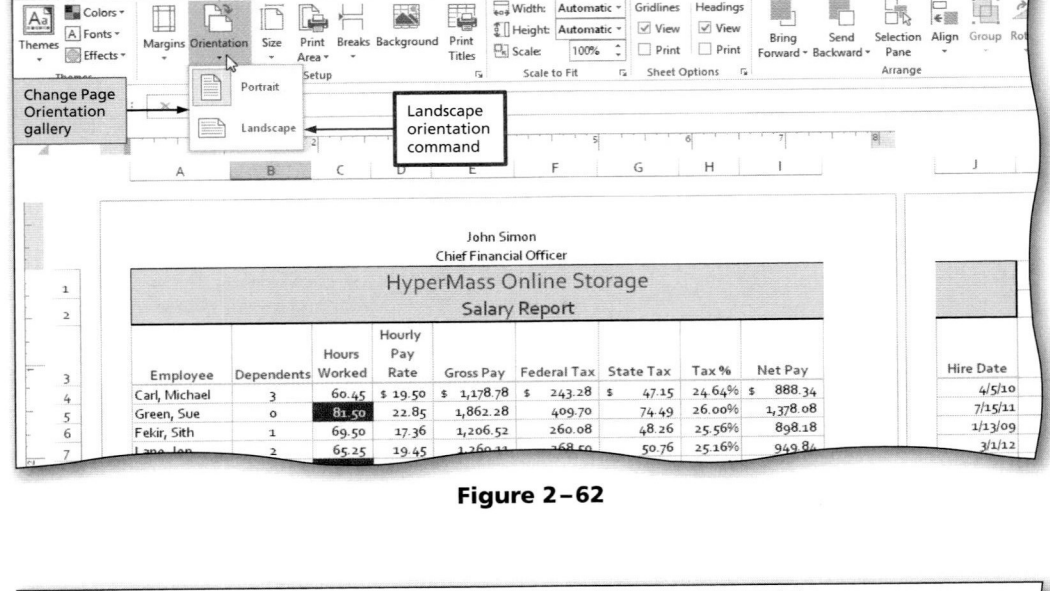

Figure 2–62

5

- Tap or click Landscape in the Change Page Orientation gallery to change the worksheet's orientation to landscape (Figure 2–63).

Q&A | Do I need to change the orientation every time I want to print the worksheet? No. Once you change the orientation and save the workbook, Excel will save the orientation setting for that workbook until you change it. When you open a new workbook, Excel sets the orientation to portrait.

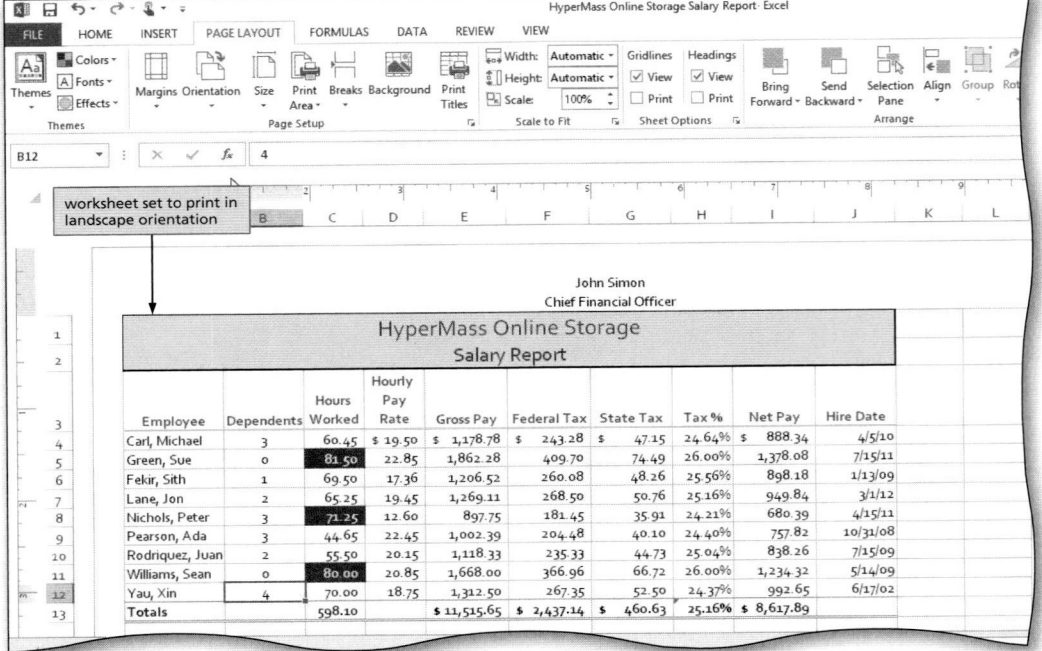

Figure 2–63

Why does the header not appear centered over the worksheet?
The header is centered between the left and right margins of the page. The worksheet contents do not extend across the page from margin to margin, which makes the header appear off center.

Other Ways

1. Tap or click Page Setup Dialog Box Launcher (PAGE LAYOUT tab | Page Setup group), tap or click Page tab (Page Setup dialog box), tap or click Portrait or Landscape, tap or click OK button

To Print a Worksheet

Excel provides other options for printing a worksheet. In the following sections, you first print the worksheet and then print a section of the worksheet. The following steps print the worksheet.

1 Tap or click FILE on the ribbon to open the Backstage view.

2 Tap or click the Print tab in the Backstage view to display the Print gallery.

3 If necessary, tap or click the Printer Status button in the Print gallery to display a list of available Printer options and then tap or click the desired printer to change the currently selected printer.

4 Tap or click the Print button in the Print gallery to print the worksheet in landscape orientation on the currently selected printer.

5 When the printer stops, retrieve the hard copy (Figure 2–64).

John Simon
Chief Financial Officer

HyperMass Online Storage
Salary Report

Employee	Dependents	Hours Worked	Hourly Pay Rate	Gross Pay	Federal Tax	State Tax	Tax %	Net Pay	Hire Date
Carl, Michael	3	60.45	$ 19.50	$ 1,178.78	$ 243.28	$ 47.15	24.64%	$ 888.34	4/5/10
Green, Sue	0	81.50	22.85	1,862.28	409.70	74.49	26.00%	1,378.08	7/15/11
Fekir, Sith	1	69.50	17.36	1,206.52	260.08	48.26	25.56%	898.18	1/13/09
Lane, Jon	2	65.25	19.45	1,269.11	268.50	50.76	25.16%	949.84	3/1/12
Nichols, Peter	3	71.25	12.60	897.75	181.45	35.91	24.21%	680.39	4/15/11
Pearson, Ada	3	44.65	22.45	1,002.39	204.48	40.10	24.40%	757.82	10/31/08
Rodriquez, Juan	2	55.50	20.15	1,118.33	235.33	44.73	25.04%	838.26	7/15/09
Williams, Sean	0	80.00	20.85	1,668.00	366.96	66.72	26.00%	1,234.32	5/14/09
Yau, Xin	4	70.00	18.75	1,312.50	267.35	52.50	24.37%	992.65	6/17/02
Totals		598.10		$ 11,515.65	$ 2,437.14	$ 460.63	25.16%	$ 8,617.89	
Highest	4	81.50	$22.85	$1,862.28	$409.70	$74.49	26.00%	$1,378.08	
Lowest	0	44.65	$12.60	$897.75	$181.45	$35.91	24.21%	$680.39	
Average	2	66.46	$19.33	$1,279.52	$270.79	$51.18		$957.54	

Figure 2–64

To Print a Section of the Worksheet

You can print portions of the worksheet by selecting the range of cells to print and then tapping or clicking the Selection option button in the Print what area in the Print dialog box. *Why? To save paper, you only want to print the portion of the worksheet you need, instead of printing the entire worksheet.* The following steps print the range A3:E16.

- Select the range to print, cells A3:E16 in this case.
- Tap or click FILE on the ribbon to open the Backstage view.
- Tap or click the Print tab to display the Print gallery.
- Tap or click 'Print Active Sheets' in the Settings area (Print tab | Print gallery) to display a list of options that determine what Excel should print (Figure 2–65).

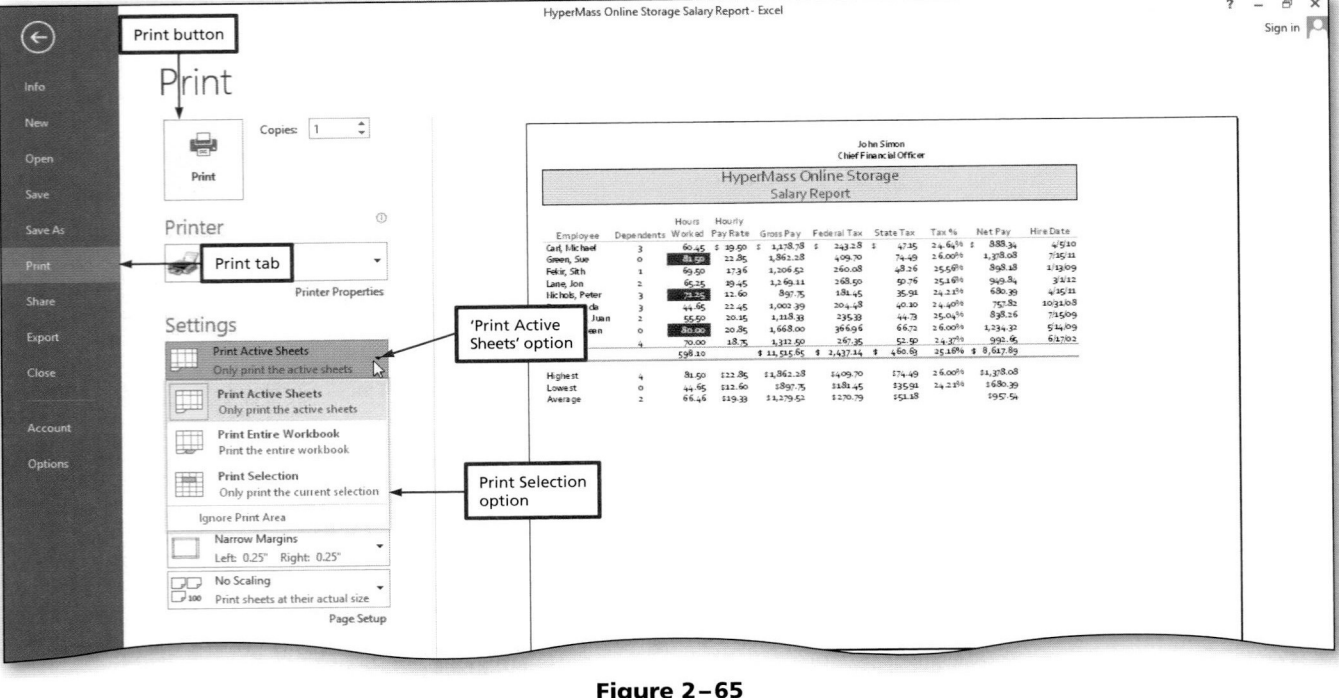

Figure 2–65

2

- Tap or click Print Selection to instruct Excel to print only the selected range.
- Tap or click the Print button in the Print gallery to print the selected range of the worksheet on the currently selected printer (Figure 2–66).
- Tap or click the Normal button on the status bar to return to Normal view.
- Tap or click cell A18 to deselect the range A3:E16.

Q&A

What are my options for telling Excel what to print?

Excel includes three options to allow you to determine what should be printed (Figure 2–65). As shown in the previous steps, the Print Selection option instructs Excel to print the selected range. The 'Print Active Sheets' option instructs Excel to print the active worksheet (the worksheet currently on the screen) or the selected worksheets. Finally, the 'Print Entire Workbook' option instructs Excel to print all of the worksheets in the workbook.

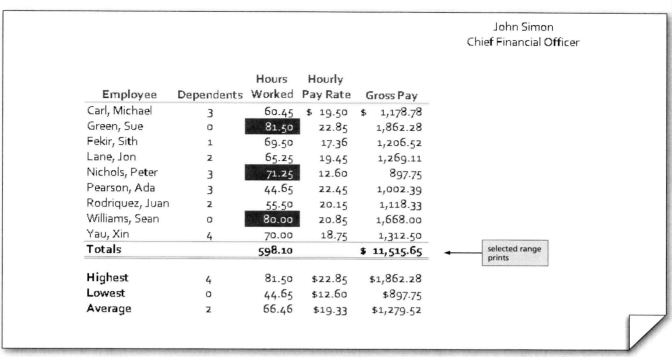

John Simon
Chief Financial Officer

Employee	Dependents	Hours Worked	Hourly Pay Rate	Gross Pay
Carl, Michael	3	60.45	$ 19.50	$ 1,178.78
Green, Sue	0	81.50	22.85	1,862.28
Fekir, Sith	1	69.50	17.36	1,206.52
Lane, Jon	2	65.25	19.45	1,269.11
Nichols, Peter	3	71.25	12.60	897.75
Pearson, Ada	3	44.65	22.45	1,002.39
Rodriquez, Juan	2	55.50	20.15	1,118.33
Williams, Sean	0	80.00	20.85	1,668.00
Yau, Xin	4	70.00	18.75	1,312.50
Totals		598.10		$ 11,515.65
Highest	4	81.50	$22.85	$1,862.28
Lowest	0	44.65	$12.60	$897.75
Average	2	66.46	$19.33	$1,279.52

selected range prints

Figure 2–66

Other Ways

1. Select range, tap or click Print Area button (PAGE LAYOUT tab | Page Setup group), tap or click 'Set Print Area', tap or click FILE tab to open Backstage view, tap or click Print tab, tap or click Print button

Displaying and Printing the Formulas Version of the Worksheet

Thus far, you have been working with the **values version** of the worksheet, which shows the results of the formulas you have entered, rather than the actual formulas. Excel also can display and print the **formulas version** of the worksheet, which shows the actual formulas you have entered, rather than the resulting values.

The formulas version is useful for debugging a worksheet. **Debugging** is the process of finding and correcting errors in the worksheet. Viewing and printing the formulas version instead of the values version makes it easier to see any mistakes in the formulas.

When you change from the values version to the formulas version, Excel increases the width of the columns so that the formulas and text do not overflow into adjacent cells on the right. The formulas version of the worksheet, thus, usually is significantly wider than the values version. To fit the wide printout on one page, you can use landscape orientation, which already has been selected for the workbook, and the Fit to option in the Page sheet in the Page Setup dialog box.

To Display the Formulas in the Worksheet and Fit the Printout on One Page

1 ENTER FORMULAS | 2 ENTER FUNCTIONS | 3 VERIFY FORMULAS
4 FORMAT WORKSHEET | 5 CHECK SPELLING | 6 PRINT WORKSHEET

The following steps change the view of the worksheet from the values version to the formulas version of the worksheet and then print the formulas version on one page. *Why? Printing the formulas in the worksheet can help you verify your formulas are correct and the worksheet is making the correct calculations.*

1

• Press CTRL+ACCENT MARK (`) to display the worksheet with formulas.

• Tap or click the right horizontal scroll arrow until column J appears (Figure 2–67).

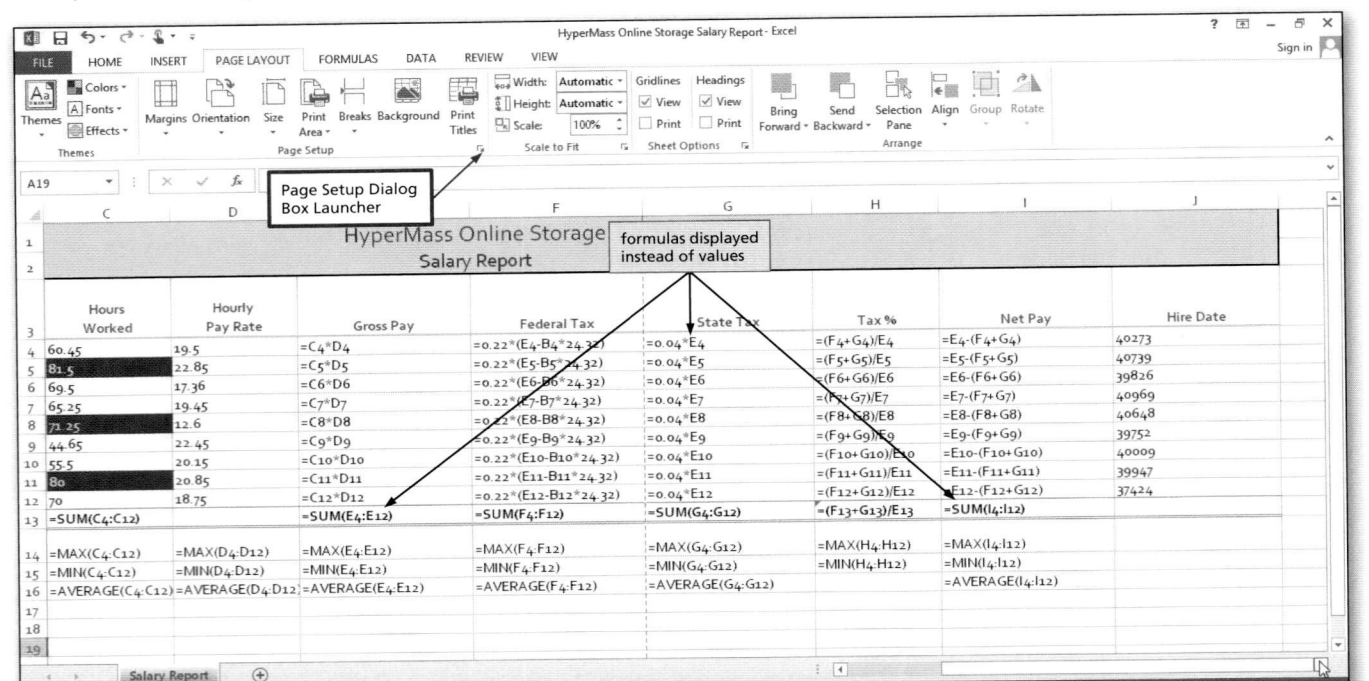

Figure 2–67

2

• Tap or click the Page Setup Dialog Box Launcher (PAGE LAYOUT tab | Page Setup group) to display the Page Setup dialog box (Figure 2–68).

• If necessary, tap or click Landscape in the Orientation area in the Page sheet to select it.

• If necessary, tap or click Fit to in the Scaling area to select it.

Figure 2–68

3

• Tap or click the Print button (Page Setup dialog box) to print the formulas in the worksheet on one page in landscape orientation (Figure 2–69). If necessary, in the Backstage view, select the Print Active Sheets option in the Settings area of the Print gallery.

• When Excel opens the Backstage view, tap or click the Print button to print the worksheet.

Figure 2-69

4

- After viewing and printing the formulas version, press CTRL+ACCENT MARK (`) to instruct Excel to display the values version.
- Tap or click the left horizontal scroll arrow until column A appears.

To Change the Print Scaling Option Back to 100%

Depending on your printer, you may have to change the Print Scaling option back to 100% after using the Fit to option. Doing so will cause the worksheet to print at the default print scaling of 100%. The following steps reset the Print Scaling option so that future worksheets print at 100%, instead of being resized to print on one page.

1 If necessary, display the PAGE LAYOUT tab and then tap or click the Page Setup Dialog Box Launcher (PAGE LAYOUT tab | Page Setup group) to display the Page Setup dialog box.

2 Tap or click Adjust to in the Scaling area to select the Adjust to setting.

3 If necessary, type 100 in the Adjust to box to adjust the print scaling to a new percentage.

4 Tap or click the OK button (Page Setup dialog box) to set the print scaling to normal.

5 Display the HOME tab.

Q&A What is the purpose of the Adjust to box in the Page Setup dialog box?
The Adjust to box allows you to specify the percentage of reduction or enlargement in the printout of a worksheet. The default percentage is 100%. When you tap or click the Fit to option, this percentage automatically changes to the percentage required to fit the printout on one page.

To Sign Out of a Microsoft Account

If you are signed in to a Microsoft account and are using a public computer or otherwise wish to sign out of your Microsoft account, you should sign out of the account from the Account gallery in the Backstage view before exiting Excel. Signing out of the account is the safest way to make sure that nobody else can access SkyDrive files or settings stored in your Microsoft account. The following steps sign out of a Microsoft account from Excel. For a detailed example of the procedure summarized below, refer to the Office and Windows chapter at the beginning of this book.

1 If you wish to sign out of your Microsoft account, tap or click FILE on the ribbon to open the Backstage view and then tap or click the Account tab to display the Account gallery.

2 Tap or click the Sign out link, which displays the Remove Account dialog box. If a Can't remove Windows accounts dialog box appears instead of the Remove Account dialog box, click the OK button and skip the remaining steps.

Q&A Why does a Can't remove Windows accounts dialog box appear?
If you signed in to Windows using your Microsoft account, then you also must sign out from Windows, rather than signing out from within Excel. When you are finished using Windows, be sure to sign out at that time.

3 Tap or click the Yes button (Remove Account dialog box) to sign out of your Microsoft account on this computer.

Q&A Should I sign out of Windows after signing out of my Microsoft account?
When you are finished using the computer, you should sign out of your account for maximum security.

4 Tap or click the Back button in the upper-left corner of the Backstage view to return to the worksheet.

To Save the Workbook and Exit Excel

With the workbook complete, the following steps save the workbook and exit Excel.

1 Tap or click the Save button on the Quick Access Toolbar.

2 Tap or click the Close button on the upper-right corner of the title bar.

3 Sign out of your account and shut down the computer as directed by your instructor.

Chapter Summary

In this chapter you have learned how to enter formulas, calculate an average, find the highest and lowest numbers in a range, verify formulas using Range Finder, add borders, align text, format numbers, change column widths and row heights, and add conditional formatting to a range of numbers. In addition, you learned to spell check a worksheet, print a section of a worksheet, and display and print the formulas version of the worksheet using the Fit to option. The items listed below include all the new Excel skills you have learned in this chapter, with the tasks grouped by activity.

Enter Formulas
Enter a Formula Using the Keyboard (EX 73)
Enter Formulas Using Point Mode (EX 76)

Enter Functions
Determine the Highest Number in a Range of Numbers Using the Insert Function Box (EX 82)
Determine the Lowest Number in a Range of Numbers Using the Sum Menu (EX 84)
Determine the Average of a Range of Numbers Using the Keyboard (EX 86)

Verify Formulas
Verify a Formula Using Range Finder (EX 89)

Format a Worksheet
Change the Workbook Theme (EX 91)
Change the Background Color and Apply a Box Border to the Worksheet Title and Subtitle (EX 93)
Format Dates and Center Data in Cells (EX 96)

Apply an Accounting Number Format and Comma Style Format Using the Ribbon (EX 97)
Apply a Currency Style Format with a Floating Dollar Sign Using the Format Cells Dialog Box (EX 98)
Apply a Percent Style Format and Use the Increase Decimal Button (EX 99)
Apply Conditional Formatting (EX 100)
Change Column Width (EX 103)
Change Row Height (EX 106)

Spell Check a Worksheet
Check Spelling on the Worksheet (EX 108)

Print a Worksheet
Change the Worksheet's Margins, Header, and Orientation in Page Layout View (EX 110)
Print a Section of the Worksheet (EX 114)
Display the Formulas in the Worksheet and Fit the Printout on One Page (EX 116)

What decisions will you need to make when creating workbooks in the future?

1. Determine the workbook structure.

 a) Determine the formulas and functions you will need for your workbook.

 b) Sketch a layout of your data and functions.

2. Create the worksheet.

 a) Enter the titles, subtitles, and headings.

 b) Enter the data, desired functions, and formulas.

3. Format the worksheet.

 a) Determine the theme for the worksheet.

 b) Format the titles, subtitles, and headings using styles.

 c) Format the totals, minimums, maximums, and averages.

 d) Format the numbers and text.

 e) Resize columns and rows.

Apply Your Knowledge

Reinforce the skills and apply the concepts you learned in this chapter.

Cost Analysis Worksheet

Note: To complete this assignment, you will be required to use the Data Files for Students. Visit www.cengage.com/ct/studentdownload for detailed instructions or contact your instructor for information about accessing the required files.

Instructions: The purpose of this exercise is to open a partially completed workbook, enter formulas and functions, copy the formulas and functions, and then format the worksheet titles and numbers. As shown in Figure 2–70, the completed worksheet analyzes the costs associated with a taxi company's fleet of vehicles.

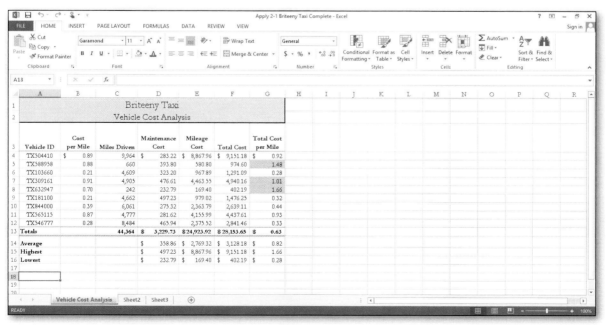

Figure 2–70

Continued >

Apply Your Knowledge *continued*

1. Run Excel. Open the workbook Apply 2–1 Briteeny Taxi.

2. Use the following formulas in cells E4, F4, and G4:

 Mileage Cost (cell E4) = Cost per Mile * Miles Driven or = B4 * C4

 Total Cost (cell F4) = Maintenance Cost + Mileage Cost or = D4 + E4

 Total Cost per Mile (cell G4) = Total Cost / Miles Driven or = F4 / C4

 Use the fill handle to copy the three formulas in the range E4:G4 to the range E5:G12.

3. Determine totals for the miles driven, maintenance cost, mileage cost, and total cost in row 13. Copy the formula in cell G12 to G13 to assign the formula in cell G12 to G13 in the total line. If necessary, reapply the Total cell style to cell G13.

4. In the range D14:D16, determine the average value, highest value, and lowest value, respectively, for the values in the range D4:D12. Use the fill handle to copy the three functions to the range E14:G16.

5. Format the worksheet as follows:

 a. Change the workbook theme to Organic by using the Themes button (PAGE LAYOUT tab | Themes group)

 b. Cell A1 — change to Title cell style

 c. Cell A2 — change to a font size of 16

 d. Cells A1:A2 — Teal, Accent 2, Lighter 80% fill color and a thick box border

 e. Cells B4, D4:G4, and D13:G13 — accounting number format with two decimal places and fixed dollar signs by using the 'Accounting Number Format' button (HOME tab | Number group)

 f. Cells B5:B12, and D5:G12 — comma style format with two decimal places by using the Comma Style button (HOME tab | Number group)

 g. Cells C4:C13 — comma style format with no decimal places

 h. Cells G4:G12 — apply conditional formatting so that cells with a value greater than 1 appear with a gold background color

6. Switch to Page Layout view. Enter your name, course, laboratory assignment number, and any other information, as specified by your instructor, in the Header area. Preview and print the worksheet in landscape orientation. Change the document properties, as specified by your instructor. Save the workbook using the file name, Apply 2-1 Briteeny Taxi Complete.

7. Use Range Finder to verify the formula in cell G13.

8. Print the range A3:D16. Press CTRL+ACCENT MARK (`) to change the display from the values version of the worksheet to the formulas version. Print the formulas version in landscape orientation on one page by using the Fit to option in the Page sheet in the Page Setup dialog box. Press CTRL+ACCENT MARK (`) to change the display of the worksheet back to the values version. Close the workbook without saving it.

9. ✳ Besides adding a header to your document, can you think of anything else that could be added when printing the worksheet?

10. Submit the workbook and results as specified by your instructor.

Extend Your Knowledge

Extend the skills you learned in this chapter and experiment with new skills. You may need to use Help to complete the assignment.

Applying Conditional Formatting to Cells

Note: To complete this assignment, you will be required to use the Data Files for Students. Visit www.cengage.com/ct/studentdownload for detailed instructions or contact your instructor for information about accessing the required files.

Instructions: Run Excel. Open the workbook Extend 2–1 Fentine Blogworld. Perform the following tasks to apply four types of conditional formatting to cells in a worksheet:

1. Select the range C4:C16. Tap or click the Conditional Formatting button (HOME tab | Styles group) and then tap or click New Rule on the Conditional Formatting menu. Select 'Format only top or bottom ranked values' in the Select a Rule Type area (New Formatting Rules dialog box), as shown in Figure 2–71. Enter any value between 10 and 30 in the text box in the Edit the Rule Description (New Formatting Rule dialog box) area, and then tap or click the '% of the selected range' check box to select it. Tap or click the Format button, and choose a purple background in the Fill sheet to assign this conditional format. Tap or click the OK button in each dialog box and view the worksheet.

2. With range C4:C16 selected, apply a conditional format to the range that uses an orange background color to highlight cells with scores that are below average.

3. With range D4:D16 selected, apply a conditional format to the range that uses a green background to highlight cells that contain a value between 200 to 400.

4. With range E4:E16 selected, apply a conditional format to the range that uses a red background color to highlight cells that contain Art or Food. (*Hint:* You need to apply two separate formats, one for Art and one for Food.)

5. ✳ When might you want to look for values above the average in a worksheet?

6. Change the document properties as specified by your instructor. Save the workbook using the file name, Extend 2-1 Fentine Blogworld Complete. Submit the revised workbook as specified by your instructor.

Figure 2–71

Analyze, Correct, Improve

Analyze a workbook and correct all errors and/or improve the design.

Correcting Formatting, Functions, and Formulas in a Worksheet

Note: To complete this assignment, you will be required to use the Data Files for Students. Visit www.cengage.com/ct/studentdownload for detailed instructions or contact your instructor for information about accessing the required files.

Instructions: Run Excel. Open the workbook ACI 2–1 Janeese Crystals. In this exercise, you will learn how to correct formatting, functions, and formula problems in a worksheet. The completed worksheet is shown in Figure 2–72.

Figure 2–72

Perform the following tasks:

1. Correct

 a. Spell check the worksheet and correct any spelling mistakes that are found, but ignore any spelling mistakes found in the worksheet title.

 b. The averages in several columns do not include the product in row 4. Adjust the functions in these cells so that all products are included in the calculation.

 c. The total profit calculations should be Total Profit = Items Sold * Profit. Adjust the formulas in the range F4:F12 so that the correct formula is used.

 d. The values for the total row were entered without using a function. Replace the values with the appropriate function.

 e. The currency values in rows 4 and 14 through 16 should be formatted with the 'Accounting Number Format' button (HOME tab | Number group). They are currently formatted with the Currency format (floating dollar sign). The accounting number format displays a fixed dollar sign.

 f. Delete the function in the cell containing the average of % Profit.

2. Improve

 a. Add a thick box border around the title and subtitle so that they appear more separated from the rest of the worksheet.

 b. Adjust the column widths of columns A, D, and F to best fit.

c. Center the column headings in row 3.

d. Format the values in C5:C12 and C14:C16 using the comma format.

e. Change the document properties as specified by your instructor. Save the workbook using the file name, ACI 2–1 Janeese Crystals Corrected. Submit the revised workbook as specified by your instructor.

3. ☼ What else could you do to improve the worksheet?

In the Labs

Design and/or create a workbook using the guidelines, concepts, and skills presented in this chapter. Labs 1 and 2, which increase in difficulty, require you to create solutions based on what you learned in the chapter; Lab 3 requires you to create a solution, which uses cloud and web technologies, by learning and investigating on your own from general guidance.

Lab 1: **Loan Balance Worksheet**

Problem: You are a part-time assistant in the accounting department at HelpToday Personal Loans, a Cincinnati-based personal loan company supplying small loans to individuals. You have been asked to use Excel to generate a report that summarizes the existing loan balances (Figure 2–73). The customer data in Table 2–6 is available for test purposes.

Instructions: Create a worksheet similar to the one shown in Figure 2–73. Include the three columns of customer data in Table 2–6 in the report, plus two additional columns to compute a monthly fee and a current balance for each customer. Assume no negative unpaid monthly balances.

Table 2–6 HelpToday Personal Loans Data

Customer	Previous Balance	Payments
Tolliver, Ralph	1,600.72	72.15
Jennings, Howard	1,518.62	382.30
Rivera, Juan	679.29	80.69
Lance, Brad	1,060.42	107.60
Yin, Yu	1,178.83	125.63
Lang, Rose	1,280.20	79.85
Tulley, Sullivan	1,253.88	389.79
Jiminez, Jose	477.11	278.52
Adams, Bettina	821.31	153.14

Figure 2–73

Continued >

In the Labs *continued*

Perform the following tasks:

1. Enter and format the worksheet title **HelpToday Personal Loans** and worksheet subtitle **Monthly Loan Balance Analysis** in cells A1 and A2. Change the theme of the worksheet to the Metropolitan theme. Apply the Title cell style to cells A1 and A2. Change the font size in cell A1 to 28 points. Merge and center the worksheet title and subtitle across columns A through E. Change the background color of cells A1 and A2 to the Orange standard color. Change the font color of cells A1 and A2 to the White theme color. Draw a thick box border around the range A1:A2.

2. Change the width of column A to 19.00 points. Change the widths of columns B through E to 15.00 points. Change the heights of row 3 to 36.00 points and row 14 to 25.50 points.

3. Enter the column titles in row 3 and row titles in the range A13:A16, as shown in Figure 2–73. Center the column titles in the range A3:E3. Apply the Heading 3 cell style to the range A3:E3. Apply the Total cell style to the range A13:E13. Bold the titles in the range A13:A16. Change the font size in the range A3:E16 to 12 points.

4. Enter the data in Table 2–6 in the range A4:C12.

5. Use the following formulas to determine the monthly fee in column D and the current balance in column E for the first customer. Copy the two formulas down through the remaining customers.
 a. Monthly Fee (cell D4) = 5% * Previous Balance
 b. Current Balance (E4) = Previous Balance – Payments + Monthly Fee

6. Determine the totals in row 13.

7. Determine the average, minimum, and maximum values in cells B14:B16 for the range B4:B12, and then copy the range B14:B16 to C14:E16.

8. Format the numbers as follows: (a) assign the currency style with a floating dollar sign to the cells containing numeric data in the ranges B4:E4 and B13:E16, and (b) assign a number style with two decimal places and a thousand's separator (currency with no dollar sign) to the range B5:E12.

9. Use conditional formatting to change the formatting to white font on a purple background in any cell in the range D4:D12 that contains a value greater than 50.

10. Change the worksheet name from Sheet1 to Loan Balance and the sheet tab color to the Orange standard color. Change the document properties, as specified by your instructor. Change the worksheet header with your name, course number, and other information as specified by your instructor.

11. Spell check the worksheet. Preview and then print the worksheet in landscape orientation. Save the workbook using the file name, Lab 2–1 HelpToday Personal Loans Report.

12. Print the range A3:D13. Print the formulas version on another page. Close the workbook without saving the changes. Submit the assignment as specified by your instructor.

13. ✹ When you created the formula for the monthly fee, you used 5%. What would you have to do if the rate changed today to, say, 10% to update the formulas?

Lab 2: **Sales Summary Worksheet**

Problem: You have been asked to build a worksheet for a start-up company, TravelUS Campers, that analyzes the financing needs for the company's first year in business. The company plans to begin operations in January with an initial investment of $700,000.00. The expected revenue and costs for the company's first year are shown in Table 2–7. The desired worksheet is shown in Figure 2–74. The initial investment is shown as the starting balance for January (cell B4). The amount of financing required by the company is shown as the lowest ending balance (cell F18).

Instructions Part 1: Perform the following tasks to build the worksheet shown in Figure 2–74.

Table 2–7 TravelUS Campers Financing Needs Data		
Month	**Incomes**	**Expenses**
January	209081	262911
February	63811	381881
March	300660	250143
April	229207	209498
May	248369	355232
June	96118	260888
July	62970	242599
August	195824	368955
September	305669	235604
October	224741	383254
November	159644	411768
December	210000	540000

Figure 2–74

1. Run Excel. Apply the Wisp theme to a new workbook.
2. Increase the width of column A to 12.00 and the width of columns B through F to 14.50.
3. Enter the worksheet title `TravelUS Campers` in cell A1 and the worksheet subtitle `Financing Needs` in cell A2. Enter the column titles in row 3, as shown in Figure 2–74. In row 3, use ALT+ENTER to start a new line in a cell.
4. Enter the financing needs data described in Table 2–7 in columns A, C, and D in rows 4 through 15. Enter the initial starting balance (cell B4) of 700000.00. Enter the row titles in the range A16:A18, as shown in Figure 2–74.
5. For the months of February through December, the starting balance is equal to the previous month's ending balance. Obtain the starting balance for February by setting the starting balance of February to the ending balance of January. Use a cell reference rather than typing in the data. Copy the formula for February to the remaining months.

Continued >

In the Labs *continued*

6. Obtain the net amounts in column E by subtracting the expenses in column D from the incomes in column C. Enter the formula in cell E4 and copy it to the range E5:E15. Obtain the ending balance amounts in column F by adding the starting balance in column B to the net in column E. Enter the formula in cell F4 and copy it to the range F5:F15.

7. In the range B16:B18, use the AVERAGE, MAX, and MIN functions to determine the average value, highest value, and lowest value in the range B4:B15. Copy the range B16:B18 to the range C16:F18.

8. One at a time, merge and center the worksheet title and subtitle across columns A through F. Select cells A1 and A2 and change the background color to light green from standard colors (column 5). Apply the Title cell style to cells A1 and A2. Change the worksheet title in cell A1 to 28-point white (column 1, row 1 on the Font Color gallery). Change the worksheet subtitle to the same color. Bold both the title and subtitle. Assign a thick box border to the range A1:A2.

9. Center the titles in row 3, columns A through F. Apply the Heading 2 cell style to the range A3:F3. Italicize and bold the row titles in the range A16:A18.

10. Assign a thick box border to the range A16:F18. Change the background and font color for cell F18 to the same colors applied to the worksheet title in Step 8.

11. Change the row heights of row 3 to 42.00 points and row 16 to 33.00 points.

12. Assign the accounting number format to the range B4:F4. Assign the comma style format to the range B5:F15. Assign a currency format with a floating dollar sign to the range B16:F18.

13. Rename the sheet tab as Financing Needs. Apply the Green color from the standard colors (column 6) to the sheet tab. Change the document properties, as specified by your instructor. Change the worksheet header with your name, course number, and other information as specified by your instructor. Save the workbook using the file name, Lab 2–2 Part 1 TravelUS Campers Report. Print the entire worksheet in landscape orientation. Next, print only the range A3:B15.

14. Display the formulas version by pressing CTRL+ACCENT MARK (`). Print the formulas version using the Fit to option button in the Scaling area in the Page sheet (Page Setup dialog box). After printing the worksheet, reset the Scaling option by selecting the Adjust to option button in the Page sheet (Page Setup dialog box) and changing the percent value to 100%. Change the display from the formulas version to the values version by pressing CTRL+ACCENT MARK (`). Do not save the workbook.

15. Submit the revised workbook as requested by your instructor.

16. ✳ In reviewing the worksheet you created, how do you think the company could obtain a positive result without increasing income or decreasing expenses?

Instructions Part 2: In this part of the exercise, you will change the revenue amounts until the lowest ending balance is greater than zero, indicating that the company does not require financing in its first year of operation. Open the workbook created in Part 1 and save the workbook as Lab 2–2 Part 2 TravelUS Campers Report. Manually increment each of the 12 values in the Incomes column by $20,000.00 until the lowest ending balance in cell F18 is greater than zero. The value of cell F18 should equal $63,361.00. All 12 values in column C must be incremented the same number of times. Update the worksheet header and save the workbook. Print the worksheet. Submit the assignment as specified by your instructor.

Instructions Part 3: In this part of the exercise, you will change the monthly costs until the lowest ending balance is greater than zero, indicating that the company does not require financing in its first year of operation. Open the workbook created in Part 1 and then save the workbook as Lab 2–2 Part 3 TravelUS Campers Report. Manually decrement each of the 12 values in the Expenses

column by $20,000.00 until the lowest ending balance in cell F18 is greater than zero. Decrement all 12 values in column D the same number of times. Your worksheet is correct when the lowest ending balance in cell F18 is $39,361.00. Update the worksheet header and save the workbook. Print the worksheet. Submit the assignment as specified by your instructor.

Lab 3: Expand Your World: Cloud and Web Technologies Online

Problem: You want to create an estimate of the cost for attending your college for four years. You decide to create the worksheet using the Excel web app so that you can share it with your friends online.

Instructions: Perform the following tasks:

1. Sign in to your Microsoft account on the web and run the Excel web app. Create a blank workbook. In the first worksheet, use row headings for each year of college (Freshman, Sophomore, Junior, and Senior). For the column headings, use your current expenses (such as car payment, rent, tuition, and so forth). Enter estimates for each year based upon estimates you find by searching the web. Include totals for each column. Also include highest, lowest, and average values for the columns. Using the techniques taught in this chapter, create appropriate titles and format the worksheet accordingly. Submit the assignment as specified by your instructor.

✳ Consider This: Your Turn

Apply your creative thinking and problem solving skills to design and implement a solution.

1: Analyze Energy Consumption

Personal

Part 1: Your parents believe that your late-night studying sessions and household appliance usage contribute to excessive electricity bills. You have decided to try to prove them wrong by analyzing your monthly electricity consumption. You research the energy consumption of your personal items and appliance usage to obtain consumption costs per hour for each item. Table 2–8 contains the data and format for the report you will create. Use the concepts and techniques presented in this project to create and format the worksheet.

Table 2–8 Appliance Electricity Usage Costs			
Appliance	Cost per Hour	Hours Used Monthly	Total Cost per Month (30 Days)
Clothes dryer	$0.447	20	
Computer	$0.08	150	
Blu-ray player	$0.061	100	
Light bulbs	$0.056	160	
Sound system	$0.05	180	
Television	$0.08	90	
Washing machine	$0.06	30	

Continued >

Consider This: **Your Turn** *continued*

Part 2: ✳ Now that you have looked over your results, did you neglect to include any appliances? How did you determine the costs you used in your calculations?

2: Analyze Profit Potential
Professional

Part 1: You work as an intern in the college student services department and have been asked to create a worksheet that will aid the clubs on campus in managing their budgets. Each club is allocated money at the beginning of the year and can hold fund-raisers to raise more money for events. Each club is required to save five percent of their income for use at the start of the next year. Table 2–9 shows the clubs that you are working with, as well as their initial allocation and estimated fund-raiser amounts. You will need

Table 2–9 Student Club Data		
Club	**Allocation**	**Fund-Raisers**
Acting Club	$40,000	$10,000
Golf Club	$25,500	$5,000
Gaming Club	$12,750	$2,000
Math Club	$5,000	$1,000
Photography Club	$3,500	$2,500
Music Club	$15,00	$7,200

to calculate how much they need to save as well as the average, lowest, and highest values for the clubs' budgets. Use the concepts and techniques presented in this chapter to create and format the worksheet.

Part 2: ✳ How did you decide on the formula to use for the amount each club needs to save? Which formats did you use and why? Which theme did you select for your worksheet?

3: Internet Service
Research and Collaboration

Part 1: You and your friends have decided to subscribe to a new Internet service provider. You would like to maximize services while keeping costs low. As a group, research and find three to five Internet service providers in your area. For each company, find the best service package as well as the basic service package. Using the cost figures you find, calculate the cost per month for each service for a year. Include totals, minimum, maximum, and average values. Use the concepts and techniques presented in this chapter to create and format the worksheet.

Part 2: ✳ Which companies did you choose for your report? Which services offered the best deals that you would be willing to use?

Learn Online

Reinforce what you learned in this chapter with games, exercises, training, and many other online activities and resources.

Student Companion Site Reinforcement activities and resources are available at no additional cost on www.cengagebrain.com. Visit www.cengage.com/ct/studentdownload for detailed instructions about accessing the resources available at the Student Companion Site.

SAM Put your skills into practice with SAM! If you have a SAM account, go to www.cengage .com/sam2013 to access SAM assignments for this chapter.

1 | Databases and Database Objects: An Introduction

Microsoft product screenshots used with permission from Microsoft Corporation.

Objectives

You will have mastered the material in this chapter when you can:

- Describe the features of the Access window
- Create a database
- Create tables in Datasheet and Design views
- Add records to a table
- Close a database
- Open a database

- Print the contents of a table
- Create and use a query
- Create and use a form
- Create and print custom reports
- Modify a report in Layout view
- Perform special database operations
- Design a database to satisfy a collection of requirements

1 | Databases and Database Objects: An Introduction

Introduction

The term **database** describes a collection of data organized in a manner that allows access, retrieval, and use of that data. Microsoft Access 2013, usually referred to as simply Access, is a database management system. A **database management system** is software that allows you to use a computer to create a database; add, change, and delete data in the database; ask and answer questions concerning the data; and create forms and reports using the data.

Project — Database Creation

Bavant Publishing Inc. is a publishing company that specializes in foreign language textbooks. Bavant sells in both the K-12 and the higher education markets. Recently, Bavant purchased a small, private publisher of Arabic, Russian, Chinese, and Japanese language textbooks. These languages are increasing in popularity with college students. All textbooks are available in hardcover and some are available as e-books. Bavant Publishing also provides ancillary materials, such as workbooks and laboratory manuals, video resources, audio resources, and companion websites.

Bavant representatives visit campuses and meet with faculty, describing the features and strengths of the textbooks and providing review materials for instructors. Bavant pays a base salary to its book reps, who can earn bonus pay based on exceeding sales goals. Customers place orders with the publisher following the organization's procedures; for example, colleges and universities place orders through their bookstores. Because institutions can cancel classes due to low enrollments, customers sometimes return unused books. At the end of an accounting period, these returns are subtracted from the current amount due.

Bavant wants to maintain records on the sales of textbooks from the newly acquired publisher separately from their other foreign language textbooks to better track profitability and market potential. Bavant organizes this data on its customers and book representatives in a database managed by Access. In this way, Bavant keeps its data current and accurate and can analyze it for trends and produce a variety of useful reports.

In a **relational database** such as those maintained by Access, a database consists of a collection of tables, each of which contains information on a specific subject. Figure 1–1 shows the database for Bavant Publishing. It consists of two tables: the Customer table (Figure 1–1a) contains information about Bavant customers, and the Book Rep table (Figure 1–1b) contains information about the book reps to whom these customers are assigned.

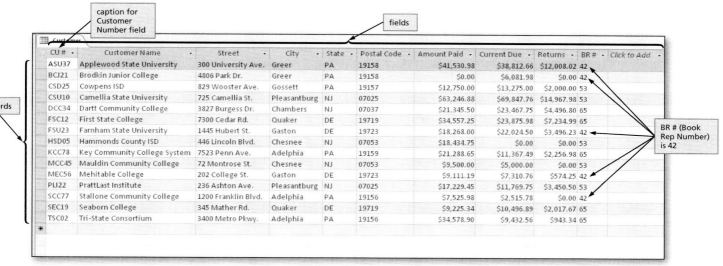

Figure 1–1 (a) Customer Table

Figure 1–1 (b) Book Rep Table

The rows in the tables are called **records**. A record contains information about a given person, product, or event. A row in the Customer table, for example, contains information about a specific customer, such as the customer's name, address information, and other data.

The columns in the tables are called fields. A **field** contains a specific piece of information within a record. In the Customer table, for example, the fourth field, City, contains the name of the city where the customer is located.

The first field in the Customer table is CU #, which is an abbreviation for Customer Number. Bavant Publishing assigns each customer a number; the Bavant customer numbers consist of three uppercase letters followed by a two-digit number.

The customer numbers are unique; that is, no two customers have the same number. Such a field is a **unique identifier**. A unique identifier, as its name suggests, is a way of uniquely identifying each record in the database. A given customer number will appear only in a single record in the table. Only one record exists, for example, in which the customer number is TSC02. A unique identifier also is called a **primary key**. Thus, the Customer Number field is the primary key for the Customer table.

BTW

BTWs
For a complete list of the BTWs found in the margins of this book, visit the BTW resource on the Student Companion Site located on www.cengagebrain.com. For detailed instructions about accessing available resources, visit www.cengage.com/ct/studentdownload or contact your instructor for information about accessing the required files.

BTW

Naming Fields

Access 2013 has a number of reserved words, words that have a special meaning to Access. You cannot use these reserved words as field names. For example, Name is a reserved word and could not be used in the Customer table to describe a customer's name. For a complete list of reserved words in Access 2013, consult Access Help.

The next eight fields in the Customer table are Customer Name, Street, City, State, Postal Code, Amount Paid, Current Due, and Returns. The Amount Paid column contains the amount that the customer has paid Bavant Publishing year to date (YTD) prior to the current period. The Current Due column contains the amount due to Bavant for the current period. The Returns column contains the dollar value of the books or other products the customer was unable to sell and has returned to Bavant in the current period. For example, customer TSC02 is Tri-State Consortium. The address is 3400 Metro Pkwy., in Adelphia, Pennsylvania. The postal code is 19156. The customer has paid $34,578.90 for products purchased so far. The amount due for the current period is $9,432.56. The customer has returned products worth $943.34.

Bavant assigns a single book rep to work with each customer. The last column in the Customer table, BR # (an abbreviation for Book Rep Number) gives the number of the customer's book rep. The book rep number for Tri-State Consortium is 65.

The first field in the Book Rep table is also BR #, for Book Rep Number. The book rep numbers are unique, so the Book Rep Number field is the primary key of the Book Rep table.

The other fields in the Book Rep table are Last Name, First Name, Street, City, State, Postal Code, Start Date, Salary, and Bonus Rate. The Start Date field gives the date the rep began working for Bavant. The Salary field gives the salary paid to the rep thus far this year. The Bonus Rate gives the potential bonus percentage based on personal performance. The bonus rate applies when the book rep exceeds a predetermined sales goal. For example, book rep 65 is Tracy Rogers. Her address is 1827 Maple Ave., in Adelphia, Pennsylvania. The postal code is 19159. Tracy started working for Bavant on July 1, 2014. So far this year, she has been paid $7,750.00 in salary. Her bonus rate is 0.18 (18%).

The book rep number appears in both the Customer table and the Book Rep table, and relates customers and book reps. Book rep 48, Michael Statnik, recently transferred from another division of the company and has not yet been assigned any customers. His book rep number, therefore, does not appear on any row in the Customer table.

CONSIDER THIS

How would you find the name of the book rep for Tri-State Consortium?

In the Customer table, you see that the book rep number for customer Tri-State Consortium is 65. To find the name of this book rep, look for the row in the Book Rep table that contains 65 in the BR # column. After you have found it, you know that the book rep for Tri-State Consortium is Tracy Rogers.

CONSIDER THIS

How would you find all the customers assigned to Tracy Rogers?

First, look in the Book Rep table to find that her number is 65. You would then look through the Customer table for all the customers that contain 65 in the BR # column. Tracy's customers are DCC34 (Dartt Community College), FSC12 (First State College), KCC78 (Key Community College System), SEC19 (Seaborn College), and TSC02 (Tri-State Consortium).

Roadmap

In this chapter, you will learn how to create and use the database shown in Figure 1–1 on page AC 3. The following roadmap identifies general activities you will perform as you progress through this chapter:

1. CREATE the FIRST TABLE, Book Rep, using Datasheet view.
2. ADD RECORDS to the Book Rep table.
3. PRINT the CONTENTS of the Book Rep table.
4. IMPORT RECORDS into the second table, Customer.
5. MODIFY the SECOND TABLE using Design view.
6. CREATE a QUERY for the Customer table.
7. CREATE a FORM for the Customer table.
8. CREATE a REPORT for the Customer table.

At the beginning of step instructions throughout the chapter, you will see an abbreviated form of this roadmap. The abbreviated roadmap uses colors to indicate chapter progress: gray means the chapter is beyond that activity, blue means the task being shown is covered in that activity, and black means that activity is yet to be covered. For example, the following abbreviated roadmap indicates the chapter would be showing a task in the 3 PRINT CONTENTS activity.

1 CREATE FIRST TABLE | 2 ADD RECORDS | **3 PRINT CONTENTS** | 4 IMPORT RECORDS | 5 MODIFY SECOND TABLE

6 CREATE QUERY | 7 CREATE FORM | 8 CREATE REPORT

Use the abbreviated roadmap as a progress guide while you read or step through the instructions in this chapter.

For an introduction to Windows and instruction about how to perform basic Windows tasks, read the Office and Windows chapter at the beginning of this book, where you can learn how to resize windows, change screen resolution, create folders, move and rename files, use Windows Help, and much more.

To Run Access

If you are using a computer to step through the project in this chapter and you want your screens to match the figures in this book, you should change your screen's resolution to 1366 × 768. For information about how to change a computer's resolution, refer to the Office and Windows chapter at the beginning of this book.

The following steps, which assume Windows is running, use the Start screen or the search box to run Access based on a typical installation. You may need to ask your instructor how to run Access on your computer. For a detailed example of the procedure summarized below, refer to the Office and Windows chapter.

1 Scroll the Start screen for an Access 2013 tile. If your Start screen contains an Access 2013 tile, tap or click it to run Access and then proceed to Step 5; if the Start screen does not contain the Access 2013 tile, proceed to the next step to search for the Access app.

2 Swipe in from the right edge of the screen or point to the upper-right corner of the screen to display the Charms bar, and then tap or click the Search charm on the Charms bar to display the Search menu.

3 Type `Access` as the search text in the Search box and watch the search results appear in the Apps list.

4 Tap or click Access 2013 in the search results to run Access.

5 If the Access window is not maximized, tap or click the Maximize button on its title bar to maximize the window.

For an introduction to Office and instruction about how to perform basic tasks in Office apps, read the Office and Windows chapter at the beginning of this book, where you can learn how to run an application, use the ribbon, save a file, open a file, exit an application, use Help, and much more.

Creating a Database

In Access, all the tables, reports, forms, and queries that you create are stored in a single file called a database. Thus, you first must create the database to hold the tables, reports, forms, and queries. You can use either the Blank desktop database option or a template to create a new database. If you already know the tables and fields you want in your database, you would use the Blank desktop database option. If not, you can use a template. Templates can guide you by suggesting some commonly used databases.

To Create a Database

Because you already know the tables and fields you want in the Bavant Publishing database, you would use the Blank desktop database option rather than using a template. The following steps assume you already have created folders for storing your files, for example, a CIS 101 folder (for your class) that contains an Access folder (for your assignments). Thus, these steps save the database in the Access folder in the CIS 101 folder on your desired save location. For a detailed example of the procedure for saving a file in a folder or saving a file on SkyDrive, refer to the Office and Windows chapter at the beginning of this book.

1 Tap or click the 'Blank desktop database' thumbnail to select the database type.

2 Type `Bavant Publishing` in the File Name text box to enter the new file name. Do not press the ENTER key after typing the file name because you do not want to create the database at this time.

3 Tap or click the 'Browse for a location to put your database' button to display the File New Database dialog box.

4 Navigate to the location for the database, for example, the Documents library, the My Documents folder, the folder identifying your class (CIS 101, in this case), and then to the Access folder.

5 Tap or click the OK button (File New Database dialog box) to select the location for the database and close the dialog box.

6 Tap or click the Create button to create the database on the selected drive in the selected folder with the file name, Bavant Publishing (Figure 1–2).

Q&A The title bar for my Navigation Pane contains All Tables rather than All Access Objects, as in the figure. Is that a problem?

It is not a problem. The title bar indicates how the Navigation Pane is organized. You can carry out the steps in the text with either organization. To make your screens match the ones in the text, tap or click the Navigation Pane arrow and then tap or click Object Type.

I do not have the Search bar that appears on the figure. Is that a problem?

It is not a problem. If your Navigation Pane does not display a Search bar and you want your screens to match the ones in the text, press and hold or right-click the Navigation Pane title bar arrow to display a shortcut menu, and then tap or click Search Bar.

One of the few differences between Windows 7 and Windows 8 occurs in the steps to run Access. If you are using Windows 7, click the Start button, type `Access` in the 'Search programs and files' box, click Access 2013, and then, if necessary, maximize the Access window. For detailed steps to run Access in Windows 7, refer to the Office and Windows chapter at the beginning of this book. For a summary of the steps, refer to the Quick Reference located at the back of this book.

BTW
Organizing Files and Folders
You should organize and store files in folders so that you easily can find the files later. For example, if you are taking an introductory computer class called CIS 101, a good practice would be to save all Access files in an Access folder in a CIS 101 folder. For a discussion of folders and detailed examples of creating folders, refer to the Office and Windows chapter at the beginning of this book.

BTW
Q&As
For a complete list of the Q&As found in many of the step-by-step sequences in this book, visit the Q&A resource on the Student Companion Site located on www.cengagebrain.com. For detailed instructions about accessing available resources, visit www.cengage.com/ct/studentdownload or contact your instructor for information about accessing the required files.

Figure 1–2

TO CREATE A DATABASE USING A TEMPLATE

Ideally, you will design your own database, create a blank database, and then create the tables you have determined that your database should contain. If you are not sure what database design you will need, you could use a template. Templates can guide you by suggesting some commonly used databases. To create a database using a template, you would use the following steps.

1. If you have another database open, close it without exiting Access by tapping or clicking FILE on the ribbon to open the Backstage view and then tapping or clicking Close.

2. If you do not see a template that you want, you can search Microsoft Office online for additional templates.

3. Tap or click the template you want to use. Be sure you have selected one that indicates it is for a desktop database.

4. Enter a file name and select a location for the database.

5. Tap or click the Create button to create the database.

The Access Window

The Access window consists of a variety of components to make your work more efficient. These include the Navigation Pane, Access work area, ribbon, shortcut menus, and Quick Access Toolbar. Some of these components are common to other Microsoft Office apps; others are unique to Access.

BTW
Naming Files
The following characters cannot be used in a file name: question mark (?), quotation mark ("), slash (/), backslash (\), colon (:), asterisk (*), vertical bar (|), greater than symbol (>), and less than symbol (<).

BTW
Available Templates
The templates gallery includes both desktop and web-based templates. If you are creating an Access database for your own use, select a desktop template. Web-based templates allow you to create databases that you can publish to a SharePoint server.

Navigation Pane and Access Work Area

BTW
The Ribbon and Screen Resolution
Access may change how the groups and buttons within the groups appear on the ribbon, depending on the computer's screen resolution. Thus, your ribbon may look different from the ones in this book if you are using a screen resolution other than 1366 × 768.

You work on objects such as tables, forms, and reports in the **Access work area**. In the work area in Figure 1–2 on the previous page, a single table, Table1, is open in the work area. **Object tabs** for the open objects appear at the top of the work area. If you have multiple objects open at the same time, you can select one of the open objects by tapping or clicking its tab. To the left of the work area is the Navigation Pane. The **Navigation Pane** contains a list of all the objects in the database. You use this pane to open an object. You also can customize the way objects are displayed in the Navigation Pane.

The **status bar**, located at the bottom of the Access window, presents information about the database object, the progress of current tasks, and the status of certain commands and keys; it also provides controls for viewing the object. As you type text or perform certain commands, various indicators may appear on the status bar. The left edge of the status bar in Figure 1–2 shows that the table object is open in **Datasheet view**. In Datasheet view, the table is represented as a collection of rows and columns called a **datasheet**. Toward the right edge are View buttons, which you can use to change the view that currently appears.

Determining Tables and Fields

Once you have created the database, you need to create the tables and fields that your database will contain. Before doing so, however, you need to make some decisions regarding the tables and fields.

Naming Tables and Fields

BTW
Naming Tables
Database users typically have their own guidelines for naming tables. Some use the singular version of the object being described while others use the prefix tbl with a table name. This book uses the singular version of the object (Customer, Book Rep).

In creating your database, you must name tables and fields. Before beginning the design process, you must understand the rules Access applies to table and field names. These rules are:

1. Names can be up to 64 characters in length.
2. Names can contain letters, digits, and spaces, as well as most of the punctuation symbols.
3. Names cannot contain periods (.), exclamation points (!), accent graves (`), or square brackets ([]).
4. Each field in a table must have a unique name.

The approach to naming tables and fields used in this text is to begin the names with an uppercase letter and to use lowercase for the other letters. In multiple-word names, each word begins with an uppercase letter, and there is a space between words (for example, Customer Number).

Determining the Primary Key

BTW
Multiple-Word Names
There are several ways to handle multiple word names. You can omit the space (CustomerNumber) or use an underscore in place of the space (Customer_Number). Another option is to use an underscore in place of a space, but use the same case for all letters (CUSTOMER_NUMBER or customer_number).

For each table, you need to determine the primary key, the unique identifier. In many cases, you will have obvious choices, such as Customer Number or Book Rep Number. If you do not have an obvious choice, you can use the primary key that Access creates automatically. It is a field called ID. It is an autonumber field, which means that Access will assign the value 1 to the first record, 2 to the second record, and so on.

Determining Data Types for the Fields

For each field in your database, you must determine the field's **data type**, that is, the type of data that can be stored in the field. Four of the most commonly used data types in Access are:

1. **Short Text** — The field can contain any characters. A maximum number of 255 characters is allowed in a field whose data type is Short Text.

2. **Number** — The field can contain only numbers. The numbers can be either positive or negative. Fields assigned this type can be used in arithmetic operations. You usually assign fields that contain numbers but will not be used for arithmetic operations (such as postal codes) a data type of Short Text.

3. **Currency** — The field can contain only monetary data. The values will appear with currency symbols, such as dollar signs, commas, and decimal points, and with two digits following the decimal point. Like numeric fields, you can use currency fields in arithmetic operations. Access assigns a size to currency fields automatically.

4. **Date & Time** — The field can store dates and/or times.

Table 1–1 shows the other data types that are available in Access.

Table 1–1 Additional Data Types	
Data Type	**Description**
Long Text	Field can store a variable amount of text or combinations of text and numbers where the total number of characters may exceed 255.
AutoNumber	Field can store a unique sequential number that Access assigns to a record. Access will increment the number by 1 as each new record is added.
Yes/No	Field can store only one of two values. The choices are Yes/No, True/False, or On/Off.
OLE Object	Field can store an OLE object, which is an object linked to or embedded in the table.
Hyperlink	Field can store text that can be used as a hyperlink address.
Attachment	Field can contain an attached file. Images, spreadsheets, documents, charts, and other elements can be attached to this field in a record in the database. You can view and edit the attached file.
Calculated	Field specified as a calculation based on other fields. The value is not actually stored.

© 2014 Cengage Learning

In the Customer table, because the Customer Number, Customer Name, Street, City, and State all can contain letters, their data types should be Short Text. The data type for Postal Code is Short Text instead of Number because you typically do not use postal codes in arithmetic operations; you do not add postal codes or find an average postal code, for example. The Amount Paid, Current Due, and Returns fields contain monetary data, so their data types should be Currency. The Book Rep Number field contains numbers, but you will not use these numbers in arithmetic operations, so its type should be Short Text.

Similarly, in the Book Rep table, the data type for the Book Rep Number, Last Name, First Name, Street, City, State, and Postal Code fields all should be Short Text. The Start Date field should be Date & Time. The Salary field contains monetary amounts, so its data type should be Currency. The Bonus Rate field contains numbers that are not dollar amounts, so its data type should be Number.

For fields whose type is Short Text, you can change the field size, that is, the maximum number of characters that can be entered in the field. If you set the field size for the State field to 2, for example, Access will not allow the user to enter more than two characters in the field. On the other hand, fields whose data type is Number often

BTW
Text Data Types
Short Text replaces the Text data type in previous editions of Access. Long Text replaces the Memo data type in previous editions.

BTW
Data Types
Different database management systems have different available data types. Even data types that are essentially the same can have different names. The Currency data type in Access, for example, is referred to as Money in SQL Server.

BTW
AutoNumber Fields
AutoNumber fields also are called AutoIncrement fields. In Design view, the New Values field property allows you to increment the field sequentially (Sequential) or randomly (Random). The default is sequential.

require you to change the field size, which is the storage space assigned to the field by Access. Table 1–2 shows the possible field sizes for Number fields.

Field Size	Description
Byte	Integer value in the range of 0 to 255
Integer	Integer value in the range of -32,768 to 32,767
Long Integer	Integer value in the range of -2,147,483,648 to 2,147,483,647
Single	Numeric values with decimal places to seven significant digits — requires 4 bytes of storage
Double	Numeric values with decimal places to more accuracy than Single — requires 8 bytes of storage
Replication ID	Special identifier required for replication
Decimal	Numeric values with decimal places to more accuracy than Single or Double — requires 12 bytes of storage

Table 1–2 Field Sizes for Number Fields

© 2014 Cengage Learning

What is the appropriate size for the Bonus Rate field?

If the size were Byte, Integer, or Long Integer, only integers could be stored. If you try to store a value that has decimal places, such as 0.18, in fields of these sizes, the portion to the right of the decimal point would be removed, giving a result of 0. To address this problem, the bonus rate should have a size of Single, Double, or Decimal. With such small numbers involved, Single, which requires the least storage of the three, is the appropriate choice.

Creating a Table

To create a table in Access, you must define its structure. That is, you must define all the fields that make up the table and their characteristics. You also must indicate the primary key.

In Access, you can use two different views to create a table: Datasheet view and Design view. In **Datasheet view**, the data in the table is presented in rows and columns, similar to a spreadsheet. Although the main reason to use Datasheet view is to add or update records in a table, you also can use it to create a table or to later modify its structure. The other view, **Design view**, is only used to create a table or to modify the structure of a table.

As you might expect, Design view has more functionality for creating a table than Datasheet view. That is, there are certain actions that only can be performed in Design view. One such action is assigning Single as the field size for the Bonus Rate field. In this chapter, you will create the first table, the Book Rep table, in Datasheet view. Once you have created the table in Datasheet view, you will use Design view to change the field size.

Whichever view you choose to use, before creating the table, you need to know the names and data types of the fields that will make up the table. You also can decide to enter a **description** for a particular field to explain important details about the field. When you select this field, this description will appear on the status bar. You also might choose to assign a **caption** to a particular field. If you assign a caption, Access will display the value you assign, rather than the field name, in datasheets and in forms. If you do not assign a caption, Access will display the field name.

When would you want to use a caption?

You would use a caption whenever you want something other than the field name displayed. One common example is when the field name is relatively long and the data in the field is relatively short. In the Book Rep table, the name of the first field is Book Rep Number, but the field contains data that is only two characters long. You will change the caption for this field to BR #, which is much shorter than Book Rep Number yet still describes the field. Doing so will enable you to greatly reduce the width of the column.

The results of these decisions for the fields in the Book Rep table are shown in Table 1–3. The table also shows the data types and field sizes of the fields as well as any special properties that need to be changed. The Book Rep Number field has a caption of BR #, enabling the width of the Book Rep Number column to be reduced in the datasheet.

Table 1–3 Structure of Book Rep Table			
Field Name	**Data Type**	**Field Size**	**Notes**
Book Rep Number	Short Text	2	Primary Key **Description:** Unique identifier of book rep **Caption:** BR #
Last Name	Short Text	15	
First Name	Short Text	15	
Street	Short Text	20	
City	Short Text	20	
State	Short Text	2	
Postal Code	Short Text	5	
Start Date	Date/Time		(This appears as Date & Time on the menu of available data types)
Salary	Currency		
Bonus Rate	Number	Single	Format: Fixed Decimal Places: 2

© 2014 Cengage Learning

If you are using your finger on a touch screen and are having difficulty completing the steps in this chapter, consider using a stylus. Many people find it easier to be precise with a stylus than with a finger. In addition, with a stylus you see the pointer. If you still are having trouble completing the steps with a stylus, try using a mouse.

How do you determine the field size?

You need to determine the maximum number of characters that can be entered in the field. In some cases, it is obvious. Field sizes of 2 for the State field and 5 for the Postal Code field are certainly the appropriate choices. In other cases, you need to determine how many characters you wish to allow. In the list shown in Table 1–3, Bavant evidently decided allowing 15 characters was sufficient for last names. This field size can be changed later if it proves to be insufficient.

CONSIDER THIS

What is the purpose of the Format and Decimal Places properties?

The format guarantees that bonus rates will be displayed with a fixed number of decimal places. Setting the decimal places property to 2 guarantees that the rates will be displayed with precisely two decimal places. Thus, a bonus rate of 0.2 will be displayed as 0.20.

CONSIDER THIS

To Modify the Primary Key

1 CREATE FIRST TABLE | 2 ADD RECORDS | 3 PRINT CONTENTS | 4 IMPORT RECORDS | 5 MODIFY SECOND TABLE
6 CREATE QUERY | 7 CREATE FORM | 8 CREATE REPORT

When you first create your database, Access automatically creates a table for you. You can immediately begin defining the fields. If, for any reason, you do not have this table or inadvertently delete it, you can create the table by tapping or clicking CREATE on the ribbon and then tapping or clicking the Table button (CREATE tab | Tables group). In either case, you are ready to define the fields.

The steps on the next page change the name, data type, and other properties of the first field to match the Book Rep Number field in Table 1–3, which is the primary key. **Why?** *Access has already created the first field as the primary key field, which it has named ID. Book Rep Number is a more appropriate choice.*

- Press and hold or right-click the column heading for the ID field to display a shortcut menu (Figure 1–3).

Why does my shortcut menu look different?
You displayed a shortcut menu for the column instead of the column heading. Be sure you press and hold or right-click the column heading.

Figure 1–3

- Tap or click Rename Field on the shortcut menu to highlight the current name.

- Type `Book Rep Number` to assign a name to the new field.

- Tap or click the white space immediately below the field name to complete the addition of the field (Figure 1–4).

Why does the full name of the field not appear?
The default column size is not large enough for Book Rep Number to be displayed in its entirety. You will address this issue in later steps.

Figure 1–4

- Because the data type needs to be changed from AutoNumber to Short Text, tap or click the Data Type arrow (TABLE TOOLS FIELDS tab | Formatting group) to display a menu of available data types (Figure 1–5).

Figure 1–5

- Tap or click Short Text to select the data type for the field (Figure 1–6).

Figure 1–6

- Tap or click the Field Size text box (TABLE TOOLS FIELDS tab | Properties group) to select the current field size, use either the DELETE or BACKSPACE keys to erase the current field size, if necessary, and then type 2 as the new field size.

- Tap or click the Name & Caption button (TABLE TOOLS FIELDS tab | Properties group) to display the Enter Field Properties dialog box.

- Tap or click the Caption text box (Enter Field Properties dialog box), and then type BR # as the caption.

- Tap or click the Description text box, and then type Unique identifier of book rep as the description (Figure 1–7).

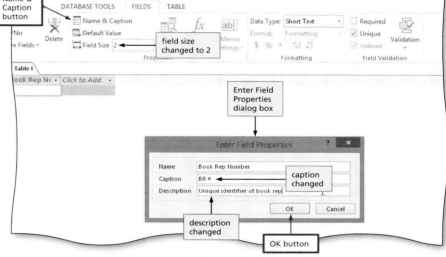

Figure 1–7

6

- Tap or click the OK button (Enter Field Properties dialog box) to change the caption and description (Figure 1–8).

Figure 1–8

To Define the Remaining Fields in a Table

1 CREATE FIRST TABLE | 2 ADD RECORDS | 3 PRINT CONTENTS | 4 IMPORT RECORDS | 5 MODIFY SECOND TABLE
6 CREATE QUERY | 7 CREATE FORM | 8 CREATE REPORT

To define an additional field, you tap or click the Click to Add column heading, select the data type, and then type the field name. This is different from the process you used to modify the ID field. The following steps define the remaining fields shown in Table 1–3 on page AC 11. These steps do not change the field size of the Bonus Rate field, however. *Why? You can only change the field size of a Number field in Design view. Later, you will use Design view to change this field size and change the format and number of decimal places.*

- Tap or click the 'Click to Add' column heading to display a menu of available data types (Figure 1–9).

Figure 1–9

- Tap or click Short Text in the menu of available data types to select the Short Text data type.

- Type `Last Name` to enter a field name.

- Tap or click the blank space below the field name to complete the change of the name. Tap or click the blank space a second time to select the field (Figure 1–10).

Q&A

After entering the field name, I realized that I selected the wrong data type. How can I correct it?
Tap or click the Data Type arrow, and then select the correct type.

I inadvertently clicked the blank space before entering the field name. How can I correct the name?
Press and hold or right-click the field name, tap or click Rename Field on the shortcut menu, and then type the new name.

Figure 1–10

3

- Change the field size to 15 just as you changed the field size of the Book Rep Number field.

- Using the same technique, add the remaining fields in the Book Rep table. For the First Name, Street, City, State, and Postal Code fields, use the Short Text data type, but change the field

Figure 1–11

sizes to match Table 1–3 on page AC 11. For the Start Date field, change the data type to Date & Time. For the Salary field, change the data type to Currency. For the Bonus Rate field, change the data type to Number (Figure 1–11).

Q&A

I have an extra row between the row containing the field names and the row that begins with the asterisk. What happened? Is this a problem? If so, how do I fix it?
You inadvertently added a record to the table by pressing a key. Even pressing the SPACEBAR would add a record. You now have an unwanted record. To fix it, press the ESC key or tap or click the Undo button to undo the action. You may need to do this more than once.

When I try to move on to specify another field, I get an error message indicating that the primary key cannot contain a null value. How do I correct this?
First, tap or click the OK button to remove the error message. Next, press the ESC key or tap or click the Undo button to undo the action. You may need to do this more than once.

Making Changes to the Structure

When creating a table, check the entries carefully to ensure they are correct. If you discover a mistake while still typing the entry, you can correct the error by repeatedly pressing the BACKSPACE key until the incorrect characters are removed. Then, type the correct characters. If you do not discover a mistake until later, you can use the following techniques to make the necessary changes to the structure:

- To undo your most recent change, tap or click the Undo button on the Quick Access Toolbar. If there is nothing that Access can undo, this button will be dim, and tapping or clicking it will have no effect.

- To delete a field, press and hold or right-click the column heading for the field (the position containing the field name), and then tap or click Delete Field on the shortcut menu.

- To change the name of a field, press and hold or right-click the column heading for the field, tap or click Rename Field on the shortcut menu, and then type the desired field name.

- To insert a field as the last field, tap or click the 'Click to Add' column heading, tap or click the appropriate data type on the menu of available data types, type the desired field name, and, if necessary, change the field size.

- To insert a field between existing fields, press and hold or right-click the column heading for the field that will follow the new field, and then tap or click Insert

BTW
Currency Symbols
To show the symbol for the Euro (€) instead of the dollar sign, change the Format property for the field whose data type is currency. To change the default symbols for currency, change the settings in Windows.

BTW
Touch Screen Differences
The Office and Windows interfaces may vary if you are using a touch screen. For this reason, you might notice that the function or appearance of your touch screen differs slightly from this chapter's presentation.

Field on the shortcut menu. Press and hold or right-click the column heading for the field, tap or click Rename Field on the shortcut menu, and then type the desired field name.

• To move a field, tap or click the column heading for the field to be moved to select the field, and then drag the field to the desired position.

As an alternative to these steps, you might want to start over. To do so, tap or click the Close button for the table, and then tap or click the No button in the Microsoft Access dialog box. Tap or click CREATE on the ribbon, and then tap or click the Table button to create a table. You then can repeat the process you used earlier to define the fields in the table.

To Save a Table

1 CREATE FIRST TABLE | 2 ADD RECORDS | 3 PRINT CONTENTS | 4 IMPORT RECORDS | 5 MODIFY SECOND TABLE
6 CREATE QUERY | 7 CREATE FORM | 8 CREATE REPORT

The Book Rep table structure is complete. The final step is to save the table within the database. As part of the process, you will give the table a name. The following steps save the table, giving it the name Book Rep. *Why?* *Bavant has decided that Book Rep is an appropriate name for the table.*

1

• Tap or click the Save button on the Quick Access Toolbar to display the Save As dialog box (Figure 1–12).

Figure 1–12

2

• Type Book Rep to change the name assigned to the table.

• Tap or click the OK button (Save As dialog box) to save the table (Figure 1–13).

Figure 1–13

Other Ways

1. Tap or click FILE on the ribbon, tap or click Save in the Backstage view	2. Press and hold or right-click tab for table, tap or click Save on shortcut menu	3. Press CTRL+S

To View the Table in Design View

Even when creating a table in Datasheet view, Design view can be helpful. *Why? You easily can view the fields, data types, and properties to ensure you have entered them correctly. It is also easier to determine the primary key in Design view.* The following steps display the structure of the Book Rep table in Design view so that you can verify the design is correct.

- Tap or click the View arrow (TABLE TOOLS FIELDS tab | Views group) to display the View menu (Figure 1–14).

Q&A Could I just tap or click the View button rather than the arrow?

Yes. Tapping or clicking the button is equivalent to tapping or clicking the command represented by the icon currently appearing on the button. Because the icon on the button in Figure 1–14 is for Design view, tapping or clicking the button would display the table in Design view. If you are uncertain, you can always tap or click the arrow and select from the menu.

Figure 1–14

- Tap or click Design View on the View menu to view the table in Design view (Figure 1–15).

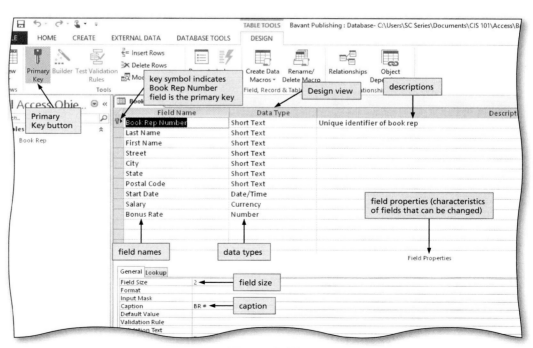

Figure 1–15

Other Ways

1. Tap or click Design View button on status bar

Checking the Structure in Design View

You should use Design view to carefully check the entries you have made. In Figure 1–15 on the previous page, for example, you can see that the Book Rep Number field is the primary key of the Book Rep table by the key symbol in front of the field name. If your table does not have a key symbol, you can tap or click the Primary Key button (TABLE TOOLS DESIGN tab | Tools group) to designate the field as the primary key. You also can check that the data type, description, field size, and caption are all correct.

For the other fields, you can see the field name, data type, and description without taking any special action. To see the field size and/or caption for a field, tap or click the field's **row selector**, the small box that precedes the field. Tapping or clicking the row selector for the Last Name field, for example, displays the properties for the field. You then can check to see that the field size is correct. In addition, if the field has a caption, you can check to see if that is correct. If you find any mistakes, you can make the necessary corrections on this screen. When you have finished, you would tap or click the Save button to save your changes.

To Change a Field Size in Design View

1 CREATE FIRST TABLE | 2 ADD RECORDS | 3 PRINT CONTENTS | 4 IMPORT RECORDS | 5 MODIFY SECOND TABLE
6 CREATE QUERY | 7 CREATE FORM | 8 CREATE REPORT

Most field size changes can be made in either Datasheet view or Design view. However, changing the field size for Number fields, such as the Bonus Rate field, can only be made in Design view. Because the values in the Bonus Rate field have decimal places, only Single, Double, or Decimal would be possible choices for the field size. The difference between these choices concerns the amount of accuracy. Double is more accurate than Single, for example, but requires more storage space. Because the rates are only two decimal places, Single is an acceptable choice.

The following steps change the field size of the Bonus Rate field to Single, the format to Fixed, and the number of decimal places to 2. **Why change the format and number of decimal places?** *To ensure that each value will appear with precisely two decimal places.*

1

• If necessary, tap or click the vertical scroll bar to display the Bonus Rate field. Tap or click the row selector for the Bonus Rate field to select the field (Figure 1–16).

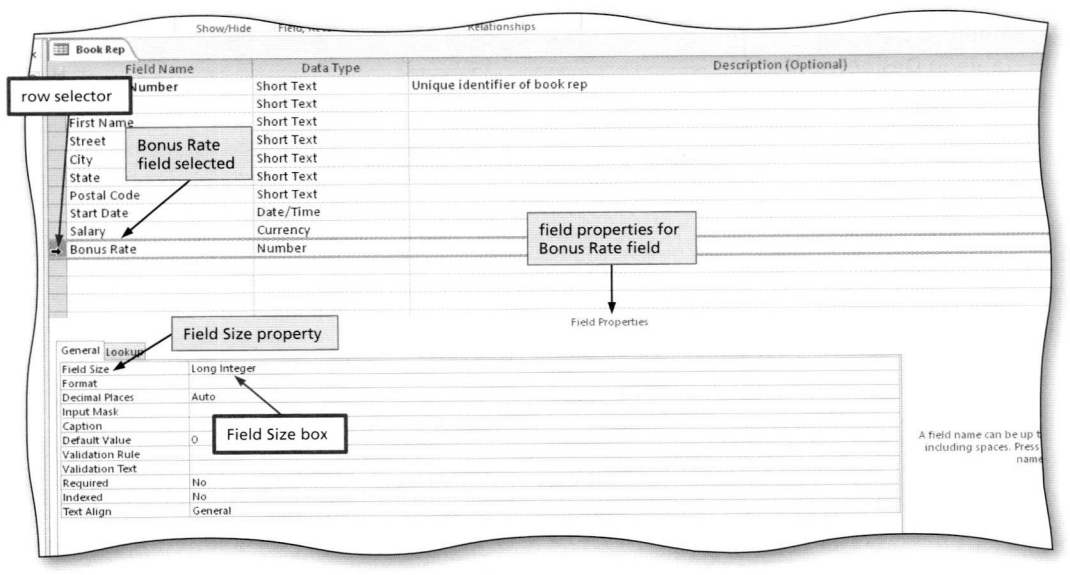

Figure 1–16

2

- Tap or click the Field Size box to display the Field Size arrow.

- Tap or click the Field Size arrow to display the Field Size menu (Figure 1–17).

Q&A What would happen if I left the field size set to Long Integer?
If the field size is Long Integer, Integer, or Byte, no decimal places can be stored. For example, a value of .10 would be stored as 0. If you enter rates and the values all appear as 0, chances are you did not change the field size property.

Figure 1–17

3

- Tap or click Single to select single precision as the field size.

- Tap or click the Format box to display the Format arrow.

- Tap or click the Format arrow to open the Format menu (Figure 1–18).

Figure 1–18

4

- Tap or click Fixed to select fixed as the format.

- Tap or click the Decimal Places box to display the Decimal Places arrow.

- Tap or click the Decimal Places arrow to enter the number of decimal places.

- Tap or click 2 to assign the number of decimal places.

- Tap or click the Save button to save your changes (Figure 1–19).

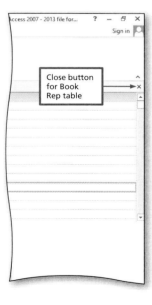

Figure 1–19

Q&A Why did the Property Update Options button appear?
You changed the number of decimal places. The Property Update Options button offers a quick way of making the same change everywhere Bonus Rate appears. So far, you have not added any data or created any forms or reports that use the Bonus Rate field, so no such changes are necessary.

To Close the Table

Once you are sure that your entries are correct and you have saved your changes, you can close the table. The following step closes the table.

1 Tap or click the Close button for the Book Rep table to close the table.

Other Ways

1. Press and hold or right-click tab for table, tap or click Close on shortcut menu

To Add Records to a Table

1 CREATE FIRST TABLE | 2 ADD RECORDS | 3 PRINT CONTENTS | 4 IMPORT RECORDS | 5 MODIFY SECOND TABLE
6 CREATE QUERY | 7 CREATE FORM | 8 CREATE REPORT

Creating a table by building the structure and saving the table is the first step in the two-step process of using a table in a database. The second step is to add records to the table. To add records to a table, the table must be open. When making changes to tables, you work in Datasheet view.

You often add records in phases. *Why? You might not have enough time to add all the records in one session, or you might not have all the records currently available.* The following steps open the Book Rep table in Datasheet view and then add the first two records in the Book Rep table (Figure 1–20).

BR #	Last Name	First Name	Street	City	State	Postal Code	Start Date	Salary	Bonus Rate
53	Chin	Robert	265 Maxwell St.	Gossett	PA	19157	6/1/2013	$26,250.00	0.19
42	Perez	Melina	261 Porter Dr.	Adelphia	PA	19156	5/14/2012	$31,500.00	0.20

Figure 1–20

1

- Press and hold or right-click the Book Rep table in the Navigation Pane to display the shortcut menu (Figure 1–21).

Figure 1–21

- Tap or click Open on the shortcut menu to open the table in Datasheet view.

- Tap or click the Shutter Bar Open/Close Button to close the Navigation Pane (Figure 1–22).

Figure 1–22

- Tap or click the first row in the BR # field if necessary to display an insertion point, and type 53 to enter the first book rep number (Figure 1–23).

Figure 1–23

4

- Press the TAB key to move to the next field.

- Enter the last name, first name, street, city, state, and postal code by typing the following entries, pressing the TAB key after each one: Chin as the last name, Robert as the first name, 265 Maxwell St. as the street, Gossett as the city, PA as the state, and 19157 as the postal code.

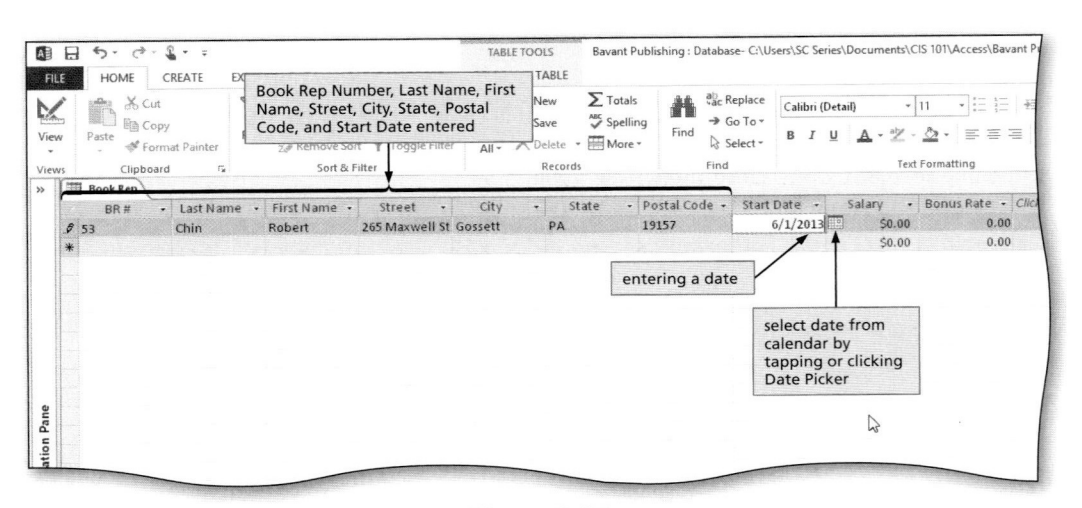

Figure 1–24

- If requested by your instructor, enter your address instead of 265 Maxwell St. as the street. If your address is longer than 20 characters, enter the first 20 characters.

- Type 6/1/2013 in the Start Date field (Figure 1–24).

5

- Press the TAB key and then type 26250 in the Salary field.

Q&A Do I need to type a dollar sign?

You do not need to type dollar signs or commas. In addition, because the digits to the right of the decimal point are both zeros, you do not need to type either the decimal point or the zeros.

- Press the TAB key to complete the entry for the Salary field.

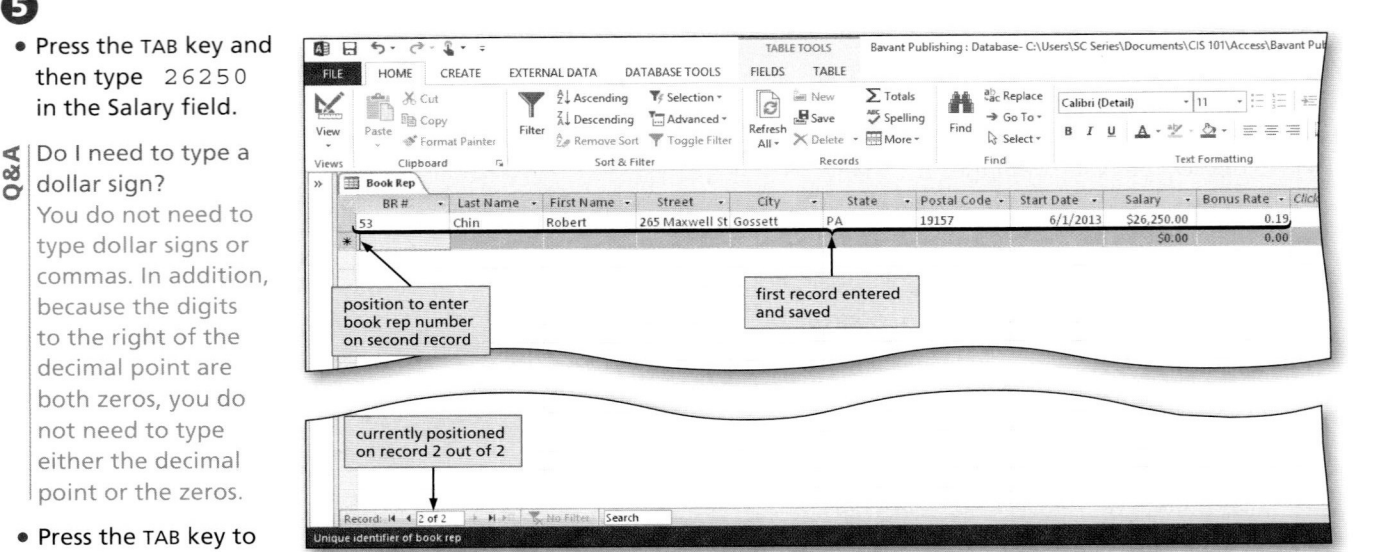

Figure 1–25

- Type 0.19 in the Bonus Rate field, and then press the TAB key to complete the entry of the first record (Figure 1–25).

Q&A Do I need to type the leading zero for the Bonus Rate?

Typing the leading zero is not necessary. You could type .19 if you prefer. In addition, you would not have to type any final zeros. For example, if you needed to enter 0.20, you could simply type .2 as your entry.

How and when do I save the record?

As soon as you have entered or modified a record and moved to another record, Access saves the original record. This is different from other applications. The rows entered in an Excel worksheet, for example, are not saved until the entire worksheet is saved.

6

- Use the techniques shown in Steps 3 through 5 to enter the data for the second record (Figure 1–26).

Q&A Does it matter that I entered book rep 42 after I entered book rep 53? Should the book rep numbers be in order?

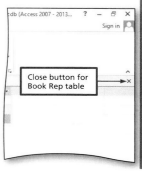

Figure 1–26

The order in which you enter the records is not important. When you close and later reopen the table, the records will be in book rep number order, because the Book Rep Number field is the primary key.

When I entered the Salary field and changed the data type to Currency, I noticed that the word Currency appeared twice. Why?

The second Currency is the format, which indicates how the data will be displayed. For the Currency data type, Access automatically sets the format to Currency, which is usually what you would want. You could change it to something else, if desired, by tapping or clicking the arrow and selecting the desired format.

Experiment

- Tap or click the Salary field on either of the records. Be sure the TABLE TOOLS FIELDS tab is selected. Tap or click the Format arrow, and then tap or click each of the formats in the Format box menu to see the effect on the values in the Salary field. When finished, tap or click Currency in the Format box menu.

Making Changes to the Data

As you enter data, check your entries carefully to ensure they are correct. If you make a mistake and discover it before you press the TAB key, correct it by pressing the BACKSPACE key until the incorrect characters are removed, and then type the correct characters. If you do not discover a mistake until later, you can use the following techniques to make the necessary corrections to the data:

- To undo your most recent change, tap or click the Undo button on the Quick Access Toolbar. If there is nothing that Access can undo, this button will be dimmed, and tapping or clicking it will have no effect.

- To add a record, tap or click the New (blank) record button, tap or click the position for the Book Rep Number field on the first open record, and then add the record. Do not worry about it being in the correct position in the table. Access will reposition the record based on the primary key, in this case, the Book Rep Number.

- To delete a record, tap or click the record selector, shown in Figure 1–26, for the record to be deleted. Then press the DELETE key to delete the record, and tap or click the Yes button when Access asks you to verify that you want to delete the record.

- To change the contents of one or more fields in a record, the record must be on the screen. If it is not, use any appropriate technique, such as the UP ARROW and DOWN ARROW keys or the vertical scroll bar, to move to the record. If the field you want to correct is not visible on the screen, use the horizontal scroll bar along the bottom of the screen to shift all the fields until the one you want appears. If the value in the field is currently highlighted, you can simply type the new value. If you would rather edit the existing value, you must have an insertion point in the field. You can place the insertion point by tapping or clicking in the field or by pressing the F2 key. You then can use the arrow keys, the DELETE key, and the BACKSPACE key for making the correction. You also can use the INSERT key to switch between Insert and Overtype mode. When you have made the change, press the TAB key to move to the next field.

BTW

AutoCorrect Feature
The AutoCorrect feature of Access corrects common data entry errors. AutoCorrect corrects two capital letters by changing the second letter to lowercase and capitalizes the first letter in the names of days. It also corrects more than 400 commonly misspelled words.

BTW

Other AutoCorrect Options
Using the Office AutoCorrect feature, you can create entries that will replace abbreviations with spelled-out names and phrases automatically. To specify AutoCorrect rules, tap or click FILE on the ribbon to open the Backstage view, tap or click Options, and then tap or click Proofing in the Access Options dialog box.

If you cannot determine how to correct the data, you may find that you are "stuck" on the record, in which case Access neither allows you to move to another record nor allows you to close the table until you have made the correction. If you encounter this situation, simply press the ESC key. Pressing the ESC key will remove from the screen the record you are trying to add. You then can move to any other record, close the table, or take any other action you desire.

To Close a Table

Now that you have created and saved the Book Rep table, you can close it. The following step closes the table.

1 Tap or click the Close button for the Book Rep table, shown in Figure 1–26 on the previous page, to close the table (Figure 1–27).

Figure 1–27

To Exit Access

The following steps exit Access. For a detailed example of the procedure summarized below, refer to the Office and Windows chapter at the beginning of this book.

1 Tap or click the Close button on the right side of the title bar to exit Access.

2 If a Microsoft Access dialog box appears, tap or click the Save button to save any changes made to the object since the last save.

Break Point: If you wish to take a break, this is a good place to do so. To resume later, continue following the steps from this location forward.

Starting Access and Opening a Database

Once you have created and later closed a database, you will need to open it in the future in order to use it. Opening a database requires that Access is running on your computer.

To Run Access

1 Scroll the Start screen for an Access 2013 tile. If your Start screen contains an Access 2013 tile, tap or click it to run Access. If the Start screen does not contain the Access 2013 tile, proceed to the next step to search for the Access app.

2 Swipe in from the right edge of the screen or point to the upper-right corner of the screen to display the Charms bar, and then tap or click the Search charm on the Charms bar to display the Search menu.

3 Type `Access` as the search text in the Search text box and watch the search results appear in the Apps list.

4 Tap or click Access 2013 in the search results to run Access.

To Open a Database from Access

Earlier in this chapter, you created the Bavant Publishing database in an appropriate storage location. The following steps open the database from the location you specified when you first created it (for example, the Access folder in the CIS 101 folder). For a detailed example of the procedure summarized below, refer to the Office 2013 and Windows chapter at the beginning of this book.

1 Tap or click FILE on the ribbon to open the Backstage view, if necessary.

2 If the database you want to open is displayed in the Recent list, tap or click the file name to open the database and display the opened database in the Access window; then skip to Step 7. If the database you want to open is not displayed in the Recent list or if the Recent list does not appear, tap or click 'Open Other Files' to display the Open Gallery.

3 If the database you want to open is displayed in the Recent list in the Open gallery, tap or click the file name to open the database and display the opened database in the Access window; then skip to Step 7.

4 Tap or click Computer, SkyDrive, or another location in the left pane and then navigate to the location of the database to be opened (for example, the Access folder in the CIS 101 folder).

5 Tap or click Bavant Publishing to select the database to be opened.

6 Tap or click the Open button (Open dialog box) to open the selected file and display the opened database in the Access window (Figure 1–28).

7 If a Security Warning appears, tap or click the Enable Content button.

BTW
Enabling Content
If the database is one that you created, or if it comes from a trusted source, you can enable the content. You should disable the content of a database if you suspect that your database might contain harmful content or damaging macros.

Figure 1–28

To Add Records to a Table that Contains Data

1 CREATE FIRST TABLE | 2 ADD RECORDS | 3 PRINT CONTENTS | 4 IMPORT RECORDS | 5 MODIFY SECOND TABLE
6 CREATE QUERY | 7 CREATE FORM | 8 CREATE REPORT

You can add records to a table that already contains data using a process almost identical to that used to add records to an empty table. The only difference is that you place the insertion point after the last record before you enter the additional data. To position the insertion point after the last record, you can use the **Navigation buttons,** which are buttons used to move within a table, found near the lower-left corner of the screen when a table is open. *Why not just tap or click the Book Rep Number (BR #) on the first open record? You could do this, but it is a good habit to use the New (blank) record button. Once a table contains more records than will fit on the screen, it is easier to tap or click the New (blank) record button.* The purpose of each Navigation button is described in Table 1–4.

Table 1–4 Navigation Buttons in Datasheet View	
Button	**Purpose**
First record	Moves to the first record in the table
Previous record	Moves to the previous record
Next record	Moves to the next record
Last record	Moves to the last record in the table
New (blank) record	Moves to the end of the table to a position for entering a new record

© 2014 Cengage Learning

The following steps add the remaining records (Figure 1–29) to the Book Rep table.

BR # ▾	Last Name ▾	First Name ▾	Street ▾	City ▾	State ▾	Postal Code ▾	Start Date ▾	Salary ▾	Bonus Rate ▾
65	Rogers	Tracy	1827 Maple Ave.	Adelphia	PA	19159	7/1/2014	$7,750.00	0.18
48	Statnik	Michael	3135 Simpson Dr.	Pleasantburg	NJ	07025	1/15/2013	$29,000.00	0.20

Figure 1–29

1

• If the Navigation Pane is closed, tap or click the Shutter Bar Open/Close Button, shown in Figure 1–27 on page AC 24, to open the Navigation Pane (Figure 1–30).

Figure 1–30

- Press and hold or right-click the Book Rep table in the Navigation Pane to display a shortcut menu.

- Tap or click Open on the shortcut menu to open the table in Datasheet view.

Q&A Why do the records appear in a different order than the order in which I entered them?
When you open the table, they are sorted in the order of the primary key. In this case, that means they will appear in Book Rep Number order.

- Close the Navigation Pane by tapping or clicking the Shutter Bar Open/Close Button (Figure 1–31).

Figure 1–31

- Tap or click the 'New (blank) record' button to move to a position to enter a new record (Figure 1–32).

Figure 1–32

- Add the records shown in Figure 1–29 using the same techniques you used to add the first two records (Figure 1–33).

Figure 1–33

Other Ways

1. Tap or click New button (HOME tab | Records group) 2. Press CTRL+PLUS SIGN (+)

To Resize Columns in a Datasheet

Access assigns default column sizes, which do not always provide space to display all the data in the field. In some cases, the data might appear but the entire field name will not. You can correct this problem by **resizing** the column (changing its size) in the datasheet. In some instances, you may want to reduce the size of a column. *Why? Some fields, such as the State field, are short enough that they do not require all the space on the screen that is allotted to them.* Changing a column width changes the **layout**, or design, of a table. The following steps resize the columns in the Book Rep table and save the changes to the layout.

1

- Point to the right boundary of the field selector for the Book Rep Number (BR #) field (Figure 1–34) so that the pointer becomes a two-headed arrow.

Q&A
I am using touch and I cannot see the pointer. Is this a problem?

It is not a problem. Remember that if you are using your finger on a touch screen, you will not see the pointer.

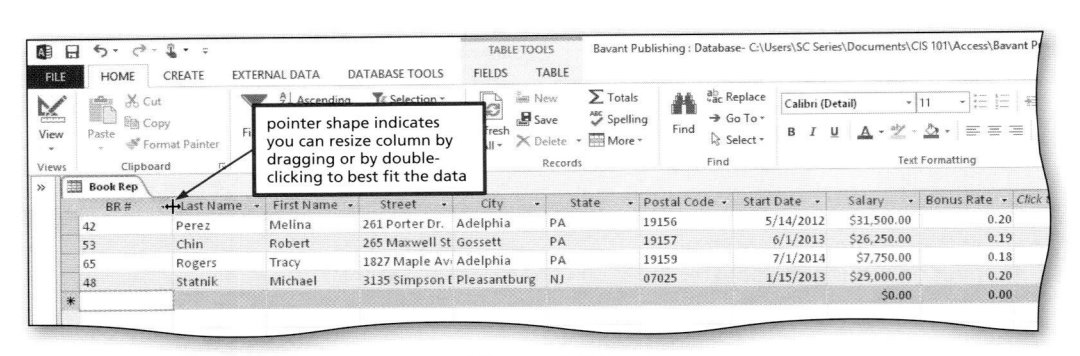

Figure 1–34

2

- Double-tap or double-click the right boundary of the field selector to resize the field so that it best fits the data.

- Use the same technique to resize all the other fields to best fit the data.

- Save the changes to the layout by tapping or clicking the Save button on the Quick Access Toolbar (Figure 1–35).

Figure 1–35

3

- Tap or click the table's Close button (shown in Figure 1–33 on the previous page) to close the table.

Q&A
What if I closed the table without saving the layout changes?

You would be asked if you want to save the changes.

Other Ways

1. Press and hold or right-click field name, tap or click Field Width

What is the best method for distributing database objects?

The traditional method of distributing database objects such as tables, reports, and forms uses a printer to produce a hard copy. A **hard copy** or **printout** is information that exists on a physical medium such as paper. Hard copies can be useful for the following reasons:

- Some people prefer proofreading a hard copy of a document rather than viewing it on the screen to check for errors and readability.

- Hard copies can serve as a backup reference if your storage medium is lost or becomes corrupted and you need to recreate the document.

Instead of distributing a hard copy, users can distribute the document as an electronic image that mirrors the original document's appearance. The electronic image of the document can be emailed, posted on a website, or copied to a portable storage medium such as a USB flash drive. Two popular electronic image formats, sometimes called fixed formats, are PDF by Adobe Systems and XPS by Microsoft. In Access, you can create electronic image files through the EXTERNAL DATA tab on the ribbon. Electronic images of documents, such as PDF and XPS, can be useful for the following reasons:

- Users can view electronic images of documents without the software that created the original document (e.g., Access). Specifically, to view a PDF file, you use a program called Adobe Reader, which can be downloaded free from Adobe's website. Similarly, to view an XPS file, you use a program called XPS Viewer, which is included in the latest versions of Windows and Internet Explorer.

- Sending electronic documents saves paper and printer supplies. Society encourages users to contribute to **green computing,** which involves reducing the electricity consumed and environmental waste generated when using computers, mobile devices, and related technologies.

Previewing and Printing the Contents of a Table

When working with a database, you often will need to print a copy of the table contents. Figure 1–36 shows a printed copy of the contents of the Book Rep table. (Yours may look slightly different, depending on your printer.) Because the Book Rep table is substantially wider than the screen, it also will be wider than the normal printed page in portrait orientation. **Portrait orientation** means the printout is across the width of the page. **Landscape orientation** means the printout is across the height of the page. To print the wide database table, you might prefer to use landscape orientation. A convenient way to change to landscape orientation is to preview what the printed copy will look like by using Print Preview. This allows you to determine whether landscape orientation is necessary and, if it is, to change the orientation easily to landscape. In addition, you also can use Print Preview to determine whether any adjustments are necessary to the page margins.

BTW

Changing Printers
To change the default printer that appears in the Print dialog box, tap or click FILE on the ribbon, tap or click the Print tab in the Backstage view, tap or click Print in the Print gallery, then tap or click the Name arrow and select the desired printer.

				Book Rep					9/15/2014
BR #	Last Name	First Name	Street	City	State	Postal Code	Start Date	Salary	Bonus Rate
42	Perez	Melina	261 Porter Dr.	Adelphia	PA	19156	5/14/2012	$31,500.00	0.20
48	Statnik	Michael	3135 Simpson Dr.	Pleasantburg	NJ	07025	1/15/2013	$29,000.00	0.20
53	Chin	Robert	265 Maxwell St.	Gossett	PA	19157	6/1/2013	$26,250.00	0.19
65	Rogers	Tracy	1827 Maple Ave.	Adelphia	PA	19159	7/1/2014	$7,750.00	0.18

Figure 1–36

To Preview and Print the Contents of a Table

The following steps use Print Preview to preview and then print the contents of the Book Rep table. *Why?* *By previewing the contents of the table in Print Preview, you can make any necessary adjustments to the orientation or to the margins before printing the contents.*

1

- If the Navigation Pane is closed, open the Navigation Pane by tapping or clicking the Shutter Bar Open/Close Button.

- Be sure the Book Rep table is selected.

Q&A Why do I have to be sure the Book Rep table is selected? It is the only object in the database. When the database contains only one object, you do not have to worry about selecting the object. Ensuring that the correct object is selected is a good habit to form, however, to make sure that the object you print is the one you want.

Figure 1–37

- Tap or click FILE on the ribbon to open the Backstage view.

- Tap or click the Print tab in the Backstage view to display the Print gallery (Figure 1–37).

2

- Tap or click the Print Preview button in the Print gallery to display a preview of what the table will look like when printed (Figure 1–38).

Q&A I cannot read the table. Can I magnify a portion of the table?
Yes. Point the pointer, whose shape will change to a magnifying glass, at the portion of the table that you want to magnify, and then tap or click. You can return to the original view of the table by tapping or clicking a second time.

Figure 1–38

❸

- Tap or click the pointer in the position shown in Figure 1–38 to magnify the upper-right section of the table (Figure 1–39).

Figure 1–39

❹

- Tap or click the Landscape button (PRINT PREVIEW tab | Page Layout group) to change to landscape orientation.

- Tap or click the Margins button (PRINT PREVIEW tab | Page Size group) and then click Normal if necessary to display all the fields (Figure 1–40).

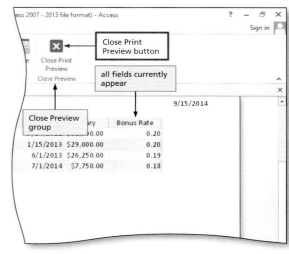

Figure 1–40

❺

- Tap or click the Print button (PRINT PREVIEW tab | Print group) to display the Print dialog box.

- Tap or click the OK button (Print dialog box) to print the table.

- When the printer stops, retrieve the hard copy of the Book Rep table.

- Tap or click the Close Print Preview button (PRINT PREVIEW tab | Close Preview group) to close the Print Preview window.

Q&A Do I have to select Print Preview before printing the table?
No. If you wish to print without previewing, you would select either Print or Quick Print rather than Print Preview.

Other Ways

1. Press CTRL+P, tap or click OK button in Print dialog box

Importing or Linking Data from Other Applications to Access

If your data for a table is stored in an Excel worksheet, you can **import** the data, which means to make a copy of the data as a table in the Access database. In this case, any changes to the data made in Access would not be reflected in the Excel worksheet.

Figure 1–41, which contains the Customer data, is an example of the type of worksheet that can be imported. In this type of worksheet, the data is stored as a **list**, that is, a collection of rows and columns in which all the entries in a column represent the same type of data. In this type of list, the first row contains **column headings**, that is, descriptions of the contents of the column, rather than data. In the worksheet in Figure 1–41, for example, the entry in the first column of the first row is Customer Number. This indicates that all the other values in this column are customer numbers. The fact that the entry in the second column of the first row is Customer Name indicates that all the other values in the second column are customer names.

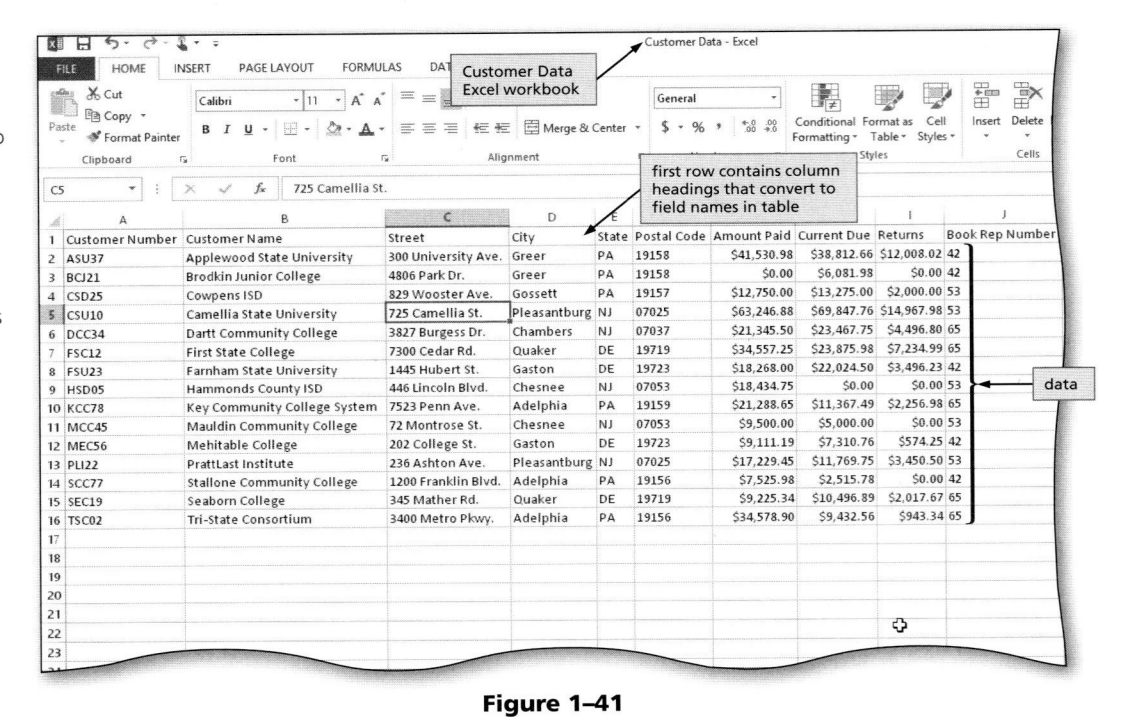

Figure 1–41

Does it matter how the data in the Excel workbook is formatted? If so, how can you be sure the Excel data is formatted in such a way you can import it?

The format of data in an Excel workbook is important when you want to import it into Access. To ensure the data is in an appropriate format:

1. Make sure the data is in the form of a list, a collection of rows and columns in which all the entries in a column represent the same type of data.

2. Make sure there are no blank rows within the list. If there are, remove them prior to importing or linking.

3. Make sure there are no blank columns within the list. If there are, remove them prior to importing or linking.

4. Determine whether the first row contains column headings that will make appropriate field names in the resulting table. If not, you might consider adding such a row. In general, the process is simpler if the first row in the worksheet contains appropriate column headings.

CONSIDER THIS

The Import process will create a table. In this table, the column headings in the first row of the worksheet become the field names. The rows of the worksheet, other than the first row, become the records in the table. In the process, each field will be assigned the data type that seems the most reasonable, given the data currently in the worksheet. When the Import process is finished, you can use Datasheet or Design view to modify these data types or to make any other changes to the structure you feel are necessary.

To Import an Excel Worksheet

1 CREATE FIRST TABLE | 2 ADD RECORDS | 3 PRINT CONTENTS | 4 IMPORT RECORDS | 5 MODIFY SECOND TABLE
6 CREATE QUERY | 7 CREATE FORM | 8 CREATE REPORT

You import a worksheet by using the Import Spreadsheet Wizard. In the process, you will indicate that the first row in the worksheet contains the column headings. ***Why? You are indicating that Access is to use those column headings as the field names in the Access table.*** In addition, you will indicate the primary key for the table. As part of the process, you could, if appropriate, choose not to include all the fields from the worksheet in the resulting table.

The following steps import the Customer worksheet.

- Tap or click EXTERNAL DATA on the ribbon to display the EXTERNAL DATA tab (Figure 1–42).

Figure 1–42

❷

- Tap or click the Excel button (EXTERNAL DATA tab | Import & Link group) to display the Get External Data - Excel Spreadsheet dialog box.

- Tap or click the Browse button in the Get External Data - Excel Spreadsheet dialog box.

- Navigate to the location containing the workbook (for example, the Access folder in the CIS 101 folder). For a detailed example of this procedure, refer to Steps 4a – 4b in the To Save a File in a Folder section in the Office and Windows chapter at the beginning of this book.

- Tap or click the Customer Data workbook, and then tap or click the Open button to select the workbook (Figure 1–43).

Figure 1–43

3

- With the option button to import the data to a new table selected, tap or click the OK button to display the Import Spreadsheet Wizard dialog box (Figure 1–44).

Q&A What happens if I select the option button to append records to an existing table?
Instead of the records being placed in a new table, they will be added to an existing table that you specify, provided the value in the primary key field does not duplicate that on an existing record.

Figure 1–44

4

- If necessary, tap or click First Row Contains Column Headings to select it.

- Tap or click the Next button (Figure 1–45).

Q&A When would I use the Field Options on the Import Spreadsheet Wizard?
You would use these options if you wanted to change properties for one or more fields. You can change the name, the data type, and whether the field is indexed. You also can indicate that some fields should not be imported.

Figure 1–45

5

- Because the Field Options need not be specified, tap or click the Next button (Figure 1–46).

Figure 1–46

6

- Tap or click the 'Choose my own primary key' option button (Figure 1–47).

 How do I decide which option button to select?

If one of the fields is an appropriate primary key, choose your own primary key from the list of fields. If you are sure you do not want a primary key, choose No primary key. Otherwise, let Access add the primary key.

Figure 1–47

7

- Because the Customer Number field, which is the correct field, is already selected as the primary key, tap or click the Next button.

- Use the DELETE or BACKSPACE keys as necessary to erase the current entry, and then type `Customer` in the Import to Table text box.

- Tap or click the Finish button to import the data (Figure 1–48).

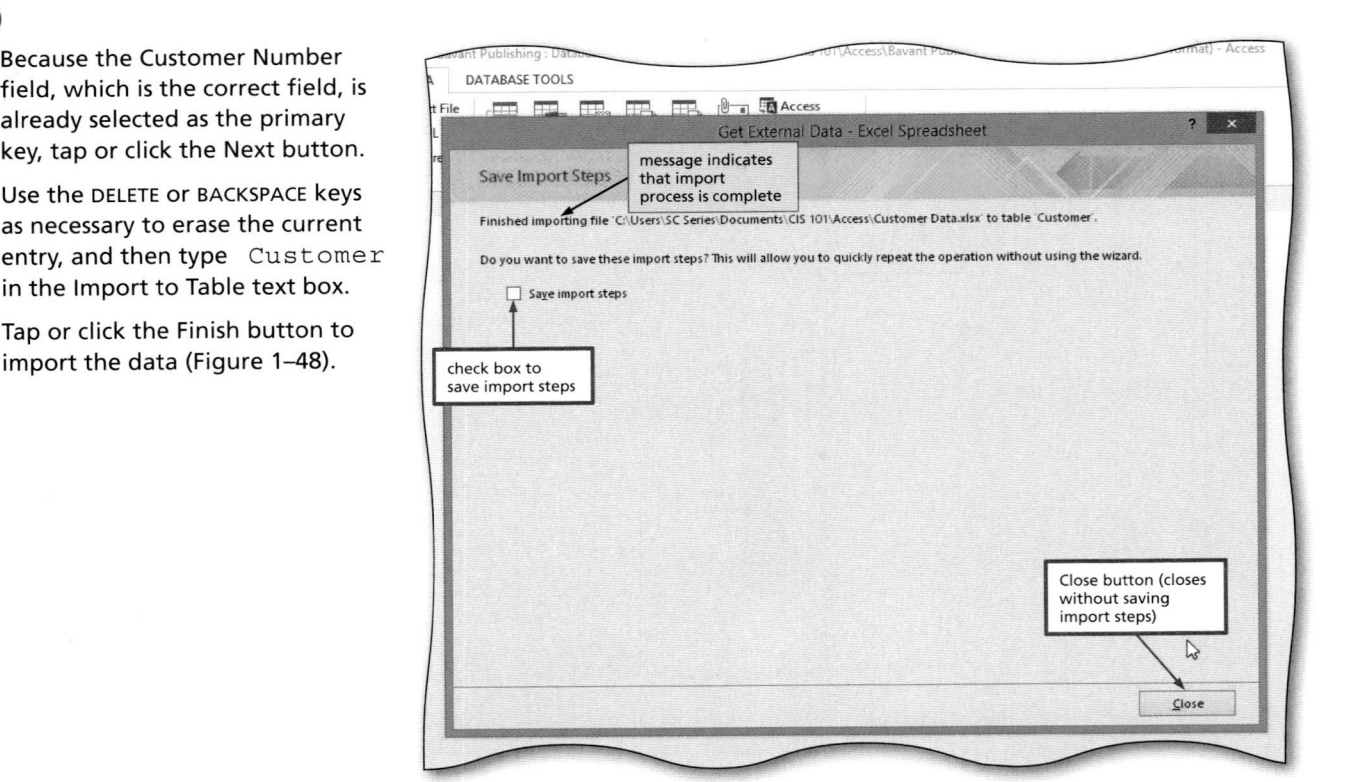

Figure 1–48

8

- Tap or click the 'Save import steps' check box to display the Save import steps options.

- If necessary, type `Import-Customer Data` in the Save as text box.

- Type `Import data from Customer Data workbook into Customer table` in the Description text box (Figure 1–49).

Q&A When would I create an Outlook task?

If the import operation is one you will repeat on a regular basis, you can create and schedule the import process just as you can schedule any other Outlook task.

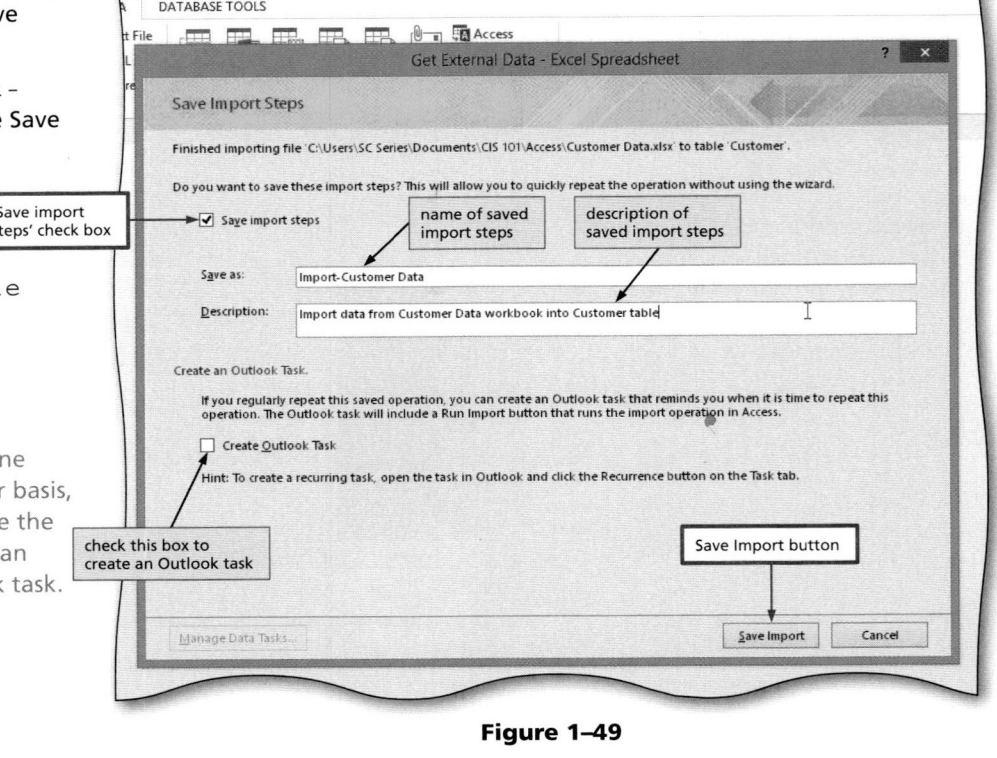

Figure 1–49

9

- Tap or click the Save Import button to save the import steps (Figure 1–50).

Q&A I saved the table as Customer Data. How can I change the name?

Press and hold or right-click the table name in the Navigation Pane. Click Rename on the shortcut menu and change the table name to Customer.

Figure 1–50

Modifying the Table

The import process has created the Customer table. The table has the correct fields and records. There are some details the process cannot handle, however. These include field sizes, descriptions, and captions. You will use Design view to make the necessary changes. The information you need is shown in Table 1–5.

BTW

Creating a Table in Design View
To create a table in Design view, display the CREATE tab, and then tap or click the Table Design button (CREATE tab | Tables group). You will then see the same screen as in Figure 1–51 on the following page, except that there will be no entries. Make all the necessary entries for the fields in your table, save the table, and assign the table a name.

Table 1–5 Structure of Customer Table

Field Name	Data Type	Field Size	Notes
Customer Number	Short Text	5	Primary Key **Description:** Customer Number (three uppercase letters followed by 2-digit number) **Caption:** CU #
Customer Name	Short Text	30	
Street	Short Text	20	
City	Short Text	20	
State	Short Text	2	
Postal Code	Short Text	5	
Amount Paid	Currency		
Current Due	Currency		
Returns	Currency		
Book Rep Number	Short Text	2	**Description:** Book Rep Number (number of book rep for customer) **Caption:** BR #

© 2014 Cengage Learning

To Modify a Table in Design View

1 CREATE FIRST TABLE | 2 ADD RECORDS | 3 PRINT CONTENTS | 4 IMPORT RECORDS | 5 MODIFY SECOND TABLE
6 CREATE QUERY | 7 CREATE FORM | 8 CREATE REPORT

You will usually need to modify the design of a table created during the import process. *Why? Some properties of a table are not specified during the import process, such as descriptions, captions, and field sizes. You also might need to change a data type.* The steps on the next page make the necessary modifications to the design of the Customer table.

1

- Open the Navigation Pane, if necessary.

- Press and hold or right-click the Customer table in the Navigation Pane to display the shortcut menu, and then tap or click Design View on the shortcut menu to open the table in Design view (Figure 1–51).

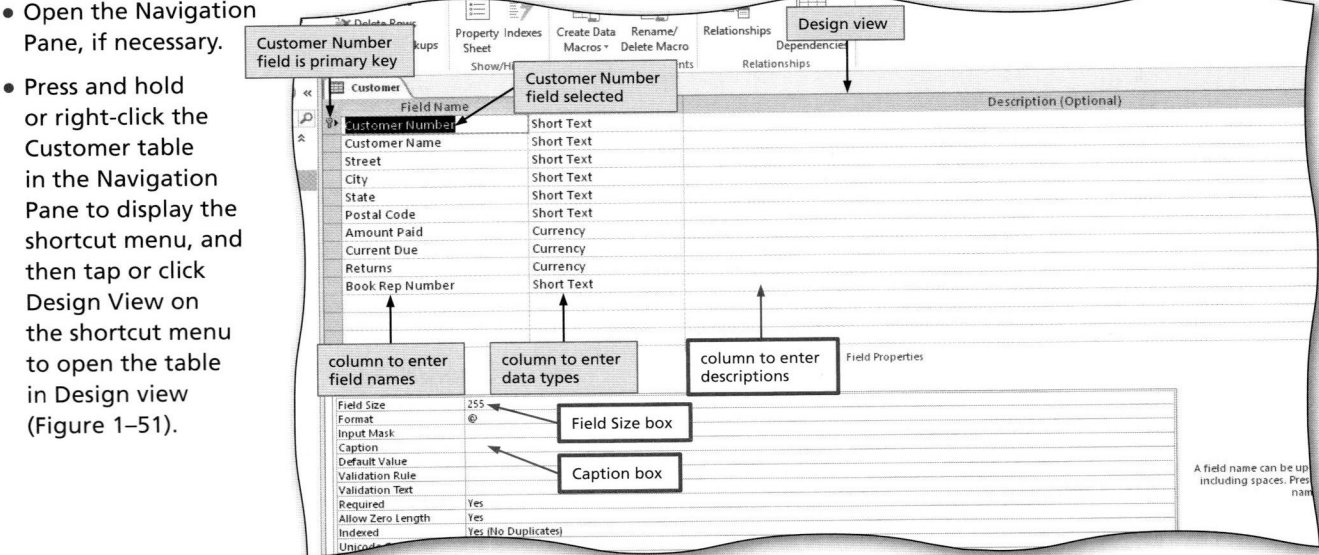

Figure 1–51

2

- Tap or click the Description (Optional) box for the Customer Number field, and then type `Customer Number (three uppercase letters followed by 2-digit number)` as the description.

- With the Customer Number field selected, tap or click the Field Size box, erase the current field size, and type `5` as the new field size.

- Tap or click the Caption box, and type `CU #` as the caption (Figure 1–52).

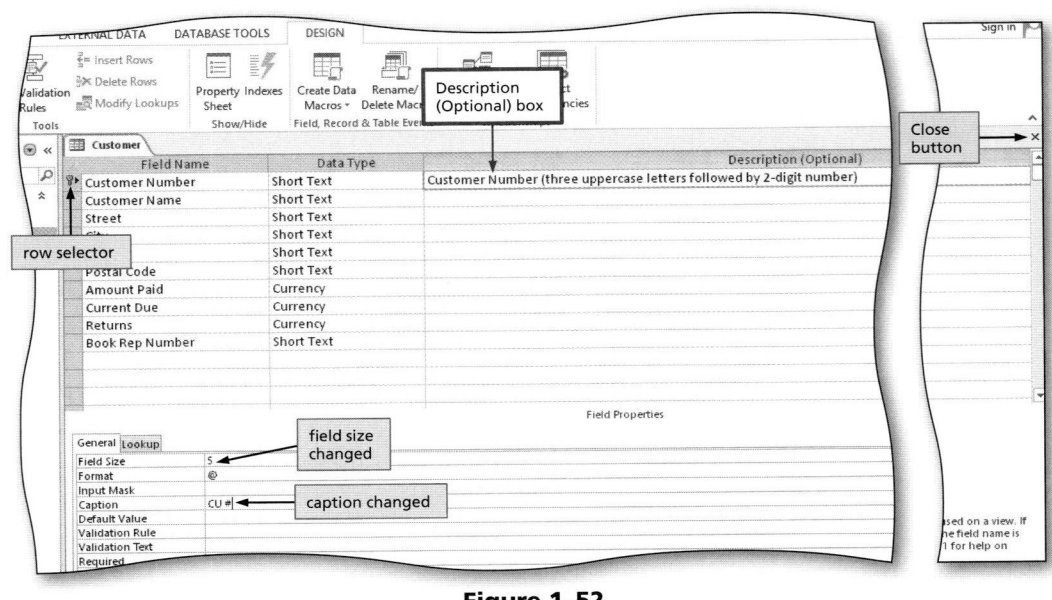

Figure 1–52

3

- Make the other changes shown in Table 1–5 on the previous page. To select a field to be changed, tap or click the field's row selector. For most fields, you only need to change the field size. For the Book Rep Number field, you also need to change the description and caption.

- Tap or click the Save button on the Quick Access Toolbar to save your changes.

- Because you know the data will satisfy the new field sizes, click the Yes button when given a message about the possibility of data loss.

Other Ways

1. Press F6 to move between upper and lower panes in Table Design window

Correcting Errors in the Structure

Whenever you create or modify a table in Design view, you should check the entries carefully to ensure they are correct. If you make a mistake and discover it before you press the TAB key, you can correct the error by repeatedly pressing the BACKSPACE key until the incorrect characters are removed. Then, type the correct characters. If you do not discover a mistake until later, you can tap or click the entry, type the correct value, and then press the ENTER key. You can use the following techniques to make changes to the structure:

- If you accidentally add an extra field to the structure, select the field by tapping or clicking the row selector (the leftmost column on the row that contains the field to be deleted). Once you have selected the field, press the DELETE key. This will remove the field from the structure.

- If you forget to include a field, select the field that will follow the one you want to add by tapping or clicking the row selector, and then press the INSERT key. The remaining fields move down one row, making room for the missing field. Make the entries for the new field in the usual manner.

- If you made the wrong field a primary key field, tap or click the correct primary key entry for the field and then tap or click the Primary Key button (TABLE TOOLS DESIGN tab | Tools group).

- To move a field, tap or click the row selector for the field to be moved to select the field, and then drag the field to the desired position.

As an alternative to these steps, you may want to start over. To do so, tap or click the Close button for the window containing the table, and then tap or click the No button in the Microsoft Access dialog box. You then can repeat the process you used earlier to define the fields in the table.

To Close the Table

Now that you have completed and saved the Customer table, you can close it. The following step closes the table.

1 Tap or click the Close button for the Customer table (see Figure 1–52) to close the table.

To Resize Columns in a Datasheet

You can resize the columns in the datasheet for the Customer table just as you resized the columns in the datasheet for the Book Rep table. The following steps resize the columns in the Customer table to best fit the data.

1 Open the Customer table in Datasheet view.

2 Double-tap or double-click the right boundary of the field selectors of each of the fields to resize the columns so that they best fit the data.

3 Save the changes to the layout by tapping or clicking the Save button on the Quick Access Toolbar.

4 Close the table.

Break Point: If you wish to take a break, this is a good place to do so. You can exit Access now. To resume at a later time, run Access, open the database called Bavant Publishing, and continue following the steps from this location forward.

Additional Database Objects

BTW
Tabbed Documents Versus Overlapping Windows
By default, Access 2013 displays database objects in tabbed documents instead of in overlapping windows. If your database is in overlapping windows mode, tap or click FILE on the ribbon, tap or click Options in the Backstage view, tap or click Current Database in the Access Options dialog box, and select the Display Document Tabs check box and the Tabbed Documents option button.

A database contains many types of objects. Tables are the objects you use to store and manipulate data. Access supports other important types of objects as well; each object has a specific purpose that helps maximize the benefits of a database. Through queries (questions), Access makes it possible to ask complex questions concerning the data in the database and then receive instant answers. Access also allows the user to produce attractive and useful forms for viewing and updating data. Additionally, Access includes report creation tools that make it easy to produce sophisticated reports for presenting data.

Creating Queries

Queries are simply questions, the answers to which are in the database. Access contains a powerful query feature that helps you find the answers to a wide variety of questions. Once you have examined the question you want to ask to determine the fields involved in the question, you can begin creating the query. If the query involves no special sort order, restrictions, or calculations, you can use the Simple Query Wizard.

To Use the Simple Query Wizard to Create a Query

1 CREATE FIRST TABLE | 2 ADD RECORDS | 3 PRINT CONTENTS | 4 IMPORT RECORDS | 5 MODIFY SECOND TABLE
6 CREATE QUERY | 7 CREATE FORM | 8 CREATE REPORT

The following steps use the Simple Query Wizard to create a query that Bavant Publishing might use to obtain financial information on its customers. *Why? The Simple Query Wizard is the quickest and easiest way to create a query.* This query displays the number, name, amount paid, current due, returns, and book rep number of all customers.

1

- If the Navigation Pane is closed, tap or click the Shutter Bar Open/Close Button to open the Navigation Pane.

- Be sure the Customer table is selected.

- Tap or click CREATE on the ribbon to display the CREATE tab.

- Tap or click the Query Wizard button (CREATE tab | Queries group) to display the New Query dialog box (Figure 1–53).

Figure 1–53

- Be sure Simple Query Wizard is selected, and then tap or click the OK button (New Query dialog box) to display the Simple Query Wizard dialog box (Figure 1–54).

Q&A What would happen if the Book Rep table were selected instead of the Customer table?
The list of available fields would contain fields from the Book Rep table rather than the Customer table.

If the list contained Book Rep table fields, how could I make it contain Customer table fields?
Tap or click the arrow in the Tables / Queries box, and then tap or click the Customer table in the list that appears.

Figure 1–54

- With the Customer Number field selected, tap or click the Add Field button to add the field to the query.

- With the Customer Name field selected, tap or click the Add Field button a second time to add the field.

- Tap or click the Amount Paid field, and then tap or click the Add Field button to add the field.

- In a similar fashion, add the Current Due, Returns, and Book Rep Number fields (Figure 1–55).

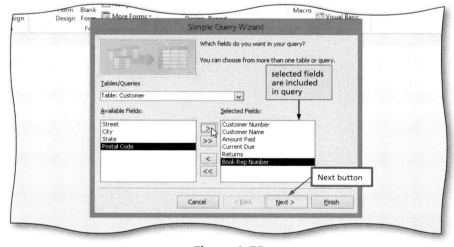

Figure 1–55

④

- Tap or click the Next button to move to the next screen.

- Ensure that the Detail (shows every field of every record) option button is selected (Figure 1–56).

Q&A What is the difference between Detail and Summary?
Detail shows all the records and fields. Summary only shows computations (for example, the total amount paid).

Figure 1–56

5

- Tap or click the Next button to move to the next screen.

- Confirm that the title of the query is Customer Query (Figure 1–57).

Q&A

What should I do if the title is incorrect? Click the box containing the title to produce an insertion point. Erase the current title and then type Customer Query.

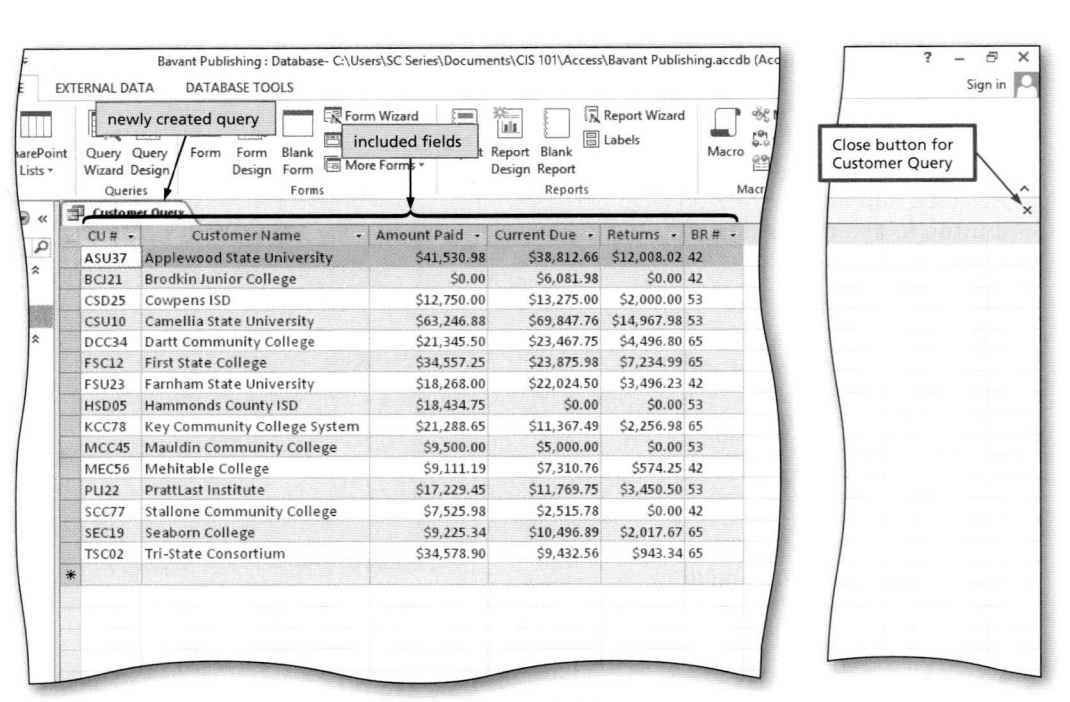

Figure 1–57

6

- Tap or click the Finish button to create the query (Figure 1–58).

7

- Tap or click the Close button for the Customer Query to remove the query results from the screen.

Q&A

If I want to use this query in the future, do I need to save the query? Normally you would. The one exception is a query created by the wizard. The wizard automatically saves the query it creates.

Figure 1–58

BTW

Access Help
At any time while using Access, you can find answers to questions and display information about various topics through Access Help. Used properly, this form of assistance can increase your productivity and reduce your frustrations by minimizing the time you spend learning how to use Access. For instruction about Access Help and exercises that will help you gain confidence in using it, read the Office and Windows chapter at the beginning of this book.

Using Queries

After you have created and saved a query, Access stores it as a database object and makes it available for use in a variety of ways:

- If you want to change the design of the query, press and hold or right-click the query in the Navigation Pane and then tap or click Design View on the shortcut menu to open the query in Design view.

- To view the results of the query from Design view, tap or click the Run button to instruct Access to **run** the query, that is, to perform the necessary actions to produce and display the results in Datasheet view.

- To view the results of the query from the Navigation Pane, open it by pressing and holding or right-clicking the query and tapping or clicking Open on the

shortcut menu. Access automatically runs the query and displays the results in Datasheet view.

- To print the results with the query open in either Design view or Datasheet view, tap or click FILE on the ribbon, tap or click the Print tab, and then tap or click either Print or Quick Print.

- To print the query without first opening it, be sure the query is selected in the Navigation Pane and tap or click FILE on the ribbon, tap or click the Print tab, and then tap or click either Print or Quick Print.

You can switch between views of a query using the View button (HOME tab | Views group). Tapping or clicking the arrow in the bottom of the button produces the View button menu. You then tap or click the desired view in the menu. The two query views you will use in this chapter are Datasheet view (which displays the query results) and Design view (for changing the query design). You also can tap or click the top part of the View button, in which case, you will switch to the view identified by the icon on the button. In the figure, the button contains the icon for Design view, so tapping or clicking the button would change to Design view. For the most part, the icon on the button represents the view you want, so you can usually simply tap or click the button.

BTW

Creating Queries
Although the Simple Query Wizard is a convenient way to create straightforward queries, you will find that many of the queries you create require more control than the wizard provides. In Chapter 2, you will use Design view to create customized queries.

To Use a Criterion in a Query

1 CREATE FIRST TABLE | 2 ADD RECORDS | 3 PRINT CONTENTS | 4 IMPORT RECORDS | 5 MODIFY SECOND TABLE
6 CREATE QUERY | **7 CREATE FORM** | **8 CREATE REPORT**

After you have determined the fields to be included in a query, you will determine whether you need to further restrict the results of the query. For example, you might want to include only those customers whose book rep number is 53. In such a case, you need to enter the number 53 as a criterion for the book rep field. *Why? A criterion is a condition that the records must satisfy in order to be included in the query results.* To do so, you will open the query in Design view, enter the criterion below the appropriate field, and then view the results of the query. The following steps enter a criterion to include only the customers of book rep 53 and then view the query results.

- Press and hold or right-click the Customer Query in the Navigation Pane to produce a shortcut menu (Figure 1–59).

Figure 1–59

2

- Tap or click Design View on the shortcut menu to open the query in Design view (Figure 1–60).

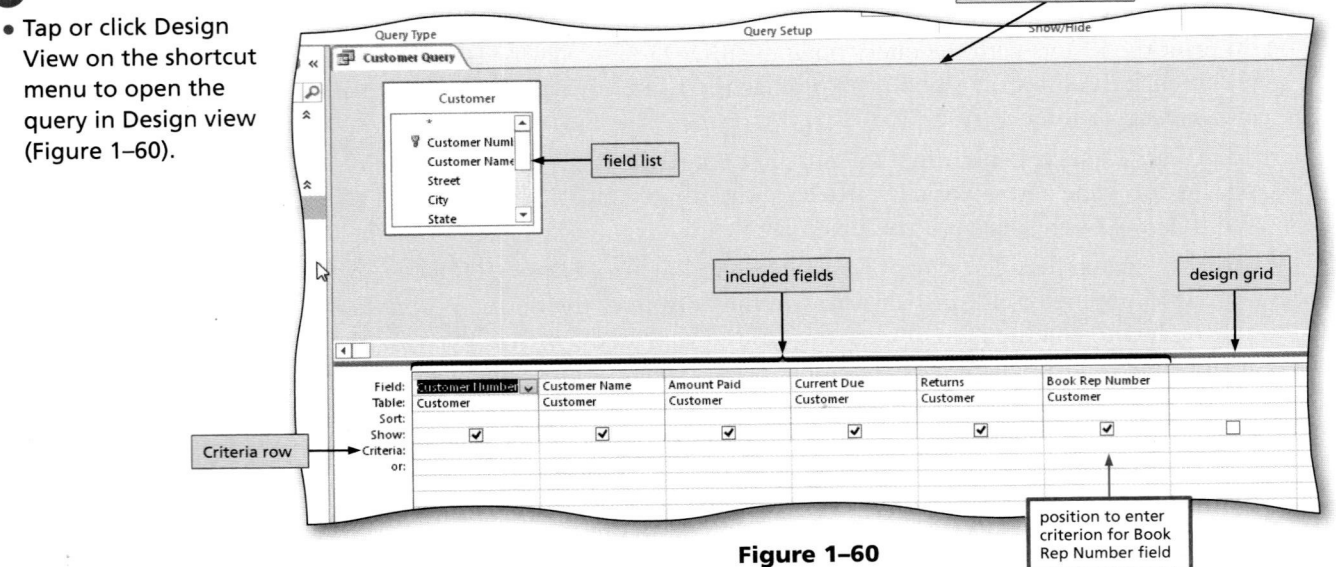

Figure 1–60

3

- Tap or click the Criteria row in the Book Rep Number column of the grid, and then type 53 as the criterion (Figure 1–61).

Q&A The Book Rep Number field is a text field. Do I need to enclose the value for a text field in quotation marks? You could, but it is not necessary, because Access inserts the quotation marks for you automatically.

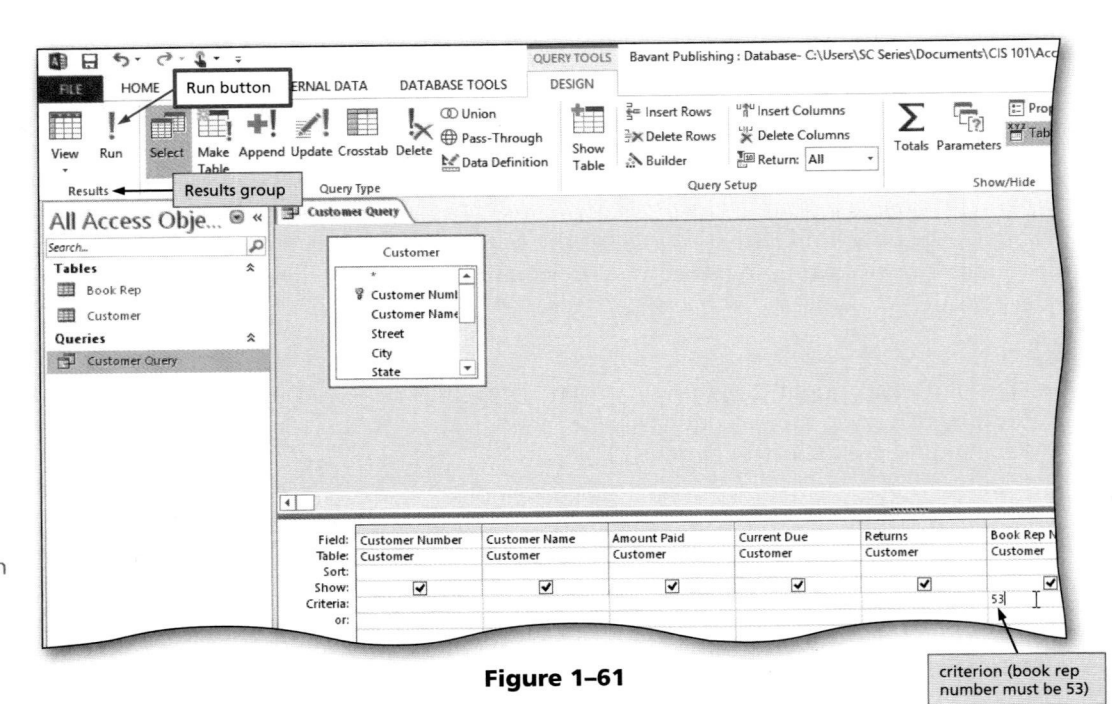

Figure 1–61

4

- Tap or click the Run button (QUERY TOOLS DESIGN tab | Results group) to run the query and display the results in Datasheet view (Figure 1–62).

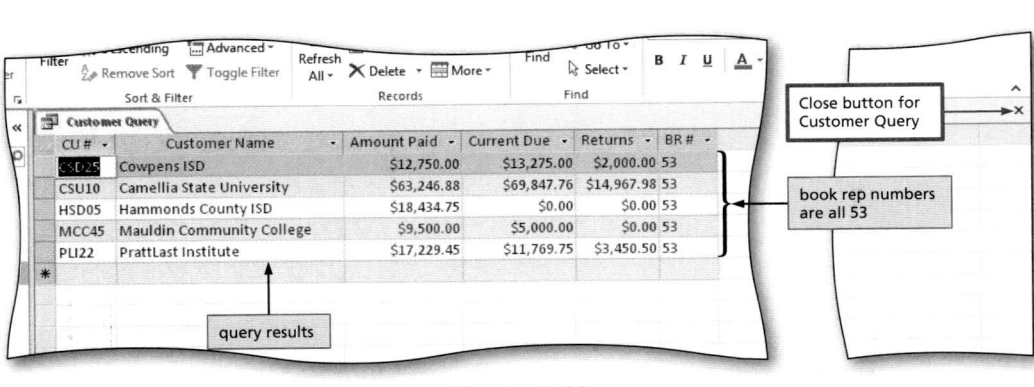

Figure 1–62

5

- Tap or click the Close button for the Customer Query to close the query.

- When asked if you want to save your changes, tap or click the No button.

Q&A If I saved the query, what would happen the next time I ran the query?
You would see only customers of book rep 53.

Could I save a query with another name?
Yes. To save a query with a different name, tap or click FILE on the ribbon, tap or click the Save As tab, tap or click Save Object As, tap or click the Save As button, enter a new file name in the Save As dialog box, and then tap or click the OK button (Save As dialog box).

Other Ways

1. Tap or click View button (QUERY TOOLS DESIGN tab | Results group) 2. Tap or click Datasheet View button on status bar

To Print the Results of a Query

The following steps print the results of a saved query.

1 With the Customer Query selected in the Navigation Pane, tap or click FILE on the ribbon to open the Backstage view.

2 Tap or click the Print tab in the Backstage view to display the Print gallery.

3 Tap or click the Quick Print button to print the query.

Creating and Using Forms

In Datasheet view, you can view many records at once. If there are many fields, however, only some of the fields in each record might be visible at a time. In **Form view**, where data is displayed in a form on the screen, you usually can see all the fields, but only for one record.

To Create a Form

1 CREATE FIRST TABLE | 2 ADD RECORDS | 3 PRINT CONTENTS | 4 IMPORT RECORDS | 5 MODIFY SECOND TABLE
6 CREATE QUERY | **7 CREATE FORM** | **8 CREATE REPORT**

Like a paper form, a **form** in a database is a formatted document with fields that contain data. Forms allow you to view and maintain data. Forms also can be used to print data, but reports are more commonly used for that purpose. The simplest type of form in Access is one that includes all the fields in a table stacked one above the other. The following steps use the Form button to create a form. *Why? Using the Form button is the simplest way to create this type of form.* The steps then use the form to view records and then save the form.

1

- Select the Customer table in the Navigation Pane.

- If necessary, tap or click CREATE on the ribbon to display the CREATE tab (Figure 1–63).

Figure 1–63

②

- Tap or click the Form button (CREATE tab | Forms group) to create a simple form (Figure 1–64).

Q&A A Field list appeared on my screen. What should I do?
Tap or click the Add Existing Fields button (FORM LAYOUT TOOLS DESIGN tab | Tools group) to remove the Field list from the screen.

Figure 1–64

③

- Tap or click the Form View button on the Access status bar to display the form in Form view rather than Layout view.

Q&A What is the difference between Layout view and Form view?
Layout view allows you to make changes to the look of the form. Form view is the view you use to examine or make changes to the data.

How can I tell when I am in Layout view?
Access identifies Layout view in three ways. The left side of the status bar will contain the words Layout View; shading will appear around the outside of the selected field in the form; and the Layout View button will be selected on the right side of the status bar.

- Tap or click the Next record button three times to move to record 4 (Figure 1–65).

Figure 1–65

- Tap or click the Save button on the Quick Access Toolbar to display the Save As dialog box (Figure 1–66).

Q&A

Do I have to tap or click the Next record button before saving?
No. The only reason you were asked to tap or click the button was so that you could experience navigation within the form.

- Type `Customer Form` as the form name, and then tap or click the OK button to save the form.

- Tap or click the Close button for the form to close the form.

Figure 1–66

Other Ways

1. Tap or click View button (FORM LAYOUT TOOLS DESIGN tab | Views group)

Using a Form

After you have saved a form, you can use it at any time by pressing and holding or right-clicking the form in the Navigation Pane and then tapping or clicking Open on the shortcut menu. In addition to viewing data in the form, you also can use it to enter or update data, a process that is very similar to updating data using a datasheet. If you plan to use the form to enter or revise data, you must ensure you are viewing the form in Form view.

Break Point: If you wish to take a break, this is a good place to do so. You can exit Access now. To resume at a later time, run Access, open the database called Bavant Publishing, and continue following the steps from this location forward.

Creating and Printing Reports

Bavant Publishing wants to create the Customer Financial Report shown in Figure 1–67. To create this report, you will first create a simple report containing all records. Then, you will modify the report to match the one shown in Figure 1–67.

Customer Financial Report		Monday, September 15, 2014 2:23:09 PM				
Customer Number	Customer Name	Amount Paid	Current Due	Returns	Book Rep Number	
ASU37	Applewood State University	$41,530.98	$38,812.66	$12,008.02	42	
BCJ21	Brodkin Junior College	$0.00	$6,081.98	$0.00	42	
CSD25	Cowpens ISD	$12,750.00	$13,275.00	$2,000.00	53	
CSU10	Camellia State University	$63,246.88	$69,847.76	$14,967.98	53	
DCC34	Dartt Community College	$21,345.50	$23,467.75	$4,496.80	65	
FSC12	First State College	$34,557.25	$23,875.98	$7,234.99	65	
FSU23	Farnham State University	$18,268.00	$22,024.50	$3,496.23	42	
HSD05	Hammonds County ISD	$18,434.75	$0.00	$0.00	53	
KCC78	Key Community College System	$21,288.65	$11,367.49	$2,256.98	65	
MCC45	Mauldin Community College	$9,500.00	$5,000.00	$0.00	53	
MEC56	Mehitable College	$9,111.19	$7,310.76	$574.25	42	
PLI22	PrattLast Institute	$17,229.45	$11,769.75	$3,450.50	53	
SCC77	Stallone Community College	$7,525.98	$2,515.78	$0.00	42	
SEC19	Seaborn College	$9,225.34	$10,496.89	$2,017.67	65	
TSC02	Tri-State Consortium	$34,578.90	$9,432.56	$943.34	65	
		$318,592.87	$255,278.86	$53,446.76		

Figure 1–67

To Create a Report

1 CREATE FIRST TABLE | 2 ADD RECORDS | 3 PRINT CONTENTS | 4 IMPORT RECORDS | 5 MODIFY SECOND TABLE
6 CREATE QUERY | 7 CREATE FORM | **8 CREATE REPORT**

You will first create a report containing all fields. **Why?** *It is easiest to create a report with all the fields and then delete the fields you do not want.* The following steps create and save the initial report. They also modify the report title.

1

- Be sure the Customer table is selected in the Navigation Pane.

- Tap or click CREATE on the ribbon to display the CREATE tab (Figure 1–68).

Q&A Do I need to select the Customer table prior to tapping or clicking CREATE on the ribbon?
You do not need to select the table at that point. You do need to select a table prior to tapping or clicking the Report button, because Access will include all the fields in whichever table or query is currently selected.

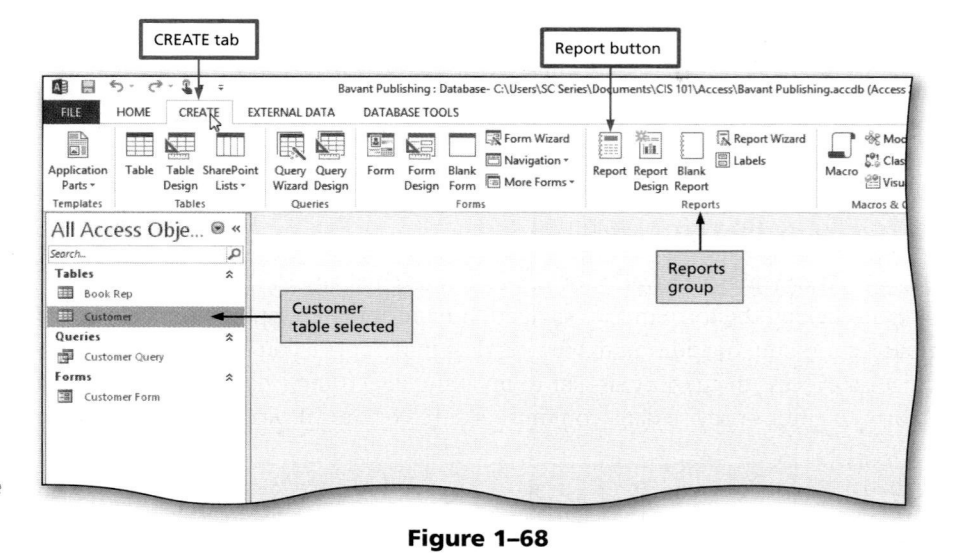

Figure 1–68

2

- Tap or click the Report button (CREATE tab | Reports group) to create the report (Figure 1–69).

Q&A Why is the report title Customer?
Access automatically assigns the name of the table or query as the title of the report. It also automatically includes the date. You can change either of these later.

Figure 1–69

3

- Tap or click the Save button on the Quick Access Toolbar to display the Save As dialog box, and then type `Customer Financial Report` as the name of the report (Figure 1–70).

Figure 1–70

4

- Tap or click the OK button (Save As dialog box) to save the report (Figure 1–71).

Q&A The name of the report changed. Why did the report title not change?
The report title is assigned the same name as the report by default. Changing the name of the report does not change the report title. You can change the title at any time to anything you like.

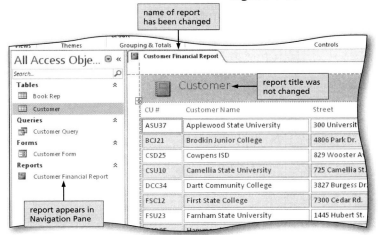

Figure 1–71

5

- Close the report by tapping or clicking its Close button.

Using Layout View in a Report

Access has four different ways to view reports: Report view, Print Preview, Layout view, and Design view. Report view shows the report on the screen. Print Preview shows the report as it will appear when printed. Layout view is similar to Report view in that it shows the report on the screen, but also allows you to make changes to the report. Layout view is usually the easiest way to make such changes. Design view also allows you to make changes, but does not show you the actual report. Design view is most useful when the changes you need to make are especially complex. In this chapter, you will use Layout view to modify the report.

To Modify Report Column Headings and Resize Columns

1 CREATE FIRST TABLE | 2 ADD RECORDS | 3 PRINT CONTENTS | 4 IMPORT RECORDS | 5 MODIFY SECOND TABLE
6 CREATE QUERY | 7 CREATE FORM | **8 CREATE REPORT**

To make the report match the one shown in Figure 1–67 on page AC 48, you need to change the title, remove some columns, modify the column headings, and also resize the columns. The following steps use Layout view to make the necessary modifications to the report. *Why? Working in Layout view gives you all the tools you need to make the desired modifications. You can view the results of the modifications immediately.*

1

- Press and hold or right-click Customer Financial Report in the Navigation Pane, and then tap or click Layout View on the shortcut menu to open the report in Layout view.

- If a Field list appears, tap or click the Add Existing Fields button (REPORT LAYOUT TOOLS DESIGN tab | Tools group) to remove the Field list from the screen.

- Close the Navigation Pane.

- Tap or click the report title once to select it.

- Tap or click the report title a second time to produce an insertion point (Figure 1–72).

Figure 1–72

Q&A

My insertion point is in the middle of Customer. How do I produce an insertion point at the position shown in the figure?

You can use the RIGHT ARROW key to move the insertion point to the position in the figure, or you can tap or click the desired position.

2

- Press the SPACEBAR to insert a space, and then type Financial Report to complete the title.

- Tap or click the column heading for the Street field to select it.

- Hold the SHIFT key down and then tap or click the column headings for the City, State, and Postal Code fields to select multiple column headings.

Figure 1–73

Q&A What happens if I do not hold down the SHIFT key?
When you tap or click another column heading, it will be the only one that is selected. To select multiple objects, you need to hold the SHIFT key down for every object after the first selection.

I selected the wrong collection of objects. What should I do?
You can tap or click somewhere else on the report so that the objects you want are not selected, and then begin the process again. Alternatively, you can repeatedly tap or click the Undo button on the Quick Access Toolbar to undo your selections. Once you have done so, you can select the objects you want.

- Tap or click ARRANGE on the ribbon to display the REPORT LAYOUT TOOLS ARRANGE tab (Figure 1–73).

3

- Tap or click the Select Column button (REPORT LAYOUT TOOLS ARRANGE tab | Rows & Columns group) to select the entire columns corresponding to the column headings you selected in the previous step.

- Press the DELETE key to delete the selected columns.

- Tap or click the column heading for the Customer Number field twice, once to select it and the second time to produce an insertion point (Figure 1–74).

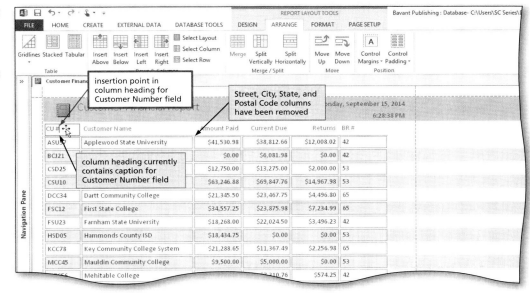

Figure 1–74

Q&A I selected the wrong field. What should I do?
Tap or click somewhere outside the various fields to deselect the one you have selected. Then, tap or click the Customer Number field twice.

4

- Use the DELETE or BACKSPACE keys as necessary to erase the current entry, and then type `Customer Number` as the new entry.

- Tap or click the heading for the Book Rep Number field twice, erase the current entry, and then type `Book Rep Number` as the new entry.

- Tap or click the Customer Number field heading to select it, point to the lower boundary of the heading for the Customer Number field so that the pointer changes to a two-headed arrow, and then drag the lower boundary to the approximate position shown in Figure 1–75 to expand the column headings.

Figure 1–75

Q&A

I did something wrong when I dragged and now my report looks strange. What should I do?

Tap or click the Undo button on the Quick Access Toolbar to undo the change. Depending on the specific action you took, you may need to tap or click it more than once.

My screen displays Book Rep Number on one line not two. Is this a problem?

No. You will adjust the column heading in a later step.

5

- Point to the right boundary of the heading for the Customer Number field so that the pointer changes to a two-headed arrow, and then drag the right boundary to the approximate position shown in Figure 1–76 to reduce the width of the column.

Figure 1–76

6

- Using the same technique, resize the other columns to the sizes shown in Figure 1–77.

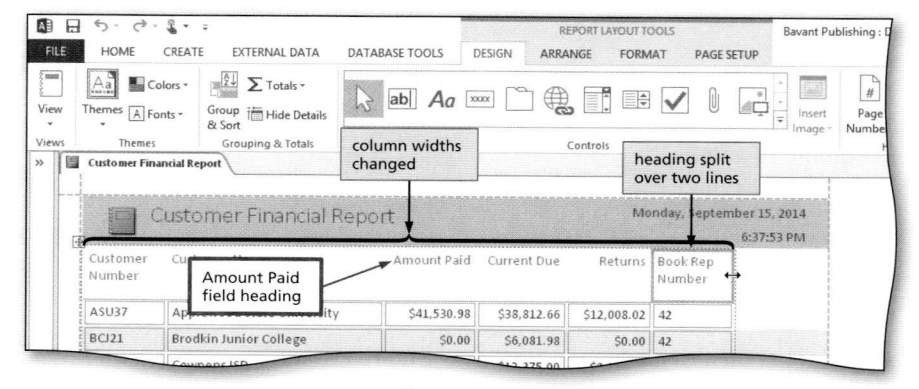

Figure 1–77

To Add Totals to a Report

The report in Figure 1–67 contains totals for the Amount Paid, Current Due, and Returns columns. You can use Layout view to add these totals. The following steps use Layout view to include totals for these three columns. *Why? In Layout view you can tap or click a single button to add totals. This button sums all the values in the field.*

- Tap or click the Amount Paid field heading (shown in Figure 1–77) to select the field.

Q&A Do I have to tap or click the heading? Could I tap or click the field on one of the records?
You do not have to tap or click the heading. You also could tap or click the Amount Paid field on any record.

- Tap or click DESIGN on the ribbon to display the DESIGN tab.

- Tap or click the Totals button (REPORT LAYOUT TOOLS DESIGN tab | Grouping & Totals group) to display the Totals menu containing a list of available calculations (Figure 1–78).

Figure 1–78

- Tap or click Sum to calculate the sum of the amount of paid values.

- Using the same technique, add totals for the Current Due and Returns columns.

Q&A When I clicked the Totals button after selecting the Returns field heading, Sum was already checked. Do I still need to tap or click Sum?
No. In fact, if you do tap or click it, you will remove the check mark, which will remove the total from the column.

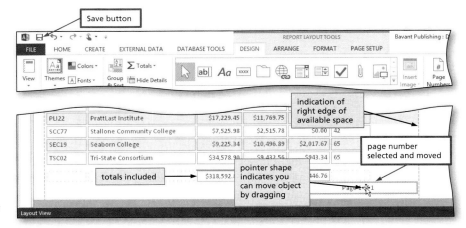

Figure 1–79

- Scroll down to the bottom of the report to verify that the totals are included. If necessary, expand the size of the total controls so they appear completely by dragging the lower boundary of the controls to the approximate position shown in Figure 1–79.

- Tap or click the page number to select it, and then drag it to the approximate position shown in Figure 1–79.

Q&A Why did I need to move the page number?
The dotted line near the right-hand edge of the screen indicates the right-hand border of the available space on the printed page, based on whatever margins and orientation are currently selected. A portion of the page number extends beyond this border. By moving the page number, it no longer extends beyond the border.

3

- Tap or click the Save button on the Quick Access Toolbar to save your changes to the report layout.

- Close the report.

To Print a Report

The following steps print the report.

1 Open the Navigation Pane if necessary, confirm that the Customer Financial Report is selected, and then tap or click FILE on the ribbon to open the Backstage view.

2 Tap or click the Print tab in the Backstage view to display the Print gallery.

3 Tap or click the Quick Print button to print the report.

When I print the report, I have pound signs (####) rather than numbers where the totals should be for the Amount Paid and Current Due columns. The report looked fine on the screen. How can I correct it?
The columns are not wide enough to display the complete number. Open the report in Layout view and slightly increase the width of the Amount Paid and Current Due columns by dragging the right boundary of the column headings.

How can I print multiple copies of my report?
Tap or click FILE on the ribbon to open the Backstage view. Tap or click the Print tab, tap or click Print in the Print gallery to display the Print dialog box, increase the number in the Number of Copies box, and then tap or click the OK button (Print dialog box).

How can I print a range of pages rather than printing the whole report?
Tap or click FILE on the ribbon to open the Backstage view. Tap or click the Print tab, tap or click Print in the Print gallery to display the Print dialog box, tap or click the Pages option button in the Print Range area, enter the desired page range, and then tap or click the OK button (Print dialog box).

BTW

Exporting a Report as a PDF or XPS File
To export a report as a PDF or XPS file, display the EXTERNAL DATA tab, and then tap or click the PDF or XPS button (EXTERNAL DATA tab | Export group). Enter the appropriate information in the Publish to PDF or XPS dialog box and tap or click the Publish button.

BTW

Report Navigation
When previewing a report, you can use the Navigation buttons on the status bar to move from one page to another.

Database Properties

Access helps you organize and identify your databases by using **database properties,** which are the details about a file. Database properties, also known as **metadata,** can include such information as the project author, title, or subject. **Keywords** are words or phrases that further describe the database. For example, a class name or database topic can describe the file's purpose or content.

Five different types of database properties exist, but the more common ones used in this book are standard and automatically updated properties. **Standard properties** are associated with all Microsoft Office documents and include author, title, and subject. **Automatically updated properties** include file system properties, such as the date you create or change a file, and statistics, such as the file size.

CONSIDER THIS

Why would you want to assign database properties to a database?
Database properties are valuable for a variety of reasons:

- Users can save time locating a particular file because they can view a file's database properties without opening the database.

- By creating consistent properties for files having similar content, users can better organize their databases.

- Some organizations require Access users to add database properties so that other employees can view details about these files.

TO CHANGE DATABASE PROPERTIES

To change database properties, you would follow these steps.

1. Tap or click FILE on the ribbon to open the Backstage view and then, if necessary, tap or click the Info tab in the Backstage view to display the Info gallery.

2. Click the 'View and edit database properties' link in the right pane of the Info gallery to display the Bavant Publishing Properties dialog box.

Q&A Why are some of the database properties already filled in?
The person who installed Office 2013 on your computer or network might have set or customized the properties.

3. If the property you want to change is displayed in the Properties dialog box, click the text box for the property and make the desired change. Skip the remaining steps.

4. If the property you want to change is not displayed in the Properties dialog box, click the appropriate tab so the property is displayed and then make the desired change.

5. Click the OK button in the Properties dialog box to save your changes and remove the dialog box from the screen.

To Sign Out of a Microsoft Account

If you are signed in to a Microsoft account and are using a public computer or otherwise wish to sign out of your Microsoft account, you should sign out of the account from the Account gallery in the Backstage view before exiting Access. Signing out of the account is the safest way to make sure that nobody else can access SkyDrive files or settings stored in your Microsoft account. The following steps sign out of a Microsoft account from Access. For a detailed example of the procedure summarized below, refer to the Office and Windows chapter at the beginning of this book.

1 If you wish to sign out of your Microsoft account, tap or click FILE on the ribbon to open the Backstage view and then tap or click the Account tab to display the Account gallery.

2 Tap or click the Sign out link, which displays the Remove Account dialog box. If a Can't remove Windows accounts dialog box appears instead of the Remove Account dialog box, click the OK button and skip the remaining steps.

Q&A Why does a Can't remove Windows accounts dialog box appear?
If you signed in to Windows using your Microsoft account, then you also must sign out from Windows, rather than signing out from within Access. When you are finished using Windows, be sure to sign out at that time.

3 Tap or click the Yes button (Remove Account dialog box) to sign out of your Microsoft account on this computer.

Q&A Should I sign out of Windows after signing out of my Microsoft account? [End Q]
When you are finished using the computer, you should sign out of your account for maximum security.

4 Tap or click the Back button in the upper-left corner of the Backstage view to return to the database.

To Exit Access

The following steps exit Access.

1 Tap or click the Close button on the right side of the title bar to close the open database, if there is one, and exit Access.

2 If a Microsoft Access dialog box appears, tap or click the Save button to save any changes made to the database since the last save.

Special Database Operations

Additional operations involved in maintaining a database are backup, recovery, compacting, and repairing.

Backup and Recovery

It is possible to damage or destroy a database. Users can enter data that is incorrect; programs that are updating the database can end abnormally during an update; a hardware problem can occur; and so on. After any such event has occurred, the database may contain invalid data or it might be totally destroyed.

Obviously, you cannot allow a situation in which data has been damaged or destroyed to go uncorrected. You must somehow return the database to a correct state. This process is called recovery; that is, you **recover** the database.

The simplest approach to recovery involves periodically making a copy of the database (called a **backup copy** or a **save copy**). This is referred to as **backing up** the database. If a problem occurs, you correct the problem by overwriting the actual database — often referred to as the **live database** — with the backup copy.

To back up the database that is currently open, you use the Back Up Database command on the Save As tab in the Backstage view. In the process, Access suggests a name that is a combination of the database name and the current date. For example, if you back up the Bavant Publishing database on October 20, 2014, Access will suggest the name, Bavant Publishing_2014-10-20. You can change this name if you desire, although it is a good idea to use this name. By doing so, it will be easy to distinguish between all the backup copies you have made to determine which is the most recent. In addition, if you discover that a critical problem occurred on October 18, 2014, you may want to go back to the most recent backup before October 18. If, for example, the database was not backed up on October 17 but was backed up on October 16, you would use Bavant Publishing_2014-10-16.

TO BACK UP A DATABASE

You would use the following steps to back up a database to a file on a hard disk or high-capacity removable disk.

1. Open the database to be backed up.
2. Tap or click FILE on the ribbon to open the Backstage view, and then tap or click the Save As tab.
3. With Save Database As selected in the File Types area, tap or click 'Back Up Database' in the Save Database As area, and then tap or click the Save As button.
4. Navigate to the desired location in the Save As box. If you do not want the name Access has suggested, enter the desired name in the File name text box.
5. Tap or click the Save button to back up the database.

Access creates a backup copy with the desired name in the desired location. Should you ever need to recover the database using this backup copy, you can simply copy it over the live version.

Compacting and Repairing a Database

As you add more data to a database, it naturally grows larger. When you delete an object (records, tables, forms, or queries), the space previously occupied by the object does not become available for additional objects. Instead, the additional objects are given new space; that is, space that was not already allocated. To remove this empty space from the database, you must **compact** the database. The same option that compacts the database also repairs problems that might have occurred in the database.

To Compact and Repair a Database

You would use the following steps to compact and repair a database.

1. Open the database to be compacted.
2. Tap or click FILE on the ribbon to open the Backstage view, and then, if necessary, select the Info tab.
3. Tap or click the Compact & Repair Database button in the Info gallery to compact and repair the database.
 The database now is the compacted form of the original.

Additional Operations

Additional special operations include opening another database, closing a database without exiting Access, and saving a database with another name. They also include deleting a table (or other object) as well as renaming an object.

When you open another database, Access will automatically close the database that previously was open. Before deleting or renaming an object, you should ensure that the object has no dependent objects; that is, other objects that depend on the object you want to delete.

To Close a Database without Exiting Access

You would use the following steps to close a database without exiting Access.

1. Tap or click FILE on the ribbon to open the Backstage view.
2. Tap or click Close.

To Save a Database with Another Name

To save a database with another name, you would use the following steps.

1. Tap or click FILE on the ribbon to open the Backstage view, and then select the Save As tab.
2. With Save Database As selected in the Database File Types area and Access Database selected in the Save Database As area, tap or click the Save As button.
3. Enter a name and select a location for the new version.
4. Tap or click the Save button.

If you want to make a backup, could you just save the database with another name?
You could certainly do that. Using the backup procedure discussed earlier has the advantage that it automatically includes the current database name and the date in the name of the file it creates.

To Delete a Table or Other Object in the Database

You would use the following steps to delete a database object.

1. Press and hold or right-click the object in the Navigation Pane.
2. Tap or click Delete on the shortcut menu.
3. Tap or click the Yes button in the Microsoft Access dialog box.

To Rename an Object in the Database

You would use the following steps to rename a database object.

1. Press and hold or right-click the object in the Navigation Pane.
2. Tap or click Rename on the shortcut menu.
3. Type the new name and press the ENTER key.

Database Design

BTW
Database Design Language (DBDL)
Database Design Language (DBDL) is a commonly accepted shorthand representation for showing the structure of a relational database. You write the name of the table and then within parentheses you list all the columns in the table. If the columns continue beyond one line, indent the subsequent lines.

This section illustrates the **database design** process, that is, the process of determining the tables and fields that make up the database. It does so by showing how you would design the database for Bavant Publishing from a set of requirements. In this section, you will use commonly accepted shorthand to represent the tables and fields that make up the database as well as the primary keys for the tables. For each table, you give the name of the table followed by a set of parentheses. Within the parentheses is a list of the fields in the table separated by commas. You underline the primary key. For example,

Product (<u>Product Code</u>, Description, On Hand, Price) represents a table called Product. The Product table contains four fields: Product Code, Description, On Hand, and Price. The Product Code field is the primary key.

Database Requirements

BTW
Determining Database Requirements
The determination of database requirements is part of a process known as systems analysis. A systems analyst examines existing and proposed documents, and examines organizational policies to determine exactly the type of data needs the database must support.

The Bavant Publishing database must maintain information on both customers and book reps. The business currently keeps this data in two Word tables and two Excel workbooks, as shown in Figure 1–80. They use Word tables for address information and Excel workbooks for financial information.

- For customers, Bavant needs to maintain address data. It currently keeps this data in a Word table (Figure 1–80a).
- Bavant also maintains financial data for each customer. This includes the amount paid, current amount due, and return amount for the customer. It keeps these amounts, along with the customer name and number, in the Excel worksheet shown in Figure 1–80b.
- Bavant keeps book rep address data in a Word table, as shown in Figure 1–80c.
- Just as with customers, it keeps financial data for book reps, including their start date, salary, and bonus rate, in a separate Excel worksheet, as shown in Figure 1–80d.

Customer Number	Customer Name	Street	City	State	Postal Code
ASU37	Applewood State University	300 University Ave.	Greer	PA	19158
BCJ21	Brodkin Junior College	4806 Park Dr.	Greer	PA	19158
CSD25	Cowpens ISD	829 Wooster Ave.	Gossett	PA	19157
CSU10	Camellia State University	725 Camellia St.	Pleasantburg	NJ	07025
DCC34	Dartt Community College	3827 Burgess Dr.	Chambers	NJ	07037
FSC12	First State College	7300 Cedar Rd.	Quaker	DE	19719
FSU23	Farnham State University	1445 Hubert St.	Gaston	DE	19723
HSD05	Hammonds County ISD	446 Lincoln Blvd.	Chesnee	NJ	07053
KCC78	Key Community College System	7523 Penn Ave.	Adelphia	PA	19159
MCC45	Mauldin Community College	72 Montrose St.	Chesnee	NJ	07053
MEC56	Mehitable College	202 College St.	Gaston	DE	19723
PLI22	PrattLast Institute	236 Ashton Ave.	Pleasantburg	NJ	07025
SCC77	Stallone Community College	1200 Franklin Blvd.	Adelphia	PA	19156
SEC19	Seaborn College	345 Mather Rd.	Quaker	DE	19719
TSC02	Tri-State Consortium	3400 Metro Pkwy.	Adelphia	PA	19156

© 2014 Cengage Learning

Figure 1–80 (a) Customer Address Information (Word Table)

	A	B	C	D	E	F	G	H
1	Customer Number	Customer Name	Amount Paid	Current Due	Returns			
2	ASU37	Applewood State University	$41,530.98	$38,812.66	$12,008.02			
3	BCJ21	Brodkin Junior College	$0.00	$6,081.98	$0.00			
4	CSD25	Cowpens ISD	$12,750.00	$13,275.00	$2,000.00			
5	CSU10	Camellia State University	$63,246.88	$69,847.76	$14,967.98			
6	DCC34	Dartt Community College	$21,345.50	$23,467.75	$4,496.80			
7	FSC12	First State College	$34,557.25	$23,875.98	$7,234.99			
8	FSU23	Farnham State University	$18,268.00	$22,024.50	$3,496.23			
9	HSD05	Hammonds County ISD	$18,434.75	$0.00	$0.00			
10	KCC78	Key Community College System	$21,288.65	$11,367.49	$2,256.98			
11	MCC45	Mauldin Community College	$9,500.00	$5,000.00	$0.00			
12	MEC56	Mehitable College	$9,111.19	$7,310.76	$574.25			
13	PLI22	PrattLast Institute	$17,229.45	$11,769.75	$3,450.50			
14	SCC77	Stallone Community College	$7,525.98	$2,515.78	$0.00			
15	SEC19	Seaborn College	$9,225.34	$10,496.89	$2,017.67			
16	TSC02	Tri-State Consortium	$34,578.90	$9,432.56	$943.34			

Figure 1–80 (b) Customer Financial Information (Excel Worksheet)

Book Rep Number	Last Name	First Name	Street	City	State	Postal Code
42	Perez	Melina	261 Porter Dr.	Adelphia	PA	19156
48	Statnik	Michael	3135 Simpson Dr.	Pleasantburg	NJ	07025
53	Chin	Robert	265 Maxwell St.	Gossett	PA	19157
65	Rogers	Tracy	1827 Maple Ave.	Adelphia	PA	19159

© 2014 Cengage Learning

Figure 1–80 (c) Book Rep Address Information (Word Table)

	A	B	C	D	E	F	G	H	I	J
1	Book Rep Number	Last Name	First Name	Start Date	Salary	Bonus Rate				
2	53	Chin	Robert	6/1/2013	$26,250	0.19				
3	42	Perez	Melina	5/14/2012	$31,500	0.20				
4	65	Rogers	Tracy	7/1/2014	$7,750	0.18				
5	48	Statnik	Michael	1/15/2013	$29,000	0.20				
6										
7										

Figure 1–80 (d) Book Rep Financial Information (Excel Worksheet)

- Finally, Bavant keeps track of which customers are assigned to which book reps. Each customer is assigned to a single book rep, but each book rep might be assigned many customers. Currently, for example, customers ASU37 (Applewood State University), BCJ21 (Brodkin Junior College), FSU23 (Farnham State University), MEC56 (Mehitable College), and SCC77 (Stallone Community College) are assigned to book rep 42 (Melina Perez). Customers CSD25 (Cowpens ISD), CSU10 (Camellia State University), HSD05 (Hammonds County ISD), MCC45 (Mauldin Community College), and PLI22 (PrattLast Institute) are assigned to book rep 53 (Robert Chin). Customers DCC34 (Dartt Community College), FSC12 (First State College), KCC78 (Key Community College System), SEC19 (Seaborn College), and TSC02 (Tri-State Consortium) are assigned to book rep 65 (Tracy Rogers). Bavant has an additional book rep, Michael Statnik, whose number has been assigned as 48, but who has not yet been assigned any customers.

Database Design Process

The database design process involves several steps.

CONSIDER THIS

What is the first step in the process?

Identify the tables. Examine the requirements for the database to identify the main objects that are involved. There will be a table for each object you identify.

In a database for one organization, for example, the main objects might be departments and employees. This would require two tables: one for departments and the other for employees. In the database for another organization, the main objects might be customers and book reps. In this case, there also would be two tables: one for customers and the other for book reps. In still another organization's database, the main objects might be books, publishers, and authors. This database would require three tables: one for books, a second for publishers, and a third for authors.

Identifying the Tables

For the Bavant Publishing database, the main objects are customers and book reps. This leads to two tables, which you must name. Reasonable names for these two tables are:

Customer
Book Rep

CONSIDER THIS

After identifying the tables, what is the second step in the database design process?

Determine the primary keys. Recall that the primary key is the unique identifier for records in the table. For each table, determine the unique identifier. In a Department table, for example, the unique identifier might be the Department Code. For a Book table, the unique identifier might be the ISBN (International Standard Book Number).

Determining the Primary Keys

The next step is to identify the fields that will be the unique identifiers, or primary keys. Customer numbers uniquely identify customers, and book rep numbers uniquely identify book reps. Thus, the primary key for the Customer table is the customer number, and the primary key for the Book Rep table is the book rep number. Reasonable names for these fields would be Customer Number and Book Rep Number, respectively. Adding these primary keys to the tables gives:

Customer (<u>Customer Number</u>)
Book Rep (<u>Book Rep Number</u>)

CONSIDER THIS

What is the third step in the database design process after determining the primary keys?

Determine the additional fields. The primary key will be a field or combination of fields in a table. A table typically will contain many additional fields, each of which contains a type of data. Examine the project requirements to determine these additional fields. For example, in an Employee table, additional fields might include Employee Name, Street Address, City, State, Postal Code, Date Hired, and Salary.

Determining Additional Fields

After identifying the primary keys, you need to determine and name the additional fields. In addition to the customer number, the Customer Address Information shown in Figure 1–80a on page AC 59 contains the customer name, street, city, state, and postal code. These would be fields in the Customer table. The Customer Financial Information shown in Figure 1–80b on page AC 59 also contains the customer number and customer name, which are already included in the Customer table. The financial information also contains the amount paid, current due, and returns. Adding the amount paid, current due, and returns fields to those already identified in the Customer table and assigning reasonable names gives:

> Customer (<u>Customer Number</u>, Customer Name, Street, City, State, Postal Code, Amount Paid, Current Due, Returns)

Similarly, examining the Book Rep Address Information in Figure 1–80c on page AC 59 adds the last name, first name, street, city, state, and postal code fields to the Book Rep table. In addition to the book rep number, last name, and first name, the Book Rep Financial Information in Figure 1–80d on page AC 59 would add the start date, salary, and bonus rate. Adding these fields to the Book Rep table and assigning reasonable names gives:

> Book Rep (<u>Book Rep Number</u>, Last Name, First Name, Street, City, State, Postal Code, Start Date, Salary, Bonus Rate)

BTW

Additional Data for Bavant Publishing
Bavant could include other types of data in the database. The Customer table could include data on a contact person at each organization, such as, name, telephone number, and email address. The Book Rep table could include the mobile telephone number, email address, and emergency contact information for the book rep.

CONSIDER THIS

What happens as the fourth step, after determining additional fields?

Determine relationships between the tables. A relationship is an association between objects. In a database containing information about departments and employees, there is an association between the departments and the employees. A department is associated with all the employees in the department, and an employee is associated with the department to which he or she is assigned. Technically, you say that a department is related to all the employees in the department, and an employee is related to his or her department.

The relationship between department and employees is an example of a **one-to-many relationship** because one employee is associated with one department, but each department can be associated with many employees. The Department table would be the "one" table in the relationship. The Employee table would be the "many" table in the relationship.

When you have determined that two tables are related, follow these general guidelines:

Identify the "one" table.

Identify the "many" table.

Include the primary key from the "one" table as a field in the "many" table.

Determining and Implementing Relationships Between the Tables

According to the requirements, each customer has one book rep, but each book rep can have many customers. Thus, the Book Rep table is the "one" table, and the Customer table is the "many" table. To implement this one-to-many relationship between book reps and customers, add the Book Rep Number field (the primary key of the Book Rep table) to the Customer table. This produces:

Customer (<u>Customer Number</u>, Customer Name, Street, City, State, Postal Code, Amount Paid, Current Due, Returns, Book Rep Number)
Book Rep (<u>Book Rep Number</u>, Last Name, First Name, Street, City, State, Postal Code, Start Date, Salary, Bonus Rate)

CONSIDER THIS

After creating relationships between tables, what is the fifth step in the database design process?
Determine data types for the fields, that is, the type of data that can be stored in the field.

Determining Data Types for the Fields

See Pages AC 9 through AC 10 for a discussion of the available data types and their use in the Bavant Publishing database. That section also discusses other properties that can be assigned, such as captions, field size, and the number of decimal places.

Identifying and Removing Redundancy

Redundancy means storing the same fact in more than one place. It usually results from placing too many fields in a table — fields that really belong in separate tables — and often causes serious problems. If you had not realized there were two objects, such as customers and book reps, you might have placed all the data in a single Customer table. Figure 1–81 shows an example of a table that includes both customer and book rep information. Notice that the data for a given book rep (number, name, address, and so on) occurs on more than one record. The data for rep 42, Melina Perez, is repeated in the figure. Storing this data on multiple records is an example of redundancy.

Customer Number	Customer Name	Street	...	Book Rep Number	Last Name	First Name
ASU37	Applewood State University	300 University Ave.	...	42	Perez	Melina
BCJ21	Brodkin Junior College	4806 Park Dr.	...	42	Perez	Melina
CSD25	Cowpens ISD	829 Wooster Ave.	...	53	Chin	Robert
CSU10	Camellia State University	725 Camellia St.	...	53	Chin	Robert
DCC34	Dartt Community College	3827 Burgess Dr.	...	65	Rogers	Tracy
...

name of Book Rep 42 appears more than once

Book Rep numbers are 42

© 2014 Cengage Learning

Figure 1–81

What problems does this redundancy cause?

Redundancy results in several problems, including:

1. Wasted storage space. The name of book rep 42, Melina Perez, for example, should be stored only once. Storing this fact several times is wasteful.

2. More complex database updates. If, for example, Melina Perez's name is spelled incorrectly and needs to be changed in the database, her name would need to be changed in several different places.

3. Possible inconsistent data. Nothing prohibits the book rep's last name from being Perez on customer ASU37's record and Perret on customer BCJ21's record. The data would be inconsistent. In both cases, the book rep number is 42, but the last names are different.

How do you eliminate redundancy?

The solution to the problem is to place the redundant data in a separate table, one in which the data no longer will be redundant. If, for example, you place the data for book reps in a separate table (Figure 1–82), the data for each book rep will appear only once.

Customer Number	Customer Name	Street	...	Book Rep Number
ASU37	Applewood State University	300 University Ave.	...	42
BCJ21	Brodkin Junior College	4806 Park Dr.	...	42
CSD25	Cowpens ISD	829 Wooster Ave.	...	53
CSU10	Camellia State University	725 Camellia St.	...	53
DCC34	Dartt Community College	3827 Burgess Dr.	...	65

Book Rep numbers are 42

Book Rep Number	Last Name	First Name	...
42	Perez	Melina	...
48	Statnik	Michael	...
53	Chin	Robert	...
65	Rogers	Tracy	...

name of Book Rep 42 appears only once

© 2014 Cengage Learning

Figure 1–82

Notice that you need to have the book rep number in both tables. Without it, there would be no way to tell which book rep is associated with which customer. The remaining book rep data, however, was removed from the Customer table and placed in the Book Rep table. This new arrangement corrects the problems of redundancy in the following ways:

1. Because the data for each book rep is stored only once, space is not wasted.

2. Changing the name of a book rep is easy. You need to change only one row in the Book Rep table.

3. Because the data for a book rep is stored only once, inconsistent data cannot occur.

Designing to omit redundancy will help you to produce good and valid database designs. You should always examine your design to see if it contains redundancy. If it does, you should decide whether you need to remove the redundancy by creating a separate table.

If you examine your design, you will see that there is one area of redundancy (see the data in Figure 1–1 on page AC 3). Cities and states are both repeated. Every customer whose postal code is 19158, for example, has Greer as the city and PA as the state. To remove this redundancy, you would create a table with the primary key Postal Code and City and State as additional fields. City and State would be removed from the Customer table. Having City, State, and Postal Code in a table is very common, however, and usually you would not take such action. No other redundancy exists in your tables.

BTW

Postal Codes
Some organizations with customers throughout the country have a separate table of postal codes, cities, and states. When placing an order, you typically are asked for your postal code (or ZIP code), rather than city, state, and postal code. You then are asked to confirm that the city and state correspond to that postal code.

Chapter Summary

In this chapter you have learned to create an Access database, create tables and add records to a database, print the contents of tables, import data, create queries, create forms, create reports, and change database properties. You also have learned how to design a database. The items listed below include all the new Access skills you have learned in this chapter, with tasks grouped by activity.

Database Object Management
Delete a Table or Other Object in the Database (AC 58)
Rename an Object in the Database (AC 58)

Database Properties
Change Database Properties (AC 55)

File Management
Run Access (AC 5)
Create a Database (AC 6)
Create a Database Using a Template (AC 7)
Exit Access (AC 24)
Open a Database from Access (AC 25)
Back Up a Database (AC 56)
Compact and Repair a Database (AC 57)
Close a Database without Exiting Access (AC 57)
Save a Database with Another Name (AC 57)

Form Creation
Create a Form (AC 45)

Import Data
Import an Excel Worksheet (AC 33)

Print Objects
Preview and Print the Contents of a Table (AC 30)

Print the Results of a Query (AC 45)
Print a Report (AC 54)

Query Creation
Use the Simple Query Wizard to Create a Query (AC 40)
Use a Criterion in a Query (AC 43)

Report Creation
Create a Report (AC 48)
Modify Report Column Headings and Resize Columns (AC 50)
Add Totals to a Report (AC 53)

Table Creation
Modify the Primary Key (AC 11)
Define the Remaining Fields in a Table (AC 14)
Save a Table (AC 16)
View the Table in Design View (AC 17)
Change a Field Size in Design View (AC 18)
Close the Table (AC 20)
Resize Columns in a Datasheet (AC 28)
Modify a Table in Design View (AC 37)

Table Update
Add Records to a Table (AC 20)
Add Records to a Table that Contains Data (AC 26)

CONSIDER THIS

What decisions will you need to make when creating your next database?
Use these guidelines as you complete the assignments in this chapter and create your own databases outside of this class.

1. Identify the tables that will be included in the database.

2. Determine the primary keys for each of the tables.

3. Determine the additional fields that should be included in each of the tables.

4. Determine relationships between the tables.

 a) Identify the "one" table.

 b) Identify the "many" table.

 c) Include the primary key of the "one" table as a field in the "many" table.

5. Determine data types for the fields in the tables.

6. Determine additional properties for fields.

 a) Determine if a special caption is warranted.

 b) Determine if a special description is warranted.

 c) Determine field sizes.

 d) Determine formats.

7. Identify and remove any unwanted redundancy.

8. Determine a storage location for the database.

9. Determine the best method for distributing the database objects.

How should you submit solutions to questions in the assignments identified with a ✳ symbol?

Every assignment in this book contains one or more questions identified with a ✳ symbol. These questions require you to think beyond the assigned database. Present your solutions to the questions in the format required by your instructor. Possible formats may include one or more of these options: write the answer; create a document that contains the answer; present your answer to the class; discuss your answer in a group; record the answer as audio or video using a webcam, smartphone, or portable media player; or post answers on a blog, wiki, or website.

Apply Your Knowledge

Reinforce the skills and apply the concepts you learned in this chapter.

Adding a Caption, Changing a Data Type, Creating a Query, a Form, and a Report

Note: To complete this assignment, you will be required to use the Data Files for Students. Visit www.cengage.com/ct/studentdownload for detailed instructions or contact your instructor for information about accessing the required files.

Instructions: Cosmetics Naturally Inc. manufactures and sells beauty and skin care products made with only natural ingredients. The company's products do not contain any synthetic chemicals, artificial fragrances, or chemical preservatives. Cosmetics Naturally has a database that keeps track of its sales representatives and customers. Each customer is assigned to a single sales rep, but each sales rep may be assigned to many customers. The database has two tables. The Customer table contains data on the customers who purchase Cosmetics Naturally products. The Sales Rep table contains data on the sales reps. You will add a caption, change a data type, create two queries, a form, and a report, as shown in Figure 1–83 on the next page.

Perform the following tasks:

1. Start Access, open the Apply Cosmetics Naturally database from the Data Files for Students, and enable the content.

2. Open the Sales Rep table in Datasheet view, add SR # as the caption for the Sales Rep Number field, and resize all columns to best fit the data. Save the changes to the layout of the table and close the table.

3. Open the Customer table in Design view and change the data type for the Postal Code field to Short Text. Change the field size for the field to 5. Save the changes to the table and close the table.

4. Use the Simple Query Wizard to create a query for the Customer table that contains the Customer Number, Customer Name, Amount Paid, Balance, and Sales Rep Number. The query is a detail query. Use the name Customer Query for the query and close the query.

5. Create a simple form for the Sales Rep table. Save the form and use the name Sales Rep for the form. Close the form.

6. Create the report shown in Figure 1–83 for the Customer table. The report includes totals for both the Amount Paid and Balance fields. Be sure the totals appear completely. You might need to expand the size of the total controls. Move the page number so that it is within the margins. Save the report as Customer Financial Report.

7. If requested by your instructor, add your last name to the title of the report, that is, change the title to Customer Financial Report LastName where LastName is your actual last name.

8. Compact and repair the database.

9. Submit the revised database in the format specified by your instructor.

10. ✳ How would you change the field name of the Balance field in the Customer table to Current Balance?

Continued >

Figure 1–83

Extend Your Knowledge

Extend the skills you learned in this chapter and experiment with new skills. You may need to use Help to complete the assignment.

Using a Database Template to Create a Contacts Database

Note: To complete this assignment, you will be required to use the Data Files for Students. Visit www.cengage.com/ct/studentdownload for detailed instructions or contact your instructor for information about accessing the required files.

Instructions: Access includes both desktop database templates and web-based templates. You can use a template to create a beginning database that can be modified to meet your specific needs. You will use a template to create a Contacts database. The database template includes sample tables, queries, forms, and reports. You will modify the database and create the Contacts Query shown in Figure 1–84.

Perform the following tasks:
1. Start Access.
2. Select the Desktop contacts template in the template gallery and create a new database with the file name Extend Contacts.
3. Enable the content. If requested to do so by your instructor, watch the videos in the Getting Started with Contacts dialog box. Close the Getting Started with Contacts dialog box.
4. Close the Contact List form.
5. Open the Contacts table in Datasheet view and delete the Fax Number field and the Attachments field in the table. The Attachments field has a paperclip as the column heading.
6. Change the data type for the ID field to Short Text, change the field name to Contact ID, and change the field size to 4. Change the column width so that the complete field name is displayed.
7. Save the changes to the Contacts table and close the table.
8. Use the Simple Query Wizard to create the Contacts Query shown in Figure 1–84. Close the query.

Figure 1–84

9. Open the Phone Book report in Layout view. Delete the control containing the date. Change the title of the report to Contact Phone List.

10. Save the changes to the report.

11. If requested to do so by your instructor, add your first and last names to the end of the title and save the changes to the report.

12. Submit the revised database in the format specified by your instructor.

13. ✳ a. Why would you use a template instead of creating a database from scratch with just the fields you need?

 b. The Attachment data type allows you to attach files to a database record. If you were using this database for a job search, what specific documents might you attach to a Contacts record?

Analyze, Correct, Improve

Analyze a database, correct all errors, and improve the design.

Correcting Errors in the Table Structure

Note: To complete this assignment, you will be required to use the Data Files for Students. Visit www.cengage.com/ct/studentdownload for detailed instructions or contact your instructor for information about accessing the required files.

Instructions: Analyze SciFi Movies is a database containing information on classic science fiction movies that your film professor would like to use for teaching. The Movie table shown in Figure 1–85 contains errors to the table structure. Your professor has asked you to correct the errors and make some improvements to the database. Start Access and open the Analyze SciFi Movies database from the Data Files for Students.

Figure 1–85

1. Correct Movie Number should be the primary key for the Movie table. The ID field should not be a field in the table. The Rating field represents a numerical rating system of one to four to indicate the quality of the movie. Your instructor wants to be able to find the average rating for films directed by a particular director. Only integers should be stored in both the Rating and the Length (Minutes) fields.

2. Improve The default field size for Short Text fields is 255. Changing the field size to more accurately represent the maximum number of characters that can be stored in a field is one way to improve the accuracy of the data. The Movie Number, Director Number, and Awards fields should have a maximum size of 3 characters. The Year Made field should have a maximum field size of 4. The Movie Name and Studio fields should have a maximum field size of 50. If instructed to do so by your instructor, rename the Movie table as Movie Last Name where Last Name is your last name. Submit the revised database in the format specified by your instructor.

3. ✳ The Awards field currently has a data type of Short Text, but the only values that will be stored in that field are Yes and No to indicate whether the movie won any awards. What would be a more appropriate data type for this field?

In the Labs

Design, create, modify, and/or use a database following the guidelines, concepts, and skills presented in this chapter. Labs are listed in order of increasing difficulty. Labs 1 and 2, which increase in difficulty, require you to create solutions based on what you learned in the chapter; Lab 3 requires you to create a solution, which uses cloud and web technologies, by learning and investigating on your own from general guidance.

Lab 1: Creating Objects for the Dartt Offsite Services Database

Problem: Dartt Offsite Services is a local company that provides offsite data services and solutions. The company provides remote data backup, disaster recovery planning and services, website backup, and offsite storage of paper documents for small businesses and nonprofit organizations. Service representatives are responsible for communicating data solutions to the client, scheduling backups and other tasks, and resolving any conflicts. The company recently decided to store its client and service rep data in a database. Each client is assigned to a single service rep, but each service rep may be assigned many clients. The database and the Service Rep table have been created, but the Monthly Salary field needs to be added to the table. The records shown in Table 1–6 must be added to the Service Rep table. The company plans to import the Client table from the Excel worksheet shown in Figure 1–86. Dartt would like to finish storing this data in a database and has asked you to help.

⊿	A	B	C	D	E	F	G	H	I	J	K
1	Client Number	Client Name	Street	City	State	Postal Code	Amount Paid	Balance Due	Service Rep Number		
2	BBF32	Babbage CPA Firm	464 Linnell Dr.	Austin	SC	28796	$3,524.00	$567.85	24		
		Theon Veterinary Services					$2,750.00	$1,200.00	37		
15	WEC05	Walburg Energy Company	12 Polk St.	Walburg	NC	28819	$1,567.45	$1,100.50	24		
16	WSC01	Wood Sports Complex	578 Central Ave.	Walburg	NC	28819	$2,250.00	$1,600.00	24		
17											

Figure 1–86

Note: To complete this assignment, you will be required to use the Data Files for Students. Visit www.cengage.com/ct/studentdownload for detailed instructions or contact your instructor for information about accessing the required files.

Instructions: Perform the following tasks:

1. Start Access and open the Lab 1 Dartt Offsite Services database from the Data Files for Students.

2. Open the Service Rep table in Datasheet view and add the Monthly Salary field to the end of the table. The field has the Currency data type. Assign the caption SR # to the Service Rep Number field.

3. Add the records shown in Table 1–6.

4. Resize the columns to best fit the data. Save the changes to the layout of the table.

Table 1–6 Data for Service Rep Table								
Service Rep Number	Last Name	First Name	Street	City	State	Postal Code	Start Date	Monthly Salary
21	Kelly	Jenna	25 Paint St.	Kyle	SC	28797	5/14/2012	$3,862.45
45	Scott	Josh	1925 Pine Rd.	Byron	SC	28795	4/28/2014	$3,062.08
24	Liu	Mia	265 Marble Dr.	Kyle	SC	28797	1/7/2013	$3,666.67
37	Martinez	Mike	31 Steel St.	Georgetown	SC	28794	5/13/2013	$3,285.00

5. Import the Lab 1–1 Client Data workbook shown in Figure 1–86 into the database. The first row of the workbook contains the column headings. Client Number is the primary key for the new table. Assign the name Client to the table. Save the Import steps, and assign the name Import-Client Data to the steps. Assign Import Client Data as the description.

6. Open the Client table in Design view and make the following changes:

 a. Change the field size for the Client Number field to 5. Change the field size for the Client Name field to 30. Change the field size for the Street and City fields to 20. Change the field size for the State field to 2 and the field size for the Postal Code field to 5. Change the field size for the Service Rep Number field to 2.

 b. Add the caption CL # to the Client Number field.

 c. Add the caption SR # to the Service Rep Number field.

7. Save the changes to the Client table. If a Microsoft Access dialog box appears with the 'Some data may be lost' message, click the Yes button.

8. Open the Client table in Datasheet view and resize all columns to best fit the data. Save the changes to the layout of the table.

9. Create a query using the Simple Query Wizard for the Client table that displays the Client Number, Client Name, Amount Paid, Balance Due, and Service Rep Number. Save the query as Client Query.

10. Create the report shown in Figure 1–87 for the Client table. The report should include the Client Number, Client Name, Amount Paid, Balance Due, and Service Rep Number fields. Include totals for the Amount Paid and Balance Due fields. Be sure to change the column headings to those shown in Figure 1–87. Save the report as Client Financial Report.

11. If requested to do so by your instructor, change the address for Jenna Kelly in the Service Rep table to your address. If your address is longer than 20 characters, simply enter as much as you can.

12. Submit the revised database in the format specified by your instructor.

13. ✳ You entered the records for the Service Rep table in the order shown in Table 1–6 on the previous page, that is service reps 21, 45, 24, 37. What order will the records be in after you close and reopen the Service Rep table? Why?

Client Financial Report		Monday, September 15, 2014 9:09:35 PM		
Client Number	Client Name	Amount Paid	Balance Due	Service Rep Number
BBF32	Babbage CPA Firm	$3,524.00	$567.85	24
		$4,445		
WSC01	Wood Sports Complex	$2,250.00	$1,600.00	24
		$31,820.85	$21,923.97	

Figure 1–87

Lab 2: Creating the Tennis Logos Database

Problem: Tennis Logos supplies customized tennis clothing and accessories for clubs and tournaments. The company purchases these items from suppliers at wholesale prices and adds the customer's logo. The final item price is determined by marking up the wholesale price and adding a fee that is based on the complexity of the logo. Tennis Logos also does graphic design work for customers. Currently, the information about the items and the suppliers is stored in two Excel workbooks. Each item is assigned to a single supplier, but each supplier may be assigned many items. You are to create a database that will store the item and supplier information. You already have determined that you need two tables, a Supplier table and an Item table, in which to store the information.

Note: To complete this assignment, you will be required to use the Data Files for Students. Visit www.cengage.com/ct/studentdownload for detailed instructions or contact your instructor for information about accessing the required files.

Continued >

In the Labs *continued*

Instructions: Perform the following tasks:

1. Use the Blank desktop database option to create a new database in which to store all objects related to the items for sale. Call the database Lab 2 Tennis Logos.

2. Import the Lab 1–2 Supplier Data Excel workbook into the database. The first row of the workbook contains the column headings. Supplier Code is the primary key for the new table. Assign the name Supplier to the table. Do not save the Import steps.

3. Open the Supplier table in Datasheet view. Change the field size for the Supplier Code field to 2; the field size for the Supplier Name field to 30; and the field size for the Telephone Number field to 12.

4. Import the Lab 1–2 Item Data Excel workbook into the database. The first row of the workbook contains the column headings. Item Number is the primary key for this table. Assign the name Item to the table. Save the Import steps, and assign the name Import-Item Data to the steps. You do not need a description.

5. Open the Item table in Design view. Change the field size for the Item Number field to 4. Change the field size for the Description field to 30. Add the caption Wholesale for the Wholesale Price field. The On Hand field should be an Integer field. Be sure that the field size for the Supplier Code in the Item table is identical to the field size for the Supplier Code in the Supplier table. Save the changes to the table and close the table.

6. Open the Item table in Datasheet view and resize the columns to best fit the data. Save the changes to the layout of the table and close the table.

7. Create a query for the Item table. Include the Item Number, Description, Wholesale Price, Base Cost, and Supplier Code. Save the query as Item Query.

8. Create a simple form for the Item table. Use the name Item for the form.

9. Create the report shown in Figure 1–88 for the Item table. Do not add any totals. Save the report as Inventory Status Report.

10. If requested to do so by your instructor, change the telephone number for Last Merchandisers to your telephone number.

11. Submit the database in the format specified by your instructor.

12. ☀ If you had designed this database, could you have used the field name, Name, for the Supplier Name? If not, why not?

Inventory Status Report		Monday, September 15, 2014	
		9:37:32 PM	
Item Number	Description	On Hand	Wholesale Price
3363	Baseball Cap	110	$4.87
3673	Cotton Visor	150	$4.59
4543	Crew Sweatshirt	75	$7.29
4583			

Figure 1–88

Lab 3: Expand Your World: Cloud and Web Technologies
Exporting Query Results and Reports

Problem: You and two of your friends have started a pet sitting business. You want to be able to share query results and reports, so you have decided to store the items on the SkyDrive. You are still learning Access, so you are going to create a sample query and the report shown in Figure 1–89, export the results, and save to the SkyDrive.

Note: To complete this assignment, you will be required to use the Data Files for Students. Visit www.cengage.com/ct/studentdownload for detailed instructions or contact your instructor for information about accessing the required files.

Customer Balance Report				Monday, September 15, 2014
				9:39:02 PM

Customer Number	Last Name	First Name	Balance	Sitter Number
AB10	Alvarez	Frances	$45.00	103
BR16		Alex	$80.00	
	Santoro	Maria	$0.00	107
TR35	Trent	Gerry	$40.00	105
			$419.00	

Figure 1–89

Instructions:

1. Open the Lab 3 Pet Sitters database from the Data Files for Students.

2. Use the Simple Query Wizard to create a query that includes the Customer Number, First Name, Last Name, Balance, and Sitter Number. Save the query as Customer Query.

3. Export the Customer Query as an XPS document to your SkyDrive in the Access folder.

4. Create the report shown in Figure 1–89. Save the report as Customer Balance Report.

5. Export the Customer Balance Report as a PDF document to your Sky Drive in the Access folder. For information about how to use the Sky Drive, refer to the Office and Windows chapter at the beginning of this book.

6. If requested to do so by your instructor, open the Sitter table and change the last name and first name for sitter 103 to your last name and your first name.

7. Submit the assignment in the format specified by your instructor.

8. ✸ Based on your current knowledge of XPS and PDF documents, which one do you think you would use most frequently? Why?

✸ Consider This: Your Turn

Apply your creative thinking and problem solving skills to design and implement a solution.

1. Creating the Craft Database

Note: To complete this assignment, you will be required to use the Data Files for Students. Visit www.cengage.com/ct/studentdownload for detailed instructions or contact your instructor for information about accessing the required files.

Personal/Academic

Part 1: You attend a college that is renowned for its school of arts and crafts. Students who major in arts and crafts can sell their designs online through the college bookstore. The bookstore has used an Excel workbook to store data on wood-crafted items as well as the students who created the items. Because you are a major in computer science and also are studying woodworking, your senior project is to create a database of these wood-crafted items. The database must keep track of the wood-crafted items for sale and maintain data on the students who created the items. Each item is created by a single student, but each student may have created several items.

Based on the information in the Your Turn 1–1 Craft workbook, use the concepts and techniques presented in this chapter to design and create a database to store the craft data. Create a Wood Crafts for Sale report that lists the item number, description, price, and student code. Submit your assignment in the format specified by your instructor.

Part 2: ✸ You made several decisions while determining the table structures and adding data to the tables in this assignment. What method did you use to add the data to each table? Are there any other methods that also would have worked?

Continued >

STUDENT ASSIGNMENTS

Consider This: Your Turn *continued*

2. Creating the Mums Landscaping Database

Professional

Part 1: Mums Landscaping is a local company that provides landscaping and lawn maintenance services to commercial customers, such as businesses, housing subdivisions, and schools. You worked for Mums part-time in both high school and in college. Mums has used an Excel workbook to store financial data on its customers but now would like to create a database that includes information on its customers and crew supervisors. Each customer is assigned to a single crew supervisor, but each supervisor may be assigned many customers.

Based on the information in the Your Turn 1–2 Mums Landscaping workbook, use the concepts and techniques presented in this chapter to design and create a database to store the data that Mums needs. Submit your assignment in the format specified by your instructor.

Part 2: ☀ You made several decisions while creating the Mums Landscaping database in this assignment. What did you decide to use as the primary key for each table? Why?

3. Creating an Electronic Assets Database

Research and Collaboration

Part 1: In today's world, most college students will own at least one electronic device, such as a cell phone. Many students have multiple electronic devices. Microsoft Access includes a desktop Asset tracking template that you can modify to keep track of your electronic devices, such as cell phone, MP3 player, and computer. Get together with your group and make a list of the electronic devices that each of you own. Use the desktop Asset tracking template to create an Electronic Assets database. Watch the video to learn how the database works. As a team, review the fields in the Assets table and decide which fields to include in the database. Delete any unwanted fields. Decide how you will describe each device, for example, will you use the term cell phone, smartphone, or mobile phone? Have each team member enter at least two devices. Create a query to find one type of device, such as cell phone. Submit your assignment in the format specified by your instructor.

Part 2: ☀ You made several decisions while creating the Electronic Assets database. Which fields did you decide to delete from the Assets table? What terms did you use to describe each device? What was the rationale for these decisions?

Learn Online

Reinforce what you learned in this chapter with games, exercises, training, and many other online activities and resources.

Student Companion Site Reinforcement activities and resources are available at no additional cost on www.cengagebrain.com. Visit www.cengage.com/ct/studentdownload for detailed instructions about accessing the resources available at the Student Companion Site.

SAM Put your skills into practice with SAM! If you have a SAM account, go to www.cengage.com/sam2013 to access SAM assignments for this chapter.

2 Querying a Database

Objectives

You will have mastered the material in this chapter when you can:

- Create queries using Design view
- Include fields in the design grid
- Use text and numeric data in criteria
- Save a query and use the saved query
- Create and use parameter queries
- Use compound criteria in queries
- Sort data in queries
- Join tables in queries
- Create a report and a form from a query
- Export data from a query to another application
- Perform calculations and calculate statistics in queries
- Create crosstab queries
- Customize the Navigation Pane

2 | Querying a Database

Introduction

One of the primary benefits of using a database management system such as Access is having the ability to find answers to questions related to data stored in the database. When you pose a question to Access, or any other database management system, the question is called a query. A **query** is simply a question presented in a way that Access can process.

To find the answer to a question, you first create a corresponding query using the techniques illustrated in this chapter. After you have created the query, you instruct Access to run the query, that is, to perform the steps necessary to obtain the answer. Access then displays the answer in Datasheet view.

BTW

Select Queries
The queries you create in this chapter are select queries. In a select query, you retrieve data from one or more tables using criteria that you specify and display the data in a datasheet.

BTW

BTWs
For a complete list of the BTWs found in the margins of this book, visit the BTW resource on the Student Companion Site located on www.cengagebrain.com. For detailed instructions about accessing available resources, visit www.cengage.com/ct/studentdownload or contact your instructor for information about accessing the required files.

Project — Querying a Database

One of the most important benefits of using Access to manage a database is easily finding the answers to questions and requests. Figure 2–1 presents examples of such queries, which concern the data in the Bavant Publishing database.

In addition to these questions, Bavant Publishing managers need to find information about customers located in a specific city, but they want to enter a different city each time they ask the question. The company can use a parameter query to accomplish this task. Bavant Publishing managers also want to summarize data in a specific way, which might involve performing calculations, and they can use a crosstab query to present the data in the desired form.

CU #	Customer Name	Amount Paid	Current Due
SCC77	Stallone Community College	$7,525.98	$2,515.78
SEC19	Seaborn College	$9,225.34	$10,496.89

Give me the number, name, amount paid, and current due for all customers whose name starts with S.

Give me the customer number, customer name, amount paid, current due, and book rep number for all customers whose returns are greater than $0.00 and whose book rep number is 42.

CU #	Customer Name	Amount Paid	Current Due	Returns	BR #
ASU37	Applewood State University	$41,530.98	$38,812.66	$12,008.02	42
FSU23	Farnham State University	$18,268.00	$22,024.50	$3,496.23	42
MEC56	Mehitable College	$9,111.19	$7,310.76	$574.25	42

Give me the customer number, customer name, amount paid, and current due for customer CSU10.

CU #	Customer Name	Amount Paid	Current Due
CSU10	Camellia State University	$63,246.88	$69,847.76

List the customer number, customer name, book rep number, and amount paid for all customers. Sort the results by book rep number. For customers with the same book rep number, further sort the results by amount paid.

Summarize the total returns by state and by book rep.

State	Total Of Retu	42	53	65
DE	$13,323.14	$4,070.48		$9,252.66
NJ	$22,915.28		$18,418.48	$4,496.80
PA	$17,208.34	$12,008.02	$2,000.00	$3,200.32

CU #	Customer Name	BR #	Amount Paid
BCJ21	Brodkin Junior College	42	$0.00
SCC77	Stallone Community College	42	$7,525.98
MEC56	Mehitable College	42	$9,111.19
FSU23	Farnham State University	42	$18,268.00
ASU37	Applewood State University	42	$41,530.98
MCC45	Mauldin Community College	53	$9,500.00
CSD25	Cowpens ISD	53	$12,750.00
PLI22	PrattLast Institute	53	$17,229.45
HSD05	Hammonds County ISD	53	$18,434.75
CSU10	Camellia State University	53	$63,246.88
SEC19	Seaborn College	65	$9,225.34
KCC78	Key Community College System	65	$21,288.65
DCC34	Dartt Community College	65	$21,345.50
FSC12	First State College	65	$34,557.25
TSC02	Tri-State Consortium	65	$34,578.90

Give me the average amount paid by customers of each book rep.

BR #	AvgOfAmou
42	$15,287.23
53	$24,232.22
65	$24,199.13

For each book rep, list the book rep number, last name, and first name. Also, list the customer number and customer name for each of the book rep's customers.

BR #	Last Name	First Name	CU #	Customer Name
42	Perez	Melina	ASU37	Applewood State University
42	Perez	Melina	BCJ21	Brodkin Junior College
42	Perez	Melina	FSU23	Farnham State University
42	Perez	Melina	MEC56	Mehitable College
42	Perez	Melina	SCC77	Stallone Community College
48	Statnik	Michael		
53	Chin	Robert	CSD25	Cowpens ISD
53	Chin	Robert	CSU10	Camellia State University
53	Chin	Robert	HSD05	Hammonds County ISD
53	Chin	Robert	MCC45	Mauldin Community College
53	Chin	Robert	PLI22	PrattLast Institute
65	Rogers	Tracy	DCC34	Dartt Community College
65	Rogers	Tracy	FSC12	First State College
65	Rogers	Tracy	KCC78	Key Community College System
65	Rogers	Tracy	SEC19	Seaborn College
65	Rogers	Tracy	TSC02	Tri-State Consortium

List the customer number, customer name, amount paid, current due, and the total amount (amount paid plus current due) for each customer.

CL #	Client Name	Amount Paid	Current Due	Total Amour
BA53	Bavant Animal Hospital	$0.00	$7,500.00	$7,500.00
BB32	Babbage CPA Firm	$1,500.00	$500.00	$2,000.00
BC76	Buda Community Clinic	$2,500.00	$750.00	$3,250.00
CJ29	Catering by Jenna	$3,000.00	$1,000.00	$4,000.00
GA74	Grant Antiques	$5,500.00	$3,200.00	$8,700.00
GF56	Granger Foundation	$0.00	$6,500.00	$6,500.00
HC10	Hendley County Hospital	$3,100.00	$1,200.00	$4,300.00
KD21	KAL Design Studio	$6,000.00	$3,200.00	$9,200.00
KG04	Kyle Grocery Cooperative	$3,200.00	$0.00	$3,200.00
ME14	Mike's Electronic Stop	$2,500.00	$1,500.00	$4,000.00
PJ34	Patricia Jean Florist	$0.00	$5,200.00	$5,200.00
SL77	Smarter Law Associates	$3,800.00	$0.00	$3,800.00
TB17	The Bikeshop	$2,750.00	$1,200.00	$3,950.00
WE05	Walburg Energy Alternatives	$4,500.00	$1,450.00	$5,950.00
WS01	Woody Sporting Goods	$2,250.00	$1,600.00	$3,850.00

Figure 2–1

Roadmap

In this chapter, you will learn how to create and use the queries shown in Figure 2–1 on the previous page. The following roadmap identifies general activities you will perform as you progress through this chapter:

1. CREATE QUERIES in Design view.
2. USE CRITERIA in queries.
3. SORT DATA in queries.
4. JOIN TABLES in queries.
5. EXPORT query RESULTS.
6. PERFORM CALCULATIONS in queries.
7. CREATE a CROSSTAB query.
8. CUSTOMIZE the NAVIGATION PANE.

For an introduction to Windows and instruction about how to perform basic Windows tasks, read the Office and Windows chapter at the beginning of this book, where you can learn how to resize windows, change screen resolution, create folders, move and rename files, use Windows Help, and much more.

At the beginning of the step instructions throughout the chapter, you will see an abbreviated form of this roadmap. The abbreviated roadmap uses colors to indicate chapter progress: gray means the chapter is beyond that activity, blue means the task being shown is covered in that activity, and black means that activity is yet to be covered. For example, the following abbreviated roadmap indicates the chapter would be showing a task in the 3 SORT DATA activity.

1 CREATE QUERIES | 2 USE CRITERIA | 3 SORT DATA | 4 JOIN TABLES | 5 EXPORT RESULTS
6 PERFORM CALCULATIONS | 7 CREATE CROSSTAB | 8 CUSTOMIZE NAVIGATION PANE

Use the abbreviated roadmap as a progress guide while you read or step through the instructions in this chapter.

To Run Access

If you are using a computer to step through the project in this chapter and you want your screens to match the figures in this book, you should change your screen's resolution to 1366×768. For information about how to change a computer's resolution, refer to the Office and Windows chapter at the beginning of this book.

The following steps, which assume Windows is running, use the Start screen or the search box to run Access based on a typical installation. You may need to ask your instructor how to run Access on your computer. For a detailed example of the procedure summarized below, refer to the Office and Windows chapter.

For an introduction to Office and instruction about how to perform basic tasks in Office programs, read the Office and Windows chapter at the beginning of this book, where you can learn how to run an app, use the ribbon, save a file, open a file, exit an app, use Help, and much more.

1 Scroll the Start screen for an Access 2013 tile. If your Start screen contains an Access 2013 tile, tap or click it to run Access and then proceed to Step 5; if the Start screen does not contain the Access 2013 tile, proceed to the next step to search for the Access app.

2 Swipe in from the right edge of the screen or point to the upper-right corner of the screen to display the Charms bar, and then tap or click the Search charm on the Charms bar to display the Search menu.

3 Type Access as the search text in the Search text box and watch the search results appear in the Apps list.

④ Tap or click Access 2013 in the search results to run Access.

⑤ If the Access window is not maximized, tap or click the Maximize button on its title bar to maximize the window.

To Open a Database from Access

In the previous chapter, you created the Bavant Publishing database in an appropriate storage location. The following steps open the database from the location you specified when you first created it (for example, the Access folder in the CIS 101 folder). For a detailed example of the procedure summarized below, refer to the Office and Windows chapter at the beginning of this book.

① Tap or click FILE on the ribbon to open the Backstage view, if necessary.

② If the database you want to open is displayed in the Recent list, tap or click the file name to open the database and display the opened database in the Access window; then skip to Step 7. If the database you want to open is not displayed in the Recent list or if the Recent list does not appear, tap or click 'Open Other Files' to display the Open Gallery.

③ If the database you want to open is displayed in the Recent list in the Open gallery, tap or click the file name to open the database and display the opened database in the Access window; then skip to Step 7.

④ Tap or click Computer, SkyDrive, or another location in the left pane and then navigate to the location of the database to be opened (for example, the Access folder in the CIS 101 folder).

⑤ Tap or click Bavant Publishing to select the database to be opened.

⑥ Tap or click the Open button (Open dialog box) to open the selected file and display the opened database in the Access window.

⑦ If a Security Warning appears, tap or click the Enable Content button.

One of the few differences between Windows 7 and Windows 8 occurs in the steps to run Access. If you are using Windows 7, click the Start button, type Access in the 'Search programs and files' box, click Access 2013, and then, if necessary, maximize the Access window. For detailed steps to run Access in Windows 7, refer to the Office and Windows chapter at the beginning of this book. For a summary of the steps, refer to the Quick Reference located at the back of this book.

Creating Queries

As you learned in Chapter 1, you can use queries in Access to find answers to questions about the data contained in the database. *Note:* In this chapter, you will save each query example. When you use a query for another task, such as to create a form or report, you will assign a specific name to a query, for example, Rep-Customer Query. In situations in which you will not use the query again, you will assign a name using a convention that includes the chapter number and a query number, for example, Ch2q01. Queries are numbered consecutively.

To Create a Query in Design View

1 CREATE QUERIES | 2 USE CRITERIA | 3 SORT DATA | 4 JOIN TABLES | 5 EXPORT RESULTS
6 PERFORM CALCULATIONS | 7 CREATE CROSSTAB | 8 CUSTOMIZE NAVIGATION PANE

In Chapter 1, you used the Simple Query Wizard to create a query. Most of the time, however, you will use Design view, which is the primary option for creating queries. *Why? Once you have created a new query in Design view, you have more options than with the wizard and can specify fields, criteria, sorting, calculations, and so on.* The following steps create a new query in Design view.

1

- Tap or click the 'Shutter Bar Open/Close Button' to close the Navigation Pane.

- Tap or click CREATE on the ribbon to display the CREATE tab (Figure 2–2).

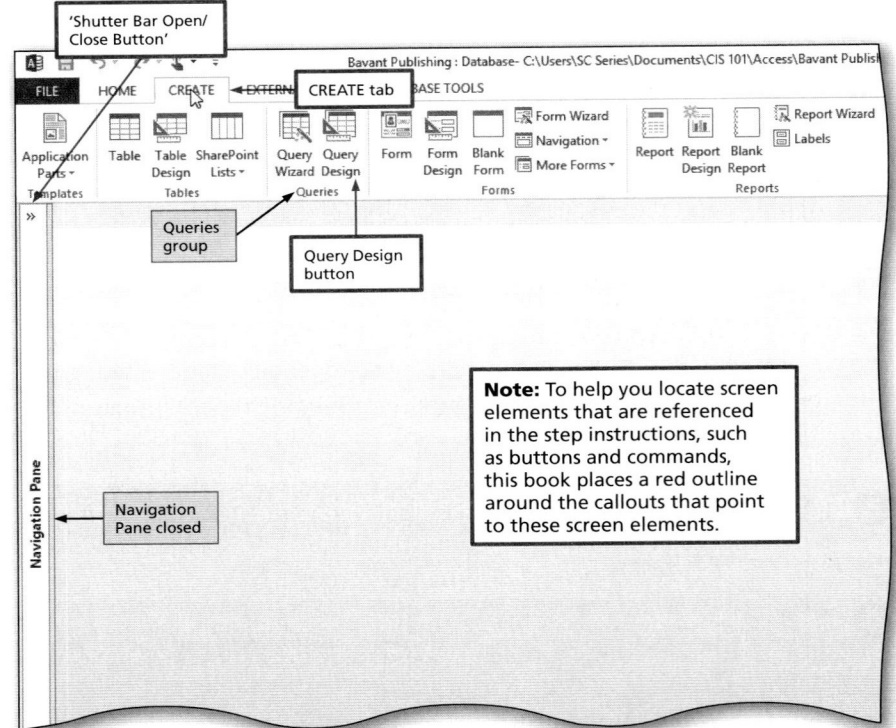

Figure 2–2

2

- Tap or click the Query Design button (CREATE tab | Queries group) to create a new query (Figure 2–3).

 Is it necessary to close the Navigation Pane?
No. Closing the pane gives you more room for the query, however, so it is usually a good practice.

Figure 2–3

- Tap or click the Customer table (Show Table dialog box) to select the table.

- Tap or click the Add button to add the selected table to the query.

- Tap or click the Close button to remove the dialog box from the screen.

Q&A What if I inadvertently add the wrong table? Press and hold or right-click the table that you added in error and tap or click Remove Table on the shortcut menu. You also can just close the query, indicate that you do not want to save it, and then start over.

Figure 2–4

In figure: field list resized so all fields appear; include asterisk (*) in design grid to display all fields in query results; drag lower edge of field list to resize field list; double-tap or double-click field in field list to add field; design grid; position to specify sort order; position to enter criteria; Customer; Customer Number, Customer Name, Street, City, State, Postal Code, Amount Paid, Current Due, Returns, Book Rep Number; Field: Table: Sort: Show: Criteria: or:

- Drag the lower edge of the field list down far enough so all fields in the table appear (Figure 2–4).

Q&A Is it essential that I resize the field list?
No. You can always scroll through the list of fields using the scroll bar. Resizing the field list so that all fields appear is usually more convenient.

To Add Fields to the Design Grid

1 CREATE QUERIES | 2 USE CRITERIA | 3 SORT DATA | 4 JOIN TABLES | 5 EXPORT RESULTS
6 PERFORM CALCULATIONS | 7 CREATE CROSSTAB | 8 CUSTOMIZE NAVIGATION PANE

Once you have a new query displayed in Design view, you are ready to make entries in the **design grid**, the portion of the window where you specify fields and criteria for the query. The design grid is located in the lower pane of the window. You add the fields you want included in the query to the Field row in the grid. *Why add fields to the grid? Only the fields that appear in the design grid will be included in the query results.* The following step begins creating a query that Bavant Publishing might use to obtain the customer number, customer name, amount paid, and current due for a particular customer.

1

- Double-tap or double-click the Customer Number field in the field list to add the field to the query.

Q&A What if I add the wrong field?
Tap or click just above the field name in the design grid to select the column and then press the DELETE key to remove the field.

- Double-tap or double-click the Customer Name field in the field list to add the field to the query.

- Add the Amount Paid field to the query.

- Add the Current Due field to the query (Figure 2–5).

Q&A What if I want to include all fields?
Do I have to add each field individually?
No. Instead of adding individual fields, you can double-tap or double-click the asterisk (*) to add the asterisk to the design grid. The asterisk is a shortcut indicating all fields are to be included.

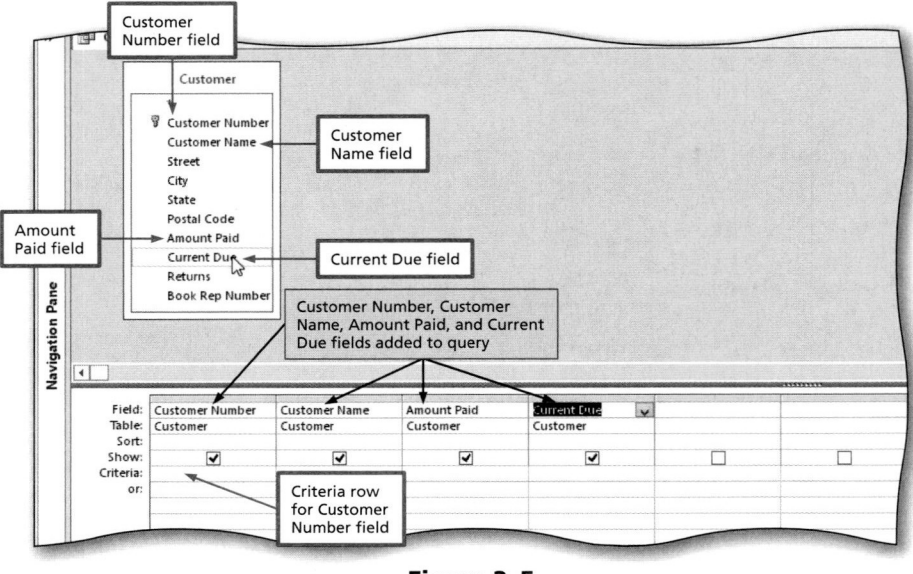

Figure 2–5

If you are using your finger on a touch screen and are having difficulty completing the steps in this chapter, consider using a stylus. Many people find it easier to be precise with a stylus than with a finger. In addition, with a stylus you see the pointer. If you still are having trouble completing the steps with a stylus, try using a mouse.

BTW
Touch Screen Differences
The Office and Windows interfaces may vary if you are using a touch screen. For this reason, you might notice that the function or appearance of your touch screen differs slightly from this chapter's presentation.

Determining Criteria

When you use queries, usually you are looking for those records that satisfy some criterion. In the simple query you created in the previous chapter, for example, you entered a criterion to restrict the records to those with the book rep number 53. In another query, you might want the name, amount paid, and current due amounts for the customer whose number is CSU10, for example, or for those customers whose names start with the letters, Gr. You enter criteria in the Criteria row in the design grid below the field name to which the criterion applies. For example, to indicate that the customer number must be CSU10, you first must add the Customer Number field to the design grid. You then would type CSU10 in the Criteria row below the Customer Number field.

Running the Query

After adding the appropriate fields and defining the query's criteria, you must run the query to get the results. To view the results of the query from Design view, tap or click the Run button to instruct Access to run the query, that is, to perform the necessary actions to produce and display the results in Datasheet view.

To Use Text Data in a Criterion

To use **text data** (data in a field whose data type is Short Text) in criteria, simply type the text in the Criteria row below the corresponding field name, just as you did in Chapter 1. In Access, you do not need to enclose text data in quotation marks as you do in many other database management systems. *Why? Access will enter the quotation marks automatically, so you can simply type the desired text.* The following steps finish creating a query that Bavant Publishing might use to obtain the customer number, customer name, amount paid, and current due amount of customer CSU10. These steps add the appropriate criterion so that only the desired customer will appear in the results. The steps also save the query.

1

- Tap or click the Criteria row for the Customer Number field to produce an insertion point.

- Type `CSU10` as the criterion (Figure 2–6).

Figure 2–6

2

- Tap or click the Run button (QUERY TOOLS DESIGN tab | Results group) to run the query (Figure 2–7).

 Can I also use the View button in the Results group to run the query?

Yes. You can tap or click the View button to view the query results in Datasheet view.

Figure 2–7

❸

- Tap or click the Save button on the Quick Access Toolbar to display the Save As dialog box.

- Type Ch2q01 as the name of the query (Figure 2–8).

Q&A Can I also save from Design view?
Yes. You can save the query when you view it in Design view just as you can save it when you view query results in Datasheet view.

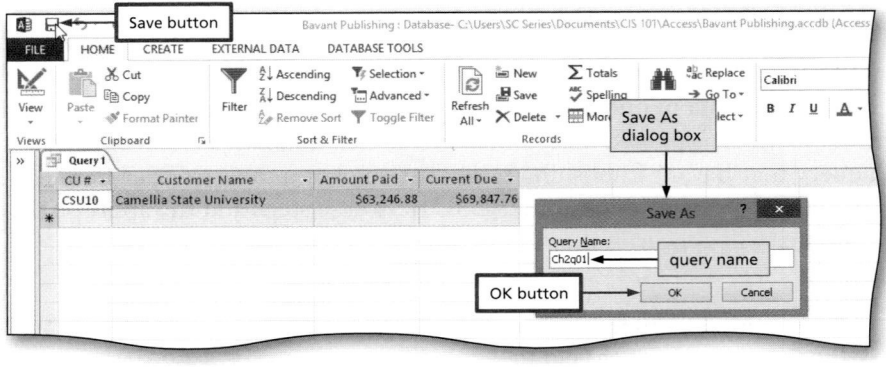

Figure 2–8

❹

- Tap or click the OK button (Save As dialog box) to save the query (Figure 2–9).

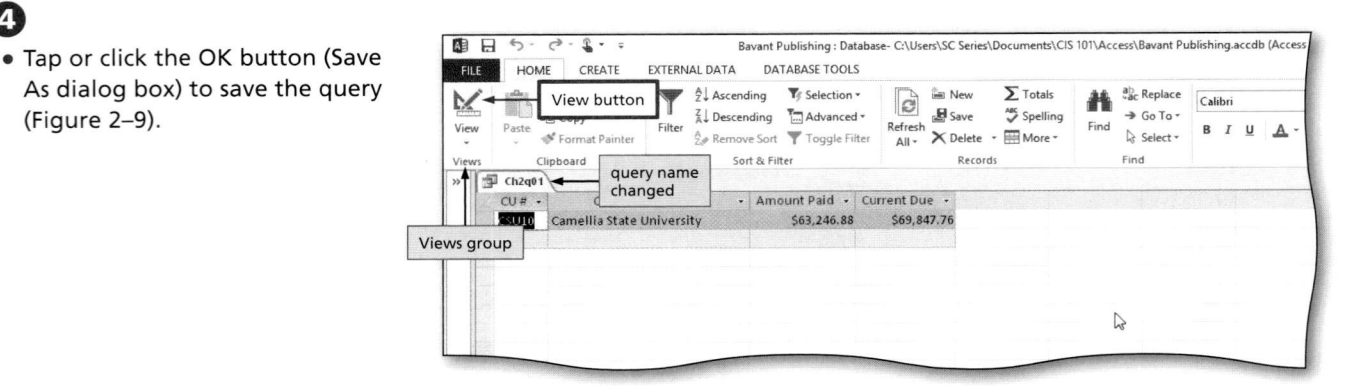

Figure 2–9

Other Ways

1. Press and hold or right-click query tab, tap or click Save on shortcut menu
2. Press CTRL + S

Using Saved Queries

After you have created and saved a query, you can use it in a variety of ways:

- To view the results of a query that is not currently open, open it by pressing and holding or right-clicking the query in the Navigation Pane and tapping or clicking Open on the shortcut menu.

- If you want to change the design of a query that is already open, return to Design view and make the changes.

- If you want to change the design of a query that is not currently open, press and hold or right-click the query in the Navigation Pane and then tap or click Design View on the shortcut menu to open the query in Design view.

- To print the results with a query open, tap or click FILE on the ribbon, tap or click the Print tab in the Backstage view, and then tap or click Quick Print.

- To print a query without first opening it, be sure the query is selected in the Navigation Pane and tap or click FILE on the ribbon, tap or click the Print tab in the Backstage view, and then tap or click Quick Print.

- You can switch between views of a query using the View button (HOME tab | Views group). Tapping or clicking the arrow at the bottom of the button produces the View button menu. You then tap or click the desired view in the menu. The two query views you use in this chapter are Datasheet view (to see the results) and Design view (to change the design). You can tap or click the top part of the

View button, in which case you will switch to the view identified by the icon on the button. In Figure 2–9, the View button displays the icon for Design view, so tapping or clicking the button would change to Design view. For the most part, the icon on the button represents the view you want, so you can usually simply tap or click the button.

BTW
On Screen Keyboard
To display the on-screen touch keyboard, tap the Touch Keyboard button on the Windows taskbar. When finished using the touch keyboard, tap the X button on the touch keyboard to close the keyboard

Wildcards

Microsoft Access supports wildcards. **Wildcards** are symbols that represent any character or combination of characters. One common wildcard, the **asterisk (*)**, represents any collection of characters. Another wildcard symbol is the **question mark (?)**, which represents any individual character.

CONSIDER THIS

What does S* represent? What does T?m represent?
S* represents the letter, S, followed by any collection of characters. T?m represents the letter, T, followed by any single character, followed by the letter, m. A search for T?m might return the names Tim or Tom.

To Use a Wildcard

1 CREATE QUERIES | 2 USE CRITERIA | 3 SORT DATA | 4 JOIN TABLES | 5 EXPORT RESULTS
6 PERFORM CALCULATIONS | 7 CREATE CROSSTAB | 8 CUSTOMIZE NAVIGATION PANE

The following steps modify the previous query to use the asterisk wildcard so that Bavant Publishing can select only those customers whose names begin with S. *Why? Because you do not know how many characters will follow the S, the asterisk wildcard symbol is appropriate.* The steps also save the query with a new name using the Save As command.

1
- Tap or click the View button (HOME tab | Views group), shown in Figure 2–9 on page AC 82, to return to Design view.
- If necessary, tap or click the Criteria row below the Customer Number field to produce an insertion point.

Q&A The text I entered now has quotation marks surrounding it. What happened?
Criteria for text data needs to be enclosed in quotation marks. You do not have to type the quotation marks; Access adds them automatically.

- Use the DELETE or BACKSPACE key as necessary to delete the current entry.
- Tap or click the Criteria row below the Customer Name field to produce an insertion point.
- Type S* as the criterion (Figure 2–10).

Figure 2–10

2

- Run the query by tapping or clicking the Run button (QUERY TOOLS DESIGN tab | Results group) (Figure 2–11).

🔍 **Experiment**

- Change the letter S to lowercase in the criteria and run the query to determine whether case makes a difference when entering a wildcard.

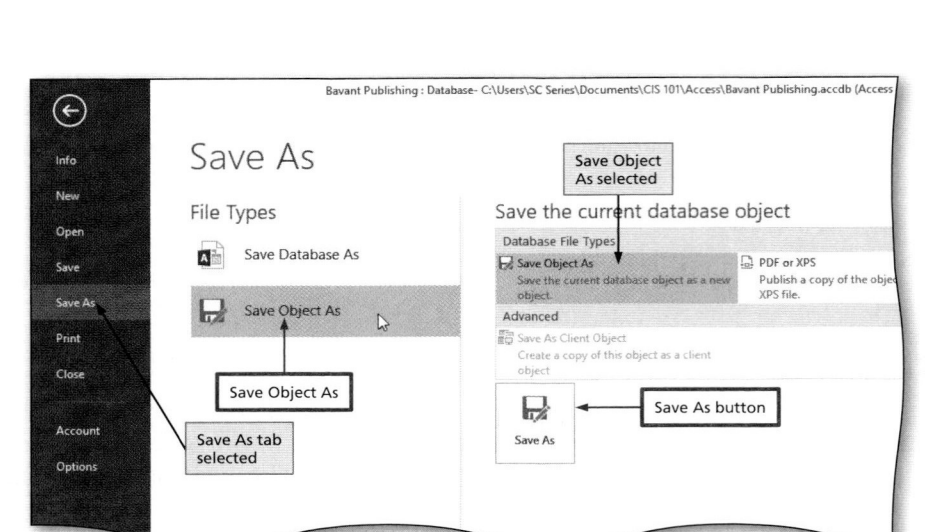

Figure 2–11

3

- Tap or click FILE on the ribbon to open the Backstage view.

- Tap or click the Save As tab in the Backstage view to display the Save As gallery.

- Tap or click Save Object As in the File Types area (Figure 2–12).

Q&A Can I just tap or click the Save button on the Quick Access Toolbar as I did when saving the previous query?
If you tapped or clicked the Save button, you would replace the previous query with the version you just created. Because you want to save both the previous query and the new one, you need to save the new version with a different name. To do so, you must use Save Object As, which is available through the Backstage view.

Figure 2–12

4

- With Save Object As selected in the File Types gallery, tap or click the Save As button to display the Save As dialog box.

- Type `Ch2q02` as the name for the saved query (Figure 2–13).

Q&A The current entry in the As text box is Query. Could I save the query as some other type of object?
Although you usually would want to save the query as another query, you also can save it as a form or report by changing the entry in the As text box. If you do, Access would create either a simple form or a simple report for the query.

Figure 2–13

5

- Tap or click the OK button (Save As dialog box) to save the query with the new name and close the Backstage view (Figure 2–14).

Q&A How can I tell that the query was saved with the new name?
The new name will appear on the tab.

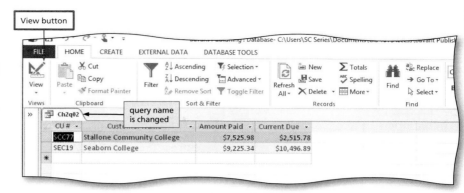

Figure 2–14

Other Ways

1. Tap or click Design View button on status bar

To Use Criteria for a Field Not Included in the Results

1 CREATE QUERIES | 2 USE CRITERIA | 3 SORT DATA | 4 JOIN TABLES | 5 EXPORT RESULTS
6 PERFORM CALCULATIONS | 7 CREATE CROSSTAB | 8 CUSTOMIZE NAVIGATION PANE

In some cases, you might require criteria for a particular field that should not appear in the results of the query. For example, you may want to see the customer number, customer name, address, and amount paid for all customers located in Gaston. The criteria involve the City field, but you do not want to include the City field in the results.

To enter a criterion for the City field, it must be included in the design grid. Normally, it would then appear in the results. To prevent this from happening, remove the check mark from its Show check box in the Show row of the grid. *Why? A check mark in the Show Check box instructs Access to show the field in the result. If you remove the check mark, you can use the field in the query but not display it in the query results.*

The following steps modify the previous query so that Bavant Publishing can select only those customers located in Gaston. Bavant does not want the city to appear in the results, however. The steps also save the query with a new name.

1

- Tap or click the View button (HOME tab | Views group), shown in Figure 2–14, to return to Design view.

Q&A The text I entered is now preceded by the word, Like. What happened?
Criteria including wildcards need to be preceded by the word, Like. However, you do not have to type it; Access adds the word automatically to any criterion involving a wildcard.

- Erase the criterion in the Criteria row of the Customer Name field.

- Add the City field to the query.

- Type Gaston as the criterion for the City field (Figure 2–15).

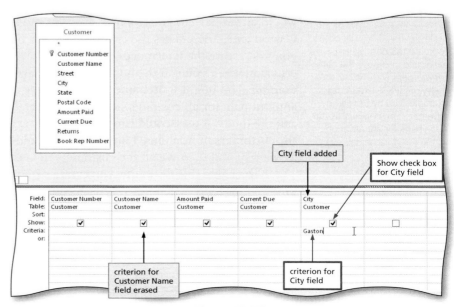

Figure 2–15

2

- Tap or click the Show check box for the City field to remove the check mark (Figure 2–16).

Q&A Could I have removed the check mark before entering the criterion?
Yes. The order in which you perform the two operations does not matter.

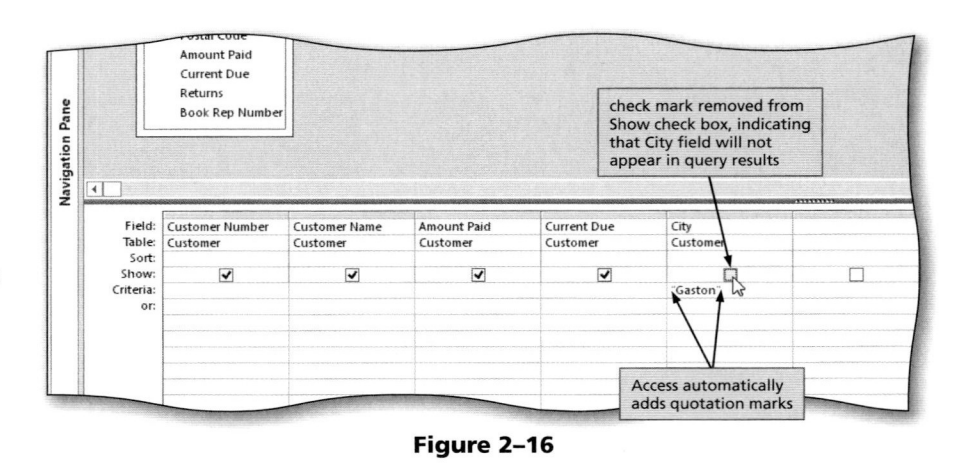

Figure 2–16

3

- Run the query (Figure 2–17).

Experiment

- Tap or click the View button to return to Design view, enter a different city name as the criterion, and run the query. Repeat this process with additional city names, including at least one city name that is not in the database. When finished, change the criterion back to Gaston.

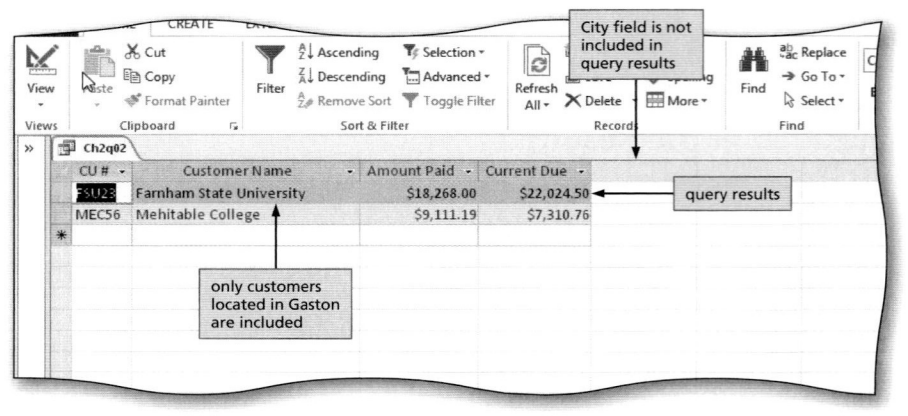

Figure 2–17

BTW
Designing Queries
Before creating queries, examine the contents of the tables involved. You need to know the data type for each field and how the data for the field is stored. If a query includes a state, for example, you need to know whether state is stored as the two-character abbreviation or as the full state name.

Creating a Parameter Query

If you wanted to find customers located in Adelphia instead of Gaston, you would either have to create a new query or modify the existing query by replacing Gaston with Adelphia as the criterion. Rather than giving a specific criterion when you first create the query, occasionally you may want to be able to enter part of the criterion when you run the query and then have the appropriate results appear. For example, you might want a query to return the customer number, customer name, and amount paid for all customers in a specific city, specifying a different city each time you run the query. A user could run the query, enter Adelphia as the city, and then see all the customers in Adelphia. Later, the user could use the same query but enter Gaston as the city, and then see all the customers in Gaston.

To enable this flexibility, you create a **parameter query**, which is a query that prompts for input whenever it is used. You enter a parameter (the prompt for the user), rather than a specific value as the criterion. You create the parameter by enclosing a value in a criterion in square brackets. It is important that the value in the brackets does not match the name of any field. If you enter a field name in square brackets, Access assumes you want that particular field and does not prompt the user for input. To prompt the user to enter the city name as the input, you could place [Enter City] as the criterion in the City field.

To Create and View a Parameter Query

The following steps create a parameter query. ***Why?*** *The parameter query will give users at Bavant the ability to enter a different city when they run the query rather than having a specific city as part of the criterion in the query.* The steps also save the query with a new name.

①

- Return to Design view.

- Erase the current criterion in the City column, and then type [Enter City] as the new criterion (Figure 2–18).

Q&A

What is the purpose of the square brackets?

The square brackets indicate that the text entered is not text that the value in the column must match. Without the brackets, Access would search for records on which the city is Enter City.

What if I typed a field name in the square brackets?

Access would simply use the value in that field. To create a parameter query, you must not use a field name in the square brackets.

Figure 2–18

②

- Tap or click the Run button (QUERY TOOLS DESIGN tab | Results group) to display the Enter Parameter Value dialog box (Figure 2–19).

Figure 2–19

③

- Type Adelphia as the parameter value in the Enter City text box, and then tap or click the OK button (Enter Parameter Value dialog box) to close the dialog box and view the query (Figure 2–20).

Experiment

- Try using other characters between the square brackets. In each case, run the query. When finished, change the characters between the square brackets back to Enter City.

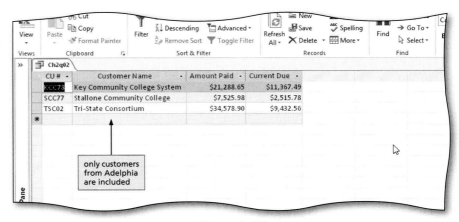

Figure 2–20

4

- Tap or click FILE on the ribbon to open the Backstage view.

- Tap or click the Save As tab in the Backstage view to display the Save As gallery.

- Tap or click Save Object As in the File Types area.

Figure 2–21

- With Save Object As selected in the File Types area, click the Save As button to display the Save As dialog box.

- Type Customer-City Query as the name for the saved query.

- Tap or click the OK button (Save As dialog box) to save the query with the new name and close the Backstage view (Figure 2–21).

5

- Tap or click the Close button for the Customer-City query to close the query.

Break Point: If you wish to take a break, this is a good place to do so. You can exit Access now. To resume later, run Access, open the database called Bavant Publishing, and continue following the steps from this location forward.

To Use a Parameter Query

1 CREATE QUERIES | 2 USE CRITERIA | 3 SORT DATA | 4 JOIN TABLES | 5 EXPORT RESULTS
6 PERFORM CALCULATIONS | 7 CREATE CROSSTAB | 8 CUSTOMIZE NAVIGATION PANE

You use a parameter query like any other saved query. You can open it or you can print the query results. In either case, Access prompts you to supply a value for the parameter each time you use the query. If changes have been made to the data since the last time you ran the query, the results of the query may be different, even if you enter the same value for the parameter. *Why? As with other queries, the query always uses the data that is currently in the table.* The following steps use the parameter query named Customer-City Query.

1

- Open the Navigation Pane.

- Press and hold or right-click the Customer-City Query to produce a shortcut menu.

- Tap or click Open on the shortcut menu to open the query and display the Enter Parameter Value dialog box (Figure 2–22).

Q&A The title bar for my Navigation Pane contains Tables and Related Views rather than All Access Objects as it did in Chapter 1. What should I do?

Tap or click the Navigation Pane arrow and then tap or click All Access Objects.

I do not have the Search bar at the top of the Navigation Pane that I had in Chapter 1. What should I do?

Press and hold or right-click the Navigation Pane title bar arrow to display a shortcut menu, and then tap or click Search Bar.

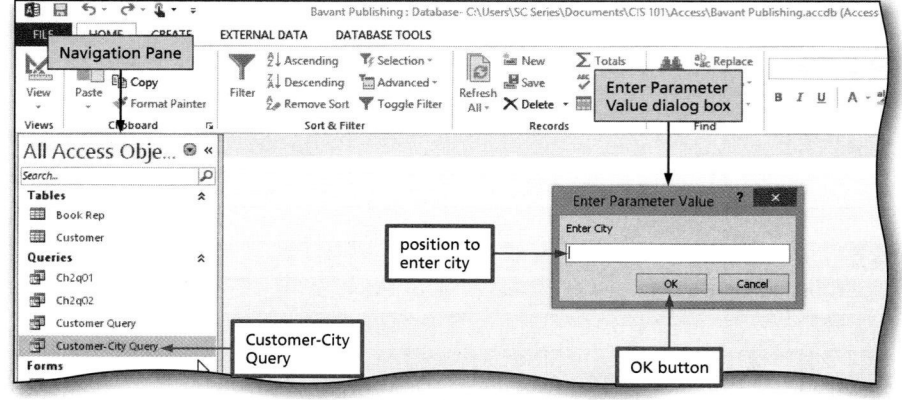

Figure 2–22

2

- Type Adelphia in the Enter City text box, and then tap or click the OK button (Enter Parameter Value dialog box) to display the results using Adelphia as the city, as shown in Figure 2–21.

- Close the query.

To Use a Number in a Criterion

To enter a number in a criterion, type the number without any dollar signs or commas. *Why? If you enter a dollar sign, Access assumes you are entering text. If you enter a comma, Access considers the criterion invalid.* The following steps create a query that Bavant Publishing might use to display all customers whose current due amount is $0. The steps also save the query with a new name.

- Close the Navigation Pane.
- Tap or click CREATE on the ribbon to display the CREATE tab.
- Tap or click the Query Design button (CREATE tab | Queries group) to create a new query.
- Tap or click the Customer table (Show Table dialog box) to select the table.

Figure 2–23

- Tap or click the Add button to add the selected table to the query.
- Tap or click the Close button to remove the dialog box from the screen.
- Drag the lower edge of the field list down far enough so all fields in the list are displayed.
- Include the Customer Number, Customer Name, Amount Paid, and Current Due fields in the query.
- Type 0 as the criterion for the Current Due field (Figure 2–23).

Q&A Do I need to enter a dollar sign and decimal point?
No. Access will interpret 0 as $0 because the data type for the Current Due field is currency.

- Run the query (Figure 2–24).

Q&A Why did Access display the results as $0.00 when I only entered 0?
Access uses the format for the field to determine how to display the result. In this case, the format indicated that Access should include the dollar sign, decimal point, and two decimal places.

Figure 2–24

- Save the query as Ch2q03.

Q&A How do I know when to use the Save button to save a query or use the Backstage view to perform a Save As?
If you are saving a new query, the simplest way is to use the Save button on the Quick Access Toolbar. If you are saving changes to a previously saved query but do not want to change the name, use the Save button. If you want to save a previously saved query with a new name, you must use the Backstage view and perform a Save Object As.

- Close the query.

Comparison Operators

Unless you specify otherwise, Access assumes that the criteria you enter involve equality (exact matches). In the last query, for example, you were requesting those customers whose current due amount is equal to 0 (zero). In other situations, you

might want to find a range of results; for example, you could request customers whose current due is greater than $1,000.00. If you want a query to return something other than an exact match, you must enter the appropriate **comparison operator**. The comparison operators are > (greater than), < (less than), >= (greater than or equal to), <= (less than or equal to), and NOT (not equal to).

To Use a Comparison Operator in a Criterion

1 CREATE QUERIES | 2 USE CRITERIA | 3 SORT DATA | 4 JOIN TABLES | 5 EXPORT RESULTS
6 PERFORM CALCULATIONS | 7 CREATE CROSSTAB | 8 CUSTOMIZE NAVIGATION PANE

The following steps use the > operator to create a query that Bavant Publishing might use to find all book reps whose start date is after 1/1/2013. *Why? A date greater than 1/1/2013 means the date comes after 1/1/2013.* The steps also save the query with a new name.

1

- Start a new query using the Book Rep table.

- Include the Book Rep Number, Last Name, First Name, and Start Date fields.

- Type >1/01/2013 as the criterion for the Start Date field (Figure 2–25).

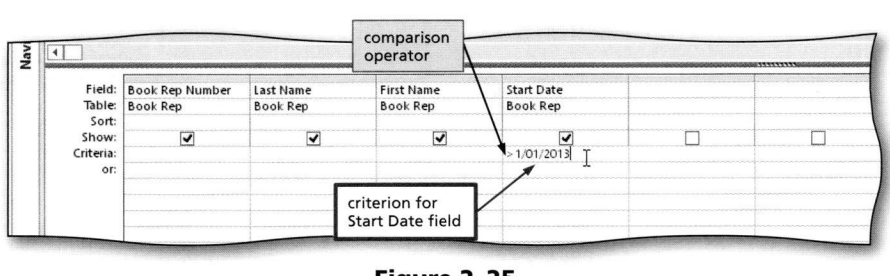

Figure 2–25

Q&A Did I have to type the leading zero in the Day portion of the date?
No. You could have typed 1/1/2013. Some people often type the day using two digits, such as 1/01/2013. You also could have typed a leading zero in the month, 01/01/2013.

2

- Run the query (Figure 2–26).

 Experiment

- Return to Design view. Try a different criterion involving a comparison operator in the Start Date field and run the query. When finished, return to Design view, enter the original criterion (>1/01/2013) in the Start Date field, and run the query.

Figure 2–26

Q&A I returned to Design view and noticed that Access changed 1/01/2013 to #1/01/2013#. Why does the date now have number signs around it?
This is the date format in Access. You usually do not have to enter the number signs because in most cases Access will insert them automatically.

My records are in a different order. Is this a problem?
No. The important thing is which records are included in the results. You will see later in this chapter how you can specify the specific order you want for cases when the order is important.

Can I use the same comparison operators with text data?
Yes. Comparison operators function the same whether you use them with number fields, currency fields, date fields, or text fields.

3

- Save the query as Ch2q04.

- Close the query.

Using Compound Criteria

Often your search data must satisfy more than one criterion. This type of criterion is called a **compound criterion** and is created using the words AND or OR.

In an **AND criterion**, each individual criterion must be true in order for the compound criterion to be true. For example, an AND criterion would allow you to find customers that have returns greater than $0.00 and whose book rep is book rep 42.

An **OR criterion** is true if either individual criterion is true. An OR criterion would allow you to find customers that have returns greater than $0.00 as well as customers whose book rep is book rep 42. In this case, any customer who has returns greater than $0.00 would be included in the answer, regardless of whether the customer's book rep is book rep 42. Likewise, any customer whose book rep is book rep 42 would be included, regardless of whether the customer has returns greater than $0.00.

BTW
Queries: Query-by-Example
Query-By-Example, often referred to as QBE, was a query language first proposed in the mid-1970s. In this approach, users asked questions by filling in a table on the screen. The Access approach to queries is based on Query-By-Example.

To Use a Compound Criterion Involving AND

1 CREATE QUERIES | 2 USE CRITERIA | 3 SORT DATA | 4 JOIN TABLES | 5 EXPORT RESULTS
6 PERFORM CALCULATIONS | 7 CREATE CROSSTAB | 8 CUSTOMIZE NAVIGATION PANE

To combine criteria with AND, place the criteria on the same row of the design grid. *Why? Placing the criteria in the same row indicates that both criteria must be true in Access.* The following steps use an AND criterion to enable Bavant to find those customers who have returns greater than $0.00 and whose book rep is rep 42. The steps also save the query.

- Start a new query using the Customer table.

- Include the Customer Number, Customer Name, Amount Paid, Current Due, Returns, and Book Rep Number fields.

- Type >0 as the criterion for the Returns field.

- Type 42 as the criterion for the Book Rep Number field (Figure 2–27).

Figure 2–27

- Run the query (Figure 2–28).

- Save the query as Ch2q05.

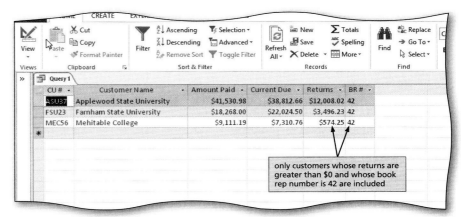

Figure 2–28

To Use a Compound Criterion Involving OR

To combine criteria with OR, each criterion must go on separate rows in the Criteria area of the grid. *Why? Placing criteria on separate rows indicates at least one criterion must be true in Access.* The following steps use an OR criterion to enable Bavant to find those customers who have returns greater than $0.00 or whose book rep is rep 42 (or both). The steps also save the query with a new name.

1

- Return to Design view.

- If necessary, tap or click the Criteria entry for the Book Rep Number field and then use the BACKSPACE key or the DELETE key to erase the entry ("42").

- Tap or click the or row (the row below the Criteria row) for the Book Rep Number field, and then type 42 as the entry (Figure 2–29).

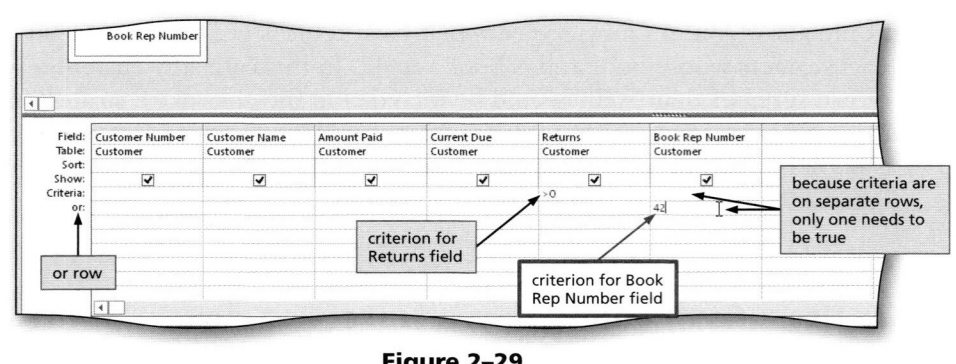

Figure 2–29

2

- Run the query (Figure 2–30).

3

- Save the query as Ch2q06.

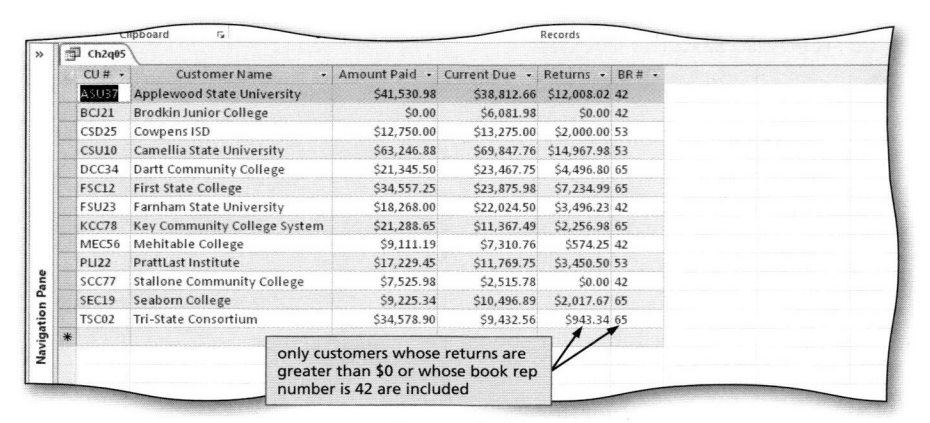

Figure 2–30

BTW
Rearranging Fields in a Query
To move a field in the design grid, tap or click the column selector for the field to select the field and drag it to the appropriate location.

BTW
Q&As
For a complete list of the Q&As found in many of the step-by-step sequences in this book, visit the Q&A resource on the Student Companion Site located on www. cengagebrain.com. For detailed instructions about accessing available resources, visit www. cengage.com/ct/studentdownload or contact your instructor for information about accessing the required files.

Special Criteria

You can use three special criteria in queries:

1. If you want to create a criterion involving a range of values in a single field, you can use the **AND operator**. You place the word AND between the individual conditions. For example, if you wanted to find all customers whose amount paid is greater than or equal to $20,000.00 and less than or equal to $40,000.00, you would enter >= 20000 AND <= 40000 as the criterion in the Amount Paid column.

2. You can select values in a given range by using the **BETWEEN operator**. This is often an alternative to the AND operator. For example, to find all customers whose amount paid is between $20,000.00 and $40,000.00, inclusive, you would enter BETWEEN 20000 AND 40000 as the criterion in the Amount Paid column.

3. You can select a list of values by using the **IN operator**. You follow the word IN with the list of values in parentheses. For example, to find customers whose book rep number is 42 and customers whose book rep is 65 using the IN operator, you would enter IN ("42","65") on the Criteria row in the Book Rep Number column. Unlike when you enter a simple criterion, you must enclose text values in quotation marks.

How would you find customers whose book rep number is 42 or 65 without using the IN operator?
Place the number 42 in the Criteria row of the Book Rep Number column. Place the number 65 in the or row of the Book Rep Number column.

Sorting

In some queries, the order in which the records appear is irrelevant. All you need to be concerned about are the records that appear in the results. It does not matter which one is first or which one is last.

In other queries, however, the order can be very important. You may want to see the cities in which customers are located and would like them arranged alphabetically. Perhaps you want to see the customers listed by book rep number. Further, within all the customers of any given book rep, you might want them to be listed by amount paid from largest amount to smallest.

To order the records in a query result in a particular way, you **sort** the records. The field or fields on which the records are sorted is called the **sort key**. If you are sorting on more than one field (such as sorting by amount paid within book rep number), the more important field (Book Rep Number) is called the **major key** (also called the **primary sort key**) and the less important field (Amount Paid) is called the **minor key** (also called the **secondary sort key**).

To sort in Microsoft Access, specify the sort order in the Sort row of the design grid below the field that is the sort key. If you specify more than one sort key, the sort key on the left will be the major sort key, and the one on the right will be the minor key.

BTW
Sorting Data in a Query
When sorting data in a query, the records in the underlying tables (the tables on which the query is based) are not actually rearranged. Instead, the DBMS determines the most efficient method of simply displaying the records in the requested order. The records in the underlying tables remain in their original order.

BTW
Clearing the Design Grid
You also can clear the design grid using the ribbon. To do so, tap or click the HOME tab, tap or click the Advanced button to display the Advanced menu, and then tap or click Clear Grid on the Advanced menu.

To Clear the Design Grid

1 CREATE QUERIES | 2 USE CRITERIA | 3 SORT DATA | 4 JOIN TABLES | 5 EXPORT RESULTS
6 PERFORM CALCULATIONS | 7 CREATE CROSSTAB | 8 CUSTOMIZE NAVIGATION PANE

Why? *If the fields you want to include in the next query are different from those in the previous query, it is usually simpler to start with a clear grid, that is, one with no fields already in the design grid.* You always can clear the entries in the design grid by closing the query and then starting over. A simpler approach to clearing the entries is to select all the entries and then press the DELETE key. The following steps return to Design view and clear the design grid.

- Return to Design view.

- Tap or click just above the Customer Number column heading in the grid to select the column.

Q&A | I clicked above the column heading, but the column is not selected. What should I do?
You did not point to the correct location. Be sure the pointer changes into a down-pointing arrow and then tap or click again.

- Hold the SHIFT key down and tap or click just above the Book Rep Number column heading to select all the columns (Figure 2–31).

Figure 2–31

- Press the DELETE key to clear the design grid.

To Sort Data in a Query

If you determine that the query results should be sorted, you will need to specify the sort key. The following steps sort the cities in the Customer table by indicating that the City field is to be sorted. The steps specify Ascending sort order. **Why?** *When sorting text data, Ascending sort order arranges the results in alphabetical order.*

1
- Include the City field in the design grid.
- Tap or click the Sort row below the City field, and then tap or click the Sort arrow to display a menu of possible sort orders (Figure 2–32).

Figure 2–32

2
- Tap or click Ascending to select the sort order (Figure 2–33).

Figure 2–33

3
- Run the query (Figure 2–34).

Experiment
- Return to Design view and change the sort order to Descending. Run the query. Return to Design view and change the sort order back to Ascending. Run the query.

Q&A Why do some cities appear more than once?

More than one customer is located in those cities.

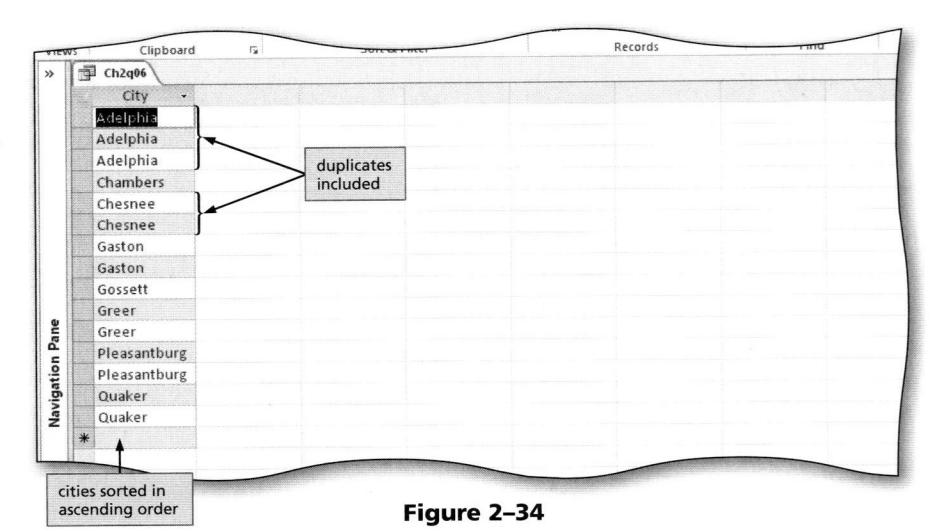

Figure 2–34

To Omit Duplicates

When you sort data, duplicates normally are included. In the query shown in Figure 2–34, for example, Adelphia appears three times. Several other cities appear twice. You eliminate duplicates using the query's property sheet. A **property sheet** is a window containing the various properties of the object. To omit duplicates, you will use the property sheet to change the Unique Values property from No to Yes.

The following steps create a query that Bavant Publishing might use to obtain a sorted list of the cities in the Customer table in which each city is listed only once. *Why? Unless you wanted to know how many customers were located in each city, the duplicates typically do not add any value.* The steps also save the query with a new name.

1

- Return to Design view.

- Tap or click the second field (the empty field to the right of City) in the design grid to produce an insertion point.

- If necessary, tap or click DESIGN on the ribbon to display the DESIGN tab.

- Tap or click the Property Sheet button (QUERY TOOLS DESIGN tab | Show/Hide group) to display the property sheet (Figure 2–35).

Q&A | My property sheet looks different. What should I do?
If your sheet looks different, close the property sheet and repeat this step.

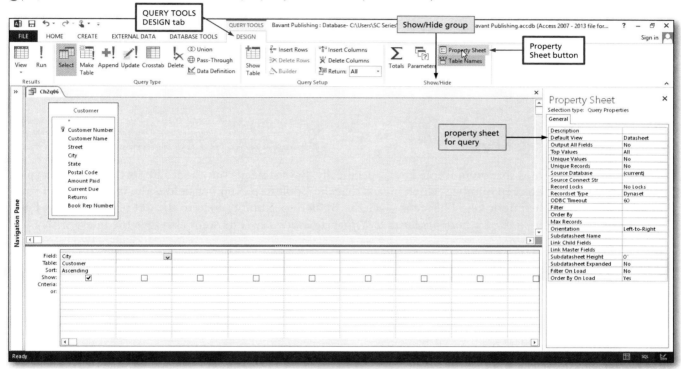

Figure 2–35

2

- Tap or click the Unique Values property box, and then tap or click the arrow that appears to display a list of available choices (Figure 2–36).

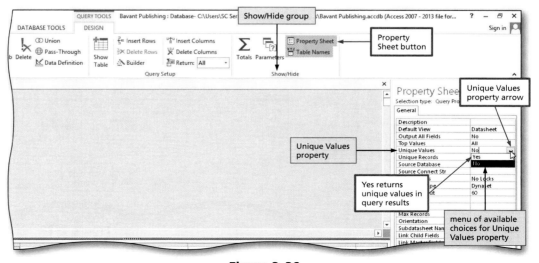

Figure 2–36

3

- Tap or click Yes to indicate that the query will return unique values, which means that each value will appear only once in the query results.

- Close the Query Properties property sheet by tapping or clicking the Property Sheet button (QUERY TOOLS DESIGN tab | Show/Hide group) a second time.

- Run the query (Figure 2–37).

4

- Save the query as Ch2q07.

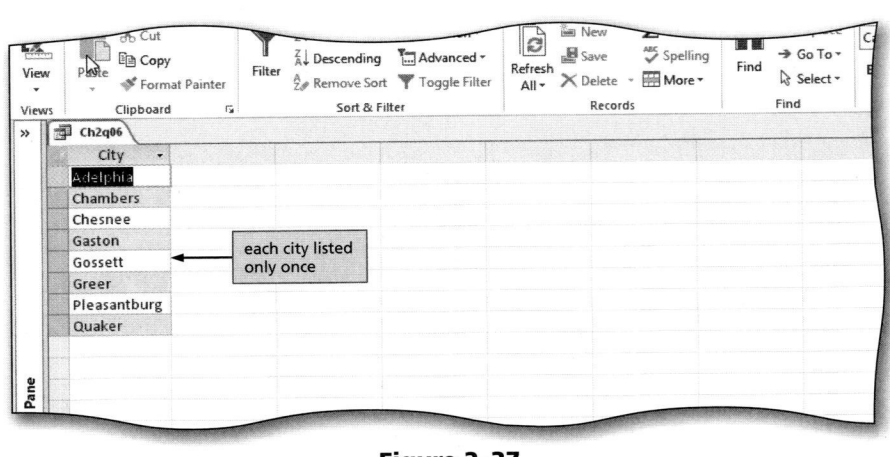

each city listed only once

Figure 2–37

Other Ways

1. Press and hold or right-click second field in design grid, tap or click Properties on shortcut menu

To Sort on Multiple Keys

1 CREATE QUERIES | 2 USE CRITERIA | 3 SORT DATA | 4 JOIN TABLES | 5 EXPORT RESULTS
6 PERFORM CALCULATIONS | 7 CREATE CROSSTAB | 8 CUSTOMIZE NAVIGATION PANE

The following steps sort on multiple keys. Specifically, Bavant needs the data to be sorted by amount paid (low to high) within book rep number, which means that the Book Rep Number field is the major key and the Amount Paid field is the minor key. The steps place the Book Rep Number field to the left of the Amount Paid field. *Why? In Access, the major key must appear to the left of the minor key.* The steps also save the query with a new name.

1

- Return to Design view. Clear the design grid by tapping or clicking the top of the first column in the grid, and then pressing the DELETE key to clear the design grid.

- In the following order, include the Customer Number, Customer Name, Book Rep Number, and Amount Paid fields in the query.

- Select Ascending as the sort order for both the Book Rep Number field and the Amount Paid field (Figure 2–38).

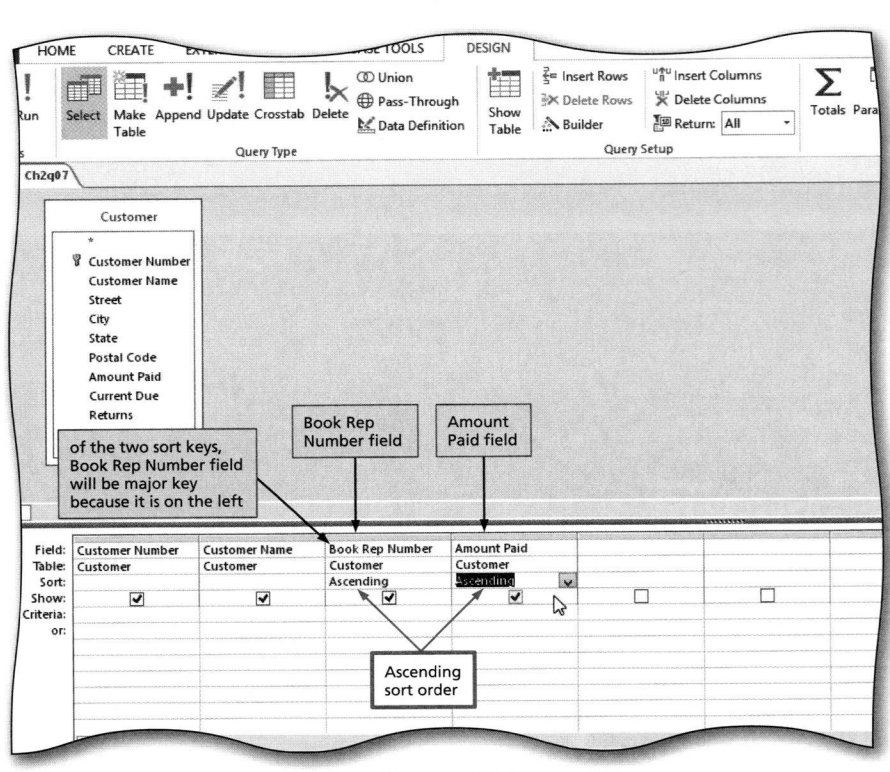

of the two sort keys, Book Rep Number field will be major key because it is on the left

Book Rep Number field

Amount Paid field

Ascending sort order

Figure 2–38

②

- Run the query (Figure 2–39).

Experiment

- Return to Design view and try other sort combinations for the Book Rep Number and Amount Paid fields, such as Ascending for Book Rep Number and Descending for Amount Paid. In each case, run the query to see the effect of the changes. When finished, select Ascending as the sort order for both fields.

 Q&A What if the Amount Paid field is to the left of the Book Rep Number field?

It is important to remember that the major sort key must appear to the left of the minor sort key in the design grid. If you attempted to sort by amount paid within book rep number, but placed the Amount Paid field to the left of the Book Rep Number field, your results would be incorrect.

CU #	Customer Name	BR #	Amount Paid
BCJ21	Brodkin Junior College	42	$0.00
SCC77	Stallone Community College	42	$7,525.98
MEC56	Mehitable College	42	$9,111.19
FSU23	Farnham State University	42	$18,268.00
ASU37	Applewood State University	42	$41,530.98
MCC45	Mauldin Community College	53	$9,500.00
CSD25	Cowpens ISD	53	$12,750.00
PLI22	PrattLast Institute	53	$17,229.45
HSD05	Hammonds County ISD	53	$18,434.75
CSU10	Camellia State University	53	$63,246.88
SEC19	Seaborn College	65	$9,225.34
KCC78	Key Community College System	65	$21,288.65
DCC34	Dartt Community College	65	$21,345.50
FSC12	First State College	65	$34,557.25
TSC02	Tri-State Consortium	65	$34,578.90

within group of customers with the same book rep number, rows are sorted by amount paid in ascending order

overall order is by book rep number in ascending order

Figure 2–39

③

- Save the query as Ch2q08.

Is there any way to sort the records in this same order, but have the Amount Paid field appear to the left of the Book Rep Number field in the query results?

Yes. Remove the check mark from the Book Rep Number field, and then add an additional Book Rep Number field at the end of the query. The first Book Rep Number field will be used for sorting but will not appear in the results. The second will appear in the results, but will not be involved in the sorting process.

How do you approach the creation of a query that might involve sorting?

Examine the query or request to see if it contains words such as *order* or *sort*. Such words imply that the order of the query results is important. If so, you need to sort the query.

If sorting is required, identify the field or fields on which the results are to be sorted. In the request, look for language such as *ordered by* or *sort the results by*, both of which would indicate that the specified field is a sort key.

If using multiple sort keys, determine the major and minor keys. If you are using two sort keys, determine which one is the more important, or the major key. Look for language such as *sort by amount paid within book rep number*, which implies that the overall order is by book rep number. In this case, the Book Rep Number field would be the major sort key and the Amount Paid field would be the minor sort key.

Determine sort order. Words such as *increasing*, *ascending*, or *low-to-high* imply Ascending order. Words such as *decreasing*, *descending*, or *high-to-low* imply Descending order. Sorting in *alphabetical order* implies Ascending order. If there were no words to imply a particular order, you would typically use Ascending.

Examine the query or request to see if there are any special restrictions. One common restriction is to exclude duplicates. Another common restriction is to list only a certain number of records, such as the first five records.

To Create a Top-Values Query

Rather than show all the results of a query, you may want to show only a specified number of records or a percentage of records. ***Why?*** *You might not need to see all the records, just enough to get a general idea of the results.* Creating a **top-values query** allows you to restrict the number of records that appear. When you sort records, you can limit results to those records having the highest (descending sort) or lowest (ascending sort) values. To do so, first create a query that sorts the data in the desired order. Next, use the Return box on the DESIGN tab to change the number of records to be included from All to the desired number or percentage.

The following steps create a query for Bavant Publishing that shows only the first five records that were included in the results of the previous query. The steps also save the resulting query with a new name.

❶

- Return to Design view.

- If necessary, tap or click DESIGN on the ribbon to display the Design tab.

- Tap or click the Return arrow (QUERY TOOLS DESIGN tab | Query Setup group) to display the Return menu (Figure 2–40).

Figure 2–40

❷

- Tap or click 5 in the Return menu to specify that the query results should contain the first five rows.

Q&A Could I have typed the 5? What about other numbers that do not appear in the list?
Yes, you could have typed the 5. For numbers not appearing in the list, you must type the number.

- Run the query (Figure 2–41).

❸

- Save the query as Ch2q09.

- Close the query.

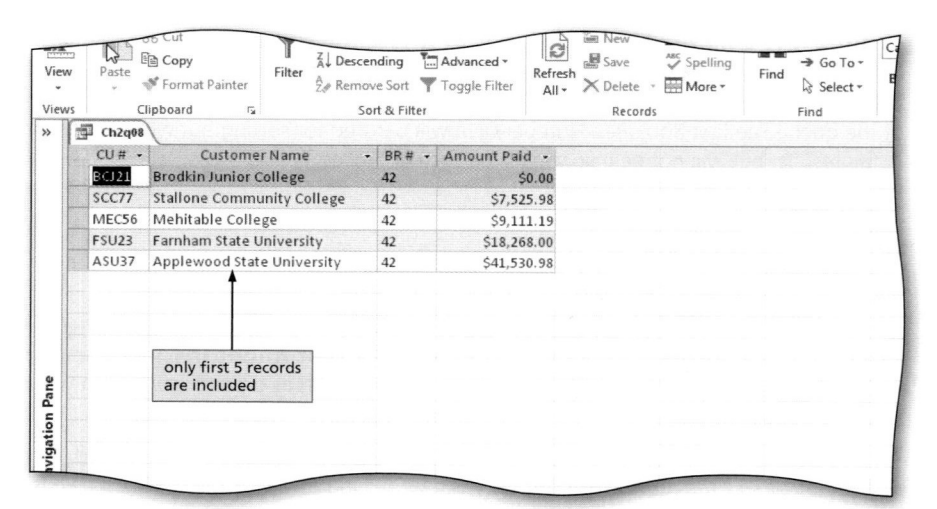

Figure 2–41

Q&A Do I need to close the query before creating my next query?
Not necessarily. When you use a top-values query, however, it is important to change the value in the Return box back to All. If you do not change the Return value back to All, the previous value will remain in effect. Consequently, you might not get all the records you should in the next query. A good practice whenever you use a top-values query is to close the query as soon as you are done. That way, you will begin your next query from scratch, which guarantees that the value is reset to All.

Break Point: If you wish to take a break, this is a good place to do so. You can exit Access now. To resume later, run Access, open the database called Bavant Publishing, and continue following the steps from this location forward.

Joining Tables

In designing a query, you need to determine whether more than one table is required. For example, if the question being asked involves data from both the Customer and Book Rep tables, then both tables are required for the query. A query might require listing the number and name of each customer (from the Customer table) along with the number and name of the customer's book rep (from the Book Rep table). Both the Customer and Book Rep tables are required for this query. You need to **join** the tables to find records in the two tables that have identical values in matching fields (Figure 2–42). In this example, you need to find records in the Customer table and the Book Rep table that have the same value in the Book Rep Number fields.

BTW
Ad Hoc Relationships
When you join tables in a query, you are creating an ad hoc relationship, that is, a relationship between tables created for a specific purpose. In Chapter 3, you will create general-purpose relationships using the Relationships window.

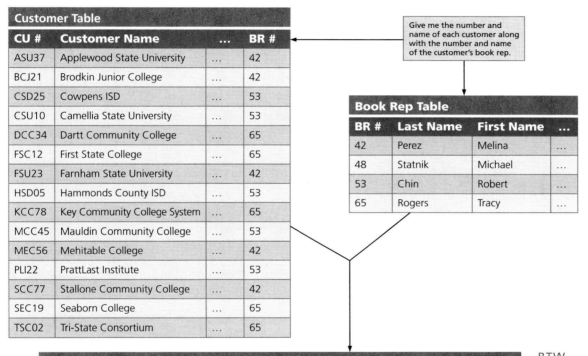

Customer Table

CU #	Customer Name	...	BR #
ASU37	Applewood State University	...	42
BCJ21	Brodkin Junior College	...	42
CSD25	Cowpens ISD	...	53
CSU10	Camellia State University	...	53
DCC34	Dartt Community College	...	65
FSC12	First State College	...	65
FSU23	Farnham State University	...	42
HSD05	Hammonds County ISD	...	53
KCC78	Key Community College System	...	65
MCC45	Mauldin Community College	...	53
MEC56	Mehitable College	...	42
PLI22	PrattLast Institute	...	53
SCC77	Stallone Community College	...	42
SEC19	Seaborn College	...	65
TSC02	Tri-State Consortium	...	65

Give me the number and name of each customer along with the number and name of the customer's book rep.

Book Rep Table

BR #	Last Name	First Name	...
42	Perez	Melina	...
48	Statnik	Michael	...
53	Chin	Robert	...
65	Rogers	Tracy	...

Customer Table

CU #	Customer Name	...	BR #	Last Name	First Name	...
ASU37	Applewood State University	...	42	Perez	Melina	...
BCJ21	Brodkin Junior College	...	42	Perez	Melina	...
CSD25	Cowpens ISD	...	53	Chin	Robert	...
CSU10	Camellia State University	...	53	Chin	Robert	...
DCC34	Dartt Community College	...	65	Rogers	Tracy	...
FSC12	First State College	...	65	Rogers	Tracy	...
FSU23	Farnham State University	...	42	Perez	Melina	...
HSD05	Hammonds County ISD	...	53	Chin	Robert	...
KCC78	Key Community College System	...	65	Rogers	Tracy	...
MCC45	Mauldin Community College	...	53	Chin	Robert	...
MEC56	Mehitable College	...	42	Perez	Melina	...
PLI22	PrattLast Institute	...	53	Chin	Robert	...
SCC77	Stallone Community College	...	42	Perez	Melina	...
SEC19	Seaborn College	...	65	Rogers	Tracy	...
TSC02	Tri-State Consortium	...	65	Rogers	Tracy	...

BTW
Join Line
If you do not get a join line automatically, there may be a problem with one of your table designs. Open each table in Design view and make sure that the data types are the same for the matching field in both tables and that one of the matching fields is the primary key in a table. Correct these errors and create the query again.

Figure 2–42

To Join Tables

If you have determined that you need to join tables, you first will bring field lists for both tables to the upper pane of the Query window while working in Design view. Access will draw a line, called a **join line**, between matching fields in the two tables, indicating that the tables are related. You then can select fields from either table. Access joins the tables automatically.

The first step is to create a new query and add the Book Rep table to the query. Then, add the Customer table to the query. A join line should appear, connecting the Book Rep Number fields in the two field lists. *Why might the join line not appear? If the names of the matching fields differ from one table to the other, Access will not insert the line. You can insert it manually, however, by tapping or clicking one of the two matching fields and dragging the pointer to the other matching field.*

The following steps create a query to display information from both the Customer table and the Book Rep table.

1

- Tap or click CREATE on the ribbon to display the CREATE tab.

- Tap or click the Query Design button (CREATE tab | Queries group) to create a new query.

- If necessary, tap or click the Book Rep table (Show Table dialog box) to select the table.

- Tap or click the Add button (Show Table dialog box) to add a field list for the Book Rep Table to the query (Figure 2–43).

Figure 2–43

2

- Tap or click the Customer table (Show Table dialog box).

- Tap or click the Add button (Show Table dialog box) to add a field list for the Customer table.

- Close the Show Table dialog box by tapping or clicking the Close button.

- Expand the size of the two field lists so all the fields in the Book Rep and Customer tables appear (Figure 2–44).

Figure 2–44

Q&A
I did not get a join line. What should I do?
Ensure that the names of the matching fields are the same, the data types are the same, and the matching field is the primary key in one of the two tables. If all of these factors are true and you still do not have a join line, you can produce one by pointing to a matching field and dragging to the other matching field.

3

- In the design grid, include the Book Rep Number, Last Name, and First Name fields from the Book Rep Table as well as the Customer Number and Customer Name fields from the Customer table.

- Select Ascending as the sort order for both the Book Rep Number field and the Customer Number field (Figure 2–45).

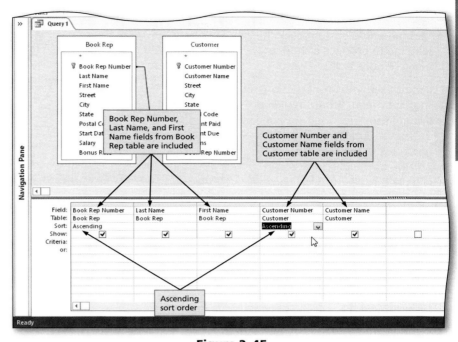

Figure 2–45

4

- Run the query (Figure 2–46).

5

- Tap or click the Save button on the Quick Access Toolbar to display the Save As dialog box.

- Type `Rep-Customer Query` as the query name.

6

- Tap or click the OK button (Save As dialog box) to save the query.

Figure 2–46

To Change Join Properties

1 CREATE QUERIES | 2 USE CRITERIA | 3 SORT DATA | 4 JOIN TABLES | **5 EXPORT RESULTS**
6 PERFORM CALCULATIONS | 7 CREATE CROSSTAB | 8 CUSTOMIZE NAVIGATION PANE

Normally, records that do not match do not appear in the results of a join query. For example, the book rep named Michael Statnik does not appear in the results. *Why? He currently does not have any customers.* To cause such a record to be displayed, you need to change the **join properties**, which are the properties that indicate which records appear in a join. The following steps change the join properties of the Rep-Customer Query so that Bavant can include all book reps in the results, rather than only those reps who have already been assigned customers.

❶

- Return to Design view.

- Press and hold or right-click the join line to produce a shortcut menu (Figure 2–47).

Q&A I do not see Join Properties on my shortcut menu. What should I do?
If Join Properties does not appear on your shortcut menu, you did not point to the appropriate portion of the join line. You will need to point to the correct (middle) portion and press and hold or right-click again.

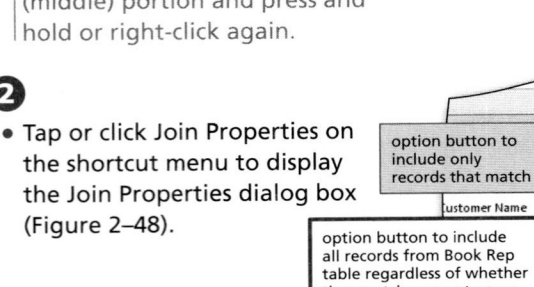

Figure 2–47

❷

- Tap or click Join Properties on the shortcut menu to display the Join Properties dialog box (Figure 2–48).

Figure 2–48

❸

- Tap or click option button 2 (Join Properties dialog box) to include all records from the Book Rep Table regardless of whether they match any customers.

- Tap or click the OK button (Join Properties dialog box) to modify the join properties.

- Run the query (Figure 2–49).

🔎 **Experiment**

- Return to Design view, change the Join properties, and select option button 3. Run the query to see the effect of this option. When done, return to Design view, change the join properties, and once again select option button 2.

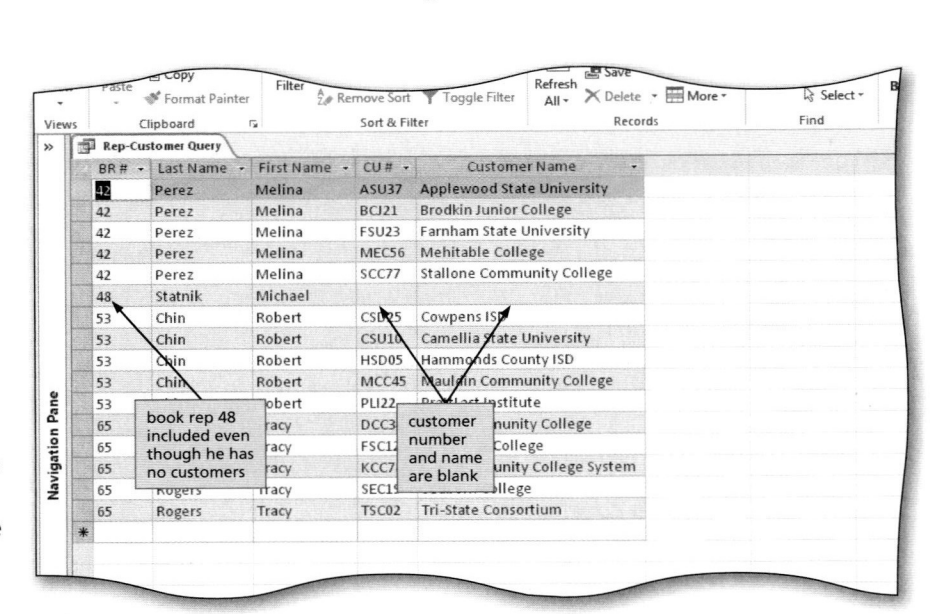

Figure 2–49

❹

- Tap or click the Save button on the Quick Access Toolbar to save the changes to the query.

- Close the Rep-Customer Query.

Q&A I see a dialog box that asks if I want to save the query. What should I do?
Tap or click the OK button to save the query.

Querying a Database **Access Chapter 2** **AC** 103

1 CREATE QUERIES | 2 USE CRITERIA | 3 SORT DATA | 4 JOIN TABLES | **5 EXPORT RESULTS**
6 PERFORM CALCULATIONS | 7 CREATE CROSSTAB | 8 CUSTOMIZE NAVIGATION PANE

Access Chapter 2

To Create a Report from a Query

You can use queries in the creation of reports. The report in Figure 2–50 involves data from more than one table. ***Why?*** *The Last Name and First Name fields are in the Book Rep table. The Customer Number and Customer Name fields are in the Customer table. The Book Rep Number field is in both tables.* The easiest way to create such a report is to base it on a query that joins the two tables. The following steps use the Report Wizard and the Rep-Customer Query to create the report.

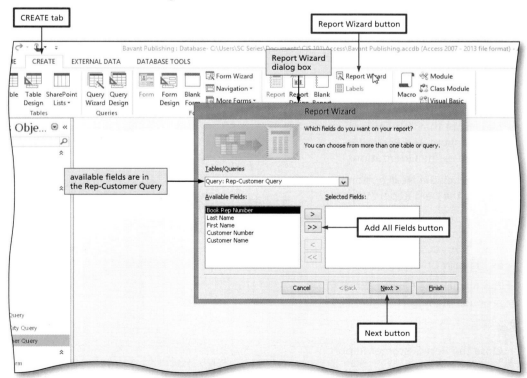

Rep-Customer Report

BR #	Last Name	First Name	CU #	Customer Name
42	Perez	Melina	ASU37	Applewood State University
42	Perez	Melina	BCJ21	Brodkin Junior College
42	Perez	Melina	FSU23	Farnham State University
42	Perez	Melina	MEC56	Mehitable College
42	Perez	Melina	SCC77	Stallone Community College
48	Statnik	Michael		
53	Chin	Robert	CSD25	Cowpens ISD
53	Chin	Robert	CSU10	Camellia State University
53	Chin	Robert	HSD05	Hammonds County ISD
53	Chin	Robert	MCC45	Mauldin Community College
53	Chin	Robert	PLI22	PrattLast Institute
65	Rogers	Tracy	DCC34	Dartt Community College
65	Rogers	Tracy	FSC12	First State College
65	Rogers	Tracy	KCC78	Key Community College System
65	Rogers	Tracy	SEC19	Seaborn College
65	Rogers	Tracy	TSC02	Tri-State Consortium

Figure 2–50

1

- Open the Navigation Pane, and then select the Rep-Customer Query in the Navigation Pane.

- Tap or click CREATE on the ribbon to display the CREATE tab.

- Tap or click the Report Wizard button (CREATE tab | Reports group) to display the Report Wizard dialog box (Figure 2–51).

Figure 2–51

2

- Tap or click the Add All Fields button (Report Wizard dialog box) to add all the fields in the Rep-Customer Query.

- Tap or click the Next button to display the next Report Wizard screen (Figure 2–52).

Figure 2–52

3

- Because you will not specify any grouping, tap or click the Next button in the Report Wizard dialog box to display the next Report Wizard screen.

- Because you already specified the sort order in the query, tap or click the Next button again to display the next Report Wizard screen.

- Make sure that Tabular is selected as the Layout and Portrait is selected as the Orientation.

- Tap or click the Next button to display the next Report Wizard screen.

- Erase the current title, and then type `Rep-Customer Report` as the new title.

- Tap or click the Finish button to produce the report (Figure 2–53).

Figure 2–53

4

- Close the Rep-Customer Report.

To Print a Report

The following steps print a hard copy of the report.

1 With the Rep-Customer Report selected in the Navigation Pane, tap or click FILE on the ribbon to open the Backstage view.

2 Tap or click the Print tab in the Backstage view to display the Print gallery.

3 Tap or click the Quick Print button to print the report.

CONSIDER THIS

How would you approach the creation of a query that might involve multiple tables?

Examine the request to see if all the fields involved in the request are in one table. If the fields are in two (or more) tables, you need to join the tables.

If joining is required, identify the matching fields in the two tables that have identical values. Look for the same column name in the two tables or for column names that are similar.

Determine whether sorting is required. Queries that join tables often are used as the basis for a report. If this is the case, it may be necessary to sort the results. For example, the Rep-Customer Report is based on a query that joins the Book Rep and Customer tables. The query is sorted by book rep number and customer number.

Examine the request to see if there are any special restrictions. For example, the user only may want customers whose current due amount is $0.00.

Examine the request to see if you only want records from both tables that have identical values in matching fields. If you want to see records in one of the tables that do not have identical values, then you need to change the join properties.

Creating a Form for a Query

In the previous chapter, you created a form for the Customer table. You also can create a form for a query. Recall that a form in a database is a formatted document with fields that contain data. Forms allow you to view and maintain data.

To Create a Form for a Query

1 CREATE QUERIES | 2 USE CRITERIA | 3 SORT DATA | 4 JOIN TABLES | **5 EXPORT RESULTS**
6 PERFORM CALCULATIONS | 7 CREATE CROSSTAB | 8 CUSTOMIZE NAVIGATION PANE

The following steps create a form, then save the form. *Why? The form will be available for future use in viewing the data in the query.*

1

- If necessary, select the Rep-Customer Query in the Navigation Pane.

- Tap or click CREATE on the ribbon to display the CREATE tab (Figure 2–54).

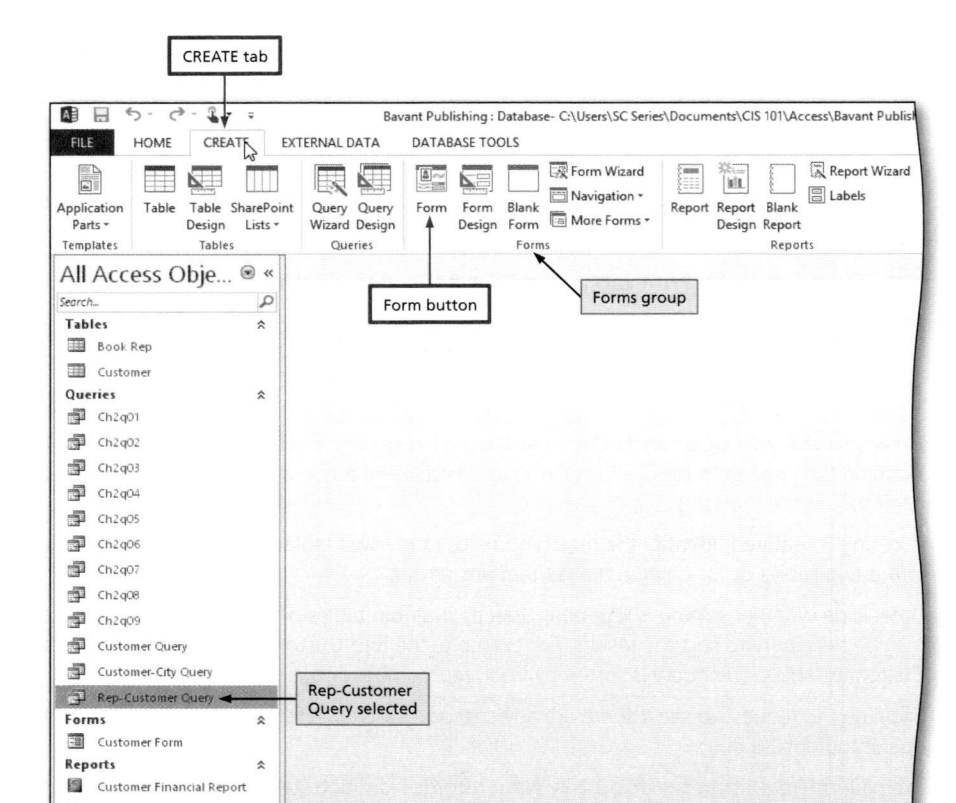

Figure 2–54

2

- Tap or click the Form button (CREATE tab | Forms group) to create a simple form (Figure 2–55).

Q&A | I see a field list also. What should I do?
Tap or click the Close button for the Field List.

3

- Tap or click the Save button on the Quick Access Toolbar to display the Save As dialog box.

- Type `Rep-Customer Form` as the form name.

4

- Tap or click the OK button to save the form.

- Tap or click the Close button for the form to close the form.

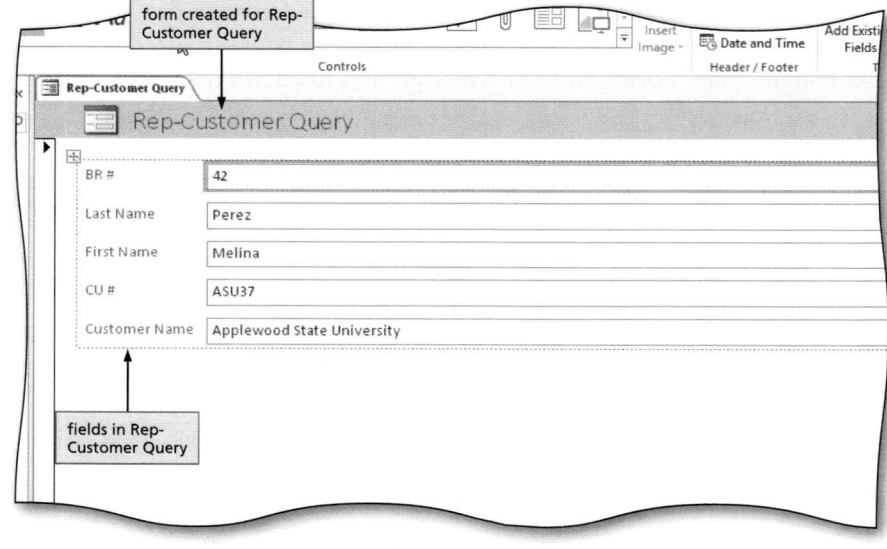

Figure 2–55

Using a Form

After you have saved a form, you can use it at any time by pressing and holding or right-clicking the form in the Navigation Pane and then tapping or clicking Open on the shortcut menu. If you plan to use the form to enter data, you must ensure you are viewing the form in Form view.

Exporting Data from Access to Other Applications

You can **export**, or copy, tables or queries from an Access database so that another application (for example, Excel or Word) can use the data. The application that will receive the data determines the export process to be used. You can export to text files in a variety of formats. For applications to which you cannot directly export data, you often can export an appropriately formatted text file that the other application can import. Figure 2–56 shows the workbook produced by exporting the Rep-Customer Query to Excel. The columns in the workbook have been resized to best fit the data.

BTW
**Distributing
a Document**
Instead of printing and distributing a hard copy of a document, you can distribute the document electronically. Options include sending the document via email; posting it on cloud storage (such as SkyDrive) and sharing the file with others; posting it on a social networking site, blog, or other website; and sharing a link associated with an online location of the document. You also can create and share a PDF or XPS image of the document, so that users can view the file in Acrobat Reader or XPS Viewer instead of in Access.

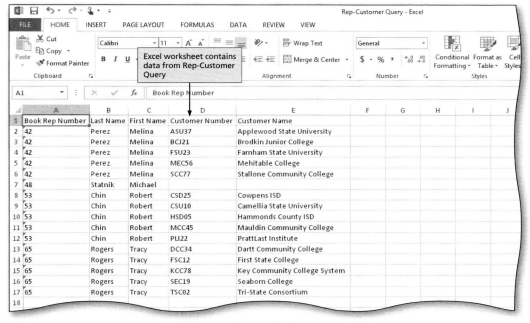

Figure 2–56

1 CREATE QUERIES | 2 USE CRITERIA | 3 SORT DATA | 4 JOIN TABLES | 5 EXPORT RESULTS
6 PERFORM CALCULATIONS | 7 CREATE CROSSTAB | 8 CUSTOMIZE NAVIGATION PANE

To Export Data to Excel

For Bavant Publishing to make the Rep-Customer Query available to Excel users, it needs to export the data. To export data to Excel, select the table or query to be exported and then tap or click the Excel button in the Export group on the EXTERNAL DATA tab. The steps on the next page export the Rep-Customer Query to Excel and save the export steps. *Why save the export steps? By saving the export steps, you could easily repeat the export process whenever you like without going through all the steps.* You would use the saved steps to export data in the future by tapping or clicking the Saved Exports button (EXTERNAL DATA tab | Export group) and then selecting the steps you saved.

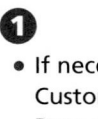

1

- If necessary, tap or click the Rep-Customer Query in the Navigation Pane to select it.

- Tap or click EXTERNAL DATA on the ribbon to display the EXTERNAL DATA tab (Figure 2–57).

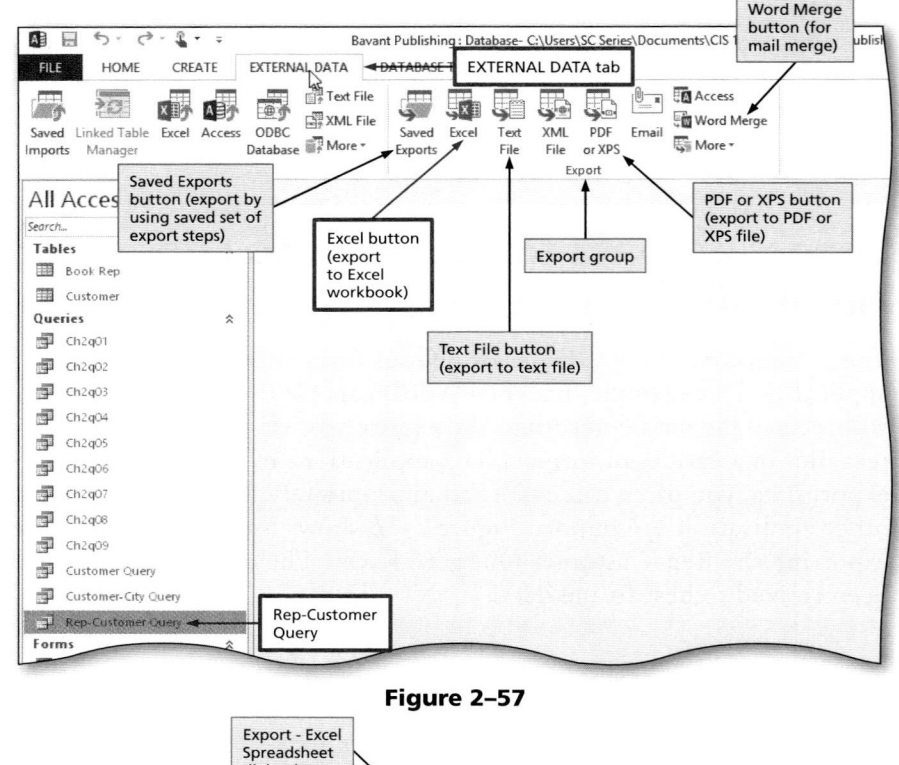

Figure 2–57

2

- Tap or click the Excel button (EXTERNAL DATA tab | Export group) to display the Export-Excel Spreadsheet dialog box.

- Tap or click the Browse button (Export-Excel Spreadsheet dialog box), and then navigate to the location where you wish to export the query (for example, the Access folder in the CIS 101 folder).

- Be sure the file name is Rep-Customer Query and then tap or click the Save button (File Save dialog box) to select the file name and location (Figure 2–58).

Figure 2–58

Q&A

Did I need to browse?
No. You could type the appropriate file location.

Could I change the name of the file?
You could change it. Simply replace the current file name with the one you want.

What if the file I want to export already exists?
Access will indicate that the file already exists and ask if you want to replace it. If you tap or click the Yes button, the file you export will replace the old file. If you tap or click the No button, you must either change the name of the export file or cancel the process.

3

- Tap or click the OK button (Export-Excel Spreadsheet dialog box) to export the data (Figure 2–59).

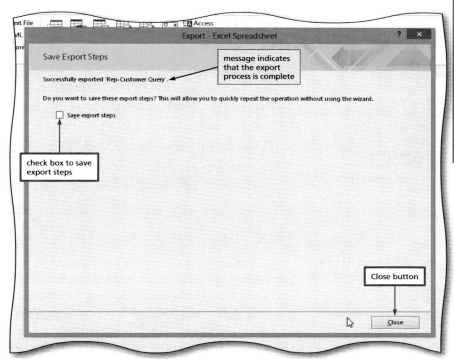

Figure 2–59

4

- Tap or click the 'Save export steps' check box (Export-Excel Spreadsheet dialog box) to display the Save Export Steps options.

- If necessary, type Export-Rep-Customer Query in the Save as text box.

- Type Export the Rep-Customer Query without formatting in the Description text box (Figure 2–60).

Q&A

How could I re-use the export steps?

You can use these steps to export data in the future by tapping or clicking the Saved Exports button (EXTERNAL DATA tab | Export group) and then selecting the steps you saved.

5

- Tap or click the Save Export button (Export-Excel Spreadsheet dialog box) to save the export steps.

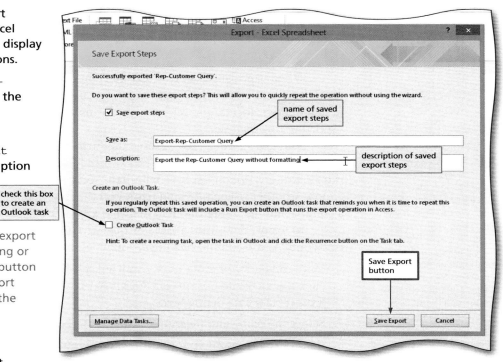

Figure 2–60

Other Ways

1. Press and hold or right-click database object in Navigation Pane, tap or click Export

TO EXPORT DATA TO WORD

It is not possible to export data from Access to the standard Word format. It is possible, however, to export the data as a rich text format (RTF) file, which Word can use. To export data from a query or table to an RTF file, you would use the following steps.

1. With the query or table to be exported selected in the Navigation Pane, tap or click the More button (EXTERNAL DATA tab | Export group) and then tap or click Word on the More menu to display the Export-RTF File dialog box.
2. Navigate to the location in which to save the file and assign a file name.
3. Tap or click the Save button, and then tap or click the OK button to export the data.
4. Save the export steps if you want, or simply tap or click the Close button in the Export-RTF File dialog box to close the dialog box without saving the export steps.

Text Files

You also can export Access data to text files, which can be used for a variety of purposes. Text files contain unformatted characters, including alphanumeric characters, and some special characters, such as tabs, carriage returns, and line feeds.

In **delimited files**, each record is on a separate line and the fields are separated by a special character, called the **delimiter**. Common delimiters are tabs, semicolons, commas, and spaces. You also can choose any other value that does not appear within the field contents as the delimiter. The comma-separated values (CSV) file often used in Excel is an example of a delimited file.

In **fixed-width files**, the width of any field is the same on every record. For example, if the width of the first field on the first record is 12 characters, the width of the first field on every other record also must be 12 characters.

TO EXPORT DATA TO A TEXT FILE

When exporting data to a text file, you can choose to export the data with formatting and layout. This option preserves much of the formatting and layout in tables, queries, forms, and reports. For forms and reports, this is the only option for exporting to a text file.

If you do not need to preserve the formatting, you can choose either delimited or fixed-width as the format for the exported file. The most common option, especially if formatting is not an issue, is delimited. You can choose the delimiter. You also can choose whether to include field names on the first row. In many cases, delimiting with a comma and including the field names is a good choice.

To export data from a table or query to a comma-delimited file in which the first row contains the column headings, you would use the following steps.

1. With the query or table to be exported selected in the Navigation Pane, tap or click the Text File button (EXTERNAL DATA tab | Export group) to display the Export-Text File dialog box.
2. Select the name and location for the file to be created.
3. If you need to preserve formatting and layout, be sure the 'Export data with formatting and layout' check box is checked. If you do not need to preserve formatting and layout, make sure the check box is not checked. Once you have made your selection, tap or click the OK button in the Export-Text File dialog box.
4. To create a delimited file, be sure the Delimited option button is selected in the Export Text Wizard dialog box. To create a fixed-width file, be sure the Fixed Width option button is selected. Once you have made your selection, tap or click the Next button.

5. a. If you are exporting to a delimited file, choose the delimiter that you want to separate your fields, such as a comma. Decide whether to include field names on the first row and, if so, tap or click the 'Include Field Names on First Row' check box. If you want to select a text qualifier, select it in the Text Qualifier list. When you have made your selections, tap or click the Next button.

 b. If you are exporting to a fixed-width file, review the position of the vertical lines that separate your fields. If any lines are not positioned correctly, follow the directions on the screen to reposition them. When you have finished, tap or click the Next button.

6. Tap or click the Finish button to export the data.

7. Save the export steps if you want, or simply tap or click the Close button in the Export-Text File dialog box to close the dialog box without saving the export steps.

Adding Criteria to a Join Query

Sometimes you will want to join tables, but you will not want to include all possible records. For example, you would like to create a report showing only those customers whose amount paid is greater than $20,000.00. In this case, you would relate the tables and include fields just as you did before. You also will include criteria. To include only those customers whose amount paid is more than $20,000.00, you will include >20000 as a criterion for the Amount Paid field.

BTW
Join Types
The type of join that finds records from both tables that have identical values in matching fields is called an inner join. An inner join is the default join in Access. Outer joins are used to show all the records in one table as well as the common records; that is, the records that share the same value in the join field. In a left outer join, all rows from the table on the left are included. In a right outer join, all rows from the table on the right are included.

To Restrict the Records in a Join

1 CREATE QUERIES | 2 USE CRITERIA | 3 SORT DATA | 4 JOIN TABLES | **5 EXPORT RESULTS**
6 PERFORM CALCULATIONS | 7 CREATE CROSSTAB | 8 CUSTOMIZE NAVIGATION PANE

The following steps modify the Rep-Customer Query so that the results for Bavant Publishing include a criterion. **Why?** *Bavant wants to include only those customers whose amount paid is more than $20,000.00.*

- Open the Navigation Pane, if necessary, and then press and hold or right-click the Rep-Customer Query to produce a shortcut menu.

- Tap or click Design View on the shortcut menu to open the Rep-Customer Query in Design view.

- Close the Navigation Pane.

- Add the Amount Paid field to the query.

- Type >20000 as the criterion for the Amount Paid field (Figure 2–61).

Figure 2–61

2
- Run the query (Figure 2–62).

3
- Close the query.
- When asked if you want to save your changes, tap or click the No button.

Q&A
What would happen if I saved the changes?
The next time you used this query, you would only see customers whose amount paid is more than $20,000.00.

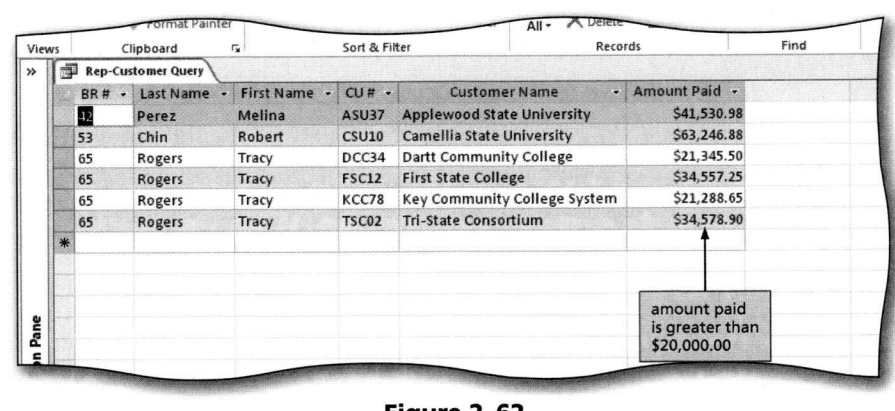

Figure 2–62

BTW

Expression Builder
Access includes a tool to help you create complex expressions. If you click Build on the shortcut menu (see Figure 2–63), Access displays the Expression Builder dialog box, which includes an expression box, operator buttons, and expression elements. You can type parts of the expression directly and paste operator buttons and expression elements into the box. You also can use functions in expressions.

Calculations

If a special calculation is required for a query, you need to determine whether the calculation is **an individual record calculation** (for example, adding the values in two fields) or a **group calculation** (for example, finding the total of the values in a particular field on all the records).

Bavant Publishing might want to know the total amount (amount paid and current due) from each customer. This would seem to pose a problem because the Customer table does not include a field for total amount. You can calculate it, however, because the total amount is equal to the amount paid plus the current due. A field that can be computed from other fields is called a **calculated field** or a **computed field**. A calculated field is an individual record calculation because each calculation only involves fields in a single record.

Bavant also might want to calculate the average amount paid for the customers of each book rep. That is, they may want the average for customers of book rep 42, the average for customers of book rep 53, and so on. This type of calculation is called a **group calculation** because each calculation involves groups of records. In this example, the customers of book rep 42 would form one group, the customers of book rep 53 would be a second group, and the customers of book rep 65 would form a third group.

To Use a Calculated Field in a Query

1 CREATE QUERIES | 2 USE CRITERIA | 3 SORT DATA | 4 JOIN TABLES | 5 EXPORT RESULTS
6 PERFORM CALCULATIONS | **7 CREATE CROSSTAB** | 8 CUSTOMIZE NAVIGATION PANE

If you need a calculated field in a query, you enter a name, or alias, for the calculated field, a colon, and then the calculation in one of the columns in the Field row of the design grid for the query. Any fields included in the expression must be enclosed in square brackets ([]). For example, for the total amount, you will type Total Amount:[Amount Paid]+[Current Due] as the expression.

You can type the expression directly into the Field row. The preferred method, however, is to select the column in the Field row and then use the Zoom command on its shortcut menu. When Access displays the Zoom dialog box, you can enter the expression. *Why use the Zoom command? You will not be able to see the entire entry in the Field row, because the space available is not large enough.*

You can use addition (+), subtraction (−), multiplication (*), or division (/) in calculations. If you have multiple calculations in an expression, you can include parentheses to indicate which calculations should be done first.

The following steps create a query that Bavant Publishing might use to obtain financial information on its customers, including the total amount (amount paid + current due), which is a calculated field.

• Create a query with a field list for the Customer table.

• Add the Customer Number, Customer Name, Amount Paid, and Current Due fields to the query.

• Press and hold or right-click the Field row in the first open column in the design grid to display a shortcut menu (Figure 2–63).

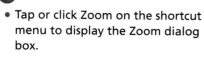

Figure 2–63

2

• Tap or click Zoom on the shortcut menu to display the Zoom dialog box.

• Type `Total Amount:[Amount Paid]+[Current Due]` in the Zoom dialog box (Figure 2–64).

Q&A | Do I always need to put square brackets around field names?
If the field name does not contain spaces, square brackets are technically not required. It is a good practice, however, to get in the habit of using the brackets in field calculations.

Figure 2–64

3

• Tap or click the OK button (Zoom dialog box) to enter the expression (Figure 2–65).

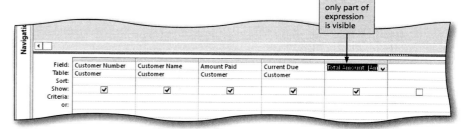

Figure 2–65

4

• Run the query (Figure 2–66).

 Experiment

• Return to Design view and try other expressions. In at least one case, omit the Total Amount and the colon. In at least one case, intentionally misspell a field name. In each case, run the query to see the effect of your changes. When finished, reenter the original expression.

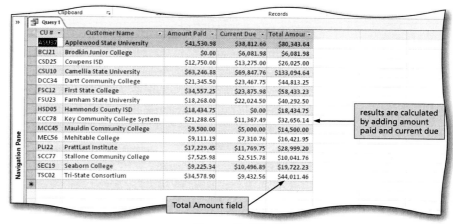

Figure 2–66

Other Ways

1. Press SHIFT+F2

To Change a Caption

In Chapter 1, you changed the caption for a field in a table. When you assigned a caption, Access displayed it in datasheets and forms. If you did not assign a caption, Access displayed the field name. You also can change a caption in a query. Access will display the caption you assign in the query results. When you omitted duplicates, you used the query property sheet. When you change a caption in a query, you use the property sheet for the field. In the property sheet, you can change other properties for the field, such as the format and number of decimal places. The following steps change the caption of the Amount Paid field to Paid and the caption of the Current Due field to Due. ***Why?*** *These changes give shorter, yet very readable, column headings for the fields.* The steps also save the query with a new name.

1

- Return to Design view.
- If necessary, tap or click DESIGN on the ribbon to display the QUERY TOOLS DESIGN tab.
- Tap or click the Amount Paid field in the design grid, and then tap or click the Property Sheet button (QUERY TOOLS DESIGN tab | Show/Hide group) to display the properties for the Amount Paid field.
- Tap or click the Caption box, and then type `Paid` as the caption (Figure 2–67).

Q&A My property sheet looks different. What should I do?
Close the property sheet and repeat this step.

Figure 2–67

2

- Close the property sheet by tapping or clicking the Property Sheet button a second time.

- Tap or click the Current Due field in the design grid, and then tap or click the Property Sheet button (QUERY TOOLS DESIGN tab | Show/Hide group).

- Tap or click the Caption box, and then type Due as the caption.

- Close the Property Sheet by tapping or clicking the Property Sheet button a second time.

- Run the query (Figure 2–68).

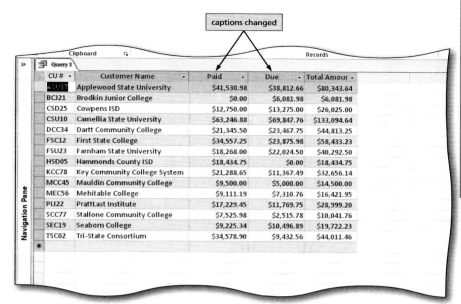

captions changed

CU #	Customer Name	Paid	Due	Total Amour
ASU37	Applewood State University	$41,530.98	$38,812.66	$80,343.64
BCJ21	Brodkin Junior College	$0.00	$6,081.98	$6,081.98
CSD25	Cowpens ISD	$12,750.00	$13,275.00	$26,025.00
CSU10	Camellia State University	$63,246.88	$69,847.76	$133,094.64
DCC34	Dartt Community College	$21,345.50	$23,467.75	$44,813.25
FSC12	First State College	$34,557.25	$23,875.98	$58,433.23
FSU23	Farnham State University	$18,268.00	$22,024.50	$40,292.50
HSD05	Hammonds County ISD	$18,434.75	$0.00	$18,434.75
KCC78	Key Community College System	$21,288.65	$11,367.49	$32,656.14
MCC45	Mauldin Community College	$9,500.00	$5,000.00	$14,500.00
MEC56	Mehitable College	$9,111.19	$7,310.76	$16,421.95
PLI22	PrattLast Institute	$17,229.45	$11,769.75	$28,999.20
SCC77	Stallone Community College	$7,525.98	$2,515.78	$10,041.76
SEC19	Seaborn College	$9,225.34	$10,496.89	$19,722.23
TSC02	Tri-State Consortium	$34,578.90	$9,432.56	$44,011.46

Figure 2–68

3

- Save the query as Ch2q10.

- Close the query.

Other Ways

1. Press and hold or right-click field in design grid, tap or click Properties on shortcut menu

To Calculate Statistics

1 CREATE QUERIES | 2 USE CRITERIA | 3 SORT DATA | 4 JOIN TABLES | 5 EXPORT RESULTS
6 PERFORM CALCULATIONS | **7 CREATE CROSSTAB** | **8 CUSTOMIZE NAVIGATION PANE**

For group calculations, Microsoft Access supports several built-in statistics: COUNT (count of the number of records), SUM (total), AVG (average), MAX (largest value), MIN (smallest value), STDEV (standard deviation), VAR (variance), FIRST (first value), and LAST (last value). These statistics are called aggregate functions. An **aggregate function** is a function that performs some mathematical function against a group of records. To use an aggregate function in a query, you include it in the Total row in the design grid. In order to do so, you must first include the Total row by tapping or clicking the Totals button on the DESIGN tab. *Why? The Total row usually does not appear in the grid.*

The following steps create a new query for the Customer table. The steps include the Total row in the design grid, and then calculate the average amount paid for all customers.

1

- Create a new query with a field list for the Customer table.

- Tap or click the Totals button (QUERY TOOLS DESIGN tab | Show/Hide group) to include the Total row in the design grid.

- Add the Amount Paid field to the query (Figure 2–69).

Figure 2–69

2

- Tap or click the Total row in the Amount Paid column to display the Total arrow.

- Tap or click the Total arrow to display the Total list (Figure 2–70).

Figure 2–70

3

- Tap or click Avg to select the calculation that Access is to perform (Figure 2–71).

Figure 2–71

4

- Run the query (Figure 2–72).

Experiment

- Return to Design view and try other aggregate functions. In each case, run the query to see the effect of your selection. When finished, select Avg once again.

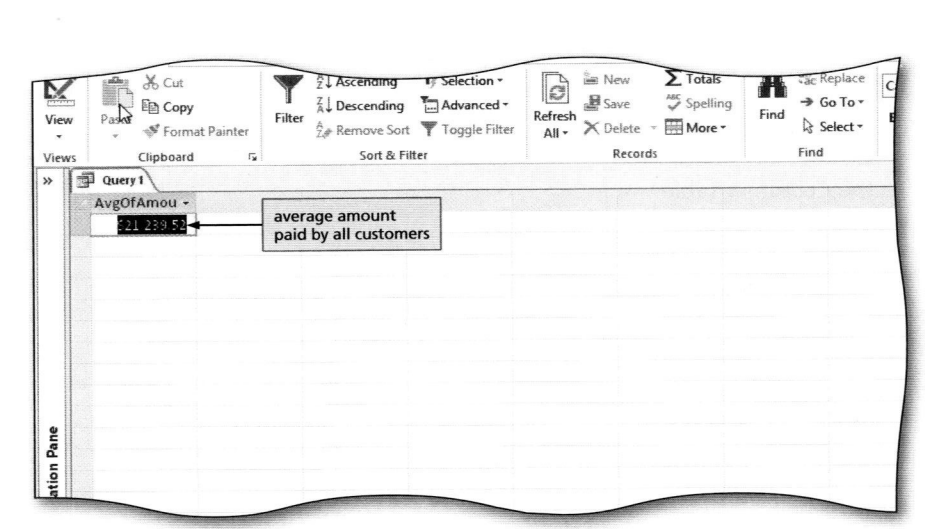

Figure 2–72

To Use Criteria in Calculating Statistics

Why? *Sometimes calculating statistics for all the records in the table is appropriate. In other cases, however, you will need to calculate the statistics for only those records that satisfy certain criteria.* To enter a criterion in a field, first you select Where as the entry in the Total row for the field, and then enter the criterion in the Criteria row. Access uses the word, Where, to indicate that you will enter a criterion. The following steps use this technique to calculate the average amount paid for customers of book rep 42. The steps also save the query with a new name.

- Return to Design view.
- Include the Book Rep Number field in the design grid.
- Tap or click the Total row in the Book Rep Number column.
- Tap or click the Total arrow in the Book Rep Number column to produce a Total list (Figure 2–73).

Figure 2–73

- Tap or click Where to be able to enter a criterion.
- Type 42 as the criterion for the Book Rep Number field (Figure 2–74).

Figure 2–74

- Run the query (Figure 2–75).

- Save the query as Ch2q11.

Figure 2–75

To Use Grouping

Why? Statistics often are used in combination with grouping; that is, statistics are calculated for groups of records. For example, Bavant could calculate the average amount paid for the customers of each book rep, which would require the average for the customers of book rep 42, the average for customers of book rep 53, and so on. **Grouping** means creating groups of records that share some common characteristic. In grouping by Book Rep Number, for example, the customers of book rep 42 would form one group, the customers of book rep 53 would form a second, and the customers of book rep 65 would form a third group. The calculations then are made for each group. To indicate grouping in Access, select Group By as the entry in the Total row for the field to be used for grouping.

The following steps create a query that calculates the average amount paid for customers of each book rep at Bavant Publishing. The steps also save the query with a new name.

①

- Return to Design view and clear the design grid.

- Include the Book Rep Number field in the query.

- Include the Amount Paid field in the query.

- Select Avg as the calculation in the Total row for the Amount Paid field (Figure 2–76).

Q&A Why was it not necessary to change the entry in the Total row for the Book Rep Number field?
Group By, which is the initial entry in the Total row when you add a field, is correct. Thus, you did not need to change the entry.

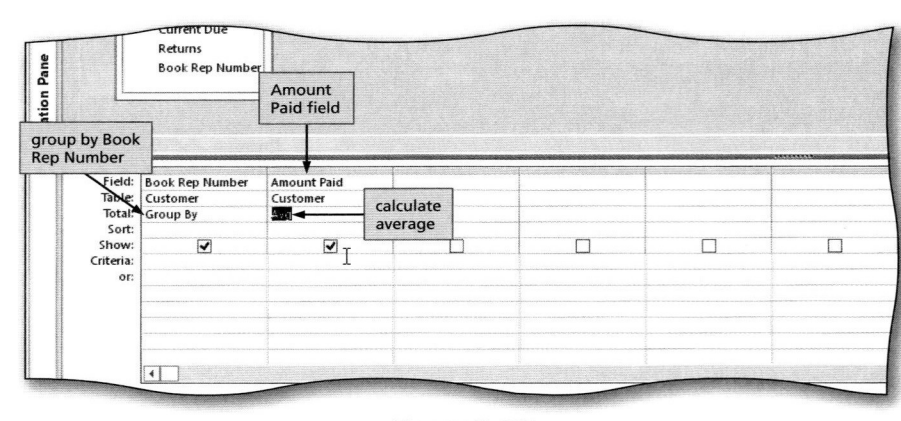

Figure 2–76

②

- Run the query (Figure 2–77).

③

- Save the query as Ch2q12.

- Close the query.

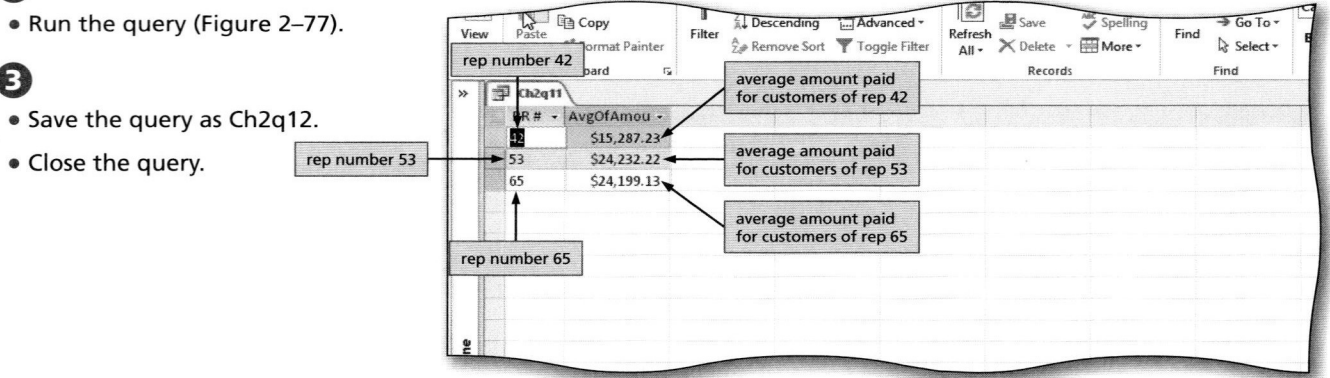

Figure 2–77

Crosstab Queries

A **crosstab query**, or simply, crosstab, calculates a statistic (for example, sum, average, or count) for data that is grouped by two different types of information. One of the types will appear down the side of the resulting datasheet, and the other will appear across the top. Crosstab queries are useful for summarizing data by category or group.

For example, if a query must summarize the sum of the returns grouped by both state and book rep number, you could have states as the row headings, that is, down the side. You could have book rep numbers as the column headings, that is, across the top. The entries within the datasheet represent the total of the returns. Figure 2–78 shows a crosstab in which the total of returns is grouped by both state and book rep number, with states down the left side and book rep numbers across the top. For example, the entry in the row labeled DE and in the column labeled 42 represents the total of the returns by all customers of book rep 42 who are located in Delaware.

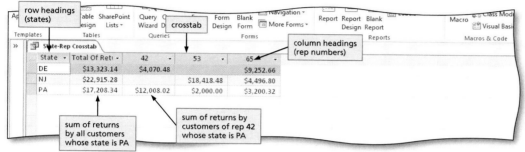

Figure 2–78

How do you know when to use a crosstab query?

If data is to be grouped by two different types of information, you can use a crosstab query. You will need to identify the two types of information. One of the types will form the row headings and the other will form the column headings in the query results.

To Create a Crosstab Query

1 CREATE QUERIES | 2 USE CRITERIA | 3 SORT DATA | 4 JOIN TABLES | 5 EXPORT RESULTS
6 PERFORM CALCULATIONS | **7 CREATE CROSSTAB** | **8 CUSTOMIZE NAVIGATION PANE**

The following steps use the Crosstab Query Wizard to create a crosstab query. *Why? Bavant Publishing wants to group data on returns by two types of information: state and book rep.*

- Tap or click CREATE on the ribbon to display the CREATE tab.
- Tap or click the Query Wizard button (CREATE tab | Queries group) to display the New Query dialog box (Figure 2–79).

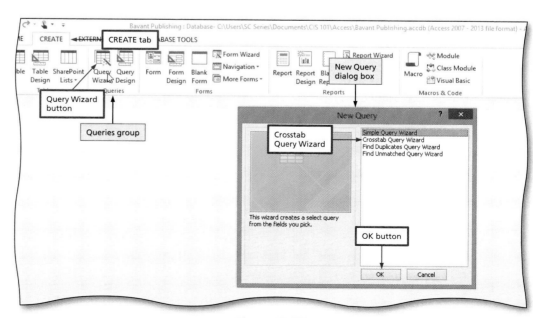

Figure 2–79

2

- Tap or click Crosstab Query Wizard (New Query dialog box).
- Tap or click the OK button to display the Crosstab Query Wizard dialog box (Figure 2–80).

Figure 2–80

3

- With the Tables option button selected, tap or click Table: Customer to select the Customer table, and then tap or click the Next button to display the next Crosstab Query Wizard screen.
- Tap or click the State field, and then tap or click the Add Field button to select the State field for row headings (Figure 2–81).

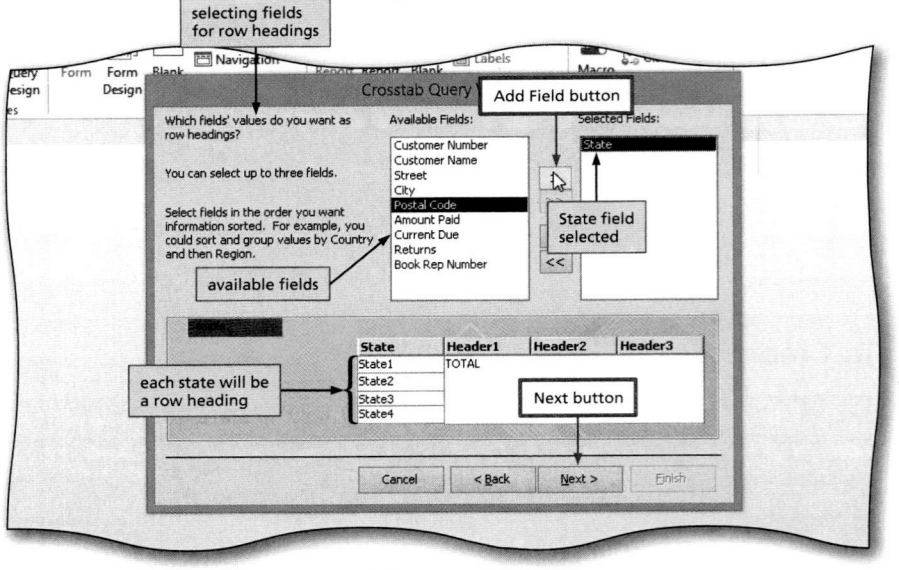

Figure 2–81

4

- Tap or click the Next button to display the next Crosstab Query Wizard screen.
- Tap or click the Book Rep Number field to select the field for column headings (Figure 2–82).

Figure 2–82

5

- Tap or click the Next button to display the next Crosstab Query Wizard screen.

- Tap or click the Returns field to select the field for calculations.

Experiment

- Tap or click other fields. For each field, examine the list of calculations that are available. When finished, tap or click the Returns field again.

- Tap or click Sum to select the calculation to be performed (Figure 2–83).

Q&A My list of functions is different. What did I do wrong?

Either you clicked the wrong field, or the Returns field has the wrong data type. For example, if you mistakenly assigned it the Short Text data type, you would not see Sum in the list of available calculations.

Figure 2–83

6

- Tap or click the Next button to display the next Crosstab Query Wizard screen.

- Erase the text in the name text box and type `State-Rep Crosstab` as the name of the query (Figure 2–84).

7

- If requested to do so by your instructor, name the crosstab query as FirstName LastName Crosstab where FirstName and LastName are your first and last names.

- Tap or click the Finish button to produce the crosstab shown in Figure 2–78 on page AC 119.

- Close the query.

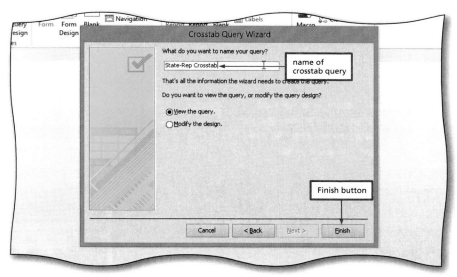

Figure 2–84

Customizing the Navigation Pane

Currently, the entries in the Navigation Pane are organized by object type. That is, all the tables are together, all the queries are together, and so on. You might want to change the way the information is organized. For example, you might want to have the Navigation Pane organized by table, with all the queries, forms, and reports associated with a particular table appearing after the name of the table. You also can use the Search bar to restrict the objects that appear to only those that have a certain collection of characters in their name. For example, if you entered the letters, Cu, only those objects containing Cu somewhere within the name will be included.

BTW

Access Help

At any time while using Access, you can find answers to questions and display information about various topics through Access Help. Used properly, this form of assistance can increase your productivity and reduce your frustrations by minimizing the time you spend learning how to use Access. For instruction about Access Help and exercises that will help you gain confidence in using it, read the Office and Windows chapter at the beginning of this book.

To Customize the Navigation Pane

The following steps change the organization of the Navigation Pane. They also use the Search bar to restrict the objects that appear. *Why? Using the Search bar, you can reduce the number of objects that appear in the Navigation Pane and just show the ones in which you are interested.*

1

• If necessary, tap or click the 'Shutter Bar Open/Close Button' to open the Navigation Pane.

• Tap or click the Navigation Pane arrow to produce the Navigation Pane menu (Figure 2–85).

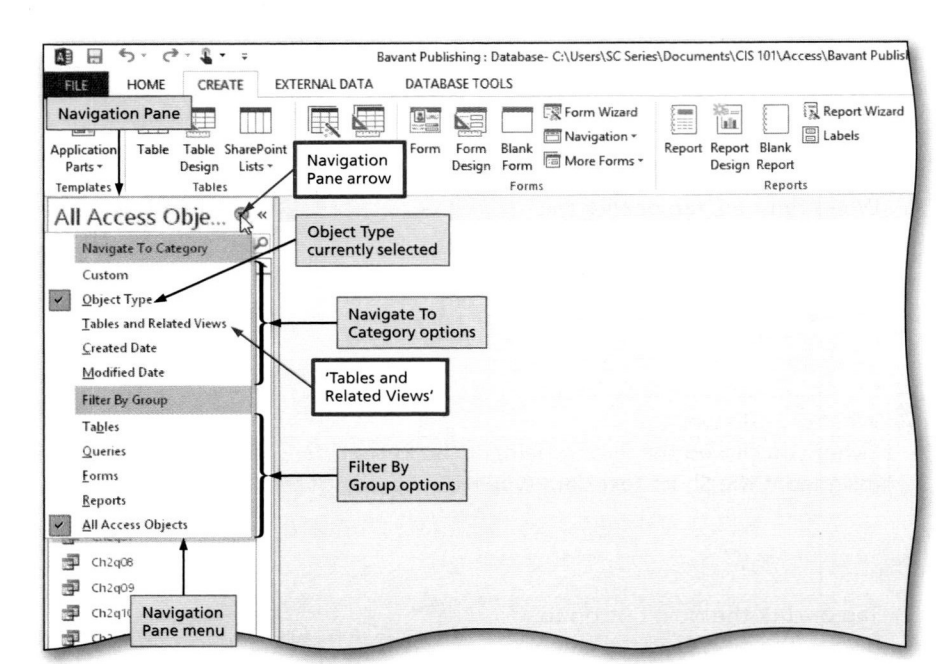

Figure 2–85

2

• Tap or click 'Tables and Related Views' to organize the Navigation Pane by table rather than by the type of object (Figure 2–86).

Figure 2–86

- Tap or click the Navigation Pane arrow to produce the Navigation Pane menu.

- Tap or click Object Type to once again organize the Navigation Pane by object type.

 Experiment

- Select different Navigate To Category options to see the effect of the option. With each option you select, select different Filter By Group options to see the effect of the filtering. When you have finished experimenting, select the 'Object Type Navigate To Category' option and the 'All Access Objects Filter By Group' option.

Figure 2–87

- If the Search bar does not appear, press and hold or right-click the Navigation Pane and tap or click Search Bar on the shortcut menu.

- Tap or click in the Search box to produce an insertion point.

- Type Cu as the search string to restrict the objects displayed to only those containing the desired string (Figure 2–87).

- Tap or click the 'Clear Search String' button to remove the search string and redisplay all objects.

Q&A Did I have to tap or click the button to redisplay all objects? Could I simply have erased the current string to achieve the same result?

You did not have to tap or click the button. You could have used the DELETE or BACKSPACE keys to erase the current search string.

To Sign Out of a Microsoft Account

If you are signed in to a Microsoft account and are using a public computer or otherwise wish to sign out of your Microsoft account, you should sign out of the account from the Account gallery in the Backstage view before exiting Access. Signing out of the account is the safest way to make sure that nobody else can access SkyDrive files or settings stored in your Microsoft account. The following steps sign out of a Microsoft account from Access. For a detailed example of the procedure summarized below, refer to the Office and Windows chapter at the beginning of this book.

1. If you wish to sign out of your Microsoft account, tap or click FILE on the ribbon to open the Backstage view and then tap or click the Account tab to display the Account gallery.

2. Tap or click the Sign out link, which displays the Remove Account dialog box. If a Can't remove Windows accounts dialog box appears instead of the Remove Account dialog box, click the OK button and skip the remaining steps.

Q&A Why does a Can't remove Windows accounts dialog box appear?

If you signed in to Windows using your Microsoft account, then you also must sign out from Windows, rather than signing out from within Access. When you are finished using Windows, be sure to sign out at that time.

BTW
Certification
The Microsoft Office Specialist (MOS) program provides an opportunity for you to obtain a valuable industry credential — proof that you have the Access 2013 skills required by employers. For more information, visit the Certification resource on the Student Companion Site located on www. cengagebrain.com. For detailed instructions about accessing available resources, visit www.cengage.com/ ct/studentdownload or contact your instructor for information about accessing the required files.

BTW
Quick Reference
For a table that lists how to complete the tasks covered in this book using touch gestures, the mouse, ribbon, shortcut menu, and keyboard, see the Quick Reference Summary at the back of this book, or visit the Quick Reference resource on the Student Companion Site located on www.cengagebrain.com. For detailed instructions about accessing available resources, visit www.cengage.com/ct/studentdownload or contact your instructor for information about accessing the required files.

3 Tap or click the Yes button (Remove Account dialog box) to sign out of your Microsoft account on this computer.

Q&A Should I sign out of Windows after signing out of my Microsoft account?
When you are finished using the computer, you should sign out of your account for maximum security.

4 Tap or click the Back button in the upper-left corner of the Backstage view to return to the database.

To Exit Access

The following steps exit Access.

1 Tap or click the Close button on the right side of the title bar to close the open database, if there is one, and exit Access.

2 If a Microsoft Access dialog box appears, tap or click the Save button to save any changes made to the database since the last save.

Chapter Summary

In this chapter you have learned to create queries, enter fields, enter criteria, use text and numeric data in queries, use wildcards, use compound criteria, create parameter queries, sort data in queries, join tables in queries, perform calculations in queries, and create crosstab queries. You also learned to create a report and a form that used a query, to export a query, and to customize the Navigation Pane. The items listed below include all the new Access skills you have learned in this chapter, with tasks grouped by activity.

Calculations in Queries
Use a Calculated Field in a Query (AC 112)
Calculate Statistics (AC 115)
Use Criteria in Calculating Statistics (AC 117)
Use Grouping (AC 118)

Crosstab Query
Create a Crosstab Query (AC 119)

Criteria in Queries
Use Text Data in a Criterion (AC 81)
Use a Wildcard (AC 83)
Use Criteria for a Field Not Included in the Results (AC 85)
Use a Number in a Criterion (AC 89)
Use a Comparison Operator in a Criterion (AC 90)
Use a Compound Criterion Involving AND (AC 91)
Use a Compound Criterion Involving OR (AC 92)

Design Grid
Clear the Design Grid (AC 93)

Export Data
Export Data to Excel (AC 107)
Export Data to Word (AC 110)
Export Data to a Text File (AC 110)

Form Creation
Create a Form for a Query (AC 105)

Join Queries
Join Tables (AC 100)
Change Join Properties (AC 101)
Restrict the Records in a Join (AC 111)

Navigation Pane
Customize the Navigation Pane (AC 122)

Parameter Query
Create and View a Parameter Query (AC 87)
Use a Parameter Query (AC 88)

Query Creation
Create a Query in Design View (AC 78)
Add Fields to the Design Grid (AC 79)
Change a Caption (AC 114)

Report Creation
Create a Report from a Query (AC 103)

Sort in Queries
Sort Data in a Query (AC 94)
Omit Duplicates (AC 94)
Sort on Multiple Keys (AC 96)
Create a Top-Values Query (AC 98)

What decisions will you need to make when creating queries?

Use these guidelines as you complete the assignments in this chapter and create your own queries outside of this class.

1. Identify the fields by examining the question or request to determine which fields from the tables in the database are involved.

2. Identify restrictions or the conditions that records must satisfy to be included in the results.

3. Determine whether special order is required.

 a) Determine the sort key(s).

 b) If using two sort keys, determine the major and minor key.

 c) Determine sort order. If there are no words to imply a particular order, you would typically use Ascending.

 d) Determine restrictions, such as excluding duplicates.

4. Determine whether more than one table is required.

 a) Determine which tables to include.

 b) Determine the matching fields.

 c) Determine whether sorting is required.

 d) Determine restrictions.

 e) Determine join properties.

5. Determine whether calculations are required.

 a) For individual record calculations, determine the calculation and a name for the calculated field.

 b) For group calculations, determine the calculation as well as the field to be used for grouping.

6. If data is to be summarized and the data is to be grouped by two different types of information, create a crosstab query.

How should you submit solutions to questions in the assignments identified with a ✻ symbol?

Every assignment in this book contains one or more questions identified with a ✻ symbol. These questions require you to think beyond the assigned database. Present your solutions to the questions in the format required by your instructor. Possible formats may include one or more of these options: write the answer; create a document that contains the answer; present your answer to the class; discuss your answer in a group; record the answer as audio or video using a webcam, smartphone, or portable media player; or post answers on a blog, wiki, or website.

Apply Your Knowledge

Reinforce the skills and apply the concepts you learned in this chapter.

Using Wildcards in a Query, Creating a Parameter Query, Joining Tables, and Creating a Report

Instructions: Start Access. Open the Apply Cosmetics Naturally database that you modified in Apply Your Knowledge in Chapter 1 on page AC 65. (If you did not complete the exercise, see your instructor for a copy of the modified database.)

Perform the following tasks:

1. Create a query for the Customer table and add the Customer Number, Customer Name, Amount Paid, and Balance fields to the design grid. Add a criterion to find all customers whose names start with the letter C. Run the query and then save it as Apply 2 Step 1 Query.

2. Create a query for the Customer table and add the Customer Number, Customer Name, Amount Paid, and Sales Rep Number fields to the design grid. Sort the records in descending order by Amount Paid. Add a criterion for the Sales Rep Number field that allows the user to enter a different sales rep each time the query is run. Run the query and enter 41 as the sales rep number to test the query. Save the query as Apply 2 Step 2 Query.

Continued >

Apply Your Knowledge *continued*

3. Create a query that joins the Sales Rep and Customer tables. Add the Sales Rep Number, Last Name, and First Name fields from the Sales Rep table and the Customer Number and Customer Name fields from the Customer table to the design grid. Sort the records in ascending order by Customer Number within Sales Rep Number. All sales reps should appear in the result, even if they currently have no customers. Run the query and save it as Rep-Customer Query.

4. Create the report shown in Figure 2–88. The report uses the Rep-Customer Query.

Rep-Customer Report

SR #	Last Name	First Name	CU #	Customer Name
34	Johnson	Bobbi	AS24	Ashley's Salon
34	Johnson	Bobbi	DB14	Della's Beauty Place
34	Johnson	Bobbi	EY07	Environmentally Yours
34	Johnson	Bobbi	NC25	Nancy's Place
34	Johnson	Bobbi	TT21	Tan and Tone
39	Gutaz	Nicholas	BL15	Blondie's on Main
39	Gutaz	Nicholas	CY12	Curlin Yoga Studio
39	Gutaz	Nicholas	JN34	Just Natural
39	Gutaz	Nicholas	LB20	Le Beauty
39	Gutaz	Nicholas	UR23	U R Beautiful
41	Orlon	Jake	BA35	Beauty for All
41	Orlon	Jake	CL09	Casual Looks
41	Orlon	Jake	FN19	Fitness Counts
41	Orlon	Jake	RD03	Rose's Day Spa
41	Orlon	Jake	TW56	The Workout Place
55	Sinson	Terry		

Figure 2–88

5. If requested to do so by your instructor, rename the Rep-Customer Report in the Navigation Pane as LastName-Customer Report where LastName is your last name.

6. Submit the revised database in the format specified by your instructor.

7. ✹ What criteria would you enter in the Customer Name field if you wanted to find all customers who had the word Beauty somewhere in their name?

Extend Your Knowledge

Extend the skills you learned in this chapter and experiment with new skills. You may need to use Help to complete the assignment.

Creating Crosstab Queries Using Criteria, and Exporting a Query

Note: To complete this assignment, you will be required to use the Data Files for Students. Visit www.cengage.com/ct/studentdownload for detailed instructions or contact your instructor for information about accessing the required files.

Instructions: Start Access. Open the Extend Janitorial Services database. Janitorial Services is a small business that provides janitorial services to commercial businesses. The owner has created an Access database in which to store information about the customers she serves and the cleaning staff she employs. You will create the crosstab query shown in Figure 2–89. You also will query the database using specified criteria, and export a query.

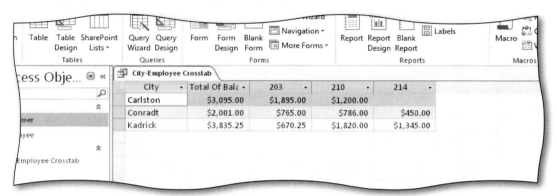

Figure 2–89

Perform the following tasks:

1. Create the crosstab query shown in Figure 2–89. The crosstab groups the total of customers' balance by city and employee number.

2. Create a query to find all customers who are not located in Kadrick. Include the Customer Number, Customer Name, and Balance fields in the query results. Save the query as Extend 2 Step 2 Query.

3. Create a query to find all employees whose first name is either Timmy or Tammy. Include the Employee Number, First Name, and Last Name in the query results. Save the query as Extend 2 Step 3 Query.

4. Create a query to find all customers where the employee number is either 210 or 214 and the balance is greater than $1,000.00. Include the Customer Number, Customer Name, Balance, and Employee Number fields in the design grid. Use the IN operator in your query design. Save the query as Extend 2 Step 4 Query.

5. Export the City-Employee Crosstab as a Word file with the name City-Employee Crosstab.rtf and save the export steps.

6. Open the Customer table and change the balance for customer AT23 to $755.

7. If requested to do so by your instructor, change the customer name of customer AT23 from Atlas Repair to Last Name Repair where Last Name is your last name.

8. Use the saved export steps to export the City-Employee Crosstab again. When asked if you want to replace the existing file, click Yes.

9. Submit the revised database and the exported RTF file in the format specified by your instructor.

10. ✳ How would you create the query in Step 4 without using the IN operator?

Analyze, Correct, Improve

Analyze a database, correct all errors, and improve the design.

Correcting Errors in the Table Structure

Note: To complete this assignment, you will be required to use the Data Files for Students. Visit www.cengage.com/ct/studentdownload for detailed instructions or contact your instructor for information about accessing the required files.

Instructions: Analyze Fitness is a database maintained by the Sports Science department at your university. Graduate students work with local residents as personal trainers to earn the necessary hours required for certification. The department chair has asked you to correct and improve two of the queries she created. Start Access and open the Analyze Fitness database from the Data Files for Students.

1. Correct The query shown in Figure 2–90 returns 0 results, and the department chair knows that is not correct. She wants to find all customers who live on Levick. Open the query in Design view, correct the errors, and save as Corrected Criteria Query.

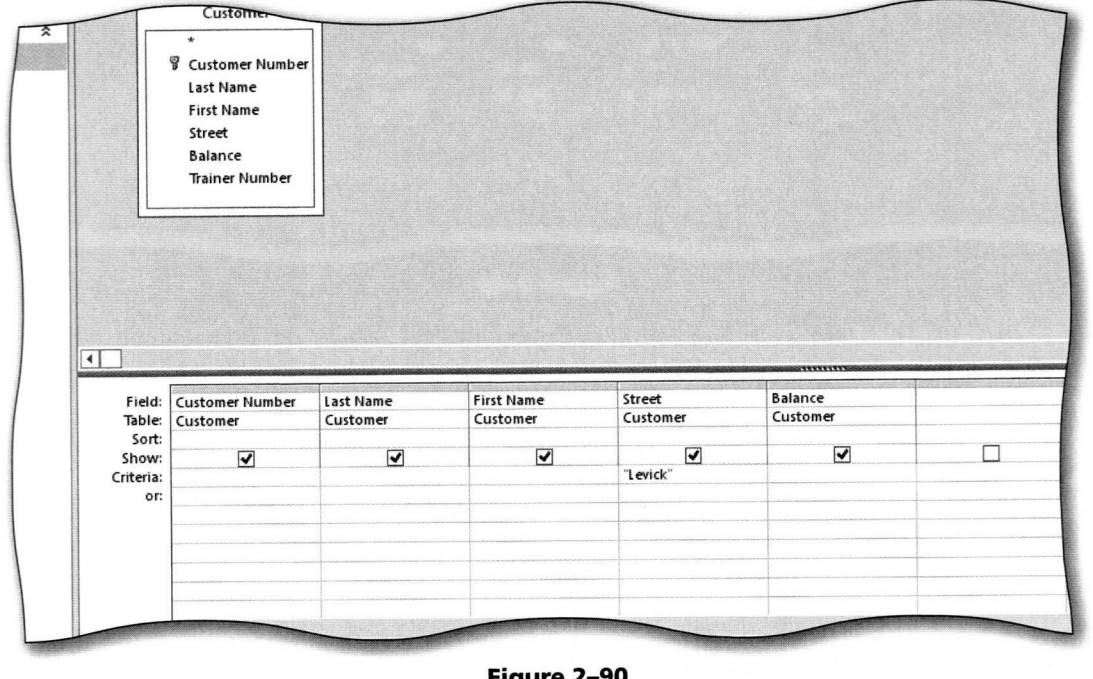

Figure 2–90

2. Improve The department chair also created the query shown in Figure 2–91. The query is sorted correctly, but she wanted Trainer Number to appear as the last field in the query result. She also would like to change the caption for the Balance field to Due. Improve the query to display the results in the desired order. Save the query as Improved Sort Query. Submit the revised database in the format specified by your instructor.

3. ✺ Why does the query shown in Figure 2–90 return 0 results?

Figure 2-91

In the Labs

Design, create, modify, and/or use a database following the guidelines, concepts, and skills presented in this chapter. Labs are listed in order of increasing difficulty. Labs 1 and 2, which increase in difficulty, require you to create solutions based on what you learned in the chapter; Lab 3 requires you to create a solution, which uses cloud and web technologies, by learning and investigating on your own from general guidance.

Lab 1: Querying the Dartt Offsite Services Database

Problem: The management of Dartt Offsite Services has determined a number of questions it wants the database management system to answer. You must obtain the answers to these questions.

Note: Use the database modified in Lab 1 of Chapter 1 on page AC 68 for this assignment, or see your instructor for information on accessing the required files.

Instructions: Perform the following tasks:
1. Start Access. Open the Lab 1 Dartt Offsite Services database and create a new query for the Client table. Add the Client Number, Client Name, Amount Paid, Balance Due, and Service Rep Number fields to the design grid, and restrict the query results to only those clients where the service rep number is 37. Save the query as Lab 2-1 Step 1 Query.
2. Create a query for the Client table that includes the Client Number, Client Name, and Balance Due fields for all clients located in North Carolina (NC) with a balance due less than $1,000.00. Save the query as Lab 2-1 Step 2 Query.
3. Create a query for the Client table that includes the Client Number, Client Name, Street, City, and State field for all clients whose names begin with Ba. Save the query as Lab 2-1 Step 3 Query.

Continued >

In the Labs *continued*

4. Create a query for the Client table that lists all cities in ascending order. Each city should appear only once. Save the query as Lab 2-1 Step 4 Query.

5. Create a query for the Client table that allows the user to type the name of the desired city when the query is run. The query results should display the Client Number, Client Name, Balance Due, and Amount Paid fields. Test the query by searching for those records where the client is located in Austin. Save the query as Lab 2-1 Step 5 Query.

6. Create a query for the Service Rep table that includes the First Name, Last Name, and Start Date for all service reps who started after May 1, 2013. Save the query as Lab 2-1 Step 6 Query.

7. Create a query that joins the Service Rep and Client tables. Include the Service Rep Number, Last Name, and First Name from the Service Rep table. Include the Client Number, Client Name, and Amount Paid from the Client table. Sort the records in ascending order by service rep's last name and client name. All service reps should appear in the result even if they currently have no clients. Save the query as Lab 2-1 Step 7 Query.

8. Open the Lab 2-1 Step 7 Query in Design view and remove the Service Rep table from the query. Add the Balance Due field to the design grid. Calculate the total of the balance and amount paid amounts. Assign the alias Total Amount to the calculated field. Change the caption for the Amount Paid field to Paid and the caption for the Balance Due field to Owe. Save the query as Lab 2-1 Step 8 Query.

9. Create a query for the Client table to display the total amount paid amount for service rep 24. Save the query as Lab 2-1 Step 9 Query.

10. Create a query for the Client table to display the average balance amount for each service rep. Save the query as Lab 2-1 Step 10 Query.

11. Create the crosstab query shown in Figure 2–92. The crosstab groups the average of clients' amount paid amounts by state and service rep number. Save the crosstab as State-Service Rep Crosstab.

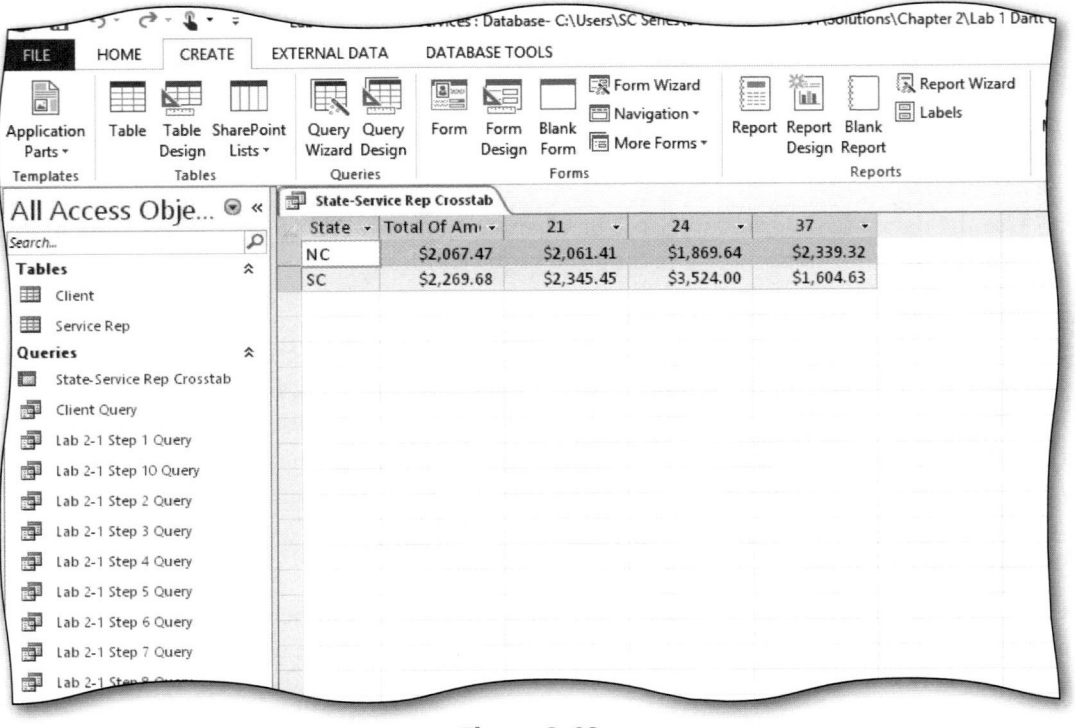

Figure 2–92

12. If requested to do so by your instructor, open the Lab 2-1 Step 1 query and change the caption for the Service Rep Number field to your last name.

13. Submit the revised database in the format specified by your instructor.

14. ✹ How would you modify the query in Step 7 to include only service reps that currently have clients?

Lab 2: **Querying the Tennis Logos Database**

Problem: The manager of Tennis Logos has determined a number of questions he wants the database management system to answer. You must obtain answers to these questions.

Note: Use the database created in Lab 2 of Chapter 1 on page AC 69 for this assignment or see your instructor for information on accessing the required files.

Instructions: Perform the following tasks:

1. Start Access. Open the Lab 2 Tennis Logos database and create a query for the Item table that includes all fields and all records in the Item table. Name the query Lab 2-2 Step 1 Query.

2. Create a query for the Item table that includes the Item Number, Description, Wholesale Price, and Supplier Code fields for all records where the supplier code is SD. Save the query as Lab 2-2 Step 2 Query.

3. Create a query for the Item table that includes the Item Number and Description fields for all items where the description starts with C. Save the query as Lab 2-2 Step 3 Query.

4. Create a query for the Item table that includes the Item Number and Description for all items with a Base Cost greater than $10.00. Save the query as Lab 2-2 Step 4 Query.

5. Create a query for the Item table that includes the Item Number, Description, and Wholesale Price fields for all items with a Wholesale Price between $1.00 and $4.00. Save the query as Lab 2-2 Step 5 Query.

6. Create a query for the Item table that includes the Item Number, Description, On Hand, and Wholesale Price fields for all items where the number on hand is less than 100 and the wholesale price is less than $3.00. Save the query as Lab 2-2 Step 6 Query.

7. Create a query for the Item table that includes the Item Number, Description, Wholesale Price, and Supplier Code for all items that have a Wholesale Price greater than $10.00 or a Supplier Code of LM. Save the query as Lab 2-2 Step 7 Query.

8. Create a query that joins the Supplier and the Item tables. Include the Supplier Code and Supplier Name from the Supplier table and the Item Number, Description, Wholesale Price, and Base Cost fields from the Item table. Sort the query in ascending order by Supplier Code and Description. Save the query as Supplier-Item Query.

9. Create a form for the Supplier-Item Query. Save the form as Supplier-Item Form.

10. If requested to do so by your instructor, rename the form in the Navigation Pane as LastName-Item Form where LastName is your last name.

11. Create the report shown in Figure 2–93. The report uses the Supplier-Item Query but does not use all the fields in the query.

12. Create a query for the Item table that includes the Item Number, Description, Base Cost, and Wholesale Price. Calculate the difference between Base Cost and Wholesale Price (Base Cost – Wholesale Price). Assign the alias Cost Difference to the calculated field. Save the query as Lab 2-2 Step 12 Query.

Continued >

In the Labs *continued*

Supplier-Item Report

Supplier Name	Description	Wholesale	Base Cost
Last Merchandisers	Baseball Cap	$4.87	$6.10
Last Merchandisers	Cotton Visor	$4.59	$5.74
Last Merchandisers	Foam Visor	$0.79	$1.00
Last Merchandisers	V-Neck Pullover	$13.60	$15.75
Last Merchandisers	V-Neck Vest	$20.85	$25.02
Pratt Clothing	Crew Sweatshirt	$7.29	$8.75
Pratt Clothing	Crew T-Shirt	$2.81	$3.38
Pratt Clothing	Fleece Vest	$28.80	$34.50
Pratt Clothing	Golf Shirt	$10.06	$12.35
Pratt Clothing	Windbreaker	$15.17	$18.20
Pratt Clothing	Zip Hoodie	$16.67	$20.04
Scryps Distributors	Drink Holder	$0.82	$1.07
Scryps Distributors	Sports Bottle	$1.04	$1.35
Scryps Distributors	Tote Bag	$1.26	$1.75
Scryps Distributors	Travel Mug	$2.47	$3.50

Figure 2–93

13. Create a query for the Item table that displays the average Wholesale Price and the average Base Cost of all items. Save the query as Lab 2-2 Step 13 Query.

14. Submit the revised database in the format specified by your instructor.

15. ✳ There are two ways to create the query in step 1. What are they? Which one did you use?

Lab 3: Expand Your World: Cloud and Web Technologies
Creating Queries, Customizing the Navigation Pane, and Using the Excel Web App

Problem: Shopper is a small business that does personal shopping for clients. You will create two queries for the owner, customize the Navigation Pane, export a query in CSV format, open the exported file, and then modify the file using the Excel Web app.

Note: To complete this assignment, you will be required to use the Data Files for Students. Visit www.cengage.com/ct/studentdownload for detailed instructions or contact your instructor for information about accessing the required files.

Instructions: Perform the following tasks:
1. Open the Lab 3 Shopper database. Create and save a query that joins the Shopper and Client tables. Include the Last Name and First Name from the Shopper table and the Client Number, Last Name, First Name, and Balance fields from the Client table. Sort the query by shopper Last Name and Client Number.

2. Create and save a query for the Client table. The query result should display the Last Name, First Name, Amount Paid, Balance, and Shopper Number in that order. Sort the query by Last Name within Shopper Number.

3. Change the organization of the Navigation Pane so that all objects associated with the Client table are grouped together and all objects associated with the Shopper table are grouped together.

4. Export the query you created in Step 2 above as a CSV file. Do not save the export steps.

5. Upload the CSV file to your SkyDrive and open the file in the Excel Web app.

6. Delete the Shopper Number column and resize the remaining columns.

7. If requested to do so by your instructor, change the last name and first name of the first client to your last name and first name.

8. Save and close the Excel workbook.

9. Submit the revised database and Excel workbook in the format specified by your instructor.

10. ✺ Study the query result from Step 2 above. What do you notice about the first name and last name field headings? Why do they appear as they do?

✺ Consider This: Your Turn

Apply your creative thinking and problem solving skills to design and implement a solution.

1: Querying the Craft Database

Personal/Academic

Instructions: Open the Craft database you created in Chapter 1 on page AC 73. If you did not create this database, contact your instructor for information about accessing the required files.

Part 1: Use the concepts and techniques presented in this chapter to create queries for the following. Save each query.

 a. Find the item number and description of all items that contain the word, Rack.

 b. Find the item number and description of all items made by students with a student code of 3962 or 7568.

 c. Find the item number, description, and price of all items that have a price between $20.00 and $40.00.

 d. Find the total price (price * on hand) of each item available for sale. Show the item number, description, price, on hand, and total price in the result. Change the caption for the On Hand field to Quantity.

 e. Find the seller of each item. Show the student's last name and first name as well as the item number, description, price, and on hand. Sort the results by description within student last name.

 f. Create a form based on the query you created in Step e.

 g. Determine the average price of items grouped by student code.

 h. Determine the two most expensive items for sale. Show the description and price.

Submit your assignment in the format specified by your instructor.

Part 2: ✺ You made several decisions while creating the queries in this assignment, including the query in Step b. What was the rationale behind your decisions? There are two ways to create the query in Step b. What are they? Which one did you use?

Continued >

Consider This: Your Turn *continued*

2: Querying the Mums Landscaping Database
Professional

Instructions: Open the Mums Landscaping database you created in Chapter 1 on page AC 73. If you did not create this database, contact your instructor for information about accessing the required files.

Part 1: Use the concepts and techniques presented in this chapter to create queries for the following. Save each query.

 a. Find all supervisors who started prior to January 1, 2013. Show the supervisor's first name, last name, and hourly rate.

 b. Find the customer name and address of all customers located on Cantor.

 c. Find the customer number, customer name, amount paid, and balance for all customers whose amount paid is $0.00 or whose balance is $0.00.

 d. Create a parameter query for the Customer table that will allow the user to enter a different postal code each time the query is run. The user should see all fields in the query result.

 e. Create a crosstab query that groups the total of customer's balance amounts by postal code and supervisor number.

 f. Find the supervisor for each customer. List the supervisor number, last name, first name, customer number, customer name, and balance. Sort the results by customer number within supervisor number.

 g. Open the query you created in Step f above and restrict retrieval to only those customers whose balance is greater than $500.00.

 h. Estimate the weekly pay for each supervisor by multiplying the hourly rate by 40. Show the supervisor's first name, last name, hourly rate, and weekly pay.

Submit your assignment in the format specified by your instructor.

Part 2: ⊛ You made several decisions while creating the queries in this assignment, including the calculation in Step h above. What was the rationale behind your decisions, and how could you modify the query in Step h if the Supervisor table included a field called Hours Worked in which the actual hours worked was stored?

3: Creating Queries to Analyze Data
Research and Collaboration

Part 1: Examine a website that contains weather data, such as weather.com or Bing weather, and, as a team, select 30 cities of interest in your state or province. Create a database that contains one table and has the following fields: City, State or Province, High Temp, Low Temp, and Conditions. Use standard weather terms for the Conditions field, such as rainy, snowy, cloudy, clear, and so on. Create queries that do the following:

 a. Display the five cities with the highest high temperature.

 b. Display the five cities with the lowest low temperature.

 c. Display the average high and low temperatures for all cities.

 d. Display the average high and low temperatures for all cities where the conditions were clear.

 e. Calculate the difference between the high and low temperatures for each city.

 f. Display the high and low temperatures for each city in both Fahrenheit and Celsius.

Submit your assignment in the format specified by your instructor.

Part 2: ☀ You made several decisions while creating the queries in this assignment, including the grouping in Steps c and d and the calculations in Steps e and f. What was the rationale behind your decisions? How would you modify the query in Step d above to show the average high and low temperatures in cities grouped by Condition?

Learn Online

Reinforce what you learned in this chapter with games, exercises, training, and many other online activities and resources.

Student Companion Site Reinforcement activities and resources are available at no additional cost on www.cengagebrain.com. Visit www.cengage.com/ct/studentdownload for detailed instructions about accessing the resources available at the Student Companion Site.

SAM Put your skills into practice with SAM! If you have a SAM account, go to www.cengage.com/sam2013 to access SAM assignments for this chapter.

Index

3-D pie charts, adding, EX 38–40

A

Access, **OFF 63**
See also databases
date format, AC 90
exiting, AC 24, AC 56
exporting data to Excel, AC 107–109
exporting data to Word, AC 110
Help, AC 42, AC 121
importing data from other
 applications into, AC 32–37
introduction to, OFF 63–64
opening databases from, AC 77
running, AC 76–77
running in Windows 7, Windows 8,
 AC 6
starting, OFF 63, AC 24–25
unique elements of, OFF 64
views, AC 49
Access window, AC 7–8
Access work area, **OFF 64**, **AC 8**
Account gallery, EX 53
accounting number format, EX 32,
 EX 33, EX 97, EX 99
accounts
 signing in to Microsoft, OFF 37–38
 signing out of Microsoft, WD 45,
 PPT 55, PPT 125, EX 53,
 EX 117–118, AC 55, AC 123–124
acknowledging all sources, WD 78
Acrobat Reader, PPT 121
actions, undoing and redoing,
 WD 24–25
active cell, **OFF 59**, OFF 60, EX 6
Active Directory Synchronization,
 CLD 8
ad hoc relationships, AC 99
adding
 See also inserting
 citations, WD 88–91
 criteria to join queries, AC 111–112
 fields to design grid, AC 79–80
 picture borders, PPT 88–90
 pie charts to worksheets, EX 37–40
 records to tables, AC 20–23
 records to tables containing data,
 AC 26–27
 shapes to slides, PPT 92–93,
 PPT 94–95
 slide transitions, PPT 45–47,
 PPT 119–120
 totals to reports, AC 53
 words to dictionary, EX 109
additions to documents, WD 46
address bar, folder windows, OFF 27

Adobe Reader, WD 51, WD 120,
 PPT 52, EX 45, **AC 29**, AC 107
Adobe Systems, WD 51, EX 45
aggregate function, **AC 115**
alignment
 centering. *See* centering
 of numbers in cells, EX 13
 right-aligning paragraphs, WD 75
 text in cells, EX 11
All Caps effect, PPT 9
American Psychological Association
 (APA), **WD 66**, WD 88
 documentation style, WD 68
AND criterion, **AC 91**
AND operator, **AC 92**
animation effects, transition, PPT 46
antivirus programs, WD 33
APA Appendix, WD 66
APA documentation style, WD 68
App bar, **OFF 8**
Apple iPads, access to Office 365,
 CLD 8
Apple iPhones, access to Office 365,
 CLD 8
Apply, Apply to All buttons, PPT 119
apps, **OFF 3**
 exiting Office, with one document
 open, OFF 42–43
 importing data from other
 applications into Access, AC 32–37
 Microsoft Office 2013, OFF 9
 pinning, unpinning, OFF 8
 running, OFF 63
 running from File Explorer, OFF 57–59
 running from Start screen,
 OFF 11–12
 running using Search box, OFF 46–48
 running using Start menu using
 Windows 7, OFF 12
 switching between Start screen and,
 OFF 13
 switching from one to another,
 OFF 30–31
arithmetic operations, EX 75
arithmetic operators
 multiplication, EX 74
 subtraction, EX 78
 summary of (table), EX 75
arranging slides, PPT 42
ascending sort order, AC 94, AC 96
assignments, OFF 83
asterisk (*)
 arithmetic operator, EX 74
 wildcard, **AC 83**
authority of sources, WD 78
Auto Fill Options button, EX 79
AutoCalculate area, **EX 48**, EX 48–49
AutoComplete feature, WD 78

AutoCorrect
 creating entries, WD 85–87
 described, **WD 84**
AutoCorrect button, EX 109
AutoCorrect dialog box, WD 87
AutoCorrect feature, **EX 9**, AC 23
AutoCorrect Options, EX 79
AutoCorrect Options button, **WD 85**
AutoFill Options button, EX 17
AutoIncrement fields, AC 9
automatic corrections, WD 87
automatic page breaks, **WD 101**
automatically updated properties,
 WD 44, **PPT 48**, **EX 44**, **AC 54**
AutoNumber fields, AC 9
AVERAGE function, EX 81,
 EX 86–87
AVG function, AC 115, AC 116

B

background colors
 changing, EX 93–94
 changing Read mode, WD 121–122
background repagination, **WD 101**
backgrounds
 formatting slide, PPT 108–112
 printing, PPT 122
backing up, **AC 56**
 databases, AC 56–57
 with different name, AC 58
Backstage view, **OFF 31**
 closing Office files using, OFF 53–54
 creating new Office documents from,
 OFF 51–52
 opening, WD 9
backup copy, **AC 56**
best fit, **EX 103**
BETWEEN operator, **AC 92**
bevel effects, WD 40, PPT 90–91
bibliographical list, **WD 106**
 creating, WD 106–107
 updating fields, WD 110
bibliography
 described, **WD 105**
 style, changing, WD 89–91
Blackberry phones, access to
 Office 365, CLD 8
blue glow effects, PPT 90–91
body copy, **WD 11**
bold
 described, **WD 29**, WD 30
 text in cells, EX 26
bolding text, PPT 21
borders
 adding page, WD 41–42
 adding picture, PPT 88–90

changing color of, PPT 89–90
troubleshooting printing, WD 52
brightness, **PPT 87**
brochures, creating, OFF 70
BTWs, OFF 4
bullet characters, PPT 16, PPT 19
bulleted lists, **WD 23**, **PPT 17**
 adding slides with, PPT 15–16
 creating text slide with multilevel,
 PPT 17–22
bulleted paragraphs, WD 14,
 WD 23–24
Bullets gallery, WD 24
business teams using Office 365 in,
 CLD 9
buttons, mouse, OFF 4

C

calculated field, **AC 112**, AC 113
calculating
 statistics, AC 115–116, AC 117
 sums, EX 14–15
 using formulas. *See* formulas
calculations
 with Access, AC 112
 using calculated fields in queries,
 AC 112–113
calendars, Office 365, CLD 7,
 CLD 10
Calibri font, WD 18, EX 23, EX 103
Cambria font, EX 25–26
Can't remove Microsoft accounts
 dialog box, PPT 55
captions
 changing field, AC 114–115
 described, **AC 10**
case, changing of selected text,
 WD 19
category names, **EX 38**
cell references, **OFF 59**
 color-coded, EX 74
 Excel's adjustments to, EX 88
 relative, **EX 78**
 verifying formulas using Range
 Finder, EX 89
cell styles, applying, EX 95
cells, **OFF 59**
 adjusting widths, EX 34
 bold text, EX 26
 centering entries across columns by
 merging, EX 29–30
 changing font color, EX 28
 changing styles, EX 24–25
 checking spelling, EX 109
 clearing entries, formatting, EX 52
 copying range of, across columns to
 adjacent ranges, EX 87–88

copying to adjacent cells in row,
 EX 16–18
 correcting errors after entering data
 into, EX 50–51
 entering text, EX 7–8
 errors in formulas, EX 79
 formatting dates and centering data
 in, EX 96
 formatting rows using cell styles,
 EX 30–32
 hiding, EX 104
 increasing font size in entries, EX 27
 number alignment in, EX 13
 selecting, EX 6
 selecting using Name box, EX 35–36
 selection commands (table), EX 36
 splitting, EX 30
 text alignment in, EX 11
 undoing last entry, EX 51
centered, **WD 15**
centering
 cell entries across columns by
 merging, EX 29–30
 data in cells, EX 96
 page contents vertically, WD 43–44
 paragraphs, WD 15, WD 33
 text, WD 106
chapter roadmaps, OFF 2
character formatting, **WD 13**
character widths, WD 11
characters
 bullet, PPT 16, PPT 19
 color, PPT 10
 formatting, WD 13–14
 formatting in presentations,
 PPT 10–15
 formatting single vs. multiple, WD 16
 keyboard shortcuts for (table),
 WD 80
chart sheet, **EX 37**
Chart Styles gallery, EX 40
charts, **OFF 55**
 adding styles to, EX 40
 moving to new sheets, EX 41–42
 pie, adding to worksheets, EX 37–39
circles in Shapes gallery, PPT 94
circular reference, **EX 73**
citations
 described, adding, WD 88–91
 editing, WD 98–99
 inserting placeholder, WD 93–94,
 WD 101
clearing
 design grid, AC 93
 worksheets, worksheet entries,
 EX 52–53
Click and Type, **WD 79**
click mouse operations, OFF 5
Click-to-Run, **CLD 6**

clip, **PPT 30**
Clip Organizer, PPT 30
clips, adding to slides, PPT 30
closing
 all documents, EX 53
 database tables, AC 20, AC 24
 databases without exiting Access,
 AC 57
 headers, WD 77
 Office files, OFF 66
 Office files using Backstage view,
 OFF 53–54
cloud computing, **CLD 2**
 Office 365. *See* Office 365
 overview of, CLD 2–3
collaboration using SharePoint,
 CLD 10
collapsing
 folders, OFF 30
 ribbon, OFF 19
color scheme, **WD 31**
colors
 applying to text, WD 26
 changing cell font, EX 28
 changing picture border, PPT 89–90
 changing Read mode, WD 121–122
 changing text, PPT 13–14
 changing WordArt outline's,
 PPT 107
 changing worksheet background,
 EX 93–94
 changing worksheet tab, EX 72–73
 character, PPT 10
 choosing when creating documents,
 WD 31
 font, EX 23
 Font Color gallery, EX 28
 formatting worksheets with, EX 93
 shading paragraphs, WD 21
 sheet tab, EX 43
 Theme Colors vs. Standard Colors,
 PPT 14
 using in flyers, WD 14
column heading, **OFF 59**
column headings, **AC 32**
columns (datasheet), resizing, AC 28,
 AC 39
columns (report), modifying headings,
 resizing, AC 50–53
columns (worksheet)
 adjusting widths, EX 34
 changing width, EX 103–105
 entering titles, EX 9–10, EX 70–71
 formatting, EX 96
 of numbers, summing, EX 14–15
 summing, EX 80
 title examples, EX 6
comma style format, EX 33, EX 97,
 EX 98

Index

commands
 Access tabs, OFF 64
 commonly used status bar (table),
 EX 48
 dimmed, OFF 61
 Excel tabs, OFF 64
 hiding from screen, OFF 20
 on mini toolbar, OFF 17
 on Quick Access Toolbar,
 OFF 17–18, OFF 22
 on ribbon, ScreenTips, OFF 16
 and shortcut menus, OFF 20–21
commas in worksheets, EX 12
compacting, repairing databases,
 AC 57
comparison operators
 described, **AC 89**
 using in criterion, AC 89–90
compound criterion, **AC 91**
 using involving AND, AC 91
 using involving OR, AC 92
computed field, **AC 112**
computers
 minimizing wrist injury, WD 12
 synchronizing to Office 365 online,
 CLD 8
conditional formatting
 applying, EX 100–102
 relational operators (table), EX 103
content placeholders, inserting pictures
 using, PPT 34–35
contextual tabs, OFF 16
contrast, **PPT 87**
converting
 fields to regular text, WD 110
 footnotes to endnotes, and visa versa,
 WD 100
copy area, **EX 15**
copying, **WD 111**
 cells to adjacent cells using fill handle,
 EX 15–18
 folders to USB flash drives,
 OFF 43–44
 formulas using fill handles, EX 78–79
 and pasting, WD 112
 and pasting shapes, PPT 101–102
 ranges of cells across columns to
 adjacent ranges, EX 87–88
 slides, PPT 41
correcting
 mistakes while typing, PPT 8
 pictures, PPT 87
 spelling mistakes, EX 107–109
 worksheet errors, EX 49–53
corrections, automatic, WD 87
costs of cloud computing, CLD 3
COUNT function, AC 115
counting words, WD 100–101
Courier New font, PPT 99

creating
 Access databases, OFF 64–66
 AutoCorrect entries, WD 85–87,
 WD 87
 bibliographical lists, WD 106–107
 blank documents, WD 4–5, WD 69
 blank Office documents, OFF 56–57
 blank Word documents, OFF 12
 blank workbook, EX 69
 brochures, OFF 70
 complex expressions with Expression
 Builder, AC 112
 crosstab queries, AC 118–121
 database tables, AC 10–15
 databases, AC 6–7
 folders, OFF 25–28
 forms, AC 45–47
 forms for queries, AC 105–106
 headers, WD 74–77
 new Office documents from Backstage
 view, OFF 51–52
 paragraphs, WD 6
 parameter queries, AC 86–88
 presentations, PPT 5–6
 Publisher documents, OFF 69–70
 queries, AC 43, AC 77–80
 reports, AC 48–49
 reports from queries, AC 103–104
 SharePoint intranet sites, CLD 11
 sources, WD 89–91, WD 103
 text slide with multilevel bulleted list,
 PPT 17–22
 Title Slide, PPT 7–8
 Title Slides, PPT 81
 top-values queries, AC 98
 websites with Office 365 Business
 Plans, CLD 8
 works cited pages, WD 104
criterion
 determining query, AC 80–82
 special, AC 92
 using comparison operator in, AC 90
 using compound, AC 91
 using for field not included in query
 results, AC 85–86
 using in calculating statistics, AC 117
 using in queries, AC 43–45
 using number in, AC 89
crosstab query, **AC 118**,
 AC 119–121
Crosstab Query Wizard, AC 119–121
CTRL key
 and keyboard shortcuts, OFF 6
 and mouse wheel, OFF 4
Currency data type, **AC 9**, AC 23,
 AC 89
currency of sources, WD 78
currency style format, EX 98, EX 98–99
currency symbols, AC 15

custom dictionaries, WD 118
custom dictionary, PPT 116
custom layout, **PPT 22**
Customize Status Bar shortcut menu,
 EX 49
customizing
 Navigation Pane, AC 121–123
 Quick Access Toolbar, OFF 22
 ribbon, OFF 59
 slide layouts, PPT 22
cutting, **WD 111**

D

Dark Blue, PPT 14
data
 entering in worksheets, EX 71
 exporting Access to other
 applications, AC 107–111
 sorting in queries, AC 93–94
 text, AC 81
data series, **EX 38**
data types, **AC 9**
 additional (table), AC 9
 determining, AC 62
database design, **AC 58**, AC 60–63
Database Design Language (DBDL),
 AC 58
database management system, **OFF 63**,
 AC 2
database properties, **AC 54**, AC 55
databases, **OFF 63**, **AC 2**
 assigning database properties to,
 AC 54
 backup and recovery, AC 56–57
 changing structure, AC 15–16
 checking structure in Design view,
 AC 18
 closing without exiting Access, AC 57
 compacting and repairing, AC 57
 correcting errors in structure, AC 39
 creating, AC 6–7
 creating Access, OFF 64–66
 deleting tables or other objects,
 AC 58
 determining requirements, AC 58
 distributing objects, AC 29
 enabling content, AC 25
 formats, OFF 65
 forms, using, AC 47
 joining tables, AC 99–102
 making changes to data, AC 23–24
 omitting duplicates, AC 94–96
 opening from Access, AC 77
 overview of, AC 2–3
 querying. See queries
 renaming objects, AC 58
 saving with another name, AC 57

Datasheet view, **AC 8**, **AC 10**, AC 20
 Navigation buttons in (table), AC 26
 switching to other views, AC 43
datasheets
 described, **AC 8**
 resizing columns in, AC 28
Date & Time data type, **AC 9**
dates
 Access format, AC 90
 Excel formats, EX 72
 formatting in cells, EX 96
 MLA formats, WD 78
debugging, **EX 115**
Decimal Places property, AC 11
deck, **PPT 2**
deleting
 See also removing
 AutoCorrect entries, WD 86
 bullets on slides, PPT 19
 database tables or other objects,
 AC 58
 files, folders, OFF 74–75
 formulas, EX 88
 notes, WD 99
 slides, PPT 79–80
 text, WD 48–49
 text from slides, PPT 43–45
deletions from documents, WD 46
delimited files, **AC 110**
delimiter, **AC 110**
demoting, **PPT 18**
description, **AC 10**
design grid
 clearing, AC 93
 described, **AC 80**
Design view, **AC 10**, AC 49
 changing field size in, AC 18–19
 checking database structure in,
 AC 18
 creating queries in, AC 78–79
 modifying tables in, AC 37–38
 New Values field property, AC 9
 switching to other views, AC 43
 viewing tables in, AC 17
designing
 databases, AC 58, AC 60–63
 queries, AC 82, AC 86
 title slides, PPT 31
 websites using SharePoint, CLD 11
desktop, **OFF 13**
destination area, **EX 15**
Dialog Box Launcher, **OFF 17**
dialog boxes, navigating in, OFF 34
dictionaries
 main and custom, WD 118
 spell checking, PPT 116
displaying
 See also viewing
 formatting marks, WD 6–7, WD 70

formulas version of worksheets,
 EX 115–117
KeyTips, OFF 18
mini toolbar, PPT 13
on-screen touch keyboard, OFF 12,
 WD 6
ribbon, OFF 20
rulers, WD 82
Search bar, AC 6
thesaurus, WD 116
distributing
 database objects, AC 29
 documents, WD 120, PPT 121, AC 107
 workbooks, EX 45
Document Information Panel, WD 45
document properties, **WD 44**,
 PPT 48, **EX 44**
 changing, WD 44–45, PPT 48,
 EX 44–45
 printing, WD 53, WD 104, EX 48
document settings, changing,
 WD 69–71
document window, **OFF 14**
documents
 See also characters, paragraphs, text
 choosing colors when creating,
 WD 31
 closing all, EX 53
 counting words, WD 100–101
 creating blank, WD 4–5, WD 69
 creating blank Office, OFF 56–57
 creating blank Word, OFF 12
 creating new, from Backstage view,
 OFF 51–52
 displaying formatting marks, WD 7
 distributing, WD 51, WD 120,
 PPT 121, AC 107
 document properties, assigning,
 WD 44–45
 entering text, WD 5–6, WD 11
 entering text in Word, OFF 23
 flyers. *See* flyers
 fonts. *See* fonts
 inserting blank lines, WD 7–8
 inserting pictures, WD 33–35
 inserting pictures into, OFF 16
 inserting text in, WD 48
 navigating, WD 12–13
 opening from Excel, EX 48
 opening from Word, WD 47
 page breaks, WD 105
 printing, WD 50–52, WD 122
 proofreading, WD 108–109
 readability statistics, WD 118
 research papers. *See* research papers
 revising, WD 46–50
 saving, WD 12–13, WD 81
 saving with same file name, WD 33,
 WD 92, WD 108

sharing with Office 365, CLD 7–8
spell- and grammar-checking,
 WD 116–117
tabbed vs. overlapping windows,
 AC 40
themes, WD 14, WD 31–32
white space, hiding and showing,
 WD 102
wordwrap, WD 8–9
zooming, WD 6, WD 35–36
Documents library, OFF 33
.docx file type, WD 15
dollar sign ($)
 in Access, AC 22
 and currency data type, AC 89
 floating, EX 98–99
 in worksheets, EX 12
domain, **CLD 11**
double-space, **WD 72**
double-tap gesture, OFF 4
Doughnut Chart gallery, EX 39
download, **WD 33**
downloading themes, PPT 77–78
drag, mouse operations, OFF 5
drag and drop, **PPT 42**
drag gesture, OFF 4
drag-and-drop editing, **WD 49–50**
dragging
 in formulas, EX 86
 to move or resize windows, OFF 75
 selection handles, WD 22
DTP (desktop publishing) software,
 OFF 69
duplicating slides, PPT 41

E

Edit mode, **EX 50**
editing
 citations, WD 98–99
 drag-and-drop, WD 49–50
 headers, WD 77
 in-cell, **EX 50**
 sources, WD 96–98, WD 103, WD 109
effects, **PPT 103**
 applying picture, WD 39–40,
 PPT 90–91
 text, applying to selected text, WD 20
email, **OFF 68**
 Office 365, CLD 7
 Office 365 using Exchange, CLD 10
endnotes
 described, **WD 92**
 working with, WD 99–100
enhancing pages, WD 40–44
equal sign (=)
 in Excel, EX 74
 and functions, formulas, **EX 20**

errors
 correcting in database structure,
 AC 39
 correcting worksheet, EX 49–53
 detecting spelling, PPT 116
 typing, OFF 23, WD 6
 wrong cell reference in formulas,
 EX 74
Excel, **OFF 55**
 See also workbooks, worksheets
 asterisk (*) arithmetic operator, EX 74
 creating documents, OFF 56–57
 exiting, EX 53, EX 118
 exporting Access data to, AC 107–109
 formatting dates, EX 72
 formulas. *See* formulas
 importing worksheet into Access,
 AC 32–37
 introduction to, OFF 55–56
 opening documents from, EX 48
 ribbon tabs, OFF 60
 running, EX 69
 running Windows 7, Windows 8,
 EX 5
 unique features of, OFF 59–60
Exchange Online, **CLD 7**, CLD 10
exiting
 Access, AC 24, AC 56
 Excel, EX 53, EX 118
 Office apps, OFF 42–43, OFF 55,
 OFF 62, OFF 67
 PowerPoint, PPT 55, PPT 125
 Word, OFF 43, WD 46, WD 53,
 WD 122
expanding
 folders, OFF 29–30
 ribbon, OFF 19
exporting
 Access data to Excel, AC 107–109
 Access data to text files, AC 110–111
 Access data to Word, AC 110
 reports as PDF or XPS files, AC 54
Expression Builder, AC 112

F

Facet theme, PPT 26
Favorites area, folder windows,
 OFF 27
fields, **WD 90**, **AC 3**
 adding to design grid, AC 79–80
 calculated, computed, AC 112
 changing captions, AC 114–115
 changing size in Design view,
 AC 18–19
 converting to regular text, WD 110
 creating reports containing,
 AC 48–49

determining additional, AC 61
determining database, AC 8,
 AC 14–15
determining maximum size, AC 11
inserting, deleting, renaming, AC 15
naming, AC 4
rearranging in queries, AC 92
sizes for Number fields (table),
 AC 10
updating, WD 110
using criteria, not included in query
 results, AC 85–86
File Explorer, OFF 35
 creating blank Office documents,
 OFF 56–57
 file management, OFF 72–74
 running apps from, OFF 57–59
file management
 described, **OFF 72**
 renaming, moving, deleting files,
 OFF 72–75
file name
 described, **OFF 24**
 invalid naming characters, OFF 32
File New Database dialog box,
 OFF 65
FILE tab, Backstage view, OFF 36
files, **OFF 13**
 See also specific type
 clip, PPT 30
 closing Office, OFF 66
 deleting, OFF 74–75
 exporting Access data to text, AC 110
 and folders, OFF 23–29
 moving, OFF 73–74
 naming, OFF 32–33, AC 7
 opening files from, OFF 57
 organizing, WD 13, WD 81, PPT 83,
 EX 23, AC 6, AC 110
 organizing and saving, OFF 23–34
 renaming, OFF 72–73
 saving in folders, OFF 31–34, OFF
 50–51, OFF 53
 saving on SkyDrive, OFF 36–38
 saving with new name, OFF 62
 sharing using Office 365, CLD 7–8
fill, **PPT 103**
 applying WordArt, PPT 106
 types of, PPT 108
fill handle, **EX 16**
fill handles
 clearing cell entries using, EX 52
 copying cells to adjacent cells,
 EX 15–18
 copying formulas using, EX 78–79
Find and Replace dialog box, WD 115
finding
 See also searching
 formatting, WD 115

and inserting synonyms, WD 116,
 PPT 114–115
and replacing text, PPT 113–114
text, WD 113–115
FIRST function, AC 115
'First Line Indent' marker, **WD 82**
first-line indent, **WD 82**
fixed-width files, **AC 110**
flagged words, WD 9
Flesch Reading Ease score, WD 118
floating dollar sign ($), EX 98–99
flyers
 See also documents
 adding page borders, WD 41–42
 areas of, WD 11
 described, WD 2–3
 formats to use, WD 14
 positioning graphics on, WD 35
folder windows, **OFF 27**, OFF 29–30
folders
 copying to USB flash drives,
 OFF 43–44
 creating, organizing, OFF 23–29
 creating using Windows 7, OFF 27
 creating within folders, OFF 27–28
 deleting, OFF 74
 expanding, scrolling through,
 collapsing, OFF 29–30
 OneNote, **OFF 71**
 organizing, WD 13, WD 81, PPT 83,
 EX 23, AC 6, AC 110
 saving files in, OFF 31–34,
 OFF 50–51, OFF 53
font, **WD 14**, **PPT 10**, **EX 23**
 changing, EX 25–26
 changing cell color, EX 28
 changing shape's, PPT 97–98
 decreasing, increasing, EX 92–93
 increasing size, PPT 12
 increasing size in cell entries, EX 27
 weight, changing, PPT 106–107
font color, WD 26, **EX 23**
Font Color gallery, EX 28
Font gallery, WD 18
font size, **WD 14**, **EX 23**
 changing for selected text, WD 17–18,
 WD 22–23
 increasing, WD 16
Font Size gallery, EX 27
font style, **EX 23**
footer, **WD 74**, WD 76
footers, **EX 110**
footnotes, **WD 92**
 deleting, renumbering, WD 99
 on research papers, WD 67
 text style, WD 94–96
 working with, WD 99–100
Form view, AC 46
format, **WD 13**, **PPT 10**, **EX 22**

Format Cells dialog box
 applying currency style format, EX 98–99
 using, EX 101–102
Format Painter, formatting text using, PPT 100–101
Format property, AC 11
formats
 Access database, OFF 65
 Access date, AC 90
 importing data in other, AC 32
 MLA date, WD 78
 style, WD 70
formatting
 characters in presentations, PPT 10–15
 conditional, EX 100–102
 dates and centering data in cells, EX 96
 finding, WD 115
 Notes pane text, PPT 116
 numbers in worksheets, EX 32–33
 numbers using ribbon, EX 97–99
 paragraphs, characters, WD 13–14
 rows using cell styles, EX 30–32
 single vs. multiple paragraphs, characters, WD 16
 slide backgrounds, PPT 108–112
 text in shapes, PPT 97–100
 text using Format Painter, PPT 100–101
 text using keyboard shortcuts, WD 81
 text using mini toolbar, WD 27–28
 text with Click and Type feature, WD 79–80
 undoing text changes, PPT 103
 worksheet titles, EX 92–93
 worksheets, EX 22–36, EX 89–96
formatting marks, **WD 6**
 displaying, WD 6, WD 14, WD 70
 hiding, WD 7
forms, **AC 45**
 creating, AC 45–47
 creating for queries, AC 105–106
 as database objects, AC 40
 using, AC 47
Formula AutoComplete list, EX 86
formula bar
 and cell entry, EX 7
 described, **OFF 60**, OFF 61
formulas, **EX 73**
 and cell references, EX 78
 copying using fill handles, EX 78–79
 deleting, EX 88
 displaying on printed worksheet, EX 115–116
 entering using keyboard, EX 20–21, EX 73–74
 entering using Point mode, EX 76–78
 examples of Excel (table), EX 75

Trace Error button, EX 79
 verifying using Range Finder, EX 89
formulas version, **EX 115**, EX 116–117
Full Screen mode, **OFF 19**
Function Arguments dialog box, EX 83
functions, **EX 66**
 asterisks (*) and, EX 74
 entering, ways of, EX 81
 learning about, EX 82
 parentheses (()) and, EX 87

G

gallery, **OFF 16**
gestures
 described, **OFF 3**
 for touch screen (table), OFF 4
glow picture effects, WD 39–40
gradient fills
 described, **PPT 108**, **PPT 111**
 inserting, PPT 111–112
grammar checking, WD 10–11, WD 116–117
graphics
 picture styles, applying, WD 38–39
 and selection rectangle, WD 35
 zooming, WD 36–37
green computing, **WD 51**, **PPT 52**, **EX 45**, **AC 29**
gridlines, **OFF 59**
group, **OFF 15**
group calculation, **AC 112**

H

handouts, speech, PPT 120
hanging indent, **WD 108**
Hanging Indent marker, **WD 108**
hard copy, **WD 51**, **PPT 52**, **EX 45**, EX 46–47, **AC 29**
hard page break, **WD 105**
headers, **WD 74**, **EX 110**
 changing worksheet's, EX 110–112
 closing, WD 77
 creating, editing, WD 74–77
 research papers, WD 67
headings
 column, row, OFF 59
 modifying report, AC 50–53
 slide, PPT 24–25
headline, **WD 11**
Help
 Access, AC 42, AC 121
 Excel, EX 37
 Office, OFF 75, OFF 77–79
 PowerPoint, PPT 35, PPT 108

Windows Help and Support, OFF 79–81
Word, WD 92
hiding
 commands from screen, OFF 20
 formatting marks, WD 7
 gridlines, OFF 59
 rulers, WD 5
 white space, WD 102
 worksheet rows, EX 107
hiding cells, **EX 104**
high-definition (HD) videoconferencing
 with Lync, CLD 13
 and Office 365, CLD 7
HOME tab, OFF 19
horizontal ruler, **WD 82**

I

identity theft, protecting your personal information, CLD 9
illustrations
 See also photos, pictures
 inserting into slides, PPT 30–35
 resizing, PPT 35–39
images, quality improvements message, OFF 42
import, **AC 32**
Import Spreadsheet Wizard, using, AC 33–37
importing
 data from other applications into Access, AC 32–37
 data in other formats, AC 32
 Excel worksheet into Access, AC 32–37
 vs. linking, AC 32
IN operator, **AC 92**
in-cell editing
 described, **EX 50**
 summary of tasks (table), EX 51
increasing font size, PPT 12
indenting
 first-line indent paragraphs, WD 82–84
 paragraphs with hanging indents, WD 108
indirect circular reference, **EX 73**
individual record calculation, **AC 112**
Info tab, Backstage view, OFF 51
information, protecting your personal, CLD 9
ink, conserving, PPT 124
Insert Function box, using, EX 82–83
Insert Media dialog box, PPT 30
Insert mode, **WD 48**, **EX 50**
Insert Options, EX 79
Insert Pictures dialog box, **PPT 30**

inserting
See also adding
blank lines, WD 7
citation placeholder, WD 93–94,
 WD 101
footnote reference mark, WD 92
gradient fill, PPT 111–112
page numbers, WD 76–77
photos, illustrations into slides,
 PPT 30–35
pictures in documents, WD 34–35
pictures in presentations, PPT 83–91
pictures into Word documents,
 OFF 16
pictures to create slide backgrounds,
 PPT 108–109
shapes in slides, PPT 91–100
slide numbers, PPT 118–119
slide transitions, PPT 119–120
text into existing documents, WD 48
texture fills, PPT 110–111
WordArt, PPT 103–104
insertion point
described, OFF 23
moving, AC 50
moving with keyboard, mouse
 (tables), WD 12
instant messaging (IM), **CLD 13**
Internet and cloud computing, CLD 2–3
Ion layout gallery (fig.), PPT 24
iPads, access to Office 365, CLD 8
iPhones, access to Office 365, CLD 8
italic, **WD 25**
italicized text, **PPT 11**
italicizing text, WD 25

J

join, **AC 99**
join line, **AC 100**
join properties
changing, AC 101–102
described, **AC 101**
join queries, adding criteria to,
 AC 111–112
join types, AC 111
joining tables, AC 99–102

K

keyboard
determining average of ranges of
 numbers, EX 86–87
entering formulas using, EX 20–21,
 EX 73–74
moving insertion point with (table),
 WD 12

on-screen touch, WD 6, AC 83
typing without, OFF 8
keyboard shortcuts, **OFF 6**, **WD 80**
for formatting characters (table),
 WD 80
for formatting paragraphs (table),
 WD 80
formatting text using, WD 81
KeyTips, **OFF 18**
keywords, **AC 54**
photo, PPT 32
theme, PPT 78
Kincaid Grade Level score, WD 118

L

landscape orientation, **OFF 49**,
 AC 29, AC 31
landscape orientation, printing
 worksheets in, EX 46–47
LAST function, AC 115
layout gallery, **PPT 22**
Layout Options button, WD 35
Layout view, AC 46, AC 49
layouts, **OFF 49**, **PPT 22**, **AC 28**
leading zeros, AC 22
Left Indent marker, **WD 82**
left-aligned, **WD 14**, WD 15
left-aligned paragraphs, WD 75
left-handed mouse functions, OFF 4
level, **PPT 8**
Libraries area, folder windows,
 OFF 27
library, **OFF 24**, OFF 25
line spacing
changing, WD 72–73
described, **WD 72**
line weight, increasing, PPT 89
lines
creating new, OFF 23
inserting blank, WD 7
selecting, WD 16
selecting multiple, WD 22
links, using Help, OFF 77
lists, PPT 17–22, **AC 32**
bibliographical, WD 106
bulleted. *See* bulleted lists
live database, **AC 56**
live preview
described, **OFF 16**, OFF 30
of picture styles, PPT 88
lock screen, **OFF 6**
logging in to user accounts, OFF 6
looking up
See also finding, searching
information, WD 119
Lync, CLD 7
Lync Online, CLD 9, CLD 11–14

M

Mac version of Office 365, CLD 6
magnifying
See also zooming
database tables, AC 30–31
major key, **AC 93**, AC 97
manual page break, **WD 105**
margins
changing worksheet's, EX 110–112
described, WD 82, WD 83, **EX 110**
MAX function, EX 81, EX 82–83,
 AC 115
meetings, connecting with Lync,
 CLD 12–13
Merge & Center menu, EX 29, EX 30
merging
cells to center entries across columns,
 EX 29–30
described, **EX 29**
metadata, **AC 54**
Microsoft Access 2013, **OFF 9**
Microsoft account area, OFF 18
Microsoft accounts
signing in, out, OFF 37–39
signing out, AC 55, AC 123–124
signing out of, WD 45, PPT 55,
 PPT 125, EX 53, EX 117–118
Microsoft Excel 2013, **OFF 9**
Microsoft InfoPath Designer 2013,
 OFF 9
Microsoft Lync, CLD 7
Microsoft Lync 2013, **OFF 9**
Microsoft Office 2013, **OFF 9**
Microsoft Office 365, **OFF 9**. *See also*
 Office 365
Microsoft Office Specialist (MOS)
 program, OFF 81, WD 46, WD
 108, PPT 55, PPT 119, EX 52,
 AC 62, AC 123
Microsoft Office Web Apps, **OFF 9**
Microsoft OneNote 2013, **OFF 9**
Microsoft Outlook 2013, **OFF 9**
Microsoft PowerPoint 2013, **OFF 9**
Microsoft Publisher 2013, **OFF 9**
Microsoft SharePoint Workspace
 2013, **OFF 9**
Microsoft Word 2013, **OFF 9**
Microsoft XPS Document Writer,
 PPT 54
MIN function, EX 81, EX 84–85,
 AC 115
mini toolbar, **OFF 17**, WD 17
formatting text using, WD 27–28
turning off, OFF 18
minimized window, **OFF 34**
minimizing
and restoring windows, OFF 34–36
wrist injury, WD 12

minor key, **AC 93**

minus sign (−), **EX 20**

misspelled words, adding to dictionary, PPT 118

misspellings, automatic corrections, WD 9

mistakes

checking cell references, EX 89

correcting while typing, PPT 8

MLA documentation style, WD 68–69, WD 74, WD 76, WD 89, WD 90, WD 94, WD 98, WD 107

mobile devices, access to Office 365, CLD 8

Modern Language Association of America (MLA), **WD 66**

documentation style, WD 68–69

parenthetical references, WD 88

Modern UI, OFF 8

modifications to documents, WD 46

mouse

moving insertion point with (table), WD 12

operations (table), OFF 5

using, OFF 3–5

Mouse mode, OFF 17–18

moving

to another slide in Normal view, PPT 29–30

charts to new sheets, EX 41–42

fields, AC 16

files, OFF 73–74

footnotes, WD 99

insertion point, WD 12, AC 50

manually through slides in slide show, PPT 50–52

page numbers, AC 53

pictures on slides, PPT 39–40

text, WD 49–50

tiles on Start screen, OFF 8

windows, OFF 75–76

multilevel bulleted list slide, **PPT 17**, PPT 18

multiplication operator (*), EX 74

N

Name box, formula bar, **OFF 60**

Name box, selecting cells using, EX 35–36

names

changing sheet tab, EX 41–43

changing worksheet tab, EX 42–43

file, OFF 24

saving workbooks with same file name, EX 45

naming

See also renaming

databases, AC 57

fields, AC 4

files, OFF 32–33, OFF 62, AC 7

presentations, PPT 14–15

queries, AC 45

reports, AC 49

workbooks, EX 21–22

navigating, **OFF 34**

in dialog boxes, OFF 34

documents, WD 12–13

navigation area, folder windows, OFF 27

Navigation buttons, **AC 26**

Navigation Pane, **WD 111**, AC 6, **AC 8**

customizing, AC 121–123

opening, AC 40

n.d. (no date), WD 107

New gallery, OFF 52

New Values field property, AC 9

nonproportionally resizing pictures, PPT 37–39

Normal style, **WD 5**, **WD 70**, WD 73, WD 105–106

Normal view

described, **PPT 28**, **EX 110**

moving to another slide in, PPT 29–30

note reference mark, **WD 92**

note taking apps. *See* Microsoft OneNote

note text, **WD 92**

notebook, **OFF 71**

notes. *See* footnotes

notes pages, **PPT 115**

Notes pane, **PPT 28**, **PPT 115**, PPT 118

number, **EX 12**

Number data type, **AC 9**

numbering slides, PPT 118–119

numbers

alignment in cells, EX 13

determining average of range of, EX 86–87

determining highest in range, EX 82–83

determining lowest in range, EX 84–85

entering, EX 12–13

formatting in worksheets, EX 32–33

formatting using ribbon, EX 97–99

O

object tabs, **OFF 64**

objects

See also specific object

database, AC 40

renaming or deleting database, AC 58

objects tabs, **AC 8**

Office 2013

compared to Office 365, CLD 4–5

overview of, CLD 4

touch screen use, OFF 4

Office 365

collaboration using SharePoint, CLD 10

compared to Office 2013, CLD 4–5

described, CLD 3–4

email, calendars, CLD 7

email using Exchange, CLD 10

file sharing, CLD 7–8

introduction to, CLD 2

Lync Online, CLD 11–14

multiple device access to, CLD 8–9

online meetings, CLD 7

teaming using in business, CLD 9

Office 365 Business Plans, CLD 6

Office 365 Enterprise and Government, CLD 5

Office 365 Home Premium, CLD 5

Office 365 Midsize Business, CLD 5, CLD 6

Office 365 Small Business, CLD 5, CLD 6

Office 365 Small Business Premium, CLD 5, CLD 6

Office 365 University for students, CLD 5

Office apps

See also apps

exiting, OFF 42–43, OFF 55, OFF 62, OFF 67

Office Help, OFF 75, OFF 79

opening Help windows in, OFF 75

Office Clipboard, **WD 111**

Office files

closing, OFF 53–54, OFF 66

opening existing, OFF 66–67

Office for Mac, CLD 6

Office Help, OFF 75, OFF 77–78

Office on Demand, **CLD 6**

Office.com, inserting pictures from, into Title Slide, PPT 31–35

Office.com Clip Art, **PPT 30**, PPT 31

offsets, **PPT 108**

on screen keyboard, AC 83

OneNote, **OFF 71**

one-to-many relationships, **AC 61**

online meetings, Office 365, CLD 7

Online Pictures button, PPT 30

on-screen touch keyboard, WD 6

opening

Backstage view, WD 9

databases from Access, AC 24–25, AC 77

documents from Excel, EX 48

documents from Word, WD 47

existing Office files, OFF 66–67
Help windows in Office apps, OFF 75
Navigation Pane, AC 40
operating system
 described, **OFF 2**
 Windows 8, OFF 2–6
operations
 in calculations, AC 112
 multiplication, EX 74
 order of, EX 75
operations, mouse (table), OFF 5
operators
 arithmetic. *See* arithmetic operators
 comparison, AC 89–90
 conditional formatting, EX 103
Option buttons in Excel (table), EX 79
OR criterion, **AC 91**, AC 92
order of operations, **EX 75**
organizing
 files, and saving, OFF 23–34
 files, folders, OFF 23–29, WD 13,
 WD 81, PPT 83, EX 23, AC 6,
 AC 110
orientation of pages
 changing worksheet's, EX 112
 portrait, landscape, AC 29
orphan, **WD 101**
outline
 described, **PPT 103**
 WordArt, changing color, PPT 107
Outlook
 described, **OFF 68**
 introduction to, OFF 68
 scheduling import procedure, AC 36
Outlook window, OFF 68
overlapping windows vs. tabbed
 documents, AC 40
Overtype mode, **EX 50**

P

page breaks, WD 105
PAGE LAYOUT tab, WD 42–43
Page Layout view, **EX 110**
page numbers
 inserting, WD 76–77
 moving, AC 53
 on research papers, WD 67
Page Setup dialog box, EX 116
page width, zooming, WD 7–8,
 WD 32
pages
 adding borders, WD 41–42
 automatic breaks, WD 101
 centering contents vertically,
 WD 43–44
 enhancing, WD 40–44
 go to specific, WD 111

works cited, WD 104
 zooming multiple, WD 120–121
pages (OneNote), **OFF 71**
paragraph formatting, **WD 13**
paragraph spacing, **WD 72**
paragraphs, **PPT 8**
 bulleted, WD 14
 bulleting lists of, WD 23–24
 centering, WD 15, WD 33
 creating, OFF 23, WD 6
 demoting, promoting, PPT 18–19
 entering on slides, PPT 8–9
 entering subtitle, PPT 9
 formatting, WD 13–14
 formatting single vs. multiple, WD 16
 formatting with hanging indents,
 WD 108
 indenting, WD 82–84
 keyboard shortcuts for (table),
 WD 80
 levels, PPT 8
 removing space after, WD 73
 right- and left-aligning, WD 75
 shading, WD 21
 spacing before, after, WD 42–43
parameter queries
 creating, AC 86–88
 described, **AC 86**
 using, AC 88
parentheses (()) and functions, EX 87
parenthetical references, WD 67,
 WD 68
password, **OFF 6**, OFF 7
Password text box, OFF 7
paste area, **EX 15**
Paste Options, EX 79
Paste Options button, WD 50
Paste Options menu, WD 113
pasting
 copying and, WD 112
 described, **WD 111**
path, **OFF 24**
pattern fill, **PPT 108**
PDF files, WD 51, WD 120, PPT 52,
 PPT 121, EX 45, AC 107
 described, **AC 29**
 exporting reports as, AC 54
percent style format, EX 99
persistent chat, **CLD 13**
personal information, protecting your,
 CLD 9
photos
 See also images, pictures
 inserting into slides, PPT 30
 resizing, PPT 35–39
 wrapping text around, PPT 42
picture effects, WD 39–40
picture effects, applying, PPT 90–91
picture fill, **PPT 108**

picture styles, applying, WD 38–39,
 PPT 87–88
pictures
 See also images, photos
 adding borders, PPT 88–90
 applying effects, WD 39–40
 changing, PPT 85–86
 correcting, PPT 87
 inserting, formatting in documents,
 WD 33–40
 inserting as slide backgrounds,
 PPT 108–109
 inserting in presentations, PPT 83–91
 inserting into Word documents,
 OFF 16
 moving on slides, PPT 39–40
 resizing, PPT 36–39
pie charts, adding to worksheets,
 EX 37–40
pinch gesture, OFF 4
pinning apps to bottom of Start screen,
 OFF 8
pixel, **EX 103**
placeholders, **OFF 49**, **PPT 7**
 deleting text in, PPT 43–45
 inserting citation, WD 93–94,
 WD 101
 selecting text, PPT 18
 title text, OFF 50
plagiarize, **WD 78**, WD 119
planning projects, OFF 82–83
point, **PPT 10**, **EX 23**
Point mode, **EX 76**, EX 77–78, EX 87
point mouse operation, OFF 5
pointer, Excel, OFF 58, OFF 60
pointers on touch screens, PPT 36
polling feature, Lync, CLD 14
portrait orientation, **AC 29**
postal codes, AC 63
PowerPoint
 See also presentations, slide shows
 difference between running Windows 7
 and Windows 8, PPT 76
 exiting, PPT 55, PPT 125
 Help, PPT 35
 Help, obtaining, PPT 108
 introduction to, OFF 45–46
 slides. *See* slide shows, slides
 views, PPT 28–30
 window, and ribbon, OFF 48–55
presentations, **OFF 45**, **PPT 2**,
 PPT 74–76
 adding slides to, PPT 15–16, PPT 23
 assigning document properties,
 PPT 48
 changing themes, PPT 26–27
 closing slides, PPT 40–41
 entering subtitle paragraph, PPT 9
 formatting characters in, PPT 10–15

inserting pictures in, PPT 83–91
making changes to slide text content, PPT 42–47
opening, closing, OFF 54–55
printing, PPT 52–54
saving, PPT 82–83, PPT 125
saving with new name, PPT 14–15
saving with same name, PPT 28
spelling, checking, PPT 117–118
themes, PPT 77–78
Title and Content layout, PPT 16
viewing in Slide Show view, PPT 49–52
Presenter view, **PPT 28**
press and hold gesture, OFF 4
press mouse wheel, OFF 5
press thumb button on mouse, OFF 5
previewing
 contents of tables, AC 29–31
 slides, PPT 121
 theme slides, PPT 77–78
 themes, PPT 6
 worksheets in landscape orientation, EX 46–47
Previous Locations arrow, folder windows, OFF 27
primary key, **AC 3**
 designating fields as, AC 18
 determining, AC 8, AC 60
 in Import Spreadsheet Wizard, AC 35–36
 modifying, AC 11–13
 record sorting and, AC 27
primary sort key, **AC 93**
Print Layout view, **OFF 14**, **WD 5**, WD 52–53, WD 102
Print Scaling option, EX 117
Print view, AC 49
printers, changing, AC 29
printing
 changing worksheet's margins, headers, EX 110–112
 conserving ink, toner, WD 50, PPT 53, PPT 124, EX 45
 contents of tables, AC 29–31
 document properties, WD 53, WD 104, PPT 48, EX 48
 documents, WD 50–52, WD 122
 presentations, PPT 52–54
 queries, query results, AC 43, AC 45, AC 82
 reports, AC 54, AC 105
 slide backgrounds, PPT 122
 speaker notes, PPT 121–124
 worksheet sections, EX 114–115
 worksheets, EX 45–47, EX 110–113
printout, **WD 51**, **PPT 52**, **EX 45**, **AC 29**

projects
 database creation, AC 2–4
 flyer with picture, WD 2–3
 planning guidelines, OFF 82–83
 presentation with bulleted list, photos, and illustration, PPT 2–3
 presentation with pictures, shapes, and WordArt, PPT 74–76
 querying a database, AC 74–75
 research paper with references, sources, WD 66–67
 worksheet and chart, EX 2–3
 worksheet with formulas and functions, EX 66–68
promoting, **PPT 18**
proofreading
 described, **WD 108**, WD 109
 workbooks, EX 107
property sheet, **AC 94**, AC 95–96, AC 114
Property Update Options button, AC 19
proportionally resizing pictures, PPT 36–37
publication types, **OFF 69**
Publisher, **OFF 69**, OFF 70
punctuation, spacing after, WD 88

Q

queries, **AC 40**
 in Access, OFF 63
 compound criterion, AC 91–92
 creating, AC 40–42, AC 43, AC 77–80
 creating forms for, AC 105–106
 creating reports from, AC 103–104
 crosstab, creating, AC 118–121
 designing, AC 86
 determining criteria, using, AC 80–82
 involving multiple tables, AC 105
 involving sorting, AC 97
 join, restricting records in, AC 111–112
 joining tables, AC 99–102
 parameter. *See* parameter queries
 printing results, AC 43
 rearranging fields in, AC 92
 saving, AC 45, AC 84, AC 89, AC 102
 sorting data in, AC 93–94
 special criteria, AC 92
 square brackets ([]) in, AC 87, AC 113
 top-values, AC 98
 using, AC 42–43
 using calculated fields in, AC 112, AC 112–113
 using criterion in, AC 43–45
 using saved, AC 82–83
query, **AC 74**
Query-By-Example (QBE), AC 91

question mark (?), **AC 83**
Quick Access Toolbar, **OFF 17**
 customizing, OFF 22
 relocating, OFF 20–21
 Start From Beginning button, PPT 49–52
 Undo and Redo buttons, PPT 8
Quick Print button, OFF 22
Quick Print option, AC 31
quotation marks (")
 and text data, AC 83
 text fields and, AC 44

R

Range Finder, **EX 89**
ranges, **EX 14**
 applying styles to cell, EX 30–32
 of cells, copying across columns to adjacent ranges, EX 87–88
 copying formulas using fill handles, EX 78–79
 copying one to another, EX 17
 determining highest number in, EX 82–83
 determining lowest number in, EX 84–85
 determining average of, of numbers, EX 86–87
 operations on, **EX 14**
Read mode, WD 52–53, WD 121–122
readability statistics, WD 118
Reading view, **PPT 28**
recent files, opening using Backstage view, OFF 54–55
recording feature, Lync, CLD 14
records, **AC 3**
 adding to tables, AC 20–23
 adding to tables containing data, AC 26–27
 restricting in joins, AC 111–112
 saving, AC 22
recover, **AC 56**
Rectangle shape, PPT 97–98
Recycle Bin, **OFF 13**, OFF 74
Redo button, WD 25, EX 51
redoing actions, WD 24–25
redundancy
 described, **AC 62**
 identifying, removing, AC 62–63
Refresh button, folder windows, OFF 27
relational database, **AC 2**
relationships
 ad hoc, AC 99
 between tables, AC 61, AC 62
relative cell references, **EX 78**
relative reference, **EX 16**

relocating
 footnotes, endnotes, WD 99
 page breaks, WD 101
 Quick Access Toolbar, OFF 20–21
removing
 See also deleting
 all effects from pictures, PPT 87
 bold format, WD 30
 bold style from cells, EX 26
 bullets from lists, paragraphs, WD 24
 fields, AC 80
 italic format, WD 25
 page borders, WD 42
 Quick Print button from Quick
 Access Toolbar, OFF 22
 redundancy from databases, AC 62–63
 ScreenTips, WD 99
 space after paragraphs, WD 73
 underlines, WD 29
renaming
 See also naming
 database objects, AC 58
 database tables, AC 37
 files, OFF 72–73
Replace All button, WD 115
Replace dialog box, PPT 113
replacing text, WD 114–115,
 PPT 113–114
Report view, AC 49
Report Wizard, AC 103–104
reports
 adding totals to, AC 53
 creating, AC 48–49
 creating from queries, AC 103–104
 as database objects, AC 40
 modifying column headings, resizing
 columns, AC 50–53
 printing, AC 54, AC 105
repositioning pictures on slides,
 PPT 39–40
research papers, **WD 66**
 citations, WD 88–89
 first drafts, parts of, WD 78
 footnotes, WD 92–94
 line, paragraph spacing, WD 72–73
 sources, WD 96–98, WD 109–110
Research task pane
 looking up information, WD 119
 options, WD 120
resizing, **WD 36, PPT 35**
 columns in datasheets, AC 28
 datasheet columns, AC 39
 field lists, AC 79
 graphics, WD 36–37
 photos, illustrations, PPT 35–39
 report columns, AC 52
 shapes, PPT 93–94
 windows, OFF 75–76
 WordArt objects, PPT 105

Restart command, OFF 7
restoring minimized windows,
 OFF 34–36
Reveal Formatting button, WD 70
reviewing, revising individual slides,
 PPT 113–124
revising documents, WD 46–50
revising papers, WD 109
ribbon, OFF 27
 Access tabs, OFF 64
 changing screen resolution and,
 OFF 40
 collapsing, expanding, OFF 19
 customizing, OFF 59
 dimmed commands, OFF 61
 displaying different tab on, OFF 18
 Excel tabs, OFF 60, EX 38
 formatting numbers using, EX 97–99
 PowerPoint, OFF 49
 and screen resolution, WD 74,
 PPT 15, AC 82
 screen resolution and, AC 8
 using, OFF 15
right-aligned, **WD 75**
right-aligning paragraphs, WD 75
right-handed mouse functions, OFF 4
roadmaps to chapters, OFF 2
rotate mouse wheel, OFF 5
row heading, **OFF 59**
row selector, **AC 18**
rows (worksheet)
 changing height, EX 106–107
 copying cells to adjacent cells in,
 EX 16–18
 entering titles, EX 11, EX 72
 formatting using cell styles,
 EX 30–32
 hiding, EX 107
 title examples, EX 6
rulers, **WD 82**
 horizontal and vertical, WD 82
 viewing, hiding, WD 5, WD 19
rules, creating conditional formatting,
 EX 100–102
run, **AC 42**
running
 Access, AC 76–77
 Access with Windows 7, Windows 8,
 AC 6
 apps, OFF 12
 apps from File Explorer,
 OFF 57–59
 apps using Search box, OFF 46–48
 Excel, EX 69
 PowerPoint, PPT 3
 Publisher, OFF 69
 queries, AC 42, AC 80–82
 Word, WD 4–5, WD 46–47
running Word, WD 69

S
Save As dialog box, WD 51
Save As gallery, OFF 31–32, OFF 37
save copy, **AC 56**
saving
 Access databases, OFF 64
 databases with another name, AC 57
 documents, OFF 24, WD 12–13,
 WD 81
 documents with same file name,
 WD 92, WD 108
 existing document with same file
 name, WD 44
 existing Office file with same or
 different name, OFF 61–62
 existing workbook with same file
 name, EX 45
 export steps, AC 110
 files in folders, OFF 31–34,
 OFF 50–51, OFF 53
 files on SkyDrive, OFF 36–38
 files to portable storage devices,
 OFF 43
 forms, AC 47
 and organizing files, OFF 23–34
 presentations, PPT 82–83, PPT 125
 presentations in folders, on SkyDrive,
 PPT 15
 presentations with new name,
 PPT 14–15
 presentations with same name,
 PPT 28
 queries, AC 45, AC 84, AC 89,
 AC 102
 records, AC 22
 tables, AC 16
 workbooks, EX 72–73
 workbooks using same file name,
 EX 88
 workbooks with new file names,
 EX 21–22
screen resolution, **OFF 39**
 changing, OFF 39–42, WD 4, PPT 4,
 EX 5, EX 69, AC 5
 and ribbon, PPT 15
 ribbon and, AC 8, AC 82
ScreenTips, **OFF 16**, WD 76
 removing, WD 99
 Undo button, PPT 8
scroll arrows, **OFF 5, PPT 28**
scroll bar, **OFF 5**, OFF 14
scroll box, **OFF 5**
scroll boxes, **PPT 28**, PPT 29
scrolling, OFF 5
Search bar, displaying, AC 6
Search box, running apps using,
 OFF 46–48
search box, folder windows, OFF 27

Search button, PPT 32
searching
 See also finding
 for online help, OFF 77
 for text, WD 113
 for themes, PPT 77–78
secondary sort key, **AC 93**
sections (OneNote), **OFF 71**
security
 Office 365, managing file sharing,
 CLD 7–8
 protecting your personal information,
 CLD 9
select, **EX 6**
selecting
 cells, EX 6, EX 35–36
 graphics, WD 36
 groups of words, WD 28, PPT 20–21
 lines, WD 16
 multiple lines, WD 22
 nonadjacent items, WD 32
 paragraphs, PPT 11
 text techniques (table), WD 32
 words, WD 49, PPT 12–13
selection handles, **WD 22**, PPT 11
selection rectangle, **WD 35**, **PPT 35**
shade, **WD 21**
shading paragraphs, WD 21
shadowing text, PPT 100
shapes
 adding, PPT 92–93, PPT 94–95
 adding, formatting text in,
 PPT 97–100
 applying styles, PPT 95–97
 changing WordArt, PPT 104
 copying and pasting, PPT 101–102
 inserting, formatting, PPT 91–100
 resizing, PPT 93–94
SharePoint, website design using,
 CLD 11
SharePoint Online, CLD 9, CLD 10
SharePoint Public Website, CLD 11
sharing information in business,
 CLD 7
sheet tab, **OFF 59**
sheet tab names, changing,
 EX 41–43
Short Text data type, **AC 9**, AC 13
shortcut, **OFF 27**
shortcut menus, **OFF 20**
 desktop commands, OFF 41
 modifying styles using, WD 94–96
Show desktop button, OFF 41
Show/Hide button, WD 7
showing
 See also displaying, viewing
 white space, WD 102
Shut down command, OFF 7
signature line, **WD 11**

sign-in screen, **OFF 6**
signing in
 to Microsoft accounts, OFF 37–38
 to user account, OFF 6, OFF 7–8
 to Windows 7 accounts, OFF 8
signing out of Microsoft accounts,
 OFF 38–39, WD 45, PPT 55,
 PPT 125, EX 53, EX 117–118,
 AC 55, AC 123–124
signing up for SkyDrive account,
 OFF 10
Simple Query Wizard, AC 40–42
size
 described, **PPT 10**
 increasing font, PPT 12
sizing
 fonts, PPT 12
 graphics, WD 36–37
 photos, illustrations, PPT 35–39
sizing handles, **WD 35**, **PPT 35**,
 PPT 37–39
SkyDrive, **OFF 10**
 saving documents to, WD 81
 saving files on, OFF 36–38
 saving presentation on, PPT 15
 signing out of Microsoft accounts,
 PPT 55
 signing up for account, OFF 10
 storage with Office 365 University,
 CLD 5
Skype
 and Office 365, CLD 7
 and Office 365 University, CLD 5
Sleep command, OFF 7
slide backgrounds, formatting,
 PPT 108–112
slide gesture, OFF 4
slide indicator, **PPT 29**
Slide pane, **PPT 28**, PPT 29
slide show, **OFF 45**, **PPT 2**
Slide Show toolbar, PPT 51
Slide Show view
 described, **PPT 49**
 viewing presentations in, PPT 49–52
slide shows
 See also presentations, slides
 ending with closing slides, PPT 40–41
 moving manually through slides in,
 PPT 50–52
Slide Sorter view, **PPT 28**
slide title, entering, PPT 17
slide transition
 adding, PPT 45–47
 described, **PPT 45**
slider, **OFF 42**
slides, **OFF 49**
 See also presentations, slide shows
 adding notes, PPT 115–116
 adding titles, headings, PPT 24–25

adding to presentations, PPT 23
adding transitions, PPT 119–120
arranging order, PPT 42
choosing words for, PPT 7
closing, ending slide shows with,
 PPT 40–41
creating text, PPT 81–82
deck, PPT 2
deleting, PPT 79–80
deleting text from, PPT 43–45
duplicating, PPT 41
formatting backgrounds,
 PPT 108–112
inserting, formatting shapes,
 PPT 91–100
inserting number, PPT 118–119
inserting photos, illustrations into,
 PPT 30–35
inserting pictures in, PPT 83–91
making changes to content,
 PPT 42–47
moving manually through,
 PPT 50–52
moving to another in Normal view,
 PPT 29–30
previewing theme, PPT 77–78
replacing text in existing, PPT 43
reviewing, revising individual,
 PPT 113–124
title. *See* Title Slide
zooming, PPT 10
Smart Guides, **PPT 39**
smartphones, access to Office 365,
 CLD 8
soft page breaks, **WD 101**
solid fill, **PPT 108**
sort, **AC 93**
sort key, **AC 93**, AC 97
sorting
 on multiple keys, AC 96–97
 overview, AC 93
 queries involving, AC 97
source area, **EX 15**
sources
 creating, WD 89–91
 details required for, WD 89
 editing, WD 96–98, WD 103
 evaluating, WD 78
 modifying, WD 109–110
 and parenthetical references,
 WD 68
 tag names, WD 93
spacing
 before, after paragraphs, WD 42–43
 line, paragraph, WD 72–73
 after punctuation, WD 88
speaker notes, printing, PPT 121–124
speech handouts, PPT 120
spell checker, **EX 107**, EX 108–109

spelling
 and AutoCorrect feature, WD 84–85
 automatic corrections, WD 9
 checking, WD 10–11, WD 116–117, PPT 116–118
 checking in presentations, PPT 116–118
Spelling and Grammar Check icon, **WD 6**, WD 9
Spelling dialog box, EX 108
Spelling pane buttons, actions (table), PPT 117
splitting, **EX 30**
square brackets ([])
 in parameter queries, AC 87
 in queries, AC 113
Standard Colors vs. Theme Colors, PPT 14
standard properties, **WD 44, PPT 48, EX 44, AC 54**
Start From Beginning button, Quick Access Toolbar, PPT 49–52
Start menu, running apps using Windows 7, OFF 12
Start screen, **OFF 3**, OFF 8, PPT 76
 running apps from, OFF 11–12
 switching between apps and, OFF 13
starting
 Access, OFF 63, AC 24–25
 PowerPoint, PPT 4, PPT 76
 presentations, PPT 49
statistics, calculating, AC 115–117
status bar, **OFF 14**, OFF 15, **AC 8**
 commonly used commands (table), EX 48
 Spelling and Grammar Check icon, WD 6
STDEV function, AC 115
stretch gesture, OFF 4
Style Inspector, WD 70
styles, **WD 38**, WD 38–39, WD 70, **PPT 10, PPT 87**
 adding to charts, EX 40
 American Psychological Association (APA), WD 66
 applying, WD 105–106
 applying shape, PPT 95–97
 applying to cell ranges, EX 30–32
 bibliography, changing, WD 89
 changing cell, EX 24–25
 default, PPT 22
 footnote text, WD 94–96
 Modern Language Association of America (MLA), WD 66
 modifying, WD 70–71
 modifying using shortcut menus, WD 94–96
 updating to match selections, WD 73
 WordArt, PPT 103

stylus for touch screens, OFF 3, WD 50, EX 5
subscription plans for Office 365, CLD 5, CLD 9
subtraction operator (–), EX 78
suites
 described, **OFF 9**
 Microsoft Office 2013, OFF 10
Sum button, EX 80
SUM function
 copying across ranges, EX 15–18
 described, **EX 14**, AC 115
Sum menu, using, EX 84–85
summarizing, WD 78
sums, calculating, EX 14–15
swipe gesture, OFF 4
switching
 between apps and Start screen, OFF 13
 to header, WD 74–75
 from one app and another, OFF 30–31
 between views of queries, AC 43, AC 82
synchronization with Office 365, CLD 8
synonyms
 described, **WD 116, PPT 114**, PPT 115
 finding and inserting, PPT 114–115

T

tab, **OFF 15**
tables (database), **OFF 55**
 adding records to, AC 20–23, AC 26–27
 changing field captions, AC 114–115
 closing, AC 20, AC 24
 creating database, AC 10–15
 as database objects, AC 40
 defining fields in, AC 14–15
 determining database, AC 8
 identifying, AC 60
 importing, linking data from other applications into Access, AC 32–37
 joining, AC 99–102
 modifying in Design view, AC 37–38
 previewing, printing contents of, AC 29–31
 relationships between, AC 61
 removing, AC 79
 renaming, AC 37
 saving, AC 16
 viewing in Design view, AC 17
tabs
 Access ribbon, OFF 64
 changing worksheet name, color, EX 72–73

displaying different, on ribbon, OFF 18
 Excel ribbon, OFF 60
 object, **OFF 64**
tag name, **WD 93**
tap gesture, OFF 4
task pane, **OFF 17**
tax percentage formula, EX 81
team portal page, Office 365, CLD 9
team websites, CLD 10
templates
 creating Access databases using, OFF 65
 creating databases using, AC 7–8
 publications, OFF 69–70
 using for website creating with Office 365, CLD 8
text, **EX 6**
 See also paragraphs, characters
 adding to shapes, PPT 97–100
 alignment in cells, EX 11
 bolding, WD 29–30, PPT 21
 centering, WD 106
 changing case of selected, WD 19
 changing color, PPT 13–14
 changing font, EX 25–26
 changing font for selected, WD 17–18, WD 22–23
 choosing words for slides, PPT 7
 coloring, WD 26
 converting fields to regular, WD 110
 copying, cutting, pasting, WD 111–115
 deleting from slides, PPT 43–45
 entering, WD 5–6, WD 11, WD 88
 entering in Word documents, OFF 23
 entering in worksheets, EX 6–8
 in Excel, **OFF 60**
 finding, WD 113–115
 finding and replacing, PPT 113–114
 formatting paragraphs, characters, WD 13
 formatting single vs. multiple paragraphs, characters, WD 16
 formatting using Format Painter, PPT 100–101
 formatting using mini toolbar, WD 27–28
 inserting into existing documents, WD 48
 italicized, PPT 11
 italicizing, WD 25
 making changes to slide content, PPT 42–47
 moving, WD 49–50
 note, WD 92
 replacing in existing slides, PPT 43
 selection techniques (table), WD 32
 shadowing, PPT 100

underlining, WD 29
wordwrap, WD 8–9
wrapping around photos, PPT 42
text box, **OFF 7**
text data, **AC 81**
 and quotation marks ("), AC 83
 using in criterion, AC 81–82
text effects, applying to selected text,
 WD 20
text fields, and quotation marks, AC 44
text files, exporting Access data to,
 AC 110
text placeholders, selecting, PPT 18
text slides, creating, PPT 81–82
texture fills
 described, **PPT 108**, PPT 106
 inserting, PPT 110–111
theme, **WD 14**, **PPT 5**
Theme Colors vs. Standard Colors,
 PPT 14
themes
 changing, PPT 26–27
 changing colors, WD 31–32
 changing variants, PPT 27–28
 changing workbook, EX 91–92
 choosing, and variants, PPT 5–6
 downloading, PPT 77–78
thesaurus, **WD 116**, **PPT 114**,
 PPT 115
Thumbnail pane, PPT 15, **PPT 28**,
 PPT 30, PPT 42, PPT 118
tiles
 described, **OFF 3**
 moving on Start screen, OFF 8
tiling options, **PPT 108**
tilt mouse wheel, OFF 5
Title and Content layout, PPT 22
Title cell style, EX 24–25
Title Only slide layout style, PPT 23
Title Slide, **OFF 49**, **PPT 7**
 creating, PPT 7–8
 designing, PPT 31
 entering content in, OFF 49–50,
 OFF 53
Title Slide layouts, PPT 79
Title Slides, creating, PPT 81
titles
 centering worksheet, EX 29
 entering column, EX 9–10
 entering row, EX 11, EX 72
 entering worksheet, EX 7–8
 entering worksheet, column, EX 70–71
 formatting worksheet, EX 92–93
 row and column, EX 6
 slide, PPT 24–25
 worksheet, OFF 60
toner, conserving, PPT 124
tool tabs, **OFF 16**
toolbars, Slide Show, PPT 51
top-values query, **AC 98**

totals
 adding to reports, AC 53
 calculating sums, EX 14–15
 determining multiple at same time,
 EX 18–20
 determining with Sum button, EX 80
 using AutoCalculate area, EX 48
touch keyboard, displaying on-screen,
 OFF 12
Touch mode, OFF 17–18
touch screen
 differences from book illustrations,
 WD 16, WD 87, PPT 17, EX 6,
 AC 15
 gestures (table), OFF 4
 insertion point, and selection handle,
 OFF 23
 on-screen touch keyboard, WD 6
 pointers on, PPT 36
 stylus and, WD 94, EX 5, AC 80
 using, OFF 3–5
Trace Error button, EX 79
trailing zeros in worksheets, EX 12
Transform effect, PPT 105
transitions, adding between slides,
 PPT 119–120
transparency, **PPT 108**, PPT 111
transparency slider, **PPT 109**
typing
 checking spelling and grammar while,
 WD 10–11
 clicking and, WD 79–80
 wordwrap while, WD 9

U

underlined, **WD 29**
underlining text, WD 29
Undo button, PPT 8, EX 51
undoing
 actions, WD 24–25, AC 15
 changes, PPT 11
 last cell entry, EX 51
 most recent changes, AC 23
 text formatting, PPT 103–104
 text replacements, WD 115,
 PPT 114
unique identifier, **AC 3**
unlocking screen, OFF 6
updating
 fields, WD 110
 styles to match selections, WD 73
USB flash drives, copying folders to,
 OFF 43–44
user account
 described, **OFF 6**
 signing in, OFF 7–8
user icon, **OFF 6**
user name, **OFF 6**, OFF 7

V

values version, **EX 115**
VAR function, AC 115
variants, **PPT 5**
 changing, PPT 27–28
 choosing, PPT 5–6
vertical ruler, **WD 82**
Vertical Scroll shape, PPT 93,
 PPT 95–96
video conferencing
 with Lync, CLD 13–14
video conferencing with Lync, CLD 12
viewing
 See also displaying
 custom dictionary entries, WD 118
 parameter queries, AC 87–88
 presentations in Slide Show view,
 PPT 49–52
 query results, AC 82
 rulers, WD 5
 tables in Design view, AC 17
views
 PowerPoint, PPT 28–30
 switching between, AC 43
virus, **WD 33**

W

Web support, **OFF 56**
Website, the, CLD 8
websites
 creating with Office 365 Business
 Plans, CLD 8
 design using SharePoint, CLD 11
 team, CLD 10
weight
 changing WordArt outline's,
 PPT 106–107
 described, **PPT 106**
white icon with arrows, PPT 24
white space, hiding and showing,
 WD 102
widow, **WD 101**
wildcards
 described, **AC 83**
 using, AC 83–85
windows
 Access, AC 7–8
 folder, OFF 27
 minimizing, restoring, OFF 34–36
 moving, resizing, OFF 75–76
 overlapping, vs. tabbed documents,
 AC 40
 PowerPoint, OFF 48–55
 Word, WD 5
Windows 7
 copying folders to USB flash drives,
 OFF 44

creating blank Office documents, OFF 57
creating folders using, OFF 27, OFF 28
deleting files, OFF 75
differences from Windows 8, AC 77
minimizing, restoring windows, OFF 36
moving files, OFF 74
renaming files, OFF 73
running Access, AC 6
running apps, OFF 63
running apps and opening files, OFF 59
running apps using Search box, OFF 46–48
running apps using Start menu, OFF 12
running Excel, EX 5
running PowerPoint, PPT 76
running Word, WD 4, WD 69
signing in to accounts using, OFF 8
starting PowerPoint from, PPT 4
Windows Help and Support, OFF 81
Windows 8, **OFF 2**
differences from Windows 7, AC 77
introduction to, OFF 2–6
running Access, AC 6
running Excel, EX 5
running PowerPoint, PPT 76
running Word, WD 4, WD 69
starting, OFF 6–8
using touch screen and mouse, OFF 3–5
Windows Help and Support, OFF 79–81
Windows desktop, OFF 13
Windows Help and Support, OFF 79–81
Windows phones, access to Office 365, CLD 8
Windows Start screen, OFF 8
Word, WD 92
Click and Type feature, WD 79–80
creating blank documents, OFF 12
documents. *See* documents
.docx files, OFF 23
entering text in documents, OFF 23
exiting, OFF 43, WD 46, WD 53, WD 122
exporting Access data to, AC 110
Help, OFF 77–78
opening documents from, WD 47
overview, OFF 10

ribbon tabs, OFF 18
running, WD 4–5, WD 46–47
running in Windows 7, Windows 8, WD 69
See also documents
Word Options dialog box, WD 10
Word window, WD 5
WordArt, **PPT 103**
applying text fill, PPT 106
changing outline color, PPT 107
changing shape, PPT 104–105
changing weight of outline, PPT 106–107
inserting in slides, PPT 103–104
words
counting, WD 100–101
finding and replacing, WD 113–115
flags described, WD 9
selecting, WD 49, PPT 12–13
selecting groups of, WD 28, PPT 20–21
wordwrap, **WD 8**
workbooks, **OFF 55**
changing themes, EX 91–92
creating blank, EX 69
distributing, EX 45
saving, EX 72–73, EX 118
saving using same file name, EX 88
saving with new file names, EX 21–22
saving with same file name, EX 45
works cited, **WD 68**, WD 69, WD 107
works cited page, **WD 104**
worksheet tab names, changing, EX 41–43
worksheets, **OFF 55**
adding pie charts to, EX 37–40
adjusting column widths, EX 34
applying cell style to column headings, formatting total rows, EX 95
applying styles to cell ranges, EX 30–32
centering cell entries across columns by merging cells, EX 29–30
changing background colors, EX 93–94
changing column width, EX 103–105
changing font, EX 25–26
changing margins, headers, EX 110–112
changing row height, EX 106–107
changing tab name, color, EX 72–73
clearing cell entries, formatting, EX 52

clearing entire, EX 52–53
copying cells to adjacent cells in rows, EX 16–18
correcting errors, EX 49–53
creating blank, OFF 56–57
determining multiple totals at same time, EX 18–20
document properties, assigning, EX 44–45
entering formulas using keyboard, EX 73–74
entering numbers, EX 12–13
entering text, EX 6–8
entering titles, OFF 60–61, EX 7–8
formatting, EX 22–36, EX 89–96
formatting numbers, EX 32–33
formatting titles, EX 92–93
formulas. *See* formulas
misspellings, checking, EX 107–109
moving charts to, EX 41–42
planning, designing, EX 4–5
previewing in landscape orientation, EX 46–47
printing, EX 45–47, EX 110–115
sheet tab, OFF 59
size of, and window, OFF 59
titles, subtitles, EX 70–71
wrapping text around photos, PPT 42
wrist injury, minimizing, WD 12

X

X Y (scatter) charts, EX 37
XPS files, WD 51, WD 120, PPT 52, PPT 121, EX 45, **AC 29**
exporting reports as, AC 54
printing presentations as, PPT 54
XPS Viewer, WD 51, WD 120, PPT 52, PPT 121, EX 45, **AC 29**, AC 107

Z

Zoom command, AC 112
zooming
100%, WD 37–38
documents, WD 6, WD 35–36
graphics, WD 36–37
multiple pages, WD 120–121
one page, WD 30
page width, WD 7–8, WD 32
slides, PPT 10

Quick Reference Summary

Microsoft Word 2013 Quick Reference Summary

Task	Page Number	Ribbon	Other On-Screen Element	Shortcut Menu	Keyboard Shortcut
All Caps	WD 19	Change Case button (HOME tab \| Font group), UPPERCASE			CTRL+SHIFT+A
AutoCorrect Entry, Create	WD 85	Options (FILE tab), Proofing (Word Options dialog box)			
AutoCorrect Options Button, Use	WD 85		Point to AutoCorrect Options button in flagged word		
AutoCorrect, Delete Entry	WD 86	Options (FILE tab), Proofing (Word Options dialog box), AutoCorrect Options button			
AutoCorrect, Set Exceptions	WD 87	Options (FILE tab), Proofing (Word Options dialog box), AutoCorrect Options button, Exceptions button (Auto Correction Exceptions dialog box)			
Bibliographical List, Create	WD 106	Bibliography button (REFERENCES tab \| Citations & Bibliography group)			
Bibliography Style, Change	WD 89	Bibliography Style arrow (REFERENCES tab \| Citations & Bibliography group)			
Bold	WD 29	Bold button (HOME tab \| Font group)	Bold button on mini toolbar	Font, Font tab (Font dialog box) Touch mode: 'Show Context Menu' button on mini toolbar, Font on shortcut menu, Font tab (Font dialog box)	CTRL+B
Bullets, Apply	WD 23	Bullets button (HOME tab \| Paragraph group)	Bullets button on mini toolbar		* (ASTERISK), SPACEBAR
Center	WD 15	Center button (HOME tab \| Paragraph group)	Center button on mini toolbar	Paragraph, Indents and Spacing tab (Paragraph dialog box)	CTRL+E

Microsoft Word 2013 Quick Reference Summary *(continued)*

Task	Page Number	Ribbon	Other On-Screen Element	Shortcut Menu	Keyboard Shortcut
Center Page Vertically	WD 43	Page Setup Dialog Box Launcher (PAGE LAYOUT tab \| Page Setup group), Layout tab (Page Setup dialog box)			
Change Case	WD 19	Change Case button (HOME tab \| Font group)		Font, Font tab (Font dialog box) Touch mode: 'Show Context Menu' on mini toolbar, Font on shortcut menu, Font tab (Font dialog box)	SHIFT+F3
Change Spacing before or after Paragraph	WD 42	Spacing Before or Spacing After box (PAGE LAYOUT tab \| Paragraph group)		Paragraph, Indents and Spacing tab (Paragraph dialog box) Touch mode: 'Show Context Menu' button on mini toolbar, Paragraph on shortcut menu, Indents and Spacing tab (Paragraph dialog box)	
Citation Placeholder, Insert	WD 93	Insert Citation button (REFERENCES tab \| Citations & Bibliography group), 'Add New Placeholder'			
Citation, Edit	WD 98		Tap or click citation, Citations Options arrow, Edit Citation		
Citation, Insert	WD 89	Insert Citation button (REFERENCES tab \| Citations & Bibliography group), 'Add New Source'			
Click and Type	WD 79		Position pointer until desired icon appears, then double-tap or double-click		
Color Text	WD 26	Font Color arrow (HOME tab \| Font group)	Font Color arrow on mini toolbar	Font, Font tab (Font dialog box) Touch mode: 'Show Context Menu' on mini toolbar, Font on shortcut menu	
Copy	WD 112	Copy button (HOME tab \| Clipboard group)		Copy	CTRL+C
Count Words	WD 100	Word Count button (REVIEW tab \| Proofing group)	Word Count indicator on status bar		CTRL+SHIFT+G

Microsoft Word 2013 Quick Reference Summary *(continued)*

Task	Page Number	Ribbon	Other On-Screen Element	Shortcut Menu	Keyboard Shortcut
Custom Dictionary, Set Default, View or Modify Entries	WD 118	Options (FILE tab), Proofing (Word Options dialog box), Custom Dictionaries button			
Document Properties, Change	WD 44	Properties button (FILE tab \| Info tab)			
Document Properties, Print	WD 104	FILE tab \| Print tab, first button in Settings area			
Double-Space	WD 72	'Line and Paragraph Spacing' button (HOME tab \| Paragraph group)		Paragraph, Indents and Spacing tab (Paragraph dialog box)	CTRL+2
Double-Underline	WD 80	Underline arrow (HOME tab \| Font group)		Font, Font tab (Font dialog box)	CTRL+SHIFT+D
Exit Word	WD 46		Close button on title bar		
Field, Convert to Regular Text	WD 110				Tap or click field, CTRL+SHIFT+F9
Field, Update	WD 110			Update Field Touch mode: 'Show Context Menu' button on mini toolbar, Update Field on shortcut menu	Tap or click field, press F9
Find Text	WD 113	Find button (HOME tab \| Editing group)	Page Number indicator on status bar		CTRL+F
Font, Change	WD 18	Font arrow (HOME tab \| Font group)	Font arrow on mini toolbar Touch mode: 'Show Context Menu' on mini toolbar, Font on shortcut menu	Font, Font tab (Font dialog box)	CTRL+D
Font Size, Change	WD 17	Font Size arrow (HOME tab \| Font group)	Font Size arrow on mini toolbar	Font, Font tab (Font dialog box) Touch mode: 'Show Context Menu' button on mini toolbar, Font on shortcut menu, Font tab (Font dialog box)	CTRL+D
Font Size, Decrease 1 point	WD 80				CTRL+[
Font Size, Increase 1 point	WD 80				CTRL+]
Footnote, Change Format	WD 99	Footnote & Endnote Dialog Box Launcher			

Microsoft Word 2013 Quick Reference Summary *(continued)*

Task	Page Number	Ribbon	Other On-Screen Element	Shortcut Menu	Keyboard Shortcut
Footnote, Delete	WD 99	Select note reference mark, Cut button (HOME tab \| Clipboard group)			CTRL+X
Footnote, Insert	WD 92	Insert Footnote button (REFERENCES tab \| Footnotes group)			ALT+CTRL+F
Footnote, Move	WD 99	Select note reference mark, Cut button (HOME tab \| Clipboard group); Paste button (HOME tab \| Clipboard group)			CTRL+X; CTRL+V
Formatting Marks	WD 6	'Show/Hide ¶' button (HOME tab \| Paragraph group)			CTRL+SHIFT+*
Go to a Page	WD 111	'Open the Navigation Pane' check box (VIEW tab \| Show group), PAGES tab	Page Number indicator on status bar, PAGES tab		CTRL+G
Graphic, Resize	WD 36	Shape Height and Shape Width boxes (PICTURE TOOLS FORMAT tab \| Size group)	Drag sizing handle	More Layout Options, Size tab (Layout dialog box)	
Hanging Indent, Create	WD 108	Paragraph Dialog Box Launcher (HOME tab \| Paragraph group), Indents and Spacing tab (Paragraph dialog box)	Drag Hanging Indent marker on ruler	Paragraph, Indents and Spacing tab (Paragraph dialog box)	CTRL+T
Hanging Indent, Remove	WD 80	Paragraph Dialog Box Launcher (HOME tab \| Paragraph group), Indents and Spacing tab (Paragraph dialog box)	Drag Hanging Indent marker on ruler	Paragraph, Indents and Spacing tab (Paragraph dialog box)	CTRL+SHIFT+T
Header and Footer, Close	WD 77	'Close Header and Footer' button (HEADER & FOOTER TOOLS DESIGN tab \| Close group)	Double-tap or double-click dimmed document text		
Header, Switch to	WD 74	'Add a Header' button (INSERT tab \| Header & Footer group)	Double-tap or double-click dimmed header	Edit Header	
Hide/Show White Space	WD 102	Options (FILE tab), Display (Word Options dialog box)	Double-tap or double-click white space between pages		
Indent, Decrease	WD 80	Decrease Indent button (HOME tab \| Paragraph group)	Drag First Line Indent marker on ruler	Paragraph, Indents and Spacing tab (Paragraph dialog box)	CTRL+SHIFT+M
Indent, First-Line	WD 82	Paragraph Settings Dialog Box Launcher (HOME tab \| Paragraph group)	Drag 'First Line Indent' marker on ruler	Paragraph, Indents and Spacing tab (Paragraph dialog box)	TAB
Indent, Increase	WD 80	Increase Indent button (HOME tab \| Paragraph group)			CTRL+M

Microsoft Word 2013 Quick Reference Summary *(continued)*

Task	Page Number	Ribbon	Other On-Screen Element	Shortcut Menu	Keyboard Shortcut	
Insertion Point, Move Down/ Up One Line	WD 12				DOWN ARROW/ UP ARROW	
Insertion Point, Move Down/ Up One Paragraph	WD 12				CTRL+DOWN ARROW/ CTRL+UP ARROW	
Insertion Point, Move Down/ Up One Screen	WD 12				PAGE DOWN/ PAGE UP	
Insertion Point, Move Left/ Right One Character	WD 12				LEFT ARROW/ RIGHT ARROW	
Insertion Point, Move Left/ Right One Word	WD 12				CTRL+LEFT ARROW/ CTRL+RIGHT ARROW	
Insertion Point, Move to Beginning/End of Document	WD 12				CTRL+HOME/ CTRL+END	
Insertion Point, Move to Beginning/ End of Line	WD 12				HOME/ END	
Insertion Point, Move to Bottom of Document Window	WD 12				ALT+CTRL+PAGE DOWN/ ALT+CTRL+PAGE UP	
Italicize	WD 25	Italic button (HOME tab	Font group)	Italic button on mini toolbar	Font, Font tab (Font dialog box) Touch mode: 'Show Context Menu' on mini toolbar, Font on shortcut menu, Font tab (Font dialog box)	CTRL+I
Justify Paragraph	WD 80	Justify button (HOME tab	Paragraph group)		Paragraph, Indents and Spacing tab (Paragraph dialog box)	CTRL+J
Left-Align Paragraph	WD 80	Align Left button (HOME tab	Paragraph group)		Paragraph, Indents and Spacing tab (Paragraph dialog box)	CTRL+L
Line Spacing, Change	WD 72	'Line and Paragraph Spacing' button (HOME tab	Paragraph group)	Touch mode: 'Show Context button' on mini toolbar, Paragraph	Paragraph, Indents and Spacing tab (Paragraph dialog box) Touch mode: 'Show Context button' on mini toolbar, Paragraph, Indents and Spacing tab (Paragraph dialog box)	CTRL+[number of desired line spacing, i.e., 2 for double-spacing]

Microsoft Word 2013 Quick Reference Summary *(continued)*

Task	Page Number	Ribbon	Other On-Screen Element	Shortcut Menu	Keyboard Shortcut
Microsoft Account, Sign Out Of	WD 45	Sign out link (FILE tab \| Account tab)			
Move Text	WD 49	Cut button (HOME tab \| Clipboard group); Paste button (HOME tab \| Clipboard group)	Drag and drop selected text	Cut, Paste	CTRL+X, CTRL+V
Normal Style, Modify	WD 70	Styles Dialog Box Launcher (HOME tab \| Styles group), style arrow, Modify		Press and hold or right-click style (HOME tab \| Styles group), Modify	
On-Screen Keyboard, Display	WD 6		Touch mode: Touch Keyboard button on Windows taskbar		
Open a Document	WD 47	Open (FILE tab)			CTRL+O
Page Border, Add	WD 41	'Borders and Shading' button (DESIGN tab \| Page Background group)			
Page Break, Insert	WD 105	'Insert a Page Break' button (INSERT tab \| Pages group)			CTRL+ENTER
Page Number, Insert	WD 76	'Add Page Numbers' button (HEADER & FOOTER TOOLS DESIGN tab \| Header & Footer group)			
Paragraph Indent, Decrease	WD 80				CTRL+SHIFT+M
Paste	WD 112	Paste arrow (HOME tab \| Clipboard group)	Paste Options button by moved/copied text	Paste	CTRL+V
Paste Options Menu, Display	WD 113		Paste Options button by moved/copied text		
Picture Effects, Apply	WD 39	Picture Effects button (PICTURE TOOLS FORMAT tab \| Picture Styles gallery)		Format Picture or Format Object Touch mode: 'Show Context Menu' button on mini toolbar, Format Object or Format Picture on shortcut menu	
Picture Style, Apply	WD 38	More button in Picture Styles gallery (PICTURE TOOLS FORMAT tab \| Picture Styles group)		'Picture Quick Styles'	
Picture, Insert	WD 34	From File button (INSERT tab \| Illustrations group)			
Print Document	WD 51	Print button (FILE tab \| Print tab)			CTRL+P
Print Layout View	WD 53	Print Layout button (VIEW tab \| Views group)	Print Layout button on status bar		

Microsoft Word 2013 Quick Reference Summary *(continued)*

Task	Page Number	Ribbon	Other On-Screen Element	Shortcut Menu	Keyboard Shortcut
Read Mode	WD 52	Read Mode button (VIEW tab \| Views group)	Read Mode button on status bar		
Read Mode, Change Color	WD 121	Page Color on View menu	Read Mode button on Status bar, Page Color on View menu		
Readability Statistics	WD 118	FILE tab \| Print tab, Proofing (Word Options dialog box)			
Redo	WD 24		Redo button on Quick Access Toolbar		CTRL+Y
Remove Character Formatting	WD 80				CTRL+SPACEBAR
Remove Paragraph Formatting	WD 80				CTRL+Q
Remove Space after Paragraph	WD 80	'Line and Paragraph Spacing' button (HOME tab \| Paragraph group)		Paragraph, Indents and Spacing tab (Paragraph dialog box)	CTRL+0 (zero)
Replace Text	WD 114	Replace button (HOME tab \| Editing group)			CTRL+H
Research Task Pane, Look Up Information	WD 119		ALT+click desired word		ALT+SHIFT+F7
Right-Align	WD 75	Align Right button (HOME tab \| Paragraph group)		Paragraph, Indents and Spacing tab (Paragraph dialog box) Touch mode: 'Show Context Menu' button on mini toolbar, Paragraph, Indents and Spacing tab (Paragraph dialog box)	CTRL+R
Rulers, Display	WD 82	View Ruler check box (VIEW tab \| Show group)			
Save	WD 12	Save (FILE tab \| Save tab)	Save button on Quick Access Toolbar		
Save Document, Same File Name	WD 33	Save (FILE tab \| Save tab)	Save button on Quick Access toolbar		
Scroll, Up/ Down One Line	WD 12		Tap or click scroll arrow at top/ bottom of vertical scroll bar		

Microsoft Word 2013 Quick Reference Summary *(continued)*

Task	Page Number	Ribbon	Other On-Screen Element	Shortcut Menu	Keyboard Shortcut	
Scroll, Up/ Down One Screen	WD 12		Tap or click above/ below scroll box on vertical scroll bar			
Select Block of Text	WD 32		Click beginning, SHIFT+click end Touch mode: Drag selection handle(s)			
Select Character(s)	WD 32		Drag pointer through characters Touch mode: Drag selection handle(s)		SHIFT+RIGHT ARROW or SHIFT+LEFT ARROW	
Select Entire Document	WD 32	Select button arrow (HOME tab	Editing group)	In left margin, triple-click		CTRL+A
Select Graphic	WD 32		Tap or click graphic			
Select Group of Words	WD 28		Drag pointer through words Touch mode: Drag selection handle(s)		CTRL+SHIFT+RIGHT ARROW OR CTRL+SHIFT+LEFT ARROW repeatedly	
Select Line	WD 16		Click in left margin Touch mode: Double-tap to left of line		SHIFT+DOWN ARROW	
Select Multiple Lines	WD 32		Drag pointer in left margin Touch mode: Drag selection handle(s)		HOME, then SHIFT+DOWN ARROW; or END, then SHIFT+UP ARROW	
Select Multiple Paragraphs	WD 32		Drag pointer in left margin Touch mode: Drag selection handle(s)		SHIFT+DOWN ARROW	
Select Nonadjacent Items	WD 32		Select first item, hold down CTRL key while selecting item(s)			
Select Paragraph	WD 32		Triple-click paragraph		CTRL+SHIFT+DOWN ARROW or CTRL+SHIFT+UP ARROW	
Select Sentence	WD 32		CTRL-click			
Select Word	WD 32		Double-tap or double-click word		CTRL+SHIFT+RIGHT ARROW or CTRL+SHIFT+LEFT ARROW	
Select Words	WD 32		Drag pointer through words Touch mode: Drag selection handle(s)		CTRL+SHIFT+RIGHT ARROW or CTRL+SHIFT+LEFT ARROW repeatedly	
Shade Paragraph	WD 21	Shading arrow (HOME tab	Paragraph group)			
Single-Space Lines	WD 80	'Line and Paragraph Spacing' button (HOME tab	Paragraph group)		Paragraph, Indents and Spacing tab (Paragraph dialog box)	CTRL+1

Microsoft Word 2013 Quick Reference Summary *(continued)*

Task	Page Number	Ribbon	Other On-Screen Element	Shortcut Menu	Keyboard Shortcut
Small Caps	WD 80	Font Dialog Box Launcher HOME Tab \| Font group), Font tab (Font dialog box)			CTRL+SHIFT+K
Source, Edit	WD 96		Tap or click citation, Citation Options arrow, Edit Source		
Source, Modify	WD 109	Manage Sources button (REFERENCES tab \| Citations & Bibliography group), Edit button			
Space after Paragraph, Remove	WD 80	'Line and Paragraph Spacing' button (HOME tab \| Paragraph group)		Paragraph Touch mode: 'Show Context Menu' on mini toolbar, Paragraph	
Spelling and Grammar, Check at Once	WD 116	'Spelling & Grammar' button (REVIEW tab \| Proofing group)	'Spelling and Grammar Check' icon on status bar, Spelling	Spelling	F7
Spelling, Check as You Type	WD 10		Tap or click word, 'Spelling and Grammar Check' icon on status bar	Press and hold or right-click error, tap or click correct word on shortcut menu	
Style, Apply	WD 105	Style name in Quick Styles gallery (HOME tab \| Styles group)			CTRL+SHIFT+S, Style Name arrow
Style, Modify	WD 70	Styles Dialog Box Launcher (HOME tab \| Styles group), select [style name], Modify		Modify	ALT+CTRL+SHIFT+S
Style, Update to Match Selection	WD 73	Styles Dialog Box Launcher (HOME tab \| Styles group), 'Update Normal to Match Selection'		'Update Normal to Match Selection'	ALT+CTRL+SHIFT+S
Subscript	WD 80	Subscript button (HOME tab \| Font group)		Font, Font tab (Font dialog box)	CTRL+EQUAL SIGN
Superscript	WD 80	Superscript button (HOME tab \| Font group)		Font, Font tab (Font dialog box)	CTRL+SHIFT+PLUS SIGN
Synonym, Find and Insert	WD 116	Thesaurus button (REVIEW tab \| Proofing group)		Tap or click desired synonym on Synonym submenu Touch Mode: 'Show Context Menu' button on mini toolbar, Synonyms on shortcut menu	SHIFT+F7
Table, Align Data in Cells	WD 80	Align [location] button (TABLE TOOLS LAYOUT tab \| Alignment group)			
Text Effect, Apply	WD 20	'Text Effects and Typography' button (HOME tab \| Font group)		Font Touch mode: 'Show Context Menu' on mini toolbar, Font on shortcut menu	

Microsoft Word 2013 Quick Reference Summary *(continued)*

Task	Page Number	Ribbon	Other On-Screen Element	Shortcut Menu	Keyboard Shortcut
Theme Colors, Change	WD 31	Theme Colors button (DESIGN tab \| Document Formatting group)			
Underline	WD 29	Underline button (HOME tab \| Font group)	Underline button on mini toolbar	Font, Font tab (Font dialog box) Touch mode: 'Show Context Menu' button on mini toolbar, Font on shortcut menu, Font tab (Font dialog box)	CTRL+U
Underline Words, Not Spaces	WD 80	Font Dialog Box Launcher (HOME tab \| Font group), Font tab (Font dialog box), Underline style arrow			CTRL+SHIFT+W
Undo	WD 24		Undo button on Quick Access Toolbar		CTRL+Z
Zoom 100%	WD 37	100% button (VIEW tab \| Zoom group)			
Zoom Document	WD 35	Zoom button (VIEW tab \| Zoom group)	Zoom Out or Zoom In button or Zoom level button on status bar Touch mode: Pinch or stretch		
Zoom Multiple Pages	WD 120	Multiple Pages button (VIEW tab \| Zoom group)			
Zoom One Page	WD 30	One Page button (VIEW tab \| Zoom group)			
Zoom Page Width	WD 7	Page Width button (VIEW tab \| Zoom group)			

Microsoft PowerPoint 2013 Quick Reference Summary

Task	Page Number	Ribbon	Other On-Screen Areas	Shortcut Menu	Keyboard Shortcut
Copy	PPT 101	Copy button (HOME tab \| Clipboard group)		Copy	CTRL+C
Document Properties, Change	PPT 48	Properties button (FILE tab \| Info tab)			
Document Properties, Print	PPT 122	FILE tab, Print tab, Print All Slides button, Document Info, Print button			
Document Theme, Change Color Variant	PPT 5	Choose color variant (DESIGN tab \| Variants group)			

Microsoft PowerPoint 2013 Quick Reference Summary

Task	Page Number	Ribbon	Other On-Screen Areas	Shortcut Menu	Keyboard Shortcut
Document Theme, Choose	PPT 5	FILE tab, New tab; More button (DESIGN tab \| Themes group)			
Exit PowerPoint	PPT 55	Exit (FILE tab)	Close button on title bar	Right-click PowerPoint app button on taskbar, click Close window	ALT+F4 or CTRL+Q
Font Size, Decrease	PPT 100	Decrease Font Size button or Font Size arrow (HOME tab \| Font group)	Decrease Font Size button or Font Size arrow on mini toolbar	Font, Size arrows (Font dialog box)	CTRL+SHIFT+LEFT CARET (<)
Font Size, Increase	PPT 12	Increase Font Size button or Font Size arrow (HOME tab \| Font group)	Increase Font Size button or Font Size arrow on mini toolbar	Font, Size arrows (Font dialog box)	CTRL+SHIFT+RIGHT CARET (>)
Font, Change	PPT 98	Font arrow or Font dialog box launcher (HOME tab \| Font group)	Font arrow on mini toolbar	Font	CTRL+SHIFT+F
Font, Change Color	PPT 13	Font Color button or Font Color arrow or Font dialog box launcher (HOME tab \| Font group)	Font Color button or Font Color arrow on mini toolbar	Font, Font Color button on Font tab (Font dialog box)	CTRL+SHIFT+F
Format Painter, Use	PPT 101	Double-click Format Painter button (HOME tab \| Clipboard group), select text with format you want to copy, select text to apply previously selected format; press ESC to turn off Format Painter	Format Painter button on mini toolbar		
Illustration, Placeholder, or Shape, Move	PPT 39		Drag		ARROW KEYS move selected image in small increments
List Level, Increase	PPT 19	Increase List Level button (HOME tab \| Paragraph group)	Increase List Level button on mini toolbar		TAB
List Level, Decrease	PPT 19	Decrease List Level button (HOME tab \| Paragraph group)	Decrease List Level button on mini toolbar		SHIFT+TAB
Move to Another Slide in Normal View	PPT 29		Next Slide or Previous Slide buttons on vertical scroll bar; drag scroll box on vertical scroll bar; click slide thumbnail in Thumbnail pane Touch Mode: Tap desired slide in Thumbnail pane		PAGE DOWN (next slide); PAGE UP (previous slide)
Move to Another Slide in Slide Show View	PPT 50		Click to display next slide; click Next Slide or Previous Slide icons on Slide Show toolbar Touch Mode: Swipe forward or backward on slide		PAGE DOWN (next slide); PAGE UP (previous slide); RIGHT ARROW or DOWN ARROW (next slide); LEFT ARROW or UP ARROW (previous slide)

Microsoft PowerPoint 2013 Quick Reference Summary *(continued)*

Task	Page Number	Ribbon	Other On-Screen Areas	Shortcut Menu	Keyboard Shortcut
Notes, Add	PPT 115		Notes icon on status bar; type notes in Notes pane		
Notes, Print	PPT 121	FILE tab, Print tab, tap or click Notes Pages (Print Layout area), tap or click Print button			CTRL+P
Open Presentation	OFF 54	Open (FILE tab)			CTRL+O
Paste	PPT 101	Paste button (HOME tab \| Clipboard group)		Paste	CTRL+V
Picture, Add Border	PPT 88	Picture Border arrow (PICTURE TOOLS FORMAT tab \| Picture Styles group)			
Picture, Change	PPT 85	Change Picture button (PICTURE TOOLS FORMAT tab \| Adjust group)		Change Picture	
Picture, Correct	PPT 87	Corrections button (PICTURE TOOLS FORMAT tab \| Adjust group)	Picture Corrections Options (Corrections gallery)	Format Picture, Picture Corrections (Format Picture dialog box)	
Picture, Insert	PPT 31	Pictures button or Online Pictures button (INSERT tab \| Images group)	Pictures icon or Online Pictures icon in slide		
Picture, Move	PPT 39		Drag		ARROW keys to move in small increments
Picture Border, Change Color or Weight	PPT 88–89	Picture Border arrow (PICTURE TOOLS FORMAT tab \| Picture Styles group)		Format Picture, Fill & Line, Line (Format Picture pane)	
Picture Effects, Apply	PPT 90	Picture Effects button (PICTURE TOOLS FORMAT tab \| Picture Styles group)		Format Picture, Effects (Format Picture pane)	
Picture Style, Apply	PPT 87	More button (PICTURE TOOLS FORMAT tab \| Picture Styles group)			
Print a Presentation	PPT 52	Print button (FILE tab \| Print tab)			CTRL+P
Resize	PPT 36, PPT 93	Enter height and width values (PICTURE TOOLS FORMAT tab \| Size group or DRAWING TOOLS FORMAT tab \| Size group or VIDEO TOOLS FORMAT tab \| Size group)	Drag sizing handles	Format Picture or Format Shape or Format Video, Size & Properties icon	
Run PowerPoint	OFF 46, PPT 4		PowerPoint 2013 tile on Start menu; search for PowerPoint 2013 using Search charm on Charms bar		
Save a Presentation	PPT 82	Save (FILE tab)	Save button on Quick Access toolbar		CTRL+S or SHIFT+F12

Microsoft PowerPoint 2013 Quick Reference Summary *(continued)*

Task	Page Number	Ribbon	Other On-Screen Areas	Shortcut Menu	Keyboard Shortcut
Save a Presentation with a New Name	PPT 15	Save As (FILE tab)			
Shape, Add	PPT 92, PPT 94	Shapes button (Insert tab \| Illustrations group); Shapes More button (HOME tab \| Drawing group) or DRAWING TOOLS FORMAT tab \| Insert Shapes group			
Shape, Apply Style	PPT 95	Quick Styles button (HOME tab \| Drawing group); Shape Styles More button or Format Shape dialog box launcher (DRAWING TOOLS FORMAT tab \| Shape Styles group)		Format Shape	
Slide, Add	PPT 15	New Slide button (HOME tab \| Slides group)		New Slide	CTRL+M
Slide, Arrange	PPT 42	Slide Sorter button (VIEW tab \| Presentation Views group), drag thumbnail to new position	Drag slide in Thumbnail pane to new position, click Slide Sorter icon on status bar, drag thumbnail to new position		
Slide, Delete	PPT 79			Delete (touch screen) or Delete Slide	DELETE
Slide, Duplicate	PPT 41	New Slide arrow (HOME tab \| Slides group), Duplicate Selected Slides		Duplicate Slide	
Slide, Format Background	PPT 109–111	Format Background button (DESIGN tab \| Customize group)		Format Background (Format Background pane)	
Slide, Insert Picture as Background	PPT 108	Format Background button (DESIGN tab \| Customize group)		Format Background, Picture or Texture Fill, Insert from File (Format Background pane)	
Slide, Select Layout	PPT 23	Layout button or New Slide arrow (HOME tab \| Slides group)			
Slide Number, Insert	PPT 118	Insert Slide Number button (INSERT tab \| Text group) or Header & Footer button (INSERT tab \| Text group), click Slide number check box			
Slide Show, Start	PPT 49	Slide Show button (SLIDE SHOW tab \| Start Slide Show group)	Slide Show button on status bar; 'Start from Beginning' button in Quick Access toolbar		F5
Slide Show, End	PPT 51		Tap or click black ending slide	End Show	ESC or HYPHEN
Spelling, Check	PPT 117	Spelling button (REVIEW tab \| Proofing group)	Spell Check icon on status bar	Spelling (or click correct word on shortcut menu)	F7

Microsoft PowerPoint 2013 Quick Reference Summary *(continued)*

Task	Page Number	Ribbon	Other On-Screen Areas	Shortcut Menu	Keyboard Shortcut
Synonym, Find and Insert	PPT 114	Thesaurus button (REVIEW tab \| Proofing group)		Synonyms	SHIFT+F7
Text, Add Shadow	PPT 100	Text Shadow button (HOME tab \| Font group)			
Text, Bold	PPT 21	Bold button (HOME tab \| Font group)	Bold button on mini toolbar	Font, Font tab (Font dialog box), Font style arrow, Bold	CTRL+B
Text, Change Color	PPT 13	Font Color button or Font Color arrow or Font dialog box launcher (HOME tab \| Font group)	Font Color button or Font Color arrow on mini toolbar	Font, Font Color button (Font dialog box)	CTRL+SHIFT+F
Text, Delete	PPT 43	Cut button (HOME tab \| Clipboard group)		Cut	DELETE or CTRL+X or BACKSPACE
Text, Find and Replace	PPT 113	Replace button (HOME tab \| Editing group)			CTRL+H
Text, Italicize	PPT 11	Italic button (HOME tab \| Font group)	Italic button on mini toolbar	Font, Font style arrow (Font dialog box), Italic	CTRL+I
Text, Select	PPT 11		Drag to select; double-click to select word; triple-click to select paragraph Touch Mode: Tap to position insertion point and drag selection handles		CTRL+SHIFT+RIGHT ARROW (select word); CTRL+SHIFT+DOWN ARROW (select paragraph)
Theme, Change	PPT 26	More button (DESIGN tab \| Themes group)			
Theme, Download	PPT 77	Choose category from Suggested searches (FILE tab, New tab), choose theme, tap or click Create button			
Transition, Add	PPT 45	More button (TRANSITIONS tab \| Transition to This Slide group)			ALT+A, T
Transition, Change Duration	PPT 46	Duration box or arrows (TRANSITIONS tab \| Timing group)			
Transparency, Change	PPT 109	Background Styles button (DESIGN tab \| Background group), Format Background, move Transparency slider		Format Background, Transparency slider	
Undo Changes	PPT 8		Undo button (Quick Access toolbar)		CTRL+Z
WordArt, Add Text Effects	PPT 104	Text Effects button (DRAWING TOOLS FORMAT tab \| WordArt Styles group)			
WordArt, Apply Text Fill	PPT 106	Text Fill arrow (DRAWING TOOLS FORMAT tab \| WordArt Styles group)			

Microsoft PowerPoint 2013 Quick Reference Summary *(continued)*

Task	Page Number	Ribbon	Other On-Screen Areas	Shortcut Menu	Keyboard Shortcut
WordArt, Change Outline Color or Weight	PPT 106–107	Text Outline arrow (DRAWING TOOLS FORMAT tab \| WordArt Styles group)			
WordArt, Insert	PPT 103	WordArt button (INSERT tab \| Text group)			
Zoom for Viewing Slides	PPT 10	Zoom button (VIEW tab \| Zoom group)	Zoom slider on status bar; Zoom In or Zoom Out buttons on Zoom slider; change percentage in Zoom level box on left side of slider Touch Mode: Pinch two fingers to zoom out; stretch two fingers apart to zoom in		

Microsoft Excel 2013 Quick Reference Summary

Task	Page Number	Ribbon	Other On-Screen Element	Shortcut Menu	Keyboard Shortcut
Accounting Number Format, Apply	EX 32	'Accounting Number Format' button (HOME tab \| Number group)	'Accounting Number Format' button on mini toolbar	Format Cells	CTRL+SHIFT+DOLLAR SIGN ($)
Auto Fill	EX 16	Fill button (HOME tab \| Editing group)	Drag fill handle		
Average	EX 86	Sum arrow (HOME tab \| Editing group) or (FORMULAS tab \| Function Library)	Insert Function box in formula bar, AVERAGE in 'Select a function' list, OK button, select range, OK button		Type **=av,** DOWN ARROW, ENTER
Background Color	EX 93	Fill Color arrow (HOME tab \| Font group)		Format Cells, Fill tab (Format Cells dialog box)	CTRL+1
Bold	EX 26	Bold button (HOME tab \| Font group)	Bold button on mini toolbar	Format Cells	CTRL+B
Border, Add	EX 93	Borders arrow (HOME tab \| Font group)			
Cell Style	EX 24	Cell Styles button (HOME tab \| Styles group)			
Chart Style, Apply	EX 40		Chart Styles button		
Chart, Add	EX 38	'Insert Pie or Doughnut Chart' button (INSERT tab \| Charts group)			
Chart, Move to New Sheet	EX 41	Move Chart button (CHART TOOLS DESIGN tab \| Location group)			

Microsoft Excel 2013 Quick Reference Summary *(continued)*

Task	Page Number	Ribbon	Other On-Screen Element	Shortcut Menu	Keyboard Shortcut
Clear Cell Entries	EX 52	Clear button (HOME tab \| Editing group)	Drag fill handle back into selected range	Clear Contents	
Clear Entire Worksheet	EX 52	Clear button (HOME tab \| Editing group), Clear All			
Column Width, Adjust	EX 34		Double-tap or double-click boundary or drag boundary	Column Width	
Comma Style, Apply	EX 32	Comma Style button (HOME tab \| Number group)		Format Cells, Number tab	
Conditional Formatting	EX 100	Conditional Formatting button (HOME tab \| Styles group)			
Copy and Paste	EX 16	Copy button (HOME tab \| Clipboard Group), select destination, Paste button (HOME tab \| Clipboard group)	Drag fill handle	Copy, select destination, Paste Touch mode: 'Show Context Menu' button on mini toolbar, Copy, select destination, Paste	CTRL+drag or CTRL+C; CTRL+V
Currency Style, Apply	EX 98	Number Format Dialog Box Launcher (HOME tab \| Number group), Currency in Category list (Format Cells dialog box)		Format Cells, Number tab	
Date, Format	EX 96			Format Cells	
Document Properties, Change	EX 44	Properties button (FILE tab \| Info tab)			
Entry, Complete	EX 7		Tap or click Enter box in formula bar		ENTER or ARROW keys
Fit on One Page	EX 115	Page Setup Dialog Box Launcher (PAGE LAYOUT tab \| Page Setup group), Fit to (Page Setup dialog box)			
Font Color, Change	EX 28	Font Color arrow (HOME tab \| Font group)	Font Color arrow on mini toolbar	Format Cells	
Font Size, Increase	EX 27	Font Size arrow (HOME tab \| Font group) or 'Increase Font Size' button (HOME tab \| Font group)	Font Size arrow on mini toolbar	Format Cells	
Font, Change	EX 25	Font arrow (HOME tab \| Font group)	Font arrow on mini toolbar Touch mode: 'Show Context Menu' button on mini toolbar, Format Cells	Format Cells	

Microsoft Excel 2013 Quick Reference Summary *(continued)*

Task	Page Number	Ribbon	Other On-Screen Element	Shortcut Menu	Keyboard Shortcut
Formulas Version, Display	EX 115				CTRL+ACCENT MARK (`)
Header, Add	EX 110	Header & Footer button (INSERT tab \| text group)	Page Layout button on status bar, tap or click in header area		
Margins, Change	EX 110	Adjust Margins button (PAGE LAYOUT tab \| Page Setup group)			
Maximum, Determine	EX 48	Sum arrow (HOME tab \| Editing group), Max	Insert Function box in formula bar, Statistical category, MAX	Maximum on Customize Status Bar shortcut menu	=max
Merge and Center	EX 29	'Merge & Center' button (HOME tab \| Alignment group)			
Minimum, Determine	EX 84	Sum arrow (HOME tab \| Editing group), Min	Insert Function box in formula bar, Statistical category, MIN		=min
Orientation, Change	EX 110	'Change Page Orientation' button (PAGE LAYOUT tab \| Page Setup group)			
Page Layout View	EX 48		Page Layout button on status bar		
Percent Style Format, Apply	EX 99	Percent Style button (HOME tab \| Number group)		Format Cells, Number tab (Format Cells dialog box)	CTRL+SHIFT+%
Print	EX 46	Print button (FILE tab \| Print tab)			CTRL+P
Print Scaling, Change Back to 100%	EX 117	Page Setup Dialog Box Launcher (PAGE LAYOUT tab \| Page Setup group), Adjust to (Page Setup dialog box)			
Print Section of Worksheet	EX 114	Print Selection option (FILE tab \| Print tab)			
Range Finder	EX 89		Double-tap or double-click cell		
Redo	EX 51		Redo button on Quick Access Toolbar		CTRL+Y
Row Height, Adjust	EX 106		Drag row boundary	Row Height	
Select Adjacent Cell	EX 36				ARROW
Select All Data in a Cell	EX 51		Double-tap or double-click (if no spaces in data)		
Select Cell One Window Down	EX 36				PAGE DOWN

Microsoft Excel 2013 Quick Reference Summary (continued)

Task	Page Number	Ribbon	Other On-Screen Element	Shortcut Menu	Keyboard Shortcut
Select Cell One Window Up	EX 36				PAGE UP
Select Cell One Worksheet Window to the Left	EX 36				ALT+PAGE UP
Select Cell One Worksheet Window to the Right	EX 36				ALT+PAGE DOWN
Select First Cell in Worksheet	EX 36				CTRL+HOME
Sheet Tab Color, Change	EX 43			Tab Color	
Sheet Tab Name, Change	EX 43		Double-tap or double-click sheet tab		

Microsoft Access 2013 Quick Reference Summary

Task	Page Number	Ribbon	Other On-Screen Areas	Shortcut Menu	Keyboard Shortcut
Back up Database	AC 56	FILE tab, Save As tab, 'Back Up Database', Save As button			
Calculated Field in Query, Use	AC 112			Press and hold or right-click field row, Zoom	
Caption, Change	AC 114	Property Sheet button (DESIGN tab \| Show/Hide group), Caption box	Select field in design grid, tap or click Properties on shortcut menu	Press and hold or right-click field in design grid, tap or click Properties on shortcut menu	
Close Object	AC 20		Close button for object	Close	
Column, Resize	AC 28		Double-click or double-tap right boundary of field selector in datasheet	Press and hold or right-click field name, Field Width	
Compact Database	AC 57	FILE tab, Info tab in Backstage view, 'Compact & Repair Database' button			
Comparison Operator, Use	AC 90		Create query, enter comparison operator on Criteria row		
Compound Criterion Involving AND, Use	AC 91				Place criteria on same line
Compound Criterion Involving OR, USE	AC 92				Place criteria on separate lines
Criteria, Use in Calculating Statistics	AC 117	Totals button (QUERY TOOLS DESIGN tab \| Show/Hide group), Total arrow, tap or click calculation			

Microsoft Access 2013 Quick Reference Summary *(continued)*

Task	Page Number	Ribbon	Other On-Screen Areas	Shortcut Menu	Keyboard Shortcut
Criterion, Use in a Query	AC 43		In Design View, tap or click Criteria row, enter criterion		
Crosstab Query, Create	AC 119	Query Wizard button (CREATE tab \| Queries group), Crosstab Query Wizard			
Data, Export to Excel	AC 107	Excel button (EXTERNAL DATA tab \| Export group)	Select object in Navigation Pane, tap or click Export		
Data, Import	AC 33	Button for imported data format (EXTERNAL DATA tab \| Import & Link group)			
Data, Sort in Query	AC 94	Select field in design grid, tap or click Sort row, tap or click Sort arrow, select order			
Database Properties, Change	AC 55	View and edit database properties link (FILE tab \| Info tab)			
Database, Create	AC 6	Blank desktop database thumbnail (FILE tab \| New tab)			
Database, Create using Template	AC 7		FILE tab, New tab, select template		
Delete Object	AC 58			Delete	
Design Grid, Clear	AC 93		In Design view, select all columns, tap or click DELETE		
Duplicates, Omit	AC 94	In Design view, Property Sheet button (QUERY TOOLS DESIGN tab \| Show/Hide group), tap or click Unique Values property, tap or click Yes			
Exit Access	AC 24		Close button on right side of title bar		
Field in Query, Add to Design Grid	AC 79		Double-click or double-tap field in field list		
Form for Query, Create	AC 105	Select query, Form button (CREATE tab \| Forms group)			
Form, Create	AC 45	Form button (CREATE tab \| Forms group)			
Grouping, Use	AC 118		Create query, select Group By in Total row, select field to group by		
Join Properties, Change	AC 101			In Design view, press and hold or right-click join line, click Join Properties	
Multiple Keys, Sort on	AC 96		Assign two sort keys in design grid		

Microsoft Access 2013 Quick Reference Summary *(continued)*

Task	Page Number	Ribbon	Other On-Screen Areas	Shortcut Menu	Keyboard Shortcut
Navigation Pane, Customize	AC 122		Navigation Pane arrow		
Number Criterion, Use	AC 89		Create query, select table, enter number as criterion in field grid		
Open Database	AC 25	Open button (FILE tab)			
Open Table	AC 21		Double-click or double-tap table in Navigation Pane	Press and hold or right-click table in Navigation Pane, tap or click Open	
Parameter Query, Create	AC 87		In Design view, type parameter in square brackets in criterion row of field grid, Run button (QUERY TOOLS DESIGN tab \| Results group)		
Parameter Query, Use	AC 87			Right-click or press and hold query in Navigation Pane, tap or click Open	
Preview or Print Object	AC 30	Print or Print Preview button (FILE tab \| Print tab)			CTRL+P, ENTER
Primary Key, Modify	AC 11	Select field, Data Type arrow (TABLE TOOLS FIELDS tab \| Formatting group), select data type			
Query, Create in Design View	AC 78	Query Design button (CREATE tab \| Queries group)			
Query, Create using Simple Query Wizard	AC 40	Query Wizard button (CREATE tab \| Queries group)			
Query, Export	AC 107		Select query in Navigation Pane, application button (EXTERNAL DATA tab \| Export group)	Press and hold or right-click query in Navigation Pane, Export	
Records in a Join, Restrict	AC 111		In Design view, enter criterion for query		
Rename Object	AC 58			Press and hold or right-click object in Navigation Pane, Rename, enter new name, press ENTER	
Report Column Headings, Modify	AC 50			Press and hold or right-click field name, Rename Field	

Microsoft Access 2013 Quick Reference Summary *(continued)*

Task	Page Number	Ribbon	Other On-Screen Areas	Shortcut Menu	Keyboard Shortcut
Report, Create	AC 48	Report button (CREATE tab \| Reports group)			
Run Access	AC 5		Access 2013 tile on Windows Start screen or display Charms bar, tap or click Search charm, type Access, tap or click Access 2013		
Save Object	AC 16	FILE tab, Save	Save button on Quick Access Toolbar		CTRL+S
Save Object As	AC 45	FILE tab, Save As tab, 'Save Object As', Save As button			
Statistics, Calculate	AC 115	Create query, Totals button (QUERY TOOLS DESIGN tab \| Show/Hide group), tap or click Total row, tap or click Total arrow, select calculation			
Table, Modify in Design View	AC 37	Table Design button (CREATE tab \| Tables group)			
Table, View in Design View	AC 17	View arrow (TABLE TOOLS FIELDS tab \| Views group), Design View	Design View button on status bar		
Tables, Join	AC 100	Query Design button (CREATE tab \| Queries group), add field lists for tables to join, add desired fields to design grid, run query			
Text Data Criterion, Use	AC 81		Create query, select table, enter text as criterion in field grid		
Top-Values Query, Create	AC 98	In Design view, Return arrow (QUERY TOOLS DESIGN tab \| Query Setup group)			
Totals, Add to a Report	AC 53	Totals button (REPORT DESIGN TOOLS DESIGN tab \| Grouping & Totals group)			
Wildcard, Use	AC 83		In Design view, tap or click Criteria row in design grid, type wildcard and text		

Important Notes for Windows 7 Users

The screen shots in this book show Microsoft Office 2013 running in Windows 8. If you are using Microsoft Windows 7, however, you still can use this book because Office 2013 runs virtually the same way on both platforms. You will encounter only minor differences if you are using Windows 7. Read this section to understand the differences.

Dialog Boxes

If you are a Windows 7 user, the dialog boxes shown in this book will look slightly different than what you see on your screen. Dialog boxes for Windows 8 have a title bar with a solid color, and the dialog box name is centered on the title bar. Beyond these superficial differences in appearance, however, the options in the dialog boxes across both platforms are the same. For instance, Figures 1 and 2 show the Font dialog box in Windows 7 and the Font dialog box in Windows 8.

Figure 1 Font Dialog Box in Windows 7

Figure 2 Font Dialog Box in Windows 8

Alternate Steps for Running an App in Windows 7

Nearly all of the steps in this book work exactly the same way for Windows 7 users; however, running an app (or program/application) requires different steps for Windows 7. The following steps show how to run an app in Windows 7.

Running an App (or Program/Application) Using Windows 7

1. Click the Start button on the taskbar to display the Start menu.
2. Click All Programs and then click the Microsoft Office 2013 folder (Figure 3).
3. If necessary, click the name of the folder containing the app you want to run.
4. Click the name of the app you want to run (such as Excel 2013).

Figure 3 Running an App Using the Windows 7 Start Menu